STATUTES, REGULATION, AND INTERPRETATION

LEGISLATION AND ADMINISTRATION IN THE REPUBLIC OF STATUTES

■ ■ ■

by

William N. Eskridge Jr.
John A. Garver Professor of Jurisprudence
Yale Law School

Abbe R. Gluck
Professor of Law
Yale Law School

Victoria F. Nourse
Professor of Law
Georgetown University Law School

AMERICAN CASEBOOK SERIES®

Mat.# 41105875

American Casebook Series is a trademark registered in the U.S. Patent and Trademark Office.

© 2014 LEG, Inc. d/b/a West Academic
    444 Cedar Street, Suite 700
    St. Paul, MN 55101
    1-877-888-1330

West, West Academic Publishing, and West Academic are trademarks of West Publishing Corporation, used under license.

Printed in the United States of America

ISBN: 978-0-314-27356-7

To Don Patron.

WNE Jr.

To my teacher, Bill Eskridge.

ARG

To Jack and Mia.

VFN

PREFACE

INTRODUCING STUDENTS TO THE REGULATORY STATE

Law school courses on "public law" have traditionally focused on judicial decisions interpreting the U.S. Constitution, the common law, and particular federal statutes, such as the Administrative Procedure Act of 1946. The big innovation for public law courses in the twentieth century was to introduce extra-judicial materials—practical and theoretical notes, problems and case studies, and excerpts from articles and books. In the new millennium, public law courses look a lot like they did fifty years ago: the primary analytical materials are still judicial decisions, the prototypical legal interpreter remains the judge, and the focus is judicially-created doctrine.

In the last generation, many law schools have started to offer, or even require, a first-year course introducing students to either Legislation or Legislation/Administrative Law ("LegAd" or "LegReg"). Surprisingly, the published materials are still dominated by the agenda and pedagogy of the 1950s. That is, the primary analytical materials are still judicial decisions, the prototypical legal interpreter remains the judge, and the focus is for the most part judicial doctrine. One of us has co-authored a Legislation casebook that is used in both upper-level and first-year courses; that book follows the traditional agenda and pedagogy and, indeed, was inspired by the Hart and Sacks materials on *The Legal Process* that were finalized in 1958.

This coursebook is a departure from tradition, because we believe that the modern regulatory state bypassed legal education and its casebooks between 30 and 80 years ago. Our premise is that it is essential for law students, preferably in their first year, to have a sophisticated introduction to basic legal structures, methods of analysis, and issues that are characteristic of the modern regulatory state. Drawing from the work of scholars who have pioneered this reconceptualization of legal education,[1] we have made three pedagogical decisions that are necessary for the education of a sophisticated lawyer in today's society:

---

[1] See especially Robert A. Katzmann, *Judging Statutes* (2014); Katzmann, *Statutes*, 87 N.Y.U. L. Rev. 637 (2012); Edward L. Rubin, *What's Wrong with Langdell's Method, and What to Do About It,* 60 Vand. L. Rev. 609 (2007); Robin West, *Toward the Study of the Legislated Constitution,* 72 Ohio St. L.J. 1343, 1348 (2011). Our own work reflects this new approach. E.g., William N. Eskridge Jr. & John Ferejohn, *A Republic of Statutes: The New American Constitution* (2010); Abbe R. Gluck & Lisa Schultz Bressman, *Statutory Interpretation from the*

First, the primary legal materials are statutes, agency regulations, as well as judicial decisions that construe and enforce those materials. This reflects the legal reality in this country since the New Deal. We live in a republic of statutes, not a common law republic. The overwhelming majority of statutory details are filled in by agency regulations and guidances, not by judicial decisions. Traditionally, even Legislation courses taught statutes through judicial decisions where learned judges dramatically debate matters of doctrinal significance. We shall often follow that pedagogical practice—this coursebook includes the canonical cases of legislation and administrative law—but our aspiration is to require students to focus also on statutes, regulations, executive orders, agency interpretive memoranda, congressional testimony, and other legal documents. Applying a statute or regulation requires different patterns of thinking and analysis than applying a judicial precedent.

Second, we take a broader view of the prototypical legal interpreter. In addition to judges, members of Congress, agency officials, and even state actors are part of the interpretive process in the modern, multi-layered legal landscape. To be sure, it is critically important for students of the regulatory state to understand how judges approach statutes and regulations, and we shall provide an ample array of enjoyable statutory debates among learned jurists. But the overwhelming majority of the official interpretations of federal statutes are supplied by agencies and not by judges. In your other courses—whether they be Torts and Contracts or Civil Procedure and Constitutional Law—you will learn how judges think. In this course, perhaps alone among your introductory law school courses, you will learn how the worlds of law-making, law-implementing, law-interpreting, and law-enforcing connect. You will learn how members of Congress and agency officials think, and how those interpreters differ from one another and from courts.

Third, we emphasize structural relationships and institution-based incentives for official actions and interactions, as well as conventional judge-recognized doctrine. Thus, each chapter is chock full of substantive doctrine, but we also emphasize how factors beyond doctrine itself explain the evolution of statutory law and its meaning. Structural relationships, such as an actor's constituency and the sequence of law-creating moves are very important to figuring out why an agency makes (or fails to make) the decisions it does. We also pay close attention to how Congress works, an innovation unique to this coursebook but most useful for advanced study of most modern subject areas. Modern lawyers cannot understand

Inside—An Empirical Study of Congressional Drafting, Delegation and the Canons: Parts I and II, 65 Stan. L. Rev. 901 (2013), 66 Stan. L. Rev. 725 (2014); Victoria F. Nourse, *A Decision Theory of Statutory Interpretation: Legislative History by the Rules,* 122 Yale L.J. 70 (2012).

statutory law without understanding the incentives, rules and processes that shape how Congress makes it.

In developing these materials for publication, the intellectual debts we owe are too numerous to list. The late Professor Philip Frickey (1953–2010) had the original idea to offer legislation, agency, and regulatory state materials in the first year of law school, and his ideas saturate this book. Many other brilliant scholars gave us ideas that helped us conceptualize this book. They include Jerry Mashaw, Jodi Short, Aaron Bruhl, Nick Parrillo, John Manning, Jim Brudney, Peter Strauss, Brian Richardson, Jayme Herschkopf, John Ferejohn, and many others.

Deans Bill Treanor (Georgetown) and Robert Post (Yale) provided both encouragement and funds for research assistants needed to advance this project. Invaluable research assistance has been provided by Molly Alarcon (Yale, 2016), Lindsay Brewer (Yale, 2016), Jeff Chen (Yale, 2016), Carter Greenbaum (Yale, 2016), Natalie Hausknecht (Yale, 2015), Alex Langlinais (Yale, 2016), Sarafina Midzik (Yale, 2016), Erika Nyborg-Burch (Yale, 2016), Chris Pagliarella (Yale, 2016), Lise Rahdert (Yale, 2015), David Simins (Yale, 2016), Xander Tabloff (Yale, 2015), Sam Thypin-Bermeo (Yale, 2015), Ben Wallace (Yale, 2016), and Katie Wynbrandt (Yale, 2016).

We fervently desire that the enterprise that follows—these teaching materials—will be relevant to the actual operation of the modern regulatory state and will facilitate the student's ability to participate in law-making and law-implementing enterprises. We hope these materials will be useful to the student. We also hope that the student will find our materials interesting, stimulating, and even fun.

WNEJr
ARG
VFN

June 2014

SUMMARY OF CONTENTS

PART 3. AGENCIES AND ADMINISTRATIVE IMPLEMENTATION

TABLE OF CONTENTS

PART 2. STATUTORY INTERPRETATION

PART 3. AGENCIES AND ADMINISTRATIVE
IMPLEMENTATION

TABLE OF CASES

The principal cases are in bold type.

STATUTES, REGULATION, AND INTERPRETATION

LEGISLATION AND ADMINISTRATION IN THE REPUBLIC OF STATUTES

INTRODUCTION TO STATUTES AND THEIR IMPLEMENTATION

"NO VEHICLES IN THE PARK"

■ ■ ■

This coursebook is designed to introduce law students to the adoption and implementation of statutes in the modern regulatory state. Statutes, agency rules and regulations, and judicial precedents interpreting statutes are not just the *primary* source of law in this country, but the *overwhelming* source of law here.

Our introduction focuses on statutes and so forth as the foundation of our *legal system*, a body of rules and practices that can be applied through careful legal reasoning by legal actors performing their roles in particular institutional contexts. Contrast our focus with that of courses where most of the law is judge-made—either the common law courses such as torts, contracts, and property, or a constitutional law course, where judicial constructions trump statutes and regulations.

Although the common law and constitutional precedents will play a role in this course, this course is fundamentally different from your common law and constitutional courses:

- *There is a relatively recent and typically detailed **text** at the center of the course*, namely, the text of the statute, as well as that of the agency regulation. Legal reasoning in this course will not involve as much reasoning by analogy as in your common law and constitutional law courses; legal reasoning will be much more text-centered, with analogies often made to other statutes, instead of other judge-made rules. The analysis of statutory text typically follows certain rules, presumptions, and principles—some relating to language and some relating to policy: the object is to apply a general text (the statute) to a specific problem using those rules, presumptions, and principles rather than to pull a "holding" out of a lengthy case opinion.

- *The key **lawmaking** players are legislators and agencies—not judges who apply common law thinking and insights to mundane real-world difficulties.* The institutional players are important, because different players bring different skill sets to the task of statutory application and because lawmaking involves the cooperation of all those officials. Judges play an important role in the modern administrative state, but they are not its primary governmental officials. On the other hand, because judges declare the law other institutional actors must follow, judicial decision-making has a pervasive effect on decisions by other institutions.

- *Legislators and agencies operate differently from judges, because they work in different institutions with different structures, players, and incentives.* Judges decide cases and, in the paradigm trial court case, need no agreement from others about how to resolve a case. Legislators and agencies tackle general problems in institutions that require agreement from many people to reach a decision. Unlike most judges, legislators and agency heads have distinct incentives based on the fact that their job exists to represent other persons, namely voters.

- *The characteristic form of reasoning by legislators and agencies differs from common law reasoning by analogy, because it is avowedly instrumental and decidedly future-oriented.* Legislators reason based on anticipated effects on the people, including electoral consequences to themselves. Administrators use cost-benefit balancing to assess anticipated effects on citizens. By contrast, judges may ignore general consequences beyond the individual case, because the common law model tells them that they are resolving a single controversy arising in the past.

The exercise that follows draws on one of the most famous hypothetical problems of statutory interpretation. We use it introduce you to the basic forms of legal reasoning that are the focus of this coursebook.

1. HOW JUDGES THINK ABOUT STATUTES

The peaceful City of Halcyon was in 1980 disrupted by a series of accidents. In each instance, a motorcyclist or (in one case) a bicyclist was racing through a public park and ran over a pedestrian in the park; in one instance, an elderly person was killed by a racing motorcycle. Responding to these incidents, the City Council enacted the following statute in December 1980:

THE PARKS SAFETY ACT OF 1980

Sec. 1. The Council finds that vehicles create safety problems when they are operated in parks and further finds that the best solution is to ban any and all vehicles from all municipal parks.

Sec. 2. No vehicles of any kind shall be allowed in any municipal park. Any person who brings or drives a vehicle into one of these parks shall be guilty of a misdemeanor, which may be punished by a fine not exceeding $500 or by a two-day incarceration in the municipal jail, or both.

Sec. 3. "Vehicle" for purposes of this law means any mechanism for conveying a person from one place to another, including motorcycles, automobiles, trucks, and motor scooters. *Provided that*, bicycles shall be allowed in the park, so long as they are being pushed or carried and not ridden.

After adoption of the Parks Safety Act of 1980, motorcycle traffic in and around municipal parks dries up, and there are no further accidents of that nature. But there are several accidents involving bicyclists zooming through parks at high rates of speed and running into elderly persons and children enjoying the parks.

A police officer observes Helen Ro pedaling her tricycle in the Hope Park, the city's largest public park and a center for children's activities. Ro pedals her tricycle down a steep hill at what the officer considers an alarming speed, and almost runs over an infant who has strayed from his inattentive father. After that near miss, the officer arrests Ro and issues her a citation for violating the Park Safety Act. Because Ro is only six years old, the officer finds her parents and presents them with a copy of the citation.

The Ro parents are both lawyers—and are outraged that their daughter has been cited. So they fight the charge in court, arguing to the Judge that the Park Safety Act does not regulate tricycles. The City Attorney argues that the law does regulate tricycles. The Judge must interpret the Park Safety Act to determine whether its prohibition of *vehicles* in the park includes *tricycles*. Jot down your answer in the margin, and consider this brief introduction to how *judges* think when they interpret statutes.

As a general matter, judges think and operate in very predictable ways. Indeed, the judge is esteemed in our society in large part because she is supposed to apply preexisting law in a predictable manner. Thus, judges will focus on concrete legal criteria and will justify their decisions by reference to such neutral criteria. But judges are also concerned with the consistency of this concrete exercise with broader norms—including the purpose of the statute being construed, the noninterference of the statute (as interpreted) with other statutory schemes developed by the legislature, and the coherence of the statute and its application with constitutional and other fundamental norms of the polity.

Federal judges and many state judges are not elected. Their comparative advantage in our system of government is their *predictable* application of preexisting law to new facts plus their *integration* of new statutes and regulations with other legal and constitutional norms plus their *neutrality* in carrying out these roles.

A. WHAT IS THE PLAIN MEANING OF THE STATUTE, AS APPLIED TO THIS CASE?

If the text of the statute admits no ambiguity, then judges will almost always apply that *plain meaning*. Is there a plain meaning of the Park Safety Act, as applied to Helen Ro? Consider some text-based considerations:

(1) Ordinary Meaning

The simplest approach is to apply ordinary rules of grammar and word usage to the phrase in question. Section 2 of the Parks Safety Act says: "No vehicles of any kind shall be allowed in any municipal park." Section 3 then defines "vehicle" as "any mechanism for conveying a person from one place to another, including motorcycles, automobiles, trucks, and motor scooters." Does a tricycle fit within that definition? The inclusion phrase, however, lists only motor vehicles. Is that a clue to the proper application of § 2?

Another kind of inquiry would be this: Would a typical speaker of the English language think that a tricycle would be included in the prohibition of "vehicles" in § 2? Engage in some self-reflection: Do you use the term vehicle that broadly? Others whom you have observed?

You might want to do some research into the ordinary meaning of "vehicle." *Webster's Third International Dictionary* defines "vehicle" as a medium (such as syrup) for administering medicine and, more pertinently, as follows:

2. an agent of transmission: CARRIER

4. a means of carrying or transporting something <planes, trains, and other *vehicles*>: as

 a : MOTOR VEHICLE * * *

The only mechanisms *Webster's* lists as examples of "vehicle" are motorized mechanisms. Other dictionaries define the term in a similar manner.

Another source might be *Wikipedia*, which includes this explanation of what "vehicle" might include:

A **vehicle** (from Latin: *vehiculum*) is a device that is designed or used to transport people or cargo. Most often vehicles are manufactured, such as bicycles, cars, motorcycles, trains, ships, boats, and aircraft.

Vehicles that do not travel on land often are called craft, such as watercraft, sailcraft, aircraft, hovercraft, and spacecraft.

Land vehicles are classified broadly by what is used to apply steering and drive forces against the ground: wheeled, tracked, railed, or skied.

Wikipedia provides a short history of vehicles, starting with ships and boats and highlighting the *draisnes*, early prototypes of the modern bicycle.

Can you think of other ways to research "ordinary meaning"? Are any of these sources relevant, however, in light of the Park Safety Act's definition of the term in § 3?

(2) Specialized Meaning Within the Legal System

"Vehicle" might have a specialized legal meaning. Section 3's definition of "vehicle" might be read to create a special legal meaning for purposes of the Parks Safety Act, and that meaning does not have to be the same as the "ordinary" meaning the term would have to a speaker of English. Also, there may be a common law consensus among judges in the state where Halcyon is located that "vehicle" as used in a regulatory statute is not limited to "motor vehicles."

Most states have laws requiring *vehicle registration* and licensing to operate various kinds of vehicles. One might research the various state vehicle-registration laws to see how far they go. Indeed, Halcyon's state may have copied the California Vehicles Code, which mainly regulates motorized vehicles and defines "vehicle" to exclude mechanisms that are propelled exclusively by human power. CVC § 670. But the California code does have a cluster of provisions regulating bicycles. CVC § 39000 defines "bicycle" for purposes of that portion of the code:

"Bicycle," for the purposes of this division, means any device upon which a person may ride, which is propelled by human power through a system of belts, chains, or gears having either two or three wheels (one of which is at least 20 inches in diameter) or having a frame size of at least 14 inches, or having four or more wheels.

How should this definition figure into your reading of the no-vehicles ordinance?

(3) Prototypical (The Best Example) v. Extensive Meaning (All Examples)?

Judges often declare a statute to be "plain," but it is fairly easy to see that words can be used in distinct ways. To think more precisely about the various ways in which words "mean," students should consider the difference between "prototypical" meanings and "extensive" meanings. A "prototypical" meaning is the core example of a term. So, in the case of the term "vehicle," the core or best example might be a car. Extensive meaning is the meaning that might cover "all examples," not just the "best" or "most typical" example. The extensive meaning of "vehicle," could include any means of transport, such as a bicycle or airplane, thus extending the meaning of the vehicle to a larger set of terms. Although "prototypical" meaning has an important role to play in statutory interpretation, judges frequently adopt a more "extensive" meaning, to give effect to the statute's purpose. Statutes are written to solve problems and limiting the meaning of the statute to prototypical meaning can undermine the purpose of the statute.

(4) Reading the Relevant Text in the Context of the Whole Statute

Another convention of legal interpretation in our culture is that the provisions of § 2, at stake in the tricycle case, should be read in light of the whole statute. If one interpretation (vehicle includes tricycle) is more consistent with the whole statute than a rival interpretation (vehicle does not include tricycle), the consistency supports the first interpretation.

For example, § 1 offers as a statutory premise for the Parks Safety Act the concern that "vehicles create safety problems when they are operated in parks." If the interpreter believes tricycles do not create safety problems, she might be reluctant to include tricycles as a "vehicle." Also, does a child "operate" a tricycle, the term the statute uses for what one does with a vehicle in the park?

Some interesting structural arguments flow from the relationship of § 3's proviso (bicycles can be brought into the park but not ridden) to the potential interpretations of vehicle. Does § 3, as a whole, contemplate that bicycles are "vehicles"? If so, that would suggest that § 3's definition does not limit the term to "motor vehicles." If not, then the case for including tricycles in the statutory domain is much harder—unless one interprets the bicycle provision to regulate tricycles. What are the arguments pro and con?

Finally, think about the *regulatory regime* created by the Parks Safety Act. Is there a logical policy structure for that regime? Is the regulation of tricycles consistent with that logical policy structure (if such can be discerned)?

B. WHICH POTENTIAL MEANING IS MOST CONSISTENT WITH THE LAW'S SUBSTANTIVE COMMITMENTS?

Another kind of judicial inquiry is substantive: Which meaning is most consistent with the legal system's substantive commitments? This kind of inquiry *can* be built into the plain meaning inquiry: Would a typical speaker of the English language *reasonably* attribute this meaning to the statute, as applied to Helen Ro? So understood, one role for a legal system is to give *notice* to the public of the laws under which it must live. Another way to approach the question is to think about the substantive commitments of this particular statute—it's *purposes*. Because the Parks Safety Act announces its statutory purpose in § 1— public safety—we can use that expression of purpose in both our textual inquiry and also in our inquiry about what the law is committed to doing.

Either way, if the interpreter concludes that public safety in municipal parks would be advanced by banning tricycles, that is a powerful argument for concluding that tricycles are vehicles, especially if the interpreter finds that statutory term ambiguous (i.e., reasonably susceptible to either reading).

Broaden the interpreter's field of vision. Consider not just the purpose of the Parks Safety Act (i.e., safety), but also the purpose of municipal parks. (There may be a municipal ordinance along those lines.) In the abstract, what is the purpose of municipal parks? How should that cut in the Case of the Tricycle? Should it even be relevant?

Broaden the field of vision further. The Parks Safety Act is not just a regulatory statute; it is a criminal statute. A misdemeanor is more serious than a traffic offense, the criminal law most of us know from first-hand experience, but it is less serious than a felony. Under the Parks Safety Act, the offender can go to jail—just two days, but jail nonetheless.

American judges have long ruled that criminal statutes too "vague" to give citizens reasonable notice as to its applications, violate the Due Process Clause of the Fifth and Fourteenth Amendments. Today, judges rarely invalidate broad criminal laws as void for vagueness—but they enforce the norm through narrowing constructions of the statute. Judges place the burden of statutory clarity on the legislature—so if the statute is ambiguous, the defendant ought to win; the government wins only when a defendant, like Helen Ro, would reasonably have thought that the "no vehicles in the park" signs included her tricycle. (See Chapter 5, discussing this presumption, called the "rule of lenity"). This presumption of narrow construction of ambiguous criminal statutes also is a mechanism for limiting the discretion of police and prosecutors. Has the park gendarmerie allowed rampant trike riding all summer—only to lower the boom against Ro?

Finally, ought the age of the youthful offender make a difference? Most states bar criminal prosecutions of six-year-olds for (at least some) "crimes," but assume that the state in which Halcyon is located has no such restriction. Should a judge nonetheless be reluctant to apply such a statute to young Ro? What is the best *legal* justification for such reluctance?

One possible legal justification is the very old canon of statutory construction that judges ought to apply the "plain meaning" of a statute—unless the plain meaning yields an "absurd result." Would the application of a misdemeanor vehicle statute to a six-year-old tricyclist be "absurd"? What criteria should determine absurdity?

PROBLEM 1: APPLYING THE "NO VEHICLES IN THE PARK" STATUTE TO A RANGE OF MECHANISMS

Think about the law's plain meaning, prototypical versus extensive meaning, and the substantive commitments of the statute. Which of the following would you include in the statute's coverage and why?

(1) Motorcycles

(2) Motorscooters

(3) Bicycles

(4) Tricycles

(5) Roller Skates

(6) Baby Carriages

(7) The Truck That the Parks Gardener Uses Every Day to Maintain the Park

Applications (1) and (2) are gimmes. Why? Because all of the different kinds of "plain" meaning and the statute's purpose cut in the same direction. Section 3 clearly includes these mechanisms as vehicles; they fall within the core, prototypical meaning of "vehicle"; and they strongly violate the safety purpose announced in § 1. Application (3) is also pretty clear, as it is squarely covered by the proviso to § 3. The question, for the judge, is *where to draw the line* between coverage and noncoverage: Is it between (3) and (4)? (4) and (5)? Right before (6)? What about (7)? The truck falls squarely within the text of the statute. Does it gel with the purpose? Would its application be absurd?

So where would you draw the line? You do not know anything else about the Parks Safety Act, but you may do outside research on matters not related to the City of Halcyon or to the State. Jot down your answer in the margin. Your Instructor might give you other possible applications of the "no vehicles in the park" rule, so be ready to address other situations.

C. IS THERE JUDICIAL PRECEDENT RELEVANT TO THE INTERPRETIVE QUESTION?

Our legal system is one where authoritative decisions by a court are considered legally binding, and must be followed by lower court judges and by the rendering court itself. Thus, if the Bliss Supreme Court has interpreted a "no vehicles in the park" statute to exclude tricycles, that *precedent* is binding on local judges unless they can *distinguish* the precedent.

For example, the Supreme Court's precedent might have construed a different city's "no vehicles in the park" statute that simply barred vehicles from municipal parks, as § 2 of the Parks Safety Act does, but that had no analogue to § 3 of the Parks Safety Act (the definition of "vehicle" and the bicycle proviso). In that event, the City Attorney can argue that the two cases are different, and therefore that the precedent is distinguishable. Ro's attorney will argue that the two statutes are not significantly different, and that the precedent's reasoning would not have been affected by the existence of § 3 in the earlier statute. Obviously, the Judge would have to decide who is right about this, for she could be reversed if she gets this wrong.

On the other hand, the applicability of the precedent might be beyond reasonable debate. Halcyon's Council might have copied its Parks Safety Act word for word from an ordinance adopted by another city in the state. If the Bliss Supreme Court has construed the parent statute to exclude tricycles, it is very likely that that precedent cannot be meaningfully distinguished, and the Judge is obligated to follow it—even if she strongly believes that the Parks Safety Act has a plain meaning that includes tricycles.

Even the Bliss Supreme Court is obligated to follow its own precedent, unless the Justices can be persuaded that it should be *overruled*. Maybe the precedent was wrongly decided, or has created conflicts with other areas of the law, or has had otherwise intolerable effects. Generally, the party arguing for an overruling has a steep uphill battle and must make a strongly persuasive case before a state supreme court will go that far. Courts will consider questions like whether others have *relied* on its precedents in structuring their actions—and such reliance makes courts quite reluctant to overturn earlier decisions. But it is much easier to distinguish a precedent than overrule it. Ironically, the two might be related: a series of decisions distinguishing a precedent, with positive professional or public feedback, will often be a prelude to an overruling.

Moreover, precedent is relevant even when it is not "on point" with the new case before the court. Thus, if the Supreme Court has ruled that a statute like the Parks Safety Act does not apply to roller skates, that precedent is relevant to the trial judge's decision whether to exclude tricycles as well. How does she figure that out? She has to reason from the Supreme Court precedent.

The *holding* of the precedent can be expressed at several levels of generality. Most narrowly, the holding of the foregoing precedent is that roller skates are not vehicles for purposes of the Parks Safety Act. More broadly, the holding excludes roller skates and other mechanisms falling within the reasoning of the opinion. Assume the precedent reasoned that roller skates are excluded because the Parks Safety Act is only aimed at *motor* vehicles and roller skates are not motor vehicles. The lower court would likely find that reasoning open to generalization and so and would rule that tricycles are likewise excluded. But if the precedent reasoned that roller skates are excluded because they are not "operated" as § 1 says, then the Judge could depart from that reasoning, finding it not on point, unless she believed that tricycles are also not "operated."

As you can see, precedent is critical to the rule of law. Specifically, precedent as a matter of aspiration renders the law more *predictable*, more *objective* (by limiting the *discretion* of judges, prosecutors, and police officers), and more *neutral*. Even though our Judge once had a bad experience with tricycles and believes them to be a menace to public safety, she will nonetheless acquit Helen Ro if the state Supreme Court has already ruled that tricycles are excluded or that roller skates are excluded because they are not motorized.

The discussion thus far involves the way *stare decisis* constrains judges *ex post*, namely, after the precedent has been handed down. But it can also constrain judges *ex ante*, namely, before any precedent is handed down. Assume that the Case of the Tricycle is the Bliss Supreme Court's first encounter with a statute like the Parks Safety Act; there is no previous roller skate decision. When the Justices decide the tricycle case, they realize that anything they write will then be binding on lower courts and on their own subsequent decisions. At the very least, this will motivate the Justices to settle on a principle for deciding the case that they think will "hold up" well over time. If the Court is uncertain how broadly to read § 3's definition of vehicle, the Justices are more likely to write a narrow opinion, focusing on the "operating" language of § 1. If the Court is certain that the purpose of the Parks Safety Act is public safety and wants to head off overenforcement of the law, then the Justices will write a broader opinion, one that would head off tricycle arrests like that of Helen Ro.

Assume, for the remainder of this chapter, that the Judge in Helen Ro's case rules that tricycles are covered by the Parks Safety Act. The Judge lectures the defendant on the importance of following the law to the bewildered defendant; remember, the defendant is only six years old.

In the end, the Judge imposes a fine of 50 cents and no jail time for the defendant, who responds with relief and promises to pay the fine the next time she receives her allowance.

2. HOW LEGISLATORS THINK ABOUT STATUTES

Legislators think about statutes much differently than judges do. First, legislators set the agenda: statutes for them are plans for solving general problems. No judge can announce tomorrow that he or she is about to solve the health care crisis with a general proposal (judges decide cases brought to them by litigants). As a result, legislators are more active and instrumental than judges in their approach to statutes: What problem are we trying to solve? How can we solve the problem at a reasonable cost? Does the solution reflect the interests of the citizens I represent?

Second, legislators operate in a very different institution. No judge has to obtain the agreement of 535 persons to decide a case. Because legislators must obtain the consent of many members (535 in the case of the Congress), they openly seek compromise. Without compromise, legislation is impossible. Legislators' strategy is thus predictable: they seek to attract wavering votes, without alienating core supporters.

Third, legislators act on behalf of other persons—they *represent* the public. No judge opens an opinion by thanking his constituency. By contrast, legislators are openly partisan: the member from the Fifth District of Texas "lives and breathes" the Fifth District of Texas. When in doubt about how their constituents will vote, legislators often identify the public interest with their party interest or with that of vocal interest groups.

In short, because of their electoral connection and the structure of the legislative process, legislators behave very differently from judges, especially those judges who are not elected and do not have to run for reelection. Consider these features in greater detail, which we shall illustrate by reference to the process by which our "no vehicles in the park" statute was debated and enacted.

In our hypothetical Halcyon City Council, the legislative process involves a number of steps, each of which might kill a proposal. Although the U.S. Congress and state legislatures have more *veto* points, our little Council, with just 15 members, has most of the major ones:

- **Committee deliberation:** New bills are typically referred to legislative committees, which often research the proposals, holding hearings on them and amending them; the chair or a committee majority can bottle up a bill in committee indefinitely.

- **Scheduling:** Even if a bill is reported out to the whole legislative body favorably by a committee, it still needs to be placed on the legislative calendar and, usually, needs to be expedited ahead of low-interest bills (in our little legislature, the Council Chair does the scheduling, based on consensus within the Council).

- **Filibuster:** Somewhat unusual in city councils but a central feature of the U.S. Senate, the filibuster allows a determined legislative minority to block a bill that does not have supermajority support (60 votes in the U.S. Senate, 10 votes in the Halcyon City Council).

- **Amendment and Voting:** Even if a bill gets out of committee, is scheduled so that it gets fair consideration, and does not generate an unbreakable filibuster, a bill is still subject to amendments that might weaken it or create ambiguity and, ultimately, subject to an up-or-down vote that might kill it.

- **[Bicameral Approval:** The U.S. Congress and all but one state legislature require that any legislation be passed in the same form by both chambers of a bicameral legislature; this process produces several more choke points but is rarely replicated in city councils. Like the New York City Council, Halcyon's City Council is unicameral.]

- **Executive Veto:** If the chief executive (President, governor, mayor) vetoes a bill, it can only become law if the legislature passes it again by a two-thirds supermajority; if supporters cannot muster such a supermajority (10 of 15 Council members in our case), they can change the bill to meet the chief executive's objections and then repass the bill.

This is the process followed by the Halcyon City Council in the abstract—now see how it plays out in connection with the regulation of vehicles in municipal parks.

The impetus for the Parks Safety Act was a serious accident in Halcyon's primary municipal park: a youth driving a motorcycle while high on LSD ran over an elderly citizen; although the victim was taken to a hospital and treated, he died of his injuries two days later. This was the tenth accident involving a motorcycle or a motor scooter in one of the municipal parks in the last five years, but it was the first fatality. (In that same time period, there were one serious accident involving the collision of a bicycle and an elderly park user and one other minor accident where a child on roller skates knocked over an elderly park user.)

In the immediate wake of the accident, Council Member Mia Kim, who also chairs the Council's Judiciary Committee, introduced a proposed Parks Safety Act in the Council. The Kim Bill was very simple, having just one provision:

> No vehicles of any kind shall be allowed in any municipal park. Any person who brings or drives a vehicle into one of these parks shall be guilty of a misdemeanor, which may be punished by a fine not exceeding $500.

The bill was referred to Kim's Judiciary Committee, which immediately held a public hearing, where several officials and experts were called to testify; several dozen citizens attended, with fifteen of them delivering public statements.

One member of the committee and a few witnesses objected that the bill was not "strong" enough to deal with the escalating public problem. In response, Chair Kim agreed to strengthen the penalties; the bill reported by the committee read:

> No vehicles of any kind shall be allowed in any municipal park. Any person who brings or drives a vehicle into one of these parks shall be guilty of a misdemeanor, which may be punished by a fine not exceeding $500 or by a two-day incarceration in the municipal jail, or both.

The committee members unanimously voted for it, and reported the bill to the Council. The two-page Committee Report said this: "The Parks Safety Act is needed to eliminate the danger that motorcycles and other vehicles pose to public safety, especially to children and the elderly."

The Council Chair scheduled the Kim Bill for an expeditious floor debate; Judiciary Chair Mia Kim managed the bill. (A bill manager answers questions and generally runs the debate because typically bill managers have more knowledge than other members about the bill's contents; committee chairs are typically bill managers). During the debate, Council Member Ryan Solomon raised a series of objections to the bill. One objection yielded the following colloquy:

> SOLOMON: It is a good idea to stop the havoc that motorcyclists have been imposing on our city's citizens as they pass time in our parks—but this bill sweeps too far. As everyone knows, I sell and fix bicycles at a store just minutes from Ruth Park. Many of my customers pedal their bikes through the park right after they purchase them from me. Will this bill subject these excellent citizens to arrest because they are operating a "vehicle" in the park? I'd say that's a fair reading of the bill's language—and for that reason I am opposed to the bill.

CHAIR KIM: May I interrupt the Member's most excellent speech with a clarification?

SOLOMON: Sure.

CHAIR KIM: The proposed bill only covers "vehicles," which everyone knows are limited to "motor vehicles." So my bill says nothing about bicycles.

SOLOMON: I am not so sure. My beloved Mother is a genius; she speaks more than a dozen languages and knows more than anyone else about words. She told me: "Ryan, if this lady's bill gets through this will ruin your business. I tell you, Ryan, *vehicle* can be anything that conveys things from one place to another. Look it up if you don't believe me, Ryan, look it up."

So I did look it up, and—no surprise to me—my Mother with the brains of Chomsky was right. That word can mean a lot of different mechanisms, and it sure includes bicycles.

CHAIR KIM: Alright, I get your point. We should make this clear. I shall offer an amendment. * * *

Solomon's was the only serious objection to the bill. The next day, Chair Kim offered to amend the committee's bill by designating the previous language as § 1 of the bill and adding a new § 2:

"Vehicle" for purposes of this law means any motorized mechanism for conveying a person from one place to another, including motorcycles, automobiles, trucks, and motor scooters.

By voice vote, the Council agreed to this amendment. CM Solomon pronounced himself satisfied, and the Kim Bill itself passed by a voice vote, with no recorded dissent.

Mayor Don Patron, however, vetoed the Kim measure. In his veto message, the Mayor objected:

The city is faced with a major safety problem, and this bill simply does not go far enough to address it. For one thing, it needs stiffer penalties—at least 30 days in jail ought to be the maximum, rather than just two days—and for another thing it needs to cover more vehicles. Motor vehicles are *not* the only vehicular threat in our city's parks. What about non-motorized vehicles that can hurt people because they can go fast? So a youth on a skateboard is just as dangerous as one on a motorscooter. Why should the skateboard kid get off—he is probably a bigger threat to public safety than the cyclist.

[The mayor had several smaller objections, and a suggestion that the proposed law include a preamble forthrightly stating its purpose.]

I VETO the proposed Park Safety Act and RETURN it to the Council to revise in light of my objections.

The Mayor's veto created quite a stir in Halcyon. In an editorial, the *New Halcyon Times* archly pronounced the original bill just fine. The editorial argued: "If the Mayor had his way, kids riding their tricycles and parents pushing baby carriages could be hauled into criminal court. This is ridiculous. The Council should override the Mayor's wrongheaded veto."

Believing they did not have the needed 10 votes, however, Chair Kim and her Committee did not try to override the veto. Instead, they put forth a revised Parks Safety Act, which provided as follows:

Sec. 1. The Council finds that vehicles create safety problems when they are operated in parks and further finds that the best solution is to ban any and all vehicles from all municipal parks.

Sec. 2. No vehicles of any kind shall be allowed in any municipal park. Any person who brings or drives a vehicle into one of these parks shall be guilty of a misdemeanor, which may be punished by a fine not exceeding $500 or by a two-day incarceration in the municipal jail, or both.

Sec. 3. "Vehicle" for purposes of this law means any mechanism for conveying a person from one place to another, including motorcycles, automobiles, trucks, and motor scooters.

In an op-ed in the *New Halcyon Times,* the Mayor opined that the revised bill is "much better, more comprehensive" and that he would consider signing it.

Not everyone was happy, however. Council Member Ryan Solomon opposed the revised bill during floor debate, on the ground that it might cover bicycles. He felt so strongly that he announced he would filibuster the bill, namely, by talking it to death and thereby preventing it from going to a vote. Under the Council's standing rules, a filibuster could only be terminated upon a vote of ten of the fifteen Council Members. Upon motion of Chair Kim, only nine Members voted to cut off Solomon's talkathon; Solomon and three other Members voted against the motion, and two Members were absent.

After further consultation with Solomon and other colleagues, Kim revised the bill once again, adding the following proviso at the end of § 3: "*Provided that*, bicycles shall be allowed in the park, so long as they are being pushed or carried and not ridden." She did not explain the point of the proviso, but Solomon announced on the floor that he was satisfied: "I would prefer a complete exclusion for bicycles, but I can live with this." Solomon withdrew his objections, and the bill was passed by a voice vote, with no recorded dissent.

The drama had not quite ended, however, for Mayor Patron had announced his opposition to the revised bill:

> My legal advisers assure me that the revised bill, with the new proviso protecting bicycles, will have the effect of exempting almost any non-motorized vehicle from the coverage of this statute. For the reasons stated in my earlier veto statement, I find this unacceptable. The City needs the strongest possible response to the problem of speedy vehicles that injure pedestrians in our parks.

The bill might have been doomed by this opposition, but Kim's Judiciary Committee immediately reported a separate bill to create another new misdemeanor for "creating a danger to the public" in any municipal space. The proposed the Municipal Safety Act was passed two days after the Council passed the Parks Safety Act. With no further comment, Mayor Patron signed both the Municipal Safety Act and the Parks Safety Act into law.

Consider some of the lessons of the foregoing thought experiment, the legislative history behind our hypothetical Parks Safety Act of 1980. First, unlike the judges discussed earlier, the legislators here are openly instrumental: they have policy goals, and they defend their stances by reference to the policy consequences of different versions of the bill. Please note that many scholars and citizens believe that judges are instrumental as well, but our point is that legislators believe it their job to be openly instrumental because this is what their constituents demand. A judge who issued an opinion exempting tricycles on the ground that the judge thought it unwise to include them in a criminal sanction would be criticized as "injudicious," but a legislator who proposed a statutory exemption for the same reason would be praised as "statesmanlike."

Second, legislators are more openly strategic than judges are, because legislators typically have to obtain the agreement of many others. *Strategic* actors have preferences about what policy or result they prefer, but in seeking to optimize their preferences strategic actors take into account the preferences of others who might block or undermine their results. Thus, Judiciary Committee Chair Kim preferred a simple bill that set a broad standard ("no vehicles in the park") and left a lot of discretion to police, prosecutors, and judges to fill in the details. But to secure the support of Council Member Solomon, she was willing to specify "motorized vehicles" as the sole object of her bill—and then to head off a mayoral veto she was willing to add the Bicycle Proviso *and* to sponsor the Municipal Safety Act. To the extent judges act strategically (on panels to gain votes of other judges, for example), they openly reject such a characterization, and their strategic actions are largely opaque, hidden from view.

Once it became clear that some kind of law was likely to be enacted, Council Member Solomon faced three possible outcomes, in order of his preference:

#1. The Parks Safety Act covers only "motorized vehicles," and so not bicycles at all.

#2. The Parks Safety Act covers all "vehicles" but has the Bicycle Proviso that allows bikes to be carried or walked across the parks.

#3. The Parks Safety Act covers all "vehicles," as defined in § 3.

Although Solomon preferred #1, he ought, rationally, to be willing to settle for #2 if he believed that #3 would pass instead. Option #2 was not Solomon's preferred option, but under these strategic conditions it was preference-maximizing for him to support the bill with the proviso.

As these examples illustrate, strategic behavior often results in *compromises* and *logrolls*. A "compromise" is collective action where each side gives up some part of what it would optimally like to have, in return for securing collective action such as the enactment of a statute. The legislative history of the Parks Safety Act contains a number of compromises, including Kim's willingness to strengthen the initial bill in an effort to assuage citizen concerns, to add language narrowing the bill to end Solomon's filibuster, and to revise the bill to avoid a mayoral veto.

Note our third lesson: the more veto points in the legislative process, the more compromises sponsors would expect to make, especially if veto points allow a determined minority (Solomon and the Mayor) to stop legislation that the majority clearly wants. So a governance structure where there is no filibuster ought to yield fewer compromises than a structure like the Halcyon City Council or the U.S. Senate.

A "logroll" is collective action where one person or group exchanges its support for a proposal in return for another person or group's agreement to support its own preferred proposal. In the foregoing legislative history, Mayor Patron and Judiciary Committee Chair Kim were engaged in a logroll: Patron got a broad misdemeanor law he and his law-and-order administration could use to enhance public safety, and Kim got a "no vehicles in the park" law that left room for kids and parents to bring at least some non-motorized mechanisms into the park.

Or did she? If there is a *legislative* compromise, there is always a danger that *judges* will not enforce it. Consider the next problem.

PROBLEM 2: RETURN TO THE CASE OF THE TRICYCLE

Now assume that you are Helen Ro's attorney. As we posited at the end of § 1, assume that the Judge interprets the Parks Safety Act to include tricycles. You, as the defendant's counsel, have text-based arguments for your appeal of this judgment against the youthful offender, but you also want to integrate the legislative history into your argument. What are your best arguments, based on the legislative history that we just set out? In thinking about this question, consider whether you think that Kim wanted the bill to cover tricycles? Would Solomon's views be different?

Step back further. Assume that there are good arguments for the proposition that the ultimate legislative compromise entailed the exclusion of tricycles from regulated "vehicles." Is this a compromise that judges should be enforcing if they do not detect it from the plain language of the statute? Say the Parks Safety Act is ambiguous: Should the legislative history demonstrating a compromise be admissible to break the tie, and decide the case for the defendant? If the Council Members were united in believing that tricycles should not be covered, shouldn't the legislative branch's views govern? Should Mayor Patron's views be considered, even though he opposed the bill, because his support was necessary to its passage?

3. HOW ADMINISTRATORS THINK ABOUT STATUTES

Like the first chapter in a novel or the mouth of a river, the enactment of a statute is just a beginning—and for landmark statutes the beginning of a long story (like a Tolstoy novel or the Mississippi River). Most of the story is worked out *not* by judges, but by those implementing the statute. The implementers of the Parks Safety Act, like most criminal statutes, are law enforcement officials, prosecutors, juries, sentencing judges, jailers, and parole and probation officers. For most civil statutes and some criminal ones, implementation occurs under the auspices of a special administrative agency or commission to which the legislature delegates lawmaking as well as law-enforcing authority.

The modern administrative state features a wide array of statutory implementers; these officials are vastly more numerous than judges and their staffs, as well as legislators and their staffs, put together. For most of us, what these administrators tell us to do is the operative law of the land. So how do implementers think about statutes?

First, like legislators and unlike judges, implementers are open about wanting their policies to work. Administrators execute the law and thus are part of the "executive" department of the government structure. They may be appointed to be neutral ("independent") parties or may be closer to policy advisors feeling themselves bound to follow the political will of the Mayor or Governor or President. Like judges and unlike legislators, administrative implementers do not create the public policy or statutory purpose they are implementing (although they frequently have informal roles in advising or lobbying legislators during the statute-making process). Instead, administrators start with the policy or purpose chosen by legislators, as well as the limits those legislators have placed on how far our polity is willing to go to implement the policy or purpose. For example, the legislature identifies public safety as the purpose of the Parks Safety Act—but various compromises in the legislation left room for further accidents. If you believe tricycles are not "vehicles" for purposes of the ordinance, that is a compromise allowing children recreational opportunities, but at some risk to elderly users of the parks. Like judges, administrative officials are supposed to enforce the compromises and deals reached in the legislature.

Unlike judges, administrative implementers, especially agencies, usually have a lot of discretion and some resources to mold the statutory scheme, within the parameters set by the legislature. For the most obvious example, administrators have a lot of room to under-enforce statutory schemes. Even if the Halcyon City Council included tricycles in the Parks Safety Act's regulatory scheme, the police or the prosecutors might choose, for institutional or even policy reasons, not to enforce that prohibition or to enforce it rarely. They have less discretion to over-enforce the Parks Safety Act, so if tricycles are not vehicles for purposes of the Parks Safety Act, the police and prosecutors do not have discretion to apply the statute to tricycles.

On the other hand, administrators, within budget constraints, have the discretion to give high priority to certain statutory schemes. If the Halcyon Police Department wanted to give motor vehicle abatement high priority, it has many options at its disposal—postings in the park, public education campaigns, a report-violators hotline, increased police surveillance, immediate police response to reported incidents, and swift prosecution and sentencing of offenders. If within the limits of the law, the police can be even more creative, for example, impounding an offender's motor scooter as "evidence" pending trial in the case and, perhaps, bargaining with the offender's parents to forfeit the motor scooter in return for no jail time.

Second, like legislators and unlike judges, administrators tend to choose the enforcement options they believe will be the most effective. Judges have a more limited array of options—deciding a single case brought to them by others—for dealing with statutory issues. To implement the Parks Safety Act, police might follow a "broken windows" policy of jumping on every infraction and subjecting citizens to the embarrassment of a misdemeanor—or the police might follow a "sliding scale" policy, enforcing the Park Safety Act against repeat offenders or park users who are being "disruptive"—or the police might just escort violators and their "vehicles" out of the park, without arresting anyone. As you can imagine, these are radically different strategies for implementing the Parks Safety Act, yet they are all available to the police. Which mix of policies the administrators choose depends on a number of soft variables, such as how pressing the vehicles problem is compared to other problems, how many officers are available and how much time they have for this, and their judgment as to the efficacy of different strategies in their community.

Like legislators, and less like judges, administrators may be highly attuned to "political" reactions to their implementation priorities. If they are political appointees, they may lose their jobs if their policies backfire and anger enough citizens. Thus, you can be sure that the Halcyon Police Department will not arrest another six-year-old minor for riding her tricycle through the park if the Department takes a lot of community heat for the Case of Helen Ro. Even if the Council were unable to amend the Parks Safety Act, the Police Department would be sensitive to community revulsion at the Case of the Tricycle, and would not want to antagonize powerful legislators like Mia Kim, who also serves on the Appropriations Committee of the Council. Moreover, the District Attorney is an elected official—and even if the police were gung ho against tricycles, the prosecutor would probably be loathe to indict youthful "offenders" given the public relations disaster such prosecutions would bring. And so on.

Third, although politically appointed administrators are often openly partisan, civil servants doing a vast amount of administrative work are often protected from political dismissals. As a result, they value nonpartisanship and government service. Civil servants, and at least some political appointees, tend to see themselves as experts in a particular area and as serving the "public interest." All administrators have a tendency to invoke expertise to justify their decisions, even when those decisions are in fact motivated by political concerns.

A.　DIVERSITY IN INSTITUTIONAL IMPLEMENTATION OF STATUTES

One of the most striking contrasts among the judicial, legislative, and executive branches of government (even local government such as Halcyon) is that the administrative branch can assume a wide array of institutional forms, while the judicial and legislative branches at all levels of American governance are structurally very similar. Thus, it is virtually impossible to present a stylized, and easily generalizable, picture of administration in this country. The structure of implementation differs from statute to statute—and structure makes a huge difference.

Consider how the implementational structure is distinctive for criminal statutes such as the "no vehicles in the park" ordinance. The Police Department dominates implementation. Notwithstanding many tensions, especially in the past, between police departments and some segments of the law-abiding community, today's police department is likely to *reflect* the community, in all its diversity. (Gone are the days when police departments were typically all-white and excluded women and gay people from service.) Police work with the community—as they must, given limited resources, which during budget crunches are severe.

Police spend only a small portion of their time arresting people or even investigating murders and such (the dramatic activities that dominate media and entertainment images of the police). Most of what the police do to enforce the law is to educate the community, warn people, break up private disputes, answer calls for help, and so forth. By now, you understand that the arrest of Helen Ro, tricycular offender, is the sort of event that would only occur in a law professor's hypothetical or a poorly conceived television comedy. If the police really thought tricycles were excluded from parks under the Parks Safety Act, they would, at most, post signs to that effect, hold community meetings to educate parents, and politely escort youngsters and their babysitters to nearby playgrounds or other spots where trike riding is permitted.

If an oddball police officer actually arrested Ro and an overly zealous prosecutor actually pursued the misdemeanor charges against the youthful offender, Ro's final line of defense would be a jury. For any offense for which she can go to jail, Ro has a Sixth Amendment right to a jury trial. (The smart prosecutor would find an offense for which she could not go to jail; then, there is no federal constitutional jury trial right.) A jury drawn from the community is most unlikely to convict her. Even if the judge told the jury that, as a matter of law, riding a tricycle in the park falls within the Parks Safety Act's prohibition, the jury would probably *nullify* the law in this case, because at least some jurors would be unwilling to apply the criminal sanction to such behavior by a child.

In a nutshell, the foregoing narrative describes the structure of implementation for criminal laws, but not most other kinds of statutes. The obvious implication of this structure is *libertarian*: the many layers of procedural protection protect the criminal defendant against hasty or erroneous determinations of culpability. Stated another way, the criminal sanction cannot formally be imposed upon Helen Ro or any other defendant unless three different kinds of implementers exercise their discretion to condemn her conduct criminally—the trained police officers, lawyers serving in the prosecutor's office, and ordinary community members serving on the jury. Informally, of course, the police and the prosecutors have other ways of exercising power, but the criminal sanction in our society is one that is not lightly imposed.

The larger lesson is that the *design* of the implementational structure makes a big difference for the success or precise implementational biases for a statutory purpose. One might argue that the criminal law and its accompanying structure (much of which is constitutionally required) are best suited for regulating conduct that is dangerous to the community and enjoys the moral condemnation of citizens. Conduct that is reckless in its disregard for other people's safety and that risks grave harm to third parties is easiest to condemn and might be the best candidate for application of the criminal sanction. Driving a motorcycle through a park filled with children and elderly persons is the kind of reckless conduct that might successfully be criminalized. In contrast, riding a tricycle in a park filled with other children is *not* the kind of inherently reckless and risky behavior that is sensibly regulated through the structure of the criminal justice system.

PROBLEM 3: LEGISLATIVE DESIGN OF AN OPTIMAL ADMINISTRATIVE STRUCTURE

Return to the very beginning—the date of the fatal motorcycle accident but before the Council responded with the Kim Bill and ultimately the Parks Safety Act. According to our earlier account, Mia Kim and her allies immediately seized upon the criminal law to structure their legislative response to the vehicles-in-the-park problem. In retrospect, that might not have been the best approach, as defensible as it might be for motorcycles.

Judiciary Committee Chair Kim and the Halcyon City Council could have chosen other regulatory structures for their governmental response to park safety. Consider a few.

First, the Council could easily have opted for a regime modeled on *traffic offenses*, which are, technically, criminal offenses, but very minor ones without jury trial rights. Police officers could issue citations to offenders, who would be required to pay a standard fine, with no jail time and little of the drama accompanying Helen Ro's arrest and trial. If the recipient disputed the citation, she or he could show up at traffic court and secure a ruling by the traffic judge.

Second, the Council could have created a new *civil standard*, "no vehicles in the parks," that could then be applied by existing regulatory bodies, including the Bliss Department of Motor Vehicles (e.g., the driver's license of an offending motorist could be suspended or revoked) and the state judges administering the common law system of tort liability (e.g., violation of the no-vehicles-in-the-park standard would be culpable per se for any injuries caused by operation of vehicles in parks).

Third, the Council could have created a *new regulatory body*, like a Recreation & Parks Commission, to devise a set of standards to improve park safety, at a reasonable cost to the community. (Cost includes opportunity cost, such as the loss of recreational opportunities by youth such as Helen Ro.)

You are a member of the Council's Judiciary Committee, and an ally of its Chair, Mia Kim. She asks you for your views on what institutional design ought to be the starting point for the committee's deliberations? How would you respond to her? You are certainly *not* limited to the various options described above. Think creatively.

B. DELEGATION OF LAWMAKING AUTHORITY TO AGENCIES AND COMMISSIONS

Pick up where Problem 3 left off and think about how the statutory scheme could have been implemented with civil administrative law, rather than criminal law. Unless state law says otherwise, the Council has discretion to enact a law that substantively just says that "no vehicles of any kind shall be allowed in any municipal park" and that delegates *both* legislative standard-setting *and* judicial adjudication to an agency or commission.

You might be surprised to know that American legislatures at the federal, state, and local level can *delegate* lawmaking authority to agencies and commissions, subject to a loosely enforced constitutional requirement that the delegation be accompanied by a legislatively announced policy, purpose, or standard (such as park safety, the standard announced by the Parks Safety Act). In the modern administrative state, most of the rules and decisions affecting people's rights are handed down by agencies and not by courts.

Take federal income tax law, for example. When you fill out your tax forms each year, you probably do not consult the Internal Revenue Code, enacted by Congress. And it is highly unlikely that you do a search for judicial opinions construing the tax code. Instead, what guides you the most are the instructions issued by the Internal Revenue Service (IRS). If there are ambiguities in the form and the instructions, you are much more likely to call the IRS Hotline or consult the IRS's regulations than read the statute or search for judicial opinions. Congress has delegated authority to make law and interpret the law (including the IRS's own regulations as well as the statute). From the taxpayer's perspective, income tax "law" is primarily text written and promulgated by the IRS, not by Congress, and certainly not by the courts. As an example from another context, the Congress set out the broad outlines for federal environmental law in the Clean Air Act and the Clean Water Act, but the actual details of what the law requires of states and private entities has been developed through rules and regulations issued by the federal agency, the Environmental Protection Agency (EPA). The same goes for Medicare and Medicaid (implemented by the Department of Health and Human Services) and so on and so on across the statutory landscape.

Why so much delegation of lawmaking authority to agencies? The main reason is that it is practically necessary. Not only are expert-filled agencies capable of filling in the details of legislation, but a rational legislature needs agencies to do this. Any important statute, such as the Parks Safety Act or the Internal Revenue Code, will be called upon to address facts and issues that did not occur to legislators drafting the statute. The process by which judges, in case-by-case elaboration, identify which mechanisms are vehicles and which are not takes too long and provides citizens with too little guidance—while agencies can announce a comprehensive list soon after the statute is adopted, and they can update that list as administrators learn more about the operation of the statutory scheme in the world.

Additionally, delegation takes some heat off of legislators, shifting it to administrators. Legislators hate making hard choices, because hard choices tend to anger one or more groups that legislators want to have on their side. Indeed, delegation might be useful to keep the enacting coalition from fracturing in the short term. It is for this reason that Judiciary Committee Chair Kim would be attracted to a delegation solution to the problem of vehicles in the park. There was a deep tension within her coalition: old people are vulnerable to injuries from bikes and trikes as well as motor scooters and motorcycles, while parents want their children to operate bikes and trikes in the park. Kim can try to avoid conflict with both groups by leaving detail to the administrative process. As a general matter, delegation can make legislation easier to secure, because it allows the hardest, most politically divisive issues to be postponed until after the statute has been enacted.

Finally, delegation may yield better and more legitimate legislation. We make this point more tentatively; many learned scholars believe that delegation of lawmaking authority undermines the legitimacy of statutes, because it creates a greater gulf between the electoral accountability of legislators and the law that citizens must obey. These scholars fear what is indeed possible: lawmaking by faceless, nameless bureaucrats. On the other hand, lawmaking by agencies may be relatively more accountable and expert than if a similar task were undertaken by Congress. Legislators often have no expertise to fill in specific details and they are often not held accountable for those details. Agencies making rules through public procedures (called "notice and comment") *are* accountable for specific details of statutory policy, Notice and comment means that the affected parties have a chance to voice their opinions on matters of specifics. Moreover, there are checks on the administrative process that may increase accountability. If agencies do something to upset a large electorate, their (elected) boss (the President, Governor or Mayor) will hear about it and do something about it. Agencies are also checked by legislatures, which exercise oversight and funding. Finally, as we will see, at least some of the time, agencies' actions are subject to judicial review to avoid arbitrary actions. Notwithstanding this last point, agencies do enjoy a fair amount of discretion when they promulgate rules to implement broadly phrased statutes such as the Parks Safety Act of 1980. Typically, however, they must, however, articulate reasons for the actions they take. Think about how that process works.

PROBLEM 4: INTERPRETATION OF STATUTES BY ADMINISTRATORS

The Halcyon City Council adopts the Parks Safety Act in the form reproduced at the beginning of this chapter, with the three sections (and including the Bicycle Proviso). But the Council also includes a fourth section that (1) creates a Recreation & Parks Commission whose members are appointed in staggered terms by the Mayor, with confirmation by the Council; (2) delegates to the Park Commission the authority to adopt "legislative rules" identifying "vehicles" that violate the Park Safety Act and a recommended schedule of penalties for different kinds of violations; and (3) specifies the procedures the Parks Commission must follow before promulgating rules that have the force of law. Thus, the Parks Commission starts by issuing a public notice of proposed rulemaking, with the text of the proposed rule(s) and a detailed justification for such rule(s); the public has an opportunity to submit comments which are publicly available for anyone's examination; and the Parks Commission must consider all comments and decide whether to issue a rule, either as proposed or with revisions. If the Commission does decide to issue the rule in final form, it must explain why it rejected serious criticisms or alternatives propounded by objectors.

Now think about how the rulemaking process might work with regard to the issue we have been exploring: What is a "vehicle" barred from municipal parks by § 2 of the Parks Safety Act? Consider this exercise in three analytical steps.

To begin with, you are the Chair of the Commission charged with developing a rule telling the public what is allowed and what is not. Motorized vehicles are, for the most part, easy calls, because the statute clearly includes them as vehicles, and they represent clear safety risks that the statute was enacted to minimize. Automobiles, motorcycles, and motor scooters are clearly covered by the Parks Safety Act. And bicycles are covered by the proviso in § 3. But how about tricycles? Skateboards? Roller skates? Baby carriages? Think through the statutory scheme and draft a short Proposed Rule Defining "Vehicles" for Purposes of the Parks Safety Act.

Assume, further, that the American Association of Retired Persons (AARP), a group representing senior citizens, has presented the following evidence to your Commission. In a survey of fifteen American cities about the size of Halcyon, the AARP tabulates the number of minor, significant, and fatal accidents reported for users of public parks involving mechanisms that might be considered "vehicles." Fatal accidents all involved motor vehicles, as did most of the significant accidents. Bicycles caused more accidents overall than any motorized vehicle, but tricycles were next highest for minor accidents. According to the report, 180 persons, most of them over the age of 65, were hospitalized because of accidents involving tricycles in parks found in those fifteen cities in the last five years. The AARP urges the Commission to include tricycles in its list of "vehicles."

How does the AARP Report affect your thinking about the tricycle issue? How should the Commission respond in its Report on the Final Rule? As you answer this question, do not forget that the City Council is watching your actions and may intervene if its legislators dislike your proposal. Your boss (the Mayor) also can fire you if you embarrass him or his administration. Consider in this context whether there is anything in the legislative history of the Act that would affect the administrators' decisions? Consider also that there may be judicial review of your answer. Does that make a difference? Continue thinking about this Problem as you read the final section of this chapter.

C. JUDICIAL REVIEW OF ADMINISTRATIVE INTERPRETATION AND IMPLEMENTATION

Most statutes are implemented by agencies—and agencies either formally make legal rules or implement statutes so creatively that they are making law in effect. But agencies make or implement law *in the shadow of judicial review*. That is, agencies realize that their discretion to make law is limited by the ability and willingness of judges not to veto their decisions. Hence, agencies need to understand "how judges think about statutes," the rules explored in Section 1.

Section 5 of our newest version of the Parks Safety Act provides for judicial review of final agency rules. The statute directs judges to *reject* any commission rule where (a) the Parks Commission does not follow the procedures mandated by § 4; (b) the Parks Commission rule is not supported by "substantial evidence" in the record, including evidence placed in the record by the Parks Commission; or (c) the Parks Commission rule is "contrary to law," namely, it reflects an incorrect legal interpretation of the Parks Safety Act.

So in the end, is it judges who ultimately call all the shots? No, for this reason: federal, state, and local judges usually *defer* to statutory interpretations by the agency charged with enforcing the statute. "Deference" means that judges will sometimes go along with agency-based interpretations that are different from those that judges would have reached on their own. Why would judges defer?

Judges are particularly prone to defer to agency interpretations when the analytical tools in the judge's interpretive toolkit—like plain meaning, statutory purpose and legislative history (§ 1)—do not yield clear answers to the judge. If the statute is "ambiguous," there is no clear "law" to apply, and any answer is going to have to rest upon a policy or even a political judgment. Agencies or commissions are in a better position to make such policy judgments, for reasons of either legitimacy or expertise. Agency interpretations of ambiguous statutes might be entitled to greater respect when the agency is more responsive to democratic pressures than judges are, or when the agency's expertise renders it a more reliable institution to make the consequentialist judgments needed to carry out the statutory purpose(s).

Additionally, judges will be more willing to defer to agency interpretations that have generated reliance interests on the part of the regulated public. If an agency has long interpreted the statute in a certain way, without disruption, courts are loathe to disturb that rule, especially when private parties have structured transactions or invested resources based upon that understanding of what the law requires. For example, if the Parks Commission issues a Final Rule allowing tricycles to be operated in the parks, and then creates special "trike paths" for youngsters, a judge years later will be more reluctant to reverse the agency's interpretation.

Are there other reasons judges might defer to agency statutory interpretations? Is there a danger that too much deference will undermine the judicial role of announcing what "the law" requires?

Following up on Problem 4, assume that the Parks Commission's Final Rule *includes* tricycles as regulated "vehicles," primarily because the AARP study persuades the Commission that tricycles are a sufficiently serious threat to public safety. If you were a judge, would you *agree* with the Commission's interpretation? Would you *defer* to it? Or would you *disagree and overrule* the agency interpretation? Compare your answer to this question, with the answer you gave at the beginning of the chapter, in response to Problem 1.

PART 1

INTRODUCTION TO CONGRESS, AGENCIES, AND COURTS

■ ■ ■

The United States Constitution creates three major federal institutions: the Congress, the Presidency, and the Supreme Court. In this Part, we will look at each of these bodies to better acquaint you with the ways in which Congress creates, the President executes, and the Supreme Court interprets laws. There are of course other critically important institutional actors. The lower courts, both state and federal, interpret federal law every day, too. And the states' central role in our constitutional structure should be clear. For purposes of this introductory Part, however, we focus on Congress, the Presidency, and the Supreme Court. We introduce the other players in future chapters.

We will consider these institutions from three perspectives:

- **formal lines**—the constitutional division of powers as "legislative," "executive," and "judicial";
- **functional competencies and capacities**—the relative capabilities of institutions, given their size, their participants, and their rules; and
- **electoral constituencies**—the audiences to whom the institutions speak and that provide an incentive for action for those seeking reelection.

The Congress. This chapter introduces you to some very basic rules. We begin with a case study of how Congress legislates, specifically how the Congress came to pass the prohibition of workplace sex discrimination in the Civil Rights Act of 1964. We then turn to consider Congress's rules—how Congress makes decisions and each of the hurdles a bill faces before it becomes a law. Just as there are rules of criminal and civil procedure, there are rules of congressional procedure. Next, we consider structural limits on Congress's authority and, in particular, Congress's ability to control the Presidency through mechanisms such as the legislative veto and the line-item veto. Finally, we consider the impact of gridlock, politics, and the modern filibuster on legislative action.

The President and Agencies. We next turn to the Executive branch. The President has the constitutional duty to faithfully execute the laws enacted by Congress. Congress creates agencies to assist the

President in executing those laws and often delegates power to the President or specific agencies to fill in gaps in the laws or otherwise effectuate them. The Executive Department consists of major departments, such as the Departments of the Treasury and State, which were founded early in our nation's history. In addition to creating such major departments, however, the Congress has created a number of agencies such as the Federal Trade Commission and the Equal Opportunity Employment Commission, among many others. Some agencies routinely enforce criminal law, like the Department of Justice, headed by the Attorney General. Other agencies have as their primary mission the job of implementing statutes—making them work on the ground—like the work undertaken by the Department of Health and Human Services to implement major federal health programs like Medicare and Medicaid. Administrative agencies do a vast amount of work in "executing" the law for the President. However, every administrative action, unless within an area of the President's own authority, must be consistent with the limits of how Congress delegated that authority to the executive branch. We will consider the President's ability to control his own officials, his ability to "take care" that the laws are executed, and the authorization of his agency's actions.

The Judiciary. Last of all, we consider how courts interact with other departments in matters of legislation. We begin by considering how courts have limited the judicial power through a variety of doctrines built upon the idea that courts decide individual cases We consider current debates about courts' role in institutional litigation stretching ancient notions of judicial power beyond the common law model of judicial decisionmaking. We then consider the power of *stare decisis*. If judges were to have a constituency, it would be the constituency of precedent: the consistency demanded by *stare decisis* is perhaps the most powerful influence on judges' decisions. Finally, we consider how agencies and Congress step in when they disagree with courts' decisions.

NOTE ON THE RELATIONSHIP AMONG LAWS, REGULATIONS, AND THE CONSTITUTION

Before you read on, remember to understand the very basic allocation of federal power under our Constitution: The Constitution trumps any law or regulation. If the law or regulation is unconstitutional, it fails. Similarly, executive (including agency) action must be authorized by law, whether under the Constitution or by statute. If the executive action is unsupported by congressional authorization, it fails unless the President is acting pursuant to an independent grant of constitutional authority. Similarly, any regulation must not only be authorized by law, but must also be consistent with the Constitution.

Constitution
- Statutes must be consistent with the Constitution
- Congress and the President must be able to cite to constitutional authority supporting their actions

Congress's Statutes
- A statute passed by Congress must have a constitutional basis
- A statute may delegate authority to an agency to execute the statute

Agency Regulations
- An agency action must trace itself to a delegated power from Congress or an independent Presidential power granted by the Constitution
- The agency action must be consistent with the statute passed by Congress

CHAPTER 1

THE CONGRESS

∎ ∎ ∎

This chapter focuses on congressional action. As you read these materials, keep in mind the central questions: How does Congress create statutes? What are the procedural limits on its action? What are the constitutional limits on its action? We introduce how Congress works through a case study of the Civil Rights Act of 1964 and an extended essay on current congressional rules. We place Congress in the context of its power to control and structure agencies. How much power does Congress have over agencies and the President?

---

1. HOW A BILL BECOMES A LAW

A. THE STORY OF THE CIVIL RIGHTS ACT OF 1964 AND SEX DISCRIMINATION[1]

In the wake of *Brown v. Board of Education* (1954), where the Supreme Court declared racially segregated schools unconstitutional, civil rights groups pressed for an end to racial discrimination in other institutions as well, including private employment. But in the decade after *Brown,* there was little tangible progress toward actual racial integration, especially in the South, where massive resistance to *Brown*

---

[1] Adapted from the Story of the Civil Rights Act in the various editions of the Eskridge and Frickey Legislation casebook, the following account draws from Charles Whalen & Barbara Whalen, *The Longest Debate: A Legislative History of the 1964 Civil Rights Act* (1985) (cited in text as "Whalens," with page numbers), and from Rachel Osterman, *Origins of a Myth: Why Courts, Scholars, and the Public Think Title VII's Ban on Sex Discrimination Was an Accident,* 20 Yale J.L. & Fem. 409 (2009) ("Osterman"). Other useful sources are Carl M. Brauer, *Women Activists, Southern Conservatives, and the Prohibition of Sex Discrimination in Title VII of the 1964 Civil Rights Act,* 49 J. S. Hist. 37 (1983) ("Brauer"); Robert A. Caro, *The Years of Lyndon Johnson: The Passage of Power* 345–46, 552–70 (2012) ("Caro"); Hugh Davis Graham, *The Civil Rights Era: Origins and Development of National Policy, 1960–1972* (1990) ("Graham"); Cynthia Harrison, *On Account of Sex: The Politics of Women's Issues, 1945–1968* (1988) ("Harrison"); James Harvey, *Civil Rights During the Kennedy Administration* (1971) ("Harvey"); Hubert Humphrey, *Beyond Civil Rights: A New Day of Equality* (1968) ("Humphrey"); Neil MacNeil, *Dirksen: Portrait of a Public Man* (1970) ("MacNeil"); John Martin, *Civil Rights and the Crisis of Liberalism: The Democratic Party, 1945–76* (1979) ("Martin"); Merle Miller, *Lyndon: An Oral Biography* (1980) ("Miller"); Edward & Frederick Schapsmeier, *Dirksen of Illinois: Senatorial Statesman* (1985) ("Schapsmeier"); Francis J. Vaas, *Title VII: Legislative History*, 7 B.C.L. Rev. 431 (1966) ("Vaas").

was initially quite successful. Civil rights groups and their allies realized that national legislation was needed to carry out their broad reading of *Brown* as a mandate to dismantle American apartheid. At the same time, a new wave of feminist energy demanded an end to what might be called the apartheid of the kitchen, where women were pervasively discriminated against in the public spheres of employment, public service, and government programs (including schools). Since 1923, women's groups had been pressing for adoption of a constitutional Equal Rights Amendment (ERA). In the 1960s, women's leaders presented the ERA as the feminist analogue to the *Brown* triumph for the civil rights movement.

In the 1950s and early 1960s, neither social movement had much success in the national legislative process. Although serious civil rights proposals were pressed in Congress, legislation enacted in 1957 and 1960 was unimpressive and marginal. Women's groups, such as the National Women's Party, were even less successful in persuading Congress to muster the two-thirds majorities needed to send the ERA to the states for ratification as an amendment.

The year 1963 was a turning point for both movements. The President's Commission on the Status of Women issued an influential report criticizing sex-based discrimination that disadvantaged women. The United States Civil Rights Commission had been issuing similar reports advocating equal treatment of racial minorities for more than a decade, and civil rights groups pressed for enactment of federal legislation requiring equal treatment by private as well as public institutions. Dramatically, civil rights groups organized a massive March on Washington in August 1963, to demonstrate solidarity in favor of broad national civil rights legislation such as that proposed earlier by President John F. Kennedy.

The President's proposed civil rights legislation concentrated on four areas of concern: discrimination in public accommodations (like restaurants and hotels), desegregation of public schools, fair employment, and discrimination by recipients of federal funds. While not addressing private discrimination, the President reaffirmed his support for legislation addressing employment discrimination in the private sector. Finally, the President's bill also proposed that recipients of federal assistance be prohibited from discriminating on the basis of race. Nothing in the President's bill barred discrimination because of sex, however.

Even the President's moderate bill seemed to have little chance of enactment in 1963, for a variety of reasons. First, both political parties were ambivalent about enacting broad anti-discrimination legislation. The Democratic Party was deeply divided, with northern liberals favoring much stronger legislation than the President proposed, and southerners opposing any legislation at all. Ironically, many of the southerners who opposed civil rights for blacks were in favor of the ERA for (white) women. The Republican Party was opposed to discrimination against racial minorities and, with more dissent, against women—but most Republicans were also reluctant to impose more "big government" regulations on small businesses and state governments.

Second, the Kennedy Administration was perceived as not firmly committed to broad civil rights legislation. As senators, President Kennedy and Vice President Lyndon B. Johnson had cooperated with southern Democrats to dilute Republican-supported civil rights legislation in 1957 and 1960. Also, President Kennedy was preoccupied with foreign relations and economic policy in the first years of his presidency (Harvey 19–20). On the other hand, in 1962 the Kennedy Administration issued an executive order barring race discrimination in federal housing policy and stood up to politicians blocking the integration of the University of Mississippi. And in 1963 the President's Committee on the Status of Women recommended that widespread discrimination against women was unfair and contrary to the public interest.

Third, and most important, civil rights legislation faced daunting obstacles in Congress. Over 90% of bills introduced in Congress—not just civil rights bills—die in the legislative labyrinth. Congress's work is organized through subject-matter committees, to which individual elected members are assigned. Virtually all bills introduced in Congress are referred initially to a committee for consideration and normally cannot be voted on until the committee has reported them out.[2] Because a committee chair controls the committee's staff and agenda, he or she effectively has the power to kill a bill by preventing the committee from considering it. Committee chairmanships have generally been awarded on the basis of seniority; at the time of the deliberations on the Civil Rights Act, many powerful chairs were held by senior congressmen from the "one-party" states of the South and Southwest (Harvey 16–17).

In the Senate, civil rights legislation fell under the jurisdiction of the Judiciary Committee. The chairman, Senator James Eastland (D–Miss.), was notorious for killing civil rights bills. The situation was little better in the House, where the Rules Committee—the committee through which almost every bill passes on its way to the floor—was headed by Howard

---

[2]   Current House Rule X, clause 1 and Senate Rule XXV, clause 1 identify the standing (permanent) committees in the two chambers and define the jurisdiction (area of exclusive authority) for each standing committee. House Rule XII, clause 2 and Senate Rule XVII, clause 3 govern referral to committees by the Speaker of the House and the Senate Majority Leader, respectively.

For current (as of 2014) versions of the Senate and House Rules, see *Standing Rules of the Senate*, in *Senate Manual*, S. Doc. No. 112–1 (2011), available at http://www.rules.senate.gov/public/index.cfm?p=RulesOfSenateHome (viewed March 1, 2014), and *Rules of the House of Representatives*, 113th Congress (2013), available at http://clerk.house.gov/legislative/house-rules.pdf (viewed March 1. 2014).

W. "Judge" Smith (D–Va.), also a foe of civil rights laws. In 1957, Smith stalled consideration of a civil rights bill simply by leaving Washington; he claimed that he needed to attend to his barn in Virginia that had recently burned down. Speaker of the House Sam Rayburn (D–Tex.) replied that he knew Smith was opposed to civil rights, but he never suspected that the Chairman would resort to arson (Martin 166)!

Even if the civil rights bill were to survive the committee process, it faced a certain *filibuster* on the floor of the Senate. Senate rules allow unlimited debate on a bill before voting, and civil rights opponents had successfully used this tactic in 1957 and 1960 to prevent consideration of civil rights legislation, by refusing to stop the debate and allowing a vote only after they had exacted tremendous concessions from the bills' supporters. The only ways to break a filibuster are by permitting it to continue until the filibusterers are physically exhausted or by invoking *cloture* (then, a two-thirds vote to end discussion; now requiring only 60 votes).[3] The former had been tried and failed in 1957, while the latter had been successfully invoked only five times in the history of the Senate and never to end debate on a civil rights bill (Whalens 126).

Notwithstanding all these obstacles, strong civil rights legislation was enacted in 1964—and it included protections against workplace sex discrimination as well. As you read the story of the bill, pay attention to the *structure of Congress;* the practical necessity of *dealmaking*; and the role of party leaders and the President in *setting the agenda* for the ultimate legislation.

(1) Passage in the House

The President's civil rights bill was introduced in both houses of Congress on June 19, 1963, but its supporters pushed for immediate consideration only in the House of Representatives. They believed that the obstacles would be less substantial in the House. If they could develop a strong record of support for the bill there, together with a large vote in favor of the bill, supporters hoped that political momentum would improve the bill's chances in the Senate. (Also, the President in mid-1963 was seeking to spring his tax cut bill from the Senate Judiciary Committee, whose Chair, Harry F. Byrd of Virginia, was expected to hold the tax legislation "hostage" once a civil rights bill came to the floor of the Senate.)

Writing a Bill the Hard Way—The Judiciary Committee. House Speaker John McCormack (D–Mass.) referred H.R. 7152 to the House Judiciary Committee, which had jurisdiction over civil rights bills.

---

[3] Under current Senate Rule XXII, clause 2, cloture can be invoked in most cases by the vote of 60 of the 100 senators, but a two-thirds vote is still required to end debate on any measure amending the Senate rules, including the rule governing cloture. See our Note on the Rules of the House and the Senate, below.

Chairman Emanuel Celler (D–N.Y.) referred the bill to Subcommittee No. 5. The chairman referred the bill to this subcommittee, which normally handled antitrust matters—not the obvious choice—because it was dominated by civil rights advocates: its chairman was Celler himself, the ranking Republican was William McCulloch (R–Ohio), and the subcommittee had no senior southern member (Harvey 60).

Starting in the early summer, Chairman Celler held twenty-two days of hearings. While Celler took testimony from Attorney General Robert Kennedy and other officials, civil rights groups and the Kennedy Administration engaged in extensive efforts to build broad grassroots support for the legislation. On August 2, the subcommittee was ready to *mark up* the bill. A mark-up is a committee's drafting session, where members consider amendments and rewrite bills. President Kennedy had asked Representative Celler to stall final consideration of the bill until his tax reform proposal was voted out of the House Ways and Means Committee, where it had been languishing since January. The highly controversial tax cut was a cornerstone in the President's economic program, and Kennedy feared that southern representatives on the Ways and Means Committee might use the bill as a target for retaliation if the civil rights bill cleared Subcommittee No. 5 first. Therefore, Celler delayed substantive mark-up of H.R. 7152 until September (Whalens 22–23). Meanwhile, public pressure for legislation mounted.[4]

On September 10, the Ways and Means Committee approved the tax bill, and Representative Celler prepared for the mark-up of H.R. 7152. Contrary to the Administration's deal with Representative McCulloch and the Republicans, the chairman chose to pursue a more aggressive approach. Anticipating that the Senate would dilute the protections of any bill the House voted for, Celler resolved to make the bill as strong as possible, so that even a diluted version would be a significant change (Whalens 30–31).

The liberal Democrats on the subcommittee proceeded to strengthen almost every title of the administration's bill. On October 2, Subcommittee No. 5 reported the new H.R. 7152 to the full Judiciary Committee. Although civil rights leaders considered the revised bill an

---

[4]   On August 28, 1963, as Congress prepared to adjourn for the Labor Day recess, almost a quarter of a million people converged on Washington, D.C., in a peaceful demonstration for equal rights—the March on Washington for Jobs and Freedom (Martin 176–77). In his address to the crowd that afternoon, Dr. King argued that, one hundred years after the Emancipation Proclamation, African Americans were still not free. "One hundred years later, the life of the Negro is still sadly crippled by the manacles of segregation and the chains of discrimination. * * * One hundred years later, the Negro is still languishing in the corners of American society and finds himself an exile in his own land." Dr. King concluded: "I have a dream that my four little children will one day live in a nation where they will not be judged by the color of their skin but by the content of their character. I have a dream today." Martin Luther King Jr., *I Have a Dream*, Aug. 28, 1963 (available at http://www.thekingcenter.org/archive/document/i-have-dream -2).

excellent product, it was not well-received elsewhere. The National Woman's Party (NWP) lobbied subcommittee members to include discrimination because of sex in the jobs title. But Representative Celler was completely unwilling to liberalize the bill in that way, partly because he feared that tackling sex discrimination would make the bill too controversial and partly because he did not view sex discrimination as a major public problem.

Southern representatives considered the mark-up a much more dangerous bill than the Administration's measure—but they also understood that the new bill might be easier to defeat or slow down. As a result, southern representatives on the subcommittee voted to send the bill to the entire committee, where Representative McCulloch pronounced it dead on arrival. House Minority Leader Charles Halleck (R–Ind.) met with Deputy Attorney General Nicholas Katzenbach and Speaker McCormack on October 8 to tell them that the Republicans would allow the strengthened bill to go to the House floor, where it would probably die—unless the liberal Democrats themselves cooperated in weakening the bill. The Administration readily agreed to the Republicans' proposal and persuaded a reluctant Representative Celler to go along (Whalens 42–44). On October 15, the Attorney General testified before the Committee to recommend weakening changes (Brauer 304). Although the changes almost failed when some liberals again wandered off the deal, the Administration bullied Representative Celler into substituting a moderate GOP–Kennedy bill for the liberal measure that Celler had crafted (Whalens 64–66). Neither the Republicans nor the Kennedy Administration suggested that sex discrimination should be added to the jobs title; all of their changes weakened the legislation.

Although civil rights leaders criticized the Administration for cutting back the subcommittee's strong proposal, the substitute bill was decidedly stronger than the original Administration bill. President Kennedy praised the new bill as "comprehensive and fair," and the Administration evenly distributed credit among Democrats and Republicans (Whalens 66).

Surviving the Rules Committee. On November 21, H.R. 7152 and the Judiciary Committee's report were conveyed to the Clerk of the House and then to the powerful Rules Committee. Each bill reported out of committee passes through the Rules Committee, where a resolution (the *rule*) governing floor debate is prepared.[5] In addition to providing that high priority bills receive expedited consideration, the rule (which must

---

[5]   Current House Rule XIII, clause 2 provides that all committee reports, including the views of the minority, shall be delivered to the Clerk for printing and reference to the proper *calendar*. Because House calendars contain many bills, and bills are to be considered in their order on the calendars, there is no assurance that the bill will be considered at all. The Rules Committee has the power to recommend a rule to expedite consideration of any bill—ahead of those previously placed on the calendars. See our Note on the Rules of the House and the Senate, below (regarding the power of the Rules Committee).

be adopted by majority vote) determines the amount of time allowed for debate, how the time for debate will be allocated, and the scope of permissible amendments.

The Rules Committee stage often constitutes a substantive consideration of the bill, and it presents an opportunity to derail a bill before the House itself has a chance to consider it. The chairman of the Rules Committee, 80-year-old former Judge Howard Smith, had spent 33 years in the House killing or eviscerating progressive legislation in the areas of labor, public housing, education, medical care, and, especially, civil rights.[6]

As he had done in the past, Judge Smith was in no hurry to provide H.R. 7152 with a special rule expediting its consideration on the House floor. Unlike previous years, however, in 1963 public opinion was focused on civil rights legislation and strongly favored it—especially after President Kennedy's assassination on November 22. (His assassination also meant that the new chief executive was the former Master of the Senate, Lyndon B. Johnson. LBJ's legislative acumen was to prove instrumental in moving civil rights legislation through the choke points of both House and Senate.)

There were three procedural options capable of dislodging Smith's stranglehold on H.R. 7152, and each was tried by the bill's supporters (Whalens 84–85). First, under House Rule XV, a petition signed by a majority of the House's members (218) can remove any bill from committee, including the Rules Committee, after it has been in committee for 30 days. On December 9, Representative Celler began circulating such a *discharge petition*, but Representatives McCulloch and Halleck refused to deliver the needed Republican signatures on the ground that such a course was antithetical to the committee process (Whalens 84; Caro 485–99). Discharge petitions have rarely been successful mechanisms for dislodging popular legislation from hostile committees.[7]

On December 11, the Republicans announced their intent to use a second device, *Calendar Wednesday*, to call up H.R. 7152. House Rule XXV allows the Speaker on each Wednesday to call the standing

---

[6] In an effort to curtail Smith's ability to bury the Administration's progressive legislative agenda, President Kennedy had worked prior to the 1961 session with then-Speaker of the House, Sam Rayburn, to enlarge the Rules Committee from ten to fifteen members (ten Democrats and five Republicans). The appointment of five new committee members allowed Rayburn and the Administration to create an 8–7 liberal majority on the Rules Committee and to increase the control of party leaders over it. While the enlargement improved prospects for the President's legislative agenda, highly controversial bills—like civil rights proposals—still faced unfavorable odds in Howard Smith's lair (Harvey 15–16).

[7] Of 563 discharge petitions initiated between 1931 and 2002, only 47 were successful in forcing floor consideration. Nineteen of the discharged bills passed the House, but only two became law, with another two resulting in changes in the House's rules. Richard Beth, Congressional Research Service Report for Congress, *The Discharge Rule in the House: Use in Historical Context* (April 17, 2003).

committees in alphabetical order to inquire whether the chairman wishes the House to consider any bill previously reported out of that committee. But with 11 committees coming alphabetically before the Judiciary Committee, including six chaired by southerners, the bill's opponents could easily defeat the tactic by calling up other bills to exhaust the available time. To prevent an embarrassing display of intraparty division, the Democratic leadership simply adjourned the House before the Calendar Wednesday maneuver could be attempted (Whalens 85).

The third mechanism was to be the key. House Rule XI permits any three members of a committee to request the chairman to call a meeting to consider a bill; if the meeting is not scheduled within three days, a majority of the committee may schedule one. Liberal Democrats numbered five on the Rules Committee, so three Republican votes were needed. The pivotal votes were controlled by 70-year-old Representative Clarence Brown (R–Ohio), the ranking minority member on the Rules Committee (Whalens 85). The conservative Brown shared the commitment to civil rights of his friend and neighboring Congressman, Bill McCulloch. Representative Brown informed his friend Judge Smith of his plans to lead a mutiny, so to head off a confrontation, the chairman announced that hearings would begin on January 9, 1964 (Whalens 86).

Between January 9 and January 30, the House Rules Committee heard testimony from 40 different members of Congress (Vaas 438). No one expected the hearings to have any effect on the outcome, but they provided the southern Democrats a forum for airing their opposition to the bill. Ironically, one of the southerners' most pointed criticisms of the Judiciary Committee's bill was that it provided no protections for female employees. On the first day of the hearings, Chairman Smith asked Representative Celler to explain why sex discrimination protections had been omitted, but Celler basically refused to answer the question, apparently assuming the issue would go away (Osterman 414).

On January 30, 1964, the Rules Committee approved House Resolution 616, governing debate on H.R. 7152, by a vote of 11–4 (Whalens 99). The bill had not only survived the Rules Committee, it had survived without a single amendment (Vaas 438). The Rules Committee had, however, declined to propose a "closed rule" that would bar amendments on the floor of the House.

Adding "Sex" to the Jobs Title on the House Floor. The House of Representatives follows a six-step process in considering a bill called up from the floor. First, the House debates and votes on the bill's rule. If the rule is accepted, the body will resolve into the *Committee of the Whole House on the State of the Union*, which is simply the full House following simplified procedures for purposes of debate. Next, pursuant to the rule, members offer amendments, which are debated and then accepted or rejected by unrecorded votes. The members will then resume sitting formally as the House and, if requested by one-fifth of the members, take recorded votes on any accepted amendments. A minority party member will be recognized to offer a motion to recommit the bill to committee. Finally, the House will vote on the bill, as amended by the Committee of the Whole (Whalens 101).

On January 3, 1964, Speaker McCormack recognized a Rules Committee member to call up House Resolution 616 (the special rule) for immediate consideration. Under the rules of the House, debate on the resolution was limited to one hour, divided equally between each party. Representative Clarence Brown spoke on behalf of the rule, and Rules Committee member William Colmer (D–Miss.) spoke against it. In a voice vote, the House ignored Representative Colmer's plea not to succumb to the violent "blackmail" of civil rights activists, and approved the rule (Whalens 102–03). The House then resolved itself into the Committee of the Whole, and Speaker McCormack stepped down and handed the gavel to Eugene Keogh (D–N.Y.), who assumed his position as Chairman of the Committee of the Whole.

Representatives Celler and McCulloch delivered the opening statements. Celler chose to describe the bill in broad dramatic terms:

> The legislation before you seeks only to honor the constitutional guarantees of equality under the law for all. It bestows no preferences on any one group; what it does is to place into balance the scales of justice so that the living force of our Constitution shall apply to all people, not only to those who by accident of birth were born with white skins.

Bill McCulloch discussed H.R. 7152 more simply, explaining the need for federal legislation and its validity under the Constitution. He argued that "this bill is comprehensive in scope, yet moderate in application."

Not surprisingly, the southern representatives cast the bill in a very different light. Representative Edwin Willis (D–La.), for example, characterized the bill as "the most drastic and far-reaching proposal and grab for power ever to be reported out of a committee of Congress in the history of our Republic." Representative Thomas Abernethy (D–Miss.) went further:

> If this bill is enacted, I predict it will precipitate upheaval that will make the sit-ins, kneel-ins, lie-ins, stand-ins, mass picketing, chanting, the march on Washington, and all the other elements of the so-called Negro revolution, all of these—I predict—will look like kindergarten play in comparison with the counter-revolution that is bound to arise and continue to grow and grow and grow.

After ten hours of such general debate, H.R. 7152 prepared to meet its ultimate test in the House—the amendment process on the floor.

Representatives McCulloch and Celler had prepared carefully for this stage of the process. Each manned a 20-foot-long table on their respective party's side of the chamber on which they had assembled an impressive array of resources. There was a lengthy manual prepared by the Justice Department, containing a section-by-section defense of the bill and responding both to the opposing views expressed by the southern Democratic minority in the Judiciary Committee's report and to expected amendments. The floor leaders had also assigned a member of the Judiciary Committee to each title with responsibility for becoming an expert on that particular area. Finally, there were eight Justice Department attorneys—one for each title of the bill—standing by for additional assistance (Whalens 103).

One concern shared by Representatives Celler and McCulloch was their ability to keep sufficient members on the floor to defeat weakening amendments during the protracted debate. Because votes taken in the Committee of the Whole were unrecorded, constituents were not likely to find out how (or even if) their representatives voted, and so marginally interested members often skipped those votes. Thus it was not unusual to find a determined minority passing substantial amendments to bills by simply waiting until enough of the bill's supporters left the floor. If such a situation arose, Celler and McCulloch planned to stall a final vote for ten minutes while they attempted to get their forces together. By objecting to the chair's call for a voice vote, they could force a standing vote. Then, with 20 members objecting to the standing vote, they could force a teller vote—a head count as the "yeas" and "nays" walked down the center aisle. During this delaying process, supporters could be rounded up.

The amendment process began at noon on Monday, February 3, and continued, title-by-title and section-by-section, until 7:00 p.m. on February 10. Over the course of that week, 124 amendments were offered, debated, and voted on, but only 34 were accepted by the Committee of the Whole. Most were technical corrections, including 12 offered by Representative Celler and the sponsoring coalition.

The most significant amendment expanded the scope of Title VII and was sponsored by none other than Judge Smith. Alice Paul and the NWP had specifically asked Judge Smith to offer an amendment protecting women against job discrimination. It is true that Smith was a longtime supporter of the ERA, but he also hoped that by transforming the civil rights bill into a law guaranteeing women equal rights with men—dramatically affecting every employer, labor union and governmental body in the country—the bill would become so controversial that it would fail, if not in the House, certainly in the Senate. On February 8, 1964, the

Rules Committee Chairman proposed the addition of the word "sex" to Title VII's list of impermissible bases for employment decisions (Vaas 441–42; Whalens 115–16). Judge Smith explained that his amendment was necessary to "prevent discrimination against another minority group, the women," and that "it is indisputable fact that all throughout industry women are discriminated against in that just generally speaking they do not get as high compensation." He then read a letter from a female citizen complaining "that women currently outnumber men, that Congress and the President have made the situation worse by engaging in wars that further the imbalance, and that the imbalance prevents women from obtaining their 'right to happiness.'" According to the record, "Smith's comments evoked laughter, though he insisted that he was serious." (Osterman 412.)

Representative Emmanuel Celler, the Democratic floor manager in support of the civil rights bill, responded to Smith's proposed amendment. "I can say as a result of 49 years of experience—and I celebrate my 50th wedding anniversary next year—that women, indeed, are not in the minority in my house. . . . I usually have the last two words, and those words are, 'Yes, dear.'" Celler then explained why he opposed the amendment, citing the "biological differences between the sexes." While Representative McCulloch and the leading GOP supporters of the civil rights bill sat on the sidelines, several other Democratic liberals joined Celler in speaking against the amendment.

The tone of good-ole-boy jocularity changed when eleven of the House's twelve female legislators rose to address Judge Smith's proposed amendment (Osterman 412–13). "I feel as a white woman when this bill has passed this House and the Senate and has been signed by the President that white women will be the last at the hiring gate," said Representative Martha W. Griffiths (D–Mich.). Representative Katharine Price Collier St. George (R–N.Y.), joined Griffiths in favor of the amendment. "Why should women be denied equality of opportunity? Why should women be denied equal pay for equal work? That is all we are asking." Representatives Frances Bolton (R–Oh.), Catherine May (R–Wash.), and Edna Kelly (D–NY) also made forceful speeches in favor of the Smith Amendment.

Representative Edith Green (D–Or.) was the only female legislator to speak against the Smith Amendment. Although she supported women's equality rights, and had voted for the Equal Pay Act of 1963, Green believed the civil rights bill should pass as it was. "For every discrimination that has been made against a woman in this country, there has been 10 times as much discrimination against the Negro." Representative Green questioned the motives of the amendment's sponsor: "[The amendment] will clutter up the bill and it may—very well—be used to help destroy this section of the bill by some of the very people who today support it." The implication was that Smith's amendment was a "killer amendment"—an amendment strategically designed to peel off critical votes.

For precisely the same reasons, the Johnson Administration was cool, at best, toward the Smith Amendment. Representative Celler read into the record a letter from the Assistant Secretary of Labor, Esther Peterson. Peterson argued that the President's Commission on the Status of Women had concluded that sex discrimination should be treated in a policy separate from race discrimination. Don't conflate the two concerns, the executive department seemed to be saying.

With a coalition of southern Democrats and pro-ERA Republicans supporting it, and the liberals divided on the apparent choice between equal rights for blacks and equal rights for women, Judge Smith's amendment passed, 168–133 (Vaas 442).

At the close of amendments on February 10, the Committee of the Whole dissolved, John McCormack reclaimed the Speaker's chair, and the members resumed sitting as the House. Chairman Keogh reported H.R. 7152, as amended, back to the House, and the Speaker prepared to complete the final three steps in the process. It was 7:00 p.m., and few were interested in prolonging the debate. Attempts to obtain recorded votes on certain substantive amendments failed to receive sufficient support, and the motion to recommit the bill to the Judiciary Committee failed on a voice vote. Finally it was time for the vote—up or down—on H.R. 7152. When the roll call was over, there were 152 Democratic votes and 138 Republican votes in favor, 96 Democratic votes and 34 Republican votes against. The civil rights bill passed overwhelmingly, 290–130 (Whalens 120–21). Now it was on to the Senate.

(2) Passage in the Senate

The euphoria that accompanied passage in the House of Representatives was short-lived. H.R. 7152 next had to face the Senate, where its supporters faced an uphill battle. In the Senate, southerners chaired the Judiciary Committee and were a cohesive block that had successfully filibustered strong civil rights bills in 1957 and 1960. They had enough votes to sustain a filibuster if they could secure support from their natural allies, namely, conservative Republicans suspicious of big government. Indeed, the Minority Leader of the Senate was Everett McKinley Dirksen (R–Ill.), a staunch supporter of small businesses and farmers; he was also publicly critical of the sex discrimination amendment added to the jobs title.

In 1964, consideration of a typical bill in the Senate followed an eight-step process. First, the bill was read for the first time. If no objections were heard, the bill would immediately be read for the second time. After the second reading, the bill was generally referred to committee, unless a majority voted to place the bill directly on the Senate calendar. The fourth step was committee consideration where, as in the House, the bill could be amended or killed. If the bill survived committee action, it was placed on the Senate calendar. The sixth step was to call up the bill for consideration, and the seventh consisted of the actual debate of the bill under the Senate's unlimited debate rules. The final step was the third reading, followed by a vote on the bill, as amended by the committee and during floor debate (Whalens 131–32).

Majority Leader Mike Mansfield (D–Mont.) had a simple strategy. First, avoid referral of H.R. 7152 to Senator James Eastland's (D–Miss.) Judiciary Committee, which would have ignored and thereby killed the bill. Second, get the 67 votes needed to invoke cloture against the southern filibuster that was sure to come. Third, pass the bill in a form that the House of Representatives would find acceptable, without the need for a Conference Committee—the process through which differences between the House and Senate versions of bills are reconciled—that would offer the southern opponents more opportunities to delay or kill the legislation.

The Longest Debate Begins. H.R. 7152 arrived in the Senate from the House on Monday, February 17, 1964. On Mike Mansfield's motion, the bill was read for the first time. However, Mansfield objected to a second reading of the bill because he wanted to delay a filibuster until the Senate had completed work on the tax bill. (Through a deft combination of flattery and budgetary logrolling, President Johnson had persuaded his old friend Senator Harry Byrd to move forward on the tax cut bill just before the civil rights bill arrived in the Senate (Caro 466–83, 552–57).)

After the tax bill had been passed, Senator Mansfield called up the civil rights bill for its second reading on February 26, 1964. Mansfield then moved to have the bill placed directly on the Senate calendar, therefore bypassing the Judiciary Committee. Senator Richard Russell (D–Ga.), leader of the southern bloc in the Senate, objected and was joined by Minority Leader Dirksen and others. Although Dirksen shared Mansfield's concern about referring a civil rights bill to Eastland's committee, he felt that a bill of this importance deserved the full legislative history that only committee consideration could provide. Mansfield persuaded 20 Republicans to join him and defeated Dirksen, 54–37, placing H.R. 7152 on the Senate calendar of pending bills (Whalens 132–35).

Senator Mansfield delayed his next motion—to call up H.R. 7152 for debate—until after the Senate voted on a pending farm bill. This two-week hiatus provided an opportunity for the Senate leadership to organize for the coming battle. Although the chairman of the committee that has jurisdiction over a bill is usually chosen to act as the primary floor leader during debate, the Majority Leader was not going to select Eastland. Instead he selected Senator Hubert Horatio Humphrey (D–Minn.), the Democrats' Senate Whip. No one was more committed to civil rights legislation than Humphrey. In 1948, it was he who led the battle for a strong civil rights plank in the Democratic platform. And the loquacious Humphrey had the energy and communication skills needed to organize the drive for 67 cloture votes.

The Republican floor manager was Thomas Kuchel (R–Cal.), that party's Senate Whip. Kuchel was an apt choice for the position because he was a progressive Republican who was still accepted in the conservative camp (Whalens 137–38). Senator Dirksen appointed seven other Republicans to assist Kuchel, selecting representatives from each region of the country to ensure that he was kept informed of the movements in all parts of his party (MacNeil 232). Senators Joseph Clark (D–Pa.) and Clifford Case (R–N.J.) were the senators responsible for handling issues involving Title VII, the equal employment title (Vaas 445).

On March 9, Majority Leader Mansfield moved to make H.R. 7152 the pending business of the Senate, a motion he knew would draw a filibuster by the southern conservatives (Vaas 444).[8] For fourteen days the Senate debated this issue—not whether to pass H.R. 7152, but simply whether to consider the bill at all. Prior to moving for immediate consideration of the bill, Mansfield had met with the southerners and had been assured that the filibuster on this preliminary issue would not last longer than four or five days. It became apparent, though, as debate dragged on, that the southerners had merely been maneuvering to convince Mansfield not to call all-night sessions. On March 23, Senator Humphrey kept the Senate in session until 10:15 p.m.—not all night, but long enough to give the filibusterers a taste of what was to come. The next day, supporters announced that they would object to the holding of any committee hearings before the Senate had finished with the civil rights bill. The southerners finally decided to allow a vote on Mansfield's motion. On March 26, 1964, the motion to take up H.R. 7152 passed 67–17, with only southern Democrats opposing (Whalens 146–47).

On March 30, 1964, the Senate began debate on the merits of H.R. 7152. Hubert Humphrey delivered the opening statement. Knowing that with another filibuster around the corner there was no need to hurry (and

---

[8]   Unlike the House, the Senate does not have a Rules Committee which recommends to the full house a rule allowing expedited consideration of important bills. Instead, the Majority Leader normally expedites consideration by negotiating a *unanimous consent agreement*, in which all interested senators agree to consider the bill on a stated date, sometimes with limitations on debate and amendments (like a House rule). But if even a single senator objects to this arrangement, it is nullified. Obviously, the southern senators in 1964 were not going to agree readily to expedited consideration of the civil rights bill. For more on this aspect of Senate procedure, see our Note on the Rules of the House and the Senate, below.

never being the sort of speaker who strove for oratorical brevity), Senator Humphrey treated the half-dozen senators present to a 55-page, three and one-half hour speech. Tom Kuchel followed with an opening of a mere one and three-quarter hours (Whalens 150–51). Rather than let the southerners monopolize debate, Humphrey decided to take the offensive early. His team held the floor for over 12 days, presenting a detailed, title-by-title defense of the bill. Senators were sent to appear on television and radio talk shows and were encouraged to send regular newsletters back to their constituents in an effort to maintain support for the bill in the press and public at large (Humphrey 89–90). Supporters of the civil rights bill emphasized the moral importance of the bill, attempting to elevate the issue above politics and appeal to a broad concept of justice (Humphrey 91–92).

Wooing the Wizard of Ooze. The southern filibusterers dominated debate after early April and seemed capable of talking the year away. Could Senators Humphrey and Kuchel muster the 67 votes needed to invoke cloture? A block of about 20 Southern Democrats were certain to vote against cloture, and about 30 liberal Democrats and 12 liberal Republicans were equally certain to vote for it. To reach the 67 votes needed for cloture, Humphrey and Kuchel needed to win the votes of 25 senators from two groups: 21 conservative Republicans and 17 moderate Democrats from western and border states. Behind the scenes, President Johnson (the Senate Majority Leader, 1955–61, and the Minority Leader, 1953–55) fed the bipartisan coalition strategic advice, twisted arms, and offered logrolls to wavering senators.

Notwithstanding bipartisan and presidential support, invoking cloture would be tough—and would depend on the endorsement of the Minority Leader, Everett Dirksen (MacNeil 230–31). Over a 29-year career, Senator Dirksen had risen to his position of power on the strength of an oratorical prowess that combined flowery language with a throatily mellifluous voice, and of an uncanny ability to turn the most difficult political situations into personal triumphs. The former earned him the sobriquet "Wizard of Ooze"; the latter, "Old Doctor Snake Oil" (Whalens 151). Publicly, Dirksen struck a delphic pose in his attitude toward the civil rights bill. When President Kennedy's bill was introduced in June 1963, Dirksen expressed doubts about either a public accommodations provision or a fair employment practices section (Humphrey 85), and as late as August he told representatives of the NAACP that a public accommodations title was not acceptable (MacNeil 223). Early in the Senate's deliberations, he expressed hostility to the sex discrimination provision in Title VII (Brauer, 54; Harrison, 181).

The momentum created by House passage and increasing public support for the bill led Senator Dirksen to soften his position, however. In early November, he assured Deputy Attorney General Katzenbach that a civil rights bill would make it to a vote in the Senate (Brauer 308). It appears that Dirksen's opposition to the sex discrimination provision also softened over time. At the urging of the NWP, Senator Margaret Chase Smith (R–Me.), one of the senior members of the Senate, worked the cloakroom with arguments for retaining the sex discrimination protection.

By the time the filibuster began in earnest, Senator Dirksen was in all probability going to support some kind of strong civil rights bill. But his support carried a price tag—namely Dirksen's own conservative stamp on the final product, especially the jobs title (MacNeil 232–33). The day after the Senate took up consideration of the bill, Senator Dirksen met with the Senate Republican Policy Committee to discuss the amendments he wanted to propose, and the next day he met with the Republican caucus. A week later he unveiled a package of 40 weakening amendments to Title VII. The amendments pleased conservative Republicans but created great concern among the party's influential liberals.

As April stretched on and Senator Dirksen found himself unable to muster sufficient bipartisan support for his amendments, he decided to approach President Johnson in an effort to bluff his way to a compromise. He met with Johnson on April 29 and offered to deliver 22 to 25 Republican votes for cloture if the Administration would go along with weakening the bill. By one account, the President and his allies refused to compromise, because they thought Dirksen had little choice but to support the civil rights bill (Whalens 171–72). Another account, however, posits that Dirksen was in a much stronger bargaining position. When he met with Mansfield, Humphrey, and the Attorney General to hammer out a compromise on May 4, Dirksen achieved much of what he wanted for the small businesses that were his primary concern. Thus, he procured the administration's support for provisions in the jobs title limiting the authority of the EEOC, protecting employers against government-required quota programs, and expanding employer defenses.[9] It is significant that he did not press the President to drop the sex discrimination protection in the jobs title, some indication that small businesses were okay with that amendment and that more Senate Republicans supported the Smith Amendment than opposed it.

Minority Leader Dirksen spent the next week selling his deal to the Republican caucus. He presented his package—the most he thought he could get the Democrats to go along with—to the Republican senators (MacNeil 234–35). Just as his earlier amendments had been attacked by his party's liberals as going too far, Dirksen's latest proposal was

---

[9]   Indispensable for understanding Dirksen's success is Daniel A. Rodriguez & Barry R. Weingast, *The Positive Political Theory of Legislative History: New Perspectives on the 1964 Civil Rights Act and Its Interpretation*, 151 U. Pa. L. Rev. 1417 (2003).

attacked by some conservatives as not going nearly far enough. Dirksen's canny response was to go public, with a *fait accompli* challenging his Republicans to follow their Minority Leader. Following the caucus, Dirksen announced to stunned reporters that the time for action had arrived, that passage of the civil rights bill had become a moral imperative and that he was resolved to see it happen. Quoting Victor Hugo, Dirksen proclaimed, "No army is stronger than an idea whose time has come" (Whalens 185).

On May 26, Dirksen presented Amendment No. 656 to the Senate, an amendment in the nature of a substitute for H.R. 7152, known as the "Mansfield-Dirksen Amendment" (Vaas 445).[10] Although the liberals were ultimately satisfied that the anti-discrimination goal of civil rights bill had not been significantly undermined (Whalens 188–89), the jobs title of the Mansfield-Dirksen substitute was in fact more business-friendly and less regulatory than the earlier version of the bill (Rodriguez & Weingast, 1487–96). Senator Dirksen characteristically termed his bill "infinitely better than what came to us from the House" (Whalens 188), but Senator Humphrey believed that he had kept his promise to Representative McCulloch not to support a weakened bill (Humphrey 85).

Apparently, by the time the Mansfield-Dirksen substitute was drafted, the sex discrimination provision of Title VII was no longer at serious risk of being dropped from the bill (Osterman 415). After opposing Judge Smith's amendment out of fears that it would make the entire legislation too controversial, the Johnson Administration came to support the amendment during the Senate's deliberations. Perhaps most critically, if that important provision were deleted in the Senate, the Johnson Administration feared that its strategy of securing quick House agreement with the bill passed by the Senate would be in peril.

Senate liberals were overwhelmingly in favor of making workplace sex discrimination illegal—and so were some conservatives. However controversial the civil rights bill was among southern senators, it would have been hated even more if it had announced that employers could no longer discriminate against black men but they could discriminate against white women.

With cloture now a tangible possibility, the bill's supporters spent the next two weeks stumping for votes. President Johnson used a combination of arm-twisting and inducements to lobby Senate Democrats from small-population states that benefitted from the filibuster. He called in markers from Senators Howard Cannon (D–Nev.), whom Majority Leader Johnson had appointed to critical Senate committees, and J.

---

[10] An *amendment in the nature of a substitute* proposes a whole new bill to replace the bill under consideration. For the importance of substitutes prior to cloture in the Senate, see our Note on the Rules of the House and the Senate, below.

Howard Edmondson (D–Okla.), whom President Johnson had supported during the state's Democratic primary. While the President only stressed the principles in the bill, his personal involvement indicated that he was calling in political debts (Whalens 187–88). Both senators would vote for cloture. A devastating earthquake had struck Alaska on March 27, and President Johnson had responded promptly, making Air Force Two available to Senators Bartlett and Gruening (both D–Alaska) and moving to free up $77.5 million in relief for the state. Although both senators had been considered questionable votes for cloture, the President's timely political favor pulled them into line (Whalens 200).

Likewise, Senators Mansfield and Humphrey concentrated on Democratic senators from the key western states, attempting to disrupt a traditional understanding between southern and western senators involving the exchange of southern votes on water projects for western votes against civil rights (Whalens 201). Meanwhile, Senator Dirksen worked to pull in the eleven or more conservative Republicans he would need for cloture. Finally, the effects of the filibuster itself were beginning to create pressure for cloture. The Senate had devoted 12 solid weeks to ducking the civil rights issue, and many senators were beginning to feel the embarrassment that came with public recognition of that fact (Whalens 202–03).

Cloture and Victory in the Senate. One by one the necessary commitments fell into place. On June 8, Senators Mansfield and Dirksen moved for cloture: "We the undersigned Senators [27 Democrats, 11 Republicans], in accordance with the provisions of Rule XXII of the Standing Rules of the Senate, hereby move to bring to a close the debate on the bill * * *." After the required two-day wait, the time came to vote. Mansfield explained the importance of the cloture motion and then listened as a weary Senator Richard Russell denounced the bill as contrary to both the spirit and the letter of the Constitution. After an uncharacteristically brief statement by Senator Humphrey, Senator Dirksen rose to make the final speech. He introduced Senate Amendment No. 1052, a second substitute for the entire bill to replace his earlier substitute amendment. Dirksen argued: "The time has come for equality of opportunity in sharing in government, in education, and in employment. It will not be stayed or denied."

The quorum call was a true formality on June 10: all 100 senators were present, including Senator Clair Engle (D–Cal.), suffering from a brain tumor and unable to speak (Humphrey 91). The roll was called alphabetically by each senator's last name. Senator Engle cast his vote from his wheelchair by feebly lifting his left hand toward his eye. Senator John Williams (R–Del.), a conservative farmer warmly supportive of the civil rights bill, cast the sixty-seventh vote for cloture. Hubert Humphrey raised his arms over his head in jubilation (Whalens 199). The final vote was 71–29, four votes more than required.

After more than 534 hours of continuous debate, spanning 58 days, the longest filibuster in the history of the Senate had been broken—and it was the first time that cloture had been achieved on a civil rights bill (Miller 368). The final breakdown was 44 Democrats and 27 Republicans in favor of cloture and 23 Democrats and 6 Republicans against cloture. President Johnson and Senator Humphrey had succeeded in capturing the votes of 19 of the 21 Democrats from western states, and Senator Dirksen had convinced 16 of the 17 Republican senators from states with public accommodations and equal employment laws on the books (as well as eight of the ten senators from states with one or the other) to vote for cloture.

Even though cloture limited senators to sixty minutes of remarks—on both the bill and proposed amendments—the southern opponents of H.R. 7152 continued to delay the bill's progress. They attempted to bog down the proceedings by calling up countless amendments, even though they knew their proposals had no chance of adoption. They slowed things down further by insisting on long roll-call votes (including a record 34 in one day) on virtually every question (Schwartz 1091).[11] But they succeeded only in delaying the inevitable for another eight days (Vaas 446). In all, 115 different amendments were defeated, 106 on roll-call votes (Miller 371), with only two amendments of substance being accepted (Schwartz 1091).

After accepting a second Mansfield-Dirksen substitute (upon a 76–18 vote), the Senate voted on H.R. 7152. The bill was read for the third time and the Clerk called the roll (Vaas 446). At 7:40 p.m., to the applause of the observers in the gallery, the Clerk of the Senate announced the final vote: 73–27 in favor of H.R. 7152, as amended by the second Mansfield-Dirksen substitute. The bill received the support of 46 Democrats and 27 Republicans, including 4 senators who had opposed cloture. Voting "no" were 21 Democrats and 6 Republicans (Whalens 215). On June 19, 1964—one year after President Kennedy had sent his civil rights bill to Congress—the landmark bill was passed by the Senate.

Most important, the bill approved by the Senate was substantially similar to the bill approved by the House in February (Miller 371). For example, of the 24 amendments to Title VII that were offered from the

---

[11] This phenomenon—the *post-cloture filibuster-by-amendment*—was possible at the time but is no longer permissible. During this period, absent a unanimous consent agreement, a senator could propose any number of amendments, including those unrelated to the subject matter of the bill. (House Rule XVI, in contrast, limits amendments to those which are *germane* to the subject of the bill.) Moreover, any senator could demand roll-call votes, not only on the amendments, but also on the normally routine motion to reconsider, and could seek repeated quorum calls. Today, Rule XXII prevents any post-cloture filibuster and amendments must be germane. See our Note on the Rules of the House and the Senate, below.

floor, only five were accepted. Even considering Senator Dirksen's important changes, the jobs title was not significantly weaker than the version delivered from the House.[12]

(3) The Bill Becomes Law

A bill does not become a law unless both chambers of Congress agree to identical legislative language. Most people do not realize that, as a result, each chamber of Congress often has to vote on legislation *twice*: any changes made to conform the respective versions passed by the House and Senate must be voted on again by each chamber. Because the Senate made a number of changes to H.R. 7152, it returned the bill to the House on June 27, 1964, together with a message asking for acquiescence in the Senate's changes. In a joint press release, Representatives Celler and McCulloch said that "none of the amendments do serious violence to the purpose of the bill. We are of a mind that a conference could fatally delay enactment of this measure" (Whalens 218). Celler and McCulloch knew that if the House refused to accept all of the Senate changes and a conference committee was called, the Senate conferees would be selected by Judiciary Chairman Eastland, guaranteeing further delay. Even if the conference committee did report out a bill, the southerners would have another opportunity to filibuster in the Senate. On balance, the best strategy was simply to accept the Senate's changes (Whalens 218–19).

The revised H.R. 7152 returned to Judge Smith's Rules Committee. This time, with the national conventions of both parties approaching, supporters would tolerate no stalling by the Chairman. After a single day of hearings, the Rules Committee voted to report House Resolution 789, expressing the House's concurrence in the Senate's amendments to H.R. 7152. The Rules Committee also voted to limit debate to one hour prior to the final vote.

On July 2, the House took up consideration of House Resolution 789. Judge Smith spoke for 15 minutes, denouncing the Rules Committee's "exercise of raw, brutal power" in limiting debate to a single hour. But he conceded that "the bell has tolled. In a few minutes you will vote this monstrous instrument of oppression upon all of the American people." As he yielded the floor, Judge Smith received applause from his southern colleagues and a handshake from Manny Celler. One wonders whether

---

[12] See Rodriguez & Weingast 1487–96. A new provision specified that preferential hiring practices to correct racial imbalances in the workforce (*affirmative action*) would not be required. The authority of the EEOC to sue in court was eliminated and replaced with a provision authorizing the Commission, when conciliation efforts failed, to refer a case to the Attorney General for possible civil suit or to authorize private suit. However, the reduction in EEOC authority was agreed to only in exchange for the inclusion of provisions allowing the courts to appoint attorneys to represent private Title VII plaintiffs and providing for an award of attorney's fees to successful plaintiffs. The new version also allowed local authorities to retain jurisdiction over cases for a short time, to attempt conciliation, before the EEOC could step in (Vaas 447–56).

Judge Smith took some pride of authorship in the bill he was wearily denouncing, for the Smith Amendment would prove to be the most far-reaching of all the additions made to the landmark statute Congress was about to enact.

Representative McCulloch, in his usual restrained manner, recommended approval of the Senate version of H.R. 7152 as a comprehensive, fair, and moderate statute. As he sat down, the House rose in a rare standing ovation. Finally, Representative Celler claimed the floor to use the remaining six minutes of the allotted hour. When he finished, the House rose once again in a standing ovation, this time led by the redoubtable Judge Smith (Whalens 224–26).

The House vote on House Resolution 789 was 289–126. After the House accepted the Senate bill, Speaker McCormack signed the official copy of H.R. 7152 and handed it to the House Clerk for return to the Senate. When the bill arrived in the other chamber, business was suspended so that Senator Carl Hayden (D–Ariz.), the Senate's President *pro tempore*, could place his signature alongside McCormack's. H.R. 7152, as amended, was now ready to be signed into law by the President. At 6:00 that evening, July 2, 1964, members of Congress and civil rights leaders arrived at the White House and, after brief remarks by President Johnson, witnessed the presidential signing of H.R. 7152 into law. H.R. 7152 had finally become "The Civil Rights Act of 1964."

Within days, Lyndon Johnson met with Nicholas Katzenbach, the new Attorney General, to discuss the President's plans for the next civil rights bill: "I want you to write me the goddamndest, toughest voting rights act that you can devise." As he had told Hubert Humphrey during the battle for the 1964 Act, "Yes, yes, Hubert, I want all of those other things—buses, restaurants, all of that—but the right to vote with no ifs, ands, or buts, that's the key. When the Negroes get that, they'll have every politician, north and south, east and west, kissing their ass, begging for their support" (Miller 371). President Johnson may have been overly optimistic (and typically crude), but he was astute enough to realize that the Civil Rights Act of 1964 was merely a start toward true equality and the end of discrimination.

PROBLEM 1–1: AFFIRMATIVE ACTION AFTER TITLE VII

The most complex, and most often litigated, portion of the Civil Rights Act has been Title VII, 78 Stat. 241, 253–66 (1964), codified as amended at 42 U.S.C. § 2000e *et seq.*, which prohibits job discrimination on the basis of race, sex, religion, or national origin. (The original text of Title VII, taken from the Statutes at Large, is reproduced as Appendix 2 to this coursebook.) Among the most controversial of the issues litigated under Title VII has been affirmative action.

Assume you are the lawyer for an employer who wishes to use affirmative action to remedy a long period of discriminating against female employees. Male employers at the firm threaten suit, saying affirmative action is not permitted under Title VII and specifically point to § 703(j) in support of their position. Women's rights groups, however, believe the law is on your side. They contend that the text of the Act makes clear its broad remedial purposes and that it does not preclude voluntary affirmative action.

We reproduce below the main provisions of the Title VII (before its amendments in 1972, 1978, and 1991), which are found in § 703(a), 42 U.S.C. § 2000e–2(a). The goal is to get your feet wet in full statutory analysis. As you resolve your position in the case, think about the structure of the act as well as its text. Which sections are the prime directives? Which sections are the exceptions? Which textual provisions are most helpful and most harmful to the case? How does § 703(j) fit into the structure of the Act? Is it similar to or different from the other provisions? Think also about the statute's legislative history. Does the fact that "sex" made it into the statute only through a "killer amendment" have any relevance? Should courts take that kind of legislative-dealmaking detail into account when decided cases involving sex discrimination under Title VII?

TITLE VII OF THE CIVIL RIGHTS ACT OF 1964
(§ 703(a), 42 U.S.C. § 2000e–2(a)).

(a) Employer practices

It shall be an unlawful employment practice for an employer—

> **(1)** to fail or refuse to hire or to discharge any individual, or otherwise to discriminate against any individual with respect to his compensation, terms, conditions, or privileges of employment, because of such individual's race, color, religion, sex, or national origin; or
>
> **(2)** to limit, segregate, or classify his employees or applicants for employment in any way which would deprive or tend to deprive any individual of employment opportunities or otherwise adversely affect his status as an employee, because of such individual's race, color, religion, sex, or national origin.

(b) Employment agency practices

It shall be an unlawful employment practice for an employment agency to fail or refuse to refer for employment, or otherwise to discriminate against, any individual because of his race, color, religion, sex, or national origin, or to classify or refer for employment any individual on the basis of his race, color, religion, sex, or national origin.

(c) Labor organization practices

It shall be an unlawful employment practice for a labor organization—

(1) to exclude or to expel from its membership, or otherwise to discriminate against, any individual because of his race, color, religion, sex, or national origin;

(2) to limit, segregate, or classify its membership or applicants for membership, or to classify or fail or refuse to refer for employment any individual, in any way which would deprive or tend to deprive any individual of employment opportunities, or would limit such employment opportunities or otherwise adversely affect his status as an employee or as an applicant for employment, because of such individual's race, color, religion, sex, or national origin; or

(3) to cause or attempt to cause an employer to discriminate against an individual in violation of this section.

(d) Training programs

It shall be an unlawful employment practice for any employer, labor organization, or joint labor-management committee controlling apprenticeship or other training or retraining, including on-the-job training programs to discriminate against any individual because of his race, color, religion, sex, or national origin in admission to, or employment in, any program established to provide apprenticeship or other training.

(e) Businesses or enterprises with personnel qualified on basis of religion, sex, or national origin; educational institutions with personnel of particular religion

Notwithstanding any other provision of this subchapter, (1) it shall not be an unlawful employment practice for an employer to hire and employ employees, for an employment agency to classify, or refer for employment any individual, for a labor organization to classify its membership or to classify or refer for employment any individual, or for an employer, labor organization, or joint labor-management committee controlling apprenticeship or other training or retraining programs to admit or employ any individual in any such program, on the basis of his religion, sex, or national origin in those certain instances where religion, sex, or national origin is a bona fide occupational qualification reasonably necessary to the normal operation of that particular business or enterprise, and (2) it shall not be an unlawful employment practice for a school, college, university, or other educational institution or institution of learning to hire and employ employees of a particular religion if such school, college, university, or other educational institution or institution of learning is, in whole or in substantial part, owned, supported, controlled, or managed by a particular religion or by a particular religious corporation, association, or society, or if the curriculum of such school, college, university, or other educational institution or institution of learning is directed toward the propagation of a particular religion.

(f) Members of Communist Party or Communist-action or Communist-front organizations

As used in this subchapter, the phrase "unlawful employment practice" shall not be deemed to include any action or measure taken by an employer, labor organization, joint labor-management committee, or employment agency with respect to an individual who is a member of the Communist Party of the United States or of any other organization required to register as a Communist-action or Communist-front organization by final order of the Subversive Activities Control Board pursuant to the Subversive Activities Control Act of 1950 [50 U.S.C.A. § 781 et seq.].

(g) National security

Notwithstanding any other provision of this subchapter, it shall not be an unlawful employment practice for an employer to fail or refuse to hire and employ any individual for any position, for an employer to discharge any individual from any position, or for an employment agency to fail or refuse to refer any individual for employment in any position, or for a labor organization to fail or refuse to refer any individual for employment in any position, if—

> **(1)** the occupancy of such position, or access to the premises in or upon which any part of the duties of such position is performed or is to be performed, is subject to any requirement imposed in the interest of the national security of the United States under any security program in effect pursuant to or administered under any statute of the United States or any Executive order of the President; and

> **(2)** such individual has not fulfilled or has ceased to fulfill that requirement.

(h) Seniority or merit system; quantity or quality of production; ability tests; compensation based on sex and authorized by minimum wage provisions

Notwithstanding any other provision of this subchapter, it shall not be an unlawful employment practice for an employer to apply different standards of compensation, or different terms, conditions, or privileges of employment pursuant to a bona fide seniority or merit system, or a system which measures earnings by quantity or quality of production or to employees who work in different locations, provided that such differences are not the result of an intention to discriminate because of race, color, religion, sex, or national origin, nor shall it be an unlawful employment practice for an employer to give and to act upon the results of any professionally developed ability test provided that such test, its administration or action upon the results is not designed, intended or used to discriminate because of race, color, religion, sex or national origin. It shall not be an unlawful employment practice under this subchapter for any employer to differentiate upon the basis of sex in determining the amount of the wages or compensation paid or to be paid to employees of such employer if such differentiation is authorized by the provisions of section 206(d) of Title 29.

(i) Businesses or enterprises extending preferential treatment to Indians

Nothing contained in this subchapter shall apply to any business or enterprise on or near an Indian reservation with respect to any publicly announced employment practice of such business or enterprise under which a preferential treatment is given to any individual because he is an Indian living on or near a reservation.

(j) Preferential treatment not to be granted on account of existing number or percentage imbalance

Nothing contained in this subchapter shall be interpreted to require any employer, employment agency, labor organization, or joint labor-management committee subject to this subchapter to grant preferential treatment to any individual or to any group because of the race, color, religion, sex, or national origin of such individual or group on account of an imbalance which may exist with respect to the total number or percentage of persons of any race, color, religion, sex, or national origin employed by any employer, referred or classified for employment by any employment agency or labor organization, admitted to membership or classified by any labor organization, or admitted to, or employed in, any apprenticeship or other training program, in comparison with the total number or percentage of persons of such race, color, religion, sex, or national origin in any community, State, section, or other area, or in the available work force in any community, State, section, or other area.

NOTE ON HOW STATUTES ARE NUMBERED

Statutes like Title VII are often referred to by the section numbers in the original bill (the so-called "public law"). Thus, in the example above, the bill as passed used the section number § 703 to designate the main directives of Title VII, and scholars and judicial opinions often refer to the provisions using that number. Type § 703 into Westlaw, however, and you will get nothing. That is because, after statutes are passed, they are "codified"— renumbered and placed into the relevant subject-matter titles of the U.S. Code. Section 703 was placed into U.S. Code Title 42—which concerns Public

Health and Welfare—at § 2000e–2(a). If you are ever stuck trying to figure out the U.S.C. section of a law whose name you know, most databases like Westlaw have a "Popular Name Table" that offers a helpful conversion index organized by the name of the bill (e.g., Civil Rights Act of 1964).

B. THE RULES OF THE HOUSE AND THE SENATE

The story of the Civil Rights Act is a story of how Congress makes decisions. Just as courts have rules for filing pleadings and motions, each house of Congress has its own set of rules for writing laws.[13] The Constitution provides that each has authority to create those rules. U.S. Const., art. I, § 5 ("Each House may determine the Rules of its Proceedings").

The standard story of lawmaking moves from introduction to committee action to floor debate to passage.

Introduction $\longrightarrow$ Committee $\longrightarrow$ Floor Debate $\longrightarrow$ Vote

The standard story is correct in general for both the House and Senate. However, it leaves out important aspects of the process.

In the House, the standard account omits the central importance of party leadership and the Rules Committee. As we saw in the case of the Civil Rights Act, the House Rules Committee is very powerful in setting the agenda for debate.

HOUSE: Introduction $\longrightarrow$ Committee $\longrightarrow$ RULES COMMITTEE $\longrightarrow$ House Resolution ("the Rule") $\longrightarrow$ Floor Debate on the Rule $\longrightarrow$ Vote on the Rule $\longrightarrow$ Floor Debate $\longrightarrow$ Vote

In the Senate, the majority and minority leaders must reach a *unanimous consent* agreement. Senate procedure, as we saw above, is dominated by the *filibuster rule*, which is really not a rule at all but the absence of a means for members of the Senate to close debate. Today, to close debate (or invoke *cloture*) under Senate Rule XXII, a bill needs 60 votes.

---

[13] The account that follows is based on the House and Senate Rules as well as a variety of sources, including David W. Brady & Craig Volden, *Revolving Gridlock: Politics and Policy from Jimmy Carter to George W. Bush* (2006); Kenneth A. Shepsle & Barry R. Weingast, eds., *Positive Theories of Congressional Institutions* (1995); Keith Krehbiel, *Information and Legislative Organization* (1992); Keith Krehbiel, *Pivotal Politics: A Theory of U.S. Lawmaking* (1998); Kenneth A. Shepsle & Mark Bonchek, *Analyzing Politics: Rationality, Behavior and Institutions* (1997). Its understanding of the rules is based on participant observation of one of the authors as well as important resources such as Barbara Sinclair, *Unorthodox Lawmaking: New Legislative Processes in the U.S. Congress* (4th ed. 2011); Walter Oleszek, *Congressional Procedures and the Policy Process* (5th ed. 2000); Charles Tiefer, *Congressional Practice and Procedure: A Reference, Research, and Legislative Guide* (1989); Gregory J. Wawro & Eric Schickler, *Filibuster: Obstructing and Lawmaking in the U.S. Senate* (2006).

Typically, before the cloture vote occurs, a new bill (called a *substitute*) will be offered which has obtained the consent of a coalition of Senators sufficient to reach the 60 vote mark.

SENATE: Introduction $\longrightarrow$ **Committee** $\longrightarrow$ **FILIBUSTER** $\longrightarrow$ **SUBSTITUTE BILL** $\longrightarrow$ **CLOTURE VOTE ON SUBSTITUTE BILL** $\longrightarrow$ **Post-Cloture Amendments** $\longrightarrow$ **Floor Debate** $\longrightarrow$ **Vote**

Ultimately, the Constitution requires, under the bicameralism clause, that both houses agree upon the text sent to the President for his approval. U.S. Const., art. I, § 7. Because of the controversy surrounding the Civil Rights Act, the House receded to the Senate's bill and that bill was sent to the President. On many major bills, however, the Senate and the House reach agreement through a *conference committee procedure* explained below, which is a central place for making final textual decisions.

House Passage $\longrightarrow$ **Senate Passage** $\longrightarrow$ **CONFERENCE COMMITTEE** $\longrightarrow$ **Returns to House to Pass CONFERENCE REPORT** $\longrightarrow$ **Senate Passes CONFERENCE REPORT** $\longrightarrow$ **President Vetoes or Signs**

We now explain these rules and procedures in greater detail.

(1) The Rules of the House

Bill Introduction (H. R. ___). Any member of the House may introduce a bill; in some cases these bills have been drafted by or with the President, as was the case for the Civil Rights Act of 1964. To introduce a bill, a legislator simply drops it into the "hopper"—a wooden box at the front of the chamber. Only members may introduce bills, although they may introduce as many as they wish. If the President wants a bill passed, such as the 1964 Civil Rights Act, he must find a member to introduce it.

88TH CONGRESS
2D SESSION

H. R. 7152

IN THE HOUSE OF REPRESENTATIVES

FEBRUARY 10, 1964
Ordered printed as passed the House

AN ACT

To enforce the constitutional right to vote, to confer jurisdiction
upon the district courts of the United States to provide
injunctive relief against discrimination in public accommodations, to authorize the Attorney General to institute suits
to protect constitutional rights in public facilities and public
education, to extend the Commission on Civil Rights, to
prevent discrimination in federally assisted programs, to
establish a Commission on Equal Employment Opportunity,
and for other purposes.

1   *Be it enacted by the Senate and House of Representa-*
2 *tives of the United States of America in Congress assembled,*
3 That this Act may be cited as "The Civil Rights Act of
4 1963".

I

Committee Referral. Standing or permanent committees have existed in the House of Representatives since the second half of the 19th century. Bills, once they are introduced, are referred to committee for consideration at the instruction of the Speaker of the House. There is a fair amount of discretion in referral; for example, the leadership steered the Civil Rights Act toward a favorable committee, the House Judiciary Committee. Multiple referrals can kill a bill because too many committees become involved. Multiple referrals may also affect later stages in the proceeding, such as a conference committee, as they will increase the number of persons who are conferees, augmenting the complexity of the conference. For example, during one conference on a savings and loan bill, 102 conferees were named (Oleszek 255). "In most Congresses since the late 1980s about three out of ten major measures were multiply referred" (Sinclair 12). Starting in 1995, however, the House began to use a process that provided for "primary referral" to one committee, and potential time limits on additional committee reports (Sinclair 14).

Subcommittee Referral. There is no requirement that a bill be considered by a committee and at different times the House has considered major measures without committee consideration. There is also no requirement that a bill be referred to subcommittee. Generally, subcommittee referral is a good deal easier than committee referral as there are fewer subcommittees within a committee than there are committees in the House as a whole. As planned, the Civil Rights Act, H.R. 7152, was referred to Manny Celler's *antitrust* subcommittee. Note that the subject matter of the referral may have little relationship to the name of the committee. (Thus, do not be surprised to find that Campaign Finance legislation was referred to the Subcommittee on the Constitution rather than a Subcommittee on Campaigns). On major legislation, supporters may actually shape the text of the bill to avoid multiple referrals or referrals to hostile committees.

Subcommittee, Committee Hearings, Mark-Up. Although there is no requirement that there be hearings on a bill, that practice is customary; indeed, lengthy hearings were held on H.R. 7152. These hearings are then produced as committee hearing documents. Hearings may include important testimony related to amendments or may be staged events producing testimony supporting the bill's proponents. Mark-ups are more useful as far as statutory language is concerned, but generally are not a matter of public record. Often a mark-up will begin with an entirely different bill than the one introduced—a "substitute" bill negotiated by the chairman and the ranking member. More controversial amendments will then be considered and voted on in the mark-up. Committee hearings are printed and appear like the following:

Committee Report. After completing bill consideration, a subcommittee or committee report may be issued (H. R. Rep ___). The report will typically describe the law's history. This provides researchers with information spanning different Congresses: if a bill was reported in 1993, but was first introduced in 1990, the committee report will typically provide that information, along with bill numbers, dates of hearings, and the like. Reports will typically reprint the bill as introduced and as reported by committee, with a section-by-section analysis of changes made in committee.

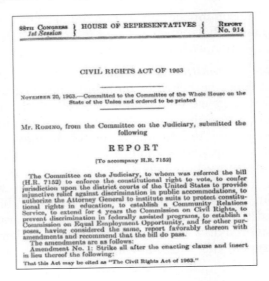

Post-Committee Changes. Even after committee consideration, the majority and minority leaders or the committee chairman and ranking member may make further changes to the bill. These changes may yield an entirely new bill, or become the bill recommended as an amendment by the Rules Committee (see below). In some cases, these changes may be added on the floor in amendment form. This is most likely to occur at the initiative of party leaders and because the bill is particularly difficult or controversial.

House Rules Committee. In the late 1880s and 1890s, the House developed a process for scheduling major floor legislation: "special rules from the Rules Committee" (Sinclair 6). A rule from the Rules Committee must be approved by the House prior to consideration of the bill. Typically, this takes the form of a House Resolution (H. Res.). An "open rule" allows all germane amendments to be offered. A "closed rule" is one which limits amendments in particular ways. Most rules today are restricted in some sense based on the nature of the amendments, or time limits. The Rules Committee is chosen by the Speaker and party leadership strongly influences the nature of the Rule.

The Rules Committee's chairman is one of the most powerful persons in the House. In the case of the civil rights bill, for example, the chairman bottled up the bill for a long time. The important point is that the Rules Committee sets the agenda: once the committee agrees, it does not agree on the bill, *but how the House will debate the bill.* For example, the Rule may say "the proponents and opponents will have 20 minutes equally divided, and there will be 7 amendments." (By contrast, in the Senate all of this must be worked out between the majority and minority leader under a "unanimous consent" agreement or UC). "One or two hours of general debate" is typically provided in a special closed rule, "although major measures occasionally are granted considerably more time" (Sinclair 25). There is no requirement that a Rule be passed; instead, the House may vote to "suspend" the rules and does so on noncontroversial legislation.

A <u>House Rule</u> As It Appears in the *Congressional Record*

> **CIVIL RIGHTS ACT OF 1963**
>
> Mr. MADDEN. Mr. Speaker, by direction of the Committee on Rules, I call up House Resolution 616 and ask for its immediate consideration.
>
> The Clerk read the resolution, as follows:
>
> *Resolved,* That upon the adoption of this resolution it shall be in order to move that the House resolve itself into the Committee of the Whole House on the State of the Union for the consideration of the bill (H.R. 7152) to enforce the constitutional right to vote, to confer jurisdiction upon the district courts of the United States to provide injunctive relief against discrimination in public accommodations, to authorize the Attorney General to institute suits to protect constitutional rights in education, to establish a Community Relations Service, to extend for four years the Commission on Civil Rights, to prevent discrimination in federally assisted programs, to establish a Commission on Equal Employment Opportunity, and for other purposes, and all points of order against said bill are hereby waived. After general debate, which shall be confined to the bill, and shall continue not to exceed ten hours, to be equally divided and controlled by the chairman and ranking minority member of the Committee on the Judiciary, the bill shall be read for amendment under the five-minute rule. It shall be in order to consider without the intervention of any points of order the substitute amendment recommended by the Committee on the Judiciary now printed in the bill, and such substitute for the purpose of amendment shall be considered under the five-minute rule as an original bill, and shall be read by titles instead of by sections. It shall also be in order to consider, without the intervention of any point of order, the text of the bill H.R. 980, 88th Congress, as an amendment to the said committee sub-

Debate on the Rule. The House may debate the Rule itself. Typically, one hour is allotted, "equally split between the chair and the ranking minority member of the committee that reported the legislation" (Sinclair 25). The majority member defends the Rule, the minority responds, and they yield time to others who might want to speak. It is possible, but rare, that the rule itself will be voted down because of underlying hostility to the bill or the Rule's procedural provisions. In any event, if the Rule fails, the bill will not be considered. It is important to recognize that debate on the Rule may well be very different from debate on the substantive merits of the bill. It is likely, for example, that there is going to be more "cheap talk" (i.e., grand statements) in the Rule debate relative to the actual debate, because there is greater incentive for both sides to exaggerate their positions if they seek to uphold or defeat a controversial Rule.

Debate and Floor Amendments. "If the House approves the [R]ule, it usually then resolves itself into the Committee of the Whole [House of the State of the Union,] where the legislation is debated and amended." (Sinclair 37.) In fact, the House does not turn itself into a smaller body, but adopts streamlined procedures allowing for a reduced quorum (100 rather than 218), and members are generally limited to five minutes to speak, subject to the Rule's provisions. The debate in the House will follow the Rule as passed. The chair of the committee or subcommittee reporting the bill manages the bill on the floor and controls the time allotted to the majority. The debate will generally begin with a statement by the floor manager explaining the legislation.

When general debate time is over, amendments will be offered only according to the Rule. In this context, the five-minute rule is somewhat misleading. A member who is permitted under the Rule to offer an amendment has five minutes to present it, unless the Rule says otherwise, and anyone who wishes to speak against it may have five minutes. In turn, another member may seek to amend that amendment with a second-degree amendment. That second-degree amendment in turn will be permitted five minutes, and any opposition five minutes. So, despite the apparent limitation of the five-minute rule, it may actually take a fairly long time to debate an amendment in the House. Unlike the Senate, however, the House has little tolerance for lengthy deliberation and may, by majority vote, close debate when it appears to be used for obstruction or delay.

After debate is completed, the House will reconvene out of the Committee on the Whole House, and repass the bill it has considered "in Committee." Typically this is done by asking for passage of the entire bill but it is possible that there may be reconsideration of specific or controversial amendments passed previously. Votes on the bill, whether "in Committee" or on final passage are computerized, allowing a member to insert a credit card type device to record his vote, which is shown on a large lighted tally board.

(2) The Rules of the Senate

Any Senator may introduce a bill by offering the bill to the appropriate clerk. The bill will be printed in the record and typically, for important bills, the Senator will introduce the bill with a speech on the floor.

Committee and Subcommittee Referral. Bills, once they are introduced, must be referred to a committee, typically by the Senate Parliamentarian's office. In the Senate, multiple referral is discouraged; a bill may be referred to one committee if the majority of its provisions relate to the committee's subject matter.

Subcommittee and Committee Mark-Up and Committee Reports. Bills may be marked up at the subcommittee and committee level. At the end of the subcommittee and committee process, the committee may issue a report (S. Rep.). Committee reports that do not carry the designation "S. Rep.," are committee documents, but may be the work of the Chairman or a group of members of the committee on a topic of interest; these reports will be denominated "S. Doc." Committee reports can be consensus documents, negotiated by the Committee Chairman and the ranking member and approved by all members; they may also be documents about which there is disagreement, typically noted by "additional" or "dissenting" views.

In the Senate, there is no rule that bills go through committee: if the majority and minority leader agree to move a bill on the floor, they may simply take it off the calendar (as they did with the civil rights bill in 1964). In cases where there is no committee consideration, there will be no committee report in the Senate. "In the Congresses of the 1990s and early 2000s, the proportion of major measures that were considered on the Senate floor without first going through committee varied widely from a low of 11 percent in the 101st Congress (1989–1990) to a high of 41 percent in the 107th (2001–02)." (Sinclair 27.) In the Senate, committees are often bypassed when matters are controversial, or there is an urgent situation; another means of bypassing the committee is by adding the bill as an amendment to another bill. There is a *no germaneness rule* in the Senate; at least in theory, a Senator can add a civil rights bill to a crime or agriculture bill.

Post-Committee Changes. A substantial number of bills are modified after introduction or committee consideration. Often individual senators or the majority leader will take the lead in these adjustments, as a means to forestall an objection or filibuster of the bill. The lead sponsor of a bill will engage with bill opponents and seek to add language that will satisfy opponents' concerns or build a coalition of at least 60 votes (see below on the necessity of a supermajority). This bill then becomes the "substitute" introduced prior to a cloture vote.

Unanimous Consent Agreements. There is no Rules Committee comparable to the one in the House of Representatives; instead, the Senate operates by unanimous consent ("UC"). The majority leader, when seeking to move to consider a particular bill, will offer a unanimous consent agreement which, like a House rule, sets forth how the Senate will proceed to debate the bill. Sometimes this UC will specify particular amendments or time limits, but it need not do so. Any senator may object to a UC. As Professor Sinclair explains, this means that "[t]he Senate is not a majority-rule chamber like the House. In the House the majority can always prevail; in the Senate minorities can often block majorities." (Sinclair 43.)

A Unanimous Consent Agreement (*Congressional Record*)

> **UNANIMOUS-CONSENT REQUEST**
>
> Mr. LOTT. Mr. President, I ask unanimous consent that the Senate stand in recess until 2 p.m. today.
>
> Mr. DASCHLE. Mr. President, on behalf of my colleagues on the Judiciary Committee, on that, too, I must object.
>
> The PRESIDING OFFICER. Objection is heard.
>
> Mr. LOTT. Mr. President, I suggest the absence of a quorum.
>
> The PRESIDING OFFICER. The clerk will call the roll.
>
> The legislative clerk proceeded to call the roll.
>
> Mr. LOTT. Mr. President, I ask unanimous consent that the order for the quorum call be rescinded.
>
> The PRESIDING OFFICER. Without objection, it is so ordered.

Filibuster/Objection to Proceed. For any controversial bill, or almost any bill today,[14] the majority leader must anticipate that the bill will be filibustered, which means that, as a practical matter, 60 votes are required for passage, because 60 votes are required to end debate ("cloture"). There was no question that the Civil Rights Act of 1964 was going to be filibustered. When the majority leader moved to proceed to the bill, a member of the opposite party "objected." In the case of the Civil Rights Act, however, there was a very lengthy debate on whether to move to proceed to the bill, a debate that is sometimes called the "longest debate."

Today, however, the reality is that no long speeches need to be made. The threat of a filibuster signaled by an objection by a single senator is enough. This is sometimes called the costless filibuster as it does not require any investment by a determined minority but simply the action of a single objecting senator. The term "filibuster" tends to conjure up images of a crusading Jimmy Stewart or senators sleeping on cots during the civil rights debate. Modern filibusters seldom require drama, and they are often simply a threat to filibuster known as a "hold." Major and minor issues may be subjected to a filibuster. Historically, nominations have been filibustered but a Fall 2013 change in Senate precedent, discussed below, allowed a majority to prevent a filibuster for all but Supreme Court nominees (at least as we write). As Professor Sinclair observes, "[h]olds are frequent, and placing them has become standard operating

---

[14] Since the 1990s, the incidence of filibusters has risen dramatically as a culture which frowned on such tactics has increasingly acceded to them. See Gregory J. Wawro & Eric Schickler, *Filibuster: Obstructing and Lawmaking in the U.S. Senate* (2007). For the latest statistics, see our Note on the Filibuster, below.

procedure in the Senate" (Sinclair 53). As Sinclair notes, holds are not a part of the Senate Rules, they are an informal custom: "What gives holds their bite is the implicit or explicit threat to filibuster." *Id.*

A "Hold/Threat to Filibuster" As It May Appear in the *Congressional Record*[15]

> Mr. MANSFIELD. Mr. President, I move to proceed to the bill at the desk, the Pregnancy Discrimination Act of 1978.
>
>
> The Presiding Officer. The clerk shall . . .
>
>
> Mr. DIRKSEN. I object.

Even before a bill is brought up, a senator may inform his or her party leader of an intention to object or "hold." The majority leader may proceed to a bill even if there is a hold, but in general he will have to anticipate that the objecting Senator will filibuster. "Especially when floor time is short—before a recess or near the end of the session," the power of the hold increases. "As time becomes scarcer, a hold increasingly becomes a veto," *even* a one-person veto (Sinclair 54).

Holds may be used on all kinds of Senate action. They have been used to strategically extract concessions on unrelated bills (sometimes known as "hostage-taking"), on nominations, or even on procedural matters. For example, when Senator Dole tried to name certain conferees to a health insurance bill that was unacceptable to Senator Kennedy, Senator Kennedy put a "hold" on the naming of conferees! Increasingly, extended debate has become a routinely employed partisan tool as well. As a consequence, controversial measures almost always need sixty votes to pass the Senate." (Sinclair 55–57.)

At the end of 2013, Senator Reid, the Majority Leader, deployed what was dubbed the "nuclear" or "constitutional" option to attempt an end to filibusters of lower court and executive nominees. Frustrated by extreme delays in the nomination process, amounting to years, the Senate created a new precedent that a majority was sufficient to end a filibuster in this select category of nominations. (It remains possible to filibuster nominees to the U.S. Supreme Court). This precedent effectively circumvented the Senate's own rules (which can only be changed with a 2/3 vote), and

---

[15] This is a fictional representation. It is offered to show that it is impossible to count "filibusters" simply by looking for the word "filibuster" in the Congressional Record as there is no requirement that a senator use that term.

invoked the power of a majority to work its will as a constitutional matter. This move did not change the normal presumption that, in all *legislative matters*, sixty votes may be necessary to pass legislation. It is also important to note that, even without the filibuster, there are other ways to block nominees (such as the "blue slip," a process by which a single senator from the nominating state may object and kill a nomination). It is also still possible to "hold" or delay nominees. Whether and how the "constitutional option" will be deployed in the future remains unknown.

Cloture and a Substitute Bill. For most of its existence, the small size of the Senate allowed it to proceed under informal norms, and obstruction was controlled by folkways in which the filibuster was frowned upon by senators, and in which there was always the threat that a determined majority might change the rules entirely to eliminate continuous debate, and provide for cloture by a mere majority. (Wawro & Schickler 117). In 1917, at the insistence of President Wilson and in light of the public's furor at obstruction of a popular bill, the Senate rules were changed to allow the closing of debate. After the debate over civil rights legislation of 1964, the threshold for cloture was changed from 67 votes to 60 votes. Today, a cloture petition requires the signatures of at least 16 senators. Typically, a cloture petition will not be filed until the majority and minority leaders have negotiated to obtain the necessary votes. This negotiated bill will then be offered as a "substitute" for the bill as originally introduced. A cloture motion will then be filed.

A Cloture Motion As It Will Appear in the
Congressional Record[16]

CLOTURE MOTION

We, the undersigned Senators, in accordance with the provisions of rule XXII of the Standing Rules of the Senate, hereby move to bring to a close debate on the nomination of John J. McConnell, Jr., of Rhode Island, to be United States District Judge for the District of Rhode Island.

Harry Reid, Patrick J. Leahy, John F. Kerry, Dianne Feinstein, Frank R. Lautenberg, Jack Reed, Sheldon Whitehouse, Robert Menendez, Amy Klobuchar, Barbara Boxer, Daniel K. Inouye, Mark Begich, Mark R. Warner, Kent Conrad, John D. Rockefeller IV, Richard J. Durbin, Ron Wyden.

Mr. REID. Mr. President, I ask unanimous consent that it be in order at this time to waive the mandatory quorums under rule XXII with respect to both cloture motions.

The PRESIDING OFFICER. Without objection, it is so ordered.

Post-Cloture Debate and Passage. If cloture is invoked, Rule XXII imposes a cap of 30 hours for debate. If cloture fails, supporters of the blocked legislation may try again. In 1987 and 1988, Majority Leader Byrd made 8 attempts to invoke cloture to advance campaign finance legislation. Almost any motion (including the motion to proceed to a bill), any amendment, motions relating to conference, and the conference report may all be filibustered. Bill supporters may file for cloture even before they know of objections to the bill as a means to force negotiations.

Debate in the Senate will typically follow a unanimous consent agreement and is thus individualized for every bill. There is a no germaneness rule in the Senate, so any amendment can be offered. If cloture is invoked, however, Rule XXII requires that amendments be germane and filed prior to cloture (a rule that did not apply to the Civil Rights Act of 1964). This rule gives opponents incentives to "relitigate" issues resolved in the substitute bill upon which cloture was invoked, in effect "testing" whether negotiators have the full Senate's support for their compromise proposal; in short, it gives opponents of the bill a "second chance" at controversial issues. At the end of consideration, the managers will typically offer a consolidated "technical" amendment which may include hundreds of provisions. Senators do not vote electronically, but instead appear on the floor of the Senate, signaling the Senate clerk of their vote, often with a thumbs up or down, as their name is read.

The Record of Debate. Debate in both the House and the Senate is recorded in the Congressional Record. The Record is just that, it records

---

[16] 157 Cong. Rec. S2573 (May 2, 2011).

the actions of the members and senators as they proceed. If the body is not conducting business, individuals may offer speeches. As a result, the Congressional Record may go from page to page on completely unrelated matters. The Record contains a vast amount of information, including a list of all bills introduced by legislators or reported from any committee in each chamber, the full text of bills considered on the legislative floor and proposed amendments to those bills, the text of conference committee reports and a full record of legislative debate and remarks. It does not, however, include most committee reports, hearings, or mark-ups.

Lawyers were once scandalized by the fact that members could insert matters into the Congressional Record even when these remarks were not given "live," without any kind of notation of the fact they were inserted. Members in both the House and Senate may "correct" their statements for errors of grammar and the like before those remarks are printed in the Daily Record, but remarks that were not made on the floor are (in theory) so designated in the Record, either by a bullet (in the Senate), a change in typeface (in the House). Sometimes, in the House, such statements appear in a section entitled "Extensions of Remarks." Below are a few examples.

House

Ms. JACKSON LEE of Texas. When we send them into battle, we have the obligation of saying there is a beginning and an end. World War I, World War II, wars that we may have liked or disliked, but we knew as they went into battle that there was an ending. And how brave they were.

As we saluted the women who participated in the Air Army Corps for Women, the WASPs today, some hundreds of them, we know that there is no doubt that they are brave. But I would say to you, end this war with Afghanistan and end this partnership with Pakistan. There are ways to be able to support the structure of both governments without our soldiers losing their lives on and on and on.

This resolution says that if the President finds it necessary to extend, he can do so. But we are asking for the troops to be out by the end of this year. So many of us have spoken to that over and over again.

Madam Speaker, this is not something unusual. This is not a cause of the fearful. This is not a cause of those who are nonpatriotic. This is a cause for people who believe in the red, white, and blue, who stand here today loving their country and believe that our soldiers are owed this respect to bring them home as heroes. We ask that you support this resolution.

Madam Speaker, I rise in solemn opposition to a war that has cost too many American lives and too many American dollars. To date, over 1,000 Americans have lost their lives in the Afghan theatre, including 70 in 2010. In 2009, 316 Americans lost their lives. The war in Afghanistan should end as safely and quickly as possible, and our troops should be brought home with honor and a national day of celebration. I strongly believe that this can

Senate

• Mr. ROCKEFELLER. Mr. President, I am sincerely disappointed about the placing of an anonymous hold on S. 2043, the "Veterans Long-Term Care and Medical Programs Enhancement Act of 2002."

There is no apparent reason why this important piece of legislation should be held up at this time. It was developed in a bipartisan manner and encompasses many vital pieces of legislation from both sides of the aisle. It is my sincere hope that the Senator responsible for this hold will realize that this is certainly not the time to be playing politics with legislation that affects our Nation's veterans.

I would like to share with my colleagues some of the key provisions of S. 2043 that seek to improve the accessibility and quality of the VA health care system.

The centerpiece of this bill is an effort to make VA's prescription drug copayment policy a bit more equitable for lower-income veterans. Mr. President, currently, veterans with incomes of less than $24,000 a year are exempt from copayments for most VA health care services. However, when it comes to prescription drugs, the income threshold for exemption is about $9,000 a year. This bill would raise the exemption level for prescription copayments to make them the same as other VA health care copayments.

Recently, however, it appears that senators have been attempting to evade the Senate's rules on publication by writing the term "LIVE" on their remarks and then submitting them for the record. (The Senate does not follow the House rule for extensions of remarks.) It is a common practice for senators, after the conclusion of a bill, to insert further remarks to thank colleagues or communicate their positions to constituents. The problem comes when the remarks are planned in an effort to sway judicial interpretation. A particularly egregious example recently surfaced involving the important Guantanamo Bay case of *Hamdan v. Rumsfeld*, 548 U.S. 547 (2006), when lawyers discovered that supposedly "live" statements directly relevant to the issue in the case did not appear on the C-Span tape of the proceedings, and so had never actually been delivered, or relied upon by others.[17] Here is an excerpt from that "live" debate. Could you have told the difference?

Mr. KYL. I would like to say a few words about the now-completed National Defense Authorization Act for fiscal year 2006, and in particular about section 1405 of that act, which expels lawsuits brought by enemy combatants from United States courts. I see that my colleague, the senior Senator from South Carolina, is also on the floor. * * *

Mr. GRAHAM. I agree entirely. If I could add one thing on this point: perhaps the best evidence that the current Rasul system undermines effective interrogation is that even the detainees' lawyers are bragging about their lawsuits' having that effect. * * *

Mr. KYL. I am glad that we have been able to work together on this issue. I would add that interrogation of these detainees is important. * * *

Mr. GRAHAM. You are absolutely correct Senator KYL. I must admit, I'm somewhat baffled by the assertion that our amendment is somehow internally inconsistent, that our provisions interfere with the McCain provisions in some way. * * *

Mr. BROWNBACK. If I might interrupt, I would like to add that I share the understanding of my colleagues from Arizona and South Carolina. I supported the McCain amendments—I think that it is important to ensure that detainees are treated

---

[17] *Compare* Emily Bazelon, *Invisible Men*, Slate Magazine (Mar. 27, 2006) & *Hamdan Hoax, Part 3* (July 26, 2006) (discussing this controversy), *with* Ramesh Ponnuru, *Snookering Stevens*, National Review Online (July 25, 2006) (disputing precisely which legislative history was given "live"). The Senate has a more flexible approach to these issues than the House: Senators have always been able to request unanimous consent that they revise and extend their remarks—in which case their remarks are not really made "live," and reading the earlier request can tip the careful reader off to that fact.

humanely. But I would not support allowing those detainees to file lawsuits against our armed forces * * *.

This has become a bigger problem thanks to technology. Westlaw, for example, does not print the bullets or the font changes even when members of Congress utilize them. If you are litigating a case involving "smoking gun" legislative history, be sure to consult a version of the *Congressional Record* as actually printed, not to mention C-Span.

(3) House and Senate Agreement: Getting to One Text

The House and the Senate may resolve their differences by sending bills back and forth until they have both passed the same text (this is sometimes called "reconciliation"). For example, in the 1964 Civil Rights Act, the House simply passed the Senate bill, without going to conference. Today this is most likely to happen when time is tight and the alternative is to let the bill die. Legislation on minor matters may shuttle back and forth with each chamber offering their proposal as a substitute. The House passes a bill and then sends it to the Senate, the Senate substitutes its version and sends it back to the House, and this can, in theory go on as long as the Congress is in session. The important point is that the same text has to be passed for the President to approve or disapprove under the Constitution's veto provision, Article I, § 7.

The most common way of resolving differing bills is to refer the bills to a conference committee: "78 percent of major measures that got to the resolution stage were sent to conference," although this dropped to "67 percent" during the early 2000s (Sinclair 76), and has dropped dramatically in recent years. See Abbe R. Gluck & Lisa Schultz Bressman, *Statutory Interpretation from the Inside—An Empirical Study of Congressional Drafting, Delegation and the Canons: Part II,* 66 Stan. L. Rev. (2014) (only 3 of 91 measures that passed in the first year of the 112th Congress went to conference).[18] Typically, a conference committee seeks to resolve the differences between bills passed in the House and the Senate. Conferees are named by the majority and minority leaders of the House and Senate and typically include the major participants in the bill's drafting and debate.

The Conference Committee typically prepares a brief report (conference committees typically work under some time pressure) explaining how the committee resolved the differences between the House and Senate language. The conference report is not a summary of the bill and is typically silent on texts agreed upon by both chambers. The

---

[18] This dip likely reflects the rise of the filibuster as an all-purpose weapon; in a world where you can filibuster the motion to go to conference or the naming of conferees, and Senators are willing to use their power in this way, it is not surprising that bills do not go to conference. What happens, instead, is a "shadow" conference where bills are compromised by the leaders and managers in advance of passage.

conference report is the language of the text of the agreed upon bill; it is accompanied by a "joint explanation" explaining the decision to choose House or Senate language or something different (conferees may not change provisions upon which both Houses have agreed, if they do, the bill is subject to a point of order in either House). Bills rarely die in conference because of the substantial amount of time already invested in their passage. A majority of the conferees from each chamber must vote for the conference report. If there is an issue about what position was taken by a House, that is determined by a majority of the conferees of that House. The Conference Report will be printed in the Congressional Record and is the "text" of the bill that is ultimately passed by both Houses.

Conference committees, as noted, are generally bound by the versions of the bill passed by both Houses, meaning they cannot add provisions that do not appear in at least one side's bill.[19] In general, conferees have an incentive to avoid a point of order when the conference report returns to the House and the Senate, because that could slow or block passage. It does happen, however, that committees violate the rule; they may violate it on noncontroversial provisions on the theory that time is short and no one will notice (Sinclair 66), or they may violate it precisely because the item is controversial.

After the conference committee, there remain three important steps toward final passage:

Repassage by House and Senate. Once the Conference Committee has agreed upon a bill, this bill, now called a Conference Report (H.R. Conf. Rep.), must be passed by the House and Senate, so that they have passed the same text. Typically, there are no amendments permitted to conference reports, but there can be debate about the new text in both the House and Senate. For example, members may raise a point of order that the conference has exceeded the scope of the bills already passed. Typically, Congress must vote on the entire bill, up or down. There are exceptions in the House involving amendments to a conference report on certain matters in appropriations bills.

Consideration by the President. Article I of the Constitution provides that the President has the right to veto a bill. This appears in the "Bicameralism and Presentment" clause, which provides that a bill passed by both houses of Congress must be submitted to the President for his signature. Sometimes, the President may issue a "signing statement" indicating his views about how the law should be interpreted.

Potential Override by 2/3 of Each House. If the President does not sign the bill, then the House and the Senate have the final say; if 2/3 of

---

[19] In theory, in the House, conferees can get around this by taking the conference report to the floor under a special rule that waives this requirement.

the members of the House and Senate vote to override, then the bill shall become law over the President's veto.

NOTE ON LEGISLATIVE VETOGATES

The most salient feature of the legislative process is that any legislative proposal must surmount many hurdles. Political scientists call these "vetogates."[20] A filibuster is a "vetogate," but so is committee consideration. If a bill cannot get voted out of committee, then it is effectively vetoed long before it gets to floor debate. Article I, § 7 of the Constitution provides that the House and the Senate must pass identical language and that this must be presented to the President. Hence, either body or any part of those bodies (subcommittees, committees, rules committees, etc.) can operate as a veto point for legislation.

The congressional process, the bodies' rules of proceeding, tell us the points at which a bill may be subject to veto. Here are only some of the ways a bill may be killed. Opponents may (1) kill the bill in subcommittee; (2) kill the bill in committee; (3) kill the bill during floor consideration, by filibuster or a "poison pill" amendment (see Judge Smith's attempt to kill the Civil Rights Act by adding "sex discrimination" to the bill), or outright defeat; (4) kill the bill in the "other" chamber, letting it die in the House if passed by the Senate or vice versa; (5) kill the bill in conference committee or when both the House and the Senate have to pass the conference report; and (6) if all else fails, persuade the President to veto the bill and work to prevent a 2/3 congressional override.

This process helps explain why very few bills do pass, and that when they are passed, they are typically passed by large vote margins: hurdling vetogates requires building a massive legislative consensus. It also means that minorities can wield a great deal of power in Congress; in fact, even a single representative may have enormous power. Any minority or individual who has control over a vetogate can, at the very least, obtain important concessions from the majority. For example, in our Civil Rights story, we saw the filibuster meant that the majority had to concede items to the minority, the Dirksen forces. Because small groups have fewer costs of getting together and negotiating than do large majorities, small groups may have a tremendous advantage if they want to "kill" a bill.

Some vetogates may be very important in understanding key textual changes in legislation and may thus be important to statutory interpreters. As noted above, in the Senate, when there is a filibuster (and since the early 1990s, there have been filibusters on nearly any bill of importance), the majority will obtain 60 votes by building a coalition, and that coalition will introduce a compromise bill called the "substitute." The "substitute" is very

---

[20] McNollgast (aka Mathew McCubbins, Roger Noll, and Barry R. Weingast), *Positive Canons: The Role of Legislative Bargains in Statutory Interpretation*, 80 Geo. L.J. 705–42 (1992); *see also* Keith Krehbiel, *Pivotal Politics: A Theory of U.S. Lawmaking* (1998); George Tsebelis, *Veto Players: How Political Institutions Work* (2002).

important—both for legislators and observers (like courts) interested in discerning the legislative deal—because it includes textual provisions necessary for bill passage. Similarly, conference committees may be very important points for textual interpreters, because the House and Senate must choose a particular text when texts differ. Often conference reports simply say things like "House recedes to Senate on section X," but this statutory change may have an important effect upon later understandings of Congress's textual decisions.

Finally, if a bill sails through without encountering these vetogates, a committee report may be a place where key textual decisions are revealed. Typically, these reports are negotiated by majority and minority staff; if you see a separate minority report, you can tell that was not the case. Committee reports are drafted by those most likely to be attentive to and expert in the text as it was introduced. Such sources, however, may lose power to persuade over time if, for example, the bill is later changed in significant ways after it leaves committee, as is the case if a substitute is offered which effectively "trumps" the committee bill.

The systemic consequences of our vetogates structure for legislation, compared with a simpler parliamentary model, are complex.[21] The obvious descriptive consequence of the vetogates structure is that federal statutes are harder to enact than they would be under a parliamentary structure. Fewer problems have been as pressing for the United States as apartheid and pervasive discrimination against persons of color, yet it took decades for Congress to adopt comprehensive legislation—and the reason was bicameralism (Senate as well as House approval) and the filibuster (southern senators were able to veto sweeping legislation before 1964). Likewise, it took Congress seventy years to adopt comprehensive national health insurance legislation, with the Affordable Care and Protection Act of 2010. The legislation finally adopted included a number of compromises to secure sixty votes in the Senate to surmount a filibuster, actions receiving considerable negative attention when the Supreme Court reviewed the law in 2012. See *National Federation of Independent Business v. Sebelius*, 132 S.Ct. 2566 (2012).

The supermajoritarian framework of vetogates affects the content of legislation as well. Theoretically, one would expect legislation under a vetogates model to involve more compromises, more logrolls and bundles, and more lawmaking delegations than legislation under a parliamentary model. Title VII of the Civil Rights Act of 1964 involved many compromises and

---

[21] William N. Eskridge Jr., *Vetogates, Preemption,* Chevron, 83 Notre Dame L. Rev. 1441 (2008). The comparison is to a simple parliamentary model where there are no bicameralism, presentment, or filibuster barriers to legislation. Under such a model, political scientists have, tentatively, concluded that there would be more legislation addressing important national problems than under the approach embedded in our Constitution and Senate/House Rules. See Sarah A. Binder, *Stalemate: Causes and Consequences of Legislative Gridlock* (2003); Arend Lijphart, *Democracies: Patterns of Majoritarian and Consensus Government in Twenty-One Countries* (1984); Sarah A. Binder, *The Dynamics of Legislative Gridlock, 1947–96*, 93 Am. Pol. Sci. Rev. 519–33 (1999).

exceptions to the nondiscrimination rule to accommodate important supporters of the bill—labor unions (§ 703(h)), businesses (§ 703(e)), and churches (§§ 702, 703(e)). There was a fair amount of blatant favor-swapping as well, where President Johnson and other supporters exchanged favors and legislative promises in order to secure votes needed to override the southern filibuster.

Sometimes this type of dealmaking occurs as part of the "textbook" legislative process, but increasingly frequently, it happens through vehicles expressly designed to get around that process and all the vetogates it includes. Bundled deals, closed-door summits, procedural tactics to avoid the dangerous conference stage are just some of the ways in which Congress now tries to leapfrog vetogates and overcome the deepening problem of gridlock. Barbara Sinclair has dubbed this new normal process as "unorthodox lawmaking."[22] In some respects, these once-unorthodox procedures have become orthodox, as controversial bills are, increasingly, bypassing committees and are being negotiated by committee chairmen, party leaders and their caucuses.

Legislative deals frequently involve delegation of authority to agencies as a way to bypass thorny substantive disagreements. Title VII created an agency (the EEOC) but did not give it lawmaking authority. In contrast, subsequent super-statutes have involved massive delegations of lawmaking authority to agencies—from the Motor Vehicle Safety Act of 1966, the Clean Air Act of 1969 and the Clean Water Act of 1972 (as well as their increasingly complicated amendments), the Endangered Species Act of 1973, the Public Utility Regulatory Policies Act of 1978, the Energy Act of 1992, the Americans with Disabilities Act of 1990, the Family and Medical Leave Act of 1993, the Telecommunications Act of 1996, the PATRIOT Act of 2001, the Family Smoking Prevention and Tobacco Control Act of 2009, and the Affordable Care Act of 2010.

The same vetogates structure that encourages delegation of lawmaking authority to agencies also ensures that agency lawmaking will be difficult for Congress to override. Of course, much agency lawmaking is subject to judicial review—thereby giving the Supreme Court ultimate authority to set statutory policy through statutory interpretations that Congress is often not able to override in the short term.[23] Notice how constitutional and institutional rules governing the *legislative process* have important effects for the power and authority of the *executive* and *judicial* organs of American government.

---

[22] On omnibus legislation, see Glen S. Krutz, *Hitching a Ride: Omnibus Legislating in the U.S. Congress* (2001). On the unorthodox procedures, see Sinclair, *Unorthodox Legislation.*

[23] Contrary to traditional assumptions, however, Congress does monitor the Supreme Court's statutory interpretation decisions and overrides a lot of them. See Mathew R. Christiansen & William N. Eskridge Jr., *Congressional Overrides of Supreme Court Statutory Interpretation Decisions, 1967–2011,* 92 Tex. L. Rev. 1317 (2014) (reporting that overrides were very common, 1975–1998 but have steeply declined since 1998).

NOTE ON INTEREST GROUPS AND THE INATTENTIVE PUBLIC

At least since the founding of our republic, political observers have been concerned that small groups of citizens will gain excessive control over the political process. We fought a revolution to free ourselves from English monarchy and aristocracy. In the *Federalist Papers*, James Madison decried factions, but believed that there could be both majority and minority factions. *Federalist* No. 10 (Madison). He hoped that the institutional structure of the government would be a way in which to channel or check factions.

Interest group politics has been decried throughout our nation's history, yet one of our great political ironies is that we are all part of "groups" that are sometimes considered "interest" groups. If you have given money to the Sierra Club or the Chamber of Commerce, you have supported an interest group. Some interest groups are huge and largely permanent, such as the American Association of Retired Persons (AARP). Other organizations, like universities or lawyers (the ABA) or your church, don't appear to be interest groups but in fact have important lobbying interests. Even federal judges have a quasi-lobbying organization, a part of the Federal Judicial Conference devoted to protecting the interests of judges.

There are many conceptions political scientists have advanced to explain the formation and importance of interest groups. Following de Tocqueville's famous discussion in *Democracy in America* (1837), Robert Dahl and other political scientists have understood interest groups as a positive feature of our governance. Citizens organize into groups for different political reasons and this results in "pluralism," or the spreading of political power over many areas. This diffuses the power of particular groups (and thus Madison's fear of factions) and yet allows a broad variety of interests to be represented. Under the rosiest versions of pluralism, politics is seen as the process by which interest groups seek to satisfy their goals, with each group securing the policies they most intensely desire, while acceding to the policies intensely desired by other groups. Under this rosy scenario, everybody gets what they want most, while compromising to allow others the same advantage.

The rosy version, however, may not be realistic. Political scientist Mancur Olson explained that small interest groups, particularly "have" groups such as lawyers and big business, enjoy disproportionate power, at the expense of "have-not" groups and even the broad middle class. It is easy for the vast majority of people, the "inattentive public" to pay no attention to politics, and "free-ride" on the efforts of others. Small groups are likely to have narrow interests at heart, for they are formed and typically cohere among the "few," who have the energy, time, money, and psychic gains to actively participate in the process. Olson argued that "[t]here is a surprising tendency for the 'exploitation' of the great by the small." Mancur Olson, *The Logic of Collective Action* 35 (1965). Some economists took Olson's insight to further extremes arguing that all legislation was the product of interest group action which aimed to obtain special advantages or "rents" from the system, at the expense of the dispersed and inattentive public.

Pushing back against this depressing account, political scientist Douglas Arnold argues that the public may be inattentive and subject to interest group manipulation, but that this is not a necessary result. R. Douglas Arnold, *The Logic of Congressional Action* 5 (1990). Politicians count votes as much as dollars and so, if they are to attain reelection, they must calculate or anticipate what the "inattentive" yet voting public are likely to think. For Arnold, you do not want to overemphasize the role of interest groups, for members of Congress are most focused on what David Mayhew dubbed "the electoral connection": more than anything else, legislators want to be reelected.[24] Indeed, politicians often resent interest groups, because groups press for selective rather than general benefits and will often oppose compromises that legislators view as essential to "getting things done" and ensuring their electoral future. At the same time, anyone who has worked in Congress will tell you that interest groups and lobbyists are valuable sources of *expertise*, and are frequently consulted by (often young or inexperienced) staffers to assist with policymaking and even the drafting of legislative language itself.

An important check on interest group power comes simply from being a competitive partisan democracy: opposing candidates are whistleblowers who can be expected to exploit an incumbent's willingness to betray the preferences of her constituents for the influence of small groups. If all of this is right, there is a check or limit on how far an interest can go, even if they lavish funding on a particular Congressman. If the Congressman thinks that most people in his voting district or state oppose that policy, they will not vote for the interest group, she will instead vote for the position of the "inattentive public." This is what one of us believes Madison was talking about in *Federalist* No. 51, when he argued that the "interest of the man" should be connected to the constitutional mission of his institution.

Based upon their survey of lobbying reports and interviews, Professor Baumgartner and his colleagues found that organized lobbying groups generally reflect a wide array of interests. Frank R. Baumgartner, Jeffrey M. Berry, Marjorie Hojnacki, David C. Kimball, and Beth L. Leech, *Lobbying and Policy Change: Who Wins, Who Loses, and Why* (2009). Thus, consumer groups and unions are well-reflected among lobbying groups arrayed around most issues of concern; although business and professional groups are even better represented and their efforts much better funded, their superior resources did not translate into an ability to dominate the legislative process. The authors found that the status quo is hard to change, and pro-business lobbyists were unable to effect change without critical support from a broader coalition, typically including government officials themselves.

---

[24] David R. Mayhew, *Congress: The Electoral Connection* (1974). As the great constitutionalist Charles Black once explained, a representative "lives and dies," based on "what [the voters] think of him [back home]." Charles L. Black Jr., *The Working Balance of the American Political Departments,* 1 Hastings Const. L. Q. 13, 16–17 (1974).

NOTE ON POLITICAL PARTIES AND LEGISLATION

Like interest groups, political parties are important in our system as ways for resolving collective action problems. Parties in the United States have a deep effect upon the organization of our electoral system; state parties help draw election districts for the federal system, and in this sense help to organize the government; at the same time, they are fairly fragmented organizations with local, state and national bodies, which operate both inside and outside government. It is important to note that, however important political parties are in America, they cannot explain some basic facts about American politics, such as why most bills are passed by large bipartisan majorities. See Keith Krehbiel, *Pivotal Politics: A Theory of U.S. Lawmaking* (1998).

Parties are helpful to voters, and because they are helpful to voters, they are helpful to members seeking reelection. Few voters are willing to invest significant time and energy to find and understand information about candidates for public office. Given their limited attention to political matters, most people vote on the basis of voting cues or shortcuts—proxies for full information about candidates and their positions. Helpful voting cues, like party affiliation, allow persons to vote competently even with limited information.[25] However, it may well be that party affiliation is not a particularly helpful cue. One result of a two-party, as opposed to a multi-party, system combined with single-member electoral districts is a convergence of the parties with respect to their positions on the issues. Sometimes "third party" tags such as the Libertarian Party or the Tea Party can provide greater information about ideology.

Parties also have sway within the institutions of government themselves. Because of the traditions and norms of the House of Representatives, parties as a general rule are more important there than in the Senate, where "unanimous consent" rules. In the House, the majority party runs the show and is known for proceeding on matters without even informing the minority of its actions.

Lawmakers who serve in party leadership positions tend to come from relatively safe districts and therefore tend to be insulated from narrow constituent pressures. The idea is that they can survive the electoral heat of authoring a compromise bill that offends the sensibilities of extremists or particular interest groups, and they may have more leeway in pursuing their vision of the public good without fearing electoral reprisals. See John Aldrich, *Why Parties? The Origin and Transformation of Political Parties in America* 205 (1995). Counterbalancing this, however, is their "desire to remain in the majority and an awareness that the reelection of some of their members may depend on legislation benefitting special interests." *Id.*

---

[25] See Elisabeth Gerber & Arthur Lupia, Voter Competence in Direct Legislation Elections, in Citizen Competence and Democratic Institutions 147 (Stephen Elkin & Koral Soltan eds., 1999).

PROBLEM 1–2: VETOGATES AND THE RULES OF CONGRESSIONAL PROCEDURE

Imagine that you want to pass legislation to veto or repeal the current health care statute, the Affordable Care Act. Such legislation could be quite easily drafted: in a single sentence, one might render the prior law null and void. Even if one were capable of drafting that sentence, to pass the bill would be quite difficult—it would require the agreement of 535 representatives and hurdling a variety of vetogates. It is one thing to know that a process is difficult, it is another to try to imagine it. Just as a trial may be difficult, you typically know the basic elements off the top of your head. See if you can do the same for legislation.

Assume that the House Majority Leader supports the bill. Outline the steps you have to go through in the House of Representatives to achieve passage. How many potential steps are there, assuming the standard process? One, five, twenty? Assume that the minority will use every power it has to stop the bill. Assume a majority of votes will ultimately favor the bill, but that a majority also supports some amendments. What will happen?

Now assume that the Senate Majority Leader also supports the bill, and he has a majority of his party caucus behind him, amounting to 48 votes. Assume there is a vocal minority devoted to stopping the bill, amounting to 10 votes, but no one knows how other senators will vote. The Senate Minority Leader has agreed to have a committee review the bill and not to use the filibuster on the initial motion to proceed to the legislation. What is likely to happen? What is going to be your strategy to gain agreement? If you knew that the way to gain ten votes was to give a single senator a filibuster-free debate on grain tariffs would you accept that compromise?

PROBLEM 1–3: CONGRESSIONAL BILL RELATING TO PREGNANCY DISCRIMINATION, CIRCA 1966

Recall that Title VII of the 1964 Act bars any "discrimination because of * * * sex" in the conditions or terms of employment. Did that rule bar covered employers from discriminating because of pregnancy? In 1965, the Equal Employment Opportunity Commission (EEOC) issued "Guidelines on Discrimination Because of Sex," but with no mention of pregnancy-based discrimination. By the end of its first year of operation, the EEOC had come to the conclusion that pregnancy was an issue that remained open for discussion:

> The prohibition against sex discrimination is especially difficult to apply with respect to the female employees who become pregnant. In all other questions involving sex discrimination, the underlying principle is the essential equality of treatment. * * * The pregnant female, however, has no analogous male counterpart and pregnancy necessarily must be treated uniquely. The Commission decided that to carry out the Congressional policy of providing truly equal

employment opportunities, including career opportunities for women, *policies would have to be devised which afforded female employees reasonable job protection during periods of pregnancy.*

EEOC, *First Annual Report* 40 (1965–66) (emphasis added). As open-ended as it was, this language was alarming to business associations, for most employers did discriminate against pregnant employees. Consider some common policies:

- **No Hire/Termination.** Airlines excluded women from becoming stewardesses (or "air hostesses," a term used by TWA) if they had ever been pregnant or had children. A more common policy, followed by many school districts for teachers, was automatic termination of employment once a teacher started showing a pregnancy.

- **Forced Leave Without Pay.** Many employers that did not automatically fire pregnant employees did require them to take unpaid leave. Moreover, many employers did not cover the medical expenses of an employee's pregnancy in the employee health and disability plans that had proliferated after World War II.

- **Refusals to Accommodate.** Employers who allowed pregnant employees to remain on the job typically did not accommodate the special needs of those employees, nor did employers usually make it easy for the nursing mother to return to work.

Within the EEOC, staff attorney Sonia Pressman, a former labor lawyer, maintained that Title VII's bar to workplace discrimination "because of * * * sex" rendered most if not all pregnancy-discriminating employment policies illegal.

Assume that the U.S. Chamber of Commerce, a leading lobbying organization representing business interests, learns in 1966 that Pressman is making this argument and becomes quite alarmed—for such an interpretation would have vast (and costly) consequences for businesses all over the country. You are their General Counsel; you assure the Chamber that the EEOC cannot impose such a policy upon employers as a matter of "law." Title VII authorizes the EEOC to provide educational, conciliation, and other facilitative services to employers, and authorizes the EEOC to bring lawsuits to enforce Title VII, see § 706, 42 U.S.C. § 2000e–5, but does not authorize the EEOC to enforce the statute against or penalize employers directly; Congress gave rulemaking authority to the EEOC only for procedural matters, § 713(a), 42 U.S.C. § 2000e–12(a).

Your client's officials take no solace in this advice, for you also tell them that the federal courts (and not the agency) will have the final say in determining the meaning of Title VII. The Chamber's President almost has a heart attack: "Earl Warren and his pack of liberal judges will make employment policy? There is nothing too far out for these people." You concede that the liberal Warren Court might indeed follow Pressman's approach and rule that pregnancy-discriminating policies violate Title VII.

The Chamber of Commerce is optimistic that it can secure legislation in 1966 to head off this possibility. All of the Republicans in the House and the Senate (about a third of each chamber) will listen to the Chamber, and such civil rights stalwarts as Bill McCulloch and Thomas Kuchel are strong allies of the Chamber, which supported the 1964 Act. And, the Chamber reminds you, many liberals opposed the sex discrimination amendment in 1964. The Chamber is confident that a majority of each chamber would support its position if it came to a vote in 1966.

(A) Suggest the outline of a draft bill heading off pregnancy discrimination claims. Generally, you want to work within the existing structure of Title VII. Are there any provisions that should be changed or deleted? Anything added? If so, where? You might even try your hand at drafting language that could be added to Title VII.

(B) What interest group allies can be attracted to the bill, and how can enemies be neutralized? Consider what allies you might have for your bill. Are there ways to expand your base of allies? What potential opponents? How can they be neutralized or their opposition diminished? (Historical note: there were few women's lobbying groups at the beginning of 1966. For example, the National Organization for Women was not formed until later that year.)

(C) How does your bill traverse all those pesky vetogates? As your client is aware, majority support in Congress usually does *not* generate legislation because of the vetogates. What are the most troublesome vetogates? What strategy can the Chamber follow to sneak through each of them?

Note to the instructor: you may want to appoint different students to be different players in Congress, and have them research their roles a little more than we have presented here. Thus, one student can be Judge Smith, another Representative Celler, another Representative Griffiths, and so on. Yet other students can represent different interests, such as the National Women's Party, led by Alice Paul. What position would Alice Paul want to take on this bill? If she is opposed, what strategy might she follow to block the Chamber's proposal?

It is also relevant that most of the participants in the great debate over the 1964 Act were still in Congress in 1966. (The main exception was Hubert Humphrey, who became Vice-President, and President of the Senate, in 1965.) Lyndon Johnson was still President—but the Women's Bureau was no longer headed by Esther Peterson, who had been cool to the sex discrimination amendment. The new Director of the Women's Bureau was Mary Dublin Keyserling (1964–69), an economist, consumer advocate, and supporter of state laws providing protections for working women.

2. STRUCTURAL LIMITS ON CONGRESSIONAL AUTHORITY

Power. The Congress has broad, but enumerated, powers to pass laws for the nation. Article I, § 8 allows the Congress to pass laws to regulate commerce, to coin money, to provide for uniform laws on bankruptcy and immigration, and to declare war, among other powers. As Constitutional Law courses teach in some detail, every exercise of congressional authority must be tied to a specific grant of authority in the Constitution; Clause 3, for a much-deployed example, authorizes Congress to adopt laws regulating interstate and international "commerce." The Constitution also provides three residual power clauses. That is, Clause 17 of Section 8 authorizes Congress "to make all Laws which shall be necessary and proper for carrying into Execution [1] the foregoing Powers, and [2] all other Powers vested by this Constitution in the Government of the United States, or [3] in any Department or Officer thereof."[26]

Competency and Capacity. Congress is a very large body made up of 535 members, 100 in the Senate and 435 in the House. By virtue simply of these numbers, it is a body created to move slowly and deliberately. At the Founding, many of the state legislatures were unicameral (one House), and many believed that this legislative structure yielded improvident, rushed laws. The remedy was a bicameral (two House) Congress.[27] The subject matter capacity of the Congress is tremendous: unlike courts which accept cases and controversies that come to them, Congress may legislate on any matter affecting the nation and the world, from the national debt to child abuse, from pregnancy discrimination to foreign affairs. The very complexity and tremendous capacity of the system make it work only with great difficulty. (Just imagine trying to write a paper or a brief with 535 authors on any topic in the world).

Representation. Relative to other institutions, the Congress is the body most directly connected to the people. The Senate is elected by state populations, with two senators for every state. This provision protects small states and is entrenched in the constitution. The House is elected by districts within a state, with the exception of small population states, where a single representative may represent an entire state. (For example, the small state of Delaware has a single representative in the House and two representatives in the Senate). Representation was one of

---

[26] See John Mikhail, *The Necessary and Proper Clauses*, 102 Geo. L.J. 1045 (2014).

[27] *See, e.g., The Federalist* No. 51 (Madison) ("In republican government, the legislative authority necessarily predominates. The remedy for this inconveniency is to divide the legislature into different branches; and to render them, by different modes of election and different principles of action, as little connected with each other as the nature of their common functions and their common dependence on the society will admit.").

the most important concerns of the Founders. Indeed, members of the Constitutional Convention often debated whether particular provisions would affect representation. For example, it was argued that the President should not be selected by the House of Representatives because this would, in effect, render the President too beholden to the local interests of House members and insufficiently attentive to the interests of the nation as a whole.

NOTE ON THE SEPARATION OF POWERS

There is no specific clause in the United States Constitution decreeing the separation of powers, as some state constitutions provide.[28] However, there are clauses at the beginning of the three main articles of the Constitution, called the "vesting" clauses, which introduce the branches and their powers. For example, Article I states that "All legislative Powers herein granted shall be vested in a Congress of the United States, which shall consist of a Senate and House of Representatives" (Art. I, § 1). Article II states that "The executive Power shall be vested in a President of the United States of America." (Art. II, § 1.) Article III states that "The judicial Power of the United States shall be vested in one supreme Court, and in such inferior Courts as the Congress may from time to time ordain and establish." (Art. III, § 1.). We will see more about these clauses later, when we consider the power of the Presidency.

The standard civics 101 account of the separation of powers is to try to imagine the Constitution as a separation of functions—executive, legislative, and judicial. This underestimates the constitutional provisions protecting our constitutional structure. Many constitutional provisions maintain the separation of powers. For example, the otherwise entirely obscure Incompatibility Clause (Art. I, § 6, cl. 2) performs a vital role in maintaining the structure of our government.[29] This clause prevents members of the Congress from sitting in the executive branch. Just imagine if the Speaker of the House could sit as the head of the Department of Defense: the Department would have enormous sway in the legislature. In a parliamentary system, however, this is precisely what happens: the Prime Minister's cabinet is taken from members of Parliament.

The incompatibility clause is not the only "stealth" separation of powers provision in the Constitution. Indeed, the Constitution's text is ripe with provisions protecting against functional disintegration. For example, the Founders rightly feared that, armed with judicial power, legislators would

---

[28] Art. XXX, Massachusetts Constitution of 1780: "In the government of this Commonwealth, the legislative department shall never exercise the executive and judicial powers, or either of them: The executive shall never exercise the legislative and judicial powers, or either of them: The judicial shall never exercise the legislative and executive powers, or either of them: to the end it may be a government of laws and not of men."

[29] Steven G. Calabresi & Joan L. Larsen, *One Person, One Office: Separation of Powers or Separation of Personnel?*, 79 Cornell L. Rev. 1045, 1050–52 (1994).

send their political enemies to jail (and they tried, unsuccessfully!)[30] The Bill of Attainder Clause (Art. I, § 9) bars Congress from punishing individuals, and the Speech and Debate Clause (Art. I, § 6, cl. 1), prohibits the President from arresting a legislator for anything she says in Congress. Even constitutional provisions involving tenure and salaries support the separation of powers: Federal judges are insulated from political pressure by constitutional provisions providing that they serve for life and their salaries may not be reduced, making them secure that, should they depart from the wishes of Congress or the President, they will retain their jobs. (Art. III, § 1). *See Federalist* No. 51 (Madison).

In fact, Articles I, II, and III are not pristinely associated only with one kind of function or power. For example, the President's veto power appears in Article I, the legislative article (Art. I, § 7), not in Article II, the executive article. Similarly, Congress's legislative power to create lower courts appears in Article III (Art. III, § 1) as well as Article I (Art. I, § 8). One might even argue that adjudicative powers are not limited to Article III, as Congress's power to impeach and "try" executive officials and judges appears in Article I (Art. I, § 3).

This functional inexactitude has been magnified in modern administrative government, as we will see later, because the President's executive branch agencies both "adjudicate" cases and "legislate" rules and regulations.[31] The executive branch is not alone bounded by functionally imprecise lines. For example, although the legislature is not supposed to "execute" the laws, it has agencies that in fact execute law for the Congress: the General Accounting Office is an investigative arm of Congress, the Capitol Police guard Congress, and the Library of Congress provides information and legal advice. This is true of the courts as well: the Judicial Department has a Judicial Conference and an Administrative Office of the Courts, not to mention a Sentencing Commission,[32] each of which serves administrative and thus executive and even legislative functions.

Functional fuzziness has divided scholars and judges: some believe there should be a more rigid adherence to formal lines of constitutional power ("formalists"). Formalists believe that the President is in charge of all executive functions, and if he tries to make rather than execute law he should be overruled; Congress does all the legislating, and if it tries to meddle in executive functions it should be overruled; the courts do all the adjudicating, and if they try to make policy they should be overruled. The problem with this approach is that it is not always that clear what boundaries the Constitution requires.

---

[30] See, e.g., Geoffrey R. Stone, *Perilous Times: Free Speech in War Time from the Sedition Act of 1798 to the War on Terrorism* 33–44 (2004).

[31] Peter L. Strauss, *Formal and Functional Approaches to Separation-of-Powers Questions—A Foolish Inconsistency?*, 72 Cornell L. Rev. 488 (1987).

[32] On the Sentencing Commission's placement within the judiciary as constitutional, see *Mistretta v. United States*, 488 U.S. 361 (1989).

In contrast, "functionalists" tolerate a good deal of concurrent power as long as the governmental innovation is "necessary."[33] The term "functionalism" is, however, somewhat misleading. Formalists depend upon the idea of functions listed in the vesting clauses.[34] So, for example, they give great meaning to the term "legislative" or "executive" in the first "vesting" clauses of Article I and Article II. But so do functionalists who simply believe that the functions can be more flexibly defined. Some scholars believe that there is really little difference between so-called formalists and functionalists because they depend upon this same concept. Mark V. Tushnet, *The Sentencing Commission and Constitutional Theory: Bowls and Plateaus in Separation of Powers Theory*, 66 S. Cal. L. Rev. 581, 596 (1992) (arguing that formal and functional approaches converge). The Supreme Court's decisions, as we will see, have tended to shift between so-called formalist and functionalist approaches.

Another standard civics 101 concept associated with the separation of powers is the notion of "checks and balances." It is often noted that the departments must work together and this means that they share power in a way that provides a check on the powers and actions of each other. The President may nominate officials to his administration but the Senate "checks" his choices because the Senate must consent to the appointment. The only problem with the "shared power" theory or the "checks" theory is that it does not tell us much about whether governmental innovations—like the line item veto or the independent counsel or the legislative veto—should fail or not. Each of these innovations can be described as creating a new "check" on Congress or the President. Simply providing checks cannot be a constitutional argument for a particular innovation, however; otherwise any "check" would be appropriate (just imagine having the Supreme Court "check" the President and Congress's decision to go to war).

Although rarely emphasized, one of the most powerful forces keeping the departments separate—representation—is written in plain sight in the Constitution. As James Madison once explained in the *Federalist Papers*, constituencies provide incentives to align individuals with the constitutional interests of their branches. *Federalist* No. 51 (Madison). At least as a relative matter, we know that the senator from Iowa cares more about Iowa than the President and that the House member from New York City cares more about

---

[33] *See, e.g.,* E. Donald Elliott, INS v. Chadha: *The Administrative Constitution, the Constitution, and the Legislative Veto*, 1983 Sup. Ct. Rev. 125.

[34] "Function-talk" appears in a variety of otherwise diverse scholarship on the separation of powers. See, e.g., Rebecca L. Brown, *Separated Powers and Ordered Liberty*, 139 U. Pa. L. Rev. 1513 (1991) (arguing that separation of powers disputes involve important questions of individual rights); Abner S. Greene, *Checks and Balances in an Era of Presidential Lawmaking*, 61 U. Chi. L. Rev. 123 (1994) (emphasizing the checks and balances between the President and Congress); Peter L. Strauss, *Formal and Functional Approaches to Separation-of-Powers Questions—A Foolish Inconsistency?*, 72 Cornell L. Rev. 488, 522 (1987) ("[C]ourts should view separation-of-powers cases in terms of the impact of challenged arrangements on the balance of power among the three named heads of American government"); Paul R. Verkuil, Separation of Powers, *The Rule of Law and the Idea of Independence*, 30 Wm. & Mary L. Rev. 301 passim (1989) (emphasizing a rule of law approach that minimizes conflicts of interest).

New York City than Hawaii. Given that the Constitution grants the branches different constituencies (and, in the case of the judiciary, no constituency at all), this tends to give individuals the incentive to serve separate masters and in this sense separates and diffuses power. This can be called the "vertical" or "representational" theory of the separation of powers.[35] Victoria F. Nourse, *The Vertical Separation of Powers*, 49 Duke L.J. 749 (1999); Victoria F. Nourse, *Toward A New Constitutional Anatomy*, 56 Stan. L. Rev. 835–900 (2004).

To comprehend the importance of representation to structure, conduct a thought experiment. Imagine a Constitution identical to the one we have today, where the branches are all performing the same functions as they do today. Make three simple changes: the House of Representatives elects the Senate; the President has no veto; Congress appoints members of the Executive Branch. *Under this Constitution, no functional changes occur, but the separation of powers will disappear.* The House will bow to the Senate; Congress will control the no-veto President and will effectively take over the Executive Branch by appointing its members to sit in the executive department, potentially creating a one-department government. The Framers knew this and rejected similar proposals because they understood that the separation of powers depended upon more than mere " 'parchment barriers.' " Victoria F. Nourse, *Toward A 'Due Foundation' for the Separation of Powers: The Federalist Papers as Political Narrative*, 74 Tex. L. Rev. 447–521 (1996).

NOTE ON THE NONDELEGATION DOCTRINE

Our Constitution requires that the branches work together, which is why the system is often called one of shared and separated powers. *Youngstown Sheet & Tube Co. v. Sawyer*, 343 U.S. 579 (1952) (Jackson, J. concurring). A proposal does not become a law unless the Congress and the President work together. This is even truer when it comes to executing the law. Congress has no troops on the ground to enforce its decrees. It must delegate power to *execute* the law to the President and his administration. This delegation, however, raises its own issues. How much power may Congress delegate? May it simply hand the reins of government over to the President's administration? As a general rule, Congress may delegate vast amounts of authority to the President and his agents as long as there is an "intelligible principle" by which the power is granted. In the 1930s, during the Depression and the New Deal, the Supreme Court signaled that it might limit the amount of power that the Congress could delegate, particularly to private parties, but this rule is now largely moribund. *A.L.A. Schecter Poultry Corp. v. United States*, 295 U.S. 495 (1935).

---

[35] This does not necessarily give any individual, however, an interest in maintaining the interest of the Congress as a whole, and it may be that Madison's "invisible hand" formula works poorly when members of Congress are elected to work "against" the body itself. See Daryl J. Levinson, Parchment and Politics: the Positive Puzzle of Constitutional Commitment, 124 Harv. L. Rev. 657 (2011) (suggesting that the "invisible hand" theory does not protect individual rights constitutionalism).

No federal statute has been invalidated by the Supreme Court on nondelegation grounds since the 1930s. For example, in *Yakus v. United States*, 321 U.S. 414 (1944), the Supreme Court upheld a broad delegation of authority to set prices of goods during World War II. More recently, in *Whitman v. American Trucking Ass'ns, Inc.*, 531 U.S. 457 (2001), the Supreme Court reversed the lower court for striking down part of the Clean Air Act on nondelegation grounds, holding that there were sufficient intelligible principles to guide the agency. If the nondelegation doctrine is considered moribund at a constitutional level, it is not necessarily moribund as a rule of statutory interpretation, however (Chapter 5). When courts see that the Congress has delegated very broad authority to an agency over particularly important questions, they have a tendency to construe the act narrowly to restrain agency discretion. See *Whitman, supra*; *MCI v. AT & T*, 512 U.S. 218 (1994); *FDA v. Brown & Williamson*, 529 U.S. 120 (2000); William N. Eskridge Jr. & Philip P. Frickey, *Quasi-Constitutional Law: Clear Statement Rules as Constitutional Lawmaking*, 45 Vand. L. Rev. 593, 607 (1992); Lisa Schultz Bressman, Schechter Poultry *at the Millennium: A Delegation Doctrine for the Administrative State*, 109 Yale L. J. 1399 (2000). (We shall come back to this point in Chapter 8).

By giving broad delegations a pass and then imposing some restraint on agencies, the Supreme Court has enabled Congress to delegate a lot of lawmaking authority to administrators. (Recall that the vetogates structure of Congress encourages such delegation.) In the modern administrative state, most of what we consider "law" consists of agency regulations rather than congressional statutes. As we shall explore in the next section of this chapter, there are a number of formats in which agencies create or interpret law, but in the last generation the primary mechanism has been notice-and-comment rulemaking. See Chapters 7 & 8 on Administrative Law.

Scholars are divided on whether broad delegations are wise. Some have argued that broad delegations give blanket authority to faceless and unaccountable bureaucrats. *Theodore Lowi, The End of Liberalism: The Second Republic of the United States* (2d ed. 1979). More recent works argue that the temptation to pass the buck to agencies is undemocratic (the unelected are making the decisions) and counterproductive (the choices may be biased if the agency is captured by industry). See David Schoenbrod, *Power Without Responsibility: How Congress Abuses the People Through Delegation* (1993). Professor Jerry Mashaw disagrees, arguing that the broad delegations to administrative agencies can sometimes ensure better policies, because they inhibit vote-trading and deal-making, allowing space for the agency to apply its experience under conditions of independence from raw politics while remaining accountable to the public interest. When agencies act, voters may hold them and the President more accountable because the actions are likely to be relatively more visible than specific deals buried in 2000-page bills. See Jerry L. Mashaw, *Greed, Chaos, and Governance: Using Public Choice to Improve Public Law* 140–157 (1997). Ultimately, the question may be one of comparative institutional competence in a particular area: sometimes the delegation may be used wisely and sometimes not. Neil K. Komesar, *Imperfect Alternatives: Choosing Institutions in Law, Economics, and Public Policy* (1994).

PROBLEM 1–4: CONGRESSIONAL DELEGATION DECISIONS

Recall from our Story of the Civil Rights Act that Congress created an agency to administer Title VII (the jobs title) of the new law—but did not give the agency significant lawmaking authority. In 1971–72, Congress revisited Title VII and ultimately amended the statute to expand its rules to state and federal employment. You are counsel for the National Organization for Women (NOW), a leading women's rights organization. The President of NOW asks you this question: During congressional deliberation regarding the Civil Rights Act Amendments of 1972, should we seek changes in Title VII's delegation structure? Among the questions entailed by this task are the following:

- **Agency Primacy Versus Court Primacy?** The 1964 Act left the details of the statute largely up to the federal courts rather than to the EEOC, which had virtually no substantive rulemaking authority and no power to enforce its internal adjudications against employers. Should NOW seek to increase the legal authority of the EEOC, at the expense of the legal authority of the federal courts? Is it relevant to your thinking that the Court is all-male and that Chief Justice Earl Warren and several liberal Justices left the Court between 1969 and 1971, replaced by more conservative (pro-business) Justices nominated by President Richard Nixon? The EEOC in 1971 has one female Commissioner (Ethel Walsh), named by President Nixon, and four male Commissioners, two named by Nixon and two by Johnson. The important question for you is this, however: In the long term, does the NAACP trust the Supreme Court more than the EEOC to set priorities and interpret Title VII?

- **What Additional Authority Should Congress Vest in the EEOC?** If you think the EEOC ought to have primary authority to interpret and implement Title VII, what structural changes would you make to the agency? What new authority would you want Congress to vest in the EEOC? Even if you favor the existing Supreme Court primacy, are there changes you would suggest to make the EEOC a more effective partner with the Court in implementing the statute aggressively?

- **Private Cause of Action?** In 1971, Title VII gave private complainants a right to seek relief for job discrimination, first, by seeking EEOC mediation of the dispute and, failing that, by a federal claim for relief brought in court; also, the EEOC can bring pattern or practice claims in federal court for groups of similarly situated workers. The latter ensures that the Supreme Court will always play an important role in construing Title VII. Do you want to change this structure?

After you have jotted down tentative answers to these questions, think about the flip side, where you are counsel to or lobbyist for the Chamber of Commerce. Assume the Chamber will oppose your changes. What vetogates might the Chamber usefully exploit in its effort to prevent NOW from expanding anti-discrimination regulation in 1971–72? Jot down your thoughts and read the next set of notes.

A.   LEGISLATIVE MECHANISMS TO CONTROL AGENCIES

1.   Detailed Legislation. The most obvious way Congress can avoid excessive delegation is to give the agency detailed statutory directives. There are obvious difficulties inherent in detailed delegation, however. As we have seen in this chapter, passing laws is exceedingly difficult. There are immense costs in gathering information, not to mention vetogates galore. The more specific the law becomes, the greater the information and bargaining costs. In fact, it may be impossible to pass extremely specific directives because of what one of us has called "structure-induced ambiguity"—the many circumstances in which the only way to pass a bill is to avoid specificity.[36] However, Congress does have other ways in which to monitor agencies, including the following.

2.   Legislative Oversight and Investigation. Congress has the power to "oversee" agency operations and it does this in a variety of ways. Typically, the elected policy entrepreneur who has spent costly electoral time on legislation will seek to make sure that the law continues to work and will have an incentive to hold hearings and gain information from the relevant agency. Oversight is sometimes formal: it may take the form of hearings where agency heads are called to account for their policies. Oftentimes, however, this happens only when there is a "crisis" atmosphere, after the policy has become salient to the public. Moreover, the committees controlling the process may not necessarily respond to the crisis if they themselves are beholden to these very interests under scrutiny. (For example, the banking committee members responsible for holding banks responsive may themselves be beholden to those same interests.) Other times oversight is less formal: Elected members and staff report utilizing a variety of methods, from phone calls, to letters, to

---

[36] Victoria F. Nourse, *Misunderstanding Congress: Statutory Interpretation, the Supermajoritarian Difficulty, and the Separation of Powers,* 99 GEO. L. J. 1119 (2011).

placing directives to agencies in legislative history (like committee reports) to influence agency behavior.[37]

3.   *Control over the Appointment of Administrators.* As you will see later, the appointment of members of the executive branch is a source of important powers for both the President and the Congress. Under Article II, the President has the power to nominate officers of his administration, but only with the advice and consent of the Senate. U.S. Const., art. II, § 2. In determining whether to confirm a particular officer, senators may attempt to secure promises from the administration or the particular officer about his conduct in office. For example, when confirming the Attorney General, the members of the Senate Judiciary Committee may secure promises that the Attorney General will seek to enforce particular laws or deploy substantial resources in furthering particular programs. None of this is binding upon the official. However, once having heard of such concerns and, if a promise is made, the committee may return to the officer in oversight hearings seeking assurance that Congress's priorities have been respected. At its most extreme, of course, Congress may simply choose not to confirm officials nominated by the President. It has been said, for example, that confirmations have in recent years become particularly difficult, requiring that nominees spend tremendous amounts of time seeking confirmation. Indeed, one way Congress may seek to advance its policy disagreements with an administration is by refusing to confirm large numbers of the President's nominees. See discussion of Senator Harkin and Alexander (2011), after Note on the Filibuster, below.

4.   *Appropriations Authority.* The power of the purse is mighty, and Congress holds that power under Article I, §§ 8 & 9 of the Constitution. If Congress does not want the President to pursue a program, it may defund that program. Congress's power of the purse is related to its oversight and appointment powers. When a congressional committee calls up the head of an agency for an oversight hearing, it often wants to hear from that agency head how the agency is spending money, and if the answers are not satisfactory, this could put the agency head's job in jeopardy. More importantly, oversight occurs when the Congress as a whole seeks to reauthorize a program. Imagine, for example, that in 1994, Congress passes the Violence Against Women Act. That law's appropriations are limited for a certain amount of time and the Act must be reauthorized, which means that Congress must pass a new statute. During reauthorization, members may inquire about how the appropriated money is being spent and if they are unsatisfied, the bill may fail.

---

[37] Abbe R. Gluck & Lisa Schultz Bressman, *Statutory Interpretation from the Inside—An Empirical Study of Congressional Drafting, Delegation and the Canons—Parts I and II,* 65 Stan. L. Rev. 901 (2013) & 66 Stan. L. Rev. 725 (2014).

Funding may affect the nature of an agency's positions. Given the incentive of agencies to want to stay in business, they may have an incentive to move their policy closer to the House or Senate position even if the agency prefers a very different policy. This is true even if the agency would be protected by a Presidential veto if the agency believes that Congress will stop funding it if it fails to change its policy. This shows the tremendous power of the purse over agency action: because the agency needs Congress to fund it, Congress has a kind of backdoor "legislative veto." If it wants to, the Congress can simply defund the agency.

In practice, however, this may be more difficult than it looks, given the nature of how Congress divides its authorization and appropriation authorities. By rule in both the Senate and the House, the power to authorize a law is in different hands than the power to appropriate money. In both chambers, it is in theory against the "rules" to "legislate" (pass substantive provisions) in an appropriations bill—but substantive change can occur under the rules simply by limiting appropriations by "legislative language" (i.e., no funds appropriated under this bill shall be spent on thus-and-so), or in the House by advance waiver of this rule by the Rules Committee. This rule allows any individual representative to "stop" an appropriations bill in its tracks by making a point of order (that is, an objection) that it violates the House or Senate Rules. Given the separate responsibility of the committees, it may be more difficult for Congress to exercise oversight over an agency by defunding: the authorizing committee worried about a substantive policy must convince the appropriating committees as well.

This division of authority may lead to a less aggressive use of the funding power through informal directives. For example, conference committee reports or committee reports accompanying appropriations bills may include directives to agencies about how money should be spent. The bills themselves may include line item provisions for particular projects or this may be included in the "joint explanation" to the conference committee report. Although report language is not binding on an agency, agencies often follow the mandates to retain the good will of the legislators and to ensure future appropriations. A recent empirical study by one of us found that staffers view appropriations legislative history as especially important for precisely this reason (Gluck & Bressman at 979–82).

5. *Design of the Implementing Agency and Procedures.* Congress may seek to control an agency through particular design of the agency. Administrative agencies may perform different functions: they may make "rules and regulations" or they may "adjudicate" cases. Congress may, for example, attempt to restrain an agency by limiting its authority in any of these areas. For example, in Title VII, Congress sought affirmatively to narrow the ability of the EEOC to issue rules and regulations. See 42 U.S.C. § 2000e–12(a). This limitation can have very important effects on the deference courts will give to the agency's actions in any future litigation. See *General Electric v. Gilbert*, 429 U.S. 125 (1976) (Chapter 3).

Congress may also seek to control or limit the power of an agency by restricting the term of the head of the agency and by limiting the President's ability to fire the agency head except for "good cause." Typically, such agencies are ones where it is claimed that expertise is central and Congress determines that it is necessary to insulate the agency head from political influence. If the President can simply fire the agent because of his political views, the fear is that the agency will not exercise "independence." For example, the head of the Nuclear Regulatory Commission and the head of the Federal Reserve are both appointed for a term of years and may not be removed by the President for purely political reasons (see *Humphrey's Executor*, discussed in Chapter 2). This creates an important constitutional question known as the "independent agency" question. Some authors and even Justices have argued for a theory known as the "unitary executive," in which Congress may not specify the terms of agency heads and that the President must have complete power to be able to fire such heads.

Finally, Congress may seek to control agencies by putting members of Congress or the judiciary on the relevant board or commission. In the first case, appointing members of Congress has run into serious constitutional problems. For example, when congressmen wanted to sit on the Board supervising the Washington, D.C. airports, the Supreme Court barred this practice under general separation of powers principles. *Metropolitan Washington Airports Authority v. Citizens for Abatement of Aircraft Noise*, 501 U.S. 252 (1991); see also *Springer v. Philippine Islands*, 277 U.S. 189 (1928). Similarly, members of Congress have on occasion attempted to put judges on various commissions. This raises its own problems, but at least in one case, the Sentencing Commission, the Supreme Court approved such a practice. *Mistretta v. United States*, 488 U.S. 361, 398 (1989); see also *Morrison v. Olson*, 487 U.S. 654 (1988) (upholding judicial appointment of independent counsel).

6. *Legislative Vetoes.* The legislative veto is any statutory mechanism rendering the implementation of agency decisions or actions subject to some further form of legislative review or control, usually for a specified time period. The purpose of the legislative veto is to provide a quick mechanism to slow down or overturn administrative actions unresponsive to the legislature's aims in the original authorizing statute, without going through the obstacle course of the full legislative process. Hence, the power to nullify an administrative decision has been vested in joint action of both chambers of the legislature, action by only one house, or action by a legislative committee. (At the state level, there have been mechanisms for suspension, rather than veto, of agency decisions by joint legislative committees.) Any of these procedures is more streamlined than the normal legislative process; even a two-house legislative veto avoids the presentment clause. Getting around the President is important because he would presumably veto most legislative nullifications of regulations passed by agencies in his government, thereby requiring a supermajority in each house to implement congressional preferences.

The legislative veto idea was used sporadically in the early part of this century and was an important part of the Reorganization Act of 1932, 47 Stat. 382. Although President Hoover objected to the legislative veto in the 1932 Act as violating the separation of powers, he accepted the provision in order to get the power to make changes in the executive branch. It was not until the 1970s that the legislative veto became a popular mechanism for greater legislative oversight of the administrative process. A Library of Congress study for the period 1932 to 1975 found 295 congressional review provisions in 196 federal statutes; for the year 1975 alone, there were 58 provisions in 21 statutes. See Clark Norton, *Congressional Review, Deferral and Disapproval of Executive Actions: A Summary and Inventory of Statutory Authority* 8–12 (1976), as well as Joseph Cooper, *The Legislative Veto in the 1980s*, in *Congress Reconsidered* 364, 367 (Lawrence Dodd & Bruce Oppenheimer eds. 3d ed. 1985) (documenting how legislative vetoes were becoming increasingly common in each decade after the 1930s).

Legislative veto provisions were attached to important legislation involving defense and foreign policy (e.g., the War Powers Resolution, 87 Stat. 555); energy and environmental policy (e.g., the Energy Policy and Conservation Act, 89 Stat. 871); consumer welfare policy (e.g., the Employee Retirement Income Security Act of 1974, 88 Stat. 829); and transportation policy (e.g., the Regional Rail Reorganization Act of 1973, 87 Stat. 985). State legislatures in the 1970s adopted a variety of legislative veto devices as well, including advisory committees to the state legislature, reviewing agency regulations and making recommendations for legislative action (18 states), legislative committees authorized to suspend the effectiveness of an agency rule pending legislative consideration of a statutory repeal (9 states), and two-house (11 states) as well as one-house (one state) vetoes of agency rules. L. Harold Levinson, *Legislative and Executive Veto of Rules of Administrative Agencies: Models and Alternatives*, 24 Wm. & Mary L. Rev. 79, 81–83 (1982).

The concept of the legislative veto also drew criticisms from political scientists, who argued that legislative vetoes created as many problems for popular government as they solved, and from legal scholars, who argued that they were hard to reconcile with the concept of separation of powers. These constitutional concerns, and the political objections, generated a series of challenges to legislative vetoes at both the state and federal level.

IMMIGRATION & NATURALIZATION SERVICE ET AL. V. JAGDISH CHADHA ET AL.

United States Supreme Court, 1983.
462 U.S. 919, 103 S.Ct. 2764, 77 L. Ed.2d 317.

CHIEF JUSTICE BURGER delivered the opinion of the Court.

[Jagdish Chadha, an East Indian born in Kenya who held a British passport, was lawfully admitted to the United States on a nonimmigrant student visa. After his visa expired and he was subject to deportation, an immigration judge, acting on behalf of the Attorney General, concluded that Chadha met the statutory grounds for a suspension of deportation: He had resided continuously in the United States for over seven years, was of good moral character, and would suffer "extreme hardship" if deported. Pursuant to the Immigration and Nationality Act, a report of this suspension of deportation was transmitted to Congress. Under § 244(c)(2) of the Act, one chamber of Congress had the authority to invalidate this decision by adopting a resolution to that effect either in the session of Congress in which the report was submitted or in the following session of Congress.]

On December 12, 1975, Representative Eilberg, Chairman of the Judiciary Subcommittee on Immigration, Citizenship, and International Law, introduced a resolution opposing "the granting of permanent residence in the United States to [six] aliens," including Chadha. The resolution was referred to the House Committee on the Judiciary. On December 16, 1975, the resolution was discharged from further consideration by the House Committee on the Judiciary and submitted to the House of Representatives for a vote. The resolution had not been printed and was not made available to other Members of the House prior to or at the time it was voted on. So far as the record before us shows, the House consideration of the resolution was based on Representative Eilberg's statement from the floor that "[i]t was the feeling of the committee, after reviewing 340 cases, that the aliens contained in the resolution [Chadha and five others] did not meet these statutory requirements, particularly as it relates to hardship; and it is the opinion of the committee that their deportation should not be suspended." The resolution was passed without debate or recorded vote.[3] Since the House

---

[3] It is not at all clear whether the House generally, or Subcommittee Chairman Eilberg in particular, correctly understood the relationship between H. Res. 926 and the Attorney General's decision to suspend Chadha's deportation. Exactly one year previous to the House veto of the Attorney General's decision in this case, Representative Eilberg introduced a similar resolution disapproving the Attorney General's suspension of deportation in the case of six other aliens. H. Res. 1518, 93d Cong., 2d Sess. (1974). The following colloquy occurred on the floor of the House:

action was pursuant to § 244(c)(2), the resolution was not treated as an Art. I legislative act; it was not submitted to the Senate or presented to the President for his action.

[Following the House action, the immigration judge ordered Chadha deported. By the time the controversy made its way to the Court of Appeals for the Ninth Circuit, the INS had agreed with Chadha and joined his arguments that the House action was unconstitutional. After entertaining amici curiae briefs from both the Senate and the House of Representatives, the Ninth Circuit held that the House action was unconstitutional. The Supreme Court affirmed.]

* * * [T]hat a given law or procedure is efficient, convenient, and useful in facilitating functions of the government, standing alone, will not save it if it is contrary to the Constitution. Convenience and efficiency are not the primary objectives—or the hallmarks—of democratic government and our inquiry is sharpened rather than blunted by the fact that congressional veto provisions are appearing with increasing frequency in statutes which delegate authority to executive and independent agencies * * *.

Explicit and unambiguous provisions of the Constitution prescribe and define the respective functions of the Congress and of the Executive in the legislative process. * * * Article I provides:

"Mr. WYLIE. Mr. Speaker, further reserving the right to object, is this procedure to expedite the ongoing operations of the Department of Justice, as far as these people are concerned. Is it in any way contrary to whatever action the Attorney General has taken on the question of deportation; does the gentleman know?

"Mr. EILBERG. Mr. Speaker, the answer is no to the gentleman's final question. These aliens have been found to be deportable and the Special Inquiry Officer's decision denying suspension of deportation has been reversed by the Board of Immigration Appeals. We are complying with the law since all of these decisions have been referred to us for approval or disapproval, and there are hundreds of cases in this category. In these six cases however, we believe it would be grossly improper to allow these people to acquire the status of permanent resident aliens.

"Mr. WYLIE. In other words, the gentleman has been working with the Attorney General's office?

"Mr. EILBERG. Yes.

"Mr. WYLIE. This bill then is in fact a confirmation of what the Attorney General intends to do?

"Mr. EILBERG. The gentleman is correct insofar as it relates to the determination of deportability which has been made by the Department of Justice in each of these cases.

"Mr. WYLIE. Mr. Speaker, I withdraw my reservation of objection." 120 Cong. Rec. 41412 (1974).

Clearly, this was an obfuscation of the effect of a veto under § 244(c)(2). Such a veto in no way constitutes "a confirmation of what the Attorney General intends to do." To the contrary, such a resolution was meant to overrule and set aside, or "veto," the Attorney General's determination that, in a particular case, cancellation of deportation would be appropriate under the standards set forth in § 244(a)(1).

All legislative Powers herein granted shall be vested in a Congress of the United States, which shall consist of a Senate *and* House of Representatives. Art. I, § 1 (Emphasis added.)

Every Bill which shall have passed the House of Representatives *and* the Senate, *shall*, before it becomes a law, be presented to the President of the United States.... Art. I, § 7, cl. 2. (Emphasis added.)

Every Order, Resolution, or Vote to which the Concurrence of the Senate and House of Representatives may be necessary (except on a question of Adjournment) *shall be* presented to the President of the United States; and before the Same shall take Effect, *shall be* approved by him, or being disapproved by him, *shall be* repassed by two thirds of the Senate and House of Representatives, according to the Rules and Limitations prescribed in the Case of a Bill. Art. I, § 7, cl. 3. (Emphasis added.)

These provisions of Art. I are integral parts of the constitutional design for the separation of powers. * * *

The decision to provide the President with a limited and qualified power to nullify proposed legislation by veto was based on the profound conviction of the Framers that the powers conferred on Congress were the powers to be most carefully circumscribed. It is beyond doubt that lawmaking was a power to be shared by both Houses and the President. In *The Federalist* No. 73, Hamilton focused on the President's role in making laws:

> If even no propensity had ever discovered itself in the legislative body to invade the rights of the Executive, the rules of just reasoning and theoretic propriety would of themselves teach us that the one ought not to be left to the mercy of the other, but ought to possess a constitutional and effectual power of self-defense. * * *

The President's role in the lawmaking process also reflects the Framers' careful efforts to check whatever propensity a particular Congress might have to enact oppressive, improvident, or ill-considered measures. The President's veto role in the legislative process was described later during public debate on ratification:

> It establishes a salutary check upon the legislative body, calculated to guard the community against the effects of faction, precipitancy, or of any impulse unfriendly to the public good, which may happen to influence a majority of that body.... The primary inducement to conferring the power in question upon the Executive is, to enable him to defend himself; the secondary

one is to increase the chances in favor of the community against the passing of bad laws, through haste, inadvertence, or design.

The Federalist No. 73, *supra*, at 458 (A. Hamilton). The Court also has observed that the Presentment Clauses serve the important purpose of assuring that a "national" perspective is grafted on the legislative process: "The President is a representative of the people just as the members of the Senate and of the House are, and it may be, at some times, on some subjects, that the President elected by all the people is rather more representative of them all than are the members of either body of the Legislature whose constituencies are local and not countrywide. . . ." *Myers v. United States, supra*, at 123.

The bicameral requirement of Art. I, §§ 1, 7, was of scarcely less concern to the Framers than was the Presidential veto and indeed the two concepts are interdependent. By providing that no law could take effect without the concurrence of the prescribed majority of the Members of both Houses, the Framers reemphasized their belief, already remarked upon in connection with the Presentment Clauses, that legislation should not be enacted unless it has been carefully and fully considered by the Nation's elected officials. * * *

Hamilton argued that a Congress comprised of a single House was antithetical to the very purposes of the Constitution. Were the Nation to adopt a Constitution providing for only one legislative organ, he warned:

> [W]e shall finally accumulate, in a single body, all the most important prerogatives of sovereignty, and thus entail upon our posterity one of the most execrable forms of government that human infatuation ever contrived. Thus we should create in reality that very tyranny which the adversaries of the new Constitution either are, or affect to be, solicitous to avert. *The Federalist* No. 22.

However familiar, it is useful to recall that apart from their fear that special interests could be favored at the expense of public needs, the Framers were also concerned, although not of one mind, over the apprehensions of the smaller states. Those states feared a commonality of interest among the larger states would work to their disadvantage; representatives of the larger states, on the other hand, were skeptical of a legislature that could pass laws favoring a minority of the people. It need hardly be repeated here that the Great Compromise, under which one House was viewed as representing the people and the other the states, allayed the fears of both the large and small states.

We see therefore that the Framers were acutely conscious that the bicameral requirement and the Presentment Clauses would serve essential constitutional functions. The President's participation in the legislative process was to protect the Executive Branch from Congress and to protect the whole people from improvident laws. The division of the Congress into two distinctive bodies assures that the legislative power would be exercised only after opportunity for full study and debate in separate settings. The President's unilateral veto power, in turn, was limited by the power of two-thirds of both Houses of Congress to overrule a veto thereby precluding final arbitrary action of one person. It emerges clearly that the prescription for legislative action in Art. I, §§ 1, 7, represents the Framers' decision that the legislative power of the Federal Government be exercised in accord with a single, finely wrought and exhaustively considered, procedure.

The Constitution sought to divide the delegated powers of the new Federal Government into three defined categories, Legislative, Executive, and Judicial, to assure, as nearly as possible, that each Branch of government would confine itself to its assigned responsibility. The hydraulic pressure inherent within each of the separate Branches to exceed the outer limits of its power, even to accomplish desirable objectives, must be resisted.

* * * When the Executive acts, he presumptively acts in an executive or administrative capacity as defined in Art. II. And when, as here, one House of Congress purports to act, it is presumptively acting within its assigned sphere.

Beginning with this presumption, we must nevertheless establish that the challenged action under § 244(c)(2) is of the kind to which the procedural requirements of Art. I, § 7, apply. Not every action taken by either House is subject to the bicameralism and presentment requirements of Art. I. Whether actions taken by either House are, in law and fact, an exercise of legislative power depends not on their form but upon "whether they contain matter which is properly to be regarded as legislative in its character and effect."

Examination of the action taken here by one House pursuant to § 244(c)(2) reveals that it was essentially legislative in purpose and effect. In purporting to exercise power defined in Art. I, § 8, cl. 4, to "establish an uniform Rule of Naturalization," the House took action that had the purpose and effect of altering the legal rights, duties, and relations of persons, including the Attorney General, Executive Branch officials and Chadha, all outside the Legislative Branch. * * * The one-House veto operated in these cases to overrule the Attorney General and mandate Chadha's deportation; absent the House action, Chadha would remain in the United States. Congress has *acted* and its action has altered Chadha's status.

The legislative character of the one-House veto in these cases is confirmed by the character of the congressional action it supplants. Neither the House of Representatives nor the Senate contends that, absent the veto provision in § 244(c)(2), either of them, or both of them acting together, could effectively require the Attorney General to deport an alien once the Attorney General, in the exercise of legislatively delegated authority,[16] had determined the alien should remain in the United States. Without the challenged provision in § 244(c)(2), this could have been achieved, if at all, only by legislation requiring deportation. * * *

The nature of the decision implemented by the one-House veto in these cases further manifests its legislative character. After long experience with the clumsy, time-consuming private bill procedure, Congress made a deliberate choice to delegate to the Executive Branch, and specifically to the Attorney General, the authority to allow deportable aliens to remain in this country in certain specified circumstances. It is not disputed that this choice to delegate authority is precisely the kind of decision that can be implemented only in accordance with the procedures set out in Art. I. Disagreement with the Attorney General's decision on Chadha's deportation—that is, Congress' decision to deport Chadha—no less than Congress' original choice to delegate to the Attorney General the authority to make that decision, involves determinations of policy that Congress can implement in only one way; bicameral passage followed by presentment to the President. Congress must abide by its delegation of authority until that delegation is legislatively altered or revoked.

Finally, we see that when the Framers intended to authorize either House of Congress to act alone and outside of its prescribed bicameral legislative role, they narrowly and precisely defined the procedure for such action. There are four provisions in the Constitution, explicit and

---

[16] Congress protests that affirming the Court of Appeals in these cases will sanction "lawmaking by the Attorney General. * * * " To be sure, some administrative agency action—rulemaking, for example—may resemble "lawmaking." * * * This Court has referred to agency activity as being "quasi-legislative" in character. *Humphrey's Executor.* Clearly, however, "[i]n the framework of our Constitution, the President's power to see that the laws are faithfully executed refutes the idea that he is to be a lawmaker." *Youngstown.* When the Attorney General performs his duties pursuant to § 244, he does not exercise "legislative" power. The bicameral process is not necessary as a check on the Executive's administration of the laws because his administrative activity cannot reach beyond the limits of the statute that created it—a statute duly enacted pursuant to Art. I, §§ 1, 7. The constitutionality of the Attorney General's execution of the authority delegated to him by § 244 involves only a question of delegation doctrine. The courts, when a case or controversy arises, can always "ascertain whether the will of Congress has been obeyed," and can enforce adherence to statutory standards. It is clear, therefore, that the Attorney General acts in his presumptively Art. II capacity when he administers the Immigration and Nationality Act. Executive action under legislatively delegated authority that might resemble "legislative" action in some respects is not subject to the approval of both Houses of Congress and the President for the reason that the Constitution does not so require. That kind of Executive action is always subject to check by the terms of the legislation that authorized it; and if that authority is exceeded it is open to judicial review as well as the power of Congress to modify or revoke the authority entirely. A one-House veto is clearly legislative in both character and effect and is not so checked; the need for the check provided by Art. I, §§ 1, 7, is therefore clear. Congress' authority to delegate portions of its power to administrative agencies provides no support for the argument that Congress can constitutionally control administration of the laws by way of a congressional veto.

unambiguous, by which one House may act alone with the unreviewable force of law, not subject to the President's veto: [the House's power to initiate impeachments, Art. I, § 2, cl. 5; the Senate's power to conduct impeachment trials, Art. I, § 3, cl. 6; the Senate's power to confirm presidential appointments, Art. II, § 2, cl. 2; and the Senate's power to ratify treaties, Art, II, § 2, cl. 2. Chief Justice Burger concluded that these "narrow, explicit, and separately justified" exceptions to bicameralism and presentment "provide further support for the conclusion that congressional authority is not to be implied."] * * *

The veto authorized by § 244(c)(2) doubtless has been in many respects a convenient shortcut; the "sharing" with the Executive by Congress of its authority over aliens in this manner is, on its face, an appealing compromise. In purely practical terms, it is obviously easier for action to be taken by one House without submission to the President; but it is crystal clear from the records of the Convention, contemporaneous writings and debates, that the Framers ranked other values higher than efficiency. The records of the Convention and debates in the States preceding ratification underscore the common desire to define and limit the exercise of the newly created federal powers affecting the states and the people. There is unmistakable expression of a determination that legislation by the national Congress be a step-by-step, deliberate and deliberative process.

The choices we discern as having been made in the Constitutional Convention impose burdens on governmental processes that often seem clumsy, inefficient, even unworkable, but those hard choices were consciously made by men who had lived under a form of government that permitted arbitrary governmental acts to go unchecked. There is no support in the Constitution or decisions of this Court for the proposition that the cumbersomeness and delays often encountered in complying with explicit constitutional standards may be avoided, either by the Congress or by the President. *See Youngstown.* With all the obvious flaws of delay, untidiness, and potential for abuse, we have not yet found a better way to preserve freedom than by making the exercise of power subject to the carefully crafted restraints spelled out in the Constitution.

[JUSTICE POWELL concurred only in the judgment. Rather than joining an opinion that "apparently will invalidate every use of the legislative veto," Justice Powell opted to decide the case on the ground that "[w]hen Congress finds that a particular person does not satisfy the statutory criteria for permanent residence in this country it has assumed a judicial function in violation of the principle of separation of powers." Justice Powell stressed the Framers' concern about the exercise of unchecked legislative power and noted that the congressional act here was surrounded by none of the traditional procedural protections that accompany adjudication. The dissenting opinion of JUSTICE REHNQUIST is also omitted. Justice Rehnquist agreed that the legislative veto was unconstitutional but would not have severed it from the remainder of the law, thereby denying Chadha any relief.]

JUSTICE WHITE, dissenting.

[Justice White first stressed that the decision "sounds the death knell for nearly 200 other statutory provisions in which Congress has reserved a 'legislative veto.'" He then emphasized the utility of the legislative veto in allowing "the President and Congress to resolve major constitutional and policy differences, assur[ing] the accountability of independent regulatory agencies, and preserv[ing] Congress' control over lawmaking."]

The history of the legislative veto also makes clear that it has not been a sword with which Congress has struck out to aggrandize itself at the expense of the other branches—the concerns of Madison and Hamilton. Rather, the veto has been a means of defense, a reservation of ultimate authority necessary if Congress is to fulfill its designated role under Art. I as the Nation's lawmaker. While the President has often objected to particular legislative vetoes, generally those left in the hands of congressional Committees, the Executive has more often agreed to legislative review as the price for a broad delegation of authority. To be sure, the President may have preferred unrestricted power, but that could be precisely why Congress thought it essential to retain a check on the exercise of delegated authority. * * *

* * * There is no question but that agency rulemaking is lawmaking in any functional or realistic sense of the term. The Administrative Procedure Act provides that a "rule" is an agency statement "designed to implement, interpret, or prescribe law or policy." When agencies are authorized to prescribe law through substantive rulemaking, the administrator's regulation is not only due deference, but is accorded "legislative effect." These regulations bind courts and officers of the Federal Government, may preempt state law, and grant rights to and impose obligations on the public. In sum, they have the force of law.

If Congress may delegate lawmaking power to independent and Executive agencies, it is most difficult to understand Art. I as prohibiting Congress from also reserving a check on legislative power for itself. Absent the veto, the agencies receiving delegations of legislative or quasi-legislative power may issue regulations having the force of law without bicameral approval and without the President's signature. It is thus not apparent why the reservation of a veto over the exercise of that legislative power must be subject to a more exacting test. In both cases, it is enough that the initial statutory authorizations comply with the Art. I requirements. * * *

The central concern of the presentment and bicameralism requirements of Art. I is that when a departure from the legal status quo is undertaken, it is done with the approval of the President and both Houses of Congress—or, in the event of a Presidential veto, a two-thirds majority in both Houses. This interest is fully satisfied by the operation of § 244(c)(2). The President's approval is found in the Attorney General's action in recommending to Congress that the deportation order for a given alien be suspended. The House and the Senate indicate their approval of the Executive's action by not passing a resolution of disapproval within the statutory period. Thus, a change in the legal status quo—the deportability of the alien—is consummated only with the approval of each of the three relevant actors. The disagreement of any one of the three maintains the alien's pre-existing status: the Executive may choose not to recommend suspension; the House and Senate may each veto the recommendation. The effect on the rights and obligations of the affected individuals and upon the legislative system is precisely the same as if a private bill were introduced but failed to receive the necessary approval. "The President and the two Houses enjoy exactly the same say in what the law is to be as would have been true for each without the presence of the one-House veto, and nothing in the law is changed absent the concurrence of the President and a majority in each House." *Atkins v. United States*, 556 F.2d 1028, 1064 (1977), cert. denied, 434 U.S. 1009 (1978). * * *

NOTES AND QUESTIONS ON THE LEGISLATIVE VETO

1. *The Holding of* Chadha? The Chief Justice's opinion invalidated the one-house veto as a violation of *both* the bicameralism *and* presentment requirements of Article I, § 7. Does *Chadha* also require the invalidation of two-house veto provisions, which only violate the Presentment Clauses? In summary orders issued soon after *Chadha*, the Supreme Court suggested that *Chadha* did cover those vetoes as well. See *Process Gas Consumers Group v. Consumer Energy Council of America*, 463 U.S. 1216 (1983) (summarily affirming invalidation of legislative veto of agency rulemaking); *United States Senate v. FTC*, 463 U.S. 1216 (1983) (summarily affirming invalidation of two-house veto of agency rulemaking). On the other hand, lower courts have ruled that *Chadha* did not invalidate "report-and-wait" or "laying over" provisions, holding off the effective date of an agency action until Congress has an opportunity to review it. E.g., *Hechinger v. Metropolitan Washington Airports Auth.*, 36 F.3d 97 (D.C. Cir. 1994).

2. *Different Functional Characterizations of the Legislative Veto.* The three *Chadha* opinions present strikingly different visions of the legislative veto. Indeed, each opinion has a different functional characterization of the veto. For the majority, the veto is *legislative*: "Examination of the action taken here by one House ... reveals that it was essentially legislative in purpose and effect." Justice Powell and Justice White characterized the veto in very different terms. Justice Powell explained that the veto was used in this case to *adjudicate* Chadha's case: "Congress ... has assumed a judicial

function in violation of the separation of powers." Justice White emphasized the veto as a restraint on *executive* action, as "reservation of a veto over the exercise of legislative power" by the executive. If the Justices cannot agree upon a functional characterization, how useful are functional arguments in deciding structural cases?

3. *Different Visions of Constitutional Structure.* The opinions also raise the two standard divisions between theories of the separation of powers, we have seen in our Note on the Separation of Powers above. Justice White's opinion took a "functional" approach toward the separation of powers, which tends to be fairly lenient about structural innovation as long as the innovation (here, the legislative veto) does not radically change existing structures. Since the veto does not gravely disrupt the executive function, it should be fine under such an approach. The President maintains his general executive power intact because it is simply "clawed back" in specific instances.

The majority opinion took a more "formal" approach toward the separation of powers, focusing on a distinct constitutional text prescribing when Congress can legislate under Article I, § 7. The Bicameralism Clause was intended to strengthen Congress vis-à-vis the President (a two-House Congress is typically more powerful against the executive than a one-House legislature), and at the same time to protect against improvident use of the legislative power. Because it is difficult for Congress to agree upon legislation, the theory is that it should produce better legislation. The formalist may concede that the legislative veto leaves the vast majority of the President's executive power substantially intact but fears that the legislative veto aggrandizes *legislative power*.

How far must we take the Court's formalism? If all actions legislative in character are subject to the bicameralism and presentment argument, is agency rulemaking unconstitutional? When an agency creates a rule that has the force of law does it not "legislate"? And if the agency is "legislating," then why should Congress not be barred by Article I, § 7 from delegating authority to agencies to make legally binding rules?

4. *Representation and the Legislative Veto.* One way to think about Congress, the President, and even the Supreme Court is this: Whom does each branch "represent"? Whom does the Attorney General represent? The nation.[38] Consider Representative Eilberg or those on his subcommittee: Whom do they represent? States and localities. What happens if we shift from one form of representation to another, in this case, from *the nation to states and localities*? In this case, the legislative veto shifts Chadha's deportation decision from a national constituency to one that may be very local indeed, particularly in the case of a one-house veto. This raises some obvious

---

[38] *Chadha,* 462 U.S. at 948: "The President is a representative of the people just as the members of the Senate and of the House are, and it may be, at some times, on some subjects, that the President elected by all the people is rather more representative of them all than are the members of either body of the Legislature whose constituencies are local and not countrywide."

questions in Chadha's case because we know that moving from larger to smaller groups increases the risk of bias against minorities. It also raises the question whether the usefulness and popularity of the legislative veto lies less in its restraint of the executive than in the increase of power to individual members of Congress. See Victoria F. Nourse, *The Vertical Separation of Powers,* 49 Duke L.J. 749 (1999).

5. *Policy Arguments For and Against the Veto. Chadha's* different opinions may reflect different policy views about the usefulness of the veto. The principal argument for the legislative veto is that once the Supreme Court has allowed Congress to delegate vast lawmaking power to agencies, Congress should be able to "claw back" its delegation, to restrain the executive, and to provide feedback about the scope of the delegation (without having to conduct oversight hearings). Congress cannot foresee all situations and so the legislative veto also allows for it to speak to issues that it did not address originally. As one scholar explains it, "By delegating a qualified authority, Congress can maintain the system's energy, while by reserving authority to review proposed rules and acts, it can restore balance and accountability." Stanley C. Brubaker, *Slouching Toward Constitutional Duty: The Legislative Veto and the Delegation of Authority*, 1 Const. Comm. 81, 85 (1984).

There are policy arguments against the veto, however. First, it may create an incentive for greater delegation because it allows for a "bailout effect." If members of Congress know that they can "take back" the delegation anytime it proves inconvenient, they will tend to delegate broadly. Second, it may yield policy deadlock. The veto may encourage Congress to avoid addressing hard questions and allow them at the same time to prevent the Administration from addressing those questions, through the exercise of the veto. Third, because the legislative veto will tend to be wielded by congressional committees and subcommittees vitally concerned with the topic, "a likely and apparently common occurrence is a significant skewing of the original legislative intent towards the interest of the congressmen on the overseeing committee or subcommittee and the groups and people most responsible for their re-election." *Id.* at 92. Put in other words, what may be the veto's virtue (updating policies) may be its vice: the ability for committees to shift outcomes when the partisan makeup of Congress changes. Michael Herz, *The Legislative Veto in Times of Political Reversal: Chadha and the 104th Congress*, 14 Const. Comm. 319 (1997); see William N. Eskridge Jr. & John Ferejohn, *The Article I, Section 7 Game,* 80 Geo. L.J. 523 (1992).

6. *The Impact of* Chadha. Congressional scholar Louis Fisher reports that many statutes enacted after *Chadha* continue to include legislative vetoes, and administrative agencies regularly attend to them as though they were the "law" by seeking committee permission for certain decisions. See Louis Fisher, *The Legislative Veto: Invalidated, It Survives*, 56 Law & Contemp. Probs. 273 (1993). On the other hand, political scientist Jessica Korn argues that other mechanisms, constitutional under *Chadha*, can and do work just as well as the legislative veto. She examines the subsequent

history of the legislative veto in the Jackson-Vanik Amendment to the Trade Act of 1974, which terminated most-favored nation (MFN) trade status upon the vote of one house of Congress. See Jessica Korn, *The Power of Separation: American Constitutionalism and the Myth of the Legislative Veto* 91–115 (1996). By Korn's account, the main value of the veto was as a fast-track vehicle for Congress to express frustration with presidential trade actions and to put pressure on the President to press congressional human rights concerns in negotiations with specific countries. Because members wanted their views considered but did not want to be seen as upsetting foreign policy, Congress did not actually "veto" any MFN status until after *Chadha*. In any event, Korn argues, joint resolutions "conditioning" MFN status upon meeting human rights conditions have been a more effective vehicle for expression of Congress's concerns. Since such resolutions can be and usually are vetoed by the President, Congress can and does express concern without hurting foreign policy.

Korn concludes that the practice was never an important weapon in the arsenal of congressional oversight. "Members did not need the legislative shortcut to force executive branch officials to attend to congressional concerns, because the most useful sources of congressional oversight power— the power to make laws, and the power to require the executive branch and independent agency officials to report [to committees] proposed actions before implementation—are well nestled in the authorities granted to members by Article I of the Constitution." Korn, *Power of Separation*, 116. Of fourteen potential oversight mechanisms, some of which we discuss in this section, the legislative veto ranked last in terms of frequency of use and ninth in terms of effectiveness, according to Joel D. Aberbach, *Keeping a Watchful Eye: The Politics of Congressional Oversight* 132 tbl. 6–1, 135 tbl. 6–2 (1990).

7.   *Severability.* The concept of severability asks whether one part of a statute may be "severed" from the rest to save the constitutionality of the remainder of the statute. Because unconstitutional legislative vetoes were included in literally hundreds of federal statutes, *Chadha* occasioned a run of cases challenging the constitutionality of the entire statutes in which such vetoes were found. The Court generally applies a "presumption in favor of severability," meaning that if the Court finds one provision of a statute unconstitutional it will not invalidate the entire statute if it can stand without the provision. This was the approach taken by the Chief Justice in *Chadha* itself (with Justices Rehnquist and White in dissent). See Chapter 6 for an in-depth discussion of the presumption of severability.

B. CONGRESS'S CONSTITUTIONAL AUTHORITY TO CONTROL THE EXECUTIVE BRANCH

We have seen Congress's attempts to control agencies through the legislative veto, and how the Supreme Court rejected this form of control as unconstitutional in *Chadha*. Are there other limits on Congress's power to structure agency action? May Congress structure the budget process, either by granting or depriving the President of power?

Charles A. Bowsher v. Mike Synar et al.
478 U.S. 714 (1986).

The Gramm-Rudman-Hollings Act sought to balance the budget by granting the Comptroller General the power to enforce budget limitations on the President. The President was required under the Act to issue a "sequestration" order mandating the spending reductions specified by the Comptroller General. A three-judge court invalidated the law, and the Supreme Court affirmed, with **Chief Justice Burger** writing for the Court, on the theory that Congress retained too much control over the Comptroller General, an official generally considered to head a congressional agency. Justice Burger wrote: "The Constitution does not contemplate an active role for Congress in the supervision of officers charged with the execution of the laws it enacts. The President appoints 'Officers of the United States' with the 'Advice and Consent of the Senate. . . .' Art. II, § 2. Once the appointment has been made and confirmed, however, the Constitution explicitly provides for removal of Officers of the United States by Congress only upon impeachment by the House of Representatives and conviction by the Senate. An impeachment by the House and trial by the Senate can rest only on 'Treason, Bribery or other high Crimes and Misdemeanors.' Art. II, § 4. A direct congressional role in the removal of officers charged with the execution of the laws beyond this limited one is inconsistent with separation of powers."

"To permit the execution of the laws to be vested in an officer answerable only to Congress would, in practical terms, reserve in Congress control over the execution of the laws. * * * The structure of the Constitution does not permit Congress to execute the laws; it follows that Congress cannot grant to an officer under its control what it does not possess."

"To permit an officer controlled by Congress to execute the laws would be, in essence, to permit a congressional veto. Congress could simply remove, or threaten to remove, an officer for executing the laws in any fashion found to be unsatisfactory to Congress. This kind of congressional control over the execution of the laws, *Chadha* makes clear, is constitutionally impermissible."

The government argued that the Comptroller General performs his duties independently and is not controlled by Congress—a contention the Chief Justice rejected, because Congress (not the President) retains the authority to remove that official. The Chief Justice rejected the government's argument that, as a practical matter, the Comptroller

General is free from influence by Congress. The Comptroller General heads the General Accounting Office (GAO), "an instrumentality of the United States Government independent of the executive departments," 31 U.S.C. § 702(a), which was created by Congress in 1921 as part of the Budget and Accounting Act of 1921. Congress created the office because it believed that it "needed an officer, responsible to it alone, to check upon the application of public funds in accordance with appropriations." H. Mansfield, *The Comptroller General: A Study in the Law and Practice of Financial Administration* 65 (1939).

"It is clear that Congress has consistently viewed the Comptroller General as an officer of the Legislative Branch. The Reorganization Acts of 1945 and 1949, for example, both stated that the Comptroller General and the GAO are 'a part of the legislative branch of the Government.' Similarly, in the Accounting and Auditing Act of 1950, Congress required the Comptroller General to conduct audits 'as an agent of the Congress.'" The Chief Justice also quoted statements from former Comptrollers General, who presented themselves as part of the Legislative Branch.

"Against this background, we see no escape from the conclusion that, because Congress has retained removal authority over the Comptroller General, he may not be entrusted with executive powers."

"The executive nature of the Comptroller General's functions under the Act is revealed in § 252(a)(3) which gives the Comptroller General the ultimate authority to determine the budget cuts to be made. Indeed, the Comptroller General commands the President himself to carry out, without the slightest variation (with exceptions not relevant to the constitutional issues presented), the directive of the Comptroller General as to the budget reductions:

"The [Presidential] order *must provide* for reductions in the manner specified in section 251(a)(3), *must incorporate* the provisions of the [Comptroller General's] report submitted under section 251(b), and *must be consistent with such report in all respects*. The President *may not modify or recalculate any of the estimates, determinations, specifications, bases, amounts, or percentages* set forth in the report submitted under section 251(b) in determining the reductions to be specified in the order with respect to programs, projects, and activities, or with respect to budget activities, within an account. . . ." § 252(a)(3) (emphasis added).

Justice Stevens (joined by Justice Marshall) concurred in the Court's judgment, based upon his reading of *Chadha*. He agreed that the Comptroller General is an agent of Congress and then argued that, "when Congress, or a component or an agent of Congress, seeks to make policy that will bind the Nation, it must follow the procedures mandated by Article I of the Constitution—through passage by both Houses and presentment to the President. In short, Congress may not exercise its fundamental power to formulate national policy by delegating that power to one of its two Houses, to a legislative committee, or to an individual agent of the Congress such as the Speaker of the House of Representatives, the Sergeant at Arms of the Senate, or the Director of the Congressional Budget Office. *Chadha.* That principle, I believe, is applicable to the Comptroller General."

Justice Stevens noted that the Court did not dispute that it would be constitutional for Congress to delegate to an executive official the authority provided to the Comptroller General in the Act. He saw the "central issue" in the case as follows: "If the delegation to a stranger is permissible, why may not Congress delegate the same responsibilities to one of its own agents?" His response was that intra-congressional delegations violate *Chadha*: "If Congress were free to delegate its policymaking authority to one of its components, or to one of its agents, it would be able to evade 'the carefully crafted restraints spelled out in the Constitution.' *Chadha.* That danger—congressional action that evades constitutional restraints—is not present when Congress delegates lawmaking power to the executive or to an independent agency."

In dissent, **Justice White** did not consider the Comptroller's authority under Gramm-Rudman to include substantial policymaking discretion and thought it sensible for Congress to entrust these duties to "an officer who is to the greatest degree possible nonpartisan and independent of the President and his political agenda and who therefore may be relied upon not to allow his calculations to be colored by political considerations." Moreover, he saw no intrusion into executive functions at work in the statute: the appropriation of funds is purely a congressional function, Congress has set a limit on the amount of appropriations, and Congress delegated the mechanics of enforcing the limitation to someone independent of the President.

"The Act vesting budget-cutting authority in the Comptroller General represents Congress' judgment that the delegation of such authority to counteract ever-mounting deficits is 'necessary and proper' to the exercise of the powers granted the Federal Government by the Constitution; and the President's approval of the statute signifies his unwillingness to reject the choice made by Congress. Under such circumstances, the role of this Court should be limited to determining whether the Act so alters the balance of authority among the branches of government as to pose a genuine threat to the basic division between the lawmaking power and the power to execute the law. Because I see no such threat, I cannot join the Court in striking down the Act."

In a separate dissent, **Justice Blackmun** would have invalidated the provisions of the 1921 statute allowing Congress to remove the Comptroller General, thereby saving the Gramm-Rudman-Hollings Act.

NOTES AND QUESTIONS ON BOWSHER AND CHADHA

Bowsher's categorization exercise is replete with logical holes and unanswered questions: Is the Comptroller General an "Executive" Official? Does Congress "control" the Comptroller? Why did *Chadha not* control this case, as Justice Stevens suggested?

The bigger question is this: How can we reconcile the various cases? Is there a principle each is enforcing? In *Checks and Balances in an Era of Presidential Lawmaking*, 61 U. Chi. L. Rev. 123, 167 (1994), Abner Greene suggests that the laws in *Bowsher* and *Chadha* were both efforts at self-aggrandizement, and the Court was right to monitor that defect. Under such a rationale, Congress can *give away* power but cannot augment its own authority. Victoria F. Nourse, in *The Vertical Separation of Powers*, 49 Duke L.J. 749, 793–95 (1999), argues that the cases can be reconciled through the vertical perspective: A shift in power is also a shift in political constituency and in popular accountability. Both *Chadha* and *Bowsher* shifted important federal decision making away from the messy but deliberative *political* process and toward less accountable insiders (*Chadha*) and bureaucrats (*Bowsher*). Both cut the President, and his national constituency, out of important public decisions. Consider both Greene's and Nourse's theory in light of the Line Item Veto Case that follows.

William J. Clinton et al. v. City of New York et al.
524 U.S. 417 (1998).

The Line Item Veto Act, Pub. L. No. 104–130, 110 Stat. 1200, codified at 2 U.S.C. § 691 *et seq.*, gave the President the authority to *cancel* certain spending and tax benefit measures after he has signed them into law. Section 691(a) of the Act provides that "the President may, with respect to any bill or joint resolution that has been signed into law pursuant to Article I, section 7, of the Constitution of the United States, cancel in whole—

(1) any dollar amount of discretionary budget authority;

(2) any item of new direct spending; or

(3) any limited tax benefit;

if the President—

(A) determines that such cancellation will—

(i) reduce the Federal budget deficit;

(ii) not impair any essential Government functions; and

(iii) not harm the national interest; and

(B) notifies the Congress of such cancellation by transmitting a special message * * * within five calendar days (excluding Sundays) after the enactment of the law [to which the cancellation applies].

The President's *cancellation* under the Act would take effect when the special message notifying Congress of the cancellation was received in the House and Senate. The Act also established expedited procedures in both Houses for the consideration of disapproval bills, § 691d. Bills or joint resolutions which, if enacted into law by the familiar procedures set out in Article I, § 7 of the Constitution, would render the President's cancellation null and void, § 691b(a).

The opinion for the Court by **Justice Stevens** ruled the line item veto authority unconstitutional. "The effect of a cancellation . . . prevents the item 'from having legal force or effect.' Thus, under the plain text of the statute, the two actions of the President that are challenged in these cases prevented one section of the Balanced Budget Act of 1997 and one section of the Taxpayer Relief Act of 1997 'from having legal force or effect.' The remaining provisions of those statutes * * * continue to have the same force and effect as they had when signed into law.

"In both legal and practical effect, the President has amended two Acts of Congress by repealing a portion of each. * * * There is no provision in the Constitution that authorizes the President to enact, to amend, or to repeal statutes." Justice Stevens contrasted the President's return of a vetoed bill, which occurs *before* the bill becomes a law and involves the entire bill. Although the Constitution, technically, says nothing explicit about the President's authority to cancel part of legislation that he or she has signed into law, the Court relied on *Chadha*'s holding that the power to enact statutes may only "be exercised in accord with a single, finely wrought and exhaustively considered, procedure." *Chadha.*

The government's main defense of this unconventional arrangement was that the substance of the authority to cancel tax and spending items "is, in practical effect, no more and no less than the power to 'decline to spend' specified sums of money, or to 'decline to implement' specified tax measures." Thus, "[t]he critical difference between this statute and all of its predecessors, however, is that unlike any of them, this Act gives the President the unilateral power to change the text of duly enacted statutes. None of the Act's predecessors could even arguably have been construed to authorize such a change."

Justice Scalia dissented, in an opinion joined by Justices O'Connor and Breyer. "Insofar as the degree of political, 'lawmaking' power conferred upon the Executive is concerned, there is not a dime's worth of difference between Congress's authorizing the President to *cancel* a spending item, and Congress's authorizing money to be spent on a particular item at the President's discretion. And the latter has been done since the Founding of the Nation." President Nixon went so far as to claim a constitutional right to impound funds authorized by Congress—a position the Court rejected in *Train v. City of New York,* 420 U.S. 35 (1975), but the Court's opinion "implicitly confirmed that Congress may confer discretion upon the Executive to withhold appropriated funds, even funds appropriated for a specific purpose." Justice Scalia complained that the Line Item Veto Act's title "has succeeded in faking out the Supreme Court. The President's action it authorizes in fact is not a line-item veto and thus does not offend Art. I, § 7; and insofar as the substance of that action is concerned, it is no different from what Congress has permitted the President to do since the formation of the Union."

Joined by Justices O'Connor and Scalia, **Justice Breyer** also dissented. Echoing Justice White's *Chadha* dissent, Justice Breyer maintained that there was no functional difference between the President's cancellation authority under the Act and an Article I, § 7 statute authorizing a particular tax, *provided that* the President does not determine that the tax is unwarranted. That is, if the President makes a particular determination, his/her certification prevents the tax from taking effect. "Whatever a person might say, or think, about the constitutionality of this imaginary law, there is one thing the English language would prevent one from saying. One could not say that a President who 'prevent[s]' the [statutory tax] language from 'having legal force or effect' has either *repealed* or *amended* this particular hypothetical statute. Rather, the President has *followed* that law to the letter. He has exercised the power it explicitly delegates to him. He has executed the law, not repealed it."

Indeed, Justice Breyer demonstrated that "this is not the first time that Congress has delegated to the President or to others this kind of power—a contingent power to deny effect to certain statutory language. [E.g.,] 28 U.S.C. § 2072 (Supreme Court is authorized to promulgate rules of practice and procedure in federal courts, and '[a]ll laws in conflict with such rules *shall be of no further force and effect*') (emphasis added); Gramm-Rudman-Hollings Act, § 252(a)(4) (authorizing the President to issue a 'final order' that has the effect of *'permanently cancell[ing]'* sequestered amounts in spending statutes in order to achieve budget compliance) (emphasis added). * * * All of these examples, like the Act, delegate a power to take action that will render statutory provisions 'without force or effect.' Every one of these examples, like the present Act, delegates the power to choose between alternatives, each of which the statute spells out in some detail. None of these examples delegates a power to "repeal" or "amend" a statute, or to "make" a new law. Nor does the Act. Rather, the delegated power to nullify statutory language was *itself* created and defined by Congress, and included in the statute books on an equal footing with (indeed, as a component part of) the sections that are potentially subject to nullification."

Speaking only for himself and Justice O'Connor, Justice Breyer rejected arguments based upon separation of powers principles: (1) Has Congress given the President the wrong kind of power, *i.e.*, "non-executive" power? No. (2) Has Congress given the President the power to "encroach" upon Congress' own constitutionally reserved territory? No. (3) Has Congress given the President too much power, violating the nondelegation doctrine? No, because the law provides "intelligible" standards to guide the President.

NOTES AND QUESTIONS ON THE LINE-ITEM VETO

The Court adheres to formalist definitions of lawmaking, under Article I, § 7, in *Chadha* and *Clinton*. Why did these cases elicit such strong opinions from the Court invalidating frequently used statutory devices (the legislative veto and the line item veto). What elements of these cases trigger this formalist analysis? Why is Justice Breyer's more functionalist dissent in *Clinton* not persuasive, especially in light of the high level of delegation permissible in the modern regulatory state? Is *Clinton,* where Congress was giving away power, not different from *Chadha*, where Congress was seeking to reassert power it had given away?

Relatedly, *Clinton* appears to cabin Congress's ability to delegate to the executive branch. Can the Court's decision be reconciled with the high level of executive delegation necessary to the modern regulatory state? Recall that delegation to agencies requires only an "intelligible principle" in order to meet constitutional standards. Prior to *Clinton,* the Office of Legal Counsel (OLC) had opined that the delegation under the Line Item Veto Act is similar to other kinds of "sweeping" discretionary powers delegated by Congress to the executive branch, including powers relating to the nation's fisc. *See* Michael J. Gerhardt, *The Bottom Line on the Line-Item Veto Act of 1996*, 6 Cornell J. L. & Pub. Pol'y 233, 236–37 (1996) (discussing the OLC opinion but predicting the Act's demise). Additionally, OLC found that the delegation under the Line Item Veto Act would satisfy the constitutional requirement of containing "intelligible principles that serve to direct executive branch action. Why did this line of argument not persuade the Court?

From a democratic point of view, one might be concerned that the item veto reflects a shift in lawmaking power away from Congress's state and local constituencies and toward national ones that elect the President. *Chadha* and *Clinton* thus raise different issues: *Chadha*'s legislative veto *reduces* the power of a national constituency while *Clinton*'s line-item veto *increases* the power of a national constituency—relative to an existing-practice baseline. Evidence from studies of governors' use of their line-item veto power suggests it has little effect on the amount of state spending but allows the executives more influence over the shape of the budget, especially when the two branches are controlled by different parties. As a matter of the Constitution's balance of representation, therefore, the item veto law significantly altered the Article I, § 7 structure—and the Court may have been right to strike it down. *See* Steven G. Calabresi, *Separation of Powers and the Rehnquist Court: The Centrality of* Clinton v. City of New York, 99 Nw. U.L. Rev. 77 (2004).

The cancellations before the Court concerned a tax provision and a spending provision. From an historical perspective, the taxing provision appears more questionable than the spending provision, which resembles impoundments.[39] Should the different provisions have been treated differently? Does *Clinton* call into question Congress's power to delegate impoundment discretion to the President?

PROBLEM 1–5: AFTER CLINTON, HOW FAR CAN CONGRESS GO IN STRUCTURING STATUTORY ENFORCEMENT?

Under the constitutional structure and the governing precedents of *Chadha, Bowsher,* and *Clinton,* consider the options Congress might have to accomplish similar goals. In other words, notwithstanding the Supreme Court's enforcement of constitutional limits, such as those drawn from Article I, § 7, does Congress not retain a great deal of power to structure statutory execution that occurs after enactment?

(A) Controlling Agency Rulemaking. In the wake of *Chadha,* what mechanisms does Congress have available to stop agencies from taking broad lawmaking delegations "too far" (from Congress's perspective anyway)? See generally Jessica Korn, *The Power of Separation: American Constitutionalism and the Myth of the Legislative Veto* 36–37 (1996); Darren A. Wheeler, *Actor Preference and the Implementation of* INS v. Chadha, 83 BYU J. Pub. L. 83 (2008).

(B) Structuring Mandatory Budget Cuts. After *Bowsher,* can Congress create a mandatory budget-cutting process that preserves a potential role for the Comptroller General? E.g., Elizabeth Garrett, *Accountability and Restraint: The Federal Budget Process and the Line Item Veto Act,* 36 Cardozo L.J. 871 (1999) (considering delegation possibilities that would "solve" the constitutional problem).

(C) Authorizing Presidential Budgetary Restraint. What options are available to Congress to give the President budget-cutting authority after *Clinton? See* Virginia A. McMurtry, Congressional Research Service, *Item*

---

[39] The definition of *cancel* is different in the context of discretionary spending. Rather than rendering a provision of law without "legal force and effect," the President "rescinds" an item of discretionary spending when he cancels it. In budget parlance, a rescission is a congressionally authorized impoundment. Since 1974, federal law has allowed the President to propose to rescind federal spending, but his proposal would not go into effect unless approved by Congress within 45 days. One way to view the Line Item Veto Act's provisions affecting appropriated money is as merely a change in the way Congress authorizes rescissions. Rather than requiring ex post congressional approval, the Line Item Veto Act delegates a continuing power to rescind spending, as long as the President complies with the standards set forth in the Act.

Veto and Expanded Impoundment Proposals: History and Current Status (June 18, 2010); Garrett, *Accountability and Restraint.*

After thinking through the answers to these questions (and there *are* answers), what hypotheses might you have about the role of the Supreme Court in the regulatory state? Is there value-added to the Court's insistence on technical lines that can be easily circumvented?

3. RETHINKING CONGRESS'S RULES

PROBLEM 1–6: IS THE SENATE FILIBUSTER UNCONSTITUTIONAL? A THREAT TO GOOD GOVERNANCE? HOW OUGHT IT BE CHANGED?

Jimmy Stewart: Wild horses aren't going to drag me off this floor until those people have heard everything I've got to say, even if it takes all winter.

Reporter: H.V. Kaltenborn speaking, half of official Washington is here to see democracy's finest show. The filibuster—the right to talk your head off.

—From the movie *Mr. Smith Goes to Washington*

Although the accounts vary, few doubt that the rise of the filibuster has been extraordinary. The following data are taken from Josh Chafetz, *The Unconstitutionality of the Filibuster*, 43 Conn. L. Rev. 1003, 1009 (2011), as well as *Examining the Filibuster: Hearings Before the Comm. on Rules and Administration, U.S. Senate*, 111th Cong., 2d Sess. (2010).[40]

Congresses	Years	Cloture Motions Filed	Cloture Votes	Cloture Invoked
66th–70th	1919–1929	11	10	4
71st–75th	1929–1939	5	3	0
76th–80th	1939–1949	8	6	0
81st–85th	1949–1959	3	3	0
86th–90th	1959–1969	22	21	4
91st–95th	1969–1979	136	97	33
96th–100th	1979–1989	197	135	54
101st–105th	1989–1999	329	221	75
106th–110th	1999–2009	411	334	169

[40] See also Gregory J. Wawro & Eric Schickler, *Filibuster: Obstruction and Lawmaking in the United States Senate* (2006); Sarah A. Binder & Steven S. Smith, *Politics or Principle? Filibustering in the United States Senate* 1 (1997). It is almost impossible to actually "count" the filibuster since a single Senator may simply "object" in private and if this is taken as a sufficient "threat," it amounts to a filibuster. The data provided above is about cloture motions, motions to close off a filibuster, which is likely to undercount the actual influence of the filibuster.

Consider the positions of Senator Harkin (opposing the filibuster as unconstitutional) and the position of Senator Alexander (supporting the filibuster) below. Who has the better argument? Does the Supreme Court's decision in *Chadha* have anything to say about the constitutionality of the filibuster? Consider the arguments of some scholars noted after the debate.

Mr. HARKIN (Excerpts from 157 Cong. Rec. S304–02 (Jan. 27, 2011).) [Senator Harkin, a Democrat from Iowa, introduced his arguments against the filibuster by noting that when he first pushed filibuster reform in 1995, his party was in the minority and therefore benefited from the filibuster.]

The filibuster was once an extraordinary tool, used in the rarest of instances. Across the entire 19th century, there were only 23 filibusters. From 1917, when the Senate first adopted rules on this until 1969, there were fewer than 50 in that whole timespan—less than one a year.

During the 104th Congress, in 1995, when I first introduced my resolution, there were 82 filibusters. But it was not until the 110th and 111th Congresses that the abuse of the filibuster would spin wildly out of control. In the 110th Congress, there were an astonishing 139 motions to end filibusters. In the 111th Congress just ended, there were 136. That is 275 filibusters in just over 4 years. It has spun out of control.

This is not just a cold statistic of 275 filibusters. It means the filibuster, instead of a rare tool to slow things down, has become an everyday weapon of obstruction, of veto. On almost a daily basis, one Senator is able to use just the threat of a filibuster to stop bills from even coming to the floor for debate and amendment, let alone a final vote.

In the last Congress, the filibuster was used to kill many pieces of legislation that enjoyed majority and often bipartisan support. The reality is, because of the way the filibuster is abused today, the minority—the minority—has unchecked veto power over public policy. * * * The power to pass legislation has been given to the minority. Reason alone would dictate there is something inherently wrong and inherently unconstitutional about this. * * *

Again, I wish to note that when I refer to the minority, I am not saying Republicans, I am saying the minority. Both parties have abused the filibuster in the past and both will, absent real reform, abuse the filibuster in the future. * * *

Let me also say, again, that for a bill to become law, it has to be passed by the House and the Senate in the same form—in the same form. Then it must go to the President. The President can veto it and then it takes a two-thirds vote to override a veto. There are a lot of checks and balances out there. So the need for the check on legislation by the minority with the ultimate power to veto that is not needed—not needed; in fact, [it is] inimical to a democratic institution. * * *

Many have argued that it is the filibuster that forces compromise and collaboration. I disagree. The fact is, right now the minority has no real incentive to compromise. Why should they if they can totally block something and then go out and campaign on a message that the majority just couldn't get anything done? Again, the minority has a great deal of power but zero incentive on compromise. * * *

I often hear opponents of reform claim that what I am proposing would turn the Senate into the House of Representatives because at the end of 8 days, 51 votes could move something. I ask my friends: When did the Senate become defined by Senate rule XXII, which is the filibuster rule? I thought the Senate was defined in the Constitution. Rule XXII, the filibuster rule, is not the essence of the Senate. Regardless, the Senate will continue to be totally different from the House. We have two senators from small States, two senators from large States. We are elected every 6 years. We have sole jurisdiction over treaties, impeachments. And the Senate operates, as we know, in so many instances based on unanimous consent. That will continue. So the power of one single Senator remains to object to any unanimous consent request. Eliminating the filibuster will not change the basic nature of this body, nor the constitutional structure of the Senate. * * *

Mr. ALEXANDER (Excerpts from 157 Cong. Rec. S304–02) (Jan. 27, 2011)

Senator HARKIN is very straightforward about his difference of opinion. He believes we ought to bring every debate eventually to 51 votes. So I would respectfully term his amendment as sort of a "hang me now or hang me later." We know that eventually it is not 60 votes we are going to require, it is 51, and he says that is the way it ought to be. I disagree. So do many others.

I will just cite two distinguished Senators who spoke on the floor of the Senate about 5 years ago when a number of Republicans got it in their minds that they would like to change the filibuster rule as it affects judges. This is what Senator HARRY REID said then:

> The filibuster is far from a procedural gimmick. It is part of the fabric of this institution that we call the Senate. For 200 years we've had the right to extend the debate. It's not a procedural gimmick. Some in this Chamber want to throw out 214 years of Senate history in the quest for absolute power. They want to do away with Mr. Smith as depicted in that great movie being able to come to Washington. They want to do away with the filibuster. They think they are wiser than our Founding Fathers. I doubt that's true.

The then-Senator from Illinois, Barack Obama, referring then to the Republican majority:

> Then if the majority chooses to end the filibuster, if they choose to change the rules and put an end to Democratic debate, then the fighting and the bitterness and the gridlock will only get worse.

I would suggest that, as a result of this discussion, we preserve the Senate as an institution, a forum for deliberation where minority rights are protected. [Senator Alexander then offered this speech as a summary of his position on the filibuster.]

THE FILIBUSTER: "DEMOCRACY'S FINEST SHOW . . . THE RIGHT TO TALK YOUR HEAD OFF," ADDRESS BY SENATOR LAMAR ALEXANDER, HERITAGE FOUNDATION
(January 4, 2011).

In the November elections, voters showed that they remember the passage of the health care law on Christmas Eve, 2009: midnight sessions, voting in the midst of a snow storm, back room deals, little time to read, amend or debate the bill, passage by a straight party line vote. It was how it was done as much as what was done that angered the American people. Minority voices were silenced. Those who didn't like it were told, "You can read it after you pass it." The majority's attitude was, "We won the election. We'll write the bill. We don't need your votes."

And of course the result was a law that a majority of voters consider to be an historic mistake and the beginning of an immediate effort to repeal and replace it. Voters remembered all this in November, but only 6 weeks later Democratic senators seemed to have forgotten it. I say this because on December 18, every returning Democratic senator sent Senator Reid a letter asking him to "take steps to bring [Republican] abuses of our rules to an end."

When the United States Senate convenes tomorrow, some have threatened to try to change the rules so it would be easier to do with every piece of legislation what they did with the health care bill: ram it through on a partisan vote, with little debate, amendment, or committee consideration, and without listening to minority voices. * * * *

Here is why Republicans who were in the majority then, and Democrats who are in the majority today, should reject a * * * rules change:

First, the proposal diminishes the rights of the minority. In his classic Democracy in America, Alexis de Tocqueville wrote that one of his two greatest fears for our young democracy was the "tyranny of the majority," the possibility that a runaway majority might trample minority voices.

Second, diluting the right to debate and vote on amendments deprives the nation of a valuable forum for achieving consensus on difficult issues. The founders knew what they were doing when they created two very different houses in Congress. Senators have six-year terms, one-third elected every two years. The Senate operates largely by unanimous consent. There is the opportunity, unparalleled in any other legislative body in the world, to debate and amend until a consensus finally is reached. This procedure takes longer, but it usually produces a better result—and a result the country is more likely to accept. For example, after the Civil Rights Act of 1964 was enacted, by a bipartisan majority over a filibuster led by Sen. Russell of Georgia, Sen. Russell went home to Georgia and said that, though he had fought the legislation with everything he had, "As long as it is there, it must be obeyed." Compare that to the instant repeal effort that was the result of jamming the health care law through in a partisan vote.

Third, such a brazen power grab by Democrats this year will surely guarantee a similar action by Republicans in two years if Republicans gain control of the Senate as many believe is likely to happen. We have seen this happen with Senate consideration of judges. Democrats began the practice of filibustering President Bush's judges even though they were well-qualified; now Democrats are unhappy because many Republicans regard that as a precedent and have threatened to do the same to President Obama's nominees. Those who want to create a freight train running through the Senate today, as it does in the House, might think about whether they will want that freight train in two years if it is the Tea Party Express. * * * *

Sen. Byrd knew the rules. I recall that when Republicans won the majority in 1981, Sen. Baker went to see Sen. Byrd and said, "Bob I know you know the rules better than I ever will. I'll make a deal with you. You don't surprise me and I won't surprise you."

Sen. Byrd said, "Let me think about it."

And the next day Sen. Byrd said yes and the two leaders managed the Senate effectively together for eight years.

What would it take to restore today's Senate to the Senate of the Baker-Byrd era?

Well, we have the answer from the master of the Senate rules himself, Sen. Byrd, who in his last appearance before the Rules Committee on May 19, 2010 said: "Forceful confrontation to a threat to filibuster is undoubtedly the antidote to the malady [abuse of the filibuster]. Most recently, Senate Majority Leader Reid announced that the Senate would stay in session around-the-clock and take all procedural steps necessary to bring financial reform legislation before the Senate. As preparations were made and cots rolled out, a deal was struck within hours and the threat of filibuster was withdrawn . . . I also know that current Senate Rules provide the means to break a filibuster.". * * * *

NOTES AND QUESTIONS ON THE FILIBUSTER

1. *Is the Filibuster Always a Minority Veto?* The Senate is made up of states with vastly different populations. A 41-vote opposition may represent a very small percent of the population, but it is also possible, depending upon the states represented by filibustering senators (think California, New York, and Florida), that the 41-vote opposition could in fact represent a majority of the population. *See* Gerard N. Magliocca, *Reforming the Filibuster*, 105 Nw. U. L. Rev. 303 (2011). Indeed, when the Republicans controlled the Senate in recent years (1995–2001, 2003–07), senators supporting many filibusters did represent a majority of the population. Note, *The Majoritarian Filibuster,* 122 Yale L.J. 980 (2013). If the filibuster is often a majority veto, does Senator Harkin's argument fail? Note that when the Democrats have controlled the Senate (1987–1995, 2001–03, after 2007), filibusters have almost always been minoritarian.

In an interesting twist on the standard constitutional arguments about the filibuster, Professor Magliocca argues that a refusal to vote for cloture should result in a "suspensory rather than an absolute veto. In other words, forty-one senators should be able to extend debate on bills or nominations that reach the floor for no more than one year." His proposal is modeled on the power of "the British House of Lords to block most bills passed by the House of Commons from becoming law for a maximum of one year." Magliocca, *Reforming the Filibuster,* 304–05. He maintains this would in fact "return the Senate to its traditional practice, which let a determined majority get its way except at the end of a Congress when claims of undue haste were more legitimate." *Id.* at 305.

2. *Is the Problem the Filibuster or the One-Person Hold?* One might argue that the biggest problem with the filibuster is not the tradition of debate, but the way in which the current "hold" practice allows individual senators to control or slow down the nation's public law agenda. One-vote vetoes were in fact the reason that we have a constitution at all. The Constitution's predecessor government, the Articles of Confederation, crumbled under a unanimous consent rule because individual states refused to follow the Confederation's dictates. (Also, the liberum veto, where one member of the legislature could block action, was supposedly one reason why the old Polish-Lithuanian Commonwealth collapsed in the eighteenth century; the once-proud but by then helpless empire was partitioned by countries with strong executives, namely, Prussia, Austria, and Russia.)

3. *Majority Strategies to Overcome Obstructive Filibusters.* Why did Senator Robert Byrd (W. Va.), who is reputed to have known the rules better than anyone else, say in 2010 that "forceful confrontation to a threat to filibuster is undoubtedly the antidote to the malady"? What non-constitutional tools are available to the Majority Leader to resist the filibuster? What does "filling the amendment tree" (the process by which the majority adds amendments in such a way as to bar further amendments by the minority) have to do with the filibuster? What might Senator Alexander

have been referring to when he mentioned votes on Friday and rolling out the cots?

4. *Is the Legislative Filibuster Unconstitutional?* The U.S. Constitution bears on the Harkin-Alexander debate in a number of important respects. For example, does the filibuster violate Article I, § 7 by adding an important vetogate to those already set forth in the Constitution?[41] What is the appropriate forum for evaluating the constitutional question. One forum for such evaluation is the Senate itself: Does the Constitution provide the Senate with an easier path toward reform of the filibuster? Some scholars have argued that the filibuster, as a "Rule" of Congress, may be immune from challenge because of the Constitution's Rules of Proceedings Clause, U.S. Const. Art. I, § 5 ("Each House may determine the Rules of its Proceedings"). *E.g.*, Michael J. Gerhardt, *The Constitutionality of the Filibuster*, 21 Const. Comm. 445 (2004). "Under the Rules of Proceedings Clause, the House may enact a rule governing its internal operations so long as the rule does not violate another provision of the Constitution." John O. McGinnis & Michael B. Rappaport, *The Constitutionality of Legislative Supermajority Requirements: A Defense*, 105 Yale L.J. 483 (1995). Accordingly, Article I, § 5 does not get us very far, for the issue that divides the commentators is whether the filibuster violates other constitutional limits implicit in Article I. Hint: consider the provisions of the Constitution requiring a two-thirds vote.

Professor Chafetz, on the other hand, maintains that the terms "passed," and "consent" in Article I bar entrenched minority obstruction. Joshua Chafetz, *The Unconstitutionality of the Filibuster*, 43 Conn. L. Rev. 1003 (2011). Chafetz starts with this hypothetical: Can the Senate adopt a rule barring the seating of new senators unless they have defeated incumbent senators by 60% or more of the vote? Although nothing in the U.S. Constitution speaks specifically to this issue, it is an unstated premise of the Seventeenth Amendment that senators are to be elected by majority vote, and the Seventeenth Amendment trumps the Rules of Proceedings Clause in this respect. What constitutional provision might trump that clause in the case of the filibuster?

If the constitutional structure supports the principle that the Senate cannot entrench *existing legislators* through supermajority electoral rules, can it not also support the principle that the Senate cannot entrench *existing legislation* through supermajority voting rules like the filibuster? "If 'elected by the people' in the Seventeenth Amendment must contain the principle that the candidate with the most votes has to win the election * * * then it is hard to understand how 'passed' in Article I's description of the legislative process, 'determine' in the Rules of Proceedings Clause, and 'consent' in the Appointments Clause can be sensibly construed so as to allow the sustained and systemic thwarting of majority will." Chafetz, *Unconstitutionality of the*

---

[41]   There is empirical support for the notion that the filibuster has a major structuring effect on the nature and product of congressional lawmaking, comparable to that of the bicameralism and presentment requirements. E.g., Sarah A. Binder, *Stalemate: Causes and Consequences of Legislative Gridlock* (2003).

Filibuster, 1013; accord, Jed Rubenfeld, *Rights of Passage: Majority Rule in Congress,* 46 Duke L.J. 73, 83 (1996) ("What it means for a bill to 'pass' the House or Senate is not open for definition by the House or Senate. It is constitutionally fixed by the implicit majority-rule meaning of 'passed.' ").

   5.   *The "Constitutional Option" for Reforming the Filibuster.* Professors Martin Gold and Dimple Gupta note that one of the Senate's most ardent proponents of the filibuster once agreed that any Senate rule could be changed by a majority under what is known as the "constitutional option" (using 51 votes). In 1979, when Senator Robert Byrd of West Virginia (the longest serving senator in American history) was Majority Leader, he faced a potential filibuster on his own rules-change proposal, and he raised the possibility that the Constitution provides the majority with a method for overriding the Senate's cloture rule:

> The Constitution in article I, section 5, says that each House shall determine the rules of its proceedings. Now we are at the beginning of Congress. This Congress is not obliged to be bound by the dead hand of the past. . . .

> The first Senate, which met in 1789, approved 19 rules by a majority vote. Those rules have been changed from time to time . . . So the Members of the Senate who met in 1789 and approved that first body of rules did not for one moment think, or believe, or pretend, that all succeeding Senates would be bound by that Senate. . . . It would be just as reasonable to say that one Congress can pass a law providing that all future laws have to be passed by two-thirds vote. Any Member of this body knows that the next Congress would not heed that law and would proceed to change it and would vote repeal of it by majority vote. [I]t is my belief—which has been supported by rulings of Vice Presidents of both parties and by votes of the Senate—in essence upholding the power and right of a majority of the Senate to change the rules of the Senate at the beginning of a new Congress.

Gold and Gupta continue: "Byrd made clear that if his rules-change proposal were filibustered, he would invoke the Senate's powers under the U.S. Constitution to force a vote. Byrd never carried out his threat to use the 'constitutional option.' He never had to. His threat to use it was enough to break the opposition and secure a vote on his rules-change proposal." Martin B. Gold & Dimple Gupta, *The Constitutional Option to Change Senate Rules and Procedures: A Majoritarian Means to Over Come the Filibuster*, 28 Harv. J. L. & Pub. Pol'y 205, 207–08 (2004) (quoting 125 Cong. Rec. 144–45 (1979) (statement of Sen. Byrd)). As discussed, in Fall 2013, Majority Leader Reid did, in fact, use the constitutional option to force a vote on administrative and lower-federal-court nominations. Does the constitutional option solve the problem of entrenchment?

In some cases, Congress has passed statutes effectively barring filibusters. The most famous of these "statutized rules," is the Budget Act, the law that allowed the Obama administration to pass the Affordable Care Act. The Budget Act is not the only such statute. Consider the implications of this case-by-case approach to filibuster reform.

Aaron-Andrew P. Bruhl, *Using Statutes to Set Legislative Rules: Entrenchment, Separation of Powers, and the Rules of Proceedings Clause*
19 J.L. & Pol. 345 (2003) (summary and selected quotations).

There are a number of exceptions to the filibuster rule, often in the form of "fast-track" statutes. In August 2002, for example, President George W. Bush signed an omnibus trade bill that included, among many other items, the Bipartisan Trade Promotion Authority Act. The "fast track" procedures at the center of this legislation empowered the Administration to negotiate trade agreements with foreign governments, and then to submit bills implementing the agreements to Congress for streamlined consideration. Under fast-track rules, Congress is required to schedule a vote within two months, neither chamber may amend the President's implementing bill, and the bill cannot be filibustered in the Senate. Fast track thus guarantees the President (and trade partners) a speedy up-or-down decision on the nation's participation in a free trade agreement.

Professor Aaron Bruhl documents that what he calls this kind of "statutized rule" for congressional process has become increasingly common in the last generation.[42] *See* Aaron-Andrew P. Bruhl, *Using Statutes to Set Legislative Rules: Entrenchment, Separation of Powers, and the Rules of Proceedings Clause* 19 J.L. & Pol. 345, 382, 385, 393,

---

[42] The fast-track procedures for trade agreements are codified at 19 U.S.C. § 2191. Other examples Professor Bruhl provides of debate-regulating statutes include 2 U.S.C. §§ 631–645a (2000) (congressional budget process); 2 U.S.C. §§ 658d-e (legislation containing unfunded mandates); 5 U.S.C. § 802 (procedures for legislation that nullifies agency regulations); 5 U.S.C. §§ 901–912 (executive reorganization plans); 15 U.S.C. § 719f (procedures for approving presidential determinations concerning Alaskan natural gas pipelines); 16 U.S.C. § 1823 (procedures for disapproving international fisheries agreements); 29 U.S.C. § 1306(b) (procedures for considering Pension Benefit Guaranty Corporation premium revisions); 42 U.S.C. § 2210(i) (procedures for nuclear accident compensation legislation); 42 U.S.C. § 6249c (legislation implementing certain petroleum contracts); 50 U.S.C. § 1622 (procedures for terminating presidentially declared states of emergency); Amtrak Reform and Accountability Act of 1997, Pub. L. No. 105–134, § 205, 111 Stat. 2570, 2582 (Senate procedures for considering Amtrak restructuring and liquidation plans); Foreign Operations, Export Financing, and Related Programs Appropriations Act, Pub. L. No. 104–208, § 518A, 110 Stat. 3009 (1997) (procedures for approving presidential findings regarding population planning funding); Defense Authorization Amendments and Base Closure and Realignment Act, Pub. L. No. 100–526, § 208, 102 Stat. 2623, 2632–33 (1988) (procedures for considering recommendations to close military bases); Anti-Drug Abuse Act of 1988, Pub. L. No. 100–690, § 7323, 102 Stat. 4181, 4467–68 (Senate procedures for habeas corpus reform legislation).

397–98 (2003). Professor Elizabeth Garrett (who calls these types of statutes "framework legislation") considers what purposes these special processes serve. *See* Elizabeth Garrett, *The Purposes of Framework Legislation*, 14 J. Contemp. Legal Issues 717, 763–64 (2005). For example, she considers the Base Realignment and Closure Acts, which set forth a process for closing naval bases in certain states—a decision no legislator wanted their fingerprints on and on which deals were unlikely to be made. The Acts delegate to an expert commission outside of Congress the authority to determine which bases to close. Once the President accepts the commission's recommendations, they are submitted to Congress and automatically take effect unless Congress affirmatively rejects the recommendations. (This ingenious procedure basically enables members of Congress to go on record with a "no" vote to oppose closing a base, but relieves any member of having to tell the voters that she voted "yes" to close.) Among other things, these laws thus facilitate legislative action on subjects too hot for Congress to handle or too-time sensitive to leave to vetogates and the filibuster in all their glory.

One way to view these rules are as mechanisms to let cowardly legislators evade accountability for tough decisions. Another way to view them is as pragmatic responses by Congress, in recognition of its own weaknesses. These statutized rules sound like a mechanism whereby Article I, § 7 (the bicameralism clause) can trump Article I, § 5 (the rules and proceedings clause), and thereby ameliorate the minority-entrenchment problem raised by the ever-expanding filibuster. Moreover, fast-track legislation is a rational response to *Chadha*: give the executive branch the first-mover role needed in areas such as international trade and immigration, but create a speedy majority-based mechanism for Congress to override executive decisions its members find objectionable. *Chadha* is satisfied, because Congress does so through a statute that is passed by both chambers and presented to the President.

Some constitutionalists might argue that such statutes violate an anti-entrenchment norm implicit in Article I, namely, that one Congress cannot "bind" another Congress's rules. Professor Bruhl points out that fast-track statutes are no more entrenching than other statutes, because the procedures they dictate can be revoked by subsequent Congresses, so long as they follow the same Article I, § 7 procedure that yielded the original fast-track legislation. Nonetheless, Professor Bruhl considers fast-track legislation constitutionally questionable, because it inserts the President's preferences into the procedural structure of Congress, the same kind of objection that sunk the Line-Item Veto in *Clinton v. New York City*.

"The Rules of Proceedings Clause simply declares that '[e]ach House may determine the Rules of its Proceedings.' Under a binding fast-track regime, a chamber could change the relevant rules only by joining together with the other house, plus the president, and amending the statute. Under such a regime, a house would be unable to set its own rules. Such a system would directly conflict with the constitutional directive that each house may determine its own Rules. Thus, fast track violates the Constitution. Or so a simple textual argument might run." Professor Bruhl immediately notes that the clause could easily be read in a more permissive fashion, as allowing each chamber to make procedural rules outside the Article I, § 7 process, but not precluding Article I, § 7 as an alternative process for rule-creation.

NOTES AND QUESTIONS ON STATUTIZED RULES

Do you find Professor Bruhl's constitutional analysis cogent? Does his argument apply more forcefully in cases where the statutized rule does not involve powers, like foreign affairs, that are primarily held by the President? Would his analysis counsel against a statutory rule that said executive or judicial nominations must be voted on by the Senate within 90 days and may not be subject to a filibuster? On the surface, as Professor Bruhl notes, the statutized trade rules appear to give the President, and his national constituency, more power relative to the baseline practice in which state and local constituencies have sole power to set the agenda (Congress sets its own rules). However, what if you knew that, without such a rule in trade cases, the President would enter into the trade deal himself as an executive agreement, evading congressional approval altogether? If that is true, the baseline changes—state and local entities are completely cut out. In that case, the statutized rule would allow Congress and its constituencies to have a greater role than they would otherwise play. This may explain why Congress would agree ex ante to such an arrangement which suggests, on the surface, that it is voting away its own power.

Not all statutized rules apply in the area of foreign affairs. One of the most important statutized rules—perhaps *the* most important rule in all legislation—is found in the Budget Act. The Act exempts from filibusters certain budget items—and is part of a slew of framework laws aimed to get around the political difficulties of the budget process. Is budget like foreign affairs, a case where there is a risk that Congress can be completely cut out? Or is the Budget Act's statutized rule a tacit acknowledgment by Congress that the filibuster is a politically dangerous tool that would not be tolerated if used repeatedly to thwart budgets and shut down the government?

Sometimes these special processes are invoked for strategic purposes. Should we care about the motivation for using them? The Affordable Care Act of 2010, for example, got through Congress only thanks to the Budget Act's exemption from the filibuster. In 2009, the Democrats had a 60–40 majority in the Senate. This enabled them to end a Republican filibuster and pass the health care reform on a strict party-line vote. Immediately after that, Democrat Ted Kennedy died and was replaced by Republican Scott Brown, thereby depriving the Democrats of their filibuster-proof majority. Because the Senate did not have the votes to go to conference (any changes in conference would have required the filibuster-proof 60 Senate votes), the House was forced to accept the Senate bill virtually unchanged. With bicameral approval of the same text, the President signed it into law. But as part of the House-Senate deal, the two chambers followed the ACA with the Health Care and Education Reconciliation Act—a series of amendments styled as *budget amendments* to take advantage of the budget exemption from the filibuster. While these parliamentary tactics got the Act passed, they also caused incidental harms of their own. Because only budget-related items could be reconciled through the special process, Congress was unable to make as many "clean up" changes as typically get made in Conference and that the ACA desperately needed. The result was a messy, 2,000 page statute with many errors.

PROBLEM 1–7: FAST TRACK FOR MEDICARE COST MANAGEMENT

The hot politics of Medicare has given birth to the most recent example of a special, fast-track legislative process. No one wants to cut health care for seniors (who are, after all, a very powerful lobby), but Congress is well aware that the escalating costs of the program must be dealt with somehow. As part of the Affordable Care Act, Congress established the Independent Payment Advisory Board (IPAB), a special commission delegated the authority to propose cuts to Medicare at the beginning of each year. 42 U.S.C. § 1395kkk. The proposed cuts automatically take effect unless the Congress passes (and the President signs) alternative cuts of the same size by August. Section 1395kkk(d) also sets forth detailed expedited processes, such as limited debate (i.e., no filibuster) in the Senate, for fast-track deliberation for proposed legislation. Section 1395kkk(d)(5) says the following:

(5) Rules of the Senate and House of Representatives

This subsection and [a previous] subsection are enacted by Congress—

> **(A)** as an exercise of the rulemaking power of the Senate and the House of Representatives, respectively, and is deemed to be part of the rules of each House, respectively, but applicable only with respect to the procedure to be followed in that House in the case of a bill under this section, and it supersedes other rules only to the extent that it is inconsistent with such rules; and

> **(B)** with full recognition of the constitutional right of either House to change the rules (so far as they relate to the procedure of that House) at any time, in the same manner, and to the same extent as in the case of any other rule of that House.

The IPAB has been extremely controversial and been called an unprecedented delegation/abdication of congressional responsibility. Critics have called it everything from unconstitutional to a death panel. Supporters say it's necessary medicine. Which is it? Is it really any different from the other examples discussed in this chapter? (You might read the entire subsection, which provides a much more detailed blueprint for legislation than anything identified in Professor Bruhl's article).

CHAPTER 2

THE PRESIDENT AND AGENCIES

■ ■ ■

This chapter focuses on executive action. As you read these materials, keep in mind the central questions: What do agencies do? What are the legal and constitutional limits on their action? How are agencies controlled by the President and Congress? We introduce you to the structure of the executive branch; the President's duty to ensure that all agencies "take care" that the law is properly executed; and the general ways in which agencies take action. These matters are intimately linked to the separation of powers: all agency action must be traceable to a statute, a link between executive action and congressional power that is central to interbranch relationships in the modern regulatory state.

The President plays a distinctive, and increasingly central, role in the creation of public policy in the modern regulatory state. Under the Constitution, the President must approve or veto all bills before they become law (Art. I, § 7), and as a practical matter he is often involved in the legislative process long before legislation reaches his desk for signature. The President is also the official charged with "executing" the law (Art. II, § 1) faithfully (§ 3). Elected by the nation as a whole (Art. II, § 1), the President represents the entire nation in a way that no other official does in our democracy. He is also the head of the largest branch of government: There are nearly *3 million* employees of the executive branch, putting together all agency personnel and White House staff. In addition to all his formal powers, the modern President is the head of one of the two major parties and has powers of agenda-setting, media attention, and quick action that threaten to leave the other organs of government to irrelevance.

Power. Outside of areas specifically delegated to the President by the Constitution, the executive branch's authority is limited to that which Congress delegates to the President and his officials in executing the law. Specifically, Congress creates the agencies through which the President executes the law. For example, when Congress created the Department of Homeland Security or the Food and Drug Administration, it prescribed rules limiting their jurisdiction and range of action. In recent years, the President has attempted to consolidate power by requiring that agency actions meet general standards set by the President's own Office of Management and Budget. In the arena of foreign relations, the President has independent constitutional authority to act and is not always constrained by the requirement of congressional delegation.

Competency and Capacity. Like Congress, the President deals with an enormous range of issues; unlike a court, the executive may act on his own initiative to address many problems through informal means, particularly in the area of foreign affairs. From the late nineteenth century through the twentieth, the President's capacity has grown through the emergence of a significant administrative apparatus. Going back to the Civil War, when the government set up an apparatus to protect veterans and their widows, the growth of the administrative state has been considerable over the twentieth century. This has been aided by Presidents of both parties. President Nixon, a Republican, for example, created the Environmental Protection Agency (EPA) and the Occupational Safety and Health Administration (OSHA). Congress has delegated wide powers to administrative agencies, from the Department of Defense to the Department of Health and Human Services.

Representation. The President serves the nation as a whole. Administrative agencies are, in theory, nationally responsive as well, because they are accountable to the President. Relative to Congress, for example, whose members are acutely aware of state and local matters, agencies tend to serve, at least remotely, a national electorate, as represented by the President. In the area of foreign affairs, the President's role as the "sole organ" of the nation is generally undisputed; however, in domestic affairs, where his authority comes from Congress, there often arise policy disputes particularly about proper decision-making authority—whether it should be the Congress or the President. There is of course one important limit on the President's relative remoteness from state and local concerns and that is the electoral college: if a sitting President seeks to remain in office, he cannot be completely aloof from the concerns of the states, as it is through state electoral votes that he is elected.

NOTE ON AGENCIES: WHAT THEY ARE AND WHERE THEY COME FROM

What is an agency? The precise term does not appear in the Constitution, but its essence does. The Framers knew that the President could not do all the work himself; he needed advisers. The Constitution contemplates that the President will have people to help him, because it gives him power to appoint officials, some who are senior "Heads of Departments" and others who are less important "inferior" officers.[1] The Heads of

---

[1] Article II, which grants the President "executive power," provides that "[t]he President . . . may require the Opinion, in writing, of the principal Officer in each of the executive

Departments are the President's major advisers—by convention, they are usually called Secretaries, such as the Secretary of State or the Secretary of Defense, and comprise the President's Cabinet. The term "agency" covers those organizations helping the President execute the law, whether the name of the agency is "Department" or "Office" or "Bureau" or "Commission." These entities are all called "administrative agencies" or "executive agencies."

The Vast Reach of Agency Government. Agencies comprise a far larger part of our government than any other. You have all read the names of agencies in the newspaper—they govern everything from cell phones to banking to war to health to education and housing. Their names include the Federal Reserve, the Department of Education, the Food & Drug Administration, the Internal Revenue Service, and the Equal Employment Opportunity Commission. *In terms of size, agencies dwarf Congress and the courts.* The largest agency is the Department of Defense: there are 1.41 million members of the armed services. All agencies combined employ an additional 2.85 million civilians, excluding an "unknown number of persons working in the intelligence agencies." By comparison, the "legislative branch employ[s] 30,900 persons and the judicial branch 32,000."[2] Put bluntly, compared to administrative agencies, Congress and the courts are tiny.

What Do Agencies Do? Agencies are the largest set of lawmakers and judges in the country. (And you thought that lawmaking was reserved to Congress, and judging to the courts—not so.) Agencies execute law by creating rules and regulations to flesh out the details of statutory implementation. For example, Congress might require that all insurance policies provide "essential health benefits" but leave it to the agency to define what exactly those benefits are, e.g., whether a colonoscopy is included. See Patient Protection and Affordable Care Act of 2010 § 1032. These rules and regulations, just like statutes, have the force of law. Unless inconsistent with a statute or the Constitution, these rules fill the gaps in law that Congress cannot, by reason of its smaller staff, attention-span, political hamstrings, or lack of expertise or foresight. So, for example, the Federal Communications Commission, created during the era of the radio, now issues rules and regulations covering cell phone towers and internet service providers. The principal idea is that the agency—as opposed to Congress—is more likely to become expert in a particular subject matter area and more capable of efficiently and flexibly responding to the needs of the country. If Congress permits, agencies also adjudicate cases. Within the Social Security

---

Departments, upon any Subject relating to the Duties of their respective Offices." U.S. CONST. art. II, § 2, cl. 1. "He shall * * * nominate, and by and with the Advice and Consent of the Senate, shall appoint Ambassadors, other public Ministers and Consuls, Judges of the supreme Court, and all other Officers of the United States, whose Appointments are not herein otherwise provided for, and which shall be established by Law: but the Congress may by Law vest the Appointment of such inferior Officers, as they think proper, in the President alone, in the Courts of Law, or in the Heads of Departments." *Id.* art. II, § 2, cl. 2.

   [2]   Administrative Conference of the United States, *Sourcebook of U.S. Executive Agencies* 12–13 (March 2013).

Administration, for example, there are a vast number of "administrative law judges" (ALJs) who decide individual claims for disability benefits; so, too, within the agencies administering our immigration and naturalization laws, ALJs decide claims for citizenship. These adjudications, like agency rulemaking, are subject to judicial review, but most embody final legal determinations.

Congress Creates Agencies by Statute. Agencies are created by law, hence through statute. In short, they owe their existence to Congress, which passes laws to authorize their conduct, names the offices inside the agency, sets the agency's organization, and appropriates funds to run the agency. Congress has created many, many different kinds of agencies, going by many, many different kinds of names (including "Corporation," "Bureau," "Commission," "Administration," "Office," etc.), and for this reason the very term "agency" is subject to debate. As the Administrative Conference (AC) (an agency itself) recently confessed, there is no single definition of agency used by the government. The AC's working definition provides that "agency" refers to a "federal executive instrumentality headed by one or more political appointees nominated by the President and confirmed by the Senate (the instrumentality itself rather than its bureaus, offices or divisions)."[3]

Political Appointees v. Career Civil Service Staff. This definition of "agency" reflects the fact that agencies are made up of two kinds of employees: a small number of "political" appointees and a large number of "career" employees. Political appointees are nominated or chosen by the President; most must be confirmed by the Senate. While political appointees see themselves as aligned with the President, and thus come and go with a particular Administration, the vast majority of government employees—including lawyers, accountants, economists, and mechanics—are civil service employees. To be part of the "civil service" means that these employees do not come and go with a particular President but continue in office throughout their "careers." Imagine if that were not the case: if 2.85 million people had to leave their job because the country elected a new President! The vast majority of government employees are "career" employees protected from political dismissal by civil service laws. Those laws aim to professionalize government employment and free it from partisan influence.

White House and Independent Agencies. Although the reach of agency government is vast, close to ninety percent of federal personnel work in one of the 15 executive departments, such as the Department of Homeland Security or the Department of Transportation. The other ten percent of employees work in two types of agency that deserve special mention because they play an important role in the materials that follow. The first is the Executive Office of the President (EOP). The EOP is, essentially, the White House. This does not mean the "West Wing"; it includes a variety of internal organs, including as we will see, the Office of Management and Budget, an agency that recent Presidents, both Republican and Democratic, have used to

---

[3]   *Id.* at 16.

centralize control over agency government. See § 3C of this chapter. The second, and more controversial, set of agencies is the group of so-called "independent agencies." See § 1 of this chapter. Again, there is no uniform definition of "independence," but the general idea is that independent agencies are designed by Congress to be independent of a particular President's, and even Congress's, political will. The classic example of an independent agency is the Federal Reserve Board, which sets monetary policy and controls our banking system. Typically, Congress tries to structure the agency to be independent, which means that the head of the agency can only be removed by the President for a good reason, or in the case of multi-member commissions, the members serve for a term of years not linked to presidential elections and are balanced politically (X number from one political party, the same number from the other political party).[4]

As we will now see, the debate about how to structure agencies, and whether they should be independent, raises important policy and constitutional questions.

1. THE STRUCTURE OF THE EXECUTIVE BRANCH

The Vesting Clause of Article II, § 1, lays all "executive" power in the hands of one person, the President. Contrast the Vesting Clause of Article I, § 1, which lays all "legislative" power in two different collective institutions (the Senate and the House). Although the President is charged with the faithful execution of the law (Art. II, § 3), obviously he cannot do all the work himself and must rely on subordinate officials, lower-level administrators, and civil service workers. He hires many of those people, with the Senate's approval. But can he fire them? This is not a small question about personnel, but a large question about whether the President has the power to control the executive branch. Think about it: If the head of a corporation could only fire his top employees when someone else approved, would the head of the corporation really be in charge? As James Madison wrote, those who control the "man" determine the constitutional rights of the "place." *Federalist* No. 51 (Madison).

Throughout history, the President and the Congress have fought over who has the last say on members of the executive branch. This is called the "removal debate" because it concerns the President's power to "remove" his personnel. The two principal questions are: Does the President have the authority to fire executive officials, with or without a good reason? Or may Congress place limitations on presidential discharge? Remember, this is not simply about who can hire or fire, but

---

[4] The Administrative Conference defines an independent agency as an administrative body that falls "outside the executive departments (i.e., is not formally a component of one of the 15 executive departments), is not subject to the direction of a departmental secretary, and often includes characteristics that limit presidential and, to a lesser extent congressional, influence over agency decisionmaking and actions."

about who controls policy. Imagine if you were an official within the executive branch and you knew that, if the President was angry with you and dismissed you, Congress could protect you. Wouldn't that personal incentive subtly or less than subtly affect the way you made hard choices?

The larger structural question is described by lawyers as the "unitary executive" question. Is the executive branch unitary (every official responsible to the President and serving at his pleasure) or is it pluralist (different organs collected under one umbrella but not one control)? As it turns out, this is both an old and continuously contentious question. It came up as early as George Washington's presidency. The House of Representatives considered a bill to create a Department of Foreign Affairs and debated who would have the power to remove the secretary heading that department. Some members thought removal power must parallel appointment power—hence, the President could remove only with the consent of the Senate (accord, *Federalist* No. 77 (Alexander Hamilton)). Other representatives thought that the President, acting alone, should have the power to remove the secretary—either because it was good policy that Congress in its discretion ought to choose or because the Constitution required such power to rest with the President alone.

During the debate that preceded the now-famous **Decision of 1789**, Madison opposed those who sought a role for the Senate in removing executive branch officers. At the start of the debate, Madison urged that the "removal power" was in its "nature" an executive power and that the Take Care Clause (Art II, § 3) meant that the President should hold the removal power. This claim, however, ran right into another textual provision—the Senate's power of advice and consent to the appointment of executive officers. See James Madison, *Removal Power of the President* (June 17, 1789), in 12 *Papers of Madison* 225–28, 232–34 (Charles F. Hobson & Robert A. Rutland eds., 1979) [hereinafter *Papers of Madison*]. Confronted with conflicting texts (neither of which explicitly resolves the issue), Madison shifted his focus to the broader precepts underlying the constitutional separation of powers. The "sacred" principle of separation was at its most important, Madison told Congress, when it "relates to officers and offices." The legislature sets the terms of office: "[it] creates the office, defines the powers, limits its duration, and annexes a compensation." This done, it "ought to have nothing to do with designating the man to fill the office." We would be "insecure" if Congress could do otherwise, Madison urges, for the practice would soon threaten the constitutional "independence of each branch of the government." *Id.* at 255–56.[5] Madison's statements have been controversial; his positions

---

[5]   Madison's views may well have varied depending upon the nature of the office. *See, e.g.,* James Madison, *Treasury Department* (June 29, 1789), in 12 *Papers of Madison*, 265–66 (noting that the comptroller of the Treasury Department, although an executive official, has duties that "partake of a judiciary quality" and thus should be insulated from political influences).

sometimes consistent with theories of a unitary executive, but other times allowing significant powers to Congress to shape administration. In 1789, the House and Senate both ultimately voted for a law that effectively left the removal power with the President alone, but with the basis for that power (the Constitution versus congressional choice) left dangling. See Gerhard Casper, *An Essay in Separation of Powers: Some Early Versions and Practices*, 30 Wm. & Mary L. Rev. 211 (1989).

The Impeachment of President Johnson over the Issue of Removal. After President Abraham Lincoln was assassinated in 1865, Vice-President Andrew Johnson became President. Johnson opposed some congressional post-war efforts to end the badges of slavery, and the Radical Republicans in Congress viewed Johnson as undermining Lincoln's anti-slavery legacy. Congress knew that Johnson could exercise policy through the executive branch—he could even fire Lincoln's major officials. To stop Johnson from changing administration policy by changing officials, Congress passed the Tenure of Office Act on March 2, 1867, 14 Stat. 430 (over the veto of the President). That law barred the President from removing presidential appointees unless the Senate approved.

This led to a major battle between the branches, with the President asserting his power to control the executive and the Congress pushing back. On August 5, 1867, President Johnson defied the Tenure of Office Act, removing Secretary of War Edwin Stanton, a Lincoln appointee popular with the Radical Republicans in Congress. Stanton refused to resign, and the Congress supported him. Under the Tenure of Office Act, which allowed his removal if the Senate approved, they voted to sustain Stanton in office by 35–16. The President ignored the Senate. He declared the Tenure of Office Act unconstitutional in that it undermined his ability to control his Administration, and he promptly named another Secretary of War, even though Stanton refused to resign. The Congress pushed back—hard. The House of Representatives voted to impeach the President for violating the law (the Tenure of Office Act). The Senate tried Johnson but acquitted him on a vote of 35–19. (Article II, § 4 requires a two-thirds vote of the Senate to convict a President and remove him from office.)

As we can see from this high-profile episode, the removal power is an important element of policy making. If the Congress was right, then the Senate could keep Lincoln's men in office and sustain their preferred policy. If the President was right, Congress gave itself too much power by declaring that they could "approve" his dismissals. Put in other words: Was the Tenure of Office Act unconstitutional? The Supreme Court, over the years, has (with some exceptions) preferred the President's position, although never without great debate about the precise basis, or implications, of its rulings.

NOTE ON THE SUPREME COURT'S DECISIONS ON
CONGRESSIONAL ATTEMPTS TO LIMIT THE
PRESIDENT'S REMOVAL AUTHORITY

Myers v. United States, 272 U.S. 52 (1926). Shortly after the Tenure of Office Act, Congress barred the President from discharging postmasters without Senate approval. Postmasters were very important political officials at the time, because Presidents could use the office as patronage—giving them out to political supporters across the nation who, in turn, could help to drum up support for the President's policies. In 1920, President Woodrow Wilson unilaterally removed the Portland, Oregon postmaster from office before the expiration of his term. The postmaster sued to retain his job. The Supreme Court ruled for the President.

Chief Justice Taft delivered the opinion for the Court, holding that the statute violated Article II of the Constitution. In an extremely long and murky opinion, the former President (1909 to 1913) held in favor of the Presidency. He started with the *Decision of 1789*, whereby a Congress filled with Framers expressed what the Chief Justice felt was a general constitutional understanding that the President must have the authority to remove executive department officers. The Chief Justice reasoned that the executive branch was a unitary one, hierarchically arrayed with the President in command of subordinate officers. He relied upon a variety of arguments including the fact that the Vesting Clause of Article II was textual evidence that all executive powers were vested in the President and a long practice in which Presidents had assumed that they had removal authority. Finally, he declared the Tenure of Office Act an aberration resulting from post-Civil War acrimony.

Subsequent scholars have agreed with the Chief Justice's opinion based upon a comparison of the texts of the Vesting Clauses of the three major Articles of the Constitution.[6] See Steven G. Calabresi & Kevin H. Rhodes, *The Structural Constitution: Unitary Executive, Plural Judiciary*, 105 Harv. L. Rev. 1153 (1992). The Vesting Clause of Article I, for example, provides that the Congress shall have all powers "herein granted," and then enumerates those powers. The Vesting Clause of Article II, by contrast, provides that "[t]he" executive power shall be granted to the President. By providing that all powers "shall" be vested in a single individual, Article II "plainly mandates full presidential control over *all* exercises of executive power." *Id.* at 1188. See also Steven G. Calabresi & Christopher S. Yoo, *The Unitary Executive: Presidential Power from Washington to Bush* (2008),

---

[6]   See U.S. Const. art. I, § 1 ("All legislative Powers herein granted shall be vested in a Congress of the United States."); *id.* art. II, § 1, cl. 1 ("The executive Power shall be vested in a President of the United States of America."); *id.* art. III, § 1 ("The judicial Power of the United States, shall be vested in one supreme Court, and in such inferior Courts as the Congress may from time to time ordain and establish.").

which concludes that every President has invoked "unitary" executive theories, at least with respect to the removal power.[7]

Justice Brandeis dissented in *Myers*, based upon a different reading of the historical practice, and based upon a logical problem in the Chief Justice's opinion: that the office of postmaster was an inferior office under the Constitution. After all, Wilson's removal of a postmaster was not the same kind of major policy clash one saw when President Johnson removed the Secretary of War. Brandeis emphasized the differences in office by explaining that the Constitution itself treats major and minor offices differently. Under the Constitution, the Congress could have vested power in the Postmaster General to remove his underlings. The Appointments Clause (Art. II, § 2, cl. 2), provides that inferior officers may be appointed by "Heads of Departments" and "Courts of Law." If Congress could grant the power to remove to heads of departments, consistent with Article II, why could it not impose limits (here, a term of office) on the President's power to remove inferior officers? Moreover, if Congress has the power to create the Post Office Department, why does it not have authority, under the Necessary and Proper Clause, to condition removals from office? Also dissenting, in separate opinions, were Justices Holmes and McReynolds.

Subsequent scholars have updated Brandeis's arguments to counter modern claims of a "unitary executive." They argue that the President has all the "executive" authority but that the Congress has the power to limit the executive as long as it does not undermine the President's ability to do his job. This would reconcile Article II with the broad authority given Congress in the Necessary and Proper Clause. Additionally, Article II lists specific powers granted to the President: Are they not superfluous if the Vesting Clause gives the President any and all control over execution? See Curtis A. Bradley & Martin S. Flaherty, *Executive Power Essentialism and Foreign Affairs*, 102 Mich. L. Rev. 545, 554–59 (2004).[8] Finally, Justice Brandeis's argument is a cogent one from a textual perspective: If the Vesting Clause gives all control to the President *and* precludes Congress from limiting the authority to remove, why does Article II, § 2, clause 2 allow Congress to vest appointments and (one assumes) removal authority for minor officials with heads of departments?

---

[7]   The book summarizes a series of articles: see Christopher S. Yoo et al., *The Unitary Executive in the Modern Era, 1945–2004*, 90 Iowa L. Rev. 601 (2005); Christopher S. Yoo et al., *The Unitary Executive During the Third Half-Century, 1889–1945*, 80 Notre Dame L. Rev. 1 (2004); Steven G. Calabresi & Christopher S. Yoo, *The Unitary Executive During the Second Half-Century*, 26 Harv. J.L. & Pub. Pol'y 667 (2003); Steven G. Calabresi & Christopher S. Yoo, *The Unitary Executive During the First Half-Century*, 47 Case W. Res. L. Rev. 1451 (1997).

[8]   For other examinations of the textual arguments, see A. Michael Froomkin, *The Imperial Presidency's New Vestments*, 88 Nw. U. L. Rev. 1346, 1362–63 (1994) (proposing that contrasting the Constitution with the Articles of Confederation will best reveal the meaning of the Vesting Clauses); see also Victoria F. Nourse & John P. Figura, *Toward a Representational Theory of the Executive*, 91 B.U. L. Rev. 273 (2011) (review of Calabresi & Yoo's book) (arguing for wide removal power for the President but rejecting the unitary executive theory as inviting aggrandizements of power in other areas).

Myers did not end the controversy, and Presidents continued to assert the power to set policy through removal. During the height of the debate over the New Deal, President Roosevelt summarily dismissed William E. Humphrey, then a member of the Federal Trade Commission (FTC), a holdover from the Hoover administration. The FTC Act permitted removal by the President for "inefficiency, neglect of duty, or malfeasance in office." Although President Roosevelt could easily have asserted a reason to remove Humphrey (who opposed his policies), the President did not, summarily dismissing him. Humphrey sued, leading to **Humphrey's Executor v. United States,** 295 U.S. 602 (1935).

The Supreme Court appeared to reverse course from *Myers,* upholding Congress's powers to limit removal as it did in the FTC Act. **Justice Sutherland**'s opinion for a unanimous Court characterized the FTC as "an administrative body created by Congress to carry into effect legislative policies." Because Congress's purpose was to create an expert body creating quasi-legislative rules and engaging in quasi-judicial adjudications, the statute provided for determinate terms. These limits, along with other protections, were designed to prevent the FTC from becoming nothing more than a political arm of the President. Hence, the Court ruled that the removal provision in the statute was a limitation on the President's authority.

Justice Sutherland distinguished *Myers.* The FTC differed from the Post Office. Because the FTC investigates, prosecutes, and adjudicates complaints of unfair trade practices, the Court characterized it as "an agency of the *legislative or judicial* departments of the government." In creating such bodies, Congress can set the terms of the commissioners' office and limit the conditions of their removal, the latter to assure their independence from the President. *Myers* was distinguishable, for it involved an "executive officer restricted to the performance of executive functions." *Humphrey's* appeared to narrow *Myers* to presidential removal of purely executive officers: "It goes no farther; much less does it include an officer who occupies no place in the executive department and who exercises no part of the executive power vested by the Constitution in the President." See also *Wiener v. United States,* 357 U.S. 349 (1958) (upholding congressional restrictions on the President's power to remove members of the War Claims Commission).

With one major case for the President and another one for the Congress, the removal question did not go away. In the late twentieth century, it would arise again in the great impeachment debates. The Nixon impeachment resulted from the use of the Presidential office for improper purposes—namely to perpetuate Nixon in office through "dirty political tricks," including a break-in at Democratic Party campaign offices. When the Justice Department tried to investigate, Nixon fired the investigator. As a result, Congress passed a statute to authorize independent officers—known as independent counsels—to investigate the President and his officers. The statute also limited the President's ability to remove those officers. Later, during the Bush 41 Administration, Congress prompted investigations of senior Justice Department officials, leading to a clash that tested the constitutionality of the "independent counsel" law and its removal provisions.

ALEXIA MORRISON V. THEODORE OLSON

United States Supreme Court, 1988.
487 U.S. 654, 108 S.Ct. 2597, 101 L.Ed.2d 569.

CHIEF JUSTICE REHNQUIST delivered the opinion of the Court.

[In response to the Watergate scandal that drove President Nixon from office, Congress adopted the Ethics in Government Act of 1978. Title VI created the office of "Independent Counsel" to investigate and, if appropriate, prosecute certain high-ranking government officials for violations of federal criminal laws. After notification of a possible federal offense, the Attorney General must decide within 90 days whether there are "reasonable grounds to believe that further investigation is warranted." If such reasonable grounds exist, the Attorney General must apply to a Special Division of the U.S. Court of Appeals for the D.C. Circuit for appointment of a special prosecutor; the judicial panel appoints the prosecutor and defines her jurisdiction. The Independent Counsel proceeds until she reports that her job is "completed," or the Special Division finds her job completed, or the Attorney General removes her (but only for "good cause," as specified in the statute). The Independent Counsel holds all the powers of the Attorney General with respect to the particular investigation subject to her jurisdiction. The law also applies in cases of investigating the President, and the independent counsel may recommend to the Congress that the President be impeached.[9]]

[Defendant Theodore Olson, then Assistant Attorney General of the Justice Department's Office of Legal Counsel, was accused of providing misleading testimony to a congressional subcommittee. Independent Counsel Alexia Morrison was appointed to investigate. Olson moved to quash her subpoenas on the ground that Title VI was unconstitutional. The Court of Appeals agreed, but the Supreme Court reversed. In Part III of his opinion, the Chief Justice first held that Morrison's manner of appointment did not violate the Appointments Clause of Article II, which reads as follows:

[The President] shall nominate, and by and with the Advice and Consent of the Senate, shall appoint Ambassadors, other public Ministers and Consuls, Judges of the supreme Court, and all other Officers of the United States, whose Appointments are not

---

[9] "This mandatory impeachment referral provision arguably makes impeachment proceedings far more likely to be initiated, and when initiated, far more threatening to the administration," because it may allow "an [Independent Counsel] to control the timing, scope, and content of impeachment inquiries." Julie R. O'Sullivan, *The Interaction Between Impeachment and the Independent Counsel Statute*, 86 Geo. L.J. 2193, 2195 (1998).

herein otherwise provided for, and which shall be established by Law: but the Congress may by Law vest the Appointment of such inferior Officers, as they think proper, in the President alone, in the Courts of Law, or in the Heads of Departments. U.S. Const., Art. II, § 2, cl. 2.

The Court held that the independent counsel was an inferior officer, even though, within her particular investigation, she wielded prosecutorial powers equivalent to those of the Attorney General. As an inferior officer, she was properly appointed because the Appointments Clause allows inferior officers to be appointed by "the Courts of Law," or "Heads of Departments."]

[In Part V of the opinion, the Chief Justice turned to the removal question and whether the Act violated the constitutional principle of separation of powers. Two related issues were distinguished: The first is whether the "good cause" removal provision is unconstitutional because it "impermissibly interferes with the President's exercise of his constitutionally appointed functions." The second is "whether, taken as a whole, the Act violates the separation of powers by reducing the President's ability to control the prosecutorial powers wielded by the independent counsel."]

Unlike both *Bowsher* [Chapter 1, § 2] and *Myers*, this case does not involve an attempt by Congress itself to gain a role in the removal of executive officials other than its established powers of impeachment and conviction. The Act instead puts the removal power squarely in the hands of the Executive Branch; an independent counsel may be removed from office "only by the personal action of the Attorney General, and only for good cause." § 596(a)(1). There is no requirement of congressional approval of the Attorney General's removal decision, though the decision is subject to judicial review. In our view, the removal provisions of the Act make this case more analogous to *Humphrey's Executor* * * * than to *Myers* or *Bowsher*. * * *

[Olson et al.] contend that *Humphrey's Executor* * * * [is] distinguishable from this case because [it] did not involve officials who performed a "core executive function." They argue that our decision in *Humphrey's Executor* rests on a distinction between "purely executive" officials and officials who exercise "quasi-legislative" and "quasi-judicial" powers. In their view, when a "purely executive" official is involved, the governing precedent is *Myers*, not *Humphrey's Executor*. * * *

We undoubtedly did rely on the terms "quasi-legislative" and "quasi-judicial" to distinguish the officials involved in *Humphrey's Executor* * * * from those in *Myers*, but our present considered view is that the determination of whether the Constitution allows Congress to impose a "good cause"-type restriction on the President's power to remove an official cannot be made to turn on whether or not that official is classified as "purely executive." The analysis contained in our removal cases is designed not to define rigid categories of those officials who may or may not be removed at will by the President, but to ensure that Congress does not interfere with the President's exercise of the "executive Power" and his constitutionally appointed duty to "take Care that the laws be faithfully executed" under Article II. *Myers* was undoubtedly correct in its holding, and in its broader suggestion that there are some "purely executive" officials who must be removable by the President at will if he is to be able to accomplish his constitutional role. * * * At the other end of the spectrum from *Myers*, the characterization of the agencies in *Humphrey's Executor* * * * as "quasi-legislative" or "quasi-judicial" in large part reflected our judgment that it was not essential to the President's proper execution of his Article II powers that these agencies be headed up by individuals who were removable at will. We do not mean to suggest that an analysis of the functions served by the officials at issue is irrelevant. But the real question is whether the removal restrictions are of such a nature that they impede the President's ability to perform his constitutional duty, and the functions of the officials in question must be analyzed in that light.

Considering for the moment the "good cause" removal provision in isolation from the other parts of the Act at issue in this case, we cannot say that the imposition of a "good cause" standard for removal by itself unduly trammels on executive authority. There is no real dispute that the functions performed by the independent counsel are "executive" in the sense that they are law enforcement functions that typically have been undertaken by officials within the Executive Branch. As we noted above, however, the independent counsel is an inferior officer under the Appointments Clause, with limited jurisdiction and tenure and lacking policymaking or significant administrative authority. Although the counsel exercises no small amount of discretion and judgment in deciding how to carry out his or her duties under the Act, we simply do not see how the President's need to control the exercise of that discretion is so central to the functioning of the Executive Branch as to require as a matter of constitutional law that the counsel be terminable at will by the President.

Nor do we think that the "good cause" removal provision at issue here impermissibly burdens the President's power to control or supervise the independent counsel, as an executive official, in the execution of his or her duties under the Act. This is not a case in which the power to remove an executive official has been completely stripped from the President, thus providing no means for the President to ensure the "faithful execution" of the laws. Rather, because the independent counsel may be terminated for "good cause," the Executive, through the Attorney General, retains ample authority to assure that the counsel is competently performing his or her statutory responsibilities in a manner that comports with the provisions of the Act. * * *

The final question to be addressed is whether the Act, taken as a whole, violates the principle of separation of powers by unduly interfering with the role of the Executive Branch. * * *

We observe first that this case does not involve an attempt by Congress to increase its own powers at the expense of the Executive Branch. Unlike some of our previous cases, most recently *Bowsher*, this case simply does not pose a "dange[r] of congressional usurpation of Executive Branch functions." [Also citing *Chadha*, Chapter 1, § 2.] Indeed, with the exception of the power of impeachment—which applies to all officers of the United States—Congress retained for itself no powers of control or supervision over an independent counsel. The Act does empower certain members of Congress to request the Attorney General to apply for the appointment of an independent counsel, but the Attorney General has no duty to comply with the request, although he must respond within a certain time limit. Other than that, Congress' role under the Act is limited to receiving reports or other information and oversight of the independent counsel's activities, functions that we have recognized generally as being incidental to the legislative function of Congress. * * *

Finally, we do not think that the Act "impermissibly undermine[s]" the powers of the Executive Branch, or "disrupts the proper balance between the coordinate branches [by] prevent[ing] the Executive Branch from accomplishing its constitutionally assigned functions." It is undeniable that the Act reduces the amount of control or supervision that the Attorney General and, through him, the President exercises over the investigation and prosecution of a certain class of alleged criminal activity. The Attorney General is not allowed to appoint the individual of his choice; he does not determine the counsel's jurisdiction; and his power to remove a counsel is limited. Nonetheless, the Act does give the Attorney General several means of supervising or controlling the prosecutorial powers that may be wielded by an independent counsel. Most importantly, the Attorney General retains the power to remove the counsel for "good cause," a power that we have already concluded provides the Executive with substantial ability to ensure that the laws are "faithfully executed" by an independent counsel. No independent counsel may be appointed without a specific request by the Attorney General, and the Attorney General's decision not to request appointment if he finds "no reasonable grounds to believe that further investigation is warranted" is committed to his unreviewable discretion. The Act thus gives the Executive a degree of control over the power to initiate an investigation by the independent counsel. In addition, the jurisdiction of the independent counsel is defined with reference to the facts submitted by the Attorney General, and once a counsel is appointed, the Act requires that the counsel abide by Justice Department policy unless it is not "possible" to do so. Notwithstanding the fact that the counsel is to some degree "independent" and free from Executive supervision to a greater extent than other federal prosecutors, in our view these features of the Act give the Executive Branch sufficient control over the independent counsel to ensure that the President is able to perform his constitutionally assigned duties.* * *

JUSTICE KENNEDY took no part in the consideration or decision of this case.

JUSTICE SCALIA, dissenting.

* * * That is what this suit is about. Power. The allocation of power among Congress, the President, and the courts in such fashion as to preserve the equilibrium the Constitution sought to establish—so that "a gradual concentration of the several powers in the same department," *Federalist* No. 51, p. 321 (J. Madison), can effectively be resisted. Frequently an issue of this sort will come before the Court clad, so to speak, in sheep's clothing: the potential of the asserted principle to effect important change in the equilibrium of power is not immediately evident, and must be discerned by a careful and perceptive analysis. But this wolf comes as a wolf. * * *

[B]y the application of this statute in the present case, Congress has effectively compelled a criminal investigation of a high-level appointee of the President in connection with his actions arising out of a bitter power dispute between the President and the Legislative Branch. Mr. Olson may or may not be guilty of a crime; we do not know. But we do know that the investigation of him has been commenced, not necessarily because the President or his authorized subordinates believe it is in the interest of the United States, in the sense that it warrants the diversion of resources from other efforts, and is worth the cost in money and in possible damage to other governmental interests; and not even, leaving aside those normally considered factors, because the President or his authorized subordinates necessarily believe that an investigation is likely to unearth a violation worth prosecuting; but only because the Attorney General cannot affirm, as Congress demands, that there are *no reasonable grounds to believe* that further investigation is warranted. The decisions regarding the scope of that further investigation, its duration, and, finally, whether or not prosecution should ensue, are likewise beyond the control of the President and his subordinates. * * *

[A]rt. II, § 1, cl. 1, of the Constitution provides: "The executive Power shall be vested in a President of the United States." * * * [T]his does not mean *some of* the executive power, but *all of* the executive power. It seems to me, therefore, that the decision of the Court of Appeals invalidating the present statute must be upheld on fundamental separation-of-powers principles if the following two questions are answered affirmatively: (1) Is the conduct of a criminal prosecution (and of an investigation to decide whether to prosecute) the exercise of purely executive power? (2) Does the statute deprive the President of the United States of exclusive control over the exercise of that power? Surprising to say, the Court appears to concede an affirmative answer to both questions, but seeks to avoid the inevitable conclusion that since the statute vests some purely executive power in a person who is not the President of the United States it is void. * * *

The utter incompatibility of the Court's approach with our constitutional traditions can be made more clear, perhaps, by applying it to the powers of the other two branches. Is it conceivable that if Congress passed a statute depriving itself of less than full and entire control over some insignificant area of legislation, we would inquire whether the matter was "*so central* to the functioning of the Legislative Branch" as really to require complete control, or whether the statute gives Congress "*sufficient* control over the surrogate legislator to ensure that Congress is able to perform its constitutionally assigned duties"? Of course we would have none of that. Once we determined that a purely legislative power was at issue we would require it to be exercised, wholly and entirely, by Congress. * * *

Is it unthinkable that the President should have such exclusive power, even when alleged crimes by him or his close associates are at issue? No more so than that Congress should have the exclusive power of legislation, even when what is at issue is its own exemption from the burdens of certain laws. No more so than that this Court should have the exclusive power to pronounce the final decision on justiciable cases and controversies, even those pertaining to the constitutionality of a statute reducing the salaries of the Justices. A system of separate and coordinate powers necessarily involves an acceptance of exclusive power that can theoretically be abused. * * * The checks against any branch's abuse of its exclusive powers are twofold: First, retaliation by one of the other branch's use of *its* exclusive powers: Congress, for example, can impeach the executive who willfully fails to enforce the laws; the executive can decline to prosecute under unconstitutional statutes; and the courts can dismiss malicious prosecutions. Second, and ultimately, there is the political check that the people will replace those in the political branches (the branches more "dangerous to the political rights of the Constitution," *Federalist* No. 78) who are guilty of abuse. Political pressures produced special prosecutors—for Teapot Dome and for Watergate, for example— long before this statute created the independent counsel.

[Justice Scalia contended that special prosecutors are in no sense "inferior" officers as they are in no sense subordinate to the President; hence, the statute violates the Appointments Clause even under the

Court's functional reading.] There are now no lines. If the removal of a prosecutor, the virtual embodiment of the power to "take Care that the laws be faithfully executed," can be restricted, what officer's removal cannot? This is an open invitation for Congress to experiment. What about a special Assistant Secretary of State, with responsibility for one very narrow area of foreign policy, who would not only have to be confirmed by the Senate but could also be removed only pursuant to certain carefully designed restrictions? * * * As far as I can discern from the Court's opinion, it is now open season upon the President's removal power for all executive officers, with not even the superficially principled restriction of *Humphrey's Executor* as cover. The Court essentially says to the President: "Trust us. We will make sure that you are able to accomplish your constitutional role." I think the Constitution gives the President—and the people—more protection than that. * * *

NOTES AND QUESTIONS ON MORRISON

1.   *What Does "Executive Power" Include?* Most scholars agree that the President heads a unitary executive branch; however, they contest the proposition that "executive Power" includes all of what we call "administration." Thus, Professor Strauss maintains that the formal *separation of powers* idea should govern relationships among the three named actors—Congress, the President, the Supreme Court—but not the inferior bodies and agencies, or what we might call "administration." Peter L. Strauss, *The Place of Agencies in Government: Separation of Powers and the Fourth Branch*, 84 Colum. L. Rev. 573, 578–80 (1984). Under this theory, the executive power would apply to require absolute presidential removal of his cabinet officials, but would permit congressional limits on the removal of mere administrators. This, of course, raises its own questions about how one draws the line between what is purely "executive" and what is "administrative." Even for "executive" officials, one wonders whether the fear of Congress's adding removal restrictions is exaggerated, given the facts that the President has the power to veto such legislation and that asserting "good cause" is not a high hurdle for removal of officials who really need to go.

2.   *Other Problems with the Statute in* Morrison. *Was Removal the Real Problem?* One of us has argued that the statute was unconstitutional for a variety of reasons having nothing to do with the so-called "unitary executive" theory. For example, if one looks at the separation of powers as a question of shifting representation, then the statute posed very serious problems. For example, a statute that allows an unelected individual (i.e., the independent counsel) to prompt the impeachment of a sitting President should give us pause. After all, no one would think of giving the federal courts power to prompt an impeachment, precisely because their members have no responsibility to the people. Why, then, should this power be potentially given to an independent counsel who has no responsibility to the people whatsoever? In this sense, *Morrison* is no different from *Bowsher*, where an

independent agent was ultimately given the authority to determine the nation's budget. Victoria F. Nourse, *The Vertical Separation of Powers,* 49 Duke L. J. 749 (1999).

3. *The Fate of the Independent Counsel Law.* It fell into bipartisan disrepute. Republicans resented use of the statute to investigate political disputes as crimes (such as Ted Olson's noncooperation with Congress) during the Reagan Administration (1981–89). The Democrats had a more favorable view—until the same abuse was turned against them during the Clinton Administration (1993–2001), with dramatic effect—prompting attempted impeachment of the President. Specifically, Independent Counsel Kenneth Starr's investigation into alleged Clinton Administration illegalities ultimately led to the exposure of the President's apparent perjury regarding his sexual relationship with a White House intern and the impeachment of President Clinton at the hands of the Republican-controlled House in 1998. Ironically, the independent counsel statute had been renewed in 1992, the same year as Clinton's election. When it came up for renewal again in 1999, both Democrats and Republicans were happy to let it lapse.

After three major cases and two presidential impeachments and acquittals, one might have thought the removal question resolved. Not so. In a 2010 case, the Supreme Court questioned Congress's power to shape presidential administration. The debate was about regulatory policy. In the wake of major financial scandals, the Congress passed a statute creating a new Board to oversee the accounting industry. Board members, like the FTC official in *Humphrey's Executor,* could only be removed for "good cause." In this case, however, it was not "good cause" as determined by the President, but "good cause" as determined by the Securities and Exchange Commission (SEC). There was a double layer of removal: The members of the SEC are appointed for a term of years, just like Humphrey, to insulate them from political pressure. As a result of this system, if the President wanted to remove a member of the accounting board, he could not; all he could do is urge the SEC to remove the board member. The Roberts Court held against the Congress, ruling that this double layer of removal was unconstitutional.

Free Enterprise Fund, Inc. v. Public Company Accounting Oversight Board
561 U.S. 477 (2010).

The Public Company Accounting Oversight Board was created as part of a series of corporate reforms in the Sarbanes-Oxley Act of 2002. The Board is composed of five members appointed by the Securities and Exchange Commission (SEC). It is a government-created entity with expansive powers to govern an entire industry. The parties stipulated that the Board is a government actor and that its members are *Officers of the United States* who exercise significant authority pursuant to the laws of the United States.

Although the SEC oversees the Board, it can remove Board members only "for good cause shown," in accordance with specified procedures. §§ 7211(e)(6), 7217(d)(3). The parties also stipulated that the SEC's Commissioners, in turn, could not themselves be removed by the President except for inefficiency, neglect of duty, or malfeasance in office, the standard in *Humphrey's Executor*. Free Enterprise and other private firms sought to invalidate the Board, on the grounds that these limits on presidential removal authority violated both the constitutional separation of powers and the Appointments Clause, Art. II, § 2, cl. 2. Delivering the opinion for the Court, **Chief Justice Roberts** ruled that the limits violate Article II's vesting all "executive" authority in the President.

The Chief Justice started with the Decision of 1789 and the Court's decisions in *Myers*, *Humphrey's Executor*, and *Morrison*. "[W]e have previously upheld limited restrictions on the President's removal power. In those cases, however, only one level of protected tenure separated the President from an officer exercising executive power. It was the President—or a subordinate he could remove at will—who decided whether the officer's conduct merited removal under the good-cause standard.

"The Act before us does something quite different. It not only protects Board members from removal except for good cause, but withdraws from the President any decision on whether that good cause exists. That decision is vested instead in other tenured officers—the Commissioners— none of whom is subject to the President's direct control. The result is a Board that is not accountable to the President, and a President who is not responsible for the Board. * * *

"A second level of tenure protection changes the nature of the President's review. Now the Commission cannot remove a Board member at will. The President therefore cannot hold the Commission fully accountable for the Board's conduct, to the same extent that he may hold the Commission accountable for everything else that it does. The Commissioners are not responsible for the Board's actions. They are only responsible for their own determination of whether the Act's rigorous good-cause standard is met. And even if the President disagrees with their determination, he is powerless to intervene—unless that determination is so unreasonable as to constitute 'inefficiency, neglect of duty, or malfeasance in office.' *Humphrey's Executor*."

The Chief Justice was concerned that "this novel structure" transformed the Board into an "executive" branch organ freed from presidential accountability, and that such a structure could easily be abused by Congress. "If Congress can shelter the bureaucracy behind two layers of good-cause tenure, why not a third? At oral argument, the Government was unwilling to concede that even *five* layers between the President and the Board would be too many. The officers of such an agency—safely encased within a Matryoshka doll of tenure protections—would be immune from Presidential oversight, even as they exercised power in the people's name."

The Chief Justice continued: "The diffusion of power carries with it a diffusion of accountability. The people do not vote for the 'Officers of the United States.' They instead look to the President to guide the 'assistants or deputies . . . subject to his superintendence.' *The Federalist* No. 72 (A. Hamilton). Without a clear and effective chain of command, the public cannot 'determine on whom the blame or the punishment of a pernicious measure, or series of pernicious measures ought really to fall.' *Id.,* No. 70. That is why the Framers sought to ensure that 'those who are employed in the execution of the law will be in their proper situation, and the chain of dependence be preserved; the lowest officers, the middle grade, and the highest, will depend, as they ought, on the President, and the President on the community.' 1 Annals of Cong., at 499 (J. Madison).

"One can have a government that functions without being ruled by functionaries, and a government that benefits from expertise without being ruled by experts. Our Constitution was adopted to enable the people to govern themselves, through their elected leaders. The growth of the Executive Branch, which now wields vast power and touches almost every aspect of daily life, heightens the concern that it may slip from the Executive's control, and thus from that of the people. This concern is largely absent from the dissent's paean to the administrative state."

The Chief Justice rejected Free Enterprise's argument that the unconstitutionality of the removal provisions required the Court to rule that the Board itself is unconstitutional and can no longer operate. Instead, the Court struck down only the unconstitutional provisions insulating the Board members from SEC removal except for good cause and let stand the rest of the provisions creating the Board and vesting it with the duties prescribed in the statute. (See Chapter 2, § 2, discussing the longstanding presumption in favor of "severability" of unconstitutional provisions). Henceforth, Board members can be removed by the SEC for any reason. The Chief Justice also rejected Free Enterprise's Appointments Clause challenge to the Board's appointment by the SEC. The Court ruled that Board members were "inferior Officers" and that the SEC (which the Court assumed to be an independent agency) is a "Department" for purposes of Article II, § 2, clause 2. Ironically, the Court's opinion failed to cite *Morrison v. Olson* for this proposition.

Justice Breyer (joined by Justices Stevens, Ginsburg, and Sotomayor) dissented. He started with a presumption in favor of the practical judgment made by Congress and the President that the Board's independence from "political" influence was important to restore public faith in the market. When he signed the Sarbanes-Oxley Act into law, President George W. Bush criticized some of its provisions as unwise or unconstitutional but had only praise for the Board's independence. Additionally, Justice Breyer argued that the Court's remedy in this case did little to solve the separation of powers concern with this arrangement. Because the SEC itself is an independent agency, the President may still not "control" the Board even if the SEC can remove its members for any reason—because the President cannot remove SEC commissioners except "for cause." Because the Court left *Humphrey's Executor* intact, its remedy in *Free Enterprise* was virtually worthless as a matter of political control and accountability. "In other words, the Court fails to show why *two* layers of 'for cause' protection—Layer One insulating the Commissioners from the President, and Layer Two insulating the Board from the Commissioners—impose any more serious limitation upon the *President's* powers than *one* layer." To the contrary, in many situations, the two-layer protections would *enhance* the President's authority, for example where the President approves of what the Board is doing while the SEC wants to discipline it. The Court's "solution" actually increased the authority of the *SEC*, not the President, to control the Board.

CONCLUSION:
SO WHAT DO WE KNOW ABOUT
WHAT THE PRESIDENT OR CONGRESS CAN DO
UNDER THESE PRECEDENTS?

We know that the Congress cannot "inject itself" into the removal process by specifically requiring that a President's firing decision is subject to their (Congress's) approval. That is *Myers*. We also know that Congress can limit removal; most particularly it can restrain the President from removal for purely partisan reasons (i.e. "I'm firing you Humphrey because you are member of the Republican Party"). Congress can require that the President come up with a good reason for the dismissal. That is *Humphrey's Executor*. To the extent this system leads to a constitutional structure in which agencies are "independent" of the President's partisan control, that system was affirmed in *Morrison*. There are limits, however: Congress cannot divert the President's removal power to another independent agency, like the SEC. *Free Enterprise*. Lest one think that there are no more issues on this topic, see the problem below, which involves an agency not governed by a "for cause" limit on removal—the EEOC.

PROBLEM 2–1: IS THE EEOC AN "INDEPENDENT" AGENCY? CAN THE PRESIDENT REMOVE EEOC COMMISSIONERS WITHOUT GOOD CAUSE?

Relatively few presidential removal cases result in a constitutional decision by the Supreme Court or any other court. One reason, noted by Chief Justice Taft in *Myers*, is that the President can get rid of most officials simply by telling them their time has expired; another reason is that finding "good cause" to dismiss an official is usually not difficult. See Neal E. Devins, *Political Will and the Unitary Executive: What Makes an Independent Agency Independent?*, 15 Cardozo L. Rev. 273 (1993). What happens, however, when there is no "good cause" limitation—when the agency's "independence" lies in the fact that the members are appointed for a period extending beyond a single presidential term?

Consider this question in connection with the EEOC, the agency created by the Civil Rights Act of 1964. Section 705(a), 42 U.S.C. § 2000e–4(a) establishes the Commission and directs that it "shall be composed of five members, not more than three of whom shall be members of the same political party. Members of the Commission shall be appointed by the President by and with the advice and consent of the Senate for a term of five years. Any individual chosen to fill a vacancy shall be appointed only for the unexpired term of the member whom he shall succeed, and all members of the Commission shall continue to serve until their successors are appointed and qualified," with two minor exceptions. Section 705(b), 42 U.S.C. § 2000e–4(b), establishes a General Counsel, appointed by the President with the advice and consent of the Senate for a term of four years. There is no provision in Title VII assuring Commissioners that they can only be discharged for good cause (the standard upheld in *Humphrey's*).

Unlike the FTC, the EEOC has no substantive rulemaking authority. The EEOC is authorized to announce rules governing procedure before the agency, § 713(a), 42 U.S.C. § 2000e–12(a), but not to issue substantive rules. Of course the EEOC (like any other agency) can issue opinions or guidances announcing its interpretation of Title VII. Likewise, the EEOC has no adjudicative authority. Instead, it is charged with educating the public about the requirements of Title VII, investigating complaints of discrimination, seeking conciliation and remedy for those it finds meritorious, and filing lawsuits against alleged violators. See §§ 705–06, 708, 42 U.S.C. §§ 2000e–4 to –5, 2000e–7. See also 29 C.F.R. Part 1601 (the EEOC's procedural regulations, governing the filing, investigation, and handling of discrimination charges with the Commission).

Given this statutory structure, as well as any illumination from the case law, does the President have the authority to remove an EEOC Commissioner without cause? The EEOC General Counsel? Imagine a great policy controversy, as might occur if the Chair and the Counsel took a position that defied the President on affirmative action. The President removes the Chair and the Counsel for taking a position contrary to his policy. Constitutional? Jot down your thoughts now and reconsider them after you have read the following opinion by the Office of Legal Counsel, which is tasked with giving constitutional advice on inter-agency matters within the executive branch but whose legal opinions may be different from those of the Counsel to the House or Senate or from the Supreme Court.

Office of Legal Counsel, U.S. Department of Justice, *President's Authority to Promulgate a Reorganization Plan Involving the Equal Employment Opportunity Commission.*
1 Op. OLC 248, 1977 WL 18064 (Oct. 20, 1977).

At the urging of EEOC Chair Eleanor Holmes Norton, President Jimmy Carter wanted to transfer administrative functions from the Department of Labor to the EEOC (including the authority to initiate pattern or practice lawsuits against private companies, as authorized by § 707 of the Civil Rights Act added in the 1972 amendments, 42 U.S.C. § 2000e–6). A broader effect of the transfer would be to make the EEOC the focal coordinator of anti-discrimination policies within the executive branch. But the transfer could not occur if inconsistent with the Reorganization Act, which only allows such transfers to an "[e]xecutive agency." *See* 5 U.S.C.A. §§ 902–903 (1977). Some independent agencies could qualify for that status, and OLC found the EEOC could qualify on that basis. However, its major conclusion was that the EEOC is an executive agency for all administrative purposes and is not an independent agency.

"EEOC was created by Title VII of the Civil Rights Act of 1964, 42 U.S.C. § 2000e–4 *et seq.* Its five members are appointed by the President with the advice and consent of the Senate, to staggered 5-year terms; no provision is made for the removal of the members from office. EEOC's functions, as contemplated in the 1964 Civil Rights Act, were largely to investigate and to conciliate. *See* 110 Cong. Rec. 7242 (1964) (remarks of Senator Case); *see, also, McGriff* v. *A. O. Smith Corporation,* 51 F.R.D. 479, 482–83 (D. S. Car. 1971). *See* 110 Cong. Rec. 6543 (1964) (remarks of Senator Humphrey); *Fekete* v. *United States Steel Corporation,* 424 F. 2d 331, 336 (3rd Cir. 1970). Moreover, while EEOC is empowered to issue guidelines, they are not regarded as regulations having the force of law. *See, General Electric Company* v. *Gilbert,* 97 S.Ct. 401, 410–11 (1976) [Chapter 3, § 3].

"The lack of any quasi-adjudicatory or quasi-legislative functions vested in EEOC leads, in our view, to a conclusion that it is a part of the executive branch. As the Supreme Court indicated in *Humphrey's Executor* and *Wiener,* the inferences to be drawn as to congressional intent on this matter rest largely on the functions that the Agency is to perform. In those cases the quasi-legislative or quasi-judicial functions lodged by Congress in the particular agencies led to a conclusion by the Court that Congress meant for the agencies to be independent; otherwise, the agencies could not perform their required duties free of Executive influence. The lack of such functions in EEOC and the consequent absence of any need to be independent of the Executive suggests that Congress meant for EEOC to be subject to Executive control.

"Other considerations support this result. First, it would raise serious constitutional problems for an agency, shorn of any quasi-judicial or quasi-legislative authority, to be set apart from the Executive; it cannot be assumed that Congress would lightly intend such a result. Moreover, there is no provision in the 1964 Civil Rights Act for the removal of EEOC members for neglect of duty or malfeasance in office. Such a provision has been customarily included in statutes setting up regulatory agencies intended to be independent of Executive control, *see, e.g.*, 29 U.S.C. § 153(a) (NLRB); 49 U.S.C. § 1321(a)(2)(CAB), except for those statutes passed in the interval between *Myers* and *Humphrey, see* 15 U.S.C. § 78d (SEC); 47 U.S.C. § 154 (FCC). While *Wiener* held that the absence of a specific provision for removal for cause does not necessarily imply that the officer is subject to Executive control, the fact that such a provision is not contained in Title VII of the Civil Rights Act seriously weakens that argument when compared to the statutes creating other regulatory agencies.

"The legislative history of the 1964 Civil Rights Act does not suggest a contrary result. Albeit, there are references in the history which could be taken to indicate a legislative belief that EEOC was to be an independent agency. For example, the House committee report states that the 'Commission will receive the usual salaries of members of independent regulatory agencies.' H.R. Rep. No. 914, 88th Cong., 1st Sess. 28 (1963). Senator Humphrey also stated that the EEOC statute would be a 'departure from the usual statutory scheme for independent regulatory agencies.' 110 Cong. Rec. 6548 (1964). These limited remarks, however, do not shed any additional light on an intent that EEOC was to be an independent Agency. If Congress had intended this result, it presumably would have so indicated more clearly and explicitly, particularly since it must have been aware that the 'most reliable factor' for drawing inferences as to independence—that of the agency's functions—would lead to a contrary conclusion. *Wiener*. In addition, it is not without significance that those opposed to the Civil Rights Act referred, without rebuttal, to EEOC as part of the executive branch. *See* 110 Cong. Rec. 7561, 7776, 8442 (1964) (remarks of Senators Thurmond, Tower, and Hill).

"We thus conclude that EEOC is an Agency within the executive branch. This conclusion is consistent with earlier opinions of this Office as to the status of EEOC."

NOTES ON PRESIDENTIAL REMOVAL AUTHORITY

1.　*What Are the Controlling Precepts of Law on This Issue?* Does the OLC opinion survive the Court's decisions in *Morrison* and *Free Enterprise*? Assume the OLC opinion survives. Does the President have the authority to discharge EEOC Commissioners without cause before their terms have expired? Could the President, as a practical matter, exercise such authority? If the President makes it clear he or she is removing an official before the end of her or his term for purely political reasons, would there not be congressional and media pushback?

2.　*The Fate of the EEOC.* After the Carter Administration's OLC ruled that the EEOC is an executive agency for purposes of the Reorganization Act, the Reagan Administration tightened White House control over the EEOC by trimming its ability to litigate its policy positions. The mechanism was the Department of Justice. The Attorney General has the authority to take a case on behalf of the United States, unless a federal statute expressly affords an agency litigation authority to represent itself. See 28 U.S.C. §§ 516, 519; *United States v. San Jacinto Tin Co.,* 125 U.S. 273 (1888). The idea is simple: to those who litigate inside the Justice Department, it seems common sense that DOJ identify a uniform "government" position for litigation.

The effect of such control can be dramatic. During the Reagan Administration, the Justice Department sought to encourage courts to rule against affirmative action. The Civil Rights Division of the Department of Justice intervened in appellate litigation involving private plaintiffs and a state institution, arguing that affirmative action was unconstitutional; the EEOC prepared an *amicus* brief defending affirmative action, and the Civil Rights Division sought to block the EEOC's brief. Building on opinions from the Office of Legal Counsel, the Department concluded that the EEOC could not even file an *amicus* brief without DOJ permission. (The behind-the-scenes story is that White House Counsel Edwin Meese worked with Brad Reynolds, Assistant Attorney General for Civil Rights, to insist that the EEOC, then headed by Clarence Thomas, agree not to file the *amicus* brief.)

Following this showdown, the Reagan and Bush 41 Administrations considered the EEOC an agency directly under the thumb of the White House—even to the point of barring the agency from filing *amicus* briefs in the Supreme Court, a privilege accorded the EEOC under prior Administrations. By 1993, the EEOC had the worst of both worlds. It was widely considered an executive agency and, as such, was under the thumb of an often skeptical White House, but enjoyed none of the insider influence enjoyed by the Civil Rights Division, part of the executive branch.

3.　*The Solicitor General's Independence Within the Executive Branch.* Independent agencies *and* executive branch agencies *and* agencies falling somewhere in between (perhaps the EEOC) are *all* subject to the centralizing features of the Solicitor General's control of virtually all federal government appellate litigation. Professor Lemos examined all Supreme Court cases between 1984 and 2006 where the Solicitor General filed a brief.

Interestingly, she found that in one-quarter of those cases, the SG was suppressing or trumping the previous views of the relevant agency. Margaret H. Lemos, *The Solicitor General as Mediator Between Court and Agency,* 2009 Mich. St. L. Rev. 185, 201–02. Professor Lemos argues that the Solicitor General wears three hats: he or she represents We the People (the United States), is an important officer of the Department of Justice and the executive branch, and is the "Tenth Justice." See Lincoln Caplan, *The Tenth Justice: The Solicitor General and the Rule of Law* (1987) (recognizing that the SG is both an advocate before and agent of the Supreme Court). As Lemos and Caplan both testify, the SG is widely considered more responsive to the Supreme Court than to the President. That is, the SG is generally resistant to White House pressure (indeed, it is not clear how often the White House even applies pressure) and is highly responsive to Supreme Court holdings, dicta, and even indirect signals.

NOTE ON PLURALITY WITHIN A "UNITARY" EXECUTIVE: IS THE EXECUTIVE/INDEPENDENT AGENCY DISTINCTION OBSOLETE?

The executive branch of government may be as much a "They" as an "It". Lisa Schultz Bressman & Michael P. Vandenbergh, *Inside the Administrative State: A Critical Look at the Practice of Presidential Control*, 105 Mich. L. Rev. 47, 49 (2006). Consider three different kinds of problems with the notion that the United States enjoys a unitary executive branch, conceptualized as a pyramid under the direct control of the President.

First, theoretical removal power does not necessarily translate into real control. Even for executive officials, whom the President may discharge without good cause, there are informal norms within our government that actually constrain the President's ability to discharge pure executive officials: Violation of those norms would raise a public ruckus, media attention and critique, and probably partisan attacks. Norms are prescriptive guidelines that people have come to accept, even though they are not codified as "law" or even nonlegal "rules." For example, there is a strong norm against presidential interference with the Solicitor General's exercise of judgment regarding appeals and the content of briefs filed with the Supreme Court. If a President fired a Solicitor General for failing to hew to the presidential agenda, there would be a firestorm of protest. Recall that the Bush-Cheney Administration sacked several U.S. Attorneys for apparently ideological reasons—a perfectly legal move—but suffered tremendous negative political consequences for that action. See John L. McKay, *Train Wreck at the Justice Department: An Eyewitness Account*, 31 Seattle U. L. Rev. 265 (2008).

Second, even when the President and top agency officials are completely in sync on matters of policy, an agency may still diverge from the President's agenda, often dramatically. The work of any agency is conducted by career staff members and experts who can slow down, undermine, or even veto official policies or priorities that the career staff believe are inconsistent with the agency's mission. (The phenomenon of a political official's "going native" is a consequence of these forces over time.) Also, Congress will exercise continuous influence through various informal, as well as formal mechanisms. An agency official who irks congressional powers because she is loyal to presidential prerogatives will face many obstacles and will usually have to resign.

Third, as to most matters of administration, even the most ideological President will not be willing to impose his or her will on agencies as to all important issues. Indeed, as to most issues faced by agencies, the White House will not have a clear vision about what is the right policy and will be susceptible to agency initiatives that enjoy broader political support. (Thus, the White House itself is a "They" and not an "It" on many issues. *See* John P. Burke, *The Institutional Presidency: Organizing and Managing the White House from FDR to Clinton* (2000).)

If this is all true, what is at stake in the debates over unitary executive authority versus a more pluralistic understanding of administration?

Scholars have demonstrated that there is no single criterion distinguishing "independent" from "executive" agencies. See, e.g., Marshall J. Breger & Gary J. Edles, *Established by Practice: The Theory and Operation of Independent Federal Agencies*, 52 Admin. L. Rev. 1111, 1128–34 (2000). Various studies suggest that, in practice, all agencies are both influenced by the President's priorities and operate independently of them. Moreover, it appears that there is no single feature, whether formal or functional, that every agency considered "independent" shares. There is a great deal of organizational diversity among agencies, and some agencies fit multiple categories. See Anne Joseph O'Connell, *Bureaucracy at the Boundary*, 162 U. Pa. L. Rev. 841 (2014). For this reason, Kirti Datla & Richard L. Revesz, *Deconstructing Independent Agencies (and Executive Agencies)*, 98 Cornell L. Rev. 769 (2013), argue that the distinction between independent and executive agencies should be retired. Inconsistent with dicta in *Humphrey's Executor*, Datla and Revesz would presumptively treat all agencies as executive ones under the plenary direction of the President—but they would follow and indeed expand *Humphrey's Executor* to allow reasonable, non-aggrandizing congressional limits on presidential control of agencies. See U.S. Const. art. I, § 8, cl. 18 (Congress has authority to adopt laws "necessary and proper" for carrying into execution the powers vested in the President and any Department).

2. THE PRESIDENT'S "TAKE CARE" DUTIES

Under Article II, § 3, the President has the duty to "take care" that Congress's laws are executed. This gives the President wide authority in the administration of the law. He administers the law through the major departments, such as the Department of State or Department of Defense, as well as through other kinds of agencies. The President may also issue "executive orders" in cases relating to the control of his administration. These orders, however, must be consistent with the Constitution and not inconsistent with any statute on point.

It is generally believed that the President has far greater leeway in exerting his national power in foreign affairs, a notion that enjoys some textual support in Article II (which charges the President with commander-in-chief duties for the armed forces and supervision of the nation's diplomatic relations as well as treaty negotiation). Some maintain that the President is the "sole organ" of the nation in international matters, based on the central case of **United States v. Curtiss-Wright Export Corp.**, 299 U.S. 304, 319 (1936) (quoting John Marshall's 1800 speech in the House of Representatives). There, the Court upheld the President's action against Curtiss-Wright for selling guns to Bolivia. Congress had by joint resolution authorized the President to place an embargo on arms sales to Bolivia and Paraguay, but **Justice Sutherland**'s opinion went far beyond that authorization. He stated not only that the President's power over external affairs is inherent and plenary, but also that the President plays a uniquely important role in foreign affairs. "In this vast external realm, with its important, complicated, delicate and manifold problems, the President alone has the power to speak or listen as a representative of the nation." *Id.*

Commentators have wondered whether Sutherland's opinion begs the central question: Even if the national government has plenary authority to act in foreign affairs, hasn't the Constitution vested primary national authority in Congress, and not the President? Especially when the President's actions violate a company's liberty of contract (as in barring the sale of weapons above), shouldn't it be the deliberative Congress, which is closer to the people, who should make the call? Consider the leading Take Care Clause case, which arose in precisely this kind of foreign affairs/national defense setting.

INTRODUCTION TO THE STEEL SEIZURE CASE[10]

Leading a United Nations-sanctioned peacekeeping force, the United States went to war with North Korea to repel its June 1950 attack on South Korea. Although Congress never declared war, it supported the war effort by authorizing a build-up of our armed forces to 3,500,000 people strong and appropriating unprecedented sums of money for national defense. In 1950, President Harry S. Truman requested authority to

---

[10] The account that follows is taken from Chief Justice Vinson's dissenting opinion, as well as Maeva Marcus, *Truman and the Steel Seizure Case: The Limits of Presidential Power* (1977); Alan Westin, *The Anatomy of a Constitutional Case* (1958); Henry M. Hart Jr. & Albert M. Sacks, *The Legal Process* 1010–46 (William N. Eskridge Jr. & Philip P. Frickey eds., 1994) (tent. ed. 1958).

requisition property and to allocate priorities for scarce goods. In Title IV of the Defense Production Act of 1950, Congress not only gave the President the powers requested, but also gave him authority to stabilize wages and prices and to provide for the settlement of labor disputes arising in the defense program. Congress extended the Act in 1951. A Senate committee expressed concern about inflation in some of the defense industries because of the strain of producing for both military and domestic markets; the committee emphasized the steel industry as the exemplar of this problem. A three-way dispute broke out among the government, the steel companies, and the unions. The unions wanted a wage increase, which the companies wouldn't grant without a hefty price increase, which the government resisted.[11]

On April 4, 1952, the union announced a nationwide strike to start on April 9. The President was in a bind. During World War II, the War Labor Disputes Act had authorized the President to seize industrial plants threatened with disruptive labor disputes. That authority ended in 1946, and Congress replaced it with a more limited authority. The Taft-Hartley Act of 1947 provided that: if in his opinion an actual or threatened strike imperiled the nation's health or safety, the President was authorized to appoint a special board to report the facts of the dispute; if the report failed to induce resolution of the dispute, the President could seek a district court order enjoining the strike for 80 days to facilitate efforts at settling the dispute (this is called a "cooling-off order"). President Truman was not willing to invoke the Taft-Hartley Act.[12] Nor was he willing to invoke the Selective Service Act of 1948, which authorized the President to take immediate possession of and operate a producer's facilities (with "just compensation" to be paid to the producer) whenever a producer failed to fill an order for goods required by the armed forces for defense purposes within a specified period of time. Nor was President Truman willing to invoke Title II of the Defense Production Act of 1950, which set up procedures for the President to

---

[11] Pursuant to Title IV, President Truman established an Economic Stabilization Agency. On January 26, 1951, the Agency issued formal wage and price controls, to stem inflationary pressures in the steel industry, among others. On November 1, 1951, the United Steelworkers Union gave notice to the major steel companies that the Union intended to demand wage increases at the end of its contract. The companies resisted these demands. On December 22, President Truman referred the union-industry dispute to the Wage Stabilization Board (WSB) for recommendation of a fair solution, also as authorized by the 1950 Act. On March 22, 1952, the WSB issued its report, recommending a modest wage increase. The union embraced the recommendation, and the companies rejected it. Yet the companies pressed the Office of Price Stabilization (OPS) for a price increase, and it is probable that favorable action on prices would have made the companies amenable to a wage increase. On March 28, the OPS suggested a modest price increase, which the companies rejected. On April 3, the companies offered the union a small wage increase, which the union rejected.

[12] In his memoirs, the President claims that both he and Congress assumed that the WSB procedures were supposed to be substitutes for the Taft-Hartley procedures; since he had already exhausted the WSB procedures, Taft-Hartley was not available. See Harry S. Truman, *Memoirs—Years of Trial and Hope* 465–78 (1956) (vol. 2). Also note that the Taft-Hartley Act itself was bitterly opposed by organized labor and enacted over President Truman's veto.

acquire by condemnation facilities necessary for the national defense. A prerequisite to condemnation was an effort by the President to acquire the facilities by negotiation.

Hours before the strike was to commence, the President issued Executive Order 10340, 17 Fed. Reg. 3139 (1952), which directed Secretary of Commerce Charles W. Sawyer to take possession of the steel industry and to keep the mills operating, "in order to assure the continued availability of steel and steel products during the existing emergency." The order invoked "the authority vested in [the President] by the Constitution and laws of the United States, and as President of the United States and Commander in Chief of the armed forces of the United States."

Executive Order 10340 had the advantage of maintaining production of an important war commodity without offending organized labor, which acquiesced in the order. It had the disadvantage of antagonizing the steel industry, which complied with the order but sued to have it overturned. On April 30, the steel companies obtained a preliminary injunction against Secretary Sawyer's action. The court of appeals stayed the effect of the injunction, pending review. In an extraordinary move, the Supreme Court took the case on certiorari on May 3; it was argued on May 12 and May 13. The Court announced its decision affirming the injunction on June 2, 1952.

YOUNGSTOWN SHEET & TUBE CO. v. SAWYER (THE STEEL SEIZURE CASE)

United States Supreme Court, 1952.
343 U.S. 579, 72 S.Ct. 863, 96 L.Ed. 1153.

JUSTICE BLACK delivered the opinion of the Court.

We are asked to decide whether the President was acting within his constitutional power when he issued an order directing the Secretary of Commerce to take possession of and operate most of the Nation's steel mills. The mill owners argue that the President's order amounts to lawmaking, a legislative function which the Constitution has expressly confided to the Congress and not to the President. The Government's position is that the order was made on findings of the President that his action was necessary to avert a national catastrophe which would inevitably result from a stoppage of steel production, and that in meeting this grave emergency the President was acting within the aggregate of his constitutional powers as the Nation's Chief Executive and the Commander in Chief of the Armed Forces of the United States. * * *

The President's power, if any, to issue the order must stem either from an act of Congress or from the Constitution itself. There is no statute that expressly authorizes the President to take possession of property as he did here. Nor is there any act of Congress to which our attention has been directed from which such a power can fairly be implied. * * * There are two statutes which do authorize the President to take both personal and real property under certain conditions * * *[, but] these conditions were not met and * * * the President's order was not rooted in either of the statutes. The Government refers to the seizure provisions of one of these statutes * * * as "much too cumbersome, involved, and time-consuming for the crisis which was at hand."

Moreover, the use of the seizure technique to solve labor disputes in order to prevent work stoppages was not only unauthorized by any congressional enactment; prior to this controversy, Congress had refused to adopt that method of settling labor disputes. When the Taft-Hartley Act was under consideration in 1947, Congress rejected an amendment which would have authorized such governmental seizures in cases of emergency. Apparently it was thought that the technique of seizure, like that of compulsory arbitration, would interfere with the process of collective bargaining. * * * Instead, the plan sought to bring about settlements by use of the customary devices of mediation, conciliation, investigation by boards of inquiry, and public reports. In some instances temporary injunctions were authorized to provide cooling-off periods. All this failing, unions were left free to strike * * *.

It is clear that if the President had authority to issue the order he did, it must be found in some provisions of the Constitution. And it is not claimed that express constitutional language grants this power to the President. The contention is that presidential power should be implied from the aggregate of his powers under the Constitution. Particular reliance is placed on provisions in Article II which say that "the executive Power shall be vested in a President * * * "; that "he shall take Care that the Laws be faithfully executed"; and that he "shall be Commander in Chief of the Army and Navy of the United States."

The order cannot properly be sustained as an exercise of the President's military power as Commander in Chief of the Armed Forces. The Government attempts to do so by citing a number of cases upholding broad powers in military commanders engaged in day-to-day fighting in a theater of war. Such cases need not concern us here. Even though "theater of war" be an expanding concept, we cannot with faithfulness to our constitutional system hold that the Commander in Chief of the Armed Forces has the ultimate power as such to take possession of private property in order to keep labor disputes from stopping production. This is a job for the Nation's lawmakers, not for its military authorities.

Nor can the seizure order be sustained because of the several constitutional provisions that grant executive power to the President. In the framework of our Constitution, the President's power to see that the laws are faithfully executed refutes the idea that he is to be a lawmaker. The Constitution limits his functions in the lawmaking process to the recommending of laws he thinks wise and the vetoing of laws he thinks bad. And the Constitution is neither silent nor equivocal about who shall make laws which the President is to execute. The first section of the first article says that "All legislative Powers herein granted shall be vested in a Congress of the United States * * * *." After granting many powers to the Congress, Article I goes on to provide that Congress may "make all Laws which shall be necessary and proper for carrying into Execution the foregoing Powers, and all other Powers vested by this Constitution in the Government of the United States, or in any Department or Officer thereof."

The President's order does not direct that a congressional policy be executed in a manner prescribed by Congress—it directs that a presidential policy be executed in a manner prescribed by the President. * * * The power of Congress to adopt such public policies as those proclaimed by the order is beyond question. It can authorize the taking of private property for public use. It can make laws regulating the relationships between employers and employees, prescribing rules designed to settle labor disputes, and fixing wages and working conditions in certain fields of our economy. The Constitution did not subject this lawmaking power of Congress to presidential or military supervision or control.

It is said that other Presidents without congressional authority have taken possession of private business enterprises in order to settle labor disputes. But even if this be true, Congress has not thereby lost its exclusive constitutional authority to make laws necessary and proper to carry out the powers vested by the Constitution "in the Government of the United States, or in any Department or Officer thereof."

The Founders of this Nation entrusted the law making power to the Congress alone in both good and bad times. It would do no good to recall the historical events, the fears of power and the hopes for freedom that lay behind their choice. Such a review would but confirm our holding that this seizure order cannot stand.

JUSTICE JACKSON, concurring in the judgment and opinion of the Court.

* * * A judge, like an executive adviser, may be surprised at the poverty of really useful and unambiguous authority applicable to concrete problems of executive power as they actually present themselves. Just what our forefathers did envision, or would have envisioned had they foreseen modern conditions, must be divined from materials almost as enigmatic as the dreams Joseph was called upon to interpret for Pharaoh. A century and a half of partisan debate and scholarly speculation yields

no net result but only supplies more or less apt quotations from respected sources on each side of any question. They largely cancel each other. And court decisions are indecisive because of the judicial practice of dealing with the largest questions in the most narrow way.

The actual art of governing under our Constitution does not and cannot conform to judicial definitions of the power of any of its branches based on isolated clauses or even single Articles torn from context. While the Constitution diffuses power the better to secure liberty, it also contemplates that practice will integrate the dispersed powers into a workable government. It enjoins upon its branches separateness but interdependence, autonomy but reciprocity. Presidential powers are not fixed but fluctuate, depending upon their disjunction or conjunction with those of Congress. We may well begin by a somewhat over-simplified grouping of practical situations in which a President may doubt, or others may challenge, his powers, and by distinguishing roughly the legal consequences of this factor of relativity.

1.   When the President acts pursuant to an express or implied authorization of Congress, his authority is at its maximum, for it includes all that he possesses in his own right plus all that Congress can delegate. In these circumstances, and in these only, may he be said (for what it may be worth) to personify the federal sovereignty. If his act is held unconstitutional under these circumstances, it usually means that the Federal Government as an undivided whole lacks power. A seizure executed by the President pursuant to an Act of Congress would be supported by the strongest of presumptions and the widest latitude of judicial interpretation, and the burden of persuasion would rest heavily upon any who might attack it.

2.   When the President acts in absence of either a congressional grant or denial of authority, he can only rely upon his own independent powers, but there is a zone of twilight in which he and Congress may have concurrent authority, or in which its distribution is uncertain. Therefore, congressional inertia, indifference or quiescence may sometimes, at least as a practical matter, enable, if not invite, measures on independent presidential responsibility. In this area, any actual test of power is likely to depend on the imperatives of events and contemporary imponderables rather than on abstract theories of law.

3.   When the President takes measures incompatible with the expressed or implied will of Congress, his power is at its lowest ebb, for then he can rely only upon his own constitutional powers minus any constitutional powers of Congress over the matter. Courts can sustain exclusive Presidential control in such a case only by disabling the Congress from acting upon the subject. Presidential claim to a power at once so conclusive and preclusive must be scrutinized with caution, for

what is at stake is the equilibrium established by our constitutional system.

Into which of these classifications does this executive seizure of the steel industry fit? It is eliminated from the first by admission, for it is conceded that no congressional authorization exists for this seizure. * * *

Can it then be defended under flexible tests available to the second category? It seems clearly eliminated from that class because Congress has not left seizure of private property an open field but has covered it by three statutory policies inconsistent with this seizure. * * *

This leaves the current seizure to be justified only by the severe tests under the third grouping, where it can be supported only by any remainder of executive power after subtraction of such powers as Congress may have over the subject. In short, we can sustain the President only by holding that seizure of such strike-bound industries is within his domain and beyond control by Congress. * * *

The Solicitor General seeks the power of seizure in three clauses of the Executive Article, the first reading, "The executive Power shall be vested in a President of the United States of America." Lest I be thought to exaggerate, I quote the interpretation which his brief puts upon it: "In our view, this clause constitutes a grant of all the executive powers of which the Government is capable." If that be true, it is difficult to see why the forefathers bothered to add several specific items, including some trifling ones.

The example of such unlimited executive power that must have most impressed the forefathers was the prerogative exercised by George III, and the description of its evils in the Declaration of Independence leads me to doubt that they were creating their new Executive in his image. Continental European examples were no more appealing. And if we seek instruction from our own times, we can match it only from the executive powers in those governments we disparagingly describe as totalitarian. I cannot accept the view that this clause is a grant in bulk of all conceivable executive power but regard it as an allocation to the presidential office of the generic powers thereafter stated.

The clause on which the Government next relies is that "The President shall be Commander in Chief of the Army and Navy of the United States" * * *. [J]ust what authority goes with the [title] has plagued Presidential advisers who would not waive or narrow it by nonassertion yet cannot say where it begins or ends. It undoubtedly puts the Nation's armed forces under Presidential command. Hence, this loose appellation is sometimes advanced as support for any Presidential action, internal or external, involving use of force, the idea being that it vests power to do anything, anywhere, that can be done with an army or navy. * * *

There are indications that the Constitution did not contemplate that the title Commander in Chief *of the Army and Navy* will constitute him also Commander in Chief of the country, its industries and its inhabitants. He has no monopoly of "war powers," whatever they are. * * *

The third clause in which the Solicitor General finds seizure powers is that "he shall take Care that the Laws be faithfully executed * * * * " That authority must be matched against words of the Fifth Amendment that "No person shall be * * * deprived of life, liberty or property, without due process of law * * * * " One gives a governmental authority that reaches so far as there is law, the other gives a private right that authority shall go no farther. These signify about all there is of the principle that ours is a government of laws, not of men, and that we submit ourselves to rulers only if under rules.

The Solicitor General lastly grounds support of the seizure upon nebulous, inherent powers never expressly granted but said to have accrued to the office from the customs and claims of preceding administrations. The plea is for a resulting power to deal with a crisis or an emergency according to the necessities of the case, the unarticulated assumption being that necessity knows no law. * * *

The appeal, however, that we declare the existence of inherent powers *ex necessitate* to meet an emergency asks us to do what many think would be wise, although it is something the forefathers omitted. They knew what emergencies were, knew the pressures they engender for authoritative action, knew, too, how they afford a ready pretext for usurpation. We may also suspect that they suspected that emergency powers would tend to kindle emergencies. Aside from suspension of the privilege of the writ of habeas corpus in time of rebellion or invasion, when the public safety may require it [U.S. Const., Art. I, § 9, cl. 2], they made no express provision for exercise of extraordinary authority because of a crisis. I do not think we rightfully may so amend their work. * * *

In view of the ease, expedition and safety with which Congress can grant and has granted large emergency powers, certainly ample to embrace this crisis, I am quite unimpressed with the argument that we should affirm possession of them without statute. Such power either has no beginning or it has no end. If it exists, it need submit to no legal restraint. I am not alarmed that it would plunge us straightway into dictatorship, but it is at least a step in that wrong direction.

As to whether there is imperative necessity for such powers, it is relevant to note the gap that exists between the President's paper powers and his real powers. The Constitution does not disclose the measure of the actual controls wielded by the modern presidential office. That instrument must be understood as an Eighteenth-Century sketch of a government hoped for, not as a blueprint of the Government that is. Vast accretions of federal power, eroded from that reserved by the States, have magnified the scope of presidential activity. Subtle shifts take place in the centers of real power that do not show on the face of the Constitution.

Executive power has the advantage of concentration in a single head in whose choice the whole Nation has a part, making him the focus of public hopes and expectations. In drama, magnitude and finality his decisions so far overshadow any others that almost alone he fills the public eye and ear. No other personality in public life can begin to compete with him in access to the public mind through modern methods of communications. By his prestige as head of state and his influence upon public opinion he exerts a leverage upon those who are supposed to check and balance his power which often cancels their effectiveness.

Moreover, rise of the party system has made a significant extra-constitutional supplement to real executive power. No appraisal of his necessities is realistic which overlooks that he heads a political system as well as a legal system. Party loyalties and interests, sometimes more binding than law, extend his effective control into branches of government other than his own and he often may win, as a political leader, what he cannot command under the Constitution. * * *

But I have no illusion that any decision by this Court can keep power in the hands of Congress if it is not wise and timely in meeting its problems. A crisis that challenges the President equally, or perhaps primarily, challenges Congress. If not good law, there was worldly wisdom in the maxim attributed to Napoleon that "The tools belong to the man who can use them." We may say that power to legislate for emergencies belongs in the hands of Congress, but only Congress itself can prevent power from slipping through its fingers.

[We omit the concurring opinions of JUSTICE DOUGLAS, JUSTICE FRANKFURTER, JUSTICE CLARK (concurring only in the judgment), and JUSTICE BURTON.]

CHIEF JUSTICE VINSON, with whom JUSTICE REED and JUSTICE MINTON join, dissenting.

* * * A review of executive action demonstrates that our Presidents have on many occasions exhibited the leadership contemplated by the Framers when they made the President Commander in Chief, and imposed upon him the trust to "take Care that the Laws be faithfully executed." With or without explicit statutory authorization, Presidents have at such times dealt with national emergencies by acting promptly and resolutely to enforce legislative programs, at least to save those programs until Congress could act. Congress and the courts have responded to such executive initiative with consistent approval. * * *

Without declaration of war, President Lincoln took energetic action with the outbreak of the War Between the States. He summoned troops and paid them out of the Treasury without appropriation therefor. He proclaimed a naval blockade of the Confederacy and seized ships violating that blockade. Congress, far from denying the validity of these acts, gave them express approval. The most striking action of President Lincoln was the Emancipation Proclamation, issued in aid of the successful prosecution of the War Between the States, but wholly without statutory authority.

In an action furnishing a most apt precedent for this case, President Lincoln without statutory authority directed the seizure of rail and telegraph lines leading to Washington. Many months later, Congress recognized and confirmed the power of the President to seize railroads and telegraph lines and provided criminal penalties for interference with Government operation. * * *

President Hayes authorized the wide-spread use of federal troops during the Railroad Strike of 1877. President Cleveland also used the troops in the Pullman Strike of 1895 and his action is of special significance. No statute authorized this action. No call for help had issued from the Governor of Illinois; indeed Governor Altgeld disclaimed the need for supplemental forces. But the President's concern was that federal laws relating to the free flow of interstate commerce and the mails be continuously and faithfully executed without interruption. To further this aim his agents sought and obtained the injunction upheld by this Court in *In re Debs*, 158 U.S. 564 (1895). The Court scrutinized each of the steps taken by the President to insure execution of the "mass of legislation" dealing with commerce and the mails and gave his conduct full approval. Congress likewise took note of this use of Presidential power to forestall apparent obstacles to the faithful execution of the laws. By separate resolutions, both the Senate and the House commended the Executive's action.

President Theodore Roosevelt seriously contemplated seizure of Pennsylvania coal mines if a coal shortage necessitated such action. In his autobiography, President Roosevelt expounded the "Stewardship Theory" of Presidential power, stating that "the executive is subject only to the people, and, under the Constitution, bound to serve the people affirmatively in cases where the Constitution does not explicitly forbid him to render the service." * * *

Beginning with the Bank Holiday Proclamation and continuing through World War II, executive leadership and initiative were characteristic of President Franklin D. Roosevelt's administration. * * * [Before, as well as after, Pearl Harbor and the declaration of war] industrial concerns were seized to avert interruption of needed production. [After war was declared,] the President directed seizure of the Nation's coal mines to remove an obstruction to the effective prosecution of the war.* * *

This is but a cursory summary of executive leadership. But it amply demonstrates that Presidents have taken prompt action to enforce the laws and protect the country whether or not Congress happened to provide in advance for the particular method of execution. * * * [T]he fact that Congress and the courts have consistently recognized and given their support to such executive action indicates that such a power of seizure has been accepted throughout our history.

NOTES AND QUESTIONS ON THE STEEL SEIZURE CASE

1. *Different Approaches to Separation of Powers.* At least three different conceptual approaches can be gleaned from the opinions in the Steel Seizure Case.

Formalist Categories. Justice Black's opinion for the Court, joined by four other Justices (Douglas, Jackson, Frankfurter, and Burton), sets forth a straightforward categorical approach. Its *ratio decidendi* seems to be that because the President's action falls under the legislative power defined in Article I and under none of the executive powers defined in Article II, the President was acting *ultra vires* (beyond his authority). This approach has the advantages of simplicity, compliance with a logical structure grounded in the constitutional text, and a clear message for future Presidents.

Constrained Functionalism. A second approach is a functional approach, which seeks to draw constitutional lines flexibly so as to allow the President to take action in emergencies, but not so flexibly as to ignore congressionally directed procedures for action. This approach is articulated in the concurring opinions of Justices Frankfurter and Jackson. These Justices were leading legal process theorists of constitutional law, who aimed to recognize how *power was shared in the constitutional scheme.* Notice that the Jackson concurring opinion rejects the Vesting Clause thesis, on the ground that if Article II, § 1 were "a grant of all the executive powers * * * it is difficult to see why the forefathers bothered to add several specific items, including some trifling ones." Jackson also rejects the view that the President has inherent authority to carry out needed policy initiatives, for such power "has no beginning or it has no end."

Evolutive Functionalism—Constitutional Adverse Possession. A third approach is a lenient functional approach, which essentially defers to the political branch taking the challenged action, so long as it has some historical precedent. Chief Justice Vinson's dissenting opinion endorsed this power and the idea that congressional acquiescence provided concrete meaning to the vague constitutional clause in question. This is a form of constitutional "adverse possession": If the President openly exercises power, with the knowledge and presumably the acquiescence of Congress, then after a certain period of time, the Constitution comes to consider this power as truly the President's. Can this be defended, in light of the background and history of separation of powers?

2. *The Jackson Concurrence as Forerunner of the Vertical as Well as Functional Approach?* Although not so recognized at the time, Justice Jackson's concurring opinion has been the most influential of those penned in the Steel Seizure Case. Jackson was one of the Justices President Truman might have expected to vote his way in the Steel Seizure Case. On June 9, 1941, President Roosevelt had ordered the U.S. Army to seize and occupy a bomber/airplane factory belonging to the North American Aviation Company, based upon threats of a wildcat strike to close down the plant. The seizure was unprecedented in peacetime. Just days before his nomination to the Court, then-Attorney General Robert Jackson defended the seizure as a measure implicitly authorized by general congressional military authorizations (89 Cong. Rec. 3992). In his concurring opinion, Justice Jackson dismissed the Government's reliance upon earlier "partisan" statements.

Justice Jackson was probably inspired to resist the 1952 seizure because of his own experience as the Chief Prosecutor at the Nuremberg Trials of Nazi war criminals.[13] What he saw in his post-mortem of Nazi Germany was the ability of determined totalitarian groups to erode liberty by chipping away at the structural protections of citizens—namely, federalism, separation of powers, and the sanctity of private property. Professor Nourse thus reads Jackson as focusing on the risks of shifting power from Congress to the President. President's Truman's actions posed minoritarian risks to personal (and corporate) liberties, as well as majoritarian risks, as it dislocated the national economy without sanction of congressional legislation (Jackson's category 3). Jackson's category 1 is least problematic because the constituencies of both the President and Congress are mobilized. The resulting policy will be most legitimate given this arrangement. For Nourse and Jackson, the hardest cases will often be those of category 2, where Congress has not asserted its authority. The President's assertion of authority may pose majoritarian or minoritarian risks, but their significance will depend on the circumstances.

3. *Consequences of the Court's Decision.* When the Supreme Court granted quick certiorari in the Steel Seizure Case, the industry and union negotiators had just reached tentative agreement at the White House to settle the controversy and head off the strike. Upon learning that the Court had granted review and stayed the effect of a takeover, the steel industry backed away from the agreement, according to Maeva Marcus, *Truman and the Steel Seizure Case: The Limits of Presidential Power* 147–48 (1977). After the Court handed the industry its victory on June 2, the union struck for 53 days; with further pressure from the President, the union and industry

---

[13] The account in text draws from Edward Reisman, *Justice Robert Jackson's Road to Youngstown Sheet & Tube Co. v. Sawyer: The Impact of Nuremberg* (Georgetown Univ. Law Center, Feb. 20, 1990).

finally agreed upon a wage increase similar to that fixed by the Wage Stabilization Board months earlier. The strike was the longest and most costly ($400 million in lost wages, 21 million tons in lost steel output) in the country's history. Historian Maeva Marcus believes that the strike did not harm the war effort—but the President was sure that it would, and a leading history of his administration concludes that the strike did impair the war effort. 2 Harry Truman, *Memoirs* 478 (1956); David McCullough, *Truman* 901–02 (1992).

PROBLEM 2–2: DO THE PRESIDENT'S RECESS APPOINTMENTS VIOLATE THE CONSTITUTION?

Traditionally, the President has used "recess appointments" to fill executive offices while the Senate was away from Washington. The idea is simple: If the Senate is not available to provide its advice and consent, the President can fill the position, and the Senate can give its advice and consent when it returns. The Constitution specifically authorizes the President to make recess appointments which expire at the end of "the[ ] next Session [of Congress]." U.S. Const. art. II, § 2, cl. 3. Thousands of appointments, over the course of history, have been made in this way.

Consider the following problem, however. The President and the Senate are at odds, with the minority in the Senate blocking many executive branch appointments. To avoid this problem, the President uses his power, under the Constitution, to fill several existing vacancies during a Senate recess during the First Session of Congress (the first year of that Congress's two-year term).

Are these appointments constitutionally valid? Consider the text of Article II, § 2, cl. 3 of the Constitution: "The President shall have Power to fill up all Vacancies that may happen during the Recess of the Senate, by granting Commissions which shall expire at the End of their next Session." Can the Senate be said to have taken a "recess" if it adjourns "within" a session of Congress as opposed to "between" sessions? The Recess Appointments Clause says "the" Recess—which could be construed to cover only a recess between sessions. (A session occurs every two years based on the election of members to the House every two years). Also, can the President make recess appointments when the vacancy did not "happen" or arise during the recess? Thus, does the Recess Appointments Clause not apply when the appointment could have been made before the Recess? How would you answer these questions, based only on the text of the Constitution? (Do not limit your consideration to this one clause.)

Would it change your mind about the text if you knew the following about the historical practice: Presidents made appointments during intra-session recesses sparingly in the nineteenth century, and Congress adopted the Pay Act in 1863 to resist that practice. But in the twentieth century, as inter-session recesses became shorter and intra-session recesses more numerous and lengthy, Presidents made many more intra-recess appointments. Congress amended the Pay Act in 1940 to allow most of these appointees to be paid, and Presidents after 1940 made thousands of appointments during intra-session recesses, without any formal congressional pushback. As regards vacancies arising before the recesses where appointments were made, the story is similar—few such appointments before the Civil War, more appointments and some congressional pushback between the Civil War and World War II, and thousands of appointments after World War II, with no formal congressional pushback. How would Chief Justice Vinson and Justices Jackson and Black have addressed this problem based on their decisions in *Steel Seizure*? For the Court's extensive internal debate over how to evaluate the historical practice, compare Justice Breyer's opinion for the Court, with Justice Scalia's opinion concurring in the Court's judgment in *NLRB v. Noel Canning*, 134 S.Ct. 2550 (2014).

NOTE ON THE IMPERIAL PRESIDENCY

Although President Washington was usually solicitous of congressional opinions when he took either domestic or foreign affairs initiatives, subsequent Presidents operated more boldly in matters of military or foreign policy. Illustrating aggressive executive department initiatives carried out without close cooperation with Congress were President Jefferson's doubling the size of the country through his agreement to purchase the Louisiana Territory from France; the "Monroe Doctrine," directing the European powers to leave Western Hemisphere matters to the United States; President Polk's leading us into the Mexican-American War; President Lincoln's leadership during the Civil War, including the Emancipation Proclamation, military trials of civilians, and suspension of the writ of habeas corpus; President Andrew Johnson's defiance of the Reconstruction Congress; President Teddy Roosevelt's deployment of "gunboat diplomacy" to protect American interests in other Western Hemisphere nations; and President Wilson's role as a founder of the League of Nations (which the Congress then refused to permit our country to join).

The birth of a grandly named "Imperial Presidency" occurred during President Franklin Delano Roosevelt's New Deal, in which an exceptionally vigorous Chief Executive met the challenges of the Great Depression and World War II with an executive activism that threatened to eclipse the other branches of the national government, as well as the states. FDR's actions did not resolve, however, the limits of the President's power. As we saw above, it was Harry Truman who brought the President's power to constitutional challenge in his seizure of the steel mills. More recently, President George W. Bush exercised a vast amount of power in what was called the "War on Terror." The vigorous deployment of presidential power in the national security arena continued under President Barack Obama.

PROBLEM 2–3: DID THE OBAMA ADMINISTRATION'S BOMBING OF LIBYA CONSTITUTE "HOSTILITIES" FOR PURPOSES OF THE WAR POWERS RESOLUTION?

Between 1954 and 1975, the United States was involved in a civil war in Vietnam. There was never a congressionally declared "war," and our involvement came about through a series of presidential decisions. During the Nixon Administration, Congress grew restive with its marginal role and with the unproductive war effort. One result was the enactment in 1973, over President Nixon's veto, of the War Powers Resolution, Pub. L. No. 93–148, 87 Stat. 555 (1973), codified at 50 U.S.C. §§ 1541 et seq. The Resolution provides, in part, as follows:

WPR § 2, codified 50 U.S.C. § 1541. Purpose and policy

(a) **Congressional declaration.** It is the purpose of this joint resolution to fulfill the intent of the framers of the Constitution of the United States and insure that the collective judgment of both the Congress and the President will apply to the introduction of United States Armed Forces into hostilities, or into situations where imminent involvement in hostilities is clearly indicated by the circumstances, and to the continued use of such forces in hostilities or in such situations.

(b) **Congressional legislative power under necessary and proper clause.** Under Article I, section 8, of the Constitution, it is specifically provided that the Congress shall have the power to make all laws necessary and proper for carrying into execution, not only its own powers but also all other powers vested by the Constitution in the Government of the United States, or in any department or officer thereof.

(c) **Presidential executive power as Commander-in-Chief; limitation.** The constitutional powers of the President as Commander-in-Chief to introduce United States Armed Forces into hostilities, or into situations where imminent involvement in hostilities is clearly indicated by the circumstances, are exercised only pursuant to (1) a declaration of war, (2) specific statutory authorization, or (3) a national emergency created by attack upon the United States, its territories or possessions, or its armed forces.

WPR § 3, codified 50 U.S.C. § 1542. Consultation; initial and regular consultations

The President in every possible instance shall consult with Congress before introducing United States Armed Forces into hostilities or into situations where imminent involvement in hostilities is clearly indicated by the circumstances, and after every such introduction shall consult regularly with the Congress until United States Armed Forces are no longer engaged in hostilities or have been removed from such situations.

WPR § 4, codified 50 U.S.C. § 1543. Reporting requirement

(a) Written report; time of submission; circumstances necessitating submission; information reported. In the absence of a declaration of war, in any case in which United States Armed Forces are introduced—

   (1) into hostilities or into situations where imminent involvement in hostilities is clearly indicated by the circumstances;

   (2) into the territory, airspace or waters of a foreign nation, while equipped for combat, except for deployments which relate solely to supply, replacement, repair, or training of such forces; or

   (3) in numbers which substantially enlarge United States Armed Forces equipped for combat already located in a foreign nation;

the President shall submit within 48 hours to the Speaker of the House of Representatives and to the President pro tempore of the Senate a report, in writing, setting forth—

   (A) the circumstances necessitating the introduction of United States Armed Forces;

   (B) the constitutional and legislative authority under which such introduction took place; and

   (C) the estimated scope and duration of the hostilities or involvement. * * *

WPR § 5, codified 50 U.S.C. § 1544. Congressional action * * *

(b) Termination of use of United States Armed Forces; exceptions; extension period. Within sixty calendar days after a report is submitted or is required to be submitted pursuant to section 4(a)(1) [50 U.S.C § 1543(a)(1)], whichever is earlier, the President shall terminate any use of United States Armed Forces with respect to which such report was submitted (or required to be submitted), unless the Congress (1) has declared war or has enacted a specific authorization for such use of United States Armed Forces, (2) has extended by law such sixty-day period, or (3) is physically unable to meet as a result of an armed attack upon the United States. Such sixty-day period shall be extended for not more than an additional thirty days if the President determines and certifies to the Congress in writing that unavoidable military necessity respecting the safety of United States Armed Forces requires the continued use of such armed forces in the course of bringing about a prompt removal of such forces.

(c) Concurrent resolution for removal by President of United States Armed Forces. Notwithstanding subsection (b), at any time that United States Armed Forces are engaged in hostilities outside the territory of the United States, its possession and territories without a declaration of war or specific statutory authorization, such forces shall be removed by the President if the Congress so directs by concurrent resolution. * * *

[**Public Law 98–164, § 1013 (1983), codified at 50 U.S.C. § 1546a**, sets forth an expedited congressional procedures for considering action pursuant to § 5(b).]

WPR § 8, codified 50 U.S.C. § 1547. Interpretation of joint resolution * * *

(a) Inferences from any law or treaty. Authority to introduce United States Armed Forces into hostilities or into situations wherein involvement in hostilities is clearly indicated by the circumstances shall not be inferred—

(1) from any provision of law (whether or not in effect before November 7, 1973), including any provision contained in any appropriation Act, unless such provision specifically authorizes the introduction of United States Armed Forces into hostilities or into such situations and states that it is intended to constitute specific statutory authorization within the meaning of this chapter; or

(2) from any treaty heretofore or hereafter ratified unless such treaty is implemented by legislation specifically authorizing the introduction of United States Armed Forces into hostilities or into such situations and stating that it is intended to constitute specific statutory authorization within the meaning of this chapter.

(b) Joint headquarters operations of high-level military commands. Nothing in this chapter shall be construed to require any further specific statutory authorization to permit members of United States Armed Forces to participate jointly with members of the armed forces of one or more foreign countries in the headquarters operations of high-level military commands which were established prior to November 7, 1973, and pursuant to the United Nations Charter or any treaty ratified by the United States prior to such date.

(c) Introduction of United States Armed Forces. For purposes of this joint resolution, the term "introduction of United States Armed Forces" includes the assignment of members of such armed forces to command, coordinate, participate in the movement of, or accompany the regular or irregular military forces of any foreign country or government when such military forces are engaged, or there exists an imminent threat that such forces will become engaged, in hostilities.

––––––––––

Acting pursuant to U.N. Security Council Resolutions 1970 and 1973, President Barack Obama mobilized American military forces on March 19, 2011, to prevent a humanitarian catastrophe and address the threat posed to international peace and security by the crisis in Libya and to protect the people of Libya from the Qadhafi regime.[14] On March 21, the President notified Congress that American and allied aircraft had commenced airstrikes against the regime; American air support was essential to create a "no fly zone" over Libya, thereby preventing Qadhafi's air force from killing civilians and crushing the insurrection. The Office of Legal Counsel (OLC) advised the President that he had the authority to act unilaterally (i.e., without a congressional declaration of war or other authorization) in this case of "limited operations." See Caroline D. Krass, Principal Deputy Assistant Attorney General (OLC), Memorandum to Eric H. Holder Jr., Attorney General: *Authority to Use Military Force in Libya* (April 1, 2011) *("Hostilities,"* 260–81). None of the leaders in Congress disputed the President's authority asserted by OLC— but questions were raised about the strategy and scope of the operation.

On June 14, House Speaker John Boehner informed the President that the American participation in Libyan hostilities was approaching the 90-day point (60 days plus a necessity extension of 30 days)—after which the WPR § 5(b) requires the President either to withdraw Americans from the hostilities or to secure congressional authorization for their continuing role. Boehner requested that the President take one of these courses of action—or explain why he was not complying with the WPR. Did he believe it was unconstitutional, as the Bush-Cheney Administration probably believed?

The President responded the next day, explaining that the United States had transferred command to NATO and that U.S. involvement had assumed a supporting role in the coalition's efforts. Since April 4, U.S. participation consisted of: (1) intelligence and logistical support to NATO; (2) deployment of aircraft in support of the no-fly zone; and (3) use of unmanned aerial vehicles (drones) "against a limited set of clearly defined targets." The President characterized American involvement as supporting "international efforts to protect civilians and civilian populated areas from the actions of the Qadhafi regime." The President emphasized that, with the exception of operations to "rescue the crew of a

––––––––––

[14] This problem draws from the excellent collection of primary materials on "Hostilities," assembled by Professor Trevor W. Morrison and published in 1 Journal of Law (1 Pub. L. Misc.) 233–311 (2011). See also Trevor W. Morrison, *Libya, "Hostilities," the Office of Legal Counsel, and the Process of Executive Branch Legal Interpretation,* 124 Harv. L. Rev. F. 62 (2011).

U.S. aircraft on March 21, 2011, the United States ha[d] deployed no ground forces to Libya." Letter from President Barack Obama to House Speaker John Boehner and Senate President Pro Tempore Daniel Inouye (June 15, 2011).

In a report accompanying the letter, the White House explained its view that the American involvement did not constitute "hostilities" under WPR §§ 4(a)(1) and 5(b):

> The President is of the view that the current U.S. military operations in Libya are consistent with the War Powers Resolution * * * because U.S. military operations are distinct from the kind of "hostilities" contemplated by the Resolution's 60 day termination provision. U.S. forces are playing a constrained and supporting role in a multinational coalition, [authorized by] a United Nations Security Council Resolution * * * to protect civilians and civilian populated areas under attack or threat of attack * * *. U.S. operations do not involve sustained fighting or active exchanges of fire with hostile forces, nor do they involve the presence of U.S. ground troops, U.S. casualties or a serious threat thereof, or any significant chance of escalation into a conflict characterized by those factors.

Because the involvement did not constitute "hostilities" under § 4(a)(1), the Administration was not bound by § 5(b)'s requirement of termination without a congressional authorization.

There were many academic critics of the President's interpretation. Jack Goldsmith, former head of OLC (2003–04), made a number of arguments supporting the proposition that the actions in Libya constituted "hostilities" under the WPR.[15] Although Congress did not define "hostilities," the relevant committee report said that Congress substituted "hostilities" for "armed conflict" without intending to change its meaning. Accord, *Presidential Power to Use the Armed Forces Abroad Without Statutory Authorization*, 4A Op. O.L.C. 185, 193–94 (1980) (OLC opinion that "hostilities" do not include defensive actions).

Additionally, presidential practice supported a broader reading, according to Goldsmith. In 1995, President Clinton submitted four different WPR reports after ordering bombing missions in Bosnia. Finally, Goldsmith argued that the President's actions fell under § 8(c), which brings within the WPR "the assignment of members of such armed forces to command, coordinate, participate in the movement of, or accompany the regular or irregular military forces of any foreign country or government when such military forces are engaged, or there exists an

---

[15] Goldsmith, *Problems with the Obama Administration's War Powers Resolution Theory*, Lawfare, June 16, 2011, http://www.lawfareblog.com/2011/06/problems-with-the-obama-administration%e2%80%99s-war-powers-resolution-theory-2/ (viewed Dec. 1, 2012).

imminent threat that such forces will become engaged, in hostilities." American "support" of the NATO campaign against Qadhafi fell under this provision, Goldsmith maintained.

The Goldsmith arguments were being made within the Obama Administration. Acting OLC Director Krass and Attorney General Holder advised the President that the Libyan operations were in fact "hostilities" as to which the WPR applied and should be followed. See Charlie Savage & Mark Landler, *White House Defends Continuing U.S. Role in Libya Operation*, N.Y. Times, June 15, 2011. Taking a contrary position were State Department Legal Adviser Harold Koh and White House Counsel Robert Bauer. All the opinions were presented to the President, a former professor of constitutional law, who made the final decision. Consider Koh's congressional testimony. Before you read it, jot down your thoughts, based upon reading the statute and the Goldsmith arguments.

Testimony by Legal Adviser Harold Hongju Koh, U.S. Department of State, On Libya and War Powers Before the Senate Foreign Relations Committee
June 28, 2011.

* * * [T]he operative term, "hostilities," is an ambiguous standard, which is nowhere defined in the statute. * * * Indeed, the legislative history of the Resolution makes clear there was no fixed view on exactly what the term "hostilities" would encompass. Members of Congress understood that the term was vague, but specifically declined to give it more concrete meaning, in part to avoid unduly hampering future Presidents by making the Resolution a "one size fits all" straitjacket * * *.

* * * Because the War Powers Resolution represented a broad compromise between competing [constitutional views], the question whether a particular set of facts constitutes "hostilities" for purposes of the Resolution has been determined more by interbranch practice than by a narrow parsing of dictionary definitions. Both branches have recognized that different situations may call for different responses, and that an overly mechanical reading of the statute could lead to unintended automatic cutoffs of military involvement in cases where more flexibility is required. * * *

[Koh recounted the legislative history of the term "hostilities." In 1975, Congress asked the State and Defense Departments to provide their "best understanding" of the term "hostilities." Monroe Leigh, then State Department Legal Adviser and Martin Hoffmann, Defense Department General Counsel responded that the executive branch understood "hostilities" to occur when "U.S. armed forces are actively engaged in exchanges of fire with opposing units of hostile forces." Letter from State

Department Legal Adviser Monroe Leigh and Department of Defense General Counsel Martin R. Hoffmann to Chairman Clement J. Zablocki (June 5, 1975) (reprinted in *"Hostilities,"* 251–55). Koh argued that the Leigh-Hoffmann letter suggested that "hostilities" did not include missions that were "limited," such as "sporadic military or paramilitary attacks," where the risk of escalation is low.]

[T]he Executive Branch has [emphasized] the distinction between full military encounters and more constrained operations, stating that "intermittent military engagements" do not require withdrawal of forces under the Resolution's 60-day rule. In the thirty-six years since Leigh and Hoffmann provided their analysis, the Executive Branch has repeatedly articulated and applied these foundational understandings. The President was thus operating within this longstanding tradition of Executive Branch interpretation when he relied on these understandings in his legal explanation to Congress on June 15, 2011.

In light of this historical practice, a combination of four factors present in Libya suggests that the current situation does not constitute the kind of "hostilities" envisioned by the War Powers Resolution's 60-day automatic pullout provision.

First, the *mission* is limited: By Presidential design, U.S. forces are playing a constrained and supporting role in a NATO-led multinational civilian protection operation, which is implementing a U.N. Security Council Resolution tailored to that limited purpose. This is a very unusual set of circumstances, not found in any of the historic situations in which the "hostilities" question was previously debated, from the deployment of U.S. armed forces to Lebanon, Grenada, and El Salvador in the early 1980s, to the fighting with Iran in the Persian Gulf in the late 1980s, to the use of ground troops in Somalia in 1993. Of course, NATO forces as a whole are more deeply engaged in Libya than are U.S. forces, but the War Powers Resolution's 60-day pullout provision was designed to address the activities of the latter.[13]

---

[13] A definitional section of the War Powers Resolution, 8(c), gives rise to a duty of Congressional notification, but not termination, upon the "assignment" of U.S. forces to command, coordinate, participate in the movement of, or accompany foreign forces that are themselves in hostilities. Section 8(c) is textually linked (through the term "introduction of United States Armed Forces") not to the "hostilities" language in section 4 that triggers the automatic pullout provision in section 5(b), but rather, to a different clause later down in that section that triggers a reporting requirement. According to the Senate report, the purpose of section 8(c) was "to prevent secret, unauthorized military support activities [such as the secret assignment of U.S. military "advisers" to South Vietnam and Laos] and to prevent a repetition of many of the most controversial and regrettable actions in Indochina," S. Rep. No. 93–220, at 24 (1973)—actions that scarcely resemble NATO operations such as this one. Indeed, absurd results could ensue if section 8(c) were read to trigger the 60-day clock, as that could require termination of the "assignment" of even a single member of the U.S. military to assist a foreign government force, unless Congress passed legislation to authorize that one-person assignment. Moreover, section 8(c) must be read together with the immediately preceding section of the Resolution, 8(b). By grandfathering in pre-existing "high-level military commands," section 8(b) not only shows

Second, the *exposure* of our armed forces is limited: To date, our operations have not involved U.S. casualties or a threat of significant U.S. casualties. Nor do our current operations involve active exchanges of fire with hostile forces, and members of our military have not been involved in significant armed confrontations or sustained confrontations of any kind with hostile forces. Prior administrations have not found the 60-day rule to apply even in situations where significant fighting plainly did occur, as in Lebanon and Grenada in 1983 and Somalia in 1993.[15]

By highlighting this point, we in no way advocate a legal theory that is indifferent to the loss of non-American lives. But here, there can be little doubt that the greatest threat to Libyan civilians comes not from NATO or the United States military, but from Qadhafi. The Congress that adopted the War Powers Resolution was principally concerned with the safety of *U.S. forces*, and with the risk that the President would entangle them in an overseas conflict from which they could not readily be extricated. In this instance, the absence of U.S. ground troops, among other features of the Libya operation, significantly reduces both the risk to U.S. forces and the likelihood of a protracted entanglement that Congress may find itself practically powerless to end.

Third, the *risk of escalation* is limited: U.S. military operations have not involved the presence of U.S. ground troops, or any significant chance of escalation into a broader conflict characterized by a large U.S. ground presence, major casualties, sustained active combat, or expanding geographical scope. Contrast this with the 1991 Desert Storm operation,

---

that Congress knew how to reference NATO operations when it wanted to, but also suggests that Congress recognized that NATO operations are generally less likely to raise the kinds of policy concerns that animated the Resolution. If anything, the international framework of cooperation within which this military mission is taking place creates a far greater risk that by withdrawing prematurely from Libya, as opposed to staying the course, we would generate the very foreign policy problems that the War Powers Resolution was meant to counteract: for example, international condemnation and strained relationships with key allies.

[15] In Lebanon, the Reagan Administration argued that U.S. armed forces were not in "hostilities," though there were roughly 1,600 U.S. marines equipped for combat on a daily basis and roughly 2,000 more on ships and bases nearby; U.S. marine positions were attacked repeatedly; and four marines were killed and several dozen wounded in those attacks. *See* Richard F. Grimmett, Congressional Research Service, *The War Powers Resolution: After Thirty Six Years* 13–15 (Apr. 22, 2010); John H. Kelly, *Lebanon: 1982–1984, in U.S. and Russian Policymaking with respect to the Use of Force* 85, 96–99 (Jeremy R. Azrael & Emily A. Payin eds., 1996). In Grenada, the Administration did not acknowledge that "hostilities" had begun under the War Powers Resolution after 1,900 members of the U.S. armed forces had landed on the island, leading to combat that claimed the lives of nearly twenty Americans and wounded nearly 100 more. *See* Grimmett, *supra*, at 15; Ben Bradlee, Jr., *A Chronology on Grenada*, Boston Globe, Nov. 6, 1983. In Somalia, 25,000 troops were initially dispatched by the President, without Congressional authorization and without reference to the War Powers Resolution, as part of Operation Restore Hope. *See* Grimmett, *supra*, at 27. By May 1993, several thousand U.S. forces remained in the country or on ships offshore, including a Quick Reaction Force of some 1,300 marines. During the summer and into the fall of that year, ground combat led to the deaths of more than two dozen U.S. soldiers. John L. Hirsch & Robert B. Oakley, *Somalia and Operation Restore Hope: Reflections on Peacemaking and Peacekeeping* 112, 124–27 (1995).

which although also authorized by a United Nations Security Council Resolution, presented "over 400,000 [U.S.] troops in the area—the same order of magnitude as Vietnam at its peak—together with concomitant numbers of ships, planes, and tanks." Prior administrations have found an absence of "hostilities" under the War Powers Resolution in situations ranging from Lebanon to Central America to Somalia to the Persian Gulf tanker controversy, although members of the United States Armed Forces were repeatedly engaged by the other side's forces and sustained casualties in volatile geopolitical circumstances, in some cases running a greater risk of possible escalation than here.

Fourth and finally, the *military means* we are using are limited: This situation does not present the kind of "full military engagement[ ] with which the [War Powers] Resolution is primarily concerned." The violence that U.S. armed forces have directly inflicted or facilitated after the handoff to NATO has been modest in terms of its frequency, intensity, and severity. The air-to-ground strikes conducted by the United States in Libya are a far cry from the bombing campaign waged in Kosovo in 1999, which involved much more extensive and aggressive aerial strike operations led by U.S. armed forces. The U.S. contribution to NATO is likewise far smaller than it was in the Balkans in the mid-1990s, where U.S. forces contributed the vast majority of aircraft and air strike sorties to an operation that lasted over two and a half years, featured repeated violations of the no-fly zone and episodic firefights with Serb aircraft and gunners, and paved the way for approximately 20,000 U.S. ground troops. Here, by contrast, the bulk of U.S. contributions to the NATO effort has been providing intelligence capabilities and refueling assets. A very significant majority of the overall sorties are being flown by our coalition partners, and the overwhelming majority of strike sorties are being flown by our partners. American strikes have been confined, on an as-needed basis, to the suppression of enemy air defenses to enforce the no-fly zone, and to limited strikes by Predator unmanned aerial vehicles against discrete targets in support of the civilian protection mission; since the handoff to NATO, the total number of U.S. munitions dropped has been a tiny fraction of the number dropped in Kosovo. All NATO targets, moreover, have been clearly linked to the Qadhafi regime's systematic attacks on the Libyan population and populated areas, with target sets engaged only when strictly necessary and with maximal precision.

Had any of these elements been absent in Libya, or present in different degrees, a different legal conclusion might have been drawn. But the unusual confluence of these four factors, in an operation that was expressly designed to be limited—limited in mission, exposure of U.S. troops, risk of escalation, and military means employed—led the President to conclude that the Libya operation did not fall within the War Powers Resolution's automatic 60-day pullout rule. * * *

NOTES AND QUESTIONS ON THE LIBYAN BOMBING CONTROVERSY

Did the Legal Adviser's argument satisfy your doubts about the President's compliance with the War Powers Resolution? Consider the following materials.

1. *Legislative History of the WPR.* Is it relevant that a lead sponsor of the WPR, Senator Jacob Javits, testified that "President Johnson's ordering of American planes into action against North Vietnam" would have been "hostilities"? *"Hostilities,"* 240 (reprinting congressional testimony). Senator Javits also opined that President Kennedy's sending airplanes over Cuba to take pictures in 1962 was not a situation where "hostilities" or "imminent hostilities" were present—but American inspection of Soviet ships sailing to Cuba would have constituted "imminent hostilities." *Id.* at 240–41.

The report of the House Committee on Foreign Affairs explained that the subcommittee substituted the word *hostilities* for *armed conflict*, "because it was considered to be somewhat broader in scope. In addition to a situation in which fighting actually has begun, *hostilities* also encompasses a state of confrontation in which no shots have been fired but where there is a clear and present danger of armed conflict. '*Imminent hostilities*' denotes a situation in which there is a clear potential either for such a state of confrontation or for actual armed conflict." House Comm. on Foreign Affairs, Report (June 15, 1973), excerpted in *"Hostilities,"* 247–48. In footnote six of his testimony (omitted in our excerpt), Koh complained that "the report provided no clear direction on what either term was understood to mean."

2. *Executive Understanding of "Hostilities."* After the WPR was passed over his veto, President Nixon challenged its constitutionality. See President Nixon's Statement regarding the Veto of the War Powers Resolution, Oct. 24, 173. One of his objections focused on WPR § 5(b), compelling the President to withdraw troops introduced into "hostilities or imminent threat of hostilities" after 60–90 days if Congress failed to pass legislation. President Nixon argued this provision was unconstitutional because it "allowed presidential powers to lapse without affirmative congressional action."[16] President Nixon's concerns were echoed by President Reagan's legal adviser in his testimony before Congress on the WPR.[17] Legal Adviser Koh did not make this argument in his testimony—in part because he and others in the Obama Administration believe the WPR to be constitutional. See Harold H. Koh, *The National Security Constitution: Sharing Power After the Iran-Contra Affair* (1990).

---

[16] See Ellen C. Collier, *The War Powers Resolution: Fifteen Years of Experience*, reprinted in *War Powers: Origins, Purposes, and Applications: Hearings before the Subcommittee on Arms, Control, Int'l Security, and Science of the House Committee on Foreign Affairs*, 100th Cong. 249 (Appendix 4) (1988).

[17] See *War Powers, Libya, and State-Sponsored Terrorism: Hearings Before the Subcommittee on Arms Control, Int'l Security and Science of the H. Comm. on Foreign Affairs*, 99th Cong. (1986) (testimony of Legal Adviser Abraham D. Sofaer).

Consider presidential practice. Between 1973 and 1988, Presidents submitted 19 reports under the WPR, but only one cited § 4(a)(1). Collier, *War Powers Resolution,* 240. The lone report was sent to Congress by President Ford after forces were already being withdrawn from the Mayaguez (a ship). However, Congress itself interpreted the requirements of § 4(a)(1) as having been met on August 29, 1983 when it passed a joint resolution to authorize the continued participation of U.S. troops in Lebanon for 18 months under the Reagan Administration. *Id.*

The Leigh-Hoffman Letter cited by Koh put forth a working definition of "hostilities" as "a situation in which units of the U.S. armed forces are actively engaged in exchanges of fire with opposing units of hostile forces, and 'imminent hostilities' [is] considered to mean a situation in which there is a serious risk from hostile fire to the safety of United States forces. In our view, neither term necessarily encompasses irregular or infrequent violence which may occur in a particular area." They conceded that under this definition the April 30, 1975 report on the evacuation of Saigon referred to "at least one incident of hostilities" and that "in the Cambodia evacuation * * * an imminent involvement in hostilities may have existed." They agreed that the suppression of North Vietnamese anti-aircraft fire would constitute hostilities, but that ground forces returning unidentified fire were not hostilities, unless there were sustained and serious engagement.[18]

3.   *The Understanding of "Hostilities" in International Law.* If the Obama Administration was not engaged in hostilities in Libya, was it violating international law when civilians were killed? Given that treaties are incorporated into U.S. domestic law, were these actions a violation of U.S. laws other than the War Powers Resolution? Professor O'Connell maintains that "the U.S. had better be involved in hostilities or else our forces are engaged in unlawful killing" due to the use of missiles and bombs. See Mary Ellen O'Connell, *U.S. Strains Credibility on Its Libya Role* (June 21, 2011). Professor O'Connell argues that international law only justifies the unintended death of civilians and killing without warning when there is value to a military objective. Such killings are not tolerated in peacetime law enforcement.[19]

---

[18] During his congressional testimony on application of the WPR, President Reagan's Legal Advisor Abraham Sofaer conceded that the introduction of armed aircraft to conduct strikes on Libyan targets triggered the WPR's consultation and reporting provisions. See *War Powers, Libya, and State-Sponsored Terrorism: Hearings Before the Subcommittee on Arms Control, Int'l Security and Science of the H. Comm. on Foreign Affairs*, 99th Cong. (1986) (testimony of Legal Adviser Abraham D. Sofaer). "Where a military action constitutes the introduction of U.S. forces into actual or imminent hostilities for the purpose of the consultation requirement of section 3 of the Resolution, the action also triggers the reporting requirement of section 4. In the case of the April 14 [Libyan] operation, the President submitted a full report consistent with the War Powers Resolution." *Id.* If the targeted air strikes, which Sofaer classified as defensive, anti-terrorism measures taken against a state-sponsor of anti-American acts, met the definition of actual or imminent hostilities, would President Obama's intervention in Libya also fit that definition?

[19] In considering this argument, consider that "[i]nternational law and international agreements of the United States are law of the United States and supreme over the law of the several States." See Restatement (Third) of Foreign Relations Law § 111 (1987). According to the

POSTSCRIPT TO THE LIBYAN BOMBING CONTROVERSY

Like most legal issues in the modern regulatory state, this one did not generate a Supreme Court opinion. After the United States and NATO established and maintained a no-fly zone by early April, General Qadhafi's regime steadily lost support to the rebels, who overthrew and killed the General in October 2011. The speedy end of the conflict mooted the WPR dispute. Note that the Obama Administration took a firm and now public legal position, while Congress did very little pushing back before General Qadhafi's demise. Was there anything Congress could have done after the fact? Does this explain the prevalent opinion among long-time Washington insiders that the War Powers Act was written for a particular conflict— Vietnam—and that it has largely become a dead letter over time, both because of the changes in the nature of warfare and because Congress has little real incentive, and it is often impracticable, to demand that troops be brought home no matter the nature of the conflict?

3. INTRODUCTION TO AGENCY STATUTORY IMPLEMENTATION

Since the Founding, the President had agents to deal with the economy, national defense, and foreign affairs. Formal departments under the direct supervision of the President were created early on in our history. By the end of the nineteenth century, however, Congress was creating more varied entities and bureaus to address national problems. In 1887, the Interstate Commerce Commission (ICC) was established to address railroad regulation. In 1914, Congress created the Federal Trade Commission (FTC) to regulate unfair competition. Other agencies followed soon thereafter, even during the relatively conservative period of the 1920s: the United States Shipping Board in 1916, the Federal Power Commission in 1920, and the Federal Radio Commission (predecessor to the Federal Communications Commission) in 1929. These were among the first modern federal independent agencies, bureaucracies set up outside the formal departments of the executive branch and with their own responsibilities for adjudication and rulemaking. Geoffrey P. Miller, *Independent Agencies,* 1986 Sup. Ct. Rev. 41.

International Committee of the Red Cross, "strong prevailing legal opinion" defines international armed conflict as "exist[ing] whenever there is *resort to armed force between two or more states*" and non-international armed conflict exists whenever there is *"protracted armed confrontations* occurring between governmental armed forces and the forces of one or more armed groups. . . ." See International Committee of the Red Cross (ICRC), *How is the Term "Armed Conflict" Defined in International Humanitarian Law?* Opinion Paper, March 2008, at 5, available at http://www.icrc.org/eng/assets/files/other/opinion-paper-armed-conflict.pdf (viewed Jan. 2014). Similarly, the *Dictionary of the International Law of Armed Conflict* defines hostilities to be "acts of violence by a belligerent against an enemy in order to put an end to his resistance and impose obedience." See P. Verri, *Dictionary of the International Law of Armed Conflict* 57 (Geneva, ICRC 1992).

During FDR's New Deal, Congress established an unprecedented array of new agencies. It was during the New Deal that the Securities and Exchange Commission (SEC) was created to prevent fraud and abuse in financial markets. The Federal Deposit Insurance Corporation (FDIC) was also a product of this period, an agency which now insures deposits in federally chartered banks to prevent runs on banks. So, too, during this period, the National Labor Relations Board (NLRB) was established as an independent entity outside the Labor Department to prevent labor strife and unfair labor practices, which were fairly common in this period of high unemployment and restrictions on labor's formal permission to strike. Since then, both Republican and Democratic Presidents have sponsored various agencies and boards throughout the government.

As independent and new executive department agencies proliferated, critics assailed the inadequacies of agency procedure and the lack of judicial review. The primary fear was that important property rights were being stripped away without proper procedural safeguards, such as trial-like hearings and meaningful judicial review. In 1945, after years of pressure from the American Bar Association, legal academics, and regulated industries, the Attorney General endorsed legislation standardizing administrative procedure thus giving birth to one of the super-statutes of the twentieth century: the Administrative Procedure Act of 1946 (APA), 60 Stat. 237, codified as amended at 5 U.S.C. §§ 551–59, 701–06 (Appendix 2; see Chapter 7). The APA defines and regulates the process by which executive and independent agencies generate "rules" and "orders," which are the kind of "quasi-legislative" and "quasi-judicial" powers that the Court referred to in *Humphrey's Executor.*

A. AGENCY TOOLS FOR IMPLEMENTING STATUTES

What regulatory tools does an agency have to implement statute(s) it is charged with enforcing? As Professor (now Dean) M. Elizabeth Magill argues, in *Agency Choice of Policymaking Form,* 71 U. Chi. L. Rev. 1383 (2004), agencies always have a choice of instruments by which to seek compliance with statutes and to influence (and usually dominate) the evolving interpretation of statutes. See also Peter L. Strauss, *The Rulemaking Continuum,* 41 Duke L. J. 1463 (1992) (very useful analysis of different kinds of "rules" agencies generate). Consider the different powers available to agencies, starting with those powers that must be granted explicitly by statute.

Substantive/Legislative Rulemaking. Substantive, or legislative, rules are like statutes, for they not only announce policy but give it legal force. These rules carry the force of law and, typically, violations of substantive rules can be subject to sanctions. This is theoretically the most powerful tool for agency regulation, because rules can set forth statutory requirements in greater detail, and violators may be subject to direct sanctions. Under most circumstances, people and corporations want to avoid even the possibility of legal sanctions, and part of your job as a lawyer is to advise clients (whether the agency itself or a regulated entity) as to what "the law" (including agency rules) requires and what the penalties are for noncompliance.

This powerful tool has its limitations, some of which will be explored later in this section and in Chapter 7, § 1 where we introduce administrative law in more detail. Most important, Congress must delegate to agencies lawmaking authority for the rules to have the force of law, and the APA sets forth an arduous process for such rulemaking. In this process, the agency must publish notice of proposed rules in the Federal Register, 5 U.S.C. § 553(b), followed by the opportunity for interested persons to submit (usually written) comments on the proposed rules, 5 U.S.C. § 553(c), which may be followed by judicial review at the behest of effected persons or companies. *Id.* §§ 701–06.

Not all agencies have this power. For example, Congress has never vested the EEOC with substantive rulemaking authority to enforce Title VII, cf. 42 U.S.C. § 2000e–12(a), though the EEOC does have substantive rulemaking authority in administering the Age Discrimination in Employment Act and part of the Americans with Disabilities Act. Other agencies rely on rulemaking as their primary mode of regulation, especially the Environmental Protection Agency (EPA), as well as the Federal Communications Commission (FCC), the Securities and Exchange Commission (SEC), the National Highway Traffic Safety Administration (NHTSA), the Occupational Safety & Health Administration (OSHA), and the Federal Energy Regulatory Commission (FERC). Because Congress has invested each of these agencies with legislative rulemaking authority, which each has deployed sometimes aggressively, they are considered more powerhouse agencies (i.e., more feared and respected) than the EEOC.

Agency Adjudication. Courts are not the only places for adjudication; in fact, much more American adjudication occurs in agencies than in courts. An agency may charge a person or company with a statutory violation; if the administrative law judge finds culpability, she may direct sanctions. This is a retail approach (isolating rulebreakers) that might complement the wholesale approach of legislative rulemaking. Note that the possibility of adjudication is also a powerful regulatory tool: the agency can build a case against an apparent lawbreaker, present some or all of its evidence to its attorneys or officers, and usually exact an agreement between the agency and the lawbreaker where the latter agrees to some kind of restitution and commitment to not violate the statute again.

Again, there are limitations. Congress must delegate the capacity to issue adjudicative orders having the force of law to the agency. If the enabling statute calls for decision "on the record after opportunity for an agency hearing," 5 U.S.C. §§ 554(a) & 556(a), the agency must provide particularized notice to the affected person or company and allow it to present its "case or defense by oral or documentary evidence, to submit rebuttal evidence, and to conduct such cross-examination as may be required for a full and true disclosure of facts." 5 U.S.C. § 556(d). The agency's decision must be based on the trial-type record and supported by reliable, probative, and substantial evidence. 5 U.S.C. § 557. Even more informal adjudications carry with them some judicial-like procedures, as demanded by the Due Process Clause. See *Mathews v. Eldridge* (Chapter 7, § 2). This is an expensive way to enforce the statute, though the costs can be reduced if the agency is able to settle before initiating charges (unfortunately the benefits can also then be reduced, especially if the settlement is secret).

As with legislative rulemaking, Congress has not delegated formal adjudication authority to the EEOC, but it has done so for other important agencies. The NLRB has adjudication authority, though it must go to court to enforce its orders. The Board also has rulemaking authority but has chosen to enforce the labor statute mainly through adjudication—a choice within the agency's discretion. In this respect, the NLRB is something of a relic from times past. In the 1950s, agency enforcement was primarily through adjudication, but since the 1970s it has been overwhelmingly through legislative rulemaking, especially by newer agencies such as the EPA, OSHA, and NHTSA.

Initiation of Litigation in Court. Agencies can bring their own lawsuits to enforce the statute they are charged with implementing if Congress has given them litigation authority. See Office of Legal Counsel, *The Attorney General's Role as Chief Litigator for the United States,* 6 Op. O.L.C. 47, 48 (1982) (by statute and custom, the Attorney General has plenary authority over federal litigation, "absent clear legislative directives to the contrary"). The main advantage of this authority is that it gives the agency a path toward powerful judicial remedies— preliminary injunctions (often swiftly granted) to preserve the status quo, injunctive relief (including structural injunctions possibly), civil and possibly criminal monetary sanctions, and so forth. During the New Deal and Great Society eras, the Antitrust Division of the Department of Justice asserted a great deal of regulatory authority by bringing Sherman Act lawsuits against large companies or alliances of firms; even the threat of suit typically brought significant changes in the way whole industries did business. Since the Reagan Administration, the Antitrust Division has been less regulatory, but it has used its *amicus* brief power to continue to dominate the evolution of antitrust law.

Likewise, the EEOC has authority to bring federal lawsuits against private employers to seek preliminary relief during an employment discrimination investigation or, more commonly, to remedy a probable discrimination that conciliation has been unable to remedy. Civil Rights Act § 6(f), 42 U.S.C. § 2000e–5(f); see also § 5(g)(6), 42 U.S.C. § 2000e–4(g)(6) (authorizing the EEOC to intervene in a lawsuit brought to enforce Title VII against nongovernmental employers). After President Carter's executive order in 1978 (Problem 2–2), the EEOC also has authority under § 707 to bring lawsuits to remedy a "pattern or practice" of statutory violations by private employers. *Id.* § 2000e–6. The Attorney General alone makes such decisions for lawsuits against public employers.

The main drawback to agency lawsuits is that they are a very expensive way to enforce the statute. Like agency rulemaking and agency adjudication, this form of enforcement rests upon the very old "command and control" model of government regulation and, for some agencies, on the less old, but even more controversial, "structural injunction" approach to regulation. These forms of regulation are what Dan Kahan calls "hard shoves." Economists are skeptical of hard shoves and favor "gentle nudges," says Kahan. See Dan M. Kahan, *Gentle Nudges vs. Hard Shoves: Solving the Sticky Norms Problem*, 67 U. Chi. L. Rev. 607 (2000). Gentle nudges include government inducements or incentives for companies to engage in socially productive conduct, information about best practices that employers might follow, and default rules that can be contracted around (perhaps with some expense) if companies find them inefficient. Lawsuits are a clunky way of nudging regulated parties, but the next three items in the regulatory toolkit will often be useful in that regard.

Agency Guidances: Policy Statements, Bulletins, etc. Agencies have a default authority (i.e., unless countermanded by Congress) to offer their opinion about what the law requires. Agencies do so through a broad range of mechanisms that extend far beyond rulemaking and adjudication. These less formal "guidances" include policy statements, agency website announcements, speeches by agency heads or commissioners at conferences or other public forums, media press releases, bulletins, question-and-answer portions of the agency's website (often called "FAQs"), and *amicus* briefs filed with the Supreme Court. See generally Chapter 7, § 3. (*Amicus* briefs at the appellate stage almost always have to be submitted by the Solicitor General, who consults with the agency but is not bound by its interpretations of law.)

The biggest problem with these informal mechanisms for statutory enforcement is that they carry no penalties for disobedience by the regulated parties. The EEOC, for example, relies extensively on guidances to enforce its understanding of Title VII, because the EEOC has no rulemaking authority. Why should a company follow such guidances? There are several possible reasons. One is that the guidance tells the company what issues the EEOC actually might bring a lawsuit to enforce, and so the EEOC's litigation authority backs up its guidance. A company openly flouting a guidance is asking for trouble. Additionally, guidances give the EEOC a first-mover advantage: the agency can canvass regulated firms as well as civil rights groups to come up with rules that are well-linked to the statute and its goals, are easy to understand, and are reasonably comprehensive. They instantly become focal points for further discussion. Employees and their lawyers will plan complaints around such rules and firms will tend to avoid clashing with them. Keep in mind that even agencies with rulemaking authority use guidances—and use them often—instead of the more formal process. Agencies have various incentives to take this course, including avoiding the special public "notice and comment" procedures that go along with rulemaking. We further explore guidances and reasons that agencies might use them in Chapter 7.

Advice-Giving. Agencies spend a lot of time giving advice. The advice-giving function of an agency helps it enforce the statute, often in combination with public guidances and policy statements. The best example of this strategy is the Internal Revenue Service (IRS), which dispenses advice to millions of Americans through its instructions book mailed to taxpayers, its website, its telephone operators, and the local offices where IRS agents answer questions and help people with their taxes in the months before April 15 (the date most of us have to file our tax returns or request extensions). Although taxpayers have a natural incentive to minimize their income taxes, they form a remarkably cooperative relationship with the tax collector because of the IRS's advice-giving culture. Tax compliance is as high as it is in the United States mostly because of our middle-class or patriotic values, but it probably also owes something to the agency's detailed advice to taxpayers. Most taxpayers pay their share of taxes more because they follow the agency's advice than because they fear a lawsuit or penalties.

Likewise, especially in its early days, the EEOC spent a lot of time answering employer inquiries about how the statute applied to common policies, such as firing or suspending employees if they became pregnant. It was such inquiries that helped initiate discussion within the EEOC about whether pregnancy-based discrimination is actionable "discrimination because of * * * sex," as Title VII uses that term. When Congress passed the Pregnancy Discrimination Act of 1978, the EEOC not only reissued its Pregnancy Discrimination Guidance, but accompanied it by twenty-four frequently posed questions and the EEOC's answers (carefully vetted by both women's and employer groups before promulgation). Employers found the questions and answers quite helpful as they struggled to comply with the new statute.

Like regular individuals, a lot of the time, companies often just want to know what the law requires of them—and agency advice-giving is a potentially useful way to induce compliance in those cases. But if a firm or an individual believes that following the law is too expensive or distasteful, advice-giving might be of no use. Put another way, the law often assumes the "bad person" standard: make rules that even bad, law-avoiding people will have to follow. Bad people and companies might listen attentively to agency advice and even solicit it (just to see how secretive they have to be), but then they will ignore the advice, cheat, and make extra profits compared to more law-abiding competitors. The existence of even a few bad apples might trigger a cascade of disobedience, as persons or companies inclined to obey the law do not want the sucker's payoff.

To be sure, the cascade might fall the other way sometimes, because of network power. See David Singh Grewal, *Network Power: The Social Dynamics of Globalization* (2008). That is, bad actors might still obey the law articulated by agencies without sanctioning power, because other firms follow the law, internalize its norms, and exclude bad actors from the benefits of their networks on the basis of a reputation for not following norms. In other words, if an agency can tie its efforts into powerful social or economic networks, network power can do much of the enforcement. For example, soon after 1964 almost no company would openly admit to discriminating on the basis of race; the EEOC played virtually no role in that overnight success, which owed its authority to the normative revolution led by the civil rights movement and the network power of the nondiscrimination idea. The EEOC proved very useful, however, in developing evidence that employers were still discriminating and that bad numbers could reveal patterns of discrimination. It has taken decades for that idea to permeate American culture, but it has done so. Even the worst firm today thinks twice before hiring that tenth white guy for an executive position filled by nine white guys.

Investigation, Information-Gathering, Promulgation, and Publicity. Another tool available to agencies is informational. Congress often assigns agencies particular informational tasks, and agencies have broad discretion to gather and promulgate information they consider useful to the public. Many kinds of information have a regulatory value. For example, the EEOC gathers information about the race and sex composition of workforces, by state and by region; this information can be very useful to target companies that may be secretly or unconsciously discriminating, because their numbers will be out of line with aggregate numbers. Publishing this information has the further regulatory value of placing local employers on notice as to the "normal" numbers, encouraging concern if their numbers are not within the normal range.

Agencies can exercise great power through promulgation of information, through their websites, informational booklets, and other forms of publicity. For example, the famous "food pyramid" suggesting a healthy balance of food groups for a day's meal, has shaped the thinking of two generations of Americans. (The federal government has recently abandoned the pyramid and has changed its mind about the most healthy balance of foods, as it turns out.) One of the most powerful regulatory tools is *normalization,* where an institution simply promulgates a standard as normal and people follow that standard because they do not want to deviate from that norm. Federal agencies have no monopoly on normalizing strategies (think about church-supported and media-publicized norms), but by collecting data and publicizing trends, agencies can contribute powerfully to social normalization.

Finally, agencies can regulate by creating systematic arrays of regimes, through menus, for example. In family law and corporate law, to take two different areas, menus can be useful channeling devices even when people and companies are not required to follow the regimes listed in the menus.

B. JURISDICTIONAL LIMITS ON AGENCY ENFORCEMENT

Step back from agency authority and strategy to consider a basic question: Is the agency acting within its statutory authority?[20] Or is the agency, like President Truman in the Steel Seizure Case, acting *ultra vires*? Almost every agency action must be traceable to a statute and not only authorized by, but consistent with, the substance of that statute. Leaving to Part III of these materials a detailed treatment of judicial review of agency rules, orders, and statutory interpretations, we focus here on the Steel Seizure question of executive authority. Our example in this section draws from a high-profile exercise of power by the Food & Drug Administration, a completely different kind of agency than the EEOC, with a lot more tools to regulate food and drugs.

We use the FDA Tobacco Case below to illustrate how issues of agency authority arise first within the executive branch of government, and how decisions by agencies to exercise their authority have important implications for the separation of powers and the Congress-agency relationship. If the White House or, especially, Congress believes an agency is acting *ultra vires,* the agency can suffer even if its actions violate only norms and not the letter of the law. Legal statutory limits are

---

[20] The Administrative Procedure Act, covered in Chapter 7 of these materials, provides that a court shall hold unlawful an agency action which is "in excess of statutory jurisdiction, authority, or limitations, or short of statutory right." 5 U.S.C. § 706(2)(C). Even without this specific statute, however, executive branch officials typically have no power to "take care that the laws are executed" without a grant of authority from Congress. See Steel Seizure Case.

generally enforced against agencies by the Department of Justice and other executive branch officials—and sometimes by the Supreme Court and lower court judges. As the FDA Tobacco Case (below) reveals, the White House will sometimes encourage rather than stop aggressive agency interpretations of their regulatory authority.

STATUTORY AND REGULATORY PREFACE TO THE FDA TOBACCO CASE

The Food & Drug Administration (FDA) is clearly not an "independent" agency, for it is situated within the Department of Health & Human Services. Moreover, unlike most other regulatory agencies, the FDA proceeds primarily through a process of categorization. That is, the agency has jurisdiction over "drugs" as well as "medical devices," so everything it regulates must fall into one of those categories. This problem will ignore the FDA's important jurisdiction over "food" and focus on its jurisdiction over drugs, an exercise much illuminated by Daniel Carpenter, *Reputation and Power: Organizational Image and Pharmaceutical Regulation at the FDA* (2010). Carpenter's argument is that an agency's formal "authority" or "power" is closely linked to the agency's "reputation" for efficacy and protecting the public. Indeed, from the very beginning of the modern statutory scheme for drug regulation, the FDA has been an excellent example of his argument.

The Pure Food & Drug Act of June 30, 1906, ch. 3915, 34 Stat. 768–72, was the first comprehensive federal law aimed at protecting the public against interstate or international sales of "adulterated or misbranded" food and drugs. The Act charged the Bureau of Chemistry (located in the Department of Agriculture) with examining foods and drugs to determine whether they were adulterated or misbranded; if so, the Act instructed the Bureau to convey the information to law enforcement officials authorized to seize offending food and drugs and prosecute dealers.

The Bureau, renamed the Food & Drug Administration in 1930, developed a great deal of expertise and no small amount of regulatory zealotry as it encountered outrageously bad drugs in its early history. The administrators were discouraged by the hydra-like nature of the problem: As soon as one quack product was suppressed, three others had arisen to take its place. Because the agency was usually *responding* to the market, it was not able to *protect* the public adequately. Most quack drugs were merely inefficacious, but some were toxic. In 1937, Dr. Massengill's Elixir generated enormous publicity as its toxicity (taking it was similar to drinking antifreeze) led to the deaths of 107 Americans, many of them children.

FDA Commissioner Walter G. Campbell (1921–24, 1927–44) seized upon the public outcry over the sulfanilamide elixir scandal to drum up public support for a drug act revision that had been languishing in Congress for several years. Feminist groups and the American Medical Association joined Campbell and his media allies, enabling the agency and its legislative allies to leapfrog opposition from the pharmaceutical industry, as well as congressional and presidential indifference, and propel into law the Food, Drug, and Cosmetics Act of 1938 (FDCA), Act of June 25, 1938, ch. 675, 52 Stat. 1040–59 (Carpenter, *Reputation and Power,* 73–117).

The FDCA's biggest innovation gave the FDA the power to define the market for drugs. Henceforth, all drugs had to go through *pre-market FDA approval* before they could be sold to the public. Before the FDCA, the agency had to track down commercial drugs, show that they were toxic or misbranded, and then take them off the market; after the FDCA, any drug that did not have the FDA's seal of approval was on the market illegally and could be seized summarily without any analysis or investigation. The FDA gained many other powers under the Act, but the pre-market approval power gave the FDA authority to define the market and required the market (i.e., pharmaceutical firms) to develop research and development laboratories that met the FDA's increasingly strict demands for science-based evidence that their drugs not only did not kill (or hurt) people, but were therapeutically effective as well.

The FDA consolidated its authority, and expanded it to include an efficacy requirement as well as a no-harm requirement, through legislative rulemaking that went well beyond the expectations of the enacting Congress (Carpenter, *Reputation and Power,* 118–227). A furious industry counterattacked in court, but the New Deal judges stood behind the agency. E.g., *Research Labs, Inc. v. United States,* 167 F.2d 410 (9th Cir. 1948) (going beyond the statute and Supreme Court precedent to uphold the FDA's authority to assert that a drug is "misbranded" if it is "ineffective" to cure the ailment it targets). And the FDA relentlessly pressed forward with new rulemaking, science-based standards, and even a science-based New Drug Application Form (further enraging the industry). The FDA also used speeches and conferences to build support for the FDA's mission among the medical community, the media, civic groups, and others.

Congressional hearings conducted in 1959–62 by Senator Estes Kefauver (D–Tenn.), an FDA ally, revealed public support for the agency's mission, including the beyond-the-letter-of-the-law efficacy requirement (which even most of the industry witnesses no longer contested). The public saw the FDA as "Their Cop Protecting the Public Against Greedy Drug Companies"—and that image received dramatic reinforcement during the hearings. In 1960, the FDA's Dr. Frances Kelsey refused to approve Kevadon, a drug that was very popular in Europe. Dr. Kelsey rejected the firm's experimental studies as so flawed in design as to be worthless and conducted a thorough literature search, which raised many red flags about possible toxicity. The drug company pressed for approval (after all every European regulator had given a green flag), but Dr. Kelsey's bosses backed her up: The FDA held firm that if it was not persuaded by the science, the consumer would not be exposed to the drug (Carpenter, *Reputation and Power*, 213–27).

In 1962, stories of hundreds of serious birth defects caused by Thalidomide (the commercial name for Kevadon) flooded the media, and American newspapers and magazines hailed Dr. Kelsey as a national savior: In standing by its science-based standards against a powerful drug company, the FDA had saved American mothers and babies from the scourge that was sweeping Europe (Carpenter, *Reputation and Power*, 228–97). Needless to say, Congress would have given the FDA almost any authority it requested in 1962. The Drug Efficacy Amendment of 1962, Pub. L. No. 87–781, confirmed the FDA's previously asserted power to keep drugs off the market on grounds of efficacy and gave the FDA new powers to recall drugs even after they had been approved. Emboldened, the FDA required more rigorous science-based evidence (e.g., clinical trials) and mandated standards for those trials in more rounds of rulemaking. For the next decade and a half, the FDA was the most admired administrative agency in the world, and it had its way on almost every issue of law that became public. The FDA's rigorous process got it into some hot water when it rejected cancer drugs in the late 1970s and proved too slow in approving AIDS drugs in the 1980s, but the agency's reputation as the protector of the nation's health remained intact. Its biggest challenge came in the 1990s.

Under the leadership of Commissioner David A. Kessler (1990–97), the FDA moved to regulate nicotine and products containing that "drug." This was one of the boldest moves in the history of a very bold agency. When the original statute was enacted in 1938, the agency did not consider tobacco or nicotine to be a "drug," in part because no one believed that it was a product designed to affect the human body; tobacco was viewed as a recreational product, not a drug. Over the years, the medical understanding of the addictive properties of nicotine found in tobacco deepened. 1960s regulators even learned that tobacco companies designed and adjusted their product to enhance its nicotine-addictive features. Based on this evidence, the FDA decided tobacco or nicotine is a "drug" and tobacco products like cigarettes are "medical devices" subject to the regulatory regime of the FDCA. For useful background overviews from different perspectives, see Richard A. Merrill, *The FDA May Not Regulate Tobacco Products as "Drugs" or as "Medical Devices,"* 47 Duke L.J. 1071 (1998); Theodore W. Ruger, *The Story of FDA v. Brown & Williamson: The Norm of Agency Continuity*, in *Statutory Interpretation Stories* 334–64 (Eskridge, Frickey & Garrett eds., 2011).

Just like the pharmaceutical industry previously, the tobacco industry fought back in court. Their argument was that the FDA did not have authority to regulate nicotine and tobacco products as drugs and medical devices under the FDCA, as amended through 1995. Before you read how the case comes out, consider some relevant statutory materials: What was the legal basis for the FDA's jurisdiction over tobacco products? What legal arguments did the tobacco companies have for thinking that the FDA did not have jurisdiction? Will the Supreme Court go along with the agency?

Food, Drug & Cosmetics Act of 1938, Pub. L. No. 75–717, 52 Stat. 1040 (1938), codified at scattered sections of 21 U.S.C.

Section 321(g)(1): The term "drug" means (A) articles recognized in the official United States Pharmacopœia, official Homœopathic Pharmacopœia of the United States, or official National Formulary, or any supplement to any of them; and (B) articles intended for use in the diagnosis, cure, mitigation, treatment, or prevention of disease in man or other animals; and (C) articles (other than food) intended to affect the structure or any function of the body of man or other animals; and (D) articles intended for use as a component of any article specified in clause (A), (B), or (C). * * *

Section 321(h)(3): The term "device" (except when used in paragraph (n) of this section and in sections 331(i), 343(f), 352(c), and 362(c) of this title) means an instrument, apparatus, implement, machine, contrivance, implant, in vitro reagent, or other similar or related article, including any component, part, or accessory, which is—

> (3) intended to affect the structure or any function of the body of man or other animals, and which does not achieve its primary intended purposes through chemical action within or on the body of man or other animals and which is not dependent upon being metabolized for the achievement of its primary intended purposes.

Section 321(n): If an article is alleged to be misbranded because the labeling or advertising is misleading, then in determining whether the labeling or advertising is misleading there shall be taken into account (among other things) not only representations made or suggested by statement, word, design, device, or any combination thereof, but also the extent to which the labeling or advertising fails to reveal facts material in the light of such representations or material with respect to consequences which may result from the use of the article to which the labeling or advertising relates under the conditions of use prescribed in the labeling or advertising thereof or under such conditions of use as are customary or usual.

Section 352(f), (j): A drug or device shall be deemed to be misbranded—

(f) Unless its labeling bears (1) adequate directions for use; and (2) such adequate warnings against use in those pathological conditions or by children where its use may be dangerous to health, or against unsafe dosage or methods or duration of administration or application, in such manner and form, as are necessary for the protection of users, * * * [or]

(j) If it is dangerous to health when used in the dosage or manner, or with the frequency or duration prescribed, recommended, or suggested in the labeling thereof.

Section 355(e)(1): The Secretary shall, after due notice and opportunity for hearing to the applicant, withdraw approval of an application with respect to any drug under this section if the Secretary finds (1) that clinical or other experience, tests, or other scientific data show that such drug is unsafe for use under the conditions of use upon the basis of which the application was approved; * * *

Federal Cigarette Labeling and Advertising Act, Pub. L. No. 89–92, 79 Stat. 282 (1965), codified at 15 U.S.C. § 1331 et seq.

Section 1331: It is the policy of the Congress, and the purpose of this chapter, to establish a comprehensive Federal program to deal with cigarette labeling and advertising with respect to any relationship between smoking and health, whereby—

(1) the public may be adequately informed about any adverse health effects of cigarette smoking by inclusion of warning notices on each package of cigarettes and in each advertisement of cigarettes; and

(2) commerce and the national economy may be (A) protected to the maximum extent consistent with this declared policy and (B) not impeded by diverse, nonuniform, and confusing cigarette labeling and advertising regulations with respect to any relationship between smoking and health.

Section 1333: It shall be unlawful for any person to manufacture, import, or package for sale or distribution within the United States any cigarettes the package for which fails to bear the following statement: "Caution: Cigarette Smoking May Be Hazardous to Your Health." Such statement shall be located in a conspicuous place on every cigarette package and shall appear in conspicuous and legible type in contrast by typography, layout, or color with other printed matter on the package.

Comprehensive Smoking Education Act of 1984, P.L. 98–474 (1984), amending 15 U.S.C. § 1331.

Section 1331(a)(1). [Congress revised § 1331 and added new warnings to cigarette packages and, in other revisions to § 1331, advertisements:]

> **SURGEON GENERAL'S WARNING:** Smoking Causes Lung Cancer, Heart Disease, Emphysema, And May Complicate Pregnancy.

> **SURGEON GENERAL'S WARNING:** Quitting Smoking Now Greatly Reduces Serious Risks to Your Health.

> **SURGEON GENERAL'S WARNING:** Smoking By Pregnant Women May Result in Fetal Injury, Premature Birth, And Low Birth Weight.

> **SURGEON GENERAL'S WARNING:** Cigarette Smoke Contains Carbon Monoxide.

FOOD & DRUG ADMINISTRATION V. BROWN & WILLIAMSON TOBACCO CORP.

United States Supreme Court, 2000.
529 U.S. 120, 120 S.Ct. 1291, 146 L.Ed.2d 121.

JUSTICE O'CONNOR delivered the opinion of the Court.

This case involves one of the most troubling public health problems facing our Nation today: the thousands of premature deaths that occur each year because of tobacco use. In 1996, the Food and Drug Administration (FDA), after having expressly disavowed any such authority since its inception, asserted jurisdiction to regulate tobacco products. The FDA concluded that nicotine is a "drug" within the meaning of the Food, Drug, and Cosmetic Act (FDCA or Act), 21 U.S.C. § 301 et seq., and that cigarettes and smokeless tobacco are "combination products" that deliver nicotine to the body. * * * [I]t promulgated regulations intended to reduce tobacco consumption among children and adolescents. * * * In this case, we believe that Congress has clearly precluded the FDA from asserting jurisdiction to regulate tobacco products. * * *

The FDCA grants the FDA, as the designee of the Secretary of Health and Human Services (HHS), the authority to regulate, among other items, "drugs" and "devices." The Act defines "drug" to include "articles (other than food) intended to affect the structure or any function of the body." 21 U.S.C. § 321(g)(1)(C). It defines "device," in part, as "an instrument, apparatus, implement, machine, contrivance, . . . or other similar or related article, including any component, part, or accessory, which is . . . intended to affect the structure or any function of the body." § 321(h). * * *

On August 28, 1996, the FDA issued a final rule entitled "Regulations Restricting the Sale and Distribution of Cigarettes and Smokeless Tobacco to Protect Children and Adolescents." The FDA determined that nicotine is a "drug" and that cigarettes and smokeless tobacco are "drug delivery devices," and therefore it had jurisdiction under the FDCA to regulate tobacco products as customarily marketed— that is, without manufacturer claims of therapeutic benefit. First, the FDA found that tobacco products " 'affect the structure or any function of the body' " because nicotine "has significant pharmacological effects." Specifically, nicotine "exerts psychoactive, or mood-altering, effects on the brain" that cause and sustain addiction, have both tranquilizing and stimulating effects, and control weight. Second, the FDA determined that these effects were "intended" under the FDCA because they "are so widely known and foreseeable that [they] may be deemed to have been intended by the manufacturers,"; consumers use tobacco products "predominantly or nearly exclusively" to obtain these effects; and the statements, research, and actions of manufacturers revealed that they "have 'designed' cigarettes to provide pharmacologically active doses of nicotine to consumers." * * * *

[II] A threshold issue is the appropriate framework for analyzing the FDA's assertion of authority to regulate tobacco products. * * * [A] reviewing court must first ask "whether Congress has directly spoken to the precise question at issue." If Congress has done so, the inquiry is at an end; the court "must give effect to the unambiguously expressed intent of Congress." But if Congress has not specifically addressed the question, a reviewing court must respect the agency's construction of the statute so long as it is permissible. * * * * With these principles in mind, we find that Congress has directly spoken to the issue here and precluded the FDA's jurisdiction to regulate tobacco products. * * *

[II.A]   [I]f tobacco products were "devices" under the FDCA, the FDA would be required to remove them from the market. * * * [T]wo distinct FDCA provisions would render cigarettes and smokeless tobacco misbranded devices. First, § 352(j) deems a drug or device misbranded "[i]f it is dangerous to health when used in the dosage or manner, or with the frequency or duration prescribed, recommended, or suggested in the labeling thereof." The FDA's findings make clear that tobacco products are "dangerous to health" when used in the manner prescribed. Second, a drug or device is misbranded under the Act "[u]nless its labeling bears . . . adequate directions for use . . . in such manner and form, as are necessary for the protection of users," except where such directions are "not necessary for the protection of the public health." § 352(f)(1). * * * Thus, were tobacco products within the FDA's jurisdiction, the Act would deem them misbranded devices that could not be introduced into interstate commerce. Contrary to the dissent's contention, the Act admits no remedial discretion once it is evident that the device is misbranded. [In 1972, the FDA itself had taken that position.]

Congress, however, has foreclosed the removal of tobacco products from the market. A provision of the United States Code currently in force states that "[t]he marketing of tobacco constitutes one of the greatest basic industries of the United States with ramifying activities which directly affect interstate and foreign commerce at every point, and stable conditions therein are necessary to the general welfare." 7 U.S.C. § 1311(a). More importantly, Congress has directly addressed the problem of tobacco and health through legislation on six occasions since 1965. When Congress enacted these statutes, the adverse health consequences of tobacco use were well known, as were nicotine's pharmacological effects. Nonetheless, Congress stopped well short of ordering a ban. Instead, it has generally regulated the labeling and advertisement of tobacco products, expressly providing that it is the policy of Congress that "commerce and the national economy may be ... protected to the maximum extent consistent with" consumers "be[ing] adequately informed about any adverse health effects." 15 U.S.C. § 1331. Congress' decisions to regulate labeling and advertising and to adopt the express policy of protecting "commerce and the national economy ... to the maximum extent" reveal its intent that tobacco products remain on the market. Indeed, the collective premise of these statutes is that cigarettes and smokeless tobacco will continue to be sold in the United States. A ban of tobacco products by the FDA would therefore plainly contradict congressional policy. * * *

Considering the FDCA as a whole, it is clear that Congress intended to exclude tobacco products from the FDA's jurisdiction. A fundamental precept of the FDCA is that any product regulated by the FDA—but not banned—must be safe for its intended use. Various provisions of the Act make clear that this refers to the safety of using the product to obtain its intended effects, not the public health ramifications of alternative administrative actions by the FDA. That is, the FDA must determine that there is a reasonable assurance that the product's therapeutic benefits outweigh the risk of harm to the consumer. According to this standard, the FDA has concluded that, although tobacco products might be effective in delivering certain pharmacological effects, they are "unsafe" and "dangerous" when used for these purposes. Consequently, if tobacco products were within the FDA's jurisdiction, the Act would require the FDA to remove them from the market entirely. But a ban would contradict Congress' clear intent as expressed in its more recent, tobacco-specific legislation. The inescapable conclusion is that there is no room for tobacco products within the FDCA's regulatory scheme. If they cannot be used safely for any therapeutic purpose, and yet they cannot be banned, they simply do not fit.

[II.B]   In determining whether Congress has spoken directly to the FDA's authority to regulate tobacco, we must also consider in greater detail the tobacco-specific legislation that Congress has enacted over the past 35 years. At the time a statute is enacted, it may have a range of plausible meanings. Over time, however, subsequent acts can shape or focus those meanings. The "classic judicial task of reconciling many laws enacted over time, and getting them to 'make sense' in combination, necessarily assumes that the implications of a statute may be altered by the implications of a later statute." *United States v. Fausto*, 484 U.S., at 453. This is particularly so where the scope of the earlier statute is broad but the subsequent statutes more specifically address the topic at hand. As we recognized recently in *United States v. Estate of Romani*, "a specific policy embodied in a later federal statute should control our construction of the [earlier] statute, even though it ha[s] not been expressly amended." 523 U.S., at 530–531.

Congress has enacted six separate pieces of legislation since 1965 addressing the problem of tobacco use and human health. Those statutes, among other things, require that health warnings appear on all packaging and in all print and outdoor advertisements, see 15 U.S.C. §§ 1331, 1333, 4402; prohibit the advertisement of tobacco products through "any medium of electronic communication" subject to regulation by the Federal Communications Commission (FCC), see §§ 1335, 4402(f); require the Secretary of HHS to report every three years to Congress on research findings concerning "the addictive property of tobacco," 42 U.S.C. § 290aa–2(b)(2); and make States' receipt of certain federal block grants contingent on their making it unlawful "for any manufacturer, retailer, or distributor of tobacco products to sell or distribute any such product to any individual under the age of 18," § 300x–26(a)(1).

In adopting each statute, Congress has acted against the backdrop of the FDA's consistent and repeated statements that it lacked authority under the FDCA to regulate tobacco absent claims of therapeutic benefit by the manufacturer. In fact, on several occasions over this period, and after the health consequences of tobacco use and nicotine's pharmacological effects had become well known, Congress considered and rejected bills that would have granted the FDA such jurisdiction. Under these circumstances, it is evident that Congress' tobacco-specific statutes have effectively ratified the FDA's long-held position that it lacks jurisdiction under the FDCA to regulate tobacco products. Congress has created a distinct regulatory scheme to address the problem of tobacco and health, and that scheme, as presently constructed, precludes any role for the FDA.

[Justice O'Connor provided detail for her claim that the FDA had consistently disclaimed jurisdiction, beginning in 1964, a position consistent with its failure to regulate from the statute's enactment in 1938.]

Moreover, before enacting the FCLAA in 1965, Congress considered and rejected several proposals to give the FDA the authority to regulate tobacco. In April 1963, Representative Udall introduced a bill "[t]o amend the Federal Food, Drug, and Cosmetic Act so as to make that Act applicable to smoking products." H.R. 5973, 88th Cong., 1st Sess., 1. Two months later, Senator Moss introduced an identical bill in the Senate. S. 1682, 88th Cong., 1st Sess. (1963). In discussing his proposal on the Senate floor, Senator Moss explained that "this amendment simply places smoking products under FDA jurisdiction, along with foods, drugs, and cosmetics." 109 Cong. Rec. 10322 (1963). In December 1963, Representative Rhodes introduced another bill that would have amended the FDCA "by striking out 'food, drug, device, or cosmetic,' each place where it appears therein and inserting in lieu thereof 'food, drug, device, cosmetic, or smoking product.'" H.R. 9512, 88th Cong., 1st Sess., § 3 (1963). And in January 1965, five months before passage of the FCLAA, Representative Udall again introduced a bill to amend the FDCA "to make that Act applicable to smoking products." H.R. 2248, 89th Cong., 1st Sess., 1. None of these proposals became law.

Congress ultimately decided in 1965 to subject tobacco products to the less extensive regulatory scheme of the FCLAA, which created a "comprehensive Federal program to deal with cigarette labeling and advertising with respect to any relationship between smoking and health." Pub. L. 89–92, § 2, 79 Stat. 282. The FCLAA rejected any regulation of advertising, but it required the warning, "Caution: Cigarette Smoking May Be Hazardous to Your Health," to appear on all cigarette packages. In the FCLAA's "Declaration of Policy," Congress stated that its objective was to balance the goals of ensuring that "the public may be adequately informed that cigarette smoking may be hazardous to health" and protecting "commerce and the national economy . . . to the maximum extent." *Id.*, § 2, 79 Stat. 282 (codified at 15 U.S.C. § 1331).

Not only did Congress reject the proposals to grant the FDA jurisdiction, but it explicitly pre-empted any other regulation of cigarette labeling: "No statement relating to smoking and health, other than the statement required by . . . this Act, shall be required on any cigarette package." Pub. L. 89–92, § 5(a), 79 Stat. 283. The regulation of product labeling, however, is an integral aspect of the FDCA, both as it existed in 1965 and today. * * * As discussed earlier, the Act requires that all products bear "adequate directions for use . . . as are necessary for the protection of users," 21 U.S.C. § 352(f)(1) (1964 ed.); requires that all products provide "adequate warnings against use in those pathological conditions or by children where its use may be dangerous to health," 21 U.S.C. § 352(f)(2) (1964 ed.); and deems a product misbranded "[i]f it is dangerous to health when used in the dosage or manner, or with the frequency or duration prescribed, recommended, or suggested in the labeling thereof," 21 U.S.C. § 352(j) (1964 ed.). In this sense, the FCLAA was—and remains—incompatible with FDA regulation of tobacco products. This is not to say that the FCLAA's preemption provision by itself necessarily foreclosed FDA jurisdiction. But it is an important factor in assessing whether Congress ratified the agency's position—that is, whether Congress adopted a regulatory approach to the problem of tobacco and health that contemplated no role for the FDA.

[Meanwhile, the FDA in the 1970s and 1980s continued to say that it lacked jurisdiction under the FDCA to regulate tobacco products, and Congress likewise acted against the backdrop of FDA assurances that tobacco products fell outside the FDCA, rejecting proposals to grant FDA jurisdiction.]

Taken together, these actions by Congress over the past 35 years preclude an interpretation of the FDCA that grants the FDA jurisdiction to regulate tobacco products. We do not rely on Congress' failure to act—its consideration and rejection of bills that would have given the FDA this authority—in reaching this conclusion. Indeed, this is not a case of simple inaction by Congress that purportedly represents its acquiescence in an agency's position. To the contrary, Congress has enacted several statutes addressing the particular subject of tobacco and health, creating a distinct regulatory scheme for cigarettes and smokeless tobacco. In doing so, Congress has been aware of tobacco's health hazards and its pharmacological effects. It has also enacted this legislation against the background of the FDA repeatedly and consistently asserting that it lacks jurisdiction under the FDCA to regulate tobacco products as customarily marketed. Further, Congress has persistently acted to preclude a meaningful role for any administrative agency in making policy on the subject of tobacco and health. Moreover, the substance of Congress' regulatory scheme is, in an important respect, incompatible with FDA jurisdiction. Although the supervision of product labeling to protect consumer health is a substantial component of the FDA's regulation of drugs and devices, see 21 U.S.C. § 352 (1994 ed. and Supp. III), the FCLAA and the CSTHEA explicitly prohibit any federal agency from imposing any health-related labeling requirements on cigarettes or smokeless tobacco products, see 15 U.S.C. §§ 1334(a), 4406(a). * * *

Although the dissent takes issue with our discussion of the FDA's change in position, our conclusion does not rely on the fact that the FDA's assertion of jurisdiction represents a sharp break with its prior interpretation of the FDCA. Certainly, an agency's initial interpretation of a statute that it is charged with administering is not "carved in stone." * * * The consistency of the FDA's prior position is significant in this case for a different reason: It provides important context to Congress' enactment of its tobacco-specific legislation. When the FDA repeatedly informed Congress that the FDCA does not grant it the authority to regulate tobacco products, its statements were consistent with the agency's unwavering position since its inception, and with the position that its predecessor agency had first taken in 1914. Although not crucial, the consistency of the FDA's prior position bolsters the conclusion that when Congress created a distinct regulatory scheme addressing the subject of tobacco and health, it understood that the FDA is without jurisdiction to regulate tobacco products and ratified that position.

The dissent also argues that the proper inference to be drawn from Congress' tobacco-specific legislation is "critically ambivalent." We disagree. In that series of statutes, Congress crafted a specific legislative response to the problem of tobacco and health, and it did so with the understanding, based on repeated assertions by the FDA, that the agency has no authority under the FDCA to regulate tobacco products. Moreover, Congress expressly pre-empted any other regulation of the labeling of tobacco products concerning their health consequences, even though the oversight of labeling is central to the FDCA's regulatory scheme. And in addressing the subject, Congress consistently evidenced its intent to preclude any federal agency from exercising significant policymaking authority in the area. Under these circumstances, we believe the appropriate inference that Congress intended to ratify the FDA's prior position that it lacks jurisdiction—is unmistakable. * * *

[II.C]   [W]e are confident that Congress could not have intended to delegate a decision of such economic and political significance to an agency in so cryptic a fashion. To find that the FDA has the authority to regulate tobacco products, one must not only adopt an extremely strained understanding of "safety" as it is used throughout the Act—a concept central to the FDCA's regulatory scheme—but also ignore the plain implication of Congress' subsequent tobacco-specific legislation. It is therefore clear, based on the FDCA's overall regulatory scheme and the subsequent tobacco legislation, that Congress has directly spoken to the question at issue and precluded the FDA from regulating tobacco products. * * *

JUSTICE BREYER, with whom JUSTICE STEVENS, JUSTICE SOUTER, and JUSTICE GINSBURG join, dissenting.

In its own interpretation, the majority nowhere denies the following two salient points. First, tobacco products (including cigarettes) fall within the scope of this statutory definition, read literally. Cigarettes achieve their mood-stabilizing effects through the interaction of the chemical nicotine and the cells of the central nervous system. Both cigarette manufacturers and smokers alike know of, and desire, that chemically induced result. Hence, cigarettes are "intended to affect" the body's "structure" and "function," in the literal sense of these words.

Second, the statute's basic purpose—the protection of public health—supports the inclusion of cigarettes within its scope. * * *

I believe that the most important indicia of statutory meaning—language and purpose—along with the FDCA's legislative history (described briefly in Part I) are sufficient to establish that the FDA has authority to regulate tobacco. The statute-specific arguments against jurisdiction that the tobacco companies and the majority rely upon (discussed in Part II) are based on erroneous assumptions and, thus, do not defeat the jurisdiction-supporting thrust of the FDCA's language and purpose. The inferences that the majority draws from later legislative history are not persuasive, since (as I point out in Part III) one can just as easily infer from the later laws that Congress did not intend to affect the FDA's tobacco-related authority at all. And the fact that the FDA changed its mind about the scope of its own jurisdiction is legally insignificant because (as Part IV establishes) the agency's reasons for changing course are fully justified. Finally, as I explain in Part V, the degree of accountability that likely will attach to the FDA's action in this case should alleviate any concern that Congress, rather than an administrative agency, ought to make this important regulatory decision.

[I] Before 1938, the federal Pure Food and Drug Act contained only two jurisdictional definitions of "drug":

"[1] medicines and preparations recognized in the United States Pharmacopoeia or National Formulary . . . and [2] any substance or mixture of substances intended to be used for the cure, mitigation, or prevention of disease." Act of June 30, 1906, ch. 3915, § 6, 34 Stat. 769.

In 1938, Congress added a third definition, relevant here:

(3) articles (other than food) intended to affect the structure or any function of the body . . . "Act of June 25, 1938, ch. 675, § 201(g), 52 Stat. 1041 (codified at 21 U.S.C. § 321(g)(1)(C)).

It also added a similar definition in respect to a "device." As I have mentioned, the literal language of the third definition and the FDCA's general purpose both strongly support a pro-jurisdiction reading of the statute. * * * This Court * * * has said that the "historical expansion of the definition of drug, and the creation of a parallel concept of devices, clearly show . . . that Congress fully intended that the Act's coverage be as broad as its literal language indicates—and equally clearly, broader than any strict medical definition might otherwise allow." * * *

In 1938, it may well have seemed unlikely that the FDA would ever bring cigarette manufacturers within the FDCA's statutory language by proving that cigarettes produce chemical changes in the body and that the makers "intended" their product chemically to affect the body's "structure" or "function." Or, back then, it may have seemed unlikely that, even assuming such proof, the FDA actually would exercise its discretion to regulate so popular a product.

But it should not have seemed unlikely that, assuming the FDA decided to regulate and proved the particular jurisdictional prerequisites, the courts would rule such a jurisdictional assertion fully authorized. Cf. *United States v. Southwestern Cable Co.*, 392 U.S. 157 (1968) (reading Communications Act of 1934 as authorizing FCC jurisdiction to regulate cable systems while noting that "Congress could not in 1934 have foreseen the development of" advanced communications systems). * * *

[In Part II.A of his dissent, Justice Breyer argued that the literal meaning of the statutory prohibition supported the agency action. In Part II.B, he maintained that the Court was wrong to revise the statutory language in light of the FDA's alleged endorsement of the tobacco companies' view that their products were not eligible for regulation.] [E]ven though the companies refused to acknowledge publicly (until only very recently) that the nicotine in cigarettes has chemically induced, and habit-forming, effects, see, e.g., Regulation of Tobacco Products (Part 1): Hearings before the House Subcommittee on Health and the Environment, 103d Cong., 2d Sess., 628 (1994) (hereinafter 1994 Hearings) (heads of seven major tobacco companies testified under oath that they believed "nicotine is *not* addictive" (emphasis added)), the FDA recently has gained access to solid, documentary evidence proving that cigarette manufacturers have long *known* tobacco produces these effects within the body through the metabolizing of chemicals, and that they have long *wanted* their products to produce those effects in this way.

For example, in 1972, a tobacco-industry scientist explained that " '[s]moke is beyond question the most optimized vehicle of nicotine,' " and " 'the cigarette is the most optimized dispenser of smoke.' " 61 Fed. Reg. 44856 (1996) (emphasis deleted). That same scientist urged company executives to

> "[t]hink of the cigarette pack as a storage container for a day's supply of nicotine. . . . Think of the cigarette as a dispenser for a dose unit of nicotine [and] [t]hink of a puff of smoke as the vehicle of nicotine." *Ibid.* (Philip Morris) (emphasis deleted).

[Justice Breyer recounted a fair amount of evidence to the same effect; none of the cited evidence had been publicly available until recent years.]

With such evidence, the FDA has more than sufficiently established that the companies "intend" their products to "affect" the body within the meaning of the FDCA.

[In Part II.C, Justice Breyer responded to the Court's argument that, if FDA were to regulate, it would have to ban cigarettes entirely.] The FDCA permits the FDA to regulate a "combination product"—*i.e.,* a "device" (such as a cigarette) that contains a "drug" (such as nicotine)— under its "device" provisions. 21 U.S.C. § 353(g)(1). And the FDCA's "device" provisions explicitly grant the FDA wide remedial discretion. For example, where the FDA cannot "otherwise" obtain "reasonable assurance" of a device's "safety and effectiveness," the agency may restrict by regulation a product's "sale, distribution, or use" upon *"such . . . conditions as the Secretary may prescribe."* § 360j(e)(1) (emphasis added). And the statutory section that most clearly addresses the FDA's power to ban (entitled "Banned devices") says that, where a device presents "an unreasonable and substantial risk of illness or injury," the Secretary *"may"*—not *must*—"initiate a proceeding . . . to make such device a banned device." § 360f(a) (emphasis added). * * *

Noting that the FDCA requires banning a "misbranded" drug, the majority also points to 21 U.S.C. § 352(j), which deems a drug or device "misbranded" if "it is dangerous to health when used" as "prescribed, recommended, or suggested in the labeling." In addition, the majority mentions § 352(f)(1), which calls a drug or device "misbranded" unless "its labeling bears . . . adequate directions for use" as "are necessary for the protection of users." But this "misbranding" language is not determinative, for it permits the FDA to conclude that a drug or device is *not* "dangerous to health" and that it *does* have "adequate" directions *when regulated so as to render it as harmless as possible.* And surely the agency can determine that a substance is comparatively "safe" (*not* "dangerous") whenever it would be *less* dangerous to make the product available (subject to regulatory requirements) than suddenly to withdraw it from the market. Any other interpretation risks substantial harm * * *. And nothing in the statute prevents the agency from adopting a view of "safety" that would avoid such harm. Indeed, the FDA already seems to have taken this position when permitting distribution of toxic drugs, such as poisons used for chemotherapy, that are dangerous for the user but are not deemed "dangerous to health" in the relevant sense. * * *

[III] In the majority's view, laws enacted since 1965 require us to deny jurisdiction, whatever the FDCA might mean in their absence. But why? Do those laws contain language barring FDA jurisdiction? The majority must concede that they do not. Do they contain provisions that are inconsistent with the FDA's exercise of jurisdiction? With one exception, the majority points to no such provision. Do they somehow repeal the principles of law (discussed in Part II, *supra*) that otherwise would lead to the conclusion that the FDA has jurisdiction in this area? The companies themselves deny making any such claim. Perhaps the later laws "shape" and "focus" what the 1938 Congress meant a generation earlier. But this Court has warned against using the views of a later Congress to construe a statute enacted many years before. And, while the majority suggests that the subsequent history "control[s] our construction" of the FDCA, this Court expressly has held that such subsequent views are not "controlling." *Haynes v. United States*, 390 U.S. 85 (1968).

Regardless, the later statutes do not support the majority's conclusion. That is because, whatever individual Members of Congress after 1964 may have assumed about the FDA's jurisdiction, the laws they enacted did not embody any such "no jurisdiction" assumption. And one cannot automatically *infer* an anti-jurisdiction intent, as the majority does, for the later statutes are both (and similarly) consistent with quite a different congressional desire, namely, the intent to proceed without interfering with whatever authority the FDA otherwise may have possessed. See, *e.g.,* Cigarette Labeling and Advertising—1965: Hearings on H.R. 2248 et al. before the House Committee on Interstate and Foreign Commerce, 89th Cong., 1st Sess., 19 (1965) (hereinafter 1965 Hearings) (statement of Rep. Fino that the proposed legislation would *not* "erode" agency authority). As I demonstrate below, the subsequent legislative history is critically ambivalent, for it can be read *either* as (a) "ratif[ying]" a no-jurisdiction assumption, *or* as (b) leaving the jurisdictional question just where Congress found it. And the fact that both inferences are "equally tenable" prevents the majority from drawing from the later statutes the firm, anti-jurisdiction implication that it needs.

Consider, for example, Congress' failure to provide the FDA with express authority to regulate tobacco—a circumstance that the majority finds significant. But cf. *Southwestern Cable Co.* (failed requests do not prove agency "did not already possess" authority). In fact, Congress *both* failed to grant express authority to the FDA when the FDA denied it had jurisdiction over tobacco *and* failed to take that authority expressly away when the agency later asserted jurisdiction. See, *e.g.,* S. 1262, 104th Cong., 1st Sess., § 906 (1995) (failed bill seeking to amend FDCA to say that "[n]othing in this Act or any other Act shall provide the [FDA] with any authority to regulate in any manner tobacco or tobacco products"); see also H.R. 516, 105th Cong., 1st Sess., § 2 (1997) (similar); H.R. Res. 980, reprinted in 142 Cong. Rec. 5018 (1996) (Georgia legislators unsuccessfully requested that Congress "rescind any action giving the FDA authority" over tobacco); H.R. 2283, 104th Cong., 1st Sess. (1995) (failed bill "[t]o prohibit the [FDA] regulation of the sale or use of tobacco"); H.R. 2414, 104th Cong., 1st Sess., § 2(a) (1995) (similar). Consequently, the defeat of various different proposed jurisdictional changes proves nothing. This history shows only that Congress could not muster the votes necessary either to grant or to deny the FDA the relevant authority. It neither favors nor disfavors the majority's position.

The majority also mentions the speed with which Congress acted to take jurisdiction away from other agencies once they tried to assert it. But such a congressional response again proves nothing. On the one hand, the speedy reply might suggest that Congress somehow resented agency assertions of jurisdiction in an area it desired to reserve for itself—a consideration that supports the majority. On the other hand, Congress' quick reaction with respect to *other* agencies' regulatory efforts contrasts dramatically with its failure to enact any responsive law (at any speed) after the FDA asserted jurisdiction over tobacco more than three years ago. And that contrast supports the opposite conclusion.

In addition, at least one post-1938 statute reveals quite a different congressional intent than the majority infers. See note following 21 U.S.C. § 321 (1994 ed., Supp. III) (FDA Modernization Act of 1997) (law "shall *[not]* be construed to affect the question of whether the [FDA] has any authority to regulate any tobacco product," and "[s]uch authority, if any, shall be exercised under the [FDCA] as in effect on the day before the date of [this] enactment"). Consequently, it appears that the only interpretation that can reconcile *all* of the subsequent statutes is the inference that Congress did not intend, either explicitly or implicitly, for its later laws to answer the question of the scope of the FDA's jurisdictional authority. See 143 Cong. Rec. S8860 (Sept. 5, 1997) (the Modernization Act will "not interfere or substantially negatively affect any of the FDA tobacco authority"). * * *

[IV] I now turn to the final historical fact that the majority views as a factor in its interpretation of the subsequent legislative history: the FDA's former denials of its tobacco-related authority.

Until the early 1990's, the FDA expressly maintained that the 1938 statute did not give it the power that it now seeks to assert. It then changed its mind. The majority agrees with me that the FDA's change of positions does not make a significant legal difference. Nevertheless, it labels those denials "important context" for drawing an inference about Congress' intent. In my view, the FDA's change of policy, like the subsequent statutes themselves, does nothing to advance the majority's position.

When it denied jurisdiction to regulate cigarettes, the FDA consistently stated *why* that was so. In 1963, for example, FDA administrators wrote that cigarettes did not satisfy the relevant FDCA definitions—in particular, the "intent" requirement—because cigarette makers did not sell their product with accompanying "therapeutic claims." Letter to Directors of Bureaus, Divisions and Directors of Districts from FDA Bureau of Enforcement (May 24, 1963), in Public Health Cigarette Amendments of 1971: Hearings on S. 1454 before the Consumer Subcommittee of the Senate Committee on Commerce, 92d

Cong., 2d Sess., 240 (1972) (hereinafter FDA Enforcement Letter). And subsequent FDA Commissioners made roughly the same assertion. One pointed to the fact that the manufacturers only "recommended" cigarettes "for smoking pleasure." Two others reiterated the evidentiary need for "health claims." Yet another stressed the importance of proving "intent," adding that "[w]e have not had sufficient evidence" of "intent with regard to nicotine." See, respectively, *id.,* at 239 (Comm'r Edwards); Letter of Dec. 5, 1977, App. 47 (Comm'r Kennedy); 1965 Hearings 193 (Comm'r Rankin); 1994 Hearings 28 (Comm'r Kessler). Tobacco company counsel also testified that the FDA lacked jurisdiction because jurisdiction "depends on . . . intended use," which in turn "depends, *in general,* on the claims and representations made by the manufacturer." Health Consequences of Smoking: Nicotine Addiction, Hearing before the Subcommittee on Health and the Environment of the House Committee on Energy and Commerce, 100th Cong., 2d Sess., 288 (1988) (testimony of Richard Cooper) (emphasis added). * * *

What changed? For one thing, the FDA obtained evidence sufficient to prove the necessary "intent" despite the absence of specific "claims." This evidence, which first became available in the early 1990's, permitted the agency to demonstrate that the tobacco companies *knew* nicotine achieved appetite-suppressing, mood-stabilizing, and habituating effects through chemical (not psychological) means, even at a time when the companies were publicly denying such knowledge.

Moreover, scientific evidence of adverse health effects mounted, until, in the late 1980's, a consensus on the seriousness of the matter became firm. That is not to say that concern about smoking's adverse health effects is a new phenomenon. It is to say, however, that convincing epidemiological evidence began to appear mid-20th century; that the first Surgeon General's Report documenting the adverse health effects appeared in 1964; and that the Surgeon General's Report establishing nicotine's addictive effects appeared in 1988. At each stage, the health conclusions were the subject of controversy, diminishing somewhat over time, until recently—and only recently—has it become clear that there is a wide consensus about the health problem. See 61 Fed. Reg. 44701–44706 (1996).

Finally, administration policy changed. Earlier administrations may have hesitated to assert jurisdiction for the reasons prior Commissioners expressed. Commissioners of the current administration simply took a different regulatory attitude.

Nothing in the law prevents the FDA from changing its policy for such reasons. By the mid-1990s, the evidence needed to prove objective intent—even without an express claim—had been found. The emerging scientific consensus about tobacco's adverse, chemically induced, health effects may have convinced the agency that it should spend its resources on this important regulatory effort. As for the change of administrations, I agree with then-Justice Rehnquist's statement in a different case, where he wrote:

> The agency's changed view . . . seems to be related to the election of a new President of a different political party. It is readily apparent that the responsible members of one administration may consider public resistance and uncertainties to be more important than do their counterparts in a previous administration. A change in administration brought about by the people casting their votes is a perfectly reasonable basis for an executive agency's reappraisal of the costs and benefits of its programs and regulations. As long as the agency remains within the bounds established by Congress, it is entitled to assess administrative records and evaluate priorities in light of the philosophy of the administration. *Motor Vehicle Mfrs. Assn. of United States, Inc. v. State Farm Mut. Automobile Ins. Co.*, 463 U.S. 29 (1983) (concurring in part and dissenting in part).

[V] One might nonetheless claim that, even if my interpretation of the FDCA and later statutes gets the words right, it lacks a sense of their "music." See *Helvering v. Gregory*, 69 F.2d 809, 810–811 (C.A.2 1934) (L. Hand, J.) ("[T]he meaning of a [statute] may be more than that of the separate words, as a melody is more than the notes . . ."). Such a claim might rest on either of two grounds.

First, one might claim that, despite the FDA's legal right to change its mind, its original statements played a critical part in the enactment of the later statutes and now should play a critical part in their interpretation. But the FDA's traditional view was largely premised on a perceived inability to prove the necessary statutory "intent" requirement. The statement, "we cannot assert jurisdiction over substance X unless it is treated as a food," would not bar jurisdiction if the agency later establishes that substance X is, and is intended to be, eaten. The FDA's denials of tobacco-related authority sufficiently resemble this kind of statement that they should not make the critical interpretive difference.

Second, one might claim that courts, when interpreting statutes, should assume in close cases that a decision with "enormous social consequences" should be made by democratically elected Members of Congress rather than by unelected agency administrators. Cf. *Kent v. Dulles*, 357 U.S. 116, 129(1958) (assuming Congress did not want to delegate the power to make rules interfering with exercise of basic human liberties). If there is such a background canon of interpretation, however, I do not believe it controls the outcome here.

Insofar as the decision to regulate tobacco reflects the policy of an administration, it is a decision for which that administration, and those politically elected officials who support it, must (and will) take responsibility. And the very importance of the decision taken here, as well as its attendant publicity, means that the public is likely to be aware of it and to hold those officials politically accountable. Presidents, just like Members of Congress, are elected by the public. Indeed, the President and Vice President are the only public officials whom the entire Nation elects. I do not believe that an administrative agency decision of this magnitude—one that is important, conspicuous, and controversial—can escape the kind of public scrutiny that is essential in any democracy. And such a review will take place whether it is the Congress or the Executive Branch that makes the relevant decision. * * *

The upshot is that the Court today holds that a regulatory statute aimed at unsafe drugs and devices does not authorize regulation of a drug (nicotine) and a device (a cigarette) that the Court itself finds unsafe. Far more than most, this particular drug and device risks the life-threatening harms that administrative regulation seeks to rectify. The majority's conclusion is counterintuitive. And, for the reasons set forth, I believe that the law does not require it.

NOTES AND QUESTIONS ON THE FDA TOBACCO CASE

The FDA's decision to regulate tobacco proceeded deliberatively and followed all the requirements for "informal" rulemaking (actually quite a formal process, as detailed in Chapter 7, § 1) found in the APA. The decision rested upon overwhelming support from science and health policy and was consistent with the plain meaning of the FDCA as well as its public health purposes; the big tobacco companies were on the defensive. Yet the Supreme Court rebuked the agency in an opinion that invoked a variety of legislative materials to reach a policy conclusion that most Americans probably thought ridiculous in the new millennium. Where, exactly, did the agency go wrong?

1.   *The Agency Took Too Big a Regulatory Step?* Did the FDA overstep the Executive Department's duty to "take care" that the FDCA be "faithfully executed"—and essentially act in a "legislative" manner? The Court majority seems to have been concerned that the FDA was not only making a big move inconsistent with its interstitial (gapfilling) powers, but a move inconsistent with regulatory decisions Congress had already made in other statutes. How would Justice Jackson's *Steel Seizure* concurring opinion analyze this matter? Would his functional approach raise red separation of powers flags about the agency's approach? How about Professor Nourse's representation-shifting view that the FDA's action improperly moved policy away from the constituencies of Congress, and toward the national science constituency and the President's own preferences, represented by the agency?

2. *The Unitary Executive.* Under Elena Kagan's account of "Presidential Administration," the FDA's story has great significance for theories of the unitary executive. It was President Clinton, not the agency, who announced the policy change, even before the FDA had finalized it. "Clinton's appropriation of regulatory product * * * sent a loud and lingering message: these were his agencies; he was responsible for their actions; and he was due credit for their successes. The public might have failed to appreciate this communication's import, but no one within the EOP or agencies could have done so. In asserting, time and again, ownership of and responsibility for the administrative sphere, Clinton may have made the prospects of substantive presidential intervention in any given regulatory matter ever more likely." Elena Kagan, *Presidential Administration*, 114 Harv. L. Rev. 2245, 2302 (2001). The idea that what may have been the President's own anti-tobacco politics could occasion a major policy shift by a scientific agency puts the question of the "unitary executive"—an executive branch controlled by the President—front and center. Anti-unitarians would argue that Congress delegated decisionmaking *to the FDA*, not to the President. On that view, to the extent that the President's actions could be understood as directing the FDA to publish the rule he wanted, as the Kagan account implies, see *id.* at 2301–02, they were possibly illegal.

3. *Were Reliance Interests Unduly Sacrificed?* Both the FDA and Congress had, for decades, taken the position that the FDCA did not cover tobacco or tobacco products—and the tobacco industry had relied on those assurances to make investments and develop its market in this country and across the world. Should agencies be able to change their positions? If you think so, on what grounds? Scientific evidence? The new President's politics? Either one? If you are drawn to the reliance argument, should private reliance interests count more than public health—especially the health of adolescents who were the primary focus of the FDA's proposed regulatory scheme?

4. *The Supreme Court's Role in Preserving Political Equilibrium and Institutional Role.* There were probably institutional reasons for the Court's decision. In a portion of her opinion, Justice O'Connor complained that the FDCA required the agency to ban tobacco products entirely if they were considered "drugs." (Justice Breyer disputed that understanding of the statute.) Neither the FDA nor the country was prepared to go so far as to ban tobacco entirely; the example of Prohibition of alcohol reminds us that a total ban could be disastrous. The Court's opinion might be read as resistance to the idea that an agency could move so far beyond the political equilibrium alone. The Court could have assumed that Congress, and not the agency, was the best forum for crafting a regulatory solution, both because of the hot politics of tobacco and also because of Congress's ability to amend the statutory scheme in ways that suited the tobacco situation better than the FDA's all-out power grab.

NOTE ON THE 2009 CONGRESSIONAL OVERRIDE OF THE FDA TOBACCO DECISION

Congress responded to *Brown & Williamson* with the Family Smoking Prevention & Tobacco Control Act of 2009, Pub. L. No. 111–31, 123 Stat. 1776 (2009). The starting point for the statute was that cigarette smoking causes devastating health effects to human beings and imposes enormous costs upon society and government. To discourage tobacco use among younger persons, Title I of the Act banned sales of tobacco products to persons under the age of 18 and authorized the FDA to develop an enforcement scheme for this ban. Title I also required the FDA to reissue its 1996 rules that had been invalidated in *Brown & Williamson*. Other provisions of the 2009 Act gave the FDA authority to set standards for the content of tobacco products (including tar and nicotine levels), to register tobacco companies, and to inspect such companies for compliance with the law. In addition, before tobacco companies can introduce new products, they must secure FDA approval (the FDA has traditionally exercised its approval power aggressively to force changes in products and marketing to satisfy health concerns). The 2009 Act also imposed limitations on the FDA's regulatory authority. Sections 906–907 bar the FDA from banning face-to-face retail sales of tobacco products entirely or from requiring a doctor's prescription to purchase these items.

Title II of the statute imposed nine new warnings for tobacco products, 15 U.S.C. § 1333, and authorized the FDA to develop the details of these warnings. After notice and comment, the FDA in 2011 announced final rules, with detailed requirements for advertisements of tobacco products. 76 Fed. Reg. 36,628 (June 22, 2011) (final rule, codified in 21 C.F.R. Part 1141, with responses to comments). Among the most controversial were new FDA requirements that packages include not only verbal warnings but also "graphic images" of smokers ravaged by lung cancer and other smoking-related illnesses. Tobacco companies successfully challenged these rules because they forced the companies to spout the government's "ideological" message, contrary to the First Amendment. *R.J. Reynolds Tobacco Co. v. Food & Drug Administration*, 696 F.3d 1205 (D.C. Cir. 2012).

Does the congressional override mean that *Brown & Williamson* was wrongly decided? On the one hand, the override vindicates the FDA's original rulemaking. Also relevant is the FDA's finding that the limitations and warnings imposed by its original rules would have saved thousands of lives between 1996 and 2010 (when the override statute took effect). On the other hand, the 2009 override statute was not only a more legitimate form of regulation (accomplished after achieving the political consensus required by the vetogate-ridden structure of Congress and bringing the tobacco industry to the table), but also went much further than the FDA had dared go in the 1990s (and remember, the Kessler FDA was a pretty daring agency). Specifically, Congress was able to reconcile the various disclosure statutes with the drug-regulatory statute—and the 2009 override was an occasion for

Congress to strengthen required disclosures and to authorize the FDA to create more effective disclosures than the abstract ones Congress had been imposing (with disappointing effects) since 1965.

Here is one way to understand the FDA Tobacco Case: Congressional delegation of lawmaking authority to an agency, in broad language ("drug"), is not an authorization for the agency to make "major" changes in statutory policy, especially when those changes reverse longstanding agency positions on which Congress has relied to develop an alternate statutory scheme. The *ex ante* argument is that this rule—that only Congress makes major changes in the statutory schemes—creates the best set of incentives for legitimate or efficient governance.

A virtue of such a rule is that it respects the vetogates structure of American constitutional governance (Chapter 1, § 1). For libertarian, pluralist, and civic republican reasons, it is presumptively better for our broadly representative Congress, rather than "expert" agencies, to make "big" political decisions that restrict consumer choice (anti-libertarian), affect significant groups in American society (tobacco farmers and companies, and states dependent on the tobacco industry), and might lack legitimacy if the process is purely bureaucratic rather than democratic (anti-republican). The 2009 Act certainly seems more consistent with the libertarian, pluralist, and civic republican premises than the 1996 FDA rulemaking. Note the parallel with the Civil Rights Act of 1964 (Chapter 1, § 1): The vetogates structure delayed enactment of major legislation, but the process and struggle to create the 1964 Act gave it legs that administrative or court decisions alone would not.

C. WHITE HOUSE COST-BENEFIT REVIEW OF AGENCY RULES

The President has many mechanisms available to influence agencies. As we have seen, the President appoints the agency heads. Although the appointment is subject to Senate rejection, the President as the "first mover" has a lot of discretion to choose someone whose regulatory philosophy is compatible with his or her own. The President's Office of Management and Budget (OMB) also prepares the budget, which the President sends to Congress, which Congress of course changes, which the President can veto, and which the President then spends. The President can use that power to punish agencies whose policies he disfavors and reward agencies the President favors. In this Section, we introduce another mechanism of presidential oversight: The White House has assumed a power to override some (executive) agency rules, a process referred to as "regulatory review."[21] We introduce the topic here and return to it in more detail in Chapter 7, § 2.

---

[21] See Thomas O. McGarity, *Reinventing Rationality: The Role of Regulatory Analysis in the Federal Bureaucracy* (1991); Richard B. Stewart, *Administrative Law in the Twenty-First*

(1) Origins and Justification for White House Regulatory Review

The process of White House regulatory review began immediately after the "new" public interest agencies (e.g., the EPA) were created. See Jim Tozzi, *OIRA's Formative Years: The Historical Record of Centralized Regulatory Review Preceding OIRA's Founding,* 63 Admin. L. Rev. 37 (2011). Thus, the Nixon Administration created a review process at OMB to facilitate interagency deliberations regarding proposed environmental regulations; President Ford directed executive branch agencies to prepare "inflation impact statements" for regulatory proposals. Going beyond these measures, President Carter's Executive Order 12,044 (Mar. 23, 1978), 43 Fed. Reg. 12,661–65 (Mar. 24, 1978), required executive agencies to accompany major regulatory proposals with analyses of their cost-effectiveness. The analyses had to include regulatory alternatives considered by agencies and a detailed explanation of reasons for choosing one option over the others.

The most important and enduring form of regulatory review, however, began within the Reagan Administration. President Reagan was elected on a platform of governmental cost-cutting, and he advanced a new constitutional order to that effect. Revoking an earlier order, President Reagan's Executive Order 12,291 (Feb. 17, 1981), 46 Fed. Reg. 13,193–98 (Feb. 1981), applied to executive department agencies but not independent regulatory agencies (§ 1(d)). Covered agencies were required to submit proposed rules and a "cost-benefit analysis" to the OMB's Office of Information and Regulatory Affairs (OIRA). Sections 2 and 3 set forth the primary requirements for these agencies, which we excerpt in part here:

> **Sec. 2.** *General Requirements.* In promulgating new regulations, reviewing existing regulations, and developing legislative proposals concerning regulation, all agencies, to the extent permitted by law, shall adhere to the following requirements:
>
> (a) Administrative decisions shall be based on adequate information concerning the need for and consequences of proposed government action;
>
> (b) Regulatory action shall not be undertaken unless the potential benefits to society for the regulation outweigh the potential costs to society;
>
> (c) Regulatory objectives shall be chosen to maximize the net benefits to society;

Century, 78 NYU L. Rev. 437 (2003); Cass R. Sunstein, *The Office of Information and Regulatory Affairs: Myths and Realities,* 126 Harv. L. Rev. 1838 (2013).

(d) Among alternative approaches to any given regulatory objective, the alternative involving the least net cost to society shall be chosen; and

(e) Agencies shall set regulatory priorities with the aim of maximizing the aggregate net benefits to society, taking into account the condition of the particular industries affected by regulations, the condition of the national economy, and other regulatory actions contemplated for the future.

Sec. 3. *Regulatory Impact Analysis and Review.* * * *

(d) To permit each proposed major rule to be analyzed in light of the requirements stated in Section 2 of this Order, each preliminary and final Regulatory Impact Analysis shall contain the following information:

(1) A description of the potential benefits of the rule, including any beneficial effects that cannot be quantified in monetary terms, and the identification of those likely to receive the benefits;

(2) A description of the potential costs of the rule, including any adverse effects that cannot be quantified in monetary terms, and the identification of those likely to bear the costs;

(3) A determination of the potential net benefits of the rule, including an evaluation of effects that cannot be quantified in monetary terms;

(4) A description of alternative approaches that could substantially achieve the same regulatory goal at lower cost, together with an analysis of this potential benefit and costs and a brief explanation of the legal reasons why such alternatives, if proposed, could not be adopted; * * *

Office of Legal Counsel, Memorandum for David Stockman, [OMB] Director: *Proposed Executive Order Entitled "Federal Regulation"*
1981 WL 30877 (Feb. 13, 1981).

This memorandum laid out the legal bases for the President's exercise of supervisory authority over agency rulemaking. "It is well established that [the Take Care Clause] authorizes the President, as head of the Executive Branch, to 'supervise and guide' executive officers in 'their construction of the statutes under which they act in order to secure that unitary and uniform execution of the laws which Article II of the Constitution evidently contemplated in vesting general executive power in the President alone.' *Myers.* * * *

"Moreover, because the President is the only elected official who has a national constituency, he is uniquely situated to design and execute a uniform method for undertaking regulatory initiatives that responds to the will of the public as a whole. In fulfillment of the President's constitutional responsibility, the proposed order promotes a coordinated system of regulation, ensuring a measure of uniformity in the interpretation and execution of a number of diverse statutes. If no such guidance were permitted, confusion and inconsistency could result as agencies interpreted open-ended statutes in differing ways.

"Nevertheless, it is clear that the President's exercise of supervisory powers must conform to legislation enacted by Congress [subject to the precept that Congress cannot 'intrude impermissibly' upon the President's inherent powers]. In issuing directives to govern the Executive Branch, the President may not, as a general proposition, require or permit agencies to transgress boundaries set by Congress. * * * When Congress delegates legislative power to executive agencies, it is aware that those agencies perform their functions subject to presidential supervision on matters of both substance and procedure." OLC distinguished independent agencies, which Congress might expect not to be subject to "presidential interference."

"Substantively, the order would require agencies to exercise their discretion, within statutory limits, in accordance with the principles of cost-benefit analysis. More complex legal questions are raised by this requirement. Some statutes may prohibit agencies from basing a regulatory decision on an assessment of the costs and benefits of the proposed action. *See*, e.g., *EPA v. National Crushed Stone Ass'n*, 449 U.S. 64 (1980). The order, however, expressly recognizes this possibility by requiring agency adherence to principles of cost-benefit analysis only 'to the extent permitted by law.'"

In an unpublished version of this opinion, OLC also considered whether the proposed executive order could legally be applied to independent agencies. The Acting Assistant Attorney General recognized that "dicta" in *Humphrey's Executor* were inconsistent with such authority and that Congress had relied on such "dicta" in creating and expanding those agencies. But OLC opined that "the Supreme Court would today [1981] retreat from these dicta." Additionally, *Humphrey's Executor* might be reconciled with the Take Care Clause in this way: "[A] frequent formulation of the President's power over the independent agencies has been that he may supervise them as necessary to ensure that they are faithfully executing the laws, although he may not displace their substantive discretion to decide particular adjudicative or rulemaking matters. Such a formulation would allow for many types of procedural supervision." In the opinion of OLC, the President can impose "procedural" requirements upon independent agencies. This would include the duty to prepare a regulatory impact analysis of proposed rules and to engage in a dialogue with OMB about the content and cogency of such analysis, so long as the agency and not the OMB made the final decision.

NOTES AND QUESTIONS ON WHITE HOUSE REGULATORY REVIEW

1.   *Was the Order Constitutional?* President Reagan's Executive Order 12,291 was immediately assailed as a violation of constitutional separation of powers, as articulated in the Steel Seizure Case. See Morton Rosenberg, *Presidential Control of Agency Rulemaking: An Analysis of Constitutional Issues That May Be Raised by Executive Order 12,291*, 23 Ariz. L. Rev. 1199 (1981). Rosenberg's argument was that OMB cost-benefit review of agency regulations is substantive remaking of law and therefore "legislative," as Justice Black used the term in the Steel Seizure Case. Reread our excerpts from President Reagan's executive order, and see how the Administration would respond to such a charge.

Additionally, the deployment of OMB for substantive review of agency rules, rather than coordination of budgetary authority, went against the history of congressional statutes in this arena, according to Rosenberg, *Beyond the Limits of Executive Power: Presidential Control of Agency Rulemaking Under Executive Order 12,291*, 80 Mich. L. Rev. 193 (1981). For counterarguments from an alumnus of OLC, see Peter M. Shane, *Presidential Regulatory Oversight and the Separation of Powers: The Constitutionality of Executive Order No. 12,291*, 23 Ariz. L. Rev. 1235 (1981).

2.   *Different Theories of the Take Care Clause.* Consider different theories of the Take Care Clause. A *procedural* or *faithful agent* theory posits that the President, when acting under the Take Care Clause, is nothing more than the faithful agent of Congress; he or she carries out statutory directives as the legislators expected and applies unclear directives in light of legislative purposes. This kind of theory would support Morton Rosenberg's skepticism about the executive order, and it receives a constitutional boost from *Humphrey's Executor* as well as the Steel Seizure Case.

A contrasting account, one held by constitutional unitarians, is a *stewardship* or *partnership* theory. Under a strong version of this theory, the Take Care President is invested with the obligation, as well as the discretion, to implement policies in a way that makes them better-suited to serve the good of the country. The President as implementing partner makes substantive judgments, not only keeping a careful eye on a program's costs relative to its benefits, but also trimming back defective programs and rethinking congressional purposes. This kind of theory would support a broad deployment of OMB to discipline agency over-regulation, and it receives a constitutional boost from *Myers* as well as *Free Enterprise*. Note that this kind of theory supports a pro-regulatory agenda just as easily as an antiregulatory one. See Nicholas Bagley & Richard Revesz, *Centralized Oversight of the Regulatory State,* 106 Colum. L. Rev. 1260 (2006).

A variation on the partnership theory asserts that the President is, in fact, the *senior partner* in American governance. His philosophy often trumps that of Congress because of the Presidency's first-mover advantages, and because of his ability to act decisively in the name of a coherent policy agenda. See Terry M. Moe & Scott A. Wilson, *Presidents and the Politics of Structure,* 57 Law & Contemp. Probs. 1 (Spring 1994). Additionally, most presidentialists claim a normative mandate for the office, as it is the only one (along with the Vice President) with a national constituency. See Elena Kagan, *Presidential Administration,* 114 Harv. L. Rev. 2245 (2001), who makes these arguments in favor of a preference for President-led policymaking.

The 1981 OLC Memorandum drew mostly from stewardship or partnership theory but was careful to accommodate the faithful agent point of view—and the published executive order was even more responsive to the latter perspective. There is a third theory suggested to us by Sheldon Jay Plager, the Administrator of OIRA from 1987–89.[22] We call this an *umpireal* theory: OIRA tries to serve the neutral umpire role of keeping all policy players on task, playing for the same team. Statutory execution now typically involves coordination among a number of agencies, and a primary umpireal duty of OIRA is to keep different agency policies from contradicting one another. Another umpireal duty is to get agencies to coordinate their activities in a more positive way. The most interesting umpireal duty is to correct for dysfunctions at the agency level. According to Plager, agencies are beset with three kinds of interrelated dysfunction: (1) turf-grabbing and increasing agency power, (2) capture by special interests, and (3) pressure from legislators and their staffs. All of these tendencies might be considered to have bad effects on policy, as they bend implementation to reflect a special agenda rather than the general interest represented by the statute. OIRA may seek opportunities to push back against agency accommodation of these special deals.

3.   *How Did OIRA Review Actually Work, 1981–1993?* As far as we can gather, early OIRA review under President Reagan mainly followed the faithful agent and the umpireal models in practice. According to OIRA Administrator Plager, the Reagan Administration felt that the legitimacy of OIRA review was fragile and that the Democrat-controlled House of Representatives would object if there was evidence that OMB was using its review authority to engage in backdoor deregulation. The Administration's blood-soaked battles with Congress over the openly dismissive attitude of EPA Administrator Anne Gorsuch toward the laws she was supposed to be implementing was disastrous from the White House's point of view. (Gorsuch

---

[22] Professor Eskridge met Jay Plager at the Duke Center for Judicial Studies' Conference on Presidential and Judicial Oversight of Administrative Agencies, April 27, 2012, and conducted two brief interviews with him. The discussion in text reflects Plager's remarks at the conference and during these two interviews.

was forced out of office and replaced with an aggressive regulator, former EPA Administrator William D. Ruckelshaus, whom Congress liked a lot better.)

On the other hand, it also appears that OIRA had substantive bite as well, consistent with the partnership theory. President Reagan had run on a platform of getting the federal government off of the back of American business, and his OIRA reflected his priorities (though Reagan himself took no interest in the operations of that organ). In particular, EPA and OSHA rules were carefully scrutinized, returned to the agencies for better justifications, sometimes killed, oftentimes amended or adjusted, and usually delayed by OIRA review. According to political scientist William West, the Reagan Administration's OIRA operated with a heavy hand on agencies that were accustomed to taking regulatory initiatives in response to congressional authorizations. See William F. West, *The Institutionalization of Regulatory Review: Organizational Stability and Responsive Competence at OIRA*, 35 Pres. Stud. Q. 76 (2005).

The institutional shock introduced by cost-benefit analysis sometimes spilled over into the courts. See *Environmental Defense Fund v. Thomas*, 627 F. Supp. 566 (D.D.C. 1986), where the court enjoined OMB from further delaying the EPA's efforts to promulgate regulations demanded by the 1984 amendments to RCRA and opined that OIRA review is no justification for an agency to miss statutorily imposed deadlines.

---

(2) White House Regulatory Review During the Clinton and Bush-Cheney Administrations

President William Clinton replaced the Reagan executive order with his own, Executive Order 12866, 58 Fed. Reg. 51735–41 (Sept. 30, 1993). Because this executive order is still in effect, we have reproduced it in Appendix 5.[23] Overall, the Clinton order continued the approach developed by his GOP predecessors, emphasizing the utility of a cost-benefit review of proposed agency rules. In its preamble, however, the Clinton order suggested a somewhat different ideal of what his administration was trying to be faithful to—namely, to carry out regulation "made necessary by compelling public need, such as material failures of private markets to protect or improve the health and safety of the public." E.O. 12866, § 1(a).

Relatedly, the Clinton order took an explicitly broader view of "cost-benefit" analysis than did the earlier order. Section 1(a) explicitly charged agencies and OMB with considering "qualitative" as well as quantifiable

---

[23] Several executive orders during the Bush-Cheney Administration amended Executive Order 12866, but President Obama's Executive Order 13497, 74 Fed. Reg. 6113 (2009), revoked the Bush-Cheney amendments and reinstated the original language of the Clinton order. On Clinton-era regulatory review, see Clinton OIRA Administrator Sally Katzen, *OIRA at Thirty: Reflections and Recommendations*, 63 Admin. L. Rev. 103 (2011).

costs and benefits, "potential" (i.e., contingent and future) costs and benefits as well as immediate ones, and the costs of inaction as well as the costs of doing something. E.O. 12866, § 1(a).

Finally, the Clinton order sought to address some criticisms of the Reagan order. Hence, the new order required a tighter timetable for OIRA review to avoid the embarrassment of the court's injunction in *EDF* (cited above). It also sought to make the process more transparent as critics claimed that the Reagan OIRA was a backdoor for industry officials to trim back some of the damage done by proposed and expensive EPA regulations. The new order required disclosure of outside contacts and information relied on by OIRA analysts.

Consistent with the executive order's pro-regulatory tenor, OIRA Administrator Sally Katzen (1993–98) brought a more cooperative relationship between OIRA and the EPA and other agencies, but her tenure also revealed more lasting institutional features. The fact that a Democratic Administration was continuing the Reagan Administration experiment gave OIRA review greater legitimacy than it had earlier. Indeed, the most outspoken defense of aggressive OIRA review was penned by Clinton Administration official Elena Kagan. In *Presidential Administration,* 114 Harv. L. Rev. 2245 (2001), she argued that presidential leadership and control over the "bureaucracy" promotes democratic accountability in governance. By taking ownership of administration (for which OIRA review is an important step), the President enables the public to respond to a government that is not working to its satisfaction.

The Bush-Cheney Administration (2001–09) left the Clinton order in place and made relatively few written changes, the most important one being the addition of "significant guidance documents" to those subject to OMB review (though it now appears that OIRA was reviewing many such documents between 1993 and 2007). Executive Order 13422, 72 Fed. Reg. 2763 (2007). The more important development during the Bush-Cheney Administration was OIRA's more aggressive deregulatory review and its more confrontational approach to the EPA and other agencies. In Circular A–4, which we examine in more detail in Chapter 7, § 2, the Bush-Cheney OIRA sought to standardize and improve the quality of data and data analysis which agencies could invoke to support proposed rules. See OMB, Circular A–4, To the Heads of Executive Agencies and Establishments: Regulatory Analysis (Sept. 17, 2003).

Through the years, OIRA has remained a powerful tool for the President to shape the major rulemaking work of his administration. Cf. Alex Acs & Charles M. Cameron, *Does White House Regulatory Review Produce A Chilling Effect and "OIRA Avoidance" in the Agencies?*, 43 Pres. Stud. Q. 443 (2013) (finding that agency appointments may have been more effective than OIRA review in shifting environmental and other policies toward the political preferences of Presidents Bush 43 and Obama).

(3) Expansion and Transformation of OIRA Review in the Obama Administration

When he took office, President Barack Obama issued Executive Order No. 13497, 74 Fed. Reg. 6113 (2009), reinstating the original language of President Clinton's executive order. Later in 2009, the President called for ideas to increase transparency and make other improvements in the OIRA process. If you were advising him, what would you urge as OIRA's priorities during President Obama's time in office? Consider the following problem, which illustrates how OIRA during the Obama Administration has been applying cost-benefit analysis.

PROBLEM 2–4: OIRA REVIEW OF PILOT FATIGUE REGULATIONS, 2010–2011

Consumer and pilot groups have complained for years that American airlines are pushing pilots to fly aircraft on very little sleep and that pilot fatigue leads to accidents. In the first airplane disaster within our borders in three years, Colgan Air Flight 3407 crashed into a farmhouse in Clarence, New York on February 12, 2009. Fifty people were killed, including both pilots, two crew, 45 passengers, and a person in the house. An important cause of the crash was pilot fatigue according to investigators. Citizen and pilot groups raised a hue and cry to Congress, which responded with the swiftness and delegation characteristic of emergency legislation. Section 212 of the Airline Safety and Federal Aviation Administration Extension Act of 2010, Pub. L. No. 111–216, 124 Stat. 2348 (2010), provides in relevant part:

SEC. 212.　　PILOT FATIGUE.

(a) FLIGHT AND DUTY TIME REGULATIONS.—

(1) IN GENERAL.—In accordance with paragraph (3), the Administrator of the Federal Aviation Administration shall issue regulations, based on the best available scientific information, to specify limitations on the hours of flight and duty time allowed for pilots to address problems relating to pilot fatigue.

(2) MATTERS TO BE ADDRESSED.—In conducting the rulemaking proceeding under this subsection, the Administrator shall consider and review the following:

(A) Time of day of flights in a duty period.

(B) Number of takeoff and landings in a duty period.

(C) Number of time zones crossed in a duty period.

(D) The impact of functioning in multiple time zones or on different daily schedules.

(E) Research conducted on fatigue, sleep, and circadian rhythms.

(F) Sleep and rest requirements recommended by the National Transportation Safety Board and the National Aeronautics and Space Administration.

(G) International standards regarding flight schedules and duty periods.

(H) Alternative procedures to facilitate alertness in the cockpit.

(I) Scheduling and attendance policies and practices, including sick leave.

(J) The effects of commuting, the means of commuting, and the length of the commute.

(K) Medical screening and treatment.

(L) Rest environments.

(M) Any other matters the Administrator considers appropriate.

(3) RULEMAKING.—The Administrator shall issue—

(A) not later than 180 days after the date of enactment of this Act, a notice of proposed rulemaking under paragraph (1); and

(B) not later than one year after the date of enactment of this Act, a final rule under paragraph (1). * * *

The Federal Aviation Administration (FAA) developed a Notice of Proposed Rulemaking within the time required and published it as *Flightcrew Member Duty and Rest Requirements*, 75 Fed. Reg. 55,852–89 (Sept. 14, 2010). Pull up the Federal Register now and read the agency's explanation of what it was doing, with a focus on pages 55,852–57, which introduce you to the lengthy history of expert recommendations that the airlines and/or the FAA adopt mandatory protocols to ensure that fatigued pilots are not operating scheduled commercial (part 121) aircraft and which explain the regulatory strategy adopted by the FAA. Part III.A (Applicability) explains the breadth of coverage and explains why the FAA rejected the demands of cargo-carrying airlines to exempt their pilots from the requirements (p. 55,857).

The FAA received more than 8,000 comments, some of them asking the agency to reconsider its inclusion of cargo pilots. According to OIRA's records, while the FAA was finalizing its rules, cargo airline officials and their association met with OIRA officials on at least four (recorded) occasions and presented them with cost-benefit analyses asserting that it was not cost-effective for the pilot fatigue regulations to be applied to cargo planes: Because of their irregular and often-shifting schedules, cargo carriers would find compliance with the rules very expensive, while the costs of the status quo were diminished by the fact that air crashes would not kill passengers. The same arguments had been presented to the FAA, which rejected them in its final draft rule submitted to OIRA on August 17, 2011; the same day, cargo industry officials again met with OIRA.[24]

At the same time the cargo carriers were lobbying OIRA to exempt them, the general carriers' association was assailing the entire regulation, arguing that nothing should be adopted because there was no cost-benefit case for any kind of intervention at this time, the Colgan disaster notwithstanding. E.g., Air Transport Association, Briefing for Office of Information and Regulatory Affairs, Federal Aviation Proposed Rule: Flightcrew Member Duty and Rest Requirements (July 25, 2011). Pilot groups also weighed in with OIRA, as did persons who lost family members in the Colgan crash. OIRA delayed issuance of a final rule by 125 days, as its staff demanded significant changes from the FAA.

After a great deal of cost-benefit pressure from the industry and from OIRA, the FAA finally acquiesced in the demands of the cargo carriers. Its Final Rule, *Flightcrew Member Duty and Rest Requirements* (Dec. 21, 2011), 77 Fed. Reg. 330–403 (Jan. 4, 2012), exempted all-cargo operations from the new pilot-fatigue rules. *Id.* at 330, 333, 335–36. Keeping the critical role of OIRA in the closet (as is typical in announcements of final rules), the FAA announced that it agreed with the industry representatives that the costs of compliance would be much higher for cargo air carriers and the benefits would be much lower; hence, extension of the regulation to those carriers would not be cost-justified.

The Independent Pilots Association (IPA) has raised a major public ruckus over the FAA's acquiescence in OIRA's and the industry's demands that so many pilots be exempted from the new regulations. IPA has pressed its objections with the FAA in a lawsuit and with Members of Congress. First, please set forth the IPA's primary arguments in response to the FAA's volte-face. How would the FAA and OIRA respond to these arguments? Second, as a policy matter, is this the sort of issue where administrators and judges can expect Congress to respond, as it did to the FDA Tobacco Case ruling?

Take a broader perspective. Does OIRA's performance regarding the Rules for Pilot Fatigue raise some questions about the application of cost-benefit analysis more broadly? If you were the President, ought you be concerned by OIRA's performance?

---

[24] The account in text is taken from James Goodwin, *Spurred on by Industry, OIRA Weakens Rule to Prevent Fatigue-Related Aviation Catastrophes*, CPR Blog, May 30, 2012, available at http://progressivereform.org/CPRBlog.cfm?idBlog=9CA2427E–B023–E297–6E9CA1731AF03E99 (viewed July 1, 2012).

If you are not concerned about OIRA's cost-benefit analysis here, you might want to consult Professor Lisa Heinzerling's analysis of the Obama Justice Department's prison rape regulations. See Heinzerling, *Cost-Benefit Jumps the Shark: The Department of Justice's Economic Analysis of Prison Rape*, Georgetown Law Faculty Blog, June 13, 2012, available at http://gulcfac.typepad.com/georgetown_university_law/2012/06/cost-benefit-jumps-the-shark.html (viewed July 1, 2012). She explains that, by statute, DOJ was required to issue regulations under the Prison Rape Elimination Act (PREA). The result, after applying cost-benefit analysis, was a 168 page document that incorporated an extensive hierarchy of rape crimes based on how much the victim would pay to avoid them (cost-benefit analysis puts a value on crimes like rape). Heinzerling noted that the PREA does not require, much less mandate, such an analysis. Is there an argument that the regulation is invalid under the statute?

NOTE ON THE OBAMA ADMINISTRATION EXPANSION OF COST-BENEFIT REVIEW

On January 18, 2011, President Obama issued Executive Order 13563, 76 Fed. Reg. 3821–23 (Jan. 21, 2011), reproduced in Appendix 5 to this coursebook. This order elaborated on President Clinton's order, which had been reinstated as written in January 2009. President Obama announced the same kind of pro-regulatory but cost-conscious philosophy that had characterized the earlier administration. Section 4 was more specific as to thinking about how to regulate "smart":

> Where relevant, feasible, and consistent with regulatory objectives, and to the extent permitted by law, each agency shall identify and consider regulatory approaches that reduce burdens and maintain flexibility and freedom of choice for the public. These approaches include warnings, appropriate default rules, and disclosure requirements as well as provision of information to the public in a form that is clear and intelligible.

Section 6(a) directed executive agencies to review existing regulations to assure that they remain cost-effective. The President's Council on Jobs and Competitiveness had urged action to reduce the number of agency regulations that imposed unnecessary costs on businesses, and President Obama was more aggressive than his predecessors in insisting that agencies review existing rules to roll back unnecessary regulatory costs. (That the economy was sluggish and job creation slower than the administration expected made this a more urgent project.)

In Executive Order 13,579, *Regulation and Independent Regulatory Agencies* (July 11, 2011), 76 Fed. Reg. 41587–88 (July 14, 2011), President Obama extended this cost-benefit reevaluation mandate to independent agencies, in the following language:

Sec. 2.   Retrospective Analyses of Existing Rules.

(a) To facilitate the periodic review of existing significant regulations, independent regulatory agencies should consider how best to promote retrospective analysis of rules that may be outmoded, ineffective, insufficient, or excessively burdensome, and to modify, streamline, expand, or repeal them in accordance with what has been learned. Such retrospective analyses, including supporting data and evaluations, should be released online whenever possible.

(b) Within 120 days of the date of this order, each independent regulatory agency should develop and release to the public a plan, consistent with law and reflecting its resources and regulatory priorities and processes, under which the agency will periodically review its existing significant regulations to determine whether any such regulations should be modified, streamlined, expanded, or repealed so as to make the agency's regulatory program more effective or less burdensome in achieving the regulatory objectives.

Does § 2's extension of White House regulatory review of independent agencies raise constitutional concerns? Regardless, is it good policy?

CHAPTER 3

THE COURTS

■ ■ ■

This chapter focuses on judicial action. As you read these materials, keep in mind the central questions: What do courts do? What kind of action can they take? What are the legal and constitutional limits on judicial action? Three issues are discussed: limits on who can sue, when they can sue, and about what questions they can sue; the enduring notion of courts as common law institutions deciding individual cases based on precedent; and how courts' failure to act can prompt other players, like agencies and Congress, to solve a problem.

Article III, § 1 of the Constitution vests the "judicial Power" in the Supreme Court and any "inferior courts" that Congress might create, as it did in the Judiciary Act of 1789. The Supreme Court and lower federal courts have the power to decide "cases and controversies" and, in such a context, to determine the constitutionality of state and federal laws. Art. III, § 2. The courts also have the power to interpret legislation and to review actions of the executive branch, including agency rules and regulations.

Power. Courts decide cases. Article III, § 2 provides federal courts with the power to decide specifically enumerated "cases or controversies." As interpreted, Article III requires that courts only decide cases in which litigants have an actual stake in the controversy. Federal courts may not issue advisory opinions, which means that, without a case, they may not express an opinion simply because the issue is timely or controversial. In fact, under "standing" and "political question" doctrines, courts are supposed to decline to exercise jurisdiction over a case that resists determination within the "case or controversy" framework. Moreover, Congress has significant power over the extent of federal court jurisdiction and authority. Congress passes statutes allocating jurisdiction, and Congress, of course, passes federal substantive laws—statutes—that themselves enlarge the terrain for federal courts by putting new "federal questions" into the public domain.

Notwithstanding all these limitations, the judiciary exercises great power through its constitutional and statutory authority to interpret the

Constitution, federal legislation, and treaties. The Supreme Court also retains "inherent" powers to remedy statutory and constitutional violations that are adjudicated by federal judges in the context of cases and controversies. Section 1 of this chapter will briefly introduce you to some basic limitations in the authority of the Supreme Court and the lower federal courts. We do not discuss state courts in this chapter, but remember that state courts sit with equal authority to the lower federal courts to hear most federal questions, including questions of federal statutory law. (The topics in this section are covered in much greater detail in your school's Federal Courts or Federal Jurisdiction course.)

Competency and Capacity. Considered by the Framers to be the "least dangerous branch," having no army and no constituency, *Federalist* No. 78 (Hamilton), the Supreme Court is a substantially different institution from Congress and the President. Related to its limited agenda-setting and case-initiation capabilities (the Article III limits noted above), the chief characteristic of the Supreme Court is that its exercise of power proceeds through case-by-case adjudication, which itself rests upon the Anglo-American common law tradition. The chief contribution the Court makes to American governance is the rule of law, the confidence that people and businesses have that there are identifiable legal rules that they can rely on and must follow, and that can be predictably elaborated by judges. Section 2 of this chapter will explore the comparative institutional advantage that the Supreme Court brings to the task of guaranteeing a neutral rule of law; the biggest advantage is the common law doctrine of *stare decisis*, whereby Supreme Court decisions not only bind lower courts but also bind the Supreme Court itself.

Representation. The federal judiciary is not a "representative" institution in the way that Congress and the President are. No judge in the federal system believes that he or she is beholden to apply the views of a particular constituency. On the other hand, there are remote links between judges and the public, particularly at the time of appointment. Typically, federal judges are not political outliers, as they must be confirmed by the Senate, which is a broadly representative body. Moreover, because the Supreme Court's interpretation of landmark and other significant statutes has political as well as legal consequences, judicial decisions play out in the political process, which sometimes overrides them. Section 3 of this chapter illustrates the Court's important role in the politics of a statutory question even when the Justices operate under outdated assumptions and beliefs, and explores the Court's possible responses to pushbacks from the political process, especially in the form of congressional overrides of Supreme Court statutory decisions.

1. THE JUDICIAL POWER OVER CASES AND CONTROVERSIES

Article III, § 1 vests the "judicial Power" in the Supreme Court and "such inferior Courts as Congress may from time to time ordain and establish." Section 2 defines the "judicial Power" as extending to "all Cases, in Law and Equity, arising under this Constitution, the Laws of the United States, and Treaties made, or which shall be made, under their Authority," as well as to a variety of other explicitly defined "Cases" and "Controversies." The Supremacy Clause, Art. VI, declares that the Constitution, federal statutes, and treaties are the "supreme Law of the Land," and that state judges are "bound thereby."

As a result of its authority to interpret the Constitution, federal statutes, and treaties, the Supreme Court often contributes to major policy debates over such issues as racial segregation, affirmative action, abortion choice, health care, immigration policy, and so forth. Yet just as striking as the frequent judicial interventions are the many examples where judges have no role to play because no parties bring a lawsuit. When the Bush-Cheney Administration was wiretapping Americans, possibly contrary to federal statutory guarantees, no one sued the lawbreakers, in part because no one knew he or she was being wiretapped. See also *Clapper v. Amnesty Int'l*, 133 S.Ct. 1138 (2013) (even after national security wiretapping became public knowledge, the Court has made it hard for plaintiffs to secure a judicial forum).

In contrast to the possibly illegal wiretapping by the Bush-Cheney Administration, there was a lawsuit challenging the Obama Administration's possibly illegal bombing missions in Libya. Although no soldier or family member sued, several members of Congress sued to enforce the War Powers Resolution—and their lawsuit was dismissed as quickly as you can spell War Powers Resolution. See *Kucinich v. Obama*, 821 F. Supp. 2d 110 (D.D.C. 2011). The reason rests in the restrained authority that the Supreme Court has read into the judicial power as articulated in Article III, § 2: such cases are "nonjusticiable" under Article III, as the Supreme Court has interpreted it.[1]

Article III, § 2 enumerates several heads of federal jurisdiction, all of which are either "Cases" or "Controversies," eighteenth century language connoting concrete clashes between competing interpretations of law. This general idea is given greater legal bite through analysis of the

---

[1] The Supreme Court's nonjusticiability cases are widely reviled within the legal academy, e.g., Owen Fiss, *The Civil Rights Injunction* (1978); Martin Redish, *The Federal Courts in the Political Order: Judicial Jurisdiction and American Political Theory* (1991), but the Justices hew to a strongly restrictive understanding of Article III, as the cases in the text will reveal. Indeed, one issue that seems to excite the passion of the current Chief Justice is justiciability. E.g., *Hollingsworth v. Perry*, 133 S.Ct. 2652 (2013) (Roberts, C.J.); *Massachusetts v. EPA*, 549 U.S. 497 (2009) (Roberts, C.J., dissenting).

structure of Article III and of the Constitution. Thus, the Vesting Clause speaks of the "judicial Power," which was understood in 1789 to entail adjudication of a concrete, active legal grievance that a court has power to redress. And the Constitution's separation of powers (as well as a comparison of the Vesting Clauses of Articles I, II, and III) suggests that the Supreme Court's "judicial" authority must be differentiated from the "legislative" (Article I) and "executive" (Article II) authorities given other branches.

The Court is sensitive to charges of usurpation of democratically accountable legislative and executive authority. We shall see that sensitivity many times over in our story of how the Court perceives its role in cases concerning statutory interpretation and implementation. In this introductory chapter, we focus not on interpretation but rather on how the courts use doctrines about judicial *power* to effectuate those concerns about separation of powers. Most importantly, the Court has inferred from Article III various doctrines of *justiciability* that the Court insists limits its power to adjudicate lawsuits in the first place. See *Valley Forge Christian College v. Americans United for Separation of Church and State*, 454 U.S. 464 (1982). Consider three kinds of persons who would like to have stopped American participation in the bombing campaign in Libya in 2011: (1) American armed forces personnel who did not want to risk their lives or the lives of men and women under their command who were participating in an illegal mission; (2) taxpayers who did not want their tax dollars funding an illegal or unwise war; and (3) Representative Dennis Kucinich and other members of Congress who wanted to make sure the President did not usurp authority he did not have under the Declare War Clause or the War Powers Resolution (see the Steel Seizure Case, Chapter 2.).

As you work through the various doctrines (below), keep in mind the larger impact of these judicial self-limits for the operation of government. From the Supreme Court's perspective, these doctrines keep the Justices from venturing too far into arenas where they have nothing useful (or strictly legal) to add and from interfering with political interactions where they can do harm. But from a broader rule-of-law perspective, these doctrines run the risk of insulating unlawful government actions from judicial review and expanding the discretion of executive officials. Yet more broadly, the Article III justiciability cases might create various biases in modern regulation.

1.   Timing: Ripeness and Mootness. Federal courts will not hear lawsuits that do not involve actual and *present* controversies between the parties. Although riddled with exceptions and uneven application, the doctrines of ripeness and mootness regulate the timing of lawsuits. A lawsuit can be too early—or it can expire before the parties' dispute is settled, often by outside events.

"Determination of the scope and constitutionality of legislation in advance of its immediate adverse effect in the context of a concrete case involves too remote and abstract an inquiry for the proper exercise of the judicial function." *International Longshoremen's & Warehousemen's Union, Local 37 v. Boyd*, 347 U.S. 222, 224 (1954). In *United Public Workers v. Mitchell*, 330 U.S. 75, 89–90 (1947), for example, government workers challenged provisions of the Hatch Act prohibiting their participation in political campaigns. While the Court found that one employee who had violated the Act had a ripe claim, those who merely wished to undertake political activities, but had not yet done so, were barred from adjudication. The Court said that the power of judicial review "arises only when the interests of litigants require the use of this judicial authority for their protection against actual interference. A hypothetical threat is not enough." Admittedly, ripeness doctrine is unevenly applied, and it has declined as a stated limit on Article III's grant of "judicial Power." For example, in First Amendment cases (like a modern day parallel to *Mitchell*), the Court is more likely to find a ripe controversy, without an actual prosecution, because of the "chilling effect" of state censorship on free speech and press rights.

" '[F]ederal courts are without power to decide questions that cannot affect the rights of litigants in the case before them.' The inability of the federal judiciary 'to review moot cases derives from the requirement of Article III of the Constitution under which the exercise of judicial power depends upon the existence of a case or controversy.'" *DeFunis v. Odegaard*, 416 U.S. 312, 316 (1974) (per curiam). Any number of things might moot a case: the plaintiff no longer objects to the defendant's conduct, the defendant agrees to conform with the plaintiff's demands, or the passage of time renders the court unable to grant the plaintiff the remedy she seeks. In *DeFunis*, the Court found the plaintiff's claim that he had been unconstitutionally denied admission to the University of Washington Law School (on the ground that the state law school's affirmative preferences for minority applicants gave his place to someone less well "qualified") moot because the school later admitted the plaintiff and he was about to graduate when the matter reached the Court. At that late point, even a judicial ruling in his favor would have no actual effect on DeFunis's rights. If the Supreme Court agreed with the district court, which had ordered DeFunis admitted, obviously DeFunis would get his degree. But everyone in the case also agreed that he would get his degree even if the Supreme Court held that the law school had acted lawfully. Over the objections of four Justices, the Court held that the case did not present a justiciable case or controversy.

There are also exceptions to the mootness rule. If DeFunis had been a plaintiff in a class action, the case would have proceeded because there only has to be one plaintiff whose case has not been mooted for a class action to present a valid case or controversy. *Sosna v. Iowa*, 419 U.S. 393 (1975). Another exception responds to the seemingly inequitable dilemma that favors defendants with the resources to stall litigation until the plaintiff's claim expires: the Court will sometimes hear a case notwithstanding its mootness where an issue is "capable of repetition, yet evading review," because the lawsuit's duration systematically tends to moot individual grievances. *Southern Pacific Terminal Co. v. ICC*, 219 U.S. 498, 515 (1911). *Roe v. Wade* and other abortion-choice cases came to the U.S. Supreme Court notwithstanding their apparent mootness, because the short time frame of abortions would render a whole class of individual rights cases nonjusticiable, which the Justices have not been willing to tolerate.

Timing issues would have bedeviled lawsuits to head off the Libyan bombing campaign. If Representative Kucinich had limited his lawsuit to WPR violations and had sued the President before the 60/90-day period, his WPR claim would not have been ripe until the President did something allegedly in violation of the 60/90-day cutoff for "hostilities" unless there was a congressional authorization. The ten members of Congress, of course, claimed that American participation in the Libyan bombing campaign was a constitutional "war" requiring a declaration from Congress under Article I, § 8—and so that claim was ripe from the commencement of hostilities.

If the plaintiffs had waited until the 90-day cutoff, WPR claims would have been ripe—but all of their claims would soon have been mooted, as General Qadhafi was overthrown by his own people (assisted by NATO-American air support) within months of the 90-day cutoff. Once President Obama halted the bombing, there was no longer a live controversy between him and his critics. Anticipating this kind of mootness problem, the plaintiffs would have wanted to move for a preliminary injunction at the beginning of their lawsuit. As above, there would have been other justiciability problems that might prevent a federal judge from adjudicating even a preliminary injunction, but such a motion could fall between the Scylla of ripeness and the Charybdis of mootness.

2. Personal Stake: Standing. Since the New Deal, federal judges have interpreted Article III to require that a plaintiff have a personal stake in the outcome of a case or controversy, so as to assure concrete adverseness that sharpens the presentation of issues upon which the court depends for illumination of difficult constitutional and statutory questions. Thus, the plaintiff in a case or controversy must be someone who has suffered an "injury in fact," an actual injury to her interests. Conversely, a defendant in a federal lawsuit who "loses" at the district court or circuit court level and desires to take an appeal must have the same kind of injury in fact, as this person or institution is the petitioning party at the appellate stage. *Hollingsworth v. Perry*, 133 S.Ct. 2652, 2661 (2013).

In addition, the Supreme Court has ruled that a plaintiff suffering from an actual injury, as required by Article III, must also make a claim that is within the "zone of interests" meant to be protected by constitutional or statutory provisions. *Association of Data Processing Service Organizations v. Camp*, 397 U.S. 150 (1970). The Supreme Court considers the injury-in-fact component of standing a constitutional requirement of Article III, but the zone-of-interests component only a prudential concern inspired by Article III. In addition, the Court considers, as a prudential matter, whether the challenging party actually brings to the case or controversy the "concrete adverseness" that Article III assumes. *See United States v. Windsor*, 133 S.Ct. 2675, 2687–89 (2013).

Doctrinally, the key concept is *injury in fact*. In *Allen v. Wright*, 468 U.S. 737, 751 (1984), the Court classically articulated what it considers an injury in fact: "A plaintiff must allege personal injury fairly traceable to the defendant's allegedly unlawful conduct and likely to be redressed by the requested relief." In this and other cases, the Court makes three inquiries: (1) whether plaintiff has suffered a legally cognizable injury distinct to that plaintiff and not universally shared, (2) whether plaintiff's injury is the result of defendant's conduct, and (3) whether plaintiff's injury can be redressed by the judicial relief she requests. *Los Angeles v. Lyons*, 461 U.S. 95 (1983); see also *Clapper v. Amnesty International*, 133 S.Ct. 1138 (2013) (also requiring that the injury be "imminent"). If a showing of any of these three elements is lacking, the court will dismiss the suit for lack of constitutional standing.

Of our three plaintiffs in the Libyan Bombing Case, a military person serving in the bombing missions is the only one with a chance of establishing constitutional standing, as the Supreme Court has interpreted Article III. Yet even soldiers might face some Article III objections. For example, they could not rely on "potential" injury; in fact, no American was killed and perhaps none was seriously injured in the Libyan bombing campaign. While they might argue that the enhanced risk of injury is sufficient, the Supreme Court has imposed an imminence requirement that might weed out some of those cases. *Clapper v. Amnesty International*, 133 S.Ct. 1138 (2013). Commanding officers with no reasonable risk of injury cannot assert the rights of "third parties" (i.e., troops serving under them), see *Tileston v. Ullman*, 318 U.S. 44 (1943) (per curiam) (doctor has no standing to litigate the rights of his patients), and would have to assert their own enhanced risk, which might be too speculative to meet the Court's requirements.

None of the plaintiffs—the soldiers, the taxpayers, or the legislators—can rely on the fact that they are American citizens wanting to make sure the President obeys the law. Agreeing that the President should obey the law, the Justices would still insist on a proper plaintiff with a "personal" stake in the case or controversy—such as the steel companies whose factories were seized by President Truman in the Steel Seizure Case. Someone whose "stake" is undifferentiated from that of a host of other people does not have standing to sue the President. Article III is not a forum for angry citizens wanting to enforce the law—such citizens are supposed to engage in the political process, and enforcement of the law is left to the executive branch and sometimes congressional pressure. Likewise, the Court has rejected generalized "taxpayer standing" for the same reason: there must be a distinct stake personal to the plaintiff. See *Frothingham v. Mellon*, 262 U.S. 447 (1923) (leading case).[2]

How about Representative Kucinich, who wants to make sure congressionally enacted statutes are not ignored? Even he has no standing, as the district court ruled in 2011, applying *Raines v. Byrd*, 521 U.S. 811 (1997). This is an important point: *Members of Congress cannot simply sue to object to how statutes they enacted are being interpreted or implemented.* In *Raines*, Senator Robert Byrd sued to enjoin the operation of the Line Item Veto Act, which Byrd had opposed on constitutional grounds. The West Virginia legislator was right about the Constitution, but he had no constitutional standing because his claimed injury was not sufficiently "personal, particularized, concrete." *Id.* at 820. He and other legislators alleged no injury to themselves as individuals: "the institutional injury they allege[d]"—how the line item veto alters the balance of lawmaking power—"is wholly abstract and widely dispersed." *Id.* at 829. The Court "attach[ed] some importance to the fact" that the plaintiffs did not have formal authority to represent either branch of Congress. It also noted that "our conclusion neither deprives Members of Congress of an adequate remedy (since they may repeal the Act or exempt appropriations bills from its reach), nor forecloses the Act from constitutional challenge (by someone who suffers judicially cognizable injury as a result of the Act)." *Id.*[3] In other words, elected members who

---

[2]   In *Flast v. Cohen*, 392 U.S. 83 (1968), the Court allowed standing for taxpayers to sue the state for providing aid to religious schools, allegedly in violation of the Establishment Clause. Since 1968, the Court has repeatedly limited the reach of *Flast*, e.g., *Arizona Christian School Tuition Organization v. Winn*, 131 S.Ct. 1436 (2011) (*Flast* did not apply to tax credits for contributions to organizations that fund scholarships for students at private schools), and several Justices have called for the Court to overrule *Flast*. See *Hein v. Freedom from Religion Foundation, Inc.*, 551 U.S. 587, 618–37 (2007) (Scalia, J., joined by Thomas, J., concurring in the judgment).

[3]   The *Byrd* Court distinguished *Coleman v. Miller*, 307 U.S. 433 (1939), in which the Court granted state legislators standing. In *Coleman*, half of the members of the Kansas Senate had voted not to ratify the proposed Child Labor Amendment, but the lieutenant governor cast the deciding vote in favor of the amendment. The *Byrd* Court ruled that *Coleman* "stands (at most)

are unhappy with a statute's operation on the ground generally must use their *own* constitutional powers—to enact, repeal and amend legislation and to oversee agencies—not the courts'.

Once President Clinton exercised the line-item veto authority that Congress (over Byrd's objections) had vested in his office, institutions denied money because of the veto successfully sued the President. A divided Supreme Court struck down the line-item veto (Chapter 1, § 2 of this coursebook), but all of the Justices agreed that at least some of the disappointed beneficiaries had standing. *Clinton v. City of New York*, 524 U.S. 417, 429–35 (1998) (all of the disappointed beneficiaries had standing); *id.* at 456–63 (Scalia, J., concurring in part and dissenting in part) (only the disappointed spending beneficiaries had standing); *id.* at 469 (Breyer, J., concurring in part and dissenting in part) (agreeing with the Court on the standing issues).

   3.   Subject Matter: Political Question Doctrine. Suggested by the Constitution's separation of legislative, executive, and judicial powers, the Supreme Court's political question doctrine posits that "courts ought not enter the political thicket." *Colegrove v. Green*, 328 U.S. 549, 556 (1946). Thus, even if Representative Kucinich's Libyan bombing lawsuit had not been dismissed for lack of standing, the district court might have dismissed it as a nonjusticiable "political question." See *Kucinich v. Bush*, 236 F. Supp. 2d 1 (D.D.C. 2002) (dismissing earlier Kucinich lawsuit on both standing and political question grounds).

What exactly makes an issue a "political question" rather than just a case with political implications? The leading exposition is the Supreme Court's decision in *Baker v. Carr*, 369 U.S. 186, 217 (1962):

> Prominent on the surface of any case held to involve a political question is found a textually demonstrable constitutional commitment of the issue to a coordinate political department; or a lack of judicially discoverable and manageable standards for resolving it; or the impossibility of deciding without an initial policy determination of a kind clearly for nonjudicial discretion;

---

for the proposition that legislators whose votes would have been sufficient to defeat (or enact) a specific legislative Act have standing to sue if that legislative action goes into effect (or does not go into effect), on the ground that their votes have been completely nullified." 521 U.S. at 823. Hence, to "uphold standing here would require a drastic extension of *Coleman*. We are unwilling to take that step." *Id.* at 826.

   Concurring, Justice Souter resolved the standing issue "under more general separation-of-powers principles underlying our standing requirements." *Id.* at 832–33. A dispute "involving only officials, and the official interests of those, who serve in the branches of the National Government" is far removed "from the model of the traditional common-law cause of action at the conceptual core of the case-or-controversy requirement." *Id.* at 833. The case presented "an interbranch controversy about calibrating the legislative and executive powers, as well as an intrabranch dispute between segments of Congress itself." *Id.* "Intervention in such a controversy" would embroil "the federal courts in a power contest nearly at the height of its political tension." *Id.*

or the impossibility of a court's undertaking independent resolution without expressing lack of the respect due coordinate branches of government; or an unusual need for unquestioning adherence to a political decision already made; or the potentiality of embarrassment from multifarious pronouncements by various departments on one question.

Unless one of these formulations is inextricable from the case at bar, there should be no dismissal for non-justiciability on the ground of a political question's presence. The doctrine of which we treat is one of "political questions," not one of "political cases."

The *Baker* Court ruled that one person-one vote claims grounded upon the Equal Protection Clause were not political questions and were justiciable under Article III. The Court expected there to be judicially manageable standards for an issue that the Constitution did not commit to the discretion of the political branches.

In contrast, the Court has consistently held that claims of partisan "gerrymandering"—the drawing of election districts to maximize party gain—are political questions that courts should not decide. See *Vieth v. Jubelirer*, 541 U.S. 267 (2004).

In another recent case, the Supreme Court considered a challenge to the Senate's practice of referring impeachment cases to special committees of senators that hear witnesses and then report to the Senate, which votes on whether to convict based upon the committee's report. The House had impeached Judge Walter Nixon for taking bribes; the Senate convicted him based upon the analysis and recommendation of a committee report. Judge Nixon argued that this was an arbitrary manner for the Senate to discharge its constitutional duties under Art. I, § 3, cl. 6. In *Nixon v. United States*, 506 U.S. 224 (1993), the Court ruled that this was a nonjusticiable political question. The majority read Clause 6 as a constitutional commitment of impeachment trials to the "sole Power" of the Senate, without any constitutional standards for judging whether the Senate was in default of its constitutional responsibilities. Judicial review of the Senate's adjudication would upset the balance of powers created by the Framers for impeachments under Article I: adding a layer of judicial review would make it harder and take a lot longer for the political process to impeach and remove corrupt officials.

The Court's most recent case involved a dispute between Congress and the State Department. Contrary to State Department practice, Congress has legislated that a person born in (disputed) Jerusalem shall be listed as born in Israel for passport purposes. Lower courts dismissed a lawsuit brought by a Jerusalem-born Israeli suing the Secretary of State to follow the statute. The Supreme Court reversed, finding the matter not to be a political question. Although complicated, the statutory and constitutional issues were susceptible to judicial decision. *Zivotofsky v. Clinton*, 132 S.Ct. 1421 (2012). In a concurring opinion, Justice Sotomayor argued that the political question doctrine is properly understood as a very narrow exception to the Court's *Marbury* authority and should only be invoked when judges are certain that the Constitution reserves decision to the political branches *or* that there are no judicially manageable standards for resolving the controversy *or* that adjudication would not be "prudent" because of unusual circumstances creating unnecessary embarrassment for other branches of government.

PROBLEM 3–1: JUSTICIABILITY OF CHALLENGES TO THE SENATE FILIBUSTER

Recall from Chapter 1, § 3, the arguments by Professor Joshua Chafetz and others that the Senate filibuster is unconstitutional. Those arguments have been bruited about within Congress and the political process but have never been addressed by the Supreme Court. Consider the following hypothetical lawsuit.

The President nominates Professor Victor Doctor to be a Supreme Court Justice. Professor Doctor is a world-renowned scholar of statutory interpretation and constitutional law; he has also drafted important civil rights legislation that secured bipartisan sponsorship and lop-sided congressional votes. But his appointment becomes embroiled in partisan politics: the President's party might lose the Presidency and the Senate in the upcoming election, and the opposing party filibusters to block deliberation and a vote on Doctor's nomination. The majority party tries to break the filibuster, and wins 58 votes out of 100 cast, but that is not enough to break the filibuster under Senate Rule XXII (requiring 60 votes). Further votes would be futile, and Doctor's nomination dies at the end of the Congress in question.

Angered by this scandal, three plaintiffs bring a federal lawsuit seeking a declaratory judgment that the filibuster is unconstitutional, as applied to Supreme Court nominations. (Recall, from Chapter 1, § 3, that the Senate in 2013 amended its Rules to render the filibuster inapplicable to nominations to lower federal courts.) The plaintiffs are Professor Doctor, the defeated nominee; Senator Doris Soaper, the floor manager for Doctor's nomination; and Joe Kim, a U.S. citizen who is depressed by the partisan politics surrounding judicial nominations and alleges that the death of Doctor's nomination has caused him "to lose faith in the integrity of the judicial nomination process."

Consider the original meaning of the Rules of Proceedings Clause, U.S. Const. Art. I, § 5 ("Each House may determine the Rules of its Proceedings"). Would that history make a difference? Reflecting most of the post-Independence state constitutions, Article I, § 5 was inspired by Parliament's procedural independence. See generally Thomas Jefferson, *Manual of*

Parliamentary Practice iii (1837) (influential explication of the Founders' understanding). Blackstone's *Commentaries*, well-known by the founding generation, explained Parliament's independence in these terms:

> [T]he whole of the law and custom of parliament has it's [sic] original from this one maxim, 'that whatever matter arises concerning either house of parliament, ought to be examined, discussed, and adjudicated in that house to which it relates, and not elsewhere.' Hence, for instance . . . [n]or will either house permit the subordinate courts of law to examine the merits of [cases involving the election of members]. . . . [T]he maxims upon which they proceed, together with the method of proceeding, rest entirely in the breast of the parliament itself.

1 Sir William Blackstone, *Commentaries on the Laws of England* 181 (1765) (St. George Tucker American ed. 1803). Consider also the structure of Article I, as well as the language actually used in Article I, § 5 (perhaps compared with Article I, § 7).

In light of the text and original meaning of Article I, § 5, as well as the Supreme Court's relevant Article III precedents, what arguments should the Attorney General make? How would a federal judge or federal court rule on this issue?

NOTE ON JUSTICIABILITY LIMITS AND GOVERNMENT FUNCTIONING

The Article III requirements for justiciability, as they have been articulated by the Supreme Court in the last generation, have potentially significant consequences for American governance. One might view the Court's understanding of "judicial Power" as assuming a common law model of the lawsuit: the plaintiff has suffered a loss cognizable at common law, the defendant has caused it, and courts can remedy the plaintiff's problem by assessing damages and/or stopping the defendant from violating the plaintiff's rights. A lot of the Court's standing decisions seem to follow this model, demanding that even public law litigation present plaintiffs who have been uniquely injured by particular action on the part of the defendant that a court can stop or assess damages. Additionally, the Supreme Court has limited procedural innovations such as class actions in light of this common law template for what adjudication ought to be. E.g., *Walmart Stores, Inc. v. Dukes*, 131 S.Ct. 2541 (2011) (reversing class action certification because there was insufficient showing that all members of the class were "discriminated" against by a common employer policy).

In the modern regulatory state, such an understanding of Article III has tremendous ramifications not only for judicial authority, but also for governance and the rule of law. Consider some potential ramifications, and evaluate whether they are causes for concern:

1. Agencies may be pressed toward underenforcing statutory mandates. From Congress's or the public's point of view, there is always the risk that agencies will either *underenforce* statutes (not applying them to core concerns or treating violators mildly) or *overenforce* statutes (applying them, way beyond legislative expectations, to trivial or controversial fact situations). *Supreme Court standing doctrine tends to raise the risk of underenforcement while reducing the risk of overenforcement.* If an agency enforces a law, those against whom the law is enforced will likely be able to sue because they will be affected by the enforcement. But if the agency ignores the law, either no one can sue or, at best, the possibility of suit is reduced. The effect of standing law is to make it more likely that agencies will underenforce statutes.

These questions get even more complicated when more players are involved. Consider *Douglas v. Independent Living Center of Southern California*, 132 S.Ct. 1204 (2012), in which medical providers alleged that the State of California was not paying doctors enough, in violation of the federal Medicaid statute. Because the federal agency that enforces Medicaid had not objected to the State's rates, the providers were between a rock and a hard place: they had no statutory hook on which to sue and no formal agency action to challenge. A post-argument change of position by the federal agency[4] allowed the Court to avoid answering the question whether providers could ever sue in such a situation, but Chief Justice Roberts's dissent for four Justices is loaded with language suggesting that he would have rejected the providers' claims. The Medicaid community has responded by raising concerns about underenforcement of the statute without accountability.

How do you feel about this? On the one hand, statutory underenforcement undermines congressional expectations embodied in statutes entrusted to agencies. And statutes devoted to public purposes are denuded of much of their power. On the other hand, the Constitution might be read as a libertarian document: Article I and related vetogates make it less likely that Congress will pass statutes in the first place; the Bill of Rights provides libertarian checks on congressional statutes; and Article III ensures that agencies and executive branch departments will be more cautious when they apply statutes than when they refrain from application.

Sometimes, the Supreme Court blinks back justiciability issues in the face of serious underenforcement problems. A recent example is *Massachusetts v. EPA*, 549 U.S. 497 (2007), where the Court ruled that the Commonwealth of Massachusetts had standing to force the EPA to confront whether rising carbon dioxide levels contribute to global warming and, therefore, fall under the EPA's protective jurisdiction. The Court relied on Congress's vesting special procedural rights of appeal in the states and upon the Commonwealth's ownership of properties that could be destroyed by global warming. A dissenting opinion claimed that the Court was bending the

---

[4] While the case was pending, the agency formally approved the State payments, allowing the Court to decide the case by remanding it on the grounds that it now needed to go through the usual procedures of challenge to federal-agency action under the Administrative Procedure Act.

justiciability precedents and that even Massachusetts did not suffer the strict injury-in-fact the Court had traditionally demanded.

The Administrative Procedure Act, which we study in Chapter 7, sets out the circumstances in which aggrieved individuals can sue an agency for interpretive or implementing action that they believe to be inconsistent with the statute (whether it be underenforcement, overenforcement or something else). The APA carves out a right to judicial review for anyone harmed by agency action, 5 U.S.C. § 702, a provision that has been interpreted by the Court as suggesting a broad presumption of judicial review. See *Abbott Labs. v. Gardner*, 387 U.S. 136 (1967). One problem is that merely charging that the agency misinterpreted the statute is not enough; the individual making the charge must suffer some concrete harm. Another potential problem is that where the statute commits a question to the agency's discretion—and most statutes do leave agencies with broad policy gaps to fill—the APA closes off the option of judicial review. See 5 U.S.C. § 701(a)(2).

2.   The President's power may increase vis-à-vis Congress's authority. If you take the Court's Article III doctrines literally, executive authority becomes more insulated from judicial review. To the extent that judicial review tends to enforce congressional preferences against executive distortion or even usurpation, Article III doctrines (such as standing) that insulate executive action from judicial review will tend to increase the discretion of the President—and certainly increase the President's ability to bend or influence the law even when Congress has not authorized such action.

For example, in *Allen v. Wright*, 468 U.S. 737 (1984), the Court held that parents of color did not have standing to sue the IRS for failing to enforce its rule that segregated academies were not entitled to tax exemptions because they were not properly deemed to be "charitable." A divided Court ruled that the parents were injured by racial discrimination against their children, but the injury was not "fairly traceable" to the IRS.[5] The plaintiffs did not claim that the IRS intended to encourage school segregation, but they did claim that the IRS placed too low a priority on enforcing the integration norm against segregated academies. The causes for such underenforcement were various, including insufficient resources, congressional committee pressure not to require monitoring information from schools, and the Reagan White House's lack of enthusiasm for the policy. In *Bob Jones University v. United States*, 461 U.S. 574 (1983), the Supreme Court had interpreted the Internal Revenue Code to deny tax exemptions to segregated private universities and colleges—over the opposition of the Reagan Administration. But by not

---

[5]   An odd feature of the case was that the plaintiff parents had not applied to enroll their children in the segregated academies. Their argument was that the segregated academies contributed to some degree of racial segregation in public schools as well, because white children were siphoned off from public schools by the private segregated academies. The *Allen* dissenters argued that the link between plaintiffs' injury and the IRS's inaction was clear, even if it required several steps: if the IRS enforced its rule, most and perhaps all of the segregated academies would either fail or have to admit students of color; in that event, there would be more racial integration of public schools.

enforcing the statutory rule, the Administration was able to trump the Court's interpretation, and *Allen v. Wright* prevents pushback from parents.

The problem of presidential authority to trump congressional directives is an important one, for it implicates the Take Care Clause of Article II. Can the President be impeached for refusing to enforce congressional directives such as the denial of tax exemptions to segregated schools? For refusing to devote resources to such enforcement? These are complicated issues—and issues with bipartisan bite. Thus, liberals complained that Presidents Reagan and Bush 43 failed to enforce environmental regulatory statutes, but conservatives make the same kind of complaint against President Obama, who has refused to enforce the nation's immigration laws as vigorously as critics maintain they should be under the Take Care Clause.

Executive branch refusals to enforce statutory directives are, of course, not always defeated by serious Article III arguments. (Even *Allen v. Wright* left room for possible lawsuits against the IRS.) The Court will sometimes allow lawsuits to go forward when an agency is accused of gross under-enforcement. *Massachusetts v. EPA* might have been such a suit, where manufacturers had pressured the White House to keep the EPA from acting in the general public interest.

3. Agency favoritism, mismanagement or incapacity may be facilitated. If an agency aggressively enforces a statute against an alleged rulebreaker, the agency can expect the rulebreaker to push back, through judicial review and the like. But if an agency uses statutory authority to reward a private group, at the expense of all taxpayers or the public interest, there will often be no one who has standing to sue the disloyal agency. Many of the environmental cases fall in this category: when an agency cuts special breaks for loggers, manufacturers, and developers, the cost-payers are often too diffuse for anyone to have standing.

The problem is also worrisome in other fields. Commentators have argued that the Department of Health and Human Services has neither the resources nor the political will to properly enforce the Medicaid program's implementation by the states, a concern evident in the *Douglas* case discussed above. In the environmental context, as another example, the Court in *Lujan v. National Wildlife Federation*, 497 U.S. 871 (1990), prevented the Federation from challenging the Bureau of Land Management's (BLM) alleged failure to follow congressionally mandated procedures for withdrawing public lands from protection against resource development. Justice Scalia's opinion for the Court faulted the Federation for not providing affidavits alleging that its members used the very lands in question, not just those in the vicinity, and also for challenging the entire BLM program and not just its review of the lands directly affecting Federation members. As in *Allen v. Wright*, the Court in this case did not foreclose standing in environmental cases entirely but did make it more expensive, thereby raising the costs for challenges to administrative sloth or incompetence.

Most dramatically, a broad reading of the Court's Article III jurisprudence would make institutional reform litigation more difficult to pursue. One important question is whether the kind of institution being reformed matters. Is there a difference when the institution being reformed is a federal agency? In the food and drug safety context, the Food and Drug Administration's (FDA) lapses have been widely chronicled. But it is doubtful that the Court would ever order wholesale structural reform of the FDA as a remedy for agency action (or inaction). On the other hand, as scholars have noted, the Court *has* used its FDA jurisprudence more subtly, in ways that recognize the agency's weaknesses and try to compensate for them—for example declining to defer to FDA policies that did not seem well thought out, or allowing parallel state enforcement actions to go forward (and avoid preemption) to fill the gaps that the FDA did not. See *Wyeth v. Levine*, 555 U.S. 555 (2009) (refusing to defer to FDA's decision to preempt state failure-to-warn claims); Gillian E. Metzger, *Federalism and Federal Agency Reform*, 111 Colum. L. Rev. 1 (2011) (arguing the Court ruled as it did in *Wyeth* as a result of the FDA's regulatory failures). Massive structural reform of the FDA, on the other hand, seems a legal impossibility, not only because it is hard to imagine the kind of case that would present such a question concretely enough for the Court to do so in light of its Article III jurisprudence, but also because so doing would be perceived as an enormous intrusion on the executive and legislative powers to oversee federal agencies.

As a contrast, school desegregation lawsuits (which have not involved challenges to federal agency actions) have often involved lengthy litigation where the original plaintiffs graduated from segregated schools long before a remedial order created a unified (integrated) school district. Hence, there was often a disconnect between the aggrieved plaintiffs and the beneficiaries of the litigation. (This problem might be solved by the class action device, where mooted-out plaintiffs can be replaced by fresh plaintiffs who meet the Article III requirements.) Even in this context, critics have been concerned that judicial orders remedying school segregation have gone too far in the direction of legislation, as federal judges seeking desegregation in the south worked out detailed remedial decrees for transitioning from a segregated to a unified system. For a defense of broad remedial decrees against procedural objections such as these, see Owen Fiss, *The Civil Rights Injunction* (1978). Federal judges have been even more aggressive in prison reform litigation, where murders of inmates as well as inhumane conditions have generated class action lawsuits and ongoing, increasingly broad judicial remedies (notably, these challenges do not involve challenges to federal agency action either). See Malcolm Feeley & Edward Rubin, *Judicial Policy Making and the Modern State: How the Courts Reformed America's Prisons* (1998). The root problems with prisons are that they are dangerous places, it is expensive to protect inmates against one another and to provide for their basic needs, and legislatures do not want to spend money on prisons even as they like to pass statutes increasing prison time for a variety of offenses. As many judges came to discover, the "harm" to individual prisoners is their enhanced risk of being murdered or seriously injured, receiving no medical care for serious or even fatal conditions, and being sexually assaulted. The enhanced risk tends to be the result of funding decisions by the legislature, high levels of executive enforcement of criminal laws, and mismanagement of prisons. Enhanced risk of death, etc., is surely an injury-in-fact—but is that risk "imminent" and fairly traceable to a particular defendant? And can a court order remedy the problem, which tends to be polycentric (sprawling) rather than focused in the way that common law disputes tend to be? Cf. Lon L. Fuller & Kenneth I. Winston, *The Forms and Limits of Adjudication*, 92 Harv. L. Rev. 353 (1978) (arguing that the moral bases for adjudication render it incapable of dealing with "polycentric" problems).

STATUTORY PREFACE TO *BROWN V. PLATA*

The Prison Litigation Reform Act of 1996, Pub. L. No. 103–322, tit. II, 108 Stat. 1827, codified at 18 U.S.C. § 3626

The political system has responded to prison reform litigation with a statute codifying a narrow version of the Court's justiciability precedents—that is, a statute with a particular vision of what the judicial role should be in these cases. The Prison Litigation Reform Act of 1996 (PLRA) imposed the requirements that follow. Evaluate the following Supreme Court decision for its compliance with these statutory requirements and with the Court's Article III jurisprudence as well.

§ 3626(a) Requirements for relief.—

(1) Prospective relief.—(A) Prospective relief in any civil action with respect to prison conditions shall extend no further than necessary to correct the violation of the Federal right of a particular plaintiff or plaintiffs. The court shall not grant or approve any prospective relief unless the court finds that such relief is narrowly drawn, extends no further than necessary to correct the violation of the Federal right, and is the least intrusive means necessary to correct the violation of the Federal right. The court shall give substantial weight to any adverse impact on public safety or the operation of a criminal justice system caused by the relief.

(B) The court shall not order any prospective relief that requires or permits a government official to exceed his or her authority under State or local law or otherwise violates State or local law, unless—**(i)** Federal law requires such relief to be ordered in violation of State or local law; **(ii)** the relief is necessary to correct the violation of a Federal right; and **(iii)** no other relief will correct the violation of the Federal right.

(C) Nothing in this section shall be construed to authorize the courts, in exercising their remedial powers, to order the construction of prisons or the raising of taxes, or to repeal or detract from otherwise applicable limitations on the remedial powers of the courts. * * *

(3) Prisoner release order.—(A) In any civil action with respect to prison conditions, no court shall enter a prisoner release order unless—

(i) a court has previously entered an order for less intrusive relief that has failed to remedy the deprivation of the Federal right sought to be remedied through the prisoner release order; and **(ii)** the defendant has had a reasonable amount of time to comply with the previous court orders. * * *

(E) The three-judge court shall enter a prisoner release order only if the court finds by clear and convincing evidence that—**(i)** crowding is the primary cause of the violation of a Federal right; and **(ii)** no other relief will remedy the violation of the Federal right.

(F) Any State or local official including a legislator or unit of government whose jurisdiction or function includes the appropriation of funds for the construction, operation, or maintenance of prison facilities, or the prosecution or custody of persons who may be released from, or not admitted to, a prison as a result of a prisoner release order shall have standing to oppose the imposition or continuation in effect of such relief and to seek termination of such relief, and shall have the right to intervene in any proceeding relating to such relief.

(b) Termination of relief. [This subsection provided for termination of prospective relief, upon motion, within two years after the date the court granted or approved the prospective relief. There are various other requirements for earlier termination of such relief.] * * *

(g) Definitions.—As used in this section * * *

(2) the term "civil action with respect to prison conditions" means any civil proceeding arising under Federal law with respect to the conditions of confinement or the effects of actions by government officials on the lives of persons confined in prison, but does not include habeas corpus proceedings challenging the fact or duration of confinement in prison * * *.

EDMUND G. BROWN, JR. v. MARCIANO PLATA

United States Supreme Court, 2011.
___ U.S. ___, 131 S.Ct. 1910, 179 L. Ed. 2d 969.

JUSTICE KENNEDY delivered the opinion of the Court. * * *

The degree of overcrowding in California's prisons is exceptional. California's prisons are designed to house a population just under 80,000, but at the time of the three-judge court's decision the population was almost double that. The State's prisons had operated at around 200% of design capacity for at least 11 years. Prisoners are crammed into spaces neither designed nor intended to house inmates. As many as 200 prisoners may live in a gymnasium, monitored by as few as two or three correctional officers. As many as 54 prisoners may share a single toilet.

The Corrections Independent Review Panel, a body appointed by the Governor and composed of correctional consultants and representatives from state agencies, concluded that California's prisons are " 'severely overcrowded, imperiling the safety of both correctional employees and inmates.' " In 2006, then-Governor Schwarzenegger declared a state of emergency in the prisons, as " 'immediate action is necessary to prevent death and harm caused by California's severe prison overcrowding.' " The consequences of overcrowding identified by the Governor include " 'increased, substantial risk for transmission of infectious illness' " and a suicide rate " 'approaching an average of one per week.' "

Prisoners in California with serious mental illness do not receive minimal, adequate care. Because of a shortage of treatment beds, suicidal inmates may be held for prolonged periods in telephone-booth sized cages without toilets. A psychiatric expert reported observing an inmate who had been held in such a cage for nearly 24 hours, standing in a pool of his own urine, unresponsive and nearly catatonic. Prison officials explained they had " 'no place to put him.' " Other inmates awaiting care may be held for months in administrative segregation, where they endure harsh and isolated conditions and receive only limited mental health services. Wait times for mental health care range as high as 12 months. In 2006, the suicide rate in California's prisons was nearly 80% higher than the national average for prison populations; and a court appointed Special Master found that 72.1% of suicides involved "some measure of inadequate assessment, treatment, or intervention, and were therefore most probably foreseeable and/or preventable."

Prisoners suffering from physical illness also receive severely deficient care. California's prisons were designed to meet the medical needs of a population at 100% of design capacity and so have only half the clinical space needed to treat the current population. A correctional officer testified that, in one prison, up to 50 sick inmates may be held together in a 12- by 20-foot cage for up to five hours awaiting treatment. The number of staff is inadequate, and prisoners face significant delays in access to care. A prisoner with severe abdominal pain died after a 5-week delay in referral to a specialist; a prisoner with "constant and extreme" chest pain died after an 8-hour delay in evaluation by a doctor; and a prisoner died of testicular cancer after a "failure of MDs to work up for cancer in a young man with 17 months of testicular pain." Doctor Ronald Shansky, former medical director of the Illinois state prison system, surveyed death reviews for California prisoners. He concluded that extreme departures from the [minimal, adequate] standard of care were "widespread," and that the proportion of "possibly preventable or preventable" deaths was "extremely high." Many more prisoners, suffering from severe but not life-threatening conditions, experience prolonged illness and unnecessary pain. * * *

[These conditions triggered class action lawsuits claiming that California state prisoners with mental or physical illnesses were incarcerated in a system that violated their Eighth (and Fourteenth) Amendment rights to be free of "cruel and unusual punishment." The state did not dispute the existence of constitutional violations and cooperated in remedial programs to improve conditions for inmates with mental and physical illnesses. After almost a decade of remedial programs, however, special masters concluded that conditions were deteriorating, in large part because of increased overcrowding in the state prisons. As required by the PLRA, a three-judge court was convened to develop a factual record that could be the basis for a remedy. The three-judge court ordered California to reduce its prison population to 137.5% of the prisons' design capacity within two years. Assuming the State does not increase capacity through new construction, the order would require a population reduction of 38,000 to 46,000 persons. In all likelihood, that would require a substantial number of prisoners to be released.]

As a consequence of their own actions, prisoners may be deprived of rights that are fundamental to liberty. Yet the law and the Constitution demand recognition of certain other rights. Prisoners retain the essence of human dignity inherent in all persons. Respect for that dignity animates the Eighth Amendment prohibition against cruel and unusual punishment. " 'The basic concept underlying the Eighth Amendment is nothing less than the dignity of man.' " *Atkins* v. *Virginia*, 536 U. S. 304, 311 (2002) (quoting *Trop* v. *Dulles*, 356 U.S. 86, 100 (1958) (plurality opinion)). * * * *

Courts faced with the sensitive task of remedying unconstitutional prison conditions must consider a range of available options, including appointment of special masters or receivers and the possibility of consent decrees. When necessary to ensure compliance with a constitutional mandate, courts may enter orders placing limits on a prison's population. By its terms, the PLRA restricts the circumstances in which a court may enter an order "that has the purpose or effect of reducing or limiting the prison population." 18 U.S.C. § 3626(g)(4). * * * [For example, the PLRA requires that such an order be grounded upon a finding that prison overcrowding is the "primary cause" of the constitutional violation. *Id.* § 3626(a)(3)(E)(i). After extensive factfinding, the three-judge court made the findings required by the PLRA, and the Supreme Court ruled that those findings were supported by the record.]

[California argued that overcrowding could not be the only "cause" of the constitutional violations, because additional measures would have to be taken to help ill inmates even if overcrowding were reduced. The Court ruled that the PLRA was satisfied by a factual demonstration that overcrowding was the "primary" even if not sole cause of the violations.] Courts should presume that Congress was sensitive to the real-world problems faced by those who would remedy constitutional violations in the prisons and that Congress did not leave prisoners without a remedy for violations of their constitutional rights. A reading of the PLRA that would render population limits unavailable in practice would raise serious constitutional concerns. A finding that overcrowding is the "primary cause" of a violation is therefore permissible, despite the fact that additional steps will be required to remedy the violation. * * *

The PLRA states that no prospective relief shall issue with respect to prison conditions unless it is narrowly drawn, extends no further than necessary to correct the violation of a federal right, and is the least intrusive means necessary to correct the violation. 18 U.S.C. § 3626(a). When determining whether these requirements are met, courts must "give substantial weight to any adverse impact on public safety or the operation of a criminal justice system." *Ibid.* [The Court found that this PLRA requirement was met, even though the remedy—reduction of overcrowding—would benefit all prisoners and not just those with mental or physical illnesses. Likewise, the Court was satisfied that the PLRA requirement that any remedial order minimize threats to public safety was met by the three-judge court's detailed factual findings and the flexibility it afforded the state to figure out the best means for meeting the 137 percent requirement.]

JUSTICE SCALIA, joined by JUSTICE THOMAS, dissenting.

Today the Court affirms what is perhaps the most radical injunction issued by a court in our Nation's history: an order requiring California to release the staggering number of 46,000 convicted criminals.

There comes before us, now and then, a case whose proper outcome is so clearly indicated by tradition and common sense, that its decision ought to shape the law, rather than vice versa. One would think that, before allowing the decree of a federal district court to release 46,000 convicted felons, this Court would bend every effort to read the law in such a way as to avoid that outrageous result. Today, quite to the contrary, the Court disregards stringently drawn provisions of the governing statute, and traditional constitutional limitations upon the power of a federal judge, in order to uphold the absurd.

The proceedings that led to this result were a judicial travesty. I dissent because the institutional reform the District Court has undertaken violates the terms of the governing statute, ignores bedrock limitations on the power of Article III judges, and takes federal courts wildly beyond their institutional capacity. * * *

[Much of Justice Scalia's objection to the Court's approach rested upon a different conception of the Eighth Amendment: unlike the Court, Justice Scalia maintained that the existence of an "inadequate" prison system does not violate anyone's Eighth Amendment rights; finding rights violations, as the Court did, was "preposterous." Such violation can only be found upon specific evidence of abuse against particular prisoners. Moreover, the Court's overbroad understanding of rights combined with an unconstitutional approach to remedies, namely the "structural injunction."]

Structural injunctions depart from [America's] historical practice, turning judges into long-term administrators of complex social institutions such as schools, prisons, and police departments. Indeed, they require judges to play a role essentially indistinguishable from the role ordinarily played by executive officials. Today's decision not only affirms the structural injunction but vastly expands its use, by holding that an entire system is unconstitutional because it *may produce* constitutional violations.

The drawbacks of structural injunctions have been described at great length elsewhere. See, *e.g., Missouri v. Jenkins,* 515 U. S. 70, 124–133 (1995) (Thomas, J., concurring); Horowitz, Decreeing Organizational Change: Judicial Supervision of Public Institutions, 1983 Duke L. J. 1265. This case illustrates one of their most pernicious aspects: that they force judges to engage in a form of factfinding-as-policymaking that is outside the traditional judicial role. The factfinding judges traditionally engage in involves the determination of past or present facts based (except for a limited set of materials of which courts may take "judicial notice") exclusively upon a closed trial record. That is one reason why a district judge's factual findings are entitled to clear-error review: because having viewed the trial first hand he is in a better position to evaluate the evidence than a judge reviewing a cold record. In a very limited category of cases, judges have also traditionally been called upon to make some predictive judgments: which custody will best serve the interests of the child, for example, or whether a particular one-shot injunction will remedy the plaintiff's grievance. When a judge manages a structural injunction, however, he will inevitably be required to make very broad empirical predictions necessarily based in large part upon policy views— the sort of predictions regularly made by legislators and executive officials, but inappropriate for the Third Branch.

This feature of structural injunctions is superbly illustrated by the District Court's proceeding concerning the decrowding order's effect on public safety. The PLRA requires that, before granting "[p]rospective relief in [a] civil action with respect to prison conditions," a court must "give substantial weight to any adverse impact on public safety or the operation of a criminal justice system caused by the relief." 18 U.S.C. § 3626(a)(1)(A). Here, the District Court discharged that requirement by making the "factual finding" that "the state has available methods by which it could readily reduce the prison population to 137.5% design capacity or less without an adverse impact on public safety or the operation of the criminal justice system." It found the evidence "clear" that prison overcrowding would "perpetuate a criminogenic prison system that itself threatens public safety," and volunteered its opinion that "[t]he population could be reduced even further with the reform of California's antiquated sentencing policies and other related changes to the laws." It "reject[ed] the testimony that inmates released early from prison would commit additional new crimes," finding that "shortening the length of stay through earned credits would give inmates incentives to participate in programming designed to lower recidivism," and that "slowing the flow of technical parole violators to prison, thereby substantially reducing the churning of parolees, would by itself improve both the prison and parole systems, and public safety." It found that "the diversion of offenders to community correctional programs has significant beneficial effects on public safety," and that "additional rehabilitative programming would result in a significant population reduction while improving public safety."

The District Court cast these predictions (and the Court today accepts them) as "factual findings," made in reliance on the procession of expert witnesses that testified at trial. Because these "findings" have support in the record, it is difficult to reverse them under a plain-error standard of review. And given that the District Court devoted nearly 10 days of trial and 70 pages of its opinion to this issue, it is difficult to dispute that the District Court has discharged its statutory obligation to give "substantial weight to any adverse impact on public safety."

But the idea that the three District Judges in this case relied solely on the credibility of the testifying expert witnesses is fanciful. *Of course* they were relying largely on their own beliefs about penology and recidivism. And *of course* different district judges, of different policy views, would have "found" that rehabilitation would not work and that releasing prisoners would increase the crime rate. I am not saying that the District Judges rendered their factual findings in bad faith. I am saying that it is impossible for judges to make "factual findings" without inserting their own policy judgments, when the factual findings *are* policy judgments. What occurred here is no more judicial factfinding in the ordinary sense than would be the factual findings that deficit spending will not lower the unemployment rate, or that the continued occupation of Iraq will decrease the risk of terrorism. Yet, because they have been branded "factual findings" entitled to deferential review, the policy preferences of three District Judges now govern the operation of California's penal system.

It is important to recognize that the dressing-up of policy judgments as factual findings is not an error peculiar to this case. It is an unavoidable concomitant of institutional-reform litigation. When a district court issues an injunction, it must make a factual assessment of the anticipated consequences of the injunction. And when the injunction undertakes to restructure a social institution, assessing the factual consequences of the injunction is necessarily the sort of predictive judgment that our system of government allocates to other government officials.

But structural injunctions do not simply invite judges to indulge policy preferences. They invite judges to indulge *incompetent* policy preferences. Three years of law school and familiarity with pertinent Supreme Court precedents give no insight whatsoever into the management of social institutions. Thus, in the proceeding below, the District Court determined that constitutionally adequate medical services could be provided if the prison population was 137.5% of design capacity. This was an empirical finding it was utterly unqualified to make. Admittedly, the court did not generate that number entirely on its own; it heard the numbers 130% and 145% bandied about by various witnesses and decided to split the difference. But the ability of judges to spit back or even average-out numbers spoon-fed to them by expert witnesses does not render them competent decisionmakers in areas in which they are otherwise unqualified. * * *

My general concerns associated with judges' running social institutions are magnified when they run prison systems, and doubly magnified when they force prison officials to release convicted criminals. As we have previously recognized:

> [C]ourts are ill equipped to deal with the increasingly urgent problems of prison administration and reform. . . . [T]he problems of prisons in America are complex and intractable, and, more to the point, they are not readily susceptible of resolution by decree. . . . Running a prison is an inordinately difficult undertaking that requires expertise, planning, and the commitment of resources, all of which are peculiarly within the province of the legislative and executive branches of government. Prison is, moreover, a task that has been committed to the responsibility of those branches, and separation of powers concerns counsel a policy of judicial restraint. Where a state penal system is involved, federal courts have . . . additional reason to accord deference to the appropriate prison authorities. *Turner v. Safley*, 482 U. S. 78, 84–85 (1987).

[We omit the separate dissenting opinion of JUSTICE ALITO (joined by CHIEF JUSTICE ROBERTS), who argued that the three-judge court order in this case was a "perfect example" of what the PLRA was enacted to prevent.]

NOTES AND QUESTIONS ON BROWN V. PLATA

In the judgment issued by the three-judge court, there is a poor fit between the injury-in-fact asserted by the plaintiffs, who have mental or physical illnesses that require treatment, and the relief granted by the court, namely, release of prisoners, many of whom will be inmates without mental or physical illnesses. Is that not a problem under Article III, as the Supreme Court has construed it? Additionally, the broad relief may violate the PLRA. How does (or should) the Court majority respond to these constitutional and statutory problems?

Justice Scalia argues that the "structural injunction" attacking the polycentric problem of poor medical care is a classic example of relief beyond the constitutional capacity of the judiciary. What is the real problem in the case? Is it that the controversy is nonjusticiable, as he maintains? What language in the Constitution or Supreme Court precedents would he be relying on? Arguably what is really driving Justice Scalia is separation of powers: Justice Scalia sees the executive and legislative branches as more competent to make predictive decisions about massive social institutions and resists the idea that judges, even if competent, should be engaged in such policy work. What kind of argument is this? A constitutional argument, as he claims it is, or a practical one?

An odd feature of this case is that the Court majority seems to hew closely to the text of the PLRA, and affirms the District Court's order, whose extensive factual findings fit the PLRA like a hand in a glove—while Justice Scalia demands that his colleagues "bend" the statutory text and disregard findings of fact in order to avoid "travesty." There is a postmodern tone to his dissenting opinion that is hard to square with the neutrality that the rule of law is supposed to embody. See Jane S. Schacter, *Text or Consequences?*, 76 Brooklyn L. Rev. 1007 (2011). Justice Scalia's point seems to be that structural injunction litigation makes it impossible for a federal judge to do his Article III duties, and so the Supreme Court ought to read the PLRA expansively and Article III narrowly, to discourage this kind of litigation. Is that not a "policy" judgment Scalia is reading into Article III? Unlike the District Court, his "policy" judgment does not rest upon any cited evidence, does it?

Justice Kennedy refuses to take the bait and writes a standard opinion applying ordinary precepts of textual interpretation and appellate review. And the District Court did the same. But these majority judges are reading highly restrictive Article III precedents and the PLRA to accommodate an unusual kind of litigation, and they arguably push the limits of the text to do so. Why would they do that? What role do they see federal courts playing in our system of governance? For some ideas, consult John Hart Ely, *Democracy and Distrust: A Theory of Judicial Review* (1980). Professor Ely argues, from the text of the Constitution, that judicial independence frees up judges to be aggressive referees when the democratic system is dysfunctional; the constitutional (and perhaps also statutory) role of judges is to be "representation-reinforcing," namely, protecting the integrity of the democratic process *and* the interests of "discrete and insular minorities" who are abused by a process in which they have little voice. Does such a democracy-enhancing theory of judicial review help explain the judges' behavior in the California Prison Case? Does it *justify* the Court's approach in that case? How would Justice Scalia respond?

Consider, also, how a representation-reinforcing theory of judicial review would play out in some of the cases examined in Chapters 1 and 2, such as *Morrison v. Olson*, the Independent Counsel Case (Chapter 2, § 1). The debate in *Morrison* focused on the nature of executive authority and the asserted requirement that the President be able to control all executive officials. But is there also a democratic dysfunction argument? Or one based upon unfair government persecution? Does the Ely theory add anything to your understanding of this case? Are there any insights that representation-reinforcement theory provides for *INS v. Chadha*, the Legislative Veto Case (Chapter 1, § 2)? See generally Victoria F. Nourse, *The Vertical Separation of Powers*, 49 Duke L.J. 749 (1999) (analyzing both *Morrison* and *Chadha* as instances where Congress proposed novel institutional arrangements that radically altered the political constituencies to which decision makers were responsible).

Finally, consider how representation-reinforcement theory might apply to issues of statutory interpretation. Professor Eskridge has argued that a representation-reinforcing judge in close cases of statutory interpretation (e.g., there is no single plain meaning; the text is ambiguous) ought to consider whether the losing group has effective access to the legislative process to press its claims for inclusion or protection. If the losing group has no access to the political process, the judge should decide in favor of that group's preferred statutory interpretation. The argument is that such interpretations not only serve the interests of pluralism (where governance is responsive to all groups), but also increase the possibility that Congress will think about an issue it did not resolve initially (the more powerful losing group is more likely to get the attention of congressional committees). See William N. Eskridge Jr., *Dynamic Statutory Interpretation* ch. 5 (1994). As we shall see in Part II of this casebook, the Court sometimes does already apply presumptions of this nature, including the rule that remedial statutes are liberally construed, and the presumption that ambiguities in criminal statutes be resolved in favor of defendants (the so-called "rule of lenity").

How does a representation-reinforcing rule of interpretation apply in practice? Recall Problem 2–6, which asked whether Title VII should be interpreted to cover discrimination against employees because they are transgender (one's chromosomes do not match one's presentation of gender or sex). The problem posed this question to the EEOC, but assume that a federal judge faced this issue as a matter of interpreting Title VII. Is this issue "close" enough to trigger a representation-reinforcing presumption? What interpretation would that presumption support? See *Schroer v. Billington*, 577 F. Supp. 2d 293 (D.D.C. 2008) (judicial ruling on this issue).

2. *STARE DECISIS*, THE RULE OF LAW, AND INSTITUTIONAL COMPETENCE

The previous section explored one set of institutional features distinctive to the Article III judiciary: federal judges do not have as much control over their agenda as legislators and agencies, cannot address polycentric problems as readily, are limited in their remedial authority, and are accountable to constitutional, statutory, and treaty texts more strictly than the other branches. Paradoxically, most thinkers believe that these very limits also vest federal judges with great power, especially a hard-earned institutional legitimacy that commands popular as well as political respect for their rulings.

Another dimension of judges' limited power that makes them more puissant derives from the distinctive nature of judicial decision-making in our culture, namely, *stare decisis* ("let the decision stand").[6] A trademark feature of common law judging, *stare decisis* requires judges not only to follow any precedent that is "on point," but also to reason from precedents when there is none precisely on point. One way of thinking about precedent is to consider the common law as something like a chain novel: the first chapter (the first case) introduces the reader to various characters and plot developments; in the second chapter (the next case), there will be new facts and the job of the narrator (the judge) is to advance the story in response to the new facts, but to make it as consistent as possible with the first chapter; in subsequent chapters, the storyline will advance in surprising ways, but the different narrators will consider themselves under an obligation to write their chapters so as to retain the overall coherence of the novel. See Ronald Dworkin, *Law's Empire* (1986).

You have seen *stare decisis* at work in your common law courses and in this coursebook. In Chapter 2, § 1, for example, we introduced you to Supreme Court precedents analyzing presidential authority to remove executive branch officials at will. We started with *Myers*, which recognized a broad removal power; continued with *Humphrey's Executor*, which interpreted *Myers* to govern purely executive officials but not commissioners of quasi-legislative and quasi-judicial agencies such as the FTC; applied those precedents to the Independent Counsel Case, *Morrison v. Olson*; and concluded with *Free Enterprise*, which refused to

---

[6] For classic treatments of the topic of *stare decisis*, start with Henry Paul Monaghan, *Stare Decisis and Constitutional Adjudication*, 88 Colum. L. Rev. 723 (1988), and Frederick Schauer, *Precedent*, 39 Stan. L. Rev. 571 (1987), and consult the varying and thoughtful perspectives offered by Gary Lawson, *The Constitutional Case Against Precedent*, 17 Harv. J.L. & Pub. Pol'y 23 (1994); Christopher J. Peters, *Foolish Consistency: On Equality, Integrity, and Justice in Stare Decisis*, 105 Yale L.J. 2031 (1996); David L. Shapiro, *The Role of Precedent in Constitutional Adjudication: An Introspection*, 86 Tex. L. Rev. 929 (2008). For a useful introduction to *stare decisis* in the executive branch, see Trevor Morrison, Stare Decisis *in the Office of Legal Counsel*, 110 Colum. L. Rev. 1448 (2010).

allow Congress to create two layers of "good cause" removal requirements for agency officials appointed by an independent agency. That path from *Myers* to *Free Enterprise* was far from predictable (like many a good novel), but the Supreme Court was at every point highly attentive to the holdings of earlier precedents and crafted rules for new situations with consideration of all the previous precedents (chapters in the novel).

Recall the Vehicles-in-the-Park Ordinance from the Introduction. The state supreme court would have final authority to interpret that ordinance and others like it. If the first case decided by that court produced a decision applying the ordinance to tricycles, that initial precedent (like the first chapter in the chain novel) would be a foundation for future applications: not only would subsequent courts routinely apply the ordinance to tricycles, but they would reason from the tricycle precedent when confronted with new mechanisms that might fall under the same piece of legislation. Thus, if the reasoning of the tricycle precedent rested upon the broad definition of "vehicle" in § 3 of the ordinance *and* on the perception that tricycles cause accidents that the Council addressed in § 1 (the purpose section), a subsequent court would be inclined to apply the ordinance also to skateboards and other nonmotorized mechanisms that transport kids at speeds that can cause harm in the event of accidents.

But even if the ordinance were applied to tricycles, skateboards, and even roller skates, a subsequent court would still be reluctant to apply the ordinance to a baby carriage. True, a baby carriage technically fits within the definition of "vehicle" in § 3, but it poses virtually no safety concerns along the lines of § 1, so much so that it might be absurd to apply the ordinance to baby carriages. However the court weighed these textual points, the subsequent court would definitely reason by analogy from precedent. That is, the court would ask: What is it about automobiles, bicycles, tricycles, and skateboards (all mechanisms clearly covered by the ordinance's text or authoritative precedents) that brings them within the ordinance?

Based upon these common features, is a baby carriage "similar" (analogous) to those mechanisms previously recognized as "vehicles"? Arguably not. So the precedent-following court is unlikely to apply the ordinance to baby carriages. How about wheelbarrows? Again, the court would ask whether the wheelbarrow is analogous to cars, tricycles, or skateboards (all covered), or is more closely analogous to baby carriages. You might say a wheelbarrow is quite unlike all these other mechanisms, but then think at a higher level of generality: Is a wheelbarrow likely to cause injury if it collides with a park user (like cars, tricycles, skateboards)—or is any collision likely to be harmless (like baby carriages)? Probably the latter.

PROBLEM 3–2: REASONING FROM PRECEDENTS ACROSS DIFFERENT SUBJECT AREAS

A potentially more difficult set of questions arises when courts use their precedents to reason across different subject-matter areas or across different statutes. Consider the following scenarios:

Scenario 1. Assume that you are in 1950 (before any kind of civil rights legislation exists), and a case arrives at the U.S. Supreme Court charging that a Veterans' Administration practice of giving female nurses shorter breaks than male nurses violates a federal common law tort duty of care to all employees. Nursing is taxing work, and the women charge that the breaks are necessary for their safety. Assume that the Court agrees, and holds that federal employers have a common law duty to not discriminate against workers with respect to safety precautions. The Court bases its opinion on its view that the common law duty of care owed to employees includes equal treatment.

The next relevant case arrives at the Court in 1960. Female employees of the Defense Department charge that they are being paid less than men for the same work, and that this violates the common law duty the Court recognized in the 1950 case. How might the Court decide this case? Would the Court decide the case differently if the employees were soldiers in the armed forces?

Scenario 2. Assume that shortly after the Civil Rights Act is passed in 1964, the U.S. Supreme Court holds (as it did in *Griggs*) that Title VII of the Civil Rights Act prohibits discrimination that is facially neutral but has a disparate impact.

Now assume that, in 2000, Manhattan Law School is sued under a different anti-discrimination statute enacted after Title VII, the Americans with Disabilities Act, on the ground that the poor acoustics of the law school that resulted from a recent renovation discriminate against faculty and students who are hearing-impaired. Assume for purposes of this hypothetical that the ADA simply prevents discrimination based on disability but (like Title VII) says nothing in the text about disparate impact. How might the Court decide this case? Are the considerations any different from Scenario 1? Why or why not?

* * *

Isn't it likely that a system where judges faithfully follow and reason from precedents will be one where the law is more **predictable**? In the common law context the answer seems clear. In the statutory context, the answer gets more complex. How would you ensure predictability in statutory cases? Is a system where judges just reason from the statutory text, without regard to previous decisions, the most predictable? Even if you favor a more text-based approach, wouldn't judges need a consistent and predictable way to interpret the text to make such efforts more predictable for the public?

Such a system might not be 100% predictable, but that is not the criterion: Is the system, relatively speaking, more predictable than an alternate system? Predictability is a big virtue in a system such as ours. If people (perhaps with the assistance of lawyers) can predict how statutes will be applied to new fact patterns and cases, there ought to be more spontaneous compliance with the rules, greater payoffs in terms of the statutory policy, and less police activity and litigation.

Another virtue of the rule of law generally and predictability in particular is that people, private institutions, and the public sector can rely on established precedents in planning their activities and in structuring legal instruments. Knowing and relying on the expectation that even tricycles are illegal in the park, older citizens will feel freer to go walking in the park, and they will make plans to do park excursions. Likewise, the police may have to adjust their protocols when they learn that baby carriages and wheelbarrows are not covered by the ordinance.

Not least important, the legislature itself can rely on precedent when it drafts new ordinances. Say the Council wants to create a safety regime for school grounds (not including the school parking lot). Its members know that if they borrow the language of the Vehicles-in-the-Park ordinance, then tricycles and skateboards will be excluded from schoolyards and school playgrounds. If the Council actually wants kids to be able to bring their tricycles and skateboards into the playground, its members know they have to draft the ordinance differently than they drafted the vehicles ordinance. And so forth.

The rule of law also requires **objectivity**, and *stare decisis* arguably contributes to that feature as well. Judicial objectivity in applying the law presumes backward-looking inquiries that (ideally) squeeze out the personal feelings of the judge: What *did* the legislature mean by the words of this statute? Which interpretation is more consistent with the precedents we have *already handed down*? With the constitutional order we *have traditionally followed*?

Ideally, *stare decisis* means that 100 judges of all ideologies, religions, sexual orientations, races, etc., would approach a new problem in roughly the same way and would often reach the same result. Thus, following precedent, judges appointed by President George W. Bush usually vote the same way as judges appointed by President Barack H. Obama. Not 100% of the time, to be sure. *Free Enterprise* is an example of an ideological split on a novel constitutional issue, namely, whether the Sarbanes-Oxley Act could prevent the SEC from removing Board members at will when the SEC's Commissioners themselves were protected from presidential removal unless there was good cause. The Bush Justices all voted with the majority to strike down that particular limitation, while the Obama Justices all voted in dissent. On that narrow issue they parted company—but it is noteworthy that all nine Justices seemed to agree that it was constitutional for Congress to limit presidential removal for SEC Commissioners (*Humphrey's Executor*), that the Appointments Clause did not deprive the President of presumptive removal-at-will authority for non-major executive branch officials (*Myers*), and that striking down the removal-only-for-cause provisions did not require invalidation of the entire statute or even of the statute's provisions creating the Board (*Alaska Airlines*)).

When Chief Justice Roberts wrote the opinion for the Court in *Free Enterprise*, he justified his answer to the novel issue presented by the 2002 statute through reasons drawn from precedent. But *stare decisis* affected his decision in another way as well. Knowing that any decision from the Court on this issue will, itself, have *stare decisis* effect, the Chief Justice was careful to develop an analysis that was closely tailored to the specific issue and did not decide "too much." A decision that reasoned too broadly might prove an embarrassment in future cases—and might generate results that would get the Court into hot water. Because the author of an opinion for the Court never knows exactly what issues future cases will present and always hopes that his or her opinion will receive full *stare decisis* effect, the author tends to write narrowly, deciding the particular issue, rather than broadly, seeking to predetermine future issues.

The following famous case concerns the intersection of professional baseball and the federal antitrust laws, which prevent restraints on free trade and competetion. As you read, consider why the court is willing to refuse to overturn its own interpretation exempting baseball from the antitrust laws when the constitutional basis of the original opinion had changed and most other major sports were not exempted. Baseball was left a glaring and, to some, absurd exception. Think about the importance of *stare decisis* as you read the case. How would you have decided?

CURTIS FLOOD V. BOWIE KUHN

United States Supreme Court, 1972.
407 U.S. 258, 92 S.Ct. 2099, 32 L. Ed. 2d 728.

MR. JUSTICE BLACKMUN delivered the opinion of the Court.

[I. *The Game*] It is a century and a quarter since the New York Nine defeated the Knickerbockers 23 to 1 on Hoboken's Elysian Fields June 19, 1846, with Alexander Jay Cartwright as the instigator and the umpire. The teams were amateur, but the contest marked a significant date in baseball's beginnings. That early game led ultimately to the development of professional baseball and its tightly organized structure.

The Cincinnati Red Stockings came into existence in 1869 upon an outpouring of local pride. With only one Cincinnatian on the payroll, this professional team traveled over 11,000 miles that summer, winning 56 games and tying one. Shortly thereafter, on St. Patrick's Day in 1871, the

National Association of Professional Baseball Players was founded and the professional league was born.

The ensuing colorful days are well known. The ardent follower and the student of baseball know of General Abner Doubleday; the formation of the National League in 1876; Chicago's supremacy in the first year's competition under the leadership of Al Spalding and with Cap Anson at third base; the formation of the American Association and then of the Union Association in the 1880's; the introduction of Sunday baseball; interleague warfare with cut-rate admission prices and player raiding; the development of the reserve "clause"; the emergence in 1885 of the Brotherhood of Professional Ball Players, and in 1890 of the Players League; the appearance of the American League, or "junior circuit," in 1901, rising from the minor Western Association; the first World Series in 1903, disruption in 1904, and the Series' resumption in 1905; the short-lived Federal League on the majors' scene during World War I years; the troublesome and discouraging episode of the 1919 Series; the home run ball; the shifting of franchises; the expansion of the leagues; the installation in 1965 of the major league draft of potential new players; and the formation of the Major League Baseball Players Association in 1966.

Then there are the many names, celebrated for one reason or another, that have sparked the diamond and its environs and that have provided tinder for recaptured thrills, for reminiscence and comparisons, and for conversation and anticipation in-season and off-season: Ty Cobb, Babe Ruth, Tris Speaker, Walter Johnson, Henry Chadwick, Eddie Collins, Lou Gehrig, Grover Cleveland Alexander, Rogers Hornsby, Harry Hooper, Goose Goslin, Jackie Robinson, Honus Wagner, Joe McCarthy, John McGraw, Deacon Phillippe, Rube Marquard, Christy Mathewson, Tommy Leach, Big Ed Delahanty, Davy Jones, Germany Schaefer, King Kelly, Big Dan Brouthers, Wahoo Sam Crawford, Wee Willie Keeler, Big Ed Walsh, Jimmy Austin, Fred Snodgrass, Satchel Paige, Hugh Jennings, Fred Merkle, Iron Man McGinnity, Three-Finger Brown, Harry and Stan Coveleski, Connie Mack, Al Bridwell, Red Ruffing, Amos Rusie, Cy Young, Smokey Joe Wood, Chief Meyers, Chief Bender, Bill Klem, Hans Lobert, Johnny Evers, Joe Tinker, Roy Campanella, Miller Huggins, Rube Bressler, Dazzy Vance, Edd Roush, Bill Wambsganss, Clark Griffith, Branch Rickey, Frank Chance, Cap Anson, Nap Lajoie, Sad Sam Jones, Bob O'Farrell, Lefty O'Doul, Bobby Veach, Willie Kamm, Heinie Groh, Lloyd and Paul Waner, Stuffy McInnis, Charles Comiskey, Roger Bresnahan, Bill Dickey, Zack Wheat, George Sisler, Charlie Gehringer, Eppa Rixey, Harry Heilmann, Fred Clarke, Dizzy Dean, Hank Greenberg, Pie Traynor, Rube Waddell, Bill Terry, Carl Hubbell, Old Hoss Radbourne, Moe Berg, Rabbit Maranville, Jimmie Foxx, Lefty Grove. The list seems endless.

And one recalls the appropriate reference to the "World Serious," attributed to Ring Lardner, Sr.; Ernest L. Thayer's "Casey at the Bat"; the ring of "Tinker to Evers to Chance"; and all the other happenings, habits, and superstitions about and around baseball that made it the "national pastime" or, depending upon the point of view, "the great American tragedy." * * *

[Curt Flood, the petitioner, was a star center fielder with the St. Louis Cardinals. Under the "reserve clause" in his contract, he was required to play for the Cardinals, the Cardinals could unilaterally assign his contract to another team, and the Cardinals could annually renew that contract so long as the minimum salary was provided.

[In October 1969, the Cards traded Flood to the Philadelphia Phillies. Flood refused to report to the Phillies and asked Bowie Kuhn, the Commissioner of Baseball, to be allowed to negotiate a contract with the team of his choice. Kuhn refused. Flood filed a lawsuit claiming, *inter alia*, that the reserve clause violated the antitrust laws because it prevented him from contracting with the team of his choice. Lower courts denied relief based on Supreme Court precedents holding baseball immune from the antitrust laws.]

[IVA. *The Legal Background*] *Federal Baseball Club v. National League*, 259 U.S. 200 (1922), was a suit for treble damages instituted by a member of the Federal League (Baltimore) against the National and American Leagues and others. The plaintiff obtained a verdict in the trial court, but the Court of Appeals reversed. The main brief filed by the plaintiff with this Court discloses that it was strenuously argued, among other things, that the business in which the defendants were engaged was interstate commerce; that the interstate relationship among the several clubs, located as they were in different States, was predominant; that organized baseball represented an investment of colossal wealth; that it was an engagement in moneymaking; that gate receipts were divided by agreement between the home club and the visiting club; and that the business of baseball was to be distinguished from the mere playing of the game as a sport for physical exercise and diversion.

Mr. Justice Holmes, in speaking succinctly for a unanimous Court, said:

> The business is giving exhibitions of base ball, which are purely state affairs. . . . But the fact that in order to give the exhibitions the Leagues must induce free persons to cross state lines and must arrange and pay for their doing so is not enough to change the character of the business. . . . [T]he transport is a mere incident, not the essential thing. That to which it is incident, the exhibition, although made, for money would not be called trade or commerce in the commonly accepted use of those

words. As it is put by the defendant, personal effort, not related to production, is not a subject of commerce. That which in its consummation is not commerce does not become commerce among the States because the transportation that we have mentioned takes place. To repeat the illustrations given by the Court below, a firm of lawyers sending out a member to argue a case, or the Chautauqua lecture bureau sending out lecturers, does not engage in such commerce because the lawyer or lecturer goes to another State.

If we are right the plaintiff's business is to be described in the same way and the restrictions by contract that prevented the plaintiff from getting players to break their bargains and the other conduct charged against the defendants were not an interference with commerce among the States. * * *

In the years that followed, baseball continued to be subject to intermittent antitrust attack. The courts, however, rejected these challenges on the authority of *Federal Baseball.* In some cases stress was laid, although unsuccessfully, on new factors such as the development of radio and television with their substantial additional revenues to baseball. For the most part, however, the Holmes opinion was generally and necessarily accepted as controlling authority. And in the 1952 Report of the Subcommittee on Study of Monopoly Power of the House Committee on the Judiciary, H.R.Rep. No. 2002, 82d Cong., 2d Sess., 229, it was said, in conclusion:

> On the other hand the overwhelming preponderance of the evidence established baseball's need for some sort of reserve clause. Baseball's history shows that chaotic conditions prevailed when there was no reserve clause. Experience points to no feasible substitute to protect the integrity of the game or to guarantee a comparatively even competitive struggle. The evidence adduced at the hearings would clearly not justify the enactment of legislation flatly condemning the reserve clause.

C.   The Court granted certiorari in [three cases], and, by a short per curiam (Warren, C.J., and Black, Frankfurter, Douglas, Jackson, Clark, and Minton, JJ.), affirmed the judgments of the respective courts of appeals in those three cases. *Toolson v. New York Yankees, Inc.*, 346 U.S. 356 (1953). *Federal Baseball* was cited as holding "that the business of providing public baseball games for profit between clubs of professional baseball players was not within the scope of the federal antitrust laws," and:

> Congress has had the ruling under consideration but has not seen fit to bring such business under these laws by legislation having prospective effect. The business has thus been left for

thirty years to develop, on the understanding that it was not subject to existing antitrust legislation. The present cases ask us to overrule the prior decision and, with retrospective effect, hold the legislation applicable. We think that if there are evils in this field which now warrant application to it of the antitrust laws it should be by legislation. Without re-examination of the underlying issues, the judgments below are affirmed on the authority of *Federal Baseball Club of Baltimore v. National League of Professional Baseball Clubs, supra,* so far as that decision determines that Congress had no intention of including the business of baseball within the scope of the federal antitrust laws.

This quotation reveals four reasons for the Court's affirmance of *Toolson* and its companion cases: (a) Congressional awareness for three decades of the Court's ruling in *Federal Baseball,* coupled with congressional inaction. (b) The fact that baseball was left alone to develop for that period upon the understanding that the reserve system was not subject to existing federal antitrust laws. (c) A reluctance to overrule *Federal Baseball* with consequent retroactive effect. (d) A professed desire that any needed remedy be provided by legislation rather than by court decree. The emphasis in *Toolson* was on the determination, attributed even to *Federal Baseball,* that Congress had no intention to include baseball within the reach of the federal antitrust laws. * * *

[Justice Blackmun recounted three subsequent opinions. In *United States v. Shubert,* 348 U.S. 222 (1955), the Court reversed a dismissal of an antitrust suit against defendants engaged in theatrical attractions across the country, indicating that *Federal Baseball* and *Toolson* provided no general antitrust exemption for businesses built around local exhibitions. Similarly, the Court in *United States v. International Boxing Club,* 348 U.S. 236 (1955), reversed a district court for dismissing the antitrust complaint; the Court denied that *Federal Baseball* gave sports other than baseball an exemption from the antitrust laws. Finally, in *Radovich v. National Football League,* 352 U.S. 445 (1957), the Supreme Court reversed the lower courts for dismissing another antitrust complaint against a football league. Justice Clark's opinion for the Court noted that *Toolson* upheld baseball's immunity, "because it was concluded that more harm would be done in overruling *Federal Base Ball* than in upholding a ruling which at best was of dubious validity." *Id.* at 450. The opinion said:]

All this, combined with the flood of litigation that would follow its repudiation, the harassment that would ensue, and the retroactive effect of such a decision, led the Court to the practical result that it should sustain the unequivocal line of authority reaching over many years.

[S]ince *Toolson* and *Federal Base Ball* are still cited as controlling authority in antitrust actions involving other fields of business, we now specifically limit the rule there established to the facts there involved, *i.e.*, the business of organized professional baseball. As long as the Congress continues to acquiesce we should adhere to—but not extend—the interpretation of the Act made in those cases. . . .

If this ruling is unrealistic, inconsistent, or illogical, it is sufficient to answer, aside from the distinctions between the businesses, that were we considering the question of baseball for the first time upon a clean slate we would have no doubts. But *Federal Base Ball* held the business of baseball outside the scope of the Act. No other business claiming the coverage of those cases has such an adjudication. We therefore, conclude that the orderly way to eliminate error or discrimination, if any there be, is by legislation and not by court decision. Congressional processes are more accommodative, affording the whole industry hearings and an opportunity to assist in the formulation of new legislation. The resulting product is therefore more likely to protect the industry and the public alike. The whole scope of congressional action would be known long in advance and effective dates for the legislation could be set in the future without the injustices of retroactivity and surprise which might follow court action.

Mr. Justice Frankfurter dissented essentially for the reasons stated in his dissent in *International Boxing*. Mr. Justice Harlan, joined by Mr. Justice Brennan, also dissented because he, too, was "unable to distinguish football from baseball." Here again the dissenting Justices did not call for the overruling of the baseball decisions. They merely could not distinguish the two sports and, out of respect for *stare decisis*, voted to affirm.

G.   Finally, in *Haywood v. National Basketball Assn.*, 401 U.S. 1204 (1971), Mr. Justice Douglas, in his capacity as Circuit Justice, reinstated a District Court's injunction *pendente lite* in favor of a professional basketball player and said, "Basketball . . . does not enjoy exemption from the antitrust laws."

H.   This series of decisions understandably spawned extensive commentary, some of it mildly critical and much of it not; nearly all of it looked to Congress for any remedy that might be deemed essential.

I.   Legislative proposals have been numerous and persistent. Since *Toolson* more than 50 bills have been introduced in Congress relative to the applicability or nonapplicability of the antitrust laws to baseball. A few of these passed one house or the other. Those that did would have expanded, not restricted, the reserve system's exemption to other professional league sports. And the Act of Sept. 30, 1961, Pub.L. 87–331, 75 Stat. 732, and the merger addition thereto effected by the Act of Nov. 8, 1966, Pub.L. 89–800, § 6(b), 80 Stat. 1515, 15 U.S.C. §§ 1291–1295, were also expansive rather than restrictive as to antitrust exemption.

[V.] In view of all this, it seems appropriate now to say that:

1.   Professional baseball is a business and it is engaged in interstate commerce.

2.   With its reserve system enjoying exemption from the federal antitrust laws, baseball is, in a very distinct sense, an exception and an anomaly. *Federal Baseball* and *Toolson* have become an aberration confined to baseball.

3.   Even though others might regard this as "unrealistic, inconsistent, or illogical," see *Radovich*, the aberration is an established one, and one that has been recognized not only in *Federal Baseball* and *Toolson*, but in *Shubert, International Boxing*, and *Radovich*, as well, a total of five consecutive cases in this Court. It is an aberration that has been with us now for half a century, one heretofore deemed fully entitled to the benefit of *stare decisis*, and one that has survived the Court's expanding concept of interstate commerce. It rests on a recognition and an acceptance of baseball's unique characteristics and needs.

4.   Other professional sports operating interstate—football, boxing, basketball, and, presumably, hockey and golf—are not so exempt.

5.   The advent of radio and television, with their consequent increased coverage and additional revenues, has not occasioned an overruling of *Federal Baseball* and *Toolson*.

6.   The Court has emphasized that since 1922 baseball, with full and continuing congressional awareness, has been allowed to develop and to expand unhindered by federal legislative action. Remedial legislation has been introduced repeatedly in Congress but none has ever been enacted. The Court, accordingly, has concluded that Congress as yet has had no intention to subject baseball's reserve system to the reach of the antitrust statutes. This, obviously, has been deemed to be something other than mere congressional silence and passivity.

7.   The Court has expressed concern about the confusion and the retroactivity problems that inevitably would result with a judicial overturning of *Federal Baseball*. It has voiced a preference that if any change is to be made, it come by legislative action that, by its nature, is only prospective in operation.

8.   The Court noted in *Radovich* that the slate with respect to baseball is not clean. Indeed, it has not been clean for half a century.

This emphasis and this concern are still with us. We continue to be loath, 50 years after *Federal Baseball* and almost two decades after *Toolson*, to overturn those cases judicially when Congress, by its positive inaction, has allowed those decisions to stand for so long and, far beyond mere inference and implication, has clearly evinced a desire not to disapprove them legislatively.

Accordingly, we adhere once again to *Federal Baseball* and *Toolson* and to their application to professional baseball. We adhere also to *International Boxing* and *Radovich* and to their respective applications to professional boxing and professional football. If there is any inconsistency or illogic in all this, it is an inconsistency and illogic of long standing that is to be remedied by the Congress and not by this Court. If we were to act otherwise, we would be withdrawing from the conclusion as to congressional intent made in *Toolson* and from the concerns as to retrospectivity therein expressed. Under these circumstances, there is merit in consistency even though some might claim that beneath that consistency is a layer of inconsistency.

* * * [W]hat the Court said in *Federal Baseball* in 1922 and what it said in *Toolson* in 1953, we say again here in 1972: the remedy, if any is indicated, is for congressional, and not judicial, action.

MR. JUSTICE WHITE joins in the judgment of the Court, and in all but Part I of the Court's opinion.

MR. JUSTICE POWELL took no part in the consideration or decision of this case.

MR. CHIEF JUSTICE BURGER, concurring.

I concur in all but Part I of the Court's opinion but, like Mr. Justice Douglas, I have grave reservations as to the correctness of *Toolson*; as he notes in his dissent, he joined that holding but has "lived to regret it." The error, if such it be, is one on which the affairs of a great many people have rested for a long time. Courts are not the forum in which this tangled web ought to be unsnarled. I agree with Mr. Justice Douglas that congressional inaction is not a solid base, but the least undesirable course now is to let the matter rest with Congress; it is time the Congress acted to solve this problem.

MR. JUSTICE DOUGLAS, with whom MR. JUSTICE BRENNAN concurs, dissenting.

This Court's decision in *Federal Baseball Club*, made in 1922, is a derelict in the stream of the law that we, its creator, should remove. Only a romantic view of a rather dismal business account over the last 50 years would keep that derelict in midstream.

In 1922 the Court had a narrow, parochial view of commerce. With the demise of the old landmarks of that era, the whole concept of commerce has changed.

Under the modern [commerce clause] decisions, the power of Congress was recognized as broad enough to reach all phases of the vast operations of our national industrial system. An industry so dependent on radio and television as is baseball and gleaning vast interstate revenues (see H.R.Rep. No. 2002, 82d Cong., 2d Sess., 4, 5 (1952)) would be hard put today to say with the Court in the *Federal Baseball Club* case that baseball was only a local exhibition, not trade or commerce.

Baseball is today big business that is packaged with beer, with broadcasting, and with other industries. The beneficiaries of the *Federal Baseball Club* decision are not the Babe Ruths, Ty Cobbs, and Lou Gehrigs.

The owners, whose records many say reveal a proclivity for predatory practices, do not come to us with equities. The equities are with the victims of the reserve clause. I use the word "victims" in the Sherman Act sense, since a contract which forbids anyone to practice his calling is commonly called an unreasonable restraint of trade.

If congressional inaction is our guide, we should rely upon the fact that Congress has refused to enact bills broadly exempting professional sports from antitrust regulation. H.R.Rep. No. 2002, 82nd Cong., 2d Sess. (1952). The only statutory exemption granted by Congress to professional sports concerns broadcasting rights. 15 U.S.C. §§ 1291–1295. I would not ascribe a broader exemption through inaction than Congress has seen fit to grant explicitly.

There can be no doubt "that were we considering the question of baseball for the first time upon a clean slate" we would hold it to be subject to federal antitrust regulation. *Radovich*. The unbroken silence of Congress should not prevent us from correcting our own mistakes.

MR. JUSTICE MARSHALL, with whom MR. JUSTICE BRENNAN joins, dissenting.

* * * This is a difficult case because we are torn between the principle of *stare decisis* and the knowledge that the decisions in *Federal Baseball Club* and *Toolson* are totally at odds with more recent and better reasoned cases. * * *

Has Congress acquiesced in our decisions in *Federal Baseball Club* and *Toolson*? I think not. Had the Court been consistent and treated all sports in the same way baseball was treated, Congress might have become concerned enough to take action. But, the Court was inconsistent, and baseball was isolated and distinguished from all other sports. In

Toolson the Court refused to act because Congress had been silent. But the Court may have read too much into this legislative inaction.

Americans love baseball as they love all sports. Perhaps we become so enamored of athletics that we assume that they are foremost in the minds of legislators as well as fans. We must not forget, however, that there are only some 600 major league baseball players. Whatever muscle they might have been able to muster by combining forces with other athletes has been greatly impaired by the manner in which this Court has isolated them. It is this Court that has made them impotent, and this Court should correct its error.

We do not lightly overrule our prior constructions of federal statutes, but when our errors deny substantial federal rights, like the right to compete freely and effectively to the best of one's ability as guaranteed by the antitrust laws, we must admit our error and correct it. We have done so before and we should do so again here. See, *e.g., Blonder-Tongue Laboratories, Inc. v. University of Illinois Foundation*, 402 U.S. 313 (1971); *Boys Markets, Inc. v. Retail Clerks Union*, 398 U.S. 235, 241 (1970).

To the extent that there is concern over any reliance interests that club owners may assert, they can be satisfied by making our decision prospective only. Baseball should be covered by the antitrust laws beginning with this case and henceforth, unless Congress decides otherwise.

NOTES AND QUESTIONS ON FLOOD V. KUHN

1.   *Was There a Rationale for* Flood? It appears that every member of the Court thought that *Federal Baseball* was wrongly decided, yet a majority nevertheless applied the wrongheaded precedent. Why should the Court reaffirm this "inconsistency and illogic of long standing"? The Court notes "retrospectivity" problems that would inhere if it were to overturn *Toolson* and *Federal Baseball*, suggesting that the industry had been "relying" on these precedents in conducting its affairs. Yet the testimony of post-*Toolson* purchasers of baseball teams indicated that they had been advised of the distinct possibility of changes in the antitrust exemption. Brief for Petitioner, at 24, *Flood v. Kuhn*.

The Chief Justice suggested that "[c]ourts are not the forum in which this tangled web ought to be unsnarled." Let Congress make the change. Do you think the Court would have issued the same opinion if one of its own common law precedents was being construed instead of a statute? Think about why a statutory case might be different. There is evidence that the Court does in fact utilize a de facto *hierarchy* of *stare decisis*: the Court applies "super-strong" *stare decisis* to its statutory decisions, like *Flood*; ordinary stare decisis to its own, common law precedents; and a lower level of stare decisis for constitutional holdings. *See CBOCS W., Inc. v. Humphries,*

553 U.S. 442 (2008) (observing that *stare decisis* "ha[s] special force in the area of statutory interpretation"). Does this make sense? The Constitution is a short, exceedingly difficult-to-amend document that is meant to stand the test of time. Statutes, on the other hand, can theoretically be amended by Congress any time and are much more detailed. How might those distinctions explain the difference for *stare decisis*? See generally William N. Eskridge Jr., *Overruling Statutory Precedents*, 76 Geo. L.J. 1361 (1988).

2. *Flood's Aftermath*. Given the history of congressional involvement, recounted by the Court, was there any reason to believe that Congress would do anything? The reaction to *Flood* in Congress was, indeed, immediate: Two bills were introduced in the House of Representatives, H.R. 12401 and H.R. 14614, 92d Cong., 2d Sess. (1972), and a hearing was held by the appropriate subcommittee, but neither bill went anywhere. Is that because Congress "liked" the Court's decision? Or didn't "dislike" it enough to revoke it? Or was lobbied very hard by the baseball owners?[7] The Court never returned to the *Flood* issue—maybe on the ground that, after *Federal Baseball, Toolson*, and *Flood*, three strikes and you're out.

Thwarted on antitrust grounds, however, players used labor law to their advantage. The players' union that had financed the *Flood* lawsuit turned to contract arbitration as a forum for change. Five years after *Flood*, an arbitrator awarded free-agent status to two players; the collective bargaining between owners and the players' union that followed, with impasses sometimes resulting in strikes, led to labor agreements that provided players with significant freedom. In the mid-1990s, following a particularly acrimonious labor conflict, management agreed with the union to approach Congress jointly and request legislation overriding *Flood*.

Congress responded by enacting the Curt Flood Act of 1998, Pub. L. No. 105–297, 112 Stat. 2824. The statute subjects any business practices "directly relating to or affecting employment of major league baseball players * * * to the antitrust laws to the same extent such * * * practices * * * would be subject to the antitrust laws if engaged in by persons in any other professional sports business affecting interstate commerce." Drafted to avoid any application of the antitrust laws to such matters as franchise relocation and the treatment of minor-league players, it is not clear that the statute changed the law in general or, in particular, provided any rights to players that they had not already achieved through collective bargaining. Nor did the override provide solace to Curt Flood, who died of cancer in 1997. For the full story, see Brad Snyder, *A Well Paid Slave: Curt Flood's Fight For Free Agency in Professional Sports* (2007).

---

[7] In the 1970s, Members of Congress were promoting the return of Major League Baseball to the nation's capital, leading one commentator to opine: "It thus appears that there is more bicameral interest in where baseball will be played than in the legalities of the sport." Philip L. Martin, *The Aftermath of Flood v. Kuhn: Professional Baseball's Exemption from Antitrust Regulation*, 3 West. St. U.L. Rev. 262, 280 (1976). For the argument that Federal Baseball was ripe for overruling, see Stephen F. Ross, *The Story of Flood v. Kuhn (1972): Dynamic Statutory Interpretation, At the Time, in Statutory Interpretation Stories* 36–57 (William N. Eskridge Jr., Philip P. Frickey & Elizabeth Garrett eds., 2011).

Consider Justice Blackmun's "Ode to Baseball" in Part I of the opinion. Was that an appropriate matter to be included in a judicial opinion? Even if not, were Chief Justice Burger and Justice White right in making a point of not joining Part I? (We think this is the only time in history that an opinion commanded a Court majority in its entirety except for its statement of facts!)

3.   *When Is It Appropriate to Overrule a Statutory Precedent?* As *Flood* suggests, the Supreme Court will not routinely overrule a prior interpretation of a statute. As noted, the Court effectively applies super-strong *stare decisis* for statutory precedents. This practice is rooted in at least two ideas: first, the "rule of law" reasons discussed above that underpin *stare decisis* in general (predictability, objectivity, and notice); and second, the idea that when courts interpret statutes, unlike in the common-law context, courts aren't in the game alone. Instead, they are in an interbranch dialogue, and the preferences of their partner in this dialogue—Congress—are generally assumed supreme ("legislative supremacy") as long as they are constitutional. A good analogy is a tennis match: The courts hit the ball and wait until Congress hits back before they move again. Even though the extra-strong presumption of *stare decisis* for statutory precedents may lack historical support in practices before the twentieth century (likely because statutes did not dominate the legal landscape as they do today), it seems to be deeply rooted at the beginning of the twenty-first. Is it ever appropriate to overrule a statutory precedent? Consider some hypotheses:

(A) Constitutionalized Recent Decisions. Some judges and scholars say the Court should terminate bad civil rights precedents before they get entrenched. The Court does sometimes overrule civil rights precedents overtaken by normative constitutional thinking, e.g., *Monell v. Department of Social Services*, 436 U.S. 658 (1978) (overruling a 1961 precedent excluding municipalities from 42 U.S.C. § 1983, which holds state governments accountable for violations of federal law), but not with unusual frequency. Overruling decisions quickly is arguably a better idea, because it reduces reliance interests. In *Flood*, for example, the whole baseball industry had developed in reliance on the antitrust exemption.

(B) Common Law Statutes. Justice Stevens once argued that certain statutes, like the Sherman Antitrust Act (*Flood*) and section 1983 (*Monell*), that deployed open-textured common law terminology were, effectively, delegations to the judiciary to develop norms, common law style, rather than requiring the focus on legislative supremacy that courts usually apply in statutory cases. Hence, ordinary, common-law-level *stare decisis* ought to apply to those decisions. Although *Flood* is inconsistent with this idea (because it involves precisely such a statute—the Sherman Act), the Court has in fact overruled Sherman Act precedents more frequently than it has done for any other federal statute. See William N. Eskridge Jr. & John Ferejohn, *A Republic of Statutes: The New American Constitution* ch. 3 (2010) (surveying the cases); Margaret H. Lemos, *Interpretive Methodology and Delegations to Courts: Are "Common-Law Statutes" Different?*, in *Intellectual Property and the Common Law* (2012).

(C) Subsequent Statutory Developments. If subsequent statutory developments support the precedent, that is a good reason not to overrule, as in *Flood*; if the subsequent developments cut against the precedent, that supports an overruling, as in *Monell*.

NOTE ON THE RETROACTIVITY OF JUDICIAL DECISIONS

Notice that Justice Marshall's *Flood* dissent recognized that there was a big reliance interest problem if the Court overruled *Federal Baseball* and *Toolson*: Major League Baseball would be subject to immediate, and possibly devastating, lawsuits for price-fixing and market division (per se illegal under the Sherman Act), as well as the reserve clause. Justice Blackmun's opinion for the Court gains traction once you realize that Congress could easily address the reliance-interest problems. Because most legislation is prospective in operation, Major League Baseball would not be liable for past anti-competitive practices; additionally, Congress could give the industry a transition period, enabling organized baseball to make the needed adjustments.

Justice Marshall's response to this problem was to suggest that the Court might overrule *Federal Baseball* and *Toolson*, but announce that the overruling was prospective only: it did not render past conduct illegal. Curt Flood would win relief from the reserve clause, and perhaps damages, but no one else could bring a Sherman Act lawsuit for past conduct. Does Article III permit federal courts to overrule precedents and announce that they have only prospective effect? The Supreme Court has addressed this issue since *Flood*.

The Warren Court had sometimes overruled constitutional criminal procedure precedents, with partial prospective effect, namely, granting relief to the fortunate petitioners but denying application of the new constitutional rule to pending cases. In **Griffith v. Kentucky**, 479 U.S. 314 (1987), the Rehnquist Court rejected that practice and eliminated limits on retroactivity in the criminal context. *Griffith* held that all "newly declared" rules must be applied retroactively to all "criminal cases pending on direct review." This holding rested on two "basic norms of constitutional adjudication." First, "the nature of judicial review" strips the Court of the quintessentially "legislat[ive]" prerogative to make rules of law retroactive or prospective as the Justices see fit. Second, the Court concluded that "selective application of new rules violates the principle of treating similarly situated [parties] the same." Because it involved criminal constitutional issues, *Griffith* left open the viability of Warren Court decisions allowing selective prospectivity when the Court overruled civil precedents.

The Court soon had an opportunity to address the issue in civil cases. In **James B. Beam Distilling Co. v. Georgia**, 501 U.S. 529 (1991), the Justices ruled that decisions overruling constitutional civil precedents, likewise, could not be given partial prospective effect. Unfortunately, there was no opinion for the Court. **Justice Souter** delivered the judgment of the

Court and wrote for himself and Chief Justice Rehnquist. They concluded that partial prospectivity is inherently unfair and "inequitable," and hence inconsistent with our regime of a neutral choice of law. Concurring, **Justice White** essentially agreed with Justice Souter.

Concurring in the judgment, **Justice Scalia** (writing also for Justices Marshall and Blackmun, who wrote the opposing opinions in *Flood v. Kuhn*) argued that the problem with selective prospectivity is constitutional and not just equitable. "If the division of federal powers central to the constitutional scheme is to succeed in its objective, it seems to me that the fundamental nature of those powers must be preserved as that nature was understood when the Constitution was enacted." * * *

Justice Scalia continued: "I am not so naive (nor do I think our forebears were) as to be unaware that judges in a real sense 'make' law. But they make it *as judges make it,* which is to say as *though* they were 'finding' it—discerning what the law *is,* rather than decreeing what it is today *changed to,* or what it will *tomorrow* be. Of course this mode of action poses 'difficulties of a . . . practical sort,' when courts decide to overrule prior precedent. But those difficulties are one of the understood checks upon judicial law-making; to eliminate them is to render courts substantially more free to 'make new law,' and thus to alter in a fundamental way the assigned balance of responsibility and power among the three branches."

In **Harper v. Virginia Department of Taxation,** 509 U.S. 86 (1993), the Court returned to this issue for civil cases. Writing for a Court majority, **Justice Thomas** (who was not on the Court for *Jim Beam*) confirmed that the point of law from *Jim Beam* is that "a rule of federal law, once announced and applied to the parties to the controversy, must be given full retroactive effect by all courts adjudicating federal law." That is, in civil as well as criminal cases, the Court cannot overrule a precedent, give the petitioning party the benefit of the new rule, and deny application of the new rule to other legally cognizable cases and controversies. "[B]oth the common law and our own decisions" have "recognized a general rule of retrospective effect for the constitutional decisions of this Court." *Robinson v. Neil*, 409 U.S. 505, 507 (1973). Nothing in the Constitution alters the fundamental rule of "retrospective operation" that has governed "[j]udicial decisions . . . for near a thousand years." *Kuhn v. Fairmont Coal Co.,* 215 U.S. 349, 372 (1910) (Holmes, J., dissenting)."

Justice Thomas concluded: "*Beam* controls this case, and we accordingly adopt a rule that fairly reflects the position of a majority of Justices in *Beam*: When this Court applies a rule of federal law to the parties before it, that rule is the controlling interpretation of federal law and must be given full retroactive effect in all cases still open on direct review and as to all events, regardless of whether such events predate or postdate our announcement of the rule. This rule extends *Griffith*'s ban against 'selective application of new rules.' Mindful of the 'basic norms of constitutional adjudication' that animated our view of retroactivity in the criminal context, we now prohibit the erection of selective temporal barriers to the application of federal law in noncriminal cases. In both civil and criminal cases, we can scarcely permit 'the substantive law [to] shift and spring' according to 'the particular equities of [individual parties'] claims' of actual reliance on an old rule and of harm from a retroactive application of the new rule. *Beam* (opinion of Souter, J.)."

After *Harper*, is there any way that the Supreme Court could have overruled *Federal Baseball*, *Toolson*, and *Flood v. Kuhn*, without upsetting huge reliance interests?

3. HOW CONGRESS AND AGENCIES REACT TO AND INTERACT WITH THE COURT

This section explores a final feature of the Supreme Court's distinctive role in American governance and its interaction with the other branches of government. As we have seen above, the Supreme Court is a largely reactive institution; it rarely has the first word in the articulation of American public policy. Its input comes after considerable deliberation and controversy in the legislative and executive branches. But once the Court has spoken, its interpretation usually sticks, and the other branches need to accommodate their policy moves to take account of what the Court has said.

Now consider this interesting asymmetry in the finality of the Court's interpretations. In constitutional cases, it is very hard, and often impossible, for the political process to override the Supreme Court's interpretations limiting governmental authority. When Congress has pushed back with its own, less restrictive constitutional views, the Court has typically shut down constitutional dissent. E.g., *City of Boerne v. Flores*, 521 U.S. 507 (1997) (invalidating the Religious Freedom Restoration Act of 1993, 42 U.S.C. §§ 2000bb to 2000bb–4, as applied to state and local governments). Constitutional decisions authorizing governmental authority need not be overridden, for they can be ignored: Congress can decide not to use any such authority recognized by the Court. After *Morrison v. Olson* upheld Congress's authority to create Independent Counsels, Congress allowed the constitutional statute to lapse.

In contrast, Supreme Court statutory interpretations—even those limiting agency authority—can be overridden by Congress, and they frequently are overridden. Between 1967 and 2011, Congress overrode 276 Supreme Court statutory interpretation decisions in 286 statutory provisions. See Matthew R. Christiansen & William N. Eskridge Jr., *Congressional Overrides of Supreme Court Statutory Interpretation Decisions, 1967–2011*, 92 Tex. L. Rev. 1317 (2014). Most of the overrides were in the areas of anti-discrimination law, civil and criminal procedure (including habeas corpus), tax, bankruptcy, environmental law, intellectual property, antitrust, and governmental affairs. Among the decisions overridden was *Flood v. Kuhn* (overridden in 1998).

From this simple structure, we can derive some surprisingly useful lessons. The creation of public policy is a *sequential process*. That is, Congress enacts important legislation, often after an arduous process to avoid or press the proposal through hostile or ambivalent vetogates; then the executive branch implements the legislation, typically through an agency Congress has created and tailored for this particular program; next, there is often judicial input, through cases interpreting the statute, reviewing the agency's interpretations, or even evaluating the statute as a matter of constitutional doctrine. However the Court construes the law, that is not the end of the process, for the agency and private interest groups will react to the Court's interpretation—and for important legislation Congress will respond to agency and court constructions with amendments to the statute, perhaps a whole new statute, and maybe lower-visibility reactions such as appropriations measures that encourage or discourage aggressive application of the law.

Within such a sequential process, each institution contributes something important. As the Framers expected, Congress makes the most important contributions, providing the authoritative statutory text and a great measure of political legitimacy to the statutory scheme, as it has received an okay or even an enthusiastic endorsement from a variety of regional and even ideological perspectives in the process of navigating the vetogates. The President and the agency fill in the details, and their contribution consists of the expertise they bring to the statutory scheme and however much muscle and inventiveness they choose to invest in it. The role of courts is to effectuate congressional intent, legitimate popular decisions, settle controversial legislative choices, integrate the statute into the larger corpus of law, and ensure that the public has notice of the laws to which it is subject. If they rule against the agency, this is likely to slow down the process by impelling more deliberation either by the agency or by Congress. Ultimately, courts can be seen as setting the line between what is considered "law" (bright line rules binding on political actors) and what is considered "politics" (matters left to the discretion of political officials).

The story of the FDA's attempt to regulate tobacco—which you will recall from the *Brown & Williamson* case in Chapter 2—provides a nice illustration. The Food Drug & Cosmetics Act of 1938 was a super-statute adopted in response to a perceived national calamity (poisonous drugs); its proponents won over skeptics and neutralized opponents not only by the perceived social need, but also by the super-effective manner in which the FDA implemented the statute, with the courts going along. The Thalidomide crisis in the early 1960s, which devastated Europe but not the United States, gave dramatic support to the FDA's aggressive regulatory program, and Congress endorsed and expanded that program in the 1963 Amendments, again with judicial acquiescence. The Clinton-administration FDA, at the direct behest of the President (recall our "unitary presidency" model from Chapter 2) tried to expand its power without Congress through regulation. The agency interpreted the FDCA's delegation of authority to the FDA over drugs and medical devices to extend to nicotine and cigarettes, respectively. The Supreme Court stopped the FDA in its tracks in *Brown & Williamson*. One interpretation of this story is that the Court was trumping the liberal agency with its own business-friendly preferences. But another explanation is that the Court was insisting upon a more democratic foundation for such a big regulatory move—a statute, not just agency action—which Congress supplied in a 2009 override statute. In the wake of the 2009 override, the FDA has attacked the problem of smoking, especially among youth, with renewed vigor, and so far the lower federal courts are going along.

The FDA's current anti-smoking campaign, requiring lurid images of smokers in the final stage of their lives, is not the end of the lawmaking process, however. Elections matter. If tobacco-friendlier politicians gain control of Congress, the FDA may face appropriations pressure or even new legislation limiting what advertisements and images on packages it can mandate. Likewise, a President friendlier to tobacco interests might install an FDA Commissioner who will slow down the agency's activism. Ironically, the Supreme Court remains an important player, even after the 2009 override law. Although the Court is generally resistant to interfering with agency statutory implementation when Congress has delegated the relevant authority to the agency, the Court still has constitutional law at its disposal. So do litigants, who are looking to find ways to challenge the FDA's moves in a legal environment that is heavily deferential to agency policy decisions. As a result, litigants are using the First Amendment instead of the doctrines of statutory interpretation and administrative review. The D.C. Circuit has ruled that the FDA's required images on cigarette packages represent compelled political speech, which can only be justified if the government compulsion is necessary to advance a compelling public interest, which the judge held it did not. *R.J. Reynolds Tobacco Co. v. FDA*, 696 F.3d 1205 (D.C. Cir. 2012). If the Supreme Court ultimately agrees with this reasoning, it will upend the FDA's regulatory scheme in very serious ways.

Consider, now, how Title VII of the Civil Rights Act has evolved, dramatically and unexpectedly, through the interaction of a Congress that did not foresee important problems, an aggressive agency, a go-slow Supreme Court, an overriding Congress, a still-aggressive agency, and further pushback from a Supreme Court closely divided along lines of sex and gender. In the following materials, the question is how to know when

Congress disagrees with courts' statutory interpretations and what to do when that happens.

PAUL JOHNSON V. TRANSPORTATION AGENCY, SANTA CLARA COUNTY

Supreme Court of the United States, 1987.
480 U.S. 616, 107 S.Ct. 1442, 94 L. Ed. 2d 613.

[*Johnson* brought the question of affirmative action for women under Title VII (recall Problem 1–2) to the Court for the first time. It also raised the important question of whether Title VII applies to public as well as private employers. Two important cases preceded *Johnson* in the Court. In *Griggs v. Duke Power Co.*, 401 U.S. 424 (1971), the Court had held that facially neutral actions that have a disparate impact on race violate the statute. The Court in *Griggs* recognized that Congress did not foresee a need for the disparate impact cause of action—Congress naively thought that merely banning discrimination would be enough—but the Court supported the cause of action as necessary to effectuate Title VII's remedial and anti-discriminatory purposes.

[The next major case was *United Steelworkers of America v. Weber*, 443 U.S. 193 (1979) (Chapter 6, § 3), which raised the question of affirmative action for racial minorities. *Weber* was a bitterly divided opinion. Justice Brennan invoked the "spirit" of Title VII to allow affirmative action under § 703(j) of Title VII, while Justice Rehnquist's dissent criticized the majority for reading in permission that the statutory text did not grant and likely violating the terms of the deal that fencesitting Senators thought they had made when they finally signed onto Title VII. Justice Blackmun's concurrence in *Weber* was most pragmatic: He believed that Title VII's text did not allow for affirmative action, but thought that affirmative action was necessary in certain situations. Otherwise (as a result of the Court's own precedents), employers were caught between a rock and a hard place; potentially liable for disparate impact actions under *Griggs* but unable to take affirmative steps to address a racial imbalance in the workplace. Against this backdrop of divided opinions and debates about what Congress knew and what Congress wanted, came Paul Johnson's case.]

JUSTICE BRENNAN delivered the opinion of the Court.

[The Transportation Agency of Santa Clara County, California promulgated an Affirmative Action Plan to remedy historic patterns of discrimination against women and minorities in some job categories. The Plan provided that, in making promotions to positions within a traditionally segregated job classification in which women had been significantly underrepresented, the Agency was authorized to consider as one factor the sex of a qualified applicant. The Agency found women significantly underrepresented in its work force generally, and virtually unrepresented in the 238 Skilled Craft Worker positions. Pursuant to the Plan, the Agency promoted Diane Joyce to the position of road dispatcher in the Agency's Roads Division. Dispatchers assign road crews, equipment, and materials, and maintain records pertaining to road maintenance jobs. One of the applicants passed over was Paul Johnson, who had a slightly higher score than Joyce based upon his paper credentials and an oral interview.

[Johnson filed a complaint with the EEOC, and subsequently a federal lawsuit. The district court granted Johnson relief, based upon its finding that Johnson was more qualified for the position than Joyce, and that sex was the "determining factor" in Joyce's selection. The Ninth Circuit reversed.]

[*Weber*] upheld the employer's decision to select less senior black applicants over the white respondent, for we found that taking race into account was consistent with Title VII's objective of "break[ing] down old patterns of racial segregation and hierarchy." As we stated:

> "It would be ironic indeed if a law triggered by a Nation's concern over centuries of racial injustice and intended to improve the lot of those who had 'been excluded from the American dream for so long' constituted the first legislative prohibition of all voluntary, private, race-conscious efforts to abolish traditional patterns of racial segregation and hierarchy." *Id.* (quoting remarks of Sen. Humphrey).[7]

---

[7]   Justice Scalia's dissent maintains that *Weber*'s conclusion that Title VII does not prohibit voluntary affirmative action programs "rewrote the statute it purported to construe." *Weber*'s decisive rejection of the argument that the "plain language" of the statute prohibits affirmative action rested on (1) legislative history indicating Congress' clear intention that employers play a major role in eliminating the vestiges of discrimination, and (2) the language and legislative history of section 703(j) of the statute, which reflect a strong desire to preserve managerial prerogatives so that they might be utilized for this purpose. As Justice Blackmun said in his concurrence in *Weber*, "[I]f the Court has misconceived the political will, it has the assurance that because the question is statutory Congress may set a different course if it so chooses." Congress has not amended the statute to reject our construction, nor have any such amendments even been proposed, and we therefore may assume that our interpretation was correct.

Justice Scalia's dissent faults the fact that we take note of the absence of Congressional efforts to amend the statute to nullify *Weber*. It suggests that Congressional inaction cannot be regarded as acquiescence under all circumstances, but then draws away from that unexceptional point the conclusion that *any* reliance on Congressional failure to act is necessarily a "canard." The fact that inaction may not always provide crystalline revelation, however, should not obscure the fact that it may be probative to varying degrees. *Weber*, for instance, was a widely-publicized decision that addressed a prominent issue of public debate. Legislative inattention thus is not a plausible explanation for Congressional inaction. Furthermore, Congress not only passed no contrary legislation in the wake of *Weber*, but not one legislator even proposed a bill to do so. The barriers of the legislative process therefore also seem a poor explanation for failure to act. By contrast, when Congress has been displeased with our interpretation of Title VII, it has not hesitated to amend the statute to tell us so. For instance, when Congress passed the Pregnancy Discrimination Act of 1978, 42 U.S.C. section 2000e(k), "it unambiguously expressed its disapproval of both the holding and the reasoning of the Court in [*General Electric v. Gilbert*, 429 U.S. 125 (1976)]." *Newport News Shipbuilding & Dry Dock v. EEOC*, 462 U.S. 669, 678

* * * *Weber* held that an employer seeking to justify the adoption of a plan need not point to its own prior discriminatory practices, nor even to evidence of an "arguable violation" on its part. Rather, it need point only to a "conspicuous ... imbalance in traditionally segregated job categories." * * *

In reviewing the employment decision at issue in this case, we must first examine whether that decision was made pursuant to a plan prompted by concerns similar to those of the employer in *Weber*. Next, we must determine whether the effect of the plan on males and nonminorities is comparable to the effect of the plan in that case. [Justice Brennan then applied these factors and determined the Agency plan to be consistent with *Weber*, holding that "[I]t is clear that the decision to hire Joyce was made pursuant to an Agency plan that directed that sex or race be taken into account for the purpose of remedying underrepresentation" and that the plan did not "unnecessarily tramme[l] the rights of male employees or created an absolute bar to their advancement."] * * *

We therefore hold that the Agency appropriately took into account as one factor the sex of Diane Joyce in determining that she should be promoted to the road dispatcher position. The decision to do so was made pursuant to an affirmative action plan that represents a moderate, flexible, case-by-case approach to effecting a gradual improvement in the representation of minorities and women in the Agency's work force. Such a plan is fully consistent with Title VII, for it embodies the contribution that voluntary employer action can make in eliminating the vestiges of discrimination in the workplace.

JUSTICE STEVENS, concurring. * * *

Prior to 1978 the Court construed the Civil Rights Act of 1964 as an absolute blanket prohibition against discrimination which neither required nor permitted discriminatory preferences for any group, minority or majority. * * * As I explained in my separate opinion in *Bakke*, and as the Court forcefully stated in *McDonald v. Santa Fe Trail Transportation Co.*, Congress intended " 'to eliminate all practices which operate to disadvantage the employment opportunities of any group protected by Title VII including Caucasians.' " If the Court had adhered to that construction of the Act, petitioner would unquestionably prevail in this case. But it has not done so.

(1983). Surely, it is appropriate to find some probative value in such radically different Congressional reactions to this Court's interpretations of the same statute.

As one scholar has put it, "When a court says to a legislature: 'You (or your predecessor) meant X,' it almost invites the legislature to answer: 'We did not.' " G. Calabresi, A Common Law for the Age of Statutes 31–32 (1982). Any belief in the notion of a dialogue between the judiciary and the legislature must acknowledge that on occasion an invitation declined is as significant as one accepted.

In the *Bakke* case in 1978 and again in *Weber,* a majority of the Court interpreted the antidiscriminatory strategy of the statute in a fundamentally different way. * * * [T]he only problem for me is whether to adhere to an authoritative construction of the Act that is at odds with my understanding of the actual intent of the authors of the legislation. I conclude without hesitation that I must answer that question in the affirmative[.]

Bakke and *Weber* have been decided and are now an important part of the fabric of our law. This consideration is sufficiently compelling for me to adhere to the basic construction of this legislation that the Court adopted in *Bakke* and in *Weber.* There is an undoubted public interest in "stability and orderly development of the law."

The logic of antidiscrimination legislation requires that judicial constructions of Title VII leave "breathing room" for employer initiatives to benefit members of minority groups. If Title VII had never been enacted, a private employer would be free to hire members of minority groups for any reason that might seem sensible from a business or a social point of view. The Court's opinion in *Weber* reflects the same approach; the opinion relied heavily on legislative history indicating that Congress intended that traditional management prerogatives be left undisturbed to the greatest extent possible. * * *

As construed in *Weber* * * * the statute does not absolutely prohibit preferential hiring in favor of minorities; it was merely intended to protect historically disadvantaged groups *against* discrimination and not to hamper managerial efforts to benefit members of disadvantaged groups that are consistent with that paramount purpose. The preference granted by respondent in this case does not violate the statute as so construed; the record amply supports the conclusion that the challenged employment decision served the legitimate purpose of creating diversity in a category of employment that had been almost an exclusive province of males in the past. Respondent's voluntary decision is surely not prohibited by Title VII as construed in *Weber.*

Whether a voluntary decision of the kind made by respondent would ever be prohibited by Title VII is a question we need not answer until it is squarely presented. Given the interpretation of the statute the Court adopted in *Weber,* I see no reason why the employer has any duty, prior to granting a preference to a qualified minority employee, to determine whether his past conduct might constitute an arguable violation of Title VII. Indeed, in some instances the employer may find it more helpful to focus on the future. Instead of retroactively scrutinizing his own or society's possible exclusions of minorities in the past to determine the outer limits of a valid affirmative-action program—or indeed, any particular affirmative-action decision—in many cases the employer will find it more appropriate to consider other legitimate reasons to give preferences to members of underrepresented groups. Statutes enacted for the benefit of minority groups should not block these forward-looking considerations. * * *

[We omit JUSTICE O'CONNOR's opinion concurring in the judgment, as well as JUSTICE WHITE's dissent. Justice White indicated that he would overrule *Weber* (an opinion he joined in 1979), because the Court's reinterpretation of it was "a perversion of Title VII."]

JUSTICE SCALIA, with whom THE CHIEF JUSTICE [REHNQUIST] joins and with whom JUSTICE WHITE joins in Parts I and II, dissenting.

With a clarity which, had it not proven so unavailing, one might well recommend as a model of statutory draftsmanship, Title VII of the Civil Rights Act of 1964 declares:

> "It shall be an unlawful employment practice for an employer—
>
> "(1) to fail or refuse to hire or to discharge any individual, or otherwise to discriminate against any individual with respect to his compensation, terms, conditions, or privileges of employment, because of such individual's race, color, religion, sex, or national origin; or
>
> "(2) to limit, segregate, or classify his employees or applicants for employment in any way which would deprive or tend to deprive any individual of employment opportunities or otherwise adversely affect his status as an employee, because of such individual's race, color, religion, sex, or national origin."

The Court today completes the process of converting this from a guarantee that race or sex will *not* be the basis for employment determinations, to a guarantee that it often *will*. Ever so subtly, without even alluding to the last obstacles preserved by earlier opinions that we now push out of our path, we effectively replace the goal of a discrimination-free society with the quite incompatible goal of proportionate representation by race and by sex in the workplace. * * *

[In Part I of his dissent, Justice Scalia argued that the Court and Justice O'Connor wrongly ignored the District Court's finding of fact that "if the Affirmative Action Coordinator had not intervened, 'the decision as to whom to promote . . . would have been made by [the Road Operations Division Director],' who had recommended that Johnson be appointed to the position"; and the further findings of fact that Johnson was "more qualified for the position" and that Joyce's gender was "the determining factor" in her selection. Justice Scalia maintained in Part II that the Court's opinion basically sanctioned affirmative action plans that remedy societal rather than employer discrimination, a holding flatly contrary to *Wygant* and in tension with the Court's holding in *Bakke*.]

[III] I have omitted from the foregoing discussion the most obvious respect in which today's decision o'erleaps, without analysis, a barrier that was thought still to be overcome. In *Weber*, this Court held that a private-sector affirmative action training program that overtly discriminated against white applicants did not violate Title VII. However, although the majority does not advert to the fact, until today the applicability of *Weber* to public employers remained an open question. In *Weber* itself, and in later decisions, this Court has repeatedly emphasized that *Weber* involved only a private employer. This distinction between public and private employers has several possible justifications. *Weber* rested in part on the assertion that the 88th Congress did not wish to intrude too deeply into private employment decisions. Whatever validity that assertion may have with respect to private employers (and I think it negligible), it has none with respect to public employers or to the 92d Congress that brought them within Title VII. Another reason for limiting *Weber* to private employers is that state agencies, unlike private actors, are subject to the Fourteenth Amendment. As noted earlier, it would be strange to construe Title VII to permit discrimination by public actors that the Constitution forbids.

In truth, however, the language of 42 U.S.C. § 2000e–2 draws no distinction between private and public employers, and the only good reason for creating such a distinction would be to limit the damage of *Weber*. It would be better, in my view, to acknowledge that case as fully applicable precedent, and to use the Fourteenth Amendment ramifications—which *Weber* did not address and which are implicated for the first time here—as the occasion for reconsidering and overruling it. It is well to keep in mind just how thoroughly *Weber* rewrote the statute it purported to construe. The language of that statute, as quoted at the outset of this dissent, is unambiguous[.] *Weber* disregarded the text of the statute, invoking instead its " 'spirit,' " and "practical and equitable [considerations] only partially perceived, if perceived at all, by the 88th Congress" (Blackmun, J., concurring). It concluded, on the basis of these intangible guides, that Title VII's prohibition of intentional discrimination on the basis of race and sex does not prohibit intentional discrimination on the basis of race and sex, so long as it is "designed to break down old patterns of racial [or sexual] segregation and hierarchy," "does not unnecessarily trammel the interests of the white [or male] employees," "does not require the discharge of white [or male] workers and their replacement with new black [or female] hirees," "does [not] create an absolute bar to the advancement of white [or male] employees," and "is a temporary measure . . . not intended to maintain racial [or sexual] balance, but simply to eliminate a manifest racial [or sexual] imbalance." In effect, *Weber* held that the legality of intentional discrimination by private employers against certain disfavored groups or individuals is to be judged not by Title VII but by a judicially crafted code of conduct, the contours of which are determined by no discernible standard, aside from (as the dissent convincingly demonstrated) the divination of congressional "purposes" belied by the face of the statute and by its legislative history. We have been recasting that self-promulgated code of conduct ever since—and what it has led us to today adds to the reasons for abandoning it.

The majority's response to this criticism of *Weber* [see note 7 of the majority opinion] asserts that, since "Congress has not amended the statute to reject our construction, . . . we . . . may assume that our interpretation was correct." This assumption, which frequently haunts our opinions, should be put to rest. It is based, to begin with, on the patently false premise that the correctness of statutory construction is to be measured by what the current Congress desires, rather than by what the law as enacted meant. To make matters worse, it assays the current Congress' desires *with respect to the particular provision in isolation*, rather than (the way the provision was originally enacted) as part of a total legislative package containing many *quids pro quo*. Whereas the statute as originally proposed may have presented to the enacting Congress a question such as "Should hospitals be required to provide medical care for indigent patients, with federal subsidies to offset the cost?," the question theoretically asked of the later Congress, in order to establish the "correctness" of a judicial interpretation that the statute provides no subsidies, is simply "Should the medical care that hospitals are required to provide for indigent patients be federally subsidized?" Hardly the same question—and many of those legislators who accepted the subsidy provisions in order to gain the votes necessary for enactment of the care requirement would not vote for the subsidy in isolation, now that an unsubsidized care requirement is, thanks to the judicial opinion, safely on the books. But even accepting the flawed premise that the intent of the current Congress, with respect to the provision in isolation, is determinative, one must ignore rudimentary principles of political science to draw any conclusions regarding that intent from the *failure* to enact legislation. The "complicated check on legislation," The Federalist No. 62, p. 378 C. Rossiter ed. 1961), erected by our Constitution creates an inertia that makes it impossible to assert with any degree of assurance that congressional failure to act represents (1) approval of the status quo, as opposed to (2) inability to agree upon how to alter the status quo, (3) unawareness of the status quo, (4) indifference to the status quo, or even (5) political cowardice * * *. I think we should admit that vindication by congressional inaction is a canard.

Justice Stevens' concurring opinion emphasizes "the underlying public interest in 'stability and orderly development of the law'" that often requires adherence to an erroneous decision. As I have described above, however, today's decision is a demonstration not of stability and order but of the instability and unpredictable expansion which the substitution of judicial improvisation for statutory text has produced. For a number of reasons, *stare decisis* ought not to save *Weber*. First, this Court has applied the doctrine of stare decisis to civil rights statutes less rigorously than to other laws. See *Maine v. Thiboutot*, 448 U.S. 1, 33 (1980) (Powell, J., dissenting); *Monroe v. Pape*, [365 U.S. 167, 221–22 (1961)] (Frankfurter, J., dissenting in part). Second, * * * *Weber* was itself a dramatic departure from the Court's prior Title VII precedents, and can scarcely be said to be "so consistent with the warp and woof of civil rights law as to be beyond question." Third, *Weber* was decided a mere seven years ago, and has provided little guidance to persons seeking to conform their conduct to the law, beyond the proposition that Title VII does not mean what it says. Finally, "even under the most stringent test for the propriety of overruling a statutory decision . . .—'that it appear beyond doubt . . . that [the decision] misapprehended the meaning of the controlling provision,'" *Weber* should be overruled.

In addition to complying with the commands of the statute, abandoning *Weber* would have the desirable side effect of eliminating the requirement of willing suspension of disbelief that is currently a credential for reading our opinions in the affirmative action field—from *Weber* itself, which demanded belief that the corporate employer adopted the affirmative action program "voluntarily," rather than under practical compulsion from government contracting agencies, to *Bakke*, a Title VI case cited as authority by the majority here, which demanded belief that the University of California took race into account as merely one of the many diversities to which it felt it was educationally important to expose its medical students, to today's opinion, which—in the face of a plan obviously designed to force promoting officials to prefer candidates from the favored racial and sexual classes, warning them that their "personal commitment" will be determined by how successfully they "attain" certain numerical goals, and in the face of a particular promotion awarded to the less qualified applicant by an official who "did little or nothing" to inquire into sources "critical" to determining the final candidates' relative qualifications other than their sex—in the face of all this, demands belief that we are dealing here with no more than a program that "merely authorizes that consideration be given to affirmative action concerns when evaluating qualified applicants." Any line of decisions rooted so firmly in naivete must be wrong. * * *

Today's decision does more, however, than merely reaffirm *Weber*, and more than merely extend it to public actors. It is impossible not to be aware that the practical effect of our holding is to accomplish *de facto* what the law—in language even plainer than that ignored in *Weber*, see 42 U.S.C. § 2000e–2(j)—forbids anyone from accomplishing *de jure*: in many contexts it effectively *requires* employers, public as well as private, to engage in intentional discrimination on the basis of race or sex. This Court's prior interpretations of Title VII, especially *Griggs*, subject employers to a potential Title VII suit whenever there is a noticeable imbalance in the representation of minorities or women in the employer's work force. Even the employer who is confident of ultimately prevailing in such a suit must contemplate the expense and adverse publicity of a trial, because the extent of the imbalance, and the "job relatedness" of his selection criteria, are questions of fact to be explored through rebuttal and counterrebuttal of a "prima facie case" consisting of no more than the showing that the employer's selection process "selects those from the protected class at a 'significantly' lesser rate than their counterparts." B. Schlei & P. Grossman, Employment Discrimination Law 91 (2d ed. 1983). If, however, employers are free to discriminate through affirmative action, without fear of "reverse discrimination" suits by their nonminority or male victims, they are offered a threshold defense against Title VII liability premised on numerical disparities. Thus, after today's decision the *failure* to engage in reverse discrimination is economic folly, and arguably a breach of duty to shareholders or taxpayers, wherever the cost of anticipated Title VII litigation exceeds the cost of hiring less capable (though still minimally capable) workers. (This situation is more likely to obtain, of course, with respect to the least skilled jobs—perversely creating an incentive to discriminate against precisely those members of the nonfavored groups *least* likely to have profited from societal discrimination in the past.) It is predictable, moreover, that this incentive will be greatly magnified by economic pressures brought to bear by government contracting agencies upon employers who refuse to discriminate in the fashion we have now approved. A statute designed to establish a color-blind and gender-blind workplace has thus been converted into a powerful engine of racism and sexism, not merely *permitting* intentional race- and sex-based discrimination, but often making it, through operation of the legal system, practically compelled.

It is unlikely that today's result will be displeasing to politically elected officials, to whom it provides the means of quickly accommodating the demands of organized groups to achieve concrete, numerical improvement in the economic status of particular constituencies. Nor will it displease the world of corporate and governmental employers (many of whom have filed briefs as amici in the present case, all on the side of Santa Clara) for whom the cost of hiring less qualified workers is often substantially less—and infinitely more predictable—than the cost of litigating Title VII cases and of seeking to convince federal agencies by nonnumerical means that no discrimination exists. In fact, the only losers in the process are the Johnsons of the country, for whom Title VII has been not merely repealed but actually inverted. The irony is that these individuals—predominantly unknown, unaffluent, unorganized—suffer this injustice at the hands of a Court fond of thinking itself the champion of the politically impotent. I dissent.

NOTES AND QUESTIONS ON JOHNSON

1. *What's Happening in Footnote 7?* Re-read footnote 7 of the Brennan opinion, and think about *stare decisis*. What is Brennan's argument for why the Court should extend *Weber* to sex in *Johnson*? Justice Scalia's dissent charges the Court with putting too much weight on the fact that Congress has not overruled *Weber*. Justice Brennan argues that this congressional inaction signifies that Congress *agreed* with the Court's decision—namely, that congressional inaction equals *congressional acquiescence*. Does that argument seem compelling to you? (By the way, Justice Brennan got his history wrong; congressional hearings were in fact held on *Weber* and an amendment was introduced to overrule it. But he was correct that nothing happened. Does this extra history strengthen or weaken his argument?)

2. *Why Would Congress Let* Weber *Stand Even if It Disagreed with It?* Justice Scalia's dissent offers a compelling picture of how interest groups and the dealmaking required to make legislation might produce fewer congressional overrides than Congress would ideally want. Justice Scalia's point is that even if prohibiting affirmative action was necessary to get Title VII passed, a misinterpretation of that deal would not necessarily be overruled. Why? He makes several different arguments for why inertia, not action, is the congressional default—arguments that range from political cowardice to vetogates.

He also reminds us about the reality of vote-trading and bundling that major statutes (including Title VII) require. Thus, in the Title VII context, the language of § 703(j) was necessary to get to 60 votes for cloture, but there were not necessarily 60 Senators who needed to see that provision. Only the fencesitters needed that commitment about preventing affirmative action. Courts consider statutory provisions in isolation (here, for instance, § 703(j)), but Congress makes statutory *deals* that include bundles of provisions (e.g., the entire Title VII statute). That disconnect potentially enables judicial opinions to unbundle deals without repercussions: If the Court misinterpreted § 703(j) in *Weber*, the fencesitters alone do not have the numbers alone to work an override to enforce the deal they agreed to.

3. *Which Congress's Intent Are We Talking About?* Justice Scalia points out that that a theory of *stare decisis* that takes solace from the inaction of the current Congress (i.e., the lack of an override) tells us nothing about what the *enacting* Congress may have intended. Justice Scalia would kill *Weber* while it is young, rather than entrench a bad precedent more deeply. Justice Stevens' opinion, on the other hand, is a classic example of super-strong *stare decisis* for statutory precedents. He believed *Weber* was

wrongly decided (he did not vote in *Weber*, but would have dissented), but he goes along in *Johnson* because of *stare decisis.*

4.   *Interest Group Theory in* Johnson. Justice Scalia's dissent ends with the criticism that *Johnson* and *Weber* will make the powerful interest groups happy and leave out in the cold what he calls the "politically impotent" Johnsons of the world, "predominantly unknown, unaffluent, unorganized." What is he getting at? He was right that the powerful political forces inside the Beltway—labor unions, civil rights groups and the Chamber of Commerce—were all satisfied with *Weber* because it allowed them to advance their goals (such as avoiding *Griggs* lawsuits). The cost-payers were the diffuse group of blue-collar males like Paul Johnson and Brian Weber—but interest groups rarely form for the "masses," as Justice Scalia's opinion implies. Small, special purpose groups have the incentive to organize and work together for common goals; it is traditionally far less likely for heterogeneous masses to organize in the same way, as people have more incentive to shirk and free-ride over the efforts they assume the many others in the group are making. See Mancur Olson, *The Logic of Collective Action* (1965) (using this theory to explain why public goods—like highways—are underprovided for this reason).

5.   *The Fate of* Johnson. After *Johnson,* voluntary affirmative action seemed entrenched in Title VII, perhaps along the same logical lines developed in *Flood v. Kuhn.* One might have thought the point was even more firmly entrenched after Congress rebuffed the Supreme Court's post-*Johnson* stingy constructions of Title VII when it enacted the Civil Rights Act of 1991, Pub. L. No. 102–166, 105 Stat. 1071. The 1991 Act not only codified the Supreme Court's disparate impact (*Griggs*) jurisprudence, which had motivated some of the Justices in *Weber* and *Johnson,* but also included, in § 116, this provision: "Nothing in the amendments made by this title shall be construed to affect court-ordered remedies, affirmative action, or conciliation agreements, that are in accordance with the law."

Nonetheless, in the next major public employer affirmative action case, the Supreme Court majority ignored the earlier precedents. The issue in *Ricci v. DeStefano,* 557 U.S. 557 (2009), was whether Title VII barred a race-motivated decision by New Haven to throw out job-test results that would have disadvantaged Latino- and African-American candidates for promotions within the fire department. Justice Kennedy's opinion for the Court conceded that race-based affirmative action is sometimes legal but ruled that "race-based action like the City's in this case is impermissible under Title VII unless the employer can demonstrate a strong basis in evidence that, had it not taken the action, it would have been liable under the disparate-impact statute." The Court ignored *Weber* and cited *Johnson* only once, for a perfunctory proposition. Were the two precedents being implicitly overruled? Narrowed? How can *Ricci* be reconciled with *Flood v. Kuhn?*

NOTE ON THE EEOC'S PREGNANCY DISCRIMINATION GUIDELINE AND THE SUPREME COURT'S INTERPRETATION OF TITLE VII

Although the EEOC cannot issue substantive rules implementing Title VII of the Civil Rights Act and having the force of law, the agency has enjoyed broad influence on employment policies in the United States. After study and internal deliberation, the EEOC took an aggressive approach to implementing the sex discrimination prohibitions in § 703, codified at 42 U.S.C. § 2000e–2, of the employment discrimination title.[8]

In 1965, the EEOC issued "Guidelines on Discrimination Because of Sex," but made no mention of pregnancy-based discrimination. By the end of its first year of operation, the Commission had come to the conclusion that pregnancy was an issue that remained open for discussion:

> The prohibition against sex discrimination is especially difficult to apply with respect to the female employees who become pregnant. In all other questions involving sex discrimination, the underlying principle is the essential equality of treatment . . . The pregnant female, however, has no analogous male counterpart and pregnancy necessarily must be treated uniquely. The Commission decided that to carry out the Congressional policy of providing truly equal employment opportunities, including career opportunities for women, *policies would have to be devised which afforded female employees reasonable job protection during periods of pregnancy.*

EEOC, *First Annual Report* 40 (1965–66) (emphasis added). As noncommittal as it was, this language was alarming to many employers, for most employers did discriminate against pregnant employees in at least one of three ways:

- **Termination of Employment/Refusals to Hire.** Some employers, admittedly a minority, terminated pregnant employees, usually without opportunity to return to their jobs after childbirth. Airlines, for example, were committed to policies excluding pregnant women or women who had borne children from becoming stewardesses (or "air hostesses," a term used by TWA). Some school districts and private employers terminated employment when a worker was pregnant; while such workers could reapply for the same jobs after the pregnancy, there was no assurance the jobs would be available, and the worker would normally lose all seniority. State unemployment and workplace disability insurance programs generally did not compensate terminated pregnant employees,

---

[8]   The account that follows draws from Barbara Allen Babcock, Ann E. Freedman, Eleanor Holmes Norton & Susan C. Ross, *Sex Discrimination and the Law: Causes and Remedies* (1975); William N. Eskridge Jr. & John Ferejohn, *A Republic of Statutes: The New American Constitution* ch. 1 (2010); Kevin Schwartz, Equalizing Pregnancy: The Birth of a Super-Statute (Yale Law School, Supervised Analytical Writing, 2006).

even though they covered male employees who lost their jobs for health reasons.

- **Forced Unpaid Maternity Leaves.** Most school districts and, probably, most employers required pregnant employees to take unpaid leaves months before their due dates (and when most of the workers were capable of doing their jobs), and continuing for several months afterwards. Indeed, six states required such maternity leaves for *all* employers as a matter of statutory law. Not only did the expecting mother lose income, but she also lost seniority and fringe benefits. Generally, employers did not require and would not allow fathers to take paternity leaves.

- **Discriminatory Health Care Coverage.** Employer-provided health and disability insurance often did not cover the costs of pregnancy and childbirth. Although any condition requiring medical treatment for men was covered by these programs, this very important medical benefit for women was generally not covered. Nor did employers provide sick leave benefits to pregnant women.

See generally Trudy Hayden, ACLU Women's Rights Project, *Punishing Pregnancy: Discrimination in Education, Employment, and Credit* (1973) (documenting these and other discriminations against pregnant women in the early 1970s).

Although the EEOC's equivocal stance did not provoke a sea change in employment policies, it did provoke questions from employers directed to the EEOC's Office of General Counsel, staffed with only five attorneys in the early years (and only one woman, Sonia Pressman, who had experience in labor law). Acting General Counsel Richard Berg wrote most of the responses to employer inquiries, opining in 1966–67 that pregnancy was "unique" to female employees; although Berg himself did not consider employer-required pregnancy leaves as "discrimination because of sex," he advised employers that they should not terminate jobs because employees took pregnancy leaves. Pressman argued that Title VII needed to be enforced against employer policies that were race- or sex-neutral but that had disparate effects on racial minorities or women—a view of the law that the Supreme Court ultimately ratified (at the behest of the EEOC and the Solicitor General) in *Griggs v. Duke Power Co.*, 401 U.S. 424 (1971). As you may recall, *Griggs* ruled that a "neutral" employer policy having a statistically significant and disparate impact upon racial minorities, thereby disproportionately disadvantaging them in the workplace, violated § 703(a)(2) of the law *unless* the employer could demonstrate that the policy was justified by "business necessity."

Pressman's internal EEOC memorandum on *"Two Conflicting Theories for Protecting Women Regarding Pregnancy"* (1967) argued that the agency ought to target policies penalizing pregnant employees as sex discrimination. There were two ways of thinking about this issue. "The first theory,"

Pressman wrote, "holds that pregnancy should be treated in the employment relationship as any other temporary disability such as sickness." This was an *equal treatment* approach to securing equality of opportunity for women, along lines of the Equal Rights Amendment that many feminists had pressed for decades. Pressman herself leaned toward a second theory, the *special treatment* approach, which "holds that pregnancy is a unique disability requiring special provision for the protection of mother and child." Under that approach, employers had to accommodate women's pregnancies, not just treat them the same as men's disabilities.

Pressman was not the only EEOC lawyer thinking about this issue. The EEOC's Office of Compliance, headed by Alfred Blumrosen, followed Pressman's approach to the pregnancy issue. Responding to complaints, the Office of Compliance generated advisory opinions that some cautious employers followed to avoid potential lawsuits. In an early decision, the Office criticized an employer's policy which made maternity leaves available to female employees on an occasional basis, depending upon the individual circumstances surrounding the incident. "We believe that to provide substantial equality of employment opportunity," Blumrosen opined, "there must be special recognition for absences due to pregnancy. [F]or this reason, a leave of absence *should* be granted for pregnancy whether or not it is granted for illness." The employer's selective pregnancy leave policy "discriminates against female employees because of their sex." EEOC Decision No. 70–360, 1970 CCH at ¶ 6084 (December 16, 1969); accord, EEOC, *Fifth Annual Report* 13 (1969–70).

Blumrosen's 1969 opinion seemed to tilt the EEOC toward the special treatment approach favored by Pressman, but new women in the agency were more impressed by the views articulated by Catherine East and her Citizens' Advisory Council on the Status of Women (an advisory group established by executive order by President Kennedy in 1963). In a statement of principle adopted on October 29, 1970, the Council concluded:

> Childbirth and complications of pregnancy are, for all *job-related purposes*, temporary disabilities and should be treated as such under any health insurance, temporary disability insurance, or sick leave plan of any employer, union, or fraternal society. * * *

> No additional or different benefit or restrictions should be applied to disability because of pregnancy or childbirth, and no pregnant woman employee should be in a better position in relation to job-related practices or benefits than an employee similarly situated suffering from other disability.

Citizens' Advisory Council on the Status of Women, *Women in 1970*, at 4 (March 1971). After Susan Deller Ross joined the General Counsel's Office in 1970, she pressed for this approach to pregnancy discrimination. (Ross had already been active in feminist politics and was a liberal feminist who believed the equal treatment approach was more likely to advance women's interests in the long term.)

The EEOC's five governing Commissioners and its General Counsel were attentive to the debate among feminists between equal treatment and special treatment—but everyone believed that this raised important sex discrimination issues that needed to be addressed in a public manner. On April 5, 1972, the EEOC issued its first Guidelines to directly interpret Title VII's meaning for pregnancy-based classifications. Under the heading "Employment policies relating to pregnancy and childbirth," 29 C.F.R. § 1604.10, the Commission, in language that Sue Ross drafted, declared:

(a) A written or unwritten employment policy or practice which excludes from employment applicants or employees because of pregnancy is a prima facie violation of title VII.

(b) Disabilities caused or contributed to by pregnancy, miscarriage, abortion, childbirth, and recovery therefrom are, for all job-related purposes, temporary disabilities and should be treated as such under any health or temporary disability insurance or sick leave plan available in connection with employment. Written and unwritten employment policies and practices involving matters such as the commencement and duration of leave, the availability of extensions, the accrual of seniority and other benefits and privileges, reinstatement, and payment under any health or temporary disability insurance or sick leave plan, formal or informal, shall be applied to disability due to pregnancy or childbirth on the same terms and conditions as they are applied to other temporary disabilities.

(c) Where the termination of an employee who is temporarily disabled is caused by an employment policy under which insufficient or no leave is available, such a termination violates the Act if it has a disparate impact on employees of one sex and is not justified by business necessity.

37 Fed. Reg. 6819, 6837 (April 5, 1972) (codified at 29 C.F.R. § 1604.10). The EEOC also opined that state laws prohibiting the employment of women for specific periods before and after childbirth were preempted by Title VII. 29 C.F.R. § 1604.2(b)(1).

The 1972 Pregnancy Guidelines, part of the EEOC's general Guidelines on Sex Discrimination, were not legislative rules having the force of law, because Congress had not delegated that authority to the EEOC. Probably most employers and insurance companies continued to follow policies that penalized pregnant employees. But the EEOC had put the issue on the nation's public law agenda, and the stakes got higher in 1972, when Congress expanded Title VII to cover state and local governments as employers. After 1972, public schoolteachers were covered by Title VII. Because most school districts required termination or leave for purposes of pregnancy, the EEOC's Pregnancy Guideline would have required a huge change in their policies, which were under constitutional attack in the late 1960s and early 1970s.

Consider the common policy among public school districts of requiring a pregnant teacher to take an unpaid leave for most of the pregnancy and for a period after childbirth. Such a policy was at war with the EEOC's Pregnancy Guidelines—and was under fire from the medical profession, as doctors insisted that most pregnant women could work much longer than the policies permitted and some were quite capable of working right up to their delivery dates. Such policies, of course, were not illegal unless the U.S. Supreme Court ruled them so. Before the EEOC Guidelines took effect, the Court ruled in *Cleveland Bd. of Ed. v. LaFleur*, 414 U.S. 632 (1974), that rigid pregnancy leave policies violated the Due Process Clause because they were arbitrary rules inconsistent with medical evidence and unjustified as a matter of the capacities of most pregnant teachers.[9]

Feminist lawyers brought a series of lawsuits challenging employer and governmental policies that discriminated against pregnant women. Most of the lawsuits followed Ross's theory and the EEOC's mandate that pregnant women receive equal treatment as other similarly situated employees. One feature of litigation is that cases are delayed or terminated unpredictably. Feminist litigators expected the Supreme Court to adjudicate a compelling Title VII case early on—but a constitutional case beat the Title VII cases to the docket. That sequence was to prove important and perhaps decisive in the Court's response to this issue.

Dwight Geduldig v. Carolyn Aiello et al.
417 U.S. 484 (1974).

An individual was eligible for disability benefits if, during a one-year base period prior to his disability, he or she had contributed one percent of a minimum income of $300 to California's Disability Fund. In the event he or she suffered a compensable disability, the individual could receive a "weekly benefit amount" of between $25 and $105, depending on the amount he earned during the highest quarter of the base period. Four women who had participated in the Disability Fund objected that the Fund did not cover their time off from work or the complications three of the women suffered during their pregnancies. (During the course of the litigation, California revoked its interpretation of its Unemployment Insurance Code that denied pregnant women coverage when their pregnancies were marked by disabling complications.)

The Supreme Court had, in *Reed v. Reed*, 404 U.S. 71 (1971), struck down a blatant sex discrimination as a violation of the Equal Protection Clause's rationality requirement. The District Court applied *Reed* to

---

[9]   The school districts would have had a better chance to win the case if they had been more honest about their policies, which were often premised on the notion that schoolchildren should not be exposed to openly pregnant women and that pregnancy should be kept in a public closet for such kids.

strike down California's discrimination against pregnancy—but the Supreme Court, in an opinion by **Justice Stewart**, reversed.

"California does not discriminate with respect to the persons or groups which are eligible for disability insurance protection under the program. The classification challenged in this case relates to the asserted underinclusiveness of the set of risks that the State has selected to insure. Although California has created a program to insure most risks of employment disability, it has not chosen to insure all such risks, and this decision is reflected in the level of annual contributions exacted from participating employees. This Court has held that, consistently with the Equal Protection Clause, a State 'may take one step at a time, addressing itself to the phase of the problem which seems most acute to the legislative mind.' * * * [T]he Equal Protection Clause does not require that a State must choose between attacking every aspect of a problem or not attacking the problem at all. * * *

"If the Equal Protection Clause were thought to compel disability payments for normal pregnancy, it is hard to perceive why it would not also compel payments for short-term disabilities suffered by participating employees. * * * The State has a legitimate interest in maintaining the self-supporting nature of its insurance program. Similarly, it has an interest in distributing the available resources in such a way as to keep benefit payments at an adequate level for disabilities that are covered, rather than to cover all disabilities inadequately. Finally, California has a legitimate concern in maintaining the contribution rate at a level that will not unduly burden participating employees, particularly low-income employees who may be most in need of the disability insurance.

"These policies provide an objective and wholly noninvidious basis for the State's decision not to create a more comprehensive insurance program than it has. There is no evidence in the record that the selection of the risks insured by the program worked to discriminate against any definable group or class in terms of the aggregate risk protection derived by that group or class from the program. There is no risk from which men are protected and women are not. Likewise, there is no risk from which women are protected and men are not."

In footnote 20, Justice Stewart said: "[T]his case is thus a far cry from * * * cases involving discrimination based upon gender as such. The California insurance program does not exclude anyone from benefit eligibility because of gender but merely removes one physical condition—pregnancy—from the list of compensable disabilities. While it is true that only women can become pregnant it does not follow that every legislative classification concerning pregnancy is a sex-based classification * * *. Normal pregnancy is an objectively identifiable physical condition with unique characteristics. Absent a showing that distinctions involving pregnancy are mere pretexts designed to effect an invidious discrimination against the members of one sex or the other, lawmakers are constitutionally free to include or exclude pregnancy from the coverage of legislation such as this on any reasonable basis, just as with respect to any other physical condition.

"The lack of identity between the excluded disability and gender as such under this insurance program becomes clear upon the most cursory analysis. The program divides potential recipients into two groups—pregnant women and nonpregnant persons. While the first group is exclusively female, the second includes members of both sexes. The fiscal and actuarial benefits of the program thus accrue to members of both sexes."

Writing also for Justices Marshall and Stevens, **Justice Brennan** dissented. He maintained that California's policy was sex discrimination that could not withstand the "stricter standard of scrutiny" he believed the Equal Protection Clause required for such classifications.

Postscript. The Court had in 1974 not settled on a standard for scrutinizing state sex discriminations. In *Craig v. Boren*, 429 U.S. 190 (1976), the Supreme Court struck down an Oklahoma statute that allowed women, but not men, between 18 and 21 years of age to purchase 2% beer. The Court ruled that a state sex discrimination such as this violated the Equal Protection Clause. Speaking for the Court, Justice Brennan's opinion held: "To withstand constitutional challenge, previous cases establish that classifications by gender must serve important governmental objectives and must be substantially related to achievement of those objectives." *Id.* at 197–98. Administrative convenience, alone, could not justify a governmental discrimination because of sex. *Craig* had no apparent effect on the viability of *Geduldig*, because the earlier opinion had ruled, in note 20, that discrimination based on pregnancy was not a constitutional sex discrimination.

When *Geduldig* was decided, there were several Title VII cases pending in the lower federal courts—and one Title VII case came to the Court shortly after *Geduldig*. When the case was argued the first time, the Court split evenly and the Chief Justice set the case down for reargument the next term.

GENERAL ELECTRIC CO. v. MARTHA V. GILBERT ET AL.

United States Supreme Court, 1976.
429 U.S. 125, 97 S.Ct. 401, 50 L. Ed. 2d 343.

MR. JUSTICE REHNQUIST delivered the opinion of the Court.

Petitioner, General Electric Co. provides for all of its employees a disability plan which pays weekly nonoccupational sickness and accident benefits. Excluded from the plan's coverage, however, are disabilities arising from pregnancy. Respondents, on behalf of a class of women employees, brought this action seeking, inter alia, a declaration that this exclusion constitutes sex discrimination in violation of Title VII of the Civil Rights Act of 1964. The District Court for the Eastern District of Virginia, following a trial on the merits, held that the exclusion of such pregnancy-related disability benefits from General Electric's employee disability plan violated Title VII. * * *

[Between the date on which the District Court's judgment was rendered and the time this case was decided by the Court of Appeals, the Supreme Court decided *Geduldig v. Aiello*. The Court of Appeals majority ruled that *Geduldig* was not controlling because it arose under the Equal Protection Clause of the Fourteenth Amendment, and not under Title VII. The dissenting opinion disagreed with the majority regarding the impact of *Geduldig*. Justice Rehnquist agreed with the dissenting opinion and reversed.]

[II] Section 703(a)(1) provides in relevant part that it shall be an unlawful employment practice for an employer

> to discriminate against any individual with respect to his compensation, terms, conditions, or privileges of employment, because of such individual's race, color, religion, sex, or national origin, 42 U.S.C. § 2000e–2(a)(1).

While there is no necessary inference that Congress, in choosing this language, intended to incorporate into Title VII the concepts of discrimination which have evolved from court decisions construing the Equal Protection Clause of the Fourteenth Amendment, the similarities between the congressional language and some of those decisions surely indicate that the latter are a useful starting point in interpreting the former. Particularly in the case of defining the term "discrimination," which Congress has nowhere in Title VII defined, those cases afford an existing body of law analyzing and discussing that term in a legal context not wholly dissimilar to the concerns which Congress manifested in enacting Title VII. We think, therefore, that our decision in *Geduldig v. Aiello,* dealing with a strikingly similar disability plan, is quite relevant in determining whether or not the pregnancy exclusion did discriminate on the basis of sex. * * *

The Court of Appeals was * * * wrong in concluding that the reasoning of *Geduldig* was not applicable to an action under Title VII. Since it is a finding of sex-based discrimination that must trigger, in a case such as this, the finding of an unlawful employment practice under § 703(a)(1), *Geduldig* is precisely in point in its holding that an exclusion of pregnancy from a disability-benefits plan providing general coverage is not a gender-based discrimination at all.

There is no more showing in this case than there was in *Geduldig* that the exclusion of pregnancy benefits is a mere "pretex(t) designed to effect an invidious discrimination against the members of one sex or the other." * * * As we noted in that opinion, a distinction which on its face is not sex related might nonetheless violate the Equal Protection Clause if it were in fact a subterfuge to accomplish a forbidden discrimination. But we have here no question of excluding a disease or disability comparable in all other respects to covered diseases or disabilities and yet confined to the members of one race or sex. Pregnancy is, of course, confined to women, but it is in other ways significantly different from the typical covered disease or disability. The District Court found that it is not a "disease" at all, and is often a voluntarily undertaken and desired condition. We do not therefore infer that the exclusion of pregnancy disability benefits from petitioner's plan is a simple pretext for discriminating against women. The contrary arguments adopted by the lower courts and expounded by our dissenting Brethren were largely rejected in *Geduldig*.

The instant suit was grounded on Title VII rather than the Equal Protection Clause, and our cases recognize that a prima facie violation of Title VII can be established in some circumstances upon proof that the effect of an otherwise facially neutral plan or classification is to discriminate against members of one class or another. For example, in the context of a challenge, under the provisions of § 703(a)(2), to a facially neutral employment test, this Court held that a prima facie case of discrimination would be established if, even absent proof of intent, the consequences of the test were "invidiously to discriminate on the basis of racial or other impermissible classification," *Griggs v. Duke Power Co.* Even assuming that it is not necessary in this case to prove intent to establish a prima facie violation of § 703(a)(1), the respondents have not made the requisite showing of gender-based effect. * * *

[III] We are told, however, that this analysis of the congressional purpose underlying Title VII is inconsistent with the guidelines of the EEOC, which, it is asserted, are entitled to "great deference" in the construction of the Act. The guideline upon which respondents rely most heavily was promulgated in 1972, and states in pertinent part:

Disabilities caused or contributed to by pregnancy, miscarriage, abortion, childbirth, and recovery therefrom are, for all job-related purposes, temporary disabilities and should be treated as such under any health or temporary disability insurance or sick leave plan available in connection with employment. . . . [Benefits] shall be applied to disability due to pregnancy or childbirth on the same terms and conditions as they are applied to other temporary disabilities. 29 CFR § 1604.10(b) (1975).

In evaluating this contention it should first be noted that Congress, in enacting Title VII, did not confer upon the EEOC authority to promulgate rules or regulations pursuant to that Title. This does not mean that EEOC guidelines are not entitled to consideration in determining legislative intent. But it does mean that courts properly may accord less weight to such guidelines than to administrative regulations which Congress has declared shall have the force of law or to regulations which under the enabling statute may themselves supply the basis for imposition of liability. The most comprehensive statement of the role of interpretative rulings such as the EEOC guidelines is found in *Skidmore v. Swift & Co.*, 323 U.S. 134, 140 (1944), where the Court said:

We consider that the rulings, interpretations and opinions of the Administrator under this Act, while not controlling upon the courts by reason of their authority, do constitute a body of experience and informed judgment to which courts and litigants may properly resort for guidance. The weight of such a judgment in a particular case will depend upon the thoroughness evident in its consideration, the validity of its reasoning, its consistency with earlier and later pronouncements, and all those factors which give it power to persuade, if lacking power to control.

The EEOC guideline in question does not fare well under these standards. It is not a contemporaneous interpretation of Title VII, since it was first promulgated eight years after the enactment of that Title. More importantly, the 1972 guideline flatly contradicts the position which the agency had enunciated at an earlier date, closer to the enactment of the governing statute. An opinion letter by the General Counsel of the EEOC, dated October 17, 1966, states: "You have requested our opinion whether the above exclusion of pregnancy and childbirth as a disability under the long-term salary continuation plan would be in violation of Title VII of the Civil Rights Act of 1964." "In a recent opinion letter regarding pregnancy, we have stated, 'The Commission policy in this area does not seek to compare an employer's treatment of illness or injury with his treatment of maternity since maternity is a temporary disability unique to the female sex and more or less to be anticipated during the working life of most women employees.' Therefore, it is our opinion that according to the facts stated above, a company's group insurance program which covers hospital and medical expenses for the delivery of employees' children, but excludes from its long-term salary continuation program those disabilities which result from pregnancy and childbirth would not be in violation of Title VII."

A few weeks later, in an opinion letter expressly issued pursuant to 29 CFR § 1601.30 (1975), the EEOC's position was that "an insurance or other benefit plan may simply exclude maternity as a covered risk, and such an exclusion would not in our view be discriminatory."

We have declined to follow administrative guidelines in the past where they conflicted with earlier pronouncements of the agency. In short, while we do not wholly discount the weight to be given the 1972 guideline, it does not receive high marks when judged by the standards enunciated in *Skidmore*. * * *

The EEOC guideline of 1972, conflicting as it does with earlier pronouncements of that agency, and containing no suggestion that some new source of legislative history had been discovered in the intervening eight years, stands virtually alone. Contrary to it are the consistent interpretation of the Wage and Hour Administrator, and the quoted language of Senator Humphrey, the floor manager of Title VII in the Senate. They support what seems to us to be the "plain meaning" of the language used by Congress when it enacted § 703(a)(1).

The concept of "discrimination," of course, was well known at the time of the enactment of Title VII, having been associated with the Fourteenth Amendment for nearly a century, and carrying with it a long history of judicial construction. When Congress makes it unlawful for an employer to "discriminate ... because of ... sex ...," without further explanation of its meaning, we should not readily infer that it meant something different from what the concept of discrimination has traditionally meant.

[JUSTICES STEWART and BLACKMUN wrote concurring opinions. Joined by Justices Marshall and Stevens, JUSTICE BRENNAN wrote a dissenting opinion, reasoning that pregnancy-based discrimination was actionable discrimination "because of sex" for purposes of Title VII.]

PROBLEM 3–3: WAS GILBERT CORRECTLY DECIDED?

To many readers today, *Gilbert* seems misguided: How can pregnancy-based exclusions *not* be discriminations "because of sex"?[10] Likewise,

---

[10] Justice Stewart's distinction between "pregnant" and "nonpregnant" persons in *Geduldig* (followed in Gilbert) seems to many laughable. Note that this analysis depends upon baseline assumptions about how to define the "class." What if you were to define the classes as "female workers wanting families" versus "male workers wanting families?" Are the former females disadvantaged in their job relative to males, if they must, in effect, quit their job for a period of time?

Geduldig may strike you as a constitutional relic, especially after *Craig v. Boren*. Was the EEOC doing a better job of constitutional and statutory interpretation than the Supreme Court?

Before you reach a firm legal conclusion, consider some broader context. Several *amicus* briefs in *Gilbert* invoked the Equal Rights Amendment (ERA) debate of the early 1970s to validate a different-treatment model of sex discrimination that would allow exclusions where there are so-called "real differences" between the sexes. In the absence of legislative history for Title VII, these *amici* turned to the ERA legislative history to argue that Congress must have intended its legislation to sanction differential treatment on the basis of sex when real differences are evident because the ERA would have done so. Although this portrait of the ERA was vigorously contested by legal feminists, a coalition of airline companies told the Court that, during the 1970 and 1971 hearings on the ERA, Congress explicitly debated the "concept of sex discrimination in a situation where members of the two sexes were *not similarly situated*." As proof that Congress had surely embraced the conception of equality sanctioning special treatment for real differences, the airline coalition pointed to a statement signed by fourteen members of the Senate Judiciary Committee:

> [T]he original resolution does not require that women must be treated in all respects the same as men. "Equality" does not mean "sameness." As a result, the original resolution would not prohibit reasonable classifications based on characteristics that are unique to one sex. For example, a law providing for payment of the medical costs of child-bearing could only apply to women.

Equal Rights for Women, S. Rep. 92–689, 92d Cong., 2d Sess. 12 (1972). Similarly, ERA advocate and Yale Law School Professor Thomas Emerson had assured the Senate that "there is one type of situation where the law may focus on a sexual characteristic . . . where the legal system deals directly with a physical characteristic that is unique to one sex." Statement of Thomas Emerson, *Hearings on S.J. RES. 61 and S.J. RES. 231 for the Sen. Comm. on the Judiciary*, 91st Cong., 2d Sess. 298–99 (1970). Thus, *amici* sought to undermine the arguments of equalitarian legal feminists by suggesting the ERA meant "that laws concerning * * * child-bearing * * * are not laws which discriminate on the basis of sex." But see Barbara A. Brown, Thomas I. Emerson, Gail Falk & Ann E. Freedman, *The Equal Rights Amendment: A Constitutional Basis for Equal Rights for Women*, 80 Yale L.J. 871, 929–32 (1971) (sharply criticizing compelled maternity leave statutes as inconsistent with the ERA).

In its briefs before the Court, General Electric demonstrated, as California had in *Geduldig*, that female employees got more benefits under the company's disability insurance program than male employees did, even when pregnancy was excluded. In *amicus* briefs filed in *Gilbert*, corporations and insurance companies argued that disability programs including pregnancy benefits would cost *a lot* more than current programs did—and this was a big change in economic rights and allocations that only our elected Congress, and not unelected administrators and judges, should make. Recall that a similar argument would later prevail in the FDA Tobacco Case.

QUERY

You are the Chair of the EEOC. After *Gilbert*, some public school systems ask the EEOC whether it is illegal for them to require pregnant teachers to take mandatory unpaid leaves starting six months before their due dates and ending no less than three months after their birth dates. How would you respond? How about airline policies that stewardesses and air hostesses must be automatically discharged if they become pregnant? Should the EEOC take the position that such policies violate Title VII? Would the *Gilbert* Court agree with that?

NOTE ON THE PREGNANCY DISCRIMINATION ACT OF 1978 (PDA)

Within days after the Court handed down its decision in *Gilbert*, Susan Deller Ross, Ruth Weyand, Wendy Williams, Mary Dunlap, Ruth Bader Ginsburg, and their allies created the "Campaign to End Discrimination Against Pregnant Workers." The Campaign ultimately included religious traditionalists as well as feminists, labor activists as well as academics, Republicans as well as Democrats. It dialogued with skeptics among employers and insurance companies as well as corporate supporters. Through legislative allies such as Senators Birch Bayh and Ted Kennedy, the Campaign petitioned Congress for an amendment to Title VII that would treat workplace discrimination because of pregnancy as a form of "sex discrimination" prohibited by the statute.

The Campaign's case to Congress was normatively the same as its brief in *Geduldig*, and many of the same lawyers (such as Wendy Webster Williams and Susan Deller Ross) were involved in both. In detailed testimony before both House and Senate committees, they made three important points.[11] First, employer discrimination against pregnant women was catastrophic for many female workers. Thirty-five million women were in the American workforce, most of them because their income was necessary to support themselves or their families. One was Sherrie O'Steen, a plaintiff in *Gilbert* and a witness before Congress. General Electric, her employer, forced her into unpaid sick leave when it learned of her pregnancy. Although G.E. had guaranteed employees insurance and leave benefits for temporary disabilities arising for virtually any medical reason, from vasectomies to hair transplants, the company made an exception—its only exception—for pregnancy.

---

[11] See Legislation to Prohibit Sex Discrimination on the Basis of Pregnancy: Hearings Before the Subcomm. on Employment Opportunities of the House Comm. on Education and Labor, 95th Cong., 1st Sess. (1977); Discrimination on the Basis of Pregnancy: Hearings Before the Subcomm. on Labor of the Senate Comm. on Human Resources, 95th Cong., 1st Sess. (1977).

As O'Steen recalls it today, her husband "got so upset with me for quitting work and us struggling that he left. He was thinking I quit because I didn't want to work." Left alone to provide for her two-year-old daughter and her pregnancy without any source of income, Sherrie's electricity and gas were cut off because she could not pay the bills. In the cold months of November and December, Sherrie and her daughter lived without any light, heat, refrigeration, or a stove. "It was devastating," she said. "It was a part of your life that you want to put in the closet and leave it there."

Second, the Campaign made a systemic point: the workplace would *never* be one where women would stand on an equal footing with men, so long as companies could discriminate against them on the basis of pregnancy. Pregnancy-based leaves or dismissals interrupted the careers of female employees, and even the possibility of pregnancy was a common excuse for not hiring or promoting women. Because there was no evidence that pregnant women were unable to do their jobs as well as men or non-pregnant women, this kind of pervasive discrimination suggested the perseverance of gender-based stereotypes or even prejudices against women in the workplace. Those old-fashioned attitudes were not only unfair to women as a group—a group who were a majority of voters, members of Congress realized—but were unproductive from an economic point of view as well. Women were in the workplace to stay, and practices that made their careers unnecessarily difficult ought not be tolerated.

Third, the Campaign argued that pregnancy-discrimination is anti-family. Both the pro-life Roman Catholic Church and pro-choice feminists like Williams and Ross pressed the norm that pregnant women doing the heavy lifting to create flourishing families should be supported rather than subject to discrimination. For Sherrie O'Steen, pregnancy-based discrimination literally destroyed her marriage and almost cost this mother the life of her child. Other women, such as Sally Armendariz, one of the *Geduldig* plaintiffs, suffered arbitrary treatment and unnecessary hardship as the result of their pregnancies. The Campaign and its allies argued that the state has an obligation to protect not only these women, but also their children and their families, against arbitrary treatment. Buried within the Campaign's case for the PDA was an overarching policy that the state should make the workplace more "family-friendly" for fathers as well as for mothers.

After extensive hearings and debate, Congress enacted the PDA as an amendment to Title VII. Its sponsors and supporters understood the PDA to be more than just correcting an oversight in the original legislation; they understood the statute to be a renunciation of a normative stance that could not understand pregnancy-based discrimination as sex discrimination and, indeed, as a form of workplace conduct that was just as objectionable as racial segregation had been. In short, Congress explicitly rejected the reasoning as well as the result of *Gilbert*.

The Pregnancy Discrimination Act of 1978, Pub. L. No. 95-555, added new § 701(k) to Title VII, 42 U.S.C. § 2000e(k):

The terms "because of sex" or "on the basis of sex" include, but are not limited to, because of or on the basis of pregnancy, childbirth, or related medical conditions; and women affected by pregnancy, childbirth, or related medical conditions shall be treated the same for all employment-related purposes, including receipt of benefits under fringe benefit programs, as other persons not so affected but similar in their ability or inability to work, and nothing in section 2000e–2(h) of this title [Title VII § 703(h)] shall be interpreted to permit otherwise. This subsection shall not require an employer to pay for health insurance benefits for abortion, except where the life of the mother would be endangered if the fetus were carried to term, or except where medical complications have arisen from an abortion: *Provided*, That nothing herein shall preclude an employer from providing abortion benefits or otherwise affect bargaining agreements in regard to abortion.

In securing the PDA, feminists were opting for the equal treatment approach advocated by the EEOC's Susan Deller Ross in the early 1970s—and not following the Sonia Pressman approach, which would have required greater employer accommodation for workers' pregnancies. What were some of the consequences of that choice? Consider the matter from the perspective of employers: What pregnancy-related policies could they *retain* without violating the new statute?

PROBLEM 3–4: APPLICATION OF THE PREGNANCY DISCRIMINATION ACT

After enactment of the PDA, Eleanor Holmes Norton, one of the first supporters of the original pregnancy guidelines and, in 1978, the Chair of the EEOC, announced that employers must now treat pregnancy the same as any other disability. The EEOC in spring 1979 reissued and expanded its earlier pregnancy discrimination guidelines. EEOC, *Employment Policies Relating to Pregnancy and Childbirth*, 44 Fed. Reg. 23804 (April 20, 1979) (codified at 29 C.F.R. § 1604.10). Anticipating issues that many employers would face under the new PDA, Chair Norton develops Questions and Answers that will be publicly available. The EEOC's "Answers" are worked out by agency lawyers, who consult with the coalition of feminist lawyers that spearheaded the PDA as well as employer groups. Norton does not want to issue Answers that will be overturned by the U.S. Supreme Court, however. How might she and her staff respond to the following issues?

(A) Accommodation of Employee Breastfeeding Under the PDA? Some female employees want the opportunity to breast-feed their infants during working hours. In some instances, this can be accomplished through two or three 15-minute sessions, without disruption of the employee's work schedule, as feminist groups argue. In their comments, employers say that a blanket rule requiring accommodation of breast-feeding would go beyond the anti-discrimination purpose of the PDA and amount to a positive accommodation or benefit, which Title VII does not generally require. Also, they point out that different employees would have different needs, depending on the ease with which they could have access to their infants and the nature of their jobs; a hard rule would introduce inefficiencies into the workplace.

Hundreds of employees file grievances with the EEOC, asking the agency to announce that a policy of complete refusal to accommodate breastfeeding violates the PDA. You are the EEOC General Counsel; the EEOC Chair tells you she thinks this is an issue the agency ought to address through an amendment to its 1978 Pregnancy Discrimination Guidelines. What procedures would you suggest for figuring out whether to issue a breastfeeding guideline? Specifically, what institutions or groups should be agency consult, if any? Should the EEOC follow particular procedures before issuing amended guidelines? Finally, sketch out a tentative provision that might be added to the EEOC's Pregnancy Discrimination Guidelines.

(B) Employer Policies Barring Pregnant or Female Employees from Work Exposing Them to Toxic Substances. Some employers have adopted a policy excluding all pregnant women and women of childbearing age from jobs with exposure to lead and other toxic substances; there is strong medical evidence that lead exposure can disrupt pregnancies and harm fetuses. What issues does the EEOC need to think about under Title VII, as amended? Do these employer policies violate the statute? See *International Union, United Automobile Workers v. Johnson Controls, Inc.*, 499 U.S. 187 (1991).

(C) Should *Geduldig v. Aiello* Be Overruled? California has legislatively repealed its exclusion of pregnancy from the state unemployment compensation regime; hence, the *Geduldig* issue has disappeared in that state and most others that likewise have repealed such laws. Assume, however, that some pregnancy-discriminating policies remain in effect in some public programs. Here is the hypothetical: Joan Kim is a public employee in a state with an unemployment compensation program exactly like the one upheld in *Geduldig*: drawing from taxes levied on employees and employers, the state provides unemployment compensation for virtually all disabilities except pregnancy. Kim sues the state official in charge of the program for an injunction requiring coverage for pregnancy-based disabilities.

Do you think Kim has a valid legal claim for a violation of Title VII? Does Kim have a claim under the Fourteenth Amendment? For the latter, the Supreme Court would have to overrule *Geduldig*. What is the best case for overruling that precedent? What contrary arguments might the state present?

PART 2

STATUTORY INTERPRETATION

▪ ▪ ▪

The process of creating and implementing statutes is ongoing, and at every stage of the ongoing story of a statute, lawyers interpret statutory language, applying it to hypothetical or actual circumstances. We saw this process in connection with the No Vehicles in the Park Law: not only did judges interpret the statute enacted by the City Council, but Members of the Council took positions based on their interpretation of the proposed legislation; officials administering the statute (police, prosecutors, the commission) acted upon their own interpretations; and, to the extent that members of the public actually read the laws, they relied on their own interpretations, too.

Basic lawyerly competence in the modern administrative state requires experience with and a deep understanding of statutory interpretation. The chapters in this part offer the introductory student a good start toward such competence. Unlike other parts of this coursebook, the focus of this part is judicial practice and doctrine. In Part III, we shall return to the multi-institutional focus with which we started these materials.

Chapter 4 is an introduction to the fundamental debates about statutory interpretation among American judges. At bottom, American judges tend to be eclectic, but various foundational theories have competed for dominance, namely, approaches giving primacy to statutory text, legislative intent, and statutory or legislative purpose. Chapter 4 sets out those debates through several canonical cases where judges grapple with philosophical as well as doctrinal issues of statutory interpretation.

Chapter 5 is an introduction to the "canons" of statutory construction, which are just the default presumptions that judges sometimes apply to resolve cases when statutes are ambiguous. Some of the canons are as old as the common law, and just as mysterious. Appendix 6 to this coursebook is our compilation of canons followed by the Rehnquist and Roberts Courts (1986–2012). Although some of these canons are unique to federal courts, some also are cited by state courts, and some have been codified by state legislatures as rules that legislatures want to *make* state judges follow. Chapter 5 itself will not cover all of the hundreds of canons represented in the appendix, but it will introduce the student to the leading presumptions about statutory language (the "textual canons"), including the presumption that statutory terms are used consistently throughout a single statute, and some of the important policy-based presumptions (the "substantive canons"), such as the presumption that ambiguities in statutes are resolved in favor of federalism values—these canons reveal a fascinating interplay between constitutional and statutory interpretation.

Chapter 6 explores the role of legislative history in statutory interpretation. At the federal level, consultation of legislative materials has been controversial in the last generation, but it is largely settled that such materials are always at least potentially relevant. In common law countries, from the United Kingdom to Canada to India to Australia, extrinsic legislative materials were long taboo but are now routinely cited and discussed. In our country, state courts increasingly rely on legislative materials, which are more readily available than ever before in American history; the trend is for such materials to become available electronically and online, a technological development that will fuel the use of legislative history among state judges.

CHAPTER 4

AN INTRODUCTION TO STATUTORY INTERPRETATION

■ ■ ■

This chapter considers how courts interpret statutes. The student should consider the differences among contemporary theories of statutory interpretation, most particularly, textualism and purposivism. The principal aim is to teach readers how to analyze texts as judges do. Students are also introduced to important theoretical problems, including the much-contested idea of legislative intent, the significance of context to meaning, and questions about how a court should best exercise "faithful" agency to Congress and about whether a court should be a faithful agent. Finally, this chapter invites consideration of some alternatives to textualism and purposivism, which can be grouped under the general umbrella of pragmatism.

When a lawyer interprets a statute, what does she consider to be the point of the enterprise? Surprisingly, this is a question as to which there is no consensus in American jurisprudence.

Today, most judges would say that the lodestar for interpretation should be statutory **text**. Many of those judges would also say that the enacted text is the best source for discerning the **purpose** of the statute (recall that our vehicles law set forth the purpose on the face of the statute). Those who emphasize statutory purpose as the best reflection of Congress's meanings tend to be "purposivists." Those who emphasize the importance of text as the best reflection of Congress's meanings tend to be "textualists." In fact these schools converge in the vast majority of cases, with textualists looking for legislative intent, and purposivists emphasizing text.

The main divide isn't over the *goal* of interpretation, it's over the *method*: Almost all interpreters agree that the role of judges in statutory interpretation should be to effectuate Congress's will, not the will of the individual judge. The serious point of contention arises, however, when it comes to the evidence one may use to determine the legislative will. Today, some judges and scholars (we will call them "new textualists") maintain that courts may never consider legislative history, only the text, and perhaps canons of interpretation, or other statutes. See Antonin Scalia, *A Matter of Interpretation* (1997) (excerpted in Section 3). New textualists refuse to cite legislative history even to confirm apparent plain meaning, because it corrupts judicial decision making and the legislative process: using extrinsic sources, some say, is like looking out over a crowd and picking out your friends; it also may take pressure off Congress to make statutes as precise as they could be and creates opportunities for strategic use of legislative history by crafty members and staff. Of course some of these same risks inhere in textualism: it is just as possible to "pick and choose" your friends in the text of the statute as well, or in the hundreds of canons at textualists' disposal, or in the many dictionaries among which textualists pick and choose. Most state and federal judges have not been persuaded to reject legislative history, a question that we address in greater detail in Chapter 6.

As you read each case in this chapter, focus on the texts that matter, and the purposes of those texts. Even new textualists look at the purpose of the statute: they simply try to glean that purpose from the face of the text rather than by delving into the details of the legislative record. Also ask yourself whether you want to know more to resolve the statute's meaning.

1. LEGISLATIVE "INTENT"

Since the beginning of our republic, courts have invoked the concept of legislative "intent" to signal that legislators, not courts, create legislative meaning. This reflects the concept of legislative supremacy, a principle grounded in the separation of powers. Even in constitutional cases, courts are wary of subverting congressional decisions, reserving judicial review for exceptional matters. But in statutory cases, legislative supremacy speaks with a much louder voice. There is nearly universal agreement that judges must not impose their own meaning on a statute, but must apply Congress's meaning.

Almost every linguist and philosopher of language believes that intent reflects a crucial bedrock principle: that the meaning of words depends upon the context in which they are uttered. Take a common example: If you tell me to "drop everything and help me" but I am holding your infant at that moment, my interpretive goal is to do what I think you intend for me to do. (I will **not** drop the poor kid on the floor.) See Lawrence M. Solan, *The Language of Statutes: Laws and Their Interpretation* (2010). When the author of a directive is the legislature, there is an additional motivation for hewing closely to legislative intent: democratic legitimacy. That federal judges are unelected and are unaccountable to voters limits their ability to move policy forward, which is the primary job of the legislature, whose members are elected by and accountable to the voters.

However, the very concept of legislative "intent," is confusing. Many students find the distinction between purpose and intent very difficult. In fact, they are right to think the matter confusing! For centuries, philosophers, linguists, and legal scholars have struggled with the notion of intent. *For our purposes, however, you should understand that there is nothing special about the term: the statutory interpreter is searching for meaning. Congress's intent is Congress's meaning.*

As you work through the materials you will get a greater sense of how judges use these terms but, at the outset, it might be useful to consider these distinctions and problems:

Purpose and intent. Sometimes intent is used synonymously with purpose. In that context, the idea is generally that interpretation should not bring about a result that will defeat the statute's purpose, or its ends. Purposive inquiries consider Congress's meanings by asking about the statute's plan. Purposivist analysis is, as we will see, quite ancient: Blackstone and others called this a search for the "mischief" prompting the statute, or the "reason" for the statute. Note, however, that purposivists, both ancient and modern, are not always clear about whether they are talking about the "core" purpose, or "any" theoretically plausible purpose for the statute.

Specific intent. Less frequently judges use the term "intent" to talk not about a statute's overarching goals but about the specific desires of a few particular elected officials. Often these are critical votes—such as fence-sitting congressmembers who cast needed votes in the final stretch. That inquiry is different—it is not about interpreting a statute in line with the problem it was designed to remedy but rather it is a more economics-inspired approach concerned with enforcing the particulars of legislative dealmaking and vote-trading. This does not mean, however, that anytime a court references the views of one particular member it is interested in specific intent. To the contrary, most often legislative history is invoked to understand the broad purposes of the statute—what it was generally trying to do.

Collective intent. Bucking a historical practice spanning centuries, some modern scholars and judges have followed Max Radin's argument (below) that Congress has no "intent." Congress is a "they"—it is made up of 535 people—and not an "it": hence, all Members are not likely to have the same idea in mind when they pass statutes. As the materials explain, however, this mental-state idea of intent fits poorly with group action. Skepticism about collective intent can be easily overstated: every organization in America is a "they" (think about corporations, for example, which enter into contracts, with "intent," all the time), and the law rarely abandons intent-based rules for such collective bodies. Very few believe that, when the organization acts, its actions are entirely meaningless or "subjective" simply because the organization is a collective (is made up of lots of people).

Intent and context. One way of thinking of "intent" is as a crude proxy for "context." As noted above, linguists and philosophers are united in believing that semantic content (the meaning of words) is not enough to determine the meaning of a communication. One needs context to determine meaning. So, for example, if someone says "I take the fifth," it may seem "plain" to lawyers that the statement is made in a trial by a witness refusing to testify under the Fifth Amendment to the Constitution. In fact, that conclusion assumes much! If one changes the context, the meaning of the statement "I take the fifth" could be entirely different. If the statement is made at a bakery, it might mean the "fifth" cookie in line. If made by a Member in Congress, it might mean the fifth amendment to an existing bill. Words alone—without context—underdetermine meaning. When interpreters look for "speaker's intent," they are often seeking context to clarify semantic content.[1]

Holy Trinity Church became one of the most famous cases in the history of statutory interpretation because of the way it used the concept of legislative intent. Below are the relevant statutory sections for the case that follows.

STATUTORY PREFACE TO *HOLY TRINITY CHURCH*

The Alien Contract Labor Act of 1885

An act to prohibit the importation and migration of foreigners and aliens under contract or agreement to perform labor in the United States, its Territories and the District of Columbia, Act of February 26, 1885, 23 Stat. 332, c. 164.

Section 1

That from and after the passage of this act it shall be unlawful for any person, company, partnership, or corporation, in any manner whatsoever, to prepay the transportation, or in any way assist or encourage the importation or migration of any alien or aliens, any foreigner or foreigners, into the United States, its Territories, or the District of Columbia, under contract or agreement, parol or special, express or implied, made previous to the importation or migration of such alien or aliens, foreigner or foreigners, to perform labor or service of any kind in the United States, its Territories, or the District of Columbia.

---

[1] So, to take a famous example, if one is told to "fetch me some soupmeat," this might mean edible soupmeat if the context is feeding the family, but not if the context is nursing a blow to the eye in which case beefsteak, edible or not, is applied to soothe the face. Since we cannot look into people's minds, context supplies evidence of likely plans.

Section 4

That the master of any vessel who shall knowingly bring within the United States on any such vessel * * * any alien, laborer, mechanic or artisan who * * * had entered into contract or agreement * * * to perform labor or service in the United States, shall be deemed guilty of a misdemeanor * * *.

Section 5

* * * [N]or shall the provisions of this act apply to professional actors, artists, lecturers, or singers, nor to persons employed strictly as personal or domestic servants[.]

RECTOR, HOLY TRINITY CHURCH V. UNITED STATES

Supreme Court of the United States, 1892.
143 U.S. 457, 12 S.Ct. 511, 36 L.Ed. 226.

MR. JUSTICE BREWER delivered the opinion of the Court.

Plaintiff in error is a corporation, duly organized and incorporated as a religious society under the laws of the State of New York. E. Walpole Warren was, prior to September, 1887, an alien residing in England. In that month the plaintiff in error made a contract with him, by which he was to remove to the city of New York and enter into its service as rector and pastor; and in pursuance of such contract, Warren did so remove and enter upon such service. It is claimed by the United States that this contract on the part of the plaintiff in error was forbidden by the act of February 26, 1885, 23 Stat. 332, c. 164, and an action was commenced to recover the penalty prescribed by that act. The circuit court held that the contract was within the prohibition of the statute, and rendered judgment accordingly, and the single question presented for our determination is whether it erred in that conclusion.

The first section describes the act forbidden, and is in these words:

Be it enacted by the Senate and House of Representatives of the United States of America in Congress assembled, That from and after the passage of this act it shall be unlawful for any person, company, partnership, or corporation, in any manner whatsoever, to prepay the transportation, or in any way assist or encourage the importation or migration of any alien or aliens, any foreigner or foreigners, into the United States, its Territories, or the District of Columbia, under contract or agreement, parol or special, express or implied, made previous to the importation or migration of such alien or aliens, foreigner or foreigners, to perform labor or service of any kind in the United States, its Territories, or the District of Columbia.

It must be conceded that the act of the corporation is within the letter of this section, for the relation of rector to his church is one of service, and implies labor on the one side with compensation on the other. Not only are the general words "labor" and "service" both used, but also, as it were to guard against any narrow interpretation and emphasize a breadth of meaning, to them is added "of any kind;" and, further, as noticed by the Circuit Judge in his opinion, the fifth section, which makes specific exceptions, among them professional actors, artists, lecturers, singers and domestic servants, strengthens the idea that every other kind of labor and service was intended to be reached by the first section. While there is great force to this reasoning, we cannot think Congress intended to denounce with penalties a transaction like that in the present case. It is a familiar rule, that a thing may be within the letter of the statute and yet not within the statute, because not within its spirit, nor within the intention of its makers. This has been often asserted, and the reports are full of cases illustrating its application. This is not the substitution of the will of the judge for that of the legislator, for frequently words of general meaning are used in a statute, words broad enough to include an act in question, and yet a consideration of the whole legislation, or of the circumstances surrounding its enactment, or of the absurd results which follow from giving such broad meaning to the words, makes it unreasonable to believe that the legislator intended to include the particular act. As said in *Stradling v. Morgan*, Plowden, 205: "From which cases, it appears that the sages of the law heretofore have construed statutes quite contrary to the letter in some appearance, and those statutes which comprehend all things in the letter they have expounded to extend to but some things, and those which generally prohibit all people from doing such an act they have interpreted to permit some people to do it, and those which include every person in the letter, they have adjudged to reach to some persons only, which expositions have always been founded upon the intent of the legislature, which they have collected sometimes by considering the cause and necessity of making the act, sometimes * * * by comparing one part of the act with another, and sometimes by foreign circumstances." * * *

* * * [T]he title of this act is, "An act to prohibit the importation and migration of foreigners and aliens under contract or agreement to perform labor in the United States, its Territories and the District of Columbia." Obviously the thought expressed in this reaches only to the work of the manual laborer, as distinguished from that of the professional man. No one reading such a title would suppose that Congress had in its mind any purpose of staying the coming into this country of ministers of the gospel, or, indeed, of any class whose toil is that of the brain. The common understanding of the terms "labor" and "laborers" does not include preaching and preachers; and it is to be assumed that words and phrases are used in their ordinary meaning. So whatever of light is thrown upon

the statute by the language of the title indicates an exclusion from its penal provisions of all contracts for the employment of ministers, rectors and pastors.

Again, another guide to the meaning of a statute is found in the evil which it is designed to remedy; and for this the court properly looks at contemporaneous events, the situation as it existed, and as it was pressed upon the attention of the legislative body. The situation which called for this statute was briefly but fully stated by Mr. Justice Brown when, as District Judge, he decided the case of *United States v. Craig*, 28 Fed. Rep. 795, 798: "The motives and history of the act are matters of common knowledge. It had become the practice for large capitalists in this country to contract with their agents abroad for the shipment of great numbers of an ignorant and servile class of foreign laborers, under contracts by which the employer agreed, upon the one hand, to prepay their passage, while, upon the other hand, the laborers agreed to work after their arrival for a certain time at a low rate of wages. The effect of this was to break down the labor market, and to reduce other laborers engaged in like occupations to the level of the assisted immigrant. The evil finally became so flagrant that an appeal was made to Congress for relief by the passage of the act in question, the design of which was to raise the standard of foreign immigrants, and to discountenance the migration of those who had not sufficient means in their own hands, or those of their friends, to pay their passage."

It appears, also, from the petitions, and in the testimony presented before the committees of Congress, that it was this cheap, unskilled labor which was making the trouble, and the influx of which Congress sought to prevent. It was never suggested that we had in this country a surplus of brain toilers, and, least of all, that the market for the services of Christian ministers was depressed by foreign competition. Those were matters to which the attention of Congress, or of the people, was not directed. So far, then, as the evil which was sought to be remedied interprets the statute, it also guides to an exclusion of this contract from the penalties of the act.

A singular circumstance, throwing light upon the intent of Congress, is found in this extract from the report of the Senate Committee on Education and Labor, recommending the passage of the bill: "The general facts and considerations which induce the committee to recommend the passage of this bill are set forth in the Report of the Committee of the House. The committee report the bill back without amendment, although there are certain features thereof which might well be changed or modified, in the hope that the bill may not fail of passage during the present session. Especially would the committee have otherwise recommended amendments, substituting for the expression 'labor and service,' whenever it occurs in the body of the bill, the words 'manual labor' or 'manual service,' as sufficiently broad to accomplish the purposes of the bill, and that such amendments would remove objections which a sharp and perhaps unfriendly criticism may urge to the proposed legislation. The committee, however, believing that the bill in its present form will be construed as including only those whose labor or service is manual in character, and being very desirous that the bill become a law before the adjournment, have reported the bill without change." Page 6059, Congressional Record, 48th Congress. And, referring back to the report of the Committee of the House, there appears this language: "It seeks to restrain and prohibit the immigration or importation of laborers who would have never seen our shores but for the inducements and allurements of men whose only object is to obtain labor at the lowest possible rate, regardless of the social and material well-being of our own citizens, and regardless of the evil consequences which result to American laborers from such immigration. This class of immigrants care nothing about our institutions, and in many instances never even heard of them; they are men whose passage is paid by the importers. They come here under contract to labor for a certain number of years. They are ignorant of our social condition, and that they may remain so, they are isolated and prevented from coming into contact with Americans. They are generally from the lowest social stratum, and live upon the coarsest food and in hovels of a character before unknown to American workmen. They, as a rule, do not become citizens, and are certainly not a desirable acquisition to the body politic. The inevitable tendency of their presence among us is to degrade American labor, and to reduce it to the level of the imported pauper labor." Page 5359, Congressional Record, 48th Congress.

We find, therefore, that the title of the act, the evil which was intended to be remedied, the circumstances surrounding the appeal to Congress, the reports of the committee of each house, all concur in affirming that the intent of Congress was simply to stay the influx of this cheap, unskilled labor.

But, beyond all these matters no purpose of action against religion can be imputed to any legislation, state or national, because this is a religious people. This is historically true. From the discovery of this continent to the present hour, there is a single voice making this affirmation. The commission to Christopher Columbus, prior to his sail westward, is from "Ferdinand and Isabella, by the grace of God, King and Queen of Castile," etc., and recites that "it is hoped that by God's assistance some of the continents and islands in the ocean will be discovered," etc. The first colonial grant, that made to Sir Walter Raleigh in 1584, was from "Elizabeth, by the grace of God, of England, Fraunce and Ireland, queene, defender of the faith," etc.; and the grant authorizing him to enact statutes of the government of the proposed colony provided that "they be not against the true Christian faith nowe professed in the Church of England." * * *

If we examine the constitutions of the various States we find in them a constant recognition of religious obligations. Every constitution of every one of the forty-four States contains language which, either directly or by clear implication, recognizes a profound reverence for religion, and an assumption that its influence in all human affairs is essential to the well being of the community. This recognition may be in the preamble, such as is found in the constitution of Illinois, 1870: "We, the people of the State of Illinois, grateful to Almighty God for the civil, political and religious liberty which He hath so long permitted us to enjoy, and looking to Him for a blessing upon our endeavors to secure and transmit the same unimpaired to succeeding generations," etc. * * *

Even the Constitution of the United States, which is supposed to have little touch upon the private life of the individual, contains in the First Amendment a declaration common to the constitutions of all the States, as follows: "Congress shall make no law respecting an establishment of religion, or prohibiting the free exercise thereof," etc. And also provides in Article 1, § 7, (a provision common to many constitutions,) that the Executive shall have ten days (Sundays excepted) within which to determine whether he will approve or veto a bill. * * *

If we pass beyond these matters to a view of American life as expressed by its laws, its business, its customs and its society, we find everywhere a clear recognition of the same truth. Among other matters note the following: The form of oath universally prevailing, concluding with an appeal to the Almighty; the custom of opening sessions of all deliberative bodies and most conventions with prayer; the prefatory words of all wills, "In the name of God, amen;" the laws respecting the observance of the Sabbath, with the general cessation of all secular business, and the closing of courts, legislatures, and other similar public assemblies on that day; the churches and church organizations which abound in every city, town, and hamlet; the multitude of charitable organizations existing everywhere under Christian auspices; the gigantic missionary associations, with general support, and aiming to establish Christian missions in every quarter of the globe. These, and many other matters which might be noticed, add a volume of unofficial declarations to the mass of organic utterances that this is a Christian nation. In the face of all these, shall it be believed that a Congress of the United States intended to make it a misdemeanor for a church of this country to contract for the services of a Christian minister residing in another nation? * * *

NOTES AND QUESTIONS ON HOLY TRINITY CHURCH

1. *The Problem of "Legislative Intent."* Does Justice Brewer think the text is clear? This is the most famous line from the case: "It is a familiar rule, that a thing may be within the letter of the statute and yet not within the statute, because not within its spirit, nor within the intention of its makers." What does that sentence mean? Justice Scalia, in a case excerpted later in this chapter, has described *Holy Trinity* as the "miraculous redeemer of lost causes." *Zuni Pub. Sch. Dist. No 89. v. Dept. Educ.*, 550 U.S. 81, 116 (2007) (Scalia, J., dissenting). In a lecture that has become the foundation for great modern debates about statutory interpretation, he expressed great skepticism about the concept of legislative intent, and called *Holy Trinity* the "prototypical case involving the triumph of 'legislative intent' (a handy cover for judicial intent) over the text of the law." Antonin Scalia, *A Matter of Interpretation* 18 (1997). "Well of course I think the act [hiring the rector] was within the letter of the statute, and was therefore within the statute: end of case." *Id.* at 19. "The decision was wrong because it failed to follow the text." *Id.* at 20.

2. *The Text of the Statute.* Did Justice Brewer concede the textual argument too quickly? The first definition of the term "labor" listed in the 1879 and 1886 editions of *Webster's Dictionary* was "[p]hysical toil or bodily exertion, * * * hard muscular effort directed to some useful end, as agriculture, manufactures, and the like." The second definition was "[i]ntellectual exertion, mental effort." *Webster's Dictionary*'s (1879 and 1886) first, and only relevant, definition of "service" was this: "The act of serving; the occupation of a servant; the performance of labor for the benefit of another, or at another's command; the attendance of an inferior, or hired helper or slave, etc., on a superior employer, master, and the like." *Black's Law Dictionary* (1891) defined service as "being employed to serve another; duty or labor to be rendered by one person to another." Is it 100% clear that the letter of the law supported the prosecution?[2]

3. *The Structure of the Statute.* Look at the other provisions of the statute. The prohibition was found in § 1 of the 1885 law. (Section 2 voided contracts made in violation of § 1, and § 3 provided for criminal penalties for such alien labor contracts.) Can we learn anything about the meaning of the word "labor" by looking at the other sections—§§ 4 and 5? Section 4, which was ignored by the Court, holds criminally accountable the master of a ship "who shall knowingly bring within the United States * * * any alien *laborer, mechanic or artisan*" who had contracted to perform "labor or service in the United States." (Emphasis added). An "artisan" was a skilled manual laborer, like a bricklayer. What light does § 4 shed on the meaning of "labor or service of any kind" in § 1? Should § 1 be read narrowly, to track the terms in § 4? What might be the counterargument? Why have § 4 at all if it tracked the

---

[2] See William N. Eskridge Jr., *Textualism, The Unknown Ideal?*, 96 Mich. L. Rev. 1509, 1517–19, 1533, 1539–40 (1998) (no!).

exact same terms as § 1? (See Chapter 5, § 1, for the canon that statutes are presumed not to use superfluous language.)

Justice Brewer did mention § 5, which provides a list of exemptions to the liabilities imposed by §§ 1–4: "[N]or shall the provisions of this act apply to professional actors, artists, lecturers, or singers, nor to persons employed strictly as personal or domestic servants." Does the omission of ministers from § 5 confirm their inclusion in § 1? Can you fit them into any of these exemptions? If you are wondering whether a minister might be an exempted "lecturer," should you infer anything about the intended meaning of "lecturer" from the words that surround it? (See Chapter 5, § 1, for the canon *noscitur a sociis*, the presumption that a statutory term takes meaning from the words around it, *but only* if the words around it form a coherent list.)

4. *Legislative Purpose.* To narrow the law's apparent plain meaning, Justice Brewer relied on the mischief against which the Act was aimed and the inapplicability to a "brain toiler" of a statute seeking to exclude "laborers." What evidence did Justice Brewer adduce to support his premise that the purpose of the statute was not to exclude brain toilers? Might the statutory purpose be understood more broadly than the Court understood it? Assume that Brewer was right about the purpose, but that he was also right that § 1 had a plain meaning that included ministers, and that the structure of the statute (e.g., § 5) reinforced the plain meaning. Under those circumstances, should judges ever read the statutory language narrowly?

5. *Internal Legislative Materials as Evidence of Legislative Intent?* This case is famous because it is the first Supreme Court case that expressly used legislative history to trump what the Court conceded (rightly or wrongly) to be clear textual meaning. Justice Brewer cited a "smoking gun" in the legislative history, specifically the Senate committee report saying that the bill was only intended to exclude people engaged in "manual labor" but that it was too late in the session to amend the statute to add that precise language. Note the two ways that Brewer deployed the idea of legislative intent: one looked to the general purpose of the law and tailored the text to meet the goal ("general intent"), and the other asked what the legislators thought they were doing as to the particular issue ("specific intent").

In light of what you know about the congressional process, can you say that Justice Brewer was right about legislative intent? Is reference to a committee report good evidence for what the "intent" of Congress might be? Would your answer change if you were told (accurately, but contrary to the committee's assumption) that the contract labor bill did not zip through the legislative process in 1884, but that it was enacted in 1885, after further debate and amendment? Does it make a difference that § 1 was not materially changed—but that § 5 was changed through the addition of new exemptions? See Adrian Vermeule, *Judging Under Uncertainty: An Institutional Theory of Legal Interpretation* 86–117 (2006) (filling in this gap in Brewer's deployment of legislative history).

6. *Subsequent Legislation.* After the federal circuit court in the Southern District of New York construed the statute to apply to Reverend Warren in the *Holy Trinity Church* litigation, Congress amended the alien contract labor law to exempt ministers and professionals generally. The amendment did not apply to pending proceedings and so did not affect the pastor in the Supreme Court case. Act of March 3, 1891, § 12, 26 Stat. 1084, 1086. Reversing the lower court, the Supreme Court in *Holy Trinity* did not mention the 1891 statute. Does this later statute vindicate, or undermine, the Court's holding? Cf. *United States v. Laws*, 163 U.S. 258, 265 (1896) (discussing the 1891 amendment).

7. *Norms: The United States as a "Christian Nation"?* Current readers might be taken aback by *Holy Trinity*'s "Christian nation" analysis. (The son of missionaries, Justice Brewer was an evangelical jurist.) Was this critical to the Court's opinion? Would Justice Brewer have exempted a doctor from the statute's coverage, for example? Cf. *Laws*, 163 U.S. 258 (interpreting the 1885 law to exempt chemists). Where does Justice Brewer get this norm? It functions here like a scale-tipping presumption, i.e., "if there were any lingering doubt, we would resolve the ambiguity in favor of the norms of our Christian Nation." It doesn't come from the *statute*. It either comes from the Justice himself, or from social context or policy, or from his understanding of fundamental constitutional principles that he believes should inform interpretation (and perhaps that he also believes it is safe to assume Congress legislated consistent with). Does this seem to you an appropriate role for judges—layering on policy/constitutional norms of this manner? Before you jump to conclusions based on the Christian Nation idea, consider that today, it would not be unusual to see a court do the same thing with federalism or free exercise values. Courts often construe statutory ambiguities in line with the presumption that we as a society value states' rights or the free exercise of religion. Keep an eye out for these presumptions, as they inform opinions. Ask yourself where they come from and how consistent they are with the idea that the goal of interpretation is to effectuate congressional intent.

F. Drew Caminetti et al. v. United States
242 U.S. 470 (1917).

A federal statute criminalized the transportation, or the inducement to travel, of "any woman or girl * * * from one place to another in interstate or foreign commerce, or in any territory or the District of Columbia, for the purpose of prostitution or debauchery, or for any other immoral purpose * * *." The case concerned a man who brought a woman from Sacramento, California, to Reno, Nevada, to "become his mistress and concubine." The Court, per **Justice Day**, stated that "[i]t is elementary that the meaning of a statute must, in the first instance, be sought in the language in which the act is framed, and if that is plain, and if the law is within the constitutional authority of the lawmaking body which passed it, the sole function of the courts is to enforce it according to its terms." The majority found the statutory meaning plain—the conduct in question was for an "immoral purpose"—and held that Caminetti violated the statute. It refused to consider the title to the Act ("the White Slave Traffic Act") or legislative history suggesting that the purpose of the statute was narrower than its plain meaning (to reach only "commercialized vice").

The majority did not cite *Holy Trinity Church*, but **Justice McKenna**, joined in dissent by two other Justices, relied on it for the proposition that "the words of the statute should be construed to execute [the statutory purpose], and they may be so construed even if their literal meaning be otherwise." The dissent also argued that the statutory text was not plain: "other immoral purpose" should not be read literally and in isolation, but in light of the limiting words preceding them. As illuminated by the legislative history and by the principle that statutes should be read with "common sense" to avoid absurd applications, the statute should not reach "the occasional immoralities of men and women," but rather the "systematized and mercenary immorality epitomized in the statute's graphic phrase 'white slave traffic.' "

Although the free-wheeling approach of *Holy Trinity Church* may seem worlds apart from the mechanical approach of *Caminetti*, one might worry that unarticulated judicial values played a heavy role in both cases. That is, the Court would stick with literalism (*Caminetti*), or trump literalism with the mischief approach and the "golden rule" that statutes should not be construed to yield absurd results (*Holy Trinity Church*), in order to reach the interpretation that better matched its sensibilities. In *Caminetti*, for example, Justice McKenna's dissent stated that "[t]here is much in the present case to tempt to a violation of the [mischief] rule. Any measure that protects the purity of women from assault or enticement to degradation finds an instant advocate in our best emotions; but the judicial function cannot yield to emotion * * *." Yet "emotion" was precisely what drove Congress to enact the Mann Act in 1910. According to David J. Langum, *Crossing Over the Line: Legislating Morality and the Mann Act* (1994), the sponsor of the statute wrote the Court, expressing hearty approval of the broad interpretation in *Caminetti*. As Professor Langum explains, the philosophical point of the statute was quite puritan: a woman who engaged in any kind of extramarital sex—whether it be fornication, adultery, or prostitution—was a corrupt woman and a corrupting influence on society.

So it might be that Justice Day, and not the dissenters, apprehended the legislative intent correctly, even if severely. In the 1920s, federal judges justified their interpretations in big statutory cases by reference to congressional intent—and when judges were imposing their own pro-business philosophy onto statutes they were most insistent that they were doing nothing more than following the intent of the legislature. E.g., *Duplex Printing Press Co. v. Deering*, 254 U.S. 443 (1921), where the Court interpreted the Clayton Act to justify an injunction against a secondary boycott by print workers against an "unfair" employer. With federal judges on both the right and the left invoking legislative intent as the lodestar for statutory interpretation, it fell to a "legal realist" academic to deflate these democracy-based claims.

MAX RADIN, *STATUTORY INTERPRETATION*
43 Harv. L. Rev. 863, 869–72 (1930).

It has frequently been declared that the most approved method is to discover the intent of the legislator. * * * On this transparent and absurd fiction it ought not to be necessary to dwell. It is clearly enough an illegitimate transference to law of concepts proper enough in literature and theology. * * *

That the intention of the legislature is undiscoverable in any real sense is almost an immediate inference from a statement of the proposition. The chances that of several hundred men each will have exactly the same determinate situations in mind as possible reductions of a given [statutory issue], are infinitesimally small. * * * In an extreme case, it might be that we could learn all that was in the mind of the draftsman, or of a committee of half a dozen men who completely approved of every word. But when this draft is submitted to the legislature and at once accepted without a dissentient voice and without debate, what have we then learned of the intentions of the four or five hundred approvers? Even if the contents of the minds of the legislature were uniform, we have no means of knowing that content except by the external utterances or behavior of these hundreds of men, and in almost every case the only external act is the extremely ambiguous one of acquiescence, which may be motivated in literally hundreds of ways, and which by itself indicates little or nothing of the pictures which the statutory descriptions imply. * * *

And if [legislative intent] were discoverable, it would be powerless to bind us. What gives the intention of the legislature obligating force? * * * [I]n law, the specific individuals who make up the legislature are men to whom a specialized function has been temporarily assigned. That function is not to impose their will even within limits on their fellow citizens, but to "pass statutes," which is a fairly precise operation. That is, they make statements in general terms of undesirable and desirable situations, from which flow certain results. * * * When the legislature has uttered the words of a statute, it is *functus officio*, not because of the Montesquieuan separation of powers, but because that is what legislating means. The legislature might also be a court and an executive, but it can never be all three things simultaneously.

And once the words are out, recorded, engrossed, registered, proclaimed, inscribed in bronze, they in turn become instrumentalities which administrators and courts must use in performing their own specialized functions. The principal use is that of "interpretation." Interpretation is an act which requires an existing determinate event—the issue to be litigated—and obviously that determinate event cannot exist until after the statute has come into force. To say that the intent of the legislature decides the interpretation is to say that the legislature interprets in advance * * * a situation which does not exist.

NOTE ON THE REALIST CRITIQUE OF "LEGISLATIVE INTENT"

Professor Radin maintained that "legislative intent" is incoherent, undiscoverable, and irrelevant. It is incoherent to the extent that a collective body cannot easily be charged with having a singular "intent." As political scientist Kenneth Shepsle subsequently put it, "Congress is a They, not an It." Kenneth Shepsle, *Congress Is a "They," Not an "It": Legislative Intent as Oxymoron*, 12 Int'l Rev. L. & Econ. 239 (1992). Intent is undiscoverable because too little evidence of collective understanding finds its way into the public record, and even when reported is hard to interpret. Also, how can the different "intents" of the House, Senate, and President be aggregated? Accord, Ronald Dworkin, *Law's Empire* 314, 335–36 (1986); Jeremy Waldron, *Law and Disagreement* (1999); John F. Manning, *The Absurdity Doctrine*, 116 Harv. L. Rev. 2387, 2410 n.81 (2003). And legislative intent is irrelevant, because the job of the interpreter is to tell us what the statute "means," not what the legislature "intended." Oliver Wendell Holmes, *The Theory of Legal Interpretation*, 12 Harv. L. Rev. 417, 417–18, 419 (1899); accord, Antonin Scalia, *A Matter of Interpretation* (1997).

Professor Radin and his many academic followers have presumed that "legislative intent" means the subjective expectations of the legislators who enacted the statute. From that presumption, Radin argued that legislative intent is incoherent, etc. Note that his skepticism would tend to eliminate the concept of collective intent from the law—which would be quite a bold move: Can corporations or other institutions never have a legal "intent"? This would be a radical move within our intellectual as well as legal traditions. See Christian List & Philip Pettit, *Group Agency* (2011). Consider other ways of thinking about legislative intent, however.

If the President or the Board of Directors of a company negotiates a contract with Joan Doe, the President's or Board's representations might be taken to be those of the company itself—and lawyers might say that the company "intended" to form a contract, with certain understandings. As both Justice Breyer and linguist and legal scholar Lawrence Solan have argued, both common sense and the law routinely attribute "intent" to collective bodies based upon the purposive declarations made by subgroups or agents publicly deputized to deliberate for the whole group. Stephen Breyer, *Making Our Democracy Work: A Judge's View* (2010); Lawrence M. Solan, *Private Language, Public Laws: The Central Role of Legislative Intent in Statutory Interpretation*, 93 Geo. L.J. 427, 437–49 (2005). In the same manner, statements by sponsors and committees might reasonably be thought to represent congressional consensus unless denied by other Members. According to a recent empirical study of congressional drafting, legislative drafters put the most weight on legislative history that is evidence of a consensus—committee reports with bipartisan support or floor colloquies (even scripted colloquies) between leaders of opposing parties about their mutual understanding of the statute. See Abbe R. Gluck & Lisa Schultz Bressman, *Statutory Interpretation from the Inside—An Empirical Study of Congressional Drafting, Delegation and the Canons: Part I*, 65 Stan. L. Rev. 901, 978 (2013). Arguably, this is an institutional convention that is reasonable, and that Congress can be expected to adjust to (through better monitoring) if it yields results that systematically fail to reflect legislative bargains or consensuses. James Landis, *A Note on "Statutory Interpretation,"* 43 Harv. L. Rev. 886, 888–90 (1930) (responding to Radin's article).[3]

Professor Nourse offers another perspective on the issue, one more focused on the procedures that Congress shares. Nourse argues that individuals within groups do not share subjective states of mind, but they do share a prior commitment to certain procedures. Those procedures are how a group plans, how it situates itself with respect to the future—a core feature of what we mean by "intent." Victoria F. Nourse, *Rethinking Legislative Intent* (Draft 2013):

> "A different meaning of intent focuses on the degree to which intent relates to action. To understand this feature of the relationship between thought and action, it is useful to consider Michael Bratman's 'planning theory of intention' [Michael E. Bratman, *Intention, Plans, and Practical Reason* (1999)]. According to this theory, individual intentions are elements of stable, partial plans of action concerning present and *future* conduct.' 'Intending,' Bratman argues, 'involves a commitment over time'. [Related to Bratman's planning theory is Christian List and Philip Pettit's *Group Agency* (2011).] They argue that group decisions emerge as a result of sequential processes involving feedback. As List and Pettit explain, 'a group's performance as an agent depends on how it is organized: on its rules and procedures for forming its propositional attitudes . . . and for putting them into action.' Procedures allow decisions that do not correspond to the intentions of any particular member but may nevertheless be said to constitute group agency.

---

[3] This is the way political scientists understand the operation of Congress. See, e.g., McNollgast, *Positive Canons: The Role of Legislative Bargains in Statutory Interpretation*, 80 Geo. L.J. 705 (1992). .

Feedback allows individuals to shift from their original preferences to ones that they 'judge . . . better for the group to accept.'

"To accept this account of group agency, it is important to recognize what the theory does not entail. It does not entail some spectral notion of intent hovering above the group, in the air, somehow divorced from individuals. Individuals pool their views through a sequential process. * * * The bottom line: one does not have to give up methodological individualism, or posit a 'group mind,' to believe that it is possible for a group to act in ways that no individual member prefers *ex ante* or even *ex post.*

"List and Pettit's insights on group agency are more than theoretical, they are also realist: it is a fact that Congress works through sequential procedures. One would need no such rules, if members could simply sit down and determine, on a moment's notice, how members would vote. That, after all, is the claim made by those who accept Radin's static, internal, notion of intent. In fact, legislation is always beset by the vagaries of time and uncertainty. *Ex ante,* members may not know the preferences of other members' and constituents' preferences about a new proposal. That uncertainty is managed by procedural means: procedures force members to reveal their preferences. With new information about preferences, other members in turn may change their views.

"In seeking to pass legislation, members must obtain the support of others—at least a majority if not a supermajority. Procedures allow for feedback as to how others will vote on a proposal or what bill changes are necessary to secure a member's vote. So, for example, let us say the Chairman of a committee proposes a bill, that bill is then heard in committee. At the markup, changes are made; the original bill may now be a collective committee effort that is no longer the preference of any single member, but which reflects the shared subplans of the committee's membership to move the legislation to the floor for debate. In fact, the bill that results may end up, as some political scientists have emphasized, to be the preference of no individual Senator or House member. This is not something about which one should be dismayed, however, it is something inherent in the process and consistent with the List/Pettit model."

So how would a focus on group agency help the statutory interpreter? Professor Nourse advances a *"decision theory"* (explored in Chapter 6 of these materials). Her theory says that the legislature forms a usable "intent" when its members and committees settle upon a final text, which is often accompanied by an explanation of how this new text was chosen. Nourse applies her theory to *Holy Trinity.* In her view, Justice Brewer's big mistake was failing to take Congress's procedures seriously: by referring to a committee report that discussed a version of the bill that was later changed, the Court was focusing on a point in time when Congress had not assumed responsibility (group agency) for the final statutory language. Professor Nourse argues that the critics, such as Professor Vermeule, make the same kinds of errors, for they criticize the straw man of legislative intent as the aggregation of static subjective individual understandings and they fail to focus on the decisions Congress has actually made, following the accepted sequence of procedures according to the rules of the lawmaking process.

Does Professor Nourse's analysis provide a more useful understanding of "legislative intent" than you found in *Holy Trinity Church* or in Professor Radin's article? Does her specific analysis of *Holy Trinity* strike you as cogent—Did it change your own thinking about that case? Do you think that judges are capable of thinking in this more sophisticated manner about the legislative process? Should they?

2. STATUTORY PURPOSE AND THE LEGAL PROCESS

Statutory interpretation in the United States was, from the beginning, an eclectic enterprise. In the twentieth century, that eclecticism came under criticism. Scholars also demanded that statutory interpretation methodology have some relationship to the reasons we have the state in the first place. During the New Deal era, 1933–45, government officials, many of whom were also past or future academics, argued that the state serves great public purposes and that statutory interpretation, therefore, must focus on those great purposes.[4]

What came out of these intellectual endeavors was the "Legal Process" movement, a view of the government as reasonable and of courts as able to discern and help to effectuate the rational purposes of law as enacted by legislators. The work of the Legal Process generation provided the conceptual foundation for modern purposivism and pragmatism alike. Below are two classic excerpts.

LON L. FULLER, *THE CASE OF THE SPELUNCEAN EXPLORERS*
62 Harv. L. Rev. 616, 619–21, 623–26, 628–40 (1949).[*]

TRUEPENNY, C.J. [The members of the Speluncean Society were amateur cave explorers. In May 4299, several members, including Roger Whetmore, were trapped in a cave because of a rockslide. Rescue efforts were delayed for various reasons, such as fresh rockslides, and the explorers were not rescued until the 32d day of their ordeal.

---

[4] For this history, see William N. Eskridge Jr. & Philip P. Frickey, *Historical and Critical Introduction*, to Henry M. Hart Jr. & Albert M. Sacks, *The Legal Process: Materials on the Making and Application of Law* (Eskridge & Frickey eds. 1994) (tent. ed. 1958).

[*] Copyright 1949 by the Harvard Law Review Association. Reprinted by permission.

Communication with the explorers was established on day 20 of the ordeal, and the explorers learned that they would not likely be rescued for another ten days, that they would probably die if they did not have sustenance within that period, and that they would probably not die if they cannibalized one of their number; the last datum was reluctantly conveyed by a doctor in response to the explorers' specific inquiry. After assimilating the doctor's predictions, all of the explorers agreed that one of them must die, and they further agreed that the person to die would be chosen by lots (rolls of the dice). Whetmore agreed to both propositions and suggested the method of lots, but before the dice were rolled he declared his withdrawal from the plan. The other explorers proceeded with the agreement, and Whetmore was the one chosen by lots. On the 23d day of their ordeal, the explorers killed and dined on Whetmore. After the surviving explorers were saved, they were indicted for the murder of Whetmore.]

[At trial, the foreman of the jury (a lawyer) asked the judge whether the jury could return a special verdict and leave it to the judge to determine guilt or innocence. With the agreement of the prosecutor and counsel for defendants, the judge agreed. The jury found the facts as related above. The trial judge ruled the defendants guilty based upon these facts and (according to the nondiscretionary requirement of the sentencing law) sentenced them to death by hanging. Both jury and judge issued communications to the Chief Executive seeking commutation of defendants' sentence to six months' imprisonment.]

* * * The language of our statute is well known: "Whoever shall willfully take the life of another shall be punished by death." N. C. S. A. (N. S.) § 12–A. This statute permits of no exception applicable to this case, however our sympathies may incline us to make allowance for the tragic situation in which these men found themselves.

In a case like this the principle of executive clemency seems admirably suited to mitigate the rigors of the law, and I propose to my colleagues that we follow the example of the jury and the trial judge by joining in the communications they have addressed to the Chief Executive. * * * I think we may therefore assume that some form of clemency will be extended to these defendants. If this is done, then justice will be accomplished without impairing either the letter or spirit of our statutes and without offering any encouragement for the disregard of law.

Foster, J. * * * If this Court declares that under our law these men have committed a crime, then our law is itself convicted in the tribunal of common sense * * *.

* * * I take the view that the enacted or positive law of this Commonwealth, including all of its statutes and precedents, is inapplicable to this case, and that the case is governed instead by what

ancient writers in Europe and America called "the law of nature." [Judge Foster argued that once the reason for law disappears, so too does the law itself. As a matter of political morality, the defendants' conduct was justified by the agreement they entered into that ensured the survival of five at the expense of one.] * * *

This concludes the exposition of the first ground of my decision. My second ground proceeds by rejecting hypothetically all the premises on which I have so far proceeded. I concede for purposes of argument that I am wrong in saying that the situation of these men removed them from the effect of our positive law, and I assume that the Consolidated Statutes have the power to penetrate five hundred feet of rock and to impose themselves upon these starving men huddled in their underground prison.

Now it is, of course, perfectly clear that these men did an act that violates the literal wording of the statute which declares that he who "shall willfully take the life of another" is a murderer. But one of the most ancient bits of legal wisdom is the saying that a man may break the letter of the law without breaking the law itself. Every proposition of positive law, whether contained in a statute or a judicial precedent, is to be interpreted reasonably, in the light of its evident purpose. * * *

The statute before us for interpretation has never been applied literally. Centuries ago it was established that a killing in self-defense is excused. There is nothing in the wording of the statute that suggests this exception. Various attempts have been made to reconcile the legal treatment of self-defense with the words of the statute, but in my opinion these are all merely ingenious sophistries. The truth is that the exception in favor of self-defense cannot be reconciled with the *words* of the statute, but only with its *purpose.*

The true reconciliation of the excuse of self-defense with the statute making it a crime to kill another is to be found in the following line of reasoning. One of the principal objects underlying any criminal legislation is that of deterring men from crime. Now it is apparent that if it were declared to be the law that a killing in self-defense is murder such a rule could not operate in a deterrent manner. A man whose life is threatened will repel his aggressor, whatever the law may say. Looking therefore to the broad purposes of criminal legislation, we may safely declare that this statute was not intended to apply to cases of self-defense. * * *

* * * [P]recisely the same reasoning is applicable to the case at bar. If in the future any group of men ever find themselves in the tragic predicament of these defendants, we may be sure that their decision whether to live or die will not be controlled by the contents of our criminal code. * * * The withdrawal of this situation from the effect of this statute

is justified by precisely the same considerations that were applied by our predecessors in office centuries ago to the case of self-defense.

* * * The line of reasoning I have applied above raises no question of fidelity to enacted law, though it may possibly raise a question of the distinction between intelligent and unintelligent fidelity. No superior wants a servant who lacks the capacity to read between the lines. The stupidest housemaid knows that when she is told "to peel the soup and skim the potatoes" her mistress does not mean what she says. She also knows that when her master tells her to "drop everything and come running" he has overlooked the possibility that she is at the moment in the act of rescuing the baby from the rain barrel. Surely we have a right to expect the same modicum of intelligence from the judiciary. The correction of obvious legislative errors or oversights is not to supplant the legislative will, but to make that will effective. * * *

TATTING, J. [This jurist responds to both arguments raised by Judge Foster. At what point, exactly, did the explorers find themselves back in a state of nature? Even if they were in a state of nature, by what authority or right can the Court resolve itself into a "Court of Nature"? Isn't the propounded code of nature a "topsy-turvy and odious" one? "It is a code in which the law of contracts is more fundamental than the law of murder." Would Whetmore have had a defense if he had shot his assailants as they set upon him? For these reasons, Judge Tatting cannot join Judge Foster's first reason. Nor can he join the second.]

* * * It is true that a statute should be applied in the light of its purpose, and that *one* of the purposes of criminal legislation is recognized to be deterrence. The difficulty is that other purposes are also ascribed to the law of crimes. It has been said that one of its objects is to provide an orderly outlet for the instinctive human demand for retribution. It has also been said that its object is the rehabilitation of the wrongdoer. Other theories have been propounded. Assuming that we must interpret a statute in the light of its purpose, what are we to do when it has many purposes or when its purposes are disputed?

[These other purposes provide a different explanation for self-defense as outside the murder prohibition. The statute requires a "willful" act, but the person who acts to repel a threat to life is not acting "willfully," according to at least one precedent, *Commonwealth v. Parry*. This purpose of the statute provides no justification for the explorers, who acted willfully. Moreover, the Court's decision in *Commonwealth v. Valjean* upheld the larceny conviction of a man who stole bread to prevent his own starvation.] If hunger cannot justify the theft of wholesome and natural food, how can it justify the killing and eating of a man? Again, if we look at the thing in terms of deterrence, is it likely that a man will starve to death to avoid a jail sentence for the theft of a loaf of bread? My brother's demonstrations would compel us to overrule *Commonwealth v. Valjean* and many other precedents that have been built on that case. * * *

There is still a further difficulty in my brother Foster's proposal to read an exception into the statute to favor this case * * *. What shall be the scope of this exception? Here the men cast lots and the victim was himself originally a party to the agreement. What would we have to decide if Whetmore had refused from the beginning to participate in the plan? Would a majority be permitted to overrule him? Or, suppose that no plan were adopted at all and the others simply conspired to bring about Whetmore's death, justifying their act by saying that he was in the weakest condition. Or again, that a plan of selection was followed but one based on a different justification than the one adopted here, as if the others were atheists and insisted that Whetmore should die because he was the only one who believed in an afterlife. These illustrations could be multiplied, but enough have been suggested to reveal what a quagmire of hidden difficulties my brother's reasoning contains. * * *

Since I have been wholly unable to resolve the doubts that beset me about the law of this case, I am with regret announcing a step that is, I believe, unprecedented in the history of this tribunal. I declare my withdrawal from the decision of this case.

KEEN, J. [This jurist insists that the Court put aside the issue, raised by the Chief Justice, of whether the Chief Executive should grant clemency. This is a "confusion of government functions," and judges should not intrude into this realm of the executive.]

The second question that I wish to put to one side is that of deciding whether what these men did was "right" or "wrong," "wicked" or "good." That is also a question that is irrelevant to the discharge of my office as a judge sworn to apply, not my conceptions of morality, but the law of the land. * * *

Whence arise all the difficulties of the case, then, and the necessity for so many pages of discussion about what ought to be so obvious? The difficulties, in whatever tortured form they may present themselves, all trace back to a single source, and that is a failure to distinguish the legal from the moral aspects of this case. To put it bluntly, my brothers do not like the fact that the written law requires the conviction of these defendants. Neither do I, but unlike my brothers I respect the obligations of an office that requires me to put my personal predilections out of my mind when I come to interpret and apply the law of this Commonwealth. * * *

[After a period in which the Commonwealth's judiciary often freely interpreted statutes,] we now have a clear-cut principle, which is the supremacy of the legislative branch of our government. From that principle flows the obligation of the judiciary to enforce faithfully the written law, and to interpret that law in accordance with its plain meaning without reference to our personal desires or our individual conceptions of justice. I am not concerned with the question whether the principle that forbids the judicial revision of statutes is right or wrong, desirable or undesirable; I observe merely that this principle has become a tacit premise underlying the whole of the legal and governmental order I am sworn to administer. * * *

My brother Foster's penchant for finding holes in statutes reminds one of the story told by an ancient author about the man who ate a pair of shoes. Asked how he liked them, he replied that the part he liked best was the holes. That is the way my brother feels about statutes; the more holes they have in them the better he likes them. In short, he doesn't like statutes.

One could not wish for a better case to illustrate the specious nature of this gap-filling process than the one before us. My brother thinks he knows exactly what was sought when men made murder a crime, and that was something he calls "deterrence." My brother Tatting has already shown how much is passed over in that interpretation. But I think the trouble goes deeper. I doubt very much whether our statute making murder a crime really has a "purpose" in any ordinary sense of the term. Primarily, such a statute reflects a deeply-felt human conviction that murder is wrong and that something should be done to the man who commits it. * * *

Now I know that the line of reasoning I have developed in this opinion will not be acceptable to those who look only to the immediate effects of a decision and ignore the long-run implications of an assumption by the judiciary of a power of dispensation. A hard decision is never a popular decision. * * * Hard cases may even have a certain moral value by bringing home to the people their own responsibilities toward the law that is ultimately their creation, and by reminding them that there is no principle of personal grace that can relieve the mistakes of their representatives.

Indeed, I will go farther and say that not only are the principles I have been expounding those which are soundest for our present conditions, but that we would have inherited a better legal system from our forefathers if those principles had been observed from the beginning. For example, with respect to the excuse of self-defense, if our courts had stood steadfast on the language of the statute the result would undoubtedly have been a legislative revision of it. Such a revision would have drawn on the assistance of natural philosophers and psychologists, and the resulting regulation of the matter would have had an understandable and rational basis, instead of the hodgepodge of verbalisms and metaphysical distinctions that have emerged from the judicial and professional treatment.

HANDY, J. * * * I never cease to wonder at my colleagues' ability to throw an obscuring curtain of legalisms about every issue presented to them for decision. * * *

* * * The problem before us is what we, as officers of the government, ought to do with these defendants. That is a question of practical wisdom, to be exercised in a context, not of abstract theory, but of human realities. When the case is approached in this light, it becomes, I think, one of the easiest to decide that has ever been argued before this Court. * * *

I have never been able to make my brothers see that government is a human affair, and that men are ruled, not by words on paper or by abstract theories, but by other men. They are ruled well when their rulers understand the feelings and conceptions of the masses. They are ruled badly when that understanding is lacking. * * *

* * * I believe that all government officials, including judges, will do their jobs best if they treat forms and abstract concepts as instruments. We should take as our model, I think, the good administrator, who accommodates procedures and principles to the case at hand, selecting from among the available forms those most suited to reach the proper result.

The most obvious advantage of this method of government is that it permits us to go about our daily tasks with efficiency and common sense. My adherence to this philosophy has, however, deeper roots. I believe that it is only with the insight this philosophy gives that we can preserve the flexibility essential if we are to keep our actions in reasonable accord with the sentiments of those subject to our rule. More governments have been wrecked, and more human misery caused, by the lack of this accord between ruler and ruled than by any other factor that can be discerned in history. Once drive a sufficient wedge between the mass of people and those who direct their legal, political, and economic life, and our society is ruined. Then neither Foster's law of nature nor Keen's fidelity to written law will avail us anything. * * *

* * * One of the great newspaper chains made a poll of public opinion on the question, "What do you think the Supreme Court should do with the Speluncean explorers?" About ninety per cent expressed a belief that the defendants should be pardoned or let off with a kind of token punishment. It is perfectly clear, then, how the public feels about the case. We could have known this without the poll, of course, on the basis of common sense, or even by observing that on this Court there are apparently four-and-a-half men, or ninety per cent, who share the common opinion.

This makes it obvious, not only what we should do, but what we must do if we are to preserve between ourselves and public opinion a reasonable and decent accord. Declaring these men innocent need not involve us in any undignified quibble or trick. No principle of statutory construction is required that is not consistent with the past practices of this Court. Certainly no layman would think that in letting these men off we had stretched the statute any more than our ancestors did when they created the excuse of self-defense. If a more detailed demonstration of the method of reconciling our decision with the statute is required, I should be content to rest on the arguments developed in the second and less visionary part of my brother Foster's opinion.

HENRY M. HART, JR. AND ALBERT M. SACKS, *THE LEGAL PROCESS: BASIC PROBLEMS IN THE MAKING AND APPLICATION OF LAW*

pp. 1374–1380 (William N. Eskridge Jr. & Philip P. Frickey eds., 1994).[*]

Note on the Rudiments of Statutory Interpretation

Consider the adequacy of the following summation:

A.   *The General Nature of the Task of Interpretation*

The function of the court in interpreting a statute is to decide what meaning ought to be given to the directions of the statute in the respects relevant to the case before it. * * *

B.   *The Mood in Which the Task Should Be Done*

In trying to discharge this function the court should:

1.   Respect the position of the legislature as the chief policy-determining agency of the society, subject only to the limitations of the constitution under which it exercises its powers; * * *

5.   Be mindful of the nature of law and of the fact that every statute is a part of the law and partakes of the qualities of law, and particularly of the quality of striving for even-handed justice.

C.   *A Concise Statement of the Task*

In interpreting a statute a court should:

1.   Decide what purpose ought to be attributed to the statute and to any subordinate provision of it which may be involved; and then

2.   Interpret the words of the statute immediately in question so as to carry out the purpose as best it can, making sure, however, that it does not give the words either—

(a) a meaning they will not bear, or

---

[*]   Reprinted by permission of the editors of the materials.

(b) a meaning which would violate any established policy of clear statement.

D.   *The Double Role of the Words as Guides to Interpretation*

* * * When the words fit with all the relevant elements of their context to convey a single meaning, as applied to the matter at hand, the mind of the interpreter moves to a confident conclusion almost instantaneously * * *.

Interpretation requires a conscious effort when the words do not fit with their context to convey any single meaning. It is in such a case that the words will be seen to play a double part, first, as a factor together with relevant elements of the context in the formulation of hypotheses about possible purposes, and, second, as a separately limiting factor in checking the hypotheses.

E.   *The Meaning the Words Will Bear*

* * * The words of the statute are what the legislature has enacted as law, and all that it has the power to enact. Unenacted intentions or wishes cannot be given effect as law.

In deciding whether words will bear a particular meaning, a court needs to be linguistically wise and not naive. It needs to understand, especially, that meaning depends upon context. But language is a social institution. Humpty Dumpty was wrong when he said that you can make words mean whatever you want them to mean.

The language belongs to the whole society and not to the legislature in office for the time being. Courts on occasion can correct mistakes, as by inserting or striking out a negative, when it is completely clear from the context that a mistake has been made. But they cannot permit the legislative process, and all the other processes which depend upon the integrity of language, to be subverted by the misuse of words. * * *

* * * [T]he proposition that words must not be given a meaning they will not bear operates almost wholly to *prevent* rather than to *compel* expansion of the scope of statutes. The meaning of words can almost always be narrowed if the context seems to call for narrowing.

F.   *Policies of Clear Statement*

* * * Like the first requirement just considered that words must bear the meaning given them, these policies of clear statement may on occasion operate to defeat the actual, consciously held intention of particular legislators, or of the members of the legislature generally. * * * But the requirement should be thought of as constitutionally imposed. The policies have been judicially developed to promote objectives of the legal system which transcend the wishes of any particular session of the legislature. * * *

Two policies of clear statement call for particular mention.

The first of these * * * requires that words which mark the boundary between criminal and non-criminal conduct should speak with more than ordinary clearness. This policy has special force when the conduct on the safe side of the line is not, in the general understanding of the community, morally blameworthy.

The second forbids a court to understand the legislature as directing a departure from a generally prevailing principle or policy of the law unless it does so clearly. This policy has special force when the departure is so great as to raise a serious question of constitutional power. * * *

G.   The Attribution of Purpose

[Professors Hart and Sacks emphasize the complexity of the task. A statute may have several purposes, each one may be of differing degrees of definiteness, and purpose includes both the immediate policy objective as well as "a larger and subtler purpose as to how the particular statute is to be fitted into the legal system as a whole."]

In determining the more immediate purpose which ought to be attributed to a statute * * * a court should try to put itself * * * in the position of the legislature which enacted the measure.

The court, however, should not do this in the mood of a cynical political observer, taking account of all the short-run currents of political expedience that swirl around any legislative session.

It should assume, unless the contrary unmistakably appears, that the legislature was made up of reasonable persons pursuing reasonable purposes reasonably. * * *

[The court should follow the approach of *Heydon's Case*.] Why would reasonable men, confronted with the law as it was, have enacted this new law to replace it? * * *

The most reliable guides to an answer will be found in the instances of unquestioned application of the statute. Even in the case of a new statute there almost invariably *are* such instances, in which, because of the perfect fit of words and context, the meaning seems unmistakable.

Once these points of reference are established, they throw a double light. The purposes necessarily implied in them illuminate facets of the general purpose. At the same time they provide a basis for reasoning by analogy to the disputed application in hand. * * * What is crucial here is the realization that law is being made, and that law is not supposed to be irrational. * * *

[Professors Hart and Sacks urge that "the whole context of the statute" should be examined, including the "state of the law" both before and after enactment, "general public knowledge" of the mischief to be remedied, and published legislative history as it sheds light on the statute's general purpose.]

The judicial, administrative, and popular construction of a statute, subsequent to its enactment, are all relevant in attributing a purpose to it.

The court's own prior interpretations of a statute in related applications should be accepted, on the principle of *stare decisis*, unless they are manifestly out of accord with other indications of purpose. * * *

H.   *Interpreting the Words to Carry Out the Purpose*

* * * The main burden of the [interpretive] task should be carried by the institution (court or administrative agency) which has the first-line responsibility for applying the statute authoritatively.

This agency should give sympathetic attention to indications in the legislative history of the lines of contemplated growth, if the history is available. It should give weight to popular construction of self-operating elements of the statute, if that is uniform. Primarily, it should strive to develop a coherent and reasoned pattern of applications intelligibly related to the general purpose. * * *

An interpretation by an administrative agency charged with first-line responsibility for the authoritative application of the statute should be accepted by the court as conclusive, if it is consistent with the purpose properly to be attributed to the statute, and if it has been arrived at with regard to the factors which should be taken into account in elaborating it.

PROBLEM 4–1: THE CASE OF THE WANDERING BASKETBALL PLAYER (A TRUE STORY)

The New York Knicks were the basketball team to beat in the 1990s. Many people (especially New Yorkers) thought that 1997 was the year they would finally capture their first championship since 1973. That (wishful) thinking was shattered when, during a critical playoff game, a fight broke out between players on the Knicks and players on the Miami Heat. Afterwards, the National Basketball Association (NBA) Commissioner suspended the players in the fight, pursuant to its rule prohibiting players from fighting or leaving the bench during a fight. More controversially, however, the Knicks super-star center, Patrick Ewing, also was suspended, even though he did not join the fight. Ewing, who had been on the bench when the fight broke out, got off the bench, and wandered a few steps onto the court in the general direction of the fight. That was enough, in the Commissioner's view, to invoke the rule. The suspensions deprived the Knicks of their best players for the next two games and the Knicks remain without their second championship trophy to this day (2014).

Here are the relevant portions of the NBA rule:

Section VIII—Fighting Fouls:

Technical fouls shall be assessed players, coaches, or trainers for fighting. No free throws will be attempted. The participants will be ejected immediately. * * *

A fine not exceeding $35,000 and/or suspension may be imposed upon such person(s) by the Commissioner at his sole discretion.

Section IX—Fines:

During an altercation, all players not participating in the game must remain in the immediate vicinity of their bench. Violators will be suspended, without pay, for a minimum of one game and fined up to $35,000. The suspensions will commence prior to the start of their next game. A team must have a minimum of eight players dressed and ready to play in every game. If five or more players leave the bench, the players will serve their suspensions alphabetically, according to the first letters of their last name. If seven bench players are suspended * * * four of them would be suspended for the first game following the altercation. The remaining three would be suspended for the second game following the altercation.

Assume you are a judge or an arbitrator reviewing the Commissioner's application of the NBA rules. (Think of the Commissioner as an agency head for purposes of this problem.) Keep in mind that the public (well, a lot of New Yorkers) are outraged. How would you rule in the following scenarios? What's the purpose of the rule? How much discretion does the Commissioner or court have? How would Judge Foster from the *Explorers* case rule? Judge Keen? Judge Handy?

a) Ewing leaves the bench, runs right up to the edge of the fight but doesn't join the fight;

b) Ewing leaves the bench during the fight to use the bathroom (which is behind the bleachers, away from the fight);

c) Ewing leaves the bench and enters the circle of the fight but only to pull one of his teammates off one of the Heat players who is being dangerously choked by one of the Knicks;

d) Ewing (as in the actual case) wanders a few steps off the bench

NOTES ON PURPOSIVE THEORY

1. *Ancient Forms of Purposivism.* Although it is generally thought that Hart & Sacks offered the most serious analysis of purposivism, the idea is quite ancient. In 1584, *Heydon's Case* focused on "the mischief and defect for which the common law did not provide." *Heydon's Case*, 30 Co. 7a, 76 Eng.

Rep. 637 (Exch, 1584). Blackstone wrote of a five-step process that has eerie reverberations in the modern world: "1. Words are generally to be understood in their usual and most known signification * * *. 2. If words happen to be still dubious, we may establish their meaning from the context * * *. 5. But, lastly the most universal and effectual way of discovering the true meaning of a law, when the words are dubious, is by considering the *reason and spirit of it*, or the cause which moved the legislator to enact it. For when this reason ceases, the law itself ought likewise to cease with it." Sir William Blackstone, 1 *Commentaries on the Laws of England* 58–61 (Cooley ed. 1876, original published 1765–69) (emphasis added). Recall that Blackstone was the leading law book in the English language during the founding period of the American republic.

2. *The Multiple Purpose Problem.* One of the problems Hart and Sacks noted was that there can be many purposes to a single statute, including the "subtler" purpose of fitting the law into the legal system. They argue that the identification of purpose is not a simple thing. Consider our vehicles in the park hypothetical. Is there one purpose? Should the interpreter consider the fact that the legal system does not generally punish children when finding the purpose of the statute? One might consider what Hart and Sacks call the "attribution" of purpose an exercise in statutory "construction" as opposed to "interpretation," which is to say that the interpreter is considering the proper legal effect of the statute rather than its meaning to those who wrote it. Consider how such an approach might change the nature of the inquiry from a focus on *congressional intent* to one focused on the *values of the legal system*—like coherence with other norms and statutes. Judges and commentators often collapse the two, but we hope you can see that these approaches do not embrace the exact same vision of what the goal and role of the judge in the statutory-interpretation endeavor should be.

NOTE ON THE FEMALE JUROR CASES

State statutes have often provided that juries are to be selected from a list of the qualified "electors" (i.e., voters) of the jurisdiction. Both the legislatures of Pennsylvania and Illinois adopted such statutes at a time when women were not allowed to vote in either state. After the ratification of the Nineteenth Amendment to the United States Constitution, which guaranteed women the right to vote, were women eligible to serve as jurors in these states by virtue of these statutes?

In *Commonwealth v. Maxwell*, 114 A. 825, 829 (Pa. 1921), the Supreme Court of Pennsylvania held that women were qualified to serve on juries:

> We then have the act of 1867, constitutionally providing that the jury commissioners are required to select "from the whole qualified electors of the respective county * * * persons, to serve as jurors in the several courts of such county," and the Nineteenth Amendment to the federal Constitution, putting women in the body of electors. * * *

"Statutes framed in general terms apply to new cases that arise, and to new subjects that are created from time to time, and which come within their general scope and policy. It is a rule of statutory construction that legislative enactments in general and comprehensive terms, prospective in operation, apply alike to all persons, subjects, and business within their general purview and scope coming into existence subsequent to their passage." 25 Ruling Case Law, 778.

But in *People ex rel. Fyfe v. Barnett*, 150 N.E. 290, 292 (Ill. 1925), the Supreme Court of Illinois reached the opposite result:

At the time of the passage by the Legislature of the act above mentioned, providing for the appointment of a jury commission and the making of jury lists, the words "voters" and "electors" were not ambiguous terms. They had a well-defined and settled meaning. [The Illinois Constitution of 1870 limited the franchise to "male citizen[s] of the United States, above the age of twenty-one."]

The legislative intent that controls in the construction of a statute has reference to the Legislature which passed the given act. 25 R.C.L. 1029. Applying the rules of construction herein mentioned, it is evident that when the Legislature enacted the law in question, which provided for the appointment of jury commissioners in counties having more than 250,000 inhabitants and imposing upon them the duty of making a jury list, using the words "shall prepare a list of all electors between the ages of twenty-one and sixty years, possessing the necessary legal qualifications for jury duty, to be known as the jury list," it was intended to use the words "electors" and "elector" as the same were then defined by the Constitution and laws of the state of Illinois. At that time the Legislature did not intend that the name of any women should be placed on the jury list, and must be held to have intended that the list should be composed of the names of male persons, only. In interpreting a statute, the question is what the words used therein meant to those using them. 25 R.C.L. 1029. The word "electors," in the statute here in question, meant male persons, only, to the legislators who used it. We must therefore hold that the word "electors," as used in the statute, means male persons, only, and that the petitioner was not entitled to have her name replaced upon the jury list of Cook County.

Accord, *Commonwealth v. Welosky*, 177 N.E. 656 (Mass. 1931) (holding that the words of a statute are controlling and are to be construed according to their common and approved usage).

Hart and Sacks's *The Legal Process* 1172–85 (1994 ed.) discusses these cases. Their critical questions suggest several reasons why a court might interpret a statute beyond or against the original legislative intent.

Consider how these courts addressed the issue of legislative intent. Is the question whether the legislature that enacted the jury-selection statute had a specific intent concerning women as jurors? What is the likelihood that there was such a specific intent? Or is the question whether the legislature intended the term "elector" to be frozen in the meaning given it by voter-qualification statutes in effect when the jury selection statutes were first enacted, or to vary as voter qualifications changed over time?

What was the purpose of the juror-qualification statutes? Would that purpose be better served by interpreting "elector" as frozen to the factual setting prior to the ratification of the Nineteenth Amendment, or alternatively as embodying later developments? If the legislature had known that the Nineteenth Amendment was going to be adopted, would its members have wanted its juror statutes to conform to the expanded concept of citizenship represented by that Amendment?

Should the court avoid an "irrational pattern of particular applications" of the statute? Hart and Sacks, *The Legal Process*, 1125. Doesn't a court have an obligation to enhance the law's overall "coherence," rather than recognizing inconsistent rules? Shouldn't the court be reluctant to interpret the juror-selection statutes in a way that runs against a fundamental legal principle or policy? Would the exclusion of women from juries have been unconstitutional when Hart and Sacks were writing? See *Hoyt v. Florida*, 368 U.S. 57 (1961) (holding that it was not unconstitutional for a state to make jury service optional for women, compulsory for men). If so, or even if the issue just raised difficult constitutional questions, would that provide a justification for construing the open-textured statute to include women?

IS THE STATUTORY INTERPRETER A "FAITHFUL AGENT" OF THE LEGISLATURE OR A "PARTNER" IN GOVERNANCE?

One important criticism of legal process theory's approach to statutory interpretation is that it represents a common law baseline, where the judge is a lawmaker and so approaches statutory interpretation as a partner with legislators. The criticism is that this metaphor is inconsistent with the structure of the modern regulatory state: most federal law is now made by Congress (federal courts retain some limited common-law making authority in special areas). On this view, legislatures are essentially the only *valid* lawmaking institutions at the federal level, and the role of the judge is to be the *faithful agent* (not the partner) of the legislature, to carry out the legislators' project and not to impose her own norms and rules. See, e.g., Thomas W. Merrill, *The Common Law Powers of Federal Courts*, 52 U. Chi. L. Rev. 1 (1985); John F. Manning, *What Divides Textualists from Purposivists?*, 106 Colum. L. Rev. 70 (2006).

This more limited view of the role of federal judges remains hotly contested. Judge Katzmann has argued that statutory interpretation by judges must be situated within an institutional context, where courts cooperate with agencies as well as legislatures to create public policy. Robert

A. Katzmann, *Judging Statutes* (2014); accord, Stephen Breyer, *Making Our Democracy Work: A Judge's View* (2010); William N. Eskridge Jr. & Philip P. Frickey, *The Supreme Court, 1993 Term—Foreword: Law as Equilibrium*, 108 Harv. L. Rev. 26 (1994) (advancing the notion that the Court and Congress are both competing and cooperating institutions in the creation of public policy).

Evening assuming that federal judges are required to be "faithful agents" of legislatures enacting statutes, does that metaphor tell you anything about what method courts should deploy when applying statutes to circumstances not contemplated by the "principal" (i.e., the legislature)? Cf. William N. Eskridge Jr., *Spinning Legislative Supremacy*, 78 Geo. L.J. 319 (1989) (deeper analysis of "agency" metaphors in statutory interpretation). Consider the following problem and analysis.

PROBLEM 4–2: FUNDING STEM CELL RESEARCH IN THE BUSH AND OBAMA ADMINISTRATIONS

Stem-cell lines are large amounts of undifferentiated cells derived from fertilized embryos; they hold enormous value for research because they have the potential to become any type of cell in the human body. They are also enormously controversial, largely due to the fact that their derivation—the creation of the line—necessarily kills the fertilized embryo. Both Presidents Bush and Obama encountered significant political heat as they developed their positions on whether federal funds could be used to support this research. Of course, there was a statute on the books that was relevant to the issue.

The Dickey-Wicker Amendment to the Balanced Budget Downpayment Act of 1996 prohibits the use of federal funds for:

(1) the creation of a human embryo or embryos for research purposes; or (2) research in which a human embryo or embryos are destroyed, discarded, or knowingly subjected to risk of injury or death greater than that allowed for research on fetuses *in utero* under [applicable federal regulations].

After much deliberation, President Bush issued an executive order interpreting Dickey-Wicker to allow federal funding to support any *existing* stem cell line but not to fund work on new lines. See Exec. Order No. 13, 435, 72 Fed. Reg. 34,591 (2007). Can you see why?

President Obama wanted to liberalize the Bush guidelines and so directed NIH to issue new guidelines, extending federal funding to research on stem cell lines created from voluntarily donated unused IVF embryos—on all but the portion of the research that involved actually deriving the stem cells (the part that kills the embryo). Exec. Order 13,505, 74 Fed. Reg. 10,667 (2009); 2009 Guidelines, 74 Fed. Reg. 32,170–75 (2009). This policy was immediately challenged in federal court. The D.C. District Court issued an injunction halting all federal funding on stem cell research, putting millions of dollars of precious scientific research in jeopardy. An appeal to the D.C. Circuit followed.

What's the best argument for each side? Is the Obama interpretation so much more offensive to the statute than the Bush interpretation? How relevant is the fact that Dickey-Wicker was passed in 1996 in response to a *totally different problem*—fears of cloning. It was not until 1998 that scientists first discovered how to derive stem cell lines from embryos.

Consider another twist. Dickey-Wicker was part of an annual *appropriations rider*, a series of annual funding authorizations for agencies that are essentially automatically renewed each year unless Congress goes in and changes them. Dickey-Wicker was renacted every year. Indeed, Obama signed a 465-page omnibus appropriations bill that contained the amendment two days after directing NIH to interpret the statute to allow the research. What do you make of this? Is it credible to assume that members of Congress were ignorant of Dickey-Wicker, as members sometimes are ignorant of matters buried in huge omnibus bills? Is it more likely that the topic was just too politically hot to touch? Does that justify or undermine the President's actions?

WILLIAM N. ESKRIDGE JR., *DYNAMIC STATUTORY INTERPRETATION*
125–128 (1994).*

[Interpretation can be viewed as an honest effort by a "faithful agent" to apply the principal's directive to unforeseen circumstances. The dynamic nature of interpretation arises, in large part, out of the agent's need for practical accommodation of the directive to new circumstances. Consider the following homely example, adapted from Francis Lieber's famous "fetch me the soup meat" hypothetical.]

* * * Williams, the head of the household, retains Diamond as a relational agent to run the household while Williams is away on business. The contract is detailed, setting forth Diamond's duties to care for Williams's two children, maintain the house, prepare the meals, and do the shopping on a weekly basis. One specific directive is that Diamond fetch five pounds of soup meat every Monday (the regular shopping day), so that he can prepare enough soup for the entire week. Diamond knows from talking to Williams that by 'soup meat' she means a certain type of nutritious beef that is sold at several local stores. When Williams leaves, Diamond has no doubt as to what he is supposed to do. But over time his interpretation of the directive will change if the social, legal, and constitutional context changes so as to affect important assumptions made in Williams's original directive.

Changes in Social Context. There are a number of changes in the world that would justify Diamond's deviation from the directive that he fetch five pounds of soup meat each Monday. For example, suppose Diamond goes to town one Monday and discovers that none of the stores has the precise kind of soup meat he knows Williams had in mind when she gave the order. Should he drive miles to other towns in search of the proper soup meat? Not necessarily. It might be reasonable for him to purchase a suitable alternative in town, especially if it appears in his judgment to be just as good for the children. One can imagine many practical reasons why, in a given week, Diamond should not follow the apparent command. The reasons for deviating are akin to the interpretive creation of "exceptions" to a statute's broad mandate based on the interpreter's judgment about the statute's goals and the extent to which other goals should be sacrificed. [Recall Justice Brewer's opinion in *Holy Trinity Church.*]

As the reasons multiply over time, one can imagine changed circumstances that would effectively nullify Williams's directive altogether * * *. Suppose Diamond discovers that one of the children has an allergy to soup meat. That child can continue to eat soup, but not with meat in it. Because Diamond realizes that one of the reasons Williams directed him to fetch soup meat every Monday was to ensure the good health and nourishment of the children, and because he believes that Williams would not want him to waste money on uneaten soup meat, he henceforth purchases only three pounds of soup meat per week. If both children are allergic to the soup meat, and Diamond does not care for it himself, he might be justified in entirely forgoing his directive to fetch it. Although he would be violating the original specific intent as well as the plain meaning of Williams's orders, Diamond could argue that his actions are consistent with her general intent that he act to protect the children's health and with her meta-intent that Diamond adapt specific directives to that end.

New Legal Rules and Policies. The relational agent might receive inconsistent directives over time. Suppose that two months after Williams embarks on her trip, she reads in a "Wellness Letter" that if children do not eat healthy foods, they will have cholesterol problems later in life. She sends Diamond a letter instructing him to place the children on a low-cholesterol diet, which should include Wendy's Bran Muffins and fresh apples. As a faithful relational agent, Diamond complies. He also reads up on the cholesterol literature, including the "Wellness Letter," and discovers that soup meat is high in cholesterol. He discontinues the weekly fetching of soup meat and fetches chicken instead because it is lower in cholesterol. Diamond's action is akin to a court's reconciliation of conflicting statutory mandates, in which one of the statutes is often given a narrow interpretation to accommodate the policies of a later statute. * * *

Changed circumstances might further alter Diamond's interpretation of Williams's inconsistent directives. Weeks after he has substituted chicken for soup meat, Diamond learns from the "Wellness Letter" that Wendy's Bran Muffins actually do not help lower cholesterol, and that they have been found to cause cancer in rats. Furthermore, Diamond discovers that 50 percent of the apples sold in his region have a dangerous chemical on them. Diamond thereupon switches from Wendy's Bran Muffins to Richard's Bran Muffins, recommended by the "Wellness Letter," and from fresh apples to fresh oranges. Thus, not only has Diamond overthrown Williams's earlier directive on soup meat because of the new policy in her later directive, but he has also altered her specific choice of low-cholesterol foods in that directive!

New Meta-Policies. The relational agent's interpretation of his orders may well be influenced over time by changing meta-policies. The new meta-policies may be endogenous or exogenous. Endogenous meta-policies are those generated by the principal herself and are just a more dramatic form of inconsistent directives. Suppose that, after several months, Williams writes to Diamond that financial reversals impel her to cut back on household expenses. Food costs must thereafter be limited to $100 per week. Although he has long been directed to fetch soup meat every Monday, and there are other ways to economize, Diamond cuts back on soup meat, in part because it is the most expensive item on the shopping list. This is akin to a court's modifying an original statutory policy to take account of supervening statutory policies.

Exogenous meta-policies are those generated by an authority greater than the principal. Suppose that Diamond has an unlimited food budget and no health concerns about soup meat, yet he stops fetching it on a weekly basis because the town is in a crisis period and meat of all sorts is being rationed; hence, Diamond could not lawfully fetch five pounds of soup meat per week. This is akin to a court construing a statute narrowly to avoid constitutional problems based on the legislature's meta-intent not to pass statutes of questionable constitutionality.

In all of these hypotheticals, Diamond, our relational agent, has interpreted Williams's soup meat directive dynamically. Quite dynamically, in fact, because in most of the variations Diamond created substantial exceptions to or even negated the original specific meaning of the directive. Notwithstanding his dynamic interpretation of the directive, I believe that Diamond has been nothing but an honest agent.

STATUTORY PREFACE FOR *MATTER OF JACOB*

New York Domestic Relations Code (1995)

Section 110.   Who May Adopt * * *

An adult unmarried person or an adult husband and his adult wife together may adopt another person. An adult married person who is living separate and apart from his or her spouse pursuant to a decree or judgment of separation or pursuant to a written agreement of separation subscribed by the parties thereto and acknowledged or proved in the form required to entitle a deed to be recorded or an adult married person who has been living separate and apart from his or her spouse for at least three years prior to commencing an adoption proceeding may adopt another person; provided, however, that the person so adopted shall not be deemed the child or step-child of the non-adopting spouse for the purposes of inheritance or support rights or obligations or for any other purposes. An adult or minor husband and his adult or minor wife together may adopt a child of either of them born in or out of wedlock and an adult or minor husband or an adult or minor wife may adopt such a child of the other spouse. No person shall hereafter be adopted except in pursuance of this article, and in conformity with section three hundred seventy-three of the social services law. * * *

An adult married person who has executed a legally enforceable separation agreement or is a party to a marriage in which a valid decree of separation has been entered or has been living separate and apart from his or her spouse for at least three years prior to commencing an adoption proceeding and who becomes or has been the custodian of a child placed in their care as a result of court ordered foster care may apply to such authorized agency for placement of said child with them for the purpose of adoption. Final determination of the propriety of said adoption of such foster child, however, shall be within the sole discretion of the court, as otherwise provided herein.

Adoption is the legal proceeding whereby a person takes another person into the relation of child and thereby acquires the rights and incurs the responsibilities of parent in respect of such other person. * * *

Section 115–b.   Special provisions relating to consents in private-placement adoptions * * *

[This section sets out the rules governing private placement adoptions, especially the rules governing the consent of the birth parent(s). The consent "may be executed or acknowledged before any judge or surrogate in this state having jurisdiction over adoption proceedings" (§ 115–b(2)(a)). "[T]he judge or surrogate shall inform such parent of the consequences of such act pursuant to the provisions of this section, including informing such parent of the right to be represented by legal counsel of the parent's own choosing; of the right to obtain supportive counseling and of any rights the parent may have * * *." Where the parent's consent is extrajudicial (through a notarized statement), § 115–c(3)–(4) requires detailed notice, in writing, of the parent's rights and what she or he is giving up, as well as a 45-day revocation period.]

8.   Notwithstanding any other provision of this section, a parent having custody of a child whose adoption is sought by his or her spouse need only consent that his or her child be adopted by a named stepfather or stepmother.

Section 117.   Effect of Adoption.

1.   **(a)** After the making of an order of adoption the birth parents of the adoptive child shall be relieved of all parental duties toward and of all responsibilities for and shall have no rights over such adoptive child or to his property by descent or succession, except as hereinafter stated.

     (b) The rights of an adoptive child to inheritance and succession from and through his natural parents shall terminate upon the making of the order of adoption except as hereinafter provided.

     (c) The adoptive parents or parent and the adoptive child shall sustain toward each other the legal relation of parent and child and shall have all the rights and be subject to all the duties of that relation including the rights of inheritance from and through each other and the natural and adopted kindred of the adoptive parents or parent.

     (d) When a natural or adoptive parent, having lawful custody of a child, marries or remarries and consents that the stepparent may adopt such child, such consent shall not relieve the parent so consenting of any parental duty toward such child nor shall such consent or the order of adoption affect the rights of such consenting spouse and such adoptive child to inherit from and through each other and the natural and adopted kindred of such consenting spouse. * * *

     (f) The right of inheritance of an adoptive child extends to the distributees of such child and such distributees shall be the same as if he were the natural child of the adoptive parent.

     (g) Adoptive children and natural children shall have all the rights of fraternal relationship including the right of inheritance from each other. Such right of inheritance extends to the distributees of such adoptive children and natural children and such distributees shall be the same as if each such child were the natural child of the adoptive parents.

(h) The consent of the parent of a child to the adoption of such child by his or her spouse shall operate to vest in the adopting spouse only the rights as distributee of a natural parent and shall leave otherwise unaffected the rights as distributee of the consenting spouse.

(i) This subdivision shall apply only to the intestate descent and distribution of real and personal property.

2.   **(a)** Except as hereinafter stated, after the making of an order of adoption, adopted children and their issue thereafter are strangers to any natural relatives for the purpose of the interpretation or construction of a disposition in any instrument, whether executed before or after the order of adoption, which does not express a contrary intention or does not expressly include the individual by name or by some classification not based on a parent-child or family relationship. * * *

New York's Social Services Law (1995).

§ 383–c. Guardianship and custody of children in foster care

[This section regulates adoptions through agencies, which enter into "surrender instruments" with a child's birth parent(s). Like § 115–b of the Domestic Relations Law, which regulates private placement adoptions, this section, governing agency adoptions, imposes detailed procedures and notice requirements to assure that birth parents understand their rights and what rights they are giving up.]

2.   **Terms.**

(a) Such guardianship shall be in accordance with the provisions of this article and the instrument shall be upon such terms and subject to such conditions as may be agreed upon by the parties thereto * * *.

(b) If a surrender instrument designates a particular person or persons who will adopt a child, such person or persons, the child's birth parent or parents, the authorized agency having care and custody of the child and the child's attorney, may enter into a written agreement providing for communication or contact between the child and the child's parent or parents on such terms and conditions as may be agreed to by the parties. If a surrender instrument does not designate a particular person or persons who will adopt the child, then the child's birth parent or parents, the authorized agency having care and custody of the child and the child's attorney may enter into a written agreement providing for communication or contact, on such terms and conditions as may be agreed to by the parties. * * * If the court before which the surrender instrument is presented for approval determines that the agreement concerning communication and contact is in the child's best interests, the court shall approve the agreement. If the court does not approve the agreement, the court may nonetheless approve the surrender; provided, however, that the birth parent or parents executing the surrender instrument shall be given the opportunity at that time to withdraw such instrument. * * *

MATTER OF JACOB
MATTER OF DANA

Court of Appeals of New York, 1995.
86 N.Y.2d 651, 636 N.Y.S.2d 716, 660 N.E.2d 397.

KAYE, C.J. [delivered the opinion for the Court.]

[The appeal involved two petitions for adoption. In the *Jacob* case, the cohabiting boyfriend, Stephen T.K., of the child's biological mother, Roseanne M.A., moved to adopt Jacob. In the *Dana* case, the cohabiting female partner, G.M., of the child's biological mother, P.I., petitioned to adopt Dana. In both cases, the family courts denied the petitions as not falling within New York's adoption statute. The Court of Appeals, by a 4–3 vote, reversed.]

[S]ince adoption in this State is "solely the creature of * * * statute," the adoption statute must be strictly construed. What is to be construed strictly and applied rigorously in this sensitive area of the law, however, is legislative purpose as well as legislative language. Thus, the adoption statute must be applied in harmony with the humanitarian principle that adoption is a means of securing the best possible home for a child. * * *

This policy would certainly be advanced in situations like those presented here by allowing the two adults who actually function as a child's parents to become the child's legal parents. The advantages which would result from such an adoption include Social Security and life insurance benefits in the event of a parent's death or disability, the right to sue for the wrongful death of a parent, the right to inherit under rules of intestacy and eligibility for coverage under both parents' health insurance policies. In addition, granting a second parent adoption further ensures that two adults are legally entitled to make medical decisions for the child in case of emergency and are under a legal obligation for the child's economic support *(see,* Domestic Relations Law § 32).

Even more important, however, is the emotional security of knowing that in the event of the biological parent's death or disability, the other parent will have presumptive custody, and the children's relationship with their parents, siblings and other relatives will continue should the coparents separate. Indeed, viewed from the children's perspective, permitting the adoptions allows the children to achieve a measure of permanency with both parent figures * * *.

A second, related point of overriding significance is that the various sections comprising New York's adoption statute today represent a complex and not entirely reconcilable patchwork. Amended innumerable times since its passage in 1873, the adoption statute was last consolidated nearly 60 years ago, in 1938 (L. 1938, ch. 606). Thus, after decades of piecemeal amendment upon amendment, the statute today contains language from the 1870's alongside language from the 1990's. * * *

Despite ambiguity in other sections, one thing is clear: section 110 allows appellants to become adoptive parents. Domestic Relations Law § 110, entitled "Who May Adopt," provides that an "adult unmarried person or an adult husband and his adult wife together may adopt another person" (Domestic Relations Law § 110). Under this language, both appellant G. M. in *Matter of Dana* and appellant Stephen T.K. in *Matter of Jacob,* as adult unmarried persons, have standing to adopt and appellants are correct that the Court's analysis of section 110 could appropriately end here. [Although Jacob's adoption was a joint petition, his mother already enjoyed parental rights, and so only Stephen T.K.'s rights were really at stake in the petition. Chief Judge Kaye faulted the dissenting opinion for reading too much into the word "together."]

The conclusion that appellants have standing to adopt is also supported by the history of section 110. The pattern of amendments since the end of World War II evidences a successive expansion of the categories of persons entitled to adopt regardless of their marital status or sexual orientation. [Section 110 was expanded in 1951 to allow adoptions by minors and in 1984 to allow adoptions by adults not yet divorced but living apart from their spouses pursuant to separation agreements.]

Supporting [the 1984] amendment was New York's "strong policy of assuring that as many children as possible are adopted into suitable family situations" (Bill Jacket, L. 1984, ch. 218, Mem. of Dept. of Social Services, at 2 [June 19, 1984]). * * *

These amendments reflect some of the fundamental changes that have taken place in the makeup of the family. Today, for example, at least 1.2 of the 3.5 million American households which consist of an unmarried adult couple have children under 15 years old, more than a six-fold increase from 1970 *(see,* Current Population Reports, Population Characteristics, U.S. Bur. of Census, Marital Status & Living Arrangements, P20–478, at IX [1993]). Yet further recognition of this transformation is evidenced by the fact that unlike the States of New Hampshire and Florida (N.H. Rev. Stat. Annot. § 170–B:4; Fla. Stat. Ann. § 63.042[3]), New York does not prohibit adoption by homosexuals.

Indeed, as noted earlier, an administrative regulation is in place in this State forbidding the denial of an agency adoption based solely on the petitioner's sexual orientation (18 NYCRR 421.16[h][2]). * * *

Appellants having standing to adopt pursuant to Domestic Relations Law § 110, the other statutory obstacle relied upon by the lower courts in denying the petitions is the provision that "[a]fter the making of an order of adoption the natural parents of the adoptive child shall be relieved of all parental duties toward and of all responsibilities for and shall have no rights over such adoptive child or to his property by descent or succession" (Domestic Relations Law § 117[l][a]). Literal application of this language would effectively prevent these adoptions since it would require the termination of the biological mothers' rights upon adoption thereby placing appellants in the "Catch-22" of having to choose one of two coparents as the child's only legal parent. * * *

Both the title of section 117 ("Effect of adoption") and its opening phrase ("After the making of an order of adoption") suggest that the section has nothing to do with the standing of an individual to adopt, an issue treated exclusively in section 110. Rather, section 117 addresses the legal effect of an adoption on the parties and their property. [This reading of section 117 is directed by the Court's precedents and commentary on the section, as well as the section's textual focus on estate law, § 117[1][i].]

[E]ven though the language of section 117 still has the effect of terminating a biological parent's rights in the majority of adoptions between strangers—where there is a need to prevent unwanted intrusion by the child's former biological relatives to promote the stability of the new adoptive family—the cases before us are entirely different. As we recognized in *Matter of Seaman* (78 N.Y.2d 451, 461), "complete severance of the natural relationship [is] not necessary when the adopted person remain[s] within the natural family unit as a result of an intrafamily adoption." [The legislature has recognized this principle by amending section 117 to allow adoptions by stepparents and to allow adoptive parents in some circumstances to agree to a continuing relationship between the child and her or his biological parents. The latter amendment, allowing "open adoptions," overrode a Court of Appeals decision construing the adoption law too narrowly.]

[Chief Judge Kaye described a 1990 amendment to Social Services Law § 383–c, which now requires agency adoptions to follow detailed procedures to assure that parents explicitly renounce their legal rights when placing a child for adoption. Likewise, a 1986 amendment to Domestic Relations Law § 115–b[1] now requires private placements to follow similar procedures.]

The procedural safeguards contained in Social Services Law § 383–c and Domestic Relations Law § 115–b—safeguards that reflect modern sensitivities as to the level of procedural protection required for waiver of parental rights—further indicate that section 117 does not invariably mandate termination in all circumstances. Under the language of section 117 alone, a biological mother's rights could theoretically be severed unilaterally, without notice as to the consequences or other procedural protections. Though arguably adequate in 1938 when the statute was enacted, such a summary procedure would be unlikely to pass muster today (see, e.g., Santosky v Kramer, 455 US 745, 768–770; Matter of Sarah K., 66 NY2d 223, 237).

A year prior to the enactment of Social Services Law § 383–c, this Court declined to sanction the concept of "open adoption" because of our belief that it was inconsistent with what we perceived to be section 117's requirement that termination of parental rights was mandatory in all cases (Matter of Gregory B., 74 NY2d 77, 91 [citations omitted]). Significantly, when enacting Social Services Law § 383–c the very next year, the Legislature saw no need to amend Domestic Relations Law § 117. Again, if section 117 automatically terminated parental rights in all circumstances, it would have the practical effect of overriding the conditional surrender/"open adoption" provisions of Social Services Law § 383–c. By passing Social Services Law § 383–c as it did, the Legislature thus necessarily rejected the reading of section 117 articulated in Matter of Gregory B.

Given the above, it is plain that an interpretation of section 117 that would limit the number of beneficial intrafamily adoptions cannot be reconciled with the legislative intent to authorize open adoptions and adoptions by minors. The coexistence of the statute's seemingly automatic termination language along with these more recent enactments creates a statutory puzzle not susceptible of ready resolution. * * *

"Where the language of a statute is susceptible of two constructions, the courts will adopt that which avoids injustice, hardship, constitutional doubts or other objectionable results" (Kauffman & Sons Saddlery Co. v. Miller, 298 N.Y. 38, 44 [Fuld, J.]; see also, McKinney's Cons. Laws of N.Y., Book 1, Statutes § 150). Given that section 117 is open to two differing interpretations as to whether it automatically terminates parental rights in all cases, a construction of the section that would deny children like Jacob and Dana the opportunity of having their two de facto parents become their legal parents, based solely on their biological mother's sexual orientation or marital status, would not only be unjust under the circumstances, but also might raise constitutional concerns in light of the adoption statute's historically consistent purpose—the best interests of the child. (See, e.g., Gomez v. Perez, 409 U.S. 535, 538 [Equal Protection Clause prevents unequal treatment of children whose parents are unmarried]; *Plyler v. Doe,* 457 U.S. 202, 220 [State may not direct the onus of parent's perceived "misconduct against his (or her) children"]; *Matter of Burns,* 55 N.Y.2d 501, 507–510 [New York statute requiring child born out of wedlock to prove "acknowledgment" by deceased parent did not further legitimate State interest].

These concerns are particularly weighty in *Matter of Dana.* Even if the Court were to rule against him on this appeal, the male petitioner in *Matter of Jacob* could still adopt by marrying Jacob's mother. Dana, however, would be irrevocably deprived of the benefits and entitlements of having as her legal parents the two individuals who have already assumed that role in her life, simply as a consequence of her mother's sexual orientation.

Any proffered justification for rejecting these petitions based on a governmental policy disapproving of homosexuality or encouraging marriage would not apply. * * * New York has not adopted a policy disfavoring adoption by either single persons or homosexuals. In fact, the most recent legislative document relating to the subject urges courts to construe section 117 in precisely the manner we have as it cautions against discrimination against "nonmarital children" and "unwed parents". An interpretation of the statute that avoids such discrimination or hardship is all the more appropriate here where a contrary ruling could jeopardize the legal status of the many New York children whose adoptions by second parents have already taken place. * * *

BELLACOSA, J., dissenting. Judges Simons, Titone and I respectfully dissent and vote to affirm in each case. * * *

Although adoption has been practiced since ancient times, the authorization for this unique relationship derives solely from legislation. It has no common-law roots or evolution. Therefore, our Court has approved the proposition that the statutory adoption charter exclusively controls. [Judge Bellacosa also emphasized that the "transcendent societal goal in the field of domestic relations is to stabilize family relationships, particularly parent-child bonds. That State interest promotes permanency planning and provides protection for an adopted child's legally secure familial placement." The state has chosen not to recognize common-law marriages or "lesbian marriages."]

Domestic Relations Law § 110, entitled "Who May Adopt," provides at its outset that *"[a]n adult unmarried person or an adult husband and his adult wife together* may adopt another person" (emphasis added). Married aspirants are directed to apply "together", i.e., jointly, as spouses, except under circumstances not applicable in these cases. [Appellant G.M., the lesbian co-parent in *Dana,* meets this requirement, but appellants Stephen T.K. and Roseanne M.A., the unmarried cohabitants in *Jacob,* do not.]

The legislative history of adoption laws over the last century also reveals a dynamic process with an evolving set of limitations. The original version enacted in 1873 provided: "Any minor child may be adopted *by any adult*" (L. 1873, ch 830 [emphasis added]). In 1896, the Legislature cut back by stating that "[a]n adult unmarried person, or an adult husband or wife, or an adult husband and his adult wife together, may adopt a minor" (L. 1896, ch. 272, § 60; *see also,* L. 1915, ch. 352; L. 1917, ch. 149). This language was further restricted, in 1920, when the Legislature omitted from the statute the language "or an adult husband or wife" *(see,* L. 1920, ch. 433). Since enactment of the 1920 amendment, the statute has provided that "[a]n adult unmarried person or an adult husband and his adult wife *together* may adopt" (Domestic Relations Law § 110 [emphasis added]). The words chosen by the Legislature demonstrate its conclusion that a stable familial entity is provided by either a one-parent family or a two-parent family when the concentric interrelationships enjoy a legal bond. The statute demonstrates that the Legislature, by express will and words, concluded that households that lack legally recognized bonds suffer a relatively greater risk to the stability needed for adopted children and families, because individuals can walk out of these relationships with impunity and unknown legal consequences. * * *

Domestic Relations Law § 117 provides: "After the making of an order of adoption the natural parents of the adoptive child *shall be relieved of all parental duties toward and of all responsibilities for and* shall have no rights over such adoptive child *or* to his [or her] property by descent or succession" (emphasis added). The plain and overarching language and punctuation of section 117 cannot be judicially blinked, repealed or rendered obsolete by interpretation. [Judge Bellacosa cited precedent where the Court of Appeals had refused to read equitable exceptions into the plain language of section 117 to ameliorate its harsh application.]

A careful examination of the Legislature's unaltered intent based on the entire history of the statute reveals the original purpose of section 117 was to enfold adoptees within the exclusive embrace of their new families and to sever all relational aspects with the former family. That goal still applies and especially to the lifetime and lifelong relationships of the affected individuals, not just to the effect of dying intestate.

[Judge Bellacosa faulted the majority's concern that the statute be construed to avoid constitutional problems because (1) that concern had not been briefed or even mentioned by appellants, nor did the Attorney General have an opportunity to present the state's views, (2) the presumption of constitutionality augurs against vague and speculative doubts about a statute's constitutionality, and (3) such a concern could not override the plain meaning of the statute.] Ambiguity cannot directly or indirectly create or substitute for the lack of statutory authorization to adopt. These adoption statutes are luminously clear on one unassailable feature: no express legislative authorization is discernible for what is, nevertheless, permitted by the holdings today. Nor do the statutes anywhere speak of de facto, functional or second parent adoptions. Frankly, if the Legislature had intended to alter the definitions and interplay of its plenary, detailed adoption blueprint to cover the circumstances as presented here, it has had ample and repeated opportunities, means and words to effectuate such purpose plainly and definitively as a matter of notice, guidance, stability and reliability. It has done so before *(see, e.g.,* L. 1984, ch. 218 [permitting adoption by adults not yet divorced]; L. 1951, ch. 211 [permitting adoption by a minor]).

Because the Legislature did not do so here, neither should this Court in this manner. Cobbling law together out of interpretative ambiguity that transforms fundamental, societally recognized relationships and substantive principles is neither sound statutory construction nor justifiable lawmaking. * * *

NOTES AND QUESTIONS ON MATTER OF JACOB

1. *Does the Court's Ruling Impose upon the Statutory Words a "Meaning They Will Not Bear"?* The dissenters' argument is that Chief Judge Kaye's interpretation is not just dynamic (way *beyond* and probably *against* the expectations of the enacting legislatures), but is also inconsistent with the statutory text. In the language of Professor Eskridge's rendition of the classic hypothetical, it is as if the legislature commanded, "Fetch me soupmeat," and the judges responded by bringing forth a dead rat. (Some New Yorkers in the 1990s would have claimed that the judges were bringing forth unhealthy or unholy relationships into state family law.) This is a serious concern under Hart and Sacks's theory: there has got to be some explanation for why the result is a plausible understanding of the statutory text. Perhaps the biggest stumbling block is § 117, which says that when an adoption occurs, the biological parent loses all parental rights—a deprivation which § 110 exempts the biological parent from if her/his spouse is the other adopting person. In *Dana*, therefore, P.I., the biological mother, wanted to retain her parental rights when G.M., her partner, secured parental rights—but §§ 110 and 117 do not seem to allow that. Is there any way out of the textual box that Judge Bellacosa puts the majority into? Can the Hart and Sacks theory provide a justification for judicial revision of the statutory language—or must that be done, under their theory, by the New York Legislature?

2. *Applying Old Codes to New Social Circumstances and Equality Norms.* When New York passed its adoption law, the idea of two women raising a child in a "lesbian" household would have been inconceivable; the legislators in 1872 might have had the women arrested for "lewd" behaviors. By 1995, lesbian unions with children were lawful and common. Moreover,

New York had taken other steps to liberalize its conception of the family. Chief Judge Kaye did not just argue her own preferences: she examined the state family law code and its legislative deliberations to identify current norms. Is this a persuasive approach? Or does it seem more like common-law judging—reasoning by analogy—than statutory interpretation? Judge Calabresi has long argued that there is no reason that judges cannot use this traditional common-law approach of analogous reasoning and ensuring cross-code legal coherence to update obsolete statutes. In fact, he argues such an approach is better for democracy: otherwise, courts turn too frequently to the Equal Protection Clause as a means of updating obsolete laws. Judge Calabresi argues that statutory interpretation, rather than constitutional lawmaking, provides for an interbranch dialogue that is better for Congress (because Congress can overrule statutory precedents, but not constitutional precedents). See Guido Calabresi, *A Common Law for the Age of Statutes* (1982).

Even if you are uncomfortable with the Calabresi argument, might the fact that Chief Judge Kaye is a state court judge make a difference? State court judges, most of whom are elected, typically have enjoyed greater lawmaking power. Even New York's judges, who are not elected, seem to have been accorded that presumption. *See* Judith S. Kaye, *State Courts at the Dawn of a New Century: Common Law Courts: Reading Statutes and Constitutions*, 70 N.Y.U. L. Rev. 1 (1995).

At the time Chief Judge Kaye wrote *Jacob,* a normative change had accompanied the social change. In 1872, legislators and judges would have considered two women raising children in the context of their own romantic relationship scandalous. By 1995, legislators would have been more tolerant of such a situation but would have been reluctant to give it the sanction of adoption law, on a par with a heterosexual marriage. The New York Court of Appeals was concerned that a family law regime withholding from lesbian families the legal protections and rights routinely afforded straight married families would be a literal violation of the constitutional admonition that states may not deny any person or persons "the equal protection of the law." This equality norm surely played a role in the Court's liberal understanding of the statutory purpose. Cf. *United States v. Windsor*, 133 S.Ct. 2675 (2013) (striking down the Defense of Marriage Act on the ground that it denied equal treatment to committed lesbian and gay couples without rational justification).

But consider this: the heterosexual couple in *Jacob* could have married, so why did they get the equality bounce afforded the lesbian couple in *Dana*? By extending second-parent adoption to cohabiting heterosexual couples, is the Court not undermining the pro-marriage policy carefully crafted by the legislature? Moreover, New York had amended its adoption law to accommodate *stepparent adoptions*, but those did not include female couples whose unions were not recognized as "marriages." Section 117 allowed adoption only if the biological mother gave up her rights; the legislature had relaxed this rule for stepparent adoptions, but not for second parents of the same sex. Which way does all this cut? Under Hart and Sacks's theory, big policy moves are supposed to be made by legislatures, and courts are supposed to engage in "interstitial lawmaking" at most. Does *Jacob* transgress this boundary? Or is the boundary an illusory one?

3. *Reversing the Burden of Legislative Inertia.* Because the legislature was slow to move on equal treatment of lesbian and gay families (just as Congress has been unable to get past the gridlock on the stem-cell issue), the New York Court of Appeals' willingness to update the statute may have been a move to *reverse the burden of legislative inertia* in these cases: second parents presumptively can adopt, until the legislature overrides that interpretation. Think of it as a gridlock-busting move. Most state supreme courts in gay-tolerant states have followed Chief Judge Kaye's dynamic reading of state adoption statutes, e.g., *Sharon S. v. Superior Court*, 31 Cal.4th 417 (2003); *Petition of K.M. and D.M.,* 653 N.E.2d 888 (Ill. 1995), but some have gone the other way, e.g., *Adoption of Baby Z*, 724 A.2d 1035 (Conn. 1999), and some states have allowed joint lesbian or gay parenting through legislation recognizing their civil unions (Colorado) or domestic partnerships (Nevada). An increasing number of states, including New York, have recognized lesbian and gay marriages.

Is this kind of political burden-shifting justifiable—or is it an example of unacceptable "judicial activism"? Drawing from representation-reinforcing theories of judicial review, Eskridge, *Dynamic Statutory Interpretation* ch. 5, argues that reversing the burden of inertia is particularly justified when the political process has traditionally been hostile to a minority group. Not only does this kind of judicial updating level the playing field a little, but it also places the burden on political groups that are actually able to attract the legislature's attention. If the will of the people is to deny lesbian and gay parents these rights, a decision granting relief in *Jacob* will probably be overridden in short order. (The converse case will not be: minorities traditionally disadvantaged in the political process find it doubly hard to persuade the legislature to do anything for them, because legislators fear backlash.)

Moreover, reversing the burden of inertia gives the persecuted minority an opportunity to falsify stereotypes—in this case, the stereotype of gay people as incapable of forming families or, indeed, as anti-family or even predatory. By allowing lesbian and gay couples to adopt children, Chief Judge Kaye was giving New Yorkers an opportunity to see that lesbian and gay families can be nurturing and productive. Not only did the New York Legislature not rebuke Chief Judge Kaye, but years of lesbian and gay family formation helped persuade the Legislature in 2011 to amend its family law code to recognize same-sex marriages. Does this "happy ending" justify the liberties the Court took with the language and structure of the statute?

BOB JONES UNIVERSITY V. UNITED STATES

Supreme Court of the United States, 1983.
461 U.S. 574, 103 S.Ct. 2017, 76 L.Ed.2d 157.

[Excerpted in Chapter 5, § 3]

3. TEXTUALIST THEORIES OF STATUTORY INTERPRETATION

Purpose-based theories of statutory interpretation have not gone unchallenged. First, the plain meaning rule is arguably more consistent with the structure of the U.S. Constitution (and most state constitutions), which vests the courts only with judicial power, while reserving lawmaking and political power to the legislative and executive branches. This constitutional separation of powers constitutes formal barriers to lawmaking that are disregarded when courts make new law. See John F. Manning, *Textualism as a Nondelegation Doctrine*, 97 Colum. L. Rev. 673 (1997). Second, and entirely within the legal process tradition, it can be argued that applying statutory plain meanings is more within the "judicial competence" than making policy or even scanning through legislative history to figure out whether the legislature "really meant" the apparent meaning of its statutory words. See Adrian Vermeule, *Legislative History and the Limits of Judicial Competence: The Untold Story of* Holy Trinity Church, 50 Stan. L. Rev. 1833 (1998).

Third, and perhaps most powerfully, the ordinary meaning of statutory language is the common understanding of what the "rule of law" is. See Antonin Scalia, *The Rule of Law as a Law of Rules*, 56 U. Chi. L. Rev. 1175 (1989). Citizens ought to be able to open up the statute books and find out what the law requires of them. Once law is understood by the cognoscenti through spirits, collective intents, and legalistic interpretive presumptions, the citizenry might lose faith in the externality of law—the objectivity of legal reasoning which provides us with some assurance that our problems are susceptible of the same rules as those of our neighbor (even if she is a rich and influential neighbor). The changes in American society since the 1960s make an external vision of the rule of law even more important than before. In a society where so many values are open to contest, using an objective criterion becomes ever more critical. But keep in mind that such a "rule of law" justification for a textual approach does not necessarily depend on the same vision of the judicial task in statutory interpretation as an approach aimed at effectuating congressional intent. Textualists often casually assume the two aims always co-exist. Congress might not intend for the word "cost" to mean the same thing in two different parts of the U.S. Code, but a "rule of law" approach might still justify interpreting the word consistently throughout.

A less complicated approach may also be democracy-enhancing in the sense of how it affects *Congress*: By placing responsibility for updating statutes on the shoulders of the people and their legislators, rather than their unelected (federal and some state) judges, such an approach would further democratic accountability. Plus, sending the responsibility back to Congress might encourage Congress to legislate more clearly in the future. Recall Judge Keen's argument that hard cases generating inequitable results should trigger a popular outrage that changes statutes more usefully and more democratically than judicial updating through a Hart and Sacks purpose approach. One way to think of this notion is as a "tough love" theory of statutory interpretation: A way to put the onus on Congress to do its own job, and do it better.

A. THE REVIVAL OF THE PLAIN MEANING RULE

At the U.S. Supreme Court, purpose-based interpretation, often drawing liberally on legislative history, dominated decision-making during the Vinson (1945–53) and Warren Courts (1953–69). This legal process approach to statutes was also prominent in landmark decisions handed down by the California Supreme Court, the New York Court of Appeals, and the New Jersey Supreme Court, traditional powerhouses of in-depth, sophisticated legal analysis. But this was not the approach followed in most state courts, where the plain meaning rule remained dominant even in many landmark opinions. (One reason for this disparity was that legislative history was not readily available in most states.) Ironically, federal circuit courts also tended to stick with the plain meaning rule, with the prominent exception of the Court of Appeals for the District of Columbia Circuit, which was more purposivist and more attentive to legislative history than the U.S. Supreme Court in the 1960s and 1970s.[5]

Starting with the Burger Court (1969–87) and continuing with the Rehnquist (1987–2005) and Roberts (2005–Present) Courts, the plain meaning rule made a big comeback at the U.S. Supreme Court and the Court of Appeals for the District of Columbia Circuit. Empirical analysis suggests that in the last generation these courts have devoted larger portions of their opinions to textual analysis and less to legislative history.[6] Qualitative analysis suggests that these judges are much less likely to admit that their decisions do not follow statutory plain meaning (virtually no *Holy Trinity* moments since 1990) and usually claim to be

---

[5] The generalizations about federal courts of appeals are drawn from the massive empirical study by our student, Glenn Bridgman, Yale Law School, Class of 2013. See Bridgman, One of These Things Is Not Like the Others: Legislative History in the U.S. Courts of Appeals (Yale Law School SAW June 2012).

[6] David S. Law, *Law Versus Ideology: The Supreme Court and the Use of Legislative History*, 51 Wm. & Mary L. Rev. 1653 (2010); Bridgman, Legislative History in the U.S. Courts of Appeals, *supra* note 5.

applying plain meaning, even when they are consulting or even emphasizing other evidence.

United States v. Madison D. Locke
471 U.S. 84 (1985).

The Federal Land Policy and Management Act (FLPMA), Pub. L. 94–579, 90 Stat. 2743, codified at 43 U.S.C. §§ 1701–1784 (1982), provided that holders of certain mining claims to federal land must, "prior to December 31" of every year, file certain documents with state officials and the federal Bureau of Land Management (BLM) or lose their claims. *Id.* § 1744. This requirement seemed like a trap for the unwary, for it seems illogical to require someone to file something, under severe penalty for default, the day *before* the last day of the year. The Locke family had been exercising rights to mine gravel on federal land since the 1960s. Knowing they were required to file papers in order to retain these rights, they sent their daughter to the nearest BLM office, which told her that claims had to be filed by December 31. The Lockes filed on that date, and the BLM rejected the papers on the ground that they were too late. The consequences were severe: loss of rights to mine gravel that the family had held for years.

Justice Marshall, for the Court, agreed with the BLM that the Lockes were out of luck. "While we will not allow a literal reading of a statute to produce a result 'demonstrably at odds with the intentions of its drafters,' with respect to filing deadlines a literal reading of Congress' words is generally the only proper reading of those words. To attempt to decide whether some date other than the one set out in the statute is the date actually 'intended' by Congress is to set sail on an aimless journey, for the purpose of a filing deadline would be just as well served by nearly any date a court might choose as by the date Congress has in fact set out in the statute. * * * [N]othing in the legislative history suggests why Congress chose December 30 over December 31 * * *, [b]ut "[d]eadlines are inherently arbitrary," while fixed dates "are often essential to accomplish necessary results." * * *

"[W]e are not insensitive to the problems posed by congressional reliance on the words 'prior to December 31.' But the fact that Congress might have acted with greater clarity or foresight does not give courts a *carte blanche* to redraft statutes in an effort to achieve that which Congress is perceived to have failed to do. 'There is a basic difference between filling a gap left by Congress' silence and rewriting rules that Congress has affirmatively and specifically enacted.' *Mobil Oil Corp. v. Higginbotham*, 436 U.S. 618, 625 (1978). * * * [D]eference to the supremacy of the Legislature, as well as recognition that Congressmen typically vote on the language of a bill, generally requires us to assume that 'the legislative purpose is expressed by the ordinary meaning of the words used.' * * * The phrase 'prior to' may be clumsy, but its meaning is clear."

Justice Stevens, joined by Justice Brennan, dissented for a variety of reasons. (1) FLPMA contained obvious drafting errors, which "should cause us to pause before concluding that Congress commanded blind allegiance to the remainder of the literal text" of the statute. (2) The BLM's implementing regulations did not repeat the statutory language, but rather stated that filing must be accomplished "on or before December 30 of each year," suggesting that the BLM itself recognized that the statutory language was unclear. (3) Indeed, the BLM once made the same mistake as the claimholders in *Locke*, for the agency had issued an information pamphlet that stated that documents must be filed "on or before December 31 of each [year]," demonstrating again that the statutory language is not "plain." Had the BLM issued regulations allowing filings on December 31, the Court surely would have upheld them, which suggests the anomaly that the agency "has more power to interpret an awkwardly drafted statute in an enlightened manner consistent with Congress' intent than does this Court."

Justice Stevens continued: "The statutory scheme requires periodic filings on a calendar-year basis. The end of the calendar year is, of course, correctly described either as 'prior to the close of business on December 31,' or 'on or before December 31,' but it is surely understandable that the author of [this statute] might inadvertently use the words 'prior to December 31' when he meant to refer to the end of the calendar year. * * * That it was in fact an error seems rather clear to me because no one has suggested any rational basis for omitting just one day from the period in which an annual filing may be made, and I would not presume that Congress deliberately created a trap for the unwary by such an omission." The dissent concluded: "I have no doubt that Congress would have chosen to adopt a construction of the statute that filing take place by the end of the calendar year if its attention had been focused on this precise issue." Do you agree?

NOTE ON LOCKE

Justice Marshall did not reverse outright. He remanded to the district court to consider the estoppel argument—namely, that the Lockes had relied to their detriment on the BLM office's own incorrect reading of the statute. Unsurprisingly, those instructions sent a clear enough signal; the government settled the case and the Lockes kept their rights. The Court thus got to have its cake and eat it too, writing a strong textual opinion but finding a way to essentially ensure a just result. Why might Justice Marshall have chosen this strategy?

It is notable that a liberal legal process Justice like Thurgood Marshall would have enforced the statutory text so strictly. Why so? Can you think of a policy reason for requiring filing before December 31? Think hard, for this is not an impossible task.

STATUTORY PREFACE FOR *TVA v. HILL*

The Endangered Species Act of 1973
(Codified at 16 U.S.C. § 1531 et seq.)

Section 2, 16 U.S.C. § 1531.   Findings, Purposes, and Policy * * *

(b) Purposes.—The purposes of this Act are to provide a means whereby the ecosystems upon which endangered species and threatened species depend may be conserved, to provide a program for the conservation of such endangered species and threatened species, and to take such steps as may be appropriate to achieve the purposes of [various species-protecting] treaties and conventions * * *.

(c) Policy.—It is further declared to be the policy of Congress that all federal departments and agencies shall seek to conserve endangered species and threatened species and shall utilize their authorities in furtherance of the purposes of this Act.

Section 4, 16 U.S.C. § 1533.   Determination of Endangered Species and Threatened Species

[This section delegates to the Secretary of the Interior the authority, after consultation, to designate species as either endangered or threatened. Private persons and other governmental agencies are bound by the Secretary's determination.]

Section 7, 16 U.S.C. § 1536.   Interagency Cooperation

The Secretary [of the Interior] shall review other programs administered by him and utilize such programs in furtherance of the purposes of this Act. All other Federal departments and agencies shall, in consultation with and with the assistance of the Secretary, utilize their authorities in furtherance of the purposes of this Act by carrying out programs for the conservation of endangered species and threatened species listed pursuant to section 4 of this Act and by taking such action necessary to insure that actions authorized, funded, or carried out by them do not jeopardize the continued existence of such endangered species and threatened species or result in the destruction or modification of habitat of such species which is determined by the Secretary, after consultation as appropriate with the affected States, to be critical.

TENNESSEE VALLEY AUTHORITY V. HIRAM G. HILL, JR.
United States Supreme Court, 1978.
437 U.S. 153, 98 S.Ct. 2279, 57 L.Ed.2d 117.

CHIEF JUSTICE BURGER delivered the opinion of the Court.

[Pursuant to § 4 of the statute, the Secretary of the Interior declared the snail darter (*Percina tanasi*) an endangered species and designated a portion of the Little Tennessee River as the only remaining natural habitat of the snail darter. That part of the river, however, would be flooded by the operation of the Tellico Dam, a $100 million Tennessee Valley Authority (TVA) project that was under way in 1973 and was almost completed by 1976, when environmentalists sought an injunction against the dam's operation. The district court denied relief. It found that the dam would destroy the snail darter's critical habitat, but it noted that Congress, though fully aware of the snail darter problem, had continued to fund the Tellico Dam after 1973. The court concluded that the Act did not justify an injunction against a project initiated before enactment. The court of appeals reversed and ordered the lower court to enjoin completion of the dam.]

It may seem curious to some that the survival of a relatively small number of three-inch fish among all the countless millions of species extant would require the permanent halting of a virtually completed dam for which Congress has expended more than $100 million. The paradox is not minimized by the fact that Congress continued to appropriate large sums of public money for the project, even after congressional Appropriations Committees were apprised of its apparent impact upon the survival of the snail darter. We conclude, however, that the explicit provisions of the Endangered Species Act require precisely that result.

One would be hard pressed to find a statutory provision whose terms were any plainer than those in § 7 of the Endangered Species Act. Its very words affirmatively command all federal agencies "to *insure* that actions *authorized, funded, or carried out* by them do not *jeopardize* the continued existence" of an endangered species or "*result* in the destruction or modification of habitat of such species. . . ." 16 U.S.C. § 1536 (1976 ed.). (Emphasis added.) This language admits of no exception. Nonetheless, petitioner urges, as do the dissenters, that the Act cannot reasonably be interpreted as applying to a federal project which was well under way when Congress passed the Endangered Species Act of 1973. To sustain that position, however, we would be forced to ignore the ordinary meaning of plain language. It has not been shown, for example, how TVA can close the gates of the Tellico Dam without "carrying out" an action that has been "authorized" and "funded" by a federal agency. Nor can we understand how such action will "*insure*" that the snail darter's habitat is not disrupted. Accepting the Secretary's determinations, as we must, it is clear that TVA's proposed operation of the dam will have precisely the opposite effect, namely the *eradication* of an endangered species. * * *

Concededly, this view of the Act will produce results requiring the sacrifice of the anticipated benefits of the project and of many millions of dollars in public funds. But examination of the language, history, and structure of the legislation under review here indicates beyond doubt that Congress intended endangered species to be afforded the highest of priorities.

When Congress passed the Act in 1973, it was not legislating on a clean slate. The first major congressional concern for the preservation of the endangered species had come with passage of the Endangered Species Act of 1966, 80 Stat. 926, repealed, 87 Stat. 903. In that legislation Congress gave the Secretary power to identify "the names of the species of native fish and wildlife found to be threatened with extinction," § 1(c), 80 Stat. 926, as well as authorization to purchase land for the conservation, protection, restoration, and propagation of "selected species" of "native fish and wildlife" threatened with extinction. §§ 2(a)–(c), 80 Stat. 926– 927. Declaring the preservation of endangered species a national policy, the 1966 Act directed all federal agencies both to protect these species and *"insofar as is practicable and consistent with the[ir] primary purposes,"* § 1(b), 80 Stat. 926, "preserve the habitats of such threatened species on lands under their jurisdiction." *Ibid.* (Emphasis added.) The 1966 statute was not a sweeping prohibition on the taking of endangered species, however, except on federal lands, § 4(c), 80 Stat. 928, and even in those federal areas the Secretary was authorized to allow the hunting and fishing of endangered species. § 4(d)(1), 80 Stat. 928.

[Notwithstanding the 1966 law, and a similar law adopted in 1969, congressional hearings in 1973 revealed that strategies encouraging species protection had not abated the "pace of disappearance of species," which appeared to be "accelerating." H.R. Rep. No. 93–412, p. 4 (1973). The dominant theme of the hearings and debates on the 1973 Act was "the overriding need to devote whatever effort and resources were necessary to avoid further diminution of national and worldwide wildlife resources." George Cameron Coggins, *Conserving Wildlife Resources: An Overview of the Endangered Species Act of 1973*, 51 N.D. L. Rev. 315, 321 (1975).]

The legislative proceedings in 1973 are, in fact, replete with expressions of concern over the risk that might lie in the loss of *any* endangered species. Typifying these sentiments is the Report of the House Committee on Merchant Marine and Fisheries on H.R. 37, a bill which contained the essential features of the subsequently enacted Act of 1973; in explaining the need for the legislation, the Report stated:

"As we homogenize the habitats in which these plants and animals evolved, and as we increase the pressure for products that they are in a position to supply (usually unwillingly) we threaten their—and our own—genetic heritage.

"The value of this genetic heritage is, quite literally, incalculable. * * *

"From the most narrow possible point of view, *it is in the best interests of mankind to minimize the losses of genetic variations.* The reason is simple: they are potential resources. They are keys to puzzles which we cannot solve, and may provide answers to questions which we have not yet learned to ask.

"To take a homely, but apt, example: one of the critical chemicals in the regulation of ovulations in humans was found in a common plant. Once discovered, and analyzed, humans could duplicate it synthetically, but had it never existed—or had it been driven out of existence before we knew its potentialities—we would never have tried to synthesize it in the first place.

"Who knows, or can say, what potential cures for <u>cancer</u> or other scourges, present or future, may lie locked up in the structures of plants which may yet be undiscovered, much less analyzed? . . . Sheer self-interest impels us to be cautious.

"*The institutionalization of that caution* lies at the heart of H.R. 37. . . ." H.R. Rep. No.93–412, pp. 4–5 (1973). (Emphasis added.)

As the examples cited here demonstrate, Congress was concerned about the *unknown* uses that endangered species might have and about the *unforeseeable* place such creatures may have in the chain of life on this planet.

In shaping legislation to deal with the problem thus presented, Congress started from the finding that "[t]he two major causes of extinction are hunting and destruction of natural habitat." S. Rep. No. 93–307, p. 2 (1973). Of these twin threats, Congress was informed that the greatest was destruction of natural habitats; see 1973 House Hearings 236 (statement of Associate Deputy Chief for National Forest System, Dept. of Agriculture); *id.,* at 241 (statement of Director of Mich. Dept. of Natural Resources); [et al.]. Witnesses recommended, among other things, that Congress require all land-managing agencies "to avoid damaging critical habitat for endangered species and to take positive steps to improve such habitat." 1973 House Hearings 241 (statement of Director of Mich. Dept. of Natural Resources). Virtually every bill introduced in Congress during the 1973 session responded to this concern by incorporating language similar, if not identical, to that found in the present § 7 of the Act. These provisions were designed, in the words of an administration witness, "for the first time [to] *prohibit* [a] federal agency from taking action which does jeopardize the status of endangered species," Hearings on S. 1592 and S. 1983 before the Subcommittee on Environment of the Senate Committee on Commerce, 93d Cong., 1st Sess., 68 (1973) (statement of Deputy Assistant Secretary of the Interior) (emphasis added); furthermore, the proposed bills would "*direc[t]* all . . . Federal agencies to utilize their authorities for carrying out programs *for the protection* of endangered animals." 1973 House Hearings 205 (statement of Assistant Secretary of the Interior). (Emphasis added.)

As it was finally passed, the Endangered Species Act of 1973 represented the most comprehensive legislation for the preservation of endangered species ever enacted by any nation. Its stated purposes were "to provide a means whereby the ecosystems upon which endangered species and threatened species depend may be conserved," and "to provide a program for the conservation of such . . . species. . . ." 16 U.S.C. § 1531(b) (1976 ed.). In furtherance of these goals, Congress expressly stated in § 2(c) that "all Federal departments and agencies *shall* seek *to conserve endangered species* and threatened species. . . ." 16 U.S.C. § 1531(c) (1976 ed.). (Emphasis added.) Lest there be any ambiguity as to the meaning of this statutory directive, the Act specifically defined "conserve" as meaning "to use and the use of *all methods and procedures which are necessary* to bring *any endangered species or threatened species* to the point at which the measures provided pursuant to this chapter are no longer necessary." § 1532(2). (Emphasis added.) Aside from § 7, other provisions indicated the seriousness with which Congress viewed this issue: Virtually all dealings with endangered species, including taking, possession, transportation, and sale, were prohibited, 16 U.S.C. § 1538 (1976 ed.), except in extremely narrow circumstances, see § 1539(b). The Secretary was also given extensive power to develop regulations and programs for the preservation of endangered and threatened species.§ 1533(d). Citizen involvement was encouraged by the Act, with provisions allowing interested persons to petition the Secretary to list a species as endangered or threatened, § 1533(c)(2), and bring civil suits in United States district courts to force compliance with any provision of the Act, §§ 1540(c) and (g).

Section 7 of the Act * * * provides a particularly good gauge of congressional intent. As we have seen, this provision had its genesis in the Endangered Species Act of 1966, but that legislation qualified the obligation of federal agencies by stating that they should seek to preserve endangered species only "*insofar as is practicable and consistent with the[ir] primary purposes. . . .*" Likewise, every bill introduced in 1973 contained a qualification similar to that found in the earlier statutes. * * *

This type of language did not go unnoticed by those advocating strong endangered species legislation. A representative of the Sierra Club, for example, attacked the use of the phrase "consistent with the primary purpose" in proposed H.R. 4758, cautioning that the qualification "could be construed to be a declaration of congressional policy that other agency purposes are necessarily more important than protection of endangered species and would always prevail if conflict were to occur."

What is very significant in this sequence is that the final version of the 1973 Act carefully omitted all of the reservations described above. [The Senate bill contained a practicability reservation; the House bill had no qualifications. The Conference Committee rejected the Senate version of § 7 and adopted the House language. Explaining the Conference action, Representative Dingell pointed out that under existing law the Secretary of Defense has discretion to ignore dangers its bombing missions posed to the near-extinct whooping crane. "[O]nce the bill is enacted, [the Secretary of Defense] *would be required to take the proper steps*." Another example was the declining population of grizzly bears, whose habitats would have to be protected by the Department of Agriculture. "The purposes of the bill included the conservation of the species and of the ecosystems upon which they depend, and every agency of government is committed to see that those purposes are carried out. * * * [T]he agencies of Government can no longer plead that they can do nothing about it. *They can and they must. The law is clear.*" 119 Cong. Rec. 42913 (1973) (emphasis added by the Chief Justice).]

It is against this legislative background that we must measure TVA's claim that the Act was not intended to stop operation of a project which, like Tellico Dam, was near completion when an endangered species was discovered in its path. While there is no discussion in the legislative history of precisely this problem, the totality of congressional action makes it abundantly clear that the result we reach today is wholly in accord with both the words of the statute and the intent of Congress. The plain intent of Congress in enacting this statute was to halt and reverse the trend toward species extinction, whatever the cost. This is reflected not only in the stated policies of the Act, but in literally every section of the statute. All persons, including federal agencies, are specifically instructed not to "take" endangered species, meaning that no one is "to harass, harm, pursue, hunt, shoot, wound, kill, trap, capture, or collect" such life forms. 16 U.S.C. §§ 1532(14), 1538(a)(1)(B) (1976 ed.). * * *

Furthermore, it is clear Congress foresaw that § 7 would, on occasion, require agencies to alter ongoing projects in order to fulfill the goals of the Act. Congressman Dingell's discussion of Air Force practice bombing, for instance, obviously pinpoints a particular activity—intimately related to the national defense—which a major federal department would be obliged to alter in deference to the strictures of § 7. A similar example is provided by the House Committee Report:

> "Under the authority of [§ 7], the Director of the Park Service would be required *to conform the practices of his agency* to the need for protecting the rapidly dwindling stock of grizzly bears within Yellowstone Park. These bears, which may be endangered, and are undeniably threatened, should at least be protected by supplying them with carcasses from excess elk within the park, *by curtailing the destruction of habitat by clearcutting National Forests surrounding the Park*, and by preventing hunting until their numbers have recovered sufficiently to withstand these pressures." H.R. Rep. No.93–412, p. 14 (1973). (Emphasis added.)

One might dispute the applicability of these examples to the Tellico Dam by saying that in this case the burden on the public through the loss of millions of unrecoverable dollars would greatly outweigh the loss of the snail darter. But neither the Endangered Species Act nor Art. III of the Constitution provides federal courts with authority to make such fine utilitarian calculations. On the contrary, the plain language of the Act, buttressed by its legislative history, shows clearly that Congress viewed the value of endangered species as "incalculable." Quite obviously, it would be difficult for a court to balance the loss of a sum certain—even $100 million—against a congressionally declared "incalculable" value, even assuming we had the power to engage in such a weighing process, which we emphatically do not.

[TVA also argued that Congress's continued funding of the Tellico Dam reflected a congressional judgment, embodied in appropriations statutes, that the dam not be shut down. Appropriations committees were aware of the effect of the dam on the snail darter.] There is nothing in the appropriations measures, as passed, which states that the Tellico Project was to be completed irrespective of the requirements of the Endangered Species Act. * * * To find a repeal of the Endangered Species Act under these circumstances would surely do violence to the " 'cardinal rule . . . that repeals by implication are not favored.' " *Morton v. Mancari*, 417 U.S. 535, 549 (1974), quoting *Posadas v. National City Bank*, 296 U.S. 497, 503 (1936). * * *

The doctrine disfavoring repeals by implication "applies with full vigor when . . . the subsequent legislation is an *appropriations* measure." *Committee for Nuclear Responsibility v. Seaborg*, 463 F.2d 783, 785 (D.C. Cir. 1971). This is perhaps an understatement since it would be more accurate to say that the policy applies with even *greater* force when the claimed repeal rests solely on an Appropriations Act. * * * When voting on appropriations measures, legislators are entitled to operate under the assumption that the funds will be devoted to purposes which are lawful and not for any purpose forbidden. [The Chief Justice also pointed to House Rule XX(2), which forbids amendments to appropriations bills which seeks to "chang[e] existing law." See also Senate Rule XVI(4).] Thus, to sustain petitioner's position, we would be obliged to assume that Congress meant to repeal *pro tanto* § 7 of the Act by means of a procedure expressly prohibited under the rules of Congress.

[Chief Justice Burger rejected TVA's urging the Court to balance the harms of shutting down the dam against the dangers to the snail darter. Not only did the Court not consider itself competent to calibrate such a balance, but Congress had already made the judgment that no cost was too high to allow the federal government to imperil a species.] [I]n our constitutional system the commitment to the separation of powers is too fundamental for us to pre-empt congressional action by judicially decreeing what accords with "common sense and the public weal." Our Constitution vests such responsibilities in the political branches.

JUSTICE POWELL, joined by JUSTICE BLACKMUN, dissenting. * * *

In my view § 7 cannot reasonably be interpreted as applying to a project that is completed or substantially completed when its threat to an endangered species is discovered. Nor can I believe that Congress could have intended this Act to produce the "absurd result"—in the words of the District Court—of this case. If it were clear from the language of the Act and its legislative history that Congress intended to authorize this result, this Court would be compelled to enforce it. It is not our province to rectify policy or political judgments by the Legislative Branch, however egregiously they may disserve the public interest. But where the statutory language and legislative history, as in this case, need not be construed to reach such a result, I view it as the duty of this Court to adopt a permissible construction that accords with some modicum of common sense and the public weal. * * *

[After securing congressional appropriations in 1966, construction of the Tellico Dam] began in 1967, and Congress has voted funds for the project in every year since. In August 1973, when the Tellico Project was half completed, a new species of fish known as the snail darter was discovered in the portion of the Little Tennessee River that would be impounded behind Tellico Dam. The Endangered Species Act was passed the following December. More than a year later, in January 1975, respondents joined others in petitioning the Secretary of the Interior to list the snail darter as an endangered species. On November 10, 1975, when the Tellico Project was 75% completed, the Secretary placed the snail darter on the endangered list and concluded that the "proposed impoundment of water behind the proposed Tellico Dam would result in total destruction of the snail darter's habitat." 40 Fed. Reg. 47506 (1975).

In respondents' view, the Secretary's action meant that completion of the Tellico Project would violate § 7 of the Act. * * * TVA nevertheless determined to continue with the Tellico Project in accordance with the prior authorization by Congress. In February 1976, respondents filed the instant suit to enjoin its completion. By that time the Project was 80% completed.

In March 1976, TVA informed the House and Senate Appropriations Committees about the Project's threat to the snail darter and about respondents' lawsuit. Both Committees were advised that TVA was attempting to preserve the fish by relocating them in the Hiwassee River, which closely resembles the Little Tennessee. It stated explicitly, however, that the success of those efforts could not be guaranteed. * * *

In 1975, 1976, and 1977, Congress, with full knowledge of the Tellico Project's effect on the snail darter and the alleged violation of the Endangered Species Act, continued to appropriate money for the completion of the Project. In doing so, the Appropriations Committees expressly stated that the Act did not prohibit the Project's completion, a view that Congress presumably accepted in approving the appropriations each year. For example, in June 1976, the Senate Committee on Appropriations released a report noting the District Court decision and recommending approval of TVA's full budget request for the Tellico Project. The Committee observed further that it did "not view the Endangered Species Act as prohibiting the completion of the Tellico project at its advanced stage," and it directed "that this project be completed as promptly as possible in the public interest." The appropriations bill was passed by Congress and approved by the President. [Nonetheless, the Sixth Circuit affirmed the district court's injunction against completing the dam.]

In June 1977, and after being informed of the decision of the Court of Appeals, the Appropriations Committees in both Houses of Congress again recommended approval of TVA's full budget request for the Tellico Project. Both Committees again stated unequivocally that the Endangered Species Act was not intended to halt projects at an advanced stage of completion:

> "[The Senate] Committee has not viewed the Endangered Species Act as preventing the completion and use of these projects which were well under way at the time the affected species were listed as endangered. If the act has such an effect, which is contrary to the Committee's understanding of the intent of Congress in enacting the Endangered Species Act, funds should be appropriated to allow these projects to be completed and their benefits realized in the public interest, the Endangered Species Act notwithstanding." [S. Rep. No.95–301, p. 99 (1977).]

"It is the [House] Committee's view that the Endangered Species Act was not intended to halt projects such as these in their advanced stage of completion, and [the Committee] strongly recommends that these projects not be stopped because of misuse of the Act." [H.R. Rep. No.95–379, p. 104 (1977).]

Once again, the appropriations bill was passed by both Houses and signed into law.

[II] Today the Court, like the Court of Appeals below, adopts a reading of § 7 of the Act that gives it a retroactive effect and disregards 12 years of consistently expressed congressional intent to complete the Tellico Project. With all due respect, I view this result as an extreme example of a literalist construction, not required by the language of the Act and adopted without regard to its manifest purpose. [Citing *Holy Trinity Church*, Justice Powell contended that the Court ought not read the broad language of § 7 so sweepingly and, instead, ought to narrow the language so as to avoid "absurd results." He would have construed the "actions" governed by § 7 to be only those taken *after* 1973, when the statute was enacted.]

If the relevant Committees that considered the Act, and the Members of Congress who voted on it, had been aware that the Act could be used to terminate major federal projects authorized years earlier and nearly completed, or to require the abandonment of essential and long-completed federal installations and edifices,[18] we can be certain that there would have been hearings, testimony, and debate concerning consequences so wasteful, so inimical to purposes previously deemed important, and so likely to arouse public outrage. The absence of any such consideration by the Committees or in the floor debates indicates quite clearly that no one participating in the legislative process considered these consequences as within the intendment of the Act.

[T]his view of legislative intent at the time of enactment is abundantly confirmed by the subsequent congressional actions and expressions. We have held, properly, that post-enactment statements by individual Members of Congress as to the meaning of a statute are entitled to little or no weight. The Court also has recognized that subsequent Appropriations Acts themselves are not necessarily entitled to significant weight in determining whether a prior statute has been

---

[18] The initial proposed rulemaking under the Act made it quite clear that such an interpretation was not intended: "Neither [the Fish and Wildlife Service of the Department of the Interior] nor [the National Marine Fisheries Service of the Department of Commerce] intends that section 7 bring about the waste that can occur if an advanced project is halted. . . . The affected agency must decide whether the degree of completion and extent of public funding of particular projects justify an action that may be otherwise inconsistent with section 7." 42 Fed.Reg. 4869 (1977).After the decision of the Court of Appeals in this case, however, the quoted language was withdrawn, and the agencies adopted the view of the court. 43 Fed. Reg. 870, 872, 875 (1978).

superseded. But these precedents are inapposite. There was no effort here to "bootstrap" a post-enactment view of prior legislation by isolated statements of individual Congressmen. Nor is this a case where Congress, without explanation or comment upon the statute in question, merely has voted apparently inconsistent financial support in subsequent Appropriations Acts. Testimony on this precise issue was presented before congressional committees, and the Committee Reports for three consecutive years addressed the problem and affirmed their understanding of the original congressional intent. We cannot assume—as the Court suggests—that Congress, when it continued each year to approve the recommended appropriations, was unaware of the contents of the supporting Committee Reports. All this amounts to strong corroborative evidence that the interpretation of § 7 as not applying to completed or substantially completed projects reflects the initial legislative intent.

[III] I have little doubt that Congress will amend the Endangered Species Act to prevent the grave consequences made possible by today's decision. Few, if any, Members of that body will wish to defend an interpretation of the Act that requires the waste of at least $53 million, and denies the people of the Tennessee Valley area the benefits of the reservoir that Congress intended to confer. There will be little sentiment to leave this dam standing before an empty reservoir, serving no purpose other than a conversation piece for incredulous tourists.

[JUSTICE REHNQUIST dissented on the ground that the legitimate debate over the statute's meaning properly informed the district court's decision not to enjoin work on the dam.]

NOTES AND QUESTIONS ON TVA V. HILL

1. *The Supreme Court's Revival of the (Soft) Plain Meaning Rule, 1976–1986.* Although most commentators of the Burger Court's statutory opinions assumed that the Court was no more interested in the plain meaning rule than the Warren Court had been, one commentator astutely observed that *Hill*'s plain meaning rule was more characteristic of the Burger Court's statutory interpretation than the legal process approach was. See Richard Pildes, Note, *Intent, Clear Statements and the Common Law: Statutory Interpretation in the Supreme Court*, 95 Harv. L. Rev. 892 (1982). To be sure, the Burger Court followed a rather "soft" version of the plain meaning rule, for it typically (as it did in *Hill*) focused on text but attempted to justify harsh textual results by using legislative history and statutory purposes to back them up. E.g., *CPSC v. GTE Sylvania*, 447 U.S. 102 (1980).

Justice Powell's dissenting opinion suggests that there is no single plain meaning when the literal meaning is so unreasonable. The Court seems to concede that possibility, by checking the legislative history to make sure its reading is not unreasonable in light of the statutory purposes. Plain meaning analysis does not necessarily stop with ordinary meaning. See Miranda McGowan, *Do as I Do, Not as I Say: An Empirical Investigation of Justice Scalia's Ordinary Meaning Method of Statutory Interpretation,* 78 Miss. L.J. 129 (2008). A statute may have a "plain meaning" that would be unavailable to ordinary readers when legal authorities impose a specialized meaning on a term or phrase. Thus, "plain meaning" might be different from an ordinary meaning when (a) Congress has defined the term in the statute; or (b) the term has been authoritatively construed by the Court, or perhaps even just by the specialized community to which the statute applies (or experts testifying about that); or (c) the ordinary meaning is inconsistent with the whole act or with the way Congress has used the term in other statutes. But see Gluck & Bressman, *Statutory Interpretation from the Inside* (arguing that the presumption against consistent usage does not reflect how Congress drafts and should be retired).

2.   *The Legislative Response to* TVA v. Hill. This case pitted the tiny snail darter against a nearly completed 100-million-dollar federal project—and the little fish won. Why would the Court do this? It seems likely that the Court thought Congress was the more institutionally appropriate actor to make this fix. All nine Justices apparently believed that Congress would override the majority's interpretation—partly because they were aware of override legislation swiftly moving through the legislative process at the same time they were deciding the case. And both majority and dissenting opinions explicitly called for a congressional override, invitations that are very highly correlated with legislative responses, according to Matthew R. Christiansen & William N. Eskridge Jr., *Congressional Overrides of Supreme Court Statutory Interpretation Decisions, 1967–2011,* 92 Tex. L. Rev. 1317 (2014). The decision, indeed, provoked an immediate legislative response. Congress overrode *TVA v. Hill* not just once, but twice, within a few years of the Court's decision.

One concern expressed in Chief Justice Burger's opinion for the Court is that any cost-benefit exemption to § 7 that the Court might have created (and that Justice Powell favored) would have been hard to administer by lower courts and would have engaged the judiciary in the kind of policy balancing that is better left to administrators. Congress's first response to *TVA v. Hill* reflected this institutional concern. The Endangered Species Act (ESA) Amendments of 1978, Pub. L. No. 95–632, § 7, 92 Stat. 3751, 3752–60 (1978), established an administrative mechanism for granting exemptions to the Act. Surprisingly, the inter-agency committee established by the 1978 Amendments refused to exempt the Tellico Dam—revealing the complexity of the policy balancing entailed in such a judgment. Pressed by the Tennessee delegation, Congress then exempted the dam specifically in Pub. L. No. 96–69, tit. IV, 93 Stat. 437, 449 (1979). For an analysis of the complicated politics of the override process in this case, and the way it intertwined with the litigation process, see Elizabeth Garrett, *The Story of* TVA v. Hill (1978): *Congress Has the Last Word,* in *Statutory Interpretation Stories* 58–91 (Eskridge, Frickey & Garrett eds. 2011).

3. *The Special Context of Appropriations.* Less institutionally realist was the Court's failure to fully grasp the significance of the fact that the purported conflict in the case involved a conflict between the ESA, on the one hand, and an appropriations statute, on the other. The *TVA* Court invoked a familiar canon, the notion that "repeals by implication are not favored," for the proposition that courts should not assume that Congress is aware of every detail buried in statutes and so should not assume that later-enacted legislation repeals earlier legislation (as would the appropriations for the dam effectively repeal the ESA with respect to the snail darter) unless Congress expressly says so. Professor Nourse has argued that this argument misunderstands how Congress works: everyone knows the money is the most important thing and everyone pays attention to where the money goes. See Nourse, *A Decision Theory of Statutory Interpretation: Legislative History by the Rules*, 122 Yale L.J. 70, 131–34 (2012).

In a portion of the opinion that we did not excerpt the Court also placed a lot of weight on the idea that the only express reference to continuing the dam project in the appropriations bill was in the *legislative history* and not in the statutory text. This, too, reveals a misunderstanding of how Congress really works. As two of us have illustrated in recent work, appropriations legislation is different from other types of legislation. First, as Nourse has shown, the House and Senate Rules bar any type of substantive language from appropriations bills; the idea is that the regulatory committees pass the substantive legislation and the appropriators simply give out the money, but do not change the laws. Thus, appropriations bills look different from ordinary legislation—they are often just a list of numbers, like this one:

H. R. 5973
June 20, 2012

Be it enacted by the Senate and House of Representatives of the United States of America in Congress assembled, That the following sums are appropriated, out of any money in the Treasury not otherwise appropriated, for Agriculture, Rural Development, Food and Drug Administration, and Related Agencies programs for fiscal year ending September 30, 2013, and for other purposes, namely:

TITLE I
AGRICULTURAL PROGRAMS

For necessary expenses of the Office of the Secretary, $89,632,000, of which not to exceed $2,959,000 shall be available for the immediate Office of the Secretary; not to exceed $439,000 shall be available for the Office of Tribal Relations; not to exceed $12,584,000 shall be available for the National Appeals Division; not to exceed $1,295,000 shall be available for the Office of Homeland Security and Emergency Coordination; not to exceed $1,185,000 shall be available for the Office of Advocacy and Outreach; not to exceed $17,867,000 shall be available for the Office of the Assistant Secretary for Administration, of which $17,118,000 shall be available for Departmental Administration to provide for necessary expenses for management support services to offices of the Department and for general administration, security, repairs and alterations, and other miscellaneous supplies and expenses not otherwise provided for and necessary for the practical and efficient work of the Department* * * *

As a result, the only place to put authorizing-type language is in the legislative history. Professors Gluck and Bressman's empirical work substantiates this claim; the majority of congressional counsels they interviewed told them that appropriations legislative history is unique and more important than non-appropriations legislative history because it explains how the money is to be spent. *See* Abbe R. Gluck & Lisa Schultz Bressman, *Statutory Interpretation from the Inside—An Empirical Study of Congressional Drafting, Delegation, and the Canons, Part I,* 65 Stan. L. Rev. 901, 980 (2013); Gluck & Bressman, *Statutory Interpretation from the Inside, Part II,* 66 Stan. L. Rev. 725, 760-69 (2014). In the context of *TVA,* this means that the legislative history was the only place possible to put a statement of Congressional intent about the dam. The only other option would have been to call up the entire Endangered Species Act for separate amendment; a wholly unrealistic proposition that would have been entirely separate from the appropriations process in any event.

How do you read *TVA v. Hill* in light of these real-world facts about appropriations? Is it possible the Court was trying to enforce the intended division between authorizing legislation and appropriations—maybe it wasn't going to let the Appropriations Committee get away with trying to do something "legislative" by funding the dam? We tend to believe the Court was simply unaware of these details of the legislative process. Apparently, the majority and dissenting Justices were also unaware that Congress enacted an appropriations statute that provided TVA with up to $2,000,000 "to relocate endangered or threatened species to other suitable habitats as may be necessary to expedite project construction." Pub. Law No. 95–96, tit. IV, 91 Stat. 797, 808 (1977). Does this statute strengthen Justice Powell's analysis and provide him with a response to the majority's opinion dismissing his legislative history? Does the statute change your mind about the proper resolution of this statutory question?

B. THE NEW TEXTUALISM

In the 1980s, a group of judges and executive officials developed a more constrained version of the plain meaning rule than that followed in cases like *TVA v. Hill.* For example, Judge Frank Easterbrook maintained in *Legal Interpretation and the Power of the Judiciary,* 7 Harv. J.L. & Pub. Pol'y 87 (1984), that courts interpreting statutes have no business figuring out "legislative intent," in part because there is no such thing in a complex body of 535 elected representatives. Judge Antonin Scalia delivered a series of speeches in 1985–86, urging courts to abandon virtually any reference to legislative history, especially the committee reports referred to in *TVA v. Hill.* The Department of Justice's Office of Legal Policy endorsed and developed these views in a document drafted by Stephen Markman, *Using and Misusing Legislative History: A Re-Evaluation of the Status of Legislative History in Statutory Interpretation* (1989) (excerpted in Chapter 6, § 1).

What we call "the new textualism"[5] is an approach to statutory interpretation developed by these judges and scholars. Although its proponents draw from legal process theory for their own purposes, their approach to statutory interpretation differs from that supported by Professors Hart, Sacks, and Fuller. Also, new textualist construction is different from the "soft" plain meaning rule of *TVA v. Hill*, as suggested by the readings and cases that follow.

Antonin Scalia, *A Matter of Interpretation: Federal Courts and the Law*
Summary and Selected Quotations (1997).

In this published version of his Tanner Lectures delivered at Princeton University, Justice Antonin Scalia presents his textualist philosophy of legal interpretation. He contends that law students (brainwashed by the first-year indoctrination in common-law methodology) and law professors (who do the brainwashing) tend to approach statutory interpretation as an exercise in applying legal authorities to new factual settings in a manner which yields both a fair result in the case and works toward a just and efficient general rule. Such an equitable common-law approach is not appropriate for construing statutes in a democracy, Justice Scalia argues, because it is fundamentally anti-democratic (pp. 9–14). A theme of the Tanner Lectures is that the common law has its place, but in a democracy it is more important that judges be constrained by, and held to, the legislatively enacted statutory law, than that they do "justice" in the individual case.

Should the lodestar for statutory interpretation, then, be legislative *intent*? Most assuredly not! "It is the *law* that governs, not the intent of the lawgiver. That seems to me the essence of the famous American ideal set forth in the Massachusetts constitution: A government of laws, not of men. Men may intend what they will; but it is only the laws that they

---

[5]   See William N. Eskridge Jr., *The New Textualism*, 37 UCLA L. Rev. 621 (1990); Jonathan Molot, *The Rise and Fall of Textualism*, 106 Colum. L. Rev. 1 (2006); Nicholas Zeppos, *Justice Scalia's Textualism and: The "New" New Legal Process*, 12 Cardozo L. Rev. 1597 (1991). For a short overview placing textualism in context with prior theories, see Philip P. Frickey, *From the Big Sleep to the Big Heat: The Revival of Theory in Statutory Interpretation*, 77 Minn. L. Rev. 241 (1992).

enact which bind us" (p. 17). Indeed, Justice Scalia argues that judges following a legislative-intent approach usually end up finding their own preferences in the statute, because "your best shot at figuring out what the legislature meant is to ask yourself what a wise and intelligent person *should* have meant; and that will surely bring you to the conclusion that the law means what you think it *ought* to mean—which is precisely how judges decide things under the common law" (p. 18). Note the implicit criticism of Hart and Sacks's purpose-based theory.

Justice Scalia then applies this critique to *Holy Trinity Church*. The Court interpreted the alien contract law contrary to its plain meaning because the Justices believed it inconsistent with legislative intent and purpose. Justice Scalia finds such an approach no more than invalid judicial lawmaking, although he would allow courts to correct scrivener's errors. "Well of course I think that the act was within the letter of the statute, and was therefore within the statute: end of case" (p. 20). "The text is the law, and it is the text which must be observed" (p. 22), says the author, citing Justice Holmes.

The apparent plain meaning of a statutory text must be the alpha and the omega in a judge's interpretation of a statute. The apparent plain meaning is that which an ordinary speaker of the English language—twin sibling to the common law's reasonable person—would draw from the statutory text. That is what textualism *is*. What it is *not*, according to Justice Scalia, is either "strict constructionism" (p. 23), which gives statutory words their stingiest ambit, nor "nihilism" (p. 24), which reads words to mean anything and everything. "A text should not be construed strictly, and it should not be construed leniently; it should be construed reasonably, to contain all that it fairly means" (p. 23). Justice Scalia also does not shy away from formalism. "Besides being accused of being simple-minded, textualism is often accused of being 'formalistic,' he writes. "The answer to that is, *of course it's formalistic!* The rule of law is *about* form" (p. 25).

Nor is textualism canonical, maintains Justice Scalia. The Tanner Lectures are skeptical of "presumptions and rules of construction that load the dice for or against a particular result" (p. 27), because they "increase the unpredictability, if not the arbitrariness of judicial decisions" (p. 28). "To the honest textualist, all of these preferential rules and presumptions are a lot of trouble," says Scalia (p. 28).

Doctrinally, the most distinctive feature of Justice Scalia's legisprudence is an insistence that judges should almost never consult, and never rely on, the legislative history of a statute (pp. 29–37). Consistent with his concurring opinion in *Bock Laundry*, *infra*, the Tanner Lectures identify several kinds of reasons for rejecting the relevance of legislative history. First, to the extent that legislative history is mined to determine legislative "intent," it must be rejected as a matter of constitutional principle. Legislative intent is not the proper goal for the statutory interpreter. This is a corollary of the rule of law: law must be objective and impersonal (the "government of laws"), not subjective and intentional ("and not of men").

Even if intent were a proper criterion and it were constitutional to consider the views of legislative subgroups, the debating history preceding statutory enactment would not be reliable evidence of such intent. For most issues, there was no collective understanding; if there were such an understanding, public statements would often point in different directions, as some representatives would find it in their interest to plant misleading evidence. Indeed, the more courts have relied on legislative history, the less reliable it has become! "In earlier days, it was at least genuine and not contrived—a real part of the legislation's *history*, in the sense that it was part of the *development* of the bill, part of the attempt to inform and persuade those who voted. Nowadays, however, when it is universally known and expected that judges will resort to floor debates and (especially) committee reports as authoritative expressions of 'legislative intent,' affecting the courts rather than informing the Congress has become the primary purpose of the exercise" (p. 34).

Justice Scalia also claims that legislators themselves do not read the committee reports (pp. 32–33). Critics respond that legislators do not read the statutes they enact, either. Justice Scalia replies that the claim to authority of the two sources is different: a committee report's (supposed) authority is bottomed on its being evidence of intent about the law, and so knowledge about its contents would seem critical; the statutory text, on the other hand, is law itself, whether or not anyone read or understood it before enactment (pp. 34–35).

In response to this reply, critics say that committee reports are authoritative evidence because of conventions by which Congress has delegated most of the detail work to committees, with the implication being that the committee product is presumptively the work of Congress. Unconstitutional!—Says Justice Scalia.[6] "The legislative power is the power to make laws, not the power to make legislators. It is nondelegable. Congress can no more authorize one committee to 'fill in the details' of a particular law in a binding fashion than it can authorize a committee to enact minor laws. * * * That is the very essence of the separation of powers [and Article I, Section 7, requiring bicameral approval and

---

[6] The following argument is supported and elaborated in detail by John F. Manning, *Textualism as a Nondelegation Doctrine*, 97 Colum. L. Rev. 673 (1997). But see Peter Strauss, *The Courts and the Congress: Should Judges Disdain Political History?*, 98 Colum. L. Rev. 242 (1998) (disagreeing with Manning and arguing in favor of the use of legislative history, particularly to discern statutory purpose). More broadly, Professor Strauss has contended that our common-law system legitimates judicial interpretive methods that range beyond textualism. See Peter Strauss, *The Common Law and Statutes*, 70 U. Colo. L. Rev. 225 (1999).

presentment to the President]. The only conceivable basis for considering committee reports authoritative, therefore, is that they are a genuine indication of the will of the entire house—which, as I have been at pains to explain, they assuredly are not" (p. 35).

Earlier scholars had called for courts to consider legislative history, so that judges might be constrained by the legislators' preferences. This was a laudable impulse, Justice Scalia concedes, but it has not worked. Legislative history has augmented rather than ameliorated the discretion of the willful judge, and this is Justice Scalia's third major quarrel with the use of legislative history. "In any major piece of legislation, the legislative history is extensive, and there is something for everybody. As Judge Harold Leventhal used to say, the trick is to look over the heads of the crowd and pick out your friends" (p. 36).

STATUTORY PREFACE FOR *GREEN V. BOCK LAUNDRY*

The Federal Rules of Evidence (P.L. 93–595 (1975))

Rule 102.   Purpose and Construction.

These Rules shall be construed to secure fairness and administration, elimination of unjustifiable expense and delay, and promotion of growth and development of the law of evidence to the end that the truth may be ascertained and proceedings justly determined.

Rule 402.   Relevant Evidence Generally Admissible; Irrelevant Evidence Inadmissible.

All relevant evidence is admissible, except as otherwise provided by the Constitution of the United States, by Act of Congress, by these Rules, or by other Rules prescribed by the Supreme Court pursuant to statutory authority. Evidence which is not relevant is not admissible.

Rule 403.   Exclusion of Relevant Evidence on Grounds of Prejudice, Confusion, or Waste of Time

Although relevant, evidence may be excluded if its probative value is substantially outweighed by the danger of unfair prejudice, confusion of the issues, or misleading the jury, or by considerations of undue delay, waste of time, or needless presentation of cumulative evidence.

Rule 404.   Character Evidence Generally Not Admissible to Prove Conduct; Exceptions; Other Crimes * * *

(b) Other Crimes, Wrongs, or Acts.—Evidence of other crimes, wrongs, or acts is not admissible to prove the character of a person in order to show that he acted in conformity therewith. It may, however, be admissible for other purposes, such as proof of motive, opportunity, intent, preparation, plan, knowledge, identity, or absence of mistake or accident.

Rule 609.   Impeachment by Evidence of Conviction of Crime.

(a) General Rule.—For the purpose of attacking the credibility of a witness, evidence that the witness has been convicted of a crime shall be admitted if elicited from the witness or established by public record during cross-examination but only if the crime (1) was punishable by death or imprisonment in excess of one year under the law under which the witness was convicted, and the court determines that the probative value of admitting this evidence outweighs its prejudicial effect to the defendant, or (2) involved dishonesty or false statement, regardless of the punishment.

(b) Time Limit.—Evidence of a conviction under this Rule is not admissible if a period of more than ten years has elapsed since the date of conviction or of the release of the witness from the confinement imposed for that conviction, whichever is the later date, unless the court determines, in the interests of justice, that the probative value of the conviction supported by specific facts and circumstances substantially outweighs its prejudicial effect. * * *

PAUL GREEN v. BOCK LAUNDRY MACHINE COMPANY

Supreme Court of the United States, 1989.
490 U.S. 504, 109 S.Ct. 1981, 104 L.Ed.2d 557.

JUSTICE STEVENS delivered the opinion of the Court.

[Paul Green, a county prisoner working at a car wash on a work-release program, reached inside a large dryer to stop it and had his arm torn off. At trial in his product liability action against the machine's manufacturer, he testified that he had been inadequately instructed about the machine's operation and dangerousness. Green admitted that he had been convicted of burglary and of conspiracy to commit burglary, both felonies, and those convictions were used by defendant to impeach his credibility. The jury returned a verdict for Bock Laundry. The Court of Appeals affirmed, rejecting Green's argument that the district court erred by denying his pretrial motion to exclude the impeaching evidence.]

[Criticism of automatic admissibility of prior felony convictions to impeach civil witnesses, particularly civil plaintiffs, has been "longstanding and widespread."] Our task in deciding this case, however, is not to fashion the rule we deem desirable but to identify the rule that Congress fashioned. * * *

[I]   Federal Rule of Evidence 609(a) provides:

"General Rule. For the purpose of attacking the credibility of a witness, evidence that the witness has been convicted of a crime shall be admitted if elicited from the witness or established by public record during cross-examination but only if the crime (1) was punishable by death or imprisonment in excess of one year under the law under which the witness was convicted, and the court determines that the probative value of admitting this evidence outweighs its prejudicial effect to the defendant, or (2) involved dishonesty or false statement, regardless of the punishment."

By its terms the Rule requires a judge to allow impeachment of any witness with prior convictions for felonies not involving dishonesty "only if" the probativeness of the evidence is greater than its prejudice "to the defendant." It follows that impeaching evidence detrimental to the prosecution in a criminal case "shall be admitted" without any such balancing.

The Rule's plain language commands weighing of prejudice to a defendant in a civil trial as well as in a criminal trial. But that literal reading would compel an odd result in a case like this. Assuming that all impeaching evidence has at least minimal probative value, and given that the evidence of plaintiff Green's convictions had some prejudicial effect on his case—but surely none on defendant Bock's—balancing according to the strict language of Rule 609(a)(1) inevitably leads to the conclusion that the evidence was admissible. In fact, under this construction of the Rule, impeachment detrimental to a civil plaintiff always would have to be admitted.

No matter how plain the text of the Rule may be, we cannot accept an interpretation that would deny a civil plaintiff the same right to impeach an adversary's testimony that it grants to a civil defendant. The Sixth Amendment to the Constitution guarantees a criminal defendant certain fair trial rights not enjoyed by the prosecution, while the Fifth Amendment lets the accused choose not to testify at trial. In contrast, civil litigants in federal court share equally the protections of the Fifth Amendment's Due Process Clause. Given liberal federal discovery rules, the inapplicability of the Fifth Amendment's protection against self-incrimination, and the need to prove their case, civil litigants almost always must testify in depositions or at trial. Denomination as a civil defendant or plaintiff, moreover, is often happenstance based on which party filed first or on the nature of the suit. Evidence that a litigant or his witness is a convicted felon tends to shift a jury's focus from the worthiness of the litigant's position to the moral worth of the litigant himself. It is unfathomable why a civil plaintiff—but not a civil defendant—should be subjected to this risk. Thus we agree with the Seventh Circuit that as far as civil trials are concerned, Rule 609(a)(1) "can't mean what it says." *Campbell v. Greer*, 831 F.2d 700, 703 (1987) [Posner, J.].

Out of this agreement flow divergent courses, each turning on the meaning of "defendant." The word might be interpreted to encompass all witnesses, civil and criminal, parties or not. It might be read to connote any party offering a witness, in which event Rule 609(a)(1)'s balance would apply to civil, as well as criminal, cases. Finally, "defendant" may refer only to the defendant in a criminal case. These choices spawn a corollary question: must a judge allow prior felony impeachment of all civil witnesses as well as all criminal prosecution witnesses, or is Rule 609(a)(1) inapplicable to civil cases, in which event Rule 403 would authorize a judge to balance in such cases?* Because the plain text does not resolve these issues, we must examine the history leading to enactment of Rule 609 as law.

[II] At common law a person who had been convicted of a felony was not competent to testify as a witness. "[T]he disqualification arose as part of the punishment for the crime, only later being rationalized on the basis that such a person was unworthy of belief." 3 J. Weinstein & M. Berger, Weinstein's Evidence paragraph 609[02], p. 609–58 (1988). As the law evolved, this absolute bar gradually was replaced by a rule that allowed such witnesses to testify in both civil and criminal cases, but also to be impeached by evidence of a prior felony conviction or a *crimen falsi* misdemeanor conviction. In the face of scholarly criticism of automatic admission of such impeaching evidence, some courts moved toward a more flexible approach.

[The American Law Institute's Model Code of Evidence and the ABA's proposed Uniform Rules of Evidence recommended that trial judges be given discretion to exclude evidence of prior convictions in appropriate circumstances. In 1969, however, the Advisory Committee's proposed Rules of Evidence included Rule 6–09, which allowed all *crimen falsi* and felony convictions evidence without mention of judicial discretion. But the Committee's second draft Rule 609(a)] authorized the judge to exclude either felony or *crimen falsi* evidence upon determination that its probative value was "substantially outweighed by the danger of unfair prejudice." The Committee specified that its primary concern was prejudice to the witness-accused; the "risk of unfair prejudice to a party in the use of [convictions] to impeach the ordinary witness is so minimal as scarcely to be a subject of comment." Yet the text of the proposal was broad enough to allow a judge to protect not only criminal defendants, but also civil litigants and nonparty witnesses, from unfair prejudice.

---

*   *Editors' note*: Rule 403 provides that relevant evidence may be excluded "if its probative value is substantially outweighed by the danger of unfair prejudice, confusion of the issues, or misleading the jury, or by considerations of undue delay, waste of time, or needless presentation of cumulative evidence."

[T]he Advisory Committee's revision of Rule 609(a) met resistance. The Department of Justice urged that the Committee supplant its proposal with the strict, amended version of the District Code. Senator McClellan objected to the adoption of the *Luck* doctrine and urged reinstatement of the earlier draft.

The Advisory Committee backed off. As Senator McClellan had requested, it submitted as its third and final draft the same strict version it had proposed in March 1969. * * * This Court forwarded the Advisory Committee's final draft to Congress on November 20, 1972.

The House of Representatives did not accept the Advisory Committee's final proposal. A Subcommittee of the Judiciary Committee recommended an amended version similar to the text of the present Rule 609(a), except that it avoided the current Rule's ambiguous reference to prejudice to "the defendant." Rather, in prescribing weighing of admissibility of prior felony convictions, it used the same open-ended reference to "unfair prejudice" found in the Advisory Committee's second draft.

The House Judiciary Committee departed even further from the Advisory Committee's final recommendation, preparing a draft that did not allow impeachment by evidence of prior conviction unless the crime involved dishonesty or false statement. Motivating the change were concerns about the deterrent effect upon an accused who might wish to testify and the danger of unfair prejudice, "even upon a witness who was not the accused," from allowing impeachment by prior felony convictions regardless of their relation to the witness' veracity. H.R. Rep. No. 93–650, p. 11 (1973). Although the Committee Report focused on criminal defendants and did not mention civil litigants, its express concerns encompassed all nonaccused witnesses.

Representatives who advocated the automatic admissibility approach of the Advisory Committee's draft and those who favored the intermediate approach proposed by the Subcommittee both opposed the Committee's bill on the House floor. Four Members pointed out that the Rule applied in civil, as well as criminal, cases. The House voted to adopt the Rule as proposed by its Judiciary Committee.

The Senate Judiciary Committee proposed an intermediate path. For criminal defendants, it would have allowed impeachment only by *crimen falsi* evidence; for other witnesses, it also would have permitted prior felony evidence only if the trial judge found that probative value outweighed "prejudicial effect against the party offering that witness." This language thus required the exercise of discretion before prior felony convictions could be admitted in civil litigation. But the full Senate, prodded by Senator McClellan, reverted to the version that the Advisory Committee had submitted. See 120 Cong. Rec. 37076, 37083 (1974).

Conflict between the House bill, allowing impeachment only by *crimen falsi* evidence, and the Senate bill, embodying the Advisory Committee's automatic admissibility approach, was resolved by a Conference Committee. The conferees' compromise—enacted as Federal Rule of Evidence 609(a)(1)—authorizes impeachment by felony convictions, "but only if" the court determines that probative value outweighs "prejudicial effect to the defendant." The Conference Committee's Report makes it perfectly clear that the balance set forth in this draft, unlike the second Advisory Committee and the Senate Judiciary Committee versions, does not protect all nonparty witnesses:

> "The danger of prejudice to a witness other than the defendant (such as injury to the witness' reputation in his community) was considered and rejected by the Conference as an element to be weighed in determining admissibility. It was the judgment of the Conference that the danger of prejudice to a nondefendant witness is outweighed by the need for the trier of fact to have as much relevant evidence on the issue of credibility as possible." H.R. Conf. Rep. No. 93–1597, pp. 9–10 (1974).

Equally clear is the conferees' intention that the rule shield the accused, but not the prosecution, in a criminal case. Impeachment by convictions, the Committee Report stated, "should only be excluded where it presents a danger of improperly influencing the outcome of the trial by persuading the trier of fact to convict the defendant on the basis of his prior criminal record."

But this emphasis on the criminal context, in the Report's use of terms such as "defendant" and "to convict" and in individual conferees' explanations of the compromise,[26] raises some doubt over the Rule's pertinence to civil litigants. The discussions suggest that only two kinds of witnesses risk prejudice—the defendant who elects to testify in a criminal case and witnesses other than the defendant in the same kind of case. Nowhere is it acknowledged that undue prejudice to a civil litigant also may improperly influence a trial's outcome. Although this omission

---

[26] Representative Dennis, who had stressed in earlier debates that the Rule would apply to both civil and criminal cases, see 120 Cong. Rec. 2377 (1974), explained the benefits of the Rule for criminal defendants and made no reference to benefits for civil litigants when he said:

> "[Y]ou can ask about all . . . felonies on cross examination, only if you can convince the court, and the burden is on the *government*, which is an important change in the law, that the probative value of the question is greater than the damage to the *defendant*; and that is damage or prejudice *to the defendant alone*." Id., at 40894 (emphases supplied).

In the same debate Representative Hogan manifested awareness of the Rule's broad application. While supporting the compromise, he reiterated his preference for a rule

> "that, for the purpose of attacking the credibility of a witness, *even if the witness happens to be the defendant in a criminal case*, evidence that he has been convicted of a crime is admissible and may be used to challenge that witness' credibility if the crime is a felony or is a misdemeanor involving dishonesty of [sic] false statement." Id., at 40895 (emphasis added).

lends support to [an] opinion that "legislative oversight" caused exclusion of civil parties from Rule 609(a)(1)'s balance, a number of considerations persuade us that the Rule was meant to authorize a judge to weigh prejudice against no one other than a criminal defendant.

A party contending that legislative action changed settled law has the burden of showing that the legislature intended such a change. Cf. *Midlantic National Bank v. New Jersey Department of Environmental Protection*, 474 U.S. 494, 502 (1986). The weight of authority before Rule 609's adoption accorded with the Advisory Committee's final draft, admitting all felonies without exercise of judicial discretion in either civil or criminal cases. Departures from this general rule had occurred overtly by judicial interpretation, as in *Luck*, or in evidence codes, such as the Model Code and the Uniform Rules. Rule 609 itself explicitly adds safeguards circumscribing the common-law rule. The unsubstantiated assumption that legislative oversight produced Rule 609(a)(1)'s ambiguity respecting civil trials hardly demonstrates that Congress intended silently to overhaul the law of impeachment in the civil context.

To the extent various drafts of Rule 609 distinguished civil and criminal cases, moreover, they did so only to mitigate prejudice to criminal defendants. Any prejudice that convictions impeachment might cause witnesses other than the accused was deemed "so minimal as scarcely to be a subject of comment." Advisory Committee's Note, 51 F.R.D., at 392. Far from voicing concern lest such impeachment unjustly diminish a civil witness in the eyes of the jury, Representative Hogan declared that this evidence ought to be used to measure a witness' moral value.[27] Furthermore, Representative Dennis—who in advocating a Rule limiting impeachment to *crimen falsi* convictions had recognized the impeachment Rule's applicability to civil trials—not only debated the issue on the House floor, but also took part in the conference out of which Rule 609 emerged. See 120 Cong.Rec. 2377–2380, 39942, 40894–40895 (1974). These factors indicate that Rule 609(a)(1)'s textual limitation of the prejudice balance to criminal defendants resulted from deliberation, not oversight.

Had the conferees desired to protect other parties or witnesses, they could have done so easily. Presumably they had access to all of Rule 609's

---

[27] "Suppose some governmental body instituted a civil action for damages, and the defendant called a witness who had been previously convicted of malicious destruction of public property. Under the committee's formulation, the convictions could not be used to impeach the witness' credibility since the crimes did not involve dishonesty or false statement. Yet, in the hypothetical case, as in any case in which the government was a party, justice would seem to me to require that the jury know that the witness had been carrying on some private war against society. Should a witness with an anti-social background be allowed to stand on the same basis of believability before juries as law-abiding citizens with unblemished records? I think not. . . . Personally I am more concerned about the moral worth of individuals capable of engaging in such outrageous acts as adversely reflecting on a witness' character than I am of thieves. . . ." *Id.*, at 2376.

precursors, particularly the drafts prepared by the House Subcommittee and the Senate Judiciary Committee, both of which protected the civil litigant as well as the criminal defendant. Alternatively, the conferees could have amended their own draft to include other parties. They did not for the simple reason that they intended that only the accused in a criminal case should be protected from unfair prejudice by the balance set out in Rule 609(a)(1).

[Finally, the Court concluded that Rule 609, as the specific provision governing the facts of the case, controlled over the general balancing provisions of Rule 403. The Court affirmed the judgment for defendant.]

JUSTICE SCALIA, concurring in the judgment.

We are confronted here with a statute which, if interpreted literally, produces an absurd, and perhaps unconstitutional, result. Our task is to give some alternate meaning to the word "defendant" in Federal Rule of Evidence 609(a)(1) that avoids this consequence; and then to determine whether Rule 609(a)(1) excludes the operation of Federal Rule of Evidence 403.

I think it entirely appropriate to consult all public materials, including the background of Rule 609(a)(1) and the legislative history of its adoption, to verify that what seems to us an unthinkable disposition (civil defendants but not civil plaintiffs receive the benefit of weighing prejudice) was indeed unthought of, and thus to justify a departure from the ordinary meaning of the word "defendant" in the Rule. For that purpose, however, it would suffice to observe that counsel have not provided, nor have we discovered, a shred of evidence that anyone has ever proposed or assumed such a bizarre disposition. The Court's opinion, however, goes well beyond this. Approximately four-fifths of its substantive analysis is devoted to examining the evolution of Federal Rule of Evidence 609 * * * all with the evident purpose, not merely of confirming that the word "defendant" cannot have been meant literally, but of determining what, precisely, the Rule does mean.

I find no reason to believe that any more than a handful of the Members of Congress who enacted Rule 609 were aware of its interesting evolution from the 1942 Model Code; or that any more than a handful of them (if any) voted, with respect to their understanding of the word "defendant" and the relationship between Rule 609 and Rule 403, on the basis of the referenced statements in the Subcommittee, Committee, or Conference Committee Reports, or floor debates—statements so marginally relevant, to such minute details, in such relatively inconsequential legislation. The meaning of terms on the statute books ought to be determined, not on the basis of which meaning can be shown to have been understood by a larger handful of the Members of Congress; but rather on the basis of which meaning is (1) most in accord with context and ordinary usage, and thus most likely to have been understood by the *whole* Congress which voted on the words of the statute (not to mention the citizens subject to it), and (2) most compatible with the surrounding body of law into which the provision must be integrated—a compatibility which, by a benign fiction, we assume Congress always has in mind. I would not permit any of the historical and legislative material discussed by the Court, or all of it combined, to lead me to a result different from the one that these factors suggest.

I would analyze this case, in brief, as follows:

(1) The word "defendant" in Rule 609(a)(1) cannot rationally (or perhaps even constitutionally) mean to provide the benefit of prejudice-weighing to civil defendants and not civil plaintiffs. Since petitioner has not produced, and we have not ourselves discovered, even a snippet of support for this absurd result, we may confidently assume that the word was not used (as it normally would be) to refer to all defendants and only all defendants.

(2) The available alternatives are to interpret "defendant" to mean (a) "civil plaintiff, civil defendant, prosecutor, and criminal defendant," (b) "civil plaintiff and defendant and criminal defendant," or (c) "criminal defendant." Quite obviously, the last does least violence to the text. It adds a qualification that the word "defendant" does not contain but, unlike the others, does not give the word a meaning ("plaintiff" or "prosecutor") it simply will not bear. The qualification it adds, moreover, is one that could understandably have been omitted by inadvertence—and sometimes is omitted in normal conversation ("I believe strongly in defendants' rights"). Finally, this last interpretation is consistent with the policy of the law in general and the Rules of Evidence in particular of providing special protection to defendants in criminal cases.[*]

(3) As well described by the Court, the "structure of the Rules" makes it clear that Rule 403 is not to be applied in addition to Rule 609(a)(1).

I am frankly not sure that, despite its lengthy discussion of ideological evolution and legislative history, the Court's reasons for both aspects of its decision are much different from mine. I respectfully decline to join that discussion, however, because it is natural for the bar to believe that the juridical importance of such material matches its prominence in our opinions—thus producing a legal culture in which,

---

[*]   Acknowledging the statutory ambiguity, the dissent would read "defendant" to mean "any party" because, it says, this interpretation "extend[s] the protection of judicial supervision to a larger class of litigants" than the interpretation the majority and I favor, which "takes protection *away* from litigants." But neither side in this dispute can lay claim to generosity without begging the policy question whether judicial supervision is better than the automatic power to impeach. We could as well say—and with much more support in both prior law and this Court's own recommendation—that our reading "extend[s] the protection of [the right to impeach with prior felony convictions] to a larger class of litigants" than the dissent's interpretation, which "takes protection *away* from litigants."

when counsel arguing before us assert that "Congress has said" something, they now frequently mean, by "Congress," a committee report; and in which it was not beyond the pale for a recent brief to say the following: "Unfortunately, the legislative debates are not helpful. Thus, we turn to the other guidepost in this difficult area, statutory language." Brief for Petitioner in *Jett v. Dallas Independent School District,* O.T.1988, No. 87–2084, p. 21.

JUSTICE BLACKMUN, with whom JUSTICE BRENNAN and JUSTICE MARSHALL join, dissenting.

* * * The majority concludes that Rule 609(a)(1) cannot mean what it says on its face. I fully agree.

I fail to see, however, why we are required to solve this riddle of statutory interpretation by reading the inadvertent word "defendant" to mean "criminal defendant." I am persuaded that a better interpretation of the Rule would allow the trial court to consider the risk of prejudice faced by any party, not just a criminal defendant. Applying the balancing provisions of Rule 609(a)(1) to all parties would have prevented the admission of unnecessary and inflammatory evidence in this case and would prevent other similar unjust results until Rule 609(a) is repaired, as it must be. The result the Court reaches today, in contrast, endorses "the irrationality and unfairness" of denying the trial court the ability to weigh the risk of prejudice to any party before admitting evidence of a prior felony for purposes of impeachment.

[A] The majority's lengthy recounting of the legislative history of Rule 609 demonstrates why almost all that history is entitled to very little weight. Because the proposed rule changed so often—and finally was enacted as a compromise between the House and the Senate—much of the commentary cited by the majority concerns versions different from the Rule Congress finally enacted.

The only item of legislative history that focuses on the Rule as enacted is the Report of the Conference Committee. Admittedly, language in the Report supports the majority's position: the Report mirrors the Rule in emphasizing the prejudicial effect on the defendant, and also uses the word "convict" to describe the potential outcome. But the Report's draftsmanship is no better than the Rule's, and the Report's plain language is no more reliable an indicator of Congress' intent than is the plain language of the Rule itself.

Because the slipshod drafting of Rule 609(a)(1) demonstrates that clarity of language was not the Conference's forte, I prefer to rely on the underlying reasoning of the Report, rather than on its unfortunate choice of words, in ascertaining the Rule's proper scope. The Report's treatment of the Rule's discretionary standard consists of a single paragraph. After noting that the Conference was concerned with prejudice to a defendant, the Report states:

> "The danger of prejudice to a witness other than the defendant (such as injury to the witness' reputation in the community) was considered and rejected by the Conference as an element to be weighed in determining admissibility. It was the judgment of the Conference that the danger of prejudice to a nondefendant witness is outweighed by the need for the trier of fact to have as much relevant evidence on the issue of credibility as possible. Such evidence should only be excluded where it presents a danger of improperly influencing the outcome of the trial by persuading the trier of fact to convict the defendant on the basis of his prior criminal record."

The Report indicates that the Conference determined that any felony conviction has sufficient relevance to a witness' credibility to be admitted, even if the felony had nothing directly to do with truthfulness or honesty. In dealing with the question of undue prejudice, however, the Conference drew a line: it distinguished between two types of prejudice, only one of which it permitted the trial court to consider.

As the Conference observed, admitting a prior conviction will always "prejudice" a witness, who, of course, would prefer that the conviction not be revealed to the public. The Report makes clear, however, that this kind of prejudice to the witness' life outside the courtroom is not to be considered in the judicial balancing required by Rule 609(a)(1). Rather, the kind of prejudice the court is instructed to be concerned with is prejudice which "presents a danger of improperly influencing the outcome of the trial." Congress' solution to that kind of prejudice was to require judicial supervision: the conviction may be admitted only if "the court determines that the probative value of admitting this evidence outweighs its prejudicial effect to the defendant." Rule 609(a)(1).

Although the Conference expressed its concern in terms of the effect on a criminal defendant, the potential for prejudice to the outcome at trial exists in any type of litigation, whether criminal or civil, and threatens all parties to the litigation. The Report and the Rule are best read as expressing Congress' preference for judicial balancing whenever there is a chance that justice shall be denied a party because of the unduly prejudicial nature of a witness' past conviction for a crime that has no direct bearing on the witness' truthfulness. In short, the reasoning of the Report suggests that by "prejudice to the defendant," Congress meant "prejudice to a party," as opposed to the prejudicial effect of the revelation of a prior conviction to the witness' own reputation.

It may be correct, as Justice Scalia notes in his opinion concurring in the judgment, that interpreting "prejudicial effect to the defendant" to include only "prejudicial effect to [a] *criminal* defendant," and not prejudicial effect to other categories of litigants as well, does the "least violence to the text," if what we mean by "violence" is the interpolation of excess words or the deletion of existing words. But the reading endorsed by Justice Scalia and the majority does violence to the logic of the only rationale Members of Congress offered for the Rule they adopted.

Certainly the possibility that admission of a witness' past conviction will improperly determine the outcome at trial is troubling when the witness' testimony is in support of a criminal defendant. The potential, however, is no less real for other litigants. Unlike Justice Scalia, I do not approach the Rules of Evidence, which by their terms govern both civil and criminal proceedings, with the presumption that their general provisions should be read to "provid[e] special protection to defendants in criminal cases." Rather, the Rules themselves specify that they "shall be construed to secure fairness in administration . . . to the end that the truth may be ascertained and proceedings justly determined" in *all* cases. Rule 102. The majority's result does not achieve that end. * * *

[D] As I see it, therefore, our choice is between two interpretations of Rule 609(a)(1), neither of which is completely consistent with the Rule's plain language. The majority's interpretation takes protection *away* from litigants—*i.e.*, civil defendants—who would have every reason to believe themselves entitled to the judicial balancing offered by the Rule. The alternative interpretation—which I favor—also departs somewhat from plain language, but does so by *extending* the protection of judicial supervision to a larger class of litigants—*i.e.*, to all parties. Neither result is compelled by the statutory language or the legislative history, but for me the choice between them is an easy one. I find it proper, as a general matter and under the dictates of Rule 102, to construe the Rule so as to avoid "unnecessary hardship," see *Burnet v. Guggenheim*, 288 U.S. 280, 285 (1933), and to produce a sensible result. * * *

NOTES AND QUESTIONS ON GREEN V. BOCK LAUNDRY

1.   *Does Textualism Work in* Bock Laundry? Why doesn't Justice Scalia join the majority opinion, given that he agrees with the result? Too much legislative history! But that does not mean that textualist Justice Scalia went with the plain meaning of the statute either. He *also* rewrote the statute, which has a perfectly "plain meaning" in this case: The felony convictions of civil plaintiffs can always be introduced to impeach them, but those of civil defendants are subject to a balancing test. Of course, such a plain meaning is probably unconstitutional, but in that event why doesn't the textualist simply strike the darn thing down? Invalidate Rule 609(a)(1) (at least as far as civil cases) and apply the Rule 403 default rule, which would probably exclude Green's conviction from evidence?

Justice Scalia disregarded plain meaning in this case because he believed that Rule 609(a)(1) was absurd as written, that the absurdity was unintended, and that an unintended absurdity justifies departure from plain meaning. See also *Brown v. Plata,* 131 S.Ct. 1910 (2011) (Scalia, J., dissenting) (Chapter 3, § 1) (urging his colleagues to "bend" the statutory text to avoid "absurd" results and judicial "travesty"). This is itself significant. By creating an exception to textualism when a statute requires unintended "absurd" consequences, is Justice Scalia not conceding that following statutory text is not all that is going on in statutory interpretation, and that current interpretive values (or at least real-world consequences) have a role to play in statutory interpretation? See Jane S. Schacter, *Text or Consequences?,* 76 Brook. L. Rev. 1007 (2011) (documenting the prominent role that public values play in Justice Scalia's statutory opinions and dissents). While Justice Scalia surely believes that plain meaning can only be sacrificed in the rare absurd-result case, why not sacrifice plain meaning when it directs an "unreasonable" result that was probably unintended by Congress? At a minimum, doesn't Justice Scalia's approach in *Bock Laundry* tell us that textualism seems to need a "safety valve"?

Recognizing an absurd results exception to the plain meaning rule has its risks: what is absurd to conservative Justice Scalia might be debatable or even reasonable to moderate conservatives such as Justice Kennedy and might be good policy to the more liberal Justice Ginsburg. (Indeed, such a divide was at issue in *Brown v. Plata.*) Isn't avoiding such judicial subjectivity one of textualism's aims? For this reason, some leading textualists in the legal academy argue that there should *not* be an "absurd results" exception to textualism at all. See John F. Manning, *The Absurdity Doctrine,* 116 Harv. L. Rev. 2387 (2003); John C. Nagle, *Textualism's Exceptions,* Issues in Legal Scholarship, Vol. 2, Iss. 2 (2002). They are willing to accept some difficult, even unjust results, as a price for the objectivity and predictability gains that a strict application of textualism has to offer. Remember the family that almost lost their livelihood in *Locke*—the mining case with the Dec. 30th filing deadline. What do you think?

2. *Justice Blackmun's Rewrite.* Although Justice Scalia agreed to rewrite the statute in *Bock Laundry*, his opinion dismissed the dissenting opinion's rewrite in favor of the majority's rewrite:

> The available alternatives [for rewriting the rule] are to interpret "defendant" to mean (a) "civil plaintiff, civil defendant, prosecutor and criminal defendant," (b) "civil plaintiff and defendant and criminal defendant," or (c) "criminal defendant." Quite obviously, the last does least violence to the text.

Is that so obvious? In essence, Justice Blackmun's dissent rewrote Rule 609(a)(1) to permit impeaching convictions only when "the court determines that the probative value of admitting this evidence outweighs its prejudicial effect to *a party*" (new language italicized). Does this do more "violence" to the text than Justice Scalia's rewrite to permit impeaching convictions only when "the court determines that the probative value of admitting this evidence outweighs its prejudicial effect to the *criminal* defendant"?

From a purely textualist perspective, Justice Blackmun's rewrite may be a better version, because Justice Scalia's rewrite leaves the statute as chaotic as it was originally. Rewritten Rule 609(a)(1) still applies in a civil case like *Bock Laundry*, and Justice Scalia's version tells the judge to follow a strange rule: Allow the witness to be impeached by his prior felony convictions, but only if its probative value outweighs its prejudice to the "criminal defendant." What criminal defendant? This is a civil case, after all. While the original Rule 609(a)(1) favored civil defendants over civil plaintiffs without apparent justification, it at least set forth a rule that could be applied by the district judge in a civil case. Under the pretense of doing "least violence" to the text, does Justice Scalia's rewrite deprive the judge of an intelligible rule?

3. *Does "Imaginative Reconstruction" Work Any Better?* Commentators sometimes use the phrase "imaginative reconstruction" to refer to the interpretive technique of trying to reconstruct what the specific elected members were thinking at the time, or how they would have responded had they been asked the question in the case. There's a lot of this in Justice Stevens's opinion. But can we really tell what the median Member of Congress thought about this issue? Recall that the House voted for a version of Rule 609(a) that would have given Green the benefit of a balancing test, and a similar version was voted out of the Senate Judiciary Committee. On the floor of the Senate, Senator McClellan proposed an amendment making all felony convictions admissible; his amendment failed by a 35–35 vote. 120 Cong. Rec. 37,080 (1974). But on immediate motion for reconsideration, his amendment was adopted, 38–34, because a couple of new senators showed up and a couple changed their votes. *Id.* at 37,083. The median senator was apparently Senator Stevens (R–Alaska): he voted against the McClellan amendment, for reconsideration, for the McClellan amendment, and then for the final conference bill, which adopted the ambiguous compromise. Why did he vote this way? What was his "intent"?

In 2006, our late colleague Philip Frickey posed these very questions to Senator Stevens, who was still representing Alaska in the Senate. Senator Stevens told Professor Frickey that the voting pattern for him and several other senators was "confused" as a matter of logic, but not as a matter of political collegiality. "As a former U.S. Attorney I favored the House and Senate Judiciary Committees' version—but McClellan was a friend. He had traveled to Alaska with me—and Jackson and Stennis were sort of mentors. This was my sixth year in the Senate—I voted with McClellan to take his 'compromise' to conference."[7]

In any event, the Senate did vote for a much more limited version of Rule 609(a) than the House, and so the key question for imaginative

---

[7]   Email from Lily Stevens (Senator Stevens's daughter) to Philip P. Frickey (April 5, 2006) (incorporating an email that Senator Stevens authorized his daughter to forward to Professor Frickey).

reconstruction is: What was the conference committee "deal" that was struck on Rule 609(a)? And of course that's completely unclear as well, since the conference report doesn't even mention civil cases, and Senator Stevens does not recall any consensus on the matter when he and other senators passed the conference bill by voice vote. Justice Scalia is probably right that no "more than a handful of Members of Congress who enacted Rule 609 were aware of its interesting evolution * * * or that any more of than a handful of them (if any) voted, with respect to their understanding of the word 'defendant' and the relationship between Rule 609 and Rule 403." What does that kind of reality-check tell us about the interpretive method judges should apply to cases like this?

4. *The Dog That Didn't Bark.* Justice Stevens finds great significance in the conference action, but only because of a judicially created canon of statutory construction, the so-called "dog that didn't bark" canon. The rule comes from a Sherlock Homes story, *Silver Blaze*, in which the great Holmes figures out that the horse-thief in question must have been someone familiar since the horse was stolen in the middle of the night without the dogs in the stable barking and awakening the sleeping stable boys. In the legislation context, the idea is that if Congress is going to make a major change, someone will bark in the legislative history. In *Bock*, Justice Stevens says, since the dog (here, Congress) didn't bark, we should assume that "nothing happened"—no radical change was made in the fabric of the law. Thus, Justice Stevens's imaginative reconstruction boils down to the application of a judicial presumption! And one that seems flimsy at best, because the common law rule was in the process of collapsing—and did collapse within the federal system the year after *Bock Laundry*. See note 5.

5. *What Happens When Text Runs Out?* One might say that the new textualist approach demands that the statutory interpreter consider the text, the whole text, and nothing but the text. This description leaves many important issues unaddressed and may be an oversimplification. Text is often ambiguous—although even that question (when exactly is meaning ambiguous?) is hard to answer. But if there is genuine ambiguity, as there often is in cases that reach appellate courts, where should a textualist turn then? For Justice Scalia, the option is to turn to sources like Supreme Court precedent *or* to defer to reasonable agency interpretations of statutes *or* to apply one of the hundred or so canons of construction that courts have at their disposal and that we shall explore in Chapter 5 *or* occasionally reason from the objective purpose of the statute. See Antonin Scalia & Bryan A. Garner, *Reading Law: The Interpretation of Legal Texts* 43–44, 63–65 (2012). In an empirical analysis of Justice Scalia's dissents, Professor McGowan concludes that Justice Scalia's textualism (especially in his dissents, which are less constrained by the process of collecting a majority) contains just as much judicial discretion and judgment as does a more purposive approach (which sometimes considers even more types of evidence!) *See* Miranda McGowan, *Do as I Do, Not as I Say: An Empirical Investigation of Justice*

Scalia's Ordinary Meaning Method of Statutory Interpretation, 78 Miss. L.J. 129 (2008).

Why not add legislative history to this list of textualist tools, at least for its *linguistic value*—namely, as evidence of how language was used at the time of the statute's enactment? One would expect new textualists who follow "original meaning" to consider legislative history carefully, for the same kinds of reasons they consider *The Federalist Papers* in determining the "original meaning" of the language used in the Constitution. Such legislative history would take the edge off of Justice Scalia's bitter critique of *Holy Trinity*. Scholars have reported that the legislative debates used the terms "labor and service" to refer only to manual work, and never to pastoral or brain work. See, e.g., Carol Chomsky, *Unlocking the Mysteries of* Holy Trinity: *Spirit, Letter, and History in Statutory Interpretation,* 100 Colum. L. Rev. 901 (2000).

6.   *Why Did the Court Go Through This Exercise?* As Justice Stevens's opinion noted, there was a proposed change to Rule 609(a) pending when the Supreme Court interpreted the Rule in *Bock Laundry*. In January 1990 (soon after the decision in *Bock Laundry*), the Supreme Court notified Congress that it had adopted an amendment to Federal Rule of Evidence 609 to take effect on December 1, 1990 (such amendments automatically take effect unless Congress disapproves them). The amendment changed Rule 609 to effectively implement Justice Blackmun's reading in *Bock Laundry* going forward. The report noted that the advisory committee had approved the proposed amendment prior to *Bock Laundry*, but had held it pending the outcome of the case (and it did not affect the outcome of that case). Congress never disapproved the revised Rule 609(a), and it went into effect on December 1, 1990.

After this amendment, Rule 609 provided:

a.   General rule.—For purposes of attacking the credibility of a witness,

> (1) evidence that a witness other than an accused has been convicted of a crime shall be admitted, subject to Rule 403, if the crime was punishable by death or imprisonment in excess of one year under the law under which the witness was convicted, and evidence that an accused has been convicted of such a crime shall be admitted if the court determines that the probative value of admitting this evidence outweighs its prejudicial effect to the accused; and

> (2) evidence that any witness has been convicted of a crime shall be admitted if it involved dishonesty or false statement, regardless of the punishment.

Under this rule, Paul Green would have gotten a new trial. Why did the Court not reach that result in *Bock Laundry*? Why would the Court have changed the rule through the Federal Rules of Evidence rather than through Mr. Green's case?

PROBLEM 4–3: THE NEW TEXTUALISM AS APPLIED TO THE VOTING RIGHTS ACT AMENDMENTS OF 1982

From his book, we know that Justice Scalia would have dissented in *Holy Trinity Church.* He probably would have voted with the majority in *TVA*—but he would have written the opinion differently or would not have joined the Court's discussion of legislative history. For another issue, consider the Voting Rights Act of 1982, which invalidates state electoral districts or rules that have a disparate impact on racial minorities. For example, in the South, at-large elections were an effective way of excluding candidates of color from elected office, because the majority white electorate would vote against any such candidate. In 1980, the Supreme Court had ruled that § 2 did not police electoral arrangements that were race-neutral and not motivated by racially exclusionary motives (which are hard to prove). To enable minority voters to challenge electoral arrangements, like at-large elections, that were not race-based on their face but that had questionable race-based effects, § 2 was amended in 1982 (Pub. Law No. 97–205) to provide as follows:

> (a) No voting qualification or prerequisite to voting or standard, practice, or procedure shall be imposed or applied by any State or political subdivision in a manner which results in a denial or abridgement of the right of any citizen of the United States to vote on account of race or color, or in contravention of the guarantees set forth in section 4(f)(2), as provided in subsection (b).

> (b) A violation of subsection (a) is established if, based on the totality of circumstances, it is shown that the political processes leading to nomination or election in the State or political subdivision are not equally open to participation by members of a class of citizens protected by subsection (a) in that its members have less opportunity than other members of the electorate to participate in the political process and to elect representatives of their choice. The extent to which members of a protected class have been elected to office in the State or political subdivision is one circumstance which may be considered: *Provided*, That nothing in this section establishes a right to have members of a protected class elected in numbers equal to their proportion in the population.

Does § 2 apply to state elections for judges? (Unlike the federal system, judges are popularly elected in many states.) How would a new textualist analyze the foregoing statutory text? Is there a plain meaning? If not, how should ambiguities be resolved? Would it make a difference to you if you knew that § 2 was applied to judicial elections before the Voting Rights Act was amended in 1982? Jot down your answer now.

RONALD CHISOM V. CHARLES E. (BUDDY) ROEMER

Supreme Court of the United States, 1991.
501 U.S. 380, 111 S.Ct. 2354, 115 L.Ed.2d 348.

JUSTICE STEVENS delivered the opinion of the Court.

[Five of the seven members of the Louisiana Supreme Court are elected from single-member districts, each of which consists of a number of parishes (counties). The other two are elected from one multimember district. In three of the four parishes in this multimember district, more than three-fourths of the registered voters are white. In the fourth parish in the multimember district, Orleans Parish, which contains about half of the population of the multimember district and has about half the registered voters in the district, more than one-half of the registered voters are African American. A class of African-American registered voters in Orleans Parish brought this action, contending that the use of the multimember district diluted the voting strength of the minority community in violation of § 2 of the Voting Rights Act, as amended in 1982. Under the controlling precedent in the Fifth Circuit, *League of United Latin American Citizens Council No. 4434 v. Clements*, 914 F.2d 620 (5th Cir. 1990) (en banc) ("*LULAC*"), section 2 was inapplicable to judicial elections.]

The text of § 2 * * * as originally enacted [in 1965] read as follows:

> "SEC. 2. No voting qualification or prerequisite to voting, or standard, practice, or procedure shall be imposed or applied by any State or political subdivision to deny or abridge the right of any citizen of the United States to vote on account of race or color." * * *

At the time of the passage of the Voting Rights Act of 1965, § 2, unlike other provisions of the Act, did not provoke significant debate in Congress because it was viewed largely as a restatement of the Fifteenth Amendment. This Court took a similar view of § 2 in *Mobile v. Bolden*, 446 U.S. 55, 60–61 (1980). * * * Section 2 protected the right to vote, and it did so without making any distinctions or imposing any limitations as to which elections would fall within its purview. * * *

Justice Stewart's opinion for the plurality in *Mobile v. Bolden*, which held that there was no violation of either the Fifteenth Amendment or § 2 of the Voting Rights Act absent proof of intentional discrimination, served as the impetus for the 1982 amendment [to § 2]. * * *

Under the amended statute, proof of intent is no longer required to prove a § 2 violation. * * * The full text of § 2 as amended in 1982 reads as follows:

> "SEC. 2. (a) No voting qualification or prerequisite to voting or standard, practice, or procedure shall be imposed or applied by

any State or political subdivision in a manner which results in a denial or abridgement of the right of any citizen of the United States to vote on account of race or color, or in contravention of the guarantees set forth in section 4(f)(2), as provided in subsection (b).

"(b) A violation of subsection (a) is established if, based on the totality of circumstances, it is shown that the political processes leading to nomination or election in the State or political subdivision are not equally open to participation by members of a class of citizens protected by subsection (a) in that its members have less opportunity than other members of the electorate to participate in the political process and to elect representatives of their choice. The extent to which members of a protected class have been elected to office in the State or political subdivision is one circumstance which may be considered: *Provided*, That nothing in this section establishes a right to have members of a protected class elected in numbers equal to their proportion in the population."

The two purposes of the amendment are apparent from its text. Section 2(a) adopts a results test, thus providing that proof of discriminatory intent is no longer necessary to establish *any* violation of the section. Section 2(b) provides guidance about how the results test is to be applied.

Respondents contend, and the *LULAC* majority agreed, that Congress' choice of the word "representatives" in the phrase "have less opportunity than other members of the electorate to participate in the political process and to elect representatives of their choice" in section 2(b) is evidence of congressional intent to exclude vote dilution claims involving judicial elections from the coverage of § 2. We reject that construction because we are convinced that if Congress had such an intent, Congress would have made it explicit in the statute, or at least some of the Members would have identified or mentioned it at some point in the unusually extensive legislative history of the 1982 amendment.[23]
* * *

The *LULAC* majority assumed that § 2 provides two distinct types of protection for minority voters—it protects their opportunity "to participate in the political process" and their opportunity "to elect representatives of their choice." Although the majority interpreted

___

[23] Congress' silence in this regard can be likened to the dog that did not bark. See A. Doyle, Silver Blaze, in The Complete Sherlock Holmes 335 (1927). Cf. *Harrison v. PPG Industries, Inc.*, 446 U.S. 578, 602 (1980) (Rehnquist, J., dissenting) ("In a case where the construction of legislative language such as this makes so sweeping and so relatively unorthodox a change as that made here, I think judges as well as detectives may take into consideration the fact that a watchdog did not bark in the night.").

"representatives" as a word of limitation, it assumed that the word eliminated judicial elections only from the latter protection, without affecting the former. In other words, a standard, practice, or procedure in a judicial election, such as a limit on the times that polls are open, which has a disparate impact on black voters' opportunity to cast their ballots under § 2, may be challenged even if a different practice that merely affects their opportunity to elect representatives of their choice to a judicial office may not. This reading of § 2, however, is foreclosed by the statutory text and by our prior cases.

Any abridgement of the opportunity of members of a protected class to participate in the political process inevitably impairs their ability to influence the outcome of an election. As the statute is written, however, the inability to elect representatives of their choice is not sufficient to establish a violation unless, under the totality of the circumstances, it can also be said that the members of the protected class have less opportunity to participate in the political process. The statute does not create two separate and distinct rights. Subsection (a) covers every application of a qualification, standard, practice, or procedure that results in a denial or abridgement of *"the right"* to vote. The singular form is also used in subsection (b) when referring to an injury to members of the protected class who have less "opportunity" than others "to participate in the political process *and* to elect representatives of their choice." 42 U.S.C. § 1973 (emphasis added). It would distort the plain meaning of the sentence to substitute the word "or" for the word "and." Such radical surgery would be required to separate the opportunity to participate from the opportunity to elect.

The statutory language is patterned after the language used by Justice White in his opinions for the Court in *White v. Regester*, 412 U.S. 755 (1973) and *Whitcomb v. Chavis*, 403 U.S. 124 (1971).* In both opinions, the Court identified the opportunity to participate and the opportunity to elect as inextricably linked. In *White v. Regester*, the Court described the connection as follows: "The plaintiffs' burden is to produce evidence . . . that its members had less opportunity than did other residents in the district to participate in the political processes *and* to elect legislators of their choice." (emphasis added). And earlier, in *Whitcomb v. Chavis*, the Court described the plaintiffs' burden as entailing a showing that they "had less opportunity than did other . . . residents to participate in the political processes *and* to elect legislators of their choice." (emphasis added).

---

*   *Editors' note: White* and *Whitcomb* were pre-*Bolden* cases in which the Court had suggested that the Constitution prohibited electoral structures or rules that had racially discriminatory effects, even without a showing that the government action in question was rooted in intentional discrimination.

The results test mandated by the 1982 amendment is applicable to all claims arising under § 2. If the word "representatives" did place a limit on the coverage of the Act for judicial elections, it would exclude all claims involving such elections from the protection of § 2. For all such claims must allege an abridgement of the opportunity to participate in the political process *and* to elect representatives of one's choice. * * *

[V] Both respondents and the *LULAC* majority place their principal reliance on Congress' use [in § 2] of the word "representatives" instead of "legislators" in the phrase "to participate in the political process and to elect representatives of their choice." When Congress borrowed the phrase from *White v. Regester*, it replaced "legislators" with "representatives."[26] This substitution indicates, at the very least, that Congress intended the amendment to cover more than legislative elections. Respondents argue, and the majority agreed, that the term "representatives" was used to extend § 2 coverage to executive officials, but not to judges. We think, however, that the better reading of the word "representatives" describes the winners of representative, popular elections. If executive officers, such as prosecutors, sheriffs, state attorneys general, and state treasurers, can be considered "representatives" simply because they are chosen by popular election, then the same reasoning should apply to elected judges.

Respondents suggest that if Congress had intended to have the statute's prohibition against vote dilution apply to the election of judges, it would have used the word "candidates" instead of "representatives." But that confuses the ordinary meaning of the words. The word "representative" refers to someone who has prevailed in a popular election, whereas the word "candidate" refers to someone who is seeking an office. Thus, a candidate is nominated, not elected. When Congress used "candidate" in other parts of the statute, it did so precisely because it was referring to people who were aspirants for an office. See, *e.g.*, 42 U.S.C. §§ 1971(b) ("any candidate for the office of President"), 1971(e) ("candidates for public office"),1973i(c) ("any candidate for the office of President"), 1973i(e)(2) ("any candidate for the office of President"), 1973l(c) ("candidates for public or party office"), 1973ff–2 ("In the case of the offices of President and Vice President, a vote for a named

---

[26] The word "representatives" rather than "legislators" was included in Senator Robert Dole's compromise, which was designed to assuage the fears of those Senators who viewed the House's version, H.R. 3112, as an invitation for proportional representation and electoral quotas. Senator Dole explained that the compromise was intended both to embody the belief "that a voting practice or procedure which is discriminatory in result should not be allowed to stand, regardless of whether there exists a discriminatory purpose or intent" and to "delineat[e] what legal standard should apply under the results test and clarif[y] that it is not a mandate for proportional representation." Hearings on S. 53 et al. before the Subcommittee on the Constitution of the Senate Committee on the Judiciary, 97th Cong., 2d Sess., 60 (1982). Thus, the compromise was not intended to exclude any elections from the coverage of subsection (a), but simply to make clear that the results test does not require the proportional election of minority candidates in *any* election.

candidate"), 1974 ("candidates for the office of President"), 1974e ("candidates for the office of President").

The *LULAC* majority was, of course, entirely correct in observing that "judges need not be elected at all," and that ideally public opinion should be irrelevant to the judge's role because the judge is often called upon to disregard, or even to defy, popular sentiment. The Framers of the Constitution had a similar understanding of the judicial role, and as a consequence, they established that Article III judges would be appointed, rather than elected, and would be sheltered from public opinion by receiving life tenure and salary protection. Indeed, these views were generally shared by the States during the early years of the Republic. Louisiana, however, has chosen a different course. It has decided to elect its judges and to compel judicial candidates to vie for popular support just as other political candidates do.

The fundamental tension between the ideal character of the judicial office and the real world of electoral politics cannot be resolved by crediting judges with total indifference to the popular will while simultaneously requiring them to run for elected office. When each of several members of a court must be a resident of a separate district, and must be elected by the voters of that district, it seems both reasonable and realistic to characterize the winners as representatives of that district. * * * Louisiana could, of course, exclude its judiciary from the coverage of the Voting Rights Act by changing to a system in which judges are appointed, and, in that way, it could enable its judges to be indifferent to popular opinion. The reasons why Louisiana has chosen otherwise are precisely the reasons why it is appropriate for § 2, as well as § 5, of the Voting Rights Act to continue to apply to its judicial elections.

The close connection between §§ 2 and 5 further undermines respondents' view that judicial elections should not be covered under § 2. Section 5 requires certain States to submit changes in their voting procedures to the District Court of the District of Columbia or to the Attorney General for preclearance. Section 5 uses language similar to that of § 2 in defining prohibited practices: "any voting qualification or prerequisite to voting, or standard, practice, or procedure with respect to voting." This Court has already held that § 5 applies to judicial elections. *Clark v. Roemer*, 500 U.S. 646 (1991). If § 2 did not apply to judicial elections, a State covered by § 5 would be precluded from implementing a new voting procedure having discriminatory effects with respect to judicial elections, whereas a similarly discriminatory system already in place could not be challenged under § 2. It is unlikely that Congress intended such an anomalous result. * * *

[VII]   Congress enacted the Voting Rights Act of 1965 for the broad remedial purpose of "rid[ding] the country of racial discrimination in voting." *South Carolina v. Katzenbach*, 383 U.S. 301, 315 (1966). In *Allen v. State Board of Elections*, 393 U.S. 544, 567 (1969), we said that the Act should be interpreted in a manner that provides "the broadest possible scope" in combatting racial discrimination. Congress amended the Act in 1982 in order to relieve plaintiffs of the burden of proving discriminatory intent, after a plurality of this Court had concluded that the original Act, like the Fifteenth Amendment, contained such a requirement. See *Mobile v. Bolden*. Thus, Congress made clear that a violation of § 2 could be established by proof of discriminatory results alone. It is difficult to believe that Congress, in an express effort to broaden the protection afforded by the Voting Rights Act, withdrew, without comment, an important category of elections from that protection. Today we reject such an anomalous view and hold that state judicial elections are included within the ambit of § 2 as amended.

The judgment of the Court of Appeals is reversed, and the case is remanded for further proceedings consistent with this opinion.

JUSTICE SCALIA, with whom THE CHIEF JUSTICE and JUSTICE KENNEDY join, dissenting.

Section 2 of the Voting Rights Act is not some all-purpose weapon for well-intentioned judges to wield as they please in the battle against discrimination. It is a statute. I thought we had adopted a regular method for interpreting the meaning of language in a statute: first, find the ordinary meaning of the language in its textual context; and second, using established canons of construction, ask whether there is any clear indication that some permissible meaning other than the ordinary one applies. If not—and especially if a good reason for the ordinary meaning appears plain—we apply that ordinary meaning.

Today, however, the Court adopts a method quite out of accord with that usual practice. It begins not with what the statute says, but with an expectation about what the statute must mean absent particular phenomena ("*[W]e are convinced* that if Congress had . . . an intent [to exclude judges] Congress would have made it explicit in the statute, or at least some of the Members would have identified or mentioned it at some point in the unusually extensive legislative history"); and the Court then interprets the words of the statute to fulfill its expectation. Finding nothing in the legislative history affirming that judges were excluded from the coverage of § 2, the Court gives the phrase "to elect representatives" the quite extraordinary meaning that covers the election of judges.

As method, this is just backwards, and however much we may be attracted by the result it produces in a particular case, we should in every case resist it. Our job begins with a text that Congress has passed and the President has signed. We are to read the words of that text as any ordinary Member of Congress would have read them, see Holmes, The Theory of Legal Interpretation, 12 Harv. L. Rev. 417 (1899), and apply the meaning so determined. In my view, that reading reveals that § 2 extends to vote dilution claims for the elections of representatives only, and judges are not representatives.

* * * I agree with the Court that [original § 2], directed towards intentional discrimination, applied to all elections, for it clearly said so:

> "No voting qualification or prerequisite to voting, or standard, practice, or procedure shall be imposed or applied by any State or political subdivision to deny or abridge the right of any citizen of the United States to vote on account of race or color."

The 1982 amendments, however, radically transformed the Act. As currently written, the statute proscribes intentional discrimination only if it has a discriminatory effect, but proscribes practices with discriminatory effect whether or not intentional. This new "results" criterion provides a powerful, albeit sometimes blunt, weapon with which to attack even the most subtle forms of discrimination. The question we confront here is how broadly the new remedy applies. The foundation of the Court's analysis, the itinerary for its journey in the wrong direction, is the following statement: "It is difficult to believe that Congress, in an express effort to broaden the protection afforded by the Voting Rights Act, withdrew, without comment, an important category of elections from that protection." There are two things wrong with this. First is the notion that Congress cannot be credited with having achieved anything of major importance by simply saying it, in ordinary language, in the text of a statute, "without comment" in the legislative history. As the Court colorfully puts it, if the dog of legislative history has not barked nothing of great significance can have transpired. Apart from the questionable wisdom of assuming that dogs will bark when something important is happening, see 1 T. Livius, The History of Rome 411–413 (1892) (D. Spillan transl.), we have forcefully and explicitly rejected the Conan Doyle approach to statutory construction in the past. See *Harrison v. PPG Industries, Inc.*, 446 U.S. 578, 592 (1980) ("In ascertaining the meaning of a statute, a court cannot, in the manner of Sherlock Holmes, pursue the theory of the dog that did not bark"). We are here to apply the statute, not legislative history, and certainly not the absence of legislative history. Statutes are the law though sleeping dogs lie.

The more important error in the Court's starting-point, however, is the assumption that the effect of excluding judges from the revised § 2 would be to "withdr[aw] . . . an important category of elections from [the] protection [of the Voting Rights Act]." There is absolutely no question here of *withdrawing* protection. Since the pre-1982 content of § 2 was coextensive with the Fifteenth Amendment, the entirety of that protection subsisted in the Constitution, and could be enforced through the other provisions of the Voting Rights Act. Nothing was lost from the prior coverage; *all* of the new "results" protection was an add-on. The issue is not, therefore, as the Court would have it, whether Congress has cut back on the coverage of the Voting Rights Act; the issue is how far it has extended it. Thus, even if a court's expectations were a proper basis for interpreting the text of a statute, while there would be reason to expect that Congress was not "withdrawing" protection, there is no particular reason to expect that the supplemental protection it provided was any more extensive than the text of the statute said.

[Justice Scalia agreed with the *LULAC* majority that § 2 created two separate rights for protected classes: (1) "to participate in the political process" and (2) "to elect representatives of their choice." On this reading, judicial elections are subject to the first right, but not the second because judges are not "representatives."] The Court, petitioners, and petitioners' *amici* have labored mightily to establish that there is *a* meaning of "representatives" that would include judges, and no doubt there is. But our job is not to scavenge the world of English usage to discover whether there is any possible meaning of "representatives" which suits our preconception that the statute includes judges; our job is to determine whether the *ordinary* meaning includes them, and if it does not, to ask whether there is any solid indication in the text or structure of the statute that something other than ordinary meaning was intended.

There is little doubt that the ordinary meaning of "representatives" does not include judges, see Webster's Second New International Dictionary 2114 (1950). The Court's feeble argument to the contrary is that "representatives" means those who "are chosen by popular election." On that hypothesis, the fan-elected members of the baseball all-star teams are "representatives"—hardly a common, if even a permissible, usage. Surely the word "representative" connotes one who is not only *elected by* the people, but who also, at a minimum, *acts on behalf of* the people. Judges do that in a sense—but not in the ordinary sense. As the captions of the pleadings in some States still display, it is the prosecutor who represents "the People"; the judge represents the Law—which often requires him to rule against the People. It is precisely because we do not *ordinarily* conceive of judges as representatives that we held judges not within the Fourteenth Amendment's requirement of "one person, one vote." *Wells v. Edwards*, 347 F.Supp. 453 (MD La.1972), aff'd, 409 U.S. 1095 (1973). The point is not that a State could not make judges in some senses representative, or that all judges must be conceived of in the Article III mold, but rather, that giving "representatives" its ordinary meaning, the ordinary speaker in 1982 would not have applied the word to judges, see Holmes, The Theory of Legal Interpretation, 12 Harv. L. Rev. 417 (1899). It remains only to ask whether there is good indication that ordinary meaning does not apply. * * *

While the "plain statement" rule may not be applicable, there is assuredly nothing whatever that points in the opposite direction, indicating that the ordinary meaning here should *not* be applied. Far from that, in my view the ordinary meaning of "representatives" gives clear purpose to congressional action that otherwise would seem pointless. As an initial matter, it is evident that Congress paid particular attention to the scope of elections covered by the "to elect" language. As the Court suggests, that language for the most part tracked this Court's opinions in *White v. Regester* and *Whitcomb v. Chavis*, but the word "legislators" was not copied. Significantly, it was replaced not with the more general term "candidates" used repeatedly elsewhere in the Act, see, *e.g.*, 42 U.S.C. §§ 1971(b), (e); 1973i(c), 19731(c); 1973ff–2; 1974; 1974e, but with the term "representatives," which appears nowhere else in the Act (except as a proper noun referring to Members of the federal lower House, or designees of the Attorney General). The normal meaning of this term is broader than "legislators" (it includes, for example, school boards and city councils as well as senators and representatives) but narrower than "candidates."

The Court says that the seemingly significant refusal to use the term "candidate" and selection of the distinctive term "representative" are really inconsequential, because "candidate" could not have been used. According to the Court, since "candidate" refers to one who has been nominated but *not yet* elected, the phrase "to elect candidates" would be a contradiction in terms. The only flaw in this argument is that it is not true, as repeated usage of the formulation "to elect candidates" by this Court itself amply demonstrates. [Citing cases.] * * * In other words, far from being an impermissible choice, "candidates" would have been the natural choice, even if it had not been used repeatedly elsewhere in the statute. It is quite absurd to think that Congress went out of its way to replace that term with "representatives," in order to convey what "candidates" naturally suggests (*viz.*, coverage of *all* elections) and what "representatives" naturally does not.

A second consideration confirms that "representatives" in § 2 was meant in its ordinary sense. When given its ordinary meaning, it causes the statute to reproduce an established, eminently logical and perhaps practically indispensable limitation upon the availability of vote dilution claims. Whatever other requirements may be applicable to elections for "representatives" (in the sense of those who are not only elected by but act on behalf of the electorate), those elections, unlike elections for *all* office-holders, must be conducted in accordance with the equal-protection principle of "one person, one vote." And it so happens—more than coincidentally, I think—that in every case in which, prior to the amendment of § 2, we recognized the possibility of a vote dilution claim, the principle of "one person, one vote" was applicable. Indeed, it is the principle of "one person, one vote" that gives meaning to the concept of "dilution." One's vote is diluted if it is not, *as it should be*, of the same practical effect as everyone else's. Of course the mere fact that an election practice satisfies the constitutional requirement of "one person, one vote" does not establish that there has been no vote dilution for Voting Rights Act purposes, since that looks not merely to equality of individual votes but also to equality of minority blocs of votes. * * * But "one person, one vote" has been the premise and the necessary condition of a vote dilution claim, since it establishes the baseline for computing the voting strength that the minority bloc *ought* to have. As we have suggested, the first question in a dilution case is whether the "one person, one vote" standard is met, and if it is, the second is whether voting structures nonetheless operate to " 'minimize or cancel out the voting strength of racial or political elements of the voting population.' "

Well before Congress amended § 2, we had held that the principle of "one person, one vote" does not apply to the election of judges, *Wells v. Edwards*, 347 F.Supp. 453 (MD La. 1972), aff'd, 409 U.S. 1095 (1973). If Congress was (through use of the extremely inapt word "representatives") making vote dilution claims available with respect to the election of judges, it was, for the first time, extending that remedy to a context in which "one person, one vote" did not apply. *That* would have been a significant change in the law, and given the need to identify some other baseline for computing "dilution," *that* is a matter which those who believe in barking dogs should be astounded to find unmentioned in the legislative history. If "representatives" is given its normal meaning, on the other hand, there is no change in the law (except elimination of the intent requirement) and the silence is entirely understandable. * * *

Finally, the Court suggests that there is something "anomalous" about extending coverage under § 5 of the Voting Rights Act to the election of judges, while not extending coverage under § 2 to the same elections. This simply misconceives the different roles of § 2 and § 5. The latter requires certain jurisdictions to preclear changes in election methods before those changes are implemented; it is a means of assuring in advance the absence of all electoral illegality, not only that which violates the Voting Rights Act but that which violates the Constitution as well. In my view, judges *are* within the scope of § 2 for nondilution claims, and thus for those claims, § 5 preclearance would enforce the Voting Rights Act with respect to judges. Moreover, intentional discrimination in the election of judges, whatever its form, is constitutionally prohibited, and the preclearance provision of § 5 gives the government a method by which to prevent that. The scheme makes entire sense without the need to bring judges within the "to elect" provision. * * *

As I said at the outset, this case is about method. The Court transforms the meaning of § 2, not because the ordinary meaning is irrational, or inconsistent with other parts of the statute, see, *e.g.*, *Green v. Bock Laundry*; *Public Citizen v. Department of Justice* (Kennedy, J., concurring in the judgment), but because it does not fit the Court's conception of what Congress must have had in mind. When we adopt a method that psychoanalyzes Congress rather than reads its laws, when we employ a tinkerer's toolbox, we do great harm. Not only do we reach the wrong result with respect to the statute at hand, but we poison the well of future legislation, depriving legislators of the assurance that ordinary terms, used in an ordinary context, will be given a predictable meaning. Our highest responsibility in the field of statutory construction is to read the laws in a consistent way, giving Congress a sure means by which it may work the people's will. We have ignored that responsibility today. I respectfully dissent.

[The dissenting opinion of JUSTICE KENNEDY is omitted.]

WEST VIRGINIA UNIVERSITY HOSPITALS, INC. v. ROBERT CASEY

Supreme Court of the United States, 1991.
499 U.S. 83, 111 S.Ct. 1138, 113 L.Ed.2d 68.

JUSTICE SCALIA delivered the opinion of the Court.

[West Virginia University Hospitals (WVUH) prevailed in its lawsuit asserting its rights under the federal Medicaid statute. The Attorneys' Fees Awards Act of 1976, 42 U.S.C. § 1988, permits the award of "a reasonable attorney's fee" to prevailing plaintiffs in federal rights cases such as this one. The question was whether § 1988 authorizes the award to prevailing plaintiffs of fees for services rendered to their attorneys by experts.]

Title 28 U.S.C. § 1920 provides:

"A judge or clerk of any court of the United States may tax as costs the following:

"(1) Fees of the clerk and marshal;

"(2) Fees of the court reporter for all or any part of the stenographic transcript necessarily obtained for use in the case;

"(3) Fees and disbursements for printing and witnesses;

"(4) Fees for exemplification and copies of papers necessarily obtained for use in the case;

"(5) Docket fees under section 1923 of this title;

"(6) Compensation of court appointed experts, compensation of interpreters, and salaries, fees, expenses, and costs of special interpretation services under section 1828 of this title."

Title 28 U.S.C. § 1821(b) limits the witness fees authorized by § 1920(3) as follows: "A witness shall be paid an attendance fee of $30 per day for each day's attendance. A witness shall also be paid the attendance fee for the time necessarily occupied in going to and returning from the place of attendance." In *Crawford Fitting Co. v. J.T. Gibbons, Inc.,* 482 U.S. 437 (1987), we held that these provisions define the full extent of a federal court's power to shift litigation costs absent express statutory authority to go further. "[W]hen," we said, "a prevailing party seeks reimbursement for fees paid to its own expert witnesses, a federal court is bound by the limits of § 1821(b), absent contract or explicit statutory authority to the contrary." *Id.* "We will not lightly infer that Congress has repealed §§ 1920 and 1821, either through [Federal Rule of Civil Procedure] 54(d) or any other provision not referring explicitly to witness fees."

As to the testimonial services of the hospital's experts, therefore, *Crawford Fitting* plainly requires, as a prerequisite to reimbursement, the identification of "explicit statutory authority." WVUH argues, however, that some of the expert fees it incurred in this case were unrelated to expert *testimony,* and that as to those fees the § 1821(b) limits, which apply only to witnesses in attendance at trial, are of no consequence. We agree with that, but there remains applicable the limitation of § 1920. *Crawford Fitting* said that we would not lightly find an implied repeal of § 1821 *or* of § 1920, which it held to be an express limitation upon the types of costs which, absent other authority, may be shifted by federal courts. None of the categories of expenses listed in § 1920 can reasonably be read to include fees for services rendered by an expert employed by a party in a nontestimonial advisory capacity. The question before us, then, is—with regard to both testimonial and nontestimonial expert fees—whether the term "attorney's fee" in § 1988 provides the "explicit statutory authority" required by *Crawford Fitting.*

[III] The record of statutory usage demonstrates convincingly that attorney's fees and expert fees are regarded as separate elements of litigation cost. While some fee-shifting provisions, like § 1988, refer only to "attorney's fees," see, *e.g.,* Civil Rights Act of 1964, 42 U.S.C. § 2000e–5(k), many others explicitly shift expert witness fees *as well as* attorney's fees. In 1976, just over a week prior to the enactment of § 1988, Congress passed those provisions of the Toxic Substances Control Act, 15 U.S.C. §§ 2618(d), 2619(c)(2), which provide that a prevailing party may recover "the costs of suit and reasonable fees for attorneys *and expert witnesses.*"

(Emphasis added.) Also in 1976, Congress amended the Consumer Product Safety Act, 15 U.S.C. §§ 2060(c), 2072(a), 2073, which as originally enacted in 1972 shifted to the losing party "cost[s] of suit, including a reasonable attorney's fee," see 86 Stat. 1226. In the 1976 amendment, Congress altered the fee-shifting provisions to their present form by adding a phrase shifting expert witness fees *in addition to* attorney's fees. See Pub. L. 94–284, § 10, 90 Stat. 506, 507. Two other significant Acts passed in 1976 contain similar phrasing: the Resource Conservation and Recovery Act of 1976, 42 U.S.C. § 6972(e) ("costs of litigation (including reasonable attorney and expert witness fees)"), and the Natural Gas Pipeline Safety Act Amendments of 1976, 49 U.S.C. App. § 1686(e) ("costs of suit, including reasonable attorney's fees and reasonable expert witnesses fees").

Congress enacted similarly phrased fee-shifting provisions in numerous statutes both before 1976, and afterwards. These statutes encompass diverse categories of legislation, including tax, administrative procedure, environmental protection, consumer protection, admiralty and navigation, utilities regulation, and, significantly, civil rights: The Equal Access to Justice Act (EAJA), the counterpart to § 1988 for violation of federal rights by federal employees, states that " 'fees and other expenses' [as shifted by § 2412(d)(1)(A)] includes the reasonable expenses of expert witnesses . . . and reasonable attorney fees." 28 U.S.C. § 2412(d)(2)(A). At least 34 statutes in 10 different titles of the United States Code explicitly shift attorney's fees *and* expert witness fees.

[Justice Scalia rejected WVUH's argument that pre-1976 practice supported the award of expert witness fees. To begin with, the cases where such fees were awarded almost always awarded attorneys' fees and costs separately from expert witness fees.] The laws that refer to fees for nontestimonial expert services are less common, but they establish a similar usage both before and after 1976: Such fees are referred to *in addition to* attorney's fees when a shift is intended. A provision of the Criminal Justice Act of 1964, 18 U.S.C. § 3006A(e), directs the court to reimburse appointed counsel for expert fees necessary to the defense of indigent criminal defendants—even though the immediately preceding provision, § 3006A(d), already directs that appointed defense counsel be paid a designated hourly rate plus "expenses reasonably incurred." WVUH's position must be that expert fees billed to a client through an attorney are "attorney's fees" because they are to be treated as part of the expenses of the attorney; but if this were normal usage, they would have been reimbursable under the Criminal Justice Act as "expenses reasonably incurred"—and subsection 3006A(e) would add nothing to the recoverable amount. The very heading of that subsection, "Services *other than* counsel" (emphasis added), acknowledges a distinction between services provided by the attorney himself and those provided to the attorney (or the client) by a nonlegal expert.

To the same effect is the 1980 EAJA, which provides: " 'fees and other expenses' [as shifted by § 2412(d)(1)(A)] includes the reasonable expenses of expert witnesses, *the reasonable cost of any study, analysis, engineering report, test, or project* which is found by the court to be necessary for the preparation of the party's case, and reasonable attorney fees." 28 U.S.C. § 2412(d)(2)(A) (emphasis added). If the reasonable cost of a "study" or "analysis"—which is but another way of describing nontestimonial expert services—is by common usage already included in the "attorney fees," again a significant and highly detailed part of the statute becomes redundant. The Administrative Procedure Act, 5 U.S.C. § 504(b)(1)(A) (added 1980), and the Tax Equity and Fiscal Responsibility Act of 1982, 26 U.S.C. § 7430(c)(1), contain similar language. Also reflecting the same usage are two railroad regulation statutes, the Regional Rail Reorganization Act of 1973, 45 U.S.C. §§ 726(f)(9) ("costs and expenses (including reasonable fees of accountants, experts, and attorneys) actually incurred"), and the Railroad Revitalization and Regulatory Reform Act of 1976, 45 U.S.C. § 854(g) ("costs and expenses (including fees of accountants, experts, and attorneys) actually and reasonably incurred").[5] * * *

WVUH further argues that the congressional purpose in enacting § 1988 must prevail over the ordinary meaning of the statutory terms. It quotes, for example, the House Committee Report to the effect that "the judicial remedy [must be] full and complete," and the Senate Committee Report to the effect that "[c]itizens must have the opportunity to recover what it costs them to vindicate [civil] rights in court." As we have observed before, however, the purpose of a statute includes not only what it sets out to change, but also what it resolves to leave alone. See *Rodriguez v. United States,* 480 U.S. 522, 525–26 (1987). The best evidence of that purpose is the statutory text adopted by both Houses of Congress and submitted to the President. Where that contains a phrase that is unambiguous—that has a clearly accepted meaning in both legislative and judicial practice—we do not permit it to be expanded or contracted by the statements of individual legislators or committees during the course of the enactment process. Congress could easily have shifted "attorney's fees and expert witness fees," or "reasonable litigation

---

[5]   WVUH cites a House Conference Committee Report from a statute passed in 1986, stating: "The conferees intend that the term 'attorneys' fees as part of the costs' include reasonable expenses and fees of expert witnesses and the reasonable costs of any test or evaluation which is found to be necessary for the preparation of the . . . case." H.R. Conf. Rep. No. 99–687, p. 5 (1986) (discussing the Handicapped Children's Protection Act of 1986, 20 U.S.C. § 1415(e)(4)(B)). In our view this undercuts rather than supports WVUH's position: The specification would have been quite unnecessary if the ordinary meaning of the term included those elements. The statement is an apparent effort to *depart* from ordinary meaning and to define a term of art.

expenses," as it did in contemporaneous statutes; it chose instead to enact more restrictive language, and we are bound by that restriction. * * *

WVUH's last contention is that, even if Congress plainly did not include expert fees in the fee-shifting provisions of § 1988, it would have done so had it thought about it. Most of the pre-§ 1988 statutes that explicitly shifted expert fees dealt with environmental litigation, where the necessity of expert advice was readily apparent; and when Congress later enacted the EAJA, the federal counterpart of § 1988, it explicitly included expert fees. Thus, the argument runs, the 94th Congress simply forgot; it is our duty to ask how they would have decided had they actually considered the question.

This argument profoundly mistakes our role. Where a statutory term presented to us for the first time is ambiguous, we construe it to contain that permissible meaning which fits most logically and comfortably into the body of both previously and subsequently enacted law. We do so not because that precise accommodative meaning is what the lawmakers must have had in mind (how could an earlier Congress know what a later Congress would enact?), but because it is our role to make sense rather than nonsense out of the *corpus juris*. But where, as here, the meaning of the term prevents such accommodation, it is not our function to eliminate clearly expressed inconsistency of policy and to treat alike subjects that different Congresses have chosen to treat differently. The facile attribution of congressional "forgetfulness" cannot justify such a usurpation. Where what is at issue is not a contradictory disposition within the same enactment, but merely a difference between the more parsimonious policy of an earlier enactment and the more generous policy of a later one, there is no more basis for saying that the earlier Congress forgot than for saying that the earlier Congress felt differently. In such circumstances, the attribution of forgetfulness rests in reality upon the judge's assessment that the later statute contains the *better* disposition. But that is not for judges to prescribe. We thus reject this last argument for the same reason that Justice Brandeis, writing for the Court, once rejected a similar (though less explicit) argument by the United States:

> "[The statute's] language is plain and unambiguous. What the Government asks is not a construction of a statute, but, in effect, an enlargement of it by the court, so that what was omitted, presumably by inadvertence, may be included within its scope. To supply omissions transcends the judicial function." *Iselin v. United States,* 270 U.S. 245, 250–51 (1926).[7]

---

[7]   WVUH at least asks us to guess the preferences of the *enacting* Congress. Justice Stevens apparently believes our role is to guess the desires of the *present* Congress, or of Congresses yet to be. "Only time will tell," he says, "whether the Court, with its literal reading of § 1988, has correctly interpreted the will of Congress." The implication is that today's holding will be proved wrong if Congress amends the law to conform with his dissent. We think not. The

For the foregoing reasons, we conclude that § 1988 conveys no authority to shift expert fees. When experts appear at trial, they are of course eligible for the fee provided by § 1920 and § 1821—which was allowed in the present case by the Court of Appeals. * * *

JUSTICE MARSHALL, dissenting.

As Justice Stevens demonstrates, the Court uses the implements of literalism to wound, rather than to minister to, congressional intent in this case. That is a dangerous usurpation of congressional power when any statute is involved. It is troubling for special reasons, however, when the statute at issue is clearly designed to give access to the federal courts to persons and groups attempting to vindicate vital civil rights. A District Judge has ably put the point in an analogous context:

> "At issue here is much more than the simple question of how much [plaintiff's] attorneys should receive as attorney fees. At issue is . . . continued full and vigorous commitment to this Nation's lofty, but as yet unfulfilled, agenda to make the promises of this land available to all citizens, without regard to race or sex or other impermissible characteristic. There are at least two ways to undermine this commitment. The first is open and direct: a repeal of this Nation's anti-discrimination laws. The second is more indirect and, for this reason, somewhat insidious: to deny victims of discrimination a means for redress by creating an economic market in which attorneys cannot afford to represent them and take their cases to court." *Hidle v. Geneva County Bd. of Ed.,* 681 F.Supp. 752, 758–759 (MD Ala.1988) (awarding attorney's fees and expenses under Title VII of the Civil Rights Act of 1964).

JUSTICE STEVENS, joined by JUSTICE MARSHALL and JUSTICE BLACKMUN, dissenting.

Since the enactment of the Statute of Wills in 1540, careful draftsmen have authorized executors to pay the just debts of the decedent, including the fees and expenses of the attorney for the estate. Although the omission of such an express authorization in a will might indicate that the testator had thought it unnecessary, or that he had overlooked the point, the omission would surely not indicate a deliberate decision by the testator to forbid any compensation to his attorney.

In the early 1970's, Congress began to focus on the importance of public interest litigation, and since that time, it has enacted numerous

---

"will of Congress" we look to is not a will evolving from Session to Session, but a will expressed and fixed in a particular enactment. Otherwise, we would speak not of "interpreting" the law but of "intuiting" or "predicting" it. Our role is to say what the law, as hitherto enacted, *is;* not to forecast what the law, as amended, *will be.*

fee-shifting statutes. In many of these statutes, which the majority cites at length, Congress has expressly authorized the recovery of expert witness fees as part of the costs of litigation. The question in this case is whether, notwithstanding the omission of such an express authorization in 42 U.S.C. § 1988, Congress intended to authorize such recovery when it provided for "a reasonable attorney's fee as part of the costs." In my view, just as the omission of express authorization in a will does not preclude compensation to an estate's attorney, the omission of express authorization for expert witness fees in a fee-shifting provision should not preclude the award of expert witness fees. We should look at the way in which the Court has interpreted the text of *this statute* in the past, as well as *this statute's* legislative history, to resolve the question before us, rather than looking at the text of the many other statutes that the majority cites in which Congress expressly recognized the need for compensating expert witnesses.

[I]   Under either the broad view of "costs" typically assumed in the fee-shifting context or the broad view of "a reasonable attorney's fee" articulated by this Court, expert witness fees are a proper component of an award under § 1988. Because we are not interpreting these words for the first time, they should be evaluated in the context that this and other courts have already created.

The term "costs" has a different and broader meaning in fee-shifting statutes than it has in the cost statutes that apply to ordinary litigation. The cost bill in this case illustrates the point. Leaving aside the question of expert witness fees, the prevailing party sought reimbursement for $45,867 in disbursements, which plainly would not have been recoverable costs under 28 U.S.C. § 1920. These expenses, including such items as travel and long-distance telephone calls, were allowed by the District Court and were not even questioned by respondents. They were expenses that a retained lawyer would ordinarily bill to his or her client. They were accordingly considered proper "costs" in a case of this kind. * * *

[In *Missouri v. Jenkins,* 491 U.S. 274 (1989), the Court, over the solo dissent of Chief Justice Rehnquist, ruled that § 1988 covered paralegal expenses as part of the recoverable "costs," even though such expenses are not "costs" under § 1920.] In *Jenkins,* the Court acknowledged that the use of paralegals instead of attorneys reduced the cost of litigation, and " 'by reducing the spiraling cost of civil rights litigation, further[ed] the policies underlying civil rights statutes.' " If attorneys were forced to do the work that paralegals could just as easily perform under the supervision of an attorney, such as locating and interviewing witnesses or compiling statistical and financial data, then "it would not be surprising to see a greater amount of such work performed by attorneys themselves, thus increasing the overall cost of litigation."

This reasoning applies equally to other forms of specialized litigation support that a trial lawyer needs and that the client customarily pays for, either directly or indirectly. Although reliance on paralegals is a more recent development than the use of traditional expert witnesses, both paralegals and expert witnesses perform important tasks that save lawyers' time and enhance the quality of their work product. * * *

[II] The Senate Report on the Civil Rights Attorney's Fees Awards Act of 1976 explained that the purpose of the proposed amendment to 42 U.S.C. § 1988 was "to remedy anomalous gaps in our civil rights laws created by the United States Supreme Court's recent decision in *Alyeska Pipeline Service Co. v. Wilderness Society,* 421 U.S. 240 (1975), and to achieve consistency in our civil rights laws." S. Rep. No. 94–1011, p. 1 (1976), 1976 U.S. Code Cong. & Admin. News 5909. The Senate Committee on the Judiciary wanted to level the playing field so that private citizens, who might have little or no money, could still serve as "private attorneys general" and afford to bring actions, even against state or local bodies, to enforce the civil rights laws. The Committee acknowledged that "[i]f private citizens are to be able to assert their civil rights, and if those who violate the Nation's fundamental laws are not to proceed with impunity, then citizens must have the opportunity to recover *what it costs them* to vindicate these rights in court." *Id.* (emphasis added). According to the Committee, the bill would create "no startling new remedy," but would simply provide "the technical requirements" requested by the Supreme Court in *Alyeska,* so that courts could "continue the practice of awarding attorneys' fees which had been going on for years prior to the Court's May decision." *Id.* * * *

The case before us today is precisely the type of public interest litigation that Congress intended to encourage by amending § 1988 to provide for fee shifting of a "reasonable attorney's fee as part of the costs." Petitioner, a tertiary medical center in West Virginia near the Pennsylvania border, provides services to a large number of Medicaid recipients throughout Pennsylvania. In January 1986, when the Pennsylvania Department of Public Welfare notified petitioner of its new Medicaid payment rates for Pennsylvania Medicaid recipients, petitioner believed them to be below the minimum standards for reimbursement specified by the Social Security Act. Petitioner successfully challenged the adequacy of the State's payment system under 42 U.S.C. § 1983.

This Court's determination today that petitioner must assume the cost of $104,133 in expert witness fees is at war with the congressional purpose of making the prevailing party whole. As we said in *Hensley v. Eckerhart,* 461 U.S. 424, 435 (1983), petitioner's recovery [under § 1988] should be "fully compensatory," or, as we expressed in *Jenkins,* petitioner's [§ 1988] recovery should be "comparable to what 'is traditional with attorneys compensated by a fee-paying client.' S.Rep. No. 94–1011, p. 6 (1976). * * *

[III] In recent years the Court has vacillated between a purely literal approach to the task of statutory interpretation and an approach that seeks guidance from historical context, legislative history, and prior cases identifying the purpose that motivated the legislation. * * *

On those occasions, however, when the Court has put on its thick grammarian's spectacles and ignored the available evidence of congressional purpose and the teaching of prior cases construing a statute, the congressional response has been dramatically different. It is no coincidence that the Court's literal reading of Title VII, which led to the conclusion that disparate treatment of pregnant and nonpregnant persons was not discrimination on the basis of sex, see *General Electric Co. v. Gilbert,* 429 U.S. 125 (1976), was repudiated by the 95th Congress; that its literal reading of the "continuous physical presence" requirement in § 244(a)(1) of the Immigration and Nationality Act, which led to the view that the statute did not permit even temporary or inadvertent absences from this country, see *INS v. Phinpathya,* 464 U.S. 183 (1984), was rebuffed by the 99th Congress; that its literal reading of the word "program" in Title IX of the Education Amendments of 1972, which led to the Court's gratuitous limit on the scope of the antidiscrimination provisions of Title IX, see *Grove City College v. Bell,* 465 U.S. 555 (1984), was rejected by the 100th Congress; or that its refusal to accept the teaching of earlier decisions in *Wards Cove Packing Co. v. Atonio,* 490 U.S. 642 (1989) (reformulating order of proof and weight of parties' burdens in disparate-impact cases), and *Patterson v. McLean Credit Union,* 491 U.S. 164 (1989) (limiting scope of 42 U.S.C. § 1981 to the making and enforcement of contracts), was overwhelmingly rejected by the 101st Congress, and its refusal to accept the widely held view of lower courts about the scope of fraud, see *McNally v. United States,* 483 U.S. 350 (1987) (limiting mail fraud to protection of property), was quickly corrected by the 100th Congress.

In the domain of statutory interpretation, Congress is the master. It obviously has the power to correct our mistakes, but we do the country a disservice when we needlessly ignore persuasive evidence of Congress' actual purpose and require it "to take the time to revisit the matter" [*Smith v. Robinson,* 468 U.S. 992, 1031 (1984) (Brennan, J., dissenting)] and to restate its purpose in more precise English whenever its work product suffers from an omission or inadvertent error. As Judge Learned Hand explained, statutes are likely to be imprecise.

"All [legislators] have done is to write down certain words which they mean to apply generally to situations of that kind. To apply these literally may either pervert what was plainly their general meaning, or leave undisposed of what there is every reason to suppose they meant to provide for. Thus it is not enough for the judge just to use a dictionary. If he should do no more, he might come out with a result which every sensible man would recognize to be quite the opposite of what was really intended; which would contradict or leave unfulfilled its plain purpose." L. Hand, How Far Is a Judge Free in Rendering a Decision?, in The Spirit of Liberty 103, 106 (I. Dilliard ed.1952).

The Court concludes its opinion with the suggestion that disagreement with its textual analysis could only be based on the dissenters' preference for a "better" statute. It overlooks the possibility that a different view may be more faithful to Congress' command. The fact that Congress has consistently provided for the inclusion of expert witness fees in fee-shifting statutes when it considered the matter is a weak reed on which to rest the conclusion that the omission of such a provision represents a deliberate decision to forbid such awards. Only time will tell whether the Court, with its literal reading of § 1988, has correctly interpreted the will of Congress with respect to the issue it has resolved today. * * *

NOTES AND QUESTIONS ON CHISOM AND CASEY

1. *Tools of the New Textualism.* We explore the most commonly-used tools of interpretation in Chapter 5, but *Chisom* and *Casey* introduce you to several of the textualists' favorites, and it is worth making a note of them here.

First, as Justice Scalia did in *Chisom*, the Court frequently uses the dictionary to provide meaning to key statutory terms. According to several studies, the use of dictionaries in Supreme Court statutory cases has skyrocketed since the legal process era—from just 23 uses over 16 opinions in the 1960s to 295 uses in 225 opinions in the 2000s. See Jeffrey L. Kirchmeier & Samuel A. Thumma, *Scaling the Lexicon Fortress: The United States Supreme Court's Use of Dictionaries in the Twenty-First Century*, 94 Marq. L. Rev. 77 (2010). And it's not just textualists who are using them. Professors Brudney and Baum report that Justices Scalia, Thomas, Breyer and Souter are the most frequent users, that dictionary use is not associated with particularly liberal or conservative outcomes, and that Justices do not seem to have a consistent method (such as the period or date of the dictionary) for choosing among the many options. See James J. Brudney & Lawrence Baum, *Oasis or Mirage: The Supreme Court's Thirst for Dictionaries in the Rehnquist and Roberts Eras*, 55 Wm. & Mary L. Rev. (2013). Such "dictionary shopping" raises questions about whether dictionaries are objective tools of interpretation (which seems to be their attraction) or are really just another way of looking over the crowd for one's friends. What are the best arguments for consulting dictionaries? The Gluck-Bressman empirical study suggests that congressional staffers do not consult them; and it is widely known that dictionaries lag behind common usage ("to google" was only recently added as a verb, for instance). Which dictionary would you consult? An ordinary desk dictionary, or something like *Black's Law Dictionary*? What edition? Note that, in *Chisom*, Justice Scalia consulted a dictionary for the ordinary meaning of representatives in 1982. But which dictionary? One from 1950!

Textualists often also argue that their methodology is contextual, not literal—that is, plain meaning is evident from the surrounding statutory context. A good example might have come from (of all places) *Holy Trinity Church*: can we understand "lecturers" from the context of other words in the § 5 exemption (which arguably all applied to entertainers, making pastors a poor fit)? On the other hand, a poor example comes from Justice Scalia himself, in *Chisom*, when he chastises the majority's reading of the term "representatives" on the ground that its reading is so broad as to potentially include members of the Major League Baseball All-Star team. What's wrong with that reading? (Google "representative" and "all-star team.")

Similarly, as in *Casey*, the Court frequently looks to evidence in the U.S. Code itself for plain meaning. If an ambiguous term is used more clearly elsewhere in the statute, or even elsewhere in the U.S. Code, the Court will draw meaning from those usages (sometimes called the "whole act" or "whole code" canons). The Court also places weight on whether its constructions of certain terms will render others redundant; in *Casey*, the Court gave significance to the fact that reading "attorneys' fees" to include the expenses of expert witnesses, would render redundant other provisions of the U.S. Code spelling out fee-shifting for the cost of studies and analyses necessary to the litigation. This so-called "rule against superfluities" is a presumption that Congress does not "waste" its words. How institutionally realist are these textualist presumptions? Professor Gluck opposes these canons on the ground that they do not reflect how Congress drafts. Congress is divided into many different subject-matter committees that do not communicate with one another when drafting, and so the idea that statutes share common-meaning across the U.S. Code is unrealistic. In *Casey*, for instance, the Court cited forty-one different statutes that contained fee-shifting provision without recognizing the fact that only four of the other statutes cited came from the same committee (Judiciary), and that the others (including the four most recent, on which the Court placed special weight) were drawn from 21 different committees that likely never communicated with Judiciary. The Gluck-Bressman empirical study also suggests that congressional staffers do repeat themselves: the majority surveyed told the authors that Congress uses redundant language to "cover the bases" or satisfy interest groups that need to see specific references to their pet causes in the statutory text. See Gluck & Bressman, *Statutory Interpretation from the Inside II*. If these textual rules do not reflect how Congress drafts, can you come up with a different justification for why textualists should use them?

2. *New Textualism v. the (Soft) Plain Meaning Rule of the Burger Court.* The relationship between the new textualism and the old plain meaning rule is evident, but they are not the same thing. Justice Scalia's

formulation of textualism at the beginning of his *Chisom* dissent, as well as his discussion in *A Matter of Interpretation*, stresses the "ordinary meaning" or "reasonable meaning" of statutory text. In his view, legislative history should never trump such ordinary meaning. In contrast, the old plain meaning rule, as exemplified by *Caminetti*, operated as an exclusionary rule concerning the use of legislative history: if the statutory text was "plain," one could not consult legislative history; if the statutory text was ambiguous, legislative history was fair game. The softer approach to plain meaning in *TVA v. Hill* and *Griffin* was even less confining, stating merely that a statutory plain meaning was presumptively the interpretation to be given to the statute, but legislative history could be consulted to confirm that understanding (and in a rare case in which the legislative history conclusively demonstrated that the textual plain meaning was not the appropriate interpretation, the plain meaning could be jettisoned).

3.   *The Arc of the New Textualism, and Where the Court Is Today*. After Justice Scalia's appointment (1986), the Court's statutory opinions more often found a "plain meaning," less often examined legislative history to confirm the existence of a plain meaning, and relied less often on legislative history to interpret a statute against what the Court felt was its plain meaning.[8] Even nontextualist Justices have relied on legislative history less, in part to garner majorities but also because the atmospheric influence of textualism has had an effect. The Justices' opinions also have tended to be more dogmatic about whether there is any ambiguity in statutes; the Court was more likely to find a plain meaning in the 1990s than it was before 1986.

But although the Court's practice has clearly been influenced by the new textualism, the Court never completely accepted its tenets. In *Wisconsin Public Intervenor v. Mortier*, 501 U.S. 597, 610 n.4 (1991), all of the other Justices joined a footnote explicitly rejecting Justice Scalia's insistence that legislative history is irrelevant to proper statutory interpretation. See Charles Tiefer, *The Reconceptualization of Legislative History in the Supreme Court*, 2000 Wis. L. Rev. 205 (arguing that the new textualism is past its peak and that its strong claims were rejected by the Court in the 1990s).[9] As in *Casey*, Justice Scalia's own opinions tend to set forth and defend the precepts of the new textualism, often with Justice Stevens, Breyer, and, more recently, Sotomayor, setting out the arguments for a more purposive

---

[8]   See William N. Eskridge Jr., *Dynamic Statutory Interpretation* ch. 7 (1994); Lawrence M. Solan, *The Language of Judges* (1993); Thomas W. Merrill, *Textualism and the Future of the Chevron Doctrine*, 72 Wash. U. L. Q. 351 (1994).

[9]   In addition, see James J. Brudney & Corey Ditslear, *The Decline and Fall of Legislative History? Patterns of Supreme Court Reliance in the Burger and Rehnquist Eras*, 89 Judicature 220 (2006); David S. Law & David Zaring, *Law Versus Ideology: The Supreme Court and the Use of Legislative History*, 51 Wm. & Mary L. Rev. 1653 (2010); Jonathan Molot, *The Rise and Fall of Textualism*, 106 Colum. L. Rev. 1 (2006); Lawrence M. Solan, *Learning Our Limits: The Decline of Textualism in Statutory Cases*, 1997 Wis. L. Rev. 235.

methodology, or at least one that considers legislative history or social context.[10]

Although textualism has not taken over, the Supreme Court has not returned to the legal process era. First, the text is now, more than it was 20 or 30 years ago, the central inquiry at the Supreme Court level and in other courts that are now following the Supreme Court's lead. A brief that starts off with, "The statute means thus-and-so because it says so in the committee report," is asking for trouble. Both advice and advocacy should start with the statutory text: "The statute means thus-and-so because that is its plain meaning," "because that is the meaning the structure of the statute supports," or "because this statute uses more narrow language than Congress purposefully used in other statutes."

Leading textualist John Manning calls this shift the "new purposivism," a more text-focused approach to purpose that is still willing to focus on legislative history. John F. Manning, *The New Purposivism*, 2011 S.Ct. Rev. 113. Manning contends this modern version of purposivism is even more faithful to Hart and Sacks than the earlier version, because the Court is more attune to the fact that "Congress legislates at different levels of generality" and so may intend different levels of judicial discretion in different cases. *Id.* at 118. Of particular interest—and as evidence of the convergence of the theories—even textualists like Manning have found room for purposivist judicial interpretation when Congress legislatives with sufficient generality.

C. PRAGMATIC APPROACHES

A third set of approaches might fall under the general umbrella of "pragmatism," although different theorists think about pragmatism in different ways. This final section introduces you to the "common sense" pragmatism of Judge Posner; the purposive pragmatism of Justice Breyer; the "practical reasoning" approach of Professors Eskridge and Frickey; and efforts by state courts to bring some order to the unpredictability of the current methodological landscape. We also return to the theme of how thinking pragmatically about the different institutions involved in any act of interpretation might affect the ultimate approach. Consider, first, the following match-up between Judge Easterbrook's textualism and Judge Posner's interpretive philosophy.

---

[10] See, for example, the debates in *MCI Telecommunications Corp. v. American Tel. & Tel. Co.*, 512 U.S. 218 (1994) (Scalia writing for the majority, Stevens in dissent); Zuni v. Pub. Sch. Dist. No 89. v. Dept. Educ., 550 U.S. 81 (2001) (Breyer for the majority, Stevens concurring, Scalia in dissent); *Graham County Soil & Water Conservation District v. United States ex rel Wilson*, 130 S.Ct. 1396, 1411 (2010) (Scalia, partially concurring, Sotomayor, in dissent).

STATUTORY PREFACE FOR *MARSHALL*

**The Controlled Substances Penalties
Amendments Act of 1984, (Public Law 98–473,
§ 502 (1984), amending 21 U.S.C. § 841(b))**

21 U.S.C. § 841(a), makes it a crime for any person knowingly to manufacture, distribute, dispense, or possess with intent to distribute a controlled substance.

§ 841(b) Penalties. Except as otherwise provided in section 859, 860, or 861 of this title, any person who violates subsection (a) of this section shall be sentenced as follows:

(1)(A) In the case of a violation of subsection (a) of this section involving—

> **(i)** 1 kilogram or more of a mixture or substance containing a detectable amount of heroin; * * *

> **(iii)** 280 grams or more of a mixture or substance described in clause (ii) which contains cocaine base;

> **(iv)** 100 grams or more of phencyclidine (PCP) or 1 kilogram or more of a mixture or substance containing a detectable amount of phencyclidine (PCP);

> **(v)** 10 grams or more of a mixture or substance containing a detectable amount of lysergic acid diethylamide (LSD); * * *

> **(vii)** 1000 kilograms or more of a mixture or substance containing a detectable amount of marijuana, or 1,000 or more marijuana plants regardless of weight; or

> **(viii)** 50 grams or more of methamphetamine, its salts, isomers, and salts of its isomers or 500 grams or more of a mixture or substance containing a detectable amount of methamphetamine, its salts, isomers, or salts of its isomers;

such person shall be sentenced to a term of imprisonment which may not be less than 10 years or more than life and if death or serious bodily injury results from the use of such substance shall be not less than 20 years or more than life, a fine not to exceed the greater of that authorized in accordance with the provisions of Title 18, or $10,000,000 if the defendant is an individual or $50,000,000 if the defendant is other than an individual, or both. [The remainder of § 841(b)(1)(A) contains further enhancements for offenders with previous convictions for a felony drug offense.]

(B) In the case of a violation of subsection (a) of this section involving—

> **(i)** 100 grams or more of a mixture or substance containing a detectable amount of heroin; * * *

(iii) 28 grams or more of a mixture or substance described in clause (ii) which contains cocaine base;

(iv) 10 grams or more of phencyclidine (PCP) or 100 grams or more of a mixture or substance containing a detectable amount of phencyclidine (PCP);

(v) 1 gram or more of a mixture or substance containing a detectable amount of lysergic acid diethylamide (LSD); * * *

(vii) 100 kilograms or more of a mixture or substance containing a detectable amount of marijuana, or 100 or more marijuana plants regardless of weight; or

(viii) 5 grams or more of methamphetamine, its salts, isomers, and salts of its isomers or 50 grams or more of a mixture or substance containing a detectable amount of methamphetamine, its salts, isomers, or salts of its isomers;

such person shall be sentenced to a term of imprisonment which may not be less than 5 years and not more than 40 years and if death or serious bodily injury results from the use of such substance shall be not less than 20 years or more than life, a fine not to exceed the greater of that authorized in accordance with the provisions of Title 18, or $5,000,000 if the defendant is an individual or $25,000,000 if the defendant is other than an individual, or both. [The remainder of § 841(b)(1)(B) contains further enhancements for offenders with previous convictions for a felony drug offense.]

UNITED STATES v. STANLEY J. MARSHALL ET AL.

United States Court of Appeals for the Seventh Circuit (en banc), 1990.
908 F.2d 1312, *aff'd sub nom. Chapman v. United States*, 500 U.S. 453 (1991).

EASTERBROOK, CIRCUIT JUDGE.

* * * Stanley J. Marshall was convicted after a bench trial and sentenced to 20 years' imprisonment for conspiring to distribute, and distributing, more than ten grams of LSD, enough for 11,751 doses. Patrick Brumm, Richard L. Chapman, and John M. Schoenecker were convicted by a jury of selling ten sheets (1,000 doses) of paper containing LSD. Because the total weight of the paper and LSD was 5.7 grams, a five-year mandatory minimum applied. The district court sentenced Brumm to 60 months (the minimum), Schoenecker to 63 months, and Chapman to 96 months' imprisonment. All four defendants confine their arguments on appeal to questions concerning their sentences.

The three questions we must resolve are these: (1) Whether 21 U.S.C. § 841(b)(1)(A)(v) and (B)(v), which set mandatory minimum terms of imprisonment—five years for selling more than one gram of a "mixture or substance containing a detectable amount" of LSD, ten years for more than ten grams—exclude the weight of the carrier medium. (2) Whether the weight tables in the sentencing guidelines likewise exclude the weight of any carrier. (3) Whether the statute and the guidelines are unconstitutional to the extent their computations are based on anything other than the weight of the pure drug. * * *

According to the Sentencing Commission, the LSD in an average dose weighs 0.05 milligrams. Twenty thousand pure doses are a gram. But 0.05 mg is almost invisible, so LSD is distributed to retail customers in a carrier. Pure LSD is dissolved in a solvent such as alcohol and sprayed on paper or gelatin; alternatively the paper may be dipped in the solution. After the solvent evaporates, the paper or gel is cut into one-dose squares and sold by the square. Users swallow the squares or may drop them into a beverage, releasing the drug. Although the gelatin and paper are light, they weigh much more than the drug. Marshall's 11,751 doses weighed 113.32 grams; the LSD accounted for only 670.72 mg of this, not enough to activate the five-year mandatory minimum sentence, let alone the ten-year minimum. The ten sheets of blotter paper carrying the 1,000 doses Chapman and confederates sold weighed 5.7 grams; the LSD in the paper did not approach the one-gram threshold for a mandatory minimum sentence. This disparity between the weight of the pure LSD and the weight of LSD-plus-carrier underlies the defendants' arguments.

If the carrier counts in the weight of the "mixture or substance containing a detectable amount" of LSD, some odd things may happen. Weight in the hands of distributors may exceed that of manufacturers and wholesalers. Big fish then could receive paltry sentences or small fish draconian ones. Someone who sold 19, 999 doses of pure LSD (at 0.05 mg per dose) would escape the five-year mandatory minimum of § 841(b)(1)(B)(v) and be covered by § 841(b)(1)(C), which lacks a minimum term and has a maximum of "only" 20 years. Someone who sold a single hit of LSD dissolved in a tumbler of orange juice could be exposed to a ten-year mandatory minimum. Retailers could fall in or out of the mandatory terms depending not on the number of doses but on the medium: sugar cubes weigh more than paper, which weighs more than gelatin. One way to eliminate the possibility of such consequences is to say that the carrier is not a "mixture or substance containing a detectable amount" of the drug. Defendants ask us to do this.

Defendants' submission starts from the premise that the interaction of the statutory phrase "mixture or substance" with the distribution of LSD by the dose in a carrier creates a unique probability of surprise results. The premise may be unwarranted. The paper used to distribute LSD is light stuff, not the kind used to absorb ink. Chapman's 1,000 doses weighed about 0.16 ounces. More than 6,000 doses, even in blotter paper, weigh less than an ounce. Because the LSD in one dose weighs about 0.05 milligrams, the combination of LSD-plus-paper is about 110 times the weight of the LSD. The impregnated paper could be described as "0.9% LSD". * * *

This is by no means an unusual dilution rate for illegal drugs. Heroin sold on the street is 2% to 3% opiate and the rest filler. Sometimes the mixture is even more dilute, approaching the dilution rate for LSD in blotter paper. Heroin and crack cocaine, like LSD, are sold on the streets by the dose, although they are sold by weight higher in the distributional chain. * * *

It is not possible to construe the words of § 841 to make the penalty turn on the net weight of the drug rather than the gross weight of carrier and drug. The statute speaks of "mixture or substance containing a detectable amount" of a drug. "Detectable amount" is the opposite of "pure"; the point of the statute is that the "mixture" is not to be converted to an equivalent amount of pure drug.

The structure of the statute reinforces this conclusion. The 10-year minimum applies to any person who possesses, with intent to distribute, "100 grams or more of phencyclidine (PCP) or 1 kilogram or more of a mixture or substance containing a detectable amount of phencyclidine (PCP)", § 841(b)(1)(A)(iv). Congress distinguished the pure drug from a "mixture or substance containing a detectable amount of" it. All drugs other than PCP are governed exclusively by the "mixture or substance" language. Even brute force cannot turn that language into a reference to pure LSD. Congress used the same "mixture or substance" language to describe heroin, cocaine, amphetamines, and many other drugs that are sold after being cut—sometimes as much as LSD. There is no sound basis on which to treat the words "substance or mixture containing a detectable amount of", repeated verbatim for every drug mentioned in § 841 except PCP, as *different* things for LSD and cocaine although the language is identical, while treating the "mixture or substance" language as meaning the *same* as the reference to pure PCP in 21 U.S.C. § 841(b)(1)(A)(iv) and (B)(iv).

Although the "mixture or substance" language shows that the statute cannot be limited to pure LSD, it does not necessarily follow that blotter paper *is* a "mixture or substance containing" LSD. That phrase cannot include all "carriers". One gram of crystalline LSD in a heavy glass bottle is still only one gram of "statutory LSD". So is a gram of LSD being "carried" in a Boeing 747. How much mingling of the drug with something else is essential to form a "mixture or substance"? The legislative history is silent, but ordinary usage is indicative.

"Substance" may well refer to a chemical compound, or perhaps to a drug in a solvent. LSD does not react chemically with sugar, blotter paper, or gelatin, and none of these is a solvent. "Mixture" is more inclusive. Cocaine often is mixed with mannitol, quinine, or lactose. These white powders do not react, but it is common ground that a cocaine-mannitol mixture is a statutory "mixture".

LSD and blotter paper are not commingled in the same way as cocaine and lactose. What is the nature of their association? The possibility most favorable to defendants is that LSD sits on blotter paper as oil floats on water. Immiscible substances may fall outside the statutory definition of "mixture". The possibility does not assist defendants—not on this record, anyway. LSD is applied to paper in a solvent; after the solvent evaporates, a tiny quantity of LSD remains. Because the fibers absorb the alcohol, the LSD solidifies inside the paper rather than on it. You cannot pick a grain of LSD off the surface of the paper. Ordinary parlance calls the paper containing tiny crystals of LSD a mixture.

United States v. Rose, 881 F.2d 386 (7th Cir. 1989), like every other appellate decision that has addressed the question, concludes that the carrier medium for LSD, like the "cut" for heroin and cocaine, is a "mixture or substance containing a detectable amount" of the drug. Although a chemist might be able to offer evidence bearing on the question whether LSD and blotter paper "mix" any more fully than do oil and water, the record contains no such evidence. Without knowing more of the chemistry than this record reveals, we adhere to the unanimous conclusion of the other courts of appeals that blotter paper treated with LSD is a "mixture or substance containing a detectable quantity of" LSD.

Two reasons have been advanced to support a contrary conclusion: that statutes should be construed to avoid constitutional problems, and that some members of the sitting Congress are dissatisfied with basing penalties on the combined weight of LSD and carrier. Neither is persuasive.

A preference for giving statutes a constitutional meaning is a reason to construe, not to rewrite or "improve". * * * "[S]ubstance or mixture containing a detectable quantity" is not ambiguous. * * * Neither the rule of lenity nor the preference for avoiding constitutional adjudication justifies disregarding unambiguous language.

The canon about avoiding constitutional decisions, in particular, must be used with care, for it is a closer cousin to invalidation than to interpretation. It is a way to enforce the constitutional penumbra, and therefore an aspect of constitutional law proper. Constitutional decisions breed penumbras, which multiply questions. Treating each as justification to construe laws out of existence too greatly enlarges the judicial power. And heroic "construction" is unnecessary, given our conclusion [in discussion omitted here] that Congress possesses the constitutional power to set penalties on the basis of gross weight.

As for the pending legislation: subsequent debates are not a ground for avoiding the import of enactments. Although the views of a subsequent Congress are entitled to respect, ongoing debates do not represent the views of Congress. * * *

CUMMINGS, CIRCUIT JUDGE, with whom BAUER, CHIEF JUDGE, and WOOD, JR., CUDAHY, and POSNER, CIRCUIT JUDGES, join, dissenting.

* * * [T]he United States District Court for the District of Columbia held that blotter paper was not a mixture or substance within the meaning of the statute. *United States v Healy*, 729 F.Supp. 140 (D.D.C. 1990). The court relied not only on ordinary dictionary definitions of the words mixture and substance but also on a November 30, 1988, Sentencing Commission publication, entitled "Questions Most Frequently Asked About the Sentencing Guidelines," which states that the Commission has not taken a position on whether the blotter paper should be weighed. The conclusion that the Commission has not yet resolved this question is further supported by a Sentencing Commission Notice issued on March 3, 1989, which requested public comments on whether the Commission should exclude the weight of the carrier for sentencing purposes in LSD cases. * * *

Two subsequent pieces of legislative history * * * shed some light on this question. In a letter to Senator Joseph R. Biden, Jr., dated April 26, 1989, the Chairman of the Sentencing Commission, William W. Wilkens, Jr., noted the ambiguity in the statute as it is currently written:

> With respect to LSD, it is unclear whether Congress intended the carrier to be considered as a packaging material, or, since it is commonly consumed along with the illicit drug, as a dilutant ingredient in the drug mixture. . . . The Commission suggests that Congress may wish to further consider the LSD carrier issue in order to clarify legislative intent as to whether the weight of the carrier should or should not be considered in determining the quantity of LSD mixture for punishment purposes.

Presumably acting in response to this query, Senator Biden added to the Congressional Record for October 5, 1989, an analysis of one of a series of technical corrections to 21 U.S.C. § 841 that were under consideration by the Senate that day. This analysis states that the purpose of the particular correction at issue was to remove an unintended "inequity" from Section 841 caused by the decisions of some courts to include the weight of the blotter paper for sentencing purposes in LSD cases. According to Senator Biden, the correction "remedie[d] this inequity by removing the weight of the carrier from the calculation of the weight of the mixture or substance." This correction was adopted as part of Amendment No. 976 to S. 1711. 135 Cong. Rec. S12749 (daily ed. Oct.

5, 1989). The amended bill was passed by a unanimous vote of the Senate (*id.* at S12765) and is currently pending before the House.

Comments in more recent issues of the Congressional Record indicate that S. 1711 is not expected to pass the House of Representatives. See 136 Cong. Rec. S943 (daily ed. Feb. 7, 1990). In the meantime, however, a second attempt to clarify Congress' intent in amending 21 U.S.C. § 841 to include the words mixture or substance has now been introduced in the Senate. On April 18, 1990, Senator Kennedy introduced an amendment to S. 1970 (a bill establishing constitutional procedures for the imposition of the death penalty) seeking to clarify the language of 21 U.S.C. § 841. That amendment, Amendment No. 1716, states:

> Section 841(b)(1) of title 21, United States Code, is amended by inserting the following new subsection at the end thereof: "(E) In determining the weight of a 'mixture or substance' under this section, the court shall not include the weight of the carrier upon which the controlled substance is placed, or by which it is transported."

136 Cong. Rec. S7069 (daily ed. May 24, 1990). [Judge Cummings argued from this evidence that the draconian penalty scheme for LSD was simply a mistake never intended by Congress and that the Seventh Circuit should follow *Healy.*]

POSNER, CIRCUIT JUDGE, joined by BAUER, CHIEF JUDGE, and CUMMINGS, WOOD, JR., and CUDAHY, CIRCUIT JUDGES, dissenting.

* * * Based as it is on weight, [the § 841 sentencing scheme] works well for drugs that are sold by weight; and ordinarily the weight quoted to the buyer is the weight of the dilute form, although of course price will vary with purity. The dilute form is the product, and it is as natural to punish its purveyors according to the weight of the product as it is to punish moonshiners by the weight or volume of the moonshine they sell rather than by the weight of the alcohol contained in it. So, for example, under Florida law it is a felony to possess one or more gallons of moonshine, and a misdemeanor to possess less than one gallon, regardless of the alcoholic content. Fla. Stat. §§ 561.01, 562.451.

LSD, however, is sold to the consumer by the dose; it is not cut, diluted, or mixed with something else. Moreover, it is incredibly light. An average dose of LSD weighs .05 milligrams, which is less than two millionths of an ounce. To ingest something that small requires swallowing something much larger. Pure LSD in granular form is first diluted by being dissolved, usually in alcohol, and then a quantity of the solution containing one dose of LSD is sprayed or eyedropped on a sugar cube, or on a cube of gelatin, or, as in the cases before us, on an inch-square section of "blotter" paper. * * * After the solution is applied to the carrier medium, the alcohol or other solvent evaporates, leaving an invisible (and undiluted) spot of pure LSD on the cube or blotter paper. The consumer drops the cube or the piece of paper into a glass of water, or orange juice, or some other beverage, causing the LSD to dissolve in the beverage, which is then drunk. * * * [A] quart of orange juice containing one dose of LSD is not more, in any relevant sense, than a pint of juice containing the same one dose, and it would be loony to punish the purveyor of the quart more heavily than the purveyor of the pint. It would be like basing the punishment for selling cocaine on the combined weight of the cocaine and of the vehicle (plane, boat, automobile, or whatever) used to transport it or the syringe used to inject it or the pipe used to smoke it. The blotter paper, sugar cubes, etc. are the vehicles for conveying LSD to the consumer.

The weight of the carrier is vastly greater than that of the LSD, as well as irrelevant to its potency. There is no comparable disparity between the pure and the mixed form (if that is how we should regard LSD on blotter paper or other carrier medium) with respect to the other drugs in section 841, with the illuminating exception of PCP. There Congress specified alternative weights, for the drug itself and for the substance or mixture containing the drug. For example, the five-year minimum sentence for a seller of PCP requires the sale of either ten grams of the drug itself or one hundred grams of a substance or mixture containing the drug. 21 U.S.C. § 841(b)(1)(B)(iv).

Ten sheets of blotter paper, containing a thousand doses of LSD, weigh almost six grams. The LSD itself weighs less than a hundredth as much. If the thousand doses are on gelatin cubes instead of sheets of blotter paper, the total weight is less, but it is still more than two grams, which is forty times the weight of the LSD. In both cases, if the carrier plus the LSD constitutes the relevant "substance or mixture" (the crucial "if" in this case), the dealer is subject to the minimum mandatory sentence of five years. One of the defendants before us (Marshall) sold almost 12,000 doses of LSD on blotter paper. This subjected him to the ten-year minimum, and the Guidelines then took over and pushed him up to twenty years. Since it takes 20,000 doses of LSD to equal a gram, Marshall would not have been subject to even the five-year mandatory minimum had he sold the LSD in its pure form. And a dealer who sold fifteen times the number of doses as Marshall—180,000—would not be subject to the ten-year mandatory minimum sentence if he sold the drug in its pure form, because 180,000 doses is only nine grams.

At the other extreme, if Marshall were not a dealer at all but dropped a square of blotter paper containing a single dose of LSD into a glass of orange juice and sold it to a friend at cost (perhaps 35 cents), he would be subject to the ten-year minimum. The juice with LSD dissolved in it would be the statutory mixture or substance containing a detectable amount of the illegal drug and it would weigh more than ten grams (one

ounce is about 35 grams, and the orange juice in a glass of orange juice
weighs several ounces). So a person who sold one dose of LSD might be
subject to the ten-year mandatory minimum sentence while a dealer who
sold 199,999 doses in pure form would be subject only to the five-year
minimum. Defendant Dean sold 198 doses, crowded onto one sheet of
blotter paper: this subjected him to the five-year mandatory minimum,
too, since the ensemble weighed slightly more than a gram. * * *

All this seems crazy but we must consider whether Congress might
have had a reason for wanting to key the severity of punishment for
selling LSD to the weight of the carrier rather than to the number of
doses or to some reasonable proxy for dosage (as weight is, for many
drugs). The only one suggested is that it might be costly to determine the
weight of the LSD in the blotter paper, sugar cube, etc., because it is so
light! That merely underscores the irrationality of basing the punishment
for selling this drug on weight rather than on dosage. But in fact the
weight is reported in every case I have seen, so apparently it can be
determined readily enough; it *has* to be determined in any event, to
permit a purity adjustment under the Guidelines. If the weight of the
LSD is difficult to determine, the difficulty is easily overcome by basing
punishment on the number of doses, which makes much more sense in
any event. To base punishment on the weight of the carrier medium
makes about as much sense as basing punishment on the weight of the
defendant. * * *

This is a quilt the pattern whereof no one has been able to discern.
The legislative history is silent, and since even the Justice Department
cannot explain the why of the punishment scheme that it is defending,
the most plausible inference is that Congress simply did not realize how
LSD is sold. The inference is reinforced by the statutory treatment of
PCP. * * *

[The] irrationality is magnified when we compare the sentences for
people who sell other drugs prohibited by 21 U.S.C. § 841. Marshall,
remember, sold fewer than 12,000 doses and was sentenced to twenty
years. Twelve thousand doses sounds like a lot, but to receive a
comparable sentence for selling heroin Marshall would have had to sell
ten kilograms, which would yield between one and two million doses. To
receive a comparable sentence for selling cocaine he would have had to
sell fifty kilograms, which would yield anywhere from 325,000 to five
million doses. While the corresponding weight is lower for crack—half a
kilogram—this still translates into 50,000 doses. * * *

Well, what if anything can we judges do about this mess? The answer
lies in the shadow of a jurisprudential disagreement that is not less
important by virtue of being unavowed by most judges. It is the
disagreement between the severely positivistic view that the content of

law is exhausted in clear, explicit, and definite enactments by or under express delegation from legislatures, and the natural lawyer's or legal pragmatist's view that the practice of interpretation and the general terms of the Constitution (such as "equal protection of the laws") authorize judges to enrich positive law with the moral values and practical concerns of civilized society. Judges who in other respects have seemed quite similar, such as Holmes and Cardozo, have taken opposite sides of this issue. Neither approach is entirely satisfactory. The first buys political neutrality and a type of objectivity at the price of substantive injustice, while the second buys justice in the individual case at the price of considerable uncertainty and, not infrequently, judicial willfulness. It is no wonder that our legal system oscillates between the approaches. The positivist view, applied unflinchingly to this case, commands the affirmance of prison sentences that are exceptionally harsh by the standards of the modern Western world, dictated by an accidental, unintended scheme of punishment nevertheless implied by the words (taken one by one) of the relevant enactments. The natural law or pragmatist view leads to a freer interpretation, one influenced by norms of equal treatment; and let us explore the interpretive possibilities here. One is to interpret "mixture or substance containing a detectable amount of [LSD]" to exclude the carrier medium—the blotter paper, sugar or gelatin cubes, and orange juice or other beverage. That is the course we rejected in *United States v. Rose, supra*, as have the other circuits. I wrote *Rose*, but I am no longer confident that its literal interpretation of the statute, under which the blotter paper, cubes, etc. are "substances" that "contain" LSD, is inevitable. The blotter paper, etc. are better viewed, I now think, as carriers, like the package in which a kilo of cocaine comes wrapped or the bottle in which a fifth of liquor is sold.

Interpreted to exclude the carrier, the punishment schedule for LSD would make perfectly good sense; it would not warp the statutory design. The comparison with heroin and cocaine is again illuminating. The statute imposes the five-year mandatory minimum sentence on anyone who sells a substance or mixture containing a hundred grams of heroin, equal to 10,000 to 20,000 doses. One gram of pure LSD, which also would trigger the five-year minimum, yields 20,000 doses. The comparable figures for cocaine are 3250 to 50,000 doses, placing LSD in about the middle. So Congress may have wanted to base punishment for the sale of LSD on the weight of the pure drug after all, using one and ten grams of the pure drug to trigger the five-year and ten-year minima (and corresponding maxima—twenty years and forty years). This interpretation leaves "substance or mixture containing" without a referent, so far as LSD is concerned. But we must remember that Congress used the identical term in each subsection that specifies the quantity of a drug that subjects the seller to the designated minimum and maximum punishments. In thus automatically including the same term in each subsection, Congress did not necessarily affirm that, for each and every drug covered by the statute, a substance or mixture containing the drug *must* be found.

The flexible interpretation that I am proposing is decisively strengthened by the constitutional objection to basing punishment of LSD offenders on the weight of the carrier medium rather than on the weight of the LSD. Courts often do interpretive handsprings to avoid having even to *decide* a constitutional question. In doing so they expand, very questionably in my view, the effective scope of the Constitution, creating a constitutional penumbra in which statutes wither, shrink, are deformed. A better case for flexible interpretation is presented when the alternative is to nullify Congress's action: when in other words there is not merely a constitutional question about, but a constitutional barrier to, the statute when interpreted literally. This is such a case.

[Judge Posner then argued that the sentencing scheme for LSD upheld by the majority violates the equal protection guarantee of the Fifth Amendment's due process clause, because of the "unequal treatment of people equally situated." That even the Justice Department could not formulate a rational basis for the distinctions it had drawn from § 841 in LSD cases was persuasive evidence that Congress had to be sent back to the drawing board.]

The literal interpretation adopted by the majority is not inevitable. All interpretation is contextual. The words of the statute—interpreted against a background that includes a constitutional norm of equal treatment, a (closely related) constitutional commitment to rationality, an evident failure by both Congress and the Sentencing Commission to consider how LSD is actually produced, distributed, and sold, and an equally evident failure by the same two bodies to consider the interaction between heavy mandatory minimum sentences and the Sentencing Guidelines—will bear an interpretation that distinguishes between the carrier vehicle of the illegal drug and the substance or mixture containing a detectable amount of the drug. The punishment of the crack dealer is not determined by the weight of the glass tube in which he sells the crack; we should not lightly attribute to Congress a purpose of punishing the dealer in LSD according to the weight of the LSD carrier. We should not make Congress's handiwork an embarrassment to the members of Congress and to us.

NOTES AND QUESTIONS ON MARSHALL

1. *Judge Posner's Pragmatism.* In *How Judges Think* (2008), Judge Richard A. Posner broadly distinguishes between "legalistic" and "pragmatic" theories of statutory interpretation. Legalistic theories claim that law is an autonomous discipline that can reach neutral interpretations through application of plain meanings (assisted perhaps with dictionaries and

linguists), following precedent, reasoning by analogy, and the like. Pragmatic theories, in contrast, openly admit that law is not (entirely) separate from politics and that interpretation carries with it discretion and policy choice. Hart and Sacks's purpose-based interpretation is, by this reading, pragmatic, and Posner's current approach, well-illustrated in the LSD case above, is an updated or more sophisticated version of legal process theory. Indeed, doesn't his dissent in the LSD case sound remarkably close to the words of Judge Foster in the Speluncean Explorers case?

2.   *The Meaning of "Mixture."* The Supreme Court affirmed *Marshall*, but was too divided to accept Judge Easterbook's argument that the "ordinary usage" of mixture included the LSD/blotter paper situation. (Judge Easterbrook's structural argument with respect to PCP might have been a stronger hook, and one that a textualist court today might have seized on. Do you see that argument?) Instead, the Supreme Court relied on a dictionary definition of mixture as "two substances blended together so that the particles of one are diffused among the particles of the other." See *Chapman v. United States*, 500 U.S. 453, 462 (1991). Because the LSD "is diffused among the fibers of the paper," the Supreme Court found a statutory "plain meaning." *Id.*

Professional linguists are willing to expand and contract meaning beyond its dictionary denotations. Words reflect categories, which are fuzzy at the margins; the necessary and sufficient conditions for membership in the category are not completely accessible to us before the fact. Professor Lawrence Solan, a Ph.D. linguist, in *When Judges Use the Dictionary*, 68 Am. Speech 50, 54–55 (1993), analyzes the *Marshall* case in this way:

> Calling the blotter paper impregnated with LSD a mixture seems odd for the same reason that it seems odd to call a pancake soaked with syrup *a pancake-syrup mixture*; or to call a wet towel *a water-cotton mixture*; or to call a towel that one has used to dry one's face during a tennis game *a cotton-sweat mixture*, or later, after the sweat has dried, *a cotton-salt mixture*. The last two of these examples I would call *a wet towel* and *a dirty towel*, respectively. In all of these examples, both substances have kept their character in a chemical sense, but one of the substances seems to have kept too much of its character for us to feel natural using the word *mixture*. * * *
>
> As an analytical matter, the Supreme Court in *Chapman* has erred by taking a concept that is fuzzy at the margins and substituting for it a definition that is subject to more refined application than the concept itself. * * *

If Professor Solan is right, Judge Posner had a stronger argument to be made with regard to the "plain meaning" of the statute. How would Judge Easterbrook respond to Professor Solan's linguistic analysis?

3. *Reasons and Coherence in Statutory Interpretation.* At oral argument in the LSD Case, Judge Posner asked the Department of Justice why the statute's drafters (lawyers in the Department) wrote the LSD provision the way they did. What reason did the drafters or the legislators have for imposing such disproportionate sentences on defendants who sold LSD on blotter paper? Even though the Solicitor General was defending the statute, the government's representative did not know the answer to this question—and that inspired Judge Posner to change his mind, renounce his opinion in *Rose,* and vote to reverse the sentence enhancement for the defendants here. Can you think of a reason Congress would have made the LSD-with-blotter-paper sentence so disproportionate to sentences given for other substances and their carrier mediums? This is precisely the inquiry Hart and Sacks contemplated. Is there an obligation to learn more about the perils of LSD, and perhaps its greater harm to young users, before concluding that there was no possible reason for treating the LSD defendants so harshly?

Piecing together the history here is not so easy, in part because of the many different institutional actors involved. You already know about the Solicitor General, the Seventh Circuit, and the Supreme Court. But there was also the U.S. Sentencing Commission, whose members are appointed by the President, with the authority to establish what are now nonbinding guidelines for federal judges to apply to criminal sentences. As Judge Cummings pointed out in his dissent in the LSD Case, the Commission for a number of years had expressed no opinion on whether blotter paper should be counted as part of the "mixture or substance" in an LSD case. But as the *Marshall* case wound its path through the courts, the Commission took a position on this issue. The mission of this agency is to create more predictability and consistency in sentencing: similar crimes ought to generate similar sentences for offenders. In light of this statutory policy, how would the Commission go about interpreting the enhancement for LSD? See 55 Fed. Reg. 19197 (May 8, 1990) (proposed amendment to Application Note 11 to Guidelines Section 2D1.1).

Of course, there was also some legislative history. The House report accompanying the Act in which the LSD penalties in *Marshall* originated explained that "One of the major goals of this bill is to give greater direction to the DEA and the U.S. Attorneys on how to focus scarce law enforcement resources. Up until 1984 the controlled substances law did not distinguish drug traffickers by the quantities of drugs they were responsible for selling or smuggling. * * * The Committee strongly believes that the Federal government's most intense focus ought to be on major traffickers, the manufacturers or the heads of organizations, who are responsible for creating and delivering very large quantities of drugs." H.R. Rep. 99–845, at § 314 (1986).

4. *System Values and Legitimacy.* Lawyers often incline textualist in *TVA* (finding the Endangered Species Act clear, they are on board with taking the dam down) and purposive or pragmatic in *Marshall,* feeling

sympathetic to the defendant. What might be the difference? One normative difference that may drive the different inclinations is what's at stake: someone's liberty—*Marshall* is a criminal case—as opposed to property and wasted money. In fact, there is a canon of statutory interpretation that captures that value, the so-called rule of lenity, which says that an ambiguous criminal statute must be interpreted in favor of the accused. As discussed in Chapter 5, § 2, the rule of lenity reflects normative concerns that defendants have fair notice before the government can lock them up for alleged crimes, that prosecutorial discretion be limited by clear legislative commands, and that legislatures announce criminal prohibitions clearly enough that unelected judges are not developing them in a common law fashion. Neither judge invoked lenity in *Marshall*, but would that have made a difference for you?

Consider another kind of normative baseline. Judge Easterbrook's first major article on statutory interpretation urged that statutes not be construed beyond the "domain" clearly demarcated by their texts. He defended this approach on the basis of a libertarian presumption akin to the standard Chicago School idea that most things should not be regulated by the state and should be left to the free operation of the market:

> Those who wrote and approved the Constitution thought that most social relations would be governed by private agreements, customs, and understandings, not resolved in the halls of government. There is still at least a presumption that people's arrangements prevail unless expressly displaced by legal doctrine. All things are permitted unless there is some contrary rule. It is easier for an agency to justify the revocation of rules (or simple nonregulation) than the creation of new rules.

Frank H. Easterbrook, *Statutes' Domains*, 50 U. Chi. L. Rev. 533, 549–50 (1983). Does this baseline support Judge Easterbrook's opinion in the LSD Case?

Stephen Breyer, *Making Our Democracy Work: A Judge's View*
Summary and Selected Quotations (2010).

Another kind of pragmatism comes from Justice Breyer, who offers a sustained response to Justice Scalia's conceptualization of the Court-Congress relationship in statutory interpretation. Justice Breyer's approach to statutory interpretation puts "purpose and consequence" ahead of text, with three primary justifications for doing so, all grounded in their benefits to democracy (p. 94).

First, Justice Breyer argues that the public does not read statutory text but, rather, understands only statutory purposes. Thus, a purposive approach furthers democratic accountability. "If courts have interpreted the statute in accordance with the legislator's purposes, there is no one to blame but the legislator. But if courts disregard the statute's purposes, it is much harder for the voter to know who is responsible when results go awry." (p. 95). Instead, a textualist approach allows "legislators to avoid responsibility for a badly written statute simply by saying that the Court reached results they did not favor. The more the Court seeks realistically to ascertain the purposes of a statute and interprets its provisions in ways that further those purposes, the harder it will be for the legislator to escape responsibility for the statute's objectives." *Id.*

Second, Justice Breyer argues that a purposive approach makes statutes "work better" for the public they are intended to serve (p. 96). Third, such an approach "help[s] Congress better accomplish its own legislative work." *Id.* Justice Breyer—former Chief Counsel to the Senate Judiciary Committee—is a congressional pragmatist. He argues that "Congress does not, cannot, and need not write statutes that precisely and exhaustively explain where and how each of the statute's provisions will apply." *Id.* Congress, which must use "general or imprecise words while relying on committee reports" and other types of legislative history "to convey intended purposes" relies on judicial "teamwork," without which "legislators and their staffs would face a drafting task that is daunting and even impractical" (p. 97).

QUERIES ON JUSTICE BREYER'S PRAGMATISM

Justice Breyer's pragmatism thus posits an active, partnering role for courts that is essential to making the legislative process work. Is this a satisfying response to Justice Scalia? How would Justice Breyer analyze the Holy Trinity Case? How would he have voted in *Chisom* and *Casey*?

William N. Eskridge Jr. and Philip P. Frickey, *Statutory Interpretation as Practical Reasoning*
42 Stan. L. Rev. 321, 345–53 (1990).

Another kind of pragmatic thinking focuses less on realistic consequences. Inspired by American pragmatic philosophers who rejected "foundationalist" thinking and urged multi-focal thinking, Professors Eskridge and Frickey criticize each of the leading "foundationalist" theories of interpretation—textualism (Justice Scalia), legislative intent (*Holy Trinity*), purpose (Professors Hart and Sacks), and instead offer a practical approach that the authors believe best reflects what the Supreme Court is actually doing in statutory cases.

"[T]he leading foundationalist theories cannot redeem their claim to [be consistent with] the very nature of majoritarian democracy, do not yield objective and determinate answers, and cannot convincingly exclude other values, including current values." Cases decided under wildly different theories—such as *Holy Trinity* (legislative intent and purpose trump plain meaning), *TVA v. Hill* (legislative intent gives way to plain meaning consistent with broad purpose), and *Casey* (plain meaning negates legislative purpose and perhaps intent as well)—"suggest that the Supreme Court does not follow any one of the foundationalist theories. We now suggest that these observations form the basis for a positive theory which refuses to privilege intention, purpose or text as the sole touchstone of interpretation, but which both explains the Supreme Court's practice in statutory interpretation and, at the same time, reflects the insights of modern theories of interpretation.

"First, statutory interpretation involves creative policymaking by judges and is not just the Court's figuring out the answer that was put 'in' the statute by the enacting legislature. An essential insight of hermeneutics is that interpretation is a dynamic process, and that the interpreter is inescapably situated historically. 'Every age has to understand a transmitted text in its own way,' says Gadamer [in *Truth and Method* 263 (1965)]. * * * Gadamer argues, following Aristotle, that one does not 'understand' a text in the abstract, without an 'application' of the text to a specific problem. American pragmatism, also influenced by Aristotle, complements this hermeneutic insight. Reasoning in human affairs does not seek abstract answers, but concretely useful results. Theories of reasoning, for [William James, in *Pragmatism* (1907)] are simply " 'mental modes of *adaptation* to reality, rather than revelations or gnostic answers.' * * *

"Second, because this creation of statutory meaning is not a mechanical operation, it often involves the interpreter's choice among several competing answers. Although the interpreter's range of choices is somewhat constrained by the text, the statute's history, and the circumstances of its application, the actual choice will not be 'objectively' determinable; interpretation will often depend upon political and other assumptions held by judges. Under [this analysis], interpretation seeks 'to make the law concrete in each specific case,' and '[t]he creative supplementing of the law that is involved is a task that is reserved to the judge.' As a practical matter, how could it be otherwise? Many statutes leave key terms ambiguous, often intentionally, and thereby delegate rulemaking authority to courts or agencies. Over time, these ambiguities and unanswered questions multiply, as society changes and background legal assumptions change with it. Hermeneutics suggests that as the interpreter's own background context—her 'tradition'—changes, so too will her interpretive choices. * * *

"Third, when statutory interpreters make these choices, they are normally not driven by any single value—adhering to majoritarian commands *or* encouraging private reliance on statutory texts *or* finding the best answer according to modern policy—but are instead driven by multiple values. Both hermeneutics and pragmatism emphasize the complex nature of human reasoning. When solving a problem, we tend to test different solutions, evaluating each against a range of values and beliefs we hold as important. The pragmatic idea that captures this concept is the 'web of beliefs' metaphor. We all accept a number of different values and propositions that, taken together, constitute a web of intertwined beliefs about, for example, the role of statutes in our public law. Each of us may accord different weight to the specific values, but almost no one excludes any of the important values altogether. Decisionmaking is, therefore, polycentric, and thus cannot be linear and purely deductive. Instead, it is spiral and inductive: We consider the consistency of the evidence for each value before reaching a final decision, and even then check our decision against the values we esteem the most. Given this web of beliefs and the spiral form of decisionmaking, an individual's reasoning will depend very much on the context of the case at hand, and specifically on the relative strength of each consideration."

Consider issues presented by the No Vehicles in the Park Act, from our Introduction, in light of the web metaphor. While tricycles and a few other mechanisms pose hard interpretive choices, what is remarkable is how easy most cases will be for the police or the commission administering the statute. Although a baby carriage might technically fall within the definition of vehicle in § 3 (they are "mechanism[s] for conveying a person from one place to another"), there are also textual reasons to doubt that they fall within the statutory ban: not only do baby carriages pose no safety concerns that § 1 of the law associates with vehicles, but the vehicles actually named in § 3 (motorcycles, bicycles, etc.) are very different from baby carriages exactly along the dimension of safety. Additionally, the legislative history of the statute reveals that legislators had no concern whatsoever for baby carriages; they were so far from even conceivable coverage that they were not mentioned. Finally, as a normative matter, judges would be reluctant to interpret a criminal law ambitiously, given the rule of lenity. Coming full circle, many judges would consider it absurd to read vehicle to include baby carriages.

"In addition to the web of beliefs idea, two other metaphors, one drawn from the pragmatist tradition and one drawn from the hermeneutical tradition, suggest more precisely how a practical reasoning approach would work. First, consider Peirce's contrast of the chain and the cable. A chain is no stronger than its weakest link, because if any of the singly connected links should break, so too will the chain. In contrast, a cable's strength relies not on that of individual threads, but upon their cumulative strength as they are woven together. Legal arguments are often constructed as chains, but they tend to be more successful when they are cable-like." Thus, a judicial decision holding that baby carriages are not vehicles draws its strength from this phenomenon: The text, one probable purpose, some legislative history, and current policy each lend some—even if not unequivocal—support to the result. Each thread standing alone is subject to quarrel and objection; woven together, the threads would persuade both a textualist such as Justice Scalia and a purposivist like Justice Breyer.

"In many cases of statutory interpretation, of course, the threads will not all run in the same direction. The cable metaphor suggests that in these cases the result will depend upon the strongest overall combination of threads. That, in turn, depends on which values the decisionmakers find most important, and on the strength of the arguments invoking each value. For most of the Supreme Court Justices, a persuasive textual argument is a stronger thread than an otherwise equally persuasive current policy or fairness argument, because of the reliance and legislative supremacy values implicated in following the clear statutory text. And a clear and convincing textual argument obviously counts more than one beclouded with doubts and ambiguities.

"Our model of practical reasoning in statutory interpretation is still not complete, for it lacks a dynamic element that is intrinsic to human reasoning in general, and interpretation in particular. The various arguments (the threads of our cable) do not exist in isolation; they interact with one another. A final metaphor that captures this interaction is the 'hermeneutical circle': A part can only be understood in the context of the whole, and the whole cannot be understood without analyzing its various parts." To interpret the No Vehicles in the Park Act, for example, the interpreter will look at the text and the legislative history and the purpose and current values. "But to evaluate the text, the interpreter will consider it in light of the whole enterprise, including the history, purpose, and current values. In other words, none of the interpretive threads can be viewed in isolation, and each will be evaluated in its relation to the other threads. * * *

"The positive metaphors of our analysis—the web of beliefs idea, the cable-versus-chain contrast, and the hermeneutical circle—suggest the contours of a practical reasoning model of statutory interpretation that roughly captures the Court's practice. Our model holds that an interpreter will look at a broad range of evidence—text, historical evidence, and the text's evolution—and thus form a preliminary view of the statute. The interpreter then develops that preliminary view by testing various possible interpretations against the multiple criteria of fidelity to the text, historical accuracy, and conformity to contemporary circumstances and values. Each criterion is relevant, yet none necessarily trumps the others. Thus while an apparently clear text, for example, will create insuperable doubts for a contrary interpretation if the other evidence reinforces it [*TVA v. Hill*], an apparently clear text may yield if other considerations cut against it [*Holy Trinity*]. As the interpreter comes to accept an interpretation (perhaps a confirmation of her preliminary view), she considers a congeries of supporting arguments, which may buttress her view much 'like the legs of a chair and unlike the links of a chain.' "

Eskridge and Frickey translate their theory into a model to reflect the evidentiary inquiries into which they expect courts will engage. "The model is, in crude imagery, a 'funnel of abstraction.' It is funnel-shaped for three reasons. First, the model suggests the hierarchy of sources that the Court has in fact assumed. For example, in formulating her preunderstanding of the statute *and* in testing it, the interpreter will value more highly a good argument based on the statutory text than a conflicting and equally strong argument based upon the statutory purpose. Second, the model suggests the degree of abstraction at each source. The sources at the bottom of the diagram involve more focused, concrete inquiries, typically with a more limited range of arguments. As the interpreter moves up the diagram, a broader range of arguments is available, partly because the inquiry is less concrete. Third, the model illustrates the pragmatistic and hermeneutical insights explained above: In formulating and testing her understanding of the statute, the interpreter will move up and down the diagram, evaluating and comparing the different considerations represented by each source of argumentation. * * * "

Below is an adapted version of the original Eskridge and Frickey diagram to reflect another practical feature, namely, precedent, that the authors believe significant. Some of us also would add canons to the mix, although they are not reflected in the diagram.

A PRACTICAL REASONING MODEL OF STATUTORY INTERPRETATION

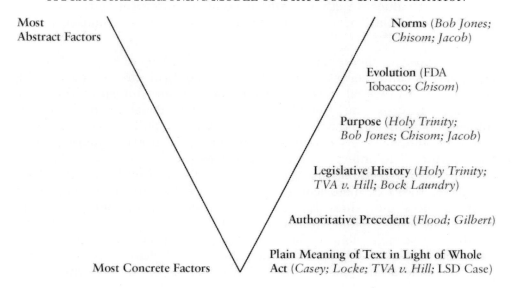

Most
Abstract Factors — Norms (*Bob Jones; Chisom; Jacob*)

Evolution (FDA Tobacco; *Chisom*)

Purpose (*Holy Trinity; Bob Jones; Chisom; Jacob*)

Legislative History (*Holy Trinity; TVA v. Hill; Bock Laundry*)

Authoritative Precedent (*Flood; Gilbert*)

Most Concrete Factors — Plain Meaning of Text in Light of Whole Act (*Casey; Locke; TVA v. Hill;* LSD Case)

On the whole, the funnel of abstraction is a descriptive theory of statutory interpretation: this is how the authors believe the judicial (or administrative) mind goes about deciding statutory cases.[11] The features of the funnel that are most important are these: First, judges will consider a variety of factors, including statutory text and structure, but also statutory purpose, legislative history, authoritative precedents, practical applications of the statute, and current norms. The funnel theory is distinctive from textualism and purposivism in the formal importance it attributes to *stare decisis* in statutory cases: Supreme Court precedents interpreting a particular statute, or words and phrases borrowed from other statutes (e.g., *Casey*), are always relevant and generally will be controlling if the statutory text is open-ended or vague. See also Miranda O. McGowan, *Do as I Do, Not as I Say: An Empirical Investigation of Justice Scalia's Ordinary Meaning Method of Statutory Interpretation,* 78 Miss. L.J. 129 (2008) (showing that even Justice Scalia ignores statutory text that he thinks delegates lawmaking authority to federal judges).

Second, the factors have varying legal force. They are hierarchical: a good text-based argument will trump a good legislative history or purpose argument, as in *Casey*. Third, and most strongly unlike more formalist theories, the funnel of abstraction posits that the various factors will *interact* with one another. Thus, a textual "plain meaning" will not become firm in the judicial mind until *after* the judge has considered all the evidence; the "authority" of a precedent will not be conclusive until the judge has thought about its consistency with statutory text and purpose; the good judge will not be firm about the relevance of "norms" until she has processed the weight of the textual and historical factors. And so forth.

Think about how the funnel helps explain the decisions in this chapter, especially *Holy Trinity, Bock Laundry, Jacob,* and *Chisom,* which openly follow the method, but also cases that don't seem to follow the method, like *Casey* and *Marshall*. Although Judge Easterbrook is not a "funnel judge," the judges who went along with his decision in *Marshall* might well have been—what might have been persuasive to them?

---

[11]   For evidence suggesting that this diagram accurately displays the factors routinely taken into account in judicial opinions interpreting statutes, see Lawrence M. Solan, *The Language of Statutes: Laws and Their Interpretation* 50–159 (2010); Nancy Staudt et al., *Judging Statutes: Interpretive Regimes,* 38 Loy. L.A. L. Rev. 1909 (2005) (empirical analysis of tax decisions); Nicholas Zeppos, *The Use of Authority in Statutory Interpretation: An Empirical Analysis,* 70 Tex. L. Rev. 1073 (1992) (earlier and broader analysis of statutory interpretation decisions). See also Frank Cross, *The Theory and Practice of Statutory Interpretation* 24–133 (2009); Robert John Araujo, *Method in Interpretation: Practical Wisdom and the Search for Meaning in Public Legal Texts,* 68 Miss. L.J. 225 (1998); Morrell Mullins, *Tools Not Rules: The Heuristic Nature of Statutory Interpretation,* 30 J. Legis. 1 (2003). Cf. Miranda O. McGowan, *Do as I Do, Not as I Say: An Empirical Investigation of Justice Scalia's Ordinary Meaning Method of Statutory Interpretation,* 78 Miss. L.J. 129 (2008) (documenting Justice Scalia's eclectic practice).

NOTE ON COURTS AS FAITHFUL AGENTS, PARTNERS, OR SYSTEMIC COHERERS? (REDUX)

Early in the chapter, we introduced you to the question of how to think of the judicial role in statutory interpretation. Almost all judges cling to the model of courts as "faithful agents of the legislature"; the idea of courts as merely implementing legislative will is attractive to federal judges because of their concerns about democratic legitimacy, legislative supremacy and judicial "activism." By now you have the tools to consider whether this is really the model that explains what courts are doing in the cases. We have seen a few judges—Breyer, Calabresi and Posner—come out and say they are doing something different, but they are outliers. We also have seen a great many textualist opinions that seem as concerned about the "rule of law" and system coherence—opinions concerned with fair notice to the public, with interpreting statutory terms consistently, etc.—as they seem concerned about effectuating actual congressional intent. And we have seen other opinions that seem to be doing something different altogether, like bringing fundamental policy or constitutional values to bear on the interpretive process. As you continue in the course and learn more of the canons that courts employ, ask yourself what role—agent, partner, system coherer—each canon is performing.

You might also want to consider whether the structure and original meaning of the U.S. Constitution support the faithful agency view against the other models. See Jerry L. Mashaw, *As if Republican Interpretation*, 97 Yale L.J. 1685, 1686 (1988) ("Any theory of statutory interpretation is at base a theory about constitutional law."). Under the Constitution, both Congress and the Supreme Court are agents of "We the People." Read this way, Articles I–III might suggest a coordinate, cooperative relationship among the three branches—and at least some of the founding generation believed that federal judges would play an active partnership role in governance, through statutory as well as constitutional interpretation. See *Federalist* No. 78 (Hamilton); William N. Eskridge Jr., *All About Words: Early Understandings of the "Judicial Power" in Statutory Interpretation, 1776–1806*, 101 Colum. L. Rev. 990 (2001). But see John F. Manning, *Textualism and the Equity of the Statute*, 101 Colum. L. Rev. 1 (2001) (maintaining that the original meaning of Article III was that judges would be nothing more than faithful agents of Congress when interpreting statutes), and *Deriving Rules of Statutory Interpretation from the Constitution*, 101 Colum. L. Rev. 1648 (2001) (responding to Eskridge's evidence of original meaning). A different broader view of the judicial role is one that sees an obligation on the part of judges to cohere the system—to make the law more predictable, for instance—even if it means exercising something like federal common lawmaking power to do so. See Abbe R. Gluck, *The Federal Common Law of Statutory Interpretation:* Erie *for the Age of* Statutes, 54 Wm. & Mary L. Rev. 753 (2013).

NOTE ON WHETHER INSTITUTIONAL CONTEXT SHOULD AFFECT STATUTORY METHODOLOGY

How does institutional context affect the methodology and answers reached by statutory interpreters? In most coursebooks (including the classic legislation text one of us introduced), virtually all of the applications and examples have been U.S. Supreme Court cases. It is easy to see why this has been the practice. The Supreme Court is a potential reviewing tribunal for any interpretation of a federal statute, and so all such interpretations occur in the "shadow" of the Court; an interpreter who ignores the Court's methodology does so at her peril. State judges must pay attention to the U.S. Supreme Court as well, not only because they apply federal statutes, but also because the Court is considered a model for other courts.

As the student knows by now, however, very few statutory rules are ratified or clarified at the Supreme Court level. Most statutory interpretation goes on elsewhere—and there is an emerging academic literature demonstrating that the kinds of methodological explorations that we see in Supreme Court opinions do not look the same when statutory interpretation is undertaken in other institutional contexts. "Happily, some scholars have begun to look beyond the Supreme Court and to produce careful positive accounts of how other [officials] actually do interpret statutes." Aaron-Andrew P. Bruhl, *Hierarchy and Heterogeneity: How to Read a Statute in a Lower Court,* 97 Cornell L. Rev. 433, 437 (2012). Consider a few variations:

1. *Statutory Interpretation by Agencies.* In this coursebook, you have already seen many examples of how agencies often apply statutes in very different ways than courts do—starting with the No Vehicles in the Park exercise in the Introduction. Although the agency we created at the end of the Introduction would surely reach the same answers as a court in most instances (a baby carriage is not barred, while a motorcycle is), the two institutions follow very different methodologies due to their different governmental functions, personnel, resources and authority. Put broadly, agencies are more purposive and energetic, while courts see their mission as ensuring predictability, protecting liberty and reliance interests, and enforcing jurisdictional and other limits. Courts are also more insulated from politics and have fewer resources than agencies.

For these reasons, scholars suggest that agency-based interpretations will typically be different from court-based interpretations in many ways. We discuss "agency statutory interpretation" at length in Chapter 8. For present purposes, consider these possible differences between agency and judicial interpretation:

- agencies are likely to be more responsive to their understanding of the statutory purpose and to their own sense of policy mission, and hence more willing to read statutory text liberally in light of that purpose and mission;

- agencies are likely to be less focused on the wide variety of textual and legalistic arguments that concern judges, often obsessively, such as dictionary-based word meaning and canons;

- agencies are likely to be more attentive to the legislative background of the statute (much of which the agency may have been responsible for), as well as the ongoing legislative deliberations (much of which may be aimed at the agency);

- agencies are likely to be more willing to revise previous interpretations due to changed political circumstances (after all, agency heads switch in new administrations and new positions are expected), in contrast to trademark judicial adherence to strict stare decisis (which is particularly stringent for statutory precedents, see Chapter 3, § 2);

Jerry L. Mashaw, *Agency Statutory Interpretation*, Issues in Legal Scholarship, Issue 3: Dynamic Statutory Interpretation (2002): Art. 9, available at www.bepress.com/ils/iss3/art9 (defending these particular differences).[12]

This kind of institutional analysis does not suggest that courts and agencies will always, or even usually, reach different results in statutory cases. In *Jacob* and *Dana*, the state social service agencies supported second-parent adoptions, the same result reached by Chief Judge Kaye, but without any of the elaborate textual and historical reasoning found in her opinion for New York's highest court. But the differences might have an impact on how courts come to understand agency positions, as we shall see in Chapter 8.

2. *Statutory Interpretation in State and Lower Federal Courts.* Professor Gluck's work on statutory interpretation in the state and lower courts has opened a new field of court-centered institutional studies that have begun to explore differences across these benches. *See* Abbe R. Gluck, *The States as Laboratories of Statutory Interpretation: Methodological Consensus and the New Modified Textualism*, 119 Yale L.J. 1750 (2010). The election of many state court judges for instance drives a wedge between a judge's constituency and the faithful agent model for statutory interpretation. See Aaron-Andrew P. Bruhl & Ethan J. Leib, *Elected Judges and Statutory Interpretation,* 79 U. Chi. L. Rev. 1215, 1243–46 (2012); Jed Handelsman Shugerman, *The Twist of Long Terms: Judicial Elections, Role Fidelity, and American Tort Law,* 98 Geo. L.J. 1349 (2010). Indeed, elected judges might best be understood as faithful agents of "We the People, with whom judges have the same kind of direct relationship as other "representatives." Professors Bruhl and Leib argue, for example, that the kind of dynamic

---

[12] Accord, Adrian Vermeule, *Judging under Uncertainty: An Institutional Theory of Legal Interpretation* 212–15 (2006); Michael Herz, *Purposivism and Institutional Competence in Statutory Interpretation*, 2009 Mich. St. L. Rev 89, 101; Jerry L. Mashaw, *Norms, Practices, and the Paradox of Deference: A Preliminary Inquiry Into Agency Statutory Interpretation*, 57 Admin. L. Rev. 501, 504–24 (2005); Peter Strauss, *When the Judge Is Not the Primary Official with Responsibility to Read: Agency Interpretation and the Problem of Legislative History*, 66 Chi. Kent L. Rev. 321 (1990).

interpretation Chief Judge Kaye applied in the *Jacob* and *Dana* appeals would have been much more democratically legitimate if the judges of the New York Court of Appeals were elected or were subject to retention votes. Bruhl & Leib, *Elected Judges,* 1262–67.

With respect to the lower federal courts, although there probably needs to be a great deal of methodological consistency between lower federal courts and the Supreme Court, Professor Bruhl argues that there is ample room for divergence, and that interpretive practice might differ in the lower courts. See Bruhl, *Hierarchy and Heterogeneity* 442–58. An obvious difference is that Congress regularly responds to and overrides Supreme Court statutory decisions, especially when the Justices invite overrides, but it rarely overrides lower court decisions, because they are less salient and perhaps less ripe for political response.[13] Hence, lower courts ought to be less attentive to institutional dialogue than the Supreme Court is, and they ought to assume that their interpretations will not provoke a political response. *Id.* at 460.

Professor Bruhl also suggests that Supreme Court review will often trigger the creation of new sources of interpretive guidance, especially in the form of *amicus* briefs. *Id.* at 464. The Solicitor General plays a major role in most Supreme Court statutory cases for this reason, and not so big a role among lower courts. Because the Solicitor General mediates, within the executive branch, purposive agency constructions, higher-level presidential policies (sometimes), and coherence and rule of law concerns, her or his advice to the Supreme Court is usually followed. But this engagement of the Solicitor General, and agency inputs into statutory interpretation decisions, usually does not occur in lower court cases.

Further, given the resource constraints on lower federal courts (fewer staff, poor briefing, a dearth of helpful *amicus* briefs), Bruhl maintains that their constructions of federal statutes will and ought to be less methodologically complex—hence less reliance on hard-to-research legislative history and elaborate examinations of the whole statute and other parts of the code. *Id.* at 470–6. Lower courts, Bruhl maintains, ought to hew closely to statutory plain meanings, the reasoning and even dicta of Supreme Court or binding appellate decisions, and agency interpretations. *Id.* at 477–84. Such a restricted approach to statutory interpretation might seem much less appropriate for federal circuit courts than for district courts, however. *Id.*

Do you think a system in which federal district courts, appellate courts, and the Supreme Court apply different methodological rules is workable? How would this affect Congress's incentives to draft in the shadow of legal rules? Think about the LSD case. You know how the Seventh Circuit and the Supreme Court handled the issue, and the different methodologies each judge applied to this contentious issue. You also know that the Department of Justice, including the Solicitor General supported the stiff penalty. Do you

---

[13] An exception is the lower court in *Holy Trinity,* whose opinion provoked Congress to amend the law in 1891; the 1891 law was inapplicable to the Supreme Court's decision on appeal.

think the trial court should have applied a different methodological approach from the Seventh Circuit? See for yourself if it did. *United States v. Marshall*, 706 F. Supp. 650 (C.D. Ill., 1989).

3. *Plain Meaning and State Courts.* Through most of the twentieth century, state courts were more likely to resolve issues of statutory interpretation merely by construing the apparent meaning of the statutory language, with attention to textual canons of statutory construction but without *any* examination of the statute's purpose or legislative history. See, e.g., *Bishop v. Linkway Stores, Inc.*, 655 S.W.2d 426 (Ark. 1983). The two most frequently mentioned reasons for state court textualism are the dearth of legislative history materials available for state statutes and a more restrained methodology practiced by many state judges, especially those who are elected by the people or subject to retention elections to remain in office (it's easier to justify statutory decisions to the voters if one argues she is constrained by the text.)

This textualist practice changed during the post-World War II era in many states. Some state high courts, like those in California and New York, are generally purposivist courts today. The California Supreme Court has often used a contextual approach to interpret legislation broadly to promote liberal social policies and fairness. For instance, *County of San Diego v. Muniz*, 583 P.2d 109 (Cal. 1978), involved a statute requiring former or present welfare recipients to reimburse the state if the person "acquires property." The California Supreme Court construed "property" *not* to include wages, because deprivation of wages would undermine the overall goal of the welfare law to assist recipients in becoming self-supporting and would be unfair and oppressive. Written or published legislative histories of state statutes are now more readily available than at any previous point in American history, and they have wider availability now that more of the materials can be found on the Internet. See Brian Barnes, *The Transformation of State Statutory Interpretation* (Yale Law School, Seminar Paper, May 10, 2010) (documenting a dramatic increase in availability of legislative materials through a state-by-state survey). This phenomenon (increased availability) has given rise to a growing body of scholarship analyzing state court use of state legislative history.[14]

On the other hand, there has been a trend toward a more textual approach in many states in recent years—perhaps as a reaction to the same types of concerns about legislative history that we have seen on the federal side or perhaps as the intersystemic ripple effect of the debates taking place in the Supreme Court. In many cases, the state courts seem motivated by a desire to bring some *predictability* to the order of the interpretation. Consider

[14] For scholarship tracing the decline of the plain meaning rule and concomitant rise of the use of legislative history, see, e.g., Shirley Abrahamson & Robert Hughes, *Shall We Dance? Steps for Legislators and Judges in Statutory Interpretation*, 75 Minn. L. Rev. 1045 (1991); Judith Kaye, *Things Judges Do: State Statutory Interpretation*, 13 Touro L. Rev. 595 (1997); Eric Lane, *How To Read a Statute in New York: A Response to Judge Kaye and Some More*, 28 Hofstra L. Rev. 85 (1999); William Popkin, *Statutory Interpretation in State Courts—A Study of Indiana Opinions*, 24 Ind. L. Rev. 1155 (1991).

the following case, which was part of Professor Gluck's study of state statutory interpretation.

STATUTORY PREFACE FOR *PORTLAND GENERAL ELECTRIC*

Oregon Revised Statutes (1992)

Section 659.360

(3) The employee seeking parental leave shall be entitled to utilize any accrued vacation leave, sick leave or other compensatory leave, paid or unpaid, during the parental leave. The employer may require the employee seeking parental leave to utilize any accrued leave during the parental leave unless otherwise provided by an agreement of the employer and the employee, by collective bargaining agreement or by employer policy.

(6) The parental leave required by subsection (1) of this section is not required to be granted with pay unless so specified by agreement of the employer and employee, by collective bargaining agreement or by employer policy.

PORTLAND GENERAL ELECTRIC CO. v. BUREAU OF LABOR AND INDUSTRIES

Supreme Court of Oregon, 1993.
317 Or. 606, 859 P.2d 1143.

VAN HOOMISSEN, J. * * *

[The issue was whether an employee taking family or medical leave could take paid sick leave even if she or he were not sick. Following the opinion of the Bureau of Labor, the Supreme Court of Oregon unanimously ruled that employees had that option, essentially converting much of the unpaid leave time into paid leave. Justice Van Hoomissen's opinion started with a statement of the interpretive approach Oregon courts are supposed to follow.] In interpreting a statute, the court's task is to discern the intent of the legislature. ORS 174.020. To do that, the court examines both the text and context of the statute. That is the first level of our analysis.

In this first level of analysis, the text of the statutory provision itself is the starting point for interpretation and is the best evidence of the legislature's intent. In trying to ascertain the meaning of a statutory provision, and thereby to inform the court's inquiry into legislative intent, the court considers rules of construction of the statutory text that bear directly on how to read the text. Some of those rules are mandated by statute, including, for example, the statutory enjoinder "not to insert what has been omitted, or to omit what has been inserted." ORS 174.010. Others are found in the case law, including, for example, the rule that words of common usage typically should be given their plain, natural, and ordinary meaning.

Also at the first level of analysis, the court considers the context of the statutory provision at issue, which includes other provisions of the same statute and other related statutes. Just as with the court's consideration of the text of a statute, the court utilizes rules of construction that bear directly on the interpretation of the statutory provision in context. Some of those rules are mandated by statute, including, for example, the principles that "where there are several provisions or particulars such construction is, if possible, to be adopted as will give effect to all," ORS 174.010, and that "a particular intent shall control a general one that is inconsistent with it," ORS 174.020. Other such rules of construction are found in case law, including, for example, the rules that use of a term in one section and not in another section of the same statute indicates a purposeful omission, and that use of the same term throughout a statute indicates that the term has the same meaning throughout the statute.

If the legislature's intent is clear from the above-described inquiry into text and context, further inquiry is unnecessary.

If, but only if, the intent of the legislature is not clear from the text and context inquiry, the court will then move to the second level, which is to consider legislative history to inform the court's inquiry into legislative intent. When the court reaches legislative history, it considers it along with text and context to determine whether all of those together make the legislative intent clear. If the legislative intent is clear, then the court's inquiry into legislative intent and the meaning of the statute is at an end and the court interprets the statute to have the meaning so determined.

If, after consideration of text, context, and legislative history, the intent of the legislature remains unclear, then the court may resort to general maxims of statutory construction to aid in resolving the remaining uncertainty. Although some of those maxims of statutory construction may be statutory, *see, e.g.*, ORS 174.030 (natural rights), others more commonly may be found in case law. Those include, for example, the maxim that, where no legislative history exists, the court will attempt to determine how the legislature would have intended the statute to be applied had it considered the issue. * * *

[Applying this structure to the issue on appeal, the Court went no further than level one.] Both of the sentences in ORS 659.360(3) are *empowerment* sentences. The second sentence *empowers* the employer to compel an employee taking parental leave "to utilize any accrued leave." Thus, if an employee has accrued leave, the employer could require the employee to utilize that accrued leave during the parental leave, "unless otherwise provided by an agreement of the employer and the employee, by collective bargaining agreement or by employer policy." ORS 659.360(3).

The reciprocal power, granted to the employee by the first sentence of ORS 659.360(3), permits the employee, at the employee's option, to do what the employer may require the employee to do. The employee may require the employer to let the employee "utilize" any accrued vacation leave, sick leave or other compensatory leave, paid or unpaid, during the parental leave. As noted, the first sentence of the statute does not contain any limitation on the employee's rights imposed under the provisions of a collective bargaining agreement.

In sum, the employer may *require* the employee seeking parental leave to utilize any accrued leave during parental leave, unless otherwise provided by an agreement of the employer and the employee, by collective bargaining agreement, or by employer policy, even if the employee is not on vacation or sick or does not wish to use accrued leave during the parental leave. Similarly, the employee may *require* the employer to let the employee utilize any accrued vacation leave, sick leave, or other compensatory leave, paid or unpaid during the parental leave, even if the employee is not on vacation or sick, and even if the employer does not want to do so. If the legislature had wanted to make the use of accrued leave during parental leave subject to any preconditions in an existing collective bargaining agreement, it easily could have done so by including in the first sentence of ORS 659.360(3) the same qualifying language that presently is found only in the second sentence of that subsection. The legislature knows how to include qualifying language in a statute when it wants to do so. It did not do so here. * * *

STATUTORY POSTSCRIPT

When the Oregon Legislature recodified its family and medical leave statute in 1995 and 2007, it created a new ORS § 659A.174, "Paid Leave":

(1) Except as provided in subsection (2) of this section, and unless otherwise provided by the terms of an agreement between the eligible employee and the covered employer, a collective bargaining agreement or an employer policy, family leave is not required to be granted with pay.

(2) An employee taking family leave is entitled to use any paid accrued sick leave or any paid accrued vacation leave during the period of family leave, or to use any other paid leave that is offered by the employer in lieu of vacation leave during the period of family leave.

(3) Subject to the terms of any agreement between the eligible employee and the covered employer or the terms of a collective bargaining agreement, the employer may determine the particular order in which accrued leave is to be used in circumstances in which more than one type of accrued leave is available to the employee.

NOTES AND QUESTIONS ON PORTLAND GENERAL ELECTRIC (PGE)

1. *A "Ranking" of the Canons: "Modified Textualism"?* The *PGE* opinion is an attempt by the Oregon Supreme Court to "rank" the general categories of interpretive rules—(1) text, (2) legislative history, then (3) canons—in a predictable order to be applied in the same way in every case. We have not seen that in our study of the federal case law. But as Professor Gluck's study shows, this is not an uncommon approach in the states. See Gluck, *States as Laboratories of Statutory Interpretation*; see *id.* at 1775–85 (detailed examination of *PGE*). Indeed, at the time of *PGE*, Oregon already had similar, tiered methodological approaches in place for constitutional, contract, and initiative interpretation. Gluck calls these state approaches "modified textualism," because they reject the new textualist exclusion of legislative history but give a formal primacy to textualist analysis that reflects a harder plain meaning rule than the Supreme Court has traditionally applied. In contrast to *TVA v. Hill*, for example, the *PGE* approach does not require judges to check their understanding of plain meaning by reference to legislative history. But this textualism is pragmatic insofar as it invites legislative history and—very rarely (by Gluck's count, almost no policy canons were deployed post *PGE*) normative analysis when the statute's meaning is not plain.

Note, also, how the *PGE* approach may alter a multi-factored approach like the Funnel of Abstraction. *PGE* retains the primary Funnel factors but "tiers" them. So for many cases the Funnel is foreshortened considerably. The factors in the second tier or level—legislative history and purpose—are considered where the text is ambiguous, but note that if there is relevant legislative history it will be briefed by the parties and considered by the judges. So you can never know whether a plain meaning has been found without any reference to legislative history (for the judges have read that part of the brief).

2. Stare Decisis *for Methodological Precedents?* Perhaps the most notable feature of *PGE* is that the Oregon Supreme Court made a self-conscious decision to set forth, in clear terms, the methodology it expected lower courts to follow in statutory cases—and that its own justices committed themselves to in subsequent supreme court cases. The House of Lords in the United Kingdom gives *stare decisis* effect to methodological precedents. Abbe Gluck and Sydney Foster have each argued that the U.S. Supreme Court should do the same. See Sydney Foster, *Should Courts Give* Stare Decisis *Effect to Statutory Interpretation Methodology?*, 96 Geo. L.J. 1863 (2008); Gluck, *States as Laboratories of Statutory Interpretation*. Consider the values of *stare decisis*: judicial economy, predictability, and reliance interests. Would consistent treatment in matters of methodology serve those interests, too?

Professor Gluck also points out that "methodological *stare decisis*" is common across many other aspects of American law. We have the parol evidence rule for contract interpretation, the tiers of scrutiny and many other decisionmaking frameworks for constitutional interpretation, and a wide array of other decisionmaking regimes, all of which receive precedential effect. In contrast, when it comes to statutory interpretation, the Court's opinion about an interpretive rule in one case (for example, whether the dog barked in legislative history is relevant) generally does not carry over to the next case, even where the same statute is being construed. Gluck questions what it is about statutory interpretation that makes judges so resistant to bind themselves and other courts. See Abbe R. Gluck, *Intersystemic Statutory Interpretation: Methodology as "Law" and the* Erie *Doctrine,* 120 Yale L.J. 1898 (2011).

Connor Raso and Professor Eskridge counter that reliance interests are not as strong in matters of methodology as they are with respect to substantive law. Connor N. Raso & William N. Eskridge Jr., Chevron *as a Canon, Not a Precedent: An Empirical Analysis of What Motivates Justices in Agency Deference Cases,* 110 Colum. L. Rev. 1727 (2010). But couldn't such an argument be made with respect to constitutional doctrine too? Namely, that litigants care about not being discriminated against, but don't rely on the tiers of scrutiny per se. Further, when it comes to statutory interpretation, perhaps the public is not the only community whose reliance matters. A consistently applied set of interpretive rules might help *Congress* do its job better too. See Abbe R. Gluck, *The Federal Common Law of Statutory Interpretation.* 54 Wm. & Mary. L. Rev. 753 (2013).

3.   *Did* PGE *work?* Consider Professor Gluck's report on the *PGE* experiment (*States as Laboratories of Statutory Interpretation,* 1779–81): "Three preliminary studies, including one conducted as part of this project, have collected data on how the *PGE* regime has been implemented since its installation. One clearly observable effect of the regime is that it has reduced the number of interpretive tools employed by the Oregon Supreme Court and so made it easier to predict which tools the court will rely on to decide cases. 'The court resolves the vast majority of statutory issues at level one,' i.e., the text-based tier. Between 1993 and 1998, for example, out of 137 statutory interpretation cases, the court looked at legislative history only thirty-three times, finding it 'useless' in one third of those cases. It consequently reached tier three—nontextual canons—only eleven times during the same period. Even more strikingly, between 1999 and 2006, the court applied the *PGE* framework 150 times, and only reached tier two (legislative history) nine times. Not a single case during that period reached the other-maxims tier (tier three). And, in a study conducted as part of this project, across the thirty-five cases in which *PGE* was cited between 2006 and May 2009, legislative history was applied six times and a substantive canon only once.

"Compare the five years before *PGE* was decided. There was no single approach: more than half of the cases resorted immediately to legislative history or policy analysis without prior consideration of text alone, and without the tiered hierarchy of sources that *PGE* later imposed. One justice called the pre-*PGE* period a 'legislative history free-for-all.'

"In contrast, under *PGE*, the court is fairly consistent with respect to which interpretive tools it relies upon. Over the four-and-a-half-year period ending in May 2009, the following eight types of textual tools were used in roughly half of the cases: 'plain meaning,' dictionaries, state court precedents, close readings of statutory definition sections, analysis of related statutes, analysis of the contested term's place in the statutory scheme, historical evolution of the statute itself, and textual canons. With respect to the textual canons, the court applied the same eight canons repeatedly throughout the cases in which textual canons were used. The only additional tools used in more than three cases were rules of grammar (ten cases) and legislative history (nine cases), making the list of the eight types of tools described above the fairly complete universe of Oregon statutory interpretation principles. All but six of the opinions over the five-year period were unanimous."

4. *Oregon's Statutory Pushback.* Professor Gluck's study of Oregon's *PGE* experiment also noted that, in 2001, the Oregon Legislature enacted a statute in direct response to *PGE*: "A court may limit its consideration of legislative history to the information that the parties provide to the court. A court shall give the weight to the legislative history that the court considers to be appropriate." Although the language of the statute was hortatory, its legislative history suggested that the legislature was reacting negatively to *PGE*. Yet it was *not until 2009* that the Oregon Supreme Court acknowledged the legislation.

By the way, the Oregon Supreme Court is not the only court that has resisted legislative attempts to codify rules of interpretation for courts to follow. Numerous state courts have ignored, or even struck down, these attempts as invasions on the judicial power—another fascinating development that raises important questions about who controls statutory interpretation. See Jacob Scott, *Codified Canons and the Common Law of Interpretation*, 98 Geo. L.J. 341 (2008). Do you think that a statute telling courts not to apply legislative history, or not to apply a particular canon is really that different from a statute defining key textual terms? *See* Linda D. Jellum, *"Which Is to Be Master," the Judiciary or the Legislature? When Statutory Directives Violate Separation of Powers*, 56 UCLA L. Rev. 837 (2009); Nicholas Quinn Rosenkranz, *Federal Rules of Statutory Interpretation*, 115 Harv. L. Rev. 2085, 2108 (2002). Courts have no problem applying statutes setting forth definitions. Where, if anywhere, would you draw the line?

In *State v. Gaines*, 206 P.3d 1042, 1046–51 (Or. 2009), the Oregon Supreme Court finally confronted the legislature's attempt to modify *PGE*. The Court held that parties are free to "proffer" legislative history as part of the level one (textual) inquiry, and that the court will consult it regardless of ambiguity, but only "where that legislative history appears useful to the court's analysis." As Professor Gluck feared in 2010, *Gaines* may have been the closing curtain for the *PGE* regime of strict tiers or levels—offering some fodder to those who have argued that once the doors open to legislative history, they become floodgates. Since *Gaines*, the Oregon Supreme Court has frequently relaxed the first level of the *PGE* approach and has considered legislative history to confirm apparent plain meanings, see, e.g., *State v. Miskell*, 351 Or. 680, 692–93 (2012); *State v. Swanson,* 266 P.3d 45, 49 (Or. 2011), *In re Marriage of Harris,* 244 P.3d 801, 809–11 (Or. 2010); *State v. Baker-Krofft,* 239 P.3d 226, 231–32 (Or. 2010), or has examined legislative history in detail before rejecting it in favor of statutory plain meanings, see, e.g., *A.G. v. Guitron,* 268 P.3d 589, 592–600 (Or. 2011), or has rested interpretation decisively on legislative history as the best means to fill in the details of a statutory provision, e.g., *Hopkins v. SAIF Corp.,* 245 P.3d 90 (Or. 2010) (seamlessly combining textual and detailed legislative history analysis). Indeed, the Oregon Supreme Court's decisions after *Gaines* look a lot more like the complicated Funnel of Abstraction (considering text, statutory and legislative history, purpose, case law, and norms) than like the strict tiers/levels announced in *PGE*. See, e.g., *State v. Glushko,* 266 P.3d 50, 54–60 (Or. 2011) (citing only *Gaines* and not *PGE*); *Arken v. City of Portland,* 263 P.3d 975, 990–92 (Or. 2011) (citing only *Gaines* and examining a wide range of evidence, including a detailed account of the legislative history); *State v. Cloutier,* 261 P.3d 1234 (Or. 2011) (similar).

What lessons might be drawn from Oregon's experiment? Consider one of the U.S. Supreme Court's most recent statements on questions about the order of interpretive tools, and the way in which it revives a favorite chestnut.

Zuni Public School District No. 89 v. Department of Education
550 U.S. 81 (2007).

The federal Impact Aid Act, 108 Stat. 3749, provides financial assistance to local school districts whose ability to finance public school education is adversely affected by a federal presence. The statute prohibits a state from offsetting this federal aid by reducing state aid to a local district. So as not to interfere with a state program that seeks to equalize per-pupil expenditures, the statute contains an exception permitting a state to reduce its own local funding on account of the federal aid where the Secretary of Education finds that the state program "equalizes expenditures" among local school districts. 20 U.S.C. § 7709(b)(1). The Secretary is required to use a formula that compares the local school district with the greatest per-pupil expenditures in a state to the school district with the smallest per-pupil expenditures. If the former does not exceed the latter by more than 25 percent, the state program qualifies as one that "equalizes expenditures." In making this determination, the Secretary must "disregard [school districts] with per-pupil expenditures * * * above the 95th percentile or below the 5th percentile of such expenditures or revenues in the State." *Id.* § 7709(b)(2)(B)(i).

Department of Education regulations first promulgated more than 30 years ago provide that the Secretary will (1) create a list of school districts ranked in order of per-pupil expenditure; then (2) identify the relevant percentile cutoff point on that list based on a specific (95th or 5th) percentile of student population (essentially identifying those districts whose students account for the 5% of the state's total student population that lies at both the high and low ends of the spending distribution); and finally (3) compare the highest spending and lowest spending of the remaining school districts to see whether they satisfy the statute's requirement that the disparity between them not exceed 25%. Two New Mexico school districts challenged this method of calculation on the ground that it was inconsistent with the plain language of the "disregard" clause. According to the districts, the clause required the Department to disregard the bottom and top 5% of school districts by number (i.e., the top 5 and the bottom 5 if there were 100 districts)—and not to consider the districts' populations, as the Department was doing.

Justice Breyer's opinion for the Court ruled that the Department's method was permissible. First, it was consistent with the evolution of the statute. Congress initially enacted an equalization law in 1974, which explicitly delegated to the Department authority to define the conditions under which equalization funds would be allowed. The Department issued regulations in 1976, essentially the same as those challenged. No one in Congress objected to those regulations, which the Department has administered consistently. "The present statutory language originated in draft legislation that the Secretary himself sent to Congress in 1994. With one minor change (irrelevant to the present calculation controversy), Congress adopted that language without comment or clarification. No one at the time—no Member of Congress, no Department of Education official, no school district or State—expressed the view that this statutory language (which, after all, was supplied by the Secretary) was intended to require, or did require, the Secretary to change the Department's system of calculation, a system that the Department and school districts across the Nation had followed for nearly 20 years, without (as far as we are told) any adverse effect."

Second, the Department's approach was consistent with the purpose of the disregard clause, to exclude "outlier" districts from the calculation. The Department originally explained why it did not follow a number-of-school-districts approach: "In States with a small number of large districts, an exclusion based on percentage of school districts might exclude from the measure of disparity a substantial percentage of the pupil population in those States. Conversely, in States with large numbers of small districts, such an approach might exclude only an insignificant fraction of the pupil population and would not exclude anomalous characteristics." 41 Fed. Reg. 26,324 (1976).

Third, the Department's approach was not inconsistent with the statutory language, which Justice Breyer thought ambiguous in light of his survey of technical and general dictionaries. The statutory language ("percentile") signifies only that the Department must divide districts into a population with a top 5% and a bottom 5%, but does not tell the Department how those "5%" figures must be calculated. "No dictionary definition we have found suggests that there is any *single* logical, mathematical, or statistical link between, on the one hand, the characterizing data (used for ranking purposes) and, on the other hand, the nature of the relevant population or how that population might be weighted for purposes of determining a percentile cutoff." When Congress has wanted to limit agency discretion in making such percentile rankings, it has phrased statutory language more precisely. For example, in another education-related law, Congress referred to "the school at the 20th percentile in the State, *based on enrollment,* among all schools *ranked by the percentage of students at the proficient level.*" 20 U.S.C. § 6311(b)(2)(E)(ii) (emphasis supplied by Justice Breyer).

Justice Breyer drew further "reassurance from the fact that no group of statisticians, nor any individual statistician, has told us directly in briefs, or indirectly through citation, that the language before us cannot be read as we have read it. This circumstance is significant, for the statutory language is technical, and we are not statisticians. And the views of experts (or their absence) might help us understand (though not control our determination of) what Congress had in mind."

Justice Scalia's dissenting opinion (joined by Chief Justice Roberts and Justices Souter and Thomas) faulted the majority for starting its analysis with the history and evolution of the statute, rather than its text. In his view, this "cart-before-the-horse approach" was inconsistent with the primary lesson of "Statutory Interpretation 101." (Writing also for Justice Alito, **Justice Kennedy** wrote a concurring opinion stating that he would be alarmed if Justice Breyer's order of treatment became "systemic." Justice Scalia responded that such deviant practices should be nipped in the bud, lest they become "systemic.")

Justice Scalia castigated the majority for finding ambiguity in a statute having a plain meaning. "This case is not a scary math problem," and judges "do not need the cadre of the Court's number-crunching *amici* to guide our way." "The question is: Whose per-pupil expenditures or revenues? Or, in the Court's terminology, what 'population' is assigned the 'characteristic' 'per-pupil expenditure or revenue'? At first blush, second blush, or twenty-second blush, the answer is abundantly clear: local educational agencies. The statute requires the Secretary to 'disregard local educational agencies with' certain per-pupil figures above or below specified percentiles of those per-pupil figures. § 7709(b)(2)(B)(i). The attribute 'per-pupil expenditur[e] or revenu[e]' is assigned to LEAs [local educational agencies]—there is no mention of student population whatsoever. And thus under the statute, 'per-pupil expenditures or revenues' are to be arrayed using a population consisting of LEAs, so that percentiles are determined from a list of (in New Mexico) 89 per-pupil expenditures or revenues representing the 89 LEAs in the State. It is just that simple."

Joining the Court's opinion, **Justice Stevens** added a concurring opinion stating that he would agree with the majority's interpretation in this case even if it were inconsistent with statutory plain meaning. "There is no reason why we must confine ourselves to, or begin our analysis with, the statutory text if other tools of statutory construction provide better evidence of congressional intent with respect to the precise point at issue. As the Court's opinion demonstrates, this is a quintessential example of a case in which the statutory text was obviously enacted to adopt the rule that the Secretary administered both before and after the enactment of the rather confusing language found in 20 U.S.C. § 7709(b)(2)(B)(i). That text is sufficiently ambiguous to justify the Court's exegesis, but my own vote is the product of a more direct route to the Court's patently correct conclusion. This happens to be a case in which the legislative history is pellucidly clear and the statutory text is difficult to fathom." Justice Stevens justified his approach by reference to cases where the Court followed statutory plain meaning consistent with its reading of the legislative history, and *Holy Trinity*, where it did not.

The *Holy Trinity* reference sparked a further response from **Justice Scalia** (in a portion of his dissent joined by Chief Justice Roberts and Justice Thomas but not by Justice Souter). *Holy Trinity*, "that miraculous redeemer of lost causes," is a dangerous precedent. "Thus, what judges believe Congress 'meant' (apart from the text) has a disturbing but entirely unsurprising tendency to be whatever judges think Congress *must* have meant, *i.e., should* have meant. In *Church of the Holy Trinity,* every Justice on this Court disregarded the plain language of a statute that forbade the hiring of a clergyman from abroad because, after all (they thought), 'this is a Christian nation,' so Congress could not have meant what it said. Is there any reason to believe that those Justices were lacking that 'intellectua[l] honest[y]' that Justice Stevens 'presume[s]' all our judges possess? Intellectual honesty does not exclude a blinding intellectual bias. And even if it did, the system of judicial amendatory veto over texts duly adopted by Congress bears no resemblance to the system of lawmaking set forth in our Constitution."

NOTE ON ZUNI

Zuni is an unusual case, both because the question about the order of interpretive tools is so explicitly considered and also because the order that Justice Breyer chose was out of the ordinary in the post-textualist era. Indeed, it would be malpractice for you to brief legislative history first in the Supreme Court these days. Moreover, Justice Stevens, who was perhaps an even more enthusiastic supporter of Breyer's history-first methodology than Breyer himself in *Zuni*, is no longer on the Court, nor is another reliable legislative-history user, Justice Souter. As noted, Justice Sotomayor (who replaced Souter) has not shied away from using legislative history, or defending its use against Justice Scalia's criticisms. As for Justice Kagan (who replaced Stevens), her propensities on this front still remain unclear.

At the same time, there are many doctrines of statutory interpretation—text- and policy-based canons most importantly—that judges of all interpretive stripes use. We introduce these doctrines in the next chapter; keep the landscape of these interpretive debates in mind as you study them and ask yourselves whether their deployment furthers textualism, purposivism, pragmatism, or something else.

CHAPTER 5

CANONS OF STATUTORY INTERPRETATION

■ ■ ■

This chapter focuses on those rules of statutory construction known as the canons of statutory interpretation. It introduces you to the "textual canons," which are based on linguistic presumptions and grammatical conventions; as well as to the "substantive canons," which are presumptions that judges have drawn from policy and constitutional values; and to the "extrinsic" canons, which are conventions about using certain sources outside the legislative process (such as the common law and other statutes) in interpretation. The chapter also sets out the debate about whether canons constrain judges, whether they should produce meanings contrary to Congress's meanings, and whether the assumptions upon which the canons rely are good approximations of how Congress really works.

The previous chapter introduced you to the history of statutory interpretation in the United States and to the major theories that have been debated. Here, we turn to more specific doctrines of statutory interpretation in the United States. Specifically, we consider the accepted and evolving *canons of statutory construction*. The canons have been the bedrock of Anglo-American interpretation for centuries. Although they were de-emphasized in federal courts after the New Deal, some canons remained important in state courts and they have made a federal comeback since the mid-1980s. Appendix 6 to this coursebook collects almost 200 different canons applied by the Rehnquist and Roberts Courts between 1986 and 2012.

Most of the nineteenth-century English and American treatises on statutory interpretation were organized around the canons, and the leading doctrinal compilation today (a descendant of an 1891 treatise) is an exhaustive canon-by-canon tour, namely, *Sutherland Statutes and Statutory Construction* (Norman Singer & J.D. Shambie Singer eds. 2008–14) (hereinafter referred to as Sutherland).[1] State legislatures have

---

[1] Sutherland is the leading American treatise. Also valuable reference works are leading treatises in the United Kingdom, see P. St. J. Langan, *Maxwell on the Interpretation of Statutes* (12th ed. 1969), and F.A.R. Bennion, *Statutory Interpretation: A Code* (4th ed. 2002); Canada, see Ruth Sullivan, *Sullivan and Driedger on the Construction of Statutes* (4th ed. 2002); Ruth

codified some of the text-based canons in their state codes, although debates continue to rage about whether legislatures can really mandate methods of judicial interpretation. E.g., Minn. Stat. ch. 645; Pennsylvania Statutory Construction Act of 1972, 1 Pa. Consol. Stat. §§ 1921–1928 (hereinafter "Pa. Stat. Constr. Act"); Jacob Scott, *Codified Canons and the Common Law of Interpretation*, 98 Geo. L.J. 341 (2010) (systematic collection of legislatively codified canons in all 50 states and the District of Columbia). On the federal side, the "Dictionary Act" provides some assumptions about word meaning that Congress has stated should apply "unless the context indicates otherwise." Dictionary Act of 1871, 16 Stat. 431, codified as amended at 1 U.S.C. §§ 1–8 (word-meaning canons, such as the rule that "person" should be construed to include a "corporation").

As Appendix 6 to this coursebook documents in some detail, there are three kinds of canons. First are the *textual canons*, which set forth inferences that are usually drawn from the drafter's choice of words, their grammatical placement in sentences, and their relationship to other parts of the statute. These are sometimes called *intrinsic aids*, for they assist the statutory interpreter in deriving probable meaning from the four corners of the statutory text. Section 1 of this chapter sets forth many of these textual canons, with illustrations from prominent cases. But keep in mind, as always, that agencies interpret statutes, too. Because legal culture has generally embraced the canons, especially the textual ones, courts seem to assume that agencies consider the canons when they interpret statutes, an assumption that some academics have strongly challenged (although agencies certainly deploy the canons when they have to defend their interpretations in court). We return to this question of agency statutory interpretation in Chapter 8.

A second genre consists of the *substantive canons*. These are presumptions about statutory meaning based upon substantive principles or policies drawn from the common law, other statutes, or the Constitution. The best-known example is the "rule of lenity," which, based in part upon principles of fair notice, postulates that criminal statutes do not outlaw behavior unless the activity clearly comes within the sweep of the statutes. Section 2 examines the substantive canons, with a focus on those that reflect constitutional values.

The third group of maxims is the *reference canons*. These are more often called *extrinsic aids* or *extrinsic canons* because they are presumptive rules telling the interpreter what other materials might be

Sullivan, *Statutory Interpretation* (2d ed. 2007); Australia, see Donald Gifford, *Statutory Interpretation* (1990), and D.C. Pearce & R.S. Geddes, *Statutory Interpretation in Australia* (3d ed. 1988); New Zealand, see Jim Evans, *Statutory Interpretation: Problems of Communication* (1988); and South Africa, see G.E. Devenish, *Interpretation of Statutes* (1992). For a compendium surveying the practice in civil law countries as well, see *Interpreting Statutes: A Comparative Study* (D. Neil MacCormick & Robert Summers eds., 1991).

consulted to figure out what the statute means. You have already been introduced to the two most important extrinsic aids, namely, *stare decisis* (Chapter 3, § 2) and legislative history (Chapter 4, with more extensive treatment in Chapter 6). Agency interpretations, which are explored in Chapter 8, are also critically important extrinsic sources that courts will typically follow, sometimes even when judges would have reached a different result otherwise. Section 3 of this chapter introduces you to other extrinsic rules, including rules about how courts look to the "horizontal" landscape of public policy to interpret statutory ambiguities, and how courts use the common law and legislative inaction as tools of interpretation.

Justice Scalia has just published a mini-treatise setting forth what he considers to be the "valid canons" the Supreme Court *should* be applying. See Antonin Scalia & Bryan Garner, *Reading Law: The Interpretation of Legal Texts* (2012). We shall situate that treatise as a useful description of many of the textual and substantive canons in §§ 1 and 2. Section 3 will examine Justice Scalia's claims in the context of the debates over the desirability of the canons. Do they provide a set of rules that constrain result-oriented judges, that usefully guide agency and legislative decisionmaking, and that (overall) render statutory interpretation more predictable? Or are the canons window-dressing for decisions reached on other grounds or, worse, camouflage for result-oriented judging?

1.   TEXTUAL CANONS

The starting point of statutory interpretation is to read the text carefully. A number of rules—based either on general notions of English composition or syntax or the structure of a statute—have emerged as guides for finding meaning from the words of the statute and nothing else. These are called "intrinsic aids" or "textual canons" of interpretation. They are normally invoked by courts as conventional benchmarks for figuring out whether a statute has a *plain meaning* or not.

Professor Solum suggests a helpful distinction. Many sentences/phrases/terms lack a plain meaning because they are *vague*: the locution covers a wide range of possible meanings; examples are statutory bars to "disorderly conduct" or "contracts in restraint of trade." Other sentences/phrases/words are *ambiguous*: the locution has alternative concrete meanings; an example would be the word "cool," which can mean chilly or hip/stylish. See Lawrence B. Solum, *The Interpretation-Construction Distinction in Constitutional Law*, 27 Const. Comm. 95, 97–98 (2010). Textual canons help interpreters identify or resolve ambiguities and enable interpreters to narrow the range of meanings for vague terms as well.

Courts do not apply the textual canons as hard-and-fast rules; they are inconsistently applied and, at best, presumptions and might be considered more like adages. See Lawrence M. Solan, *The Language of Judges* ch. 2 (1993) (linguistic analysis of several textual canons), as well as Solan, *The Language of Statutes: Laws and Their Interpretation* (2010), and Antonin Scalia & Bryan Garner, *Reading Law: The Interpretation of Legal Texts* (2012). One of us believes the canons should be treated more like ordinary legal doctrines, such as the parol evidence rule,[2] but that position is controversial. Regardless of their formal legal status, when courts do invoke the canons, as we shall see, they often carry a lot of weight in deciding cases.

A good way to learn the textual canons is to explore them in the context of familiar statutory problems. This section uses our no-vehicles law from the Introduction and the *Holy Trinity Church* case from Chapter 4 to introduce the most important rules. Recall the questions from those cases: Is a tricycle a "vehicle" for purposes of the law prohibiting vehicles in the park? Does a pastor fall under the law prohibiting employers from bringing foreigners to the United States to perform "labor or service of any kind in the United States"?

A. MAXIMS OF WORD MEANING AND ASSOCIATION

Plain meaning is the legal meaning a statute has in light of the provision's ordinary meaning, the statutory purpose and structure, and any specialized definition the term has acquired over the years. Miranda McGowan, *Do as I Do, Not as I Say: An Empirical Investigation of Justice Scalia's Ordinary Meaning Method of Statutory Interpretation*, 78 Miss. L.J. 129 (2008). Consider the relevance of the canons of word meaning and association to resolve ambiguity in cases like that of the tricycle (Introduction) or the pastor in *Holy Trinity* (Chapter 4, § 1).

(1) Ordinary Versus Technical Meaning of Words

Typically, interpreters will assume that the legislature uses words like "vehicle" in their ordinary sense: What would these words convey to the "ordinary" or "reasonable" reader? To figure this out, judges, increasingly and perhaps paradoxically, consult dictionaries,[3] but they

---

[2] See Abbe R. Gluck, *Intersystemic Statutory Interpretation: Methodology as "Law" and the* Erie *Doctrine*, 120 Yale L. J. 1898 (2011).

[3] See Ellen P. Aprill, *The Law of the Word: Dictionary Shopping in the Supreme Court*, 30 Ariz. St. L.J. 275 (1998); James J. Brudney & Lawrence Baum, *Oasis or Mirage: The Supreme Court's Thirst for Dictionaries in the Rehnquist and Roberts Eras*, 55 William & Mary L. Rev. 483 (2013); Clark D. Cunningham et al., *Plain Meaning and Hard Cases*, 103 Yale L.J. 1561 (1994); Lawrence M. Solan, *When Judges Use the Dictionary*, 68 Am. Speech 50 (1993); Samuel A. Thumma & Jeffrey L. Kirchmeier, *The Lexicon Has Become a Fortress: The United States Supreme Court's Use of Dictionaries*, 47 Buff. L. Rev. 227 (1999); Note, *Looking It Up: Dictionaries and Statutory Interpretation*, 107 Harv. L. Rev. 1437 (1994); Rickie Sonpal, Note, *Old Dictionaries and New Textualists*, 71 Fordham L. Rev. 2177 (2003).

will often just rely on their own linguistic experience or intuition to decide the most reasonable meaning of the words given the context in which they are being used and applied. Linguists suggest that the interpreter start with the *prototypical* meaning of statutory words.[4] What is the core idea associated with a word or phrase? For example, this was the approach implicitly followed by Justice Brewer in *Holy Trinity*, where he essentially confined the statutory terms "labor or service of any kind" to manual work, the prototypical form of "labor."

Is this linguistic exercise necessary when the statute (like our no-vehicles law) has a definitional section? As Scalia and Garner say, interpreters should "carefully follow" definitional sections, *Reading Law,* 225–33, but statutory definitions themselves might be unclear. Section 3 of the no-vehicles law ("[v]ehicle for purposes of this law means any mechanism for conveying a person from one place to another, including motorcycles, automobiles, trucks and motor scooters") has that quality: a tricycle may literally be a mechanism that conveys a person from one place to another, but should that be the end of inquiry? Not necessarily. The "normal" prototypical meaning of the term remains relevant, and is often dispositive, when the statutory definition leaves room for reasonable debate. *Id.* at 228–33.

What if the statute is an old one? In that event, judges sometimes consult dictionaries and other evidence from the era in which the statute was enacted. For example, the Supreme Court in *St. Francis College v. Al-Khazraji*, 481 U.S. 604 (1987), interpreted the Civil Rights Act of 1866 to apply to discrimination against a person of Arab ancestry. Defendant had argued that any discrimination against an ethnic Arab was not actionable, because the statute only required the same protections as are "enjoyed by white citizens" and Arabs are ethnographically Caucasian. The Court invoked nineteenth-century dictionaries and encyclopedias to demonstrate that defendant's conception of race was not the one held in the nineteenth century, which viewed different ethnic "stock" and family "lineage" as different "races." Thus, these sources referred to Finns, Greeks, Basques, Arabs, Norwegians, Jews, and Hungarians as identifiable "races."

In addition to special meanings that words may have had historically, words often have meanings limited to parlance in a trade, academic discipline, or technical area. Where the statute itself deals with a technical, specialized subject, courts tend to adopt the specialized meaning of words used in the statute, unless that leads to an absurd result. Scalia & Garner, *Reading Law,* 73–77. For a hoary, and perhaps

---

[4] See Lawrence M. Solan, *Learning Our Limits: The Decline of Textualism in Statutory Cases*, 1997 Wis. L. Rev. 235, 270–75 (explaining linguists' "prototype" theory and applying it to several statutory interpretation cases).

amusing, example of this maxim, consider ***Nix v. Hedden***, 149 U.S. 304, 305–07 (1893):

> This was an action, brought February 4, 1887, against the collector of the port of New York, to recover back duties paid under protest on tomatoes imported by the plaintiff from the West Indies in the spring of 1886, which the collector assessed under "Schedule G.—Provisions," of the Tariff Act of March 3, 1883, chap. 121, imposing a duty on "vegetables in their natural state, or in salt or brine, not specially enumerated or provided for in this Act, ten per centum *ad valorem;*" and which the plaintiffs contended came within the clause in the free list of the same act, "Fruits, green, ripe or dried, not specially enumerated or provided for in this act." 22 Stat. 504, 519.

> At the trial the plaintiff's counsel, after reading in evidence definitions of the words "fruit" and "vegetables" from Webster's Dictionary, Worchester's Dictionary and the Imperial Dictionary, called two witnesses, who had been for 30 years in the business of selling fruit and vegetables, and asked them, after hearing these definitions, to say whether these words had "any special meaning in trade or commerce, different from those read."

> One of the witnesses answered as follows: "Well, it does not classify all things there, but they are correct as far as they go. It does not take all kinds of fruit or vegetables; it takes a portion of them. I think the words 'fruit' and 'vegetable' have the same meaning in trade today that they had on March 1, 1883. I understand that the term 'fruit' is applied in trade only to such plants or parts of plants as contain the seeds. There are more vegetables than those in the enumeration given in Webster's Dictionary under the term 'vegetable,' as 'cabbage, cauliflower, turnips, potatoes, peas, beans, and the like,' probably covered by the words 'and the like.'"

> The other witnesses testified: "I don't think the term 'fruit' or the term 'vegetables' had in March 1883, and prior thereto, any special meaning in trade and commerce in this country different from that which I have read here from the dictionaries."

> The plaintiff's counsel then read in evidence from the same dictionaries the definitions of the word "tomato."

> The defendant's counsel then read in evidence from Webster's dictionary the definitions of the words "pea," "eggplant," "cucumber," "squash," and "pepper."

The plaintiff then read in evidence from Webster's and Worcester's dictionaries the definitions of "potato," "turnip," "parsnip," "cauliflower," "cabbage," "carrot," and "bean."

No other evidence was offered by either party. The court, upon the defendant's motion, directed a verdict for him, which was returned, and judgment rendered therein. The plaintiffs duly excepted to the instruction, and sued out this writ of error. * * *

There being no evidence that the words "fruit" and "vegetables" have acquired any special meaning in trade or commerce, they must receive their ordinary meaning. Of that meaning the court is bound to take judicial notice, as it does in regard to all words in our own tongue; and upon such a question dictionaries are admitted, not as evidence, but only as aids to the memory and understanding of the court.

Botanically speaking, tomatoes are the fruit of a vine, just as are cucumbers, squashes, beans and peas. But in the common language of the people, whether sellers or consumers of provisions, all these are vegetables, which are grown in kitchen gardens, and which, whether eaten cooked or raw, are, like potatoes, carrots, parsnips, turnips, beets, cauliflower, cabbage, celery and lettuce, usually served at dinner in, with, or after the soup, fish or meats which constitute the principal part of the repast, and not, like fruits generally, as dessert.

The attempt to class tomatoes as fruit is not unlike a recent attempt to class beans as seeds, of which Mr. Justice Bradley, speaking for this court, said: "We do not see why they should be classified as seeds, any more than walnuts should be so classified. Both are seeds in the language of botany or natural history, but not in commerce nor in common parlance. On the other hand in speaking generally of provisions, beans may well be included under the term 'vegetables.' As an article of food on our tables, whether baked or boiled, or forming the basis of soup, they are used as a vegetable, as well as when ripe as when green. This is the principal use to which they are put. Beyond the common knowledge which we have on this subject, very little evidence is necessary, or can be produced." *Robertson v. Salomon*, 130 U.S. 412, 414 (1889).

Do you agree with the Supreme Court?

For a different kind of specialized meaning, courts sometimes look to the common law for the meaning of ambiguous terms. "Where Congress uses terms that have accumulated settled meaning under either equity or the common law, a court must infer, unless the statute otherwise dictates, that Congress means to incorporate the established meaning of these terms." *NLRB v. Amax Coal Co.*, 453 U.S. 322, 329 (1981); accord, *Buckhannon Bd. & Care Home, Inc. v. W. Va. Dep't of Health and Human Resources*, 532 U.S. 598 (2001); *Morissette v. United States,* 342 U.S. 246, 250 (1952) (leading case). Thus, courts assume—realistically or not—that Congress knows the common law (i.e., that Congress knows and absorbs the holdings of judicial decisions on non-statutory matters) and legislates against its backdrop. (We come back to this assumption in § 3 of this chapter). If the technical term originates outside the common-law domain, courts instead start with the presumption that "where Congress has used technical words or terms of art, it [is] proper to explain them by reference to the art or science to which they [are] appropriate." *Corning Glass Works v. Brennan*, 417 U.S. 188, 201 (1974).

(2) *Noscitur a Sociis* and *Ejusdem Generis*

Words are social creatures: they travel in packs. Section 3 of the no-vehicles law says that a "vehicle" is "any mechanism for conveying a person from one place to another, including motorcycles, automobiles, trucks, and motor scooters." Does the society of terms illustrating what mechanisms are included (i.e., "motorcycles," etc.) tell us anything about what other "mechanisms" might be included or not included in the statutory definition? Several canons suggest that there are permissible inferences from the company that words keep.

"*Noscitur a sociis*" translates as "[i]t is known from its associates." Light may be shed on the meaning of an ambiguous word by reference to words associated with it. "Thus, when two or more words are grouped together, and ordinarily have a similar meaning, but are not equally comprehensive, the general word will be limited and qualified by the special word." 2A Sutherland § 47.16. For example, in *Jarecki v. G. D. Searle & Co.*, 367 U.S. 303 (1961), a federal income tax statute allowed allocation to other years of income "resulting from exploration, discovery, or prospecting." A drug manufacturer and a camera manufacturer argued that they should be allowed to take advantage of the allocation statute with respect to income from the sale of patented products because by definition such a products resulted from a "discovery." The Court disagreed. When interpreted in light of the associated words "exploration" and "prospecting," the term "discovery" meant "only the discovery of mineral resources."

Consider the exceptions provided in the *Holy Trinity* statute. Section 5 sets out the following exemptions from the immigration ban: "[N]or shall the provisions of this act apply to professional actors, artists, lecturers, or singers, nor to persons employed strictly as personal or domestic servants." Assume that you have your eye on the term "lecturer." Is it possible that "lecturer" includes pastor? Using *noscitur a sociis* you might conclude that these exceptions apply to *entertainers* coming from abroad, and that the pastor might be out of luck.

The vehicles in the park statute offers a different kind of list problem. Section 3 defines vehicles as "mechanisms," etc. *including* motorcycles, automobiles, trucks, and motor scooters." This manner of phrasing the definition renders *noscitur a sociis* inapplicable—that canon works to shed light on an ambiguous term in a list, like "lecturer." In the vehicles problem, the ambiguity is not in terms of the list itself, but in what the list is trying to illustrate. Here another word association canon is possibly relevant.

"*Ejusdem generis*," a sibling of *noscitur a sociis*, translates as "[o]f the same kind, class, or nature." "Where general words follow specific words in a statutory enumeration, the general words are construed to embrace only objects similar in nature to those objects enumerated by the preceding specific words. Where the opposite sequence is found, i.e., specific words following general ones, the doctrine is equally applicable, and restricts application of the general term to things that are similar to those enumerated." 2A Sutherland § 47.17. The purpose of this rule is to give effect to all the words—the particular words indicate the class and the general words extend the provisions of the statute to everything else in the class (even though not enumerated by the specific words). So, for example, assume there exists a statute that prohibits citizens from "leaving in the street any newspapers, trash bags, food items or any other item obstructing the gutters or drains in the street." You park your car on the street, with the tire exactly on top of the street drain. Are you in violation of the statute? *Ejusdem generis* tells you that "any other item" gets at garbage-type items, not cars.

Return to the vehicles in the park statute. Because § 3's definition of "vehicle" starts with a general term ("mechanism") followed by specific examples ("motorcycles, etc."), *ejusdem generis* might be applicable: the general term is limited to the feature most obviously common among the specific terms, namely, motorization. Justice Scalia and Professor Garner reject the statement in the Sutherland treatise that *ejusdem generis* applies to a text where specific terms follow a general one and insist that the rule only applies when the text has this structure: [specific term], [specific term], and all other [general term]. Scalia & Garner, *Reading Law*, 203–05. If they are right about that, *ejusdem generis* would have no application in the Case of the Tricycle. Does that strike you as correct?

Another important limitation for *ejusdem generis* (as well as *noscitur a sociis*) is that the interpreter needs to figure out what is the common feature shared by the specific terms that should be imputed as a limitation on the general term. We have assumed that the common feature for "motorcycle, etc." is that they are all motorized—but one might also say that a common feature is that they all pose safety dangers to park users. Nonmotorized bicycles might then be included in the term "mechanism" if this is the better understanding.

Circuit City Stores, Inc. v. Adams, 532 U.S. 105 (2001), provides a real-world example of this problem. Section 1 of the Federal Arbitration Act of 1926 (FAA) excludes from coverage "contracts of employment of seamen, railroad employees, or any other class of workers engaged in foreign or interstate commerce." 9 U.S.C. § 1. The issue in *Circuit City* was whether the exclusion was limited to contracts involving *transportation* but not other kinds of employment contracts. Workers suing their employers generally want a court, not an arbitrator, especially for discrimination claims such as those in *Circuit City*. So the plaintiff argued that his job at a retail store, obviously engaged in "interstate commerce," fell within the exclusion: Congress, he argued, meant to exclude employment contracts generally, and used language tied to the jurisdictional basis of the FAA, the Commerce Clause. Justice Kennedy's majority opinion rejected that reading, on the ground that *ejusdem generis* suggested that Congress meant the exclusion to be limited to contracts "like" those involving seamen and railroad workers—namely, transportation contracts. But the dissenters found the common feature to be "employment contracts within Congress's Commerce Clause power." See generally 2A Sutherland § 47.17–.22 (discussing *ejusdem generis* and qualifications to its use).

Another challenge for both *noscitur a sociis* and *ejusdem generis* is that not every list has commonality. Some statutory lists are just grab bags of unrelated terms, in which case you cannot draw meaning from their association. As a practicing lawyer, this is a great defense against the use of these canons. Consider the *Holy Trinity* exemption again: "[N]or shall the provisions of this act apply to professional actors, artists, lecturers, or singers, nor to persons employed strictly as personal or domestic servants." A savvy lawyer for the pastor, hoping to convince a court that "lecturers" does indeed include pastors, could try to defeat the *noscitur* argument that lecturers are only intended to be entertainers by pointing to the inclusion of personal and domestic servants in the prohibition to argue that the association of words in the list has neither rhyme nor reason.

(3) *Expressio (Inclusio) Unius*

Words omitted may be just as significant as words set forth. The maxim "*expressio* [or *inclusio*] *unius est exclusio alterius*" means "expression [or inclusion] of one thing indicates exclusion of the other." The notion is one of negative implication: the enumeration of certain things in a statute suggests that the legislature had no intent to include things not listed or embraced. "When a statute limits a thing to be done in a particular mode, it includes a negative of any other mode." *Raleigh & Gaston R.R. Co. v. Reid*, 13 Wall. 269, 270 (1872); see *Tate v. Ogg*, 195 S.E. 496 (Va. 1938) (statute covering "any horse, mule, cattle, hog, sheep or goat" did not cover turkeys); Sutherland § 47.25 (discussing the limitations of the canon). The canon also is relevant to exceptions—when Congress goes to the trouble of listing exceptions in a statute, we assume that it did not mean to include any additional exceptions not mentioned.

In *Holy Trinity*, assuming for the moment that "lecturers" does not include pastors, application of *expressio unius* would have led the Court to conclude that the exceptions specifically listed were the only ones not covered by the prohibition. As that case illustrates, courts feel free to refuse to apply the maxim when they believe it would lead to a result Congress did not intend. One basic problem is that this canon, like many of the others, assumes that the legislature thinks through statutory language carefully, considering every possible variation. Some critics have suggested that the maxim is unreliable because legislators do not consider all possible alternatives when they adopt statutes.[5]

Another way of looking at this issue is to consider context, including normative context. If Mother tells Sally, "Don't hit, kick, or bite your sister Anne," Sally is *not* authorized by *expressio unius* to pinch her little sister. The reason is that the normative baseline (discerned from prior practice or just family culture) is "no harming sister," and the directive was an expression of such a baseline that ought to be broadly applied and not easily overridden. Contrariwise, where the directive in question is a departure from the normative baseline, the canon ought to have greater force. For example, if Mother tells Sally, "You may have a cookie and a scoop of ice cream," Sally has implicitly been forbidden to snap up that candy bar lying on the kitchen table. For cases where normative statutory baselines augured against application of *expressio unius*, see, e.g., *Marrama v. Citizens Bank of Mass.*, 549 U.S. 365, 374–75 (2007) (Stevens, J.); *Christensen v. Harris County*, 529 U.S. 576, 583–84 (2000) (Thomas, J.).

Does *expressio unius* have any bearing on your interpretation of the no-vehicles law? Recall the bicycle proviso at the end of § 2 ("*Provided that*, bicycles shall be allowed in the park, so long as they are being pushed or carried and not ridden"). By providing a special rule for bicycles, did the Council thereby exclude tricycles from the proviso? Or are tricycles "included" within the general category of bicycles? How would you answer these questions? Does your answer have significant bearing on how you would apply the law to tricycles?

---

[5] A recent empirical study of the congressional process, however, found that staff are aware of *expressio unius* and do draft statutes with that canon in mind. See Abbe R. Gluck & Lisa Schultz Bressman, *Statutory Interpretation from the Inside: An Empirical Study of Congressional Drafting, Delegation, and the Canons: Part I*, 65 Stan. L. Rev. 901 (2013).

B. GRAMMAR CANONS

Although "justice should not be the handmaiden of grammar," *Value Oil Co. v. Irvington*, 377 A.2d 1225, 1231 (N.J. Super. 1977), the legislature is presumed to know and follow basic conventions of grammar and syntax. Sometimes, the grammar canons help us see that there is a single, grammatically correct reading of a phrase or a sentence. Other times, grammar canons help us see that there is an ambiguity in language, making a phrase or sentence susceptible to either of two meanings. As we shall see, however, the grammar canons provide some interesting arguments in the Case of the Tricycle that we have been considering.

(1) Punctuation Rules

"The punctuation canon in America * * * has assumed at least three forms: (1) adhering to the strict English rule that punctuation forms no part of the statute; (2) allowing punctuation as an aid in statutory construction; and (3) looking on punctuation as a less-than-desirable, last-ditch alternative aid in statutory construction. The last approach * * * seems to have prevailed as the majority rule." Ray Marcin, *Punctuation and the Interpretation of Statutes*, 9 Conn. L. Rev. 227, 240 (1977). "[A]n act should be read as punctuated unless there is some reason to do otherwise," such as an indication that reading a statute according to its punctuation would defeat the apparent intent of the legislature. "This is especially true where a statute has been repeatedly reenacted with the same punctuation, or has been the subject of numerous amendments without alteration of punctuation." 2A Sutherland § 47.15; see Pa. Stat. Constr. Act § 1923(b): "In no case shall the punctuation of a statute control or affect the intention of the General Assembly in the enactment thereof but punctuation may be used in aid in the construction thereof * * *."

Consider *Tyrrell v. City of New York*, 53 N.E. 1111 (N.Y. 1899). A state statute provided that the salaries for persons employed as street cleaners "shall not exceed the following: * * * of the section foremen, one thousand dollars each; * * * of the hostlers, seven hundred and twenty dollars each, and extra pay for work on Sundays." (A "hostler" is someone who tends the horses in the stables.) The court ruled that a foreman was not entitled to extra pay for work on Sundays:

> The punctuation of this statute is of material aid in learning the intention of the legislature. While an act of parliament is enacted as read, and the original rolls contain no marks of punctuation, a statute of this state is enacted as read and printed, so that the punctuation is a part of the act as passed, and appears in the roll when filed with the secretary of state.

The punctuation canon has *not* played a major role in the legisprudence of the U.S. Supreme Court. The Court did find the punctuation rule decisive in *United States v. Ron Pair Enterprises, Inc.*, 489 U.S. 235 (1989). Justice Scalia, a fan of the canon, admits that it is rarely dispositive. Scalia & Garner, *Reading Law*, 161–66. In *United States National Bank of Oregon v. Independent Insurance Agents*, 508 U.S. 439 (1993), the Court in effect repunctuated a statute after concluding that a scrivener's error had occurred.

(2) Referential and Qualifying Words: The Rule of the Last Antecedent

A basic rule of grammar is that referential and qualifying words or phrases refer only to the last antecedent, unless such a reading is contrary to the apparent legislative intent derived from the sense of the entire enactment. For example, in the sentence, "I would like the shoes in white, blue and pink with yellow flowers," the qualifying words—the yellow flowers—refer only to the pink shoes (pink is the last antecedent). Courts apply this rule too. E.g., *Jama v. Immigration & Customs Enforcement*, 543 U.S. 335 (2005). Similarly, a proviso (such as the bicycle proviso to § 3 of our no-vehicles law) applies only to the provision, clause, or word immediately preceding it.

Consider this recent example. The Social Security Act's disability benefits program is available to a worker who meets the following requirement:

> [His] physical or mental impairment or impairments are of such severity that he is not only unable to do his previous work but cannot, considering his age, education, and work experience, engage in any other kind of substantial gainful work which exists in the national economy." 42 U.S.C. § 423(d)(2)(A).

Pauline Thomas was an elevator operator until that job was eliminated from the economy; she claimed to be disabled, saying she could not do other jobs in the economy. The Third Circuit, through then-Judge Alito, ruled for Thomas. It rejected the agency's argument that, as long as she could still do her "previous work," she was not disabled. Alito reasoned that "previous work" (like "any other kind of substantial gainful work") had to exist "in the national economy." The Supreme Court unanimously reversed, based upon the rule of the last antecedent. Only the "other kind" of work—and *not* the "previous work"—had to exist in the national economy. *Barnhart v. Thomas*, 540 U.S. 20, 26 (2003).[6]

---

[6] Judge Alito did not dispute that "which exists in the national economy" modified "any other kind of substantial gainful work," the last antecedent point. Alito's argument was that by using "*any other* kind of work," Congress was demanding a parallelism between these other jobs which exist in the national economy and the applicant's "previous work." The Supreme Court responded: "Consider, for example, the case of parents who, before leaving their teenage son

The last antecedent rule can be trumped by the punctuation rule. "Evidence that a qualifying phrase is supposed to apply to all antecedents instead of only to the immediately preceding one may be found in the fact that it is separated from the antecedents by a comma." 2A Sutherland § 47.33. Thus, if the statutory definition in *Thomas* had included a comma before "which exists in the national economy," Pauline Thomas would have had a better chance of success with the textually-oriented Supreme Court.

(3) Some Particular Grammar Rules: The And/Or and May/Shall Rules

The nature of the conjunctions connecting different words or phrases may be significant. The word "or" technically means "and/or." As linguists point out, when I say "I want this or that," I might be saying I want either one item or the other, but I might also be saying I want both items. See Solan, *Language of Judges*, 45–53.

In the courts, terms connected by the disjunctive "or" are often read to have separate meanings and significance. For instance, 21 U.S.C. § 881(a) subjects to forfeiture any property used as part of a drug crime, but exempts property "established by th[e] owner to have been committed or omitted without the knowledge or consent of that owner." What if the owner knows, but does not consent? See *U.S. v. 141st Street Corp. by Hersh*, 911 F.2d 870, 878 (2d Cir. 1990) ("Congress's use of the disjunctive 'or' suggests that a claimant should succeed by establishing either lack of knowledge or lack of consent.").

When a statute uses mandatory language ("shall" rather than "may"), courts typically interpret the statute to exclude discretion to take account of equitable or policy factors. See *Escondido Mutual Water Co. v. La Jolla Indians*, 466 U.S. 765 (1984); *Dunlop v. Bachowski*, 421 U.S. 560 (1975). But see *In re Cartmell's Estate*, 138 A.2d 588 (Vt. 1958) ("The word 'may' can be construed as 'shall' or 'must' when such was the legislative intention.") Compare *Lopez v. Davis*, 531 U.S. 230 (2001) (a law providing that the sentence of a nonviolent offender "may be reduced" by the Bureau of Prisons vested discretion with the Bureau not only to deny or grant this benefit to specific nonviolent offenders, but also to create a new category of nonviolent offenders (those whose crime involved a firearm) who could not receive the benefit of its discretion).

---

alone in the house for the weekend, warn him, 'You will be punished if you throw a party or engage in any other activity that damages the house.' If the son nevertheless throws a party and is caught, he should hardly be able to avoid punishment by arguing that the house was not damaged. The parents proscribed (1) a party, and (2) any other activity that damages the house." Is this a persuasive answer?

(4) Conventions Trumping Ordinary Grammar: Singular and Plural Numbers; Male and Female Pronouns

One grammar rule that is *not* often followed by statutory interpreters is the difference between singular and plural nouns. "In determining the meaning of any Act of Congress, unless the context indicates otherwise, words importing the singular include and apply to several persons, parties, or things; words importing the plural include the singular * * *." 1 U.S.C. § 1. Many states have analogous provisions. For example, the N.Y. Gen. Constr. Law § 35 (West 2013) provides: "Words in the singular number include the plural, and in the plural number include the singular." Like other rules of construction, however, New York courts will not consider this one decisive where it seems contrary to the apparent legislative purpose or intent. See, e.g., *Moynahan v. New York*, 98 N.E. 482 (N.Y. 1912).

A grammar rule even less often followed is the pronoun gender rule: "He" means a male referent, "she" a female referent. Because most statutes were drafted in eras when the main legal actors who counted were men, the male pronoun includes the female. 1 U.S.C. § 1. Unlike the U.S. Code, many states and the District of Columbia make the rule reciprocal: male references include female, and vice-versa.

(5) The *De Dicto/De Re* Distinction

An underappreciated rule of grammar is the distinction between *opaque* and *transparent* sentences. A transparent sentence is one in which the object of the activity is a particular, identifiable object. An opaque sentence is one in which the object of the activity may be either a particular, identifiable object *or* a more generic category of objects. Drawing from the work of Professor Anderson, who first brought this to the attention of the legal academy,[7] we may express the difference in this way:

(1) Bill loves his vehicle (car).

(2) Bill wants to buy a vehicle (car).

Sentence (1) is transparent: the reference is to a particular, identifiable vehicle, i.e., Bill's trusty 20-year-old Toyota Camry that always starts in the morning. Sentence (2) is opaque: the reference might be to a particular, identifiable vehicle (Bill would like to buy the Honda Accord his mechanic is offering for sale)—or the reference might be to a generic category (some kind of vehicle, yet to be determined) without specification.

---

[7] See Jill C. Anderson, *Just Semantics: The Lost Readings of the Americans with Disabilities Act*, 117 Yale L.J. 992 (2008), and Anderson, *Misreading Like a Lawyer: Cognitive Bias in Statutory Interpretation,* 127 Harv. L. Rev. 1521 (2014).

The punch line of this insight is that opaque sentences are linguistically "ambiguous": the term "vehicle" in Sentence (2) may either be a specific vehicle (the *de re* reading) or a generic vehicle (the *de dicto* reading). To be sure, additional context might clear up the ambiguity— but the baseline is linguistic ambiguity. As Professor Anderson demonstrates, lawyers and judges often read opaque sentences as though they had a single plain meaning that permits the interpreter to ignore context. As a matter of linguistics, and perhaps also as a matter of law, that is incorrect. Consider an example.

A statute made it an offense to fraudulently "personate any person entitled to vote." The defendant voted in the name of his neighbor, whose name was on the voter rolls but who was dead. In *Whiteley v. Chappell* (1868) L.R. 4 Q.B. 147, the court ruled that the defendant was not guilty of violating the statute, the judges lamenting that they could not bring the case "within the words of the enactment." After all, a dead person is not "a person entitled to vote." The court blamed the drafters: "[T]he legislature has not used words wide enough to make the personation of a dead person an offence." Professor Anderson provides a cogent critique of the court's approach:

"In linguistic terms, the *Whiteley* court's error was to miss a literal, *de dicto* reading of the statute, one that would have accorded well with its purpose of prohibiting election fraud by impersonation. The verb '(im)personate' is opaque. * * * [O]ne can 'impersonate' a doctor (a basketball player, a queen, etc.), but no particular one. We can paraphrase two different readings of the offense of 'personat[ing] any person entitled to vote' this way:

> *de re:*   pretending to be some particular individual, who is in fact entitled to vote
>
> *de dicto:*   pretending to belong in the category, 'entitled to vote'

The *de re* reading is satisfied only if 'there is some X, such that X is a person entitled to vote, and the defendant impersonated X.' In this case, there was no such X, because X was dead and therefore not entitled to vote. This was exactly the court's reasoning in finding that the statutory text did not apply. The *de dicto* reading, on the other hand, is satisfied where the defendant has pretended to belong in the category of eligible voters. That is just what the defendant did. The statute on its *de dicto* reading would therefore have easily supported the conviction that the court sought." Anderson, *Misreading Like a Lawyer*.

(6) The Golden Rule (The Rule Against Absurdity)

English-speaking jurisdictions have a few catch-all rules providing a mental check for the technical process of word-parsing and grammar-crunching. You were introduced to a prominent one in Chapter 4: The *golden rule* is that interpreters should "adhere to the ordinary meaning of the words used, and to the grammatical construction, unless that * * * leads to any manifest absurdity or repugnance, in which case the language may be varied or modified, so as to avoid such inconvenience, but no further." *Becke v. Smith*, 150 Eng. Rep. 724, 726 (U.K. Exch. 1836). For example, an early admiralty statute required purchasers of a vessel to register it immediately and barred them from receiving favorable duty treatment until they did so. In *United States v. Willings*, 8 U.S. 48 (1807), Chief Justice Marshall allowed favorable duty treatment for purchasers who had bought the vessel at sea and therefore could not have registered the purchase until their return. A strict application of the statute under those circumstances would have been manifestly unreasonable, the Chief Justice reasoned.

The golden rule is, in short, an *absurd results* exception to the plain meaning rule. In *Thomas* (the disabled elevator operator case), then-Judge Alito thought it absurd for the government to consider the applicant not disabled from working her previous job when it no longer existed in the national economy. Writing for the Supreme Court, Justice Scalia disagreed. A claimant who is concededly able to do her previous job is *probably* able to perform a job *somewhere* in the national economy. Hence, the agency's position was at most stingy, but by no means an absurd rule for a program with limited resources. You also saw this rule in *Bock Laundry* (the case about the word "defendant" in Fed. R. Evid. 609 in Chapter 4, § 3B), when Justice Scalia used it as an escape-valve from the absurd result that would have occurred by reading "defendant" literally to exclude a civil plaintiff and thereby providing extra evidentiary protection to an otherwise-similarly situated civil defendant. See generally Scalia & Garner, *Reading Law*, 234–39 (recognizing the absurd results exception, but only if "no reasonable person" would have meant the apparent plain meaning).[8]

Arguably, courts should be even more willing to revise *scrivener's errors*—obvious mistakes, typos, or "cutting and pasting" errors in the transcription of statutes into the law books. *Green v. Bock Laundry* (Chapter 2, § 3B) (all Justices agreeing to rewrite statute to correct an absurd provision that must have been the result of a scrivener's error); *Schooner Paulina's Cargo v. United States*, 11 U.S. 52, 67–68 (1812) (Marshall, C.J., revising statute to clean up scrivener's error). The

---

[8] See Jane S. Schacter, *Text or Consequences?*, 76 Brooklyn L. Rev. 1007 (2011) (demonstrating that Justice Scalia in statutory cases often demands that judges avoid absurd or even unreasonable interpretations).

current text-oriented Court has been stingier than Courts of the past in applying this rule. See, e.g., *Lamie v. U.S. Trustee*, 540 U.S. 526, 530–31 (2004) (refusing to rewrite Bankruptcy Act to fix what the Court agreed was an obvious drafting error).

C. THE WHOLE ACT RULE

Other rules or maxims of statutory interpretation are based upon the context within the statute of the relevant language. The Sutherland treatise endorses the *whole act rule* as "the most realistic in view of the fact that a legislature passes judgment upon the act as an entity, not giving one portion of the act any greater authority than another. Thus any attempt to segregate any portion or exclude any other portion from consideration is almost certain to distort the legislative intent." 2A Sutherland § 47.2; accord, Scalia & Garner, *Reading Law,* 167–82 (whole act rule and various corollaries).

From its earliest cases, the U.S. Supreme Court has followed the whole act rule in construing statutes. E.g., *United States v. Fisher*, 6 U.S. (2 Cranch) 358 (1805); *United States v. Priestman*, 4 U.S. (Dall.) 28 (1800) (per curiam). The whole act rule remains prevalent in modern Supreme Court jurisprudence: "Statutory interpretation * * * is a holistic endeavor. A provision that may seem ambiguous in isolation is often clarified by the remainder of the statutory scheme—because the same terminology is used elsewhere in a context that makes its meaning clear, or because only one of the permissible meanings produces a substantive effect that is compatible with the rest of the law." *United Savings Ass'n of Texas v. Timbers of Inwood Forest Assocs.*, 484 U.S. 365, 371 (1988) (Scalia, J.). "When interpreting a statute, the court will not look merely to a particular clause in which general words may be used, but will take in connection with it the whole statute * * * and the objects and policy of the law, as indicated by its various provisions, and give to it such a construction as will carry into execution the will of the legislature." *Kokoszka v. Belford*, 417 U.S. 642, 650 (1974) (internal quotation marks omitted). A critical assumption of the whole act approach is *coherence*: the interpreter presumes that the legislature drafted the statute as a document that is internally consistent in its use of language and in the way its provisions work together.[9] Note similarities to interpretation of contracts and sacred texts like the Bible.

The presumption of coherence is an unrealistic one: the legislature does not always approach statute-drafting the way God is thought to have dictated the Bible. Instead, statutes are often assembled the way Christmas trees are decorated, with ornaments being added or subtracted

---

[9]   See, e.g., *Ledbetter v. Goodyear Tire & Rubber Co.*, 550 U.S. 618 (2007); *Gonzales v. Oregon*, 546 U.S. 243 (2006); *Conroy v. Aniskoff*, 507 U.S. 511 (1993); *King v. St. Vincent's Hosp.*, 502 U.S. 215 (1991).

willy-nilly and at the last minute, just to satisfy enough interest groups and legislators to gain the majorities needed to get through various legislative vetogates (recall Chapter 1, § 2). Staff and drafting offices are supposed to clean up legislation to make it appropriate for inclusion in the code, but even the best drafters cannot always meld all the deals into a coherent whole. The structure of Congress contributes to the problem: statutes are often drafted by multiple committees, and those committees do not always communicate with one another. See Abbe R. Gluck & Lisa Schultz Bressman, *Statutory Interpretation from the Inside: An Empirical Study of Congressional Drafting, Delegation, and the Canons: Part I*, 65 Stan. L. Rev. 901, 933, 936–37 (2013) (finding that majority of congressional counsels surveyed knew of the whole act rule but said that the realities of lawmaking make it an inaccurate assumption of how Congress drafts). Nonetheless, courts all over the world operate under the coherence assumption. Can you think of a normative defense of it?

Think about the no-vehicles statute as a whole. Is an interpretation of § 3's definition of "vehicle" to include tricycles consistent with the whole statute? Or is the opposite interpretation (tricycles are not vehicles) a better one? Consider some corollaries to the whole act rule and how they might influence your analysis in the Case of the Tricycle.

(1) Titles

Our no-vehicles statute has a title, "The Parks Safety Act of 1980." In modern American history, the title is part of the statutory text voted upon by Congress and presented to the President under Article I, § 7. Hence, it is part of the statutory text and might be relevant to the application of the statute to tricycles and other mechanisms. Thus, one argument that might be made by the defendant in the Case of the Tricycle is that these little contraptions are not dangers to "Parks Safety." Hence, this is an important reason not to apply the law to tricycles. Will such an argument be persuasive?

According to the Sutherland treatise, the "title cannot control the plain words of the statute," but "[i]n case of ambiguity the court may consider the title to resolve uncertainty in the purview [the body] of the act or for the correction of obvious errors." 2A Sutherland § 47.3. The Supreme Court in *Holy Trinity* considered the statute's long title as cogent evidence of its purpose and indeed reworked the statutory provision to be consistent with it. Today's Supreme Court does occasionally rely on statutory titles as important evidence of statutory meaning, e.g., *Almendarez-Torres v. United States*, 523 U.S. 224, 234 (1998), and Justices will sometimes quote the title as relevant context. E.g., *Porter v. Nussle*, 534 U.S. 516, 524 (2002).

(2) Preambles and Purpose Clauses

Section 1 of the no-vehicles law is a preamble or purpose clause[10]: "The Council finds that vehicles create safety problems when they are operated in parks and further finds that the best solution is to ban any and all vehicles from all municipal parks." If this provision were admissible, one can draw a number of interesting arguments from it. For the defendant, § 1 provides the same kind of purpose argument made above to defend the tricycle defendant. For the prosecution, however, there may be significance in the Council's statement that the solution to the problem is a ban of "any and all vehicles," which might support a broad reading of the definition of "vehicle" in § 3. Does any of this count?

Traditional English practice gave great weight to statutory preambles, because they were considered the best source for determining statutory purpose. The modern rule is more modest. American courts following the whole act approach have declined to give the preamble any greater weight than other parts of the statute (the title, purview, individual sections). "Thus the settled principle of law is that the preamble cannot control the enacting part of the statute in cases where the enacting part is expressed in clear, unambiguous terms" but "may be resorted to [to] help discover the intention of the law maker." 2A Sutherland § 47.4; accord, Scalia & Garner, *Reading Law*, 217–20 (endorsing the preamble canon but cautioning that the purpose expressed in the preamble cannot add to the specific dispositions of the specific statutory text).

To the extent that the interpreter is able to find ambiguity, the preamble will often be a valuable source of insight. A preamble played a key interpretive role in *Sutton v. United Airlines, Inc.*, 527 U.S. 471 (1999). The Americans with Disabilities Act (ADA) prohibits job discrimination against people with disabilities. The airline had refused to consider hiring Karen Sutton and Kimberly Hinton as pilots because of their eyesight, which was severely myopic. The airline argued that the two women (twins) were not persons with a disability under the statute. Because poor eyesight could be completely corrected by eyeglasses, Sutton, Hinton, and other myopics did not have a "physical or mental impairment that substantially limits one or more . . . major life activities." 42 U.S.C. § 12102(1)(A). This was an ironic construction of the ADA, for it would allow the airline to refuse to hire the sisters because of an impairment that the airline conceded was correctable. Yet the Supreme Court agreed, in part because the ADA's preamble found that 43 million people in the U.S. had disabilities, 42 U.S.C. § 12101(a)(1)—a much smaller number than Congress could have found if it counted people with

---

[10] A *preamble* sets out the important facts or considerations that gave rise to the legislation. A *purpose clause* sets out the objectives the legislation seeks to achieve or the problems it tries to solve. In text, we shall refer to both as preambles.

correctable vision problems. *Sutton*, 527 U.S. at 484–86; see *id*. at 494–95 (Ginsburg, J., concurring especially for this reason).

(3) Provisos

Provisos restrict the effect of statutory provisions or create exceptions to general statutory rules. They typically follow the provision being restricted or excepted. Classical provisos are conditions that apply to the material preceding them. Thus, "Sally may have a cookie, *Provided that* she babysits her sister Anne for the afternoon." Because they are exceptions to the general rule, classic provisos are supposed to be narrowly construed. 2A Sutherland § 47.8.

Few statutory drafters use provisos this way anymore; they are usually tacked onto general language to create exceptions or exemptions to its rule. Thus, § 3 of the no-vehicles law defined "vehicle" and concluded with a non-classical proviso: "*Provided that*, bicycles shall be allowed in the park, so long as they are being pushed or carried and not ridden." What bearing might this proviso have on the Case of the Tricycle? If "bicycle" includes tricycles, the proviso provides the rule for decision, and the defendant loses, because she was riding the tricycle and not pushing or carrying it. If "bicycle" does not include tricycles, what bearing might the proviso have in this case?

(4) The Rule to Avoid Redundancy (or Surplusage)

Under the whole act rule, the presumption is that every word and phrase adds something to the statutory command. Accordingly, it is a "cardinal rule of statutory interpretation that no provision should be construed to be entirely redundant." *Kungys v. United States*, 485 U.S. 759, 778 (1988) (plurality opinion by Scalia, J.). A construction that would leave without effect any part of the language of a statute will normally be rejected. See Scalia & Garner, *Reading Law*, 174–79 (strong endorsement of the canon against surplusage).

In the *Holy Trinity* statute, § 4 held criminally accountable the master of a ship "who shall knowingly bring within the United States * * * any alien laborer, mechanic or artisan." (An "artisan" is a skilled manual laborer.) Think about how § 4 and the rule against superfluities help us to understand the immigration ban on those who perform "labor or service of any kind" in § 1? If §§ 1 and 4 both covered only manual laborers, why was the text of the two provisions so different? ? This use of the rule against superfluities cuts against the pastor; construing § 1 to extend beyond manual laborers prevents the specification in § 4 from being superfluous.

The rule against surplusage or redundancy, however, is more at odds with the legislative drafting process than most of the other whole act rules, as words and phrases are added to important legislation right up to the last minute. Congress sometimes uses redundancies intentionally, for emphasis and to satisfy supporters and interest groups that the statute will meet their needs. See Gluck & Bressman, *Statutory Interpretation from the Inside: Part I*, 65 Stan. L. Rev. at 933-36 (documenting congressional staff view of this use of redundancies).

Nonetheless, the rule against redundancy or surplusage plays a more important role in Supreme Court opinions in the new millennium than it did in the old. *Circuit City v. Adams*, 532 U.S. 105 (2001), is but one example. Responding to Justice Souter's textual argument that "seamen, railroad employees, or any other class of workers engaged in foreign or interstate commerce" included all contract employees, Justice Kennedy's *Circuit City* opinion fell back on the rule against surplusage: "there would be no need for Congress to use the phrases 'seamen' and 'railroad employees' if those same classes of workers were subsumed within the meaning of the 'engaged in . . . commerce' residual clause." *Id.* at 114. Interestingly, the D.C. Circuit, through Judge Kavanaugh, recently took the more realistic view, rejecting the rule against superfluities: "Lawmakers, like Shakespeare characters, sometimes employ overlap or redundancy so as to remove any doubt and make doubly sure. *Loving* v. *IRS*, 742 F.3d 1014, 1019 (D.C. Cir. 2014) ("Interpreting Section 330(a)(2) [of the tax code] to have some modest overlap is far more reasonable than interpreting the statute, as the IRS does, to mean 'or' when it says 'and' ").

(5) Presumption of Consistent Usage—and of Meaningful Variation

Under the holistic assumptions of the whole act rule, courts presume that the same meaning is implied by the use of the same expression or statutory term in every part of the statute. Similarly, where a statutory word has been used in other statutes dealing with the same subject matter and has a settled meaning in those statutes, interpreters will presumptively follow the settled meaning. In other words, courts presume that Congress means the same thing each time it uses a statutory term in a single statute or even across the U.S. Code.

Consider a leading example. The Equal Access to Justice Act, 28 U.S.C. § 2412(d)(1)(A), provides that a party prevailing in a lawsuit against the United States should be awarded attorney's fees "unless the court finds that the position of the United States was substantially justified or that special circumstances make an award unjust." The prevailing private party argued that the government had to pay unless its position was "justified to a high degree." The Supreme Court in *Pierce v. Underwood*, 487 U.S. 552 (1988), found this a plausible construction of the words but accepted the government's interpretation, that it could avoid counsel fees if its position were reasonable, or "justified in substance or in the main." Justice Scalia's opinion found a plain meaning, because the term "substantially justified" is used elsewhere in the U.S. Code and in the Federal Rules of Civil Procedure, especially Rule 37. *Id.* at 565. Courts had never interpreted the term from the Federal Rules to require a higher degree of justification, and Justice Scalia accepted that as dispositive.

The rule of consistent usage implies a corollary presumption of meaningful variation: "From the general presumption that the same expression is presumed to be used in the same sense throughout an Act or a series of cognate Acts, there follows the further presumption that a change of wording denotes a change in meaning." P. St. J. Langan, *Maxwell on the Interpretation of Statutes* 282 (12th ed. 1969); cf. *id.* at 286 (but this is a weak presumption). The leading American case for this presumption of meaningful variation is Chief Justice Marshall's opinion in *United States v. Fisher*, 6 U.S. (2 Cranch) 358, 388–97 (1805). A statute whose first four sections regulated the relationship between the United States and "receivers of public money" had a fifth section which said that "where any revenue officer, or other person, hereafter becoming indebted to the United States * * * shall become insolvent, * * * the debt due to the United States shall be first satisfied." A competing creditor argued that § 5 should have been limited to receivers of public moneys, like §§ 1–4 and the title of the law, but Marshall found no reason to think that Congress intended a narrower ambit for § 5 and therefore read it without the limitation. Accord, *Lawrence v. Florida*, 549 U.S. 327 (2007); *Hamdan v. Rumsfeld*, 548 U.S. 557 (2006).

West Virginia Hospitals v. Casey, the expert witness fee case from Chapter 4, § 3, provides another example. Justice Scalia's opinion cited forty-one different statutes that contained explicit expert witness fee-shifting provisions to support his presumption that Congress intended to omit such fees in *Casey*—i.e., that the textual variation was meaningful. But cf. *Gutierrez v. Ada*, 528 U.S. 250 (2000) (declining to apply a rule of meaningful variation when a later amendment used different terminology from the provision at issue); Scalia & Garner, *Reading Law,* 170–73 (similar).

If the legislature changes a statute when reenacting it, the rule has renewed bite, as in *Osborn v. Bank of the United States*, 22 U.S. (9 Wheat.) 738, 817–18 (1824). The statute creating the first Bank of the United States contained a provision allowing the Bank to "sue and be sued * * * in Courts of record." The Supreme Court in 1810 construed that provision to afford no basis for federal jurisdiction in lawsuits involving the Bank. When the second Bank was established in 1816, the "sue and be sued" provision was changed to allow suits "in all State Courts having competent jurisdiction, and in any Circuit Court of the United States."

Chief Justice Marshall construed the new language—pointedly expanding the language that was the focus of the earlier case—to be a congressional vesting of jurisdiction in circuit courts to hear lawsuits where the Bank was a party.

A wedding of *expressio unius* and consistent usage is the rule that "[w]here Congress includes particular language in one section of a statute but omits it in another * * * it is generally presumed that Congress acts intentionally and purposely in the disparate inclusion or exclusion." *Keene Corp. v. United States*, 508 U.S. 200, 208 (1993) (a leading case). The Court refined this canon in *Field v. Mans*, 516 U.S. 59, 67–76 (1995), where it held that this negative implication rule was inapplicable when there was a reasonable explanation for the variation. "The more apparently deliberate the contrast, the stronger the inference, as applied, for example, to contrasting statutory sections originally enacted simultaneously in relevant respects. * * * The rule is weakest when it suggests results strangely at odds with other textual pointers, like the common-law language at work in the [bankruptcy] statute here." *Id.* at 75–76.

The presumption against meaningful variation is subject to the same criticisms about how well it reflects the realities of legislative drafting as the coherence assumptions that begot it. Return to *Casey.* Of the forty-one fee-shifting statutes that Justice Scalia relied upon, only four of the other cited statutes came from the same judiciary committees that drafted the statute at issue in the case. The others (including the four most recent, on which the Court placed special weight) were drawn from twenty-one different committees that likely never communicated with the judiciary committees. Even beyond the fact that Congress works in subject-matter silos, some statutes are very long; others are very short. (The Sherman Antitrust Act is one paragraph long; the health care legislation, the Affordable Care Act, is 2000 pages.) Some statutes are written quickly, on the floor; others are deliberated for weeks or months in committee. Some are omnibus bills—bundled deals cobbling together many diverse legislative acts to satisfy a majority of supporters; others essentially involve a single subject. Does it make sense that the same presumptions of textual consistency apply? See Gluck & Bressman, *Statutory Interpretation from the Inside: Part I* (documenting that legislative drafters recognize such differences across statutes and how this affects the likelihood of consistency). Can you come up with a different justification for why courts should apply them nonetheless?

(6) Rule Against Interpreting a Provision in Derogation of Other Provisions

An important corollary of the whole act rule is that one provision of a statute should not be interpreted in such a way as to derogate from other provisions of the statute (to the extent this is possible). An interpretation of provision 1 might derogate from other parts of the statute in one or more of the following ways:

- *Operational conflict.* As interpreted, provision 1's operation conflicts with that of provision 2. For example, a citizen cannot obey provision 1 without violating provision 2.

- *Philosophical tension.* As interpreted, provision 1 is in tension with an assumption of provision 2. For example, provision 2 might reflect a legislative compromise inconsistent with a broad reading of provision 1.

- *Structural derogation.* Sharing elements of both operational conflict and philosophical tension, provision 1's interpretation might be at odds with the overall structure of the statute. Thus, provisions 2 and 3 might reflect a legislative policy that certain kinds of violations be handled administratively rather than judicially, which a broad view of judicially enforceable provision 1 might undermine.

For an example of cross-cutting derogations, see *Robinson v. Shell Oil Co.,* 519 U.S. 337, 345–46 (1997). See generally Scalia & Garner, *Reading Law,* 180–82 (setting forth a "harmonious-reading" canon).

In our Case of the Tricycle, the defendant might argue that the best, most harmonious way to read the entire statute is to exclude tricycles from the definition of "vehicle." See if you can construct such an argument—and then identify the prosecution's response to it. After that, consider the following problem in administrative harmonization.

STATUTORY PREFACE TO *BABBITT V. SWEET HOME*

Endangered Species Act of 1973, P.L. 93–205, as amended in 1978 and 1982

ESA § 2, 16 U.S.C. § 1531.   Findings, Purposes, and Policy

(b) Purposes.—The purposes of this chapter are to provide a means whereby the ecosystems upon which endangered species and threatened species depend may be conserved, to provide a program for the conservation of such endangered species and threatened species, and to take such steps as may be appropriate to achieve the purposes of [species-protective] treaties and conventions * * *.

(c) Policy.—It is further declared to be the policy of Congress that all Federal Departments and Agencies shall seek to conserve endangered species and threatened species and shall utilize their authorities in furtherance of the purposes of this chapter.

ESA § 3, 16 U.S.C. § 1532. Definitions.

> **(14)** The term "take" means to harass, harm, pursue, hunt, shoot, wound, kill, trap, capture, or collect, or to attempt to engage in any such conduct.

ESA § 4, 16 U.S.C. § 1533. Determination of Endangered Species and Threatened Species. [Under subsections (a)–(c), the Secretary of the Interior has the responsibility to designate endangered and threatened species, and this section sets out the procedures and standards she is supposed to apply.]

(d) Protective Regulations.—Whenever any species is listed as a threatened species pursuant to subsection (c) of this Section, the Secretary shall issue such regulations as he deems necessary and advisable to provide for the conservation of such species. The Secretary may by regulation prohibit with respect to any threatened species any act prohibited under Section 1538(a)(1) * * *.

ESA § 5, 16 U.S.C. § 1534.   Land Acquisition.

(a) Program.—The Secretary of the Interior shall establish and implement a program to conserve (a) fish and wildlife which are listed as endangered species or threatened species pursuant to Section 1533 of this title; or [specified plants]. To carry out such program, he—

> **(1)** shall utilize the land acquisition and other authority under the Fish and Wildlife Act of 1956, as amended, the Fish and Wildlife Coordination Act, as amended, and the Migratory Bird Conservation Act, as appropriate; and

> **(2)** is authorized to acquire by purchase, donation, or otherwise, lands, waters, or interest therein, and such authority shall be in addition to any other land acquisition authority vested in him.

(b) Acquisitions.—Funds made available pursuant to the Land and Water Conservation Fund Act of 1965, as amended, may be used for the purpose of acquiring lands, waters, or interests therein under subsection (a) of this Section.

ESA § 7, 16 U.S.C. § 1536.   Interagency Cooperation.

(a) Federal agency actions and consultations.

> **(1)** The Secretary shall review other programs administered by him and utilize such programs in furtherance of the purposes of this Act. All other Federal agencies shall, in consultation with and with the assistance of the Secretary, utilize their authorities in furtherance of the purposes of this Act by carrying out programs for the conservation of endangered species and threatened species listed pursuant to Section 1533 of this title.

(2) Each Federal agency shall, in consultation with and with the assistance of the Secretary, insure that any action authorized, funded, or carried out by such agency (hereinafter in this section referred to as an "agency action") is not likely to jeopardize the continued existence of any endangered species or threatened species or result in the destruction or adverse modification of habitat of such species which is determined by the Secretary, after consultation as appropriate with affected States, to be critical, unless such agency has been granted an exemption for such action by the Committee pursuant to subsection (h) of this section. In fulfilling the requirements of this paragraph each agency shall use the best scientific and commercial data available.

(3) Subject to such guidelines as the Secretary may establish, a Federal agency shall consult with the Secretary on any prospective agency action at the request of, and in cooperation with, the prospective permit or license applicant if the applicant has reason to believe that an endangered species or a threatened species may be present in the area affected by his project and that implementation of such action will likely affect such species.

(4) Each Federal agency shall confer with the Secretary on any agency action which is likely to jeopardize the continued existence of any species proposed to be listed under Section 1533 of this title or result in the destruction or adverse modification of critical habitat proposed to be designated for such species. This paragraph does not require a limitation on the commitment of resources as described in subsection (d) of this section.* * *

ESA § 9(a)(1), 16 U.S.C. § 1538(a)(1). Prohibited Activities.

(a) General.—**(1)** Except as provided in Sections 1535(g)(2) and 1539 of this title, with respect to any endangered species of fish or wildlife listed pursuant to Section 1533 of this title, it is unlawful for any person subject to the jurisdiction of the United States to—

> **(A)** import any such species into, or export any such species from the United States;
>
> **(B)** take any such species within the United States or the territorial sea of the United States;
>
> **(C)** take any such species upon the high seas;
>
> **(D)** possess, sell, deliver, carry, transport or ship, by any means whatsoever, any such species taken in violation of subparagraphs (B) and (C);

(E) deliver, receive, carry, transport, or ship in interstate or foreign commerce, by any means whatsoever and in the course of a commercial activity, any such species;

(F) sell or offer for sale in interstate or foreign commerce any such species; or

(G) violate any regulation pertaining to such species or to any threatened species of fish or wildlife listed pursuant to section 1533 of this title and promulgated by the Secretary pursuant to authority provided by this chapter. * * *

ESA § 10, 16 U.S.C. § 1539 (as amended 1982).   Exceptions.

(a) Permits

(1) The Secretary may permit, under such terms and conditions as he shall prescribe—

(A) any act otherwise prohibited by section 1538 of this title for scientific purposes or to enhance the propagation or survival of the affected species, including, but not limited to, acts necessary for the establishment and maintenance of experimental populations pursuant to subsection (j) of this section; or

(B) any taking otherwise prohibited by section 1538(a)(1)(B) of this title if such taking is incidental to, and not the purpose of, the carrying out of an otherwise lawful activity.

(2)   (A) No permit may be issued by the Secretary authorizing any taking referred to in paragraph (1)(B) unless the applicant therefor submits to the Secretary a conservation plan that specifies—

(i) the impact which will likely result from such taking;

(ii) what steps the applicant will take to minimize and mitigate such impacts, and the funding that will be available to implement such steps;

(iii) what alternative actions to such taking the applicant considered and the reasons why such alternatives are not being utilized; and

(iv) such other measures that the Secretary may require as being necessary or appropriate for purposes of the plan.

(B) If the Secretary finds, after opportunity for public comment, with respect to a permit application and the related conservation plan that—

(i) the taking will be incidental;

(ii) the applicant will, to the maximum extent practicable, minimize and mitigate the impacts of such taking;

(iii) the applicant will ensure that adequate funding for the plan will be provided;

(iv) the taking will not appreciably reduce the likelihood of the survival and recovery of the species in the wild; and

(v) the measures, if any, required under subparagraph (A)(iv) will be met; and he has received such other assurances as he may require that the plan will be implemented, the Secretary shall issue the permit. The permit shall contain such terms and conditions as the Secretary deems necessary or appropriate to carry out the purposes of this paragraph, including, but not limited to, such reporting requirements as the Secretary deems necessary for determining whether such terms and conditions are being complied with.

(C) The Secretary shall revoke a permit issued under this paragraph if he finds that the permittee is not complying with the terms and conditions of the permit.

[Section 10(b) allows the Secretary to grant "hardship exemptions" where a landowner enters into a contract before the listing of an endangered species and would suffer great hardship if he could not have some leeway to violate § 9(a).]

(d) Permit and exemption policy

The Secretary may grant exceptions under subsections (a)(1)(A) and (b) of this section only if he finds and publishes his finding in the Federal Register that (1) such exceptions were applied for in good faith, (2) if granted and exercised will not operate to the disadvantage of such endangered species, and (3) will be consistent with the purposes and policy set forth in section 1531 of this title.

ESA § 11, 16 U.S.C. § 1540. Penalties. [Section 11 provides for potential civil and criminal penalties for "knowing" (civil) or "willful" (criminal) violations of § 9(a) and other prohibitions in the Act.]

BRUCE BABBITT v. SWEET HOME CHAPTER OF COMMUNITIES FOR A GREAT OREGON

Supreme Court of the United States, 1995.
15 U.S. 687, 115 S.Ct. 2407, 132 L. Ed. 2d 597.

JUSTICE STEVENS delivered the opinion of the Court.

The Endangered Species Act of 1973 (ESA or Act), 87 Stat. 884, 16 U.S.C. § 1531 (1988 ed. and Supp. V), contains a variety of protections designed to save from extinction species that the Secretary of the Interior designates as endangered or threatened. Section 9 of the Act makes it unlawful for any person to "take" any endangered or threatened species. The Secretary has promulgated a regulation that defines the statute's prohibition on takings to include "significant habitat modification or degradation where it actually kills or injures wildlife." This case presents the question whether the Secretary exceeded his authority under the Act by promulgating that regulation. * * *

The Interior Department regulations that implement the statute, however, define the statutory term "harm":

> "*Harm* in the definition of "take" in the Act means an act which actually kills or injures wildlife. Such act may include significant habitat modification or degradation where it actually kills or injures wildlife by significantly impairing essential behavioral patterns, including breeding, feeding, or sheltering." 50 CFR § 17.3 (1994).

This regulation has been in place since 1975.

A limitation on the § 9 "take" prohibition appears in § 10(a)(1)(B) of the Act, which Congress added by amendment in 1982. That section authorizes the Secretary to grant a permit for any taking otherwise prohibited by § 9(a)(1)(B) "if such taking is incidental to, and not the purpose of, the carrying out of an otherwise lawful activity." 16 U.S.C. § 1539(a)(1)(B).

In addition to the prohibition on takings, the Act provides several other protections for endangered species. Section 4, 16 U.S.C. § 1533, commands the Secretary to identify species of fish or wildlife that are in danger of extinction and to publish from time to time lists of all species he determines to be endangered or threatened. Section 5, 16 U.S.C. § 1534, authorizes the Secretary, in cooperation with the States, see § 1535, to acquire land to aid in preserving such species. Section 7 requires federal agencies to ensure that none of their activities, including the granting of licenses and permits, will jeopardize the continued existence of endangered species "or result in the destruction or adverse modification of habitat of such species which is determined by the Secretary . . . to be critical." 16 U.S.C. § 1536(a)(2).

[A group of small landowners, logging companies, and families dependent on the forest products industries and organizations that represent their interests brought this action to challenge the Secretary's definition of "harm" to include habitat modification and degradation. They specifically objected to the application of the regulation to protect the red-cockaded woodpecker and the spotted owl by prohibiting changes in their natural habitat that would have the effect of injuring or killing those animals. The court of appeals agreed with respondents' challenge, but the Supreme Court reversed.]

The text of the Act provides three reasons for concluding that the Secretary's interpretation is reasonable. First, an ordinary understanding of the word "harm" supports it. The dictionary definition of the verb form of "harm" is "to cause hurt or damage to: injure." Webster's Third New International Dictionary 1034 (1966). In the context of the ESA, that definition naturally encompasses habitat modification that results in actual injury or death to members of an endangered or threatened species.

Respondents argue that the Secretary should have limited the purview of "harm" to direct applications of force against protected species, but the dictionary definition does not include the word "directly" or suggest in any way that only direct or willful action that leads to injury constitutes "harm." Moreover, unless the statutory term "harm" encompasses indirect as well as direct injuries, the word has no meaning that does not duplicate the meaning of other words that § 3 uses to define "take." A reluctance to treat statutory terms as surplusage supports the reasonableness of the Secretary's interpretation.

Second, the broad purpose of the ESA supports the Secretary's decision to extend protection against activities that cause the precise harms Congress enacted the statute to avoid. In *TVA v. Hill*, 437 U.S. 153 (1978) [Chapter 7, § 2C], we described the Act as "the most comprehensive legislation for the preservation of endangered species ever enacted by any nation." Whereas predecessor statutes enacted in 1966 and 1969 had not contained any sweeping prohibition against the taking of endangered species except on federal lands, the 1973 Act applied to all land in the United States and to the Nation's territorial seas. As stated in § 2 of the Act, among its central purposes is "to provide a means whereby the ecosystems upon which endangered species and threatened species depend may be conserved. . . ."

In *Hill*, we construed § 7 as precluding the completion of the Tellico Dam because of its predicted impact on the survival of the snail darter. Both our holding and the language in our opinion stressed the importance of the statutory policy. "The plain intent of Congress in enacting this statute," we recognized, "was to halt and reverse the trend toward species extinction, whatever the cost. This is reflected not only in the stated policies of the Act, but in literally every section of the statute." Although the § 9 "take" prohibition was not at issue in *Hill*, we took note of that prohibition, placing particular emphasis on the Secretary's inclusion of habitat modification in his definition of "harm." In light of that provision for habitat protection, we could "not understand how TVA intends to operate Tellico Dam without 'harming' the snail darter." Congress' intent to provide comprehensive protection for endangered and threatened species supports the permissibility of the Secretary's "harm" regulation. * * *

Third, the fact that Congress in 1982 authorized the Secretary to issue permits for takings that § 9(a)(1)(B) would otherwise prohibit, "if such taking is incidental to, and not the purpose of, the carrying out of an otherwise lawful activity," 16 U.S.C. § 1539(a)(1)(B), strongly suggests that Congress understood § 9(a)(1)(B) to prohibit indirect as well as deliberate takings. The permit process requires the applicant to prepare a "conservation plan" that specifies how he intends to "minimize and mitigate" the "impact" of his activity on endangered and threatened species, 16 U.S.C. § 1539(a)(2)(A), making clear that Congress had in mind foreseeable rather than merely accidental effects on listed species. No one could seriously request an "incidental" take permit to avert § 9 liability for direct, deliberate action against a member of an endangered or threatened species, but respondents would read "harm" so narrowly that the permit procedure would have little more than that absurd purpose. "When Congress acts to amend a statute, we presume it intends its amendment to have real and substantial effect." Congress' addition of the § 10 permit provision supports the Secretary's conclusion that activities not intended to harm an endangered species, such as habitat modification, may constitute unlawful takings under the ESA unless the Secretary permits them.

[The court of appeals had come to a contrary conclusion on the basis of the *noscitur a sociis* canon: the surrounding words—such as "pursue," "hunt," "shoot"—connoted application of force directed at a particular animal. But other words, such as "harass," do not so connote, and the lower court's construction would effectively write "harm" out of the statute entirely. That would violate the rule against surplusage.]

We need not decide whether the statutory definition of "take" compels the Secretary's interpretation of "harm," because our conclusions that Congress did not unambiguously manifest its intent to adopt respondents' view and that the Secretary's interpretation is reasonable suffice to decide this case. See generally *Chevron, U.S.A., Inc. v. Natural Resources Defense Council* [Chapter 9, § 2]. The latitude the ESA gives the Secretary in enforcing the statute, together with the degree of regulatory expertise necessary to its enforcement, establishes that we owe some degree of deference to the Secretary's reasonable interpretation. See Breyer, Judicial Review of Questions of Law and Policy, 38 Admin. L. Rev. 363, 373 (1986). [Justice Stevens also rejected application of the rule of lenity, see § 2B1 below. Although there is a separate criminal sanction for "knowing" violations of the ESA, the Court had never applied the rule of lenity to review agency rules implementing a civil statute that has parallel criminal sanctions.]

Our conclusion that the Secretary's definition of "harm" rests on a permissible construction of the ESA gains further support from the legislative history of the statute. The Committee Reports accompanying the bills that became the ESA do not specifically discuss the meaning of "harm," but they make clear that Congress intended "take" to apply broadly to cover indirect as well as purposeful actions. The Senate Report stressed that " '[t]ake' is defined . . . in the broadest possible manner to include every conceivable way in which a person can 'take' or attempt to 'take' any fish or wildlife." S. Rep. No. 93–307, p. 7 (1973). The House Report stated that "the broadest possible terms" were used to define restrictions on takings. H.R. Rep. No. 93–412, p. 15 (1973). The House Report underscored the breadth of the "take" definition by noting that it included "harassment, *whether intentional or not.*" *Id.*, at 11 (emphasis added). The Report explained that the definition "would allow, for example, the Secretary to regulate or prohibit the activities of birdwatchers where the effect of those activities might disturb the birds and make it difficult for them to hatch or raise their young." *Ibid.* * * *

The definition of "take" that originally appeared in S. 1983 differed from the definition as ultimately enacted in [this] significant respect: It included "the destruction, modification, or curtailment of [the] habitat or range" of fish and wildlife. Respondents make much of the fact that the Commerce Committee removed this phrase from the "take" definition before S. 1983 went to the floor. See 119 Cong. Rec. 25663 (1973). We do not find that fact especially significant. The legislative materials contain no indication why the habitat protection provision was deleted. That provision differed greatly from the regulation at issue today. Most notably, the habitat protection in S. 1983 would have applied far more broadly than the regulation does because it made adverse habitat modification a categorical violation of the "take" prohibition, unbounded by the regulation's limitation to habitat modifications that actually kill or injure wildlife. The S. 1983 language also failed to qualify "modification" with the regulation's limiting adjective "significant." We do not believe the Senate's unelaborated disavowal of the provision in S. 1983 undermines the reasonableness of the more moderate habitat protection in the Secretary's "harm" regulation. [In footnote 19, Justice Stevens rejected the argument that statements by Senate and House sponsors

supported the idea that the § 5 land acquisition provision and not § 9 was
expected to be the ESA's remedy for habitat modification.]

The history of the 1982 amendment that gave the Secretary
authority to grant permits for "incidental" takings provides further
support for his reading of the Act. The House Report expressly states that
"[b]y use of the word 'incidental' the Committee intends to cover
situations in which it is known that a taking will occur if the other
activity is engaged in but such taking is incidental to, and not the purpose
of, the activity." H.R. Rep. No. 97–567, p. 31 (1982). This reference to the
foreseeability of incidental takings undermines respondents' argument
that the 1982 amendment covered only accidental killings of endangered
and threatened animals that might occur in the course of hunting or
trapping other animals. Indeed, Congress had habitat modification
directly in mind: Both the Senate Report and the House Conference
Report identified as the model for the permit process a cooperative state-
federal response to a case in California where a development project
threatened incidental harm to a species of endangered butterfly by
modification of its habitat. See S. Rep. No. 97–418, p. 10 (1982); H.R.
Conf. Rep. No. 97–835, pp. 30–32 (1982). Thus, Congress in 1982 focused
squarely on the aspect of the "harm" regulation at issue in this litigation.
Congress' implementation of a permit program is consistent with the
Secretary's interpretation of the term "harm." * * *

JUSTICE SCALIA, with whom the CHIEF JUSTICE [REHNQUIST] and
JUSTICE THOMAS join, dissenting.

I think it unmistakably clear that the legislation at issue here (1)
forbade the hunting and killing of endangered animals, and (2) provided
federal lands and federal funds *for the acquisition of private lands*, to
preserve the habitat of endangered animals. The Court's holding that the
hunting and killing prohibition incidentally preserves habitat on private
lands imposes unfairness to the point of financial ruin—not just upon the
rich, but upon the simplest farmer who finds his land conscripted to
national zoological use. I respectfully dissent.

[Justice Scalia objected to three features of the regulation, which, as
he saw it, (1) failed to consider whether death or injury to wildlife is an
intentional or even foreseeable effect of a habitat modification, (2) covered
omissions as well as acts, and (3) considered injuries to future as well as
present animal populations, and not just specific animals.] None of these
three features of the regulation can be found in the statutory provisions
supposed to authorize it. The term "harm" in § 1532(19) has no legal force
of its own. An indictment or civil complaint that charged the defendant
with "harming" an animal protected under the Act would be dismissed as
defective, for the only *operative* term in the statute is to "take." If "take"
were not elsewhere defined in the Act, no one could dispute what it

means, for the term is as old as the law itself. To "take," when applied to wild animals, means to reduce those animals, by killing or capturing, to human control. [Citing dictionaries, cases, and Blackstone.] This is just the sense in which "take" is used elsewhere in federal legislation and treaty. See, e.g., Migratory Bird Treaty Act, 16 U.S.C. § 703 (1988 ed., Supp. V) (no person may "pursue, hunt, take, capture, kill, [or] attempt to take, capture, or kill" any migratory bird); Agreement on the Conservation of Polar Bears, Nov. 15, 1973, Art. I, 27 U.S.T. 3918, 3921, T.I.A.S. No. 8409 (defining "taking" as "hunting, killing and capturing"). And that meaning fits neatly with the rest of § 1538(a)(1), which makes it unlawful not only to take protected species, but also to import or export them (§ 1538(a)(1)(A)); to possess, sell, deliver, carry, transport, or ship any taken species (§ 1538(a)(1)(D)); and to transport, sell, or offer to sell them in interstate or foreign commerce (§§ 1538(a)(1)(E), (F)). The taking prohibition, in other words, is only part of the regulatory plan of § 1538(a)(1), which covers all the stages of the process by which protected wildlife is reduced to man's dominion and made the object of profit. It is obvious that "take" in this sense—a term of art deeply embedded in the statutory and common law concerning wildlife—describes a class of acts (not omissions) done directly and intentionally (not indirectly and by accident) to particular animals (not populations of animals).

[Although "harm" has a range of meaning, the most likely in this statutory context is one that focuses on specific and intentional harming.] "Harm" is merely one of 10 prohibitory words in § 1532(19), and the other 9 fit the ordinary meaning of "take" perfectly. To "harass, pursue, hunt, shoot, wound, kill, trap, capture, or collect" are all affirmative acts (the provision itself describes them as "conduct," see § 1532(19)) which are directed immediately and intentionally against a particular animal—not acts or omissions that indirectly and accidentally cause injury to a population of animals. * * * What the nine other words in § 1532(19) have in common—and share with the narrower meaning of "harm" described above, but not with the Secretary's ruthless dilation of the word—is the sense of affirmative conduct intentionally directed against a particular animal or animals.

I am not the first to notice this fact, or to draw the conclusion that it compels. In 1981 the Solicitor of the Fish and Wildlife Service delivered a legal opinion on § 1532(19) that is in complete agreement with my reading:

> The Act's definition of "take" contains a list of actions that illustrate the intended scope of the term. . . . With the possible exception of "harm," these terms all represent forms of conduct that are directed against and likely to injure or kill *individual wildlife*. Under the principle of statutory construction, *ejusdem generis*, . . . the term "harm" should be interpreted to include

only those actions that are directed against, and likely to injure or kill, individual wildlife. [Memorandum of April 17, 1981 (emphasis in original).]

I would call it *noscitur a sociis*, but the principle is much the same: The fact that "several items in a list share an attribute counsels in favor of interpreting the other items as possessing that attribute as well." * * * [Moreover,] the Court's contention that "harm" in the narrow sense adds nothing to the other words underestimates the ingenuity of our own species in a way that Congress did not. To feed an animal poison, to spray it with mace, to chop down the very tree in which it is nesting, or even to destroy its entire habitat in order to take it (as by draining a pond to get at a turtle), might neither wound nor kill, but would directly and intentionally harm.

The penalty provisions of the Act counsel this interpretation as well. Any person who "knowingly" violates § 1538(a)(1)(B) is subject to criminal penalties under § 1540(b)(1) and civil penalties under § 1540(a)(1); moreover, under the latter section, any person "who otherwise violates" the taking prohibition (i.e., violates it *un*knowingly) may be assessed a civil penalty of $500 for each violation, with the stricture that "[e]ach such violation shall be a separate offense." This last provision should be clear warning that the regulation is in error, for when combined with the regulation it produces a result that no legislature could reasonably be thought to have intended: A large number of routine private activities— for example, farming, ranching, roadbuilding, construction and logging— are subjected to strict-liability penalties when they fortuitously injure protected wildlife, no matter how remote the chain of causation and no matter how difficult to foresee (or to disprove) the "injury" may be (*e.g.*, an "impairment" of breeding). * * *

So far I have discussed only the immediate statutory text bearing on the regulation. But the definition of "take" in § 1532(19) applies "[f]or the purposes of this chapter," that is, it governs the meaning of the word *as used everywhere in the Act*. Thus, the Secretary's interpretation of "harm" is wrong if it does not fit with the use of "take" throughout the Act. And it does not. In § 1540(e)(4)(B), for example, Congress provided for the forfeiture of "[a]ll guns, traps, nets, and other equipment . . . used to aid the taking, possessing, selling, [etc.]" of protected animals. This listing plainly relates to "taking" in the ordinary sense. If environmental modification were part (and necessarily a major part) of taking, as the Secretary maintains, one would have expected the list to include "plows, bulldozers, and backhoes." * * * The Act is full of like examples. See, *e.g.*, § 1538(a)(1)(D) (prohibiting possession, sale, and transport of "species taken in violation" of the Act). "[I]f the Act is to be interpreted as a symmetrical and coherent regulatory scheme, one in which the operative words have a consistent meaning throughout," *Gustafson v. Alloyd Co.,* 513 U.S. 561, 569 (1995), the regulation must fall.

The broader structure of the Act confirms the unreasonableness of the regulation. Section 1536 provides:

> Each Federal agency shall . . . insure that any action authorized, funded, or carried out by such agency . . . is not likely to jeopardize the continued existence of any endangered species or threatened species or *result in the destruction or adverse modification of habitat* of such species which is determined by the Secretary . . . to be critical. 16 U.S.C. § 1536(a)(2) (emphasis added).

The Act defines "critical habitat" as habitat that is "essential to the conservation of the species," §§ 1532(5)(A)(i), (A)(ii), with "conservation" in turn defined as the use of methods necessary to bring listed species "to the point at which the measures provided pursuant to this chapter are no longer necessary." § 1532(3).

These provisions have a double significance. Even if §§ 1536(a)(2) and 1538(a)(1)(B) were totally independent prohibitions—the former applying only to federal agencies and their licensees, the latter only to private parties—Congress's explicit prohibition of habitat modification in the one section would bar the inference of an implicit prohibition of habitat modification in the other section. "[W]here Congress includes particular language in one section of a statute but omits it in another . . . , it is generally presumed that Congress acts intentionally and purposely in the disparate inclusion or exclusion." *Keene Corp. v. United States*, 508 U.S. 200, 208 (1993). And that presumption against implicit prohibition would be even stronger where the one section which uses the language carefully defines and limits its application. That is to say, it would be passing strange for Congress carefully to define "critical habitat" as used in § 1536(a)(2), but leave it to the Secretary to evaluate, willy-nilly, impermissible "habitat modification" (under the guise of "harm") in § 1538(a)(1)(B).

In fact, however, §§ 1536(a)(2) and 1538(a)(1)(B) do *not* operate in separate realms; federal agencies are subject to *both*, because the "person[s]" forbidden to take protected species under § 1538 include agencies and departments of the Federal Government. See § 1532(13). This means that the "harm" regulation also contradicts another principle of interpretation: that statutes should be read so far as possible to give independent effect to all their provisions. See *Ratzlaf v. United States*, 510 U.S. 135, 140–41 (1994). By defining "harm" in the definition of "take" in § 1538(a)(1)(B) to include significant habitat modification that injures populations of wildlife, the regulation makes the habitat-modification restriction in § 1536(a)(2) almost wholly superfluous. As "critical habitat" is habitat "essential to the conservation of the species," adverse modification of "critical" habitat by a federal agency would also constitute habitat modification that injures a population of wildlife. * * *

The Court makes * * * other arguments. First, "the broad purpose of the [Act] supports the Secretary's decision to extend protection against activities that cause the precise harms Congress enacted the statute to avoid." I thought we had renounced the vice of "simplistically . . . assum[ing] that *whatever* furthers the statute's primary objective must be the law." *Rodriguez v. United States*, 480 U.S. 522, 526 (1987) (*per curiam*) (emphasis in original). Deduction from the "broad purpose" of a statute begs the question if it is used to decide by what *means* (and hence to what *length*) Congress pursued that purpose; to get the right answer to that question there is no substitute for the hard job (or in this case, the quite simple one) of reading the whole text. "The Act must do everything necessary to achieve its broad purpose" is the slogan of the enthusiast, not the analytical tool of the arbiter.

Second, the Court maintains that the legislative history of the 1973 Act supports the Secretary's definition. Even if legislative history were a legitimate and reliable tool of interpretation (which I shall assume in order to rebut the Court's claim); and even if it could appropriately be resorted to when the enacted text is as clear as this, but see *Chicago v. Environmental Defense Fund*, 511 U.S. 328, 337 (1994); here it shows quite the opposite of what the Court says. I shall not pause to discuss the Court's reliance on such statements in the Committee Reports as " '[t]ake' is defined . . . in the broadest possible manner to include every conceivable way in which a person can 'take' or attempt to 'take' any fish or wildlife." [S. Rep. No. 93–307, p. 7 (1973)]. This sort of empty flourish—to the effect that "this statute means what it means all the way"—counts for little even when enacted into the law itself. See *Reves v. Ernst & Young*, 507 U.S. 170, 183–84 (1993).

Much of the Court's discussion of legislative history is devoted to two items: first, the Senate floor manager's introduction of an amendment that added the word "harm" to the definition of "take," with the observation that (along with other amendments) it would " 'help to achieve the purposes of the bill' "; second, the relevant Committee's removal from the definition of a provision stating that "take" includes " 'the destruction, modification or curtailment of [the] habitat or range' " of fish and wildlife. The Court inflates the first and belittles the second, even though the second is on its face far more pertinent. But this elaborate inference from various pre-enactment actions and inactions is quite unnecessary, since we have *direct* evidence of what those who brought the legislation to the floor thought it meant—evidence as solid as any ever to be found in legislative history, but which the Court banishes to a footnote [footnote 19, omitted here].

Both the Senate and House floor managers of the bill explained it in terms which leave no doubt that the problem of habitat destruction on private lands was to be solved principally by the land acquisition program of § 1534, while § 1538 solved a different problem altogether—the problem of takings. Senator Tunney stated:

> *Through [the] land acquisition provisions, we will be able to conserve habitats necessary to protect fish and wildlife from further destruction.*
>
> Although most endangered species are threatened primarily by the destruction of their natural habitats, a significant portion of these animals are subject to *predation by man for commercial, sport, consumption, or other purposes.* The provisions of [the bill] would prohibit the commerce in or the importation, exportation, or taking of endangered species . . . [119 Cong. Rec. 25669 (1973) (emphasis added).]

The House floor manager, Representative Sullivan, put the same thought in this way:

> [T]he principal threat to animals stems from destruction of their habitat. . . . *[The bill] will meet this problem by providing funds for acquisition of critical habitat.* . . . It will also enable the Department of Agriculture to cooperate with willing landowners who desire to assist in the protection of endangered species, *but who are understandably unwilling to do so at excessive cost to themselves.*
>
> Another hazard to endangered species arises from those who *would capture or kill them for pleasure or profit.* There is no way that the Congress can make it less pleasurable for a person to take an animal, but we can certainly make it less profitable for them to do so. [*Id.*, at 30162 (emphasis added).]

Habitat modification and takings, in other words, were viewed as different problems, addressed by different provisions of the Act. [Justice Scalia argued that these statements destroyed the Court's legislative history case.]

Third, the Court seeks support from a provision that was added to the Act in 1982, the year after the Secretary promulgated the current regulation [in its amended form]. The provision states:

> [T]he Secretary may permit, under such terms and conditions as he shall prescribe—. . . .
>
> any taking otherwise prohibited by section 1538(a)(1)(B) . . . if such taking is incidental to, and not the purpose of, the carrying out of an otherwise lawful activity. [16 U.S.C. § 1539(a)(1)(B).]

This provision does not, of course, implicate our doctrine that reenactment of a statutory provision ratifies an extant judicial or administrative interpretation, for neither the taking prohibition in § 1538(a)(1)(B) nor the definition in § 1532(19) was reenacted. The Court claims, however, that the provision "strongly suggests that Congress understood [§ 1538(a)(1)(B)] to prohibit indirect as well as deliberate takings." That would be a valid inference if habitat modification were the only substantial "otherwise lawful activity" that might incidentally and nonpurposefully cause a prohibited "taking." Of course it is not. This provision applies to the many otherwise lawful takings that incidentally take a protected species—as when fishing for unprotected salmon also takes an endangered species of salmon. * * *

This is enough to show, in my view, that the 1982 permit provision does not support the regulation. I must acknowledge that the Senate Committee Report on this provision, and the House Conference Committee Report, clearly contemplate that it will enable the Secretary to permit environmental modification. But the *text* of the amendment cannot possibly bear that asserted meaning, when placed within the context of an Act that must be interpreted (as we have seen) not to prohibit private environmental modification. The neutral language of the amendment cannot possibly alter that interpretation, nor can its legislative history be summoned forth to contradict, rather than clarify, what is in its totality an unambiguous statutory text. There is little fear, of course, that giving no effect to the relevant portions of the Committee Reports will frustrate the real-life expectations of a majority of the Members of Congress. If they read and relied on such tedious detail on such an obscure point (it was not, after all, presented as a revision of the statute's prohibitory scope, but as a discretionary-waiver provision) the Republic would be in grave peril. * * *

[JUSTICE O'CONNOR wrote a separate concurring opinion, responding to some of Justice Scalia's concerns. "[T]he regulation's application is limited by ordinary principles of proximate causation, which introduce notions of foreseeability." For example, she disapproved of an application of the statute where the grazing of sheep was found to be a "taking" of palila birds, as the sheep destroyed seedlings which would have grown into trees needed by the bird for nesting. The chain of causation was simply too attenuated, Justice O'Connor concluded. Justice Scalia responded that this was Justice O'Connor's gloss on the statute, not the agency's. He chided his colleague for trying to have it both ways—deferring to the agency but then rewriting the regulation to suit her fancy. Justice Scalia concluded: "We defer to reasonable agency interpretations of ambiguous statutes precisely in order that agencies, rather than courts, may exercise policymaking discretion in the interstices of statutes. See *Chevron*. Just as courts may not exercise an agency's power to adjudicate, and so may not affirm an agency order on discretionary grounds the agency has not advanced, so also this Court may not exercise the Secretary's power to regulate, and so may not uphold a regulation by adding to it even the most reasonable of elements it does not contain."]

NOTES AND QUESTIONS ON SWEET HOME

1.   *How Many Canons Can You Count?* Notice how many of the textual canons are relevant to the Court's deliberations about the plain meaning of text in this case: the ordinary meaning rule and its corollaries regarding dictionaries and technical meaning, *noscitur a sociis* and (possibly) *ejusdem generis, expressio unius* and other rules of negative implication, the rule against redundancy, the rule of consistent usage and meaningful variation, and the anti-derogation rule. The anti-derogation rule supports in particular the structural arguments made by both sides. Justice Scalia emphasized the conflict between Congress's asserted allocation of responsibilities in §§ 5 and 7, while Justice Stevens emphasized the philosophical and structural conflict between a narrow reading of § 9 and the statutory scheme established in § 10.

A problem immediately apparent from this case is that different canons cut in different directions. How can one resolve the conflicting canonical signals? Count who has the most? Who makes the most elegant case? Another tiebreaker might be to defer to the *political equilibrium*—the position favored by the agency.

2.   *Easy Case or Hard Case?* One of us has argued that this case is a hard case, because the Justices offered strong legal arguments on both sides of the issue and ultimately had to implicitly rely on normative conceptions, because legal canons and rules do not bring closure on this issue, especially under the 1973 Act (before its amendment in 1982).[11] Note that Justice Scalia, who is the epitome of the "neutral" rule-following jurist, did not start off his dissenting opinion with a denunciation of the agency and the majority for violating the rule of law. Instead, he expressed outrage that the property of the "simplest farmer" was being "conscripted" for "national zoological use"! This barb was not just an expression of personal ideology (anti-socialism), but was *also* an announcement of the following legal baseline: the Blackstonian common law, which defined "take" as an active targeting and capture/shooting of a particular animal and which understood property rights as well-nigh absolute, unless the owner were imposing tangible harms on his neighbor. Reread Scalia's dissent in light of this normative baseline, which (by the way) is consistent with the philosophical baseline of modern conservative classics, such as Frederick Hayek, *The Constitution of Liberty* (1960). See Robert Westmoreland, *Hayek: The Rule of Law or the Law of Rules?*, 17 Law & Phil. 77 (1998).

---

[11] William N. Eskridge Jr, *Nino's Nightmare: Legal Process Theory as a Jurisprudence of Toggling Between Facts and Norms*, 57 St. Louis U. L.J. 865 (2012).

Conversely, Justice Stevens's opinion was framed by the norms reflecting America's "green revolution." See J. Peter Byrne, *Green Property,* 7 Const. Comm. 239 (1990). His baseline was that property is held subject to the public good—and biodiversity is a public good that justifies regulation of property use. Notice, however, that the modern regulatory state also provides that when the government "takes" your property, it must provide compensation—as ESA § 5 provides. Justice Stevens accepted a broad view of "take" for purposes of the ESA, but a narrow view for purposes of the Takings Clause of the Fifth Amendment. Reread his majority opinion in this light— the "law" is refracted through the lens of the New Deal.

Another of us has argued that the Justices made the case harder than it might have been precisely for the purpose of engaging in this larger debate about the role of regulation and environmentalism.[12] Certainly, if one takes the opinions as they are written, the Justices seemed to believe the case "hard," and there is no question that there is evidence they indulged in rhetoric extolling and/or denigrating environmental regulation. But is there not another way of looking at it? Does the statutory text "incidental taking" not make a strong textual argument for Justice Stevens's position? What is Justice Scalia's response to the 1982 statute?

3. *The Bill's History.* In 1973, the original Senate bill included language in the definition of "take" that specifically referred to "the destruction, modification, or curtailment of [the] habitat or range of fish and wildlife." Before the bill reached the floor, however, the Senate Commerce Committee took out this language and added the term "harm" to the definition of "take." 119 Cong. Rec. 25663 (1973). Justice Scalia noted this history in support of his theory that the original law aimed to resolve habitat degradation through a land acquisition program. Assume that the 1973 text supported Justice Scalia's understanding of the ESA, as not reaching private habitat destruction—but of course the statutory text changed in 1982. Congress in 1982 amended the ESA to give the Secretary the power to issue grants for "incidental" takings, especially the takings by private property holders who destroyed habitat as a consequence of developing their property. If later language trumps earlier language, then why did the Justices not begin with the "incidental takings" language? What was Justice Scalia's view of the meaning of "incidental" takings?

The majority invoked committee reports in support of its position. In response, Justice Scalia emphasized 1973 sponsor statements suggesting that habitat modification was to be cured by government land acquisition programs under § 5, not by the application of § 9. Should sponsor statements trump committee reports in general? Under what theory should these statements trump the 1973 committee reports? Senator Tunney stated on the same page cited by Justice Scalia that the 1973 Act was intended to prevent "harmful" actions to endangered species. 119 Cong. Rec. 25669 (statement of

---

[12] Victoria F. Nourse, *Decision Theory and* Babbitt v. Sweet Home: *Skepticism about Norms, Discretion, and the Virtues of Purposivism,* 57 St. Louis U. L.J. 909 (2013).

Senator Tunney). Does this change your view of Justice Scalia's argument or the validity of the regulation? Is this debate relevant after the 1982 amendments? Notice also Justice Scalia's sarcastic remark about whether Members of Congress should pay attention to representations in committee reports. Does the statement reflect a proper appreciation of the role of Congress under the Constitution?

4. *The 1982 Conference Report.* Remember that Conference is the critical legislative stage—where bills are changed for the last time and where remaining House-Senate disagreements are resolved. Do the following excerpts from the 1982 Conference's joint explanation seal the case for the majority's interpretation of the statute?

> This provision [referring to the incidental takings provision] is modeled after a *habitat conservation plan* that has been developed by three Northern California cities in the County of San Mateo, and *private* landowners and developers to provide the conservation of the *habitat* of three endangered species and other unlisted species of concern within the San Bruno Mountain area of San Mateo County.

H.R. Conf. Rep. 97–835, at 30–31 (Sept. 17, 1982) (emphasis added). The joint explanation continues:

> This provision will measurably reduce conflicts under the Act and will provide the institutional framework to permit cooperation between the public and *private* sectors in the interest of endangered species and habitat conservation.

> The terms of this provision require a unique partnership between the public and *private* sectors in the interest of species and *habitat conservation.* However, it is recognized that significant development projects often take many years to complete and permit applicants may need long-term permits.

Id. at 31 (emphasis added). "The Secretary, in determining whether to issue a long-term permit to carry out a conservation plan should consider the extent to which the conservation plan is likely to enhance the *habitat* of the listed species or increase the long-term survivability of the species or its *ecosystem.*" *Id.*

The Conference dubbed the San Bruno project involving endangered butterflies as a model for "incidental takings":

> Because the San Bruno Mountain plan is the model for this long term permit and because the adequacy of similar conservation plans should be measured against the San Bruno plan, the Committee believes that the elements of this plan should be clearly understood. Large portions of the *habitat* on San Bruno Mountain are privately owned. * * *

> 1. The Conservation Plan addresses the *habitat* throughout the area and preserves sufficient *habitat* to allow for enhancement of

the survival of the species. The plan protects in perpetuity at least 87 percent of the *habitat* of the listed butterflies.

2.   The establishment of a funding program which will provide permanent on-going funding for important *habitat* management and enhancement activities. Funding is to be provided through direct interim payments from landowners and developers and through permanent assessments on development units within the area.

How would you have ruled?

PROBLEM 5–1: AFTER SWEET HOME: HOW SHOULD SECRETARY BABBITT DEAL WITH SAGEBRUSH RESISTANCE?

So Secretary Babbitt won the case—but there was a danger he was losing the war to protect the habitat of endangered species.

Confronted with the Department's "harm" regulation, Chuck Cushman, Executive Director of the American Land Rights Association, insisted upon the Blackstonian rights of ranchers and farmers. Defiantly, he publicly urged this response: When landowners find an endangered animal on their property, the best solution under current law is to "shoot, shovel and shut up." Mark Sagoff, *Muddle or Muddle Through? Takings Jurisprudence Meets the Endangered Species Act,* 38 Wm. & Mary L. Rev. 825, 826 (1997) (quoting Cushman). According to Cushman, "[a] private-property owner is thinking to himself, 'I find a spotted owl on my property, I'm going to lose everything I've worked for all my life.' " *Id.* at 827. Perhaps a more common response than this abrasive one was that of Betty Orem, one of the property owners who were plaintiffs in the *Sweet Home* litigation. Quietly and during the course of the litigation, without the knowledge of the regulators, Orem went ahead and cut the trees on her land, destroying habitat needed by the spotted owl. *Id.* at 853–854.

You are the head of the Fish & Wildlife Service, the agency administering the ESA within the Interior Department. Secretary Babbitt asks you what the agency should do in light of its broad authority to address such a strong private resistance to regulation. What should you tell the Secretary?

2.   SUBSTANTIVE CANONS

Most of the canons discussed in the previous section are linguistic or syntactic guidelines that purport to be policy-neutral. (Section 3 will question whether even these textual canons are policy-neutral on their face or in practice.) Other canons represent decisions that are transparently substantive, and hence their application does not purport to be policy-neutral. Traditionally, the main substantive canons were directives to interpret different types of statutes "liberally" or "strictly." The old Anglo-American rule was that "remedial" statutes were to be liberally interpreted, while statutes in derogation of the common law were to be strictly interpreted. (But those canons are often at war: What remedial statute is not in derogation of the common law?)

More modern typologies of the liberal-versus-strict construction canons have emerged. Certain statutes (such as civil rights, securities, and antitrust statutes) are supposed to be liberally construed—in other words, applied expansively to new situations.[13] As Appendix 6, reporting the Court's deployment of canons from the 1986 through the 2011 Terms, demonstrates, these liberal construction canons have not often been invoked by the Rehnquist and Roberts Courts. Other statutes are to be strictly construed—in other words, applied stingily. The rule of lenity, requiring strict construction of criminal penal statutes, is the best example—and you might have followed something like the rule of lenity when you worked through the Case of the Tricycle. (The no-vehicles law is a criminal statute; although the penalty is modest, the rule of lenity applies to misdemeanor laws as well as the most serious felony statutes.)

Consider examples of other canons reflecting substantive judgments about how broadly to read the statute's text:

- *Strict Construction of Statutes in Derogation of Sovereignty.* If a statute is written in general language, it is presumed that it only applies to private parties; governments and their agencies are presumptively not included unless the statute clearly says so. See *Nevada Dep't of Human Resources v. Hibbs*, 538 U.S. 721 (2003) (finding such clarity); Scalia & Garner, *Reading Law,* 281–90 (no waiver unless "unequivocally clear"). This canon is based upon the old idea of sovereign immunity: the state cannot be sued or otherwise regulated without its consent. See 3 Sutherland § 62.1-4.

- *Strict Construction of Public Grants.* Similarly, public grants by the government to private parties are to be construed narrowly, that is, in favor of the government. 3 Sutherland § 63.4.

- *Strict Construction of (Some) Revenue Provisions?* 3 Sutherland § 66.1, writes that "courts have settled the rule that tax laws are strictly construed against the state and in favor of the taxpayer. Where there is reasonable doubt as to the meaning of a revenue statute, the doubt is resolved in favor of those taxed." See *Gould v. Gould*, 245 U.S. 151

---

[13] See generally William N. Eskridge Jr. & John Ferejohn, *A Republic of Statutes: The New American Constitution* ch. 1 (2010) (arguing that super-statutes whose policy or principle comes to be entrenched in the public culture over time will be interpreted liberally, especially by agencies, with courts going along, to advance their policies or principles, and expansively vis-a-vis more ordinary statutes). Examples include the Sherman Act of 1890, see *id.* ch. 3; the Social Security Act of 1935, see *id.* ch. 4; the Voting Rights Act of 1965, see *id.* ch. 2; and the Endangered Species Act of 1973, see *id.* ch. 6.

(1917). Taxpayers who have lost lawsuits against the Internal Revenue Service over fine points of statutory interpretation would dispute that generalization. Courts today do not follow the old rule because of the necessary public purpose implicated in the system of taxation. See 3 Sutherland § 66.2. Indeed, courts usually apply the opposite rule—that *exemptions* to the tax code are narrowly construed. See *United States v. Wells Fargo Bank*, 485 U.S. 351, 357 (1988); 3 Sutherland § 66.9; see also *United States v. Fior D'Italia,* 536 U.S. 238, 242–43 (2002) (presuming that IRS-generated tax assessments are correct).

Substantive canons are also formulated as presumptions that cut across different types of statutes and statutory schemes. These represent policies that the Court will "presume" Congress intends to incorporate into statutes, but such presumptions are rebuttable ones. These presumptions have various levels of strength, often depending on a particular case. A substantive canon can be treated as a starting point for discussion, a balancing factor, or a decisive tiebreaker at the end of a discussion. The policies underlying interpretive presumptions have been derived from the Constitution, federal statutes, and the common law. Some examples of substantive presumptions:

- Presumption against congressional reduction of American Indian rights. See *Hagen v. Utah*, 510 U.S. 399 (1994); *Montana v. Blackfeet Tribe*, 471 U.S. 759 (1985).

- Presumption of Indian tribal immunity from state regulation. See *Bryan v. Itasca County*, 426 U.S. 373 (1976).

- Presumption that Congress does not intend to pass statutes that violate international law. See *Sosa v. Alvarez-Machain*, 542 U.S. 692 (2004); *Weinberger v. Rossi*, 456 U.S. 25, 32 (1982); *Murray v. The Charming Betsy*, 6 U.S. (2 Cranch) 64, 118 (1804).

- Presumption that Congress does not intend to pass statutes that violate treaty obligations. See *Hamdan v. Rumsfeld*, 548 U.S. 557 (2006).

- Presumption that Congress does not intend that statutes have extraterritorial application. See *Foley Bros. v. Filardo*, 336 U.S. 281 (1949).

- Presumption that Congress does not intend that substantive statutes be applied retroactively. See *Landgraf v. USI Film Products*, 511 U.S. 244, 259–60 (1994).

- Presumption that Congress does not intend that federal regulations unnecessarily intrude into traditional state responsibilities (any more than is necessary to serve national objectives). See *Rush Prudential HMO v. Moran*, 536 U.S. 355 (2002); *Cipollone v. Liggett Group, Inc.*, 505 U.S. 504 (1992); *Ray v. Atl. Richfield Co.*, 435 U.S. 151, 157 (1978).

- Presumption that ambiguous federal statutes do not preempt (displace) existing state law. *Rice v. Santa Fe Elevator Corp.*, 331 U.S. 218 (1947).

- Presumption that Congress will not withdraw the courts' traditional equitable discretion. See *Weinberger v. Romero-Barcelo*, 456 U.S. 305, 320 (1982); *Hecht Co. v. Bowles*, 321 U.S. 321, 330 (1944).

- Presumption that Congress will not withdraw all remedies or judicial avenues of relief when it recognizes a statutory right. See *South Carolina v. Regan*, 465 U.S. 367 (1984).

- Presumption of judicial review. See *Demore v. Kim*, 538 U.S. 510 (2003); *Dunlop v. Bachowski*, 421 U.S. 560 (1975); *Abbott Labs. v. Gardner*, 387 U.S. 136 (1967).

- Presumption against derogation of the President's traditional powers. See *Dep't of Navy v. Egan*, 484 U.S. 518, 527 (1988); *Haig v. Agee*, 453 U.S. 280 (1981).

Courts have formulated these canons in different ways. Sometimes they formulate them as *clear statement rules*, which are presumptions that can only be rebutted by express language in the text of the statute. See *Astoria Fed. Sav. & Loan Ass'n v. Solimino*, 501 U.S. 101, 108–09 (1991) (contrasting presumptions and clear statement rules). Clear statement rules have been developed by the Supreme Court as expressions of quasi-constitutional values. For example, the Court has held that Congress cannot impose liability and process directly against the states unless the statutory text clearly says so (§ 2B below).

There is some mobility in the Court's articulation of these substantive canons. For example, in *EEOC v. Arabian Am. Oil Co.*, 499 U.S. 244, 258–59 (1991), a majority of the Court transformed the old *Foley Brothers* presumption against extraterritorial application (of Title VII in that case) into a clear statement rule, requiring explicit statutory language in order for a law to apply outside the United States. Justice Marshall's dissenting opinion objected to the Court's transformation. *Id.* at 263. (Note here how the general rule that civil rights laws, like Title VII, should be liberally construed was itself trumped by the more specific canon against extraterritorial regulation.) The mobility goes in both directions. In the federalism context for example, the Court moves between using presumptions and requiring clear statements when it interprets statutes that are ambiguous with respect to their effect on the states.

Don't let the labels trip you up. The substantive canons vary in their impact upon interpretation. The labels, and how the canons are deployed, help to identify how a court is using a canon, but do not necessarily tell you how the courts will use them in the next case. By way of review, consider the three possibilities alluded to above. First, sometimes courts will treat a substantive canon as a *tiebreaker* that affects the outcome only if, at the end of the basic interpretive process, the court is left unable to choose between the two competing interpretations put forward by the parties. Second, courts might treat substantive canons as *presumptions* that, at the beginning of the interpretive process, set up a presumptive outcome, which can be overcome by persuasive support for the contrary interpretation. Typically, the party attempting to overcome the presumption may use any potential evidence of statutory meaning (e.g., statutory text, legislative history, statutory purposes, policy arguments, and so on) to rebut the presumption. On this understanding, a presumption simply adds weight to one side of the balancing process captured by eclectic statutory interpretation. Third, courts may treat substantive canons as *clear statement rules*, which purport to compel a particular interpretive outcome unless there is a clear statement to the contrary. Sometimes we even see what we will call "super-strong" clear statement rules, presumptions that only may be overcome by extremely clear statutory text (where the "clear statement" is a targeted statement of textual meaning—a "magic words" rule, in effect). Pay attention to how these various approaches are deployed to implement the canons that are discussed in the remainder of this Part.

A. THE RULE OF LENITY

One of the hoariest canons of statutory interpretation states that laws whose purpose is to punish (usually by fine or imprisonment) must be construed strictly. This is called the "rule of lenity" in construing penal statutes: If the punitive statute does not clearly outlaw private conduct, the private actor cannot be penalized. While criminal statutes are the most obvious and common type of penal law, many civil statutes (such as the Endangered Species Act) have criminal penalties as well.

What is the purpose of the rule of lenity? The leading justification has been *fair notice*. The state may not impose penalties upon people without clearly warning them about unlawful conduct and its consequences. A classic reference for this rationalization is *McBoyle v. United States*, 283 U.S. 25 (1931). A 1919 federal statute prohibited the transportation of stolen *motor vehicles* in interstate commerce. The law defined motor vehicle to "include an automobile, automobile truck, automobile wagon, motor cycle, or any other self-propelled vehicle not designed for running on rails." *Id.* at 25. The issue in the case was whether defendant's transportation of a stolen airplane fell within the statute. Because *airplane* was not within the popular (or what linguists today call the prototypical) meaning of *motor vehicle*, Justice Holmes's opinion for the Court held that it did not. He justified lenity on grounds of notice:

> Although it is not likely that a criminal will carefully consider the text of the law before he murders or steals, it is reasonable that a fair warning should be given to the world in language that the common world will understand, of what the law intends to do if a certain line is passed. To make the warning fair, so far as possible the line should be clear. When a rule of conduct is laid down in words that evoke in the common mind only the picture of the vehicles moving on land, the statute should not be extended to aircraft, simply because it may seem to us that a similar policy applies, or upon the speculation that if the legislature had thought of it, very likely broader words would have been used.

Id. at 27. Accord, *United States v. Lanier*, 520 U.S. 259, 265–66 (1997) (excellent elaboration of *McBoyle* and the various fair warning doctrines). See also Lawrence M. Solan, *Law, Language, and Lenity*, 40 Wm. & Mary L. Rev. 57 (1998) (contrasting prototypical meaning of words with broader understandings).

A justification related to fair notice might be the Anglo-American emphasis on *mens rea* as a presumptive requirement for criminal penalties. Although ignorance of the law is no defense to a crime, the inability of the reasonable defendant to know that his actions are criminal undermines the justice of inferring a criminal intent in some cases. It also suggests a corollary of the rule of lenity, namely, the presumption that criminal statutes carry with them a *mens rea*, or intentionality, requirement.

One illustration of this rationale is *Ratzlaf v. United States*, 510 U.S. 135 (1994), which construed the Money Laundering Control Act of 1986. Prior law required banks to report cash transactions in excess of $10,000; to prevent people from "structuring" their transactions to avoid the reporting requirement, the 1986 law made it illegal to make lower deposits for the purpose of evading the reporting requirements. The Court interpreted the statute to require *double scienter*: not only must the government prove that defendants Waldemar and Loretta Ratzlaf intended to evade the bank reporting law, but also that they knew about and intended to evade the anti-structuring law as well.[14] Justice

---

[14] The Supreme Court similarly read special *scienter* requirements into a statute making it a crime to possess a "machine gun," *Staples v. United States*, 511 U.S. 600 (1994) (government must prove defendant knew the gun was a machine gun), or to distribute images of minors

Ginsburg's opinion for the Court emphasized that there were many benign reasons people would want to structure their transactions to avoid bank reporting requirements, including fear of burglary and a desire to secrete assets from a spouse or tax inspectors. According to Justice Ginsburg, "structuring is not inevitably nefarious." *Id.* at 144. Four dissenting Justices argued that a *double scienter* requirement was not justified by the statutory language, rendered the statute a nullity, and focused on unduly extreme cases.

Under this type of fair warning rationale, the rule of lenity is most appropriately applied to criminal statutes that create offenses that are *malum prohibitum* (bad only because they are prohibited) rather than *malum in se* (bad by their very nature). Oliver Wendell Holmes Jr., *The Common Law* 50 (1881); James Willard Hurst, *Dealing with Statutes* 64–65 (1982). Understood through the lens of fair warning, the rule of lenity weighs strongly in favor of the defendant in the Case of the Tricycle: few parents and virtually no children would read a "No VEHICLES in the Park" sign and think that it applied to tricycles and other children's toys.

A third justification for the rule of lenity was originally suggested by Chief Justice Marshall in *United States v. Wiltberger*, 18 U.S. 76, 92 (1820): separation of powers. The Chief Justice ruled that Congress cannot delegate to judges and prosecutors power to make common law crimes, because the moral condemnation inherent in crimes ought only to be delivered by the popularly elected legislature. If the legislature alone has the authority to define crimes, it is inappropriate for judges to elaborate on criminal statutes so as to expand them beyond the clear words adopted by the legislature. There is also a separation of powers concern that judicial expansion of criminal statutes, common-law style, threatens to expand prosecutorial discretion beyond that contemplated by the legislature. See Herbert L. Packer, *The Limits of the Criminal Sanction* 79–96 (1968).

Yet another justification is the rule's "sheer antiquity." Antonin Scalia, *A Matter of Interpretation* (1997). Justice Scalia has argued that the rule has such a long history that we can safely assume Congress knows about it, agrees with it, and drafts in its shadow. This type of Congress-oriented justification has attractions for judges like Justice Scalia, whose emphasis on neutrality and formalism leads them to justify the policy canons as something *other* than the imposition of mere judicial or other external preferences.

---

engaged in sexually explicit conduct, *United States v. X-Citement Video, Inc.*, 513 U.S. 64 (1994) (government must prove defendant knew the performer was actually a minor). See also *Cheek v. United States*, 498 U.S. 192 (1991) (taxpayer's honest but unreasonable belief that he did not have to pay taxes was a valid defense to a charge of willful failure to pay taxes).

Notwithstanding the antiquity and multiple rationales for the rule of lenity, many distinguished scholars say it has fallen into decline since the New Deal. See generally Francis Allen, *The Erosion of Legality in American Criminal Justice: Some Latter-Day Adventures of the* Nulla Poena *Principle*, 29 Ariz. L. Rev. 385 (1987). As many as twenty-eight states have abolished or even reversed the rule of lenity by statute.[15] Typical is Arizona Criminal Code § 13–104: "The general rule that a penal statute is to be strictly construed does not apply to this title, but the provisions herein must be construed according to the fair meaning of their terms to promote justice and effect the objects of the law * * *." The primary explanation for these anti-lenity statutes is that state legislatures in the late twentieth century were prone to invoke the criminal sanction liberally, and did not want judges obstructing such an expansion (legislators like to be seen as "tough on crime"). If this rationale holds up, does that provide a reason *favoring* the rule of lenity? Do the rule's constitutional overtones trump such statutes under some circumstances? Cf. *State v. Pena*, 683 P.2d 744, 748–49 (Ariz. App. 1983), aff'd, 683 P.2d 743 (Ariz. 1984) (applying rule of lenity notwithstanding the legislative abrogation).

Criticism of the rule of lenity has not been limited to legislators. Dan Kahan, *Lenity and Federal Common Law Crimes*, 1994 Sup. Ct. Rev. 345, maintains that the nondelegation reason is the only coherent justification for the rule of lenity, at least for federal criminal statutes, but further argues that the rule of lenity should be abolished as a canon of construction because the polity would be better off without the rule of lenity. Normal interpretation of criminal statutes, without a judicial thumb on either side of the scale, would promote a more orderly and less costly development of criminal law (common-law style, the way commercial law has developed, for example), without much in the way of unfairness, especially if the Department of Justice cleared up ambiguities by authoritative interpretations of federal criminal statutes. Consider this thesis in light of the following case and problem. Is there a coherent rationale for the rule of lenity? Does it serve useful purposes? Or does it impose needless costs on the system?

---

[15] See Robert Yablon, "Lenity Without Strict Construction: Matching the Rule to Its Purposes" (Yale Law School Supervised Analytical Writing 2006) (collecting state statutes) (on file with the editors).

Frank J. Muscarello v. United States

Supreme Court of the United States, 1998.
524 U.S. 125, 118 S.Ct. 1911, 141 L. Ed. 2d 111.

Justice Breyer delivered the opinion of the Court.

[Section 924(c)(1) of 18 U.S.C. provides that "[w]hoever, during and in relation to any crime of violence or drug trafficking crime * * * uses or carries a firearm, shall, in addition to the punishment provided for such crime of violence or drug trafficking crime, be sentenced to a term of imprisonment of not less than five years[.]" The practical consequence of this provision is that someone who possessed a gun at the time of a drug offense gets a mandatory additional five-year sentence if § 924(c)(1) was violated; if that provision was not violated, the possession of the gun would be taken into account under the federal sentencing guidelines and would add some time to the sentence (perhaps a 30–40% enhancement) unless the gun was clearly not involved in the drug offense. Apparently it is almost always in the interest of the defendant to be subjected to the sentencing guidelines in this way rather than receive the mandatory additional sentence provided by § 924(c)(1). Accordingly, there has been much litigation concerning what the government must show beyond the mere possession of a gun during a drug offense to satisfy § 924(c)(1).

[In *Smith v. United States*, 508 U.S. 223 (1993), the Court held that when a person traded a gun for drugs, he "used" the gun in violation of § 924(c)(1). Justice Scalia's dissenting opinion contended that the ordinary meaning of § 924(c)(1), read in context, is that "uses a firearm" means "uses the firearm as a weapon," and that in any event the issue was sufficiently doubtful for the rule of lenity to control the outcome in favor of the defendant. In *Bailey v. United States*, 516 U.S. 137 (1995), a unanimous Court held that the "use" element requires active employment of the firearm by the defendant, such that it did not apply to a defendant who had a gun in the trunk of his car in which illegal drugs were found or to a defendant who had a gun locked in a trunk in a closet in a bedroom where illegal drugs were stored.

[Muscarello unlawfully sold marijuana from his truck and confessed that he "carried" a gun in the truck's locked glove compartment " 'for protection in relation' to the drug offense." In a companion case, Donald Cleveland and Enrique Gray-Santana were arrested for stealing and dealing drugs; they had bags of guns in the locked trunk of their car at the scene. The issue was whether these defendants had "carrie[d]" a firearm within the meaning of § 924(c)(1).]

We begin with the statute's language. The parties vigorously contest the ordinary English meaning of the phrase "carries a firearm." Because they essentially agree that Congress intended the phrase to convey its ordinary, and not some special legal, meaning, and because they argue the linguistic point at length, we too have looked into the matter in more than usual depth. Although the word "carry" has many different meanings, only two are relevant here. When one uses the word in the first, or primary, meaning, one can, as a matter of ordinary English, "carry firearms" in a wagon, car, truck, or other vehicle that one accompanies. When one uses the word in a different, rather special, way, to mean, for example, "bearing" or (in slang) "packing" (as in "packing a gun"), the matter is less clear. But, for reasons we shall set out below, we believe Congress intended to use the word in its primary sense and not in this latter, special way.

Consider first the word's primary meaning. The Oxford English Dictionary gives as its *first* definition "convey, originally by cart or wagon, hence in any vehicle, by ship, on horseback, etc." 2 Oxford English Dictionary 919 (2d ed. 1989); see also Webster's Third New International Dictionary 343 (1986) (*first* definition: "move while supporting (*as in a vehicle* or in one's hands or arms)"); The Random House Dictionary of the English Language Unabridged 319 (2d ed. 1987) (*first* definition: "to take or support from one place to another; convey; transport").

The origin of the word "carries" explains why the first, or basic, meaning of the word "carry" includes conveyance in a vehicle. See The Barnhart Dictionary of Etymology 146 (1988) (tracing the word from Latin "carum," which means "car" or "cart"); 2 Oxford English Dictionary, *supra*, at 919 (tracing the word from Old French "carier" and the late Latin "carricare," which meant to "convey in a car") * * *.

The greatest of writers have used the word with this meaning. See, e.g., the King James Bible, 2 Kings 9:28 ("[H]is servants carried him in a chariot to Jerusalem"); *id.*, Isaiah 30:6 ("[T]hey will carry their riches upon the shoulders of young asses"). Robinson Crusoe says, "[w]ith my boat, I carry'd away every Thing." D. Defoe, Robinson Crusoe 174 (J. Crowley ed. 1972). And the owners of Queequeg's ship, Melville writes, "had lent him a [wheelbarrow], in which to carry his heavy chest to his boardinghouse." H. Melville, Moby Dick 43 (U. Chicago 1952). This Court, too, has spoken of the "carrying" of drugs in a car or in its "trunk." [Citations omitted.]

These examples do not speak directly about carrying guns. But there is nothing linguistically special about the fact that weapons, rather than drugs, are being carried. * * * And, to make certain that there is no special ordinary English restriction (unmentioned in dictionaries) upon the use of "carry" in respect to guns, we have surveyed modern press usage, albeit crudely, by searching computerized newspaper databases— both the New York Times data base in Lexis/Nexis, and the "US News" data base in Westlaw. We looked for sentences in which the words "carry," "vehicle," and "weapon" (or variations thereof) all appear. We found thousands of such sentences, and random sampling suggests that many, perhaps more than one third, are sentences used to convey the meaning at issue here, *i.e.*, the carrying of guns in a car. [Justice Breyer gave several examples of such newspaper stories.] * * *

Now consider a different, somewhat special meaning of the word "carry"—a meaning upon which the linguistic arguments of petitioners and the dissent must rest. The Oxford English Dictionary's *twenty-sixth* definition of "carry" is "bear, wear, hold up, or sustain, as one moves about; habitually to bear about with one." Webster's [Third New International Dictionary] defines "carry" as "to move while supporting," not just in a vehicle, but also "in one's hands or arms." And Black's Law Dictionary defines the entire phrase "carry arms or weapons" as "[t]o wear, bear or carry them upon the person or in the clothing or in a pocket, for the purpose of use, or for the purpose of being armed and ready for offensive or defensive action in case of a conflict with another person."

These special definitions, however, do not purport to *limit* the "carrying of arms" to the circumstances they describe. No one doubts that one who bears arms on his person "carries a weapon." But to say that is not to deny that one may also "carry a weapon" tied to the saddle of a horse or placed in a bag in a car.

Nor is there any linguistic reason to think that Congress intended to limit the word "carries" in the statute to any of these special definitions. To the contrary, all these special definitions embody a form of an important, but secondary, meaning of "carry," a meaning that suggests support rather than movement or transportation, as when, for example, a column "carries" the weight of an arch. 2 Oxford English Dictionary, *supra*, at 919, 921. In this sense a gangster might "carry" a gun (in colloquial language, he might "pack a gun") even though he does not move from his chair. It is difficult to believe, however, that Congress intended to limit the statutory word to this definition—imposing special punishment upon the comatose gangster while ignoring drug lords who drive to a sale carrying an arsenal of weapons in their van.

We recognize, as the dissent emphasizes, that the word "carry" has other meanings as well. But those other meanings, (e.g., "carry all he knew," "carries no colours") are not relevant here. And the fact that speakers often do *not* add to the phrase "carry a gun" the words "in a car" is of no greater relevance here than the fact that millions of Americans did *not* see Muscarello carry a gun in his car. The relevant linguistic facts are that the word "carry" in its ordinary sense includes carrying in a car and that the word, used in its ordinary sense, keeps the same meaning whether one carries a gun, a suitcase, or a banana. * * *

We now explore more deeply the purely legal question of whether Congress intended to use the word "carry" in its ordinary sense, or whether it intended to limit the scope of the phrase to instances in which a gun is carried "on the person." We conclude that neither the statute's basic purpose nor its legislative history support circumscribing the scope of the word "carry" by applying an "on the person" limitation.

This Court has described the statute's basic purpose broadly, as an effort to combat the "dangerous combination" of "drugs and guns." *Smith v. United States*, 508 U.S. 223, 240 (1993). And the provision's chief legislative sponsor has said that the provision seeks "to persuade the man who is tempted to commit a Federal felony to leave his gun at home." 114 Cong. Rec. 22231 (1968) (Rep. Poff); see *Busic v. United States*, 446 U.S. 398, 405 (1980) (describing Poff's comments as "crucial material" in interpreting the purpose of § 924(c)); *Simpson v. United States*, 435 U.S. 6, 13–14 (1978) (concluding that Poff's comments are "clearly probative" and "certainly entitled to weight"); see also 114 Cong. Rec. 22243–22244 (statutes would apply to "the man who goes out taking a gun to commit a crime") (Rep. Hunt); *id.*, at 22244 ("Of course, what we are trying to do by these penalties is to persuade the criminal to leave his gun at home") (Rep. Randall); *id.*, at 22236 ("We are concerned . . . with having the criminal leave his gun at home") (Rep. Meskill).

From the perspective of any such purpose (persuading a criminal "to leave his gun at home"), what sense would it make for this statute to penalize one who walks with a gun in a bag to the site of a drug sale, but to ignore a similar individual who, like defendant Gray-Santana, travels to a similar site with a similar gun in a similar bag, but instead of walking, drives there with the gun in his car? How persuasive is a punishment that is without effect until a drug dealer who has brought his gun to a sale (indeed has it available for use) actually takes it from the trunk (or unlocks the glove compartment) of his car? It is difficult to say that, considered as a class, those who prepare, say, to sell drugs by placing guns in their cars are less dangerous, or less deserving of punishment, than those who carry handguns on their person.

We have found no significant indication elsewhere in the legislative history of any more narrowly focused relevant purpose. * * * One legislator indicates that the statute responds in part to the concerns of law enforcement personnel, who had urged that "carrying short firearms in motor vehicles be classified as carrying such weapons concealed." *Id.*, at 22242 (Rep. May). Another criticizes a version of the proposed statute by suggesting it might apply to drunken driving, and gives as an example a drunken driver who has a "gun in his car." *Id.*, at 21792 (Rep. Yates). Others describe the statute as criminalizing gun "possession"—a term that could stretch beyond both the "use" of a gun and the carrying of a gun on the person. See *id.*, at 21793 (Rep. Casey); *id.*, at 22236 (Rep. Meskill); *id.*, at 30584 (Rep. Collier); *id.*, at 30585 (Rep. Skubitz).

We are not convinced by petitioners' remaining arguments to the contrary. First, they say that our definition of "carry" makes it the equivalent of "transport." Yet, Congress elsewhere in related statutes used the word "transport" deliberately to signify a different, and broader, statutory coverage. The immediately preceding statutory subsection, for example, imposes a different set of penalties on one who, with an intent to commit a crime, "ships, transports, or receives a firearm" in interstate commerce. 18 U.S.C. § 924(b). Moreover, § 926A specifically "entitle[s]" a person "not otherwise prohibited . . . from transporting, shipping, or receiving a firearm" to "transport a firearm . . . from any place where he may lawfully possess and carry" it to "any other place" where he may do so. Why, petitioners ask, would Congress have used the word "transport," or used both "carry" and "transport" in the same provision, if it had intended to obliterate the distinction between the two?

The short answer is that our definition does not equate "carry" and "transport." "Carry" implies personal agency and some degree of possession, whereas "transport" does not have such a limited connotation and, in addition, implies the movement of goods in bulk over great distances. See Webster's Third New International Dictionary 343 (noting that "carry" means "moving to a location some distance away while supporting or maintaining off the ground" and "is a natural word to use in ref. to cargoes and loads on trucks, wagons, planes, ships, or even beasts of burden," while "transport refers to carriage in bulk or number over an appreciable distance and, typically, by a customary or usual carrier agency"); see also Webster's Dictionary of Synonyms 141 (1942). If Smith, for example, calls a parcel delivery service, which sends a truck to Smith's house to pick up Smith's package and take it to Los Angeles, one might say that Smith has shipped the package and the parcel delivery service has transported the package. But only the truck driver has "carried" the package in the sense of "carry" that we believe Congress intended. Therefore, "transport" is a broader category that includes "carry" but also encompasses other activity.

The dissent refers to § 926A and to another statute where Congress used the word "transport" rather than "carry" to describe the movement of firearms. 18 U.S.C. § 925(a)(2)(B). According to the dissent, had Congress intended "carry" to have the meaning we give it, Congress would not have needed to use a different word in these provisions. But as we have discussed above, we believe the word "transport" is broader than the word "carry."

And, if Congress intended "carry" to have the limited definition the dissent contends, it would have been quite unnecessary to add the proviso in § 926A requiring a person, to be exempt from penalties, to store her firearm in a locked container not immediately accessible. See § 926A (exempting from criminal penalties one who transports a firearm from a place where "he may lawfully possess and carry such firearm" but not exempting the "transportation" of a firearm if it is "readily accessible or is directly accessible from the passenger compartment of transporting vehicle"). The statute simply could have said that such a person may not "carry" a firearm. But, of course, Congress did not say this because that is not what "carry" means.

As we interpret the statutory scheme, it makes sense. Congress has imposed a variable penalty with no mandatory minimum sentence upon a person who "transports" (or "ships" or "receives") a firearm knowing it will be used to commit any "offense punishable by imprisonment for [more than] . . . one year," § 924(b), and it has imposed a 5-year mandatory minimum sentence upon one who "carries" a firearm "during and in relation to" a "drug trafficking crime," § 924(c). The first subsection imposes a less strict sentencing regime upon one who, say, ships firearms by mail for use in a crime elsewhere; the latter subsection imposes a mandatory sentence upon one who, say, brings a weapon with him (on his person or in his car) to the site of a drug sale.

Second, petitioners point out that, in *Bailey v. United States*, 516 U.S. 137 (1995), we considered the related phrase "uses . . . a firearm" found in the same statutory provision now before us. We construed the term "use" narrowly, limiting its application to the "active employment" of a firearm. Petitioners argue that it would be anomalous to construe broadly the word "carries," its statutory next-door neighbor.

In *Bailey*, however, we limited "use" of a firearm to "active employment" in part because we assumed "that Congress . . . intended each term to have a particular, non-superfluous meaning." A broader interpretation of "use," we said, would have swallowed up the term "carry." But "carry" as we interpret that word does not swallow up the term "use." "Use" retains the same independent meaning we found for it in *Bailey*, where we provided examples involving the displaying or the bartering of a gun. "Carry" also retains an independent meaning, for, under *Bailey*, carrying a gun in a car does not necessarily involve the gun's "active employment." More importantly, having construed "use" narrowly in *Bailey*, we cannot also construe "carry" narrowly without undercutting the statute's basic objective. For the narrow interpretation would remove the act of carrying a gun in a car entirely from the statute's reach, leaving a gap in coverage that we do not believe Congress intended.

Third, petitioners say that our reading of the statute would extend its coverage to passengers on buses, trains, or ships, who have placed a firearm, say, in checked luggage. To extend this statute so far, they argue, is unfair, going well beyond what Congress likely would have thought possible. They add that some lower courts, thinking approximately the same, have limited the scope of "carries" to instances where a gun in a car is immediately accessible, thereby most likely excluding from coverage a gun carried in a car's trunk or locked glove compartment. * * *

In our view, this argument does not take adequate account of other limiting words in the statute—words that make the statute applicable only where a defendant "carries" a gun *both* "during *and* in relation to" a drug crime. § 924(c)(1) (emphasis added). Congress added these words in part to prevent prosecution where guns "played" no part in the crime. See S. Rep. No. 98–225, at 314, n.10.

Once one takes account of the words "during" and "in relation to," it no longer seems beyond Congress' likely intent, or otherwise unfair, to interpret the statute as we have done. If one carries a gun in a car "during" and "in relation to" a drug sale, for example, the fact that the gun is carried in the car's trunk or locked glove compartment seems not only logically difficult to distinguish from the immediately accessible gun, but also beside the point.

At the same time, the narrow interpretation creates its own anomalies. The statute, for example, defines "firearm" to include a "bomb," "grenade," "rocket having a propellant charge of more than four ounces," or "missile having an explosive or incendiary charge of more than one-quarter ounce," where such device is "explosive," "incendiary," or delivers "poison gas." 18 U.S.C. § 921(a)(4)(A). On petitioners' reading, the "carry" provision would not apply to instances where drug lords, engaged in a major transaction, took with them "firearms" such as these, which most likely could not be carried on the person.

Fourth, petitioners argue that we should construe the word "carry" to mean "immediately accessible." * * * That interpretation, however, is difficult to square with the statute's language, for one "carries" a gun in the glove compartment whether or not that glove compartment is locked. Nothing in the statute's history suggests that Congress intended that limitation. And, for reasons pointed out above, we believe that the words "during" and "in relation to" will limit the statute's application to the harms that Congress foresaw.

Finally, petitioners and the dissent invoke the "rule of lenity." The simple existence of some statutory ambiguity, however, is not sufficient to warrant application of that rule, for most statutes are ambiguous to some degree. " 'The rule of lenity applies only if, "after seizing everything from which aid can be derived," . . . we can make "no more than a guess as to what Congress intended." ' " *United States v. Wells*, 519 U.S. 482, 499 (1997) [quoting earlier cases]. To invoke the rule, we must conclude that there is a " 'grievous ambiguity or uncertainty' in the statute." *Staples v. United States*, 511 U.S. 600, 619 n.17 (1994) (quoting *Chapman v. United States*, 500 U.S. 453, 463 (1991). Certainly, our decision today is based on much more than a "guess as to what Congress intended," and there is no "grievous ambiguity" here. The problem of statutory interpretation [in this case] is indeed no different from that in many of the criminal cases that confront us. Yet, this Court has never held that the rule of lenity automatically permits a defendant to win. * * * [Affirmed.]

JUSTICE GINSBURG, with whom THE CHIEF JUSTICE [REHNQUIST], JUSTICE SCALIA, and JUSTICE SOUTER join, dissenting.

[Justice Ginsburg explained that defendants' gun possession would have adverse consequences even if § 924(c)(1) were held to be inapplicable. For example, the federal sentencing guidelines provided Muscarello a 6–12 month presumptive sentence for his involvement in the distribution of 3.6 kilograms of marijuana. The "two-level enhancement" under the guidelines for possession of a gun would increase the sentencing range to 10–16 months. If, instead, as the majority held, Muscarello violated § 924(c)(1), his sentence would reflect the underlying drug offense (6–12 months) *plus* the five-year mandatory additional sentence provided by § 924(c)(1).]

* * * Unlike the Court, I do not think dictionaries, surveys of press reports, or the Bible[4] tell us, dispositively, what "carries" means embedded in § 924(c)(1). On definitions, "carry" in legal formulations could mean, *inter alia*, transport, possess, have in stock, prolong (carry over), be infectious, or wear or bear on one's person.[5] At issue here is not "carries" at large but "carries a firearm." The Court's computer search of newspapers is revealing in this light. Carrying guns in a car showed up as the meaning "perhaps more than one third" of the time. One is left to wonder what meaning showed up some two thirds of the time. Surely a most familiar meaning is, as the Constitution's Second Amendment ("keep and *bear* Arms") (emphasis added) and Black's Law Dictionary, at 214, indicate: "wear, bear, or carry . . . upon the person or in the clothing or in a pocket, for the purpose . . . of being armed and ready for offensive or defensive action in a case of conflict with another person."

On lessons from literature, a scan of Bartlett's and other quotation collections shows how highly selective the Court's choices are. If "[t]he greatest of writers" have used "carry" to mean convey or transport in a

---

4   The translator of the Good Book, it appears, bore responsibility for determining whether the servants of Ahaziah "carried" his corpse to Jerusalem. Compare [majority opinion] with, e.g., The New English Bible, 2 Kings 9:28 ("His servants *conveyed* his body to Jerusalem."); Saint Joseph Edition of the New American Bible ("His servants *brought* him in a chariot to Jerusalem."); Tanakh: The Holy Scriptures ("His servants *conveyed* him in a chariot to Jerusalem."); see also *id.*, Isaiah 30:6 ("They *convey* their wealth on the backs of asses."); The New Jerusalem Bible ("[T]hey *bear* their riches on donkeys' backs.") (emphasis added in all quotations).

5   The dictionary to which this Court referred in *Bailey v. United States* contains 32 discrete definitions of "carry," including "[t]o make good or valid," "to bear the aspect of," and even "[t]o bear (a hawk) on the fist." See Webster's New International Dictionary of English Language 412 (2d ed. 1949).

vehicle, so have they used the hydra-headed word to mean, *inter alia,* carry in one's hand, arms, head, heart, or soul, sans vehicle. [Justice Ginsburg quoted Isaiah 40:11, poems by Oliver Goldsmith and Rudyard Kipling, and Theodore Roosevelt's famous advice to "[s]peak softly and carry a big stick."][6]

These and the Court's lexicological sources demonstrate vividly that "carry" is a word commonly used to convey various messages. Such references, given their variety, are not reliable indicators of what Congress meant, in § 924(c)(1), by "carries a firearm."

Noting the paradoxical statement, " 'I *use* a gun to protect my house, but I've never had to *use* it,' " the Court in *Bailey* emphasized the importance of context—the statutory context. Just as "uses" was read to mean not simply "possession," but "active employment," so "carries," correspondingly, is properly read to signal the most dangerous cases—the gun at hand, ready for use as a weapon. It is reasonable to comprehend Congress as having provided mandatory minimums for the most life-jeopardizing gun-connection cases (guns in or at the defendant's hand when committing an offense), leaving other, less imminently threatening, situations for the more flexible guidelines regime. As the Ninth Circuit suggested, it is not apparent why possession of a gun in a drug dealer's moving vehicle would be thought more dangerous than gun possession on premises where drugs are sold: "A drug dealer who packs heat is more likely to hurt someone or provoke someone else to violence. A gun in a bag under a tarp in a truck bed [or in a bedroom closet] poses substantially less risk." *United States v. Foster*, 133 F.3d 704, 707 (1998) (en banc).

For indicators from Congress itself, it is appropriate to consider word usage in other provisions of Title 18's chapter on "Firearms." The Court, however, does not derive from the statutory complex at issue its thesis that " '[c]arry' implies personal agency and some degree of possession, whereas 'transport' does not have such a limited connotation and, in addition, implies the movement of goods in bulk over great distances." [Quoting majority opinion.] Looking to provisions Congress enacted, one finds that the Legislature did not acknowledge or routinely adhere to the distinction the Court advances today; instead, Congress sometimes employed "transports" when, according to the Court, "carries" was the right word to use.

Section 925(a)(2)(B), for example, provides that no criminal sanction shall attend "the transportation of [a] firearm or ammunition carried out

---

[6] Popular films and television productions provide corroborative illustrations. * * * [I]n the television series "M*A*S*H," Hawkeye Pierce (played by Alan Alda) presciently proclaims: "I will not carry a gun. . . . I'll carry your books, I'll carry a torch, I'll carry a tune, I'll carry on, carry over, carry forward, Cary Grant, cash and carry, carry me back to Old Virginia, I'll even 'hari-kari' if you show me how, but I will not carry a gun!" See http://www.geocities.com/Hollywood/8915/mashquotes.html.

to enable a person, who lawfully received such firearm or ammunition from the Secretary of the Army, to engage in military training or in competitions." The full text of § 926A, rather than the truncated version the Court presents, is also telling:

> Notwithstanding any other provision of any law or any rule or regulation of a State or any political subdivision thereof, any person who is not otherwise prohibited by this chapter from transporting, shipping, or receiving a firearm shall be entitled to transport a firearm for any lawful purpose from any place where he may lawfully possess and carry such firearm to any other place where he may lawfully possess and carry such firearm if, during such transportation the firearm is unloaded, and neither the firearm nor any ammunition being transported is readily accessible or is directly accessible from the passenger compartment of such transporting vehicle: *Provided*, That in the case of a vehicle without a compartment separate from the driver's compartment the firearm or ammunition shall be contained in a locked container other than the glove compartment or console.

In describing when and how a person may travel in a vehicle that contains his firearm without violating the law, §§ 925(a)(2)(B) and 926A use "transport," not "carry," to "impl[y] personal agency and some degree of possession." [Again quoting majority opinion.][10]

Reading "carries" in § 924(c)(1) to mean "on or about [one's] person" is fully compatible with these and other "Firearms" statutes. For example, under § 925(a)(2)(B), one could carry his gun to a car, transport it to the shooting competition, and use it to shoot targets. Under the conditions of § 926A, one could transport her gun in a car, but under no circumstances could the gun be readily accessible while she travels in the car. "[C]ourts normally try to read language in different, but related, statutes, so as best to reconcile those statutes, in light of their purposes and of common sense." [*United States v. McFadden*, 13 F.3d 463, 467 (1st Cir. 1994) (Breyer, C.J., dissenting).] So reading the "Firearms" statutes, I would

---

[10] The Court asserts that "'transport' is a broader category that includes 'carry' but encompasses other activity." "Carry," however, is not merely a subset of "transport." A person seated at a desk with a gun in hand or pocket is carrying the gun, but is not transporting it. Yes, the words "carry" and "transport" often can be employed interchangeably, as can the words "carry" and "use." But in *Bailey*, this Court settled on constructions that gave "carry" and "use" independent meanings. Without doubt, Congress is alert to the discrete meanings of "transport" and "carry" in the context of vehicles, as the Legislature's placement of each word in § 926A illustrates. The narrower reading of "carry" preserves discrete meanings for the two words, while in the context of vehicles the Court's interpretation of "carry" is altogether synonymous with "transport." Tellingly, when referring to firearms traveling in vehicles, the "Firearms" statutes routinely use a form of "transport"; they never use a form of "carry."

not extend the word "carries" in § 924(c)(1) to mean transports out of hand's reach in a vehicle.[12]

Section 924(c)(1), as the foregoing discussion details, is not decisively clear one way or another. The sharp division in the Court on the proper reading of the measure confirms, "[a]t the very least, . . . that the issue is subject to some doubt. Under these circumstances, we adhere to the familiar rule that, 'where there is ambiguity in a criminal statute, doubts are resolved in favor of the defendant.'" *Adamo Wrecking Co. v. United States*, 434 U.S. 275, 284–285 (1978); see *United States v. Granderson*, 511 U.S. 39, 54 (1994) ("[W]here text, structure, and history fail to establish that the Government's position is unambiguously correct—we apply the rule of lenity and resolve the ambiguity in [the defendant's] favor."). "Carry" bears many meanings, as the Court and the "Firearms" statutes demonstrate.[13] The narrower "on or about [one's] person" interpretation is hardly implausible nor at odds with an accepted meaning of "carries a firearm."

Overlooking that there will be an enhanced sentence for the gun-possessing drug dealer in any event, the Court asks rhetorically: "How persuasive is a punishment that is without effect until a drug dealer who has brought his gun to a sale (indeed has it available for use) actually takes it from the trunk (or unlocks the glove compartment) of his car?" Correspondingly, the Court defines "carries a firearm" to cover "a person who knowingly possesses and conveys firearms [anyplace] in a vehicle . . . which the person accompanies." Congress, however, hardly lacks competence to select the words "possesses" or "conveys" when that is what

---

[12] The Court places undue reliance on Representative Poff's statement that § 924(c)(1) seeks "'to persuade the man who is tempted to commit a Federal felony to leave his gun at home.'" See [majority opinion] (quoting 114 Cong. Rec. 22231 (1968)). As the Government argued in its brief to this Court in *Bailey*:

> In making that statement, Representative Poff was not referring to the "carries" prong of the original Section 924(c). As originally enacted, the "carries" prong of the statute prohibited only the "unlawful" carrying of a firearm while committing an offense. The statute would thus not have applied to an individual who, for instance, had a permit for carrying a gun and carried it with him when committing an offense, and it would have had no force in "persuading" such an individual "to leave his gun at home." Instead, Representative Poff was referring to the "uses" prong of the original Section 924(c). [Quoting U.S. Brief in *Bailey*.]

Representative Poff's next sentence confirms that he was speaking of "uses," not "carries": "Any person should understand that if he *uses* his gun and is caught and convicted, he is going to jail." 114 Cong. Rec., at 22231 (emphasis added).

[13] Any doubt on that score is dispelled by examining the provisions in the "Firearms" chapter, in addition to § 924(c)(1), that include a form of the word "carry": 18 U.S.C. § 922(a)(5) ("*carry out* a bequest"); §§ 922(s)(6)(B)(ii), (iii) ("*carry out* this subsection"); § 922(u) ("*carry away* [a firearm]"); 18 U.S.C.A. § 924(a)(6)(B)(ii) (Supp.1998) ("*carry* or otherwise possess or discharge or otherwise use [a] handgun"); 18 U.S.C. § 924(e)(2)(B) ("*carrying* of a firearm"); § 925(a)(2) ("*carried out* to enable a person"); § 926(a) ("*carry out* the provisions of this chapter"); § 926A ("lawfully possess and *carry* such firearm to any other place where he may lawfully possess and *carry* such firearm"); § 929(a)(1) ("uses or *carries* a firearm and is in possession of armor piercing ammunition"); § 930(d)(3) ("lawful *carrying* of firearms . . . in a Federal facility incident to hunting or other lawful purposes") (emphasis added in all quotations).

the Legislature means.[14] Notably in view of the Legislature's capacity to speak plainly, and of overriding concern, the Court's inquiry pays scant attention to a core reason for the rule of lenity: "[B]ecause of the seriousness of criminal penalties, and because criminal punishment usually represents the moral condemnation of the community, legislatures and not courts should define criminal activity. This policy embodies 'the instinctive distaste against men languishing in prison unless the lawmaker has clearly said they should.' " *United States v. Bass* (quoting H. Friendly, Mr. Justice Frankfurter and the Reading of Statutes, in Benchmarks 196, 209 (1967)). * * *

NOTES AND QUESTIONS ON THE RULE OF LENITY

1. *The Textual Canons and the Rule of Lenity.* Notice how Justices Breyer and Ginsburg deploy the textual canons surveyed in § 1 of this chapter. Among the canons that see action in this battle are the ordinary meaning rule, the dictionary rule, the purpose rule, the absurd results rule, the presumption of consistent usage, the presumption of meaningful variation, the whole act rule, and the whole code rule. In addition, Justice Ginsburg invokes what might be called the "pet fish canon": some words in combination produce a meaning much narrower than one would expect from analyzing the words separately. (A pet is a dog or cat; a fish is salmon or cod; a "pet fish" is a goldfish.)

Notice also the significantly different role played by the rule of lenity in the two opinions. For Justice Ginsburg, lenity is the baseline, and the government has the burden of showing that defendants were not "carrying" guns in connection with their crimes. It is a rather strong baseline in fact, as she agrees that one can "carry" a gun in one's getaway car; her point seems to be that this is not the prototypical meaning of "carry." For Justice Breyer, lenity is the tiebreaker, if needed, after analysis of the statute's text, structure, purpose, and legislative history.

Finally, notice the unusual alignment of Justices. This is not the typical liberal-conservative split. The values enshrined in the rule of lenity— protection of liberty and the nondelegation precept—are ones that cut across ideological lines. And the regulatory values supporting the majority—get guns off the streets and tough punishments against potentially violent criminals—likewise cut across different political commitments.

2. *Does the Rule of Lenity Have Any Bite?* The rule of lenity is both broader and narrower than its distinguished tradition would have it. On the

---

[14] See, e.g., 18 U.S.C.A. § 924(a)(6)(B)(ii) (1994 ed., Supp. II) ("if the person sold . . . a handgun . . . to a juvenile knowing . . . that the juvenile intended to *carry or otherwise possess* . . . the handgun . . . in the commission of a crime of violence"); 18 U.S.C. § 926A ("may lawfully *possess and carry* such firearm to any other place where he may lawfully *possess and carry* such firearm"); § 929(a)(1) ("uses or *carries a firearm and is in possession* of armor piercing ammunition"); § 2277 ("brings, *carries, or possesses* any dangerous weapon") (emphasis added in all quotations).

one hand, it is notable that all the Justices believed the rule of lenity applicable in *Muscarello*, a sentencing case. For most of American history, the rule of lenity was applied only in the context of substantive criminal law, because sentencing was largely a matter of judicial discretion within well-defined statutory confines. In the last 20 years, the law of sentencing has become more complex and less discretionary with judges—and the Supreme Court applied the rule of lenity to criminal sentencing in *United States v. R.L.C.*, 503 U.S. 291 (1992). For an argument that the Court should not apply lenity in this context, see Phillip Spector, *The Sentencing Rule of Lenity*, 33 U. Toledo L. Rev. 511 (2002). The Court has also applied the rule of lenity to civil cases penalizing defendants for violating a criminal-type statute. See, e.g., *Hughey v. United States*, 495 U.S. 411 (1990); *Crandon v. United States*, 494 U.S. 152 (1990).

On the other hand, the Supreme Court does not even mention the rule of lenity in most cases where it clearly applies. Between 1984 and 2006, the Court heard 114 statutory criminal cases and invoked the rule of lenity in only 34 of them (32.5% of the potential cases). Interestingly, when the Court invoked the rule of lenity, the government won 37.8% of the time—in contrast to its win rate of 74.0% when the Court ignored the rule of lenity. See William N. Eskridge Jr. & Lauren E. Baer, *The Continuum of Deference: Supreme Court Treatment of Agency Statutory Interpretations from* Chevron *to* Hamdan, 96 Geo. L.J. 1083, 1115–17 (2008) (empirical study). It is unclear which result "causes" the other—whether the Court only cites the rule of lenity when the defendant loses or whether the rule of lenity actually affects the willingness of the Justices to read criminal statutes the government's way. Because the government's overall win rate in criminal cases (62.2%) is significantly lower than its win rate in civil cases (69.6%), see *id.* at 1117, we are inclined to think that the rule of lenity (or the values/norms it reflects) does have some effect at the Supreme Court level.

3. *The Rule of Lenity and the Dialogue Between Court and Congress.* Perhaps unique among the Court's substantive canons, the rule of lenity serves to create a useful dialogue between the Court and Congress. The reason is that the defendants who benefit from the rule of lenity have poor access to Congress, while the Department of Justice can almost always secure congressional deliberation for its proposals to override the Court when it loses criminal cases. See William N. Eskridge Jr., *Dynamic Statutory Interpretation* 151–54 (1994), and Matthew R. Christiansen & William N. Eskridge Jr., *Congressional Overrides of Supreme Court Statutory Interpretation Decisions, 1967–2011,* 92 Tex. L. Rev. 1317 (2014). Accord, Scalia & Garner, *Reading Law* 299. Thus, even if congressional drafters do not know the rule,[16] the Department of Justice monitors its losses in court and can be trusted to bring important matters to Congress's attention. This

---

[16] The Gluck-Bressman empirical study of congressional drafters found some evidence suggesting the rule of lenity is not widely known to statutory drafters or utilized by them as a background principle. See Gluck & Bressman, *Statutory Interpretation from the Inside: Part I,* 65 Stan. L. Rev. at 946.

political process justification for the rule of lenity seems, on first glance, to support Justice Ginsburg's dissenting view in *Muscarello.* Consider the subsequent history of this issue.

Recall that, just before *Muscarello,* the Court had interpreted the "uses a gun" language of § 924 narrowly in *Bailey.* Soon after the Court's opinion in *Muscarello,* Congress overrode *Bailey* (and *Muscarello,* to some extent) in "An Act to Throttle Criminal Use of Guns," Pub. L. No. 105–386, 112 Stat. 3469 (1998). The new law amended 18 U.S.C. § 924(c)(1) to read as follows:

(c)(1)(A) Except to the extent that a greater minimum sentence is otherwise provided by this subsection or by any other provision of law, any person who, during and in relation to any crime of violence or drug trafficking crime (including a crime of violence or drug trafficking crime that provides for an enhanced punishment if committed by the use of a deadly or dangerous weapon or device) for which the person may be prosecuted in a court of the United States, uses or carries a firearm, or who, in furtherance of any such crime, possesses a firearm, shall, in addition to the punishment provided for such crime of violence or drug trafficking crime—

> (i) be sentenced to a term of imprisonment of not less than 5 years;
>
> (ii) if the firearm is brandished, be sentenced to a term of imprisonment of not less than 7 years; and
>
> (iii) if the firearm is discharged, be sentenced to a term of imprisonment of not less than 10 years.

(B) If the firearm possessed by a person convicted of a violation of this subsection—

> (i) is a short-barreled rifle, short-barreled shotgun, or semiautomatic assault weapon, the person shall be sentenced to a term of imprisonment of not less than 10 years; or
>
> (ii) is a machinegun or a destructive device, or is equipped with a firearm silencer or firearm muffler, the person shall be sentenced to a term of imprisonment of not less than 30 years.

(C) In the case of a second or subsequent conviction under this subsection, the person shall—

> (i) be sentenced to a term of imprisonment of not less than 25 years; and
>
> (ii) if the firearm involved is a machinegun or a destructive device, or is equipped with a firearm silencer or firearm muffler, be sentenced to imprisonment for life.

Brandish is defined in the new § 924(c)(4): "to display all or part of the firearm, or otherwise to make the presence of the firearm known to another person, in order to intimidate that person, regardless of whether the firearm is directly visible to that person." Has the statute been improved? Consider the following problem.

PROBLEM 5–2: APPLYING THE NEW GUN-ENHANCEMENT LAW TO THROTTLE THE CRIMINAL USE OF GUNS

You are the U.S. Attorney for the Southern District of the State of Bliss. The FBI has apprehended, and you are prosecuting, three alleged malefactors who are pleading guilty to various crimes involving the criminal possession and sale of cocaine. For each defendant, the FBI has seized firearms that its agents believe are associated with the crimes in question. You need to figure out whether your office wants to include a sentencing enhancement for each defendant; this can be very useful in plea bargaining with the defendants. What enhancements, if any, apply to the following defendants?

(A) Bartering Defendant. Defendant 1 traded a dozen long-barreled rifles for cocaine; the FBI apprehended him after he had handed over the rifles and taken the money. Does he get an enhancement? If so, how long?

(B) Defendant with a Gun in the Trunk. Defendant 2 drove to a garage, parked his car in the garage, and walked two blocks to an abandoned warehouse, where he sold 100 kilos of cocaine to undercover FBI agents. In the trunk of his car were a dozen long-barreled rifles. Does he get an enhancement? If so, how long?

(C) Butterfingered Defendant. Defendant 3 delivered 100 kilos of cocaine to an abandoned warehouse and sold them to undercover FBI agents. In the process of completing the deal, Defendant 3 became nervous and took a pistol out of his pocket. When he did so, 27 hidden FBI agents all emerged from behind crates and barrels; several of them cried, "Drop your weapon!" Startled, Defendant 3 dropped his gun, and it discharged when it fell on the ground, hitting another drug dealer in the right buttock. Defendant 3 certainly gets an enhancement—but how long?

B. INTERPRETATION TO AVOID CONSTITUTIONAL PROBLEMS

The next substantive canon we introduce, the *canon of constitutional avoidance*, likewise finds its justification in longstanding constitutional values. The canon operates as a presumption that Congress does not intend to enact unconstitutional legislation. The result of applying this presumption is that courts will interpret ambiguous, but potentially unconstitutional, statutes in ways that avoid the constitutional problem. The canon is grounded in separation of powers, respect for Congress's workproduct and the idea that courts should err on the side of saving statutes, rather than striking them down. These values have play outside the statutory interpretation sphere too. In *Ashwander v. TVA*, 345–38 (1936) (Brandeis, J., joined by Stone, Roberts & Cardozo, JJ., concurring), Justice Brandeis famously listed seven different jurisprudential rules that the Court had developed to avoid unnecessary constitutional decisions. See Henry Paul Monaghan, *Of Avoidance, Agenda Control and Other Matters*, 112 Colum. L. Rev. 665 (2012). Apart from the avoidance canon, the best known of the *Ashwander* rules are rules against advisory opinions on constitutional matters and the rule that the Court will always decide a case on statutory grounds instead of constitutional grounds if possible.

You should see the link between the avoidance canon and the rule of lenity. One way to think of the rule of lenity is as a constitutional avoidance rule: We presume that the legislature is loathe to enact unconstitutional criminal statutes, and so will construe criminal penalties narrowly enough so that there is no question that the statute is constitutional as it is construed. Like the rule of lenity, the canon of constitutional avoidance has both proponents and detractors. Consider a couple of recent constitutional avoidance cases, beginning with one in which the link to lenity is explicit.

Jeffrey Skilling v. United States
561 U.S. 358 (2010).

Founded in 1985, Enron Corporation swiftly became the seventh highest-revenue-grossing company in America. Jeffrey Skilling was a longtime Enron officer, its chief executive officer for most of 2001. Less than four months after he resigned, Enron crashed into bankruptcy, and its stock plummeted in value. After an investigation uncovered a conspiracy to prop up Enron's stock prices by overstating the company's financial well-being, the federal government prosecuted dozens of Enron employees, culminating in prosecutions of Skilling and two other top executives. The indictment charged that these three defendants violated several federal criminal statutes when they allegedly engaged in a scheme to deceive investors about Enron's true financial performance by manipulating its publicly reported financial data and making false and misleading statements. Count 1 of the indictment charged Skilling with conspiracy to commit "honest-services" wire fraud, 18 U.S.C. §§ 371, 1343, 1346, by depriving Enron and its shareholders of the intangible right of his honest services. Skilling was convicted of these and other charges, and his conviction was upheld on appeal to the Fifth Circuit.

Section 1343 provided in relevant part:

> Whoever, having devised or intending to devise any scheme or artifice to defraud, or for obtaining money or property by means of false or fraudulent pretenses, representations, or promises, transmits or causes to be transmitted by means of wire, radio, or television communication in interstate or foreign commerce, any

writings, signs, signals, pictures, or sounds for the purpose of executing such scheme or artifice, shall be fined under this title or imprisoned not more than 20 years, or both. * * *

Section 1346, added in 1990 to override a Supreme Court decision narrowly interpreting "scheme to defraud," provided that the statutory " term 'scheme or artifice to defraud' includes a scheme or artifice to deprive another of the intangible right of honest services."

The Supreme Court reversed Skilling's conviction for violating §§ 1343 and 1346. **Justice Ginsburg**'s opinion for the Court on this issue (joined by Chief Justice Roberts and Justices Stevens, Breyer, Alito, and Sotomayor) interpreted § 1346 to be limited to schemes to defraud of honest services only where there have been bribes and kickbacks. Justice Ginsburg started with a review of pre-1987 mail and wire fraud lower-court cases prosecuted under §§ 1341 and 1343 that expanded "scheme to defraud" crimes to include losses of "honest services" and not just losses of tangible property.

As Justice Ginsburg noted, in *McNally v. United States*, 483 U.S. 350 (1986), the Supreme Court had stopped the lower- court development of the intangible rights doctrine "in its tracks"—and Congress "responded swiftly," with new § 1346. Skilling argued that the swift response was too vague to satisfy the Due Process Clause, however. "To satisfy due process, 'a penal statute [must] define the criminal offense [1] with sufficient definiteness that ordinary people can understand what conduct is prohibited and [2] in a manner that does not encourage arbitrary and discriminatory enforcement.' *Kolender* v. *Lawson*, 461 U.S. 352, 357 (1983)." Skilling claimed that § 1346 does not clearly define what behavior it prohibits and its "standardless sweep allows policemen, prosecutors, and juries to pursue their personal predilections," and sought a judgment invalidating the statute. No court of appeals had ruled that § 1346 was void for vagueness, and the Supreme Court agreed that the better path was a narrowing construction rather than striking the statute down entirely.

"It has long been our practice, * * * before striking a federal statute as impermissibly vague, to consider whether the prescription is amenable to a limiting construction. See, e.g., *Hooper v. California,* 155 U.S. 648, 657 (1895) ('The elementary rule is that *every reasonable construction* must be resorted to, in order to save a statute from unconstitutionality.' (emphasis added)). We have accordingly instructed 'the federal courts . . . to avoid constitutional difficulties by [adopting a limiting interpretation] if such a construction is fairly possible.' *Boos,* 485 U.S., at 331; see *United States v. Harriss,* 347 U.S. 612, 618 (1954) ('[I]f the general class of offenses to which the statute is directed is plainly within its terms, the statute will not be struck down as vague. . . . And if this general class of offenses can be made constitutionally definite by a reasonable construction of the statute, this Court is under a duty to give the statute that construction.').'"

Justice Ginsburg then explored the possibility of a narrowing construction based upon the law. "First, we look to the doctrine developed in pre-*McNally* cases in an endeavor to ascertain the meaning of the phrase 'the intangible right of honest services.' Second, to preserve what Congress certainly intended the statute to cover, we pare that body of precedent down to its core: In the main, the pre-*McNally* cases involved fraudulent schemes to deprive another of honest services through bribes or kickbacks supplied by a third party who had not been deceived. Confined to these paramount applications, § 1346 presents no vagueness problem."

Finally, Justice Ginsburg turned to the rule of lenity, holding that if the constitutional analysis left any question, "[f]urther dispelling doubt on this point is the familiar principle that ambiguity concerning the ambit of criminal statutes should be resolved in favor of lenity." Justice Ginsburg rejected the government's suggestion that § 1346 be interpreted also to include cases where there is "undisclosed self-dealing by a public official or private employee—i.e., the taking of official action by the employee that furthers his own undisclosed financial interests while purporting to act in the interests of those to whom he owes a fiduciary duty." Because Skilling's alleged misbehavior did not include charges that he received bribes or kickbacks, Justice Ginsburg reversed his § 1346 conviction and remanded to the lower courts to determine whether the other convictions could stand.

Justice Scalia (joined by Justices Thomas and Kennedy) concurred in the Court's judgment but would have declared § 1346 void for vagueness and therefore would have struck the statute down as unconstitutional. He viewed the Court's surgery on § 1346 to be "not interpretation but invention," the equivalent of judicial crafting of a common law crime, which our nation's constitutional culture has long abjured. *E.g., United States v. Hudson*, 11 U.S. (7 Cranch) 32, 34 (1812). He rejected the canon of constitutional avoidance as inapplicable because the statutory text could not fairly be read to offer a competing constitutional interpretation. "When the constitutionality of a statute is assailed, if the statute be reasonably susceptible of two interpretations, by one of which it would be unconstitutional and by the other valid, it is our plain duty to adopt that construction which will save the statute from constitutional infirmity. * * * Here there is no choice to be made between two 'fair alternatives.' Until today, no one has thought (and there is no basis for thinking) that the honest-services statute prohibited only bribery and kickbacks." Additionally, Justice Scalia wondered what the rewritten/narrowed § 1346 now covered: Does it apply to private officials, such as Skilling, at all? What would constitute a "bribe" or "kickback" (terms that do not appear in the statute but that are now interpolated into it by the majority) in future cases?

National Federation of Independent Business v. Kathleen Sebelius
132 S.Ct. 2566 (2012).

One of the most salient, and controversial, deployments of the avoidance canon in recent years came in the litigation against President Obama's health reform legislation, the Patient Protection and Affordable Care Act of 2010 (ACA). Challengers argued, among other things, that Congress exceeded its powers under the Commerce Clause when it included in the ACA a mandate requiring almost all Americans either to hold health insurance or to pay the IRS a penalty. The Obama Administration justified this exercise of power on the ground that failure to purchase health insurance has ripple effects throughout the national economy (including distorting the insurance market, requiring charity care institutions to pay for health care for the uninsured, and affecting employees' ability to work). The Commerce Clause argument met resistance in the lower federal courts and at oral argument in the Supreme Court, because some jurists were skeptical that Congress's power extended to what they called "inaction" (failure to purchase insurance). The Administration then argued in the alternative: Because the mandate was also a tax, enforceable by the IRS, it could be upheld under Congress's constitutional taxing power, which might be applied to a taxpayer's failure to do something.

Chief Justice Roberts, writing for five Justices, turned to the tax argument to save the statute. "The text of a statute can sometimes have more than one possible meaning. To take a familiar example, a law that reads 'no vehicles in the park' might, or might not, ban bicycles in the park. And it is well established that if a statute has two possible meanings, one of which violates the Constitution, courts should adopt the meaning that does not do so." The Chief Justice found that the "most straightforward reading of the mandate" was a "command" to maintain health insurance. But because he had concluded that Congress did not have such power under the Commerce Clause, the Chief Justice reasoned that it was "therefore necessary to ask whether the Government's alternative reading of the statute—that it only imposes a tax on those without insurance—is a reasonable one."

"The question is not whether that is the most natural interpretation of the mandate, but only whether it is a 'fairly possible' one. * * * As we have explained, 'every reasonable construction must be resorted to, in order to save a statute from unconstitutionality.' *Hooper v. California,*

155 U.S. 648, 657 [1895]. The Government asks us to interpret the mandate as imposing a tax, if it would otherwise violate the Constitution. Granting the Act the full measure of deference owed to federal statutes, it can be so read * * *."

The **Joint Dissent** (by Justices Scalia, Kennedy, Thomas, and Alito) charged the Chief Justice with "sav[ing] a statute Congress did not write," an act of "vast judicial overreaching." The dissenters also charged the Chief Justice with perverting the avoidance canon: "The Court's disposition, invented and atextual as it is, does not even have the merit of avoiding constitutional difficulties. It creates them. The holding that the Individual Mandate is a tax raises a difficult constitutional question (what is a direct tax?) that the Court resolves with inadequate deliberation."

NOTES AND QUESTIONS ON THE AVOIDANCE CANON

1.   *Different Ways of Framing the Avoidance Canon, and the Problem of Advisory Opinions.* Judges and scholars have identified several different ways in which the avoidance canon might be expressed. Most commentators prefer what Professor Nagle calls "classic avoidance," followed by judges in the nineteenth century:[17] When one interpretation of an ambiguous statute *would be* unconstitutional, choose another one that would pass constitutional muster. *Murray v. The Schooner Charming Betsy*, 6 U.S. (2 Cranch) 64 (1804). Chief Justice Roberts' approach in the health reform case exemplifies classic avoidance: Writing only for himself on this issue, the Chief Justice *decided* the constitutional question under the Commerce Clause in the negative and then (with the support of a Court majority) moved onto another interpretation that would avoid the need to strike down an important statute. Since the New Deal, however, what scholars call "modern avoidance" has been deployed by federal judges far more frequently. The modern approach states: When one interpretation *might* raise serious constitutional *problems or doubts*, choose the one that would not. Under modern avoidance, the court does not actually decide the constitutional question before moving to an alternative interpretation. Rather, the court flags a *potential* constitutional question and so moves to an alternative interpretation to avoid having to address it. *United States ex rel. Attorney General v. Delaware & Hudson Co.*, 213 U.S. 366 (1909). Justice Ginsburg's opinion in the Enron case (*Skilling*) articulates the doctrine in precisely this way.

One common justification for the avoidance doctrine is that it avoids unnecessary constitutional holdings and advisory opinions by the Court. Can you see how modern avoidance (*Skilling*) might accomplish this better than classic avoidance (*Sebelius*)? For example, Chief Justice Roberts *did* issue an advisory opinion—he reached the Commerce Clause question even though he

---

[17] John Copeland Nagle, Delaware & Hudson *Revisited*, 72 Notre Dame L. Rev. 1495 (1997). See also Trevor W. Morrison, *Constitutional Avoidance in the Executive Branch*, 106 Colum. L. Rev. 1189 (2006); Adrian Vermeule, *Saving Constructions*, 85 Geo. L.J. 1945 (1997).

did not have to reach it to apply the avoidance doctrine. We now know that there likely are five votes on the Court (Roberts plus the Joint Dissent) for the proposition that Congress cannot regulate inaction through the Commerce Clause, even though that wasn't the "holding" of the case. One risk associated with advisory opinions is that they can be constitutional lawmaking on the cheap. Didn't Roberts get to articulate a very important rule of constitutional law without being stuck with its consequences?

Modern avoidance, on the other hand, often requires the Court to engage in interpretive gymnastics to save a statute that might not really need saving. Finding a constitutional "doubt" is not the same thing as finding a statute unconstitutional. In a case like *Skilling*, the Court effectively decided that the statute *might be* unconstitutional and so rewrote it. But what if the Court had gone ahead and decided the question? If the statute had survived constitutional scrutiny, wouldn't Congress have preferred the original version to stand? (And if you believe that any Court finding a constitutional doubt has really concluded that one interpretation *is* unconstitutional, then there is no real difference between the two formulations of the avoidance doctrine.)

2. *Other Values Underlying the Avoidance Canon.* Consider three other potentially important values that support the avoidance canon, even the broader modern version. First, it may be a rule of thumb for ascertaining legislative meaning. The avoidance interpreter assumes that the legislature would *not* have wanted to press constitutional limits. Fred Schauer, Ashwander *Revisited*, 1995 Sup. Ct. Rev. 71, finds such a theory most implausible. In the average case, why shouldn't the enacting legislature prefer that its work product be given full force—and if it's unconstitutional the Court should say so openly so that there can be a full-blown constitutional controversy? See Jerry L. Mashaw, *Greed, Chaos, and Governance: Using Public Choice Theory To Improve Public Law* 105 (1997). Consider the Enron Case: Is it plausible that Congress would have wanted the Court to trim back the statute in the way that it did in *Skilling*?

A second value of the avoidance canon is that it might provide a low-salience mechanism for giving effect to what Larry Sager calls "underenforced constitutional norms."[18] *Skilling* is an excellent example of this idea: Judges are loathe to strike down statutes on grounds of vagueness, but applying the avoidance canon (or the rule of lenity) allows the Court to enforce an anti-vagueness norm without actually striking down the law. And so the norm is vindicated—but Congress can (re)assert a broader result after deliberation and debate over a statutory amendment that clearly overrides the norm-adhering interpretation.

---

[18] William N. Eskridge Jr. & Philip P. Frickey, *Quasi-Constitutional Law: Clear Statement Rules as Constitutional Lawmaking*, 45 Vand. L. Rev. 593 (1992), drawing from Lawrence Sager, *Fair Measure: The Legal Status of Underenforced Constitutional Norms*, 91 Harv. L. Rev. 1212 (1978); see also Neal Katyal, *Judges as Advicegivers*, 50 Stan. L. Rev. 1709 (1998); Ronald J. Krotoszynski, Jr., *Constitutional Flares: On Judges, Legislatures, and Dialogue*, 83 Minn. L. Rev. 1 (1998); Ernest Young, *Constitutional Avoidance, Resistance Norms, and the Preservation of Judicial Review*, 78 Tex. L. Rev. 1549, 1585–87 (2000).

A third value for the avoidance canon is suggested by Professor Bickel's theory of the passive virtues.[19] One way that courts conserve their institutional capital is by techniques of avoidance. Standard techniques are for the Court to divest itself of constitutional cases whose resolution is premature by dismissing the complaint on procedural grounds such as standing, ripeness, etc. The avoidance canon represents a middle ground between pure passive virtues and constitutional invalidation. That middle ground allows the Court to slow down a political process that is moving too hastily and overriding human rights, but without incurring the full wrath of a political process that doesn't like to be thwarted. See Philip P. Frickey, *Getting from Joe to Gene (McCarthy): The Avoidance Canon, Legal Process Theory, and Narrowing Statutory Interpretations in the Early Warren Court*, 93 Calif. L. Rev. 397 (2005). How might this theory apply to the Enron and ACA Cases?

3. *Criticisms of the Avoidance Canon.* The leading critique of the avoidance canon remains Judge Henry Friendly, *Mr. Justice Frankfurter and the Reading of Statutes*, in *Benchmarks* 211–12 (1967):

> Although questioning the doctrine of construction to avoid constitutional doubts is rather like challenging Holy Writ, the rule has always seemed to me to have almost as many dangers as advantages. For one thing, it is one of those rules that courts apply when they want and conveniently forget when they don't—some, perhaps, would consider that to be a virtue. * * * Some considerations advanced in its favor, such as the awesome consequences of "a decree of unconstitutionality," overlook that if the Court finds the more likely construction to be unconstitutional, another means of rescue—the principle of construing to avoid unconstitutionality—will be at hand. The strongest basis for the rule is thus that the Supreme Court ought not to indulge in what, if adverse, is likely to be only a constitutional advisory opinion. While there is force in this, the rule of "construing" to avoid constitutional doubts should, in my view, be confined to cases where the doubt is exceedingly real. Otherwise this rule, whether it be denominated one of statutory interpretation or, more accurately, of constitutional adjudication—still more accurately, of constitutional nonadjudication—is likely to become one of evisceration and tergiversation.

Judge Friendly's charge is that the avoidance canon will be an occasion for *stealth judicial activism*, which is both anti-democratic and unhealthy for the

---

[19] Alexander M. Bickel, *The Least Dangerous Branch: The Supreme Court at the Bar of Politics* 156–69 (1962). Bickel's ideas about statutory interpretation are set forth in Alexander M. Bickel & Harry H. Wellington, *Legislative Purpose and the Judicial Process: The* Lincoln Mills *Case*, 71 Harv. L. Rev. 1 (1957).

judiciary. This is a serious concern that has been echoed by generations of commentators.[20]

4. *Avoidance and Textual Clarity.* The question of when canons apply is an important one, and most of the time canons are invoked only when statutory text is ambiguous, often as a tiebreaker. In *Skilling*, Justice Ginsburg used lenity and avoidance precisely that way. Justice Scalia opposed those canons in *Skilling* because, in his view, the statutory text wasn't ambiguous but rather was clearly unconstitutional. In a recent case involving the legality of a "straw purchase" of firearms, the positions were reversed, with Justice Scalia finding statutory ambiguity and calling for lenity in dissent, while the majority (through Justice Kagan this time) did not apply the rule because it found the statutory design clear. See *Abramski v. United* States, 134 S.Ct. 2259 (2014).

Consider *Zadvydas v. Davis*, 533 U.S. 678 (2001), a common citation for the avoidance doctrine. *Zadvydas* concerned the removal of noncitizens unlawfully present in the United States. A statute had authorized detention beyond the normal 90-day holding period for certain noncitizens "beyond the removal period." The question in the case was whether this statute authorized the Attorney General to detain a removable noncitizen "indefinitely"—which the majority believed would be unconstitutional, or merely for a period "reasonably necessary to secure the alien's removal." Justice Breyer applied the avoidance canon to save the law, "constru[ing] the statute to contain an implicit 'reasonable time' limitation, the application of which is subject to federal-court review." Justice Kennedy's dissent chastised the majority for applying the avoidance rule where the statutory text was totally clear. The majority, he wrote, "announces it will reject the Government's argument 'that the statute means what it literally says,' but then declines to offer any other acceptable textual interpretation." Was the avoidance doctrine invoked properly in *Zadvydas*?

5. *Avoidance in the Executive Branch.* Judge Friendly's critique of avoidance above takes on greater bite when one considers the fact that most statutory interpretation is accomplished by the executive and not by the judicial branch of government. As explained in Trevor Morrison, *Constitutional Avoidance in the Executive Branch*, 106 Colum. L. Rev. 1189 (2006), presidential, executive, and agency officials rely on the avoidance doctrine when it suits their purposes. Consider the following problem. Which side has the more supportable interpretation of the statute? What light does this exercise shed on the avoidance canon?

---

[20] See, e.g., Richard A. Posner, *The Federal Courts: Crisis and Reform* 285 (1985); Lisa Kloppenberg, *Avoiding Constitutional Questions*, 35 B.C. L. Rev. 1003 (1994); John F. Manning, *The Nondelegation Doctrine as a Canon of Avoidance,* 2000 Sup. Ct. Rev. 223; John Copeland Nagle, Delaware & Hudson *Revisited*, 72 Notre Dame L. Rev. 1495 (1997).

PROBLEM 5–3: PRESIDENTIAL AUTHORITY TO EAVESDROP FOR NATIONAL SECURITY PURPOSES

In the wake of the al Qaeda-organized attacks on the World Trade Center and the Pentagon on September 11, 2001, President George W. Bush authorized the National Security Agency (NSA) to intercept international communications into and out of the United States of persons linked to al Qaeda or related terrorist organizations. The President subsequently explained that his purpose was to "establish an early warning system to detect and prevent another catastrophic terrorist attack on the United States." Department of Justice White Paper, *Legal Authorities Supporting the Activities of the National Security Agency Described by the President*, Jan. 19, 2006, at 5. "[A] two-minute phone conversation between somebody linked to al Qaeda here and an operative overseas could lead directly to the loss of thousands of lives." Presidential Press Conference, Dec. 19, 2005. (Since 9/11, al Qaeda leaders had repeatedly promised to deliver another attack on American soil. The group has done so successfully in Spain, Indonesia, and the United Kingdom since 9/11.)

Because terrorists pose such a huge threat and move quickly from place to place, the President maintained that protocols Congress set in place in 1978 for long-term electronic communications monitoring were no longer appropriate and had to be supplemented with emergency shorter-term measures. NSA activities are "carefully reviewed approximately every 45 days to ensure [they are] being used properly." *Id.* The Attorney General monitors for legality, and NSA officials themselves monitor to assure protection of civil liberties. Civil libertarians assailed the NSA wiretapping program, and Members of Congress expressed concern.

You are the General Counsel to the Senate Judiciary Committee, chaired in 2006 by Senator Arlen Specter (R–PA). Senator Specter wonders whether the NSA program is legal. Senator Specter asks you to tell him whether the NSA program is a legitimate exercise of the President's authority, especially in light of prior legislation. The following materials will help you frame an answer to Senator Specter.[21]

January 9, 2006 Letter from Scholars and Former Government Officials [Curtis A. Bradley et al.] to Congressional Leadership in Response to Justice Department Letter of December 22, 2005.[22] In 1978, Congress enacted the Foreign Intelligence Surveillance Act (FISA). "With minor exceptions, FISA authorizes electronic surveillance only upon certain specified showings, and only if approved by a court. The statute specifically allows for warrantless *wartime* domestic electronic surveillance—

---

[21] These materials are taken from the appendices to David Cole & Martin Lederman, *The National Security Agency's Domestic Spying Program: Framing the Debate*, 81 Ind. L.J. 1363–1424 (2006).

[22] This Letter, 81 Ind. L.J. at 1364–72, was a response to the December 22, 2005 Letter from Department of Justice to the Leadership of the Senate Select Committee on Intelligence and House Permanent Select Committee on Intelligence, *id.* at 1360–63.

but only for the first fifteen days of a war. 50 U.S.C. § 1811. It makes criminal any electronic surveillance not authorized by statute, *id.* § 1809; and it expressly establishes FISA and specified provisions of the federal criminal code (which govern wiretaps for criminal investigation) as the *'exclusive* means by which electronic surveillance . . . may be conducted.' 18 USC § 2511(2)(f) (emphasis added)."

The Department of Justice conceded that FISA did not authorize the NSA program, but argued that the AUMF [Authorization for the Use of Military Force] did. Signed on September 18, 2001, the AUMF empowered the President to use "all necessary and appropriate force against" al Qaeda. According to the DOJ, collecting "signals intelligence" on the enemy, including U.S. phone tapping, is a "fundamental incident of war" authorized by the AUMF.

The scholars advanced several reasons they thought the President was wrong about that: (1) The statute specifically addressing the matter of wiretaps (FISA) governs the more generally phrased law (AUMF), under accepted principles of statutory interpretation. Also, (2) repeals by implication, the effect of the DOJ's broad AUMF interpretation, are disfavored in the law. Finally, (3) Members of Congress advised the Attorney General that legislation amending the FISA to allow this program would not be feasible. "It is one thing, however, to say that foreign battlefield capture of enemy combatants is an incident of waging war that Congress intended to authorize. It is another matter entirely to treat unchecked warrantless *domestic* spying as included in that authorization, especially where an existing statute specifies that other laws are the 'exclusive means' by which electronic surveillance may be conducted and provides that even a declaration of war authorizes such spying only for a fifteen-day emergency period.

" * * * [T]he [old] federal law involving wiretapping specifically provided that '[n]othing contained in this chapter or in section 605 of the Communications Act of 1934 shall limit the constitutional power of the President . . . to obtain foreign intelligence information deemed essential to the security of the United States.' 18 U.S.C. § 2511(3) (1976).

"But FISA specifically *repealed* that provision, FISA § 201(c), 92 Stat. 1797, and replaced it with language dictating that FISA and the criminal code are the 'exclusive means' of conducting electronic surveillance. In doing so, Congress did not deny that the President has constitutional power to conduct electronic surveillance for national security purposes; rather, Congress properly concluded that 'even if the President has the inherent authority *in the absence of legislation* to authorize warrantless electronic surveillance for foreign intelligence purposes, Congress has the power to regulate the conduct of such surveillance by legislating a reasonable procedure, which then becomes the exclusive means by which such surveillance can be conducted.' H.R. Rep. No. 95–1283, pt 1, at 24 (1978).
* * *

"Congress plainly has authority to regulate domestic wiretapping by federal agencies under its Article I powers, and the DOJ does not suggest otherwise. Indeed, when FISA was enacted, the Justice Department agreed that Congress had power to regulate such conduct, and could require judicial approval of foreign intelligence surveillance. [S. Rep. No. 95–604, pt. 1, at 16 (1977), et al.] * * *

U.S. Department of Justice, "Legal Authorities Supporting the Activities of the National Security Agency Described by the President," January 19, 2006.[23] "As Congress expressly recognized in the AUMF, 'the President has authority under the Constitution to take action to deter and prevent acts of international terrorism against the United States,' AUMF pmbl., especially in the context of the current conflict. Article II of the Constitution vests in the President all executive power of the United States, including the power to act as Commander in Chief of the Armed Forces, see U.S. Const. art. II, § 2, and authority over the conduct of the Nation's foreign affairs. As the Supreme Court has explained, '[t]he President is the sole organ of the nation in its external relations, and its sole representative with foreign nations.' *United States v. Curtiss-Wright Export Corp.*, 299 U.S. 304, 319 (1936). In this way, the Constitution gives the President inherent power to protect the Nation from foreign attack, see, e.g., *The Prize Cases*, 67 U.S. (2 Black) 635, 668 (1863), and to protect national security information, *see, e.g.*, *Department of the Navy v. Egan*, 484 U.S. 518, 527 (1988).

"To carry out these responsibilities, the President must have authority to gather information necessary for the execution of his office. The Founders, after all, intended the federal Government to be clothed with all authority necessary to protect the Nation. See, e.g., *The Federalist* * * * No. 41, at 269 (James Madison) ('Security against foreign danger is one of the primitive objects of civil society . . . The powers requisite for attaining it must be effectually confided to the federal councils.'). Because of the structural advantages of the Executive Branch, the Founders also intended that the President would have the primary responsibility and necessary authority as Commander in Chief and Chief Executive to protect the Nation and to conduct the Nation's foreign affairs. See, e.g., *The Federalist* No. 70, at 471–72 (Hamilton); see also *Johnson v. Eisentrager*, 339 U.S. 763, 788 (1950) ('this [constitutional] grant of war power includes all that is necessary and proper for carrying these powers into execution'). Thus, it has long been recognized that the President has the authority to use secretive means to collect intelligence necessary for the conduct of foreign affairs and military campaigns. [*Curtiss-Wright* et al.]

"In reliance on these principles, a consistent understanding has developed that the President has inherent constitutional authority to conduct warrantless searches and surveillance within the United States for foreign intelligence purposes. Wiretaps for such purposes have been authorized by

---

[23] This White Paper, 81 Ind. L.J. at 1374–1414 was a white paper presented by the Department of Justice outlining the legal authority underlying President Bush's expansion of the NSA's surveillance power after September 11.

Presidents at least since the administration of Franklin Roosevelt in 1940. *See, e.g., United States v. United States District Court*, 444 F.2d 651, 669–71 (6th Cir. 1971) (reproducing, as an appendix, memoranda from Presidents Roosevelt, Truman, and Johnson). In a Memorandum to Attorney General Jackson, President Roosevelt wrote on May 21, 1940:

> You are, therefore, authorized and directed in such cases as you may approve, after investigation of the need in each case, to authorize the necessary investigation agents that they are at liberty to secure information by listening devices directed to the conversation or other communications of persons suspected of subversive activities against the Government of the United States, including suspected spies. You are requested furthermore to limit these investigations so conducted to a minimum and limit them insofar as possible to aliens. *Id.* at 670 (appendix A).

President Truman approved a memorandum drafted by Attorney General Tom Clark in which the Attorney General advised that 'it is as necessary as it was in 1940 to take the investigative measures' authorized by President Roosevelt to conduct electronic surveillance 'in cases vitally affecting the domestic security.' *Id.* Indeed, while the FISA was being debated during the Carter Administration, Attorney General Griffin Bell testified that 'the current bill recognizes no inherent power of the President to conduct electronic surveillance, and I want to interpolate here to say that *this does not take away the power [of] the President under the Constitution.*' Foreign Intelligence Electronic Surveillance Act of 1978: Hearings on H.R. 5764 [et al.] Before the Subcomm. on Legislation of the House Comm. on Intelligence, 95th Cong., 2d Sess. 15 (1978) (emphasis added) * * *.

"On September 14, 2001, in its first legislative response to the attacks of September 11th, Congress gave its express approval to the President's military campaign against al Qaeda and, in the process, confirmed the well-accepted understanding of the President's Article II powers. *See* AUMF § 2(a). In the preamble to the AUMF, Congress stated that 'the President has authority under the Constitution to take action to deter and prevent acts of international terrorism against the United States,' AUMF pmbl., and thereby acknowledged the President's inherent constitutional authority to defend the United States. This clause 'constitutes an extraordinarily sweeping recognition of independent presidential *constitutional* power to employ the war power to combat terrorism.' Michael Stokes Paulsen, Youngstown *Goes to War*, 19 Const. Comment. 215, 252 (2002). This striking recognition of presidential authority cannot be discounted as the product of excitement in the immediate aftermath of September 11th, for the same terms were repeated by Congress more than a year later in the Authorization for the Use of Military Force Against Iraq Resolution of 2002. Pub. L. No. 107–243, pmbl., 116 Stat. 1498, 1500 (Oct. 16, 2002) ('The President has authority under the Constitution to take action in order to deter and prevent acts of international terrorism against the United States. . . .'). In the context of the conflict with al Qaeda and related terrorist organizations, therefore, Congress has acknowledged a broad executive authority to 'deter and prevent' further attacks against the United States.

"The AUMF passed by Congress on September 14, 2001, does not lend itself to a narrow reading. Its expansive language authorizes the President 'to use all *necessary and appropriate force* against those nations, organizations, or persons *he determines* planned, authorized, committed, or aided the terrorist attacks that occurred on September 11, 2001.' AUMF § 2(a) (emphasis added). In the field of foreign affairs, and particularly that of war powers and national security, congressional enactments are to be broadly construed where they indicate support for authority long asserted and exercised by the Executive Branch. * * * This authorization transforms the struggle against al Qaeda and related terrorist organizations from what Justice Jackson called 'a zone of twilight,' in which the President and Congress may have concurrent powers whose 'distribution is uncertain,' *Youngstown* (Jackson, J., concurring), into a situation in which the President's authority it at its maximum because 'it includes all that he possesses in his own right plus all that Congress can delegate,' *id.* at 635. With regard to these fundamental tools of warfare—and, as demonstrated below, warrantless electronic surveillance against the declared enemy is one such tool—the AUMF places the President's authority at its zenith under *Youngstown.* * * *

"The Supreme Court's interpretation of the scope of the AUMF in *Hamdi v. Rumsfeld*, 542 U.S. 507 (2004), strongly supports this reading of the AUMF. In *Hamdi*, five members of the Court found that the AUMF authorized the detention of an American within the United States, notwithstanding a statute that prevents the detention of U.S. citizens 'except pursuant to an Act of Congress.' 18 U.S.C. § 4001(a). Drawing on historical materials and 'longstanding law-of-war principles,' a plurality of the Court [Justice O'Connor, writing also for the Chief Justice and Justices Rehnquist and Breyer] concluded that detention of combatants who fought against the United States as part of an organization 'known to have supported' al Qaeda 'is so fundamental and accepted an incident to war as to be an exercise of the "necessary and appropriate force" Congress has authorized the President to use.' *Id.* at 518; *see also id.* at 587 (Thomas, J., dissenting) (agreeing with the plurality that the joint resolution authorized the President to 'detain those arrayed against our troops'); *accord Quirin*, 317 U.S. at 26–29, 38 (recognizing the President's authority to capture and try agents of the enemy in the United States even if they had never 'entered the theatre or zone of active military operations'). Thus, even though the AUMF does not say anything expressly about detention, the Court nevertheless found that it satisfied section 4001(a)'s requirement that detention be congressionally authorized. * * *

"The history of warfare—including the consistent practice of Presidents since the earliest days of the Republic—demonstrates that warrantless intelligence surveillance against the enemy is a fundamental incident of the use of military force, and this history confirms the statutory authority provided by the AUMF. Electronic surveillance is a fundamental tool of war that must be included in any natural reading of the AUMF's authorization to use 'all necessary and appropriate force.' "

The Department argued that, from General Washington onward, American leaders have "intercepted communications for wartime intelligence purposes and, if necessary, ha[ve] done so within [our] own borders." This practice continued during World War II and, according to one historian, "helped to shorten the war by perhaps two years."

" * * * [S]ection 109 of FISA prohibits any person from intentionally 'engag[ing] . . . in electronic surveillance under color of law *except as authorized by statute.*' 50 U.S.C. § 1809(a)(1) (emphasis added). * * * The AUMF qualifies as a 'statute' authorizing electronic surveillance within the meaning of section 109 of FISA. * * * As explained above, it is not necessary to demarcate the outer limits of the AUMF to conclude that it encompasses electronic surveillance targeted at the enemy. Just as a majority of the Court concluded in *Hamdi* that the AUMF authorizes detention of U.S. citizens who are enemy combatants without expressly mentioning the President's long-recognized power to detain, so too does it authorize the use of electronic surveillance without specifically mentioning the President's equally long-recognized power to engage in communications intelligence targeted at the enemy. And just as the AUMF satisfies the requirement in 18 U.S.C. § 4001(a) that no U.S. citizen be detained 'except pursuant to an Act of Congress,' so too does it satisfy section 109's requirement for statutory authorization of electronic surveillance. * * * "

Section 111 of FISA, 50 U.S.C. § 1811, which capped presidential surveillance even in time of war without court authorization at fifteen days, "cannot reasonably be read as Congress's final word on electronic surveillance during wartime. * * * Rather, section 111 represents Congress's recognition that it would likely have to return to the subject and provide additional authorization to conduct warrantless electronic surveillance outside FISA during time of war. * * * Nothing in the terms of section 111 disables Congress from authorizing such electronic surveillance as a traditional incident of war through a broad, conflict-specific authorization for the use of military force, such as the AUMF. * * *

" * * * Nevertheless, some might argue that sections 109 and 111 of the FISA, along with section 2511(2)(f)'s 'exclusivity' provision and section 2511(2)(e)'s liability exception for officers engaged in FISA-authorized surveillance, are best read to suggest that FISA requires that subsequent authorizing legislation specifically amend FISA in order to free the Executive from FISA's enumerated procedures. As detailed above, this is not the better reading of FISA. But even if these provisions were ambiguous, any doubt as to whether the AUMF and FISA should be understood to allow the President to make tactical military decisions to authorize surveillance outside the parameters of FISA must be resolved to avoid the serious constitutional questions that a contrary interpretation would raise.

"It is well established that the first task of any interpreter faced with a statute that may present an unconstitutional infringement on the powers of the President is to determine whether the statute may be construed to avoid the constitutional difficulty. '[I]f an otherwise acceptable construction of a statute would raise serious constitutional problems, and where an alternative interpretation of the statute is "fairly possible," then we are obligated to construe the statute to avoid such problems.' *INS v. St. Cyr*, 533 U.S. 289, 299–300 (2001); *Ashwander v. TVA*, 297 U.S. 288, 345–48 (1936) (Brandeis, J., concurring). Moreover, the canon of constitutional avoidance has particular importance in the realm of national security, where the President's constitutional authority is at its highest. See *Department of the Navy v. Egan*, 484 U.S. 518, 527, 530 (1988); William N. Eskridge Jr., *Dynamic Statutory Interpretation* 325 (1994) (describing '[s]uper-strong rule against congressional interference with the President's authority over foreign affairs and national security')." Therefore, the AUMF should be interpreted broadly, and FISA narrowly, to avoid constructions where FISA would unconstitutionally obstruct the President's commander-in-chief powers.

February 2, 2006 Letter from Scholars and Former Government Officials to Congressional Leadership in Response to Justice Department White Paper of January 19, 2006. The Scholars found no authorization for illegal wiretapping in the AUMF, especially in light of section 111. "An amendment to FISA of the sort that would presumably be required to authorize the NSA program here would be a momentous statutory development, undoubtedly subject to serious legislative debate. It is decidedly *not* the sort of thing that Congress would enact *inadvertently*. As the Supreme Court recently noted, ' "Congress . . . does not alter the fundamental details of a regulatory scheme in vague terms or ancillary provisions—it does not, one might say, hide elephants in mouseholes." ' *Gonzales v. Oregon*, 126 S.Ct. 904, 921 (2006) (quoting *Whitman v. American Trucking Ass'ns*, 531 U.S. 457, 468 (2001))."

Section 111 also distinguishes this situation from that in *Hamdi*. The detention statute in *Hamdi* did not mention detention of citizens in wartime. "Had there been a statute on the books providing that when Congress declares war, the President may detain Americans as 'enemy combatants' *only* for the first fifteen days of the conflict, the Court could not reasonably have read the AUMF to authorize silently what Congress had specifically sought to limit. Yet that is what the DOJ's argument would require here. [See also 18 U.S.C. § 2511(2)(f), which specifies that FISA and the criminal code are the 'exclusive means' by which electronic surveillance can be conducted. DOJ concedes that its interpretation requires an implicit repeal of § 2511, which is strongly disfavored in the law.]

"The argument that conduct undertaken by the Commander in Chief that has some relevance to 'engaging the enemy' is immune from congressional regulation finds no support in, and is directly contradicted by, both case law and historical precedent. *Every* time the Supreme Court has confronted a statute limiting the Commander-in-Chief's authority, it has upheld the statute. No precedent holds that the President, when acting as Commander in Chief, is free to disregard an Act of Congress, much less a *criminal statute* enacted by Congress, that was designed specifically to restrain the President as such. [See, e.g., *Little v. Barreme*, 6 U.S. (2 Cranch) 170 (1804), holding unlawful a presidential seizure of a ship coming *from* France during the Quasi-War with France, when Congress authorized seizure only of ships going *to* France.]

"In fact, as cases such as *Hamdi* and *Rasul* demonstrate, Congress has routinely enacted statutes regulating the Commander-in-Chief's 'means and methods of engaging the enemy.' It has subjected the Armed Forces to the Uniform Code of Military Justice, which expressly restricts the means they use in 'engaging the enemy.' It has enacted statutes setting forth the rules for governing occupied territory. And, most recently, it has enacted statutes prohibiting torture under all circumstances, 18 U.S.C. §§ 2340–2340A, and prohibiting the use of cruel, inhuman, and degrading treatment. Pub. L. No. 109–148, Div. A, tit X, § 1003, 119 Stat. 2739–2740 (2005). These limitations make ample sense in light of the overall constitutional structure. Congress has the explicit power 'To make Rules for the Government and Regulation of the land and naval Forces.' US Const., art. I, § 8, cl. 14. The President has the explicit constitutional obligation to 'take Care that the Laws be faithfully executed,' U.S. Const., art. II, § 3—including FISA. And Congress has the explicit power to 'make all Laws which shall be necessary and proper for carrying into Execution * * * all * * * Powers vested by this Constitution in the Government of the United States, or in any Department or Officer thereof.' U.S. Const., art. I, [§ 8, cl. 18].

"If the DOJ were correct that Congress cannot interfere with the Commander in Chief's discretion in 'engaging the enemy,' all of these statutes would be unconstitutional. Yet the President recently conceded that Congress may constitutionally bar him from engaging in torture. Torturing a suspect, no less than wiretapping an American, might provide information about the enemy that could conceivably help prevent a terrorist attack, yet the President has now conceded that Congress can prohibit that conduct. * * * "

The Letter also argued that FISA does not unduly interfere with the President's ability to gather intelligence. FISA only applies if the target is a U.S. person in the U.S., or where the surveillance "acquisition" occurs in the U.S. 50 U.S.C. § 1801(f)(1)–(2). FISA does not prohibit wiretapping; it only requires approval, including after-the-fact approval so long as the petition is filed within 72 hours. 50 U.S.C. § 1805(f). "As such, the statute cannot reasonably be said to intrude impermissibly upon the President's ability to 'engage the enemy,' and certainly does not come anywhere close to 'prohibit[ing] the President from undertaking actions necessary to fulfill his constitutional obligation to protect the Nation from foreign attack.' DOJ Memo at 35."

NOTES AND QUESTIONS ON THE FISA PROBLEM

Notice how both the Bush-Cheney Administration and its critics were able to muster a large number of textual and substantive canons to support their respective positions. Do the canons line up strongly one way or the other? Notice that the avoidance canon might cut both ways on this issue. The Administration argued that a broad construction of FISA will avoid serious separation of powers problems—but the Scholars argued (in a portion of their letters we have omitted) that a narrow construction of FISA's limits avoided serious Fourth Amendment problems. The Supreme Court has construed the Fourth Amendment to require warrants and probable cause for wiretaps, see e.g., *Katz v. United States*, 389 U.S. 347 (1967), but the Court has never definitively ruled on the Fourth Amendment validity of surveillance to investigate foreign-sponsored terrorist activities. See *United States v. United States District Court*, 407 U.S. 297 (1972) (reserving this issue). Is the avoidance issue a wash in this case?

All things considered, what would be your legal advice to Senator Specter? Did the NSA wiretapping program violate FISA, properly construed? If you suggest to the Chair that the program violated FISA, how might Specter respond to the Administration's unlawful assertion of authority? Can Specter sue an Administration official to stop the program? Are there remedies for illegality available through the legislative process?

Ultimately, Congress expanded the President's statutory authority in the FISA Amendments Act of 2008, Public Law No. 110–261, 122 Stat. 2436 (July 10, 2008). According to classified documents leaked by Edward Snowden in 2013, the Obama Administration's NSA acted in excess of its authority under the 2008 FISA Amendments. Even when the executive branch engages in serious constitutional analysis, its officials may be tempted to color outside the lines. Is there any cure for such actions?

NOTE ON SEVERABILITY

The first cousin of the avoidance doctrine is the *presumption in favor of severability*. This canon states that, if a court finds a portion of a statute unconstitutional, it should presumptively "sever" only the unconstitutional portion, and let as much as possible of the remaining statute stand. The Supreme Court's doctrine regarding severability, however, has followed an unsteady path. Early in the twentieth century, the Court frequently refused to sever unconstitutional portions of regulatory legislation, thereby sweeping the whole statute away. See, e.g., *Carter v. Carter Coal Co.*, 298 U.S. 238 (1936). The New Deal Court abandoned that practice. After 1938, the Court followed a strong presumption of severability and rarely refused to sever unconstitutional provisions from statutes. See, e.g., *Regan v. Time*, 468 U.S. 641 (1984) (plurality opinion).

Nevertheless, the severability doctrine remains something of a puzzle. The Court has not always applied consistent criteria to decide these questions and, instead, applies what have been identified as multiple tests.

Sometimes the Court looks to whether the statute *works* without the severed portion in the way that Congress *intended*. Other times it asks whether Congress would have *enacted* the law absent the severed provisions. Still other times the Court asks whether the remaining provisions are *capable of functioning independently*. And sometimes the Court looks to the presence or absence of a *severability clause* in the statute itself declaring Congress's intentions on this question. (Here is an example of a severability clause: "Any provision of this chapter held to be invalid or unenforceable by its terms, or as applied to any person or circumstance, shall be construed so as to give it the maximum effect permitted by law, unless such holding shall be one of utter invalidity or unenforceability, in which event such provision shall be deemed severable from this chapter and shall not affect the remainder thereof * * *." 6 U.S.C. § 102 (chapter on Homeland Security Organization)).

It should be evident to you that each of these inquiries is not the same. There is a big difference, for instance, between the Court exercising the judgment necessary to decide whether the remaining provisions still function rationally and the Court asking whether Congress would have enacted the statute in the first place without the provision. Are judges competent to evaluate complex policy questions like whether thousand-page statutes can function when a portion is removed? Is it a fair inquiry to ask whether Congress would have enacted the statute without the provision in question?

Take the health reform case as an example. One question briefed by the litigants was whether the insurance mandate could be severed from the rest of the ACA if the Court found the mandate to be unconstitutional. Would removing the mandate distort the insurance market provisions in the Act? This question divided economists as well as lawyers. Asking whether Congress would have enacted the statute without the mandate was a false question—without the mandate, no one thought Congress wouldn't have tried to enact health reform; it simply would have used a different mechanism to get people insured. (Although a Court majority ultimately upheld the individual mandate, the Court struck down a key provision in the Medicaid funding section of the Act, but ruled it severable from the remainder of the law. See *Sebelius,* 132 S.Ct. at 2607–08 (Roberts, C.J., for the Court)).

The leading severability case of the modern era is *Alaska Airlines v. Brock*, 480 U.S. 678 (1987), in which the Court held that an unconstitutional legislative veto provision found in the employee protections title of the Airline Deregulation Act of 1978, 92 Stat. 1705, was severable from the remainder of the title. The Court held:

> [The] relevant inquiry in evaluating severability is whether the statute will function in a *manner* consistent with the intent of Congress. In considering this question in the context of a legislative veto, it is necessary to recognize that the absence of the veto necessarily alters the balance of powers between the Legislative and Executive Branches of the Federal Government. Thus, it is not only appropriate to evaluate the importance of the veto in the original

legislative bargain, but also to consider the nature of the delegated authority that Congress made subject to a veto. Some delegations of power to the Executive or to an independent agency may have been so controversial or so broad that Congress would have been unwilling to make the delegation without a strong oversight mechanism. The final test, for legislative vetos as well as for other provisions, is the traditional one: the unconstitutional provision must be severed unless the statute created in its absence is legislation that Congress would not have enacted. *Id.* at 684.

This seems like a sensible formulation, but its application might be questioned. A unanimous Court in *Alaska Airlines* severed the legislative veto from the employee protections title, even though that title was the only one out of twenty-five in the statute to have a legislative veto attached to it; there was great concern about the title because it would be administered by the Secretary of Labor, not under the normal oversight responsibility of the transportation committees; a primary House sponsor specifically spoke to the importance of the legislative veto to the employee protection title and no one spoke against it. Contrary to the Court, it seems implausible that Congress would have adopted the title without the legislative veto.

Is the *Alaska Airlines* presumption of severability the best baseline under separation of powers precepts? *See* Michael Shumsky, *Severability, Inseverability, and the Rule of Law*, 41 Harv. J. Legis. 227 (2004) (no). One might argue that the presumption facilitates judicial activism. Because the Court can strike down marginal provisions and sever them from the rest of the statute, the dramatic consequences of its judgment are diminished, muting public outrage in cases of judicial usurpation. Also, severability leaves in force a statute that Congress did not pass and the President did not sign. Does that fall athwart *Chadha*? Wouldn't presumptive nullification of the entire statute, or title, often be more appropriate, so that Congress itself could readjust the statutory scheme? See *Califano v. Westcott*, 443 U.S. 76, 93 (1979) (Powell, J., dissenting). Can the presumption of severability be defended as useful to protect private reliance interests that would be unsettled if entire statutes fell because of the invalidity of minor provisions? Another possible justification in favor of the presumption is accountability: Isn't Congress the more appropriate branch to make the tough decisions about what happens to big statutes when a piece is invalidated?

Another angle deepens the mystery. The statute in *Alaska Airlines* had a severability clause. There was some question whether the severability clause covered the title under consideration, but it is significant that the Supreme Court did not resolve that question first and announced its broad test without reference to a severability clause. Isn't it a violation of Article I, § 7 (as construed in *Chadha*) for the Court to ignore a controlling statutory provision? Why shouldn't the "presumption" of severability be conclusive when there is a statutory provision on point? Are there any circumstances under which a court might ignore a severability clause and strike down an entire statute? Cf. *Warren v. Mayor of Charlestown*, 68 Mass. (2 Gray) 84

(1854) (Shaw, C.J.) (refusing to sever when invalid and valid provisions were "so mutually connected with and dependent on each other, as conditions, considerations or compensations for each other" that it would be unreasonable to sever).

C. THE NEW FEDERALISM CANONS

Congress legislates against the backdrop of state law, which traditionally has governed most of our everyday affairs. The Supremacy Clause allows an otherwise constitutional federal statute to displace or "preempt" state law that gets in the way of the operation of those federal schemes. As a result (perhaps surprisingly), a fair amount of statutory litigation involves questions of potential preemption of state law by federal law. See, e.g., *Arizona v. United States,* 132 S.Ct. 2492 (2012) (involving a contentious and well-publicized showdown between the Obama Administration and Arizona's Governor on enforcing federal immigration laws). Although Arizona lost most of its claims to federal preemption, the Supreme Court's lodestar for these cases is a *presumption against federal preemption of traditional state regulatory regimes.* See *Cipollone v. Liggett Group, Inc.,* 505 U.S. 504 (1992) (tort law); *Rose v. Rose,* 481 U.S. 619, 636–37 (1987) (O'Connor, J., concurring) (family law); *BFP v. Resolution Trust Corp.,* 511 U.S. 531 (1994) (property law).

The presumption is an important one. "Absent a clear statutory requirement to the contrary, we must assume the validity of this state-law regulatory background and take due account of its effect." *BFP*, 511 U.S. at 539–40. Furthermore, "[f]ederal statutes impinging upon important state interests 'cannot . . . be construed without regard to the implications of our dual system of government. . . . [W]hen the Federal Government takes over . . . local radiations in the vast network of our national economic enterprise and thereby radically readjusts the balance of state and national authority, those charged with the duty of legislating [must be] reasonably explicit.' " *Id.* at 544 (quoting Felix Frankfurter, *Some Reflections on the Reading of Statutes*, 47 Colum. L. Rev. 527, 539–40 (1947)); accord, *Bond v. United States*, 134 S.Ct. 2077 (2014). Thus, the presumption is based on both congressional intent and democratic accountability: The Court assumes that Congress legislates against the backdrop of state law and puts the onus on Congress to be clear when it intends to disrupt the traditional allocation between state and federal responsibility.

The presumption against preemption is the primary and oldest of the federalism canons (and even it is less than a century old, developed after the New Deal in *Rice v. Santa Fe Elevator Corp., 331 U.S. 218 (1947)*), but new ones have sprouted like wildflowers since 1980. In the last generation, the Court has created or clarified "clear statement rules" or even "super-strong clear statement rules" that reflect constitutional norms of federalism.[24] See *Pennhurst State School & Hospital v. Halderman*, 451 U.S. 1 (1981) (conditions attached to federal funding for state programs must be clear); *Atascadero State Hospital v. Scanlon*, 473 U.S. 234 (1985) (super-strong clear statement rule against congressional abrogation of state Eleventh Amendment immunity from suit in federal courts). As in the case of the other canons, sometimes the Court formulates these doctrines as presumptions or tiebreakers and other times the Court creates a higher burden for preemption, requiring a "clear statement" of Congress's intent to intrude on state authority. Understand these nuances, but also realize that they all aim to effectuate the same constitutionally-derived value. The following case is one of the most dramatic examples of the Court's activity in protecting state sovereignty through the use of canons.

Consider some background first. In *National League of Cities v. Usery*, 426 U.S. 833 (1976), by a 5–4 vote, the Court overruled an earlier precedent and refused to apply the Fair Labor Standards Act's minimum wage and maximum hours provisions to state and municipal employees, on the ground that the Constitution prohibits federal regulation of traditional state functions. *National League of Cities* then met its own apparent demise in *Garcia v. San Antonio Metropolitan Transit Authority*, 469 U.S. 528 (1985), another 5–4 constitutoinal case, which explicitly overruled that nine-year-old precedent and allowed such federal regulation. As the next case demonstrates, what the Court taketh away as constitutional protection it can revive as canonical interpretive protection.

STATUTORY PREFACE TO *GREGORY*

Age Discrimination in Employment Act
29 U.S.C. §§ 621–34

ADEA § 623. Prohibition of Age Discrimination.

(a) Employer practices. It shall be unlawful for an employer—

(1) to fail or refuse to hire or to discharge any individual or otherwise discriminate against any individual with respect to his compensation, terms, conditions, or privileges of employment, because of such individual's age;

---

[24] Recall our terminology: a "clear statement rule" requires that a statute be interpreted a certain way unless the contrary interpretation is clearly required by statutory text; a "super-strong clear statement rule" requires that the statutory text target the issue unmistakably, especially through specific language. See generally William N. Eskridge Jr. & Philip P. Frickey, *Quasi-Constitutional Law: Clear Statement Rules as Constitutional Lawmaking*, 45 Vand. L. Rev. 593 (1992).

(2) to limit, segregate, or classify his employees in any way which would deprive or tend to deprive any individual of employment opportunities or otherwise adversely affect his status as an employee, because of such individual's age; or

(3) to reduce the wage rate of any employee in order to comply with this chapter. * * *

ADEA § 630. Definitions. * * *

(f) The term "employee" means an individual employed by any employer except that the term "employee" shall not include any person elected to public office in any State or political subdivision of any State by the qualified voters thereof, or any person chosen by such officer to be on such officer's personal staff, or an appointee on the policymaking level or an immediate adviser with respect to the exercise of the constitutional or legal powers of the office. The exemption set forth in the preceding sentence shall not include employees subject to the civil service laws of a State government, governmental agency, or political subdivision. The term "employee" includes any individual who is a citizen of the United States employed by an employer in a workplace in a foreign country.

ELLIS GREGORY JR. v. JOHN D. ASHCROFT
Supreme Court of the United States, 1991.
501 U.S. 452, 111 S.Ct. 2395, 115 L. Ed. 2d 410.

JUSTICE O'CONNOR delivered the opinion of the Court.

[It is a *prima facie* violation of the federal Age Discrimination in Employment Act (ADEA), 29 U.S.C. §§ 621–34, for an "employer" covered by the Act to specify a mandatory retirement age for "employees" over forty years of age who are covered by the Act. State and local governments are "employers" covered by the ADEA. In this case, the Missouri Constitution provided a mandatory retirement age of seventy for most state judges. Petitioners were state judges seeking to obtain a declaration that the mandatory retirement age violates the ADEA. The district court dismissed the action, concluding that the judges were "appointees on the policymaking level," a category of state officials excluded from the definition of "employees" covered by the Act. The Court of Appeals affirmed. What follows is Part II of Justice O'Connor's opinion.]

    [II.A]   As every schoolchild learns, our Constitution establishes a system of dual sovereignty between the States and the Federal Government. This Court also has recognized this fundamental principle. In *Tafflin v. Levitt*, 493 U.S. 455, 458 (1990), "[w]e beg[a]n with the axiom that, under our federal system, the States possess sovereignty concurrent with that of the Federal Government, subject only to limitations imposed by the Supremacy Clause." Over 120 years ago, the Court described the constitutional scheme of dual sovereigns:

> " '[T]he people of each State compose a State, having its own government, and endowed with all the functions essential to separate and independent existence,' . . . '[W]ithout the States in union, there could be no such political body as the United States.' Not only, therefore, can there be no loss of separate and independent autonomy to the States, through their union under the Constitution, but it may be not unreasonably said that the preservation of the States, and the maintenance of their governments, are as much within the design and care of the Constitution as the preservation of the Union and the maintenance of the National government. The Constitution, in all its provisions, looks to an indestructible Union, composed of indestructible States." *Texas v. White*, 7 Wall. 700, 725 (1869), quoting *Lane County v. Oregon*, 7 Wall. 71, 76 (1869).

The Constitution created a Federal Government of limited powers. "The powers not delegated to the United States by the Constitution, nor prohibited by it to the States, are reserved to the States respectively, or to the people." U.S. Const., Amdt. 10. The States thus retain substantial sovereign authority under our constitutional system. As James Madison put it:

> "The powers delegated by the proposed Constitution to the federal government are few and defined. Those which are to remain in the State governments are numerous and indefinite. . . . The powers reserved to the several States will extend to all the objects which, in the ordinary course of affairs, concern the lives, liberties, and properties of the people, and the internal order, improvement, and prosperity of the State." The Federalist No. 45, pp. 292–293 (C. Rossiter ed. 1961).

This federalist structure of joint sovereigns preserves to the people numerous advantages. It assures a decentralized government that will be more sensitive to the diverse needs of a heterogenous society; it increases opportunity for citizen involvement in democratic processes; it allows for more innovation and experimentation in government; and it makes government more responsive by putting the States in competition for a mobile citizenry.

Perhaps the principal benefit of the federalist system is a check on abuses of government power. "The 'constitutionally mandated balance of power' between the States and the Federal Government was adopted by the Framers to ensure the protection of 'our fundamental liberties.' " *Atascadero State Hospital v. Scanlon*, 473 U.S. 234, 242 (1985), quoting *Garcia v. San Antonio Metropolitan Transit Authority*, 469 U.S. 528, 572

(1985) (Powell, J., dissenting). Just as the separation and independence of the coordinate Branches of the Federal Government serve to prevent the accumulation of excessive power in any one branch, a healthy balance of power between the States and the Federal Government will reduce the risk of tyranny and abuse from either front. Alexander Hamilton explained to the people of New York, perhaps optimistically, that the new federalist system would suppress completely "the attempts of the government to establish a tyranny":

> "[I]n a confederacy the people, without exaggeration, may be said to be entirely the masters of their own fate. Power being almost always the rival of power, the general government will at all times stand ready to check usurpations of the state governments, and these will have the same disposition towards the general government. The people, by throwing themselves into either scale, will infallibly make it preponderate. If their rights are invaded by either, they can make use of the other as the instrument of redress." The Federalist No. 28, pp. 180–181 (C. Rossiter ed. 1961).

James Madison made much the same point:

> "In a single republic, all the power surrendered by the people is submitted to the administration of a single government; and the usurpations are guarded against by a division of the government into distinct and separate departments. In the compound republic of America, the power surrendered by the people is first divided between two distinct governments, and then the portion allotted to each subdivided among distinct and separate departments. Hence a double security arises to the rights of the people. The different governments will control each other, at the same time that each will be controlled by itself." The Federalist No. 51, p. 323.

One fairly can dispute whether our federalist system has been quite as successful in checking government abuse as Hamilton promised, but there is no doubt about the design. If this "double security" is to be effective, there must be a proper balance between the States and the Federal Government. These twin powers will act as mutual restraints only if both are credible. In the tension between federal and state power lies the promise of liberty.

The Federal Government holds a decided advantage in this delicate balance: the Supremacy Clause. U.S. Const., Art. VI, cl. 2. As long as it is acting within the powers granted it under the Constitution, Congress may impose its will on the States. Congress may legislate in areas traditionally regulated by the States. This is an extraordinary power in a federalist system. It is a power that we must assume Congress does not exercise lightly.

The present case concerns a state constitutional provision through which the people of Missouri establish a qualification for those who sit as their judges. This provision goes beyond an area traditionally regulated by the States; it is a decision of the most fundamental sort for a sovereign entity. Through the structure of its government, and the character of those who exercise government authority, a State defines itself as a sovereign. * * *

Congressional interference with this decision of the people of Missouri, defining their constitutional officers, would upset the usual constitutional balance of federal and state powers. For this reason, "it is incumbent upon the federal courts to be certain of Congress' intent before finding that federal law overrides" this balance. *Atascadero*. We explained recently:

> "[I]f Congress intends to alter the 'usual constitutional balance between the States and the Federal Government,' it must make its intention to do so 'unmistakably clear in the language of the statute.' *Atascadero*; see also *Pennhurst State School and Hospital v. Halderman*, 465 U.S. 89, 99 (1984). *Atascadero* was an Eleventh Amendment case, but a similar approach is applied in other contexts. Congress should make its intention 'clear and manifest' if it intends to pre-empt the historic powers of the States. . . . 'In traditionally sensitive areas, such as legislation affecting the federal balance, the requirement of clear statement assures that the legislature has in fact faced, and intended to bring into issue, the critical matters involved in the judicial decision.'" *Will v. Michigan Dept. of State Police*, 491 U.S. 58, 65 (1989).

This plain statement rule is nothing more than an acknowledgment that the States retain substantial sovereign powers under our constitutional scheme, powers with which Congress does not readily interfere.

In a recent line of authority, we have acknowledged the unique nature of state decisions that "go to the heart of representative government." [Here Justice O'Connor referred to cases holding that, although state exclusion of noncitizens from public employment generally raises serious equal protection questions, the Court has created a "political function" exception and upheld state programs limiting to citizens employment in positions that are "intimately related to the process of democratic self-government."] * * *

These cases stand in recognition of the authority of the people of the States to determine the qualifications of their most important government officials. It is an authority that lies at " 'the heart of representative government.' " It is a power reserved to the States under the Tenth Amendment and guaranteed them by that provision of the Constitution under which the United States "guarantee[s] to every State in this Union a Republican Form of Government." U.S. Const., Art. IV, § 4.

The authority of the people of the States to determine the qualifications of their government officials is, of course, not without limit. Other constitutional provisions, most notably the Fourteenth Amendment, proscribe certain qualifications; our review of citizenship requirements under the political-function exception is less exacting, but it is not absent. Here, we must decide what Congress did in extending the ADEA to the States, pursuant to its powers under the Commerce Clause. See *EEOC v. Wyoming*, 460 U.S. 226 (1983) (the extension of the ADEA to employment by state and local governments was a valid exercise of Congress' powers under the Commerce Clause). As against Congress' powers "[t]o regulate Commerce . . . among the several States," U.S. Const., Art. I, § 8, cl. 3, the authority of the people of the States to determine the qualifications of their government officials may be inviolate.

We are constrained in our ability to consider the limits that the state-federal balance places on Congress' powers under the Commerce Clause. See *Garcia v. San Antonio Metropolitan Transit Authority*, 469 U.S. 528 (1985) (declining to review limitations placed on Congress' Commerce Clause powers by our federal system). But there is no need to do so if we hold that the ADEA does not apply to state judges. Application of the plain statement rule thus may avoid a potential constitutional problem. Indeed, inasmuch as this Court in *Garcia* has left primarily to the political process the protection of the States against intrusive exercises of Congress' Commerce Clause powers, we must be absolutely certain that Congress intended such an exercise. "[T]o give the state-displacing weight of federal law to mere congressional *ambiguity* would evade the very procedure for lawmaking on which *Garcia* relied to protect states' interests." Lawrence Tribe, American Constitutional Law § 6–25, p. 480 (2d ed. 1988).

[II.B]   In 1974, Congress extended the substantive provisions of the ADEA to include the States as employers. At the same time, Congress amended the definition of "employee" to exclude all elected and most high-ranking government officials. Under the Act, as amended:

> "The term 'employee' means an individual employed by any employer except that the term 'employee' shall not include any person elected to public office in any State or political subdivision of any State by the qualified voters thereof, or any person chosen by such officer to be on such officer's personal

staff, or an appointee on the policymaking level or an immediate adviser with respect to the exercise of the constitutional or legal powers of the office." 29 U.S.C. § 630(f).

Governor Ashcroft contends that the § 630(f) exclusion of certain public officials also excludes judges, like petitioners, who are appointed to office by the Governor and are then subject to retention election. The Governor points to two passages in § 630(f). First, he argues, these judges are selected by an elected official and, because they make policy, are "appointee[s] on the policymaking level."

Petitioners counter that judges merely resolve factual disputes and decide questions of law; they do not make policy. Moreover, petitioners point out that the policymaking-level exception is part of a trilogy, tied closely to the elected-official exception. Thus, the Act excepts elected officials and: (1) "any person chosen by such officer to be on such officer's personal staff"; (2) "an appointee on the policymaking level"; and (3) "an immediate advisor with respect to the constitutional or legal powers of the office." Applying the maxim of statutory construction *noscitur a sociis*—that a word is known by the company it keeps—petitioners argue that since (1) and (3) refer only to those in close working relationships with elected officials, so too must (2). Even if it can be said that judges may make policy, petitioners contend, they do not do so at the behest of an elected official.

Governor Ashcroft relies on the plain language of the statute: It exempts persons appointed "at the policymaking level." [The Governor argued that state judges make policy through common law decisions and supervisory authority over the state bar. Moreover, state appellate judges have additional policymaking responsibilities: supervising inferior courts, establishing rules of procedure for the state courts, and developing disciplinary rules for the bar.]

The Governor stresses judges' policymaking responsibilities, but it is far from plain that the statutory exception requires that judges actually make policy. The statute refers to appointees "on the policymaking level," not to appointees "who make policy." It may be sufficient that the appointee is in a position requiring the exercise of discretion concerning issues of public importance. This certainly describes the bench, regardless of whether judges might be considered policymakers in the same sense as the executive or legislature.

Nonetheless, "appointee at the policymaking level," particularly in the context of the other exceptions that surround it, is an odd way for Congress to exclude judges; a plain statement that judges are not "employees" would seem the most efficient phrasing. But in this case we are not looking for a plain statement that judges are excluded. We will not read the ADEA to cover state judges unless Congress has made it clear that judges are *included*. This does not mean that the Act must mention judges explicitly, though it does not. Rather, it must be plain to anyone reading the Act that it covers judges. In the context of a statute that plainly excludes most important state public officials, "appointee on the policymaking level" is sufficiently broad that we cannot conclude that the statute plainly covers appointed state judges. Therefore, it does not.

The ADEA plainly covers all state employees except those excluded by one of the exceptions. Where it is unambiguous that an employee does not fall within one of the exceptions, the Act states plainly and unequivocally that the employee is included. It is at least ambiguous whether a state judge is an "appointee on the policymaking level." * * *

[II.C]   The extension of the ADEA to employment by state and local governments was a valid exercise of Congress' powers under the Commerce Clause. *EEOC v. Wyoming,* 460 U.S. 226 (1983). In *Wyoming,* we reserved the questions whether Congress might also have passed the ADEA extension pursuant to its powers under § 5 of the Fourteenth Amendment, and whether the extension would have been a valid exercise of that power. We noted, however, that the principles of federalism that constrain Congress' exercise of its Commerce Clause powers are attenuated when Congress acts pursuant to its powers to enforce the Civil War Amendments. This is because those "Amendments were specifically designed as an expansion of federal power and an intrusion on state sovereignty." One might argue, therefore, that if Congress passed the ADEA extension under its § 5 powers, the concerns about federal intrusion into state government that compel the result in this case might carry less weight.

By its terms, the Fourteenth Amendment contemplates interference with state authority: "No State shall . . . deny to any person within its jurisdiction the equal protection of the laws." U.S. Const. Amdt. 14. But this Court has never held that the Amendment may be applied in complete disregard for a State's constitutional powers. Rather, the Court has recognized that the States' power to define the qualifications of their officeholders has force even as against the proscriptions of the Fourteenth Amendment.

We return to the political-function cases. In *Sugarman* [*v. Dougall,* 413 U.S. 634, 642 (1973)], the Court noted that "aliens as a class 'are a prime example of a "discrete and insular" minority * * * and that classifications based on alienage are 'subject to close judicial scrutiny.'" The *Sugarman* Court held that New York City had insufficient interest in preventing aliens from holding a broad category of public jobs to justify the blanket prohibition. At the same time, the Court established the rule that scrutiny under the Equal Protection Clause "will not be so demanding where we deal with matters resting firmly within a State's constitutional prerogatives." Later cases have reaffirmed this practice. See [cases concerning the "political-function" exception from strict scrutiny of state classifications disadvantaging aliens]. These cases demonstrate that the Fourteenth Amendment does not override all principles of federalism.

Of particular relevance here is *Pennhurst State School and Hospital v. Halderman*, 451 U.S. 1 (1981). The question in that case was whether Congress, in passing a section of the Developmentally Disabled Assistance and Bill of Rights Act, 42 U.S.C. § 6010 (1982 ed.), intended to place an obligation on the States to provide certain kinds of treatment to the disabled. Respondent Halderman argued that Congress passed § 6010 pursuant to § 5 of the Fourteenth Amendment, and therefore that it was mandatory on the States, regardless of whether they received federal funds. Petitioner and the United States, as respondent, argued that, in passing § 6010, Congress acted pursuant to its spending power alone. Consequently, § 6010 applied only to States accepting federal funds under the Act.

The Court was required to consider the "appropriate test for determining when Congress intends to enforce" the guarantees of the Fourteenth Amendment. 452 U.S. at 16. We adopted a rule fully cognizant of the traditional power of the States: "Because such legislation imposes congressional policy on a State involuntarily, and because it often intrudes on traditional state authority, we should not quickly attribute to Congress an unstated intent to act under its authority to enforce the Fourteenth Amendment." *Ibid.* Because Congress nowhere stated its intent to impose mandatory obligations on the States under its § 5 powers, we concluded that Congress did not do so.

The *Pennhurst* rule looks much like the plain statement rule we apply today. In *EEOC v. Wyoming*, the Court explained that *Pennhurst* established a rule of statutory construction to be applied where statutory intent is ambiguous. In light of the ADEA's clear exclusion of most important public officials, it is at least ambiguous whether Congress intended that appointed judges nonetheless be included. In the face of such ambiguity, we will not attribute to Congress an intent to intrude on state governmental functions regardless of whether Congress acted pursuant to its Commerce Clause powers or § 5 of the Fourteenth Amendment.

[The Court also held that the mandatory retirement requirement for judges did not violate the Equal Protection Clause of the Fourteenth Amendment, rejecting arguments that it was irrational to distinguish between judges who have reached age 70 and younger judges, and between judges 70 and over and other state employees of the same age who are not subject to mandatory retirement.]

JUSTICE WHITE, with whom JUSTICE STEVENS joins, concurring in part, dissenting in part, and concurring in the judgment.

[I]   * * * While acknowledging [the] principle of federal legislative supremacy, the majority nevertheless imposes upon Congress a "plain statement" requirement. The majority claims to derive this requirement from the plain statement approach developed in our Eleventh Amendment cases, see, *e.g., Atascadero,* and applied two Terms ago in *Will.* The issue in those cases, however, was whether Congress intended a particular statute to extend to the States *at all.* In *Atascadero,* for example, the issue was whether States could be sued under § 504 of the Rehabilitation Act of 1973, 29 U.S.C. § 794. Similarly, the issue in *Will* was whether States could be sued under 42 U.S.C. § 1983. In the present case, by contrast, Congress has expressly extended the coverage of the ADEA to the States and their employees. Its intention to regulate age discrimination by States is thus "unmistakably clear in the language of the statute." *Atascadero.* The only dispute is over the precise details of the statute's application. We have never extended the plain statement approach that far, and the majority offers no compelling reason for doing so.

The majority also relies heavily on our cases addressing the constitutionality of state exclusion of aliens from public employment. In those cases, we held that although restrictions based on alienage ordinarily are subject to strict scrutiny under the Equal Protection Clause, the scrutiny will be less demanding for exclusion of aliens "from positions intimately related to the process of democratic self-government." This narrow "political function" exception to the strict scrutiny standard is based on the "State's historical power to exclude aliens from participation in its democratic political institutions." *Sugarman.*

It is difficult to see how the "political function" exception supports the majority's plain statement rule. First, the exception merely reflects a determination of the scope of the rights of aliens under the Equal Protection Clause. Reduced scrutiny is appropriate for certain political functions because "the right to govern is reserved to citizens." This conclusion in no way establishes a method for interpreting rights that are statutorily created by Congress, such as the protection from age discrimination in the ADEA. Second, it is one thing to limit *judicially created* scrutiny, and it is quite another to fashion a restraint on *Congress'* legislative authority, as does the majority; the latter is both counter-majoritarian and an intrusion on a coequal branch of the Federal Government. Finally, the majority does not explicitly restrict its rule to "functions that go to the heart of representative government," 413 U.S. at 647, and may in fact be extending it much further to all "state governmental functions." [Quoting majority opinion.]

The majority's plain statement rule is not only unprecedented, it directly contravenes our decisions in *Garcia v. San Antonio Metropolitan Transit Authority* and *South Carolina v. Baker*, 485 U.S. 505 (1988). In those cases we made it clear "that States must find their protection from congressional regulation through the national political process, not through judicially defined spheres of unregulable state activity." *Id.* at 512. We also rejected as "unsound in principle and unworkable in practice" any test for state immunity that requires a judicial determination of which state activities are "traditional," "integral," or "necessary." *Garcia,* 469 U.S. at 546. The majority disregards those decisions in its attempt to carve out areas of state activity that will receive special protection from federal legislation.

The majority's approach is also unsound because it will serve only to confuse the law. First, the majority fails to explain the scope of its rule. Is the rule limited to federal regulation of the qualifications of state officials? Or does it apply more broadly to the regulation of any "state governmental functions"? [Quoting majority opinion.] Second, the majority does not explain its requirement that Congress' intent to regulate a particular state activity be "plain to anyone reading [the federal statute]." Does that mean that it is now improper to look to the purpose or history of a federal statute in determining the scope of the statute's limitations on state activities? If so, the majority's rule is completely inconsistent with our pre-emption jurisprudence. See, *e.g.,* *Hillsborough County v. Automated Medical Laboratories, Inc.,* 471 U.S. 707, 715 (1985) (pre-emption will be found where there is a "clear and manifest *purpose*" to displace state law) (emphasis added). The vagueness of the majority's rule undoubtedly will lead States to assert that various federal statutes no longer apply to a wide variety of State activities if Congress has not expressly referred to those activities in the statute. Congress, in turn, will be forced to draft long and detailed lists of which particular state functions it meant to regulate.

The imposition of such a burden on Congress is particularly out of place in the context of the ADEA. Congress already has stated that all "individual[s] employed by any employer" are protected by the ADEA unless they are expressly excluded by one of the exceptions in the definition of "employee." See 29 U.S.C. § 630(f). The majority, however, turns the statute on its head, holding that state judges are not protected by the ADEA because "Congress has [not] made it clear that judges are included." * * *

The majority asserts that its plain statement rule is helpful in avoiding a "potential constitutional problem." It is far from clear, however, why there would be a constitutional problem if the ADEA applied to state judges, in light of our decisions in *Garcia* and *Baker,* discussed above. As long as "the national political *process* did not operate in a defective manner, the Tenth Amendment is not implicated." *Baker.* There is no claim in this case that the political process by which the ADEA was extended to state employees was inadequate to protect the States from being "unduly burden[ed]" by the Federal Government. In any event, as discussed below, a straightforward analysis of the ADEA's definition of "employee" reveals that the ADEA does not apply here. Thus, even if there were potential constitutional problems in extending the ADEA to state judges, the majority's proposed plain statement rule would not be necessary to avoid them in this case. Indeed, because this case can be decided purely on the basis of statutory interpretation, the majority's announcement of its plain statement rule, which purportedly is derived from constitutional principles, *violates* our general practice of avoiding the unnecessary resolution of constitutional issues.

My disagreement with the majority does not end with its unwarranted announcement of the plain statement rule. Even more disturbing is its treatment of Congress' power under § 5 of the Fourteenth Amendment. Section 5 provides that "[t]he Congress shall have power to enforce, by appropriate legislation, the provisions of this article." Despite that sweeping constitutional delegation of authority to Congress, the majority holds that its plain statement rule will apply with full force to legislation enacted to enforce the Fourteenth Amendment. The majority states: "In the face of . . . ambiguity, we will not attribute to Congress an intent to intrude on state governmental functions *regardless of whether Congress acted pursuant to its Commerce Clause powers or § 5 of the Fourteenth Amendment.*" (Emphasis added).

The majority's failure to recognize the special status of legislation enacted pursuant to § 5 ignores that, unlike Congress' Commerce Clause power, "[w]hen Congress acts pursuant to § 5, not only is it exercising legislative authority that is plenary within the terms of the constitutional grant, it is exercising that authority under one section of a constitutional Amendment whose other sections by their own terms embody limitations on state authority." *Fitzpatrick v. Bitzer,* 427 U.S. 445, 456 (1976). Indeed, we have held that "principles of federalism that might otherwise be an obstacle to congressional authority are necessarily overridden by the power to enforce the Civil War Amendments 'by appropriate legislation.' Those Amendments were specifically designed as an expansion of federal power and an intrusion on state sovereignty." *City of Rome v. United States,* 446 U.S. 156, 179 (1980).

The majority relies upon *Pennhurst State School and Hospital v. Halderman,* but that case does not support its approach. There, the Court merely stated that "we should not quickly attribute to Congress an unstated intent to act under its authority to enforce the Fourteenth Amendment." In other words, the *Pennhurst* presumption was designed only to answer the question whether a particular piece of legislation was enacted pursuant to § 5. That is very different from the majority's apparent holding that even when Congress *is* acting pursuant to § 5, it nevertheless must specify the precise details of its enactment.

The majority's departures from established precedent are even more disturbing when it is realized, as discussed below, that this case can be affirmed based on simple statutory construction.

[II] The statute at issue in this case is the ADEA's definition of "employee," which provides:

> "The term 'employee' means an individual employed by any employer except that the term 'employee' shall not include any person elected to public office in any State or political subdivision of any State by the qualified voters thereof, or any person chosen by such officer to be on such officer's personal staff, or an appointee on the policymaking level or an immediate adviser with respect to the exercise of the constitutional or legal powers of the office. The exemption set forth in the preceding sentence shall not include employees subject to the civil service laws of a State government, governmental agency, or political subdivision." 29 U.S.C. § 630(f).

A parsing of that definition reveals that it excludes from the definition of "employee" (and thus the coverage of the ADEA) four types of (non-civil service) state and local employees: (1) persons elected to public office; (2) the personal staff of elected officials; (3) persons appointed by elected officials to be on the policymaking level; and (4) the immediate advisers of elected officials with respect to the constitutional or legal powers of the officials' offices.

The question before us is whether petitioners fall within the third exception. * * * [I] conclude that petitioners are "on the policymaking level."

"Policy" is defined as "a definite course or method of action selected (as by a government, institution, group, or individual) from among alternatives and in the light of given conditions to guide and usu[ally] determine present and future decisions." Webster's Third New International Dictionary 1754 (1976). Applying that definition, it is clear that the decisionmaking engaged in by common-law judges, such as petitioners, places them "on the policymaking level." In resolving disputes, although judges do not operate with unconstrained discretion, they do choose "from among alternatives" and elaborate their choices in order "to guide and . . . determine present and future decisions." * * *

Moreover, it should be remembered that the statutory exception refers to appointees "on the policymaking level," not "policymaking employees." Thus, whether or not judges actually *make* policy, they certainly are on the same *level* as policymaking officials in other branches of government and therefore are covered by the exception. * * *

Petitioners argue that the "appointee[s] on the policymaking level" exception should be construed to apply "only to persons who advise or work closely with the elected official that chose the appointee." In support of that claim, petitioners point out that the exception is "sandwiched" between the "personal staff" and "immediate adviser" exceptions in § 630(f), and thus should be read as covering only similar employees.

Petitioners' premise, however, does not prove their conclusion. It is true that the placement of the "appointee" exception between the "personal staff" and "immediate adviser" exceptions suggests a similarity among the three. But the most obvious similarity is simply that each of the three sets of employees [is] connected in some way with elected officials: the first and third sets have a certain working relationship with elected officials, while the second is *appointed* by elected officials. There is no textual support for concluding that the second set must *also* have a close working relationship with elected officials. Indeed, such a reading would tend to make the "appointee" exception superfluous since the "personal staff" and "immediate adviser" exceptions would seem to cover most appointees who are in a close working relationship with elected officials.

Petitioners seek to rely on legislative history, but it does not help their position. There is little legislative history discussing the definition of "employee" in the ADEA, so petitioners point to the legislative history of the identical definition in Title VII, 42 U.S.C. § 2000e(f). If anything, that history tends to confirm that the "appointee[s] on the policymaking level" exception was designed to exclude from the coverage of the ADEA all high-level appointments throughout state government structures, including judicial appointments. * * *

[The dissenting opinion of JUSTICE BLACKMUN, joined by JUSTICE MARSHALL, is omitted.]

NOTES AND QUESTIONS ON THE FEDERALISM CANON

1. *Where Did the "Federalism Canon" in* Gregory *Come From?* Justice O'Connor created the new "plain statement rule"—that "[i]n the face of * * * ambiguity, we will not attribute to Congress an intent to intrude on state governmental functions"—herself! Much like a common-law judge, she reasoned from other federalism-protecting rules, such as the *Pennhurst* rule that Congress must be clear if it wishes to attach strings to states' receipt of federal programmatic funds, to extend analogous protection to "state governmental functions." Does the Court have the power to make up new canons as it goes along? What has come to be known as *Gregory*'s "federalism canon" is not so different from the presumption against preemption. The

main differences are that the federalism canon, because it is phrased as a clear statement rule, may be a stronger formulation and that the presumption against preemption generally only applies when there is existing state law out there for the federal statute to displace, whereas the federalism canon applies whenever Congress treads into the arena of state government functions regardless of whether state law already governs it.

2. *Did the Court Need the Federalism Canon at All?* As Justice O'Connor noted, there is a respectable textual argument that the ADEA exceptions do not apply to appointed judges, in part because of the *noscitur a sociis* canon. But note that every other potential source of statutory meaning points in the other direction. See Philip P. Frickey, *Lawnet: The Case of the Missing (Tenth) Amendment*, 75 Minn. L. Rev. 755 (1990).

Consider first the absurd-result exception to the plain meaning approach. On the face of it, the exceptions provision to the ADEA seems to take elected judges completely out of the statute (and thus they can be required to step down at age 70), but protects appointed judges against any retirement requirement. This seems absolutely backwards from any public policy perspective: if superannuated judges are to remain in authority, presumably that judgment should be made by the voters on a judge-by-judge basis, not as a categorical decision made by Congress. Why would Congress want to hogtie states in this manner? On the other hand, is this result "absurd" or just "unreasonable"? Is the apparent distinction between elected and appointed judges so irrational as to raise a serious constitutional question that should be avoided through statutory construction?

Other sources strongly cut against the apparent plain meaning of the ADEA exceptions provision as well. The statutory purpose, irrelevant to Justice O'Connor's super-strong clear statement approach, seems narrower than the plain meaning of the exception. The ADEA was designed to protect workers from being replaced by younger employees who would accept lower pay, and had little to do with persons who possess guaranteed tenure and who would be replaced by persons receiving the same salary. From the standpoint of public values, as Justice O'Connor suggests, the people of the state ought to be able to choose how to structure important governmental positions. But this need not lead to the creation of a clear statement rule: any kind of canon, like an ordinary presumption, would surely be sufficient to tip the case to the conclusion Justice O'Connor desired. Why create the canonical equivalent of a nuclear weapon when a fly swatter would have been sufficient?

3. *When Does the Canon Apply? What Does It Require?* As Justice White stressed, it is by no means clear what Congress must do to comply with the *Gregory* canon. Must Congress rely upon its legislative authority under § 5 of the Fourteenth Amendment, or may it rely upon its commerce power as well? To what kinds of state governmental operations does the canon apply? In *Garcia,* one justification for overruling *National League of Cities* was that the standard identified there for state immunity from federal regulation—the

federal government could not "directly displace the States' freedom to structure integral operations in areas of traditional government functions"—proved too vague for any consistent application in the lower courts. Is the *Gregory* canon any easier for lower courts to apply?

One would think that, at a minimum, the canon applies with full force to federal regulation of state judges. One would be wrong. In *Chisom v. Roemer* (Chapter 4, § 3), the Court applied § 2 of the Voting Rights Act to the election of state judges without any mention of the *Gregory* canon. Justice O'Connor was in the majority in *Chisom* (and, of course, the author of *Gregory*). Ironically, *Gregory* and *Chisom* were decided on the same day! Justice Scalia's *Chisom* dissent, however, discussed *Gregory*:

> If the [*Gregory*] principle were applied here, we would have double reason to give "representatives" its ordinary meaning. It is true, however, that in *Gregory* interpreting the statute to include judges would have made them the only high-level state officials affected, whereas here the question is whether judges were excluded from a general imposition upon state elections that unquestionably exists; and in *Gregory* it was questionable whether Congress was invoking its powers under the Fourteenth Amendment (rather than merely the Commerce Clause), whereas here it is obvious. Perhaps those factors suffice to distinguish the two cases. Moreover, we tacitly rejected a "plain statement" rule as applied to unamended § 2 in *City of Rome v. United States*, 446 U.S. 156 (1980), though arguably that was before the rule had developed the significance it currently has. I am content to dispense with the "plain statement" rule in the present case[,] but it says something about the Court's approach to today's decision that the possibility of applying that rule never crossed its mind.

Fairly read, is *Gregory* susceptible to the potential distinctions between it and *Chisom* that Justice Scalia suggests? If not, are the two cases simply irreconcilable? By the way, what is Justice Scalia doing when he joins the values-packed O'Connor opinion, rather than the more simply textualist White concurring opinion?[25]

4. *New Federalism Canons: Stealth Judicial Activism?* Another concern is whether the use of such rules may actually encourage judicial activism because it seems far easier to use them than to do constitutional

---

[25] Critics could suggest that cases like *Gregory* demonstrate that textualism fails to live up to its promise of providing objective interpretive methods in the face of outcomes judges cannot tolerate. In other words, every human interpretive technique, including textualism, needs a "safety valve" of some sort. For liberals, the *Holy Trinity* "purpose trumps plain meaning" approach sometimes serves this purpose. For conservative textualists who care about federalism, the safety valve when textualism gets them boxed in, as in *Gregory*, is the creation of a canon that tips the scales or, in the case of super-strong clear statement rule, is a trump card. Is it fair to say that *Gregory* undercuts the textualist principle of constraining judicial discretion in interpretation? Is it fair to go even further and suggest that *Gregory* and *Chisom*, when read together, undermine the very notion of predictability and coherence in interpretation?

decisionmaking.[26] If the Supreme Court had struck down the ADEA provision as a violation of the Tenth Amendment, you can be sure that the *New York Times* would have given the case front-page treatment; probably, a certain amount of controversy would have ensued. By announcing results such as this in statutory, rather than constitutional decisions, the Court avoided any serious public scrutiny or controversy.

There is also a practical concern with the Court's aggressive application of the federalism canons. One important factor in assessing any theory of statutory interpretation is whether it is compatible with the assumptions about law held by other legal actors (the Congress, the President, attorneys, citizens). The federalism canons, as currently deployed, fare poorly, according to the empirical study of congressional drafters conducted by Abbe R. Gluck & Lisa Schultz Bressman, *Statutory Interpretation from the Inside: An Empirical Study of Congressional Drafting, Delegation, and the Canons: Part I*, 65 Stan. L. Rev. 901 (2013). According to Gluck and Bressman, only 28.4% of the professional staff said they could name a single one of the clear statement rules—and when asked to name one, only 4% of those staff members were able to correctly identify such a rule, with none able to identify any of the federalism clear statement rules. Even the preemption canon was not well understood; a mere 5.84% of the respondents correctly identified the presumption as protecting state law, with double that number (11.68%) believing the presumption went the other way (in favor of federal law), and the rest stating they did not know in which direction the presumption cut. *Id.* at 942–45.

The new federalism canons have another important effect, from a democratic perspective. That is, earlier Congresses arguably relied on the Court's normal approach, before the Justices gave sharper teeth to the federalism canons. When the Court changes the rules applicable to statutes along important dimensions like this, it may be betraying congressional reliance interests. Consider an example. The Education of the Handicapped Act (EHA) is a comprehensive statutory scheme to assure that disabled children may receive a free public education appropriate to their needs. The Act guarantees parental rights to participate in state planning of their children's educational needs and to challenge state plans they don't like. The statute imposes pervasive obligations on state and local governments, and it provides that "[a]ny party aggrieved by the findings and decision [made in the state or local administrative process] shall have the right to bring a civil action . . . in any State court of competent jurisdiction or in a district court of the United States without regard to the amount in controversy." 20 U.S.C. § 1415(i)(2)(A). EHA's sponsor made it clear "that a parent or guardian may present a complaint alleging that a State or local educational agency has refused to provide services to which a child may be entitled" and may sue

---

[26] *See* William N. Eskridge Jr. & Philip P. Frickey, *The Supreme Court, 1993 Term—Foreword: Law as Equilibrium*, 108 Harv. L. Rev. 4 (1994), criticizing *BFP* and related decisions as examples of stealth constitutionalism.

state and local governments in state or federal court. 121 Cong. Rec. 37415 (1975).

When the EHA was enacted in 1975, the above-noted evidence would probably have sufficed to abrogate the states' Eleventh Amendment immunity from suit in federal court, pursuant to *Employees v. Missouri Dep't of Public Health & Welfare*, 411 U.S. 279 (1973) (general jurisdictional grant plus explicit legislative history would be sufficient to abrogate Eleventh Amendment immunity). In *Atascadero State Hospital v. Scanlon*, 473 U.S. 234, 241 (1985), however, the Court changed the rule for congressional abrogation of Eleventh Amendment immunity: "Congress may abrogate the States' constitutionally secured immunity from suit in federal court only by making its intention unmistakably clear in the language of the statute." The Court held that the Rehabilitation Act of 1973, another statute protecting the disabled, did not abrogate states' immunity, because there was no clear textual indication of such abrogation.

Sensing that the rules had changed, and reacting to the Court's restrictive interpretation of the Rehabilitation Act, Congress in 1986 enacted the following: "A State shall not be immune under the Eleventh Amendment * * * from suit in Federal Court for a violation of [enumerated provisions of the Rehabilitation Act], or the provisions of any other Federal statute prohibiting discrimination by recipients of Federal financial assistance." The latter clause clearly covers the EHA. Then, in *Dellmuth v. Muth*, 491 U.S. 223 (1989), a case that arose before the 1986 amendment, the Court held that the EHA did not abrogate state immunity. The Court pointed to the 1986 statute as a good example of the drafting clarity needed to abrogate immunity, and held that there was no abrogation before 1986.

Poor Congress. It thought it had abrogated state immunity in 1975, and given precedent in 1975 it probably had done so. Then it reiterated its intent in 1986, but the new statute was used by the Court to confirm Congress's failure to abrogate in 1975. This might be amusing if important rights were not involved.[27] This type of bait-and-switch is an issue every time the Court changes its interpretive rules but insists on applying the new interpretive rules to old statutes. As another example, whereas the Court used to take a more purposive approach to finding private rights of action in federal statutes, it now applies a very textual approach, and not one consistent with the assumptions underlying the drafting of older statutes.

As the Court mentioned, a slew of federalism-favoring canons accompany *Gregory*'s doctrine. What is important to recognize is that, unlike constitutional doctrines, which have hard boundaries, these statutory interpretation norms *do not prevent Congress from legislating in state domains*; instead they put a burden on Congress to be extra *clear*—effectively

---

[27] Congress immediately overrode *Dellmuth* in the Education of the Handicapped Act of 1990, Pub. L. No. 101–476, § 103, 104 Stat. 1103, 1106, again with complaints that its expectations had been thwarted. It took Congress three statutes to effectuate a policy it thought had been effectuated in 1975.

requiring an additional vetogate or extra deliberation. *Atascadero*'s clear statement rule requires abrogation of state immunity in the statute's text, without regard to legislative history, but the abrogation must be explicit and really clear. See, e.g., *Kiobel v. Royal Dutch Petroleum Co.*, 133 S.Ct. 1659 (2013); *Hoffman v. Conn. Dep't of Income Maintenance*, 492 U.S. 96 (1989); *Will v. Mich. Dep't of State Police*, 491 U.S. 58 (1989). Other new canons that the Court has created include a toughened rule against waivers of federal sovereign immunity, *United States v. Nordic Village*, 503 U.S. 30 (1992); the recently fortified rule against extraterritorial application of federal statutes, *EEOC v. Arabian Am. Oil Co.*, 499 U.S. 244 (1991); the rule against congressional derogation of traditional presidential powers, *Japan Whaling Ass'n v. Am. Cetacean Society*, 478 U.S. 221 (1986); and the rule that congressional conditions of grants to the states be explicit and clear, *Pennhurst State Sch. and Hosp. v. Halderman*, 451 U.S. 1 (1981).

5. *The Federalism Canon and Ambiguity.* Just as we saw in our discussion of the rule of lenity, the question of when the canon is to be triggered arises in the federalism context, too. Consider the Court's recent decision in *Bond v. United States*, 134 S.Ct. 2077 (2014), which concerned the reach of the Chemical Weapons Convention Implementation Act to violence attempted in the context of a local love triangle. The case was closely watched by constitutional lawyers and foreign affairs experts, who were expecting a major separation of powers opinion. Instead, the Court went down a similar path as it did in *Gregory*, resolving the high-profile matter through the much lower-profile route of applying the federalism canon. In dissent, Justice Scalia, generally a supporter of the canon, argued that the statutory text was clear, leaving no room for what the Court presented as a presumption. Note the importance of how the canon is framed: Had the federalism canon in *Bond* been set out as a super-strong clear statement rule, Justice Scalia would have been looking for a specific statement that local crimes were included. Instead, by framing the canon as basic presumption , as in the lenity context, ambiguity becomes the trigger.

6. *Federalism from Federal Statutes.* Professor Young embraces canons like the *Gregory* canon, finding them to form the fabric of what he calls "Constitution outside the Constitution"—a set of "soft" constitutional norms that inform our everyday understandings of the structure of our government and the allocation of power. Ernest A. Young, *The Constitution Outside the Constitution*, 117 Yale L.J. 408, 424 (2007). Decisions about the reach of federal statutes, Young argues, "are "no less 'constitutive' of our governmental structure" than the lines drawn in constitutional law cases." *Id.* at 432; *see* William N. Eskridge Jr. & John Ferejohn, *A Republic of Statutes* (2010) (arguing how some statutes have come to function as "small c" constitutional law).

Professor Gluck goes further, arguing that the states' continuing relevance in the post-New Deal Era comes from not from constitutional divisions of state and federal authority but, rather, from the role that states play *from the inside of federal statutes* in implementing them. Because

Congress can preempt state law as long as the federal statute is clear, Gluck argues that federal statutes can now extend virtually anywhere and so states exert their greatest leverage when they have roles to play in federal schemes. So understood, in Gluck's view, federalism now comes from federal statutes; at the grace of a Congress that can design statutes with a prominent role for the states or that can leave states out in the cold entirely. See Abbe R. Gluck, *Our [National] Federalism*, 123 Yale L.J. 1996 (2014); Abbe R. Gluck, *Federalism from Federal Statutes*, 81 Fordham L. Rev. 1749 (2013). If Gluck is right, then the future of federalism may depend on even more—and better—interpretive rules of statutory federalism.

3. DO THE CANONS CONTRIBUTE POSITIVELY TO A PREDICTABLE AND COHERENT RULE OF LAW?

A fundamental debate has bedeviled the canons for more than half a century. Their defenders and fans hail the canons, especially the textual canons, as contributing to the predictability, objectivity, and transparency of the rule of law. One way of putting the case is this: as a collection of presumptions and rules, the canons form an *interpretive regime* within which lawyers in our culture can approach statutes. See William N. Eskridge Jr. & John Ferejohn, *Politics, Interpretation, and the Rule of Law*, in *The Rule of Law* 265, 281–85 (Ian Shapiro ed., 1994).

Critics of the canons view them as little or nothing more than window-dressing for dispositions made for other reasons, often hidden ones. As post-hoc add-ons, the canons do not constrain—instead, they conceal the real reasons judges or agencies are interpreting statutes in a particular way. Let us start our examination with the most famous law review article ever written about statutory interpretation.

KARL LLEWELLYN, *REMARKS ON THE THEORY OF APPELLATE DECISION AND THE RULES OR CANONS ABOUT HOW STATUTES ARE TO BE CONSTRUED*
3 Vand. L. Rev. 395, 401–06 (1950).[28]

When it comes to presenting a proposed construction in court, there is an accepted conventional vocabulary. As in argument over points of case-law, the accepted convention still, unhappily, requires discussion as if only one single correct meaning could exist. Hence there are two opposing canons on almost every point. An arranged selection is appended. Every lawyer must be familiar with them all: they are still needed tools of argument. At least as early as Fortescue the general picture was clear, on this, to any eye which would see.

---

[28] Reprinted by permission.

Plainly, to make any canon take hold in a particular instance, the construction contended for must be sold, essentially, by means other than the use of the canon: The good sense of the situation and a *simple* construction of the available language to achieve that sense, *by tenable means, out of the statutory language.*

Canons of Construction

Statutory interpretation still speaks a diplomatic tongue. Here is some of the technical framework for maneuver.

Thrust	**But**	**Parry**
1. A statute cannot go beyond its text.		1. To effect its purpose a statute may be implemented beyond its text.
2. Statutes in derogation of the common law will not be extended by construction.		2. Such acts will be liberally construed if their nature is remedial.
3. Statutes are to be read in the light of the common law and a statute affirming a common law rule is to be construed in accordance with the common law.		3. The common law gives way to a statute which is inconsistent with it and when a statute is designed as a revision of a whole body of law applicable to a given subject it supersedes the common law.
4. Where a foreign statute which has received construction has been adopted, previous construction is adopted too.		4. It may be rejected where there is conflict with the obvious meaning of the statute or where the foreign decisions are unsatisfactory in reasoning or where the foreign interpretation is not in harmony with the spirit or policy of the laws of the adopting state.
5. Where various states have already adopted the statute, the parent state is followed.		5. Where interpretations of other states are inharmonious, there is no such restraint.
6. Statutes *in pari materia* must be construed together.		6. A statute is not *in pari materia* if its scope and aim are distinct or where a legislative design to depart from the general purpose or policy of previous enactments may be apparent.

7. A statute imposing a new penalty or forfeiture, or a new liability or disability, or creating a new right of action will not be construed as having a retroactive effect.

8. Where design has been distinctly stated no place is left for construction.

9. Definitions and rules of construction contained in an interpretation clause are part of the law and binding.

10. A statutory provision requiring liberal construction does not mean disregard of unequivocal requirements of the statute.

11. Titles do not control meaning; preambles do not expand scope; section headings do not change language.

12. If language is plain and un-ambiguous it must be given effect.

13. Words and phrases which have received judicial construction before enactment are to be understood according to that construction.

14. After enactment, judicial decision upon interpretation of particular terms and phrases controls.

7. Remedial statutes are to be liberally construed and if a retroactive interpretation will promote the ends of justice, they should receive such construction.

8. Courts have the power to inquire into real—as distinct from ostensible—purpose.

9. Definitions and rules of construction in a statute will not be extended beyond their necessary import nor allowed to defeat intention otherwise manifested.

10. Where a rule of construction is provided within the statute itself the rule should be applied.

11. The title may be consulted as a guide when there is doubt or obscurity in the body; preambles may be consulted to determine rationale, and thus the true construction of terms; section headings may be looked upon as part of the statute itself.

12. Not when literal interpretation would lead to absurd or mischievous consequences or thwart manifest purpose.

13. Not if the statute clearly requires them to have a different meaning.

14. Practical construction by executive officers is strong evidence of true meaning.

15. Words are to be taken in their ordinary meaning unless they are technical terms or words of art.

15. Popular words may bear a technical meaning and technical words may have a popular signification and they should be so construed as to agree with evident intention or to make the statute operative.

16. Every word and clause must be given effect.

16. If inadvertently inserted or if repugnant to the rest of the statute, they may be rejected as surplusage.

17. The same language used repeatedly in the same connection is presumed to bear the same meaning throughout the statute.

17. This presumption will be disregarded where it is necessary to assign different meanings to make the statute consistent.

18. Words are to be interpreted according to the proper grammatical effect of their arrangement within the statute.

18. Rules of grammar will be disregarded where strict adherence would defeat purpose.

19. Exceptions not made cannot be read.

19. The letter is only the "bark." Whatever is within the reason of the law is within the law itself.

20. Expression of one thing excludes another.

20. The language may fairly comprehend many different cases where some only are expressly mentioned by way of example.

21. General terms are to receive a general construction.

21. They may be limited by specific terms with which they are associated or by the scope and purpose of the statute.

22. It is a general rule of construction that where general words follow an enumeration they are to be held as applying only to persons and things of the same general kind or class specifically mentioned (*ejusdem generis*).

22. General words must operate on something. Further, *ejusdem generis* is only an aid in getting the meaning and does not warrant confining the operations of a statute within narrower limits than were intended.

23. Qualifying or limiting words or clauses are to be referred to the next preceding antecedent.

23. Not when evident sense and meaning require a different construction.

24. Punctuation will govern when a statute is open to two constructions.

24. Punctuation marks will not control the plain and evident meaning of language.

25. It must be assumed that language has been chosen with due regard to grammatical propriety and is not interchangeable on mere conjecture.

25. "And" and "or" may be read interchangeably whenever the change is necessary to give the statute sense and effect.

26. There is a distinction between words of permission and mandatory words.

26. Words imparting permission may be read as mandatory and words imparting command may be read as permissive when such construction is made necessary by evident intention or by the rights of the public.

27. A proviso qualifies the provision immediately preceding.

27. It may clearly be intended to have a wider scope.

28. When the enacting clause is general, a proviso is construed strictly.

28. Not when it is necessary to extend the proviso to persons or cases which come within its equity.

NOTES ON THE ACADEMIC DEBATE ABOUT THE VALUE OF THE CANONS

1. *Assault on the Canons by Legal Realists and Critical Scholars.* Professor Llewellyn's *tour de farce* is a celebrated exposure of the many facets of the canons of statutory construction, and it is representative of the legal realists' tendency to debunk legal formalisms. Their view was that nothing turned on formalist rules such as the canons. Canons of construction, for example, "are useful only as facades, which for an occasional judge may add luster to an argument persuasive for other reasons." Frank C. Newman & Stanley S. Surrey, *Legislation: Cases and Materials* 654 (1955).

Although critical scholars of the 1970s and 1980s did not focus on the canons, the perspective of many of them (intellectual heirs to the most skeptical realists) would go one step further. The canons are just part of the mystifying game that is played with legal logic, which is ultimately indeterminate. Critical scholars argue that legal reasoning can be oppressive by denying its own contingency, i.e., denying that there are other ways of looking at the situation. Perhaps the canons of construction might be deemed similarly oppressive, for they adhere to the linguistic and logical premise that the legislature goes about its work in a methodical, rational way and that judicial interpreters can scientifically discern the proper statutory meaning through simple rules.

2. *Legal Process Defense of the Canons.* Legal process thinkers have tended to defend at least some of the canons against the mockery of the realists. For example, Henry M. Hart Jr. & Albert M. Sacks, *The Legal Process* 1191 (Eskridge & Frickey eds., 1994) (tent. ed. 1958), responded to Llewellyn as follows:

> All this [skepticism], it is ventured, involves a misunderstanding of the function of the canons, and at bottom the problem of interpretation itself. Of course, there are pairs of maxims susceptible of being invoked for opposing conclusions. Once it is understood that meaning depends upon context and that contexts vary, how could it be otherwise? Maxims should not be treated, any more than a dictionary, as saying what meaning a word or group of words *must* have in a given context. They simply answer the question whether a particular meaning is linguistically permissible, if the context warrants it. Is this not a useful function?

Professor Dickerson suggests that some of the canons "reflect the probabilities generated by normal usage or legislative behavior. These represent either (1) lexicographical judgments of how legislatures tend to use language and its syntactical patterns, or (2) descriptions of how legislatures tend to behave. They serve as useful presumptions of supposed actual legislative intent and are, therefore, modestly useful in carrying [out] legislative meaning." Reed Dickerson, *The Interpretation and Application of Statutes* 228 (1975).

3. *The Law and Economics Debate over the Canons.* The canons were subjected to sharp criticism by Judge Richard A. Posner in *Statutory Interpretation—In the Classroom and in the Courtroom*, 50 U. Chi. L. Rev. 800, 806–07 (1983). Judge Posner complained that "most of the canons are just plain wrong" in that (1) they do not reflect a code by which legislatures draft statutes, (2) they are not even common-sense guides to interpretation, (3) they do not operate to constrain the discretion of judges, and (4) they do not force legislatures to draft statutes with care. Judge Posner blasted one canon after another—from the plain meaning rule to *expressio unius* to the whole act rule—by showing that the canons rest on wholly unrealistic conceptions of the legislative process. For example, many of the canons erroneously assume legislative omniscience (*id.* at 811):

> Most canons of statutory construction go wrong not because they misconceive the nature of judicial interpretation or of the legislative or political process but because they impute omniscience to Congress. Omniscience is always an unrealistic assumption, and particularly so when one is dealing with the legislative process. The basic reason why statutes are so frequently ambiguous in application is not that they are poorly drafted—though many are— and not that the legislators failed to agree on just what they wanted

to accomplish in the statute—though often they do fail—but that a statute necessarily is drafted in advance of, and with imperfect appreciation for the problems that will be encountered in, its application.

For a contrary position, Einer Elhauge, *Preference-Estimating Statutory Default Rules*, 102 Colum. L. Rev. 2027, 2030 (2002), argues that many of the canons actually "minimize political dissatisfaction with statutory results." Congress, Elhauge suggests, is perfectly happy that the Court smooths over statutory potholes, integrates statutes with the larger legal terrain, and even sends some sensitive issues back for more work. Which is the more credible understanding of what Congress would want? Does it matter what Congress wants?

In their survey of more than 130 congressional drafters, Abbe R. Gluck & Lisa Schultz Bressman, *Statutory Interpretation from the Inside: Part I*, 65 Stan. L. Rev. 901 (2013), reported some findings that would support Judge Posner. Statutory drafters were of course aware that the Supreme Court follows the ordinary meaning of statutory words, but they were largely ignorant of clear statement rules and emphatically rejected other canons, including the whole act rule and its many corollaries, as unrealistic assumptions about how Congress drafts.

From an economic point of view, it may be better to view the canons ex ante rather than ex post. Under an ex ante perspective, it may not matter whether a canon reflects legislative realities. Instead, the question is this: Does the legal process, including the lawmaking process, work *better* with this set of rules than with another set or with no rules at all? The canons might also be defended from an economic point of view as an *interpretive regime* that affords greater predictability for statutory interpreters. See Eskridge & Ferejohn, *Politics, Interpretation, and the Rule of Law*, as well as Appendix 6 to this coursebook (a complex array of more than two hundred canons followed by the Rehnquist-Roberts Court). So understood, the canons would not be viewed as reflecting congressional expectations or practice (the typical "faithful agent" model). Instead, the canons would be seen as effectuating a "rule of law" regime designed to give notice to the legal system and the public about how statutes will be interpreted, and to make such interpretation more predictable. Be acutely aware that this is *not* the system we have now. Even formalist judges do not justify the canons as legal rules wholly divorced from congressional practice, even when formalists invoke such rule of law values. Nor could they. Federal courts do not rank the canons or treat them as precedential law, and they do not apply them consistently—pre-requisites that at least one of us believes are required before courts could deploy the canons in a "rule of law" way.[29]

---

[29] *See* Abbe R. Gluck, *Intersystemic Statutory Interpretation: Methodology as "Law" and the* Erie *Doctrine*, 120 Yale L.J. 1898 (2011).

Antonin Scalia and Bryan Garner, *Reading Law: The Interpretation of Legal Texts*

Summary and Selected Quotations (2012).

Justice Scalia has, in the past, expressed the skeptical view that "all of these preferential rules and presumptions are a lot of trouble." Antonin Scalia, *A Matter of Interpretation* 28 (1997). Teaming up with linguist Bryan Garner, however, Justice Scalia has had a change of heart. In their new book, Scalia and Garner depict current statutory interpretation practice as turning judges loose to read anything they want into statutes. In contrast, the proper approach, they say, "will curb—even reverse—the tendency of judges to imbue authoritative texts with their own policy preferences" (p. xxviii) and "will provide greater certainty in the law, and hence greater predictability and greater respect for the rule of law" (p. xxix).

The thesis of the book is that there are "valid canons" of statutory interpretation (p. 9) and that if all judges followed these valid canons they would be more constrained and law would be more predictable. The meat of the book consists of these "valid canons" that, by Scalia and Garner's account, reflect "sound principles of interpretation": thirty-seven "principles applicable to all texts" (pp. 49–239), plus twenty "principles applicable specifically to governmental prescriptions" when judges interpret statutes (pp. 241–339), plus thirteen "falsities exposed" by the authors (pp. 341–410). While the authors suggest that their list may be as few as one-third of the total number of "valid canons," they are satisfied that following these rules will make judging "easier," even if not completely "easy" (p. xxviii).

The canons endorsed by Scalia and Garner are, essentially, those discussed in §§ 1 and 2 of this chapter, together with some further "stabilizing canons" discussed in the Note on Continuity-Based Canons below. Most of the "valid" canons are textual ones, like the ordinary meaning canon, the various Latin canons, and the whole act canons. The primary substantive canons endorsed by Scalia and Garner are the rule of lenity, the avoidance canon, and the federalism canons. They maintain that any judge who honestly follows these "valid canons" will complete statutory interpretations that are more predictable and objective—and less influenced by judicial value judgments.

Scalia and Garner are aware of Llewellyn's criticisms and find them unpersuasive. "Llewellyn's supposed demonstration, however, treats as canons some silly (and deservedly contradicted) judicial statements that are so far from having acquired canonical status that most lawyers have never heard of them. And some are not [valid] canons of interpretation because they reject textual interpretation as the basis of decision." (p. 59). As examples of "silly" canons, the authors list the Llewellyn Parries 1, 8,

19. Of course, most of the canons that Llewellyn invokes are neither silly nor anti-textual, but Scalia and Garner are not bothered in the least by the thrust and parry, for they "are not contradictions at all, but merely indications that different (noncontradictory) canons may sometimes provide differing indications of meaning" (pp. 59–60).

If Scalia and Garner are right that Llewellyn's thrust-and-parry columns do not prove that the canons are manipulable by unscrupulous judges, it is not clear that Scalia and Garner show how their fifty-seven "valid canons" will improve the predictability or objectivity of statutory interpretation. See William N. Eskridge Jr., *The New Textualism and Normative Canons,* 113 Colum. L. Rev. 531 (2013). Professor Eskridge recasts Llewellyn's arguments about how judges can cherry-pick the canons to support results they desire for other reasons. Rather than suggesting that every canon has a counter-canon, Eskridge suggests that for any difficult case there will be as many as a dozen or more relevant canons and that applying each canon requires normative judgments. (He uses the statutory debate in *Sweet Home* above to illustrate the numerous cross-cutting canons applicable in hard cases.) So the cherry-picking problem is even worse than Llewellyn suggested.

Are Professors Llewellyn and Eskridge right in suggesting that the canons, at least as currently deployed, do not restrict judges in the hard cases? Or are Justice Scalia and Professor Garner right that the canons do constrain judges? Consider also the fact that Scalia and Garner leave out of their book the more than 100 canons, described at the outset of this chapter and identified in Appendix 6 to this coursebook, that are subject specific (for example, the canon that ambiguities in the bankruptcy laws are construed in favor of the debtor). Are those canons more or less justifiable than the others? Are they closer to the imposition of judicial policy values than other canons—such as those made up by the Court (but drawn from constitutional norms (think, *Gregory*)? Isn't there something bizarre about the fact that the canons take on such great importance in the cases but there remains uncertainty, even judicial sloppiness, about what justifies them and where they come from? Think about this debate in light of the following Supreme Court decision and some preliminary empirical evidence.

Circuit City Stores, Inc. v. Saint Clair Adams
532 U.S. 105 (2001).

Saint Clair Adams sued his employer, Circuit City, for employment discrimination under California law. Circuit City moved to dismiss the lawsuit, on the ground that Adams had signed an agreement referring any job disputes to arbitration. Under the Federal Arbitration Act of 1925

(FAA), 9 U.S.C. §§ 1–16, federal courts are barred from adjudicating controversies subject to valid agreements to arbitrate, so long as those are agreements "involving [interstate] commerce." *Id.* § 2; cf. U.S. Const. art. I, § 7, cl. 3 (authority of Congress to pass laws regulating interstate commerce). The lower court, however, ruled that Adams's lawsuit was exempted from these requirements by § 1 of the law, which says that the FAA shall not apply "to contracts of employment of seamen, railroad employees, or any other class of workers engaged in foreign or interstate commerce." 9 U.S.C. § 1. Following the lower court, Adams maintained that § 1 exempted all employment contracts that were covered by § 2.

Justice Kennedy's opinion for the Court rejected this argument and ruled that § 2 only exempted employment contracts for transportation workers engaged in foreign or interstate commerce. "Unlike the 'involving commerce' language in § 2, the words 'any other class of workers engaged in . . . commerce' constitute a residual phrase, following, in the same sentence, explicit reference to 'seamen' and 'railroad employees.' Construing the residual phrase to exclude all employment contracts fails to give independent effect to the statute's enumeration of the specific categories of workers which precedes it; there would be no need for Congress to use the phrases 'seamen' and 'railroad employees' if those same classes of workers were subsumed within the meaning of the 'engaged in . . . commerce' residual clause. The wording of § 1 calls for the application of the maxim *ejusdem generis,* the statutory canon that '[w]here general words follow specific words in a statutory enumeration, the general words are construed to embrace only objects similar in nature to those objects enumerated by the preceding specific words.' 2A N. Singer, Sutherland on Statutes and Statutory Construction § 47.17 (1991); see also *Norfolk & Western R. Co. v. Train Dispatchers,* 499 U.S. 117, 129 (1991). Under this rule of construction the residual clause should be read to give effect to the terms 'seamen' and 'railroad employees,' and should itself be controlled and defined by reference to the enumerated categories of workers which are recited just before it; the interpretation of the clause pressed by respondent fails to produce these results.

"Canons of construction need not be conclusive and are often countered, of course, by some maxim pointing in a different direction. The application of the rule *ejusdem generis* in this case, however, is in full accord with other sound considerations bearing upon the proper interpretation of the clause. For even if the term 'engaged in commerce' stood alone in § 1, we would not construe the provision to exclude all contracts of employment from the FAA. Congress uses different modifiers to the word 'commerce' in the design and enactment of its statutes. The phrase 'affecting commerce' indicates Congress' intent to regulate to the outer limits of its authority under the Commerce Clause. [*Allied-Bruce Terminix v. Dobson,* 513 U.S. 265, 277 (1995).]"

The "involving commerce" phrase, the operative words for the reach of the basic coverage provision in § 2, had been at issue in *Allied-Bruce*. Based upon the usual meaning of the word "involving," *Allied-Bruce* held that the "word 'involving,' like 'affecting,' signals an intent to exercise Congress' commerce power to the full." In contrast, Justice Kennedy reasoned that the general words "in commerce" and the specific phrase "engaged in commerce" had a more limited reach. *Allied-Bruce* said that the words "in commerce" are "often-found words of art" that the Court had not read as expressing congressional intent to regulate to the outer limits of authority under the Commerce Clause. The Court also relied upon the observation in *Allied-Bruce*, and a host of other cases, that the overriding purpose of the FAA was to reverse the longstanding judicial skepticism of arbitration as an appropriate remedial system.

In dissent, **Justice Stevens** (joined by Justices Souter, Ginsburg, and Breyer) argued that the original meaning of § 1 excluded all "employment contracts." Introduced in 1922, the original arbitration bill was aimed at commercial and maritime contracts—but labor feared that its broad language could be applied to employment contracts as well. In response to those concerns, Secretary of Commerce Herbert Hoover, suggested that "[i]f objection appears to the inclusion of workers' contracts in the law's scheme, it might be well amended by stating 'but nothing herein contained shall apply to contracts of employment of seamen, railroad employees, or any other class of workers engaged in interstate or foreign commerce.' The legislation was reintroduced in the next session of Congress with Secretary Hoover's exclusionary language added to § 1, and the amendment eliminated organized labor's opposition to the proposed law."

Also in dissent, **Justice Souter** (joined by Justices Stevens, Ginsburg, and Breyer) disputed the majority's reliance on *ejusdem generis*. "[I]t is imputing something very odd to the working of the congressional brain to say that Congress took care to bar application of the Act to the class of employment contracts it most obviously had authority to legislate about in 1925, contracts of workers employed by carriers and handlers of commerce, while covering only employees 'engaged' in less obvious ways, over whose coverage litigation might be anticipated with uncertain results. It would seem to have made more sense either to cover all coverable employment contracts or to exclude them all. In fact, exclusion might well have been in order based on concern that arbitration could prove expensive or unfavorable to employees, many of whom lack the bargaining power to resist an arbitration clause if their prospective employers insist on one. And excluding all employment contracts from the Act's enforcement of mandatory arbitration clauses is consistent with Secretary Hoover's suggestion that the exemption language would respond to any 'objection . . . to the inclusion of workers' contracts.' "

Justice Kennedy's opinion for the Court held that the legislative history invoked by the dissenters and by Adams was irrelevant, because § 1 had a plain meaning. In response, Justice Souter pointed to the Court's precedents holding that *ejusdem generis*, in particular, could be rebutted by legislative history as well as by text-based arguments. In *Watt v. Western Nuclear, Inc.,* 462 U.S. 36 44, n. 5 (1983), for example, the Court concluded that the *ejusdem generis* canon did not justify a limiting construction for Congress's identification of "coal and other minerals" where "[t]here were special reasons for expressly addressing coal that negate any inference that the phrase 'and other minerals' was meant to reserve only substances *ejusdem generis,*" namely, that Congress wanted "to make clear that coal was reserved even though existing law treated it differently from other minerals." Both dissenting opinions argued that Congress in 1925 made clear that employment contracts covered by its then-existing labor relations statutes were exempt from the requirements of the FAA.

James J. Brudney and Corey Ditslear, *Canons of Construction and the Elusive Quest for Neutral Reasoning*
58 Vand. L. Rev. 1 (2005) (summary and selected quotations).

This article is a more systematic approach to the Court's deployment of the canons than any previous work of scholarship. The authors (a labor law and legislation professor and a political scientist) collected 630 Supreme Court workplace-law decisions between 1969 and 2003 and coded them by result (pro-labor liberal and pro-business conservative) and mode of reasoning. Using multiple regression analyses that control for other variables, Professors Brudney and Ditslear found that the Rehnquist Court relied on textual canons (such as *ejusdem generis*) much more, and legislative history much less, than the Burger Court had done.

Exemplary of the new trend is the *Circuit City* case, excerpted above. Justice Kennedy's majority opinion relied on the canon *ejusdem generis* to hold that Congress meant to limit the exclusion from arbitration to contracts "like" those involving seamen and railroad workers—namely, transportation contracts. This canon enabled the Court majority to ignore legislative history that supported the worker's argument that the executive branch proponents and congressional sponsors wanted the exception to cover all employment contracts within Congress's Commerce Clause power. Brudney and Ditslear were troubled by the Court's refusal even to consider congressional materials based upon an abstract canon that probably no one in Congress was familiar with in 1926.

Professors Brudney and Ditslear also found that this methodological development has been serving ideological purposes (pp. 53–69). As the authors summarized their findings (p. 6), "canon usage by Justices identified as liberals tends to be linked to liberal outcomes, and canon reliance by conservative Justices to be associated with conservative outcomes. We also found that canons are often invoked to justify conservative results in close cases—those decided by a one-vote or two-vote margin. Indeed, closely divided cases in which the majority relies on substantive canons are more likely to reach conservative results than close cases where those canons are not invoked." *Circuit City* illustrates that pattern: the Court's five most conservative Justices invoked the textual canon to impose a business-friendly reading on the exception, while the four most liberal Justices relied on legislative materials, but to no avail.

"In addition, we identified a subset of cases in which the majority relies on canons while the dissent invokes legislative history: these cases, almost all decided since 1988, have yielded overwhelmingly conservative results. [E.g., *Circuit City*.] Doctrinal analysis of illustrative decisions indicates that conservative members of the Rehnquist Court are using the canons in such contested cases to ignore—and thereby undermine—the demonstrable legislative preferences of Congress. Taken together, the association between canon reliance and outcomes among both conservative and liberal justices, the distinctly conservative influence associated with substantive canon reliance in close cases, and the recent tensions in contested cases between conservative majority opinions that rely on canons and liberal dissents that invoke legislative history, suggest that the canons are regularly used in an instrumental if not ideologically conscious manner."

In subsequent work, Professor Brudney has controlled for other variables and has found that "liberal" (pro-labor) Justices vote more neutrally when they look at legislative history, while "conservative" (pro-business) Justices vote more conservatively when they ignore legislative history and find "plain meanings" by using the canons. See James J. Brudney, *Liberal Justices' Reliance on Legislative History: Principle, Strategy, and the Scalia Effect*, 29 Berkeley J. Emp. & Lab. L. 117 (2008), as well as James J. Brudney, *Canon Shortfalls and the Virtues of Political Branch Interpretive Assets*, 98 Calif. L. Rev. 1199 (2010).

Professors Brudney and Ditslear applied their empirical findings to the theoretical debate over the utility of the canons. First, the authors were skeptical that the canons form an interpretive regime that can provide an ordering mechanism for legislators and lawyers to make statutory interpretation more predictable (pp. 95–102). Aside from the fact that legislators do not rely on the canons when drafting statutes, see Gluck & Bressman, *Statutory Interpretation from the Inside: Part I*;

Victoria F. Nourse & Jane S. Schacter, *The Politics of Legislative Drafting: A Congressional Case Study,* 77 N.Y.U. L. Rev. 575 (2002), legislators and lawyers cannot rely on the canons in predicting how statutes will be applied, because the canons are deployed in such an ideological way by both liberal and conservative judges. A neutral observer who just read the statute and the legislative history in *Circuit City*, for example, would have expected the Court to read the labor exemption much more expansively than the five-Justice majority in fact did. Brudney and Ditslear offer almost two dozen equally dramatic canon surprises from their dataset.

Second, and relatedly, Brudney and Ditslear's study lends empirical support to relatively cynical accounts of the canons (pp. 77–95). They found much wisdom in the views of Stephen Ross, *Where Have You Gone Karl Llewellyn? Should Congress Turn Its Lonely Eyes to You?,* 45 Vand. L. Rev. 561 (1992), and Edward L. Rubin, *Modern Canons, Loose Canons, and the Limits of Practical Reason: A Response to Farber and Ross*, 45 Vand. L. Rev. 579 (1992), who maintain that Supreme Court Justices use the canons strategically, to justify judicial policy preferences or to frustrate legislative intent. The malleability noted by Professor Llewellyn not only undermines canonical predictability, but also allows the canons to be manipulated by result-oriented jurists. Brudney and Ditslear argue that their evidence is consistent with, though does not conclusively prove, this claim. Is their hypothesis consistent with your reaction to the problems and cases we have presented in this coursebook? Does their skeptical view of the canons strike you as more plausible than Scalia and Garner's faith that the canons constrain statutory decision-making?

Third, Professors Brudney and Ditslear found some support for the hypothesis, first advanced by Jonathan R. Macey and Geoffrey P. Miller, *The Canons of Construction and Judicial Preferences*, 45 Vand. L. Rev. 647 (1992), that the canons are substitutes for judicial expertise and can reduce error costs in areas (such as ERISA and the procedural complexities of Title VII) where judicial knowledge and preferences are low (pp. 70–77). E.g., *Adams Fruit Co. v. Barrett*, 494 U.S. 638 (1990) (*expressio unius* provides the ground for a conservative Court to allow, without dissent, a private right of action under a technical migrant workers' law). Brudney and Ditslear add that such cases may be more strongly influenced by legislative purpose analysis and, most important, agency views than by canon reliance. In short, there is a correlation between canon invocation and technical issues but not necessarily any causal link.

These conclusions suggest that in the most technical areas of law—such as bankruptcy, civil procedure, energy regulation, intellectual property, taxation, telecommunications—canon usage would be more important and less ideologically slanted than in labor law. In less technical and more normatively charged areas—such as civil rights, criminal law and procedure, freedom of information, and perhaps federal land law—canon usage would be less frequent and more ideologically slanted.

NOTE ON THE COMMON LAW, THE RULE AGAINST IMPLIED REPEALS AND OTHER CONTINUITY-BASED AND COHERENCE CANONS

David L. Shapiro, in *Continuity and Change in Statutory Interpretation*, 67 N.Y.U. L. Rev. 921, 925 (1992), has provided a different justification for many of the canons: they promote legal stability, as they presume "that close questions of statutory interpretation should be resolved in favor of continuity and against change." Notice that most of the canons mentioned or discussed in Section 2 are, essentially, continuity canons. The rule of lenity assures all of us that our conduct is not criminal unless the legislature has given us clear notice. The federalism-effecting canons preserve the traditional role for state law unless otherwise clearly demanded by the legislature.

The most important continuity canon is the one we introduced in Chapter 3: the super-strong presumption of correctness for statutory precedents. E.g., *Flood v. Kuhn* (Chapter 3, § 2). *Stare decisis* assures all of us that old interpretations will persist and that new issues will be evaluated predictably from established precedents, at least insofar as courts are involved. But see Chapter 8 (discussing different *stare decisis* rules when agencies are the primary interpreters).

There are many other canons, most not yet mentioned in this chapter, that similarly rest on continuity and coherence values. Some concern which "extrinsic" sources (sources outside the statute) courts might look to, including the common law and the rest of the regulatory and policy landscape. Others rest on assumptions about congressional intent when Congress legislates in the wake of previous judicial statutory decisions. We introduce you to the most important such canons here, followed by two illustrative cases.

1. *The Reenactment and Borrowed Statute Rules, and Other Presumptions Based on Legislative Inaction.* One important set of canons presumes that Congress is aware of the administrative or judicial constructions of provisions it is reenacting or borrowing, and means to follow those constructions when it does not act to change them. Assume the Court interprets "vehicle" in a 2010 case to include a tricycle. In 2012, assume that Congress reenacts the Vehicles in the Park Law, perhaps amending other sections, but not touching the definition of "vehicle." When Congress reenacts without changing a statutory provision that has previously been construed by the Court, courts infer congressional agreement with the judicial construction. This *Reenactment Rule* should remind you of the *Legislative*

Acquiescence Canon that we saw in the *Johnson* case in Chapter 3. Because Congress did not act to change the Court's earlier construction of Title VII (in *Weber*) to permit race-based affirmative action by private employers, the Court assumed Congress acquiesced in its decision when it came time to extend that precedent to sex discrimination and public employers in *Johnson*. Also of the same feather is the *Dog that Didn't Bark Canon*, which we introduced in the *Bock Laundry* case in Chapter 4: Courts presume that Congress did not intend to make a major change to the status quo if no one mentioned it in the legislative history.

A similar presumption is known as the *Borrowed Statute Rule*, and the idea is that when Congress borrows language from an existing statute to use in a new statute, it is safe to assume that Congress intended to incorporate judicial constructions of the old statutes in the new statute's meaning. In *Lorillard v. Pons*, 434 U.S. 575 (1978), for example, the Court found that Congress had modeled the enforcement provisions of the Age Discrimination in Employment Act on those in the Fair Labor Standards Act. Because the Court had previously interpreted the borrowed language from the FLSA to include a right to a jury trial in private actions under the act, the Court concluded that the Congress intended that interpretation to carry over to the new ADEA provisions. In other words, Congress did not have to add the words from the Court's interpretation—the interpretation of the old was effectively assumed to have been incorporated into the new statute. Related is the *in Pari Materia* Rule, where similar provisions in different statutes are presumed to be construed in the same way.

A slightly more active relative of these rules is the *Rejected Proposal Rule*: Courts will not construe ambiguous statutes in ways that Congress already has rejected. This presumption usually applies when Congress has voted down an amendment that would reach the same result as the interpretation in question, but sometimes courts apply it simply when Congress lets proposals die in Committee or elsewhere in the vetogates. Recall *Flood v. Kuhn*, the baseball case from Chapter 3, § 2. One reason the Court was reluctant to overrule baseball's antitrust exemption was that Congress had rejected approximately 50 such proposals itself.

These presumptions impute a whole lot of knowledge to Congress about judicial work. For that reason, the most common formulations of these rules assume that they apply only when the previous interpretation comes from the Supreme Court or, in the state context, a state's highest court, because those decisions are more salient. Do you think it is realistic to assume that Congress keeps abreast of even all of those cases? The canons also put a lot of weight on legislative *inaction*—e.g., why Congress doesn't bark in legislative history, or why Congress doesn't re-open a statute for fresh amendments when reenacting it. After all that you've learned about vetogates in this coursebook, is it wise to attribute so much legislative intent to Congress's failure to act? Another way to view these canons is as *judicial power grabs*—they place a heavy thumb on the scale privileging the continuing of judicial statutory interpretations and the status quo, even in the face of new legislation.

2. *The Presumption Against Implied Repeals.* Similarly, courts presume that later-coming legislation does not trump (effectively, repeal) earlier legislation unless Congress so clearly states. This rule, too, perhaps naively assumes legislative omniscience—legislators and their staff members do not search the statute books to ensure that new legislation will interfere minimally with established legislation. And why should they? Shouldn't new legislative policy be applied to full effect, liberally supplanting outdated prior statutes? On the other hand, the canon against implied repeals might be defended, "not only to avoid misconstruction of the law effecting the putative repeal, but also to preserve the intent of later Congresses that have already enacted laws that are dependent on the continued applicability of the law whose implicit repeal is in question." *Smith v. Robinson*, 468 U.S. 992, 1026 (1984) (Brennan, J., dissenting); accord, Scalia & Garner, *Reading Law*, 327–33. *Morton v. Mancari*, excerpted below, is the key citation for this canon.

3. *Presumption That Statutes Are Construed to Be Consistent with the Common Law.* Courts also presume congressional familiarity with the judge-made common law and presume that Congress intends for common law terms and concepts to carry their traditional common law meanings even in legislation, e.g., *Isbrandtsen Co. v. Johnson*, 343 U.S. 779 (1952), possibly updated to reflect the evolving common law, e.g., *Smith v. Wade,* 461 U.S. 30 (1983). A corollary to this canon is the presumption that statutes are not to be construed in derogation of the common law—in other words, when statutes are ambiguous courts should interpret them not to disturb common-law holdings. Scalia and Garner called this canon "a relic of the courts' historical hostility to the emergency of statutory law," *Reading Law*, 318. Judge Posner has called it a "fossil remnant of the traditional hostility of English judges to legislation," *Liu v. Mund*, 686 F. 3d 418, 421 (7th Cir. 2012). Can you see why?

4. *Horizontal Coherence: Reasoning from Policy and the Regulatory Landscape.* Finally, courts sometimes will draw inferences about statutory meaning from the surrounding *horizontal landscape* of the law. Chief Judge Kaye's opinion in *In re Jacob*, the New York State same-sex adoption case in Chapter 4, offers a good example. Chief Judge Kaye looked around and saw that many other aspects of New York family law had been updated to reflect an enlarged and liberal vision of the family. Reasoning from those other statutes, she effectively updated the adoption statute to cohere with the modern regulatory landscape. See Guido Calabresi*, A Common Law for the Age of Statutes* (1982) (arguing that judges can use their common-law capacities of reasoning by analogy and for "fit" to bring obsolete statutes in line with the current legal landscape); William N. Eskridge Jr. *Dynamic Statutory Interpretation* (1994) (developing a theory of when courts should construe statutes in line with public policy). On rare occasion, courts will go even further, reasoning from not only statutes, but also from cases, regulations and other public values to bring a statute into the political and

legal equilibrium. *Bob Jones*, the second case below, offers a prominent example.

Read the cases below and consider whether their continuity-based approaches form a better foundation for an interpretive regime than, for example, the canons in *Circuit City*.

ROGERS C.B. MORTON v. C.R. MANCARI

Supreme Court of the United States, 1974.
417 U.S. 535, 94 S.Ct. 2474, 41 L.Ed.2d 290.

MR. JUSTICE BLACKMUN delivered the opinion of the Court.

The Indian Reorganization Act of 1934, also known as the Wheeler-Howard Act, 48 Stat. 984, 25 U.S.C. § 461 *et seq.*, accords an employment preference for qualified Indians in the Bureau of Indian Affairs (BIA or Bureau). Appellees, non-Indian BIA employees, challenged this preference as contrary to the anti-discrimination provisions of the Equal Employment Opportunity Act of 1972, 86 Stat. 103, 42 U.S.C. § 2000e *et seq.* (1970 ed., Supp. II), and as violative of the Due Process Clause of the Fifth Amendment. * * *

[I] Section 12 of the Indian Reorganization Act, 48 Stat. 986, 25 U.S.C. § 472, provides:

> "The Secretary of the Interior is directed to establish standards of health, age, character, experience, knowledge, and ability for Indians who may be appointed, without regard to civil-service laws, to the various positions maintained, now or hereafter, by the Indian Office, in the administration of functions or services affecting any Indian tribe. Such qualified Indians shall hereafter have the preference to appointment to vacancies in any such positions."

In June 1972, pursuant to this provision, the Commissioner of Indian Affairs, with the approval of the Secretary of the Interior, issued a directive (Personnel Management Letter No. 72–12) stating that the BIA's policy would be to grant a preference to qualified Indians not only, as before, in the initial hiring stage, but also in the situation where an Indian and a non-Indian, both already employed by the BIA, were competing for a promotion within the Bureau. The record indicates that this policy was implemented immediately.

Shortly thereafter, appellees, who are non-Indian employees of the BIA at Albuquerque, instituted this class action, on behalf of themselves and other non-Indian employees similarly situated, in the United States District Court for the District of New Mexico, claiming that the "so-called 'Indian Preference Statutes'" were repealed by the 1972 Equal

Employment Opportunity Act and deprived them of rights to property without due process of law, in violation of the Fifth Amendment. * * *

After a short trial focusing primarily on how the new policy, in fact, has been implemented, the District Court concluded that the Indian preference was implicitly repealed by § 11 of the Equal Employment Opportunity Act of 1972, Pub. L. 92–261, 86 Stat. 111, 42 U.S.C. § 2000e–16(a) (1970 ed., Supp. II), proscribing discrimination in most federal employment on the basis of race.[6] Having found that Congress repealed the preference, it was unnecessary for the District Court to pass on its constitutionality. The court permanently enjoined appellants "from implementing any policy in the Bureau of Indian Affairs which would hire, promote, or reassign any person in preference to another solely for the reason that such person is an Indian." * * *

[II] The federal policy of according some hiring preference to Indians in the Indian service dates at least as far back as 1834. Since that time, Congress repeatedly has enacted various preferences of the general type here at issue.[8] The purpose of these preferences, as variously expressed in the legislative history, has been to give Indians a greater participation in their own self-government; to further the Government's trust obligation toward the Indian tribes[9]; and to reduce the negative effect of having non-Indians administer matters that affect Indian tribal life.

The preference directly at issue here was enacted as an important part of the sweeping Indian Reorganization Act of 1934. The overriding

---

[6]   Section 2000e–16(a) reads:

"All personnel actions affecting employees or applicants for employment (except with regard to aliens employed outside the limits of the United States) in military departments as defined in section 102 of Title 5, in executive agencies (other than the General Accounting Office) as defined in section 105 of Title 5 (including employees and applicants for employment who are paid from nonappropriated funds), in the United States Postal Service and the Postal Rate Commission, in those units of the Government of the District of Columbia having positions in the competitive service, and in those units of the legislative and judicial branches of the Federal Government having positions in the competitive service, and in the Library of Congress shall be made free from any discrimination based on race, color, religion, sex, or national origin."

[8]   Act of May 17, 1882, § 6, 22 Stat. 88, and Act of July 4, 1884, § 6, 23 Stat. 97, 25 U.S.C. § 46 (employment of clerical, mechanical, and other help on reservations and about agencies); Act of Aug. 15, 1894, § 10, 28 Stat. 313, 25 U.S.C. § 44 (employment of herders, teamsters, and laborers, "and where practicable in all other employments" in the Indian service); Act of June 7, 1897, § 1, 30 Stat. 83, 25 U.S.C. § 274 (employment as matrons, farmers, and industrial teachers in Indian schools); Act of June 25, 1910, § 23, 36 Stat. 861, 25 U.S.C. § 47 (general preference as to Indian labor and products of Indian industry).

[9]   A letter, contained in the House Report to the 1934 Act, from President F. D. Roosevelt to Congressman Howard states:

"We can and should, without further delay, extend to the Indian the fundamental rights of political liberty and local self-government and the opportunities of education and economic assistance that they require in order to attain a wholesome American life. This is but the obligation of honor of a powerful nation toward a people living among us and dependent upon our protection." H.R.Rep. No. 1804, 73d Cong., 2d Sess., 8 (1934).

purpose of that particular Act was to establish machinery whereby Indian tribes would be able to assume a greater degree of self-government, both politically and economically. Congress was seeking to modify the then-existing situation whereby the primarily non-Indian-staffed BIA had plenary control, for all practical purposes, over the lives and destinies of the federally recognized Indian tribes. Initial congressional proposals would have diminished substantially the role of the BIA by turning over to federally chartered self-governing Indian communities many of the functions normally performed by the Bureau.[13] Committee sentiment, however, ran against such a radical change in the role of the BIA. The solution ultimately adopted was to strengthen tribal government while continuing the active role of the BIA, with the understanding that the Bureau would be more responsive to the interests of the people it was created to serve.

One of the primary means by which self-government would be fostered and the Bureau made more responsive was to increase the participation of tribal Indians in the BIA operations. In order to achieve this end, it was recognized that some kind of preference and exemption from otherwise prevailing civil service requirements was necessary.[16] Congressman Howard, the House sponsor, expressed the need for the preference:

> "The Indians have not only been thus deprived of civic rights and powers, but they have been largely deprived of the opportunity to enter the more important positions in the service of the very bureau which manages their affairs. Theoretically, the Indians have the right to qualify for the Federal civil service. In actual practice there has been no adequate program of training to qualify Indians to compete in these examinations, especially for technical and higher positions; and even if there were such training, the Indians would have to compete under existing law, on equal terms with multitudes of white applicants. . . . The various services on the Indian reservations are actually local rather than Federal services and are comparable to local municipal and county services, since they are dealing with purely local Indian problems. It should be possible for Indians with the requisite vocational and professional training to enter

---

[13] Hearings on H.R. 7902, Readjustment of Indian Affairs, 73d Cong., 2d Sess., 1–7 (1934) (hereafter House Hearings).

[16] "The bill admits qualified Indians to the position [*sic*] in their own service.

"Thirty-four years ago, in 1900, the number of Indians holding regular positions in the Indian Service, in proportion to the total of positions, was greater than it is today.

"The reason primarily is found in the application of the generalized civil service to the Indian Service, and the consequent exclusion of Indians from their own jobs." House Hearings 19 (memorandum dated Feb. 19, 1934, submitted by Commissioner Collier to the Senate and House Committees on Indian Affairs).

the service of their own people without the necessity of competing with white applicants for these positions. This bill permits them to do so." 78 Cong. Rec. 11729 (1934).

Congress was well aware that the proposed preference would result in employment disadvantages within the BIA for non-Indians.[17] Not only was this displacement unavoidable if room were to be made for Indians, but it was explicitly determined that gradual replacement of non-Indians with Indians within the Bureau was a desirable feature of the entire program for self-government.[18] Since 1934, the BIA has implemented the preference with a fair degree of success. The percentage of Indians employed in the Bureau rose from 34% in 1934 to 57% in 1972. This reversed the former downward trend, see n.16, *supra*, and was due, clearly, to the presence of the 1934 Act. The Commissioner's extension of the preference in 1972 to promotions within the BIA was designed to bring more Indians into positions of responsibility and, in that regard, appears to be a logical extension of the congressional intent.

[III] It is against this background that we encounter the first issue in the present case: whether the Indian preference was repealed by the Equal Employment Opportunity Act of 1972. Title VII of the Civil Rights Act of 1964 was the first major piece of federal legislation prohibiting discrimination in private employment on the basis of "race, color, religion, sex, or national origin." 42 U.S.C. § 2000e–2(a). Significantly, §§ 701(b) and 703(i) of that Act explicitly exempted from its coverage the preferential employment of Indians by Indian tribes or by industries located on or near Indian reservations. 42 U.S.C. §§ 2000e(b) and 2000e–2(i).[19] This exemption reveals a clear congressional recognition, within the framework of Title VII, of the unique legal status of tribal and reservation-based activities. The Senate sponsor, Senator Humphrey, stated on the floor by way of explanation:

---

[17] Congressman Carter, an opponent of the bill, placed in the Congressional Record the following observation by Commissioner Collier at the Committee hearings:

> "[W]e must not blind ourselves to the fact that the effect of this bill if worked out would unquestionably be to replace white employees by Indian employees. I do not know how fast, but ultimately it ought to go very far indeed." 78 Cong. Rec. 11737 (1934).

[18] "It should be possible for Indians to enter the service of their own people without running the gauntlet of competition with whites for these positions. Indian progress and ambition will be enormously strengthened as soon as we adopt the principle that the Indian Service shall gradually become, in fact as well as in name, an Indian service predominantly in the hands of educated and competent Indians." *Id.*, at 11731 (remarks of Cong. Howard).

[19] Section 701(b) excludes "an Indian Tribe" from the Act's definition of "employer." Section 703(i) states:

> "Nothing contained in this subchapter shall apply to any business or enterprise on or near an Indian reservation with respect to any publicly announced employment practice of such business or enterprise under which a preferential treatment is given to any individual because he is an Indian living on or near a reservation."

"This exemption is consistent with the Federal Government's policy of encouraging Indian employment and with the special legal position of Indians." 110 Cong. Rec. 12723 (1964).[20]

The 1964 Act did not specifically outlaw employment discrimination by the Federal Government. Yet the mechanism for enforcing longstanding Executive Orders forbidding Government discrimination had proved ineffective for the most part. In order to remedy this, Congress, by the 1972 Act, amended the 1964 Act and proscribed discrimination in most areas of federal employment. See n. 6, *supra*. In general, it may be said that the substantive anti-discrimination law embraced in Title VII was carried over and applied to the Federal Government. As stated in the House Report:

"To correct this entrenched discrimination in the Federal service, it is necessary to insure the effective application of uniform, fair and strongly enforced policies. The present law and the proposed statute do not permit industry and labor organizations to be the judges of their own conduct in the area of employment discrimination. There is no reason why government agencies should not be treated similarly. . . ." H.R.Rep. No. 92–238, on H.R. 1746, pp. 24–25 (1971).

Nowhere in the legislative history of the 1972 Act, however, is there any mention of Indian preference.

Appellees assert * * * that since the 1972 Act proscribed racial discrimination in Government employment, the Act necessarily, albeit *sub silentio*, repealed the provision of the 1934 Act that called for the preference in the BIA of one racial group, Indians, over non-Indians:

"When a conflict such as in this case, is present, the most recent law or Act should apply and the conflicting Preferences passed some 39 years earlier should be impliedly repealed." Brief for Appellees 7.

We disagree. For several reasons we conclude that Congress did not intend to repeal the Indian preference and that the District Court erred in holding that it was repealed.

First: There are the above-mentioned affirmative provisions in the 1964 Act excluding coverage of tribal employment and of preferential treatment by a business or enterprise on or near a reservation. These 1964 exemptions as to private employment indicate Congress' recognition of the longstanding federal policy of providing a unique legal status to Indians in matters concerning tribal or "on or near" reservation

---

[20] Senator Mundt supported these exemptions on the Senate floor by claiming that they would allow Indians "to benefit from Indian preference programs now in operation or later to be instituted." 110 Cong.Rec. 13702 (1964).

employment. The exemptions reveal a clear congressional sentiment that an Indian preference in the narrow context of tribal or reservation-related employment did not constitute racial discrimination of the type otherwise proscribed. In extending the general anti-discrimination machinery to federal employment in 1972, Congress in no way modified these private employment preferences built into the 1964 Act, and they are still in effect. It would be anomalous to conclude that Congress intended to eliminate the longstanding statutory preferences in BIA employment, as being racially discriminatory, at the very same time it was reaffirming the right of tribal and reservation-related private employers to provide Indian preference. Appellees' assertion that Congress implicitly repealed the preference as racially discriminatory, while retaining the 1964 preferences, attributes to Congress irrationality and arbitrariness, an attribution we do not share.

Second: Three months after Congress passed the 1972 amendments, it enacted two *new* Indian preference laws. These were part of the Education Amendments of 1972, 86 Stat. 235, 20 U.S.C. §§ 887c(a) and (d), and § 1119a (1970 ed., Supp. II). The new laws explicitly require that Indians be given preference in Government programs for training teachers of Indian children. It is improbable, to say the least, that the same Congress which affirmatively approved and enacted these additional and similar Indian preferences was, at the same time, condemning the BIA preference as racially discriminatory. In the total absence of any manifestation of supportive intent, we are loathe to imply this improbable result.

Third: Indian preferences, for many years, have been treated as exceptions to Executive Orders forbidding Government employment discrimination. The 1972 extension of the Civil Rights Act to Government employment is in large part merely a codification of prior anti-discrimination Executive Orders that had proved ineffective because of inadequate enforcement machinery. There certainly was no indication that the substantive proscription against discrimination was intended to be any broader than that which previously existed. By codifying the existing anti-discrimination provisions, and by providing enforcement machinery for them, there is no reason to presume that Congress affirmatively intended to erase the preferences that previously had co-existed with broad anti-discrimination provisions in Executive Orders.

Fourth: Appellees encounter head-on the "cardinal rule . . . that repeals by implication are not favored." *Posadas v. National City Bank*, 296 U.S. 497, 503 (1936). They and the District Court read the congressional silence as effectuating a repeal by implication. There is nothing in the legislative history, however, that indicates affirmatively any congressional intent to repeal the 1934 preference. Indeed, as explained above, there is ample independent evidence that the legislative intent was to the contrary.

This is a prototypical case where an adjudication of repeal by implication is not appropriate. The preference is a longstanding, important component of the Government's Indian program. The anti-discrimination provision, aimed at alleviating minority discrimination in employment, obviously is designed to deal with an entirely different and, indeed, opposite problem. Any perceived conflict is thus more apparent than real.

In the absence of some affirmative showing of an intention to repeal, the only permissible justification for a repeal by implication is when the earlier and later statutes are irreconcilable. *Georgia v. Pennsylvania R. Co.*, 324 U.S. 439, 456–457 (1945). Clearly, this is not the case here. A provision aimed at furthering Indian self-government by according an employment preference within the BIA for qualified members of the governed group can readily coexist with a general rule prohibiting employment discrimination on the basis of race. Any other conclusion can be reached only by formalistic reasoning that ignores both the history and purposes of the preference and the unique legal relationship between the Federal Government and tribal Indians.

Furthermore, the Indian preference statute is a specific provision applying to a very specific situation. The 1972 Act, on the other hand, is of general application. Where there is no clear intention otherwise, a specific statute will not be controlled or nullified by a general one, regardless of the priority of enactment. See, e.g., *Bulova Watch Co. v. United States*, 365 U.S. 753, 758 (1961); *Rodgers v. United States*, 185 U.S. 83, 87–89 (1902).

The courts are not at liberty to pick and choose among congressional enactments, and when two statutes are capable of co-existence, it is the duty of the courts, absent a clearly expressed congressional intention to the contrary, to regard each as effective. "When there are two acts upon the same subject, the rule is to give effect to both if possible. . . . The intention of the legislature to repeal 'must be clear and manifest.' " *United States v. Borden Co.*, 308 U.S. 188, 198 (1939). In light of the factors indicating no repeal, we simply cannot conclude that Congress consciously abandoned its policy of furthering Indian self-government when it passed the 1972 amendments.

We therefore hold that the District Court erred in ruling that the Indian preference was repealed by the 1972 Act. * * *

STATUTORY PREFACE TO *BOB JONES*

Internal Revenue Code of 1954
(Income Tax Advantages for Educational Institutions)

26 U.S.C. § 170. Charitable, etc., contributions and gifts

(a) Allowance of deduction.

> **(1) General rule.**—There shall be allowed as a deduction any charitable contribution (as defined in subsection (c)) payment of which is made within the taxable year. A charitable contribution shall be allowable as a deduction only if verified under regulations prescribed by the Secretary. * * *

(c) Charitable contribution defined.—For purposes of this section, the term "charitable contribution" means a contribution or gift to or for the use of * * *

> **(2)** A corporation, trust, or community chest, fund, or foundation * * *

> > **(A)** created or organized in the United States or in any possession thereof, or under the law of the United States, any State, the District of Columbia, or any possession of the United States;

> > **(B)** organized and operated exclusively for religious, charitable, scientific, literary, or educational purposes, or to foster national or international amateur sports competition (but only if no part of its activities involve the provision of athletic facilities or equipment), or for the prevention of cruelty to children or animals;

> > **(C)** no part of the net earnings of which inures to the benefit of any private shareholder or individual; and

> > **(D)** which is not disqualified for tax exemption under section 501(c)(3) by reason of attempting to influence legislation, and which does not participate in, or intervene in (including the publishing or distributing of statements), any political campaign on behalf of (or in opposition to) any candidate for public office.

> > A contribution or gift by a corporation to a trust, chest, fund, or foundation shall be deductible by reason of this paragraph only if it is to be used within the United States or any of its possessions exclusively for purposes specified in subparagraph (B). * * *

> **(4)** In the case of a contribution or gift by an individual, a domestic fraternal society, order, or association, operating under

the lodge system, but only if such contribution or gift is to be used exclusively for religious, charitable, scientific, literary, or educational purposes, or for the prevention of cruelty to children or animals. * * *

26 U.S.C. § 501. Exemption from tax on corporations, certain trusts, etc.

(a) Exemption from taxation.—An organization described in subsection (c) or (d) or section 401(a) shall be exempt from taxation under this subtitle unless such exemption is denied under section 502 or 503. * * *

(c) List of exempt organizations.—The following organizations are referred to in subsection (a): * * *

(3) Corporations, and any community chest, fund, or foundation, organized and operated exclusively for religious, charitable, scientific, testing for public safety, literary, or educational purposes, or to foster national or international amateur sports competition (but only if no part of its activities involve the provision of athletic facilities or equipment), or for the prevention of cruelty to children or animals, no part of the net earnings of which inures to the benefit of any private shareholder or individual, no substantial part of the activities of which is carrying on propaganda, or otherwise attempting, to influence legislation (except as otherwise provided in subsection (h)), and which does not participate in, or intervene in (including the publishing or distributing of statements), any political campaign on behalf of (or in opposition to) any candidate for public office.

(4) **(A)** Civic leagues or organizations not organized for profit but operated exclusively for the promotion of social welfare, or local associations of employees, the membership of which is limited to the employees of a designated person or persons in a particular municipality, and the net earnings of which are devoted exclusively to charitable, educational, or recreational purposes.

(B) Subparagraph (A) shall not apply to an entity unless no part of the net earnings of such entity inures to the benefit of any private shareholder or individual.

(5) Labor, agricultural, or horticultural organizations.

(6) Business leagues, chambers of commerce, real-estate boards, boards of trade, or professional football leagues (whether or not administering a pension fund for football players), not organized for profit and no part of the net earnings of which inures to the benefit of any private shareholder or individual.

(7) Clubs organized for pleasure, recreation, and other nonprofitable purposes, substantially all of the activities of which are for such purposes and no part of the net earnings of which inures to the benefit of any private shareholder.

(8) Fraternal beneficiary societies, orders, or associations—

(A) operating under the lodge system or for the exclusive benefit of the members of a fraternity itself operating under the lodge system, and

(B) providing for the payment of life, sick, accident, or other benefits to the members of such society, order, or association or their dependents. * * *

(i) Prohibition of discrimination by certain social clubs.— Notwithstanding subsection (a), an organization which is described in subsection (c)(7) shall not be exempt from taxation under subsection (a) for any taxable year if, at any time during such taxable year, the charter, bylaws, or other governing instrument, of such organization or any written policy statement of such organization contains a provision which provides for discrimination against any person on the basis of race, color, or religion. The preceding sentence to the extent it relates to discrimination on the basis of religion shall not apply to—

(1) an auxiliary of a fraternal beneficiary society if such society—

(A) is described in subsection (c)(8) and exempt from tax under subsection (a), and

(B) limits its membership to the members of a particular religion, or

(2) a club which in good faith limits its membership to the members of a particular religion in order to further the teachings or principles of that religion, and not to exclude individuals of a particular race or color. * * *

BOB JONES UNIVERSITY V. UNITED STATES
Supreme Court of the United States, 1983.
461 U.S. 574, 103 S.Ct. 2017, 76 L.Ed.2d 157.

CHIEF JUSTICE BURGER delivered the opinion of the Court.

We granted certiorari to decide whether petitioners, nonprofit private schools that prescribe and enforce racially discriminatory admissions standards on the basis of religious doctrine, qualify as tax-exempt organizations under § 501(c)(3) of the Internal Revenue Code of 1954.

[I]   Until 1970, the Internal Revenue Service granted tax-exempt status to private schools, without regard to their racial admissions policies, under § 501(c)(3) of the Internal Revenue Code, 26 U.S.C. § 501(c)(3),[1] and granted charitable deductions for contributions to such schools under § 170 of the Code, 26 U.S.C. § 170.[2]

On January 12, 1970, a three-judge District Court for the District of Columbia issued a preliminary injunction prohibiting the IRS from according tax-exempt status to private schools in Mississippi that discriminated as to admissions on the basis of race. *Green v. Kennedy*, 309 F. Supp. 1127, *app. dismissed sub nom. Cannon v. Green*, 398 U.S. 956 (1970). Thereafter, in July 1970, the IRS concluded that it could "no longer legally justify allowing tax-exempt status [under § 501(c)(3)] to private schools which practice racial discrimination." IRS News Release July 7, 1970. At the same time, the IRS announced that it could not "treat gifts to such schools as charitable deductions for income tax purposes [under § 170]." By letter dated November 30, 1970, the IRS formally notified private schools, including those involved in this case, of this change in policy, "applicable to all private schools in the United States at all levels of education."

On June 30, 1971, the three-judge District Court issued its opinion on the merits of the Mississippi challenge. *Green v. Connally*, 330 F.Supp. 1150 (D.D.C.), *aff'd sub nom. Coit v. Green*, 404 U.S. 997 (1971). That court approved the IRS's amended construction of the Tax Code. The court also held that racially discriminatory private schools were not entitled to exemption under § 501(c)(3) and that donors were not entitled to deductions for contributions to such schools under § 170. The court permanently enjoined the Commissioner of Internal Revenue from approving tax-exempt status for any school in Mississippi that did not publicly maintain a policy of nondiscrimination.

---

[1]   Section 501(c)(3) lists the following organizations, which, pursuant to § 501(a), are exempt from taxation unless denied tax exemptions under other specified sections of the Code:

Corporations, and any community chest, fund, or foundation, *organized and operated exclusively for religious, charitable*, scientific, testing for public safety, literary, *or educational purposes*, or to foster national or international amateur sports competition (but only if no part of its activities involve the provision of athletic facilities or equipment), or for the prevention of cruelty to children or animals, no part of the net earnings of which inures to the benefit of any private shareholder or individual, no substantial part of the activities of which is carrying on propaganda, or otherwise attempting, to influence legislation . . . , and which does not participate in, or intervene in (including the publishing or distributing of statements), any political campaign on behalf of any candidate for public office. (Emphasis added.)

[2]   Section 170(a) allows deductions for certain "charitable contributions." Section 170(c)(2)(B) includes within the definition of "charitable contribution" a contribution or gift to or for the use of a corporation "organized and operated exclusively for religious, charitable, scientific, literary, or educational purposes. . . ."

The revised policy on discrimination was formalized in Revenue Ruling 71–447, 1971–2 Cum. Bull. 230:

> "Both the courts and the Internal Revenue Service have long recognized that the statutory requirement of being 'organized and operated exclusively for religious, charitable, ... or educational purposes' was intended to express the basic common law concept [of 'charity']. ... All charitable trusts, educational or otherwise, are subject to the requirement that the purpose of the trust may not be illegal or contrary to public policy."

Based on the "national policy to discourage racial discrimination in education," the IRS ruled that "a private school not having a racially nondiscriminatory policy as to students is not 'charitable' within the common law concepts reflected in sections 170 and 501(c)(3) of the Code."
* * *

[IIA]   In Revenue Ruling 71–447, the IRS formalized the policy, first announced in 1970, that § 170 and § 501(c)(3) embrace the common law "charity" concept. Under that view, to qualify for a tax exemption pursuant to § 501(c)(3), an institution must show, first, that it falls within one of the eight categories expressly set forth in that section, and second, that its activity is not contrary to settled public policy.

Section 501(c)(3) provides that "[c]orporations ... organized and operated exclusively for religious, charitable ... or educational purposes" are entitled to tax exemption. Petitioners argue that the plain language of the statute guarantees them tax-exempt status. They emphasize the absence of any language in the statute expressly requiring all exempt organizations to be "charitable" in the common-law sense, and they contend that the disjunctive "or" separating the categories in § 501(c)(3) precludes such a reading. Instead, they argue that if an institution falls within one or more of the specified categories it is automatically entitled to exemption, without regard to whether it also qualifies as "charitable." The Court of Appeals rejected that contention and concluded that petitioners' interpretation of the statute "tears section 501(c)(3) from its roots."

It is a well-established canon of statutory construction that a court should go beyond the literal language of a statute if reliance on that language would defeat the plain purpose of the statute. * * *

Section 501(c)(3) therefore must be analyzed and construed within the framework of the Internal Revenue Code and against the background of the congressional purposes. Such an examination reveals unmistakable evidence that, underlying all relevant parts of the Code, is the intent that entitlement to tax exemption depends on meeting certain common-law standards of charity—namely, that an institution seeking tax-exempt status must serve a public purpose and not be contrary to established public policy.

This "charitable" concept appears explicitly in § 170 of the Code. That section contains a list of organizations virtually identical to that contained in § 501(c)(3). It is apparent that Congress intended that list to have the same meaning in both sections.[10] In § 170, Congress used the list of organizations in defining the term "charitable contributions." On its face, therefore, § 170 reveals that Congress' intention was to provide tax benefits to organizations serving charitable purposes. The form of § 170 simply makes plain what common sense and history tell us: in enacting both § 170 and § 501(c)(3), Congress sought to provide tax benefits to charitable organizations, to encourage the development of private institutions that serve a useful public purpose or supplement or take the place of public institutions of the same kind.

Tax exemptions for certain institutions thought beneficial to the social order of the country as a whole, or to a particular community, are deeply rooted in our history, as in that of England. The origins of such exemptions lie in the special privileges that have long been extended to charitable trusts.[12]

More than a century ago, this Court announced the caveat that is critical in this case:

> "[I]t has now become an established principle of American law, that courts of chancery will sustain and protect . . . a gift . . . to public charitable uses, *provided the same is consistent with local laws and public policy. . . .*" *Perin v. Carey*, 24 How. 465, 501 (1861) (emphasis added).

Soon after that, in 1878, the Court commented:

---

[10] The predecessor of § 170 originally was enacted in 1917, as part of the War Revenue Act of 1917, ch. 63, § 1201(2), 40 Stat. 300, 330 (1917), whereas the predecessor of § 501(c)(3) dates back to the income tax law of 1894, Act of Aug. 27, 1894, ch. 349, 28 Stat. 509. There are minor differences between the lists of organizations in the two sections. Nevertheless, the two sections are closely related; both seek to achieve the same basic goal of encouraging the development of certain organizations through the grant of tax benefits. The language of the two sections is in most respects identical, and the Commissioner and the courts consistently have applied many of the same standards in interpreting those sections. To the extent that § 170 "aids in ascertaining the meaning" of § 501(c)(3), therefore, it is "entitled to great weight," *United States v. Stewart*, 311 U.S. 60, 64–65 (1940).

[12] The form and history of the charitable exemption and deduction sections of the various income tax acts reveal that Congress was guided by the common law of charitable trusts. See Simon, *The Tax-Exempt Status of Racially Discriminatory Religious Schools*, 36 Tax L.Rev. 477, 485–489 (1981). Congress acknowledged as much in 1969. The House Report on the Tax Reform Act of 1969, Pub.L. 91–172, 83 Stat. 487, stated that the § 501(c)(3) exemption was available only to institutions that served "the specified charitable purposes," H.R.Rep. No. 91–413, pt. 1, p. 35 (1969), and described "charitable" as "a term that has been used in the law of trusts for hundreds of years." *Id.*, at 43. We need not consider whether Congress intended to incorporate into the Internal Revenue Code any aspects of charitable trust law other than the requirements of public benefit and a valid public purpose.

"A charitable use, *where neither law nor public policy forbids*, may be applied to almost any thing *that tends to promote the well-doing and well-being of social man.*" *Ould v. Washington Hospital for Foundlings*, 95 U.S. 303, 311 (1878) (emphasis added). * * *

When the Government grants exemptions or allows deductions all taxpayers are affected; the very fact of the exemption or deduction for the donor means that other taxpayers can be said to be indirect and vicarious "donors." Charitable exemptions are justified on the basis that the exempt entity confers a public benefit—a benefit which the society or the community may not itself choose or be able to provide, or which supplements and advances the work of public institutions already supported by tax revenues. History buttresses logic to make clear that, to warrant exemption under § 501(c)(3), an institution must fall within a category specified in that section and must demonstrably serve and be in harmony with the public interest. The institution's purpose must not be so at odds with the common community conscience as to undermine any public benefit that might otherwise be conferred.

[IIB]   We are bound to approach these questions with full awareness that determinations of public benefit and public policy are sensitive matters with serious implications for the institutions affected; a declaration that a given institution is not "charitable" should be made only where there can be no doubt that the activity involved is contrary to a fundamental public policy. But there can no longer be any doubt that racial discrimination in education violates deeply and widely accepted views of elementary justice. Prior to 1954, public education in many places still was conducted under the pall of *Plessy v. Ferguson*, 163 U.S. 537 (1896); racial segregation in primary and secondary education prevailed in many parts of the country.[20] This Court's decision in *Brown v. Board of Education*, 347 U.S. 483 (1954), signalled an end to that era. Over the past quarter of a century, every pronouncement of this Court and myriad Acts of Congress and Executive Orders attest a firm national policy to prohibit racial segregation and discrimination in public education.

An unbroken line of cases following *Brown v. Board of Education* establishes beyond doubt this Court's view that racial discrimination in

---

[20] In 1894, when the first charitable exemption provision was enacted, racially segregated educational institutions would not have been regarded as against public policy. Yet contemporary standards must be considered in determining whether given activities provide a public benefit and are entitled to the charitable tax exemption. In *Walz v. Tax Comm'n*, 397 U.S. 664, 673 (1970), we observed: "Qualification for tax exemption is not perpetual or immutable; some tax-exempt groups lose that status when their activities take them outside the classification and new entities can come into being and qualify for exemption." Charitable trust law also makes clear that the definition of "charity" depends upon contemporary standards. See, *e.g.*, Restatement (Second) of Trusts § 374, comment a (1959).

education violates a most fundamental national public policy, as well as rights of individuals.

> "The right of a student not to be segregated on racial grounds in schools . . . is indeed so fundamental and pervasive that it is embraced in the concept of due process of law." *Cooper v. Aaron*, 358 U.S. 1, 19 (1958).

In *Norwood v. Harrison*, 413 U.S. 455, 468–469 (1973), we dealt with a nonpublic institution:

> "[A] private school—even one that discriminates—fulfills an important educational function; *however, . . . [that] legitimate educational function cannot be isolated from discriminatory practices . . . [D]iscriminatory treatment exerts a pervasive influence on the entire educational process.*" (Emphasis added.)

Congress, in Titles IV and VI of the Civil Rights Act of 1964, Pub.L. 88–352, 78 Stat. 241, 42 U.S.C. §§ 2000c et seq., 2000c–6, 2000d et seq., clearly expressed its agreement that racial discrimination in education violates a fundamental public policy. Other sections of that Act, and numerous enactments since then, testify to the public policy against racial discrimination. See, *e.g.*, the Voting Rights Act of 1965; Title VIII of the Civil Rights Act of 1968; [the Emergency School Aid Acts of 1972 and 1978].

The Executive Branch has consistently placed its support behind eradication of racial discrimination. Several years before this Court's decision in *Brown v. Board of Education*, President Truman issued Executive Orders prohibiting racial discrimination in federal employment decisions, Exec. Order No. 9980, 3 CFR 720 (1943–1948 Comp.), and in classifications for the Selective Service, Exec. Order No. 9988, 3 CFR 726, 729 (1943–1948 Comp.). In 1957, President Eisenhower employed military forces to ensure compliance with federal standards in school desegregation programs. Exec. Order No. 10730, 3 CFR 389 (1954–1958 Comp.). And in 1962, President Kennedy announced:

> "[T]he granting of Federal assistance for . . . housing and related facilities from which Americans are excluded because of their race, color, creed, or national origin is unfair, unjust, and inconsistent with the public policy of the United States as manifested in its Constitution and laws." Exec. Order No. 11063, 3 CFR 652 (1959–1963 Comp.).

These are but a few of numerous Executive Orders over the past three decades demonstrating the commitment of the Executive Branch to the fundamental policy of eliminating racial discrimination.

Few social or political issues in our history have been more vigorously debated and more extensively ventilated than the issue of racial discrimination, particularly in education. Given the stress and anguish of the history of efforts to escape from the shackles of the "separate but equal" doctrine of *Plessy v. Ferguson*, it cannot be said that educational institutions that, for whatever reasons, practice racial discrimination, are institutions exercising "beneficial and stabilizing influences in community life," *Walz v. Tax Comm'n*, 397 U.S. 664, 673 (1970), or should be encouraged by having all taxpayers share in their support by way of special tax status.

There can thus be no question that the interpretation of § 170 and § 501(c)(3) announced by the IRS in 1970 was correct. That it may be seen as belated does not undermine its soundness. It would be wholly incompatible with the concepts underlying tax exemption to grant the benefit of tax-exempt status to racially discriminatory educational entities, which "exer[t] a pervasive influence on the entire educational process." *Norwood v. Harrison, supra*. Whatever may be the rationale for such private schools' policies, and however sincere the rationale may be, racial discrimination in education is contrary to public policy. Racially discriminatory educational institutions cannot be viewed as conferring a public benefit within the "charitable" concept discussed earlier, or within the Congressional intent underlying § 170 and § 501(c)(3).

[IIC]	[Chief Justice Burger rejected the argument that the IRS did not have the authority to issue the 1970 rule and that its longstanding prior policy could only be overturned by legislative amendment of the Code. He reasoned that the IRS had been given broad rulemaking power by Congress and, moreover, that the policy adopted by the IRS was fully consistent with national policy since *Brown* and the Civil Rights Act of 1964.]

[IID]	The actions of Congress since 1970 leave no doubt that the IRS reached the correct conclusion in exercising its authority. It is, of course, not unknown for independent agencies or the Executive Branch to misconstrue the intent of a statute; Congress can and often does correct such misconceptions, if the courts have not done so. Yet for a dozen years Congress has been made aware—acutely aware—of the IRS rulings of 1970 and 1971. As we noted earlier, few issues have been the subject of more vigorous and widespread debate and discussion in and out of Congress than those related to racial segregation in education. Sincere adherents advocating contrary views have ventilated the subject for well over three decades. Failure of Congress to modify the IRS rulings of 1970 and 1971, of which Congress was, by its own studies and by public discourse, constantly reminded; and Congress' awareness of the denial of tax-exempt status for racially discriminatory schools when enacting other and related legislation make out an unusually strong case of legislative acquiescence in and ratification by implication of the 1970 and 1971 rulings.

Ordinarily, and quite appropriately, courts are slow to attribute significance to the failure of Congress to act on particular legislation. We have observed that "unsuccessful attempts at legislation are not the best of guides to legislative intent." Here, however, we do not have an ordinary claim of legislative acquiescence. Only one month after the IRS announced its position in 1970, Congress held its first hearings on this precise issue. *Equal Educational Opportunity: Hearings before the Senate Select Comm. on Equal Educational Opportunity*, 91st Cong., 2d Sess. 1991 (1970). Exhaustive hearings have been held on the issue at various times since then. These include hearings in February 1982, after we granted review in this case. *Administration's Change in Federal Policy Regarding the Tax Status of Racially Discriminatory Private Schools: Hearing before the House Comm. on Ways and Means*, 97th Cong., 2d Sess. (1982).

Non-action by Congress is not often a useful guide, but the non-action here is significant. During the past 12 years there have been no fewer than 13 bills introduced to overturn the IRS interpretation of § 501(c)(3). Not one of these bills has emerged from any committee, although Congress has enacted numerous other amendments to § 501 during this same period, including an amendment to § 501(c)(3) itself. Tax Reform Act of 1976, Pub. L. 94–455, § 1313(a), 90 Stat. 1730. It is hardly conceivable that Congress—and in this setting, any Member of Congress—was not abundantly aware of what was going on. In view of its prolonged and acute awareness of so important an issue, Congress' failure to act on the bills proposed on this subject provides added support for concluding that Congress acquiesced in the IRS rulings of 1970 and 1971.

The evidence of Congressional approval of the policy embodied in Revenue Ruling 71–447 goes well beyond the failure of Congress to act on legislative proposals. Congress affirmatively manifested its acquiescence in the IRS policy when it enacted the present § 501(i) of the Code, Act of Oct. 20, 1976, Pub. L. 94–568, 90 Stat. 2697 (1976). That provision denies tax-exempt status to social clubs whose charters or policy statements provide for "discrimination against any person on the basis of race, color, or religion." Both the House and Senate Committee Reports on that bill articulated the national policy against granting tax exemptions to racially discriminatory private clubs. S. Rep. No. 94–1318, p. 8 (1976); H.R. Rep. No. 94–1353, p. 8 (1976).

Even more significant is the fact that both reports focus on this Court's affirmance of *Green v. Connally*, [330 F.Supp. 1150 (D.D.C 1971)], as having established that "discrimination on account of race is inconsistent with an *educational institution's* tax-exempt status." S. Rep. No. 94–1318 at 7–8, and n. 5; H.R. Rep. No. 94–1353 at 8, and n. 5 (emphasis added). These references in congressional Committee Reports on an enactment denying tax exemptions to racially discriminatory private social clubs cannot be read other than as indicating approval of the standards applied to racially discriminatory private schools by the IRS subsequent to 1970, and specifically of Revenue Ruling 71–447.[27]

[In Part III, Chief Justice Burger rejected the argument that the IRS ruling violated the Free Exercise Clause of the First Amendment, and in Part IV he rejected the argument that the IRS ruling was not properly applied to the petitioners.]

JUSTICE POWELL, concurring in the judgment.

[Justice Powell found much to admire in the dissenting opinion's analysis of the statutory text but agreed with the Court's result, based upon the reasoning in Part II.B–D of the opinion for the Court. He did not agree with the reasoning in Part II.A.] I am unconvinced that the critical question in determining tax-exempt status is whether an individual organization provides a clear "public benefit" as defined by the Court. Over 106,000 organizations filed § 501(c)(3) returns in 1981. I find it impossible to believe that all or even most of those organizations could prove that they "demonstrably serve and [are] in harmony with the public interest" or that they are "beneficial and stabilizing influences in community life." Nor I am prepared to say that petitioners, because of their racially discriminatory policies, necessarily contribute nothing of benefit to the community. It is clear from the substantially secular character of the curricula and degrees offered that petitioners provide educational benefits.

Even more troubling to me is the element of conformity that appears to inform the Court's analysis. The Court asserts that an exempt organization must "demonstrably serve and be in harmony with the public interest," must have a purpose that comports with "the common community conscience," and must not act in a manner "affirmatively at

---

[27] Reliance is placed on scattered statements in floor debate by Congressmen critical of the IRS' adoption of Revenue Ruling 71–447. Those views did not prevail. That several Congressmen, expressing their individual views, argued that the IRS had no authority to take the action in question, is hardly a balance for the overwhelming evidence of Congressional awareness of and acquiescence in the IRS rulings of 1970 and 1971. Petitioners also argue that the Ashbrook and Dornan Amendments to the Treasury, Postal Service, and General Government Appropriations Act of 1980, Pub. L. 96–74, §§ 103, 614, 615, 93 Stat. 559, 562, 576–577 (1979), reflect Congressional opposition to the IRS policy formalized in Revenue Ruling 71–447. Those amendments, however, are directly concerned only with limiting more aggressive enforcement procedures proposed by the IRS in 1978 and 1979 and preventing the adoption of more stringent substantive standards. The Ashbrook Amendment, § 103 of the Act, applies only to procedures, guidelines, or measures adopted after August 22, 1978, and thus in no way affects the status of Revenue Ruling 71–447. In fact, both Congressman Dornan and Congressman Ashbrook explicitly stated that their amendments would have no effect on prior IRS policy, including Revenue Ruling 71–447, see 125 Cong. Rec. H5982 (1979) (Cong. Dornan: "[M]y amendment will not affect existing IRS rules which IRS has used to revoke tax exemptions of white segregated academies under Revenue Ruling 71–447. . . ."); id., at 18446 (Cong. Ashbrook: "My amendment very clearly indicates on its face that all the regulations in existence as of August 22, 1978, would not be touched"). These amendments therefore do not indicate Congressional rejection of Revenue Ruling 71–447 and the standards contained therein.

odds with [the] declared position of the whole government." Taken together, these passages suggest that the primary function of a tax-exempt organization is to act on behalf of the Government in carrying out governmentally approved policies. In my opinion, such a view of § 501(c)(3) ignores the important role played by tax exemptions in encouraging diverse, indeed often sharply conflicting, activities and viewpoints. * * * [P]rivate, nonprofit groups receive tax exemptions because "each group contributes to the diversity of association, viewpoint, and enterprise essential to a vigorous, pluralistic society." [*Walz v. Tax Comm'n*, 397 U.S. 664, 689 (1970) (Brennan, J., concurring).] Far from representing an effort to reinforce any perceived "common community conscience," the provision of tax exemptions to nonprofit groups is one indispensable means of limiting the influence of governmental orthodoxy on important areas of community life. Given the importance of our tradition of pluralism, "[t]he interest in preserving an area of untrammeled choice for private philanthropy is very great." *Jackson v. Statler Foundation*, 496 F.2d 623, 639 (CA2 1974) (Friendly, J., dissenting from denial of reconsideration en banc).

[Judgments about whether a class of institutions advances the public interest is a judgment best left to Congress, reasoned Justice Powell. The IRS has, by its own admission, no special expertise in making the kind of determinations the Court upholds in this case.] The contours of public policy should be determined by Congress, not by judges or the IRS.

JUSTICE REHNQUIST, dissenting.

The Court points out that there is a strong national policy in this country against racial discrimination. To the extent that the Court states that Congress in furtherance of this policy could deny tax-exempt status to educational institutions that promote racial discrimination, I readily agree. But, unlike the Court, I am convinced that Congress simply has failed to take this action and, as this Court has said over and over again, regardless of our view on the propriety of Congress' failure to legislate we are not constitutionally empowered to act for them.

In approaching this statutory construction question the Court quite adeptly avoids the statute it is construing. This I am sure is no accident, for there is nothing in the language of § 501(c)(3) that supports the result obtained by the Court. Section 501(c)(3) provides tax-exempt status for:

"Corporations, and any community chest, fund, or foundation, organized and operated exclusively for religious, charitable, scientific, testing for public safety, literary, or educational purposes, or to foster national or international amateur sports competition (but only if no part of its activities involve the provision of athletic facilities or equipment), or for the prevention of cruelty to children or animals, no part of the net earnings of which inures to the benefit of any private shareholder or individual, no substantial part of the activities of which is carrying on propaganda, or otherwise attempting, to influence legislation (except as otherwise provided in subsection (h)), and which does not participate in, or intervene in (including the publishing or distributing of statements), any political campaign on behalf of any candidate for public office." 26 U.S.C. § 501(c)(3).

With undeniable clarity, Congress has explicitly defined the requirements for § 501(c)(3) status. An entity must be (1) a corporation, or community chest, fund, or foundation, (2) organized for one of the eight enumerated purposes, (3) operated on a nonprofit basis, and (4) free from involvement in lobbying activities and political campaigns. Nowhere is there to be found some additional, undefined public policy requirement.

The Court first seeks refuge from the obvious reading of § 501(c)(3) by turning to § 170 of the Internal Revenue Code which provides a tax deduction for contributions made to § 501(c)(3) organizations. In setting forth the general rule, § 170 states:

"There shall be allowed as a deduction any charitable contribution (as defined in subsection (c)) payment of which is made within the taxable year. A charitable contribution shall be allowable as a deduction only if verified under regulations prescribed by the Secretary." 26 U.S.C. § 170(a)(1).

The Court seizes the words "charitable contribution" and with little discussion concludes that "[o]n its face, therefore, § 170 reveals that Congress' intention was to provide tax benefits to organizations serving charitable purposes," intimating that this implies some unspecified common-law charitable trust requirement.

The Court would have been well advised to look to subsection (c) where, as § 170(a)(1) indicates, Congress has defined a "charitable contribution":

"For purposes of this section, the term 'charitable contribution' means a contribution or gift to or for the use of . . . [a] corporation, trust, or community chest, fund, or foundation . . . organized and operated exclusively for religious, charitable, scientific, literary, or educational purposes, or to foster national or international amateur sports competition (but only if no part of its activities involve the provision of athletic facilities or equipment), or for the prevention of cruelty to children or animals; . . . no part of the net earnings of which inures to the benefit of any private shareholder or individual; and . . . which is not disqualified for tax exemption under section 501(c)(3) by reason of attempting to influence legislation, and which does not participate in, or intervene in (including the publishing or distributing of statements), any political campaign on behalf of any candidate for public office." 26 U.S.C. § 170(c).

Plainly, § 170(c) simply tracks the requirements set forth in § 501(c)(3). Since § 170 is no more than a mirror of § 501(c)(3) and, as the Court points out, § 170 followed § 501(c)(3) by more than two decades, it is at best of little usefulness in finding the meaning of § 501(c)(3).

Making a more fruitful inquiry, the Court next turns to the legislative history of § 501(c)(3) and finds that Congress intended in that statute to offer a tax benefit to organizations that Congress believed were providing a public benefit. I certainly agree. But then the Court leaps to the conclusion that this history is proof Congress intended that an organization seeking § 501(c)(3) status "must fall within a category specified in that section *and must demonstrably serve and be in harmony with the public interest.*" (Emphasis added). To the contrary, I think that the legislative history of § 501(c)(3) unmistakably makes clear that *Congress has decided* what organizations are serving a public purpose and providing a public benefit within the meaning of § 501(c)(3) and has clearly set forth in § 501(c)(3) the characteristics of such organizations. In fact, there are few examples which better illustrate Congress' effort to define and redefine the requirements of a legislative act.

The first general income tax law was passed by Congress in the form of the Tariff Act of 1894. A provision of that Act provided an exemption for "corporations, companies, or associations organized and conducted solely for charitable, religious, or educational purposes." The income tax portion of the 1894 Act was held unconstitutional by this Court, see *Pollock v. Farmers' Loan & Trust Co.*, 158 U.S. 601 (1895), but a similar exemption appeared in the Tariff Act of 1909 which imposed a tax on corporate income. The 1909 Act provided an exemption for "any corporation or association organized and operated exclusively for religious, charitable, or educational purposes, no part of the net income of which inures to the benefit of any private stockholder or individual."

With the ratification of the Sixteenth Amendment, Congress again turned its attention to an individual income tax with the Tariff Act of 1913. And again, in the direct predecessor of § 501(c)(3), a tax exemption was provided for "any corporation or association organized and operated exclusively for religious, charitable, scientific, or educational purposes, no part of the net income of which inures to the benefit of any private stockholder or individual." In subsequent Acts Congress continued to broaden the list of exempt purposes. The Revenue Act of 1918 added an exemption for corporations or associations organized "for the prevention of cruelty to children or animals." The Revenue Act of 1921 expanded the groups to which the exemption applied to include "any community chest, fund, or foundation" and added "literary" endeavors to the list of exempt purposes. The exemption remained unchanged in the Revenue Acts of 1924, 1926, 1928, and 1932. In the Revenue Act of 1934 Congress added the requirement that no substantial part of the activities of any exempt organization can involve the carrying on of "propaganda" or "attempting to influence legislation." Again, the exemption was left unchanged by the Revenue Acts of 1936 and 1938.

The tax laws were overhauled by the Internal Revenue Code of 1939, but this exemption was left unchanged. When the 1939 Code was replaced with the Internal Revenue Code of 1954, the exemption was adopted in full in the present § 501(c)(3) with the addition of "testing for public safety" as an exempt purpose and an additional restriction that tax-exempt organizations could not "participate in, or intervene in (including the publishing or distributing of statements), any political campaign on behalf of any candidate for public office." Ch. 1, § 501(c)(3), 68A Stat. 163 (1954). Then in 1976 the statute was again amended adding to the purposes for which an exemption would be authorized, "to foster national or international amateur sports competition," provided the activities did not involve the provision of athletic facilities or equipment. Tax Reform Act of 1976, Pub. L. 94–455, § 1313(a), 90 Stat. 1520, 1730 (1976).

One way to read the opinion handed down by the Court today leads to the conclusion that this long and arduous refining process of § 501(c)(3) was certainly a waste of time, for when enacting the original 1894 statute Congress intended to adopt a common law term of art, and intended that this term of art carry with it all of the common law baggage which defines it. Such a view, however, leads also to the unsupportable idea that Congress has spent almost a century adding illustrations simply to clarify an already defined common law term. * * *

Perhaps recognizing the lack of support in the statute itself, or in its history, for the 1970 IRS change in interpretation, the Court finds that "[t]he actions of Congress since 1970 leave no doubt that the IRS reached the correct conclusion in exercising its authority," concluding that there is "an unusually strong case of legislative acquiescence in and ratification by implication of the 1970 and 1971 rulings." The Court relies first on several bills introduced to overturn the IRS interpretation of § 501(c)(3). But we have said before, and it is equally applicable here, that this type of congressional inaction is of virtually no weight in determining legislative intent. See *United States v. Wise*, 370 U.S. 405, 411 (1962); *Waterman S.S. Corp. v. United States*, 381 U.S. 252, 269 (1965). These bills and related hearings indicate little more than that a vigorous debate has existed in Congress concerning the new IRS position.

The Court next asserts that "Congress affirmatively manifested its acquiescence in the IRS policy when it enacted the present § 501(i) of the Code," a provision that "denies tax-exempt status to social clubs whose charters or policy statements provide for" racial discrimination. Quite to the contrary, it seems to me that in § 501(i) Congress showed that when it wants to add a requirement prohibiting racial discrimination to one of the tax-benefit provisions, it is fully aware of how to do it.

The Court intimates that the Ashbrook and Dornan Amendments also reflect an intent by Congress to acquiesce in the new IRS position. The amendments were passed to limit certain enforcement procedures proposed by the IRS in 1978 and 1979 for determining whether a school operated in a racially nondiscriminatory fashion. The Court points out that in proposing his amendment, Congressman Ashbrook stated: " 'My amendment very clearly indicates on its face that all the regulations in existence as of August 22, 1978, would not be touched.' " The Court fails to note that Congressman Ashbrook also said:

> "The IRS has no authority to create public policy. . . . So long as the Congress has not acted to set forth a national policy respecting denial of tax exemptions to private schools, it is improper for the IRS or any other branch of the Federal Government to seek denial of tax-exempt status. . . . There exists but a single responsibility which is proper for the Internal Revenue Service: To serve as tax collector." 125 Cong. Rec. H5879–80 (1979).

In the same debate, Congressman Grassley asserted: "Nobody argues that racial discrimination should receive preferred tax status in the United States. However, the IRS should not be making these decisions on the agency's own discretion. Congress should make these decisions." *Id.*, at 5884. The same debates are filled with other similar statements. While on the whole these debates do not show conclusively that Congress believed the IRS had exceeded its authority with the 1970 change in position, they likewise are far less than a showing of acquiescence in and ratification of the new position.

This Court continuously has been hesitant to find ratification through inaction. This is especially true where such a finding "would result in a construction of the statute which not only is at odds with the language of the section in question and the pattern of the statute taken as a whole, but also is extremely far reaching in terms of the virtually untrammeled and unreviewable power it would vest in a regulatory agency." *SEC v. Sloan*, 436 U.S. 103, 121 (1978). Few cases would call for more caution in finding ratification by acquiescence than the present one. The new IRS interpretation is not only far less than a long-standing administrative policy, it is at odds with a position maintained by the IRS, and unquestioned by Congress, for several decades prior to 1970. The interpretation is unsupported by the statutory language, it is unsupported by legislative history, the interpretation has led to considerable controversy in and out of Congress, and the interpretation gives to the IRS a broad power which until now Congress had kept for itself. Where in addition to these circumstances Congress has shown time and time again that it is ready to enact positive legislation to change the Tax Code when it desires, this Court has no business finding that Congress has adopted the new IRS position by failing to enact legislation to reverse it.

I have no disagreement with the Court's finding that there is a strong national policy in this country opposed to racial discrimination. I agree with the Court that Congress has the power to further this policy by denying § 501(c)(3) status to organizations that practice racial discrimination. But as of yet Congress has failed to do so. Whatever the reasons for the failure, this Court should not legislate for Congress. * * *

NOTES AND QUESTIONS ON MANCARI AND BOB JONES

1. *Continuity Canons in* Mancari *and* Bob Jones. Although Justice Blackmun voiced several reasons to support the result in *Mancari,* the continuity norm of the presumption against implied repeals was apparently the tiebreaker in that case. For example, the Court's first reason is subject to the reply that Congress showed itself able to exempt Indians from the operation of antidiscrimination laws in 1964; the absence of any express exemption in the 1972 Act, then, gives a strong *expressio unius* argument to plaintiffs. Likewise, the fact that Congress enacted explicit Native American preferences in two other 1972 statutes (Justice Blackmun's second reason) provides a textual reason to reach the opposite result: Under the meaningful variation canon, Congress's explicit carve-out in these other laws is a meaningful contrast with the general nondiscrimination rule in the 1972 Amendments. The third argument, grounded in prior interpretation of executive orders, is based on the same continuity norm and reliance interests as the rule against implied repeals. The rule against implied repeals is a mighty powerful canon (as these canons go). The Supreme Court almost *never* finds that one statute has implicitly repealed another one altogether. The Court's normal approach when there is an apparent conflict between two statutes is to figure out whether there is way to interpret them to leave both in effect—but if the statutes are truly "irreconcilable" then the earlier one must be deemed repealed. For a recent example of the Court's practice, see *Pom Wonderful LLC v. Coca-Cola Co.,* 134 S.Ct. 2228 (2014) (reconciling a potential conflict between the Lanham Act and the Federal Food, Drug and Cosmetic Act in a drink labeling dispute).

Bob Jones is a leading cite for several other continuity canons. First, the case stands for the principle of *legislative acquiescence*: the Court relied on the failure of Congress to overrule the 1971 revenue ruling and concluded that Congress—by doing nothing—acquiesced in the agency's action. Justice Powell was also persuaded by this justification. (In our opinion, however, the Court was inconsistent in its application of this rule. Congress failed to overrule the IRS policy *before* 1971, too. Why didn't that count in the Court's view?) The case also stands for the *rejected proposal rule*. The Court placed great weight on the fact that more than a dozen bills had been introduced to overturn the IRS's interpretation, but they never got anywhere in Congress. The imputation of congressional intent to such rejected proposals, in the Court's view, was even more powerful because Congress had amended § 501 in other ways numerous times since the 1970s.

2.   *Other Canons in* Bob Jones. *Bob Jones* provides a cornucopia of other familiar canons for your review. Did you notice the whole act rule (the Court drew meaning from the appearance of the same list of organizations in a different section of the Tax Code, § 170), or the presumption that statutes are to be construed in accordance with the common law (the Court emphasized that the common law of charitable trusts requires that they be consistent with public policy)? Chief Justice Burger even cited *Holy Trinity* for this proposition: "It is a well-established canon of statutory construction that a court should go beyond the literal language of a statute if reliance on that language would defeat the plain purpose of the statute." Justice Rehnquist's dissent relied on other canons, namely, plain meaning and an *expressio unius*-type argument about the evolution of the Tax Code: Congress's long history of amending the tax code—making minor refinements and adding new categories—to the list of exemptions illustrates that Congress knows how to refine § 501(c)(3), and so any omissions should be assumed intentional. Justice Rehnquist also asserted a powerful *expressio* argument in the fact that Congress added § 501(i) to deny tax exempt statues to racially discriminatory social clubs. Do you find the reasoning persuasive?

3.   *Reading Statutes in Light of Larger Statutory and Constitutional Policy.* Even if Justice Rehnquist were right that the statutory text lends support to Bob Jones's position, Chief Justice Burger maintained that the public policy context requires a clearer statement from Congress in order to consider a racially discriminatory institution to be "charitable." Mayer G. Freed and Daniel D. Polsby, in *Race, Religion & Public Policy*: Bob Jones University v. United States, 1983 Sup. Ct. Rev. 1, 5, object to Chief Justice Burger's reliance on general "public policy"—the Constitution, Title VI and other provisions of the Civil Rights Act—to rewrite § 501. We count even more sources of public policy used by the Court as part of its horizontal coherence and continuity approach: In addition to the Constitution and other statutes, Chief Justice Burger also invoked other judicial precedents (an unbroken line of cases since *Brown* showing that discrimination in education violates public policy), executive actions (anti-discrimination executive orders), regulations, and even subsequent statutes as evidence of the current political equilibrium that the Court uses to help it interpret the statute.

Yet none of the sources cited by Chief Justice Burger actually prohibited Bob Jones University's private race discrimination. Is there something anomalous about "expanding" these constitutional and statutory authorities beyond their well-defined ambit? Do judges have a comparative advantage over Congress to update statutes in this way? How is a Court to choose among the range of "public values"? Is there any concern that such a dynamic approach might, over time, politicize and undermine judicial legitimacy—or encourage Congress to be lazy and let the Court do the hard work?

As Professor Johnson points out, an earlier draft of the Chief Justice's opinion did note that federal law barred private schools from discriminating on the basis of race—but Burger dropped that highly relevant reference in the final opinion. See Olatunde Johnson, *The Story of* Bob Jones University v. United States (1983): *Race, Religion, and Congress's Extraordinary Acquiescence*, in *Statutory Interpretation Stories* 126, 151 (Eskridge, Frickey & Garrett eds., 2011). In fact, Bob Jones was violating 42 U.S.C. § 1981, which bars race discrimination in private contracting, and which the Supreme Court had interpreted to bar private schools from discriminating on the basis of race. Does § 1981 provide a cogent response to the Freed and Polsby concerns? Why might the Chief Justice have dropped reference to § 1981 in his opinion for the Court?

4. *Horizontal Versus Vertical Coherence.* Notice how Chief Justice Burger's public-policy oriented approach in *Bob Jones* might come into tension with another coherence value; namely the vertical coherence value of *stare decisis.* In our baseball case from Chapter 3, for example, *Flood v. Kuhn*, a horizontal coherence approach like the one taken in *Bob Jones* would have led the Court to update the antitrust rule for baseball, bringing it in line with all of the other professional sports. But the Court favored vertical coherence (*stare decisis*) over horizontal coherence (consistency with current statutory and constitutional norms). What considerations would you take into account in considering how to resolve this kind of tension?

5. *Public Values or Public Hypocrisy? Bob Jones* reads like a very high-minded opinion: How can we as a society subsidize segregated schools? We cannot! That sounds great, a ringing reaffirmation of *Brown v. Board of Education.* But the reality is a great deal less inspiring. See Johnson, *Story of* Bob Jones (detailed account from which we draw). The Carter Administration's IRS issued regulations in 1978–79 placing burdens on schools with low minority percentages to "prove" their nondiscrimination. Congress reacted with the Dornan and Ashbrook Amendments, which effectively barred the IRS from implementing the new regulations. (Justice Rehnquist relied on these amendments in objecting to the acquiescence argument. Did he have a point?) When *Bob Jones* was decided, IRS enforcement depended heavily on "self-reporting": Institutions that admitted to race discrimination were the only ones to lose their tax exemptions. In short, only those institutions that discriminated as a matter of principle—like Bob Jones—lost their tax exemption. Institutions that deceived the IRS (or themselves) did not. Is this a "public value"?

At the same time Bob Jones was suing to recover its tax-exempt status, African-American parents were suing the IRS to enforce the nondiscrimination rule more effectively. Then-judge Ruth Bader Ginsburg of the D.C. Circuit wrote an opinion favorable to the parents, but the Supreme Court reversed. A year after the Court decided *Bob Jones*, it held (by a slender 5–4 majority) that these parents lacked "standing" to sue the IRS, thereby failing to satisfy the Court's "case or controversy" requirement, discussed in Chapter 3, § 1. See *Allen v. Wright*, 468 U.S. 737 (1984). The grudging approach to standing taken in *Allen* is an ironic contrast to the expansive approach to the antidiscrimination principle taken in *Bob Jones*. The contrast is all the more striking when it is noted that there were significant justiciability problems in *Bob Jones* itself. While *Bob Jones* was pending on appeal to the Supreme Court, the Reagan Administration switched sides and announced that it agreed with Bob Jones and wanted to change the regulation back to its pre-1970 status. Because the two parties in *Bob Jones University v. United States* both agreed that Bob Jones should be exempt, why was the case not moot? Was there an ongoing "case or controversy" as required by the Court's reading of Article III? See Chapter 3, § 1. As it has done in other cases, the Court kept the appeal alive by appointing William Coleman, a former Secretary of Transportation, "to brief and argue this case, as *amicus curiae*, in support of the judgments below." 456 U.S. 922 (1982) (order of Court). Of course, Coleman, who represented neither party, won the case!

After 1984, the IRS was left with few incentives to enforce *Bob Jones*: Congress in the Ashbrook Amendment had signaled that it didn't want vigorous enforcement, President Reagan had formally abandoned the policy until it was forced back upon him by the Supreme Court, and private citizens who might object to the virtual abandonment of the policy were not easily able to get into court, while any segregated school that loses its exemption of course has standing to sue the IRS. Is this a scenario likely to promote "public values"?

Consider a final historical irony. Bob Jones University has in the new millennium not only revoked its race-discriminatory admissions policy, but has also issued a public apology for the race discrimination it practiced for most of its history. See Johnson, *The Story of* Bob Jones, 157. What do you make of that?

NOTE ON LEGISLATED CANONS OF STATUTORY INTERPRETATION

Sometimes the legislature attempts to direct the court in how to interpret a particular statute. For example, a provision of the federal Racketeer Influenced and Corrupt Organizations Act (RICO), 18 U.S.C. § 1961, which contains criminal sanctions, contains precisely such a *rule of construction*: "[t]he provisions of this title shall be liberally construed to effectuate its remedial purposes." Some constitutional objections to such a provision could conceivably be raised—the most straightforward would be that it violates the separation of powers because it invades the court's power to say what the law is—but leaving that problem aside, what should a court do with this rule of construction? In *Russello v. United States*, 464 U.S. 16, 26–27 (1983), the Court cited the RICO provision as well as legislative history to support a broad construction of the statute. In contrast, in *Reves v. Ernst & Young*, 507 U.S. 170, 183–84 (1993), the Court said the following about the RICO clause:

> This clause obviously seeks to ensure that Congress' intent is not frustrated by an overly narrow reading of the statute, but it is not an invitation to apply RICO to new purposes that Congress never intended. Nor does the clause help us to determine what purposes Congress had in mind. Those must be gleaned from the statute through the normal means of interpretation. The clause "only serves as an aid for resolving an ambiguity; it is not to be used to beget one."

Does this approach leave any role for the interpretive clause at all?

Congress has also adopted the Dictionary Act, which codifies a few generic canons of statutory construction, such as the rules that singular terms include the plural, and male pronouns also include females. See 1 U.S.C. § 1 *et seq.* By its terms, the Dictionary Act does not apply where context indicates otherwise, and so the Act has traditionally been relatively toothless) (2014) (relying on the Dictionary Act's definition of "person" as including "corporations" to hold that for-profit, closely held corporations are "persons" protected by the Religious Freedom Restoration Act).

All 50 states and the District of Columbia have adopted more ambitious interpretation acts legislating canons to guide judicial interpretation for all statutes. Chapter 645 of the Minnesota Statutes, for example, contains the following provisions:

645.16.   LEGISLATIVE INTENT CONTROLS

The object of all interpretation and construction of laws is to ascertain and effectuate the intention of the legislature. Every law shall be construed, if possible, to give effect to all its provisions.

When the words of a law in their application to an existing situation are clear and free from all ambiguity, the letter of the law shall not be disregarded under the pretext of pursuing the spirit.

When the words of a law are not explicit, the intention of the legislature may be ascertained by considering, among other matters:

    (1)   The occasion and necessity for the law;

    (2)   The circumstances under which it was enacted;

    (3)   The mischief to be remedied;

(4)   The object to be attained;

(5)   The former law, if any, including other laws upon the same or similar subjects;

(6)   The consequences of a particular interpretation;

(7)   The contemporaneous legislative history; and

(8)   Legislative and administrative interpretations of the statute.

645.17. PRESUMPTIONS IN ASCERTAINING LEGISLATIVE INTENT

In ascertaining the intention of the legislature the courts may be guided by the following presumptions:

(1)   The legislature does not intend a result that is absurd, impossible of execution, or unreasonable;

(2)   The legislature intends the entire statute to be effective and certain;

(3)   The legislature does not intend to violate the constitution of the United States or of this state;

(4)   When a court of last resort has construed the language of a law, the legislature in subsequent laws on the same subject matter intends the same construction to be placed upon such language; and

(5)   The legislature intends to favor the public interest as against any private interest.

Notice that Minnesota's legislated canons provide (1) a general theory of statutory interpretation, (2) an indication of the sources judges should consult and when they might consult them, and (3) specific presumptions of statutory meaning.

In a pathbreaking study, Jacob Scott, *Codified Canons and the Common Law of Interpretation*, 98 Geo. L.J. 341 (2010), collected and categorized the statutory canons for all 50 states and the District of Columbia. Scott then analyzed the patterns he found across the nationwide sample. Among the patterns he reported are the following:

- **Plain Meaning.** Fifteen legislatures, including that of Minnesota, have codified the plain meaning rule, but with explicit inclusion of exceptions for "absurd results" and/or "scrivener's errors" (Table 1, p. 357). Thirty-four legislatures have codified the dictionary canon and the canon that "ordinary usage" should normally be applied (Table 1). No legislature has codified *expressio unius*, and only two have codified *ejusdem generis* or *noscitur a sociis*.

- **Whole Act.** Thirty legislatures (including Minnesota's) have codified the whole act rule *and* the presumption of consistent usage of terms within a statute (Table 3, p. 368). Thirty-one have codified the rule against interpreting one provision in a way that is inconsistent with the structure of the statute (Table 3). Ten states (including Minnesota) have codified the rule against surplusage (Table 3).

- **Consistency Across Statutes.** Twenty-six states (including Minnesota) have codified the presumption that the same term should be interpreted consistently across different statutes (Table 6, p. 378). Fifteen states have codified the canon against implied repeals (Table 10, p. 397).

- **Legislative History.** Eleven states (including Minnesota) have codified the rule that legislative history "may" be considered under various circumstances; no state has legislated against consideration of legislative history (Table 7, p. 383). Like Minnesota's codification, most of these codifications require the statute to be ambiguous, but a few states (such as Texas) say legislative history can be consulted under any circumstances.

- **Constitutional Canons.** Minnesota is unusual in not codifying any of the policy or constitutional canons. Five states have codified the avoidance canon; none has rejected it (Table 8, p. 388). Thirty-five states have codified the presumption of severability (Table 8). Twenty-four states have codified the presumption against statutory retroactivity (Table 9, p. 391).

- **Purposive Canons.** Like Minnesota, 21 other states have codified the canon that ambiguous statutes should be interpreted to carry out the legislative purpose (Table 10, p. 397). Nineteen state legislatures say that remedial statutes should be liberally construed, and 17 states say that all statutes should be liberally construed (Table 11, p. 402). Eleven states have codified the presumption that the legislature intends "reasonable" results (Table 11).

Scott argues that there is thus a "common law" of canons of statutory construction—a common law to which legislatures and not just courts are contributing. He suggests that judges ought to be chary of deploying canons, such as *expressio unius* or *ejusdem generis*, that legislatures have uniformly failed to embrace. If statutory interpretation is supposed to be attentive to legislative intent, as most judges are, is it not relevant that legislated canons never include *expressio unius* or *ejusdem generis* and overwhelmingly endorse the absurd results exception to plain meaning and the importance of legislative purpose in resolving statutory ambiguities? Conversely, Scott suggests that the pattern of codification lends legislative, and perhaps democratic, support and legitimacy to the pragmatic approach laid out in

William N. Eskridge Jr. & Philip P. Frickey, *Statutory Interpretation as Practical Reasoning*, 42 Stan. L. Rev. 321 (1990) (Chapter 4, § 3(C)).

Of course, this point has traction for general theories of statutory interpretation, too. If Congress does not know, or even consciously rejects, the canons that courts deploy, how can these methodologies of statutory interpretation continue to be justified—as most commentators and judges justify them—under the rubric that judges are acting as "faithful agents of the legislature"? See *Gluck & Bressman, Statutory Interpretation from the Inside: Part I* (documenting many canons that congressional drafters do not know or that they reject).

For an argument that Congress has and should exercise the authority to enact more ambitious federal rules of statutory interpretation (more like those of Minnesota and other states), see Nicholas Quinn Rosenkranz, *Federal Rules of Statutory Interpretation*, 115 Harv. L. Rev. 2085 (2002). For assessments of this approach, see Linda D. Jellum, *"Which Is to Be Master," the Judiciary or the Legislature? When Statutory Directives Violate Separation of Powers*, 56 UCLA L. Rev. 837 (2009), Adam W. Kiracofe, Note, *The Codified Canons of Statutory Construction: A Response and Proposal to Nicholas Rosenkranz's* Federal Rules of Statutory Interpretation, 84 B.U. L. Rev. 571 (2004). For a critique and counter-proposal suggesting that an organization like the American Law Institute formulate a restatement of statutory interpretation, see Gary E. O'Connor, *Restatement (First) of Statutory Interpretation*, 7 N.Y.U. J. Legis. & Pub. Pol'y 333 (2003–2004).

Justice Scalia and Professor Garner contend that these debates about whether legislators have the power to impose statutory interpretation canons on courts are merely "academic," because these legislated rules do not exist in the real world. Scalia & Garner, *Reading Law*, 245. But it is not only the state-law landscape that proves Scalia and Garner wrong. Federal legislation is littered with rules of construction, like the RICO rule set out at the beginning of this note. A Westlaw search for the phrase "shall be construed," for example, returns more than 5000 such rules. It is clear that the story of the canons—what they are, how they apply, and where they come from—is not settled yet.

CHAPTER 6

LEGISLATIVE HISTORY AND LAWMAKING CONTEXT

■ ■ ■

In this chapter, we address questions focusing on statutory and legislative history, offering a more sophisticated account of how Congress works. We contend that this legislative-context-focused approach illuminates both text and purpose. The chapter introduces a method of "reverse" engineering, using Congress's rules, one that offers a more efficient and reliable way to understand the legislative process and the materials that come out of it. This approach reflects a more general theory, also developed in this chapter, that different lawmaking contexts may affect interpretation, from the differences between statutes drafted by a single Senator to statutes drafted in committee, to statutes enacted through direct democracy. The chapter also sets out the major conceptual debates about the use of legislative history, the very idea of legislative "intent," as well as arguments based on the Constitution.

The history of a statute will often provide useful context for interpreting that law. Recall the "no vehicles in the park" statute from the Introduction. Does the statute ban tricycles from the park? The law's *statutory history* (the formal evolution of the statutory code) might provide important clues. For example, assume that the no-vehicles law said "vehicles" but was later amended to add the word "motor" before "vehicles." In that case, it is very clear that the bill should be read to be limited to motorized transportation. The lawmaking history of the statutory language is thus relevant to its meaning. Strict textualists, as well as most other kinds of interpreters, will in theory consider a law's statutory history, although practice is less consistent.

Contrast *statutory history* with *legislative history*, namely, the internal institutional progress of a bill to enactment and the deliberation accompanying that progress. Recall the normal process of legislation laid out in Chapter 1, § 1. Each stage of the process usually produces records of public deliberation regarding not only the desirability of the proposed legislation but also what it is trying to accomplish and, sometimes, how it will be applied to particular circumstances. These documents, as well as the record of chamber debates, will often contain declarations of purpose or application that are potentially relevant to an interpretive issue. For example, consider a case where the statute says "vehicle" but the committee report consistently identifies mechanisms that triggered the statute as "motorized." That evidence might count strongly against an application of the statute to tricycles as an example of the contextual assumptions made by the statute's drafters.

The larger theoretical point here is about lawmaking context. If you change the lawmaking context, should that affect interpretation? This applies to changes in the type of process at a macro and micro level. For example, as we will see, law made in parliamentary as opposed to presidential systems, or in the states versus the federal system, might yield different answers. Finally, differences within a body, such as the variety of different lawmaking contexts within Congress, may matter. So, for example, appropriations committee work is very different from that of authorization committees, and their products often interact in unique ways that may be relevant to the meaning of statutes.

At the outset, students should recognize that when one uses the term "legislative history," one is likely to ignite a fairly serious public debate. In the wake of the revival of the plain meaning rule in *TVA v. Hill* (Chapter 4, § 3A), the U.S. Supreme Court reduced its reliance on legislative history—and during the Reagan Administration (1981–89) lawyers, judges, and academics questioned the value of legislative history. Soon supported by Justice Scalia's pointed opinions in the Supreme Court, "new textualists" argued that "legislative history" should never be consulted, that it might be "shameful" or "wrong" to do so, and that it was even "unconstitutional."[1] We consider these more general arguments at length—reprinting the Reagan Administration's Justice Department position below. Having said that, however, it would not be accurate for readers to believe that courts do not use legislative history or that the Supreme Court blinds itself to that history even after two decades of public dispute. Legislative history is regularly briefed in federal and state courts[2] although practice varies as to how much weight it is given. We

---

[1] For in-depth analyses of the new textualism, see, e.g., William N. Eskridge Jr., *The New Textualism*, 37 UCLA L. Rev. 621 (1990); John F. Manning, *Textualism as a Nondelegation Doctrine*, 97 Colum. L. Rev. 673 (1997); Jonathan Molot, *The Rise and Fall of Textualism*, 106 Colum. L. Rev. 1, 23–29 (2006).

[2] In a Westlaw search conducted on September 16, 2011 in the Westlaw U.S. Courts of Appeals database using the term "legislative history" at least 5 times in a single case resulted in over 5000 appellate cases; at least 4 times, yields over 7000 cases; and at least 3 times, yields over 10,000 cases (in a database retrieving cases from 1891). It would thus be quite premature for lawyers not to learn, cite, or be prepared to rebut claims drawn from legislative history. For recent examples, see *DePierre v. United States*, 131 S.Ct. 2225 (2011); *Bruesewitz v. Wyeth LLC*, 131 S.Ct. 1068 (2011); *Los Angeles County v. Humphries*, 131 S.Ct. 447 (2010); *Bilski v. Kappos*, 130 S.Ct. 3218 (2010); *Recovery Grp, Inc. v. C.I.R.*, 652 F.3d 122 (1st Cir. 2011); *Cohen v. United States*, 650 F.3d 717 (D.C. Cir. 2011).

conclude the chapter by outlining larger theoretical and constitutional debates about legislative history.

A final note on terminology: the term "legislative history" itself deserves some clarification.[3] Those inclined toward textualism should ask themselves as they read the cases in the chapter whether textualist judges are actively tracing statutory, as opposed to legislative, history and whether that might improve their analysis. They should also ask whether statutory history changes their views about the proper text at issue. By contrast, those inclined toward purposivism should ask themselves if their analysis might be improved by greater attention to the relevant lawmaking context.

1.   SHOULD JUDGES OR AGENCIES CONSULT LEGISLATIVE CONTEXT?

Although everyone agrees that judges should start with text and even textualists agree that text may reveal purpose, there is no such agreement about legislative history. Deep conceptual divisions remain. When it comes to the relevance of the broader legislative context, such as the structure of Congress and differences across types of statutes, we see the opposite problem—almost no attention has been paid to that question, by either textualists or purposivists.

We begin here with the debate that does exist, over legislative history, and introduce the broader contextual factors, which we think also highly relevant, in Section 2 and 3 of this chapter. Many textualists believe that interpreters should not give any weight to legislative history. *E.g.*, Antonin Scalia, *A Matter of Interpretation* 23 (1997); Antonin Scalia & Bryan Garner, *Reading Law: The Interpretation of Legal Texts* (2012). Purposivists and pragmatic interpreters, by contrast, agree that one should begin with the text but are happy to look at the legislative history to complement the text's indications of purpose. E.g., Stephen Breyer, *On the Uses of Legislative History in Interpreting Statutes*, 65 S. Cal. L. Rev. 845, 864–65 (1992); Stephen Breyer, *Active Liberty* ch. 8 (2005).

A central criticism advanced by legislative history skeptics is that judges should not supplant plain meaning with a ragbag of external evidence favoring their own ideological views. Textualists sometimes argue that Congress's statutes are like contracts where external evidence is generally disallowed. In the 1980s, however, even legislative history's advocates raised doubts about whether judges were capable of using legislative history in a sophisticated manner. In one of the most quoted articles on the topic, Judge Patricia Wald, in *Some Observations on the*

---

[3]   For an intensive inquiry into the question of what constitutes legislative history, see Victoria F. Nourse, *Elementary Statutory Interpretation: Rethinking Statutory Intent and History* (forthcoming)).

Use of Legislative History in the 1981 Supreme Court Term, 68 Iowa L. Rev. 195, 214 (1983), opined that "consistent and uniform rules for statutory construction and use of legislative materials are not being followed today. It sometimes seems that citing legislative history is still, as my late colleague Harold Leventhal once observed, akin to 'looking over a crowd and picking out your friends.' "

Although jurists like Scalia and Breyer have contributed a good deal to the debate, the biggest governmental users of legislative history are agencies. The regulatory agencies routinely look to legislative history as evidence of Congress's directions for implementation. Enforcement agencies, too, especially the U.S. Department of Justice, are frequently users, including in litigation. Interestingly, it is the Office of Legal Policy in the Department of Justice that published the most extensive critique of legislative history, in a document it produced during the Reagan Administration, which appointed many of the new textualist judges to the federal bench. This critique has provided the conceptual foundation for many of the textualist objections.

Office of Legal Policy, *Using and Misusing Legislative History: A Re-Evaluation of the Status of Legislative History in Statutory Interpretation*

(Department of Justice, January 5, 1989) (summary and selected quotations).

During the Reagan Administration, the Office of Legal Policy (OLP) advanced a sophisticated, and influential, array of reasons why courts and agencies (including the Department) should not rely on legislative materials when interpreting statutes.[4]

Starting with first principles, OLP posited that the proper object of statutory interpretation is the *actual meaning* of the words Congress enacts. Actual meaning is "the meaning that the words of the statute convey to the typical members of the audience" (p. 21). The Office conceded that intended meaning might often vary from actual meaning— and took the position that actual meaning must always prevail (pp. 21–26).

One set of justifications for preferring actual meaning over intended meaning (and hence for disregarding internal legislative materials) is that the former is much more coherent and easily discoverable. "Legislative intent" for a body as large and diverse as Congress, the Office maintained, is not a coherent notion (p. ii). Thus, political scientists tell

---

[4] The analysis in text also draws from William N. Eskridge Jr., *The New Textualism*, 37 UCLA L. Rev. 621 (1990); John F. Manning, *Textualism as a Nondelegation Doctrine*, 97 Colum. L. Rev. 673 (1997); Jonathan Molot, *The Rise and Fall of Textualism*, 106 Colum. L. Rev. 1, 23–29 (2006).

us that Congress is a "they" and not an "it."[5] So even if one could aggregate the likely preferences of 218 House Members and 51 (or 60) Senators, the exercise in and of itself would miss the point of the institution: the very essence of Congress is its multiplicity, its "535–ness."[6]

Even if legislative intent were a coherent idea, it would be unknowable for virtually any piece of legislation (p. ii). Rarely do the legislative materials tell us what more than a handful of representatives thought about an issue; indeed, in most cases the legislative discussion is vaguer than the statutory language and tells us nothing about the expectations of a handful. And even when legislative materials are packed with speeches by various Members of Congress, it is impossible to aggregate the individual expectations of 435 House Members and match them up with an aggregation of as many as 100 Senators and with the President's intent when he or she signs the measure into law. Max Radin, *Statutory Interpretation*, 43 Harv. L. Rev. 863 (1930).

OLP advanced a second set of reasons for focusing only on a statute's actual meaning and, therefore, ignoring intended meaning and excluding legislative history; these reasons were explicitly grounded in the Office's understanding of the U.S. Constitution. "The Constitution and the legislative process it establishes *assume* an approach to statutory interpretation that focuses on the actual rather than the intended meaning of the statutory text" (p. 26). As a matter of faithfully executing the law (agencies) or authoritatively interpreting the law (judges), interpreters must never lose sight of the text, which is formally all that Congress enacts into "law" under the process described by Article I, § 7. "This [actual meaning] approach is implicit in the establishment of a bicameral legislature and in the requirement that bills be presented to the President and be subject to a qualified veto," by Article I, § 7 (p. 26). Thus, the bicameralism requirement requires a focus on statutory text, because that text is the only thing both chambers of Congress actually vote on (pp. 27–30). If the House and Senate pass versions of a bill that have exactly the same intent but slightly different language, the bicameralism requirement is not met; "the Constitution does not consider Congress' legislative task to be complete until a single text is agreed upon, even though the intended meaning of the two versions is identical" (p. 27). Likewise, the presentment requirement in Article I, § 7 presumes that the President is handed a *text*, and not a statement of intentions, and has the option of signing or vetoing a *text*, and not a statement of intentions (pp. 30–33).

---

[5]   E.g., Kenneth Shepsle, *Congress Is a "They," Not an "It": Legislative Intent as Oxymoron*, 12 Int'l Rev. L. & Econ. 239 (1992).

[6]   Jeremy Waldron, *Law and Disagreement* 99 (1999).

OLP also read Article I, § 7 to create a nondelegation rule: the notions that inspire a committee to report a bill cannot constitutionally be attributed to Congress as a whole.[7] In *INS v. Chadha* (Chapter 1, § 2), the Supreme Court broadly invalidated legislative vetoes because they sought to create legislation without obtaining the approval of both houses of Congress (the bicameralism requirement) and of the President (the presentment requirement). For these same reasons, the Office read *Chadha* to represent a hard constitutional rule against delegation of lawmaking authority to a legislative subgroup (pp. 48–49).

Relatedly, OLP maintained that judicial treatment of committee reports as authoritative sources of law would violate the Constitution's separation of legislative and judicial powers. "Intended meaning is a form of extra-statutory legislative interpretation of a statute, and judicial reliance upon it allows the legislature to exercise essentially judicial power," in violation of the separation of the legislative and the judicial powers in Articles I and III of the Constitution (p. 34). Among the most important functions of the Article III judiciary is ensuring *stability* in the law, and the only methodology that consistently delivers stable rules is a consistent judicial inquiry into actual meaning (pp. 34–37). The Office was certain that judicial reliance on legislative history undermines law's stability and reduces the ability of private companies and persons to plan their activities (pp. 51–52).

A third set of reasons advanced by OLP to focus on actual meaning, and to ignore intended meaning and legislative history, were pragmatic: legislative history is not useful, and in fact it is often misleading or can be used to mislead. Legislative materials are not useful because they are, paradoxically, both highly incomplete and typically voluminous (pp. 56–57). Any interpretive statement found in legislative debates and reports has got to be understood critically: Was the speaker being strategic, and therefore trying to distort rather than explain the statutory language? Was the speaker or author idiosyncratic? Did the statement come too early in the legislative process to reflect the final compromise needed to pass the statute through the vetogates? Given the complexities of the legislative process, which judges do not understand very well, it is easy for courts to make mistakes. Recall that the Supreme Court in *Holy Trinity* missed the most relevant legislative materials and mischaracterized the timing of the committee report on which the Justices relied (Chapter 4, § 1, Note to *Holy Trinity*).

Even worse, some legislative history is inserted for "political" reasons, such as to please an interest group (p. 53). Indeed, "much

---

[7]   Manning, *Textualism as a Nondelegation Doctrine*. But see Victoria F. Nourse, *Toward a "Due Foundation" for the Separation of Powers: The Federalist Papers as Political Narrative*, 74 Tex. L. Rev. 447 (1996) (noting that self-delegation is common among the departments of government and that the framers did not consider this to violate the separation of powers).

legislative history is 'planted' in the record to influence executive or judicial interpretation without having to achieve a bicameral congressional consensus or to risk a presidential veto" (p. 53). According to the Office, the "planting" and other manipulative use of legislative history is often accomplished by congressional staff rather than by the elected representatives themselves (p. 56).

Because it is inherently manipulable, legislative history invites or enables unelected administrators and judges to read their own policy preferences into statutes.[8] The rule of law requires predictability, objectivity, and transparency in the interpretation and application of statutes—and reliance on legislative history encourages interpreters to read their own values into statutes, which undermines predictability (because you do not know what kind of judicial ideology will dominate) and transparency (because phony or hard-to-falsify reasons are being advanced). As a practical matter, invocation of legislative history corrupts both the judicial process (because it invites interpretive cherry-picking) and the legislative process (because it invites legislators to speak to future interpreters rather than to other legislators and the public).

Given all these difficulties, OLP opined that both executive and judicial branch statutory interpreters ought to hew carefully to a strict version of the plain meaning rule: if a statute has a plain meaning, interpretation is at an end, without any reference to legislative materials (pp. 57–65). Specifically, legislative materials cannot be used to find or argue for ambiguity in the text adopted by Congress. Nor may legislative history be used to fill in statutory "gaps"; according to the Office, when there is a "gap" in statutory coverage, federal judges have no "law" to apply at all (pp. 97–104).

Some textualists (such as Antonin Scalia when he was a judge on the D.C. Circuit) have suggested that interpreters might sometimes find guidance in the proposals *rejected* in the legislative process. (Recall that Justice Scalia joined the Court's opinion in the FDA Tobacco Case [Chapter 2, § 3B], which relied heavily on rejected proposals.) OLP denied any utility for rejected proposals, because Congress's failure to do something can have no legal significance (pp. 107–08). Thus, OLP would have been sharply critical of the Supreme Court opinions in the FDA Tobacco Case, as well as the Bob Jones Case [Chapter 5, § 3].

Finally, OLP endorsed a limited utility for legislative materials. If there is ambiguity on the face of the statute, the interpreter might consult legislative materials—but *only as evidence of actual meaning*, and not as evidence of intended meaning (pp. 74–77). For example, OLP

---

[8]   This has been a major theme of Justice Scalia's critique. See Scalia & Garner, *Reading Law*, xxviii–xxix; *Hamdan v. Rumsfeld*, 548 U.S. 557, 667 (2006) (Scalia, J. dissenting); Daniel A. Farber & Philip P. Frickey, *Legislative Intent and Public Choice*, 74 Va. L. Rev. 423 (1988).

emphatically rejected the relevance of the committee reports invoked by the Supreme Court in *Holy Trinity* and opined that the 1885 immigration law had a plain meaning that included ministers. OLP did not consider the text-based argument that a minister might be a "lecturer" exempted from the statutory bar by § 5. If "lecturer" were ambiguous, OLP might consider legislative discussions that stated or assumed that the term lecturers included ministers.

NOTES ON THE NEW TEXTUALIST CRITIQUE OF LEGISLATIVE HISTORY

OLP had no formal authority over the remainder of the executive branch; the arguments were hortatory. The Solicitor General's Office of the Department of Justice never adopted OLP's advice and continued to rely, heavily, on legislative history in its influential briefs filed with the Supreme Court. Nonetheless, the OLP memorandum has been influential in other ways. At the same time the Reagan Administration's Department of Justice was working on this memorandum, Reagan-appointed federal judges (*i.e.,* Judges Scalia and Starr on the D.C. Circuit, Easterbrook on the Seventh Circuit, and Kozinski on the Ninth Circuit) were advancing similar arguments against the use of legislative history in statutory interpretation.[9] When President Reagan named Judge Scalia to the Supreme Court in 1986, the critique of legislative history became (and remains) a live issue within the nation's highest tribunal. Although Justice Scalia rails against any reliance upon, and sometimes even mention of, legislative history, the Supreme Court does still cite to these materials.[10] On occasion, the majority of the Court has issued statements in opinions squarely rejecting Justice Scalia's position that legislative history should not be consulted, e.g., *Wisconsin Public Intervenor v. Mortier*, 501 U.S. 597, 610 n.4 (1991). Nevertheless, those moments have not served to end the debate.

1.   *The Epistemic Argument Against "Intended Meaning": Congress Is a They, Not an It.* Recall from Chapter 4, § 1, that Max Radin first made this argument, that Congress is too complex and heterogeneous to have a discoverable "intent." As political scientist Kenneth Shepsle put it, the Radin idea that Congress is a "They" and not an "It" means that legislative intent is an "oxymoron."[11] This argument raises deep questions about what we mean by "intent" for a group. Some have dismissed this claim as one about

---

[9]   The articles and opinions are surveyed and analyzed in Eskridge, *New Textualism*, and Farber & Frickey, *Legislative Intent.*

[10]   Frank B. Cross, *The Theory and Practice of Statutory Interpretation* 142–43 (2009); David S. Law & David T. Zaring, *Law Versus Ideology: The Supreme Court and the Use of Legislative History,* 51 Wm. & Mary L. Rev. 1653 (2010).

[11]   Shepsle, *Congress Is a "They," Not an "It."* Other political scientists disagree that an aggregated congressional intent is unknowable. For a sophisticated approach to aggregation, see Daniel B. Rodriguez & Barry R. Weingast, *The Positive Political Theory of Legislative History: New Perspectives on the 1964 Civil Rights Act and Its Interpretation,* 151 U. Pa. L. Rev. 1417 (2003).

metaphor: "intent" is simply being used as a heuristic.[12] But this is unsatisfying, for the term "intent" carries with it notions of subjectivity.

Is it inadmissible to say that Congress, as a body, has a subjective intent? Can we say that corporations, such as General Electric Co. or Georgetown University, have subjective intents? Some theorists argue that corporate bodies and institutions do have this kind of intent, e.g., Lawrence M. Solan, *Private Language, Public Laws: The Central Role of Legislative Intent in Statutory Interpretation*, 93 Geo. L.J. 427, 437–49 (2005), but another kind of response, advanced by Professor Nourse, considers the notion that institutional "intent" has a more objective content: it is not the aggregation of individual subjective intents to create a corporate intent, but is rather the product of accepted procedures whereby institutions work out agreement to adopt plans and rules (Chapter 4, § 1).[13]

Thus, Nourse suggests that there is such a thing as legislative intent, but only if we define intent in a way that does not carry with it embedded assumptions that, by definition, only apply to individuals. Congress has the functional equivalent of intent by acting through its sequential procedures. So when we ask about Congress's "intent," what we are asking for is not a mental state, but an elaboration of the context in which Congress acted. The importance of the "intent" metaphor is not to show some kind of subjective expectation, but instead to establish a collective authorship and responsibility for a directive.

For example, suppose that a group of senators file a cloture petition. Those senators have signed their name to a document, acting to close debate. From this action, we can infer that the members share a "we-intention." This does not require that the senators communicate with each other or that the signatories have precisely similar mental pictures in their heads of what it means to say "we want cloture." Signing may be a thoughtless act. But if the members act in parallel, even without a mental event or communication, it is permissible to infer that they had the we-intention to do the act.

Group agency of any entity, whether it is a church, a corporation, or a university, depends upon agreed-upon procedures to plan future action. Acting pursuant to congressional procedure reflects a group intent to allow any particular piece of legislation to constitute the act of the group. Think of the rules as a signpost saying: "Any act that follows according to these procedures is now stamped as legitimate group action and when you (individual representative) act in this way, you have acted with group intention." This applies to all steps within the congressional process legitimated by the rules. There is nothing terribly exotic about this: when we agree to abide by a Supreme Court decision or an election, even if we disagree with the outcome, we do so because we have made a commitment to procedures we believe are legitimate.

---

[12] E.g., James Willard Hurst, *Dealing with Statutes* 32–33 (1982).

[13] See Victoria Nourse, *Elementary Concepts in Statutory Interpretation* (forthcoming 2014); on group agency more generally, see Christian List & Philip Pettit, *Group Agency* (2011).

To summarize: Group intent may be inferred from group action. Group action happens because of sequential procedures. This is how the group plans for the future. If this is correct, then when one looks for "congressional intent," one is not looking for any special mental state behind text or action—whether of individuals or groups. Instead, one is looking for crucial context for interpreting group action. One is looking for the public meaning of public acts done according to the rules. Congress has no mind, but it has the functional equivalent of intent—a way to plan for the future. And that "way" is essential context for understanding its actions. We explore this type of approach in further detail in section 2.)

2. *Article I, Section 7 Arguments Against "Intended Meaning."* The principal constitutional argument against legislative history is that it violates Article I, § 7.[14] Some textualists now say that "second-generation" textualism has shifted away from political theory arguments against legislative history and toward ones based on the Constitution. E.g., John F. Manning, *Second-Generation Textualism,* 98 Calif. L. Rev. 1287 (2010).

The OLP booklet makes two arguments from Article I, § 7. Because each chamber must agree on the same statutory text to meet the bicameralism requirement and because only the text is presented to the President, OLP concludes that the interpretive task *must* be to read the words adopted by both chambers and presented to the President. The problem with this argument is that this process does not tell the interpreter what sources might illuminate what the text would have meant to the enacting Congress. Indeed, the purpose of Article I, § 7, was to encourage congressional deliberation, see *INS v. Chadha.* Given that purpose, shouldn't interpreters consider the deliberative materials, such as committee reports, to help figure out what Congress enacted? See William N. Eskridge Jr., *The New Textualism,* 37 UCLA L. Rev. 621, 671–73 (1990).

In the alternative, OLP maintains that consideration of committee reports violates the bicameralism requirement of Article I, § 7, because it treats a congressional subgroup as announcing "authoritative" meaning. But considering committee reports to figure out what statutory language might mean does not treat those materials as authoritative any more than citing a dictionary would constitute a delegation of lawmaking authority to private institutions (e.g., the Merriam-Webster enterprises). There are also textual answers to the bicameralism claim,[15] most notably in Article I, § 5, which

---

[14] U.S. Const., art. I, § 7, cl. 2 ("Every Bill * * * shall, before it becomes a Law, be presented to the President of the United States; If he approve he shall sign it, but if not he shall return it, with his Objections"). "Simply put, if the statute and the legislative history genuinely conflict, Article I, Section 7 of the Constitution itself gives the text a greater claim to authoritativeness." John F. Manning, *The New Purposivism,* 2011 S.CT. REV. 113, 167–68 (2011).

[15] For other articles on the constitutional arguments, see James J. Brudney, *Canon Shortfalls and the Virtues of Political Branch Interpretive Assets,* 98 Cal. L. Rev. 1199, 1218–24 (2010) (arguing from the original meaning of the Journal Clause, Article I, § 5, that statutory interpreters ought to pay attention to legislative history); Jonathan Siegel, *The Use of Legislative History in a System of Separated Powers,* 53 Vand. L. Rev. 1537, 1534–35 (2000) (rejecting textualists' nondelegation argument); John C. Roberts, *Are Congressional Committees*

allows "each house to set the rules of its proceedings." Giving Congress power over its own proceedings prevents other departments from controlling, and perhaps even destroying, Congress from within. Section 5 provides support for Congress to set up rules and presumably for it to act according to those rules. Thus, no one could argue that congressional creation of committees and debate procedures themselves violate the Constitution. Since the founding, when the Constitutional Convention created rules, and delegated authority to committees for important drafting tasks, legislative bodies have been held to have wide power to create their own procedures.[16] Indeed, given that committees are delegated responsibility for drafting statutory text too, shouldn't the textualist critique of committee delegation apply as much to enacted text as legislative history?[17]

The question, then, is whether *Chadha*'s bicameralism argument against the legislative veto also indicts legislative history. To be sure, Congress cannot set up procedures that violate *other* parts of the constitution, a position the lower courts and the Supreme Court have upheld in a number of cases. See, e.g., *Powell v. McCormack*, 395 U.S. 486 (1969). On the other hand, when the Constitution authorizes an action, presumably the results of that action are cognizable in a court of law. "Imagine if the Constitution gave courts the express power to create 'rules for X.' Could another department constitutionally blind itself to the rules or the resulting work the judiciary had created pursuant to such a constitutional authorization? There can be no question that the courts would, if given an express power to create rules or procedures, demand respect for that power from other branches." Victoria F. Nourse, *The Constitution and Legislative History* (forthcoming 2014).

As Professor Nourse also argues, statutes often involve conflicting texts. For example, in *Holy Trinity,* there might be a conflict between § 1, which regulates companies importing noncitizens to perform "labor or service of any kind," and § 4, which regulates the transportation of "artisans, laborers, and mechanics." What is the relationship between §§ 1 and 4? (Or § 5, which includes as an exempted group "lecturers"?) Any two conflicting provisions are part of the Article I, § 7 deal, but the statutory text does not tell us how they are related. The legislative history might show us how the provisions relate to one another. Recall from Chapter 4, § 1, that the sponsor repeatedly described §§ 1 and 4 as relating to the same classes of noncitizens, a point that supports the majority's reading of the words in *Holy Trinity*. Note that

---

Constitutional? Radical Textualism, Separation of Powers, and the Enactment Process, 52 Case W. Res. L. Rev. 489, 491 (2001).

[16] 1 Joseph Story, *Commentaries on the Constitution of the United States* § 837 (1873 ed.): "No person can doubt the propriety of the provision authorizing each house to determine the rules of its own proceedings. If the power did not exist, it would be utterly impracticable to transact the business of the nation, either at all, or at least with decency, deliberation, and order. The humblest assembly of men is understood to possess this power, and it would be absurd to deprive the councils of the nation of a like authority."

[17] Frances Lieber, the great theorist of statutory interpretation, called the rules of any legislative body its "law" essential to legislative "liberty" and part of the "common law" of legislative bodies. Francis Lieber, *On Civil Liberty and Self-Government* 188–89 (1879 ed.).

Justice Scalia's assault on *Holy Trinity* in *Matter of Interpretation* (1997) did not even mention § 4; one reason he "missed" an essential statutory text is that he did not consult the legislative history of the 1885 law. To the extent legislative history is necessary to find how the text developed according to the rules, it may be necessary to find the appropriate text and in this sense may be necessary to bicameralism!

Finally, Article I, § 5 helps us address the problem that textualists themselves have long recognized about the bicameralism argument—what Professor Manning has called the bicameralism "paradox."[18] One of the easiest responses to the bicameral argument is its overreach. Vast amounts of agency lawmaking (for example) do not satisfy the Bicameralism Clause. Under an expansive reading of the Bicameralism Clause, judicial precedents (as lawmaking) might be unconstitutional. However, if we limit bicameralism to actions taken under Article I, including the Rules of Proceedings Clause, then the paradox disappears. Only legislative law-making, leading to legislative "bills," according to Congress's Rules of Proceeding, requires bicameral approval.

To be sure, OLP responds with the *Chadha* point: Even if Congress may constitutionally delegate lawmaking authority to executive bodies (like agencies), Congress cannot delegate lawmaking authority to legislative bodies (like committees). See Manning, *Nondelegation,* 683. Self-delegation breeds a conflict of interest and risks congressional self-aggrandizement. "Although neither a preenactment Supreme Court case nor a committee report formally goes through bicameralism and presentment, crediting a legislatively created source of meaning offers Congress a more substantial temptation to shift the specification of detail outside the legislative process." *Id.* at 707.

Professor Nourse counters: "On its surface, the non-delegation argument cannot supplant the Rules of Proceedings Clause. That clause amounts to a constitutional license for congressional self-delegation. Indeed, to the extent the Constitution gives each house the power to decide its own rules, it performs delegation—it delegates to a part of Congress ('each House') what might otherwise require bicameralism (that all rules would have to be passed by both Houses and submitted to the President). It is simply not accurate to say, as a matter of constitutional text, that 'the' legislative power under

---

[18] John F. Manning, *Textualism as a Nondelegation Doctrine*, 97 Colum. L. Rev. 673, 695 (1997): "The nondelegation rationale * * * leads to a potential paradox requiring explanation. * * * [T]extualists accept that the details of statutory meaning may derive from sources outside the text of the enacted legislation. * * * [A]gencies and courts, acting pursuant to explicit or implied delegations of authority, routinely defin[e] the specific meaning of general statutory texts. In those instances, specific and binding legal rules emerge from a process other than bicameralism and presentment. * * *[T]extualists often rely on extrinsic sources, such as judicial decisions and legal treatises, to determine the specific meaning of codified terms of art. There too, textualists derive meaning from sources that have not undergone the legitimating process of bicameralism and presentment. Despite their devotion to bicameralism and presentment, textualists hardly believe that every detail of statutory meaning must emerge from the constitutionally-prescribed legislative process."

Article I cannot be delegated if in fact Article I, section 5 delegates power to a part of the Congress to create its own rules and procedures.

"Let us assume that Congress does have a conflict of interest when it comes to legislative history. On what ground does this distinguish legislators from judges or members of the executive branch? When executive agents rely upon their own interpretation of rules, they have a conflict of interest, and they have an incentive as well to push their authority to its limits. When judges rely upon their own canons or common law, they have a conflict of interest. Departments tend to rely upon the materials they themselves produce and this applies whether the department is legislative, executive, or judicial." Nourse, *The Constitution and Legislative History* (forthcoming 2014).

Ultimately, it may be that the conflict of interest argument is less a constitutional argument than a pragmatic one. Professor Manning contends that if courts use "legislative history," Congress will have a greater incentive to put materials in legislative history rather than text. The empirical assumption here—that Congress actually creates legislative history in response to what courts say about interpretive rules—is belied by what we know about Congress and most collective bodies. Whatever rules courts create, Congress will continue to create legislative history, just as any corporation delegates and creates records of its delegations.[19] Every empirical study to date, the most recent being the comprehensive Gluck-Bressman study[20], supports the claim that Congress's procedures are not responses to judicial action; they are created to allow a large group of 535 to manage its business.

3.   *Rule of Law and Judicial Power Arguments Against Intended Meaning.* One of the most prominent constitutional debates about statutory interpretation concerns the meaning of the "judicial Power" in Article III of the Constitution. Article III vests the "judicial Power" in the Supreme Court and other inferior courts as Congress may establish. U.S. Const., art. I, § 1. Compare William N. Eskridge Jr., *All About Words: Early Understandings of the "Judicial Power" in Statutory Interpretation* 1776–1806, 101 Colum. L. Rev. 990 (2001), with John F. Manning, *Textualism and the Equity of the Statute,* 101 Colum. L. Rev. 1 (2001). Professor Eskridge maintains that the founding generation understood the "judicial Power" to entail statutory interpretation that considered statutory texts in light of a variety of contextual factors including ordinary language, judicial precedents, statutory purposes, equity, constitutional norms, and the law of nations. Professor

---

[19] Thomas Conyngton, R.J. Bennett & Paul W. Pinkerton, *Corporation Procedure: Law, Finance, and Accounting* § 294, at 245 (1922) ("Power of the Board to Delegate Authority to Committees"), *id.* at § 300, at 250–51 ("[M]inutes should be kept containing a faithful record of all committee proceedings.").

[20] Abbe R. Gluck & Lisa Schultz Bressman, *Statutory Interpretation from the Inside—An Empirical Study of Congressional Drafting, Delegation, and the Canons: Part I*, 65 Stan. L. Rev. 901 (2013) (affirming in far more extensive study original findings of Nourse and Schacter on the question whether Congress is capable of not creating legislative history).

Manning maintains that the founding generation applied the "judicial Power" to hew closely to statutory text, and text alone, for the most part.

Professor Manning articulates the challenge that the original meaning of Article III might pose to strict textualists. He argues that the most significant challenge to the textualist approach is the "ancient common law doctrine of the equity of the statute," which "authorized courts to extend a clear statute to reach omitted cases that fell within its ratio or purpose, and conversely, to imply exceptions to such a statute when the text would inflict harsh results that did not serve the statutory purpose. [A] number of scholars have tried to invoke [the equity of the statute] as the basis for a distinct theory of judicial power * * * *. In particular, this scholarship assumes that Article III of the Constitution does not confine federal judges to decoding legislative intent, but assigns to them all the ancient common law powers of interpretation. * * * * By grounding this method in a theory of broad judicial power, rather than legislative intent, the new scholarship would render much, if not all, of the textualists' critique of strong purposivism beside the point."

Professors Manning and Eskridge read the original materials differently. Manning argues that the Constitution marked a sharp break with English practice: "in contrast with relevant English practice, the U.S. Constitution self-consciously separated the judicial from the legislative power and, in so doing, sought to differentiate sharply the functions performed by these two distinct branches." Manning, *Textualism and Equity of the Statute.* Eskridge, on the other hand, after an exhaustive survey of Blackstone and other sources of British practice, reaches a strikingly different conclusion: "the original materials surrounding Article III's judicial power assume an eclectic approach to statutory interpretation, open to understanding the letter of a statute in pursuance of the spirit of the law and in light of fundamental values. Furthermore, the original materials suggest that the founding generation expected judges certainly to trim the letter of the law to protect common law liberties and probably sometimes to expand the letter of the law to unprovided-for cases." With respect to legislative history in particular, Eskridge concludes that "the materials shed little light on the debate about the utility of legislative history, in part because judges in the founding era often knew that history and usually had no published reports which could be cited."

For Eskridge, "[t]he central lesson of the early period, best embodied in the work of John Marshall, is that statutory interpretation is all about words, but words are about much more than dictionaries and ordinary usage; they also involve policies chosen by the legislature and enduring principles suggested by the common law, the law of nations, and the Constitution. Just as the United States created a new kind of constitutionalism, popular and written, so its new constitutionalism inspired a new kind of statutory interpretivism, text-based but principled, sometimes equitable, and frequently dynamic." That contextual approach today would include legislative history. Eskridge, *All About Words.*

With regard to the specific practice of citing legislative history, there is evidence that legislative journals were cited very early on by lawyers and courts. See, e.g., James J. Brudney, *Canon Shortfalls and the Virtues of Political Branch Interpretive Assets*, 98 Cal. L. Rev. 1199, 1218–24 (2010); Nourse, *The Constitution and Legislative History* (forthcoming 2014). For example, in *The Venus, Rae, Master*, 8 Cranch 253, 264 (1814), the reporter finds counsel citing the statement of "Mr. Russell in a committee report" from the House journal. Also, counsel reportedly cited an amendment in the Senate for the proposition that Congress did not mean to authorize the capture of property belonging to mere inhabitants of a hostile country because the law had been amended in the Senate to cover "subjects" of hostile nations.[21] Likewise, judges cited the journals. For example, Justice M'Kean, a celebrated Justice of the Pennsylvania Supreme Court, referred to a "legislative construction" of a statute—a series of statutes in fact—as to the amount to be paid for a military uniform, citing to state legislative journals. *Roach v. Commonwealth*, 2 U.S. 206 (1793). The journals were also referred to in constitutional cases. In *Worcester v. Georgia*, 31 U.S. 515, 549 (1832), Chief Justice Marshall said that "[t]he early journals of congress exhibit the most anxious desire to conciliate the Indian nations."[22]

Perhaps the most important argument made by OLP and by the new textualists generally is that examination of statutory text, and only the text, is the method that imposes discipline on judges to prevent their personal beliefs from affecting their statutory readings. Critics of the new textualism dispute the foregoing propositions. They maintain that an interpreter relying just on statutory text, and ignoring legislative context, will be no more constrained, and perhaps less so, than an interpreter who considers legislative materials. E.g., William N. Eskridge Jr., *The New Textualism and Normative Canons*, 113 Colum. L. Rev. 531 (2013) (reviewing Scalia & Garner, *Reading Law*). Thus far, there is no strong empirical evidence supporting or refuting these rule of law claims for the new textualists.

4.   *The Debate in Other Courts.* A number of state courts have been influenced by the textualist critique of legislative history. See Abbe R. Gluck, *The States as Laboratories of Statutory Interpretation: Methodological Consensus and the New Modified Textualism*, 119 Yale L.J. 1750 (2010). Indeed, the author of the OLP report, Stephen Markman, has been a justice on the Michigan Supreme Court since 1998. In that capacity, he has brought

---

[21]   See also *Commonwealth v. Franklin*, 4 U.S. 255, 261 (1802) (counsel citing journals of old Congress on question of land grant); *Anderson v. Dunn*, 19 U.S. 204, 214 (1821) (counsel referring to House and Senate Journals on the practice of issuing contempt orders); *Menard v. Aspasia*, 30 U.S. 505, 509 (1831) (counsel referring to journals of Congress on knowledge of slavery in passing northwest ordinance).

[22]   See also *Cherokee Nation v. Georgia*, 30 U.S. 1, 60 (1831) ("the journals of congress, from the year 1775 down to the adoption of the present constitution abundantly demonstrate this fact"—the Cherokees as a foreign nation) (Thompson, J. dissenting in an opinion concurred in by Story, J.); see *id.* at 63 ("on examining the journals of the old congress * * * the terms 'nation' and 'tribe' are frequently used indiscriminately"); *Wheaton v. Peters*, 33 U.S. 591, 681 (1834) (Thompson, J., dissenting) (referring to journals of the 1783 Congress to determine whether copyright was a common law right).

a stringent version of the critique to that court, which has had a textualist majority most of the last fifteen years. Justice Markman's most famous decision, in the Michigan Domestic Partnership Case, is reproduced in § 3 of this chapter.

On the other hand, some courts outside the United States have gone in the opposite direction. Britain's House of Lords for years had in place an "exclusionary rule" that Justice Scalia and the Reagan-Era OLP would love—a rule prohibiting judicial consultation with Hansard, the British legislative history materials. Consider Problem 6–1 below. Facts analogous to the problem produced a decision by the British House of Lords (which follows the problem), moving British statutory interpretation methodology away from the strict textualist position.

PROBLEM 6–1: THE CASE OF THE OVER-TAXED TEACHER

The State of Bliss taxes the incomes of its citizens. Theresa Teacher earns a healthy salary but also enjoys a great fringe benefit from the Bliss private school where she is employed: her two children could be (and are) educated at the school for 5% of the tuition normally charged. The Bliss Revenue Service levies a tax on the "cash equivalent" of such fringe benefits, which the statute defines as "an amount equal to the *cost* of the benefit, less so much (if any) of it as is made good by the employee to those providing the benefit." The statute defines "the cost of the benefit" as "the amount of any expense incurred in or in connection with its provision, and (here and in those subsections) includes a proper proportion of any expense relating partly to the benefit and partly to other matters."

The Revenue Service includes in Teacher's income $95,000 as the "cash equivalent" of the fringe benefit: normal tuition is $50,000 per pupil; Teacher is able to enroll her children at $2500 apiece. The Service assumes, and Teacher does not challenge, that the $50,000 per pupil tuition represents the *average cost* of educating each pupil at the school. But Teacher maintains that she should only be assessed the *marginal cost* (i.e., the additional costs incurred by the school to add her two kids), minus her $5000 contribution. The marginal cost for each child is $2500; hence, under this reading, Teacher would owe no tax on this fringe benefit.

As a matter of pure text-based interpretation, how would a judge rule in the Case of the Over-Taxed Teacher? Jot down your answer in the margin—and then read the following case.

STATUTORY PREFACE TO THE BRITISH CASE
ON LEGISLATIVE HISTORY

The Finance Act of 1976, § 63

A "cash equivalent of the benefit," which was the measure of taxable benefit, is defined as follows:

(1) The cash equivalent of any benefit chargeable to tax under section 61 above is an amount equal to the cost of the benefit, less so much (if any) of it as is made good by the employee to those providing the benefit.

(2) Subject to the following subsections, the cost of a benefit is the amount of any expense incurred in or in connection with its provision, and (here and in those subsections) includes a proper proportion of any expense relating partly to the benefit and partly to other matters.

DEREK PEPPER V. JOHN HART

House of Lords for the United Kingdom, 1992.
[1992] 3 W.L.R. 1032, [1993] 1 All E.R. 42.

[Malvern College gave its employees a "fringe benefit"—it allowed employees to send their children to the school for 20% of the fees paid by other parents. Because the school in question had not been able to fill all its seats, its marginal costs in providing education to these children were minimal. The employees argued that they had received no actual income at all, because the fringe benefit they received, measured as the (marginal) expense incurred by their employer, was less than the fees they had paid. The tax collector disagreed, arguing that the "expense incurred" should be the average cost per pupil incurred by the school. When the Lords first heard the case, they found the statute's meaning "plain," and the taxpayers lost. When they reheard it with a larger panel, they reversed, after looking at the legislative history. *Pepper* changed centuries old British practice in which judges refused to look to Hansard, the report of parliamentary debates.

British cases involve seriatim opinions. Do not let that confuse you. Also do not let the tax law confuse you. The basic question is about how to tax fringe benefits, as in Problem 6–1.]

LORD MACKAY OF CLASHFERN [LORD CHANCELLOR].

[F]or the first time this House has been asked to consider a detailed argument on the extent to which reference can properly be made before a court of law in the United Kingdom to proceedings in Parliament recorded in Hansard.

For the appellant [taxpayers] Mr. Lester submits that it should now be appropriate for the courts to look at Hansard in order to ascertain the intention of the legislators as expressed in the proceedings on the Bill which has then been enacted in the statutory words requiring to be construed. This submission appears to me to suggest a way of making more effective proceedings in Parliament by allowing the court to consider what has been said in Parliament as an aid to resolving an ambiguity which may well have become apparent only as a result of the attempt to apply the enacted words to a particular case. * * *

The principal difficulty I have on this aspect of the case is that in Mr. Lester's submission reference to Parliamentary material as an aid to interpretation of a statutory provision should be allowed only with leave of the court and where the court is satisfied that such a reference is justifiable:

> (a) to confirm the meaning of a provision as conveyed by the text, its object and purpose;

> (b) to determine a meaning where the provision is ambiguous or obscure; or

> (c) to determine the meaning where the ordinary meaning is manifestly absurd or unreasonable.

I believe that practically every question of *statutory* construction that comes before the courts will involve an argument that the case falls under one or more of these three heads. It follows that the parties' legal advisors will require to study Hansard [the official collection of parliamentary debates] in practically every such case to see whether or not there is any help to be gained from it. I believe this is an objection of real substance. It is a practical objection not one of principle * * *. Such an approach appears to me to involve the possibility at least of an immense increase in the cost of litigation in which statutory construction is involved. * * * [T]he Law Commission and the Scottish Law Commission, in their joint report on *The Interpretation of Statutes* (1969) (Law Com. no. 21) (Scot. Law Com. no. 11) and the Renton Committee Report on *The Preparation of Legislation* ((1975) Cmnd. 6053), advised against a relaxation on the practical grounds to which I have referred. * * *

[We omit the separate opinions of LORD BRIDGE OF HARWICH, LORD GRIFFITHS, LORD OLIVER OF AYLMERTON, LORD KEITH OF KINKEL, and LORD ACKNER. With varying degrees of enthusiasm, all five agreed with the following opinion by LORD BROWNE-WILKINSON. Lords Bridge and Oliver had voted in the first hearing to dismiss the appeal, but the Hansard materials impelled them to change their votes. Finding the statute ambiguous, Lord Griffiths had voted with the taxpayer in the first hearing.]

LORD BROWNE-WILKINSON. * * *

* * * [I]t is necessary first to refer to the legislation affecting the taxation of benefits in kind before 1975. Under the Finance Act 1948, section 39(1), directors and employees of bodies corporate earning more than £2,000 per annum were taxed under Schedule E on certain benefits in kind. The amount charged was the expense incurred by the body corporate "in or in connection with the provision" of the benefit in kind. By section 39(6) it was provided that references to expenses "incurred in or in connection with any matter includes a reference to a proper proportion of any expense incurred partly in or in connection with that matter." Employment by a school or charitable organisation was expressly excluded from the charge: sections 41(5) and 44. These provisions were re-enacted in the Income and Corporation Taxes Act 1970.

Those provisions covered in-house benefits as well as external benefits. We were told that after 1948 the Revenue sought to tax at least two categories of employees in receipt of in-house benefits. Higher-paid employees of the railways enjoy free or concessionary travel on the railways. The Revenue reached an agreement that such employees should be taxed on 20% (later 25%) of the full fare. Airline employees also enjoy concessionary travel. We were told that in the 1960s the Revenue sought to tax such employees on that benefit on the basis of the average cost to the airline of providing a seat, not merely on the marginal cost. The tax commissioners rejected such claim: the Revenue did not appeal. Therefore in practice from 1948 to 1975 the Revenue did not seek to extract tax on the basis of the average cost to the employer of providing in-house benefit.

In 1975 the government proposed a new tax on vouchers provided by an employer to his employees which could be exchanged for goods or services. Clause 33(1) of the Finance (No. 2) Bill 1975 provided that the employee was to be treated, on receipt of a voucher, as having received an emolument from his employment of an amount "equal to the expense incurred by the person providing the voucher in or in connection with the provision of the voucher and the money, goods or services for which it is capable of being exchanged." The statutory wording of the Bill was therefore similar to that in the Act of 1948 and in section 63(2) of the Finance Act 1976. On 1 July 1975 in the Standing Committee on the Bill (Standing Committee H), the Financial Secretary was asked about the impact of the clause on railwaymen. He gave the following answer:

> "Similarly, the railwayman travelling on his normal voucher will not be taxable either. The clause deals with the situation where a number of firms produce incentives of various kinds. In one or two instances, there is likely to be some liability concerning rail

vouchers of a special kind, but in general, the position is as I have said and they will not be taxable."

He was then asked to explain why they would not be taxable and replied:

"Perhaps I can make clear why there is no taxable benefit in kind, because the provision of the service that he provides falls upon the employer. Clearly, the railways will run in precisely the same way whether the railwaymen use this facility or not, so there is no extra charge to the Railways Board itself therefore there would be no taxable benefits." * * *

The Finance Bill 1976 sought to make a general revision of the taxation of benefits in kind. The existing legislation on fringe benefits was to be repealed. Clause 52 of the Bill as introduced eventually became section 61 of the Act of 1976 and imposed a charge to tax on benefits in kind for higher-paid employees, i.e., those paid more than £5,000 per annum. Clause 54 of the Bill eventually became section 63 of the Act of 1976. As introduced, clause 54(1) provided that the cash equivalent of any benefit was to be an amount equal to "the cost of the benefit." Clause 54(2) provided that, except as provided in later subsections "the cost of a benefit is the amount of any expense incurred in or in connection with its provision." Crucially, clause 54(4) of the Bill sought to tax in-house benefits on a different basis from that applicable to external benefits. It provided that the cost of a benefit consisting of the provision of any service or facility which was also provided to the public (i.e., in-house benefits) should be the price which the public paid for such facility or service. Employees of schools were not excluded from the new charge.

Thus if the 1976 Bill had gone through as introduced, railway and airline employees would have been treated as receiving benefits in kind from concessionary travel equal to the open market cost of tickets and schoolmasters would have been taxed for concessionary education on the amount of the normal school fees.

After second reading, clause 52 of the Bill was committed to a committee of the whole House and clause 54 to Standing Committee E. On 17 May 1976, the House considered clause 52 and strong representations were made about the impact of clause 52 on airline and railway employees. At the start of the meeting of Standing Committee E on 17 June 1976 (before clause 54 was being discussed) the Financial Secretary to the Treasury, Mr. Robert Sheldon, made an announcement (Hansard, columns 893–895) in the following terms:

"The next point I wish to make concerns services and deals with the position of employees of organisations, bodies, or firms which provide services, where the employee is in receipt of those services free or at a reduced rate. Under Clause 54(4) the taxable benefit is to be based on the arm's length price of the benefit received. At present the benefit is valued on the cost to the employer. Representations have been made concerning airline travel and railway employees. . . . It was never intended that the benefit received by the airline employee would be the fare paid by the ordinary passenger. The benefit to him would never be as high as that, because of certain disadvantages that the employee has. Similar considerations, although of a different kind, apply to railway employees.

I have had many interviews, discussions and meetings on this matter and I have decided to withdraw Clause 54(4). I thought I would mention this at the outset because so many details, which would normally be left until we reached that particular stage, will be discussed with earlier parts of the legislation. I shall give some reasons which weigh heavily in favour of the withdrawal of this provision.

The first is the large difference between the cost of providing some services and the amount of benefit which under the Bill would be held to be received. There are a number of cases of this kind, and I would point out that air and rail journeys are only two of a number of service benefits which have a number of problems attached to them. But there is a large difference between the cost of the benefit to the employer and the value of that benefit as assessed. It could lead to unjustifiable situations resulting in a great number of injustices and I do not think we should continue with it. . . .

The second reason for withdrawing Clause 54(4) is that these services would tend to be much less used. The problem would then arise for those who had advocated the continuation of this legislation that neither the employer nor the employee nor the Revenue would benefit from the lesser use of these services. This factor also weighed with me.

The third reason is the difficulty of enforcement and administration which both give rise to certain problems.

Finally, it was possible to withdraw this part of the legislation as the services cover not only a more difficult area, but a quite distinct area of these provisions, without having repercussions on some of the other areas. . . .

A Member: I, too, have talked to many airline employees about this matter, and I am not completely clear as to the purport of my Hon. Friend's remarks. Is he saying that these benefits will remain taxable but that the equivalent cost of the benefit will be calculated on some different basis? Or is he saying that these benefits will not be taxable at all?

Financial Secretary: The existing law which applies to the taxation of some of these benefits will be retained. The position will subsequently be unchanged from what it is now before the introduction of this legislation."

[His Lordship quoted several further references where the Financial Secretary insisted that the government's intent was not to change the tax treatment previously afforded to railway and airline employees; they would and should be allowed to receive free travel and be assessed only for the extra cost to the employer.]

Simultaneously with the announcement to the standing committee, a press release was issued announcing the withdrawal of clause 54(4). It referred to the same matters as the Financial Secretary had stated to the Committee and concluded:

"The effect of deleting this subclause will be to continue the present basis of taxation of services, namely the cost to the employer of providing the service."

The point was further debated in committee on 22 June 1976. A member is reported as saying, at column 1013, that

"Like many others, I welcome the concession that has been made to leave out the airline staff and the railway employees and all the others that are left out by the dropping of clause 54(4)."

Another member, after referring to the particular reference in the Financial Secretary's statement to airline and railway employees, asked (at col 1023) whether the same distinction applied to services provided by hotel companies to their employees—that is, to rooms which are freely available for the general public in hotels being offered at a concessionary rate to employees of the hotel group. In response, the Financial Secretary said (at col 1024) of the position of such employees:

"The position is, as he probably expected, the same as that which, following my announcement last week about the withdrawal of Clause 54(4), applies to other employees in service industries; the benefit is the cost to the employer. It is a good illustration of one of the reasons why I withdrew this subsection, in that the cost to the employer in this instance could be much less than the arm's length cost to the outside person taking advantage of such a service." (Column 1024.) * * *

The very question which is the subject matter of the present appeal was also raised. A member said, at columns 1091–1092:

"I should be grateful for the Financial Secretary's guidance on these two points. . . . The second matter applies particularly to private sector, fee-paying schools where, as the Financial Secretary knows, there is often an arrangement for the children of staff in these schools to be taught at less than the commercial fee in other schools. I take it that because of the deletion of Clause 54(4) that is not now caught. Perhaps these examples will help to clarify the extent to which the Government amendment goes."

The Financial Secretary responded to this question as follows:

"He mentioned the children of teachers. The removal of clause 54(4) will affect the position of a child of one of the teachers at the child's school, because now the benefit will be assessed on the cost to the employer, which would be very small indeed in this case." (Column 1095.)

Thereafter, clause 54 was not the subject of further debate and passed into law as it now stands as section 63 of the Act. * * *

Under present law, there is a general rule that reference to Parliamentary material as an aid to statutory construction is not permissible ("the exclusionary rule") * * *. The exclusionary rule was probably first stated by Willes J. in *Millar v. Taylor* (1769) 4 Burr. 2303, 2332. [Lord Browne-Wilkinson provided a brief history of the exclusionary rule and possible loopholes as well as criticisms that developed over time.]

My Lords, I have come to the conclusion that, as a matter of law, there are sound reasons for making a limited modification to the existing rule (subject to strict safeguards) unless there are constitutional or practical reasons which outweigh them. In my judgment, subject to the questions of the privileges of the House of Commons, reference to Parliamentary material should be permitted as an aid to the construction of legislation which is ambiguous or obscure or the literal meaning of which leads to an absurdity. Even in such cases references in court to Parliamentary material should only be permitted where such material clearly discloses the mischief aimed at or the legislative intention lying behind the ambiguous or obscure words. In the case of statements made in Parliament, as at present advised I cannot foresee that any statement other than the statement of the minister or other promoter of the Bill is likely to meet these criteria.

I accept Mr. Lester's submissions [for the taxpayers], but my main reason for reaching this conclusion is based on principle. Statute law consists of the words that Parliament has enacted. It is for the courts to construe those words and it is the court's duty in so doing to give effect to the intention of Parliament in using those words. It is an inescapable fact that, despite all the care taken in passing legislation, some statutory provisions when applied to the circumstances under consideration in any specific case are found to be ambiguous. One of the reasons for such ambiguity is that the members of the legislature in enacting the statutory provision may have been told what result those words are intended to achieve. Faced with a given set of words which are capable of conveying that meaning it is not surprising if the words are accepted as having that meaning. Parliament never intends to enact an ambiguity. Contrast with that the position of the courts. The courts are faced simply with a set of words which are in fact capable of bearing two meanings. The courts are ignorant of the underlying Parliamentary purpose. Unless something in other parts of the legislation discloses such purpose, the courts are forced to adopt one of the two possible meanings using highly technical rules of construction. In many, I suspect most, cases references to Parliamentary materials will not throw any light on the matter. But in a few cases it may emerge that the very question was considered by Parliament in passing the legislation. Why in such a case should the courts blind themselves to a clear indication of what Parliament intended in using those words? The court cannot attach a meaning to words which they cannot bear, but if the words are capable of bearing more than one meaning why should not Parliament's true intention be enforced rather than thwarted?

A number of other factors support this view. As I have said, the courts can now look at white papers and official reports for the purpose of finding the "mischief" sought to be corrected, although not at draft clauses or proposals for the remedying of such mischief. A ministerial statement made in Parliament is an equally authoritative source of such information: why should the courts be cut off from this source of information as to the mischief aimed at? In any event, the distinction between looking at reports to identify the mischief aimed at but not to find the intention of Parliament in enacting the legislation is highly artificial. Take the normal Law Commission Report which analyses the problem and then annexes a draft Bill to remedy it. It is now permissible to look at the report to find the mischief and at the draft Bill to see that a provision in the draft was *not* included in the legislation enacted. There can be no logical distinction between that case and looking at the draft Bill to see that the statute as enacted reproduced, often in the same words, the provision in the Law Commission's draft. Given the purposive approach to construction now adopted by the courts in order to give effect to the true intentions of the legislature, the fine distinctions between looking for the mischief and looking for the intention in using words to provide the remedy are technical and inappropriate. Clear and unambiguous statements made by ministers in Parliament are as much the background to the enactment of legislation as white papers and Parliamentary reports. * * *

It is said that Parliamentary materials are not readily available to, and understandable by, the citizen and his lawyers who should be entitled to rely on the words of Parliament alone to discover his position. It is undoubtedly true that Hansard and particularly records of Committee debates are not widely held by libraries outside London and that the lack of satisfactory indexing of Committee stages makes it difficult to trace the passage of a clause after it is redrafted or renumbered. But such practical difficulties can easily be overstated. It is possible to obtain Parliamentary materials and it is possible to trace the history. The problem is one of expense and effort in doing so, not the availability of the material. In considering the right of the individual to know the law by simply looking at legislation, it is a fallacy to start from the position that all legislation is available in a readily understandable form in any event: the very large number of statutory instruments made every year are not available in an indexed form for well over a year after they have been passed. Yet, the practitioner manages to deal with the problem albeit at considerable expense. Moreover, experience in New Zealand and Australia (where the strict rule has been relaxed for some years) has not shown that the non-availability of materials has raised these practical problems.

Next, it is said that lawyers and judges are not familiar with Parliamentary procedures and will therefore have difficulty in giving proper weight to the Parliamentary materials. Although, of course, lawyers do not have the same experience of these matters as members of the legislature, they are not wholly ignorant of them. If, as I think, significance should only be attached to the clear statements made by a minister or other promoter of the Bill, the difficulty of knowing what weight to attach to such statements is not overwhelming. In the present case, there were numerous statements of view by members in the course of the debate which plainly do not throw any light on the true construction of section 63. What is persuasive in this case is a consistent series of answers given by the minister, after opportunities for taking advice from his officials, all of which point the same way and which were not withdrawn or varied prior to the enactment of the Bill.

Then it is said that court time will be taken up by considering a mass of Parliamentary material and long arguments about its significance, thereby increasing the expense of litigation. In my judgment, though the introduction of further admissible material will inevitably involve some increase in the use of time, this will not be significant as long as courts insist that Parliamentary material should only be introduced in the limited cases I have mentioned and where such material contains a clear indication from the minister of the mischief aimed at, or the nature of the cure intended, by the legislation. Attempts to introduce material which does not satisfy those tests should be met by orders for costs made against those who have improperly introduced the material. Experience in the United States of America, where legislative history has for many years been much more generally admissible than I am now suggesting, shows how important it is to maintain strict control over the use of such material. That position is to be contrasted with what has happened in New Zealand and Australia (which have relaxed the rule to approximately the extent that I favour): there is no evidence of any complaints of this nature coming from those countries.

There is one further practical objection which, in my view, has real substance. If the rule is relaxed legal advisers faced with an ambiguous statutory provision may feel that they have to research the materials to see whether they yield the crock of gold, i.e., a clear indication of Parliament's intentions. In very many cases the crock of gold will not be discovered and the expenditure on the research wasted. This is a real objection to changing the rule. However, again it is easy to overestimate the cost of such research: if a reading of Hansard shows that there is nothing of significance said by the minister in relation to the clause in question, further research will become pointless.

In sum, I do not think that the practical difficulties arising from a limited relaxation of the rule are sufficient to outweigh the basic need for the courts to give effect to the words enacted by Parliament in the sense that they were intended by Parliament to bear. Courts are frequently criticised for their failure to do that. This failure is due not to cussedness but to ignorance of what Parliament intended by the obscure words of the legislation. The courts should not deny themselves the light which Parliamentary materials may shed on the meaning of the words Parliament has used and thereby risk subjecting the individual to a law which Parliament never intended to enact. * * *

The Attorney General raised a further constitutional point, namely, that for the court to use Parliamentary material in construing legislation would be to confuse the respective roles of Parliament as the maker of law and the courts as the interpreter. I am not impressed by this argument. The law, as I have said, is to be found in the words in which Parliament has enacted. It is for the courts to interpret those words so as to give effect to that purpose. The question is whether, in addition to other aids to the construction of statutory words, the courts should have regard to a further source. Recourse is already had to white papers and official reports not because they determine the meaning of the statutory words but because they assist the court to make its own determination. I can see no constitutional impropriety in this. * * *

I therefore reach the conclusion, subject to any question of Parliamentary privilege, that the exclusionary rule should be relaxed so as to permit reference to Parliamentary materials where:

(a) Legislation is ambiguous or obscure, or leads to an absurdity;

(b) The material relied on consists of one or more statements by a minister or other promoter of the Bill together if necessary with such other Parliamentary material as is necessary to understand such statements and their effect;

(c) The statements relied on are clear.

[In the present case, the statute was ambiguous and the Hansard materials clearly resolved the ambiguity in favor of the taxpayers.]

The question then arises whether it is right to attribute to Parliament as a whole the same intention as that repeatedly voiced by the Financial Secretary. In my judgment it is. It is clear from reading Hansard that the committee was repeatedly asking for guidance as to the effect of the legislation once subclause (4) of clause 54 was abandoned. That Parliament relied on the ministerial statements is shown by the fact that the matter was never raised again after the discussions in committee, that amendments were consequentially withdrawn and that no relevant amendment was made which could affect the correctness of the Minister's statement. * * *

Having once looked at what was said in Parliament, it is difficult to put it out of mind. I have the advantage that, after the first hearing and before seeing the Parliamentary materials, I had reached the conclusion, in agreement with Vinelott J. and the Court of Appeal, that the Revenue's submissions were correct. If it is not permissible to take into account what was said by the Financial Secretary, I remain of the same view. * * *

NOTES ON THE UNITED KINGDOM'S EMBRACE OF LEGISLATIVE HISTORY

1. *The Abandonment of the Exclusionary Rule in English-Speaking Countries.* In the United Kingdom, *Pepper v. Hart* created quite a stir, and unleashed a fair amount of interest in legislative history by lower courts and the House of Lords. An excellent survey by James J. Brudney, *Below the Surface: Comparing Legislative History Usage by the House of Lords and the Supreme Court*, 85 Wash. U. L. Rev. 1 (2007), demonstrates that much of the Lords' reliance on Hansard cites to minister (floor manager) explanations and *not* to committee reports, which are not routinely generated in Parliament. On the other hand, Professor Brudney found that during the post-*Pepper* period, the Lords have greatly increased their references to government white papers and commission reports, background documents with some similarity to our committee reports. In short, the Lords are explicitly considering a lot more background materials than they did twenty years ago. See James J. Brudney, *The Story of* Pepper v. Hart (1992): *Examining Legislative History Across the Pond*, in *Statutory Interpretation Stories* 258–293 (Eskridge, Frickey & Garrett eds. 2011).

The House of Lords' decision has had echoes throughout the Commonwealth countries. Even before *Pepper,* the leading Canadian treatise observed that "the [exclusionary] rule has been eroding at a rapid rate. Some courts have ignored it while other courts have carved out significant exceptions and qualifications. * * * The exclusionary rule in its traditional form is clearly dead." Elmer Driedger, *The Construction of Statutes* 486 (1983). See also David Duff, *Interpreting the Income Tax Act*, 47 Can. Tax. J. 464 & 741 (1999) (reviewing the use of legislative history in tax cases). The exclusionary rule had previously been abandoned in Australia, see Commonwealth Acts Interpretation Act 1901 § 15AB, and other Commonwealth countries. Many civil-law countries still follow such a rule or practice, however.

2. *When Should Legislative Materials Be Admissible? The Potato Chip Problem.* The key opinion by Lord Browne-Wilkinson admits legislative materials, but only in limited circumstances. How must one characterize the holding of the case? This is more difficult than appears on first glance.

(A) Sponsor Statements May Be Consulted When the Statute Is Ambiguous. This appears to be the holding as articulated by Lord Browne-Wilkinson, and the U.S. Supreme Court sometimes says it follows a similar rule. See, e.g., *Director, OWCP v. Greenwich Collieries*, 512 U.S. 267 (1994). Isn't this a problem when the ambiguity is not apparent on the face of the statute? The first committee of Law Lords found the statute unambiguous against the taxpayer; on the original panel, only Lord Griffith found ambiguity. Other Lords, including Browne-Wilkinson, found ambiguity only after they consulted the Hansard materials.

(B) Hansard Materials May Be Consulted to Confirm Statutory Plain Meaning. The narrowest interpretation of *Pepper*, embraced by Lord Steyn and others, is that Hansard materials can only be introduced for textualist reasons. Namely, they can be admitted to suggest or confirm standard usage of statutory terms or the plain meaning they have to reasonable speakers of the English language.

(C) Hansard May Be Invoked to Clear Up Any Statutory Matters. In the aftermath of *Pepper*, some Law Lords used the decision as a Magna Carta for browsing parliamentary debates for what they were worth, essentially ignoring Lord Browne-Wilkinson's suggested limits. See David Miers, *Taxing Perks and Interpreting Statutes:* Pepper v. Hart, 56 Mod. L. Rev. 695, 705–06 (1993). Few Lords in the new millennium openly endorse this position, and there are procedural hurdles in place, but there is some indication that some lower court judges are running wild with legislative materials. Should this have been expected?

Aside from the precise limits suggested in this case, consider a *potato chip theory*, suggested by American judicial practice after *Holy Trinity*: once a court starts looking at the "best" legislative history, like the Law Lords' view of sponsor statements, other kinds of history will get smuggled in. Before long, everything becomes relevant and might be considered "for what it is worth" (the trend in modern evidence law). Just as you can never eat just one potato chip, you can never admit just one bit of legislative history. It might take decades for the potato chip process to develop, but the theory is that Hansard reliance will grow by fits and starts until there is some kind of crisis that pushes in the other direction. For a real-world example, recall our discussion in Chapter 4 of the evolution in Oregon, from an approach that excluded legislative history when the text was clear to one that attempted to admit legislative history only in limited fashion. Once the Oregon Supreme Court opened the door to legislative history, however, there was no stopping it—and it quickly grew fat on potato chips.

3.   *Relevance for the U.S. Debate?* Should *Pepper* suggest to the new textualists that they should adopt a more moderate skepticism about legislative materials? If you were Justice Scalia, how would you have voted in *Pepper*? (Hint: Consider the *statutory history* of the treatment of in-house benefits, from 1948 to 1993, nicely laid out in Lord Browne-Wilkinson's opinion. You can be a textualist and consider the formal evolution of the statutory scheme. What argument might a textualist draw from that?)

Professor Brudney argues that the U.S. Supreme Court should conclude from the Parent Country's post-*Pepper* practice that the most fruitful debates focus not on the tired admissibility debate (i.e., legislative history or no legislative history), but rather on *when* legislative history would be useful, *which* legislative history should be consulted, and *how much* weight it should be accorded. "[S]hould legislative history be regarded as presumptively more valuable to help resolve textual ambiguities that stem from lack of foresight rather than lack of political consensus? Is legislative history accompanying omnibus bills generally less suitable for judicial use because congressional deals on such a grand scale are simply indecipherable? Should legislative history in certain subject areas be presumed to have less weight where the law is administered primarily by a federal agency rather than private parties, or where the statutory text tends to be detailed and technical rather than open-ended and of more general public interest?" Brudney, *Below the Surface,* 85 Wash. U.L. Rev. at 63.

Or perhaps there is no lesson for the American debate over legislative history. It is possible that this result makes sense in a parliamentary democracy as opposed to a presidential system like that in the United States. In the United States, members of Congress do not serve at the side of the President to effectuate his policies. In a system where the ministers (the executors) sit in the parliament, might it not be easier for them to understand legislative policies; might the ministers feel more "accountable" to legislators? This is an example of what we mentioned in the introduction about lawmaking "context" at a higher level. We will see other examples below when we consider lawmaking in the specific contexts of Congress and the states.

2. CONGRESSIONAL PROCEDURE AND READING STATUTES "BY THE RULES"

As Judge Katzmann has explained, most judges are "neither wholly textualists nor purposivists."[23] To be effective and parsimonious in their use of legislative materials, Katzmann argues, lawyers must have a clearer understanding of congressional procedure and learn how to identify congressional decisions without engaging in unnecessary effort. In fact, as we try to show in this chapter, careful understanding of *the legislative process should be useful to textualists, too, as it can focus interpreters on the central texts at issue* and can provide useful information about how words were being used by the legislature. It can be just as helpful to purposivists as it limits available legislative history and can discipline the tendency to seize upon unreliable materials in an ad hoc fashion.

Critics of legislative materials as a source of guidance complain about the complexity of the legislative process; hence, it is simply too difficult to find legislative materials. Of course, there are almost no courses in law school that teach legislative process in any but the most rudimentary ways, so it is not surprising that it would seem a daunting venture. Perhaps this is not surprising given that most law professors themselves have no familiarity with legislatures,[24] even as law professors have long worried that Congress is not sufficiently attentive to process values, like deliberation and transparency. E.g., Hans Linde, *Due Process of Lawmaking*, 55 Neb. L. Rev. 197 (1976). In our view, any method of interpretation that is based on some link to Congress—and textualism and purposivism certainly fall in that category—is incomplete, nay, even irresponsible—if it does not incorporate some understanding of the context in which Congress drafts.

In the remainder of this chapter, we will recall for you the congressional rules and procedures described in Chapter 1, § 1, and introduce you to other structural features of congressional drafting. We derive from those procedures what we consider the proper methodology for using both text and legislative materials by agencies and courts when they interpret statutes. Ours is in some respects a novel approach, but it is not unduly complex. We shall not take you on a fishing expedition, but rather will introduce several objective rules that serve to clarify statutory meaning and the relevant legislative materials. To get you comfortable with this approach, we will return throughout the chapter to some of the

---

[23] Robert A. Katzmann, *Statutes*, 87 N.Y.U. L. Rev. 637, 667 (2012). See Katzmann, *Judging Statutes* (2014).

[24] Dakota S. Rudesill, *Closing the Legislative Experience Gap: How A Legislative Law Clerk Program Will Benefit the Legal Profession and Congress*, 87 Wash. U. L. Rev. 699, 706–08 (2010) (empirical study showing what the author calls a "virtual non-existence of legislative work experience" among judges and top legal faculty members).

cases from earlier in the coursebook as examples of how a process-focused approach could have been deployed.

A. THE STANDARD HIERARCHY OF LEGISLATIVE MATERIALS AND CONGRESS'S RULES

The standard hierarchy ranks legislative materials according to their purported *reliability,* namely, the likelihood that statements in those materials reflect the views of the legislative coalition that enacts the statute. By the conventional wisdom, the most reliable sources of legislative history are (1) committee reports, including conference committee[25] reports, followed by (2) on the record speeches by the measure's sponsors and floor managers, and then (3) statements by other supporters and even drafters. Least reliable are post-enactment statements, whether they be in committee reports or speeches made on the floor of the House or Senate.

Figure 6–1. The Conventional Hierarchy of Legislative History

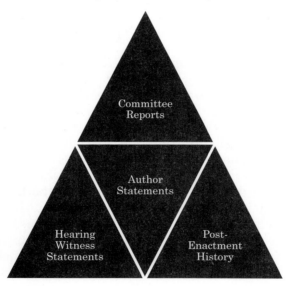

In this section, we argue that this conventional hierarchy of interpretive evidence should yield to Congress's own rules and procedures as sources of reliability and interpretive canons. By our account, the best legislative history is usually the history most proximate to the text, and proximity to textual decision requires an understanding of congressional

---

[25] Sometimes authors and judges have recognized that conference committee reports were in fact different from committee reports and should be part of the "gold standard" for legislative history; on the other hand, there are just as many judicial opinions and secondary resources which do not make any distinction between the two.

processes and rules. Rather than a pyramid, we should view the question as one of sequential process, like a trial, where there are motions to dismiss, summary judgment, trial instructions and a verdict. Often, the most important textual decisions are made *at the end of the process.* Legislative history is in this sense a misnomer: one is not really looking for the history of a statute, but instead one searches for the last decisions made by the enacting coalition to arrive at the relevant statutory text. The last decision may be made early in the process, akin to a motion to dismiss at trial (i.e., committee consideration), or during the trial (i.e., floor debate), or at the end of trial (i.e., conference committee).

Rather than a hierarchy, it is best to see this as an internal legislative dynamic in which the statutory interpreter is searching for meaning by "reverse engineering" the text of the statute. A bill begins with introduction in the House and Senate (like pleadings); it moves on to be considered in committee (like a motion to dismiss or summary judgment, it may well die there), where there may be hearings and markup. In the Senate, any major bill typically poses a threat of a filibuster, requiring 60 votes to break it. This typically causes the text to be revised in a "substitute," aimed to garner the support of 60, which is then introduced to amend the bill before post-cloture debate.

> *Senate Bill* $\longrightarrow$ *Committee (Hearings; Markup)* $\longrightarrow$ *Committee Text* $\longrightarrow$ *Floor* $\longrightarrow$ *Cloture Motion* $\longrightarrow$ *Substitute Text; Cloture Vote* $\longrightarrow$ *Debate & Amendments* = *Final Senate Text*

The House has a slightly different procedure. As there are many more members and committees, a bill is more frequently referred to multiple committees in the House than in the Senate (which causes various problems in drafting). More importantly, the bill must not only pass through committees, it must pass through the Rules Committee, which can kill a bill. The Rules Committee creates a resolution for debate and amendment to the bill; an "open rule" allows any amendments, but it is increasingly rare; typically amendments and the time for debate is specified in a closed Rule. Note that this House rule is only for the purposes of debating a particular bill. It is a one-time rule unlike the "standing" rules, which govern all legislation.

> *House Bill* $\longrightarrow$ *Committee (Hearings; Markup)* $\longrightarrow$ *Committee Text* $\longrightarrow$ *Rules Committee (Rules for Debate)* $\longrightarrow$ *Debate & Amendments* = *Final House Text*

Once House and Senate have passed texts, they must be reconciled, either by passing the bill back and forth between the Houses or by going to Conference. The Conference's charge is to resolve disagreement on text.

Under the Rules of both the House and Senate, the Conference cannot itself change the language that both Houses have passed. Once the Conference agrees on a text, this text must then be repassed by both the House and the Senate, but may not be further amended at that time.

In this chapter, we will perform the "reverse engineering" we have described. We begin at the end—with conference committee reports, which are the text of the statute brought to the Senate and House for consideration and unification. We will then go back to consider legislative debate and committee reports. Along the way, we emphasize statutes as forms of elections in which there are winners and losers.

B. REVERSE-ENGINEERING: CONFERENCE COMMITTEE REPORTS

However a bill begins, its text often ends with a Conference Report, because the House and Senate have passed different bills. A Conference Report is the text of the bill agreed to by House and Senate conferees; once it is sent back to the House and the Senate, it can no longer be amended. Barbara Sinclair reports that, from the 1960s to the 1990s, over three-quarters of all *major* legislation went to conference committee. *See* Barbara Sinclair, *Unorthodox Lawmaking: New Legislative Processes in the U.S. Congress* 91 (4th ed. 2011). The number of conferences has plummeted in recent years, likely due to heightened gridlock. Nevertheless, issues about conference committees still find their way to legislative briefs and important Supreme Court cases, especially because the vast majority of older statutes were the product of conference. See, for example, the competing *amicus* briefs filed by former Republican staff and legislators and by former Democratic staff and legislators in the hotly contested securities law controversy, *Erica P. John Fund v. Halliburton Co.*, 131 S.Ct. 2179 (2011) (No. 13–317) (unanimous Court adopts a compromise resolution, following neither *amicus* entirely).

Note that the Conference Report is the *text of the proposed bill:* a conference committee has agreed upon language about which the House and Senate versions of a bill disagree. The "Joint Explanation" to the Conference Report is the legislative history accompanying the Conference Report's text; because the committee's charge is to reconcile differences, and time is of the essence, the Joint Explanation is typically short and focuses on differences in the bills, not similarities. This is an important point, and one courts overlook: Just because something is not mentioned in the Joint Explanation does not mean that Congress was not attuned to it or that it was not significant; the very fact that it is not discussed may indicate that the House and Senate passed precisely the same language. The rules of Conference dictate what is relevant to the Conference Report's legislative history. The report and the text return to each chamber for approval; no member can add amendments. A sample conference report is an appendix to this chapter.

It should be noted that there are other ways to reach a single text than through a conference committee. Minor bills tend not to go to conference; instead, Congress reaches a single text by flip-flopping the bill from chamber to chamber until a single text is achieved. Very rarely, major statutes are passed by one chamber in the precise form they were passed by the other, also to avoid conference. For example, the Senate version of the Civil Rights Act of 1964 was accepted by the House because of the difficulty of passing the bill in the Senate and the fear that this difficulty would simply be repeated in conference. Also unusual (although increasingly important), a major bill will be completed by a special process known as "budget reconciliation." The Budget Act includes a "statutized rule" (see Chapter 1, § 3)—a special procedure that allows for reconciling House and Senate differences without filibuster, ensuring that budgets can be enacted when they need to be. Sometimes party leaders will use budget reconciliation to get around a filibuster for a statute that otherwise appears to be something other than a "budget" measure—the recent health reform legislation is a primary example. This workaround is not without risk: In reconciliation, only budget-related changes can be made, which means that non-budget statutes that use reconciliation do not receive the further review that Conference allows.

In considering conference reports, it is important to remember their position in the process. *They are not, emphasis on **not**, the same as committee reports.* Committee reports are documents generated in the early part of a bill's consideration; conference committee reports come at the end of the process. Typically, under the Rules of the House and Senate, conference committees cannot change the text in significant ways; otherwise the bill will be subject to a point of order (or objection on the floor). Moreover, a Conference Report is not subject to amendment. It must be accepted all or nothing. After you consider Figure 6–2, turn to the following case and note: (1) the text of the bill passed by the House; (2) the text of the bill passed by the Senate; and (3) the language of the Conference Report.

Figure 6–2. Creation and Passage of Final Text via Conference

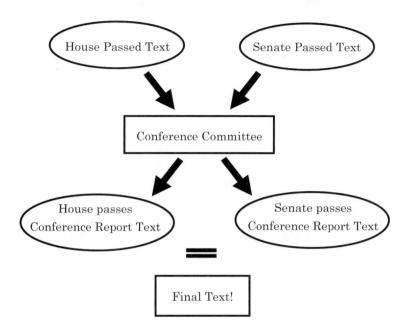

STATUTORY PREFACE TO *PUBLIC CITIZEN*

**Federal Advisory Committee Act (FACA),
5 U.S.C. App. § 3(2)**

For the purpose of this Act—

(2) The term 'advisory committee' means any committee, board, commission, council, conference, panel, task force, or other similar group, or any subcommittee or other subgroup thereof (hereafter in this paragraph referred to as 'committee'), which is—

(A) established by statute or reorganization plan, or

(B) established or utilized by the President, or

(C) established or utilized by one or more agencies, in the interest of obtaining advice or recommendations for the President or one or more agencies or officers of the Federal Government, except that such term excludes (i) the Advisory Commission on Intergovernmental Relations, (ii) the Commission on Government Procurement, and (iii) any committee which is composed wholly of full-time officers or employees of the Federal Government.

PUBLIC CITIZEN V. UNITED STATES DEPARTMENT OF JUSTICE

United States Supreme Court, 1989.
491 U.S. 440, 109 S.Ct. 2558, 105 L.Ed.2d 377.

JUSTICE BRENNAN delivered the opinion of the Court.

[Public Citizen challenged the practice of the Department of Justice seeking opinions about judicial nominees from the American Bar Association (ABA). The Department sought a declaration that the ABA was not subject to the FACA which requires that certain advisory committees be balanced, deliberate openly, and advise Congress on their activities. The ABA and DOJ contended that the Act did not apply to the ABA. In the Supreme Court, the debate focused on whether the ABA group was "utilized" by the president within the meaning of § 3(2) of the Federal Advisory Committee Act (FACA).]

* * * [III.A] There is no doubt that the Executive makes use of the ABA Committee, and thus "utilizes" it in one common sense of the term. As the District Court recognized, however, "reliance on the plain language of FACA alone is not entirely satisfactory." "Utilize" is a woolly verb, its contours left undefined by the statute itself. Read unqualifiedly, it would extend FACA's requirements to any group of two or more persons, or at least any formal organization, from which the President or an Executive agency seeks advice. We are convinced that Congress did not intend that result. A nodding acquaintance with FACA's purposes, as manifested by its legislative history and as recited in § 2 of the Act, reveals that it cannot have been Congress' intention, for example, to require the filing of a charter, the presence of a controlling federal official, and detailed minutes any time the President seeks the views of the National Association for the Advancement of Colored People (NAACP) before nominating Commissioners to the Equal Employment Opportunity Commission, or asks the leaders of an American Legion Post he is visiting for the organization's opinion on some aspect of military policy.

Nor can Congress have meant—as a straightforward reading of "utilize" would appear to require—that all of FACA's restrictions apply if a President consults with his own political party before picking his Cabinet. It was unmistakably *not* Congress' intention to intrude on a political party's freedom to conduct its affairs as it chooses, or its ability to advise elected officials who belong to that party, by placing a federal employee in charge of each advisory group meeting and making its minutes public property. FACA was enacted to cure specific ills, above all the wasteful expenditure of public funds for worthless committee meetings and biased proposals; although its reach is extensive, we cannot believe that it was intended to cover every formal and informal consultation between the President or an Executive agency and a group rendering advice.[9] As we said in *Church of the Holy Trinity v. United States*: "[F]requently words of general meaning are used in a statute, words broad enough to include an act in question, and yet a consideration of the whole legislation, or of the circumstances surrounding its enactment, or of the absurd results which follow from giving such broad meaning to the words, makes it unreasonable to believe that the legislator intended to include the particular act."

Where the literal reading of a statutory term would "compel an odd result," *Green v. Bock Laundry Machine Co.*, we must search for other evidence of congressional intent to lend the term its proper scope. "The circumstances of the enactment of particular legislation," for example, "may persuade a court that Congress did not intend words of common meaning to have their literal effect." Even though, as Judge Learned Hand said, "the words used, even in their literal sense, are the primary, and ordinarily the most reliable, source of interpreting the meaning of any writing," nevertheless "it is one of the surest indexes of a mature and developed jurisprudence not to make a fortress out of the dictionary; but to remember that statutes always have some purpose or object to accomplish, whose sympathetic and imaginative discovery is the surest guide to their meaning." Looking beyond the naked text for guidance is perfectly proper when the result it apparently decrees is difficult to fathom or where it seems inconsistent with Congress' intention, since the plain-meaning rule is "rather an axiom of experience than a rule of law, and does not preclude consideration of persuasive evidence if it exists." *Boston Sand & Gravel Co. v. United States*, 278 U.S. 41 (1928) (Holmes, J.).

Consideration of FACA's purposes and origins in determining whether the term "utilized" was meant to apply to the Justice Department's use of the ABA Committee is particularly appropriate here, given the importance we have consistently attached to interpreting

---

[9] Justice Kennedy agrees with our conclusion that an unreflective reading of the term "utilize" would include the President's occasional consultations with groups such as the NAACP and committees of the President's own political party. Having concluded that groups such as these are covered by the statute when they render advice, however, Justice Kennedy refuses to consult FACA's legislative history—which he later denounces, with surprising hyperbole, as "unauthoritative materials," although countless opinions of this Court, including many written by the concurring Justices, have rested on just such materials—because this result would not, in his estimation, be "absurd." Although this Court has never adopted so strict a standard for reviewing committee reports, floor debates, and other nonstatutory indications of congressional intent, and we explicitly reject that standard today, even if "absurdity" were the test, one would think it was met here. The idea that Members of Congress would vote for a bill subjecting their own political parties to bureaucratic intrusion and public oversight when a President or Cabinet officer consults with party committees concerning political appointments is outlandish. Nor does it strike us as in any way "unhealthy," or undemocratic, to use all available materials in ascertaining the intent of our elected representatives, rather than read their enactments as requiring what may seem a disturbingly unlikely result, provided only that the result is not "absurd." Indeed, the sounder and more democratic course, the course that strives for allegiance to Congress' desires in all cases, not just those where Congress' statutory directive is plainly sensible or borders on the lunatic, is the traditional approach we reaffirm today.

statutes to avoid deciding difficult constitutional questions where the text fairly admits of a less problematic construction. * * *

[III.B]   Close attention to FACA's history is helpful, for FACA did not flare on the legislative scene with the suddenness of a meteor. Similar attempts to regulate the Federal Government's use of advisory committees were common during the 20 years preceding FACA's enactment. An understanding of those efforts is essential to ascertain the intended scope of the term "utilize."

In 1950, the Justice Department issued guidelines for the operation of federal advisory committees in order to forestall their facilitation of anticompetitive behavior by bringing industry leaders together with Government approval. Several years later, after the House Committee on Government Operations found that the Justice Department's guidelines were frequently ignored, Representative Fascell sponsored a bill that would have accorded the guidelines legal status. H.R. 7390, 85th Cong., 1st Sess. (1957). Although the bill would have required agencies to report to Congress on their use of advisory committees and would have subjected advisory committees to various controls, it apparently would not have imposed any requirements on private groups, not established by the Federal Government, whose advice was sought by the Executive. See H.R. Rep. No. 576, 85th Cong., 1st Sess., 5–7 (1957); 103 Cong. Rec. 11252 (1957) (remarks of Rep. Fascell and Rep. Vorys).

Despite Congress' failure to enact the bill, the Bureau of the Budget issued a directive in 1962 incorporating the bulk of the guidelines. Later that year, President Kennedy issued Executive Order No. 11007, 3 CFR 573 (1959–1963 Comp.), which governed the functioning of advisory committees until FACA's passage. Executive Order No. 11007 is the probable source of the term "utilize" as later employed in FACA. The Order applied to advisory committees "formed by a department or agency of the Government in the interest of obtaining advice or recommendations," or "not formed by a department or agency, but only during any period when it is being *utilized* by a department or agency in the same manner as a Government-formed advisory committee." § 2(a) (emphasis added). To a large extent, FACA adopted wholesale the provisions of Executive Order No. 11007. For example, like FACA, Executive Order No. 11007 stipulated that no advisory committee be formed or utilized unless authorized by law or determined as a matter of formal record by an agency head to be in the public interest, § 3; that all advisory committee meetings be held in the presence of a Government employee empowered to adjourn the meetings whenever he or she considered adjournment to be in the public interest, § 6(b); that meetings only occur at the call of, or with the advance approval of, a federal employee, § 6(a); that minutes be kept of the meetings, §§ 6(c), (d); and that committees terminate after two years unless a statute or an agency head decreed otherwise § 8.

There is no indication, however, that Executive Order No. 11007 was intended to apply to the Justice Department's consultations with the ABA Committee. Neither President Kennedy, who issued the Order, nor President Johnson, nor President Nixon apparently deemed the ABA Committee to be "utilized" by the Department of Justice in the relevant sense of that term. Notwithstanding the ABA Committee's highly visible role in advising the Justice Department regarding potential judicial nominees, and notwithstanding the fact that the Order's requirements were established by the Executive itself rather than Congress, no President or Justice Department official applied them to the ABA Committee.

Although FACA's legislative history evinces an intent to widen the scope of Executive Order No. 11007's definition of "advisory committee" by including "Presidential advisory committees," which lay beyond the reach of Executive Order No. 11007, see H.R. Rep. No. 91–1731, pp. 9–10 (1970); H.R. Rep. No. 92–1017, p. 4 (1972); S. Rep. No. 92–1098, pp. 3–5, 7 (1972), as well as to augment the restrictions applicable to advisory committees covered by the statute, there is scant reason to believe that Congress desired to bring the ABA Committee within FACA's net. FACA's principal purpose was to enhance the public accountability of advisory committees established by the Executive Branch and to reduce wasteful expenditures on them. That purpose could be accomplished, however, without expanding the coverage of Executive Order No. 11007 to include privately organized committees that received no federal funds. Indeed, there is considerable evidence that Congress sought nothing more than stricter compliance with reporting and other requirements—which were made more stringent—by advisory committees already covered by the Order and similar treatment of a small class of publicly funded groups created by the President.

The House bill which in its amended form became FACA applied exclusively to advisory committees "established" by statute or by the Executive, whether by a federal agency or by the President himself. H.R. 4383, 92d Cong., 2d Sess. § 3(2) (1972). Although the House Committee Report stated that the class of advisory committees was to include "committees which may have been organized before their advice was sought by the President or any agency, but which are used by the President or any agency in the same way as an advisory committee formed by the President himself or the agency itself," H.R. Rep. No. 92–1017, *supra,* at 4, it is questionable whether the Report's authors believed that the Justice Department used the ABA Committee in the same way as it used advisory committees it established. The phrase "used . . . in the same way" is reminiscent of Executive Order No. 11007's reference to advisory committees "utilized . . . in the same manner" as a committee established by the Federal Government, and the practice of three administrations demonstrates that Executive Order No. 11007 did not encompass the ABA Committee.

This inference draws support from the earlier House Report which instigated the legislative efforts that culminated in FACA. That Report complained that committees "utilized" by an agency—as opposed to those established directly by an agency—rarely complied with the requirements of Executive Order No. 11007. See H.R. Rep. No. 91–1731, *supra*, at 15. But it did not cite the ABA Committee or similar advisory committees as willful evaders of the Order. Rather, the Report's paradigmatic example of a committee "utilized" by an agency for purposes of Executive Order No. 11007 was an advisory committee established by a quasi-public organization in receipt of public funds, such as the National Academy of Sciences. There is no indication in the Report that a purely private group like the ABA Committee that was not formed by the Executive, accepted no public funds, and assisted the Executive in performing a constitutionally specified task committed to the Executive was within the terms of Executive Order No. 11007 or was the type of advisory entity that legislation was urgently needed to address.

Paralleling the initial House bill, the Senate bill that grew into FACA defined "advisory committee" as one "established or organized" by statute, the President, or an Executive agency. S. 3529, 92d Cong., 2d Sess. §§ 3(1), (2) (1972). Like the House Report, the accompanying Senate Report stated that the phrase "established or organized" was to be understood in its "most liberal sense, so that when an officer brings together a group by formal or informal means, by contract or other arrangement, and whether or not Federal money is expended, to obtain advice and information, such group is covered by the provisions of this bill." S. Rep. No. 92–1098, *supra*, at 8. While the Report manifested a clear intent not to restrict FACA's coverage to advisory committees funded by the Federal Government, it did not indicate any desire to bring all private advisory committees within FACA's terms. Indeed, the examples the Senate Report offers—"the Advisory Council on Federal Reports, the National Industrial Pollution Control Council, the National Petroleum Council, advisory councils to the National Institutes of Health, and committees of the national academies where they are utilized and officially recognized as advisory to the President, to an agency, or to a Government official," *ibid.*—are limited to groups organized by, or closely tied to, the Federal Government, and thus enjoying quasi-public status. Given the prominence of the ABA Committee's role and its familiarity to Members of Congress, its omission from the list of groups formed and maintained by private initiative to offer advice with respect to the President's nomination of Government officials is telling. If the examples offered by the Senate Committee on Government Operations are representative, as seems fair to surmise, then there is little reason to think that there was any support, at least at the committee stage, for going beyond the terms of Executive Order No. 11007 to regulate comprehensively the workings of the ABA Committee.

It is true that the final version of FACA approved by both Houses employed the phrase "established or utilized," and that this phrase is more capacious than the word "established" or the phrase "established or organized." But its genesis suggests that it was not intended to go much beyond those narrower formulations. The words "or utilized" were added by the Conference Committee to the definition included in the House bill. See H.R. Conf. Rep. No. 92–1403, p. 2 (1972). The Joint Explanatory Statement, however, said simply that the definition contained in the House bill was adopted "with modification." *Id.* at 9. The Conference Report offered no indication that the modification was significant, let alone that it would substantially broaden FACA's application by sweeping within its terms a vast number of private groups, such as the Republican National Committee, not formed at the behest of the Executive or by quasi-public organizations whose opinions the Federal Government sometimes solicits. Indeed, it appears that the House bill's initial restricted focus on advisory committees established by the Federal Government, in an expanded sense of the word "established," was retained rather than enlarged by the Conference Committee. In the section dealing with FACA's range of application, the Conference Report stated: "The Act does not apply to persons or organizations which have contractual relationships with Federal agencies *nor to advisory committees not directly established by or for such agencies.*" *Id.,* at 10 (emphasis added). The phrase "or utilized" therefore appears to have been added simply to clarify that FACA applies to advisory committees established by the Federal Government in a generous sense of that term, encompassing groups formed indirectly by quasi-public organizations such as the National Academy of Sciences "for" public agencies as well as "by" such agencies themselves.

Read in this way, the term "utilized" would meet the concerns of the authors of House Report No. 91–1731 that advisory committees covered by Executive Order No. 11007, because they were "utilized by a department or agency in the same manner as a Government-formed advisory committee" such as the groups organized by the National Academy of Sciences and its affiliates which the Report discussed—would be subject to FACA's requirements. And it comports well with the initial House and Senate bills' limited extension to advisory groups "established," on a broad understanding of that word, by the Federal Government, whether those groups were established by the Executive Branch or by statute or whether they were the offspring of some organization created or permeated by the Federal Government. Read in this way, however, the word "utilized" does not describe the Justice Department's use of the ABA Committee. Consultations between the Justice Department and the ABA Committee were not within the purview of Executive Order No. 11007, nor can the ABA Committee be said to have been formed by the Justice Department or by some semiprivate entity the Federal Government helped bring into being.

[In Part III.C. of his opinion, Justice Brennan applies the canon of constitutional avoidance [see Chapter 5, § 2B] to resolve any lingering doubts. Finding that "construing FACA to apply to the Justice Department's consultations with the ABA Committee would present formidable constitutional difficulties," because it might infring[e] unduly on the President's Article II power to nominate federal judges and violat[e] the doctrine of separation of powers, Justice Brennan concluded that "[w]here the competing arguments based on FACA's text and legislative history, though both plausible, tend to show that Congress did not desire FACA to apply to the Justice Department's confidential solicitation of the ABA Committee's views on prospective judicial nominees, sound sense counsels adherence to our rule of caution. Our unwillingness to resolve important constitutional questions unnecessarily thus solidifies our conviction that FACA is inapplicable."]

JUSTICE SCALIA took no part in the consideration or decision of these cases.

JUSTICE KENNEDY, with whom THE CHIEF JUSTICE [REHNQUIST] and JUSTICE O'CONNOR join, concurring in the judgment.

* * * I cannot join the Court's conclusion that the Federal Advisory Committee Act (FACA), does not cover the activities of the American Bar Association's Standing Committee on Federal Judiciary in advising the Department of Justice regarding potential nominees for federal judgeships. * * * I cannot accept the method by which the Court arrives at its interpretation of FACA, which does not accord proper respect to the finality and binding effect of legislative enactments. The second question in the case is the extent to which Congress may interfere with the President's constitutional prerogative to nominate federal judges. On this issue, which the Court does not reach because of its conclusion on the statutory question, I think it quite plain that the application of FACA to the Government's use of the ABA Committee is unconstitutional.

There is a ready starting point, which ought to serve also as a sufficient stopping point, for this kind of analysis: the plain language of the statute. Yet the Court is unwilling to rest on this foundation, for several reasons. One is an evident unwillingness to define the application of the statute in terms of the ordinary meaning of its language. We are told that "utilize" is "a woolly verb," and therefore we cannot be content to rely on what is described, with varying levels of animus, as a "literal reading," a "literalistic reading," and "a dictionary reading" of this word. We also are told in no uncertain terms that we cannot rely on (what I happen to regard as a more accurate description) "a straightforward reading of 'utilize.'" Reluctance to working with the basic meaning of words in a normal manner undermines the legal process. These cases demonstrate that reluctance of this sort leads instead to woolly judicial construction that mars the plain face of legislative enactments.

The Court concedes that the Executive Branch "utilizes" the ABA Committee in the common sense of that word. Indeed, this point cannot be contested. As the Court's own recitation of the facts makes clear, the Department of Justice has, over the last four decades, made regular use of the ABA Committee to investigate the background of potential nominees and to make critical recommendations regarding their qualifications. This should end the matter. The Court nevertheless goes through several more steps to conclude that, although "it seems to us a close question," Congress did not intend that FACA would apply to the ABA Committee.

Although I believe the Court's result is quite sensible, I cannot go along with the unhealthy process of amending the statute by judicial interpretation. Where the language of a statute is clear in its application, the normal rule is that we are bound by it. There is, of course, a legitimate exception to this rule, which the Court invokes, citing *Church of the Holy Trinity v. United States* (Chapter 4, § 1), and with which I have no quarrel. Where the plain language of the statute would lead to "patently absurd consequences," * * * we need not apply the language in such a fashion. When used in a proper manner, this narrow exception to our normal rule of statutory construction does not intrude upon the lawmaking powers of Congress, but rather demonstrates a respect for the coequal Legislative Branch, which we assume would not act in an absurd way.

This exception remains a legitimate tool of the Judiciary, however, only as long as the Court acts with self-discipline by limiting the exception to situations where the result of applying the plain language would be, in a genuine sense, absurd, *i.e.,* where it is quite impossible that Congress could have intended the result, see *ibid.,* and where the alleged absurdity is so clear as to be obvious to most anyone. A few examples of true absurdity are given in the *Holy Trinity* decision cited by the Court, such as where a sheriff was prosecuted for obstructing the mails even though he was executing a warrant to arrest the mail carrier for murder, or where a medieval law against drawing blood in the streets was to be applied against a physician who came to the aid of a man who had fallen down in a fit. In today's opinion, however, the Court disregards the plain language of the statute not because its application would be patently absurd, but rather because, on the basis of its view of the legislative history, the Court is "fairly confident" that "FACA should [not] be construed to apply to the ABA Committee." I believe the Court's loose invocation of the "absurd result" canon of statutory construction creates too great a risk that the Court is exercising its own "WILL instead of JUDGMENT," with the consequence of "substituti[ng] [its own] pleasure to that of the legislative body." The Federalist No. 78, p. 469 (C. Rossiter ed. 1961) (A. Hamilton).

The Court makes only a passing effort to show that it would be absurd to apply the term "utilize" to the ABA Committee according to its commonsense meaning. It offers three examples that we can assume are meant to demonstrate this point: the application of FACA to an American Legion Post should the President visit that organization and happen to ask its opinion on some aspect of military policy; the application of FACA to the meetings of the National Association for the Advancement of Colored People (NAACP) should the President seek its views in nominating Commissioners to the Equal Employment Opportunity Commission; and the application of FACA to the national committee of the President's political party should he consult it for advice and recommendations before picking his Cabinet.

None of these examples demonstrate the kind of absurd consequences that would justify departure from the plain language of the statute. A commonsense interpretation of the term "utilize" would not necessarily reach the kind of ad hoc contact with a private group that is contemplated by the Court's American Legion hypothetical. Such an interpretation would be consistent, moreover, with * * * the General Services Administration (GSA) regulation interpreting the word "utilize," which the Court in effect ignores. As for the more regular use contemplated by the Court's examples concerning the NAACP and the national committee of the President's political party, it would not be at all absurd to say that, under the Court's hypothetical, these groups would be "utilized" by the President to obtain "advice or recommendations" on appointments, and therefore would fall within the coverage of the statute. Rather, what is troublesome about these examples is that they raise the very same serious constitutional questions that confront us here (and perhaps others as well). The Court confuses the two points. The fact that a particular application of the clear terms of a statute might be unconstitutional does not, in and of itself, render a straightforward application of the language absurd, so as to allow us to conclude that the statute does not apply.

* * * Unable to show that an application of FACA according the plain meaning of its terms would be absurd, the Court turns instead to the task of demonstrating that a straightforward reading of the statute would be inconsistent with the congressional purposes that lay behind its passage. To the student of statutory construction, this move is a familiar one. It is,

as the Court identifies it, the classic *Holy Trinity* argument. "[A] thing may be within the letter of the statute and yet not within the statute, because not within its spirit, nor within the intention of its makers." *Holy Trinity*. I cannot embrace this principle. Where it is clear that the unambiguous language of a statute embraces certain conduct, and it would not be patently absurd to apply the statute to such conduct, it does not foster a democratic exegesis for this Court to rummage through unauthoritative materials to consult the spirit of the legislation in order to discover an alternative interpretation of the statute with which the Court is more comfortable. It comes as a surprise to no one that the result of the Court's lengthy journey through the legislative history is the discovery of a congressional intent not to include the activities of the ABA Committee within the coverage of FACA. The problem with spirits is that they tend to reflect less the views of the world whence they come than the views of those who seek their advice.

Lest anyone think that my objection to the use of the *Holy Trinity* doctrine is a mere point of interpretive purity divorced from more practical considerations, I should pause for a moment to recall the unhappy genesis of that doctrine and its unwelcome potential. * * * * I should think the potential of this doctrine to allow judges to substitute their personal predelictions for the will of the Congress is so self-evident from the case which spawned it as to require no further discussion of its susceptibility to abuse.

Even if I were inclined to disregard the unambiguous language of FACA, I could not join the Court's conclusions with regard to Congress' purposes. I find the Court's treatment of the legislative history one sided and offer a few observations on the difficulties of perceiving the true contours of a spirit.

The first problem with the Court's use of legislative history is the questionable relevance of its detailed account of Executive practice before the enactment of FACA. This background is interesting but not instructive, for as the Court acknowledges, even the legislative history as presented by the Court "evinces an intent to widen the scope of" the coverage of prior Executive Orders, and in any event the language of the statute is "more capacious" than any of the previous "narrower formulations." Indeed, Congress would have had little reason to legislate at all in this area if it had intended FACA to be nothing more than a reflection of the provisions of Executive Order No. 11007, 3 CFR 573 (1959–1963 Comp.), which was already the settled and governing law at the time this bill was introduced, considered, and enacted. In other words, the background to FACA cannot be taken to illuminate its breadth precisely because FACA altered the landscape to address the many concerns Congress had about the increasing growth and use of advisory committees.

Another problem with the Court's approach lies in its narrow preoccupation with the ABA Committee against the background of a bill that was intended to provide comprehensive legislation covering a widespread problem in the organization and operation of the Federal Government. The Court's discussion takes portentous note of the fact that Congress did not mention or discuss the ABA Committee by name in the materials that preceded the enactment of FACA. But that is hardly a remarkable fact. The legislation was passed at a time when somewhere between 1,800 and 3,200 target committees were thought to be in existence, see S. Rep. No. 92–1098, pp. 3, 4 (1972), and the congressional Reports mentioned few committees by name. More to the point, its argument reflects an incorrect understanding of the kinds of laws Congress passes: it usually does not legislate by specifying examples, but by identifying broad and general principles that must be applied to particular factual instances. And that is true of FACA.

Finally, though the stated objective of the Court's inquiry into legislative history is the identification of Congress' purposes in passing FACA, the inquiry does not focus on the most obvious place for finding those purposes, which is the section of the Conference Committee Report entitled "Findings and Purposes." That section lists six findings and purposes that underlie FACA:

"(1) the need for many existing advisory committees has not been adequately reviewed;

"(2) new advisory committees should be established only when they are determined to be essential and their number should be kept to the minimum necessary;

"(3) advisory committees should be terminated when they are no longer carrying out the purposes for which they were established;

"(4) standards and uniform procedures should govern the establishment, operation, administration, and duration of advisory committees;

"(5) the Congress and the public should be kept informed with respect to the number, purpose, membership, activities, and cost of advisory committees; and

"(6) the function of advisory committees should be advisory only, and that all matters under their consideration should be determined, in accordance with law, by the official, agency, or officer involved." H.R. Conf. Rep. No. 92–1403, pp. 1–2 (1972).

The most pertinent conclusion to be drawn from this list of purposes is that all of them are implicated by the Justice Department's use of the ABA Committee. In addition, it shows that Congress' stated purposes for addressing the use of advisory committees went well beyond the amount of public funds devoted to their operations, which in any event is not the sole component in the cost of their use; thus the Court errs in focusing on this point.

It is most striking that this section of the Conference Committee Report, which contains Congress' own explicit statement of its purposes in adopting FACA, receives no mention by the Court on its amble through the legislative history. The one statement the Court does quote from this Report, that FACA does not apply " 'to advisory committees not directly established by or for [federal] agencies,' " quoting H.R. Conf. Rep. 92–1403, *supra,* at 10, U.S. Code Cong. & Admin. News 1972, p. 3509 (emphasis deleted), is of uncertain value. It is not clear that this passage would exclude the ABA Committee, which was established in 1946 and began almost at once to advise the Government on judicial nominees. It also is not clear why the reasons a committee was formed should determine whether and how they are "utilized by" the Government, or how this consideration can be squared with the plain language of the statute. The Court professes puzzlement because the Report says only that the Conference Committee modified the definition of "advisory committee" to include the phrase "or utilized," but does not explain the extent of the modification in any detail. One would have thought at least that the Court would have been led to consider how the specific purposes Congress identified for this legislation might shed light on the reasons for the change. * * *

In sum, it is quite desirable not to apply FACA to the ABA Committee. I cannot, however, reach this conclusion as a matter of fair statutory construction. The plain and ordinary meaning of the language passed by Congress governs, and its application does not lead to any absurd results. An unnecessary recourse to the legislative history only confirms this conclusion. And the reasonable and controlling interpretation of the statute adopted by the agency charged with its implementation is also in accord.

[Justice Kennedy then rejects the canon of constitutional avoidance on the ground that the statute is clear. In Part II of his concurring opinion, Justice Kennedy nonetheless agrees with the Court's judgment, because he finds that the FACA cannot be constitutionally applied to regulate the President's consultation with the ABA and other advisors in connection with his appointment of judges and other officials.]

NOTES AND QUESTIONS ON PUBLIC CITIZEN

Within the field of statutory interpretation, *Public Citizen* is known as a *difficult case.* For Justice Kennedy, the language of "utilize" is plain, and that should be the end of the case. The Court's result seems to require it to use "judicial surgery," rewriting the statute, a function typically best left to the legislature. Also, the majority uses the rule against absurdities, prompting an emphatic response from Justice Kennedy that this textualist escape hatch should not be applied as liberally as the Court tends to do (recall *Bock Laundry*). Finally, there is a lurking constitutional question—whether the President's power to nominate judges has been infringed—that implicates the constitutional avoidance canon. Justice Brennan's opinion also cites a good deal of legislative (and other) history. Did the case need all of these interpretive gymnastics? The purpose of this set of notes is to explore the case, and its statutory history, from a different angle.

1.   Write a list of all the kinds of legislative history the majority opinion uses (including evidence not from Congress as well as evidence of prior bills or texts). Note that "H.R." refers to a House bill; "S." refers to a Senate bill; "H.R. Rep" refers to a committee report generated in the House and "Sen. Rep." refers to a committee report generated in the Senate; "H. Conf. Rep." or "S. Conf. Rep." refers to a conference committee report.

2.   Now look at the text of the statute that was passed by the House, and the text of the statute as passed by the Senate. (Both can be found in the opinion itself). Note that both chambers passed similar language on the question of "establish." Now consider the Conference language (i.e., the text agreed upon by the conferees). Where did the word "utilize" come from?

3.   Congress's rules say that members of a Conference cannot change language that was passed by both the House and the Senate.[26] Assuming that Congress sought to follow the rules, then a faithful member of Congress would have to believe that "utilize" did not make a substantial change to the existing text. If that is right, does the Court's result follow from Congress's rules more easily than it does from the majority's legislative history analysis?

4.   Could a textualist apply the foregoing analysis consistently with her views about legislative history? Construct a textualist's best argument that this approach does not violate the rules against relying on legislative history. (Or that this approach does not violate the concerns invoked by OLP as reasons to eschew "intended meaning" when interpreting statutes.) Is Justice Brennan's intentionalist/purposivist analysis strengthened by this methodology? Construct a purposivist's best argument that reliance on the rules is the best approach to *Public Citizen*.

5.   Should the Supreme Court have wasted its time with the legislative history in the majority opinion? Did it have to contend with the absurdity canon or constitutional avoidance? Was the legislative history a good deal less voluminous than the majority suggested? The relevant portion of the

---

[26] See Senate Manual, S. Doc. No. 106–1, 197 (2000) (Senate Rule 28: "Conferees may not include in their report matters not committed to them by either House. In the House, in case such matter is included, the conference report may be ruled out on a point of order. In the Senate, in case such matter is included, the custom is to submit the question of order to the Senate."); *see id.* Rule 30 ("Conferees may not strike out in conference anything in a bill agreed to and passed by both Houses" (citing Jefferson's Manual, § XLV.)).

Conference Report was roughly a single page, and the entire report only four pages. *See* the report reprinted as an appendix to this chapter.

6.   Why consider Congress's rules if Congress passed the language "utilize" as part of its bicameral procedures? Does it really matter what happened in Conference? On the one hand, because textualists care about text because it is passed by the whole, one might wonder whether they should be giving credit to text coming from less than the whole. On the other hand, because the whole Congress embraced "utilize" why should we not assume they meant "utilize"? Given all of the other interpretive rules to which Court looks (absurdities, avoidance, etc.), might it be the case that relying upon Congress's rules would be a more democratically legitimate and less intrusive means of dealing with the statute?

PAUL GREEN V. BOCK LAUNDRY MACHINE COMPANY

Supreme Court of the United States, 1989.
490 U.S. 504, 109 S.Ct. 1981, 104 L.Ed.2d 557.

[Excerpted in Chapter 4, § 3B]

NOTE AND PROBLEM ON GREEN V. BOCK LAUNDRY

Public Citizen is not the only famous statutory interpretation case that involves a hidden question of legislative process. Read or reread *Green v. Bock Laundry*, where the Court interpreted Rule 609 of the Federal Rules of Evidence, with a new textualist concurring opinion by Justice Scalia. In *Bock Laundry*, the question appeared to be one of absurdity. Could Congress possibly have meant to impeach civil defendants and *not* civil plaintiffs? All of the Justices noted this, including Justice Scalia, who even conceded that such an absurdity might cause him to look to legislative history to "verify that what seems to us an unthinkable disposition * * * was indeed unthought of."

The *Bock Laundry* Court focused almost exclusively on the term "defendant." After a very long exegesis on the legislative history, Justice Stevens's opinion concluded that all witnesses but criminal defendants should be subject to the old common law rule, which would mean that a civil plaintiff like Green in *Bock Laundry*, would not be covered by Congress's new balancing test for felony impeachment. Justice Scalia refused to look at the legislative history but inserted the word "criminal" in the statute as the best ordinary meaning reading of the term "defendant." Justice Blackmun believed that the best alternative was to include all "parties" under the balancing test.

Query whether all the Justices missed the same process point absent from *Public Citizen*. In *Bock Laundry*, both houses passed bills in which Rule 609 covered civil and criminal cases; neither passed the word "defendant," a term that appears for the first time in the Conference Report. In *Public Citizen*, the "absurd" text turns out to be text added at the last minute in conference committee negotiations. Although decidedly more difficult than

Public Citizen, this case raises many of the same concerns: None of the Justices paid much attention to the evolution of the statutory text, or to the fact that the central text at issue was added in *conference,* which might make any investigation into prior legislative history irrelevant. At a minimum, anyone wishing to save energy and research would have focused on the conference report (compare, for example, Justice Stevens's 13-year history)!

Focusing on the Conference Report substantially reduces the amount of work one must undertake to find the legislative history, but it does not resolve the case, unless the interpreter is willing to consider the effect of Congress's own rules about language inserted at conference. If we apply the legislative canon we considered in the notes to *Public Citizen,* changes made in conference should be disfavored because, based on congressional rules, conference-added language cannot "significantly" change the underlying bills passed by both Houses. Because both chambers passed bills covering civil cases, the conference could not change that coverage. Under this approach, one would read "defendant" to include "civil" witnesses, or as Justice Blackmun did, as a proxy for civil "parties." Both views mean that Green wins! Notice however that it leaves open questions about the categories of witnesses unresolved (see footnote 27 below on special concerns in criminal cases).

PROBLEM 6–2: TRYING YOUR HAND AT REVERSE ENGINEERING

1. *Trace the Process Outlined in the Note Above.* Find the statutory language as passed by the House and the language as passed by the Senate. (The bills passed by the Senate and House are repeated in the case.) Compare the language with the statute as it was passed after conference, set forth in the statutory preface to the case. Now determine the point during the legislative process where the balancing act language and the term "defendant" were added.

2. *Review the Joint Explanation to the Conference Report.* The "joint explanation" is the legislative history to the Conference Report's textual changes. Remember that the "joint explanation" will not address matters that are not in dispute, as for example, if everyone agreed that the bill covered "witnesses." Reprinted at the end of this Problem is the relevant portion of the joint explanation to the Conference Report on Rule 609. It is sometimes said that legislative history repeats the ambiguities of text, and this may be a very good example of that adage. Read the following report and write down the ways in which the term "defendant" is used. Is it used to mean "witness," "criminal defendant," "party," "someone else?" Note that the joint explanation uses the term "accused" to refer to the rule that allows impeachment for all witnesses and all parties for false statement crimes. Does the report suggest, contrary to linguistic intuition, that one could use the term "defendant" when one really meant "party" or "witness"?

3.   *Other Explanations for the Statutory Language. Bock Laundry* is a more difficult case than *Public Citizen,* because there are other ways one might explain what happened at conference. The conference "split" the baby on balancing: the House bill was all balancing for all witnesses; the Senate bill had no balancing for any witness; and the Conference bill compromised by giving the balancing test to criminal defendants, the parties with the greatest stake. This sounds highly plausible to lawyers, but consider the congressional context. Why would a typically tough-on-crime Congress grant more protections to criminal defendants than to seemingly more-reputable civil defendants and plaintiffs? Similarly, why would a typically pro-prosecution Congress disadvantage prosecutors by having their cases undermined through the impeachment of confidential-informants? Then, too, does this explanation reflect an even split of the "balancing" baby? Why would the House accept a bill that returned to the common law rule for the vast majority of witnesses with one exception (see the list below), when the House passed a bill that was a complete repudiation of the common law? See if you think this explanation is supported by the "joint explanation" reprinted below.[27]

---

[27] Keep in mind, there are seven different kinds of witnesses in the cases covered by Rule 609. All seven may be impeached by their own false statement crimes, but only one obtains the benefit of a balancing test for impeachment by a felony under Rule 609. As a policy matter, should criminal defendants enjoy this benefit more than other witnesses?

	Felony Admissible, but Only After Balancing	False Statement Crime Admissible?
Criminal Defendant (Party)	Yes	Yes
Criminal Prosecution Witness	?	Yes
Criminal Defense Witness	?	Yes
Civil Defendant (Party)	?	Yes
Civil Plaintiff (Party)	?	Yes
Civil Defendant Witness	?	Yes
Civil Plaintiff Witness	?	Yes

There may be good reasons why criminal cases should be treated differently. For example, the conferees may have decided to treat criminal defendants more favorably than prosecution witnesses. For example, the prosecution is often aided by "confidential informants," with criminal records. One might want a rule, as some members of Congress did, in which the criminal defendant (who should be proven guilty only upon a showing of evidence beyond a reasonable doubt) could only be impeached with safeguards but which would allow the prosecution witnesses to be easily impeached (after all, those witnesses were not going to jail and typically had avoided jail by offering to testify). Query whether the same calculus should operate in civil cases, where the civil plaintiff has the burden of proof. Does one have to decide the question about prosecution witnesses or criminal defendants to decide Green's case?

JOINT EXPLANATION TO THE CONFERENCE REPORT ON FEDERAL RULES OF EVIDENCE

[H.R. Conf. Rep. 93–1597, pp. 9–10 (1974)]

RULE 609. IMPEACHMENT BY EVIDENCE OF CONVICTION OF CRIME

Rule 609 defines when a party may use evidence of a prior conviction in order to impeach a witness. The Senate amendments make changes in two subsections of Rule 609.

A. Rule 609(a)—General Rule

The House bill provides that the credibility of a witness can be attacked by proof of prior conviction of a crime only if the crime involves dishonesty or false statement. The Senate amendment provides that a witness' credibility may be attacked if the crime (1) was punishable by death or imprisonment in excess of one year under the law under which he was convicted or (2) involves dishonesty or false statement, regardless of the punishment.

The Conference adopts the Senate amendment with an amendment. The Conference amendment provides that the credibility of a witness, whether a defendant or someone else, may be attacked by proof of a prior conviction but only if the crime: (1) was punishable by death or imprisonment in excess of one year under the law under which he was convicted and the court determines that the probative value of the conviction outweighs its prejudicial effect to the defendant; or (2) involved dishonesty or false statement regardless of the punishment.

By the phrase "dishonesty and false statement" the Conference means crimes such as perjury or subornation of perjury, false statement, criminal fraud, embezzlement, or false pretense, or any other offense in the nature of crimen falsi, the commission of which involves some element of deceit, untruthfulness, or falsification bearing on the accused's propensity to testify truthfully.

The admission of prior convictions involving dishonesty and false statement is not within the discretion of the Court. Such convictions are peculiarly probative of credibility and, under this rule, are always to be admitted. Thus, judicial discretion granted with respect to the admissibility of other prior convictions is not applicable to those involving dishonesty or false statement.

With regard to the discretionary standard established by paragraph (1) of rule 609(a), the Conference determines that the prejudicial effect to be weighed against the probative value of the conviction is specifically the prejudicial effect to the defendant. The danger of prejudice to a witness other than the defendant (such as injury to prejudice to a witness other than the defendant (such as injury to the witness' reputation in his community) was considered and rejected by the Conference as an element to be weighed in determining admissibility. It was the judgment of the Conference that the danger of prejudice to a nondefendant witness is outweighed by the need for the trier of fact to have as much relevant evidence on the issue of credibility as possible. Such evidence should only be excluded where it presents a danger of improperly influencing the outcome of the trial by persuading the trier of fact to convict the defendant on the basis of his prior criminal record.

> B.   Rule 609(b)—Time Limit

The House bill provides in subsection (b) that evidence of conviction of a crime may not be used for impeachment purposes under subsection (a) if more than ten years have elapsed since the date of the conviction or the date the witness was released from confinement imposed for the conviction, whichever is later. The Senate amendment permits the use of convictions older than ten years, if the court determines, in the interests of justice, that the probative value of the conviction, supported by specific facts and circumstances, substantially outweighs its prejudicial effect.

The Conference adopts the Senate amendment with an amendment requiring notice by a party that he intends to request that the court allow him to use a conviction older than ten years. The Conferees anticipate that a written notice, in order to give the adversary a fair opportunity to contest the use of the evidence, will ordinarily include such information as the date of the conviction, the jurisdiction, and the offense or statute involved. In order to eliminate the possibility that the flexibility of this provision may impair the ability of a party-opponent to prepare for trial, the Conferees intend that the notice provision operate to avoid surprise.

C.   LEGISLATIVE DEBATE AND COMMITTEE REPORTS

In this part, we look at the legislative process occurring before any Conference Report: legislative debate and committee reports. We first revisit *Holy Trinity Church* (excerpted in Chapter 4, § 1), a classic opinion depending on these type of materials. We then provide *United Steelworkers v. Weber,* a modern classic in discrimination law and statutory interpretation, in which the Justices' debate over whether the Civil Rights Act of 1964 allowed affirmative action focused on statutory meaning supported by legislative history. You will note that if one applies the "reverse-engineering" method, questions arise not only about the proper legislative history, but about the proper *text*—i.e., which amendment or which statutory text should have mattered most.

RECTOR, HOLY TRINITY CHURCH V. UNITED STATES

Supreme Court of the United States, 1892.
143 U.S. 457, 12 S.Ct. 511, 36 L.Ed. 226.

[Excerpted in Chapter 4, § 1]

NOTES ON LEGISLATIVE HISTORY IN HOLY TRINITY

As we saw above, there is a conventional hierarchy of legislative materials. At the top of that hierarchy, along with conference reports, sit committee reports and statements by the sponsor or floor manager of the legislation. Reliance on committee reports has a long pedigree, reaching back to *Holy Trinity* and other nineteenth century cases. Committee reports deserve their reputation for their reliability, on the theory that Congress delegates to its committees the difficult work of drafting legislation. In the early twentieth century, Professor (later President) Woodrow Wilson argued that Congress's committees were where work was done. *Holy Trinity* seems to be the first case where the Supreme Court rewrote a statute based upon the conclusions in a committee report. A revised edition of the leading treatise cited it repeatedly and endorsed its proposition that courts could consider legislative records to figure out what the intent of the legislature was on a particular issue. See J.G. Sutherland, *Statutes and Statutory Construction* 879–83 (John Lewis ed., 2d ed. 1904). (The first edition of the Sutherland treatise, published in 1891, followed the English practice of excluding extrinsic legislative materials from consideration in statutory cases.) The federal courts in the twentieth century cited an increasing amount and variety of legislative history.

As you know from Chapter 4, § 3, and from § 1 of this chapter, the Supreme Court has been more skeptical about the value of committee reports since the mid-1970s—and *Holy Trinity* has been Exhibit "A" in the new textualists' case against reliance on legislative history of any sort. In his Tanner Lectures, Justice Scalia outlined a purely textualist theory of statutory interpretation—and offered *Holy Trinity* as the classic example of what the Court should *never* do in statutory interpretation, namely, depart from the plain meaning of the statutory text because of judges' understanding of "legislative intent." See Antonin Scalia, *A Matter of Interpretation* (1997). Recall the relevant statutory language, which barred the "importation of such alien or aliens, foreigner or foreigners, to perform labor or service of any kind in the United States." § 1.

Assume that Justice Scalia is wrong that the plain meaning of the 1885 Alien Contract Labor Law included Christian ministers. Professor Adrian Vermeule argues that the statute's legislative history provides no cogent justification for reading the statute narrowly—because the Court got the legislative history totally backwards. See Adrian Vermeule, *Judging Under Uncertainty* 86–117 (2006). As we noted in Chapter 4, the committee report invoked by the Court did *not* come at the end of the process, for the alien contract labor bill was debated and amended after the committee report.

Moreover, as Vermeule reports, some of the debate (excerpted below) indicates that the sponsors represented to the Senate that the bill was all-embracing and would include "toilers of the brain" as well as manual laborers. Although Professor Carol Chomsky disagrees with Vermeule's conclusions based upon her documentation of congressional agreement about the statute's purpose,[28] the backwards induction method we are introducing in this chapter lends support to Vermeule's account: start at the end, trace the legislative process leading from the final text, and apply your conclusions to solve the Mystery of *Holy Trinity*.

1. *The Importance of Subsequent Debates and Amendments.* Remember that Congress operates on bills in sequential fashion: introduction, committee referral, floor consideration, conference committee, etc. In light of this process, consider the committee report for the alien contract labor bill, issued in 1884. Contrary to the expectations of the committee, the bill was *not* passed at the end of the second session of the 85th Congress in 1884—but during the third session of that Congress in 1885 (the Congress reflecting the results of the 1884 election did not start until March 1885 in those days, and so Congress often did business in those winter months). Importantly, as Professor Vermeule first observed, the bill was extensively debated in the third session (1885), and it was amended to add and subtract exemptions now found in § 5. Does that render the 1884 committee report completely irrelevant? Well, that depends on whether the subsequent debates and amendments rendered the report irrelevant.

2. *Reading Debates with an Understanding of Winners (Who Won) and Losers (Who Lost).* Professor Vermeule cites portions of the legislative history, of which there is a fair amount, where some senators supporting the legislation complained that the bill was broadly drafted and covered a wide array of workers. Conversely, Professor Chomsky cites other portions of the debate showing that the supporters were only concerned with excluding those workers imported in slave labor type conditions, and that Congress relied upon a prior statute, the Chinese Exclusion Act, in which courts had held that labor applied only to manual labor. "[I]t is difficult to read page after page of this House debate without concluding that the bill was meant to address the 'contract labor system,' the practice by industrialists of importing large numbers of workers from abroad to take the place of American laborers at reduced wages, and that this was understood by all legislators considering the bill." Chomsky, *Unlocking the Mysteries,* 927.

Reading legislative history correctly, who is right? Consider in this light the following two exchanges in the debate on the bill. First, consider an exchange in the House between a sponsor of the bill and a friendly representative:

[28] See Carol Chomsky, *The Story of* Holy Trinity Church v. United States (1892): *Spirit and History in Statutory Interpretation*, in *Statutory Interpretation Stories* 2–35 (William N. Eskridge, Philip P. Frickey & Elizabeth Garrett eds., 2011), as well as Chomsky, *Unlocking the Mysteries of* Holy Trinity: *Spirit, Letter, and History in Statutory Interpretation*, 100 Colum. L. Rev. 901 (2000).

> Mr. O'Neill, of Missouri. It is not intended by this bill to keep away skilled mechanics or laborers from coming to the country who come here voluntarily. It is for the purpose of preventing pauper laborers from being brought here from abroad for the purpose of breaking down the efforts of the workingmen of this country to secure their just rights.
>
> Mr. Adams, of New York. Why do you not insert "day laborers?"
>
> Mr. O'Neill, of Missouri. Because they are not day laborers; they are liable to work by the week or the month.
>
> Now there is one thing I will refer back to, because I want to bring it to the ears of this House, that you mean to protect American labor here is where you can show your sympathy in the best way.
>
> Never mind about these *hair-splitting technicalities* with reference to the bill; but remedy any defects that you believe to exist in it. If we all had to run as constitutional lawyers, few of us would get elected [laughter], and remember that what the workingmen ask you to do for them is simply that this Congress shall give, so far as it can, protection to them against this infamous contract system.

15 Cong. Rec. 5358 (1884) (emphasis added). Now consider the exchange in the Senate, between a sponsor and a fierce critic, that Professor Vermeule believes is decisive evidence that the law applied broadly and not just to manual workers:

> Senator Morgan, a critic of the bill: "[I]f [the alien] happens to be a lawyer, an artist, a painter, an engraver, a sculptor, a great author, or what not, and he comes under employment to write for a newspaper, or to write books, or to paint pictures * * * he comes under the general provisions of the bill. * * * I shall propose when we get to it to put an amendment in there I want to associate with the lecturers and singers, and actors, painters, sculptors, engravers, or other artists, farmers, farm laborers, gardeners, orchardists, herders, farriers, druggists and druggists' clerks, shopkeepers, clerks, book-keepers, or any person having special skill in any business, art, trade or profession."
>
> Senator Blair, the bill's Senate sponsor, replied: "The Senator will observe that it is only the importation of such people under contract to labor that is prohibited. * * * *If that class of people are liable to become the subject-matter of such importation, then the bill applies to them. Perhaps the bill ought to be further amended.*"

15 Cong. Rec. 5358 (1884) (emphasis added by Vermeule).

Professor Vermeule reads the Senate debate as demonstrating that legislators knew the bill was overbroad. Professor Chomsky reads the House debate as demonstrating that the bill only applied to the core prototype of importation, under conditions typical of "contract labor." Both Vermeule and Chomsky fail to take account of what political scientists tell us: statutes are like elections.[29] There are some versions of the statute that win, and others that lose. For over two decades, positive political theorists have argued that statements of both winners and losers are likely to be suspect: winners will exaggerate the intended benefits of the law and losers will exaggerate the law's potential pitfalls.[30] These theorists are correct to be more cautious about winners' statements than the standard approach to legislative history. The authoritative meaning of the bill cannot be taken only from winners' statements (a likely pitfall of purposivist interpretation). At the same time, there is much greater difficulty, if legislative history is based on losers' history—particularly in the case of a minority filibuster. Were a court to accept the losers' statements as authoritative, judges would be changing the statute to enact the meaning that could not have been passed.

If one reads the congressional debate in 1884–85 with the notion of "winners and losers" in mind, one sees several patterns.[31] *All* of the supporters emphasized the need to protect manual labor markets from being flooded by inexpensive laborers from abroad. They resisted the addition of the term "manual" to § 1, as that might have excluded "skilled" labor imported under slave-labor conditions (they were particularly concerned about "glassblowers"). The supporters appeared to care little about professional individuals, because they could not imagine them being imported en masse in slave labor conditions. Those who opposed the bill insisted that the bill applied universally and ridiculed the bill for its poor drafting and overbreadth—indeed they implied that the bill had been drafted by labor unions and must therefore have been flawed. To emphasize the bill's broad ambit in § 1, and at the same time limit the bill's reach, the opposition emphasized the amendment excluding professionals, such as lecturers.

3.   *More New Evidence.* Professor Vermeule's best point is that § 5's list of exemptions for "professional actors, artists, lecturers, or singers" as well as "persons employed strictly as personal or domestic servants" was extensively debated and amended several times, supporting Justice Scalia's *inclusio unius* argument that the list of exemptions in § 5 was exhaustive. As Scalia says, § 1 should be read in light of other provisions of the statute—but that also includes § 4, which makes a shipmaster liable for knowingly transporting "any alien laborer, mechanic, or artisan." When he delivered his Tanner Lectures, Justice Scalia made no mention of § 4. Had he read the

---

[29] Kenneth Shepsle, *Analyzing Politics: Rationality, Behavior, and Institutions* 127 (2d ed. 2010) ("We think of pure majority-rule legislative choice as an 'election writ small.' ").

[30] E.g., McNollgast, *Legislative Intent: The Use of Positive Political Theory in Statutory Interpretation,* 57 Law & Contemp. Probs. 3, 5 (1994); McNollgast, *Positive Canons: The Role of Legislative Bargains in Statutory Interpretation,* 80 Geo. L.J. 705, 741 (1992); Daniel B. Rodriguez & Barry R. Weingast, *The Paradox of Expansionist Statutory Interpretations,* 101 Nw. U. L. Rev. 1207, 1219–22 (2007); Daniel B. Rodriguez & Barry R. Weingast, *The Positive Political Theory of Legislative History: New Perspectives on the 1964 Civil Rights Act and Its Interpretation,* 151 U. Pa. L. Rev. 1417, 1442–48 (2003).

[31] Nourse, *Rule-Based Decision Theory,* 122–25.

statute closely, he would surely have argued that the narrow language of § 4 supported his broad reading of § 1, based upon the canon of meaningful variation: Congress *knew* how to draft a narrow statute (§ 4) but purposely chose the broader language of § 1. Yet when you read the legislative history, Congress "knew" no such thing. Senator Blair, the floor manager invoked by Professor Vermeule, repeatedly assured his colleagues that § 4 was aimed at "the man who knowingly brings an immigrant * * * who comes here under and by virtue of a contract such as is prohibited by [§ 1] of the bill." 16 Cong. Rec. 1630 (1885). Should this evidence influence the Court's understanding of the relationship between §§ 1 and 4? See William N. Eskridge Jr., *No Frills Textualism*, 119 Harv. L. Rev. 2041, 2065–70 (2006).

4. *Reverse-Engineering: The Lecturer Amendment Versus the Committee Report.* From the perspective of the "last" acts on the bill, amendments made to it in 1885 are far closer to the text than the committee report from 1884. Very little analysis of the exemption amendment has characterized the legislative history debate. The exemption was added in the House, and then debated in the Senate. Should not statements on that amendment be relevant to the meaning of the term "lecturer"? Even opponents of the bill conceded that the lecturer exception would indeed cover lectures on religious topics. Senator Morgan stated that "[p]eople who can instruct us in morals and religion and in every species of elevation by lectures . . . are not prohibited." 16 Cong. Rec. 1633 (1885). Although Senator Morgan was an opponent of the bill, he was a supporter (a winner) of the lecturer exemption, and his concession was what positive political theorists call a "costly signal" and therefore a reliable statement, because it was against Senator Morgan's interest (he would have preferred to have no bill at all). He argued that the bill was overbroad, including all labor, but sought exemptions reducing the law's application. If the statute is ambiguous, does this legislative history resolve the matter? Or does the legislative history remain ambiguous as well?

Query: Does any of the foregoing legislative history help resolve your doubts about the correct result in *Holy Trinity*?

STATUTORY PREFACE TO *WEBER*

The Civil Rights Act of 1964 (as amended in 1972)

CRA § 703, 42 U.S.C. § 2000e–2:

(a) Employer Practices

It shall be an unlawful employment practice for an employer—

> (1) to fail or refuse to hire or to discharge any individual, or otherwise to discriminate against any individual with respect to his compensation, terms, conditions, or privileges of employment, because of such individual's race, color, religion, sex, or national origin; or

(2) to limit, segregate, or classify his employees or applicants for employment in any way which would deprive or tend to deprive any individual of employment opportunities or otherwise adversely affect his status as an employee, because of such individual's race, color, religion, sex, or national origin.

(d) Training programs

It shall be an unlawful employment practice for any employer, labor organization, or joint labor-management committee controlling apprenticeship or other training or retraining, including on-the-job training programs to discriminate against any individual because of his race, color, religion, sex, or national origin in admission to, or employment in, any program established to provide apprenticeship or other training.

(j) Preferential treatment not to be granted on account of existing number or percentage imbalance

Nothing contained in this subchapter shall be interpreted to require any employer, employment agency, labor organization, or joint labor-management committee subject to this subchapter to grant preferential treatment to any individual or to any group because of the race, color, religion, sex, or national origin of such individual or group on account of an imbalance which may exist with respect to the total number or percentage of persons of any race, color, religion, sex, or national origin employed by any employer, referred or classified for employment by any employment agency or labor organization, admitted to membership or classified by any labor organization, or admitted to, or employed in, any apprenticeship or other training program, in comparison with the total number or percentage of persons of such race, color, religion, sex, or national origin in any community, State, section, or other area, or in the available work force in any community, State, section, or other area.

UNITED STEELWORKERS OF AMERICA ET AL. V. BRIAN WEBER

Supreme Court of the United States, 1979.
443 U.S. 193, 99 S.Ct. 2721, 61 L.Ed.2d 480.

MR. JUSTICE BRENNAN delivered the opinion of the Court. * * *

In 1974, petitioner United Steelworkers of America (USWA) and petitioner Kaiser Aluminum & Chemical Corp. (Kaiser) entered into a master collective-bargaining agreement covering terms and conditions of employment at 15 Kaiser plants. The agreement contained, inter alia, an affirmative action plan designed to eliminate conspicuous racial imbalances in Kaiser's then almost exclusively white craft-work forces. Black craft-hiring goals were set for each Kaiser plant equal to the percentage of blacks in the respective local labor forces. To enable plants to meet these goals, on-the-job training programs were established to teach unskilled production workers—black and white—the skills necessary to become craftworkers. The plan reserved for black employees 50% of the openings in these newly created in-plant training programs.

This case arose from the operation of the plan at Kaiser's plant in Gramercy, La. Until 1974, Kaiser hired as craftworkers for that plant only persons who had had prior craft experience. Because blacks had long been excluded from craft unions, few were able to present such credentials. As a consequence, prior to 1974 only 1.83% (5 out of 273) of the skilled craftworkers at the Gramercy plant were black, even though the work force in the Gramercy area was approximately 39% black.

Pursuant to the national agreement Kaiser altered its craft-hiring practice in the Gramercy plant. Rather than hiring already trained outsiders, Kaiser established a training program to train its production workers to fill craft openings. Selection of craft trainees was made on the basis of seniority, with the proviso that at least 50% of the new trainees were to be black until the percentage of black skilled craftworkers in the Gramercy plant approximated the percentage of blacks in the local labor force.

During 1974, the first year of the operation of the Kaiser-USWA affirmative action plan, 13 craft trainees were selected from Gramercy's production work force. Of these, seven were black and six white. The most senior black selected into the program had less seniority than several white production workers whose bids for admission were rejected. Thereafter one of those white production workers, respondent Brian Weber (hereafter respondent), instituted this class action in the United States District Court for the Eastern District of Louisiana.

The complaint alleged that the filling of craft trainee positions at the Gramercy plant pursuant to the affirmative action program had resulted in junior black employees' receiving training in preference to senior white employees, thus discriminating against respondent and other similarly situated white employees in violation of §§ 703(a) and (d) of Title VII. The District Court held that the plan violated Title VII, entered a judgment in favor of the plaintiff class, and granted a permanent injunction prohibiting Kaiser and the USWA "from denying plaintiffs, Brian F. Weber and all other members of the class, access to on-the-job training programs on the basis of race." A divided panel of the Court of Appeals for the Fifth Circuit affirmed, holding that all employment preferences based upon race, including those preferences incidental to bona fide affirmative action plans, violated Title VII's prohibition against racial discrimination in employment. * * * We reverse.

We emphasize at the outset the narrowness of our inquiry. * * * [S]ince the Kaiser-USWA plan was adopted voluntarily, we are not concerned with what Title VII requires or with what a court might order to remedy a past proved violation of the Act. The only question before us is the narrow statutory issue of whether Title VII forbids private employers and unions from voluntarily agreeing upon bona fide affirmative action plans that accord racial preferences in the manner and for the purpose provided in the Kaiser-USWA plan. * * *

Respondent argues that Congress intended in Title VII to prohibit all race-conscious affirmative action plans. Respondent's argument rests upon a literal interpretation of §§ 703(a) and (d) of the Act. Those sections make it unlawful to "discriminate . . . because of . . . race" in hiring and in the selection of apprentices for training programs. Since, the argument runs, *McDonald v. Santa Fe Trail Transp. Co.*, [427 U.S. 273, 281 n.8 (1976)], settled that Title VII forbids discrimination against whites as well as blacks, and since the Kaiser-USWA affirmative action plan operates to discriminate against white employees solely because they are white, it follows that the Kaiser-USWA plan violates Title VII.

Respondent's argument is not without force. But it overlooks the significance of the fact that the Kaiser-USWA plan is an affirmative action plan voluntarily adopted by private parties to eliminate traditional patterns of racial segregation. In this context respondent's reliance upon a literal construction of §§ 703(a) and (d) and upon McDonald is misplaced. It is a "familiar rule, that a thing may be within the letter of the statute and yet not within the statute, because not within its spirit, nor within the intention of its makers." *Holy Trinity Church v. United States*, 143 U.S. 457, 459 (1892). The prohibition against racial discrimination in §§ 703(a) and (d) of Title VII must therefore be read against the background of the legislative history of Title VII and the historical context from which the Act arose. Examination of those sources makes clear that an interpretation of the sections that forbade all race-conscious affirmative action would "bring about an end completely at variance with the purpose of the statute" and must be rejected. *United States v. Public Utilities Comm'n*, 345 U.S. 295, 315 (1953).

Congress's primary concern in enacting the prohibition against racial discrimination in Title VII of the Civil Rights Act of 1964 was with "the plight of the Negro in our economy." 110 Cong. Rec. 6548 (1964) (remarks of Sen. Humphrey). Before 1964, blacks were largely relegated to "unskilled and semi-skilled jobs." *Ibid.* (remarks of Sen. Humphrey); *id.*, at 7204 (remarks of Sen. Clark); *id.*, at 7379–7380 (remarks of Sen. Kennedy). Because of automation the number of such jobs was rapidly decreasing. See *id.*, at 6548 (remarks of Sen. Humphrey); *id.*, at 7204 (remarks of Sen. Clark). As a consequence, "the relative position of the Negro worker [was] steadily worsening." * * *

Congress feared that the goals of the Civil Rights Act—the integration of blacks into the mainstream of American society—could not be achieved unless this trend were reversed. And Congress recognized that that would not be possible unless blacks were able to secure jobs "which have a future." *Id.*, at 7204 (remarks of Sen. Clark). See also *id.*, at 7379–7380 (remarks of Sen. Kennedy). As Senator Humphrey explained to the Senate:

> "What good does it do a Negro to be able to eat in a fine restaurant if he cannot afford to pay the bill? What good does it do him to be accepted in a hotel that is too expensive for his modest income? How can a Negro child be motivated to take full advantage of integrated educational facilities if he has no hope of getting a job where he can use that education?" *Id.*, at 6547. * * *

Accordingly, it was clear to Congress that "[t]he crux of the problem [was] to open employment opportunities for Negroes in occupations which have been traditionally closed to them," 10 Cong. Rec. 6548 (1964) (remarks of Sen. Humphrey), and it was to this problem that Title VII's prohibition against racial discrimination in employment was primarily addressed.

It plainly appears from the House Report accompanying the Civil Rights Act that Congress did not intend wholly to prohibit private and voluntary affirmative action efforts as one method of solving this problem. The Report provides:

> "No bill can or should lay claim to eliminating all of the causes and consequences of racial and other types of discrimination against minorities. There is reason to believe, however, that national leadership provided by the enactment of Federal legislation dealing with the most troublesome problems *will create an atmosphere conducive to voluntary or local resolution of other forms of discrimination.*" H.R. Rep. No. 914, 88th Cong., 1st Sess., pt. 1, p. 18 (1963). (Emphasis supplied.) * * *

Given this legislative history, we cannot agree with respondent that Congress intended to prohibit the private sector from taking effective steps to accomplish the goal that Congress designed Title VII to achieve. * * * It would be ironic indeed if a law triggered by a Nation's concern over centuries of racial injustice and intended to improve the lot of those who had "been excluded from the American dream for so long," 110 Cong. Rec. 6552 (1964) (remarks of Sen. Humphrey), constituted the first legislative prohibition of all voluntary, private, race-conscious efforts to abolish traditional patterns of racial segregation and hierarchy.

Our conclusion is further reinforced by examination of the language and legislative history of § 703(j) of Title VII. Opponents of Title VII raised two related arguments against the bill. First, they argued that the Act would be interpreted to *require* employers with racially imbalanced work forces to grant preferential treatment to racial minorities in order to integrate. Second, they argued that employers with racially imbalanced work forces would grant preferential treatment to racial minorities, even if not required to do so by the Act. See 110 Cong. Rec. 8618–8619 (1964) (remarks of Sen. Sparkman). Had Congress meant to prohibit all race-conscious affirmative action, as respondent urges, it easily could have answered both objections by providing that Title VII would not require or *permit* racially preferential integration efforts. But Congress did not choose such a course. Rather, Congress added § 703(j) which addresses only the first objection. The section provides that nothing contained in Title VII "shall be interpreted to *require* any employer . . . to grant preferential treatment . . . to any group because of the race . . . of such . . . group on account of" a *de facto* racial imbalance in the employer's work force. The section does *not* state that "nothing in Title VII shall be interpreted to permit" voluntary affirmative efforts to correct racial imbalances. The natural inference is that Congress chose not to forbid all voluntary race-conscious affirmative action.

The reasons for this choice are evident from the legislative record. Title VII could not have been enacted into law without substantial support from legislators in both Houses who traditionally resisted federal regulation of private business. Those legislators demanded as a price for their support that "management prerogatives, and union freedoms . . . be left undisturbed to the greatest extent possible." H.R. Rep. No. 914, 88th Cong., 1st Sess., pt. 2, p. 29 (1963). Section 703(j) was proposed by Senator Dirksen to allay any fears that the Act might be interpreted in such a way as to upset this compromise. The section was designed to prevent § 703 of Title VII from being interpreted in such a way as to lead to undue "Federal Government interference with private businesses because of some Federal employee's ideas about racial balance or racial imbalance." 110 Cong. Rec. 14314 (1964) (remarks of Sen. Miller). See also *id.*, at 9881 (remarks of Sen. Allott); *id.*, at 10520 (remarks of Sen. Carlson); *id.*, at 11471 (remarks of Sen. Javits); *id.*, at 12817 (remarks of Sen. Dirksen). Clearly, a prohibition against all voluntary, race-conscious, affirmative action efforts would disserve these ends. Such a prohibition would augment the powers of the Federal Government and diminish traditional management prerogatives while at the same time impeding attainment of the ultimate statutory goals. In view of this legislative history and in view of Congress's desire to avoid undue federal regulation of private businesses, use of the word "require" rather than the phrase "require or permit" in § 703(j) fortifies the conclusion that Congress did not intend to limit traditional business freedom to such a degree as to prohibit all voluntary, race-conscious affirmative action.[7]

---

[7]   Respondent argues that our construction of § 703 conflicts with various remarks in the legislative record. See, e.g., 110 Cong. Rec. 7213 (1964) (Sens. Clark and Case); id., at 7218 (Sens.

We therefore hold that Title VII's prohibition in §§ 703(a) and (d) against racial discrimination does not condemn all private, voluntary, race-conscious affirmative action plans. * * * [The Court held that the Kaiser plan was lawful under Title VII because both its purpose and effect were permissible: it was "designed to eliminate conspicuous racial imbalance in traditionally segregated job categories," and it "does not unnecessarily trammel the interests of white employees" because no white employees lost their jobs, half of those trained in the program will be white, and it was a temporary measure ending when "the percentage of black skilled craft workers in the Gramercy plant approximates the percentage of blacks in the local labor force."]

MR. JUSTICE POWELL and MR. JUSTICE STEVENS took no part in the consideration or decision of these cases.

MR. JUSTICE BLACKMUN, concurring.

While I share some of the misgivings expressed in Mr. Justice Rehnquist's dissent concerning the extent to which the legislative history of Title VII clearly supports the result the Court reaches today, I believe that additional considerations, practical and equitable, only partially perceived, if perceived at all, by the 88th Congress, support the conclusion reached by the Court today, and I therefore join its opinion as well as its judgment.

[In the remainder of his opinion, Justice Blackmun explains why, as a matter of pragmatism and fairness, if not of statutory text and intent, Justice Brennan's approach was the right one. The crux of his argument was that, because an earlier Supreme Court precedent had made employers liable for past discrimination, leaving employers without a

---

Clark and Case); id., at 6549 (Sen. Humphrey); id., at 8921 (Sen. Williams). We do not agree. In Senator Humphrey's words, these comments were intended as assurances that Title VII would not allow establishment of systems "to maintain racial balance in employment." Id., at 11848 (emphasis added). They were not addressed to temporary, voluntary, affirmative action measures undertaken to eliminate manifest racial imbalance in traditionally segregated job categories. Moreover, the comments referred to by respondent all preceded the adoption of § 703(j), 42 U.S.C. § 2000e–2(j). After § 703(j) was adopted, congressional comments were all to the effect that employers would not be required to institute preferential quotas to avoid Title VII liability, see, e.g., 110 Cong. Rec. 12819 (1964) (remarks of Sen. Dirksen); id., at 13079–13080 (remarks of Sen. Clark); id., at 15876 (remarks of Rep. Lindsay). There was no suggestion after the adoption of § 703(j) that wholly voluntary, race-conscious, affirmative action efforts would in themselves constitute a violation of Title VII. On the contrary, as Representative MacGregor told the House shortly before the final vote on Title VII:

"Important as the scope and extent of this bill is, it is also vitally important that all Americans understand what this bill does not cover.

"Your mail and mine, your contacts and mine with our constituents, indicates a great degree of misunderstanding about this bill. People complain about * * * preferential treatment or quotas in employment. There is a mistaken belief that Congress is legislating in these areas in this bill. When we drafted this bill we excluded these issues largely because the problems raised by these controversial questions are more properly handled at a governmental level closer to the American people and by communities and individuals themselves." 110 Cong. Rec. 15893 (1964).

remedy puts them on a "high tightrope without a net beneath them." Thus, "[i]f Title VII is read literally, on the one hand they face liability for past discrimination against blacks, and on the other they face liability to whites for any voluntary preferences adopted to mitigate the effects of prior discrimination against blacks."]

MR. JUSTICE REHNQUIST, with whom the CHIEF JUSTICE joins, dissenting.

In a very real sense, the Court's opinion is ahead of its time: it could more appropriately have been handed down five years from now, in 1984, a year coinciding with the title of a book from which the Court's opinion borrows, perhaps subconsciously, at least one idea. Orwell describes in his book a governmental official of Oceania, one of the three great world powers, denouncing the current enemy, Eurasia, to an assembled crowd:

> "It was almost impossible to listen to him without being first convinced and then maddened. . . . The speech had been proceeding for perhaps twenty minutes when a messenger hurried onto the platform and a scrap of paper was slipped into the speaker's hand. He unrolled and read it without pausing in his speech. Nothing altered in his voice or manner, or in the content of what he was saying, but suddenly the names were different. Without words said, a wave of understanding rippled through the crowd. Oceania was at war with Eastasia! . . . The banners and posters with which the square was decorated were all wrong! . . .

> "[T]he speaker had switched from one line to the other actually in mid-sentence, not only without a pause, but without even breaking the syntax."

—G. Orwell, Nineteen Eighty-Four 181–182 (1949).

Today's decision represents an equally dramatic and equally unremarked switch in this Court's interpretation of Title VII. * * *

[II] Were Congress to act today specifically to prohibit the type of racial discrimination suffered by Weber, it would be hard pressed to draft language better tailored to the task than that found in § 703(d) of Title VII:

> "It shall be an unlawful employment practice for any employer, labor organization, or joint labor-management committee controlling apprenticeship or other training or retraining, including on-the-job training programs to discriminate against any individual because of his race, color, religion, sex, or national origin in admission to, or employment in, any program established to provide apprenticeship or other training." 78 Stat. 256, 42 U.S.C. § 2000e–2(d).

Equally suited to the task would be § 703(a)(2), which makes it unlawful for an employer to classify his employees "in any way which would deprive or tend to deprive any individual of employment opportunities or otherwise adversely affect his status as an employee, because of such individual's race, color, religion, sex, or national origin." 78 Stat. 255, 42 U.S.C. § 2000e–2(a)(2).

Entirely consistent with these two express prohibitions is the language of § 703(j) of Title VII, which provides that the Act is not to be interpreted "to require any employer . . . to grant preferential treatment to any individual or to any group because of the race . . . of such individual or group" to correct a racial imbalance in the employer's work force. 42 U.S.C. § 2000e–2(j). Seizing on the word "require," the Court infers that Congress must have intended to "permit" this type of racial discrimination. Not only is this reading of § 703(j) outlandish in the light of the flat prohibitions of §§ 703(a) and (d), but also, as explained in Part III, it is totally belied by the Act's legislative history.

Quite simply, Kaiser's racially discriminatory admission quota is flatly prohibited by the plain language of Title VII. This normally dispositive fact, however, gives the Court only momentary pause. An "interpretation" of the statute upholding Weber's claim would, according to the Court, "'bring about an end completely at variance with the purpose of the statute.'" To support this conclusion, the Court calls upon the "spirit" of the Act, which it divines from passages in Title VII's legislative history indicating that enactment of the statute was prompted by Congress's desire "'to open employment opportunities for Negroes in occupations which [had] been traditionally closed to them.'" But the legislative history invoked by the Court to avoid the plain language of §§ 703(a) and (d) simply misses the point. To be sure, the reality of employment discrimination against Negroes provided the primary impetus for passage of Title VII. But this fact by no means supports the proposition that Congress intended to leave employers free to discriminate against white persons. In most cases, "[l]egislative history . . . is more vague than the statute we are called upon to interpret." [*United States v. Public Utilities Comm'n*, 345 U.S. 295, 320 (1953) (Jackson, J., concurring)] Here, however, the legislative history of Title VII is as clear as the language of §§ 703(a) and (d), and it irrefutably demonstrates that Congress meant precisely what it said in §§ 703(a) and (d)—that *no* racial discrimination in employment is permissible under Title VII, not even preferential treatment of minorities to correct racial imbalance.

[III] In undertaking to review the legislative history of Title VII, I am mindful that the topic hardly makes for light reading, but I am also fearful that nothing short of a thorough examination of the congressional debates will fully expose the magnitude of the Court's misinterpretation of Congress' intent.

[A] Introduced on the floor of the House of Representatives on June 20, 1963, the bill—H.R. 7152—that ultimately became the Civil Rights Act of 1964 contained no compulsory provisions directed at private discrimination in employment. The bill was promptly referred to the Committee on the Judiciary, where it was amended to include Title VII. With two exceptions, the bill reported by the House Judiciary Committee contained §§ 703(a) and (d) as they were ultimately enacted. Amendments subsequently adopted on the House floor added § 703's prohibition against sex discrimination and § 703(d)'s coverage of "on-the-job training."

After noting that "[t]he purpose of [Title VII] is to eliminate . . . discrimination in employment based on race, color, religion, or national origin," the Judiciary Committee's Report simply paraphrased the provisions of Title VII without elaboration. H.R. Rep., pt. 1, p. 26. In a separate Minority Report, however, opponents of the measure on the Committee advanced a line of attack which was reiterated throughout the debates in both the House and Senate and which ultimately led to passage of § 703(j). Noting that the word "discrimination" was nowhere defined in H.R. 7152, the Minority Report charged that the absence from Title VII of any reference to "racial imbalance" was a "public relations" ruse and that "the administration intends to rely upon its own construction of 'discrimination' as including the lack of racial balance. . . ." H.R. Rep., pt. 1, pp. 67–68. To demonstrate how the bill would operate in practice, the Minority Report posited a number of hypothetical employment situations, concluding in each example that the employer *may be forced to hire according to race*, to 'racially balance' those who work for him *in every job classification* or be in violation of Federal law." *Id.*, at 69 (emphasis in original).

When H.R. 7152 reached the House floor, the opening speech in support of its passage was delivered by Representative Celler, Chairman of the House Judiciary Committee and the Congressman responsible for introducing the legislation. A portion of that speech responded to criticism "seriously misrepresent[ing] what the bill would do and grossly distort[ing] its effects":

> "[T]he charge has been made that the Equal Employment Opportunity Commission to be established by title VII of the bill would have the power to prevent a business from employing and promoting the people it wished, and that a 'Federal inspector' could then order the hiring and promotion only of employees of certain races or religious groups. This description of the bill is entirely wrong. . . .

"Even [a] court could not order that any preference be given to any particular race, religion or other group, but would be limited to ordering an end of discrimination. The statement that a Federal inspector could order the employment and promotion only of members of a specific racial or religious group is therefore patently erroneous.

" . . . The Bill would do no more than prevent . . . employers from discriminating against or *in favor* of workers because of their race, religion, or national origin.

"It is likewise not true that the Equal Employment Opportunity Commission would have power to rectify existing 'racial or religious imbalance' in employment by requiring the hiring of certain people without regard to their qualifications simply because they are of a given race or religion. Only actual discrimination could be stopped." 110 Cong. Rec. 1518 (1964) (emphasis added).

Representative Celler's construction of Title VII was repeated by several other supporters during the House debate.

Thus, the battle lines were drawn early in the legislative struggle over Title VII, with opponents of the measure charging that agencies of the Federal Government such as the Equal Employment Opportunity Commission (EEOC), by interpreting the word "discrimination" to mean the existence of "racial imbalance," would "require" employers to grant preferential treatment to minorities, and supporters responding that the EEOC would be granted no such power and that, indeed, Title VII prohibits discrimination "in favor of workers because of their race." Supporters of H.R. 7152 in the House ultimately prevailed by a vote of 290 to 130, and the measure was sent to the Senate to begin what became the longest debate in that body's history.

[B] The Senate debate was broken into three phases: the debate on sending the bill to Committee, the general debate on the bill prior to invocation of cloture, and the debate following cloture. * * *

Formal debate on the merits of H.R. 7152 began on March 30, 1964. Supporters of the bill in the Senate had made elaborate preparations for this second round. Senator Humphrey, the majority whip, and Senator Kuchel, the minority whip, were selected as the bipartisan floor managers on the entire civil rights bill. Responsibility for explaining and defending each important title of the bill was placed on bipartisan "captains." Senators Clark and Case were selected as the bipartisan captains responsible for Title VII. Vaas, Title VII: Legislative History, 7 B.C. Ind. & Com. L. Rev. 431, 444–445 (1966) (hereinafter Title VII: Legislative History).

In the opening speech of the formal Senate debate on the bill, Senator Humphrey addressed the main concern of Title VII's opponents, advising that not only does Title VII not require use of racial quotas, *it does not permit* their use. "The truth," stated the floor leader of the bill, "is that this title forbids discriminating against anyone on account of race. This is the simple and complete truth about title VII." 110 Cong. Rec. 6549 (1964). Senator Humphrey continued:

> "Contrary to the allegations of some opponents of this title, there is nothing in it that will give any power to the Commission or to any court to require hiring, firing, or promotion of employees in order to meet a racial 'quota' or to achieve a certain racial balance.

> "That bugaboo has been brought up a dozen times; but it is nonexistent. In fact, *the very opposite is true. Title VII prohibits discrimination.* In effect, it says that race, religion and national origin are not to be used as the basis for hiring and firing. Title VII is designed to encourage hiring on the basis of ability and qualifications, not race or religion." *Ibid.* (emphasis added).

At the close of his speech, Senator Humphrey returned briefly to the subject of employment quotas: "It is claimed that the bill would require racial quotas for all hiring, when in fact it provides that race shall not be a basis for making personnel decisions." *Id.,* at 6553. * * *

A few days later the Senate's attention focused exclusively on Title VII, as Senators Clark and Case rose to discuss the title of H.R. 7152 on which they shared floor "captain" responsibilities. In an interpretative memorandum submitted jointly to the Senate, Senators Clark and Case took pains to refute the opposition's charge that Title VII would result in preferential treatment for minorities. * * * Of particular relevance to the instant litigation were their observations regarding seniority rights. As if directing their comments at Brian Weber, the Senators said:

> "Title VII would have no effect on established seniority rights. Its effect is prospective and not retrospective. Thus, for example, if a business has been discriminating in the past and as a result has an all-white working force, when the title comes into effect the employer's obligation would be simply to fill future vacancies on a nondiscriminatory basis. He would not be obliged—*or indeed permitted*—to fire whites in order to hire Negroes, *or to prefer Negroes for future vacancies, or, once Negroes are hired, to give them special seniority rights at the expense of the white workers hired earlier." Ibid.* (emphasis added).

[In addition, Senator Kuchel made similar comments. Southern opponents to the bill were still not satisfied, though. Senator Robertson

(D–Va.) argued that the bill would mandate quotas. Senator H. Williams (D–N.J.) responded:]

> "Those opposed to H.R. 7152 should realize that to hire a Negro solely because he is a Negro is racial discrimination, just as much as a 'white only' employment policy. Both forms of discrimination are prohibited by title VII of this bill. The language of that title simply states that race is not a qualification for employment. . . . Some people charge that H.R. 7152 favors the Negro, at the expense of the white majority. But how can the language of equality favor one race or one religion over another? Equality can have only one meaning, and that meaning is self-evident to reasonable men. Those who say that equality means favoritism do violence to common sense." *Id.*, at 8921. * * *

While the debate in the Senate raged, a bipartisan coalition under the leadership of Senators Dirksen, Mansfield, Humphrey, and Kuchel was working with House leaders and representatives of the Johnson administration on a number of amendments to H.R. 7152 designed to enhance its prospects of passage. The so-called "Dirksen-Mansfield" amendment was introduced on May 26 by Senator Dirksen as a substitute for the entire House-passed bill. The substitute bill, which ultimately became law, left unchanged the basic prohibitory language of §§ 703(a) and (d), as well as the remedial provisions in § 706(g). It added, however, several provisions defining and clarifying the scope of Title VII's substantive prohibitions. One of those clarifying amendments, § 703(j), was specifically directed at the opposition's concerns regarding racial balancing and preferential treatment of minorities, providing in pertinent part: "Nothing contained in [Title VII] shall be interpreted to require any employer . . . to grant preferential treatment to any individual or to any group because of the race . . . of such individual or group on account of" a racial imbalance in the employer's work force. 42 U.S.C. § 2000e–2(j). * * *

Contrary to the Court's analysis, the language of § 703(j) is precisely tailored to the objection voiced time and again by Title VII's opponents. Not once during the 83 days of debate in the Senate did a speaker, proponent or opponent, suggest that the bill would allow employers *voluntarily* to prefer racial minorities over white persons. In light of Title VII's flat prohibition on discrimination "against any individual . . . because of such individual's race," § 703(a), 42 U.S.C. § 2000e–2(a), such a contention would have been, in any event, too preposterous to warrant response. Indeed, speakers on both sides of the issue, as the legislative history makes clear, recognized that Title VII would tolerate no voluntary racial preference, whether in favor of blacks or whites. The complaint consistently voiced by the opponents was that Title VII, particularly the word "discrimination," would be *interpreted* by federal agencies such as the EEOC to *require* the correction of racial imbalance through the granting of preferential treatment to minorities. Verbal assurances that Title VII would not require—indeed, would not permit—preferential treatment of blacks having failed, supporters of H.R. 7152 responded by proposing an amendment carefully worded to meet, and put to rest, the opposition's charge. Indeed, unlike §§ 703(a) and (d), which are by their terms directed at entities—*e.g.*, employers, labor unions—whose actions are restricted by Title VII's prohibitions, the language of § 703(j) is specifically directed at entities—federal agencies and courts—charged with the responsibility of interpreting Title VII's provisions.

In light of the background and purpose of § 703(j), the irony of invoking the section to justify the result in this case is obvious. The Court's frequent references to the "voluntary" nature of Kaiser's racially discriminatory admission quota bear no relationship to the facts of this case. Kaiser and the Steelworkers acted under pressure from an agency of the Federal Government, the Office of Federal Contract Compliance, which found that minorities were being "underutilized" at Kaiser's plants. That is, Kaiser's work force was racially imbalanced. Bowing to that pressure, Kaiser instituted an admissions quota preferring blacks over whites, thus confirming that the fears of Title VII's opponents were well founded. Today, § 703(j), adopted to allay those fears, is invoked by the Court to uphold imposition of a racial quota under the very circumstances that the section was intended to prevent. * * *

[Justice Rehnquist also pointed to Senator Ervin's June 9 amendment to delete Title VII. Responding for the sponsors, Senator Clark emphasized that the bill "establishes no quotas." Senator Cotton (R–N.H.) offered an amendment to limit Title VII to firms having more than 100 employees. He opined that Title VII would forbid quotas. Although his amendment was defeated, Justice Rehnquist observed that the sponsors did not dispute the Cotton view.]

[When cloture was invoked June 10, 1964, debate was limited, but several post-cloture statements by the bill's supporters reinforced the earlier view that Title VII imposed no quotas. The substitute bill was passed June 19. In final form, the bill was passed by the House on July 2 and signed by the President the same day.]

[V] Our task in this case, like any other case involving the construction of a statute, is to give effect to the intent of Congress. To divine that intent, we traditionally look first to the words of the statute and, if they are unclear, then to the statute's legislative history. Finding the desired result hopelessly foreclosed by these conventional sources, the Court turns to a third source—the "spirit" of the Act. But close examination of what the Court proffers as the spirit of the Act reveals it as the spirit animating the present majority, not the 88th Congress. For if the spirit of the Act eludes the cold words of the statute itself, it rings out with unmistakable clarity in the words of the elected representatives who made the Act law. It is *equality*. Senator Dirksen, I think, captured that spirit in a speech delivered on the floor of the Senate just moments before the bill was passed:

> " . . . [T]oday we come to grips finally with a bill that advances the enjoyment of living; but, more than that, it advances the equality of opportunity.

> "I do not emphasize the word 'equality' standing by itself. It means equality of opportunity in the field of education. It means equality of opportunity in the field of employment. It means equality of opportunity in the field of participation in the affairs of government. . . .

> "That is it.

> "Equality of opportunity, if we are going to talk about conscience, is the mass conscience of mankind that speaks in every generation, and it will continue to speak long after we are dead and gone." 110 Cong. Rec. 14510 (1964).

There is perhaps no device more destructive to the notion of equality than the *numerus clausus*—the quota. Whether described as "benign discrimination" or "affirmative action," the racial quota is nonetheless a creator of castes, a two-edged sword that must demean one in order to prefer another. In passing Title VII, Congress outlawed all racial discrimination, recognizing that no discrimination based on race is benign, that no action disadvantaging a person because of his color is affirmative. With today's holding, the Court introduces into Title VII a tolerance for the very evil that the law was intended to eradicate, without offering even a clue as to what the limits on that tolerance may be. We are told simply that Kaiser's racially discriminatory admission quota "falls on the permissible side of the line." By going not merely *beyond*, but directly *against* Title VII's language and legislative history, the Court has sown the wind. Later courts will face the impossible task of reaping the whirlwind.

NOTES AND QUESTIONS ON WEBER

1. *The Conventional Wisdom.* A rough academic consensus considers Justice Brennan's opinion a flawed exercise in statutory interpretation. "With all due respect for Justice Brennan * * * the opinion is a failure: it so lacks persuasive methodological power as to raise questions * * * about the Court's candor." Philip P. Frickey, *Wisdom on* Weber, 74 Tul. L. Rev. 1169, 1177 (2000). In dissent, Justice Rehnquist engaged in an extraordinarily lengthy legislative history of the 1964 Civil Rights Act. Many commentators have

agreed with Justice Rehnquist that the Court "changed" the meaning of the statute by judicial fiat, and "[t]hat change goes to the roots of the bargain struck by the 88th Congress, and to the roots of our color-blind aspiration." Bernard D. Meltzer, *The* Weber *Case: The Judicial Abrogation of the Antidiscrimination Standard in Employment*, 47 U. Chi. L. Rev. 423, 456 (1980).[32] Do you concur?

2.   *The Meaning of "Discriminate."* We will not dwell on the textual arguments in this set of notes. (You may recall that we introduced you to this statute, and some of those arguments in Problem 1–2 of this coursebook.) But ask yourself whether Justice Rehnquist overstated the clarity of § 703(d). Is the language enacted by Congress amenable to another plausible interpretation supporting Justice Brennan's decision? Is there a single "plain meaning" of "discriminate"? Are there other text-based arguments that Justice Rehnquist should have emphasized? See William N. Eskridge Jr., *Dynamic Statutory Interpretation* 42–43 (1994) (laying out arguments for Justice Rehnquist's position based on the structure of § 703).

3.   *The Evolution of the Civil Rights Bill.* Did Justice Rehnquist properly represent the internal evolution of the civil rights bill? He begins his historical analysis by emphasizing that §§ 703(a) and (d) were included in the early House bills, and then provides a lengthy discussion of the House debate. As a matter of congressional procedure, this is not highly relevant if later amendments changed the bill in ways limiting or clarifying these provisions. The House sponsors knew that the bill would go to the Senate and be filibustered (Chapter 1, § 1). So why is the House consideration relevant? The House could not have debated § 703(j), because that critical provision was added much later, as part of the Dirksen-Mansfield deal that broke the Senate filibuster.[33] Section 703(j) says that nothing in the bill was to "require" preferential hiring. Does this tell us something about the relevant *text* as well as the relevant history? How can §§ 703(a) and (d) be the central texts, and why is their legislative history relevant, if § 703(j) trumps them?

4.   *Winners and Losers.* After focusing on the early debate, Justice Rehnquist goes on to cite a separate "Minority Report" put forth in the House. This report was penned long before the Senate debate, but more importantly it relied upon minority views. Is it the Court's job to try to enforce the views of a minority, in this case a Senate minority that filibustered the bill? Loser's history is not reliable evidence of a legislative deal. Recall that Justice Stevens also made this error in reading the legislative history for *Bock Laundry*. It is usually a bad idea to rely on the loser's point of view when interpreting a statute that rejected their position. See Victoria F. Nourse, *A*

---

[32] Accord, Nelson Lund, *The Law of Affirmative Action In and After the Civil Rights Act of 1991: Congress Invites Judicial Reform*, 6 Geo. Mason L. Rev. 87, 90–101 (1997); Daniel B. Rodriguez & Barry R. Weingast, *The Positive Political Theory of Legislative History: New Perspectives on the 1964 Civil Rights Act and Its Interpretation*, 151 U. Pa. L. Rev. 1417 (2003).

[33] Cloture was voted on June 10, 1964, 110 Cong. Rec. 13,327 (1964); 110 Cong. Rec. 13,314 (1964) (reporting substitute bill including § 703(j)). The original bill was H.R. 7152, 88th Cong. (1963).

Decision Theory of Statutory Interpretation: Legislative History by the Rules, 122 Yale L. J. 70 (2012).

5. *Senate Cloture and Legislative History.* In the Senate, as we have emphasized, the crucial moment in any controversial bill is obtaining the votes needed for cloture (60 today, 67 in 1964 when all senators were present). Cloture is usually preceded by a "substitute" bill whose provisions are different from the bill as introduced; provisions must be added to assuage the skeptics and moderates needed to produce a supermajority coalition. The substitute bill is basically a large amendment that effectively replaces the original text. In this case, the pre-cloture debate (again relied upon by Justice Rehnquist) did not include the central provision at issue: § 703(j), which speaks directly to the question of quotas, but was added in the substitute bill, trumping prior text. Justice Rehnquist's treatment of the Senate is at its most persuasive when he cites post-cloture statements from the Act's proponents, who made statements against quotas and said that the bill would not permit discrimination. This discussion is marred, however, by the repeated invocation of legislative statements of those who opposed the bill.[34]

6. *Reversing the Conventional Wisdom.* As noted above, the conventional wisdom is that Justice Rehnquist got the legislative history right, while Justice Brennan had no cogent response and lamely relied on the statutory purpose and a strained reading of § 703(j). But Justice Rehnquist's opinion would have been much stronger had it been a good deal shorter, focusing on the text and discussion of § 703(j). Homing in on the most relevant legislative history may well have reduced his account to a few pages. Meanwhile, Justice Brennan, much criticized for his opinion's failure to attend to text, relied on the key statutory provision, § 703(j), and in footnote 7 cited highly relevant legislative discussion of the compromise that § 703(j) represented to conservative, farm-state Republicans (such as Representative MacGregor of Minnesota).

NOTE ON OTHER LEGISLATIVE MATERIALS

The legislative process produces many other legislative materials in addition to those singled out by the conventional hierarchy. This note provides a brief introduction to several of them:

Hearing Transcripts. Congressional committees frequently hold hearings on proposed bills, which result in transcripts that are sometimes deployed in litigation. Although these transcripts can provide valuable background materials—for example, the nature of the policy question that Congress is trying to address or the views of various interests groups or experts called into testify—for the most part, hearings do not provide "reliable" evidence of statutory meaning. Instead, they are often political performances, and more importantly, occur long before statutory text is

---

[34] Nourse, *A Decision Theory of Statutory Interpretation,* 106–08 (criticizing Justice Rehnquist for relying on Minority house reports and pre-filibuster legislative history).

finalized. Hearings can provide some useful evidence of statutory drafting when the witness is a drafter, particularly members of the executive branch.

Markups. In contrast, the "markup"—the record of the deliberations and decisions made to the text of a bill before it leaves committee—seems to us a potentially highly valuable piece of legislative history, *if* the bill is not substantially amended after it leaves committee. Staffers concur that the markup is where important deals are often reflected, and it is something of a puzzle that markups have rarely found their way into litigation or court opinions. A likely reason is that early markup transcripts were not recorded, and until recently they were not accessible on legal databases; interested parties had to specially request them from the relevant committee. Increasingly, however, committees are making them available on their websites. For an early critique of how markups have been overlooked by lawyers and judges in court cases, see Patricia M. Wald, *Some Observations on the Use of Legislative History in the 1981 Supreme Court Term*, 68 Iowa L. Rev. 195, 202 (1983).

Scripted Colloquies. Slightly different from ordinary floor statements made by a single member of Congress are scripted colloquies—essentially staged exchanges of words on the floor of the chamber designed to create a record of statutory meaning. These colloquies have long been observed with a high degree of skepticism, precisely because of their scripted nature. A recent empirical study, however, offers a different view of those colloquies between leaders of opposing parties. A substantial number of congressional staffers interviewed reported such colloquies to be particularly *persuasive* evidence of a legislative "deal" if there was a *bipartisan* agreement and the colloquy aimed to get the bipartisan deal in the record, through the scripted conversation. See Gluck & Bressman, *Statutory Interpretation from the Inside: Part I*, 65 Stan. L. Rev. at 987. The jury is still out on these materials, but bipartisan colloquies may be the fine middle line between winners' and losers' history.

Subsequent (Post-Enactment) Legislative History. Sometimes legislative materials are produced *after* a statute is enacted. This so-called "subsequent legislative history" has been viewed with a high degree of suspicion. If the point is to find the text, and the text has already been passed, one might argue that post-enactment history is entirely irrelevant. It also might be a sneaky way for members to add legislative history into the record after congressional attention has moved elsewhere and when it is too late for clarifying amendments to the statute. The Court does not generally give weight to these materials, although there have been notable exceptions. See, for example, The FDA Tobacco Case from Chapter 2 (relying on legislative history that came *after* the Food, Drug & Cosmetics Act of 1938 was passed, in order to show that Congress did not intend to permit the agency to regulate tobacco).

Presidential Signing and Veto Statements. This chapter has focused on legislative materials produced by Congress, but recall that the President is the last stop in the legislative process (absent a veto override). The President produces his own legislative materials, in the form of "signing statements," which are written memoranda issued by the President at his option to accompany the legislation he signs. For controversial pieces of legislation, these signing statements sometimes include statements of *interpretation*—that is, how the President understands certain (sometimes controversial) provisions of the statute. Beginning in the Reagan Administration, modern Presidents began to use these opportunities more aggressively. President George W. Bush's statements came under particular scrutiny because they offered controversial interpretations of high-profile legislation related to the War on Terror. For example, when signing the Detainee Treatment Act of 2005, which banned inhumane treatment of detainees, Bush said he would construe the Act "in a manner consistent with the authority of the President to supervise the unitary executive branch and as Commander in Chief and consistent with the constitutional limitations on the judicial power." This language was reminiscent of prior views expressed by the Bush Administration that presidential agents are immune from prosecution for torture of suspects. Should courts rely on signing statements as evidence of meaning? Given that a statute cannot be passed (absent a veto override) without the President's signature, isn't the President's understanding relevant? Like sponsors of legislation, whose statements are often relied upon by courts, presidents are also repeat-players in legislation and sometimes front-movers in shaping major statutes. On the other hand, presidential signing statements have the scent of "subsequent legislative history"—one person's view, made after the gates have shut on the legislative process and not subject to effective public rebuttal. How would you decide?

"Veto statements"—statements accompanying the President's decision to veto legislation—pose similar questions. If Congress overrides the President's veto, then an interpreter might infer that Congress rejected the President's preferences. On the other hand, if in subsequent legislation, Congress modifies the bill to respond to the veto message, the later-enacted bill might be construed consistent with the President's earlier-stated views.

3. LAWMAKING CONTEXT: MICRO TO MACRO

Whereas legislative history has been the subject of intense attention by judges and academics, the rest of the congressional lawmaking context has received surprisingly little attention. The first goal of this section is to introduce you to some important structural features inside Congress that affect how statutes are put together and understood by those who write them. The second goal is to pose the question whether those features, even if they do affect legislation, should or can be incorporated into our methods of interpretation. The final part of this section moves outside of Congress and applies these questions to a form of lawmaking unique to the states—direct democracy.

A. CONGRESSIONAL CONTEXT: HOW CONGRESS'S STRUCTURE AND PROCESSES AFFECT LEGISLATION

When courts interpret statutes, should it matter how many people worked on the drafts or how quickly the statute was enacted? For example, the initial Hurricane Katrina relief legislation was introduced in both chambers, passed by Congress, and signed by the President on a single day, just three days after the Hurricane ended; it is one page long and was passed with less than a quorum of the Senate present. See Barbara Sinclair, *Unorthodox Lawmaking: New Legislative Processes in the U.S. Congress* (4th ed. 2011). The Affordable Care Act of 2010 is more than 2,000 pages long. It was worked on by five different congressional committees with overlapping jurisdiction, and was passed after two years of hearings, using the Budget Act procedure of "reconciliation" (discussed in § 2) that limits amendments and filibuster to avoid a conference committee. The Farm Bill of 2014 briefly went through the Agriculture Committees in House and Senate; each chamber passed different versions of the bill; the bill then went to conference, where it spent about eight months before being reported out and passed. It is 300 pages long. These process differences affected the look and content of the underlying legislation but are not the kinds of factors that courts typically consider when interpreting statutes.[35] Should they?

Who drafts legislation? The question of who drafts statutes is intensely complicated. At the most basic level, statutes are drafted by everyone, including citizens, lobbyists, White House staff, agency officials, academics, congressional committees, Members of Congress and their staff, and anyone in between—and often by many of these stakeholders at once. Ask anyone in Washington—the President, the Vice President, Senators, Members of the House, lobbyists, lawyers, staffers, academics— and they will all claim (with some legitimacy) to draft legislation. When it comes down to the nitty-gritty process of drafting the actual text to be enacted, the story is quite complex.

Committees have traditionally been thought to have played the most important role in legislation. Congress is organized into more than forty committees (more than 200 if one includes subcommittees), and the committee system has long served as Congress's way of dividing responsibility and encouraging the development of policy expertise among Members and staff. But multiple committees are often involved in drafting different parts of a single statute. One potential problem for statutory interpretation is that different committees do not regularly communicate with one another when drafting statutes, and so the

---

[35] The discussion in this section is drawn from Gluck & Bressman, *Statutory Interpretation from the Inside: Parts I and II*, 65 Stan. Law. Rev. 901 (2013) and 66 Stan. L. Rev. 725 (2014).

structural fragmentation of Congress is an impediment to consistent drafting, even though courts presume that such consistency exists.

Party Leaders and the President also have had an increasingly important role in legislation. As Barbara Sinclair has pointed out, the growing problem of gridlock has led to more statutes being taken out of the "textbook" legislative process. Sinclair, *Unorthodox Lawmaking.* Instead of committee-to-floor-to-conference, we now have statutes that are negotiated with the President in closed door "summits," or by specially constituted groups of Members (e.g., the "Gang of 14"). What Sinclair calls "unorthodox" legislative processes have multiple implications for interpretation. Statutes drafted outside of committee may not have robust legislative history (no committee report, for instance), and often have a less transparent record—for example, no markup available for public review. Some argue that statutes negotiated by political leaders also lose the benefit of the deep policy expertise that committee staff offers, although it seems possible that executive branch agencies may act as surrogates at least some of the time. Even if this kind of lawmaking has increased over time, one might wonder how different it is from major legislation that does go through committee; typically, a bill never reaches the Senate floor unless there are negotiations between the Majority and Minority Leaders in the Senate or major negotiations among party leaders in the House. So, too, when there is an impasse in bills that seem to have followed the proper process, off-the-floor negotiations are common.

House and Senate Legislative Counsel. For decades, Congress has employed a staff of non-partisan professional drafters, housed in the Offices of House and Senate Legislative Counsel. There are approximately seventy-five such staffers today, split across the two chambers. They are the self-described "technicians" of statutory drafting and their role, in many statutes, is to take statutory deals (often captured by Members or high-level policy and committee staff in policy memoranda)) and turn them into statutory text. See Jarrod Shobe, *Intertemporal Statutory Interpretation and the Evolution of Legislative Drafting,* 114 Colum. L. Rev. 807 (2014). There is no requirement that staffers use Legislative Counsel, and there is some evidence that some staffers and some committees use them more or less than others. The lawyer-heavy judiciary committees, for example appear to use Legislative Counsel less often than other committees.

In addition to drafting the text of some statutes, Legislative Counsel staff also flag legal and interpretive issues and read statutory provisions with an eye toward consistency and coherence. As promising as this sounds for those concerned with well-drafted and consistent statutory text, the effectiveness of the Offices of Legislative Counsel is limited by a few key factors. First, other staff and committees are not required to use

Legislative Counsel and so there is inconsistency of practice in that regard. Second, Legislative Counsel is required to remain nonpartisan and cannot interfere in any political disputes, even where political disputes or considerations are responsible for statutory ambiguity or other interpretive issues. Although non-partisanship may sound good, it sometimes can provide a disincentive for staff to use professional drafters on controversial matters as staff may be reluctant to share sensitive political information. Third, individual staff attorneys are themselves subject-matter experts, so tend to review statutes for consistency within a single subject-matter areas, but not across the U.S. Code. Fourth, the Senate and House Offices of Legislative Counsel have different traditions and staffs—even different drafting manuals! Fifth, there is not always time to consult the professional drafters on last-minute deals.

Individual Members and Their Staff. Smaller bills are, on rare occasion, drafted by individual members, outside of committee by their "personal" (in-office) staff. These statutes tend to be simple bills, or bills that primarily affect a particular state or district. The professional drafters in House and Senate Legislative Counsel Offices play an especially large role in statutes drafted by personal staff, because such staff often includes many non-lawyers who lack the technical expertise of committee staff.

Different types of legislation. Some statutes are long, some statutes are short. Some are drafted quickly, others are drafted with years of deliberation and care. Some involve multiple subjects, and some are single subject bills. But even beyond these obvious differences, there are formal differences across different types of statutes. We highlight below two types of statutes that differ significantly from ordinary legislation.

Omnibus statutes are laws approved as a single bill but that include many unrelated topics, often unrelated "mini-bills" within a single statute. The Emergency Economic Stabilization Act of 2008, for instance, included not only the financial stimulus required to pull the nation from the brink of depression after the 2008 fiscal crisis, but also included the Paul Wellstone and Pete Domenici Mental Health Parity and Addiction Equity Act of 2008—a bill long sought by advocates of equal insurance coverage for mental health conditions. Omnibus bills often have something for everyone—a bunch of mini-deals (or "Christmas tree ornaments," as they are sometimes called)—designed to garner the votes needed to pass the package. This meta-logrolling process is a very common feature of modern bills. The process has been facilitated by the structure of the Senate; there is no "germaneness" rule in the Senate, which means the Senate has the ability to attach unrelated matters on *any* bill, regardless of its subject. From a statutory interpretation perspective, what is critical about omnibus legislation is that, because it includes many unrelated subjects, the text of the different parts of the bill tends to be drafted by many different staffers or committees, who may not be talking to one another or checking one another for consistency. Further, because omnibus legislation often pastes together many smaller bills, some of which were drafted years earlier, as in the case of the Wellstone Act above, the proper legislative history can be hard to find, nonexistent, or outdated.

Appropriations statutes are laws in which Congress provides funds. Often appropriations bills are omnibus in nature, but they have a very different look and feel. As we set out in Chapter 4, appropriations bills are a list of numbers with the agencies and programs to which those funds must be directed. Congressional rules prevent Congress from "legislating through appropriations," an effort to leave the substantive legal provisions to the policy committees, and let the appropriations committee determine the amount of the funds. As we noted in Chapter 4, it would be naïve to assume that this is always the way Congress works. Everyone follows the money, and so the appropriators have enormous power, even to the point of refusing to appropriate any money for highly popular bills. One other aspect of appropriations is especially important for our purposes. Because of the rule against legislating through appropriations, appropriations *legislative history* is very important inside of Congress and the federal agencies. That is where the appropriators direct how they expect agencies to spend the money. Staffers report that appropriation legislative history is therefore more significant than other legislative history—especially for agencies, who ignore it at their peril.

Different legislative processes. We have detailed the ways in which veto points in the legislative process affect a bill's ability to survive and the number of (often-clarity-challenging) compromises this structure induces. Think of how the process may affect the product. For example, statutes that proceed straight to the floor instead of going to committee bypass one veto point (committee consideration) and thus lose the transparency that is the result of public reports, and other legislative history that come out of the committee process. In some circumstances, bypassing the committee stage can deprive a bill of what might be months of expert debate, hearings, and study on a particular issue. Similarly, bills that bypass conference out of fear that any additional veto point would be treacherous may get through Congress but miss the opportunity that conference provides to clarify ambiguities and clean up mistakes in the statute. Statutes are often amended quickly, on the floor, or late at night, because Members of Congress demand it, and may be amended in ways that do harm to the overall structure of the statute—for example creating inconsistencies within the statutory text. But absent a vigilante staff or sharp-eyed outside interest group, such harm may go unnoticed until it is too late.

There are other features of the legislative process that have different, profound effects on statutes. A final important example is the "budget score." Congress is required to seek estimates of the budgetary impact of most proposed legislation from the Congressional Budget Office. See Office of Management & Budget, *The Statutory Pay-as-You-Go Act of 2010, available at* http://www.whitehouse.gov/omb/paygo_description. The score has an enormous impact on the drafting process, especially for major statutes, where the cost of legislation is often a source of concern and media attention. Staffers describe an iterative process with CBO, in which they go back and forth with the budget experts about how to write certain provisions. Statutory language is routinely changed and "tweaked" to affect the bottom line, and it seems likely that everyday staffers think a lot more about how the words they draft will affect the budget score than about whether they will invoke a particular judge-made canon of statutory construction.

NOTES AND QUESTIONS ABOUT LEGISLATIVE PRACTICE AND STATUTORY INTERPRETATION

1. *The Undeniability of Unorthodox Lawmaking.* Political scientist Barbara Sinclair coined the term "unorthodox lawmaking" to describe the increasingly frequent deviations from the textbook lawmaking process we have described. Barbara Sinclair, *Unorthodox Lawmaking: New Legislative Processes in the U.S. Congress* (4th ed. 2011). Over four editions of her work, she painstakingly traces a trend of ever-fewer statutes going through committee, or being drafting by single, coordinated groups, or going to Conference. By our count, in the first year of the 112th Congress (2011), only 7 (8%) of the 91 measures that passed went through the "textbook" process in both houses, passing through committees on each side, while 37 measures (41%) did not go through the committee process in either house before final passage. Only 3 of those 91 measures went to conference.

2. *Due Process of Lawmaking.* Professor Sinclair documents unorthodox lawmaking but does not criticize it. Instead she sees it as a pragmatic solution to congressional gridlock. Without party leaders twisting arms and making big deals, statutes wouldn't get passed at all. But what about the flip side of this story? Consider as an example the proposed "Cap and Trade" climate-change legislation that passed the House in 2009. It was widely reported that, at the last minute, Democratic party leaders replaced the entire 1,000 page bill with a different 1,200 page text designed to garner more votes. Two hundred more pages were added in the wee hours of the morning, just moments before the final vote. According to some reports, there was no complete copy of the bill in existence when the House was asked to vote. The story may be even more complicated; it is possible that the added 200 pages were taken from bills that already had been under consideration and so perhaps more widely known. But how should a court deal with such information? Assume the bill had passed. Would it be any less legitimate—

any less of a "law"—because it was passed without being read? Or because it was read in different pieces at different times?

The Supreme Court has chosen to stay out of such matters. The Court has resisted enforcing any notion of "due process of lawmaking," the idea—famously suggested by Oregon Supreme Court Chief Justice Hans Linde—that legislation that does not go through a deliberative, transparent or otherwise proper process is not legitimate in a democracy. See Hans Linde *Due Process of Lawmaking*, 55 Neb. L. Rev. 197, 243 (1976). Instead, the Court generally does not evaluate the adequacy of Congress's procedures (although, in our view, some of the canons do seem to be under-the-radar attempts to affect how Congress drafts). Do you think courts should consider, when interpreting statutes, how "unorthodoxly" a particular statute was passed? How does one measure "unorthodox"? Is the Civil Rights Act of 1964 "unorthodox," because it bypassed the Senate Judiciary Committee? How would courts implement such considerations? Ask yourself what constitutes adequate deliberation and democratically legitimate legislation. Must every Member have read the bill? It is enough that a small group of expert Members worked very hard on it for a long time? What if party leaders allow a certain number of amendments but then deploy procedural maneuvers to block more? How much, and what kind, of process would be enough?

3.   *The Importance of Staff in Statutory Drafting.* One recurring textualist critique of legislative history is that legislative history is a "staff" operation, a position that implies that text is more attributable to elected members. See, e.g., *In re Sinclair*, 870 F.2d 1340 (7th Cir. 1989) (Easterbrook, J.) (stating, in response to the argument that legislative history evinces members' intent that "[on]e may say in reply that legislative history is a poor guide to legislators' intent because it is written by the staff rather than by members of Congress"). To be sure, the Members *vote* on the text, but they do not draft it (and they might not even read it). Every study of Congress substantiates the role played by staff in the drafting of statutory text. How, then, does this fact affect the textualist critique? Does the fact that Members are not involved with the minor textual details—but rather only the broader policy deals—undermine the textualist argument that text is the ballgame? The granular manner in which many current Supreme Court opinions focus on text—often focusing on the meaning of a single word—seems quite disconnected from the more general way in which elected officials themselves interact with the text. Do any of these factors affect your view?

4.   *Congress's Obligations as a "Faithful Principal" to the Courts.* Does Congress have an obligation to get its act together? Should we tolerate a system in which different congressional committees draft single statutes together but do not communicate or try to make their drafting consistent? Or a system in which there is so much diversity of practice that a standardized account is impossible? The various different committees—and even the two Offices of Legislative Counsel—have different drafting manuals and different checklists! Committees also adopt different practices with respect to legislative history. The Senate Finance Committee, for example, produces a

"conceptual mark" a policy (not text) version of the bill being voted out of Committee that seems to have received no attention in litigation but could be extremely valuable. The Joint Tax Committee, in contrast, publishes its legislative history *after* the statute enacted in a document known as the Blue Book (the Blue Book is heavily relied upon by agencies and tax practitioners, but rejected by courts because courts distrust "subsequent" legislative history even though "official" subsequent history is unique to the tax context).

It is possible we have been too hard on courts. We have critiqued many of the unrealistic assumptions that judicial doctrine makes about how statutes are put together. But looking from the other side, at least some of the fault lies with Congress. Statutes are *law*, after all. Shouldn't Congress, as law's creator, do its own job furthering "rule of law" values—like transparency, consistency, predictability and notice—the same values we expect from courts? Is this realistic?

PROBLEM 6–3: REVISITING SOME OF OUR FAVORITE CASES IN LIGHT OF CONGRESSIONAL CONTEXT

1.   Recall *West Va. Hospitals v. Casey*, the attorneys' fee case from Chapter 4, § 3. Justice Scalia's super-textualist opinion for the Court looked to 41 different statutes to glean meaning for the fee-shifting provisions of the civil rights statute at issue in that case. How relevant is it that only four of the other statutes cited came from the same committee (judiciary), and that the others (including the four most recent, on which the Court placed special weight) were drawn from twenty-one different committees?

2.   Recall *TVA v. Hill*—the snail darter case—also from Chapter 4, § 3. Chief Justice Burger's "soft plain meaning" opinion halted a $100 million project to save a little fish, pursuant to the plain language of the Endangered Species Act. The Court refused to give credit to the fact that the most recent relevant appropriations legislation did specifically mention the dam project—because it was only mentioned in the legislative history not in the statutory text itself. Was it right to do so? (What if you knew, as we pointed out in Chapter 4, that the Court got it wrong and a later appropriations bill actually referenced the dam in a rider?)[36]

3.   Recall the Health Reform Case discussed in Chapter 5. The Affordable Care Act (ACA) is a very long statute, with nine different titles. The first three titles of the statute introduced some of the key insurance and health-care delivery reforms. Some of the later titles included a "mini-statute," the Class Act (written years earlier by Senator Kennedy to establish a long-term-care insurance system, and rolled into the ACA), a title having to do with biologic drugs, and another having to do with doctor training. Recall that the Supreme Court used the constitutional avoidance canon to uphold the statute's requirement that every American must hold health insurance or pay a tax. But the Court struck down another part of the statute as

---

[36]   As we noted in Chapter 4, the Court may have been incorrect about its own facts. A later statute appears to have mentioned the dam in the text.

unconstitutional—the requirement that the states significantly expand Medicaid or lose all prior Medicaid funding. The majority held the Medicaid portions *severable*—excising only those portions from the statute and letting the rest of the statute stand. The Joint Dissent, however, would have struck down the *entire* 2,000-page Act. The dissenters opined: "When we are confronted with such a so-called 'Christmas tree,' a law to which many nongermane ornaments have been attached, we think the proper rule must be that when the tree no longer exists the ornaments are superfluous. We have no reliable basis for knowing which pieces of the Act would have passed on their own. It is certain that many of them would not have, and it is not a proper function of this Court to guess which. To sever the statute in that manner would be to make a new law, not to enforce an old one. This is not part of our duty.'" *National Fed. of Indep. Bus. (NFIB) v. Sebelius,* 132 S.Ct. 2566, 2675–76 (2012) (joint dissent). What would you have done? What if you knew that omnibus legislation of this sort has been quite common for several decades?

4.   Related to *NFIB*, and currently winding its way through the courts are four related cases, *Halbig v. Burwell*, 2014 WL 3579745 (D.C. Cir. July 22, 2014); *King v. Burwell*, 2014 WL 3582800 (4th Cir. July 22, 2014); *Indiana v. IRS* (pending in District Court in Indiana); and *Pruitt v. Burwell* (pending in District Court in Oklahoma), which involve a potential drafting error in the ACA. Specifically, the statute sets up health insurance "exchanges" (marketplaces) with subsidies, and allows those marketplaces to be operated by either the states or the federal government (at the states' option) in each state. Throughout the debates on the ACA, there is not a single mention that the subsidies would be available to one type of marketplace but not the other. The statute as a whole refers in many places to the exchanges, without singling out one type or the other. However, the provision that introduces the subsidies provides they shall be available "through an Exchange established by the State under section 1311" and does not mention the federal-exchange provision. This has provided an opening for opponents to argue that, based on the plain language of the ACA, the subsidies should not be given on the federal marketplaces—a construction that would be lethal to the statute's effective operation. On July 22, 2014, a panel of the Fourth Circuit held that subsidies are available in the federal exchanges (*King v. Burwell*), and on the same day a panel of the D.C. Circuit held that subsidies were not available in the federal exchanges (*Halbig v. Burwell*).

Consider the potential relevance of three additional facts: (1) the ACA did not go to conference; (2) another provision of the statute specifically requires each exchange to report to the IRS about all individuals receiving subsidies on state and federal exchanges (would this make any sense if there were no subsidies on federal exchanges?); and (3) at the time the statute was passed, CBO scored the statute without differentiating among subsidies offered on either set of exchanges and without singling out either one, perhaps because most people were assuming at the time that most of the states would choose to operate their own exchanges. How do you decide this issue? How will the Supreme Court resolve this issue, if it agrees to hear the case?

B. DIRECT DEMOCRACY

We conclude this chapter with a more dramatic example of how lawmaking context affects legislation: direct democracy. Twenty-four states allow for the form of popular lawmaking known as the "initiative"—the method whereby a certain percentage of the electorate may petition to place proposed legislation or state-constitutional amendments on the ballot for a popular vote.

Consider four important differences between initiatives and legislation enacted in Congress or state legislatures:

Sponsors. Sponsors of ordinary legislation are accountable to the people. They also are "repeat players," meaning they cannot adopt a "scorched earth" approach to legislation if they hope to pass more legislation in the future. Some initiatives are backed by repeat-player political organizations, but others are backed by single-issue groups who care about their single issue above anything that might happen in the future.

Amendments. Unlike ordinary legislation, initiatives approved for placement on the ballot cannot be amended to respond to concerns or ambiguities raised during public debate over the proposal before the election. Instead, voters must be content with assurances, from experts, policymakers, and advocates about what the proposed bill will do.

Legislative History. What is the equivalent of legislative history when it comes to initiatives? There are no hearings, committee reports or anything of that nature. Sponsors speak to the public through the media, through promotional materials they produce to educate (and convince) the public, and sometimes through official explanatory documents (sometimes put together by the government, other times by the initiative's proponents) sent to the voters in advance of election day.

Audience. Legislation passed by initiatives is approved by the citizenry, not by elected officials working in a professional institution designed to support them in that process. Most voters will be uneducated about the particulars of the question at hand, and almost none will have lawyers working for them to help them understand the statutes they are being asked to consider.

How might these differences affect what statutes passed by initiative look like, how they are understood by the public, and how they should be interpreted by the courts? Should courts use the same interpretive methodologies that they use for other statutes when they interpret initiatives? Formulate your answers to these questions, before reading the next case, which involved a state constitutional amendment, passed by initiative in Michigan.

NATIONAL PRIDE AT WORK, INC. V. GOVERNOR OF MICHIGAN

Michigan Supreme Court, 2008.
481 Mich. 56, 748 N.W.2d 524.

MARKMAN, J., for the Court [joined by the CHIEF JUSTICE and three other Justices].

We granted leave to appeal to consider whether the marriage amendment, Const. 1963, art. 1, § 25, which states that "the union of one man and one woman in marriage shall be the only agreement recognized as a marriage or similar union for any purpose," prohibits public employers from providing health-insurance benefits to their employees' qualified same-sex domestic partners. Because we agree with the Court of Appeals that providing such benefits does violate the marriage amendment, we affirm its judgment. * * *

On March 16, 2005, in response to a state representative's request for an opinion regarding the marriage amendment's effect on the city of Kalamazoo's ability to provide same-sex domestic-partner health-insurance benefits to its employees, the Attorney General issued a formal opinion, concluding that the city's policy did violate the amendment. The Attorney General asserted that "Const. 1963, art. 1, § 25 prohibits state and local governmental entities from conferring benefits on their employees on the basis of a 'domestic partnership' agreement that is characterized by reference to the attributes of a marriage." OAG, 2005–2006, No. 7,171, p. 17 (March 16, 2005), 2005 Mich. Reg. 5, p. 35.

[Pursuant to the terms of its collective bargaining agreement with a public employees union, Kalamazoo's public policy entitled municipal employees to include their "domestic partners" in their health insurance coverage that came with their employment package. Married employees could include their legal spouses. Nonmarried employees could include their domestic partners, so long as they met the following requirements:

- the partners were of the same sex;
- the partners were at least 18 years old and mentally competent to enter into a contract;
- the partners shared a common residence and had done so for at least six (6) months;
- the partners were unmarried and not related by blood closer than would prevent marriage;

– the partners shared financial arrangements and daily living expenses related to their common welfare; and

– the partners had filed a statement of termination of previous domestic partnership at least six (6) months prior to signing another Certification of Domestic Partnership.

[The city's official policy provided: "It is the intent of this program to provide insurance coverage and other benefits to domestic partners of the City of Kalamazoo identical to those provided to spouses of City employees." The declaratory judgment lawsuit involved other domestic partnership benefits provided for the employees of other governmental entities, such as the University of Michigan.]

The primary objective in interpreting a constitutional provision is to determine the original meaning of the provision to the ratifiers, "we the people," at the time of ratification. * * * Thus, the primary objective of constitutional interpretation, not dissimilar to any other exercise in judicial interpretation, is to faithfully give meaning to the intent of those who enacted the law. This Court typically discerns the common understanding of constitutional text by applying each term's plain meaning at the time of ratification. *Wayne Co. v. Hathcock*, 684 N.W.2d 765 (Mich. 2004).

Plaintiffs argue that "the only thing that is prohibited by the [marriage] amendment is the recognition of a same-sex relationship as a marriage" and that the public employers here are not recognizing a domestic partnership "as a marriage." We respectfully disagree. First, the amendment prohibits the recognition of a domestic partnership "as a marriage or similar union. . . ." That is, it prohibits the recognition of a domestic partnership as a marriage or as a union that is similar to a marriage. Second, just because a public employer does not refer to, or otherwise characterize, a domestic partnership as a marriage or a union similar to a marriage does not mean that the employer is not recognizing a domestic partnership as a marriage or a union similar to a marriage.

The pertinent question is not whether public employers are recognizing a domestic partnership as a marriage or whether they have declared a domestic partnership to be a marriage or something similar to marriage; rather, it is whether the public employers are recognizing a domestic partnership as a union similar to a marriage. A "union" is "something formed by uniting two or more things; combination; . . . a number of persons, states, etc., joined or associated together for some common purpose." *Random House Webster's College Dictionary* (1991). Certainly, when two people join together for a common purpose and legal consequences arise from that relationship, i.e., a public entity accords legal significance to this relationship, a union may be said to be formed. When two people enter a domestic partnership, they join or associate together for a common purpose, and, under the domestic-partnership policies at issue here, legal consequences arise from that relationship in the form of health-insurance benefits. Therefore, a domestic partnership is most certainly a union.

The next question is whether a domestic partnership is similar to a marriage. Plaintiffs and the dissent argue that because the public employers here do not bestow upon a domestic partnership all the legal rights and responsibilities associated with marriage, the partnership is not similar to a marriage. Again, we respectfully disagree. "Similar" means "having a likeness or resemblance, [especially] in a general way; having qualities in common[.]" A union does not have to possess all the same legal rights and responsibilities that result from a marriage in order to constitute a union "similar" to that of marriage.* * * If the marriage amendment were construed to prohibit only the recognition of a union that possesses legal rights and responsibilities identical to those that result from a marriage, the language "or similar union" would be rendered meaningless, and an interpretation that renders language meaningless must be avoided. Further, the dissimilarities identified by plaintiffs are not dissimilarities pertaining to the nature of the marital and domestic-partnership unions themselves, but are merely dissimilarities pertaining to the legal effects that are accorded these relationships. However, given that the marriage amendment prohibits the recognition of unions similar to marriage "for any purpose," the pertinent question is not whether these unions give rise to all the same legal effects; rather, it is whether these unions are being recognized as unions similar to marriage "for any purpose."[6] * * *

All the domestic-partnership policies at issue here require the partners to be of a certain sex, i.e., the same sex as the other partner. Similarly, Michigan law requires married persons to be of a certain sex, i.e., a different sex from the other. MCL 551.1 ("Marriage is inherently a unique relationship between a man and a woman."). In addition, each of the domestic-partnership policies at issue in this case requires that the partners not be closely related by blood. Similarly, Michigan law requires that married persons not be closely related by blood. MCL 551.3 and MCL 551.4. Although there are, of course, many different types of relationships in Michigan that are accorded legal significance—e.g., debtor-creditor,

---

[6] Plaintiffs argue that the marriage amendment was adopted in response to *Baker v. State*, 744 A.2d 864 (Vt. 1999), in which the Vermont Supreme Court held that that state is constitutionally required to extend to same-sex couples in a civil union all the same benefits and protections that are provided to married couples. Thus, plaintiffs contend that the amendment only prohibits the establishment of "civil unions" that confer the same rights and obligations as does a marriage. However, as explained earlier, a union does not have to confer all the same rights and obligations as does a marriage in order to be "similar" to a marriage. Moreover, it is no less plausible that the amendment was adopted in response to a series of judicial decisions holding that public employers can extend health-insurance benefits to employees' domestic partners. See, e.g., *Tyma v. Montgomery Co.*, 801 A.2d 148 (Md. 2002); [et al.].

parent-child, landlord-tenant, attorney-client, employer-employee—marriages and domestic partnerships appear to be the only such relationships that are defined in terms of both gender and the lack of a close blood connection. As discussed earlier, "similar" means "having a likeness or resemblance, [especially] in a general way; having qualities in common[.]" *Random House Webster's College Dictionary* (1991). Marriages and domestic partnerships share two obviously important, and apparently unique (at least in combination), qualities in common. Because marriages and domestic partnerships share these "similar" qualities, we believe that it can fairly be said that they "resembl[e]" one another "in a general way." Therefore, although marriages and domestic partnerships are by no means identical, they are similar. Because marriages and domestic partnerships are the only relationships in Michigan defined in terms of both gender and lack of a close blood connection, and, thus, have these core "qualities in common," we conclude that domestic partnerships are unions similar to marriage. * * *

Plaintiffs and the dissent argue that Citizens for the Protection of Marriage, an organization responsible for placing the marriage amendment on the 2004 ballot and a primary supporter of this initiative during the ensuing campaign, published a brochure that indicated that the proposal would not preclude public employers from offering health-insurance benefits to their employees' domestic partners. However, such extrinsic evidence can hardly be used to contradict the unambiguous language of the constitution. * * *

In *Michigan Civil Rights Initiative v. Bd. of State Canvassers*, 475 Mich. 903, 903, 716 N.W.2d 590 (2006) (Markman, J., concurring), in which it was alleged that numerous petition signatures had been obtained in support of placing the Michigan Civil Rights Initiative (MCRI) on the ballot by circulators who misrepresented the MCRI, it was emphasized that "the signers of these petitions did not sign the oral representations made to them by circulators; rather, they signed written petitions that contained the actual language of the MCRI." Similarly, the voters here did not vote for or against any brochure produced by Citizens for the Protection of Marriage; rather, they voted for or against a ballot proposal that contained the actual language of the marriage amendment.[22]

---

[22] As an aside, this brochure did not render a verdict on the instant controversy. Rather, it stated:

> Marriage is a union between a husband and wife. Proposal 2 will keep it that way. This is not about rights or benefits or how people choose to live their life. This has to do with family, children and the way people are. It merely settles the question once and for all what marriage is—for families today and future generations.

We do not read this language as resolving that the marriage amendment would not prohibit domestic partners from obtaining health-insurance benefits. Moreover, statements made by other supporters of the amendment stated that partnership benefits would, in fact, be prohibited by the amendment.

Moreover, like the Citizens for the Protection of Marriage, the Michigan Civil Rights Commission issued a statement asserting:

> If passed, Proposal 2 would result in fewer rights and benefits for unmarried couples, both same-sex and heterosexual, by banning civil unions and overturning existing domestic partnerships. Banning domestic partnerships would cause many Michigan families to lose benefits such as health and life insurance, pensions and hospital visitation rights.[23]

* * * [A]ll that can reasonably be discerned from the extrinsic evidence is this: before the adoption of the marriage amendment, there was public debate regarding its effect, and this debate focused in part on whether the amendment would affect domestic-partnership benefits. The people of this state then proceeded to the polls, they presumably assessed the actual language of the amendment in light of this debate, and a majority proceeded to vote in favor. The role of this Court is not to determine who said what about the amendment before it was ratified, or to speculate about how these statements may have influenced voters. Instead, our responsibility is, as it has always been in matters of constitutional interpretation, to determine the meaning of the amendment's actual language. * * *

In addition to the brochure, plaintiffs and the dissent rely on statements made by counsel for Citizens for the Protection of Marriage to the Board of State Canvassers in which he apparently asserted that the amendment would not prohibit public employers from providing health-insurance benefits to domestic partners. Whatever the accuracy of this characterization, it should bear little repeating that the people ultimately did not cast their votes to approve or disapprove counsel's, or any other person's, statements concerning the amendment; they voted to approve or disapprove the language of the amendment itself.

[23] Other opponents made similar statements concerning the adverse consequences of the amendment. See, generally, *amicus curiae* brief of the American Family Association of Michigan, pp. 9–12. The dissent contends that "[i]t is reasonable to assume that the public relied heavily on the proponents of the amendment to explain its meaning and scope." We see no basis for this argument. Contrary to the dissent, it is no more likely that the voters relied on proponents' views rather than opponents' views of the amendment. Indeed, one might conceivably think that at least some of the people would be significantly more likely to rely on an assessment of the amendment from an official agency of the government than from a private organization with an obvious stake in the passage of the amendment. Similarly, it might be expected that at least some might be influenced by the characterizations of newspapers such as the *Detroit Free Press*, in which its political columnist stated in a question-answer format on September 13, 2004:

Q. What about employee benefits accorded to domestic partners and their dependents by some municipalities and public universities?

A. Proponents and opponents of the amendment say they would be prohibited to the extent they mimic benefits for married employees.

Because we cannot read voters' minds to determine whose views they relied on and whose they ignored—and because in the end this would not be relevant—we must look to the actual language of the amendment. The dissent inadvertently illustrates the principal infirmity of reliance upon legislative history, namely that it affords a judge essentially unchecked discretion to pick and choose among competing histories in order to select those that best support his own predilections. In relying on what she describes as the "wealth of extrinsic information available," the dissenting justice refers only to information supporting her own viewpoint, while disregarding the abundant "wealth of extrinsic information" that does not.

KELLY, J., joined by CAVANAUGH, J., dissenting.

* * First, the language of the amendment itself prohibits nothing more than the recognition of same-sex marriages or similar unions. It is a perversion of the amendment's language to conclude that, by voluntarily offering the benefits at issue, a public employer recognizes a union similar to marriage. Second, the circumstances surrounding the adoption of the amendment strongly suggest that Michigan voters did not intend to prohibit public employers from offering health-care benefits to their employees' same-sex partners. The majority decision does not represent "the law which the people have made, [but rather] some other law which the words of the constitution may possibly be made to express." Accordingly, I dissent. * * *

As always, when interpreting the Michigan Constitution, this Court's "duty is to enforce the law which the people have made, and not some other law which the words of the constitution may possibly be made to express." The initial step in determining what law the people have made is to examine the specific language used. In so doing, "it is not to be supposed that [the people] have looked for any dark or abstruse meaning in the words employed, but rather that they have accepted them in the sense most obvious to the common understanding, and ratified the instrument in the belief that that was the sense designed to be conveyed." And, since our task is a search for intent, it is often necessary to "consider the circumstances surrounding the adoption of the provision and the purpose it is designed to accomplish.

Beginning in 1993 with the Hawaii Supreme Court case of *Baehr v. Lewin*, a number of state courts and state legislatures joined in a national discussion on the constitutionality of barring same-sex marriages. In *Baehr*, the court held that Hawaii's statute limiting marriage to one man and one woman was presumptively unconstitutional under the Hawaii Constitution. It held that the state had the burden of showing a compelling state interest in limiting marriage to male/female unions. Following *Baehr*, the Vermont Supreme Court issued a decision in 1999 ordering the state legislature to create a legal form that would afford same-sex couples a status similar to that of married couples. Then, in 2003, in the famous case of *Goodridge v. Dep't of Pub. Health*, the Massachusetts Supreme Judicial Court held that barring two people of the same sex from marrying violated the equal protection guarantees of the Massachusetts Constitution. That same year, the California Legislature granted registered domestic partners "the same rights, protections, and benefits . . . as are granted to and imposed upon spouses."

It was against this background that the Michigan Christian Citizens Alliance commenced an initiative to amend the Michigan Constitution to bar same-sex marriage. The alliance formed the Citizens for the Protection of Marriage committee (CPM) "in response to the debate taking place across the country over the definition of marriage." The committee's stated goal was to place the issue of same-sex marriage on the ballot so that Michigan voters would have the ultimate say in the matter.

During CPM's campaign, concerns arose regarding exactly what the amendment would prohibit. CPM attempted to address these concerns at an August 2004 public certification hearing before the Board of State Canvassers. Specifically, CPM addressed whether the amendment, which it had petitioned to place on the ballot, would bar public employers from providing benefits to their employees' same-sex domestic partners. CPM's representative, attorney Eric E. Doster, assured the board that it would not. Mr. Doster stated:

> [T]here would certainly be nothing to preclude [a] public employer from extending [health-care] benefits, if they so chose, as a matter of contract between employer and employee, to say domestic dependent benefits . . . [to any] person, and it could be your cat. So they certainly could extend it as a matter of contract. * * *

> [A]n employer, as a matter of contract between employer and employee, can offer benefits to whomever the employer wants to. And if it wants to be my spouse, if it wants to be my domestic partner—however that's defined under the terms of your contract or my cat, the employer can do that. . . .

* * * In its campaign to win over voters, CPM made a number of additional public statements that were consistent with Mr. Doster's testimony before the Board of State Canvassers. For example, Marlene Elwell, the campaign director for CPM, was quoted in USA Today as stating that "[t]his has nothing to do with taking benefits away. This is about marriage between a man and a woman." Similarly, CPM communications director Kristina Hemphill was quoted as stating that "[t]his Amendment has nothing to do with benefits. . . . It's just a diversion from the real issue."

CPM also made clear on its webpage that it was "not against anyone, [CPM is] for defining marriage as the union of one man and one woman. Period." Instead, CPM contended that its reason for proposing the amendment was its belief that "[n]o one has the right to redefine marriage, to change it for everyone else. Proposal 2 will keep things as they are and as they've been. And by amending Michigan's constitution, we can settle this question once and for all."

CPM even distributed a brochure that asserted that the amendment would not affect any employer health-benefit plan already in place. The brochure stated:

Proposal 2 is Only About Marriage

Marriage is a union between a husband and wife. Proposal 2 will keep it that way. This is not about rights or benefits or how people choose to live their life. This has to do with family, children and the way people are. It merely settles the question once and for all what marriage is—for families today and future generations.

It can be assumed that the clarifications offered by CPM, the organization that successfully petitioned to place the proposal on the ballot, carried considerable weight with the public. Its statements certainly encouraged voters who did not favor a wide-ranging ban to vote for what they were promised was a very specific ban on same-sex marriage.

And a poll conducted shortly before the election indicates that CPM's public position was in line with public opinion. The poll results indicated that, whereas the public was in favor of banning same-sex marriage, it was not opposed to employer programs granting benefits to same-sex domestic partners.

In an August 2004 poll of 705 likely voters, 50 percent of respondents favored the amendment while only 41 percent planned to vote against it. But 70 percent specifically disapproved of making domestic partnerships and civil unions illegal. Sixty-five percent disapproved of barring cities and counties from providing domestic-partner benefits. And 63 percent disapproved of prohibiting state universities from offering domestic-partner benefits.

Accordingly, the circumstances surrounding the adoption of the amendment indicate that the lead proponents of the amendment worked hard to convince voters to adopt it.[34] CPM told voters that the "marriage amendment" would bar same-sex marriage but would not prohibit public employers from providing the benefits at issue. It is reasonable to conclude that these statements led the ratifiers to understand that the

---

[34] * * * The majority attempts to justify its disregard of the extrinsic sources available by concluding that the "marriage amendment" is unambiguous. As can be discerned by any reader of the amendment, the vague language used is ambiguous in regard to the resolution of the question presented by this case. Clearly, the amendment does not unambiguously state whether public employers are barred from providing health benefits to their employees' same-sex partners. It says nothing about these benefits. Accordingly, it is necessary to engage in judicial construction to resolve that question.

Since the amendment is ambiguous in regard to the proper resolution of the issue presented, I disagree with the majority's choice to ignore the extrinsic sources available. Because our goal is to discern the law that the people have made, when extrinsic sources exist that shed light on this intent, I believe it is essential to consider them. * * *

amendment's purpose was limited to preserving the traditional definition of marriage. And it seems that a majority of likely voters favored an amendment that would bar same-sex marriage but would go no further. Therefore, this Court's majority errs by holding that the amendment not only bars same-sex marriage but also prohibits the benefits at issue. The error of the majority decision is confirmed by examining the amendment's language.

The employer benefit programs at issue do not grant same-sex couples the rights, responsibilities, or benefits of marriage. The most that can be said is that the programs provide health-insurance coverage to same-sex partners. But health coverage is not a benefit of marriage. Although many benefits are conferred on the basis of the status of being married, health benefits are not among them. Notably absent is any state or federal law granting health benefits to married couples. Instead, the health coverage at issue is a benefit of employment. And the fact that the coverage is conferred on the employee's significant other does not transform it into a benefit of marriage; the coverage is also conferred on other dependents, such as children.

But even if health coverage were a benefit of marriage, it is the only benefit afforded to the same-sex couples in this case. The same-sex couples are not granted any of the other rights, responsibilities, or benefits of marriage. It is an odd notion to find that a union that shares only one of the hundreds of benefits that a marriage provides is a union similar to marriage. It follows that the amendment is not violated because the employee-benefit programs do not constitute recognition of same-sex "marriage or [a] similar union." * * *

The Attorney General makes much of the fact that the amendment uses the phrase "for any purpose." The Attorney General contends that, as long as one benefit is provided to same-sex couples in the same way that it is provided to married couples, the amendment is violated. The majority accepts this argument. The majority's interpretation of the amendment is problematic because it essentially reads the word "similar" out of the amendment. It construes the amendment to read: "the union of one man and one woman in marriage shall be the only agreement recognized as a marriage or union for any purpose." * * *

NOTES AND QUESTIONS ON PRIDE AT WORK AND INTERPRETING LAWMAKING INITIATIVES

1. *Interpreting Popular Lawmaking Initiatives.* As Justice Markman says, and the dissenters agree, the Michigan Supreme Court follows the same precepts when it construes an initiative-based constitutional amendment as when it construes an initiative-based statute. This point can be generalized to some other states, according to Jane S. Schacter, *The Pursuit of "Popular Intent: Interpretive Dilemmas in Direct Democracy*, 105 Yale L.J. 107 (1995).

A few states have special rules for initiatives, but it is not evident they are very different. The Oregon Supreme Court, for instance, has held that, for initiatives, "our task is to discern the intent of the voters. The best evidence of the voter's intent is the text of the provision itself. The context of the language of the ballot measure may also be considered; however, if the intent is clear based on the text and context of the [provision] the court does not look further." *Ecumenical Ministries v. Or. State Lottery Comm'n*, 871 P.2d 106, 110–11 (Or. 1994). In that spirit, consider the interpretive issues posed by this case.

2.   *Ought the Concessions by the Initiative's Proponents Be Persuasive to the Court?* The main argument by the dissenters is adapted from Glen Staszewski, *The Bait-and-Switch in Direct Democracy*, 2006 Wis. L. Rev. 17. Professor Staszewski claims that these initiative proponents engaged in a bait-and-switch game, where during the campaign they denied their initiative would preempt domestic partnership benefits—only to take the opposite position once the initiative had been adopted. Staszewski argues the formal proponents of an initiative should be treated as sponsors accountable for their representations to the electorate, especially ones that appeal to popular prejudices (for purposes of judicial review) or that claim a narrow effect of their proposals if enacted (for purposes of statutory interpretation). Glen Staszewski, *Rejecting the Myth of Popular Sovereignty and Applying an Agency Model to Direct Democracy*, 56 Vand. L. Rev. 395 (2003). Accord, Glenn Smith, *Solving the "Initiatory Construction" Puzzle (and Improving Direct Democracy) by Appropriate Refocusing on Sponsor Intent*, 78 U. Colo. L. Rev. 257 (2007), and D. Zachary Hudson, Note, *Interpreting the Products of Direct Democracy*, 28 Yale L. & Pol'y Rev. 223, 224 (2009).

The majority has a number of answers. One is that there is a plain meaning, and so all these representations are not relevant. We discuss those arguments in the next note. But if the proponents themselves said, repeatedly, that the plain meaning of the initiative would not cover domestic partnership employment benefits, is that not evidence of how a reasonable speaker of the English language might have understood these words and phrases?

Moreover, the court, accurately, points out that opponents worried that the initiative would be broadly construed: Should their representations count just as much, and therefore cancel out the claims of the proponents? (Or are they losers' history"?) Do the dissenters have a cogent response to this argument?

3.   *Was There a Plain Meaning?* The majority and dissent agree that judges must apply a plain meaning if there is one—and then they disagree about whether the initiative had a plain meaning that covered the Kalamazoo health benefit plan. The initiative provided that "the union of one man and one woman in marriage shall be the only agreement recognized as a marriage or similar union for any purpose." There are a number of technical objections to the majority's extended effort to insist upon a plain meaning

here. (It is no coincidence that author of the opinion, Justice Markman, was the same Stephen Markman who, while at the Department of Justice's Office of Legal Policy, authored the foundational defense of textualism set out at the beginning of this chapter.)

First, what "agreement" was being enforced by Kalamazoo? That city did not require employees to have an "agreement" to be domestic partners; instead, the city required the municipal employee and his or her partner to "certify" that they met the requirements quoted in Justice Markman's opinion. So was Kalamazoo recognizing an "agreement" as a marriage or similar union? Or was the city acting upon a "certification" signed by the employee and by the domestic partner? Is there a single "plain meaning" here, or is there ambiguity?

Second, was Kalamazoo "recognizing" whatever it is that the majority thought to be an "agreement"? Marriages, civil unions, and many municipal domestic partnership laws create a registry where couples present themselves, secure an official authorization for their civil status (as married or partnered), and are recorded as such; once their union is recorded, the couple is entitled to specific legal benefits. The Kalamazoo policy was not a domestic partnership registry; it was an employment benefit, given out to employees who could make the certification. We understand how the majority saw this process as "recognition," but is it not possible to say that official "recognition" comes only when there is an official registry? Is there a single "plain meaning" here, or is there ambiguity?

Third, if there was an agreement recognized by the city, was this recognition "as a marriage or similar union"? In 2004, civil *unions* were a term of art, based upon the 2000 Vermont statute giving same-sex couples all the same legal benefits and duties of marriage—but that is a far cry from the Kalamazoo employment benefit. Does the majority have a good response? Is there a single "plain meaning" here, or is there ambiguity?

Consider this literary analogy to the majority's central argument, i.e., that the employment benefit was "similar" to marriage. In Jane Austen's *Northanger Abbey* (1817), Henry Tilney is dancing with Catherine Morland. When a rival suitor tries to cut in, Henry compares the intrusion to an effort by an outsider to break up a marriage. Catherine expresses surprise: "But they are very different things!" In marriage, there is a lifetime commitment, she insists, while a dance is just a short interlude. Henry responds:

> "Taken in that light certainly, their resemblance is not striking; but I think I could place them in such a view.—You will allow, that in both, man has the advantage of choice, woman only the power of refusal; that in both, it is an engagement between man and woman, formed for the advantage of each; and that when once entered into, they belong exclusively to each other till the moment of its dissolution; that it is their duty, each to endeavour to give the other no cause for wishing that he or she had bestowed themselves elsewhere, and their best interest to keep their own imaginations

from wandering towards the perfections of their neighbours, or fancying that they should have been better off with anyone else. You will allow all this?"

Like the dissenters in the Michigan case, Catherine concedes there is an analogy, but that the differences are more striking. Like the majority in the Michigan case, Henry insists on the similarities. Is this not an example of how a reader can extract a variety of meanings from the same words?

Jane Austen provides a deeper lesson, however. She suggests that Henry is a motivated interpreter; he has an ulterior motive for treating a country dance like a marriage. He says:

"This disposition on your side is rather alarming. You totally disallow any similarity in the obligations; and may I not thence infer that your notions of the duties of the dancing state are not so strict as your partner might wish? Have I not reason to fear that if the gentleman who spoke to you just now were to return, or if any other gentleman were to address you, there would be nothing to restrain you from conversing with him as long as you chose?"

Edging closer toward the analogy to marriage, Catherine protests her disinterest in the interloper and affirms her devotion to Henry, who pronounces himself satisfied with her concession. (Read the novel to find out what happens to their relationship after this exquisite exchange.)

4.   *Broader Implications for the Relevance of Lawmaking Context.* Cases like *Pride at Work* bring the question of lawmaking context into sharp focus. If you are convinced that there should be special interpretive rules for initiatives based on their particular lawmaking context, how does that conclusion fit into your view whether we should have similarly tailored rules to reflect Congress's internal context? Throughout this chapter we have introduced considerations such as the rules and processes followed by Congress, or other contextual factors such as the type of statute involved. Is the case for tailoring interpretation to context as strong in Congress as it is in the initiative context? Why or why not?

APPENDIX TO CHAPTER 6: SAMPLE CONFERENCE REPORT

| 92D CONGRESS
 2d Session | HOUSE OF REPRESENTATIVES | REPORT
 No. 92–1403 |

EXECUTIVE BRANCH ADVISORY COMMITTEES

SEPTEMBER 18, 1972.—Ordered to be printed

Mr. HOLIFIELD, from the committee of conference,
submitted the following

CONFERENCE REPORT

[To accompany H.R. 4383]

The committee of conference on the disagreeing votes of the two Houses on the amendment of the Senate to the bill (H.R. 4383) to authorize the establishment of a system governing the creation and operation of advisory committees in the executive branch of the Federal Government, and for other purposes, having met, after full and free conference, have agreed to recommend and do recommend to their respective Houses as follows:

That the House recede from its disagreement to the amendment of the Senate to the text of the bill and agree to the same with an amendment as follows:

In lieu of the matter proposed to be inserted by the Senate amendment insert the following:

That this Act may be cited as the "Federal Advisory Committee Act".

FINDINGS AND PURPOSES

SEC. 2. (a) The Congress finds that there are numerous committees, boards, commissions, councils, and similar groups which have been established to advise officers and agencies in the executive branch of the Federal Government and that they are frequently a useful and beneficial means of furnishing expert advice, ideas, and diverse opinions to the Federal Government.

(b) The Congress further finds and declares that—

(1) the need for many existing advisory committees has not been adequately reviewed;

(2) new advisory committees should be established only when they are determined to be essential and their number should be kept to the minimum necessary;

(3) advisory committees should be terminated when they are no longer carrying out the purposes for which they were established;

2

(4) standards and uniform procedures should govern the establishment, operation, administration, and duration of advisory committees;

(5) the Congress and the public should be kept informed with respect to the number, purpose, membership, activities, and cost of advisory committees; and

(6) the function of advisory committees should be advisory only, and that all matters under their consideration should be determined, in accordance with law, by the official, agency, or officer involved.

DEFINITIONS

SEC. 3. *For the purpose of this Act—*

(1) The term "Director" means the Director of the Office of Management and Budget.

(2) The term "advisory committee" means any committee, board, commission, council, conference, panel, task force, or other similar group, or any subcommittee or other subgroup thereof (hereafter in this paragraph referred to as "committee"), which is—

(A) established by statute or reorganization plan, or

(B) established or utilized by the President, or

(C) established or utilized by one or more agencies,

in the interest of obtaining advice or recommendations for the President or one or more agencies or officers of the Federal Government, except that such term excludes (i) the Advisory Commission on Intergovernmental Relations, (ii) the Commission on Government Procurement, and (iii) any committee which is composed wholly of full-time officers or employees of the Federal Government.

(3) The term "agency" has the same meaning as in section 551(1) of title 5, United States Code.

(4) The term "Presidential advisory committee" means an advisory committee which advises the President.

APPLICABILITY

SEC. 4. *(a) The provisions of this Act or of any rule, order, or regulation promulgated under this Act shall apply to each advisory committee except to the extent that any Act of Congress establishing any such advisory committee specifically provides otherwise.*

(b) Nothing in this Act shall be construed to apply to any advisory committee established or utilized by—

(1) the Central Intelligence Agency; or

(2) the Federal Reserve System.

(c) Nothing in this Act shall be construed to apply to any local civic group whose primary function is that of rendering a public service with respect to a Federal program, or any State or local committee, council, board, commission, or similar group established to advise or make recommendations to State or local officials or agencies.

RESPONSIBILITIES OF CONGRESSIONAL COMMITTEES

SEC. 5. *(a) In the exercise of its legislative review function, each standing committee of the Senate and the House of Representatives shall make a continuing review of the activities of each advisory committee under its jurisdiction to determine whether such advisory committee should be abolished or merged with any other advisory committee, whether the responsi-*

3

bilities of such advisory committee should be revised, and whether such advisory committee performs a necessary function not already being performed. Each such standing committee shall take appropriate action to obtain the enactment of legislation necessary to carry out the purpose of this subsection.

(b) In considering legislation establishing, or authorizing the establishment of any advisory committee, each standing committee of the Senate and of the House of Representatives shall determine, and report such determination to the Senate or to the House of Representatives, as the case may be, whether the functions of the proposed advisory committee are being or could be performed by one or more agencies or by an advisory committee already in existence, or by enlarging the mandate of an existing advisory committee. Any such legislation shall—

(1) contain a clearly defined purpose for the advisory committee;

(2) require the membership of the advisory committee to be fairly balanced in terms of the points of view represented and the functions to be performed by the advisory committee;

(3) contain appropriate provisions to assure that the advice and recommendations of the advisory committee will not be inappropriately influenced by the appointing authority or by any special interest, but will instead be the result of the advisory committee's independent judgment;

(4) contain provisions dealing with authorization of appropriations, the date for submission of reports (if any), the duration of the advisory committee, and the publication of reports and other materials, to the extent that the standing committee determines the provisions of section 10 of this Act to be inadequate; and

(5) contain provisions which will assure that the advisory committee will have adequate staff (either supplied by an agency or employed by it), will be provided adequate quarters, and will have funds available to meet its other necessary expenses.

(c) To the extent they are applicable, the guidelines set out in subsection (b) of this section shall be followed by the President, agency heads, or other Federal officials in creating an advisory committee.

RESPONSIBILITIES OF THE PRESIDENT

SEC. 6. (a) The President may delegate responsibility for evaluating and taking action, where appropriate, with respect to all public recommendations made to him by Presidential advisory committees.

(b) Within one year after a Presidential advisory committee has submitted a public report to the President, the President or his delegate shall make a report to the Congress stating either his proposals for action or his reasons for inaction, with respect to the recommendations contained in the public report.

(c) The President shall, not later than March 31 of each calendar year (after the year in which this Act is enacted), make an annual report to the Congress on the activities, status, and changes in the composition of advisory committees in existence during the preceding calendar year. The report shall contain the name of every advisory committee, the date of and authority for its creation, its termination date or the date it is to make a report, its functions, a reference to the reports it has submitted, a statement of whether it is an ad hoc or continuing body, the dates of its meetings, the names and occupations of its current members, and the total estimated

4

annual cost to the United States to fund, service, supply, and maintain such committee. Such report shall include a list of those advisory committees abolished by the President, and in the case of advisory committees established by statute, a list of those advisory committees which the President recommends be abolished together with his reasons therefor. The President shall exclude from this report any information which, in his judgment, should be withheld for reasons of national security, and he shall include in such report a statement that such information is excluded.

RESPONSIBILITIES OF THE DIRECTOR, OFFICE OF MANAGEMENT AND BUDGET

SEC. 7. *(a) The Director shall establish and maintain within the Office of Management and Budget a Committee Management Secretariat, which shall be responsible for all matters relating to advisory committees.*

(b) The Director shall, immediately after the enactment of this Act, institute a comprehensive review of the activities and responsibilities of each advisory committee to determine—

(1) whether such committee is carrying out its purpose;

(2) whether, consistent with the provisions of applicable statutes, the responsibilities assigned to it should be revised;

(3) whether it should be merged with other advisory committees; or

(4) whether it should be abolished.

The Director may from time to time request such information as he deems necessary to carry out his functions under this subsection. Upon the completion of the Director's review he shall make recommendations to the President and to either the agency head or the Congress with respect to action he believes should be taken. Thereafter, the Director shall carry out a similar review annually. Agency heads shall cooperate with the Director in making the reviews required by this subsection.

(c) The Director shall prescribe administrative guidelines and management controls applicable to advisory committees, and, to the maximum extent feasible, provide advise, assistance, and guidance to advisory committees to improve their performance. In carrying out his functions under this subsection, the Director shall consider the recommendations of each agency head with respect to means of improving the performance of advisory committees whose duties are related to such agency.

(d)(1) The Director, after study and consultation with the Civil Service Commission, shall establish guidelines with respect to uniform fair rates of pay for comparable services of members, staffs, and consultants of advisory committees in a manner which gives appropriate recognition to the responsibilities and qualifications required and other relevant factors. Such regulations shall provide that—

(A) no member of any advisory committee or of the staff of any advisory committee shall receive compensation at a rate in excess of the rate specified for GS–18 of the General Schedule under section 5332 of title 5, United States Code; and

(B) such members, while engaged in the performance of their duties away from their homes or regular places of business, may be allowed travel expenses, including per diem in lieu of subsistence, as authorized by section 5703 of title 5, United States Code, for persons employed intermittently in the Government service.

(2) Nothing in this subsection shall prevent—

(A) an individual who (without regard to his service with an advisory committee) is a full-time employee of the United States, or

5

(B) an individual who immediately before his service with an advisory committee was such an employee,
from receiving compensation at the rate at which he otherwise would be compensated (or was compensated) as a full-time employee of the United States.

(e) The Director shall include in budget recommendations a summary of the amounts he deems necessary for the expenses of advisory committees, including the expenses for publication of reports where appropriate.

RESPONSIBILITIES OF AGENCY HEADS

SEC. 8. (a) Each agency head shall establish uniform administrative guidelines and management controls for advisory committees established by that agency, which shall be consistent with directives of the Director under section 7 and section 10. Each agency shall maintain systematic information on the nature, functions, and operations of each advisory committee within its jurisdiction.

(b) The head of each agency which has an advisory committee shall designate an Advisory Committee Management Officer who shall—

(1) exercise control and supervision over the establishment, procedures, and accomplishments of advisory committees established by that agency;

(2) assemble and maintain the reports, records, and other papers of any such committee during its existence; and

(3) carry out, on behalf of that agency, the provisions of section 552 of title 5, United States Code, with respect to such reports, records, and other papers.

ESTABLISHMENT AND PURPOSE OF ADVISORY COMMITTEES

SEC. 9. (a) No advisory committee shall be established unless such establishment is—

(1) specifically authorized by statute or by the President; or

(2) determined as a matter of formal record, by the head of the agency involved after consultation with the Director, with timely notice published in the Federal Register, to be in the public interest in connection with the performance of duties imposed on that agency by law.

(b) Unless otherwise specifically provided by statute or Presidential directive, advisory committees shall be utilized solely for advisory functions. Determinations of action to be taken and policy to be expressed with respect to matters upon which an advisory committee reports or makes recommendations shall be made solely by the President or an officer of the Federal Government.

(c) No advisory committee shall meet or take any action until an advisory committee charter has been filed with (1) the Director, in the case of Presidential advisory committees, or (2) with the head of the agency to whom any advisory committee reports and with the standing committees of the Senate and of the House of Representatives having legislative jurisdiction of such agency. Such charter shall contain the following information:

(A) the committee's official designation;

(B) the committee's objectives and the scope of its activity;

(C) the period of time necessary for the committee to carry out its purposes;

6

(D) *the agency or official to whom the committee reports;*

(E) *the agency responsible for providing the necessary support for the committee;*

(F) *a description of the duties for which the committee is responsible, and, if such duties are not solely advisory, a specification of the authority for such functions;*

(G) *the estimated annual operating costs in dollars and man-years for such committee;*

(H) *the estimated number and frequency of committee meetings;*

(I) *the committee's termination date, if less than two years from the date of the committee's establishment; and*

(J) *the date the charter is filed.*

A copy of any such charter shall also be furnished to the Library of Congress.

ADVISORY COMMITTEE PROCEDURES

SEC. 10. (a) (1) Each advisory committee meeting shall be open to the public.

(2) Except when the President determines otherwise for reasons of national security, timely notice of each such meeting shall be published in the Federal Register, and the Director shall prescribe regulations to provide for other types of public notice to insure that all interested persons are notified of such meeting prior thereto.

(3) Interested persons shall be permitted to attend, appear before, or file statements with any advisory committee, subject to such reasonable rules or regulations as the Director may prescribe.

(b) Subject to section 552 of title 5, United States Code, the records, reports, transcripts, minutes, appendixes, working papers, drafts, studies, agenda, or other documents which were made available to or prepared for or by each advisory committee shall be available for public inspection and copying at a single location in the offices of the advisory committee or the agency to which the advisory committee reports until the advisory committee ceases to exist.

(c) Detailed minutes of each meeting of each advisory committee shall be kept and shall contain a record of the persons present, a complete and accurate description of matters discussed and conclusions reached, and copies of all reports received, issued, or approved by the advisory committee. The accuracy of all minutes shall be certified to by the chairman of the advisory committee.

(d) Subsections (a)(1) and (a)(3) of this section shall not apply to any advisory committee meeting which the President, or the head of the agency to which the advisory committee reports, determines is concerned with matters listed in section 552(b) of title 5, United States Code. Any such determination shall be in writing and shall contain the reasons for such determination. If such a determination is made, the advisory committee shall issue a report at least annually setting forth a summary of its activities and such related matters as would be informative to the public consistent with the policy of section 552(b) of title 5, United States Code.

(e) There shall be designated an officer or employee of the Federal Government to chair or attend each meeting of each advisory committee. The officer or employee so designated is authorized, whenever he determines it to be in the public interest, to adjourn any such meeting. No

7

advisory committee shall conduct any meeting in the absence of that officer or employee.

(f) Advisory committees shall not hold any meetings except at the call of, or with the advance approval of, a designated officer or employee of the Federal Government, and in the case of advisory committees (other than Presidential advisory committees), with an agenda approved by such officer or employee.

AVAILABILITY OF TRANSCRIPTS

SEC. 11. (a) *Except where prohibited by contractual agreements entered into prior to the effective date of this Act, agencies and advisory committees shall make available to any person, at actual cost of duplication, copies of transcripts of agency proceedings or advisory committee meetings.*

(b) As used in this section "agency proceeding" means any proceeding as defined in section 551(12) of title 5, United States Code.

FISCAL AND ADMINISTRATIVE PROVISIONS

SEC. 12. (a) *Each agency shall keep records as will fully disclose the disposition of any funds which may be at the disposal of its advisory committees and the nature and extent of their activities. The General Services Administration, or such other agency as the President may designate, shall maintain financial records with respect to Presidential advisory committees. The Comptroller General of the United States, or any of his authorized representatives, shall have access, for the purpose of audit and examination, to any such records.*

(b) Each agency shall be responsible for providing support services for each advisory committee established by or reporting to it unless the establishing authority provides otherwise. Where any such advisory committee reports to more than one agency, only one agency shall be responsible for support services at any one time. In the case of Presidential advisory committees, such services may be provided by the General Services Administration.

RESPONSIBILITIES OF LIBRARY OF CONGRESS

SEC. 13. Subject to section 552 of title 5, United States Code, the Director shall provide for the filing with the Library of Congress of at least eight copies of each report made by every advisory committee and, where appropriate, background papers prepared by consultants. The Librarian of Congress shall establish a depository for such reports and papers where they shall be available to public inspection and use.

TERMINATION OF ADVISORY COMMITTEES

SEC. 14. (a)(1) *Each advisory committee which is in existence on the effective date of this Act shall terminate not later than the expiration of the two-year period following such effective date unless—*

(A) in the case of an advisory committee established by the President or an officer of the Federal Government, such advisory committee is renewed by the President or that officer by appropriate action prior to the expiration of such two-year period; or

(B) in the case of an advisory committee established by an Act of Congress, its duration is otherwise provided for by law.

(2) Each advisory committee established after such effective date shall

8

terminate not later than the expiration of the two-year period beginning on the date of its establishment unless—

(A) in the case of an advisory committee established by the President or an officer of the Federal Government such advisory committee is renewed by the President or such officer by appropriate action prior to the end of such period; or

(B) in the case of an advisory committee established by an Act of Congress, its duration is otherwise provided for by law.

(b)(1) Upon the renewal of any advisory committee, such advisory committee shall file a charter in accordance with section 9(c).

(2) Any advisory committee established by an Act of Congress shall file a charter in accordance with such section upon the expiration of each successive two-year period following the date of enactment of the Act establishing such advisory committee.

(3) No advisory committee required under this subsection to file a charter shall take any action (other than preparation and filing of such charter) prior to the date on which such charter is filed.

(c) Any advisory committee which is renewed by the President or any officer of the Federal Government may be continued only for successive two-year periods by appropriate action taken by the President or such officer prior to the date on which such advisory committee would otherwise terminate.

EFFECTIVE DATE

Sec. 15. Except as provided in section 7(b), this Act shall become effective upon the expiration of ninety days following the date of enactment.

And the Senate agree to the same.

CHET HOLIFIELD,
JOHN S. MONAGAN,
DANTE B. FASCELL,
SAM STEIGER,
GARRY BROWN,
Managers on the Part of the House.

EDMUND S. MUSKIE,
HUBERT H. HUMPHREY,
LAWTON CHILES,
LEE METCALF,
CHARLES PERCY,
W. V. ROTH, Jr.,
BILL BROCK,
Managers on the Part of the Senate.

JOINT EXPLANATORY STATEMENT OF THE COMMITTEE OF CONFERENCE

The managers on the part of the House and the Senate at the conference on the disagreeing votes of the two Houses on the amendment of the Senate to the bill (H.R. 4383) to authorize the establishment of a system governing the creation and operation of advisory committees in the executive branch of the Federal Government, and for other purposes, submit the following joint statement to the House and the Senate in explanation of the effect of the action agreed upon by the managers and recommended in the accompanying conference report:

1. SHORT TITLE

The Senate amendment changed the short title of the House bill to the "Federal Advisory Committee Act" The conference substitute conforms to the Senate amendment.

2. FINDINGS AND PURPOSES

The Senate amendment contained a more lengthy statement of of findings and purposes than did the House bill, but did not differ substantially from the House bill. The conference substitute adopts a compromise between the two provisions.

3. DEFINITIONS

The Senate amendment contained definitions of "agency advisory committee", "Presidential advisory committee", and "advisory committee", while the House bill contained definitions of "advisory committee" and "Presidential advisory committee"

The conference substitute adopts the House definition of "Presidential advisory committee" without any change and adopts the House definition of "advisory committee" with modification.

The conference substitute definition of "advisory committee" includes committees which are established or utilized by the President or by one or more agencies or officers of the Federal Government. The conference substitute excludes from the definition of "advisory committee" the Advisory Commission on Intergovernmental Relations, the Commission on Government Procurement, and any committee which is composed wholly of full-time officers or employees of the Federal Government.

The conference substitute deletes the Senate amendment definitions of "officer" and "employee"

4. APPLICABILITY OF THE PROVISIONS OF THE ACT

The Senate amendment contained a provision setting forth the applicability of provisions of the Act, while the House bill contained

10

no comparable provision. The conference substitute adopts the language of the Senate amendment with modifications. The conference substitute specifically exempts from the applicability of the provisions of the Act any advisory committee established or utilized by the Central Intelligence Agency or by the Federal Reserve System.

The Act does not apply to persons or organizations which have contractual relationships with Federal agencies nor to advisory committees not directly established by or for such agencies.

5. RESPONSIBILITIES OF CONGRESSIONAL COMMITTEES

The Senate amendment and the House bill contained minor differences regarding the legislative review functions of the standing committees of Congress. The conference substitute adopts the language of the Senate amendment.

The Senate amendment and the House bill differed regarding the duties of the standing committees of Congress when considering legislation establishing advisory committees. The conference substitute adopts the House bill with minor modifications.

The House bill provides that when the President, any agency head, or any other Federal official establishes an advisory committee, he shall follow the guidelines which are set forth in the House bill for standing committees of the Congress when they are considering legislation establishing advisory committees. The Senate amendment contained no comparable provision. The conference substitute adopts the House bill.

6. RESPONSIBILITIES OF THE PRESIDENT

The Senate amendment and the House bill differed with respect to the responsibilities of the President. The conference substitute adopts a compromise provision which provides that the President may delegate responsibility for evaluating and taking action with respect to the public recommendations of Presidential advisory committees. The conference substitute further provides that the President or his delegate shall submit a report to Congress stating his proposals for action or his reasons for inaction with respect to such public recommendations.

The House bill required the President to make an annual report to Congress regarding advisory committees. The Senate amendment required the Director of the Office of Management and Budget to make a similar annual report. The conference substitute adopts the House bill with modifications. The modifications include the adoption of a provision similar to a provision contained in the Senate amendment excluding from such annual report information which should be withheld for reasons of national security.

7. RESPONSIBILITIES OF THE DIRECTOR OF THE OFFICE OF MANAGEMENT AND BUDGET

The Senate amendment contained several differences from the House bill with respect to the responsibilities of the Director of the Office of Management and Budget.

As noted above, the Senate amendment required the Director to make an annual report to Congress on advisory committees. The

11

conference substitute provides that the President shall make such annual reports, as did the House bill.

With respect to the other duties of the Director, the conference substitute adopts the language of the Senate amendment with slight modification.

The conference substitute requires the Director to include in budget recommendations a summary of amounts necessary for the expenses of advisory committees.

8. RESPONSIBILITIES OF AGENCY HEADS

The Senate amendment differed from the House bill in that it provided that each agency head should designate an Advisory Committee Management Officer with specified duties, and the House bill contained no comparable provision. The conference substitute adopts the Senate amendment with slight modifications.

9. ESTABLISHMENT AND PURPOSE OF ADVISORY COMMITTEES

The Senate amendment set forth a procedure to be followed when advisory committees are established and provided that advisory committees be utilized solely for advisory functions. The House bill had no comparable provision. The conference substitute adopts the Senate amendment with modifications.

10. ADVISORY COMMITTEE PROCEDURES

With regard to the availability of the records and other papers of advisory committees and public access to their meetings, the Senate amendment differed from the House bill. The conference substitute provides for publication in the Federal Register of timely notice of advisory committee meetings, except where the President determines otherwise for reasons of national security. The conference substitute further provides for public access to advisory committee meetings subject to restrictions which may be imposed by the President or the head of any agency to which an advisory committee reports. Such restrictions may be imposed after it is determined that an advisory committee meeting is concerned with matters listed in section 552(b) of title 5, United States Code. The conference substitute also provides that subject to section 552 of title 5, United States Code, the records and other papers of advisory committees shall be available for public inspection and copying.

The conference substitute requires that each advisory committee keep detailed minutes of its meetings.

The conference substitute requires that a designated officer or employee of the Government attend each advisory committee meeting. No such meeting may be conducted in his absence or without his approval. Except in the case of Presidential advisory committees the agenda of such meeting must be approved by him.

12

11. AVAILABILITY OF TRANSCRIPTS

The Senate amendment provided that agencies and advisory committees should make any transcripts of their proceedings or meetings available to the public at actual cost of duplication. The House bill contained no comparable provision. The conference substitute adopts the Senate amendment with modification.

12. COLLECTION OF INFORMATION

The Senate amendment contained a provision relating to procedures followed by the Office of Management and Budget in carrying out its duties under the Federal Reports Act. The House bill contained no such provision.

The conference substitute contains no provision on this subject.

13. FISCAL AND ADMINISTRATIVE PROVISIONS

The Senate amendment and the House bill differ slightly regarding the requirement that records be kept concerning the disposition of funds and the nature and extent of activities of advisory committees. The conference substitute provides that each agency shall keep financial and other records regarding the advisory committees under its jurisdiction and that either the General Services Administration or such agency as the President may designate shall maintain financial records of Presidential advisory committees.

The conference substitute adopts the provision of the Senate amendment concerning support services for advisory committees.

14. RESPONSIBILITIES OF THE LIBRARY OF CONGRESS

The Senate amendment and the House bill differed with respect to the responsibilities of the Library of Congress as a depository of the reports and other materials of advisory committees. The conference substitute adopts the House bill with modifications.

15. TERMINATION OF ADVISORY COMMITTEES

The Senate amendment differed from the House bill in that it provided for the termination of advisory committees created by Act of Congress before the effective date of the bill and further differed in that it provided for the termination of all advisory committees not later than December 31, 1973. The House bill provided for the termination of all advisory committees, other than those created by Act of Congress before the date of enactment of the bill, within two years after the effective date of the bill.

The conference substitute adopts the Senate amendment with modifications. An important modification to the Senate amendment is the substitution of a termination date which occurs two years after the effective date of the bill.

13

The Senate amendment and the House bill differed slightly with respect to effective date. The conference substitute adopts the Senate amendment with modifications.

CHET HOLIFIELD,
JOHN S. MONAGAN,
DANTE B. FASCELL,
SAM STEIGER,
GARRY BROWN,
Managers on the Part of the House.

EDMUND S. MUSKIE,
HUBERT H. HUMPHREY,
LAWTON CHILES,
LEE METCALF,
CHARLES PERCY,
W. V. ROTH, Jr.,
BILL BROCK,
Managers on the Part of the Senate.

○

PART 3

AGENCIES AND ADMINISTRATIVE IMPLEMENTATION

■ ■ ■

As we have seen, most of the work of the modern administrative state is conducted by administrative agencies. Indeed, most directives that have the force of law and allow for immediate sanctions for violations are issued by agencies, not by legislatures. Chapter 2 examined characteristic forms of agency action. Given different substantive directives, different problems to solve, and different legislative delegations of authority, different agencies regulate in a variety of different ways.

But agencies are subject to constraint: their regulatory decisions are always made in the shadow of rules that limit their range of action; such rules of constraint find their legal basis in the Constitution, statutes, executive orders, and administrative manuals. Relatedly, agency decisions are always made with other officials—legislators, judges, and executive officials—watching and reacting. Chapter 7 introduces you to these constraints upon agency action. This chapter broadly covers statutory and constitutional restrictions that fall under conventional understandings of "administrative law" and that judges sometimes enforce, but it also introduces you to rules and restrictions grounded in executive orders and presidential directives, a newer form of administrative law.

Chapter 7 surveys the rules agencies must abide by in deference to judicial or executive oversight, and Chapter 8 is an introduction to the deference that judges pay to agency interpretations of statutes. Thus, not only do agencies generate the vast majority of official interpretations of federal statutes, but the relatively few agency interpretations that do come before judges are presumptively accepted by those judges as they perform their core judicial duties to say what the "law" is. As with many other areas of law, the most interesting problems tend to be those where at least some judges believe that agency interpretations should *not* be followed, and Chapter 8 offers an interesting array of such problems.

Concluding this part, and this book, is Chapter 9 on "administrative constitutionalism," the articulation and application of important public values by administrative and executive officials, working together with legislators. An important, and underappreciated, theme of the modern regulatory state is that the public values and legal frameworks that most profoundly affect our lives are set forth in super-statutes and implemented, dynamically, by agencies. While the Supreme Court and the judicial branch are most famously engaged in the process of ascertaining Large "C" Constitutional frameworks and values, in landmark cases like *Brown v. Board of Education*, small "c" constitutional frameworks and values are established by Congress in super-statutes, such as the Civil Rights Act of 1964, which are then implemented and elaborated after great normative deliberation by agencies—these actions carried forth, deepened, and radically altered the anti-discrimination norm announced in *Brown* and other Supreme Court cases. Chapter 9 will explore administrative constitutionalism through the prism of several different small "c" constitutional revolutions, namely, (1) the understanding of employment disadvantages because of pregnancy as a malign form of "discrimination"; (2) the entrenchment of social security insurance as the core for retirement support; and (3) the civil rights movement for lesbian, gay, bisexual, and transgender (LGBT) persons, culminating in marriage equality for same-sex couples.

CHAPTER 7

INTRODUCTION TO ADMINISTRATIVE LAW

■ ■ ■

This chapter addresses the basic elements of the Administrative Procedure Act (APA) and its limits on agency action. It considers the difference between agency *rulemaking* and agency *adjudication*, and the APA's requirements for each. This chapter also focuses on how APA rulemaking differs from less formal agency action as well as agency inaction (the failure to act). Finally, it considers the importance of White House control over agencies through presidential executive orders and the Office of Information and Regulatory Affairs (OIRA).

"Administrative law" is usually conceptualized as rules governing agency action that are enforced by judges. The framework statute for this understanding of administrative law is the Administrative Procedure Act of 1946 (APA), 60 Stat. 237, codified as amended at 5 U.S.C. §§ 551–559, 701–706 *et al.* (Appendix 3 to this coursebook). A key distinction in the APA is between agency *rules* and agency *orders*. Rules are like statutes, for they are "designed to implement, interpret, or prescribe law or policy." 5 U.S.C. § 551(4).[1] Orders are like judicial decisions, for they constitute the "final disposition" of a controversy involving the statutory or agency rules. § 551(6). Both orders and rules have the force of law—meaning they function like statutes—unless Congress overrules them or the agency changes them.

The APA as well as agency-specific laws set forth the procedures agencies must use when they promulgate rules and orders. See §§ 553–554, 556–557. Administrative law distinguishes between *informal* and *formal* rulemaking. Section 553 lays out detailed procedures, including requirements for public notice and a right to comment on proposed rules, for "informal" rulemaking. Where the statute requires rulemaking decisions "on the record," §§ 556–557 set forth more detailed trial-like procedures for "formal" rulemaking.[2] Both types of rulemaking

---

[1] Ironically, § 551(4) is considered a poorly drafted law, and courts have supplemented its vague and unhelpful text. See Ronald M. Levin, *The Case for (Finally) Fixing the APA's Definition of "Rule,"* 56 Admin. L. Rev. 1077 (2004).

[2] See *United States v. Florida East Coast Ry. Co.,* 410 U.S. 224 (1973) (essentially requiring the magic words "on the record" to trigger the more burdensome formal rulemaking

procedures can support "rules" that have the force of law. Almost all the rules you will encounter in this coursebook, including some pretty ambitious acts of agency lawmaking (such as the FDA Tobacco Rules), are the result of "informal" rulemaking.

Likewise, the APA contemplates different procedures for *formal* and *informal* adjudication. Where the statute the agency is implementing requires adjudication "on the record after agency hearing," APA §§ 554 and 556–557 impose a highly detailed procedural apparatus for "formal" adjudications. Where the underlying statute does not require a hearing "on the record," the APA sets forth no minimal procedures for "informal" adjudications, though procedures such as notice and a right to a meaningful hearing are often required by the Due Process Clause. As with rulemaking, the "informal" processes are more commonly used.[3]

From the enactment of the APA in 1946 until the 1960s, most agencies relied on formal as well as informal adjudications to develop policies. See M. Elizabeth Magill, *Agency Choice of Policymaking Form*, 71 U. Chi. L. Rev. 1383, 1398 (2004). Since the 1960s, however, agency policymaking has proceeded largely through informal rulemaking. This reflected more congressional delegation of rulemaking authority, especially to newer agencies such as the Environmental Protection Agency, as well as a shift of perspective in some of the older agencies, such as the Securities and Exchange Commission, to effectuate their statutory missions through broader rules rather than a series of orders.

Sections 701–706 of the APA provide for judicial review of final agency rules, orders, and other actions. "Any person suffering legal wrong because of agency action, or adversely affected or aggrieved by agency action within the meaning of a relevant statute, is entitled to judicial review thereof," § 702, unless "(1) statutes preclude judicial review; or (2) agency action is committed to agency discretion by law." § 701(a). Courts will not review administrative reports or recommendations that do not represent the agency's "final" decision having a direct effect on the parties. *Franklin v. Massachusetts*, 505 U.S. 788 (1992) (holding that an agency recommendation to the President is not a final agency action). Although courts interpret the APA to recognize a presumption in favor of judicial review, the Supreme Court has found a great deal of agency action unreviewable under § 701(a)(1)–(2). See *Lincoln v. Vigil,* 508 U.S. 182, 191–92 (1993) (surveying the cases and holding that agencies have unreviewable discretion in how they spend congressional lump-sum appropriations).

---

proceedings). The vast amount of agency work is done through informal mechanisms rather than this formal process.

[3]   See *Chemical Waste Management, Inc. v. EPA*, 873 F.2d 1477 (D.C. Cir. 1989) (statutory requirement of "public hearing" does not trigger procedures required for formal adjudication).

The APA also sets forth standards for judicial examination of agency decisions that are reviewable. In an action for judicial review, the court "shall" under § 706:

(1) compel agency action unlawfully withheld or unreasonably delayed; and

(2) hold unlawful and set aside agency action, findings, and conclusions found to be—

(A) arbitrary, capricious, an abuse of discretion, or otherwise not in accordance with law;

(B) contrary to constitutional right, power, privilege, or immunity;

(C) in excess of statutory jurisdiction, authority, or limitations, or short of statutory right;

(D) without observance of procedure required by law;

(E) unsupported by substantial evidence in a case subject to sections 556 and 557 of this title or otherwise reviewed on the record of an agency hearing provided by statute; or

(F) unwarranted by the facts to the extent that the facts are subject to trial de novo by the reviewing court.

The APA was essentially designed to recognize the legislative and adjudicative roles of independent agencies and executive departments (both of which are included in the APA definition of "agency," § 551(1)), but also to rein in the bureaucratic state with procedural safeguards and judicial review to prevent arbitrary or unlawful action.

Most of this chapter will outline the established constitutional and statutory doctrine governing federal agency decisions and actions, including less formal actions and even failures to act. But federal "administrative law" also includes an expanding body of procedures and directives promulgated not by Congress, but by executive department officials, and enforced by executive department officials, not by federal judges. Thus, agencies themselves usually establish detailed procedural protocols in handbooks, guidance documents, and official websites that inform the public as well as agency officials of what steps need to be taken in response to particular problems and what substantive criteria should be followed in resolving those problems. While the agency's own procedures are not necessarily judicially enforceable against the agency, they are "enforceable" by agency officials themselves, who take them seriously and do not want to appear "irregular." A subordinate agency official might get into trouble if she does not follow the protocols duly established by the agency heads.

An agency's freedom of action is also constrained by other agencies. Consider a simple but important example. If an agency promulgates a controversial legislative rule that regulated companies sue to overturn, the agency usually cooperates with the Department of Justice in the course of the lawsuit. If the companies are successful at the trial level, the agency cannot appeal its loss without the agreement of the Solicitor General (the SG, an official in the Department of Justice). If the agency wants to file an *amicus* brief with a court of appeals or with the Supreme Court, in most cases the agency must persuade the SG to file it. Thus, the agency needs the cooperation of the Office of the Solicitor General: if the lawyers in that office disagree with the agency's interpretation of the law, then the agency will not be able to defend its rule, order, or interpretation in court. This is a genuine constraint upon agency decisionmaking at the policymaking level.

Finally, the White House itself constrains agency policymaking, even when Congress has delegated lawmaking authority to the agency, and not to the President. Executive Order 12,866, 58 Fed. Reg. 51,735–44 (Sept. 30, 1993) (Appendix 4 to this coursebook) provides a legal framework for executive branch promulgation and review of legislative rules. Recall from Chapter 2 that President Barack Obama has expanded upon E.O. 12,866 with a more aggressive directive to executive agencies—and with a new executive order directing independent agencies to reconsider rules in light of the cost-benefit analysis indicated in E.O. 12,866.

1. AGENCY RULEMAKING

As defined by the APA, agency rules are "designed to implement, interpret, or prescribe law or policy." 5 U.S.C. § 551(4); see Ronald M. Levin, *The Case for (Finally) Fixing the APA's Definition of "Rule,"* 56 Admin. L. Rev. 1077 (2004). Today, the most important form of agency action is legislative rules, namely, those rules having the force of law upon their final promulgation by the agency. (Interpretive rules, often called guidances, do not have the force of law.) Agencies can promulgate legislative rules *only* if authorized by an explicit delegation of lawmaking authority from Congress. Congress for most of the twentieth century followed a precise formula for such delegations; for example, statutes would establish legal penalties for violations of agency orders or rules. In the last generation, however, the Supreme Court and lower federal courts have followed the approach of *National Petroleum Refiners Ass'n v. FTC*, 482 F.2d 672 (D.C. 1973), which found such a delegation in a statutory authorization for the FTC to issue "rules and regulations for the purpose of carrying out the provisions" of the statute.[4]

---

[4] For the pre-1973 convention, which was much more restrictive than the *National Petroleum* formulation, see Thomas W. Merrill & Kathryn Tongue Watts, *Agency Rules with the Force of Law: The Original Convention*, 116 Harv. L. Rev. 467 (2002).

Most legislative rules are promulgated through the APA's process of *informal (notice-and-comment) rulemaking.* In this process, the agency must publish notice of proposed rules in the Federal Register, followed by the opportunity for interested persons to submit comments, usually written, on these proposed rules. § 553.[5] When the agency promulgates its final rule, it must respond to the major comments and explain why it did or did not make material changes to the proposed rule. *Formal rulemaking,* on the other hand requires agency rulemaking "on the record." APA §§ 556–557 impose further requirements that effectively impose trial-like procedures on the rulemaking process. Agencies rarely use formal rulemaking unless so directed by statute. Section 706 of the APA subjects legislative rules to judicial review. In addition to the explicit requirements of the APA, federal judges have developed an administrative common law of precepts applicable to agency decisionmaking. The Supreme Court proclaims itself limited to the precepts found in the APA and has abrogated at least some of the administrative common law generated by the Court of Appeals for the D.C. Circuit. More important, as noted at the beginning of this chapter, there is a significant amount of executive department rulemaking, common law, and practice placing limits on agency decisionmaking.

Perhaps after you have read the complicated body of doctrine in the following materials, step back and consider: What is the purpose of these legal and practical restrictions? There are at least three different kinds of purposes:

- *Libertarian.* Agency action usually impinges on the liberty of people and corporations. Restrictions on agency action may operate to protect liberty, along the same lines as the vetogates that prevent legislatures from over-regulating, at least in theory. Yet like vetogates, restrictions on agencies operate in an anti-libertarian manner when they prevent agencies from deregulating or easing the costs of government regulation.

- *Democratic Legitimacy.* Congress has delegated agencies a lot of lawmaking power, yet agency lawmaking is not made by elected representatives accountable to We the People in the same way as legislative lawmaking. To be sure, executive department agencies are accountable to the President, who is elected by the entire nation, but the President is not accountable as deeply as Congress. At least some of this "democratic deficit" might be addressed by processes that

---

[5]   See Cornelius Kerwin, *Rulemaking: How Government Agencies Write Law and Policy* (4th ed. 2010) (comprehensive description and analysis of notice-and-comment rulemaking); Peter L. Strauss, *The Rulemaking Continuum,* 41 Duke L.J. 1463 (1992) (the variety of rulemaking options).

increase agency accountability to We the People. Both the APA and Executive Order 12,866 require openness and opportunities for public participation that may improve the democratic legitimacy of agency rulemaking.

- *Efficiency.* Many constraints on agency decisionmaking are justified on simple efficiency grounds. These constraints attempt to ensure that the benefits of agency rules are justified by their probable costs. Public participation may check agency tendencies to impose costly rules, and the agenda of Executive Order 12,866 and related presidential directives is explicitly cost-effectiveness.

Consider also the costs of constraint and of judicial review. The main cost is *agency ossification*: just as Congress is paralyzed by too many vetogates, so critics maintain that agencies can be paralyzed by too many procedural restrictions that "ossify" agency capacities to solve public problems.[6] For example, Jerry Mashaw and David Harfst's book, *The Struggle for Auto Safety* (1990), examines the implementation of the National Traffic and Motor Vehicle Safety Act of 1966, Pub. L. No. 89–563, 80 Stat. 718, currently codified at 49 U.S.C. § 31010 *et seq.* The 1966 Act created the National Traffic Safety Agency, later renamed the National Highway Traffic Safety Administration (NHTSA) within the new Department of Transportation. Congress vested the agency (since 1994, the Department) with the authority to promulgate rules to establish "motor vehicle safety standards" that are "reasonable, practicable, and appropriate, * * * to meet the need for motor vehicle safety, and * * * [are] stated in objective terms." (NTMVSA § 103(a), now codified with new language in 49 U.S.C. § 30111.) No one can sell or import into the United States motor vehicles or equipment not in conformity with these standards (NTMVSA § 105(b), now codified with new language in 49 U.S.C. § 30112).

Like the FDA (Chapter 2, § 3), the NHTSA and the Department of Transportation enjoy congressionally-delegated authority to structure the automobile market by establishing minimum safety standards for cars sold in this country. Prior efforts to affect auto safety, such as speed limits and drunk-driving punishments, sought to *avoid accidents.* Epidemiologists noted that injuries and deaths were more proximately caused by the passenger's collision with parts of his own car, and not just

---

[6]   See Jerry L. Mashaw & David L. Harfst, *The Struggle for Auto Safety* (1990); R. Shep Melnick, *Administrative Law and Bureaucratic Reality*, 44 Admin. L. Rev. 245 (1992); Mark Seidenfeld, *Demystifying Deossification: Rethinking Recent Proposals to Modify Judicial Review of Notice and Comment Rulemaking*, 75 Tex. L. Rev. 483 (1997) (surveying and analyzing arguments and reform proposals). But see William S. Jordan, *Ossification Revisited: Does Arbitrary and Capricious Review Significantly Interfere with Agency Ability to Achieve Regulatory Goals Through Informal Rulemaking?*, 94 Nw. U. L. Rev. 393 (2000) (arguing that review for arbitrary and capricious decisionmaking has not significantly impeded agencies in pursuit of policy goals).

the collisions of two cars. Hence, they proposed a new strategy for reducing death and injury: *redesign the automobile* to make it safer when accidents do occur. Mechanisms that hold the passenger in place (today's seatbelts and shoulder harnesses) or cushion the passenger from the chassis (today's airbags) can prevent or ameliorate injuries from the "second collision."

The auto safety law, passed without a single negative vote in Congress, had a fast start out of the garage but has run out of gas since then. Mashaw and Harfst place most of the blame on the institutional actors that have meddled with the agency's application of expertise to improve auto design in a cost-effective way—legislators who overreacted to high visibility problems and derailed the agency's agenda, executive department officials who paid off interest groups by sacrificing traffic safety, and (especially) well-intentioned judges who slowed down the agency and discouraged needed experimentation by demanding too much empirical support for rulemaking.

Dramatically, Mashaw and Harfst provide what they consider a frightening example of ossification. Too much judicial review of agency standard-setting has, they maintain, discouraged the NHTSA from setting and tightening standards and has resulted in the wasteful strategy of relying on ex post recalls rather than ex ante design-forcing standards. This section will conclude with the leading Supreme Court case evaluating the agency's long-running effort to impose "passive restraints" like airbags and automatic seat belts on automakers for the protection of passengers involved in accidents. We shall also examine other points of view, which reject the ossification themes of Professor Mashaw's work.

A. PROCEDURAL REQUIREMENTS FOR LEGISLATIVE RULEMAKING

*1. **Requirements Imposed by Statute.*** The Magna Carta for the modern administrative state, the APA is the main source of procedures that agencies must follow when they adopt legislative rules. Section 553 of the APA requires the agency to notify the public that it is considering a proposed rule, and to invite public comments. Only after reviewing the public comments can the agency issue a final rule, which is subject to judicial review to weed out any requirement that federal judges find to be "arbitrary and capricious." APA § 706(2)(A). Other procedural requirements might be deduced from the APA. For example, it is reasonable to conclude, from these requirements, that when the agency issues its final rule it must include an explanation of how the final rule reflects (or does not reflect) significant, substantive comments.

In addition to these generic requirements of APA § 553, the specific statute delegating authority to or otherwise directing the relevant agency sometimes imposes additional requirements before the agency can issue legislative rules. E.g., Consumer Products Safety Act Amendments of 1981, codified at 15 U.S.C. § 2058, which imposes new requirements before the Consumer Product Safety Commission (CPSC) issues regulations, including a major curtailment in the role of consumer groups and the accountability of the CPSC to such groups.

Section 553(c) prescribes more formal trial-type procedures "when rules are required by statute to be made on the record after opportunity for an agency hearing." Contrast this trial-type "formal" rulemaking with the notice-and-comment "informal" rulemaking that is the APA's default. The Supreme Court has construed this "on the record" requirement narrowly, however. In *United States v. Allegheny-Ludlum Steel Corp.*, 406 U.S. 742 (1972), and *United States v. Florida East Coast Railway Co.*, 410 U.S. 224 (1973), the Court ruled that statutes authorizing agency rules "after hearing" or after considering specified factors do *not* trigger the formal rulemaking procedures of § 553(c).

In the wake of *Allegheny-Ludlum* and *Florida East Coast Railway*, formal rulemaking based upon statute-specific directives has virtually disappeared—but agencies often operate under congressional directives to consider particular factors when they promulgate rules. As amended in 1966, the Interstate Commerce Act, construed in *Florida East Coast Railway*, required the ICC to "give consideration to the national level of ownership of such type of freight car and to other factors affecting the adequacy of the national freight car supply" in rate-setting proceedings. Federal laws authorizing legislative rulemaking in such disparate areas as auto safety and corporate regulation have similarly imposed substantive considerations for agency rulemaking, but these requirements do not trigger the more formal rulemaking process.

Other general statutes impose additional procedural requirements on agency rulemaking. For example, the Regulatory Flexibility Act of 1980, 5 U.S.C. § 601 *et seq.*, requires a "regulatory flexibility" analysis for agency action imposing significant costs on small businesses. The Unfunded Mandates Reform Act of 1995 (UMRA), 2 U.S.C. § 658 *et seq.*, requires agencies to disclose new costs its rules will impose on private parties or state/local governments and to consider alternatives to those "unfunded" costs. (UMRA also makes similar requirements of legislators proposing bills). The Congressional Review Act of 1995, 5 U.S.C. § 801, requires agencies to report new rules to Congress and prevents their taking effect for 60 days so that Congress can overturn them through a resolution that must be adopted by both chambers and presented to the President but is not subject to the Senate filibuster.

Experts believe the APA requirements strongly affect agency rulemaking but that these other statutory requirements usually do not. See Connor A. Raso, *Procedural Constraints on Agency Rulemaking* (Ph.D. Dissertation, Stanford University, Political Science Dep't, 2010). One statute that has had a strong effect on agency decisionmaking is the National Environmental Policy Act (NEPA), 1969, 42 U.S.C. § 4321 *et seq.*, which requires environmental impact statements (EIS) before federal projects can proceed. Agencies take NEPA's requirements very seriously; the process of securing an EIS is time-consuming and frequently educational.

2. *Requirements Imposed by Judicial Decisions.* Responding to concerns about "agency capture" by special interest groups, the D.C. Circuit considered procedural ways to open up legislative rulemaking, a process ostensibly halted by the Supreme Court in *Vermont Yankee Nuclear Power Co. v. Natural Resources Defense Council, Inc. (NRDC)*, 435 U.S. 519 (1978). See Gillian E. Metzger, *The Story of* Vermont Yankee*: A Cautionary Tale of Judicial Review and Nuclear Waste*, in *Administrative Law Stories* 124–67 (Peter L. Strauss ed., 2006) (excellent account, from which we liberally draw).

In 1971, Vermont Yankee applied to the Atomic Energy Commission for a license to operate a nuclear plant in Vernon, Vermont. The NRDC opposed the application, in part because of alleged environmental effects of operations to reprocess fuel or to dispose of waste resulting from these reprocessing operations. The environmental issue was excluded from consideration by the Licensing Board which conducted the adjudicatory hearing, but in 1972 the Commission itself began rulemaking proceedings on the issue of what consideration the Licensing Board should give to the environmental effects of the uranium fuel cycle. The Commission's notice set forth two possible rules. In 1973, the Commission scheduled a hearing on the alternative rules and made available to the public an Environmental Survey prepared by its staff. Both written and oral comments were received, and the Commission in 1974 issued a rule requiring consideration of such environmental impact. Although that rule was inconsistent with the practice of the Licensing Board in the Vermont Yankee proceeding, the Commission affirmed the grant of an operating license to Vermont Yankee. Although the Commission had followed all the § 553 procedures for informal rulemaking, the D.C. Circuit found the procedures inadequate overall and remanded for the agency to follow procedures permitting greater public scrutiny of information upon which the Commission relied.

The Supreme Court unanimously reversed. Justice Rehnquist's opinion for the Court criticized the D.C. Circuit's "Monday morning quarterbacking" of the agency's procedures. The Court ruled that § 553 of the APA "established the maximum procedural requirements which

Congress was willing to have the courts impose upon agencies in conducting rulemaking procedures." While "[t]his is not to say necessarily that there are no circumstances which would ever justify a court in overturning agency action because of a failure to employ procedures beyond those required by statute * * * such circumstances, if they exist, are extremely rare." Moreover, apart from the APA, "this Court has for more than four decades emphasized that the formulation of procedures was basically to be left within the discretion of the agencies to which Congress had confided the responsibility for substantive judgments." See also *Florida East Coast Railway* (an earlier opinion by Justice Rehnquist, rejecting lower court efforts to impose more formal processes than required by statute upon agency rulemakers).

Notwithstanding *Vermont Yankee*, federal courts of appeals have sometimes imposed procedural requirements on informal rulemaking— but under cover of liberally "interpreting" the notice-and-comment requirements of § 553, rather than imposing them as a matter of administrative common law. See *United States v. Nova Scotia Food Prods.,* 568 F.2d 240 (2d Cir. 1977), excerpted below; see generally Gary Lawson, *Federal Administrative Law* 240–83 (4th ed. 2007) (disapproving); Gillian E. Metzger, *Story of* Vermont Yankee (acquiescent).

3. *Requirements Imposed by the Agency or by Executive Order.* Just as the D.C. Circuit's procedural experiments were being repudiated within the judicial branch, the executive branch was imposing more aggressive procedural requirements onto agency rulemaking, through a series of presidential executive orders, culminating in Executive Order 12,866 (Sept. 30, 1993) (Appendix 5 to this coursebook). Section 1(a) generally requires agencies to perform a cost-benefit analysis to justify any rules they adopt; presumably, as a matter of procedure, this means that the agency must gather information, perhaps including expert information, about the costs and benefits of a proposed rule and then perform a written analysis justifying any costs the rule will impose. Section 1(b)(3) requires the agency to consider and assess alternative forms of regulation before adopting a particular rule. Section 1(b)(9) requires consultation with state, local, and tribal officials "[w]herever feasible" for any rule imposing burdens on those governmental bodies.

Section 6 is considerably more specific and is a departure from past practice. Section 6(a)(1) requires agencies, *before* notice of proposed rulemaking, to consult with "interested" parties, especially state, local, and tribal officials, who would benefit from or be burdened by the requirements of such proposed rule. Agencies are instructed to negotiate, where possible, with affected parties to produce a broadly acceptable rule.

For "significant regulatory actions," § 6(a)(3)(A) requires agencies to submit draft regulations and supporting cost-benefit analysis to the Office of Information and Regulatory Affairs (OIRA), which under § 6(b) will examine those regulations to determine whether the benefits of the rule justify its costs for society and other governmental units. OIRA is an office within the Office of Management and Budget that, in addition to its regulatory review responsibilities, plays an important role in coordinating and overseeing major rulemaking efforts. OIRA itself does not have veto power over proposed regulations that are not cost-justified, but it may return regulations to the agency with comments and objections. Ultimately, § 7 of the Executive Order vests with the President and the Vice President the power to decide what to do about the regulation if the agency and OIRA cannot resolve the matter.

B. SUBSTANTIVE REVIEW BY THE EXECUTIVE

"Hard look" review (i.e., close and often critical scrutiny) of agency rulemaking remains alive and well in the federal government—but such hard looks are most often conducted within the executive branch and not as often by federal judges. Much of this review is centralized within the White House, with input from more than a dozen organs working directly under the President, usually steps from the Oval Office. We provided an introduction to White House regulatory review in Chapter 2, § 2; in this chapter, we examine the actual operation of such review and its relationship to judicial review of agency rules.[7]

The process of White House regulatory review began immediately after the new public interest agencies (like the EPA) were created; the Office of Management and Budget (OMB) under Presidents Nixon, Ford, and Carter asked some agencies for cost-benefit justifications for their legislative rules. In a major initiative, President Ronald Reagan's Executive Order 12,291, 3 C.F.R. 127 (1981), required agencies to submit proposed rules and a cost-benefit analysis to OIRA. OIRA not only reviewed the rules, but also delayed rules that did not meet its cost-benefit specifications. During the Reagan and Bush 41 Administrations, OSHA and EPA were the main objects of OIRA's cost-cutting analyses. Presidents Clinton, Bush 43, and Obama have tweaked this Reagan-era policy in various ways but have also continued the practice of OIRA substantive review of proposed agency regulations. President Clinton's

---

[7] For useful scholarly examinations of White House/OMB regulatory review, see Jerry L. Mashaw, Richard A. Merrill & Peter M. Shane, *Administrative Law—The American Public Law System: Cases and Materials* 266–307 (6th ed. 2009); Steven P. Croley, *White House Review of Agency Rulemaking: An Empirical Investigation*, 70 U. Chi. L. Rev. 821 (2003); Elena Kagan, *Presidential Administration,* 114 Harv. L. Rev. 2245 (2001); Peter L. Strauss, *Presidential Rulemaking*, 72 Chi.–Kent L. Rev. 965 (1997); Cass R. Sunstein, *Commentary, The Office of Information and Regulatory Affairs: Myths and Realities*, 126 Harv. L. Rev. 1838 (2013).

Executive Order 12,866 (Sept. 30, 1993) (Appendix 5) is the governing directive today.

The substantive command of Executive Order 12,866 is that the costs imposed upon business and government by agency regulations must be justified by the regulatory benefits. Additionally, agencies are under a duty to consider regulatory approaches such as disclosure requirements that tend to be less expensive than command-and-control rules of the past. Dan Kahan has helpfully distinguished between a "gentle nudges" approach to regulation, like disclosure requirements and default rules, from a "hard shoves" approach, such as mandatory rules. See Dan M. Kahan, *Gentle Nudges vs. Hard Shoves: Solving the Sticky Norms Problem*, 67 U. Chi. L. Rev. 607 (2000). In the last thirty years, the White House has, across different administrations and political ideologies, stressed gentle nudges over hard shoves, and most agencies have responded accordingly.

OFFICE OF MANAGEMENT AND BUDGET CIRCULAR A–4 TO HEADS OF EXECUTIVE DEPARTMENTS AND ESTABLISHMENTS REGULATORY ANALYSIS

http://www.whitehouse.gov/omb/circulars_a004_a-4 (Sept. 17, 2003).

[This memorandum, generated by OIRA Administrator James Graham, was "designed to assist analysts in the regulatory agencies by defining good regulatory analysis * * * and standardizing the way benefits and costs of Federal regulatory actions are measured and reported," for purposes of Executive Order 12,866.]

The Need for Analysis of Proposed Regulatory Actions

Regulatory analysis is a tool regulatory agencies use to anticipate and evaluate the likely consequences of rules. It provides a formal way of organizing the evidence on the key effects, good and bad, of the various alternatives that should be considered in developing regulations. The motivation is to (1) learn if the benefits of an action are likely to justify the costs or (2) discover which of various possible alternatives would be the most cost-effective.

A good regulatory analysis is designed to inform the public and other parts of the Government (as well as the agency conducting the analysis) of the effects of alternative actions. Regulatory analysis sometimes will show that a proposed action is misguided, but it can also demonstrate that well-conceived actions are reasonable and justified.

Benefit-cost analysis is a primary tool used for regulatory analysis. Where all benefits and costs can be quantified and expressed in monetary units, benefit-cost analysis provides decision makers with a clear indication of the most efficient alternative, that is, the alternative that generates the largest net benefits to society (ignoring distributional effects). This is useful information for decision makers and the public to receive, even when economic efficiency is not the only or the overriding public policy objective.

It will not always be possible to express in monetary units all of the important benefits and costs. When it is not, the most efficient alternative will not necessarily be the one with the largest quantified and monetized net-benefit estimate. In such cases, you should exercise professional judgment in determining how important the non-quantified benefits or costs may be in the context of the overall analysis. If the non-quantified benefits and costs are likely to be important, you should carry out a "threshold" analysis to evaluate their significance. Threshold or "break-even" analysis answers the question, "How small could the value of the non-quantified benefits be (or how large would the value of the non-quantified costs need to be) before the rule would yield zero net benefits?" In addition to threshold analysis you should indicate, where possible, which non-quantified effects are most important and why.

Key Elements of a Regulatory Analysis

A good regulatory analysis should include the following three basic elements: (1) a statement of the need for the proposed action, (2) an examination of alternative approaches, and (3) an evaluation of the benefits and costs—quantitative and qualitative—of the proposed action and the main alternatives identified by the analysis.

To evaluate properly the benefits and costs of regulations and their alternatives, you will need to do the following:

- Explain how the actions required by the rule are linked to the expected benefits. For example, indicate how additional safety equipment will reduce safety risks. A similar analysis should be done for each of the alternatives.
- Identify a baseline. Benefits and costs are defined in comparison with a clearly stated alternative. This normally will be a "no action" baseline: what the world will be like if the proposed rule is not adopted. Comparisons to a "next best" alternative are also especially useful.
- Identify the expected undesirable side-effects and ancillary benefits of the proposed regulatory action and the alternatives. These should be added to the direct benefits and costs as appropriate. * * *

When there are important non-monetary values at stake, you should also identify them in your analysis so policymakers can compare them with the monetary benefits and costs. * * *

As you design, execute, and write your regulatory analysis, you should seek out the opinions of those who will be affected by the regulation as well as the views of those individuals and organizations who may not be affected but have special knowledge or insight into the regulatory issues. Consultation can be useful in ensuring that your analysis addresses all of the relevant issues and that you have access to all pertinent data. Early consultation can be especially helpful. * * *

The Need for Federal Regulatory Action

Before recommending Federal regulatory action, an agency must demonstrate that the proposed action is necessary. If the regulatory intervention results from a statutory or judicial directive, you should describe the specific authority for your action, the extent of discretion available to you, and the regulatory instruments you might use. Executive Order 12866 states that "Federal agencies should promulgate only such regulations as are required by law, are necessary to interpret the law, or are made necessary by compelling need, such as material failures of private markets to protect or improve the health and safety of the public, the environment, or the well being of the American people. . . ."

Executive Order 12866 also states that "Each agency shall identify the problem that it intends to address (including, where applicable, the failures of private markets or public institutions that warrant new agency action) as well as assess the significance of that problem." Thus, you should try to explain whether the action is intended to address a significant market failure or to meet some other compelling public need such as improving governmental processes or promoting intangible values such as distributional fairness or privacy. If the regulation is designed to correct a significant market failure, you should describe the failure both qualitatively and (where feasible) quantitatively. You should show that a government intervention is likely to do more good than harm. For other interventions, you should also provide a demonstration of compelling social purpose and the likelihood of effective action. Although intangible rationales do not need to be quantified, the analysis should present and evaluate the strengths and limitations of the relevant arguments for these intangible values.

Market Failure or Other Social Purpose

The major types of market failure include: externality, market power, and inadequate or asymmetric information. Correcting market failures is a reason for regulation, but it is not the only reason. Other possible justifications include improving the functioning of government, removing distributional unfairness, or promoting privacy and personal freedom.

1.   Externality, common property resource and public good

An externality occurs when one party's actions impose uncompensated benefits or costs on another party. Environmental problems are a classic case of externality. For example, the smoke from a factory may adversely affect the health of local residents while soiling the property in nearby neighborhoods. If bargaining were costless and all property rights were well defined, people would eliminate externalities through bargaining without the need for government regulation. From this perspective, externalities arise from high transactions costs and/or poorly defined property rights that prevent people from reaching efficient outcomes through market transactions.

Resources that may become congested or overused, such as fisheries or the broadcast spectrum, represent common property resources. "Public goods," such as defense or basic scientific research, are goods where provision of the good to some individuals cannot occur without providing the same level of benefits free of charge to other individuals.

2.   Market Power

Firms exercise market power when they reduce output below what would be offered in a competitive industry in order to obtain higher prices. They may exercise market power collectively or unilaterally. Government action can be a source of market power, such as when regulatory actions exclude low-cost imports. Generally, regulations that increase market power for selected entities should be avoided. However, there are some circumstances in which government may choose to validate a monopoly. If a market can be served at lowest cost only when production is limited to a single producer, * * * a natural monopoly is said to exist. In such cases, the government may choose to approve the monopoly and to regulate its prices and/or production decisions. Nevertheless, you should keep in mind that technological advances often affect economies of scale. This can, in turn, transform what was once considered a natural monopoly into a market where competition can flourish.

3.   Inadequate or Asymmetric Information

Market failures may also result from inadequate or asymmetric information. Because information, like other goods, is costly to produce and disseminate, your evaluation will need to do more than demonstrate the possible existence of incomplete or asymmetric information. Even though the market may supply less than the full amount of information, the amount it does supply may be reasonably adequate and therefore not require government regulation. Sellers have an incentive to provide information through advertising that can increase sales by highlighting distinctive characteristics of their products. Buyers may also obtain reasonably adequate information about product characteristics through other channels, such as a seller offering a warranty or a third party providing information.

Even when adequate information is available, people can make mistakes by processing it poorly. Poor information-processing often occurs in cases of low probability, high-consequence events, but it is not limited to such situations. For instance, people sometimes rely on mental rules-of-thumb that produce errors. If they have a clear mental image of an incident which makes it cognitively "available," they might overstate the probability that it will occur. Individuals sometimes process information in a biased manner, by being too optimistic or pessimistic, without taking sufficient account of the fact that the outcome is exceedingly unlikely to occur. When mistakes in information processing occur, markets may overreact. When it is time-consuming or costly for consumers to evaluate complex information about products or services (e.g., medical therapies), they may expect government to ensure that minimum quality standards are met. However, the mere possibility of poor information processing is not enough to justify regulation. If you think there is a problem of information processing that needs to be addressed, it should be carefully documented.

4.   Other Social Purposes

There are justifications for regulations in addition to correcting market failures. A regulation may be appropriate when you have a clearly identified measure that can make government operate more efficiently. In addition, Congress establishes some regulatory programs to redistribute resources to select groups. Such regulations should be examined to ensure that they are both effective and cost-effective. Congress also authorizes some regulations to prohibit discrimination that conflicts with generally accepted norms within our society. Rulemaking may also be appropriate to protect privacy, permit more personal freedom or promote other democratic aspirations.

Showing That Regulation at the Federal Level Is the Best Way to Solve the Problem

Even where a market failure clearly exists, you should consider other means of dealing with the failure before turning to Federal regulation. Alternatives to Federal regulation include antitrust enforcement, consumer-initiated litigation in the product liability system, or administrative compensation systems.

In assessing whether Federal regulation is the best solution, you should also consider the possibility of regulation at the State or local level. In some cases, the nature of the market failure may itself suggest the most appropriate governmental level of regulation. For example, problems that spill across State lines (such as acid rain whose precursors are transported widely in the atmosphere) are probably best addressed by

Federal regulation. More localized problems, including those that are common to many areas, may be more efficiently addressed locally.

The advantages of leaving regulatory issues to State and local authorities can be substantial. If public values and preferences differ by region, those differences can be reflected in varying State and local regulatory policies. Moreover, States and localities can serve as a testing ground for experimentation with alternative regulatory policies. One State can learn from another's experience while local jurisdictions may compete with each other to establish the best regulatory policies. You should examine the proper extent of State and local discretion in your rulemaking context.

A diversity of rules may generate gains for the public as governmental units compete with each other to serve the public, but duplicative regulations can also be costly. Where Federal regulation is clearly appropriate to address interstate commerce issues, you should try to examine whether it would be more efficient to retain or reduce State and local regulation. The local benefits of State regulation may not justify the national costs of a fragmented regulatory system. For example, the increased compliance costs for firms to meet different State and local regulations may exceed any advantages associated with the diversity of State and local regulation. Your analysis should consider the possibility of reducing as well as expanding State and local rulemaking.

The role of Federal regulation in facilitating U.S. participation in global markets should also be considered. Harmonization of U.S. and international rules may require a strong Federal regulatory role. Concerns that new U.S. rules could act as non-tariff barriers to imported goods should be evaluated carefully.

The Presumption Against Economic Regulation

Government actions can be unintentionally harmful, and even useful regulations can impede market efficiency. For this reason, there is a presumption against certain types of regulatory action. In light of both economic theory and actual experience, a particularly demanding burden of proof is required to demonstrate the need for any of the following types of regulations:

- price controls in competitive markets;
- production or sales quotas in competitive markets;
- mandatory uniform quality standards for goods or services if the potential problem can be adequately dealt with through voluntary standards or by disclosing information of the hazard to buyers or users; or
- controls on entry into employment or production, except (a) where indispensable to protect health and safety (e.g., FAA tests for commercial pilots) or (b) to manage the use of

common property resources (e.g., fisheries, airwaves, Federal lands, and offshore areas).

Alternative Regulatory Approaches

Once you have determined that Federal regulatory action is appropriate, you will need to consider alternative regulatory approaches. Ordinarily, you will be able to eliminate some alternatives through a preliminary analysis, leaving a manageable number of alternatives to be evaluated according to the formal principles of the Executive Order. The number and choice of alternatives selected for detailed analysis is a matter of judgment. There must be some balance between thoroughness and the practical limits on your analytical capacity. With this qualification in mind, you should nevertheless explore modifications of some or all of a regulation's attributes or provisions to identify appropriate alternatives. The following is a list of alternative regulatory actions that you should consider.

Different Choices Defined by Statute

When a statute establishes a specific regulatory requirement and the agency is considering a more stringent standard, you should examine the benefits and costs of reasonable alternatives that reflect the range of the agency's statutory discretion, including the specific statutory requirement. * * *

Different Enforcement Methods

Compliance alternatives for Federal, State, or local enforcement include on-site inspections, periodic reporting, and noncompliance penalties structured to provide the most appropriate incentives. When alternative monitoring and reporting methods vary in their benefits and costs, you should identify the most appropriate enforcement framework. For example, in some circumstances random monitoring or parametric monitoring will be less expensive and nearly as effective as continuous monitoring.

Different Degrees of Stringency

In general, both the benefits and costs associated with a regulation will increase with the level of stringency (although marginal costs generally increase with stringency, whereas marginal benefits may decrease). You should study alternative levels of stringency to understand more fully the relationship between stringency and the size and distribution of benefits and costs among different groups.

Different Requirements for Different Sized Firms

You should consider setting different requirements for large and small firms, basing the requirements on estimated differences in the expected costs of compliance or in the expected benefits. The balance of benefits and costs can shift depending on the size of the firms being regulated. Small firms may find it more costly to comply with regulation, especially if there are large fixed costs required for regulatory compliance. On the other hand, it is not efficient to place a heavier burden on one segment of a regulated industry solely because it can better afford the higher cost. This has the potential to load costs on the most productive firms, costs that are disproportionate to the damages they create. You should also remember that a rule with a significant impact on a substantial number of small entities will trigger the requirements set forth in the Regulatory Flexibility Act. (5 U.S.C. 603(c), 604).

Different Requirements for Different Geographic Regions

Rarely do all regions of the country benefit uniformly from government regulation. It is also unlikely that costs will be uniformly distributed across the country. Where there are significant regional variations in benefits and/or costs, you should consider the possibility of setting different requirements for the different regions.

Performance Standards Rather than Design Standards

Performance standards express requirements in terms of outcomes rather than specifying the means to those ends. They are generally superior to engineering or design standards because performance standards give the regulated parties the flexibility to achieve regulatory objectives in the most cost-effective way. In general, you should take into account both the cost savings to the regulated parties of the greater flexibility and the costs of assuring compliance through monitoring or some other means.

Market-Oriented Approaches Rather than Direct Controls

Market-oriented approaches that use economic incentives should be explored. These alternatives include fees, penalties, subsidies, marketable permits or offsets, changes in liability or property rights (including policies that alter the incentives of insurers and insured parties), and required bonds, insurance or warranties. One example of a market-oriented approach is a program that allows for averaging, banking, and/or trading (ABT) of credits for achieving additional emission reductions beyond the required air emission standards. ABT programs can be extremely valuable in reducing costs or achieving earlier or greater benefits, particularly when the costs of achieving compliance vary across production lines, facilities, or firms. ABT can be allowed on a plant-wide, firm-wide, or region-wide basis rather than vent by vent, provided this does not produce unacceptable local air quality outcomes (such as "hot spots" from local pollution concentration).

Informational Measures Rather than Regulation

If intervention is contemplated to address a market failure that arises from inadequate or asymmetric information, informational remedies will often be preferred. Measures to improve the availability of information include government establishment of a standardized testing and rating system (the use of which could be mandatory or voluntary), mandatory disclosure requirements (e.g., by advertising, labeling, or enclosures), and government provision of information (e.g., by government publications, telephone hotlines, or public interest broadcast announcements). A regulatory measure to improve the availability of information, particularly about the concealed characteristics of products, provides consumers a greater choice than a mandatory product standard or ban.

Specific informational measures should be evaluated in terms of their benefits and costs. Some effects of informational measures are easily overlooked. The costs of a mandatory disclosure requirement for a consumer product will include not only the cost of gathering and communicating the required information, but also the loss of net benefits of any information displaced by the mandated information. The other costs also may include the effect of providing information that is ignored or misinterpreted, and inefficiencies arising from the incentive that mandatory disclosure may give to overinvest in a particular characteristic of a product or service.

Where information on the benefits and costs of alternative informational measures is insufficient to provide a clear choice between them, you should consider the least intrusive informational alternative sufficient to accomplish the regulatory objective. To correct an informational market failure it may be sufficient for government to establish a standardized testing and rating system without mandating its use, because competing firms that score well according to the system should thereby have an incentive to publicize the fact.

PROBLEM 7–1: COST-BENEFIT EVALUATION OF THE DEPARTMENT OF JUSTICE'S IMPLEMENTATION OF THE PRISON RAPE ELIMINATION ACT OF 2003

Responding to the pervasive problem of rape within federal and state prisons, now housing more than two million persons, Congress unanimously enacted the Prison Rape Elimination Act of 2003 (PREA), Pub. L. No. 108–79, 117 Stat. 972 (Sept. 4, 2003), codified at 42 U.S.C. § 15601 *et seq.* Congress estimated that more than ten percent of the prison population is raped each year and sought to protect inmates against this harm. Section 7 of the law established a Commission to study the problem and make recommendations for reform. Section 8 directed the Attorney General to publish a final rule adopting "national standards for the detection, prevention, reduction, and punishment of prison rape * * * based upon the independent judgment of the Attorney General, after giving due consideration to the recommended national standards provided by the Commission * * * and being informed by such data, opinions, and proposals that the Attorney General determines to be appropriate to consider." 42 U.S.C. § 15607(a)(1)–(2). However, the standards may not "impose substantial additional costs compared to the costs presently expended by Federal, State, and local prison authorities." 42 U.S.C. § 15607(a)(3).

After notice of proposed rulemaking and a period for public comment, Attorney General Eric Holder promulgated a final rule on May 16, 2012: "National Standards to Prevent, Detect, and Respond to Prison Rape," 28 C.F.R. Part 115. The standards are binding on the Federal Bureau of Prisons, but are voluntary for state and local facilities. 42 U.S.C. § 15607(b). A state whose governor does not certify full compliance with the standards is subject to the loss of five percent of any Department of Justice grant funds that it would otherwise receive for prison purposes, unless the governor submits an assurance that such five percent will be used only to achieve and certify full compliance with the standards in future years. 42 U.S.C. § 15607(e)(2)(A)–(B).

The DOJ's standards are process-oriented rather than result- or performance-oriented. They require facilities to (1) designate a point person responsible for coordinating protective measures, (2) develop a plan to upgrade staffing and video monitoring to prevent and detect rape, (3) create special protections for juvenile inmates, (4) ban cross-gender searches, (5) implement special training protocols for staff, (6) establish a process for coordinating the actions of first responders, medical persons, and investigators involved in any given incident of prison rape, (7) implement policies to protect against any retaliation for reporting or cooperating in the investigation of prison rapes, (8) implement no-tolerance policies for inmates who commit rape and officials who approve such behaviors, and (9) provide lesbian, gay, bisexual, transgender, and intersex inmates as well as inmates with disabilities with protections against rape and sexual abuse because of their status.

The DOJ's final rule was accompanied by a detailed cost-benefit analysis, United States Dep't of Justice, Regulatory Impact Assessment for PREA Final Rule (May 17, 2012), available at http://www.ojp.usdoj.gov/programs/pdfs/prea_ria.pdf (viewed July 1, 2014). Skim that analysis, which is an example of the cost-benefit analysis contemplated in OMB Circular A–4. The Department estimated that full nationwide compliance with the final standards would cost confinement facilities approximately $468.5 million per year, when annualized over 15 years at a 7% discount rate, or 0.6% of total annual correctional expenditures in 2008. (Recall that full nationwide compliance is not likely, as the states have the option of not participating.) DOJ opined that this figure met the statutory requirement that rape reform costs not be "substantial."

The more difficult part of the analysis went to the benefits of the standards, if implemented. DOJ estimated from 2008 data that 209,400 persons (including 78,500 in prisons or jails) were raped or sexually assaulted in detention facilities each year. DOJ then estimated the monetizable benefit to an adult of *avoiding* the most severe category of prison sexual misconduct (nonconsensual sexual acts involving injury or force, or no injury or force but high incidence) to be about $310,000 per victim using the willingness to pay model (i.e., how much does society invest in preventing particular crimes) and $480,000 per victim using the victim compensation model (i.e., what amount of money would the victim "accept" in return for being raped). For juveniles, who typically experience significantly greater injury from sexual abuse than adults, DOJ valued the corresponding category as worth $675,000 per victim. The Department estimated that the cost to society for (and therefore the benefit of eliminating) prison rape each year is between $26.9 billion and $51.9 billion.

At the end of its impact analysis (pp. 157–63), the Department conducted a break-even analysis: How many prison rapes would the new standards have to eliminate each year to justify the estimated costs? (The analysis assumes full compliance at both state and federal level for both cost and benefit calculations.) DOJ concludes that if the regulations prevent between 25,000 and 35,000 rapes each year, they are cost-justified; preventing more rapes would obviously be an even better result. Based on this statute and the resulting cost-benefit analysis, consider the following questions:

(A) Monetization and Methodology. Focus on how the DOJ calculates the costs of the prison rape prevention standards and, especially, on the benefits of those standards. Is the DOJ analysis a rigorous application of the empirical methodology suggested by the cost-benefit executive orders and required by OMB's Circular A–4? Does the DOJ analysis suggest analytical problems with cost-benefit analysis as envisioned by the executive orders and the OMB circular? For one critical analysis, see Lisa Heinzerling, *Cost-Benefit Jumps the Shark: The Department of Justice's Economic Analysis of Prison Rape*, Georgetown Law Faculty Blog, June 13, 2012, http://gulcfac. typepad.com/georgetown_university_law/2012/06/cost-benefit-jumps-the-shark.html (viewed July 1, 2014). Jot down your own thoughts before you consult the Heinzerling analysis.

(B) Legitimacy and Statutory Purpose. PREA's stated purposes are very broad, and they include "establish[ing] a zero-tolerance standard for the incidence of prison rape in prisons in the United States" and "mak[ing] the prevention of prison rape a top priority in each prison system." PREA § 3(1)–(2), codified at 42 U.S.C. § 15602(1)–(2). Do the DOJ standards faithfully implement this purpose? More bluntly, is there any reason to believe that the DOJ standards will actually reduce the incidence of prison rape in the United States? Are there rape-prevention options that the DOJ did not consider, but should have?

(C) Reevaluation and Revision. Recall President Obama's Executive Order 13,563 (Appendix 5), directing executive agencies to review existing regulations to assure that they remain cost-effective. Assume that a new President takes office in January 2017, and that her first executive order is something like Executive Order 13,563. You are the DOJ's point person for

PREA and its regulations, so you must reevaluate its standards under a cost-benefit approach. Assume that (1) most state prison systems have implemented the DOJ standards, as has the federal Bureau of Prisons; (2) the prison system still incarcerates about two million persons, pretty much the same number of inmates as in 2003, when Congress enacted the statute, and as in 2012, when DOJ issued its regulations; and (3) the estimated number of prison rapes has increased by about ten percent since 2013, when federal prisons and most state prisons implemented the PREA standards. You are authorized to retain the RAND Corporation to help you figure out the cost-effectiveness of the PREA standards. What questions do you pose to RAND? (You can ask RAND to engage in empirical research, informed speculation from known facts, and policy analysis.)

C. SUBSTANTIVE JUDICIAL REVIEW OF AGENCY RULES

APA § 702 provides that "[a] person suffering a legal wrong because of agency action, or adversely affected or aggrieved by agency action within a meaning of a relevant statute, is entitled to judicial review thereof." The Supreme Court has construed this language to "embod[y] a basic presumption of judicial review," *Abbott Laboratories v. Gardner*, 387 U.S. 136, 140 (1967).

Judicial review of agency rules is quite different from OIRA and other forms of executive department review. To begin with, courts are reactive institutions: judges will only review rules if a person or institution actually injured by the rule files a lawsuit challenging the rule (Chapter 3, § 1 of this book). Even when there is an Article III case or controversy, however, judges will decline to review issues that are rendered unreviewable, either because the statute precludes review, § 701(a)(1), or because the issues are "committed to agency discretion by law," § 701(a)(2). For these reasons, many legislative rules are, in practice, not subject to judicial review.

When courts do examine those rules, the criteria for review are very different from those followed within the executive branch. Unless there is a statutory requirement to do so, judges will not review rules for cost-effectiveness or regulatory alternatives and will, instead, only review them for consistency with both substantive and procedural requirements of law. APA § 706(2)(A) provides that a reviewing court is supposed to invalidate agency action that is "arbitrary, capricious, an abuse of discretion, or otherwise not in accordance with law." What does this mean in the context of informal rulemaking? How wrong or misguided does an agency rule have to be for a court to strike it down as arbitrary etc.?

Finally, the process of judicial review is somewhat different from the OIRA process and other forms of executive branch review. Review within the executive branch is much more like a negotiation, where suggestions and resistance flow back and forth among administrative officials. Judicial review is more formal, like judicial review of trial court decisions. For example, judges focus on the "record" created by the agency and can only affirm the agency if its *stated* reasons pass muster; the Supreme Court has admonished federal judges that they cannot sustain agency action justified by "*post hoc* rationalizations." *SEC v. Chenery Corp.*, 318 U.S. 80 (1943). Timing is another distinction: OIRA review of an agency rule comes *before* the rule has been finalized and promulgated, while judicial review necessarily comes only *after* the rule has been finalized and promulgated. Hence, the remedy is different: OIRA's remedy is to delay or sometimes veto the issuance of a rule, while the court's remedy is to vacate the rule or (increasingly) to leave the rule in place and require the agency to reconsider the rule. See *NRDC v. EPA,* 489 F.3d 1250 (D.C. Cir. 2007) (circuit judges debate the appropriate remedy when disapproving an agency rule).

UNITED STATES V. NOVA SCOTIA FOOD PRODUCTS CORP.

United States Court of Appeals for the Second Circuit, 1977.
568 F.2d 240.

GURFEIN, CIRCUIT JUDGE.

[The Food and Drug Administration (FDA) found that hot smoked whitefish is "adulterated" under the Food, Drug and Cosmetics Act §§ 302(a) and 301(k), as well as 21 U.S.C. §§ 332(a) and 331(k), unless it is processed in accordance with time-temperature-salinity (T–T–S) regulations contained in 21 C.F.R. Part 122 (1977). The regulations required that hot-process smoked fish be heated by a controlled heat process that provides a monitoring system positioned in as many strategic locations in the oven as necessary. This monitoring system would assure a continuous temperature through each fish of not less than 180 degrees for a minimum of 30 minutes for fish that have been brined to contain 3.5% water phase salt, or at 150 degrees for a minimum of 30 minutes if the salinity was at 5%. Nova Scotia maintained that the regulation was invalid (1) because it was beyond the authority delegated by the statute; (2) because the FDA improperly relied upon undisclosed evidence in promulgating the regulation and because it is not supported by the administrative record; and (3) because there was no adequate statement setting forth the basis of the regulation.

[The hazard that the FDA sought to minimize was the outgrowth and toxin formation of spores of the bacteria which sometimes inhabit fish and which cause botulism in humans. After a notice-and-comment period, the FDA adopted an important suggestion tendered by the National Institute of Fisheries (NIF) but did not accept the NIF proposal that the standard be species-by-species rather than a single general standard. The Bureau of Commercial Fisheries of the Department of the Interior endorsed that idea and also objected to the general application of the T–T–S requirement on the ground that application of the regulation to all species of fish being smoked was not commercially feasible, and that the regulation should therefore specify time-temperature-salinity requirements, as developed by research and study, on a species-by-species basis. The Bureau suggested that "wholesomeness considerations could be more practically and adequately realized by reducing processing temperature and using suitable concentrations of nitrite and salt." The Commissioner took cognizance of the suggestion, but decided, nevertheless, to impose the T–T–S requirement on all species of fish (except chub, which were regulated by 21 C.F.R. 172.177 (1977) (dealing with food additives)). The Second Circuit found the regulation within the authority delegated by the statute, but invalidated it because of "serious inadequacies in the procedure followed in the promulgation of the regulation."]

[The FDA's Commissioner] did acknowledge, however, in his "basis and purpose" statement required by the APA, 5 U.S.C. § 553(c), that "adequate times, temperatures and salt concentrations have not been demonstrated for each individual species of fish presently smoked." 35 F.R. 17,401 (Nov. 13, 1970). The Commissioner concluded, nevertheless, that "the processing requirements of the proposed regulations are the safest now known to prevent the outgrowth and toxin formation of C. botulinum Type E." He determined that "the conditions of current good manufacturing practice for this industry should be established without further delay." Id.

The Commissioner did not answer the suggestion by the Bureau of Fisheries that nitrite and salt as additives could safely lower the high temperature otherwise required, a solution which the FDA had accepted in the case of chub. Nor did the Commissioner respond to the claim of Nova Scotia through its trade association, the Association of Smoked Fish Processors, Inc., Technical Center that "[t]he proposed process requirements suggested by the FDA for hot processed smoked fish are neither commercially feasible nor based on sound scientific evidence obtained with the variety of smoked fish products to be included under this regulation." * * *

[II] Appellants contend that there is an inadequate administrative record upon which to predicate judicial review, and that the failure to disclose to interested persons the factual material upon which the agency was relying vitiates the element of fairness which is essential to any kind of administrative action. Moreover, they argue that the "concise general statement of . . . basis and purpose" by the Commissioner was inadequate.

The question of what is an adequate "record" in informal rulemaking has engaged the attention of commentators for several years. The extent of the administrative record required for judicial review of informal rulemaking is largely a function of the scope of judicial review. Even when the standard of review is whether the promulgation of the rule was "arbitrary, capricious, an abuse of discretion, or otherwise not in accordance with law," as specified in 5 U.S.C. § 706(2)(A), judicial review must nevertheless, be based on the "whole record" (*id.*). Adequate review of a determination requires an adequate record, if the review is to be meaningful. What will constitute an adequate record for meaningful review may vary with the nature of the administrative action to be reviewed. Review must be based on the whole record even when the judgment is one of policy, except that findings of fact such as would be required in an adjudicatory proceeding or in a formal "on the record" hearing for rulemaking need not be made. Though the action was informal, without an evidentiary record, the review must be "thorough, probing, [and] in depth".

This raises several questions regarding the informal rulemaking procedure followed here: (1) What record does a reviewing court look to? (2) How much of what the agency relied on should have been disclosed to interested persons? (3) To what extent must the agency respond to criticism that is material?

[II.A]   With respect to the content of the administrative "record," the Supreme Court has told us that in informal rulemaking, "the focal point for judicial review should be the administrative record already in existence, not some new record made initially in the reviewing court." See *Camp v. Pitts*, 411 U.S. 138, 142 (1973).

No contemporaneous record was made or certified. When, during the enforcement action, the basis for the regulation was sought through pretrial discovery, the record was created by searching the files of the FDA and the memories of those who participated in the process of rulemaking. This resulted in what became Exhibit D at the trial of the injunction action. Exhibit D consists of (1) Tab A containing the comments received from outside parties during the administrative "notice-and-comment" proceeding and (2) Tabs B through L consisting of scientific data and the like upon which the Commissioner now says he relied but which were not made known to the interested parties.

Appellants object to the exclusion of evidence in the District Court "aimed directly at showing that the scientific evidence relied upon by the FDA was inaccurate and not based upon a realistic appraisal of the true facts. Appellants attempted to introduce scientific evidence to demonstrate that in fixing the processing parameters FDA relied upon tests in which ground fish were injected with many millions of botulism [sic] spores and then tested for outgrowth at various processing levels whereas the spore levels in nature are far less and outgrowth would have been prevented by far less stringent processing parameters." (Br. p. 33). The District Court properly excluded the evidence.

In an enforcement action, we must rely exclusively on the record made before the agency to determine the validity of the regulation. The exception to the exclusivity of that record is that "there may be independent judicial fact-finding when issues that were not before the agency are raised in a proceeding to *enforce* non-adjudicatory agency action." [*Citizens to Preserve Overton Park v. Volpe*, 401 U.S. 402, 415 (1971) (emphasis added by Judge Gurfein).]

Though this is an enforcement proceeding and the question is close, we think that the "issues" were fairly before the agency and hence that de novo evidence was properly excluded * * *. Our concern is, rather, with the manner in which the agency treated the issues tendered.

[II.B]   The key issues were (1) whether, in the light of the rather scant history of botulism in whitefish, that species should have been considered separately rather than included in a general regulation which failed to distinguish species from species; (2) whether the application of the proposed T–T–S requirements to smoked whitefish made the whitefish commercially unsaleable; and (3) whether the agency recognized that prospect, but nevertheless decided that the public health needs should prevail even if that meant commercial death for the whitefish industry. The procedural issues were whether, in the light of these key questions, the agency procedure was inadequate because (i) it failed to disclose to interested parties the scientific data and the methodology upon which it relied; and (ii) because it failed utterly to address itself to the pertinent question of commercial feasibility.

[**The History of Botulism in Whitefish**] The history of botulism occurrence in whitefish, as established in the trial record, which we must assume was available to the FDA in 1970, is as follows. Between 1899 and 1964 there were only eight cases of botulism reported as attributable to hot-smoked whitefish. In all eight instances, vacuum-packed whitefish was involved. All of the eight cases occurred in 1960 and 1963. The industry has abandoned vacuum-packing, and there has not been a single case of botulism associated with commercially prepared whitefish since 1963, though 2,750,000 pounds of whitefish are processed annually. Thus, in the seven-year period from 1964 through 1970, 17.25 million pounds of whitefish have been commercially processed in the United States without a single reported case of botulism. The evidence also disclosed that defendant Nova Scotia has been in business some 56 years, and that there has never been a case of botulism illness from the whitefish processed by it.

[**The Scientific Data**] Interested parties were not informed of the scientific data, or at least of a selection of such data deemed important by the agency, so that comments could be addressed to the data. Appellants argue that unless the scientific data relied upon by the agency are spread upon the public records, criticism of the methodology used or the meaning to be inferred from the data is rendered impossible.

We agree with appellants in this case, for although we recognize that an agency may resort to its own expertise outside the record in an informal rulemaking procedure, we do not believe that when the pertinent research material is readily available and the agency has no special expertise on the precise parameters involved, there is any reason to conceal the scientific data relied upon from the interested parties. As Judge Leventhal said in *Portland Cement Ass'n v. Ruckelshaus*, 486 F.2d 375, 393 ([D.C. Cir.] 1973): "It is not consonant with the purpose of a rulemaking proceeding to promulgate rules on the basis of inadequate data, or on data that [in] critical degree, is known only to the agency." This is not a case where the agency methodology was based on material supplied by the interested parties themselves. Cf. *International Harvester Co. v. Ruckelshaus*, 478 F.2d 615, 632 ([D.C. Cir.] 1973). Here all the scientific research was collected by the agency, and none of it was disclosed to interested parties as the material upon which the proposed rule would be fashioned. Nor was an articulate effort made to connect the scientific requirements to available technology that would make commercial survival possible, though the burden of proof was on the agency. This required it to "bear a burden of adducing a reasoned presentation supporting the reliability of its methodology." *International Harvester*.

Though a reviewing court will not match submission against counter-submission to decide whether the agency was correct in its conclusion on scientific matters (unless that conclusion is arbitrary), it will consider whether the agency has taken account of all "relevant factors and whether there has been a clear error of judgment." *Overton Park.* * * *

If the failure to notify interested persons of the scientific research upon which the agency was relying actually prevented the presentation of relevant comment, the agency may be held not to have considered all "the relevant factors." We can think of no sound reasons for secrecy or reluctance to expose to public view (with an exception for trade secrets or national security) the ingredients of the deliberative process. Indeed, the FDA's own regulations now specifically require that every notice of proposed rulemaking contain "references to all data and information on which the Commissioner relies for the proposal (copies or a full list of which shall be a part of the administrative file on the matter . . .)." 21 C.F.R. § 10.40(b) (1) (1977). And this is, undoubtedly, the trend. * * *

[II.C] Appellants additionally attack the "concise general statement" required by APA, 5 U.S.C. § 553, as inadequate. We think that, in the circumstances, it was less than adequate. It is not in keeping with the rational process to leave vital questions, raised by comments which are of cogent materiality, completely unanswered. The agencies certainly have a good deal of discretion in expressing the basis of a rule, but the agencies do not have quite the prerogative of obscurantism reserved to legislatures. "Congress did not purport to transfer its legislative power to the unbounded discretion of the regulatory body." *F.C.C. v. RCA Communications, Inc.*, 346 U.S. 86, 90 (1953) (Frankfurter, J.). * * *

The test of adequacy of the "concise general statement" was expressed by Judge McGowan in the following terms:

> "We do not expect the agency to discuss every item of fact or opinion included in the submissions made to it in informal rulemaking. We do expect that, if the judicial review which Congress has thought it important to provide is to be meaningful, the 'concise general statement of . . . basis and purpose' mandated by Section 4 will enable us to see what major issues of policy were ventilated by the informal proceedings and why the agency reacted to them as it did." *Automotive Parts & Accessories Ass'n v. Boyd*, 407 F.2d 330, 338 ([D.C. Cir.] 1968).

* * * The Secretary was squarely faced with the question whether it was necessary to formulate a rule with specific parameters that applied to all species of fish, and particularly whether lower temperatures with the addition of nitrite and salt would not be sufficient. Though this alternative was suggested by an agency of the federal government, its suggestion, though acknowledged, was never answered.

Moreover, the comment that to apply the proposed T–T–S requirements to whitefish would destroy the commercial product was neither discussed nor answered. We think that to sanction silence in the face of such vital questions would be to make the statutory requirement of a "concise general statement" less than an adequate safeguard against arbitrary decision-making. * * *

One may recognize that even commercial infeasibility cannot stand in the way of an overwhelming public interest. Yet the administrative process should disclose, at least, whether the proposed regulation is considered to be commercially feasible, or whether other considerations prevail even if commercial infeasibility is acknowledged. This kind of forthright disclosure and basic statement was lacking in the formulation of the T–T–S standard made applicable to whitefish. It is easy enough for an administrator to ban everything. In the regulation of food processing, the worldwide need for food also must be taken into account in formulating measures taken for the protection of health. In the light of the history of smoked whitefish to which we have referred, we find no articulate balancing here sufficient to make the procedure followed less than arbitrary.

[Judge Gurfein ruled the regulation invalid and suggested that the FDA review the T–T–S regulations in light of the scientific evidence and, if it still wanted to regulate this matter, promulgate a new notice for comment by interested parties.]

NOTES AND QUESTIONS ON AGENCY RECORDS FOR PURPOSES OF JUDICIAL REVIEW

1. *What Must Be Disclosed in the Agency "Record"?* According to APA § 553(b)(3), the notice of proposed rulemaking that appears in the Federal Register "shall include * * * either the terms or substance of the proposed rule or a description of the subjects and issues involved." After this notice, § 553(c) affords interested persons "an opportunity to participate in the rule making through submission of written data, views, or arguments." Notwithstanding the APA's failure to require inclusion of an evidentiary basis for proposed rules, reviewing courts have devoted considerable attention to the adequacy of informal rulemaking records pursuant to the Supreme Court's holding that under § 706, judicial review of agency action must be based on the "whole record" compiled by the agency. *Citizens to Preserve Overton Park v. Volpe*, 401 U.S. 402, 419 (1971).

Professors McMillan and Peterson identify five guidelines courts have followed for determining what constitutes a whole or complete record: (1) the record should include all documents the agency considers, not just those on which the agency relies; (2) the record should include all documents considered or relied on by agency personnel whose work and recommendations reached the agency decisionmaker; (3) bona fide confidential business information ordinarily need not be included in the record; (4) deliberative intra-agency memoranda and staff reports should ordinarily be excluded from the record, although a court may require their inclusion to supply a contemporaneous explanation for the decision if the agency has made no findings to explain its decision or its findings are incomplete; (5) materials that provide factual support for materials in the record need not be part of the record unless they were reviewed or considered by the agency personnel involved in the decision. Richard McMillan Jr. & Todd D. Peterson, *The Permissible Scope of Hearings, Discovery, and Additional Fact-Finding During Judicial Review of Informal Agency Action*, 1982 Duke L.J. 333, 341–43. Why do courts want the record to include documents *considered,* rather than simply *relied on,* by the agency?

2. *When Must Information Be Disclosed?* In *Nova Scotia*, the agency's failure occurred during the period before the FDA began soliciting comments. What are the agency's disclosure obligations with respect to information or data received during the comment period or after the period ends? Should the APA be interpreted to require the agency to disclose all new material by issuing an amended notice of proposed rulemaking setting a further period

for comments? Is it relevant whether the after-acquired information was generated by the agency itself or by a potentially affected party? If the latter, does it matter whether the information was produced at the party's initiative or in response to an agency request or invitation? Should it make a difference whether the information contributes genuinely new evidence as opposed to supporting or confirming data already in the record?

In *Rybacheck v. EPA*, 904 F.2d 1276 (9th Cir. 1990), the Ninth Circuit held that the agency could add 6,000 pages of "supporting documentation for a final rule in response to public comments," without providing notice and a chance for further comment. The court worried that a new notice requirement would unduly delay the rulemaking process. But in *Ober v. EPA*, 84 F.3d 304 (9th Cir. 1996), the Ninth Circuit ruled that the agency was required to notify commenters when the agency requested additional material from the state of Arizona after the time period for comments had closed and then relied on this additional information in its final plan. That the later information materially affected the EPA's final rules also distinguished this case from *Rybachek*.

3.   *Agency Responses to Criticism*. According to Judge McGowan, an agency is not "expect[ed] to discuss every item of fact or opinion included in the submissions made to it in informal rulemaking," but at the same time the statement should "enable [courts] to see what major issues of policy were ventilated by the informal proceedings and why the agency reacted to them as it did." *Automotive Parts & Accessories Ass'n v. Boyd*, 407 F.2d 330, 338 (D.C. Cir. 1968). In Judge Gurfein's words, "[i]t is not in keeping with the rational process to leave vital questions, raised by comments which are of cogent materiality, completely unanswered." *Nova Scotia*. How does an agency determine which questions raised by the comments are "vital," thus requiring a response? Once it has determined which questions are vital, how expansive must an agency be in discussing each question? Should the agency be obligated to dispel the criticism in full or simply say enough to show that it considered the comment?

Professor Fontana proposes that the APA require agencies to include as part of their general statement a "democratic participation statement (DPS) * * * indicat[ing] the number of relevant and non-repetitive comments received during rulemaking, and break[ing] down by category and by individual or institutional interest who precisely submitted these comments." Comments that are unresponsive or that duplicate other comments would not be counted. Courts would have jurisdiction to review the DPS (under a flexible standard) to make sure it is truthful. Fontana contends that the number of relevant and non-repetitive comments submitted should form the basis for determining whether the agency rule is entitled to special deference from a reviewing court. He recognizes various criticisms, but argues that individual counting of comments would be relatively objective while screening out repetitive comments would minimize the risks of agency capture from organized interest group campaigns. David Fontana, *Reforming the Administrative Procedure Act: Democracy Index Rulemaking*, 74 Fordham L. Rev. 81, 89–90, 99, 120–21 (2005). Does this proposal seem like an improvement on the current judicial review process? Does it adequately account for considerations of equality or for public choice-related concerns?

MOTOR VEHICLE MANUFACTURERS ASS'N v. STATE FARM MUTUAL AUTOMOBILE INS. CO.
Supreme Court of the United States, 1983.
463 U.S. 29, 103 S.Ct. 2856, 77 L. Ed. 2d 443.

JUSTICE WHITE delivered the opinion of the Court.

The development of the automobile gave Americans unprecedented freedom to travel, but exacted a high price for enhanced mobility. Since 1929, motor vehicles have been the leading cause of accidental deaths and injuries in the United States. * * * Congress responded by enacting the National Traffic and Motor Vehicle Safety Act of 1966. The Act, created for the purpose of "reduc[ing] traffic accidents and deaths and injuries to persons resulting from traffic accidents," 15 U.S.C. § 1381, directs the Secretary of Transportation or his delegate to issue motor vehicle safety standards that "shall be practicable, shall meet the need for motor vehicle safety, and shall be stated in objective terms." 15 U.S.C. § 1392(a). In issuing these standards, the Secretary is directed to consider "relevant available motor vehicle safety data," whether the proposed standard "is reasonable, practicable and appropriate" for the particular type of motor vehicle, and the "extent to which such standards will contribute to carrying out the purposes" of the Act. 15 U.S.C. § 1392(f)(1), (3), (4).

The Act also authorizes judicial review under the provisions of the Administrative Procedure Act (APA), 5 U.S.C. § 706, of all "orders establishing, amending, or revoking a Federal motor vehicle safety standard," 15 U.S.C. § 1392(b). Under this authority, we review today whether NHTSA acted arbitrarily and capriciously in revoking the requirement in Motor Vehicle Safety Standard 208 that new motor vehicles produced after September 1982 be equipped with passive restraints to protect the safety of the occupants of the vehicle in the event of a collision. Briefly summarized, we hold that the agency failed to present an adequate basis and explanation for rescinding the passive restraint requirement and that the agency must either consider the matter further or adhere to or amend Standard 208 along lines which its analysis supports.

[I] * * * As originally issued by the Department of Transportation in 1967, Standard 208 simply required the installation of seatbelts in all automobiles. 32 Fed.Reg. 2408, 2415 (Feb. 3, 1967). It soon became apparent that the level of seatbelt use was too low to reduce traffic injuries to an acceptable level. The Department therefore began consideration of "passive occupant restraint systems"—devices that do not depend for their effectiveness upon any action taken by the occupant except that necessary to operate the vehicle. Two types of automatic crash protection emerged: automatic seatbelts and airbags. The automatic seatbelt is a traditional safety belt, which when fastened to the interior of the door remains attached without impeding entry or exit from the vehicle, and deploys automatically without any action on the part of the passenger. The airbag is an inflatable device concealed in the dashboard and steering column. It automatically inflates when a sensor indicates that deceleration forces from an accident have exceeded a preset minimum, then rapidly deflates to dissipate those forces. The life-saving potential of these devices was immediately recognized, and in 1977, after substantial on-the-road experience with both devices, it was estimated by NHTSA that passive restraints could prevent approximately 12,000 deaths and over 100,000 serious injuries annually. 42 Fed.Reg. 34,298.

In 1969, the Department formally proposed a standard requiring the installation of passive restraints, 34 Fed.Reg. 11,148 (July 2, 1969), thereby commencing a lengthy series of proceedings. In 1970, the agency revised Standard 208 to include passive protection requirements, 35 Fed.Reg. 16,927 (Nov. 3, 1970), and in 1972, the agency amended the standard to require full passive protection for all front seat occupants of vehicles manufactured after August 15, 1975. 37 Fed.Reg. 3911 (Feb. 24, 1972). In the interim, vehicles built between August 1973 and August 1975 were to carry either passive restraints or lap and shoulder belts coupled with an "ignition interlock" that would prevent starting the vehicle if the belts were not connected. On review, the agency's decision to require passive restraints was found to be supported by "substantial evidence" and upheld. *Chrysler Corp. v. Dep't of Transportation*, 472 F.2d 659 ([6th Cir.] 1972).

In preparing for the upcoming model year, most car makers chose the "ignition interlock" option, a decision which was highly unpopular, and led Congress to amend the Act to prohibit a motor vehicle safety standard from requiring or permitting compliance by means of an ignition interlock or a continuous buzzer designed to indicate that safety belts were not in use. Motor Vehicle and Schoolbus Safety Amendments of 1974, Pub. L. 93–492, § 109, 88 Stat. 1482, 15 U.S.C. § 1410b(b). The 1974 Amendments also provided that any safety standard that could be satisfied by a system other than seatbelts would have to be submitted to Congress where it could be vetoed by concurrent resolution of both houses. 15 U.S.C. § 1410b(b)(2).

The effective date for mandatory passive restraint systems was extended for a year until August 31, 1976. 40 Fed.Reg. 16,217 (April 10, 1975); *id.*, at 33,977 (Aug. 13, 1975). But in June 1976, Secretary of Transportation William T. Coleman, Jr., initiated a new rulemaking on the issue, 41 Fed.Reg. 24,070 (June 9, 1976). After hearing testimony and reviewing written comments, Coleman extended the optional alternatives indefinitely and suspended the passive restraint requirement. Although he found passive restraints technologically and economically feasible, the Secretary based his decision on the expectation that there would be widespread public resistance to the new systems. He instead proposed a demonstration project involving up to 500,000 cars installed with passive restraints, in order to smooth the way for public acceptance of mandatory passive restraints at a later date. Department of Transportation, The Secretary's Decision Concerning Motor Vehicle Occupant Crash Protection (December 6, 1976).

Coleman's successor as Secretary of Transportation disagreed. Within months of assuming office, Secretary Brock Adams decided that the demonstration project was unnecessary. He issued a new mandatory passive restraint regulation, known as Modified Standard 208. 42 Fed.Reg. 34,289 (July 5, 1977); 42 CFR § 571.208 (1977). The Modified Standard mandated the phasing in of passive restraints beginning with large cars in model year 1982 and extending to all cars by model year 1984. The two principal systems that would satisfy the Standard were airbags and passive belts [i.e., seatbelts that operated automatically and therefore did not require the passenger's affirmative action]; the choice of which system to install was left to the manufacturers. In *Pacific Legal Foundation v. Dep't of Transportation*, 593 F.2d 1338 ([D.C. Cir.]), *cert. denied*, 444 U.S. 830 (1979), the Court of Appeals upheld Modified Standard 208 as a rational, nonarbitrary regulation consistent with the agency's mandate under the Act. The standard also survived scrutiny by Congress, which did not exercise its authority under the legislative veto provision of the 1974 Amendments.

Over the next several years, the automobile industry geared up to comply with Modified Standard 208. As late as July, 1980, NHTSA reported:

"On the road experience in thousands of vehicles equipped with airbags and automatic safety belts has confirmed agency estimates of the life-saving and injury-preventing benefits of such systems. When all cars are equipped with automatic crash protection systems, each year an estimated 9,000 more lives will be saved and tens of thousands of serious injuries will be prevented."

NHTSA, Automobile Occupant Crash Protection, Progress Report No. 3, p. 4. In February 1981, however, Secretary of Transportation Andrew Lewis reopened the rulemaking due to changed economic circumstances and, in particular, the difficulties of the automobile industry. 46 Fed.Reg. 12,033 (Feb. 12, 1981). Two months later, the agency ordered a one-year delay in the application of the standard to large cars, extending the deadline to September 1982, 46 Fed.Reg. 21,172 (April 9, 1981) and at the same time, proposed the possible rescission of the entire standard. 46 Fed.Reg. 21,205 (April 9, 1981). After receiving written comments and holding public hearings, NHTSA issued a final rule (Notice 25) that rescinded the passive restraint requirement contained in Modified Standard 208.

[II] In a statement explaining the rescission, NHTSA maintained that it was no longer able to find, as it had in 1977, that the automatic restraint requirement would produce significant safety benefits. Notice 25, 46 Fed.Reg. 53,419 (Oct. 29, 1981). This judgment reflected not a change of opinion on the effectiveness of the technology, but a change in plans by the automobile industry. In 1977, the agency had assumed that airbags would be installed in 60% of all new cars and automatic seatbelts in 40%. By 1981 it became apparent that automobile manufacturers planned to install the automatic seatbelts in approximately 99% of the new cars. For this reason, the life-saving potential of airbags would not be realized. Moreover, it now appeared that the overwhelming majority of passive belts planned to be installed by manufacturers could be detached easily and left that way permanently.[8] Passive belts, once detached, then required "the same type of affirmative action that is the stumbling block to obtaining high usage levels of manual belts." 46 Fed.Reg., at 53421. For this reason, the agency concluded that there was no longer a basis for reliably predicting that the standard would lead to any significant increased usage of restraints at all.

In view of the possibly minimal safety benefits, the automatic restraint requirement no longer was reasonable or practicable in the agency's view. The requirement would require approximately $1 billion to implement and the agency did not believe it would be reasonable to impose such substantial costs on manufacturers and consumers without more adequate assurance that sufficient safety benefits would accrue. In addition, NHTSA concluded that automatic restraints might have an adverse effect on the public's attitude toward safety. Given the high expense and limited benefits of detachable belts, NHTSA feared that many consumers would regard the standard as an instance of ineffective regulation, adversely affecting the public's view of safety regulation and, in particular, "poisoning popular sentiment toward efforts to improve occupant restraint systems in the future." 46 Fed.Reg., at 53424.

[The United States Court of Appeals for the District of Columbia Circuit invalidated the agency's rule rescinding the passive restraint

---

[8]   [Eds.] There are three kinds of seatbelts: (1) manual seatbelts that require the passenger to make an affirmative effort to buckle up; (2) automatic seatbelts (also called "passive restraints") that operate automatically but can be detached by the passenger and thereby transformed into manual seatbelts; and (3) automatic seatbelts that cannot be detached by the passenger. Secretary Lewis concluded that seatbelts in category (2) are no more effective in ensuring passenger safety than those in category (1), and so it was not cost-effective for the agency to impose those extra costs on the auto industry.

requirement, on the ground that it was arbitrary and capricious and therefore in violation of the APA. 680 F.2d 206 (1982).] * * *

[In Part III, the Court held that the APA fully applied to NHTSA's rulemaking proceeding, and that a reviewing court has an obligation to set aside any rule found to be "arbitrary, capricious, an abuse of discretion, or otherwise not in accordance with law." 5 U.S.C. § 706(2)(A). The Court rejected Motor Vehicle's argument that an agency's rescission of a rule should be governed by the same narrow standard as the agency's refusal to issue a rule in the first place.]

[Justice White explained the "arbitrary and capricious" standard of review.] [T]he agency must examine the relevant data and articulate a satisfactory explanation for its action including a "rational connection between the facts found and the choice made." *Burlington Truck Lines Inc. v. United States*, 371 U.S. 156, 168 (1962). In reviewing that explanation, we must "consider whether the decision was based on a consideration of the relevant factors and whether there has been a clear error of judgment." *Bowman Transp. Inc. v. Arkansas-Best Freight System*, [419 U.S. 281, 285 (1974)]. Normally, an agency rule would be arbitrary and capricious if the agency has relied on factors which Congress has not intended it to consider, entirely failed to consider an important aspect of the problem, offered an explanation for its decision that runs counter to the evidence before the agency, or is so implausible that it could not be ascribed to a difference in view or the product of agency expertise. The reviewing court should not attempt itself to make up for such deficiencies: "We may not supply a reasoned basis for the agency's action that the agency itself has not given." * * * For purposes of these cases, it is also relevant that Congress required a record of the rulemaking proceedings to be compiled and submitted to a reviewing court, 15 U.S.C. § 1394, and intended that agency findings under the Motor Vehicle Safety Act would be supported by "substantial evidence on the record considered as a whole." S.Rep. No. 1301, 89th Cong., 2d Sess. 8 (1966); H.R.Rep. No. 1776, 89th Cong., 2d Sess. 21 (1966).

[In Part IV, Justice White rejected the lower court's requirement that NHTSA was obligated to provide "increasingly clear and convincing reasons" for its action. The Court of Appeals relied on post-1974 congressional signals (such as Congress's failure to override the Carter-era NHTSA initiatives) to infer a "congressional commitment to the concept of automatic crash protection devices for vehicle occupants." Justice White found the lower court's reading of the materials misguided. Also, "this Court has never suggested that the *standard* of review is enlarged or diminished by subsequent congressional action. While an agency's interpretation of a statute may be confirmed or ratified by subsequent congressional failure to change that interpretation, in the cases before us, even an unequivocal ratification—short of statutory incorporation—of the passive restraint standard would not connote approval or disapproval of an agency's later decision to rescind the regulation. That decision remains subject to the arbitrary and capricious standard."] * * *

[V] The ultimate question before us is whether NHTSA's rescission of the passive restraint requirement of Standard 208 was arbitrary and capricious. We conclude, as did the Court of Appeals, that it was. We also conclude, but for somewhat different reasons, that further consideration of the issue by the agency is therefore required. * * *

[V.A]   The first and most obvious reason for finding the rescission arbitrary and capricious is that NHTSA apparently gave no consideration whatever to modifying the Standard to require that airbag technology be utilized. Standard 208 sought to achieve automatic crash protection by requiring automobile manufacturers to install either of two passive restraint devices: airbags or automatic seatbelts. There was no suggestion in the long rulemaking process that led to Standard 208 that if only one of these options were feasible, no passive restraint standard should be promulgated. Indeed, the agency's original proposed Standard contemplated the installation of inflatable restraints in all cars. Automatic belts were added as a means of complying with the standard because they were believed to be as effective as airbags in achieving the goal of occupant crash protection. 36 Fed.Reg. 12,858, 12,859 (July 8, 1971). At that time, the passive belt approved by the agency could not be detached. Only later, at a manufacturer's behest, did the agency approve of the detachability feature—and only after assurances that the feature would not compromise the safety benefits of the restraint. Although it was then foreseen that 60% of the new cars would contain airbags and 40% would have automatic seatbelts, the ratio between the two was not significant as long as the passive belt would also assure greater passenger safety.

The agency has now determined that the detachable automatic belts will not attain anticipated safety benefits because so many individuals will detach the mechanism. Even if this conclusion were acceptable in its entirety, standing alone it would not justify any more than an amendment of Standard 208 to disallow compliance by means of the one technology which will not provide effective passenger protection. It does not cast doubt on the need for a passive restraint standard or upon the efficacy of airbag technology. In its most recent rulemaking, the agency again acknowledged the lifesaving potential of the airbag:

> "The agency has no basis at this time for changing its earlier conclusions in 1976 and 1977 that basic airbag technology is sound and has been sufficiently demonstrated to be effective in those vehicles in current use. . . ."

NHTSA Final Regulatory Impact Analysis (RIA) at XI–4 [(Oct. 1981)]. Given the effectiveness ascribed to airbag technology by the agency, the mandate of the Act to achieve traffic safety would suggest that the logical response to the faults of detachable seatbelts would be to require the installation of airbags. At the very least this alternative way of achieving the objectives of the Act should have been addressed and adequate reasons given for its abandonment. But the agency not only did not require compliance through airbags, it also did not even consider the possibility in its 1981 rulemaking. Not one sentence of its rulemaking statement discusses the airbags-only option. * * * [W]hat we said in *Burlington Truck Lines v. United States* is apropos here:

> "There are no findings and no analysis here to justify the choice made, no indication of the basis on which the [agency] exercised its expert discretion. We are not prepared to and the Administrative Procedure Act will not permit us to accept such . . . practice. . . . Expert discretion is the lifeblood of the administrative process, but 'unless we make the requirements for administrative action strict and demanding, *expertise*, the strength of modern government, can become a monster which rules with no practical limits on its discretion.' *New York v. United States*, 342 U.S. 882, 884 (1951)."

We have frequently reiterated that an agency must cogently explain why it has exercised its discretion in a given manner, and we reaffirm this principle again today.

The automobile industry has opted for the passive belt over the airbag, but surely it is not enough that the regulated industry has eschewed a given safety device. For nearly a decade, the automobile industry waged the regulatory equivalent of war against the airbag and lost—the inflatable restraint was proved sufficiently effective. Now the automobile industry has decided to employ a seatbelt system which will not meet the safety objectives of Standard 208. This hardly constitutes cause to revoke the Standard itself. Indeed, the Motor Vehicle Safety Act was necessary because the industry was not sufficiently responsive to safety concerns. The Act intended that safety standards not depend on current technology and could be "technology-forcing" in the sense of inducing the development of superior safety design. If, under the statute, the agency should not defer to the industry's failure to develop safer cars, which it surely should not do, *a fortiori* it may not revoke a safety standard which can be satisfied by current technology simply because the industry has opted for an ineffective seatbelt design. * * *

[In Part V.B, Justice White ruled that NHTSA was "too quick to dismiss the safety benefits of automatic seatbelts." Although an agency may decline to issue and may revoke a safety standard on the basis of "serious uncertainties" about its efficacy, those uncertainties must be supported in the administrative record and reasonably explained. In this case, there was no direct evidence in the record supporting NHTSA's finding that detachable automatic belts cannot be predicted to substantially increase in usage. Evidence in the record revealed more than a doubling of seat belt use under those circumstances. For one example, Volkswagen between 1975 and 1980 sold 350,000 Rabbits equipped with passive seatbelts guarded by an ignition interlock. NHTSA found that seatbelt use in Rabbits averaged 34% where the cars had regular manual belts, and 84% for the detachable passive belts. Although Justice White maintained that the agency had discretion to refuse to generalize from studies of Rabbit drivers to the general population of drivers, the agency was required to consider a fact that it neglected but that critically distinguishes detachable automatic belts and ordinary manual ones: a detachable passive belt requires an affirmative act to detach it, while a manual belt can be simply ignored. "Thus, inertia—a factor which the agency's own studies have found significant in explaining the current low usage rates for seatbelts—works in *favor* of, not *against*, use of the protective device." This would suggest that seatbelt use by occasional users would be substantially increased by detachable passive belts. "Whether this is in fact the case is a matter for the agency to decide, but it must bring its expertise to bear on the question."]

The agency is correct to look at the costs as well as the benefits of Standard 208. The agency's conclusion that the incremental costs of the requirements were no longer reasonable was predicated on its prediction that the safety benefits of the regulation might be minimal. Specifically, the agency's fears that the public may resent paying more for the automatic belt systems is expressly dependent on the assumption that detachable automatic belts will not produce more than "negligible safety benefits." 46 Fed.Reg., at 53,424. When the agency reexamines its findings as to the likely increase in seatbelt usage, it must also reconsider its judgment of the reasonableness of the monetary and other costs associated with the Standard. In reaching its judgment, NHTSA should bear in mind that Congress intended safety to be the preeminent factor under the Motor Vehicle Safety Act. [Quoting committee reports for the Safety Act.] * * *

JUSTICE REHNQUIST, with whom THE CHIEF JUSTICE [BURGER], JUSTICE POWELL, and JUSTICE O'CONNOR join, concurring in part and dissenting in part.

I join Parts I, II, III, IV, and V–A of the Court's opinion. In particular, I agree that, since the airbag and continuous spool automatic seatbelt were explicitly approved in the standard the agency was rescinding, the agency should explain why it declined to leave those requirements intact. In this case, the agency gave no explanation at all.

Of course, if the agency can provide a rational explanation, it may adhere to its decision to rescind the entire standard.

I do not believe, however, that NHTSA's view of detachable automatic seatbelts was arbitrary and capricious. The agency adequately explained its decision to rescind the standard insofar as it was satisfied by detachable belts.

The statute that requires the Secretary of Transportation to issue motor vehicle safety standards also requires that "[e]ach such . . . standard shall be practicable [and] shall meet the need for motor vehicle safety." 15 U.S.C. § 1392(a). The Court rejects the agency's explanation for its conclusion that there is substantial uncertainty whether requiring installation of detachable automatic belts would substantially increase seatbelt usage. The agency chose not to rely on a study showing a substantial increase in seatbelt usage in cars equipped with automatic seatbelts and an ignition interlock to prevent the car from being operated when the belts were not in place *and* which were voluntarily purchased with this equipment by consumers. It is reasonable for the agency to decide that this study does not support any conclusion concerning the effect of automatic seatbelts that are installed in all cars whether the consumer wants them or not and are not linked to an ignition interlock system.

The Court rejects this explanation because "there would seem to be grounds to believe that seatbelt use by occasional users will be substantially increased by the detachable passive belts," and the agency did not adequately explain its rejection of these grounds. It seems to me that the agency's explanation, while by no means a model, is adequate. The agency acknowledged that there would probably be some increase in belt usage, but concluded that the increase would be small and not worth the cost of mandatory detachable automatic belts. 46 F.R. 53421–54323 (1981). The agency's obligation is to articulate a " 'rational connection between the facts found and the choice made.' " I believe it has met this standard. * * *

The agency's changed view of the standard seems to be related to the election of a new President of a different political party. It is readily apparent that the responsible members of one administration may consider public resistance and uncertainties to be more important than do their counterparts in a previous administration. A change in administration brought about by the people casting their votes is a perfectly reasonable basis for an executive agency's reappraisal of the costs and benefits of its programs and regulations. As long as the agency remains within the bounds established by Congress, it is entitled to assess administrative records and evaluate priorities in light of the philosophy of the administration.

NOTES AND QUESTIONS ON STATE FARM AND ARBITRARY AND CAPRICIOUS REVIEW

Did the Court do the right thing in this case—as a matter of law? As a matter of good governance? Write down your answer in the margin, and read on.

1. *What Is the Proper Role of the Judiciary in the Implementation of Public Policy?* In reviewing agency rulemaking, what do you think the role of the federal judiciary should be: (1) Agent of Congress? If so, which Congress—the enacting one, the amending one, or the current one? (2) Independent principal, imposing the court's own values, thwarting agencies implementing bad policies, and rewarding agencies that protect the court's conception of the public interest? (3) Independent principal, imposing rule of law values? If so, what does the rule of law require in *State Farm*?

Both Justice White and Justice Rehnquist present themselves as enforcing the rule of law found in APA § 706(2)(A), but what does the "arbitrary and capricious" standard of review require in this case? Justice Rehnquist argues that it requires more explanation from the agency. Justice White argues that it *also* requires the agency to make a judgment that is consistent with both logic and with the evidence brought to the agency's attention by the public commenters. This is a harder look at the agency's decision than Justice Rehnquist would have required. Which view is more consistent with the APA? Was Judge Gurfein's scrutiny in *Nova Scotia* consistent with the Court's approach? In other words, if the agency relied on new scientific studies to reject regulatory alternatives, would the *State Farm* Court have required the agency to provide fresh notice of these studies, so objecting interested parties could comment?

Notice, however, that all nine Justices (as well as the Second Circuit judges in *Nova Scotia*) agreed that (1) the agency could alter the safety regulation to take into account changed circumstances, (2) including a new political philosophy represented by the Reagan Administration, but (3) needed to explain, with reference to objective evidence, why the new circumstances justified the new rule. Although the Supreme Court has never addressed the matter, the D.C. Circuit has made the same point regarding the influence of Members of Congress on agency rulemaking: the agency can consult with Members of Congress and consider their views, but the agency cannot rely on current congressional preferences and must announce (instead) a sound fact-based justification tied to the statutory purposes. See *Aera Energy LLC v. Salazar*, 642 F.3d 212, 220–23 (D.C. Cir. 2011) (summarizing the cases).

2. *Does the Participation of the Judiciary in the Statutory Implementation Process Advance the Public Interest?* Step back and evaluate the role of APA judicial review in the evolution of the statutory scheme. Does the (moderately) hard look review reflected in Justice White's opinion for the Court protect the statutory scheme against agency backsliding? (This is the perspective of those supporting hard look review.) Or does it impose an undue

burden on agency experimentation or measured deregulation? (This is the perspective of those who fear that hard look review contributes to ossification of agency action.)

Mashaw and Harfst, in *Struggle for Auto Safety*, doubt that the Court performs a useful role, on balance. The judiciary is the forum of choice whenever the government tries to upset traditional ways of doing things (ways easily translated into "vested rights"). Thus, the courts were a natural forum for the auto industry to harass the agency and delay implementation of its rules. The proceduralization of the rulemaking process rendered it less decisive and more vulnerable to shifts in public opinion and presidential leadership. According to Mashaw and Harfst, adverse judicial decisions in the 1970s directly contributed to agency paralysis and contributed less directly to an increasingly cautious attitude toward regulation by agency officials. Judges demanded "objective" testing standards for auto regulation that prevented the sort of experimentation and technology-forcing rules that the early experts thought necessary to reduce auto injuries and fatalities.

More generally, the adverse judicial decisions discouraged NHTSA from proceeding by rulemaking, which had been the agency's original mandate and was probably its only hope for regulatory success. Favorable judicial decisions in response to NHTSA's recall campaigns, on the other hand, encouraged the agency to rely more and more heavily on that less effective regulatory mechanism. Like a Pavlovian dog, NHTSA was trained by the judiciary to quail at the thought of rules and salivate at the prospect of recalls. So officials recalled millions of cars but issued only a handful of new rules and standards.

Mashaw and Harfst are pessimistic about the role of the "legal culture" and of multiple principals in our administrative state of separated powers. "[T]he combination of congressional oversight and appropriations, Executive Office intervention and monitoring, and judicial review, has sharply limited the degree to which NHTSA could translate [its regulatory] aspirations into concrete technological requirements." Mashaw & Harfst, *Auto Safety*, 228. Do you find this level of pessimism persuasive? Arguing to the contrary is Kevin McDonald, *Shifting Out of Park: Moving Auto Safety from Recalls to Reason* (2006), who maintains that judicial review has prevented the agency from engaging in excessive regulation and has not driven it toward what McDonald agrees is the wasteful recall strategy, which from early on has been the NHSTA's primary regulatory device.

Which account makes the most sense to you? What would you expect to be the consequence of the Court's remand in *State Farm*? Jot down your initial thoughts in the margin, and then read the next note.

3.   *The Aftermath of* State Farm. Transportation Secretary Elizabeth Dole initiated rulemaking to answer the Court's inquiries, and 7,800 comments were filed. On July 17, 1984, Dole issued the final rule, which (1) dropped mandatory airbags like a lead balloon and (2) required phasing in "automatic occupant restraints" (including airbags as an option for the

manufacturer) between 1986 and 1989, unless (3) before April 1, 1989, two-thirds of the U.S. population are covered by state mandatory seat belt use laws meeting NHTSA's conditions. 49 Fed. Reg. 28,962–63 (1984).

By endorsing state mandatory seat belt laws as the preferred form of regulation, the agency seemed to revert to the old command-and-control regime that had been ineffective and to retreat from the proven-to-be-effective mandatory-redesign regime. State Farm challenged this rule, but the D.C. Circuit held the lawsuit premature. *State Farm Mutual Automobile Ins. Co. v. Dole*, 802 F.2d 474 (D.C. Cir. 1986).

With the support of the auto industry as well as new groups such as Mothers Against Drunk Driving (MADD), almost all the states adopted mandatory seatbelt laws—but most were careful *not* to satisfy the requirements of the Dole rule. "As a consequence, the American public got both airbags and mandatory use laws." Jerry L. Mashaw, *The Story of* Motor Vehicles Manufacturers Association v. State Farm Insurance Co.: *Law, Science, and Politics in the Administrative State*, in *Administrative Law Stories* 385 (Peter L. Strauss ed. 2006). Perhaps surprisingly, *both* kinds of regulations captured the imagination of Americans. We the People started buckling up in record numbers *and* demanded more airbags from manufacturers than the law required.

The 1984 Dole Regulation was superseded by the Intermodal Transportation Efficiency Act of 1991, which required all new cars to have airbags, starting no later than the 1998 model year. The Department of Transportation has implemented the law through a revised regulation, which lays out a detailed set of requirements for airbags in various kinds of vehicles. 49 C.F.R. § 571.208 (2012). So automobiles sold in the United States in the new millennium will generally have both airbags that automatically inflate in the event of an accident *and* seat belts that every state now requires drivers and at least front-seat passengers to use.

Looking back on more than a generation of expensive federal regulation of auto safety, Kevin McDonald argues that the government's focus on passive standards has reduced occupant fatality risk by about 15–20%, which he argues is not an impressive amount given the tens of billions of dollars in cost and the much greater traffic safety achieved in Canada, Europe, and Australia, which focus on seat belts and prophylactic rules to reduce driver errors. See McDonald, *Shifting Out of Park*, 18–19; Leonard Evans, *Traffic Safety* 117 (2004). Indeed, he maintains that, in the United States, reducing the speed limit has had greater safety effects than all the design changes posed by the NHTSA. McDonald, *Shifting Out of Park,* 42 n.65. Under President Obama's Executive Order 13,563, should the Department of Transportation reconsider the costly approach represented by Standard 208 and focus instead on the regulatory strategy suggested by McDonald?

Business Roundtable v. Securities and Exchange Commission
647 F.3d 1144 (D.C. Cir. 2011).

The proxy process is the means by which shareholders of a publicly traded corporation elect the company's board of directors. Typically, incumbent directors nominate a candidate for each vacancy. Before the annual meeting where officers are elected, the company puts information about each nominee in the set of "proxy materials"—a proxy voting card and a proxy statement—it distributes to all shareholders. Almost all shareholders who participate will vote by proxy. A shareholder who wishes to nominate a different candidate may separately file his own proxy statement and solicit votes from shareholders, thereby initiating a "proxy contest."

The SEC's Rule 14a–11 provided shareholders an alternative path for nominating and electing directors. Facilitating Shareholder Director Nominations, 74 Fed. Reg. 29,024, 29,025–26 (2009). Finding that the proxy process is too heavily weighted in favor of incumbent management, the SEC after notice and comment issued a rule that required a company subject to the Securities Exchange Act proxy rules to include in its proxy materials "the name of a person or persons nominated by a [qualifying] shareholder or group of shareholders for election to the board of directors." *Id.* at 56,682–83. Business Roundtable and other institutions challenged this rule as inconsistent with the APA and with the governing statute.

Writing for the D.C. Circuit, **Judge Douglas Ginsburg** set forth the APA requirements as interpreted in *State Farm* and added that, under the Exchange Act, "the Commission has a unique obligation to consider the effect of a new rule upon 'efficiency, competition, and capital formation,' 15 U.S.C. §§ 78c(f), 78w(a)(2), 80a–2(c), and its failure to 'apprise itself—and hence the public and the Congress—of the economic consequences of a proposed regulation' makes promulgation of the rule arbitrary and capricious and not in accordance with law. [*Chamber of Commerce v. SEC,* 412 F.2d 133, 144 (D.C. Cir. 2005).]" Under these criteria, Judge Ginsburg invalidated Rule 14a–11 as arbitrary, because "the Commission inconsistently and opportunistically framed the costs and benefits of the rule; failed adequately to quantify the certain costs or to explain why those costs could not be quantified; neglected to support its predictive judgments; contradicted itself; and failed to respond to substantial problems raised by commenters."

The Commission predicted Rule 14a–11 would lead to "[d]irect cost savings" for shareholders in part due to "reduced printing and postage costs" and reduced expenditures for advertising compared to those of a "traditional" proxy contest. The Commission also found that the rule "will mitigate collective action and free-rider concerns," which can discourage a shareholder from exercising his right to nominate a director in a traditional proxy contest. Because more dissident nominees would be offered and more would be chosen by the shareholders, the SEC found that the rule "has the potential of creating the benefit of improved board performance and enhanced shareholder value." "The Commission anticipated the rule would also impose costs upon companies and shareholders related to 'the preparation of required disclosure, printing and mailing . . ., and [to] additional solicitations,' and could have 'adverse effects on company and board performance,' for example, by distracting management." The Commission nonetheless concluded the rule would promote the "efficiency of the economy on the whole," and the benefits of the rule would "justify the costs" of the rule.

Judge Ginsburg agreed with the challengers that the SEC underestimated the costs of Rule 14a–11. The Commission acknowledged that "company boards may be motivated by the issues at stake to expend significant resources to challenge shareholder director nominees" but concluded that a company's solicitation and campaign costs "may be limited by two factors." First, "to the extent that the directors' fiduciary duties prevent them from using corporate funds to resist shareholder director nominations for no good-faith corporate purpose," they may decide "simply [to] include the shareholder director nominees . . . in the company's proxy materials." Second, the "requisite ownership threshold and holding period" would "limit the number of shareholder director nominations that a board may receive, consider, and possibly contest."

The challengers objected that "the Commission failed to appreciate the intensity with which issuers would oppose nominees and arbitrarily dismissed the probability that directors would conclude their fiduciary duties required them to support their own nominees. The [challengers] also argue it was arbitrary for the Commission not to estimate the costs of solicitation and campaigning that companies would incur to oppose candidates nominated by shareholders, which costs commenters expected to be quite large. The Chamber of Commerce submitted a comment predicting boards would incur substantial expenditures opposing shareholder nominees through 'significant media and public relations efforts, advertising . . . , mass mailings, and other communication efforts, as well as the hiring of outside advisors and the expenditure of significant time and effort by the company's employees.' It pointed out that in recent proxy contests at larger companies costs 'ranged from $14 million to $4 million' and at smaller companies 'from $3 million to $800,000.' In its brief the Commission maintains it did consider the commenters' estimates of the costs, but reasonably explained why those costs 'may prove less than these estimates.'

"We agree with the [challengers] that the Commission's prediction [that] directors might choose not to oppose shareholder nominees had no basis beyond mere speculation. Although it is possible that a board, consistent with its fiduciary duties, might forgo expending resources to oppose a shareholder nominee—for example, if it believes the cost of opposition would exceed the cost to the company of the board's preferred candidate losing the election, discounted by the probability of that happening—the Commission has presented no evidence that such forbearance is ever seen in practice. To the contrary, the American Bar Association Committee on Federal Regulation of Securities commented:

> If the [shareholder] nominee is determined [by the board] not to be as appropriate a candidate as those to be nominated by the board's independent nominating committee . . . , then the board will be compelled by its fiduciary duty to make an appropriate effort to oppose the nominee, as boards now do in traditional proxy contests. Letter from Jeffrey W. Rubin, Chair, Comm. on Fed. Regulation of Secs., Am. Bar Ass'n, to SEC 35 (August 31, 2009).

"The Commission's second point, that the required minimum amount and duration of share ownership will limit the number of directors nominated under the new rule, is a reason to expect election contests to be infrequent; it says nothing about the amount a company will spend on solicitation and campaign costs when there is a contested election. Although the Commission acknowledged that companies may expend resources to oppose shareholder nominees, it did nothing to estimate and quantify the costs it expected companies to incur; nor did it claim estimating those costs was not possible, for empirical evidence about expenditures in traditional proxy contests was readily available. Because the agency failed to 'make tough choices about which of the competing estimates is most plausible, [or] to hazard a guess as to which is correct,' we believe it neglected its statutory obligation to assess the economic consequences of its rule."

Judge Ginsburg also agreed with the challengers that the SEC overestimated the expected benefits of Rule 14a–11. As to the agency's prediction that the rule would trigger the election of more directors sponsored by dissidents and that this kind of corporate democracy would benefit shareholders, "the Commission acknowledged the numerous studies submitted by commenters that reached the opposite result. One commenter, for example, submitted an empirical study showing that 'when dissident directors win board seats, those firms underperform peers by 19 to 40% over the two years following the proxy contest.' Elaine Buckberg, NERA Econ. Consulting, & Jonathan Macey, Yale Law School, Report on Effects of Proposed SEC Rule 14a–11 on Efficiency, Competitiveness and Capital Formation 9 (2009). The Commission completely discounted those studies 'because of questions raised by subsequent studies, limitations acknowledged by the studies' authors, or [its] own concerns about the studies' methodology or scope.'

"The Commission instead relied exclusively and heavily upon two relatively unpersuasive studies, one concerning the effect of 'hybrid boards' (which include some dissident directors) and the other concerning the effect of proxy contests in general, upon shareholder value. [74 Fed. Reg.] at 56,762 & n. 921 (citing Chris Cernich et al., IRRC Inst. for Corporate Responsibility, Effectiveness of Hybrid Boards (May 2009), and J. Harold Mulherin & Annette B. Poulsen, *Proxy Contests & Corporate Change: Implications for Shareholder Wealth*, 47 J. Fin. Econ. 279 (1998)). Indeed, the Commission 'recognize[d] the limitations of the Cernich (2009) study,' and noted 'its long-term findings on shareholder value creation are difficult to interpret.' In view of the admittedly (and at best) 'mixed' empirical evidence, we think the Commission has not sufficiently supported its conclusion that increasing the potential for election of directors nominated by shareholders will result in improved board and company performance and shareholder value."

The challengers also maintained that the SEC acted arbitrarily and capriciously by "entirely fail[ing] to consider an important aspect of the problem," *State Farm:* namely, how union and state pension funds might use Rule 14a–11. Commenters objected that these employee benefit funds would impose costs upon companies by using Rule 14a–11 as leverage to gain concessions, such as additional benefits for unionized employees, unrelated to shareholder value. The Commission claimed that it did consider this problem when it concluded that "the totality of the evidence and economic theory" both indicate the rule "has the potential of creating the benefit of improved board performance and enhanced shareholder value." Thus, "companies could be negatively affected if shareholders use the new rules to promote their narrow interests at the expense of other shareholders," but the Commission reasoned that these potential costs "may be limited" because the ownership and holding requirements would "allow the use of the rule by only holders who demonstrated a significant, long-term commitment to the company," and who would therefore be less likely to act in a way that would diminish shareholder value. The SEC concluded that costs may be limited because other shareholders may be alerted, through the disclosure requirements, "to the narrow interests of the nominating shareholder." But the challengers argued that the SEC failed to respond to the costs companies would incur even when a shareholder nominee is not ultimately elected: a board might succumb to the demands of a special interest shareholder threatening to nominate a director. Judge Ginsburg ruled: "The Commission did not completely ignore these potential costs, but neither did it adequately address them."

"Notwithstanding the ownership and holding requirements, there is good reason to believe institutional investors with special interests will be able to use the rule and, as more than one commenter noted, 'public and union pension funds' are the institutional investors 'most likely to make use of proxy access.' Nonetheless, the Commission failed to respond to comments arguing that investors with a special interest, such as unions and state and local governments whose interests in jobs may well be greater than their interest in share value, can be expected to pursue self-interested objectives rather than the goal of maximizing shareholder value, and will likely cause companies to incur costs even when their nominee is unlikely to be elected. [Citing Business Roundtable's Comments and Leo E. Strine, Jr., *Toward a True Corporate Republic: A Traditionalist Response to Bebchuk's Solution for Improving Corporate America*, 119 Harv. L. Rev. 1759, 1765 (2006).] By ducking serious evaluation of the costs that could be imposed upon companies from use of the rule by shareholders representing special interests, particularly union and government pension funds, we think the Commission acted arbitrarily."

Judge Ginsburg also found that the SEC's proposed rule arbitrarily included investment companies, without adequate supporting evidence. The Court vacated Rule 14a–11 as arbitrary and capricious.

NOTES AND QUESTIONS ON BUSINESS ROUNDTABLE

Does Judge Ginsburg's opinion go beyond arbitrariness review under *State Farm* and venture into policymaking by the D.C. Circuit? According to critics, Judge Ginsburg's opinion created "empirical" difficulties for the SEC's rule that had not been briefed by the parties and that provided a misleading account of what independent "empirical" studies suggested. See Bruce R. Kraus & Connor Raso, *Rational Boundaries to SEC Cost-Benefit Analysis*, 30 Yale J. Reg. 289, 314–17 (2013). For example, the NERA study relied on by Judge Ginsburg was not an independent empirical analysis, but rather one commissioned by the Business Roundtable. According to Kraus and Raso, a number of independent empirical studies, not cited by Judge Ginsburg, supported the SEC.

Does the securities statute justify the level of judicial scrutiny here? Did the SEC follow the statutory mandate to "consider" the effect of a new rule upon "efficiency, competition, and capital formation"? Has Judge Ginsburg transformed the statutory "consideration" mandate into a "requirement" mandate, so that any SEC must now show the D.C. Circuit that the rule would have a positive net effect on "efficiency, competition, and capital formation"? Note that the D.C. Circuit has not applied this level of scrutiny in non-corporate cases. E.g., *Association of Private Sector Colleges and Universities v. Duncan*, 681 F.3d 427 (D.C. Cir. 2012).

The SEC did not appeal its loss in *Business Roundtable* to the Supreme Court. Why not? If you were the Solicitor General, who must approve and handle any such appeal, would you seek Supreme Court review? Why or why not?

Judge Ginsburg was the OIRA Administrator during part of the Reagan Administration. Does his opinion in *Business Roundtable* look more like OIRA review than *State Farm* judicial review? Because it is an "independent" agency, the SEC is not subject to OIRA review (as of 2014)—but in response to *Business Roundtable* the SEC has revamped its rulemaking process to incorporate the agency's highly credentialed economics experts into the rulemaking process and to add new economics Ph.Ds. to its staff; in a 2012 Guidance the agency adopted rules for cost-benefit analysis that are similar to those followed by executive agencies subject to OIRA review. See Kraus & Raso, *Rational Boundaries*, 325–36; Catherine M. Sharkey, State Farm *"With Teeth": Heightened Judicial Review in the Absence of Executive Oversight*, 90 N.Y.U. L. Rev. (forthcoming 2014) (arguing that courts should give a stronger form of hard look review when the agency is independent or the policy in question was not reviewed by OIRA). Does this process suggest value to Judge Ginsburg's opinion?

2. ADMINISTRATIVE ADJUDICATION

Adjudication is the "agency process for the formulation of an order," and orders are like judicial decisions, for they constitute the "final disposition" of a controversy involving the statutory or agency rules. 5 U.S.C. § 551(6)–(7). As noted in the introduction to this chapter, adjudications can be either formal or informal.

The procedure for *formal adjudications* is similar to trial in a court. If the enabling statute calls for decision "on the record after opportunity for agency hearing," APA §§ 554(a), 556(a); *Chemical Waste Management, Inc. v. EPA*, 873 F.2d 1477 (D.C. Cir. 1989), the agency must not only provide particularized notice to the affected person, but it must also allow him or her "to present his [or her] case or defense by oral or documentary evidence, to submit rebuttal evidence, and to conduct such cross-examination as may be required for a full and true disclosure of facts." § 556(d). The agency's decision must be based on the trial-type record and supported by reliable, probative, and substantial evidence. § 557. APA §§ 554 and 556–557 mandate at least a partial separation of functions between the prosecutorial staff and agency decisionmakers, particularly in formal adjudications. For example, formal adjudications are usually handled by *administrative law judges*, who have their own staff and are monitored and rewarded by the Office of Personnel Management and not by the agency itself. Therefore, these administrative law judges will not be beholden to the agency whose interests may ultimately be at stake.

What process is required for *informal adjudications,* where there is no statutory requirement for a decision on the record after opportunity for a formal agency hearing? The agency has a great deal of discretion in constructing procedures for such orders, see *Chemical Waste Management,* but some minimal process is mandatory when the government engages in informal adjudications that affect people's liberties or their entitlements to government benefits. In *Goldberg v. Kelly*, 397 U.S. 254 (1970), the Supreme Court interpreted the Due Process Clause to require notice, a right to be heard in person and to cross-examine witnesses, a right to be represented by counsel, and a reasoned decision by an impartial decisionmaker, before the government can deprive a person of "property." *Goldberg* involved the state's termination of welfare benefits, which the Court held to be "property" triggering due process protections. Under *Goldberg*, some of the procedural requirements of APA §§ 556–557 are also applicable to many less formal governmental decisions, including decisions that involve governmental entitlements. Part A of this section will explore the implications of *Goldberg*.

Many agencies, such as the National Labor Relations Board (NLRB) and the Federal Communications Commission (FCC), are authorized by statute to proceed through either rulemaking or adjudication. Agencies have a great deal of discretion as to how they might proceed; courts have been loathe to overturn an agency decision based solely upon the mode of proceeding—but the mode of proceeding may have important legal consequences for what relief the agency might grant and how broadly its policy pronouncements might be. Part B will consider these issues through a case study involving the FCC's mixed history of rulemaking and adjudication with regard to the issue of "profane" or "indecent" expletives on broadcast television.

Finally, agency orders, like agency rules, are subject to judicial review under the criteria in APA § 706(2), including the "arbitrary and capriciousness" standard of § 706(2)(A). Part C will consider whether the FCC's justifications for its new policy regarding "fleeting expletives" satisfied § 706(2)(A). The Supreme Court decision rejecting the APA challenge to the FCC's action is an important application, and clarification, of the *State Farm* interpretation of § 706(2)(A), especially as applied to agency shifts in policy.

A. DUE PROCESS CLAUSE REQUIREMENTS

The Due Process Clauses of the Fifth Amendment (applicable to the federal government) and the Fourteenth Amendment (applicable to the states) provide that "persons" cannot be "deprived of life, liberty, or property, without due process of law." Any time the government takes away our liberty or property, it must provide at least minimal procedures.

Goldberg v. Kelly, 397 U.S. 254 (1970), held that asserted "entitlements" to an income stream of government benefits (specifically, welfare benefits in that case) are "property" whose termination triggers the protections of the Due Process Clauses. Additionally, *Goldberg* held that most of the procedures required by the APA for formal adjudications are constitutionally required for many informal adjudications and benefit terminations. Consider the leading case applying, and narrowing, *Goldberg*.

F. DAVID MATHEWS V. GEORGE H. ELDRIDGE

United States Supreme Court, 1976.
424 U.S. 319, 96 S.Ct. 893.

MR. JUSTICE POWELL delivered the opinion of the Court.

The issue in this case is whether the Due Process Clause of the Fifth Amendment requires that prior to the termination of Social Security disability benefit payments the recipient be afforded an opportunity for an evidentiary hearing.

[I]   Cash benefits are provided to workers during periods in which they are completely disabled under the disability insurance benefits program created by the 1956 amendments to Title II of the Social Security Act. 70 Stat. 815, 42 U.S.C. § 423. Respondent Eldridge was first awarded benefits in June 1968. In March 1972, he received a questionnaire from the state agency charged with monitoring his medical condition. Eldridge completed the questionnaire, indicating that his condition had not improved and identifying the medical sources, including physicians, from whom he had received treatment recently. The state agency then obtained reports from his physician and a psychiatric consultant. After considering these reports and other information in his file the agency informed Eldridge by letter that it had made a tentative determination that his disability had ceased in May 1972. The letter included a statement of reasons for the proposed termination of benefits, and advised Eldridge that he might request reasonable time in which to obtain and submit additional information pertaining to his condition.

In his written response, Eldridge disputed one characterization of his medical condition and indicated that the agency already had enough evidence to establish his disability.[2] The state agency then made its final determination that he had ceased to be disabled in May 1972. This

---

[2]   Eldridge originally was disabled due to chronic anxiety and back strain. He subsequently was found to have diabetes. The tentative determination letter indicated that aid would be terminated because available medical evidence indicated that his diabetes was under control, that there existed no limitations on his back movements which would impose severe functional restrictions, and that he no longer suffered emotional problems that would preclude him from all work for which he was qualified. App. 12–13. In his reply letter he claimed to have arthritis of the spine rather than a strained back.

determination was accepted by the Social Security Administration (SSA), which notified Eldridge in July that his benefits would terminate after that month. The notification also advised him of his right to seek reconsideration by the state agency of this initial determination within six months.

Instead of requesting reconsideration Eldridge commenced this action challenging the constitutional validity of the administrative procedures established by the Secretary of Health, Education, and Welfare (HEW) for assessing whether there exists a continuing disability. [Reasoning from *Goldberg v. Kelly*, the district court agreed with Eldridge and ruled that the Due Process Clause required a pre-termination (of benefits) evidentiary hearing. Specifically, HEW (now Health and Human Services) could not terminate Eldridge's benefits until after he had an opportunity to appear, in person, before an impartial decisionmaker and to confront the evidence against him.]

[III.A] Procedural due process imposes constraints on governmental decisions which deprive individuals of "liberty" or "property" interests within the meaning of the Due Process Clause of the Fifth or Fourteenth Amendment. The Secretary does not contend that procedural due process is inapplicable to terminations of Social Security disability benefits. He recognizes, as has been implicit in our prior decisions, that the interest of an individual in continued receipt of these benefits is a statutorily created "property" interest protected by the Fifth Amendment. Rather, the Secretary contends that the existing administrative procedures, detailed below, provide all the process that is constitutionally due before a recipient can be deprived of that interest.

This Court consistently has held that some form of hearing is required before an individual is finally deprived of a property interest. The "right to be heard before being condemned to suffer grievous loss of any kind, even though it may not involve the stigma and hardships of a criminal conviction, is a principle basic to our society." *Joint Anti-Fascist Comm. v. McGrath*, 341 U.S. 123, 168 (1951) (Frankfurter, J., concurring). The fundamental requirement of due process is the opportunity to be heard "at a meaningful time and in a meaningful manner." *Armstrong v. Manzo*, 380 U.S. 545, 552 (1965). Eldridge agrees that the review procedures available to a claimant before the initial determination of ineligibility becomes final would be adequate if disability benefits were not terminated until after the evidentiary hearing stage of the administrative process. The dispute centers upon what process is due prior to the initial termination of benefits, pending review.

In recent years this Court increasingly has had occasion to consider the extent to which due process requires an evidentiary hearing prior to the deprivation of some type of property interest even if such a hearing is provided thereafter. In only one case, *Goldberg v. Kelly*, has the Court held that a hearing closely approximating a judicial trial is necessary. In other cases requiring some type of pretermination hearing as a matter of constitutional right the Court has spoken sparingly about the requisite procedures. * * *

These decisions underscore the truism that " '[d]ue process,' unlike some legal rules, is not a technical conception with a fixed content unrelated to time, place and circumstances." *Cafeteria Workers v. McElroy*, 367 U.S. 886, 895 (1961). "[D]ue process is flexible and calls for such procedural protections as the particular situation demands." *Morrissey v. Brewer*, 408 U.S. 471, 481 (1972). Accordingly, resolution of the issue whether the administrative procedures provided here are constitutionally sufficient requires analysis of the governmental and private interests that are affected. More precisely, our prior decisions indicate that identification of the specific dictates of due process generally requires consideration of three distinct factors: First, the private interest that will be affected by the official action; second, the risk of an erroneous deprivation of such interest through the procedures used, and the probable value, if any, of additional or substitute procedural safeguards; and finally, the Government's interest, including the function involved and the fiscal and administrative burdens that the additional or substitute procedural requirement would entail. See, e.g., *Goldberg v. Kelly*.

We turn first to a description of the procedures for the termination of Social Security disability benefits and thereafter consider the factors bearing upon the constitutional adequacy of these procedures.

[III.B]   The disability insurance program is administered jointly by state and federal agencies. State agencies make the initial determination whether a disability exists, when it began, and when it ceased. 42 U.S.C. § 421(a). The standards applied and the procedures followed are prescribed by the Secretary, see § 421(b), who has delegated his responsibilities and powers under the Act to the SSA. See 40 Fed. Reg. 4473 (1975).

In order to establish initial and continued entitlement to disability benefits a worker must demonstrate that he is unable

"to engage in any substantial gainful activity by reason of any medically determinable physical or mental impairment which can be expected to result in death or which has lasted or can be expected to last for a continuous period of not less than 12 months. . . ." 42 U.S.C. § 423(d)(1)(A).

To satisfy this test the worker bears a continuing burden of showing, by means of "medically acceptable clinical and laboratory diagnostic techniques," § 423(d)(3), that he has a physical or mental impairment of such severity that

> "he is not only unable to do his previous work but cannot, considering his age, education, and work experience, engage in any other kind of substantial gainful work which exists in the national economy, regardless of whether such work exists in the immediate area in which he lives, or whether a specific job vacancy exists for him, or whether he would be hired if he applied for work." § 423(d)(2)(A).

The principal reasons for benefits terminations are that the worker is no longer disabled or has returned to work. As Eldridge's benefits were terminated because he was determined to be no longer disabled, we consider only the sufficiency of the procedures involved in such cases.

The continuing-eligibility investigation is made by a state agency acting through a "team" consisting of a physician and a nonmedical person trained in disability evaluation. The agency periodically communicates with the disabled worker, usually by mail in which case he is sent a detailed questionnaire or by telephone, and requests information concerning his present condition, including current medical restrictions and sources of treatment, and any additional information that he considers relevant to his continued entitlement to benefits. CM § 6705.1; Disability Insurance State Manual (DISM) § 353.3 (TL No. 137, Mar. 5, 1975).

Information regarding the recipient's current condition is also obtained from his sources of medical treatment. DISM § 353.4. If there is a conflict between the information provided by the beneficiary and that obtained from medical sources such as his physician, or between two sources of treatment, the agency may arrange for an examination by an independent consulting physician. *Ibid.* Whenever the agency's tentative assessment of the beneficiary's condition differs from his own assessment, the beneficiary is informed that benefits may be terminated, provided a summary of the evidence upon which the proposed determination to terminate is based, and afforded an opportunity to review the medical reports and other evidence in his case file. He also may respond in writing and submit additional evidence. Id., § 353.6.

The state agency then makes its final determination, which is reviewed by an examiner in the SSA Bureau of Disability Insurance. 42 U.S.C. § 421(c); CM §§ 6701(b), (c). If, as is usually the case, the SSA accepts the agency determination it notifies the recipient in writing, informing him of the reasons for the decision, and of his right to seek de novo reconsideration by the state agency. 20 CFR §§ 404.907, 404.909 (1975). Upon acceptance by the SSA, benefits are terminated effective two months after the month in which medical recovery is found to have occurred. 42 U.S.C. (Supp. III) § 423(a) (1970 ed., Supp. III).

If the recipient seeks reconsideration by the state agency and the determination is adverse, the SSA reviews the reconsideration determination and notifies the recipient of the decision. He then has a right to an evidentiary hearing before an SSA administrative law judge. 20 CFR §§ 404.917, 404.927 (1975). The hearing is nonadversary, and the SSA is not represented by counsel. As at all prior and subsequent stages of the administrative process, however, the claimant may be represented by counsel or other spokesmen. § 404.934. If this hearing results in an adverse decision, the claimant is entitled to request discretionary review by the SSA Appeals Council, § 404.945, and finally may obtain judicial review. 42 U.S.C. § 405(g); 20 CFR § 404.951 (1975).

Should it be determined at any point after termination of benefits, that the claimant's disability extended beyond the date of cessation initially established, the worker is entitled to retroactive payments. 42 U.S.C. § 404. If, on the other hand, a beneficiary receives any payments to which he is later determined not to be entitled, the statute authorizes the Secretary to attempt to recoup these funds in specified circumstances. 42 U.S.C. § 404.

[III.C] Despite the elaborate character of the administrative procedures provided by the Secretary, the courts below held them to be constitutionally inadequate, concluding that due process requires an evidentiary hearing prior to termination. In light of the private and governmental interests at stake here and the nature of the existing procedures, we think this was error.

Since a recipient whose benefits are terminated is awarded full retroactive relief if he ultimately prevails, his sole interest is in the uninterrupted receipt of this source of income pending final administrative decision on his claim. His potential injury is thus similar in nature to that of the welfare recipient in Goldberg [and other claimants whose due process rights were recognized by the Court].

Only in *Goldberg* has the Court held that due process requires an evidentiary hearing prior to a temporary deprivation. It was emphasized there that welfare assistance is given to persons on the very margin of subsistence:

> "The crucial factor in this context a factor not present in the case of . . . virtually anyone else whose governmental entitlements are ended is that termination of aid pending resolution of a controversy over eligibility may deprive an eligible recipient of the very means by which to live while he waits."

Eligibility for disability benefits, in contrast, is not based upon financial need. Indeed, it is wholly unrelated to the worker's income or support from many other sources, such as earnings of other family members, workmen's compensation awards, tort claims awards, savings, private insurance, public or private pensions, veterans' benefits, food stamps, public assistance, or the "many other important programs, both public and private, which contain provisions for disability payments affecting a substantial portion of the work force. . . ." *Richardson v. Belcher*, 404 U.S. at 85–87 (Douglas, J., dissenting). See Staff of the House Committee on Ways and Means, Report on the Disability Insurance Program, 93d Cong., 2d Sess., 9–10, 419–429 (1974) (hereinafter Staff Report).

As *Goldberg* illustrates, the degree of potential deprivation that may be created by a particular decision is a factor to be considered in assessing the validity of any administrative decisionmaking process. The potential deprivation here is generally likely to be less than in *Goldberg*, although the degree of difference can be overstated. As the District Court emphasized, to remain eligible for benefits a recipient must be "unable to engage in substantial gainful activity." 42 U.S.C. § 423. Thus, in contrast to the discharged federal employee in Arnett, there is little possibility that the terminated recipient will be able to find even temporary employment to ameliorate the interim loss.

As we recognized last Term in *Fusari v. Steinberg*, 419 U.S. 379, 389 (1975), "the possible length of wrongful deprivation of . . . benefits [also] is an important factor in assessing the impact of official action on the private interests." The Secretary concedes that the delay between a request for a hearing before an administrative law judge and a decision on the claim is currently between 10 and 11 months. Since a terminated recipient must first obtain a reconsideration decision as a prerequisite to invoking his right to an evidentiary hearing, the delay between the actual cutoff of benefits and final decision after a hearing exceeds one year.

In view of the torpidity of this administrative review process, and the typically modest resources of the family unit of the physically disabled worker,[26] the hardship imposed upon the erroneously terminated disability recipient may be significant. Still, the disabled worker's need is likely to be less than that of a welfare recipient. In addition to the possibility of access to private resources, other forms of government assistance will become available where the termination of disability benefits places a worker or his family below the subsistence level. In view of these potential sources of temporary income, there is less reason here

---

[26] Amici cite statistics compiled by the Secretary which indicate that in 1965 the mean income of the family unit of a disabled worker was $3,803, while the median income for the unit was $2,836. The mean liquid assets i.e., cash, stocks, bonds of these family units was $4,862; the median was $940. These statistics do not take into account the family unit's nonliquid assets i.e., automobile, real estate, and the like. Brief for AFL-CIO et al. as Amici Curiae App. 4a.

than in *Goldberg* to depart from the ordinary principle, established by our decisions, that something less than an evidentiary hearing is sufficient prior to adverse administrative action.

[III.D]   An additional factor to be considered here is the fairness and reliability of the existing pretermination procedures, and the probable value, if any, of additional procedural safeguards. Central to the evaluation of any administrative process is the nature of the relevant inquiry. *See Mitchell v. W. T. Grant Co.*, 416 U.S. 600, 617 (1974); Friendly, *Some Kind of Hearing*, 123 U. Pa. L. Rev. 1267, 1281 (1975). In order to remain eligible for benefits the disabled worker must demonstrate by means of "medically acceptable clinical and laboratory diagnostic techniques," 42 U.S.C. § 423(d)(3), that he is unable "to engage in *any* substantial gainful activity by reason of any medically determinable physical or mental impairment. . . ." § 423(d)(1)(A) (emphasis supplied). In short, a medical assessment of the worker's physical or mental condition is required. This is a more sharply focused and easily documented decision than the typical determination of welfare entitlement. In the latter case, a wide variety of information may be deemed relevant, and issues of witness credibility and veracity often are critical to the decisionmaking process. *Goldberg* noted that in such circumstances "written submissions are a wholly unsatisfactory basis for decision."

By contrast, the decision whether to discontinue disability benefits will turn, in most cases, upon "routine, standard, and unbiased medical reports by physician specialists," *Richardson v. Perales*, concerning a subject whom they have personally examined. In *Richardson* the Court recognized the "reliability and probative worth of written medical reports," emphasizing that while there may be "professional disagreement with the medical conclusions" the "specter of questionable credibility and veracity is not present." To be sure, credibility and veracity may be a factor in the ultimate disability assessment in some cases. But procedural due process rules are shaped by the risk of error inherent in the truthfinding process as applied to the generality of cases, not the rare exceptions. The potential value of an evidentiary hearing, or even oral presentation to the decisionmaker, is substantially less in this context than in *Goldberg*.

The decision in *Goldberg* also was based on the Court's conclusion that written submissions were an inadequate substitute for oral presentation because they did not provide an effective means for the recipient to communicate his case to the decisionmaker. Written submissions were viewed as an unrealistic option, for most recipients lacked the "educational attainment necessary to write effectively" and could not afford professional assistance. In addition, such submissions would not provide the "flexibility of oral presentations" or "permit the recipient to mold his argument to the issues the decision maker appears to regard as important." In the context of the disability-benefits-entitlement assessment the administrative procedures under review here fully answer these objections.

The detailed questionnaire which the state agency periodically sends the recipient identifies with particularity the information relevant to the entitlement decision, and the recipient is invited to obtain assistance from the local SSA office in completing the questionnaire. More important, the information critical to the entitlement decision usually is derived from medical sources, such as the treating physician. Such sources are likely to be able to communicate more effectively through written documents than are welfare recipients or the lay witnesses supporting their cause. The conclusions of physicians often are supported by X-rays and the results of clinical or laboratory tests, information typically more amenable to written than to oral presentation. *Cf.* W. Gellhorn & C. Byse, *Administrative Law Cases and Comments* 860–863 (6th ed. 1974).

A further safeguard against mistake is the policy of allowing the disability recipient's representative full access to all information relied upon by the state agency. In addition, prior to the cutoff of benefits the agency informs the recipient of its tentative assessment, the reasons therefor, and provides a summary of the evidence that it considers most relevant. Opportunity is then afforded the recipient to submit additional evidence or arguments, enabling him to challenge directly the accuracy of information in his file as well as the correctness of the agency's tentative conclusions. These procedures, again as contrasted with those before the Court in *Goldberg*, enable the recipient to "mold" his argument to respond to the precise issues which the decisionmaker regards as crucial.

Despite these carefully structured procedures, amici point to the significant reversal rate for appealed cases as clear evidence that the current process is inadequate. Depending upon the base selected and the line of analysis followed, the relevant reversal rates urged by the contending parties vary from a high of 58.6% for appealed reconsideration decisions to an overall reversal rate of only 3.3%.[29] Bare statistics rarely provide a satisfactory measure of the fairness of a decisionmaking process. Their adequacy is especially suspect here since the administrative review system is operated on an open-file basis. A

[29] By focusing solely on the reversal rate for appealed reconsideration determinations amici overstate the relevant reversal rate. As we indicated last Term in *Fusari v. Steinberg*, 419 U.S. 379, 383 n.6 (1975), in order fully to assess the reliability and fairness of a system of procedure, one must also consider the overall rate of error for all denials of benefits. Here that overall rate is 12.2%. Moreover, about 75% of these reversals occur at the reconsideration stage of the administrative process. Since the median period between a request for reconsideration review and decision is only two months, Brief for AFL-CIO et al. as Amici Curiae App. 4a, the deprivation is significantly less than that concomitant to the lengthier delay before an evidentiary hearing. Netting out these reconsideration reversals, the overall reversal rate falls to 3.3%. *See* Supplemental and Reply Brief for Petitioner 14.

recipient may always submit new evidence, and such submissions may result in additional medical examinations. Such fresh examinations were held in approximately 30% To 40% Of the appealed cases, in fiscal 1973, either at the reconsideration or evidentiary hearing stage of the administrative process. Staff Report 238. In this context, the value of reversal rate statistics as one means of evaluating the adequacy of the pretermination process is diminished. Thus, although we view such information as relevant, it is certainly not controlling in this case.

[III.E]   In striking the appropriate due process balance the final factor to be assessed is the public interest. This includes the administrative burden and other societal costs that would be associated with requiring, as a matter of constitutional right, an evidentiary hearing upon demand in all cases prior to the termination of disability benefits. The most visible burden would be the incremental cost resulting from the increased number of hearings and the expense of providing benefits to ineligible recipients pending decision. No one can predict the extent of the increase, but the fact that full benefits would continue until after such hearings would assure the exhaustion in most cases of this attractive option. Nor would the theoretical right of the Secretary to recover undeserved benefits result, as a practical matter, in any substantial offset to the added outlay of public funds. The parties submit widely varying estimates of the probable additional financial cost. We only need say that experience with the constitutionalizing of government procedures suggests that the ultimate additional cost in terms of money and administrative burden would not be insubstantial.

Financial cost alone is not a controlling weight in determining whether due process requires a particular procedural safeguard prior to some administrative decision. But the Government's interest, and hence that of the public, in conserving scarce fiscal and administrative resources is a factor that must be weighed. At some point the benefit of an additional safeguard to the individual affected by the administrative action and to society in terms of increased assurance that the action is just, may be outweighed by the cost. Significantly, the cost of protecting those whom the preliminary administrative process has identified as likely to be found undeserving may in the end come out of the pockets of the deserving since resources available for any particular program of social welfare are not unlimited. *See* Friendly, supra, 123 U.Pa.L.Rev., at 1276, 1303.

But more is implicated in cases of this type than ad hoc weighing of fiscal and administrative burdens against the interests of a particular category of claimants. The ultimate balance involves a determination as to when, under our constitutional system, judicial-type procedures must be imposed upon administrative action to assure fairness. We reiterate the wise admonishment of Mr. Justice Frankfurter that differences in the origin and function of administrative agencies "preclude wholesale transplantation of the rules of procedure, trial and review which have evolved from the history and experience of courts." *FCC v. Pottsville Broadcasting Co.*, 309 U.S. 134, 143 (1940). The judicial model of an evidentiary hearing is neither a required, nor even the most effective, method of decisionmaking in all circumstances. The essence of due process is the requirement that "a person in jeopardy of serious loss (be given) notice of the case against him and opportunity to meet it." *Joint Anti-Fascist Comm. v. McGrath* (Frankfurter, J., concurring). All that is necessary is that the procedures be tailored, in light of the decision to be made, to "the capacities and circumstances of those who are to be heard," *Goldberg v. Kelly*, to insure that they are given a meaningful opportunity to present their case. In assessing what process is due in this case, substantial weight must be given to the good-faith judgments of the individuals charged by Congress with the administration of social welfare programs that the procedures they have provided assure fair consideration of the entitlement claims of individuals. This is especially so where, as here, the prescribed procedures not only provide the claimant with an effective process for asserting his claim prior to any administrative action, but also assure a right to an evidentiary hearing, as well as to subsequent judicial review, before the denial of his claim becomes final.

We conclude that an evidentiary hearing is not required prior to the termination of disability benefits and that the present administrative procedures fully comport with due process.

[JUSTICE STEVENS did not participate in the case.]

JUSTICE BRENNAN, with whom JUSTICE MARSHALL concurs, dissenting.

For the reasons stated in my dissenting opinion in *Richardson v. Wright*, 405 U.S. 208, [212–27] (1972), I agree with the District Court and the Court of Appeals that, prior to termination of benefits, Eldridge must be afforded an evidentiary hearing of the type required for welfare beneficiaries under Title IV of the Social Security Act, 42 U.S.C. § 601 et seq. *See Goldberg v. Kelly.* I would add that the Court's consideration that a discontinuance of disability benefits may cause the recipient to suffer only a limited deprivation is no argument. It is speculative. Moreover, the very legislative determination to provide disability benefits, without any prerequisite determination of need in fact, presumes a need by the recipient which is not this Court's function to denigrate. Indeed, in the present case, it is indicated that because disability benefits were terminated there was a foreclosure upon the Eldridge home and the family's furniture was repossessed, forcing Eldridge, his wife, and their children to sleep in one bed. Tr. of Oral Arg. 39, 47–48. Finally, it is also no argument that a worker, who has been placed in the untenable position of having been denied disability benefits, may still seek other forms of public assistance.

NOTES AND QUESTIONS ON ADMINISTRATIVE DUE PROCESS

1. *Statutory and Administrative Due Process.* Notice that the social security statute and the agency regulations provide a detailed roadmap for claimants like Eldridge to challenge their benefit terminations. Indeed, the regulations afford a considerable amount of due process for Eldridge. Although he does not get a formal adjudicatory hearing before termination of his benefits, he is supposed to be consulted, to be given notice of what the agency is considering and what he can do, to be afforded multiple opportunities to supplement his record, and so forth. In footnote 29, Justice Powell suggests that this administrative due process is working quite well, with "true" reversal rates of either 12.2% or 3.3%. In his dissenting opinion in *Richardson v. Wright,* Justice Brennan sharply disputes these numbers, observing that 37% of the requests for agency reconsideration are granted and that the claimants who receive a post-termination oral hearing win 55% of the time. See 405 U.S. at 221 (data taken from the government's brief). Is this a system that operates with an acceptable number of errors?

The larger point is that administrative due process is set, first, by Congress in the APA and various substantive statutes and, secondarily, by agencies in their own rules. If the agency had not followed the statutory or even its own legal procedures, Eldridge would have had a different (and likely successful) legal claim: courts will typically require agencies to follow not only procedures mandated by statute but also those the agencies themselves have publicized and written into their manuals and the Code of Federal Regulations. Courts enforce due process at a tertiary level (after Congress and the agency have set policy), based upon constitutional due process considerations. As in *Mathews,* the Supreme Court is very reluctant to add further procedures to those established, after due deliberation, by Congress and the agency, *unless* the Court has strong concerns about the operation of that process.

2. *The Balancing Process: What Values Are at Stake?* A key question posed by both *Goldberg* and *Mathews* is this: What is the value of "extra" process? In other words, why should government give claimants like Eldridge an oral hearing *before* his benefits are terminated? There are various ways of understanding the value of the extra process:[9]

(A) Reduction in Error Costs. Consistent with the premises of the "cost-benefit state" (OIRA and such), one might say that the extra process

---

[9]   For excellent treatments, from a variety of perspectives, see Tom R. Tyler, *Why People Obey the Law* (rev. ed. 2006); Henry J. Friendly, *Some Kind of Hearing,* 121 U. Pa. L. Rev. 1267 (1975); Jerry L. Mashaw, *The Supreme Court's Due Process Calculus for Administrative Adjudication in* Mathews v. Eldridge: *Three Factors in Search of a Theory of Value,* 44 U. Chi. L. Rev. 28 (1976); William H. Simon, *The Rule of Law and Two Realms of Welfare Administration,* 56 Brooklyn L. Rev. 777 (1990).

will reduce the costs of error: claimants who are unjustly denied benefits will be saved from having their safety nets cut, which can be devastating to their lives. The premise of this kind of thinking is that policy should optimize overall social utility: if the state can spend $5 to save $10 for the average claimant, the state should spend the money because society is better off by $5. Are the benefits of a pre-termination hearing greater than the costs of such a hearing? If so, the state should provide it.

This was the calculus that undergirded Justice Powell's opinion—which conceded there were large error costs involved in the challenged administrative practice, where there was only a post-termination hearing. Implicitly, however, Justice Powell was concerned that there would be big costs if the Court required a pre-termination hearing—not only the costs of the process itself (more claimants would demand oral hearings), but also new error costs of allowing nonqualified claimants to continue to receive benefits that should be going to persons who are actually disabled. How does the Court figure out whether the first kind of error costs are greater than the second kind (plus the cost of extra hearings)?

(B) Dignitary Interests. Another way of looking at the point of process is dignitary: confronted with the possibility of a severe state penalty (including the termination of important economic benefits), every human being is entitled to respectful treatment, regardless of the economic cost-benefit analysis. Such a precept might be supported either by a humanistic philosophy or by theories of democracy. It probably inspired much of the Court's analysis in *Goldberg*, as well as Justice Brennan's dissent in *Mathews* and *Richardson* (though Brennan framed his dissents in the cost-benefit terms laid down by Justice Powell's majority opinion).

One might object that debates about dignitary interests are matters for philosophers, not judges, but one could frame a dignitary analysis in terms of Anglo-American tradition: as a general matter, citizens have demanded, and received, the opportunity to contest serious government deprivations in person, with a chance to confront witnesses and refute evidence supporting the deprivations in question. (See the Bill of Rights for such guarantees when the government is pressing criminal charges.)

(C) Legitimacy and Social Stability. Another value of process is legitimacy. A defective process generates skepticism that the result should be obeyed. As Tom Tyler has demonstrated empirically, people are much more likely to obey the law if they believe they have been treated fairly by the system—and they are less likely to obey the law if they feel they have been treated unfairly. See Tom R. Tyler, *Why People Obey the Law* (rev. ed. 2006). Multiplied by tens of thousands of disappointed claimants, an unfair process for distribution (and deprivation) of government benefits might generate a lot of social dissatisfaction.

Indeed, *Goldberg* emphasized the widespread social turmoil that roiled the nation's large cities in the late 1960s and suggested that government needs to be attentive to the needs of poor people, lest they depart en masse from the social contract. One way to distinguish *Mathews*, as a cultural document, is that the election of Richard Nixon as President in 1968 meant that the nation was more willing to "crack down" on dissatisfied poor people than accommodate them. (Moreover, Nixon, who ran on a law and order platform, named Powell to the Supreme Court, as well as three other conservative Justices who joined Powell's opinion in *Mathews*. The three *Mathews* dissenters were holdovers from the more liberal Warren Court.)

3.   *The New Property.* One issue that is easy to overlook in *Mathews* is the government's concession that termination of a stream of state disability benefits is *property* for purposes of the Due Process Clause. This concession had also been made in *Goldberg*, which cited Charles Reich's landmark article, *The New Property*, 73 Yale L.J. 733 (1964). See *Goldberg*, 397 U.S. at 262 n.8. Professor Reich argued that old property (land, cold cash, jewels) is being eclipsed in the modern regulatory state by government entitlements like social security pension and disability benefits, welfare benefits, and the like. (Today, we'd add old-age medical insurance benefits and others.)

After *Goldberg* and *Mathews*, the Burger Court expanded the concept of due process "property" to include also contractual assurances of continued public employment, see *Perry v. Sindermann*, 408 U.S. 593 (1972); *Cleveland Bd. of Educ. v. Loudermill*, 470 U.S. 532 (1985), as well as the continued enjoyment of driver's licenses, see *Bell v. Burson*, 402 U.S. 535 (1971), and professional licenses, see *Gibson v. Berryhill*, 411 U.S. 564 (1973).

PROBLEM 7–2: DUE PROCESS PROTECTIONS FOR CITIZENS ACCUSED OF BEING "ENEMY COMBATANTS"?

After the al Qaeda-orchestrated terrorist attacks of 9/11/2001, Congress passed a resolution—the Authorization for Use of Military Force (AUMF)—authorizing the President to "use all necessary and appropriate force" against "nations, organizations, or persons" that he determines "planned, authorized, committed, or aided" in the attacks. As part of this response, President George W. Bush ordered an invasion of Afghanistan to attack al Qaeda and the Taliban regime that harbored al Qaeda. The President also ordered the detention of hundreds of persons as "enemy combatants" that the Bush Administration thought were connected with al Qaeda or other terrorist groups.

Yaser Hamdi was an American citizen, captured by American forces in Afghanistan and after some intermediate stops detained at a naval brig in Charleston, S.C. No charges were filed against him. His father filed a habeas corpus petition to secure his release from detention. Hamdi was not allowed any contact with outsiders, and hence was unable to file the petition himself or to communicate with his father. His father asserted that Hamdi went to Afghanistan to do "relief work" less than two months before September 11, 2001, and could not have received military training. In response to the petition, the government filed a declaration from Michael Mobbs, a Defense Department official. The Mobbs Declaration alleged various details regarding

Hamdi's trip to Afghanistan, his affiliation there with a Taliban unit during a time when the Taliban was battling U.S. allies, and his subsequent surrender of an assault rifle. Several legal issues were presented by the federal government's detention of Hamdi:

(A) Can an American citizen be detained without charges? As a general matter, no. "No citizen shall be imprisoned or otherwise detained by the United States except pursuant to an Act of Congress." 18 U.S.C. § 4001(a). Congress passed § 4001(a) in 1971 as part of a bill to repeal the Emergency Detention Act of 1950, which provided procedures for executive detention, during times of emergency, of individuals deemed likely to engage in espionage or sabotage. Congress was particularly concerned about the possibility that the Act could be used to reprise the Japanese internment camps of World War II. Hamdi argued that he could not be detained at all, based on § 4001(a). Over fierce dissents, however, the Supreme Court in *Hamdi v. Rumsfeld*, 542 U.S. 507 (2004), ruled that the AUMF constituted an authorization for the President to detain suspected terrorists such as Hamdi.

(B) Can suspected "enemy combatants" be detained indefinitely? A virtually unanimous Supreme Court ruled in *Hamdi* that suspected enemy combatants *cannot* be detained indefinitely. Justice O'Connor's plurality opinion ruled that "indefinite detention for the purpose of interrogation is not authorized. Further, we understand Congress' grant of authority for the use of 'necessary and appropriate force' to include the authority to detain for the duration of the relevant conflict, and our understanding is based on longstanding law-of-war principles. * * * If the record establishes that United States troops are still involved in active combat in Afghanistan, those detentions are part of the exercise of 'necessary and appropriate force,' and therefore are authorized by the AUMF." Four Justices (Stevens, Scalia, Souter, and Ginsburg) maintained that Hamdi could not be detained at all, and one Justice (Thomas) believed there was no limit on the term of Hamdi's detention.

(C) What procedures must be made available to Hamdi to contest the claim that he is an enemy combatant? Joined by a majority of the Court, Justice O'Connor's opinion in *Hamdi* required the Bush-Cheney Administration to provide some kind of process to Hamdi. She explicitly framed her analysis in terms of the factors laid out in *Mathews v. Eldridge*. What process would *Mathews* require, as a matter of due process, in this kind of proceeding? See Jenny S. Martinez, *Process and Substance in the "War on Terror,"* 108 Colum. L. Rev. 1013, 1061–79 (2008).

Consider another way of putting this question—as administrative due process rather than constitutional due process. In the wake of *Hamdi*, the Bush Administration established Combat Status Review Tribunals (CSRTs) to determine whether Hamdi and all other Guantanamo detainees should continue to be detained as suspected enemy combatants. Memorandum of the Secretary of the Navy, Implementation of Combatant Status Review Tribunal Procedures for Enemy Combatants Detained at Guantanamo Bay Naval Base

(July 9, 2004). What kind of procedures should the President establish for these tribunals? Assume that the President follows *Mathews v. Eldridge* in thinking that the value of procedure is reduction of error costs, including errors associated with releasing guilty terrorists as well as errors associated with keeping innocent people in prison. What procedures should the CSRTs follow?

B. ADJUDICATION VS. RULEMAKING

Agency adjudications of social security benefits in *Mathews v. Eldridge* and of detainee liberty interests in *Hamdi v. Rumsfeld*, analyzed in the previous part, necessarily involve the application of general principles of law to particular factual circumstances. In *Mathews*, the Social Security Act provided a statement of the substantive law to be applied to evaluate disability claims. In contrast, there was no statutory foundation for the principles of substantive law that the executive branch was supposed to apply in determining whether Guantanamo detainees should be released.

An intermediate case is presented below, namely the FCC's enforcement of the statutory mandates that the broadcast media not carry "obscene," "indecent," or "profane" expression. Like *Mathews*, agency adjudications involving network violations applied statutory criteria—but like *Hamdi*, the substantive details come mainly from the agency adjudicators, proceeding in common law (i.e., case by case) fashion. Like common law courts, agencies applying open-textured statutory principles will proceed dynamically: as the adjudicators learn from the cases, as society changes, and as the decisionmakers themselves change, so will the legal applications derived from highly general principles.

There are several important issues presented by this phenomenon. One is whether the agency has some kind of responsibility (not necessarily a responsibility that courts will enforce) to announce significant shifts in policy through notice-and-comment rulemaking rather than through case-by-case adjudication. The advantages of rulemaking include the following:

- *Broad Participation.* Notice-and-comment rulemaking usually generates much greater participation among citizens and interest groups. (These days, the participation occurs through the Internet.) This may ensure that the agency entertains more perspectives, more information, and more critical presentations of evidence.

- *Legitimacy.* A proceeding that yields a legislative policy affecting rights and duties of companies and people might be more legitimate if it proceeded through notice-and-comment rulemaking, which looks more like the legislative process than does agency adjudication.

- *Reliance.* Especially when an agency is advancing a new policy, or altering an established or longstanding policy, companies and people have probably relied on that policy. Rulemaking not only alerts all the regulated community that a change is in the works, but also gives a broad array of interests and perspectives the opportunity to oppose the change and/or suggest transition rules.

See David L. Shapiro, *The Choice of Rulemaking or Adjudication in the Development of Administrative Policy*, 78 Harv. L. Rev. 921, 929–42 (1965).

As Professor Shapiro points out, the potential advantages of rulemaking should not be overstated. For example, rulemaking does not necessarily yield clearer or more precise legal formulations than adjudications: rules can be vague and orders can lay out a precise roadmap for compliance with the statutory regime. In the course of adjudicating a particular controversy, an agency may develop detailed rules to which it subsequently ascribes precedential status. These adjudicatory rules will affect if not control the resolution of future cases presenting identical or comparable issues. The agency may, for example, amplify the meaning of crucial yet ambiguous statutory terms (see *Town & Country Elec. Co.*, 309 N.L.R.B. 1250 (1992)), or it may set forth burdens of proof with respect to certain statutorily protected activities (see *Levitz Furniture Co.*, 333 N.L.R.B. 717 (2001)). These types of adjudicatory rules effectively make policy, facilitating resolution of similar issues in later cases.

Thus, adjudication can be an effective way for an agency to advance legally binding directives. And it has other potential advantages for regulatory institutions, including:

- *Trial and Error, with Feedback.* Proceeding case by case allows the agency to avoid committing itself to a broad policy before it is certain about what that policy should be. Indeed, congressional, public, and expert reactions to particular decisions might provide the agency with useful feedback as it proceeds gradually toward a broader policy formulation.

- *Flexibility.* A related advantage is that case-by-case adjudication gives the agency more flexibility to adapt policy to changing circumstances, whether they be technological or evolving social mores. As *State Farm* may reflect, regulations might be harder for the agency to alter or to tailor to unforeseen circumstances than precedent-based principles.

- *Retroactivity.* There may often be fairness or other policy advantages to adjudication, which presumptively applies retroactively (unlike rulemaking, which presumptively applies prospectively). Retroactivity may help ensure that similar situations are treated similarly and that agency common law proceeds in a "principled" matter, and not just as the result of changing political climate.

Shapiro, *Rulemaking or Adjudication*, 942–57.

Consider a famous pair of Supreme Court cases that illustrate the agency's discretion in such matters. In *SEC v. Chenery Corp.*, 318 U.S. 80 (1943), the Supreme Court overturned the agency's refusal to approve a corporate reorganization, because the agency misconstrued the Supreme Court's precedents governing equity rules applicable to corporate reorganizations. On remand, the SEC accomplished the same result by applying its context-dependent "expertise" to the transaction—that is, it re-issued the same order but based it on policy justifications rather than arguing the order was simply applying existing Court precedents. See *SEC v. Chenery*, 332 U.S. 194 (1947). In *Chenery II*, the Court discussed the asserted advantages, from the perspective of the regulated institutions, of judicial nudges for agencies to announce legislative rules (after notice-and-comment) and thereby gave regulated institutions a clearer idea of what is required of them. The Court held that "the choice made between proceeding by general rule or by individual, ad hoc litigation is one that lies primarily in the informed discretion of the administrative agency." Accord, *NLRB v. Bell Aerospace Corp.*, 416 U.S. 267 (1974) (quoting *Chenery II* and following this directive).

Under the current structure of executive branch oversight, recall that OIRA review generally focuses on actions that are "economically significant" and that are expected to lead to the promulgation of a rule or regulation. Accordingly, agencies can choose adjudication (as well as other strategies like guidance documents, non-significant rules or simple inaction) as an instrument that is likely to escape OIRA review. See Jennifer Nou, *Agency Self-Insulation Under Presidential Review*, 126 Harv. L. Rev. 1755, 1783–85 (2013). Of course, agencies also have many ways to avoid OIRA review of their rules, such as breaking up proposed mega-rules into smaller rulemaking initiatives. See Note, *OIRA Avoidance*, 124 Harv. L. Rev. 994 (2011).

Now, consider the application of these general ideas to a specific agency problem, namely, the FCC's regulation of obscene, indecent, and profane utterances on television and radio. Obviously, the FCC's regulation implicates the First Amendment, which limits Congress's (and the FCC's) ability to "abridge" free expression. The Supreme Court has ruled that "obscenity" is not "speech" protected by the First Amendment, see *Miller v. California*, 413 U.S. 15 (1973) (defining "obscenity" for constitutional purposes), and that the First Amendment also allows the FCC to regulate "indecent" speech on the broadcast media because it might be heard by minors. See *FCC v. Pacifica*, 438 U.S. 726 (1978). In the new millennium, the FCC expanded its understanding of indecent and profane speech and regulated it more aggressively, as reflected in the following opinion of the Commission.

IN THE MATTER OF COMPLAINTS AGAINST VARIOUS BROADCAST LICENSEES REGARDING THEIR AIRING OF THE "GOLDEN GLOBE AWARDS" PROGRAM

Federal Communications Commission, File No. EB–03–IH–0110.
Adopted: March 3, 2004 and Released: March 18, 2004.

MEMORANDUM OPINION AND ORDER BY THE COMMISSION

[In this proceeding, the Commission granted an Application for Review filed by the Parents Television Council ("PTC") on November 3, 2003. PTC had sought reversal of an October 3, 2003 Order issued by the Chief, Enforcement Bureau ("Bureau") that denied their complaint that various licensees violated indecency and profanity restrictions regarding the broadcast of obscene and indecent material by airing the "Golden Globe Awards" on January 19, 2003.]

Background * * *

3.   The Commission received numerous complaints from individuals associated with PTC alleging that the licensees named on the complaints broadcast the "Golden Globe Awards" program, during which the performer Bono uttered a phrase allegedly in violation of the FCC's rules restricting the broadcast of indecent material. The Golden Globe Awards are sponsored by the Hollywood Foreign Press Association. Bono made the statement in response to winning the award for "Best Original Song." The complainants maintained that such language was obscene and/or indecent, and requested that the Commission levy sanctions against the licensees for broadcasting the subject material. The Bureau, however, concluded that the material was not obscene or indecent, finding in particular with respect to indecency that the language used by Bono did not describe, in context, sexual or excretory organs or activities and that the utterance was fleeting and isolated. In its Application for Review, PTC maintains that the *Bureau Order* is legally incorrect, that it is "'patently offensive' to use the 'F–Word' in any shape, form or meaning on broadcast network television," and requests that the Commission levy a forfeiture against each licensee that aired the "Golden Globe Awards" program. NBC opposes the Application for Review and argues that the *Bureau Order* is consistent with precedent.

Discussion

4.   The Federal Communications Commission is authorized to license radio and television broadcast stations and is responsible for enforcing the Commission's rules and applicable statutory provisions concerning the operation of those stations. The Commission's role in overseeing program content is very limited. The First Amendment to the United States Constitution and section 326 of the Communications Act of 1934, as amended (the "Act"), prohibit the Commission from censoring program material and from interfering with broadcasters' freedom of expression. The Commission does, however, have the authority to enforce statutory and regulatory provisions restricting obscenity, indecency and profanity. Specifically, it is a violation of federal law to broadcast obscene, indecent or profane programming. Title 18 of the United States Code, Section 1464 prohibits the utterance of "any obscene, indecent or profane language by means of radio communication." Consistent with a subsequent statute and court case, section 73.3999 of the Commission's rules provides that radio and television stations shall not broadcast obscene material at any time, and shall not broadcast indecent material during the period 6 a.m. through 10 p.m. The Commission may impose a monetary forfeiture, pursuant to Section 503(b)(1) of the Act, upon a finding that a licensee has broadcast indecent material in violation of 18 U.S.C. § 1464 and section 73.3999 of the rules.

5.   Any consideration of government action against allegedly indecent or profane programming must take into account the fact that such speech is protected under the First Amendment. The federal courts consistently have upheld Congress's authority to regulate the broadcast of indecent speech, as well as the Commission's interpretation and implementation of the governing statute. Nevertheless, the First Amendment is a critical constitutional limitation that demands that, in such determinations, we proceed cautiously and with appropriate restraint.

6.   The Commission defines indecent speech as language that, in context, depicts or describes sexual or excretory activities or organs in terms patently offensive as measured by contemporary community standards for the broadcast medium.[15]

> Indecency findings involve at least two fundamental determinations. First, the material alleged to be indecent must fall within the subject matter scope of our indecency definition— that is, the material must describe or depict sexual or excretory organs or activities. . . . Second, the broadcast must be *patently*

---

[15] *Infinity Broadcasting Corporation of Pennsylvania*, 2 FCC Rcd 2705 (1987) (citing *Pacifica Foundation*, 56 FCC 2d 94, 98 (1975), *aff'd sub nom. FCC v. Pacifica Foundation*, 438 U.S. 726 (1978)).

offensive as measured by contemporary community standards for the broadcast medium.[16]

7.   In making indecency determinations, the Commission has indicated that the *"full context* in which the material appeared is critically important," and has articulated three "principal factors" for its analysis: "(1) the *explicitness or graphic nature* of the description or depiction of sexual or excretory organs or activities; (2) whether the material *dwells on or repeats at length* descriptions of sexual or excretory organs or activities; (3) *whether the material appears to pander or is used to titillate,* or *whether the material appears to have been presented for its shock value."*[18] In examining these three factors, we must weigh and balance them to determine whether the broadcast material is patently offensive because "[e]ach indecency case presents its own particular mix of these, and possibly, other factors." In particular cases, one or two of the factors may outweigh the others, either rendering the broadcast material patently offensive and consequently indecent, or, alternatively, removing the broadcast material from the realm of indecency.

8.   With respect to the first step of the indecency analysis,[22] we disagree with the Bureau and conclude that use of the phrase at issue is within the scope of our indecency definition because it does depict or describe sexual activities. We recognize NBC's argument that the "F–Word" here was used "as an intensifier." Nevertheless, we believe that, given the core meaning of the "F–Word," any use of that word or a variation, in any context, inherently has a sexual connotation, and therefore falls within the first prong of our indecency definition. This conclusion is consistent with the Commission's original *Pacifica* decision, affirmed by the Supreme Court, in which the Commission held that the "F–Word" does depict or describe sexual activities.[24]

9.   We now turn to the second step of the analysis—whether the broadcast of the phrase at issue here is patently offensive under contemporary community standards for the broadcast medium and therefore indecent. We conclude that the answer to this question is yes.

---

[16] *Industry Guidance on the Commission's Case Law Interpreting 18 U.S.C. § 1464 and Enforcement Policies Regarding Broadcast Indecency ("Indecency Policy Statement"),* 16 FCC Rcd 7999, 8002 (2001) (emphasis in original).

[18] *Indecency Policy Statement,* 16 FCC Rcd at 8003 (emphasis in original).

[22] PTC does not allege in the Application for Review that the language was obscene. In any case, we agree with the Bureau's conclusion that the language was not obscene since it did not meet the three-prong test set forth in *Miller v. California. Miller v. California,* 413 U.S. 15, 24 (1973) (holding that, to be obscene, the material must meet the following three-prong test: (1) the average person, applying contemporary community standards, must find that the material, as a whole, appeals to the prurient interest; (2) the material must depict or describe, in a patently offensive way, sexual conduct specifically defined by applicable law; and (3) the material, taken as a whole, must lack serious literary, artistic, political or scientific value).

[24] *Citizen's Complaint Against Pacifica Foundation Station WBAI(FM), New York, New York,* 56 FCC 2d 94, 99 (1975), *recon. granted in part,* 59 FCC 2d 892 (1976), *aff'd sub nom. FCC v. Pacifica Foundation,* 438 U.S. 726 (1978).

The "F–Word" is one of the most vulgar, graphic and explicit descriptions of sexual activity in the English language. Its use invariably invokes a coarse sexual image. The use of the "F–Word" here, on a nationally telecast awards ceremony, was shocking and gratuitous. In this regard, NBC does not claim that there was any political, scientific or other independent value of use of the word here, or any other factors to mitigate its offensiveness. If the Commission were routinely not to take action against isolated and gratuitous uses of such language on broadcasts when children were expected to be in the audience, this would likely lead to more widespread use of the offensive language. Neither Congress nor the courts have ever indicated that broadcasters should be given free rein to air any vulgar language, including isolated and gratuitous instances of vulgar language.[27] The fact that the use of this word may have been unintentional is irrelevant; it still has the same effect of exposing children to indecent language. Our action today furthers our responsibility to safeguard the well-being of the nation's children from the most objectionable, most offensive language.

10. We also note that in this case NBC and other licensees were on notice that an award presenter or recipient might use offensive language during the live broadcast, and it could have taken appropriate steps to ensure that it did not broadcast such language. In this regard, this is not the first case where such language has been used by an award recipient in a live program. For example, we note that, during the broadcast of the 2002 Billboard Awards Ceremony, Cher, in receiving an award, reportedly used the "F–Word." Indeed, Bono himself reportedly used the "F–Word" on the 1994 Grammy Awards broadcast.

11. We note also that technological advances have made it possible as a general matter to prevent the broadcast of a single offending word or action without blocking or disproportionately disrupting the message of the speaker or performer. NBC and other licensees could have easily avoided the indecency violation here by delaying the broadcast for a period of time sufficient for them to effectively bleep the offending word. Indeed, we encourage networks and broadcasters to undertake such technological measures. The ease with which broadcasters today can block even fleeting words in a live broadcast is an element in our decision to act upon a single and gratuitous use of a vulgar expletive.

12. While prior Commission and staff action have indicated that isolated or fleeting broadcasts of the "F–Word" such as that here are not indecent or would not be acted upon, consistent with our decision today we conclude that any such interpretation is no longer good law. In *Pacifica Foundation, Inc.*, 2 FCC Rcd 2698, 2699 (1987) (subsequent history

---

[27] That the statute applies to whoever "utters" any obscene, indecent, or profane language, without reference to repeated or sustained utterances, seems to imply that a single, isolated use is sufficient.

omitted), for example, the Commission stated as follows: "If a complaint focuses solely on the use of expletives, we believe that . . . deliberate and repetitive use in a patently offensive manner is a requisite to a finding of indecency." The staff has since found that the isolated or fleeting use of the "F–Word" is not indecent in situations arguably similar to that here. We now depart from this portion of the Commission's 1987 *Pacifica* decision as well as all of the cases [following *Pacifica*] and any similar cases holding that isolated or fleeting use of the "F–Word" or a variant thereof in situations such as this is not indecent and conclude that such cases are not good law to that extent. We now clarify, as we have made clear with respect to complaints going beyond the use of expletives, that the mere fact that specific words or phrases are not sustained or repeated does not mandate a finding that material that is otherwise patently offensive to the broadcast medium is not indecent.

13. We also find, as an independent ground, that the use of the phrase at issue here in the context and at the time of day here constitutes "profane" language under 18 U.S.C. § 1464. The term "profanity" is commonly defined as "vulgar, irreverent, or coarse language."[34] The Seventh Circuit, in its most recent decision defining "profane" under section 1464, stated that the term is "construable as denoting certain of those personally reviling epithets naturally tending to provoke violent resentment or denoting language so grossly offensive to members of the public who actually hear it as to amount to a nuisance."[35] We find that the broadcast of the phrase at issue here in the context and at the time of day qualifies as "profane" under the Seventh Circuit nuisance rationale. Use of the "F–Word" in the context at issue here is also clearly the kind of vulgar and coarse language that is commonly understood to fall within the definition of "profanity."[36]

14. We recognize that the Commission's limited case law on profane speech has focused on what is profane in the context of blasphemy, but nothing in those cases suggests either that the statutory definition of profane is limited to blasphemy, or that the Commission could not also apply the definition articulated by the Seventh Circuit. Broadcasters are on notice that the Commission in the future will not limit its definition of

---

[34] Black's Law Dictionary 1210 (6th ed. 1990) (citing 18 U.S.C. § 1464). *See also* American Heritage College Dictionary 1112 (4th ed. 2002) (definition of profane includes "[v]ulgar, coarse.")

[35] *Tallman v. United States*, 465 F.2d 282, 286 (7th Cir. 1972). In *United States v Simpson*, 561 F.2d 53 (7th Cir. 1977), the court called into question the nuisance rationale for the regulation of offensive speech set forth in *Tallman*, suggesting that it might not survive cases such as *Cohen v California*, 403 U.S. 15 (1971). *Id.* at 58 & n.7. But the Supreme Court's *Pacifica* decision subsequently upheld an indecency finding that "rested entirely on a nuisance rationale." 438 U.S. at 750. See also 12 Am. Jur. 2d Blasphemy and Profanity 9 (citing *Tallman* standard in connection with section 1464).

[36] Nuisance has been defined as including "a condition of things which is prejudicial to the . . . sense of decency or morals of the citizens at large. . . ." Ballentine's Law Dictionary (3d ed. 1969).

profane speech to only those words and phrases that contain an element of blasphemy or divine imprecation, but, depending on the context, will also consider under the definition of "profanity" the "F–Word" and those words (or variants thereof) that are as highly offensive as the "F–Word," to the extent such language is broadcast between 6 a.m. and 10 p.m. We will analyze other potentially profane words or phrases on a case-by-case basis.

15. But for the fact that existing precedent would have permitted this broadcast, it would be appropriate to initiate a forfeiture proceeding against NBC and other licensees that broadcast the program prior to 10 p.m. Given, however, that Commission and staff precedent prior to our decision today permitted the broadcast at issue, and that we take a new approach to profanity, NBC and its affiliates necessarily did not have the requisite notice to justify a penalty.[40]

16. Finally, our decision is not inconsistent with the Supreme Court ruling in *Pacifica*. The Court explicitly left open the issue of whether an occasional expletive could be considered indecent. Just as the Court held that Pacifica's broadcast of the George Carlin routine "could have enlarged a child's vocabulary in an instant," we believe that even isolated broadcasts of the "F–Word" in situations such as that here could do so as well, in a manner that many, if not most, parents would find highly detrimental and objectionable. Thus, finding broadcast of this word indecent and profane here is consistent with the "well-being of [the country's] youth" and "supporting parents' claims to authority in their own household," which the Court used as a basis for its decision in *Pacifica,* in combination with the "ease with which children may obtain access to broadcast material. . . ."

Conclusion

17. We conclude, therefore, that NBC and other licensees that broadcast Bono's use of the "F–Word" during the live broadcast of the Golden Globe Awards violated 18 U.S.C. § 1464. By our action today, broadcasters are on clear notice that, in the future, they will be subject to potential enforcement action for any broadcast of the "F–Word" or a variation thereof in situations such as that here. We also take this opportunity to reiterate our recent admonition (which took place after the behavior at issue here) that serious multiple violations of our indecency rule by broadcasters may well lead to the commencement of license revocation

---

[40] See *Trinity Broadcasting of Florida, Inc. v. FCC*, 211 F.3d 618 (D.C. Cir. 2000) (court reversed Commission decision that denied a renewal application for abuse of process in connection with the Commission's minority ownership rules because the court found the Commission had not provided sufficiently clear notice of what those rules required). In addition, given that existing precedent would have permitted this broadcast, we will not require any of the stations that broadcast the program to report our finding here to us as part of its renewal application and we will not consider the broadcast of this program adversely to such licensees as part of the renewal process.

proceedings, and that we may issue forfeitures for each indecent utterance in a particular broadcast. We note that one way broadcasters can easily ensure that they are not subject to enforcement action under our decision today is to adopt and successfully implement a delay/bleeping system for live broadcasts.

STATEMENT OF CHAIRMAN MICHAEL K. POWELL * * *

For the first time, the Commission has applied the profanity section of the statute for the broadcast of this highly offensive word, an application I fully support. The Commission has an important obligation to punish those who violate our law. In administering our authority, the Commission must afford parties fair warning and due process and not let our zeal trample these fundamental protections. Given that today's decision clearly departs from past precedent in important ways, I could not support a fine retroactively against the parties. Prospectively, parties are on notice that they could now face significant penalties for similar violations.

Going forward, as instructed by the Supreme Court, we must use our enforcement tools cautiously. As I have said since becoming a Commissioner, government action in this area can have a potential chilling effect on free speech. We guard against this by ruling when a clear line has been crossed and the government has no choice but to act.

We will continue to respect the delicate balance of protecting the interests of the First Amendment with the need to protect our children.

[**COMMISSIONERS KATHLEEN Q. ABERNATHY** and **JONATHAN ADELSTEIN** issued similar statements, supporting the Chairman's view that sanctions were not appropriate because of the notice problem.]

[**COMMISSIONER KEVIN J. MARTIN** issued a statement approving in part and dissenting in part.]

I am pleased that the Commission finally is making clear that the use of the "F-word" during this prime-time broadcast was both indecent and profane, regardless of whether used as an adjective, adverb, or gerund. I am particularly pleased that, at long last, the Commission is enforcing the statutory prohibition against the broadcast of profanity. Better late than never.

I firmly support these conclusions, and approve these aspects of this Order.

I disagree, however, with the Order's characterization of our precedent on indecency, and the corresponding conclusion that licensees were not on notice that the F-word is indecent.

Even more troubling is the conclusion that we cannot issue a fine for the use of profanity. The majority argues that there is no notice. How ironic that the majority relies on the Commission's own failure to enforce its statutory mandate as the basis for NBC not knowing that the F-word is prohibited profanity. Taking a step back, I can't help but think NBC was "on notice" that the F-word was profane. In fact, *NBC* hasn't even claimed that they were not on notice that the F-word was profane. Yet the majority concludes otherwise, and issues no fine. I cannot support this analysis, and therefore dissent in part.

[COMMISSIONER MICHAEL J. COPPS issued a similar statement, agreeing with the finding of a violation and urging the Commission to impose penalties.]

NOTES AND QUESTIONS ON THE FCC'S GOLDEN GLOBES DECISION

1. *Another Account of the Evolution of the FCC's Policy.* The following account is taken from Judge Pooler's subsequent opinion in *Fox Television Stations, Inc. v. FCC*, 613 F.3d 317 (2d Cir. 2010). "In the years after *Pacifica*, the FCC did indeed pursue a restrained enforcement policy, taking the position that its enforcement powers were limited to the seven specific words in the Carlin monologue. No enforcement actions were brought between 1978 and 1987. Then, in 1987, the FCC abandoned its focus on specific words, concluding that 'although enforcement was clearly easier under the standard, it could lead to anomalous results that could not be justified.' [*Infinity Broadcasting Corp., et al.*, 3 F.C.C.R. 930, at ¶ 5 (1987).] The FCC reasoned that under the prior standard, patently offensive material was permissible as long as it avoided certain words. This, the Commission concluded, 'made neither legal nor policy sense.' *Id.* The Commission instead decided to utilize the definition it had used in *Pacifica,* adopting a contextual approach to indecent speech." [Despite its move to a more flexible standard, the FCC repeatedly held that a single, non-literal use of an expletive was not actionably indecent.]

"In 2001, in an attempt to 'provide guidance to the broadcast industry regarding . . . [its] enforcement policies with respect to broadcast indecency,' the FCC issued a policy statement in which it set forth its indecency standard in more detail. *Industry Guidance on the Commission's Case Law Interpreting 18 U.S.C. § 1464*, 16 F.C.C.R. 7999, at ¶ 1 (2001). In *Industry Guidance*, the FCC explained that an indecency finding involved the following two determinations: (1) whether the material 'describe[s] or depict[s] sexual or excretory organs or activities'; and (2) whether the broadcast is 'patently offensive as measured by contemporary community standards for the broadcast medium.' *Id.* at ¶¶ 7–8 (emphasis omitted). The FCC further explained that it considered the following three factors in determining whether a broadcast is patently offensive: (1) 'the explicitness or graphic nature of the description or depiction'; (2) 'whether the material dwells on or repeats at length' the description or depiction; and (3) 'whether the material appears to pander or is used to titillate, or whether the materials appears to have been presented for its shock value.' *Id.* at ¶ 10 (emphasis omitted). The *Industry Guidance* reiterated that under the second prong of the patently offensive test, 'fleeting and isolated' expletives were not actionably indecent. *Id.* at ¶ 18."

The 2004 decision in *Golden Globes* was, by this account, a sharper departure from prior policy than is reflected in the Commission's decision above. Does this different account affect the way you evaluate the FCC's action and its new rules? Consider, also, the fact that all five Commissioners in *Golden Globes* were appointed to the FCC by President George W. Bush. As required by statute, the Commissioners were bipartisan: three were Republicans and two were Democrats from the Midwest and South. Chairman Michael Powell, a Republican, was originally appointed by President Clinton, but President Bush elevated him to the chairmanship in 2001. During his tenure, and that of his successor as Chairman (Kevin Martin, 2005–09), the FCC issued record fines and penalties against the networks and radio broadcasters for violation of statutory indecency standards.

2. *Constitutional Concerns.* The Commission was aware of First Amendment concerns with aggressive regulation of the airwaves but dismissed them without much doctrinal analysis. The First Amendment protects "indecent" (but not "obscene") speech, *Reno v. ACLU*, 521 U.S. 844, 874–75 (1997), and so fleeting expletives can only be regulated if they are the least restrictive means to serve a compelling governmental interest. *Sable Communications v. FCC*, 492 U.S. 115 (1989). In *Pacifica* and other cases, the Supreme Court has given the government more regulatory leeway for the broadcast media because it is, the Court asserts, a scarce resource that the government can regulate in the public interest. Although the Supreme Court has itself been unclear as to the level of scrutiny for broadcast media, federal courts generally assume that content regulations should be evaluated under an intermediate level of scrutiny: the content regulation must serve an important public interest and be reasonably necessary to effectuate that interest.

Also, the First Amendment does not tolerate "vague" regulation, because it tends to "chill" protected speech. In *Reno v. ACLU*, the Court struck down § 223(a), (d) of the Communications Decency Act of 1996 on this ground. Section 223(a) prohibited the transmission of "indecent" material to minors over the Internet; § 223(d) prohibited material that "in context, depicts or describes, in terms patently offensive as measured by contemporary community standards, sexual or excretory activities or organs." In addition to finding that the statute was not narrowly tailored, the Court found the statute unconstitutionally vague because "the many ambiguities concerning the scope of its coverage render[ed] it problematic for purposes of the First Amendment." The statute's use of the "general, undefined terms 'indecent' and 'patently offensive' cover[ed] large amounts of nonpornographic material with serious educational or other value." Because of the "vague contours" of the regulation, the Court held that "it unquestionably silence[d] some speakers whose messages would be entitled to constitutional protection."

The *Golden Globes Case* was not the same as *Reno v. ACLU*, for the FCC had tried to tailor its anti-expletive policy more carefully to avoid regulation of protected expression. But when popular musician Bono uttered the word "fuck" in the heat of the moment, was he not expressing himself in a distinctive way? Is there a compelling governmental interest in shielding minors from ever hearing the word "fuck"? Is this interest served by punishing NBC for not bleeping the word out of the broadcast of the Golden Globes? Would minors also be served by bleeping out the entire broadcast of the Golden Globes, on the ground that the banality of the show is harmful to impressionable minds?

Consider also the FCC's 2001 policy, as applied here and in the future, from the perspective of NBC and other networks. Under the 2001 policy, the FCC told ABC that its program *NYPD Blue* could not use the word "bullshit" but that "dick" and "dickhead" were permissible. If at the next year's Golden Globes show the popular entertainer Bono returned and said, "The FCC is a bunch of dickheads," can NBC be sure it would not be penalized? In short, does the FCC policy provide sufficient guidance to broadcasters? Would a bright-line policy of prohibited words (the original *Pacifica* era policy) better meet the vagueness problems of the FCC's new standard?

If you were an FCC Commissioner in 2004, would these constitutional concerns affect your approach to the Golden Globes controversy or to the FCC's 2001 Policy Statement? How would you balance your regulatory responsibilities with the free speech protections of the First Amendment? Should this issue be left to the courts and not figure into the FCC's decisionmaking?

3.   *Predict the Answer to This Episode.* Fox Television once ran a show called "The Simple Life," in which socialites Paris Hilton and Nicole Richie "roughed" it in rural locales, where they encountered situations not common in the Upper East Side of Manhattan. In one episode, Hilton found that her couture purse had been soiled and exclaims, "Have you ever tried to get cow shit off of a Prada purse?" Does this violate the FCC's indecency rules? Would it be a violation if Hilton added, "It's not so fucking simple!" How about if Hilton had said, "Have you ever tried to get bovine excrement off a Prada purse? It's not so fornicating simple!"

C. JUDICIAL REVIEW OF AGENCY ADJUDICATIONS

Section 706 of the APA governs judicial review of agency orders just as it governs review of agency rules. The main standard of review for orders as well as rules is § 706(2)(A)'s "arbitrary and capricious" standard. (Section 706(2)(E) requires formal agency decisions based on a trial-type record to be supported by "substantial evidence in the record.")

Consider the Supreme Court's further elaboration of that standard in a follow-up to the FCC's action against NBC; soon after the *Golden Globes* case, the FCC entered orders against Fox for not bleeping out fleeting expletives by Cher and Paris Hilton on television shows that were aired before the *Golden Globes* decision by the FCC.

Federal Communications Commission v. Fox Television Stations, Inc.
556 U.S. 502 (2009).

Federal law prohibits broadcasting "any . . . indecent . . . language," 18 U.S.C. § 1464, which includes expletives referring to sexual or excretory activity or organs, as we saw in the *Golden Globes* case. As narrowed by the courts, the Public Telecommunications Act of 1992, § 16(a), 106 Stat. 954, directs the FCC to enforce this ban between the hours of 6 a.m. and 10 p.m. Congress has given the Commission various means of enforcing the indecency ban, including civil fines, *see* § 503(b)(1), and license revocations or the denial of license renewals, *see* §§ 309(k), 312(a)(6).

For many years, the FCC followed an announced regulatory approach that banned sexual or excretory "expletives" only if their use was "deliberate and repetitive"; mere "fleeting" expletives would generally be allowed. See the 2001 Policy Statement discussed in the *Golden Globes* case. Even as the FCC expanded its indecency standard to encompass ever more words and phrases, it preserved this approach—until the 2004 FCC ruling against NBC in the *Golden Globes* decision and then again in a 2006 FCC ruling against Fox in the present case.

The *Fox Television* adjudication involved two incidents, both occurring before the FCC's *Golden Globes* decision. One was the Fox broadcast of the 2002 Billboard Music Awards, when the singer Cher exclaimed, "I've also had critics for the last 40 years saying that I was on my way out every year. Right. So f * * * 'em." The other episode involved a segment of the 2003 Billboard Music Awards, during the presentation of an award by Nicole Richie and Paris Hilton, principals in a Fox television series called "The Simple Life." On stage, Hilton reminded Richie to "watch the bad language," but Richie then asked the audience, "Why do they even call it 'The Simple Life?' Have you ever tried to get cow s * * * out of a Prada purse? It's not so f * * *ing simple." Following each of these broadcasts, the Commission received numerous complaints from parents whose children were exposed to the language. In 2006, the Commission ruled that Fox violated the statutory prohibitions in both instances, but (as it had done in *Golden Globes*) declined to impose sanctions.

Fox Television appealed the FCC's 2006 order on the ground that its departure from the prior agency policy was "arbitrary and capricious" under APA § 706(2)(A). Invoking the Supreme Court's decision in *State Farm*, the Second Circuit overturned the agency's order against Fox, on the ground that the FCC had not adequately explained why it was jettisoning its longstanding rule against regulating fleeting expletives.

The Supreme Court reversed, in an opinion by **Justice Scalia**. "We find no basis in the Administrative Procedure Act or in our opinions for a requirement that all agency [action that changes prior policy] be subjected to more searching review. The Act mentions no such heightened standard. And our opinion in *State Farm* neither held nor implied that every agency action representing a policy change must be justified by reasons more substantial than those required to adopt a policy in the first instance. That case, which involved the rescission of a prior regulation, said only that such action requires 'a reasoned analysis for the change beyond that which may be required when an agency *does not act* in the first instance.' ([E]mphasis added). Treating failures to act and rescissions of prior action differently for purposes of the standard of review makes good sense, and has basis in the text of the [APA], which likewise treats the two separately. It instructs a reviewing court to 'compel agency action unlawfully withheld or unreasonably delayed,' 5 U.S.C. § 706(1), and to 'hold unlawful and set aside agency action, findings, and conclusions found to be [among other things] . . . arbitrary [or] capricious,' § 706(2)(A). The statute makes no distinction, however, between initial agency action and subsequent agency action undoing or revising that action.

"To be sure, the requirement that an agency provide reasoned explanation for its action would ordinarily demand that it display awareness that it *is* changing position. An agency may not, for example, depart from a prior policy *sub silentio* or simply disregard rules that are still on the books. And of course the agency must show that there are good reasons for the new policy. But it need not demonstrate to a court's satisfaction that the reasons for the new policy are *better* than the reasons for the old one; it suffices that the new policy is permissible under the statute, that there are good reasons for it, and that the agency *believes* it to be better, which the conscious change of course adequately indicates. This means that the agency need not always provide a more detailed justification than what would suffice for a new policy created on a blank slate. Sometimes it must—when, for example, its new policy rests upon factual findings that contradict those which underlay its prior policy; or when its prior policy has engendered serious reliance interests that must be taken into account. It would be arbitrary or capricious to ignore such matters. In such cases it is not that further justification is demanded by the mere fact of policy change; but that a reasoned explanation is needed for disregarding facts and circumstances that underlay or were engendered by the prior policy."

Under this understanding of the law, Justice Scalia ruled that the FCC's order was not "arbitrary and capricious." The FCC had "forthrightly acknowledged" that it was creating new policy and repudiating inconsistent prior actions taken by the Commission and staff. Also, the FCC's reasons for its decision were "entirely rational." It was reasonable for the FCC to conclude that the literal-expletive distinction was nonsensical given that both kinds of uses could cause offense and subject children to a harmful "first blow" of indecency; given technological advances, it was reasonable for the FCC to expect broadcasters to "bleep out" even fleeting expletives.

Justice Kennedy joined Justice Scalia's opinion but issued a concurring opinion, which took a somewhat different approach. "The question whether a change in policy requires an agency to provide a more-reasoned explanation than when the original policy was first announced is not susceptible, in my view, to an answer that applies in all cases." For Justice Kennedy, the issue "is whether the agency's reasons for the change, when viewed in light of the data available to it, and when informed by the experience and expertise of the agency, suffice to demonstrate that the new policy rests upon principles that are rational, neutral, and in accord with the agency's proper understanding of its authority."

"Where there is a policy change the record may be much more developed because the agency based its prior policy on factual findings. In that instance, an agency's decision to change course may be arbitrary and capricious if the agency ignores or countermands its earlier factual findings without reasoned explanation for doing so. An agency cannot simply disregard contrary or inconvenient factual determinations that it made in the past, any more than it can ignore inconvenient facts when it writes on a blank slate." This is the lesson Justice Kennedy drew from *State Farm.* "The present case does not raise the concerns addressed in *State Farm,*" because the FCC had based its prior policy not on factual findings, but on its interpretation of the Court's *Pacifica* ruling, and had given appropriate reasons for changing its policy.

Justice Stevens dissented in an opinion emphasizing the FCC's status as an independent agency, which, he believed, should be relatively free from political influence. "The FCC, like all agencies, may revise its regulations from time to time, just as Congress amends its statutes as circumstances warrant. But the FCC is constrained by its congressional mandate. There should be a strong presumption that the FCC's initial views, reflecting the informed judgment of independent commissioners with expertise in the regulated area, also reflect the views of the Congress that delegated the Commission authority to flesh out details not fully defined in the enacting statute. The rules adopted after *Pacifica* have been in effect for decades and have not proved unworkable in the intervening years. * * * [B]roadcasters have a substantial interest in regulatory stability; the threat of crippling financial penalties looms large over these entities. The FCC's shifting and impermissibly vague indecency policy only imperils these broadcasters and muddles the regulatory landscape. It therefore makes eminent sense to require the Commission to justify why its prior policy is no longer sound before allowing it to change course. The FCC's congressional charter, the Administrative Procedure Act, § 706(2)(A) (instructing courts to 'hold unlawful and set aside . . . arbitrary [or] capricious' agency action), and the rule of law all favor stability over administrative whim."

Justice Breyer (joined by Justices Stevens, Souter, and Ginsburg) dissented. He started with the premise that, as an independent agency, the FCC was relatively insulated from political oversight. "That insulation helps to secure important governmental objectives, such as the constitutionally related objective of maintaining broadcast regulation that does not bend too readily before the political winds. But that agency's comparative freedom from ballot-box control makes it all the more important that courts review its decisionmaking to assure compliance with applicable provisions of the law—including law requiring that major policy decisions be based upon articulable reasons." Additionally, Justice Breyer wrote, the agency must act consistently, and when it changes its own rules the agency "must focus on the fact of change and explain the basis for that change."

"To explain a change requires more than setting forth reasons why the new policy is a good one. It also requires the agency to answer the question, 'Why did you change?' And a rational answer to this question typically requires a more complete explanation than would prove satisfactory were change itself not at issue." *State Farm* "requires the agency here to focus upon the reasons that led the agency to adopt the initial policy, and to explain why it now comes to a new judgment.

"I recognize that *sometimes* the ultimate explanation for a change may have to be, 'We now weigh the relevant considerations differently.' But at other times, an agency can and should say more. Where, for example, the agency rested its previous policy on particular factual findings; or where an agency rested its prior policy on its view of the governing law; or where an agency rested its previous policy on, say, a special need to coordinate with another agency, one would normally expect the agency to focus upon those earlier views of fact, of law, or of policy and explain why they are no longer controlling. Regardless, to say that the agency here must answer the question 'why change' is not to require the agency to provide a justification that is '*better* than the reasons for the old [policy].' It is only to recognize the obvious fact that *change* is sometimes (not always) a relevant background feature that sometimes (not always) requires focus (upon prior justifications) and explanation lest the adoption of the new policy (in that circumstance) be 'arbitrary, capricious, an abuse of discretion.' "

Like the Second Circuit, Justice Breyer concluded that the FCC's decision violated the *State Farm* requirement that an agency making a policy change "consider [ ] important aspect[s] of the problem." In particular, he faulted the FCC for failing adequately to consider its new policy's First Amendment implications and potential impact on local broadcasters, many of whom might not be able to afford the technology necessary to "bleep out" fleeting expletives. Justice Breyer dismissed as inadequate the various reasons the FCC had adduced for its policy change—in particular, the claim that the literal-expletive distinction was nonsensical and the claim that the new policy better protects children against "the first blow" of broadcast indecency. Neither of these claims, Justice Breyer argued, could justify the FCC's policy *change* since both claims remained conclusory, failing to address the rationales underlying the prior policy.

NOTES AND QUESTIONS ON CHANGING AGENCY POLICIES

State Farm can be read as trying to strike a balance between two kinds of risks attending judicial review of agency policy changes. On the one hand, if courts are too deferential, there is the risk that agencies will "yo-yo" such that their policies will fluctuate too frequently. On the other hand, if courts are too scrutinizing, there is the "ossification" risk that agencies will become too loath to change their policies. While the *State Farm* Court and the *Fox* dissenters were more troubled by the yo-yo risk than the ossification risk, the *Fox* Court seemed to have the opposite concern. Is *Fox* therefore inconsistent with *State Farm*? If so, can the inconsistency be justified?

1. *Independent Versus Executive Agencies?* The agency in *State Farm* was an executive department directly accountable to the President, while the agency in *Fox* was an independent agency. The *Fox* dissenters argued that, because of the relative insulation of independent agencies from political pressures, policy changes made by independent agencies should be subject to *more* stringent judicial scrutiny than those made by executive agencies and, consequently, that *State Farm* applies *a fortiori* to *Fox*. Cf. Sharkey, *State Farm "With Teeth"* (arguing for more judicial review for independent agency decisions). But might the opposite be true? Might the relative insulation of independent agencies from political pressures lead one to expect their decisions to be generally *more* reasoned than the decisions of executive agencies and thus to merit *more* deference from courts?

Writing for a plurality of Justices (Part III.E of his opinion, which Justice Kennedy did not join), Justice Scalia argued that independent agencies like the FCC are subject to significant political pressures exerted by Congress through its oversight authority. Thus, "independent" agencies are not necessarily free from politics; the political pressure just comes from different branches of government. (In fact, Justice Scalia argued that the FCC's new policy in *Fox Television* was a direct consequence of congressional complaints that families were being subjected to inappropriate language during prime-time television.) Accordingly, not-so-independent agencies might be entitled to some leeway, to accommodate the evolving political landscape. But once again, might the opposite be true? Might the political accountability of independent agencies lead one to expect their decisions to be *as poorly* reasoned as those of executive agencies and thus to merit *as much* scrutiny from courts?

Should APA judicial review in any way distinguish between the types of agencies promulgating the evolving policy that is being reviewed? Relatedly, should judicial review be attentive to "political" pressure from senators, representatives, and oversight committees? Cf. *Aera Energy LLC v. Salazar*, 642 F.3d 212, 220–23 (D.C. Cir. 2011) (even if there is congressional "pressure" on an agency, APA review is satisfied so long as the agency has articulated a rational basis for its rule).

2.   *Facts Versus Norms.* Rather than trying to distinguish *State Farm* and *Fox* based on the different kinds of *agencies* involved in each, one might try to distinguish them based on the different kinds of *policies* involved in each: Whereas the policy in *State Farm* was based on a relatively technical cost-benefit analysis, the policy in *Fox* was based more on a social or moral judgment. Also recall the D.C. Circuit's decision in *Business Roundtable*, which is more like *State Farm* in this respect.

This difference might help to explain Justice Scalia's observation about the difficulty of obtaining data about the harmfulness of fleeting expletives in broadcasts and the comparative ease of obtaining data about the benefits of passive restraints in automobiles. Perhaps the FCC's policy change rested on the judgment that, whatever the tangible harm caused by fleeting expletives, it was simply *wrong* or *immoral* to expose the public—and especially children—to such indecency. If this was in fact the nature of the FCC's judgment, should courts be more or less willing to defer to it than they would be to defer to a more technical cost-benefit analysis?

Note also that the moral judgment represented in *Fox* raises important First Amendment concerns not present in the cost-benefit judgment represented in *State Farm*: Isn't a "fleeting expletive" a classic example of free expression? Cf. *Cohen v. California*, 403 U.S. 15 (1971) (invalidating state censorship of a young man, standing in a public courthouse and wearing a jacket embroidered with the phrase "Fuck the Draft"). As *Pacifica* held, Congress has greater leeway to regulate indecent speech on the radio and television than in newspapers and the print media—but the regulatory authority is not unlimited. Should there be more specific guidance from Congress as to such important matters—or is Justice Scalia right, that Congress was behind the FCC's tighter rule?

3.   *The Difference Process Might Make?* Should process distinguish *State Farm* from *Fox Television*? The obvious process difference is that the

former was an informal rulemaking proceeding, while the latter was an agency adjudication—but that difference might just as easily cut the other way. That is, a shift in agency policy might be more legitimate in the kind of rulemaking that *State Farm* overturned than in an adjudication that *Fox Television* sanctioned. In notice-and-comment rulemaking, for example, a greater variety of interests will submit analyses, and the agency must consider them—in contrast to adjudication, where the agency must only respond to the parties' presentations.

Another possible process distinction is that the DOT's auto safety policy had been a political football through several administrations, and the *State Farm* Court might have felt that the agency needed to buckle down and take its law work more seriously. In contrast, perhaps, the FCC's policy was more stable over several administrations. Although the FCC was moving policy toward greater regulation in *Fox Television*, it was making a small step (expanding the longstanding policy to include "fleeting" expletives), and a step that was arguably justified by proliferation of fleeting expletives during prime time (when more children are watching TV) and by technology allowing networks to bleep out fleeting expletives. Are any of these distinctions persuasive—or is *Fox Television* simply a precedent-narrowing reading of *State Farm*? Should *State Farm* be reframed, or even overruled?

Federal Communications Commission v. Fox Television Stations, Inc.
132 S.Ct. 2307 (2012).

On remand, the Second Circuit in **Fox II** reached the constitutional issues that Justice Scalia's opinion left open in **Fox I**. See *Fox Television, Inc. v. FCC*, 613 F.3d 317 (2d Cir. 2010). Judge Pooler's opinion found the FCC's policy too vague and malleable to pass First Amendment scrutiny and pointed to a number of instances where protected speech had been chilled by the threat of FCC censorship. The FCC again appealed to the Supreme Court, which consolidated the Fox Television appeal with a similar one involving an FCC order penalizing ABC for airing "fleeting nudity" (brief exposure of the buttocks of a female character) in its acclaimed police series *NYPD Blue*. The Supreme Court rebuked the agency in all three appeals and remanded the cases to the Second Circuit.

Justice Kennedy's opinion for the Court started with a review of the Commission's indecency policy that closely tracked Judge Pooler's review in the court below (and quoted in our first note after *Fox I*). In a nutshell, the George Carlin Seven Dirty Words Case was the agency's only indecency prosecution until 1987. After 1987, the FCC announced heightened concerns over indecency during hours that children might be watching television but continued to say that "deliberate and repetitive use in a patently offensive manner is a requisite to a finding of indecency." In its 2001 policy statement, the Commission said that "[r]epetition of and persistent focus on sexual or excretory material have been cited consistently as factors that exacerbate the potential offensiveness of broadcasts. In contrast, where sexual or excretory references have been made once or have been passing or fleeting in nature, this characteristic has tended to weigh against a finding of indecency." The Commission gave examples of material that was not found indecent because it was fleeting and isolated (e.g., *L.M. Communications of South Carolina, Inc. (WYBB(FM))*, 7 FCC Rcd. 1595 (MMB 1992) (finding "a fleeting and isolated utterance" in the context of live and spontaneous programming not actionable)), and contrasted it with fleeting references that were found patently offensive in light of other factors (e.g., *Temple Radio, Inc. (KUPD-FM)*, 12 FCC Rcd. 21828 (MMB 1997) (finding fleeting language that clearly refers to sexual activity with a child to be patently offensive)).

In *Golden Globes*, the FCC clarified its new, hard-line policy against "fleeting expletives" and found NBC in violation but did not impose penalties. Because the Cher and Paris Hilton incidents occurred before the clarification in *Golden Globes*, the FCC did not assess penalties against Fox Television but did rule that it had broadcast indecent material in violation of the statute. Notwithstanding the lack of explicit penalties, Justice Kennedy ruled that the FCC's order against Fox violated the Due Process Clause of the Fifth Amendment.

"A fundamental principle in our legal system is that laws which regulate persons or entities must give fair notice of conduct that is forbidden or required. *See Connally v. General Constr. Co.*, 269 U.S. 385, 391 (1926) ('[A] statute which either forbids or requires the doing of an act in terms so vague that men of common intelligence must necessarily guess at its meaning and differ as to its application, violates the first essential of due process of law') * * *. This requirement of clarity in regulation is essential to the protections provided by the Due Process Clause of the Fifth Amendment. *See United States v. Williams*, 553 U.S. 285, 304 (2008). It requires the invalidation of laws that are impermissibly vague. A conviction or punishment fails to comply with due process if the statute or regulation under which it is obtained 'fails to provide a person of ordinary intelligence fair notice of what is prohibited, or is so standardless that it authorizes or encourages seriously discriminatory enforcement.' *Ibid.* As this Court has explained, a regulation is not vague because it may at times be difficult to prove an incriminating fact but rather because it is unclear as to what fact must be proved. See *id.*, at 306.

"Even when speech is not at issue, the void for vagueness doctrine addresses at least two connected but discrete due process concerns: first, that regulated parties should know what is required of them so they may act accordingly; second, precision and guidance are necessary so that those enforcing the law do not act in an arbitrary or discriminatory way. *See Grayned v. City of Rockford,* 408 U.S. 104, 108–109 (1972). When speech is involved, rigorous adherence to those requirements is necessary to ensure that ambiguity does not chill protected speech.

"These concerns are implicated here because, at the outset, the broadcasters claim they did not have, and do not have, sufficient notice of what is proscribed. And leaving aside any concerns about facial invalidity, they contend that the lengthy procedural history set forth above shows that the broadcasters did not have fair notice of what was forbidden. Under the 2001 Guidelines in force when the broadcasts occurred, a key consideration was 'whether the material dwell[ed] on or repeat[ed] at length' the offending description or depiction. In the 2004 *Golden Globes* Order, issued after the broadcasts, the Commission changed course and held that fleeting expletives could be a statutory violation. In the challenged orders now under review the Commission applied the new principle promulgated in the *Golden Globes* Order and determined fleeting expletives and a brief moment of indecency were actionably indecent. This regulatory history, however, makes it apparent that the Commission policy in place at the time of the broadcasts gave no notice to Fox or ABC that a fleeting expletive or a brief shot of nudity could be actionably indecent; yet Fox and ABC were found to be in violation. The Commission's lack of notice to Fox and ABC that its interpretation had changed so the fleeting moments of indecency contained in their broadcasts were a violation of § 1464 as interpreted and enforced by the agency 'fail[ed] to provide a person of ordinary intelligence fair notice of what is prohibited.' *Williams.* This would be true with respect to a regulatory change this abrupt on any subject, but it is surely the case when applied to the regulations in question, regulations that touch upon 'sensitive areas of basic First Amendment freedoms,' *Baggett v. Bullitt,* 377 U.S. 360, 372 (1964); *see also Reno v. American Civil Liberties Union,* 521 U.S. 844, 870–871 (1997) ('The vagueness of [a content-based regulation of speech] raises special First Amendment concerns because of its obvious chilling effect')."

The Government argued that there was no constitutional harm, because Fox suffered no immediate penalty from the FCC's finding. "Though the Commission claims it will not consider the prior indecent broadcasts 'in any context,' it has the statutory power to take into account 'any history of prior offenses' when setting the level of a forfeiture penalty. *See* 47 U.S.C. § 503(b)(2)(E). Just as in the First Amendment context, the due process protection against vague regulations 'does not leave [regulated parties] . . . at the mercy of *noblesse oblige.' United States v. Stevens,* 559 U.S. 460, 471 (2010). Given that the Commission found it was 'not inequitable to hold Fox responsible for [the 2003 broadcast],' and that it has the statutory authority to use its finding to increase any future penalties, the Government's assurance it will elect not to do so is insufficient to remedy the constitutional violation.

"In addition, when combined with the legal consequence described above, reputational injury provides further reason for granting relief to Fox. *Cf. Paul v. Davis*, 424 U.S. 693, 708–709 (1976) (explaining that an 'alteration of legal status . . . combined with the injury resulting from the defamation' justifies the invocation of procedural safeguards). As respondent CBS points out, findings of wrongdoing can result in harm to a broadcaster's 'reputation with viewers and advertisers.' This observation is hardly surprising given that the challenged orders, which are contained in the permanent Commission record, describe in strongly disapproving terms the indecent material broadcast by Fox, *see, e.g.*, 21 FCC Rcd., at 13310–13311, ¶ 30 (noting the 'explicit, graphic, vulgar, and shocking nature of Ms. Richie's comments'), and Fox's efforts to protect children from being exposed to it, *see id.*, at 13311, ¶ 33 (finding Fox had failed to exercise 'reasonable judgment, responsibility, and sensitivity to the public's needs and tastes to avoid [a] patently offensive broadcas[t]'). Commission sanctions on broadcasters for indecent material are widely publicized. The challenged orders could have an adverse impact on Fox's reputation that audiences and advertisers alike are entitled to take into account.

"With respect to ABC, the Government with good reason does not argue no sanction was imposed. The fine against ABC and its network affiliates for the seven seconds of nudity was nearly $1.24 million. The Government argues instead that ABC had notice that the scene in *NYPD Blue* would be considered indecent in light of a 1960 decision where the Commission declared that the 'televising of nudes might well raise a serious question of programming contrary to 18 U.S.C. § 1464.' This argument does not prevail. An isolated and ambiguous statement from a 1960 Commission decision does not suffice for the fair notice required when the Government intends to impose over a $1 million fine for allegedly impermissible speech. The Commission, furthermore, had released decisions before sanctioning ABC that declined to find isolated and brief moments of nudity actionably indecent. *See, e.g.,* * * * *In re WPBN/WTOM License Subsidiary, Inc.*, 15 FCC Rcd. 1838, 1840 (2000) (finding full frontal nudity in Schindler's List not indecent). This is not to say, of course, that a graphic scene from *Schindler's List* involving nude concentration camp prisoners is the same as the shower scene from *NYPD Blue*. It does show, however, that the Government can point to nothing that would have given ABC affirmative notice that its broadcast would be considered actionably indecent. It is likewise not sufficient for the Commission to assert, as it did in its order, that though 'the depiction [of nudity] here is not as lengthy or repeated' as in some cases, the shower scene nonetheless 'does contain more shots or lengthier depictions of nudity' than in other broadcasts found not indecent. This broad language fails to demonstrate that ABC had fair notice that its broadcast could be found indecent. In fact, a Commission ruling prior to the airing of the *NYPD Blue* episode had deemed 30 seconds of nude buttocks 'very brief' and not actionably indecent in the context of the broadcast. In light of this record of agency decisions, and the absence of any notice in the 2001 Guidance that seven seconds of nude buttocks would be found indecent, ABC lacked constitutionally sufficient notice prior to being sanctioned.

"The Commission failed to give Fox or ABC fair notice prior to the broadcasts in question that fleeting expletives and momentary nudity could be found actionably indecent. Therefore, the Commission's standards as applied to these broadcasts were vague, and the Commission's orders must be set aside."

Because the Court was invalidating the FCC's actions on due process grounds, Justice Kennedy expressed no opinion on whether the FCC's indecency policy expressed in *Golden Globes* violated the First Amendment or whether the Court should at some point revisit the First Amendment reasoning in *Pacifica* (given technological change and the wider availability of bandwidth than the Court had assumed in the earlier decision). **Justice Ginsburg** concurred in the Court's judgment, as she believed that *Pacifica* should be overruled. **Justice Sotomayor** did not participate in the Court's deliberations in these appeals.

PROBLEM 7–3: THE FCC'S OPTIONS AFTER FOX TELEVISION

With no Justice in dissent, the Supreme Court delivered a rebuke to the FCC's *Golden Globes* policy as applied to broadcasts before that policy was announced. First Amendment arguments against the indecency policy are still available, and it appears that *Pacifica* is easily distinguishable, because George Carlin hammered listeners over the head with the Seven Dirty Words. Also, ominously (for the agency), Justice Thomas in *Fox I* and Justice Ginsburg in *Fox II* expressed a willingness to reconsider *Pacifica*.

All of the *Golden Globe* Commissioners have left the agency. You are the new General Counsel for the FCC, and the new Chair asks you (1) whether the agency ought to adopt a rule or a guidance setting forth precisely what its "expletives" policy is; (2) what the FCC ought to do with the thousands of complaints now pending by parents and institutions complaining about fleeting expletives and nudity on various television programs; and (3) what options apart from the fleeting expletives ban the FCC has to protect children against indecent programming before 10pm (the accepted cutoff point for the FCC's children-protecting rules). The Solicitor General tells you that he thinks *Pacifica* can survive, for the time being, but has no prediction beyond that. What regulatory options can you suggest to the Chair? What procedures ought the FCC to follow in implementing these options? Jot down your thoughts now, and revisit them after you consider the materials in the next section.

3. INFORMAL ADJUDICATIONS, GUIDANCES, AND INACTION

Most administrative decisionmaking does not take the form of APA rulemaking or formal adjudication. Although unencumbered with a great deal of process, such decisions may reflect important policy judgments on the part of the agency, which might publicize those decisions through guidance documents, policy statements, press releases, *amicus* briefs or might issue no public statement whatsoever. As a current example, in the context of the ongoing implementation of the Affordable Care Act, the Department of Health & Human Services has utilized a variety of guidance documents, including letters to state officials, "Frequently Asked Questions," bulletins, and memoranda to implement central aspects of the statute. Although conveying agency policy pronouncements, the foregoing mechanisms avoid notice-and-comment, OIRA review, and the threat of imminent judicial review. See Nicholas Bagley & Helen Levy, *Essential Health Benefits and the Affordable Care Act: Law and Process*, 39 J. Health Pol. Pol'y & L. 443 (2014).

Many of these kinds of decisions are unreviewable because they are "committed to agency discretion by law," APA § 706(a)(2). For example, decisions by prosecutors *not* to seek indictments of alleged lawbreakers are not subject to judicial review for this reason. Applying § 706(a)(2), the Supreme Court has held that judges cannot review agency decisions to terminate programs funded under lump-sum congressional appropriations, *Lincoln v. Vigil*, 508 U.S. 182 (1993). In addition, the Court has held unreviewable agency refusals to reconsider decisions for material errors, *ICC v. Locomotive Engineers*, 482 U.S. 270 (1987), as well as agency decisions involving national security, *Webster v. Doe*, 486 U.S. 592 (1988). As the Court held in *Webster*, judges will still consider constitutional issues even when the statute precludes them from considering challenges grounded upon the statutory goals.

In Parts A and B of this section, we examine some prominent cases where complainants were successful in securing judicial review of agency decisions that are neither rules nor formal adjudications. The section concludes with administrative guidance documents (statements like the FCC's famous 2001 policy statement on broadcast indecency, explored above), which are usually not subjected to immediate judicial review but often are subject to subsequent evaluation by judges.

A. JUDICIAL REVIEW OF ADMINISTRATIVE ACTIONS THAT DO NOT RESULT IN RULES

CITIZENS TO PRESERVE OVERTON PARK, INC. V. JOHN VOLPE

United States Supreme Court, 1971.
401 U.S. 402, 91 S.Ct. 814, 28 L.Ed.2d 136.

Opinion of the Court by MR. JUSTICE MARSHALL, announced by MR. JUSTICE STEWART.

The growing public concern about the quality of our natural environment has prompted Congress in recent years to enact legislation[1] designed to curb the accelerating destruction of our country's natural beauty. We are concerned in this case with § 4(f) of the Department of Transportation Act of 1966, as amended,[2] and § 18(a) of the Federal-Aid Highway Act of 1968, 82 Stat. 823, 23 U.S.C. § 138 (hereafter § 138).[3] These statutes prohibit the Secretary of Transportation from authorizing the use of federal funds to finance the construction of highways through public parks if a "feasible and prudent" alternative route exists. If no such route is available, the statutes allow him to approve construction through

---

[1] *See, e.g.,* The National Environmental Policy Act of 1969, 83 Stat. 852, 42 U.S.C. § 4321 et seq. (1964 ed., Supp. V); Environmental Education Act, 84 Stat. 1312, 20 U.S.C. § 1531 et seq. (1970 ed.); Air Quality Act of 1967, 81 Stat. 485, 42 U.S.C. § 1857 et seq. (1964 ed., Supp. V); Environmental Quality Improvement Act of 1970, 84 Stat. 114, 42 U.S.C. §§ 4371–4374 (1970 ed.).

[2] "It is hereby declared to be the national policy that special effort should be made to preserve the natural beauty of the countryside and public park and recreation lands, wildlife and waterfowl refuges, and historic sites. The Secretary of Transportation shall cooperate and consult with the Secretaries of the Interior, Housing and Urban Development, and Agriculture, and with the States in developing transportation plans and programs that include measures to maintain or enhance the natural beauty of the lands traversed. After August 23, 1968, the Secretary shall not approve any program or project which requires the use of any publicly owned land from a public park, recreation area, or wildlife and waterfowl refuge of national, State, or local significance as determined by the Federal, State, or local officials having jurisdiction thereof, or any land from an historic site of national, State, or local significance as so determined by such officials unless (1) there is no feasible and prudent alternative to the use of such land, and (2) such program includes all possible planning to minimize harm to such park, recreational area, wildlife and waterfowl refuge, or historic site resulting from such use." 82 Stat. 824, 49 U.S.C. § 1653(f) (1964 ed., Supp. V).

[3] "It is hereby declared to be the national policy that special effort should be made to preserve the natural beauty of the countryside and public park and recreation lands, wildlife and waterfowl refuges, and historic sites. The Secretary of Transportation shall cooperate and consult with the Secretaries of the Interior, Housing and Urban Development, and Agriculture, and with the States in developing transportation plans and programs that include measures to maintain or enhance the natural beauty of the lands traversed. After the effective date of the Federal-Aid Highway Act of 1968, the Secretary shall not approve any program or project which requires the use of any publicly owned land from a public park, recreation area, or wildlife and waterfowl refuge of national, State, or local significance as determined by the Federal, State, or local officials having jurisdiction thereof, or any land from an historic site of national, State, or local significance as so determined by such officials unless (1) there is no feasible and prudent alternative to the use of such land, and (2) such program includes all possible planning to minimize harm to such park, recreational area, wildlife and waterfowl refuge, or historic site resulting from such use." 23 U.S.C. § 138 (1964 ed., Supp. V).

parks only if there has been "all possible planning to minimize harm" to the park.

Petitioners, private citizens as well as local and national conservation organizations, contend that the Secretary has violated these statutes by authorizing the expenditure of federal funds for the construction of a six-lane interstate highway through a public park in Memphis, Tennessee. Their claim was rejected by the District Court, which granted the Secretary's motion for summary judgment, and the Court of Appeals for the Sixth Circuit affirmed. After oral argument, this Court granted a stay that halted construction and, treating the application for the stay as a petition for certiorari, granted review. We now reverse the judgment below and remand for further proceedings in the District Court.

Overton Park is 342-acre city park located near the center of Memphis. The park contains a zoo, a nine-hole municipal golf course, an outdoor theater, nature trails, a bridle path, an art academy, picnic areas, and 170 acres of forest. The proposed highway, which is to be a six lane, high-speed, expressway, will sever the zoo from the rest of the park. Although the roadway will be depressed below ground level except where it crosses a small creek, 26 acres of the park will be destroyed. The highway is to be a segment of Interstate Highway I–40, part of the National System of Interstate and Defense Highways. I–40 will provide Memphis with a major east-west expressway which will allow easier access to downtown Memphis from the residential areas on the eastern edge of the city.

Although the route through the park was approved by the Bureau of Public Roads in 1956 and by the Federal Highway Administrator in 1966, the enactment of § 4(f) of the Department of Transportation Act prevented distribution of federal funds for the section of the highway designated to go through Overton Park until the Secretary of Transportation determined whether the requirements of § 4(f) had been met. Federal funding for the rest of the project was, however, available; and the state acquired a right-of-way on both sides of the park. In April 1968, the Secretary announced that he concurred in the judgment of local officials that I–40 should be built through the park. And in September 1969 the State acquired the right-of-way inside Overton Park from the city. Final approval for the project—the route as well as the design—was not announced until November 1969, after Congress had reiterated in § 138 of the Federal-Aid Highway Act that highway construction through public parks was to be restricted. Neither announcement approving the route and design of I–40 was accompanied by a statement of the Secretary's factual findings. He did not indicate why he believed there were no feasible and prudent alternative routes or why design changes could not be made to reduce the harm to the park.

Petitioners contend that the Secretary's action is invalid without such formal findings and that the Secretary did not make an independent determination but merely relied on the judgment of the Memphis City Council. They also contend that it would be "feasible and prudent" to route I–40 around Overton Park either to the north or to the south. And they argue that if these alternative routes are not "feasible and prudent," the present plan does not include "all possible" methods for reducing harm to the park. Petitioners claim that I–40 could be built under the park by using either of two possible tunneling methods, and they claim that, at a minimum, by using advanced drainage techniques the expressway could be depressed below ground level along the entire route through the park including the section that crosses the small creek.

Respondents argue that it was unnecessary for the Secretary to make formal findings, and that he did, in fact, exercise his own independent judgment which was supported by the facts. In the District Court, respondents introduced affidavits, prepared specifically for this litigation, which indicated that the Secretary had made the decision and that the decision was supportable. These affidavits were contradicted by affidavits introduced by petitioners, who also sought to take the deposition of a former Federal Highway Administrator who had participated in the decision to route I–40 through Overton Park.

The District Court and the Court of Appeals found that formal findings by the Secretary were not necessary and refused to order the deposition of the former Federal Highway Administrator because those courts believed that probing of the mental processes of an administrative decisionmaker was prohibited. And, believing that the Secretary's authority was wide and reviewing courts' authority narrow in the approval of highway routes, the lower courts held that the affidavits contained no basis for a determination that the Secretary had exceeded his authority.

We agree that formal findings were not required. But we do not believe that in this case judicial review based solely on litigation affidavits was adequate.

A threshold question—whether petitioners are entitled to any judicial review—is easily answered. Section 701 of the Administrative Procedure Act, 5 U.S.C. § 701, provides that the action of "each authority of the Government of the United States," which includes the Department of Transportation, is subject to judicial review except where there is a statutory prohibition on review or where "agency action is committed to agency discretion by law." In this case, there is no indication that Congress sought to prohibit judicial review and there is most certainly no "showing of 'clear and convincing evidence' of a . . . legislative intent" to restrict access to judicial review. *Abbott Laboratories v. Gardner*, 387 U.S. 136, 141 (1967).

Similarly, the Secretary's decision here does not fall within the exception for action "committed to agency discretion.'" This is a very narrow exception. Berger, *Administrative Arbitrariness and Judicial Review*, 65 Col. L. Rev. 55 (1965). The legislative history of the Administrative Procedure Act indicates that it is applicable in those rare instances where "statutes are drawn in such broad terms that in a given case there is no law to apply." S.Rep. No. 752, 79th Cong., 1st Sess., 26 (1945).

Section 4(f) of the Department of Transportation Act and § 138 of the Federal-Aid Highway Act are clear and specific directives. Both the Department of Transportation Act and the Federal-Aid to Highway Act provide that the Secretary "shall not approve any program or project" that requires the use of any public parkland "unless (1) there is no feasible and prudent alternative to the use of such land, and (2) such program includes all possible planning to minimize harm to such park. . . ." 23 U.S.C. § 138; 49 U.S.C. § 1653(f). This language is a plain and explicit bar to the use of federal funds for construction of highways through parks—only the most unusual situations are exempted.

Despite the clarity of the statutory language, respondents argue that the Secretary has wide discretion. They recognize that the requirement that there be no 'feasible' alternative route admits of little administrative discretion. For this exemption to apply the Secretary must find that as a matter of sound engineering it would not be feasible to build the highway along any other route. Respondents argue, however, that the requirement that there be no other "prudent" route requires the Secretary to engage in a wide-ranging balancing of competing interests. They contend that the Secretary should weigh the detriment resulting from the destruction of parkland against the cost of other routes, safety considerations, and other factors, and determine on the basis of the importance that he attaches to these other factors whether, on balance, alternative feasible routes would be "prudent."

But no such wide-ranging endeavor was intended. It is obvious that in most cases considerations of cost, directness of route, and community disruption will indicate that parkland should be used for highway construction whenever possible. Although it may be necessary to transfer funds from one jurisdiction to another, there will always be a smaller outlay required from the public purse when parkland is used since the public already owns the land and there will be no need to pay for right-of-way. And since people do not live or work in parks, if a highway is built on parkland no one will have to leave his home or give up his business. Such factors are common to substantially all highway construction. Thus, if Congress intended these factors to be on an equal footing with preservation of parkland there would have been no need for the statutes.

Congress clearly did not intend that cost and disruption of the community were to be ignored by the Secretary. [Citations to legislative history.] But the very existence of the statutes[29] indicates that protection of parkland was to be given paramount importance. The few green havens that are public parks were not to be lost unless there were truly unusual factors present in a particular case or the cost or community disruption resulting from alternative routes reached extraordinary magnitudes. If the statutes are to have any meaning, the Secretary cannot approve the destruction of parkland unless he finds that alternative routes present unique problems.

Plainly, there is "law to apply" and thus the exemption for action "committed to agency discretion" is inapplicable. But the existence of judicial review is only the start: the standard for review must also be determined. For that we must look to § 706 of the Administrative Procedure Act, which provides that a "reviewing court shall ... hold unlawful and set aside agency action, findings, and conclusions found" not to meet six separate standards. In all cases agency action must be set aside if the action was "arbitrary, capricious, an abuse of discretion, or otherwise not in accordance with law" or if the action failed to meet statutory, procedural, or constitutional requirements. 5 U.S.C. §§ 706(2)(A), (B), (C), (D). In certain narrow, specifically limited situations, the agency action is to be set aside if the action was not supported by "substantial evidence." And in other equally narrow circumstances the reviewing court is to engage in a de novo review of the action and set it aside if it was "unwarranted by the facts." 5 U.S.C. §§ 706(2)(E), (F).

Petitioners argue that the Secretary's approval of the construction of I–40 through Overton Park is subject to one or the other of these latter two standards of limited applicability. First, they contend that the "substantial evidence" standard of § 706(2)(E) must be applied. In the alternative, they claim that § 706(2)(F) applies and that there must be a de novo review to determine if the Secretary's action was "unwarranted by the facts." Neither of these standards is, however, applicable.

---

[29] The legislative history of both § 4(f) of the Department of Transportation Act, 49 U.S.C. § 1653(f), and § 138 of the Federal-Aid Highway Act, 23 U.S.C. § 138, is ambiguous. The legislative committee reports tend to support respondents' view that the statutes are merely general directives to the Secretary requiring him to consider the importance of parkland as well as cost, community disruption, and other factors. See, e.g., S. Rep. No. 1340, 90th Cong., 2d Sess., 19; H.R. Rep. No. 1584, 90th Cong., 2d Sess., 12. Statements by proponents of the statutes as well as the Senate committee report on § 4(f) indicate, however, that the Secretary was to have limited authority. See, e.g., 114 Cong. Rec. 24033–24037; S. Rep. No.1659, 89th Cong., 2d Sess., 22. See also H.R. Conf. Rep. No. 2236, 89th Cong., 2d Sess., 25. Because of this ambiguity it is clear that we must look primarily to the statutes themselves to find the legislative intent.

Review under the substantial-evidence test is authorized only when the agency action is taken pursuant to a rulemaking provision of the Administrative Procedure Act itself, 5 U.S.C. § 553, or when the agency action is based on a public adjudicatory hearing. *See* 5 U.S.C. §§ 556, 557. The Secretary's decision to allow the expenditure of federal funds to build I–40 through Overton Park was plainly not an exercise of a rulemaking function. And the only hearing that is required by either the Administrative Procedure Act or the statutes regulating the distribution of federal funds for highway construction is a public hearing conducted by local officials for the purpose of informing the community about the proposed project and eliciting community views on the design and route. The hearing is nonadjudicatory, quasi-legislative in nature. It is not designed to produce a record that is to be the basis of agency action—the basic requirement for substantial-evidence review. *See* H.R. Rep. No. 1980, 79th Cong., 2d Sess.

Petitioners' alternative argument also fails. De novo review of whether the Secretary's decision was "unwarranted by the facts" is authorized by § 706(2)(F) in only two circumstances. First, such de novo review is authorized when the action is adjudicatory in nature and the agency factfinding procedures are inadequate. And, there may be independent judicial factfinding when issues that were not before the agency are raised in a proceeding to enforce nonadjudicatory agency action. H.R. Rep. No. 1980, 79th Cong., 2d Sess. Neither situation exists here.

Even though there is no de novo review in this case and the Secretary's approval of the route of I–40 does not have ultimately to meet the substantial-evidence test, the generally applicable standards of § 706 require the reviewing court to engage in a substantial inquiry. Certainly, the Secretary's decision is entitled to a presumption of regularity. But that presumption is not to shield his action from a thorough, probing, in-depth review.

The court is first required to decide whether the Secretary acted within the scope of his authority. *Schilling v. Rogers*, 363 U.S. 666 (1960). This determination naturally begins with a delineation of the scope of the Secretary's authority and discretion. As has been shown, Congress has specified only a small range of choices that the Secretary can make. Also involved in this initial inquiry is a determination of whether on the facts the Secretary's decision can reasonably be said to be within that range. The reviewing court must consider whether the Secretary properly construed his authority to approve the use of parkland as limited to situations where there are no feasible alternative routes or where feasible alternative routes involve uniquely difficult problems. And the reviewing court must be able to find that the Secretary could have reasonably believed that in this case there are no feasible alternatives or that alternatives do involve unique problems.

Scrutiny of the facts does not end, however, with the determination that the Secretary has acted within the scope of his statutory authority. Section 706(2)(A) requires a finding that the actual choice made was not "arbitrary, capricious, an abuse of discretion, or otherwise not in accordance with law." To make this finding the court must consider whether the decision was based on a consideration of the relevant factors and whether there has been a clear error of judgment. Although this inquiry into the facts is to be searching and careful, the ultimate standard of review is a narrow one. The court is not empowered to substitute its judgment for that of the agency.

The final inquiry is whether the Secretary's action followed the necessary procedural requirements. Here the only procedural error alleged is the failure of the Secretary to make formal findings and state his reason for allowing the highway to be built through the park.

Undoubtedly, review of the Secretary's action is hampered by his failure to make such findings, but the absence of formal findings does not necessarily require that the case be remanded to the Secretary. Neither the Department of Transportation Act nor the Federal-Aid Highway Act requires such formal findings. Moreover, the Administrative Procedure Act requirements that there be formal findings in certain rulemaking and adjudicatory proceedings do not apply to the Secretary's action here. And, although formal findings may be required in some cases in the absence of statutory directives when the nature of the agency action is ambiguous, those situations are rare. Plainly, there is no ambiguity here; the Secretary has approved the construction of I–40 through Overton Park and has approved a specific design for the project.

* * * The lower courts based their review on the litigation affidavits that were presented. These affidavits were merely "post hoc" rationalizations, which have traditionally been found to be an inadequate basis for review. *SEC v. Chenery Corp.*, 318 U.S. 80, 87 (1943). And they clearly do not constitute the "whole record" compiled by the agency: the basis for review required by § 706 of the Administrative Procedure Act.

Thus it is necessary to remand this case to the District Court for plenary review of the Secretary's decision. That review is to be based on the full administrative record that was before the Secretary at the time he made his decision. But since the bare record may not disclose the factors that were considered or the Secretary's construction of the evidence it may be necessary for the District Court to require some explanation in order to determine if the Secretary acted within the scope of his authority and if the Secretary's action was justifiable under the applicable standard.

The court may require the administrative officials who participated in the decision to give testimony explaining their action. Of course, such inquiry into the mental processes of administrative decisionmakers is usually to be avoided. *United States v. Morgan*, 313 U.S. 409, 422 (1941). And where there are administrative findings that were made at the same time as the decision, as was the case in *Morgan*, there must be a strong showing of bad faith or improper behavior before such inquiry may be made. But here there are no such formal findings and it may be that the only way there can be effective judicial review is by examining the decisionmakers themselves.

The District Court is not, however, required to make such an inquiry. It may be that the Secretary can prepare formal findings including the information required by DOT Order 5610.1 that will provide an adequate explanation for his action. Such an explanation will, to some extent, be a 'post hoc rationalization' and thus must be viewed critically. If the District Court decides that additional explanation is necessary, that court should consider which method will prove the most expeditious so that full review may be had as soon as possible.

[MR. JUSTICE DOUGLAS took no part in the consideration or decision of this case. MR. JUSTICE BLACK, joined by MR. JUSTICE BRENNAN, concurred in most of the Court's opinion but would have remanded the case directly to the Secretary of Transportation. We also omit MR. JUSTICE BLACKMUN's concurring opinion.]

NOTES ON REVIEWABILITY OF LESS FORMAL AGENCY ACTION

1.   *The Presumption of Reviewability. Overton Park* is a leading statement of the "presumption of reviewability," even of highly informal decisions, so long as the reviewing court has statute-based "law to apply." But the Court had to torture the statute long and hard to extract "law to apply"— and one commentator claims that the Court got the law wrong. See Peter L. Strauss, Citizens to Preserve Overton Park v. Volpe—*Of Politics and Law, Young Lawyers and the Highway Goliath*, in *Administrative Law Stories* 258– 332 (Peter L. Strauss ed., 2006). Professor Strauss found the statutory directive much less clear than Justice Marshall did and credited legislative history which assumed that the Secretary would consider the importance of the parkland, along with cost, community disruption, and other factors. The Secretary did consider park values, and plans were changed several times in response to park concerns. By requiring that parklands be given paramount rather than ordinary consideration, the Court was imposing values by judicial decree on the Secretary that were not clearly those Congress had put into the statute. Strauss maintains that the political balance between park values and efficient road-building values was disrupted by the Court's hurried decision.

2.   *The Remedy for Arbitrary Agency Action.* The *Overton Park* Court's mandate was to remand the case to the trial court, with directions to create a record through a judicial hearing. That remedy would be highly unusual today; instead, the Court has repeatedly admonished lower federal courts to remand unlawful decisions to the agency. E.g., *Florida Power & Light Co. v. Lorion*, 470 U.S. 729, 744–45 (1985) (discussing post-*Overton Park* case law). A related issue has been debated in the D.C. Circuit, especially in environmental law cases: Should the reviewing court *vacate* the unlawful agency decision and *remand* the matter to the agency, or might the court leave the agency decision in place and simply *remand* the matter for the agency to reconsider (with the decision remaining in place during the reconsideration). Compare *NRDC v. EPA*, 489 F.3d 1250, 1262–64 (D.C. Cir. 2007) (Randolph, J., concurring) (urging that the court always vacate and remand unlawful agency decisions), with *id.* at 1264–67 (Rogers, J., dissenting in part) (urging the court to remand without vacatur in cases where there would be public harm to the lapse in an agency rule).

3.   *The Proceedings on Remand in* Overton Park. The Secretary on remand was ultimately unable to justify his decision and so declined to approve the parkland route. See *Citizens to Preserve Overton Park, Inc. v. Brinegar*, 494 F.2d 1212 (6th Cir. 1974), *cert. denied*, 421 U.S. 991 (1975). After more back-and-forth between local authorities and the Nixon, Ford, and Carter Administrations, the whole idea of an east-west expressway through Memphis was abandoned. Because most of I–40's east-west path had already been completed, the interstate now dead-ends when it reaches the park.

B. JUDICIAL REVIEW OF ADMINISTRATIVE INACTION?

Agencies implement statutes and affect public policy by what they do *not* do—yet agency inaction is usually not subject to judicial review. For example, prosecutorial decisions not to bring charges against an alleged lawbreaker are not reviewable: even victims of the legal violation often do not have Article III standing to get into federal court (Chapter 3, § 1), and judges believe that prosecutorial discretion insulates decisions not to charge from judicial review even if there were a justiciable case or controversy.

Yet, sometimes, judicial review is available. In *Dunlop v. Bachowski*, 421 U.S. 560 (1975), for example, the Supreme Court ruled that the losing candidate could sue the Secretary of Labor for his refusal to challenge the results of a union election that allegedly violated the Landrum-Griffin Act of 1959. (Title IV of the Act vests the Secretary with the exclusive authority to sue to overturn an election violating the statutory guarantee of a free and fair election according to statutory standards.) As in *Overton Park*, the Court in *Bachowski* ruled that the injured party could require a statement of reasons from the Secretary; the district court could then review the statement of reasons to determine whether it was, on its face, "arbitrary and capricious" under the APA.

After *Bachowski*, the Secretary of Labor has issued detailed statements of reasons when he or she has decided not to seek invalidation of challenged union elections, see 29 C.F.R. § 458.64(b), and challengers have sometimes sued the Secretary for judicial review of those statements of reasons. Federal courts have usually dismissed challenges to such decisions based upon the reasonableness of the statements. E.g., *Corner v. U.S. Dep't of Labor*, 219 F. App'x 492 (7th Cir. 2007); *Madonado v. Brock*, 661 F. Supp. 548 (S.D.N.Y. 1987). Sometimes, a reviewing court has remanded the matter to the Secretary for a more detailed statement of reasons if the Secretary failed to address a significant, plausible claim of statutory violation made by the losing candidate. See *Harrington v. Chao*, 280 F.3d 50 (1st Cir. 2002) (also requiring the Secretary to explain whether she was altering the rule adopted by regulation and, if so, why that was justifiable); *Balanoff v. Donovan*, 549 F. Supp. 102 (N.D. Ill. 1982). Generally, the Secretary has provided a fresh statement of reasons answering all relevant questions, and the reviewing courts have then dismissed the claim. E.g., *Creese v. Dole*, 776 F. Supp. 1474 (D. Colo. 1991). In *Doyle v. Brock*, 641 F. Supp. 223 (D.D.C. 1986) *aff'd*, 821 F.2d 778 (D.C. Cir. 1987), however, the district judge found the Secretary's supplemental statement of reasons arbitrary and directed the Secretary to file suit to overturn the challenged election. Can a court order an executive official to file suit? Are there separation of powers problems with such a move? (Reconsider your answer after reading the next case.)

As the *Bachowski* line of cases suggests, the *Overton Park* liberality toward judicial review of informal agency decisions can generate statements of reasons exposing legal and factual flaws in the agency's decisionmaking. As in *State Farm*, judicial review that requires agencies to explain why they did not accept significant arguments can have considerable bite. How far should the *Overton Park-Bachowski* line of cases go toward subjecting agency inaction to judicial review?

Margaret M. Heckler v. Larry Leon Chaney
470 U.S. 821 (1985).

Prison inmates convicted of capital offenses and sentenced to death by lethal injection under the laws of Oklahoma and Texas petitioned the Food and Drug Administration (FDA) to intervene to stop the use of drugs to carry out the executions; the inmates alleged that under the circumstances the use of these drugs for capital punishment violated the Federal Food, Drug, and Cosmetic Act, 52 Stat. 1040, 21 U.S.C. § 301 *et seq.* (FDCA). They alleged that the drugs had not been tested for the purpose for which they were to be used, and that, given that the drugs would likely be administered by untrained personnel, it was also likely that the drugs would not induce the quick and painless death intended. Accordingly, use of these drugs for human execution was the "unapproved use of an approved drug" and constituted a violation of the Act's prohibitions against "misbranding." 21 U.S.C. § 352(f).

The FDA Commissioner refused to take the requested actions. The Commissioner concluded that FDA jurisdiction in the area was generally unclear but in any event should not be exercised to interfere with this particular aspect of state criminal justice systems. Even if the agency had jurisdiction, the Commissioner would have declined the petition, because this use of drugs did not pose the serious danger to public health that the agency usually required before it would devote resources to a major intervention.

The trial court found the FDA's refusal to act unreviewable, but the D.C. Circuit ruled that under the APA there is a presumption in favor of judicial review, see *Abbott Laboratories v. Gardner*, 387 U.S. 136, 139–141 (1967); 5 U.S.C. §§ 701 (judicial review unless precluded by statute or when action is "committed to agency discretion"), 551(13) (judicial review extends to agency refusals to act), and found the presumption not rebutted in the context of this challenge. The court invoked a FDA policy statement indicating that the agency was "obligated" to investigate the unapproved use of an approved drug when such use became "widespread" or "endanger[ed] the public health." 37 Fed. Reg. 16504 (1972). The court held that this policy statement constituted a "rule" and was considered binding by the FDA. Given the policy statement indicating that the FDA should take enforcement action in this area, and the strong presumption that all agency action is subject to judicial review, the court concluded that review of the agency's refusal was not foreclosed. It then proceeded to assess whether the agency's decision not to act was "arbitrary, capricious, or an abuse of discretion." Citing evidence that the FDA assumed jurisdiction over drugs used to put animals to sleep and the unapproved uses of drugs on prisoners in clinical experiments, the court found that the FDA's refusal was irrational, and that the inmates' evidence that use of the drugs could lead to a cruel and protracted death was entitled to more searching consideration. The Supreme Court reversed.

Justice Rehnquist's opinion for the Court examined the APA's provisions governing judicial review of agency action, 5 U.S.C. §§ 701–706 (Appendix 2). Before any review at all may be undertaken, a party must first clear the hurdle of § 701(a). That section provides that the chapter on judicial review "applies, according to the provisions thereof, except to the extent that—(1) statutes preclude judicial review; or (2) agency action is committed to agency discretion by law." The FDA argued that its decision to refuse enforcement is "committed to agency discretion by law" under § 701(a)(2).

"This Court has not had occasion to interpret this second exception in § 701(a) in any great detail. On its face, the section does not obviously lend itself to any particular construction; indeed, one might wonder what difference exists between § (a)(1) and § (a)(2). The former section seems easy in application; it requires construction of the substantive statute involved to determine whether Congress intended to preclude judicial review of certain decisions. * * * But one could read the language 'committed to agency discretion *by law*' in § (a)(2) to require a similar inquiry. In addition, commentators have pointed out that construction of § (a)(2) is further complicated by the tension between a literal reading of § (a)(2), which exempts from judicial review those decisions committed to agency 'discretion,' and the primary scope of review prescribed by § 706(2)(A)—whether the agency's action was 'arbitrary, capricious, or an *abuse of discretion.*' How is it, they ask, that an action committed to agency discretion can be unreviewable and yet courts still can review agency actions for abuse of that discretion? * * * The APA's legislative history provides little help on this score. Mindful, however, of the common-sense principle of statutory construction that sections of a statute generally should be read 'to give effect, if possible, to every clause . . . ,' we think there is a proper construction of § (a)(2) which satisfies each of these concerns."

Justice Rehnquist discussed the Court's previous decision in *Overton Park*, which he read to support the following distinction between § 701(a)(1) and § 701(a)(2): "The former applies when Congress has expressed an intent to preclude judicial review. The latter applies in different circumstances; even where Congress has not affirmatively precluded review, review is not to be had if the statute is drawn so that a court would have no meaningful standard against which to judge the agency's exercise of discretion. In such a case, the statute ('law') can be taken to have 'committed' the decisionmaking to the agency's judgment absolutely. This construction avoids conflict with the 'abuse of discretion' standard of review in § 706—if no judicially manageable standards are available for judging how and when an agency should exercise its discretion, then it is impossible to evaluate agency action for 'abuse of discretion.' In addition, this construction satisfies the principle of statutory construction mentioned earlier, by identifying a separate class of cases to which § 701(a)(2) applies. * * *

"*Overton Park* did not involve an agency's refusal to take requested enforcement action. It involved an affirmative act of approval under a statute that set clear guidelines for determining when such approval should be given. Refusals to take enforcement steps generally involve precisely the opposite situation, and in that situation we think the presumption is that judicial review is not available. This Court has recognized on several occasions over many years that an agency's decision not to prosecute or enforce, whether through civil or criminal process, is a decision generally committed to an agency's absolute discretion. * * * This recognition of the existence of discretion is attributable in no small part to the general unsuitability for judicial review of agency decisions to refuse enforcement.

"The reasons for this general unsuitability are many. First, an agency decision not to enforce often involves a complicated balancing of a number of factors which are peculiarly within its expertise. Thus, the agency must not only assess whether a violation has occurred, but whether agency resources are best spent on this violation or another, whether the agency is likely to succeed if it acts, whether the particular enforcement action requested best fits the agency's overall policies, and, indeed, whether the agency has enough resources to undertake the action at all. An agency generally cannot act against each technical violation of the statute it is charged with enforcing. The agency is far better equipped than the courts to deal with the many variables involved in the proper ordering of its priorities. Similar concerns animate the principles of administrative law that courts generally will defer to an agency's construction of the statute it is charged with implementing, and to the procedures it adopts for implementing that statute. * * *

"In addition to these administrative concerns, we note that when an agency refuses to act it generally does not exercise its *coercive* power over an individual's liberty or property rights, and thus does not infringe upon areas that courts often are called upon to protect. Similarly, when an agency *does* act to enforce, that action itself provides a focus for judicial review, inasmuch as the agency must have exercised its power in some manner. The action at least can be reviewed to determine whether the agency exceeded its statutory powers. * * * Finally, we recognize that an agency's refusal to institute proceedings shares to some extent the characteristics of the decision of a prosecutor in the Executive Branch not to indict—a decision which has long been regarded as the special province of the Executive Branch, inasmuch as it is the Executive who is charged by the Constitution to 'take Care that the Laws be faithfully executed.' U.S. Const., Art. II, § 3.

"We of course only list the above concerns to facilitate understanding of our conclusion that an agency's decision not to take enforcement action should be presumed immune from judicial review under § 701(a)(2). For good reasons, such a decision has traditionally been 'committed to agency discretion,' and we believe that the Congress enacting the APA did not intend to alter that tradition. * * * In so stating, we emphasize that the decision is only presumptively unreviewable; the presumption may be rebutted where the substantive statute has provided guidelines for the agency to follow in exercising its enforcement powers.[4] Thus, in establishing this presumption in the APA, Congress did not set agencies free to disregard legislative direction in the statutory scheme that the agency administers. Congress may limit an agency's exercise of enforcement power if it wishes, either by setting substantive priorities, or by otherwise circumscribing an agency's power to discriminate among issues or cases it will pursue. How to determine when Congress has done so is the question left open by *Overton Park*."

The Court then examined the statutory structure. "The Secretary is *authorized* to conduct examinations and investigations" (21 U.S.C. § 372) and may seek remedies for statutory violations through injunctions (§ 332), criminal sanctions (§§ 333 and 335), and seizure (§ 334). Justice Rehnquist concluded: "The Act's enforcement provisions thus commit complete discretion to the Secretary to decide how and when they should be exercised." Although the FDA had issued a policy statement that it considered itself "obligated" to take certain investigative actions, the Court observed that the policy statement "was attached to a rule that was never adopted. Whatever force such a statement might have, and leaving to one side the problem of whether an agency's rules might under certain circumstances provide courts with adequate guidelines for informed judicial review of decisions not to enforce, we do not think the language of the agency's 'policy statement' can plausibly be read to override the agency's express assertion of unreviewable discretion contained in the above rule."

In a concurring opinion, **Justice Brennan** emphasized that judicial review was *not* foreclosed by the Court's opinion "in cases where (1) an agency flatly claims that it has no statutory jurisdiction to reach certain conduct [the Court's footnote 4]; (2) an agency engages in a pattern of nonenforcement of clear statutory language [footnote 4]; (3) an agency has refused to enforce a regulation lawfully promulgated and still in effect; or (4) a nonenforcement decision violates constitutional rights." In addition, judicial review might be justified where there has been agency "nonenforcement in return for a bribe."

Justice Marshall concurred in the judgment and argued "for a different basis of decision: that refusals to enforce, like other agency actions, are reviewable in the absence of a 'clear and convincing' congressional intent to the contrary, but that such refusals warrant

---

[4] We do not have in this case a refusal by the agency to institute proceedings based solely on the belief that it lacks jurisdiction. Nor do we have a situation where it could justifiably be found that the agency has 'consciously and expressly adopted a general policy' that is so extreme as to amount to an abdication of its statutory responsibilities. *See, e.g., Adams v. Richardson*, 480 F.2d 1159 (D.C. Cir. 1973) (en banc). Although we express no opinion on whether such decisions would be unreviewable under § 701(a)(2), we note that in those situations the statute conferring authority on the agency might indicate that such decisions were not 'committed to agency discretion.'

deference when, as in this case, there is nothing to suggest that an agency with enforcement discretion has abused that discretion." Section 553(e) of the APA required the FDA to provide a statement of reasons for denying the requested action, and the FDA provided such a statement here:

> "[W]e believe we would be authorized to decline to exercise [jurisdiction] under our inherent discretion to decline to pursue certain enforcement matters. The unapproved use of approved drugs is an area in which the case law is far from uniform. Generally, enforcement proceedings in this area are initiated only when there is a serious danger to the public health or a blatant scheme to defraud. We cannot conclude that those dangers are present under State lethal injection laws. . . . [W]e decline, as a matter of enforcement discretion, to pursue supplies of drugs under State control that will be used for execution by lethal injection."

Justice Marshall believed that this statement was subject to judicial review—and that it passed with flying colors. "As long as the agency is choosing how to allocate finite enforcement resources, the agency's choice will be entitled to substantial deference, for the choice among valid alternative enforcement policies is precisely the sort of choice over which agencies generally have been left substantial discretion by their enabling statutes. *On the merits*, then, a decision not to enforce that is based on valid resource-allocation decisions will generally not be 'arbitrary, capricious, an abuse of discretion, or otherwise not in accordance with law,' 5 U.S.C. § 706(2)(A). The decision in this case is no exception to this principle."

Justice Marshall rejected the Court's broader rationale. The Court's novel "presumption of unreviewability" is inconsistent with the structure of the APA, with the legislative history of that landmark statute,[10] and with the Court's precedents requiring a broad availability of judicial review. E.g., *Abbott Laboratories v. Gardner,* 387 U.S. 136 (1967) (Harlan, J.).

NOTES AND QUESTIONS ON THE ACTION-INACTION DISTINCTION

Justice Rehnquist's opinion rejected the presumption of reviewability when the agency is not acting. But the Court's *action-inaction* distinction flies in the face of APA § 553(e), the structure of the APA, its relevant legislative history, and a number of Supreme Court precedents, such as *Dunlop v. Bachowski.* At a deeper level, it is in tension with *Overton Park,* as *Chaney* rests upon the notion that the Constitution is primarily concerned with

---

[10] H.R. Rep. No. 1980, 79th Cong., 2d Sess., 41 (1946) (to preclude APA review, a statute "must upon its face give clear and convincing evidence of an intent to withhold it").

protecting against governmental deprivations of people's liberties (negative rights) and is not concerned with protecting against governmental failures to affirmatively protect people's liberties (positive rights). If read broadly, Justice Rehnquist's idea would be quite radical. From Thomas Hobbes's *Leviathan* (1660) onward, social contract theorists who inspired the framers of the Constitution saw the central role of the state as being the *positive* protection of liberty (the "brutish" state of nature is one where we can be victimized by our neighbors, and the state is created to prevent that). So the primary role of a constitution is to ensure the positive liberties that are the foundation of the state; a secondary role is to ensure those negative liberties against excessive state regulation or oppression. Thus, the nation's long campaign against southern apartheid was, at bottom, a campaign to assure citizens of color their positive liberties: stopping private lynchings was as important as assuring due process in state trials; school desegregation was justified to avoid feelings of social inferiority as well as denial of equal resources; assuring a positive right to vote, and not just removing overt discrimination, was the basis for future progress in the south.

Does Justice Rehnquist's opinion require a reconsideration of the premises of the modern regulatory state, which has expanded upon Hobbes's positive guarantees? Not necessarily. As Justice Brennan's concurring opinion makes clear, the presumption of nonreviewability for agency inaction does not apply if the petitioners are claiming that the agency (1) erroneously claims that it has no statutory jurisdiction (legal error); (2) engages in a pattern of nonenforcement of clear statutory or regulatory language; (3) has adopted a policy that violates constitutional rights or has acted corruptly. Thus, where a statute requires an agency to take action under specified circumstances, the agency's failure to do so might be reviewable—perhaps via judicial examination of the agency's statement of reasons to determine whether it is arbitrary or capricious. Compare *Bachowski* and the lower court decisions implementing that judicial review precedent. But note that § 553(e) *did* require the FDA to take action in response to the prisoners' petition. How can Justice Rehnquist get around that statutory fact? Is the action-inaction rule one that can be neutrally applied?[11]

---

[11] Lower courts read *Chaney* to allow judicial review where the agency's inaction was grounded on inaccurate statutory interpretations or was an effort by the agency to alter established understandings of statutory requirements. E.g., *International Union, United Automobile, Aerospace & Agricultural Implement Workers of America v. Dole*, 869 F.2d 616 (D.C. Cir. 1989); *Davis Enterprises v. EPA*, 877 F.2d 1181 (3d Cir. 1989); *Dina v. Attorney General*, 793 F.2d 473 (2d Cir. 1986); *Electricities of N.C. v. Southeastern Power Admin.*, 774 F.2d 1262 (4th Cir. 1985).

Gale Norton v. Southern Utah Wilderness Alliance (SUWA)
542 U.S. 55 (2004).

Almost half of Utah is federal land administered by the Bureau of Land Management (BLM), an agency within the Department of Interior. For nearly 30 years, BLM's management of public lands has been governed by the Federal Land Policy and Management Act of 1976 (FLPMA), 90 Stat. 2744, 43 U.S.C. § 1701 *et seq.*, which "established a policy in favor of retaining public lands" for "multiple use management."

The agency was charged with striking a balance among the many competing uses to which land can be put, " 'including, but not limited to, recreation, range, timber, minerals, watershed, wildlife and fish, and [uses serving] natural scenic, scientific and historical values.' 43 U.S.C. § 1702(c). A second management goal, sustained yield, requires BLM to control depleting uses over time, so as to ensure a high level of valuable uses in the future. § 1702(h). To these ends, FLPMA establishes a dual regime of inventory and planning. Sections 1711 and 1712, respectively, provide for a comprehensive, ongoing inventory of federal lands, and for a land use planning process that 'project[s]' 'present and future use,' § 1701(a)(2), given the lands' inventoried characteristics."

Congress also directed that "some lands should be set aside as wilderness at the expense of commercial and recreational uses. * * * [T]he Wilderness Act of 1964, 78 Stat. 890, provides that designated wilderness areas, subject to certain exceptions, 'shall [have] no commercial enterprise and no permanent road,' no motorized vehicles, and no manmade structures. 16 U.S.C. § 1133(c)." Under § 1782(a), the Secretary of the Interior has identified a number of "wilderness study areas" (WSAs), roadless lands of 5,000 acres or more that possess "wilderness characteristics," as determined by the Secretary. "In 1991, out of 3.3 million acres in Utah that had been identified for study, 2 million were recommended by BLM as suitable for wilderness designation. 1 U.S. Dept. of Interior, BLM, Utah Statewide Wilderness Study Report 3 (Oct. 1991). This recommendation was forwarded to Congress, which had not yet acted upon it. Until Congress acts one way or the other, FLPMA provides that 'the Secretary shall continue to manage such lands . . . in a manner so as not to impair the suitability of such areas for preservation as wilderness.' 43 U.S.C. § 1782(c). This nonimpairment mandate applies to all WSAs identified under § 1782, including lands considered unsuitable by the Secretary.

"Aside from identification of WSAs, the main tool that BLM employs to balance wilderness protection against other uses is a land use plan— what BLM regulations call a 'resource management plan.' 43 CFR § 1601.0–5(k) (2003). Land use plans, adopted after notice and comment, are 'designed to guide and control future management actions, § 1601.0–

2. *See* 43 U.S.C. § 1712; 43 CFR § 1610.2 (2003). Generally, a land use plan describes, for a particular area, allowable uses, goals for future condition of the land, and specific next steps. § 1601.0–5(k). Under FLPMA, "[t]he Secretary shall manage the public lands under principles of multiple use and sustained yield, in accordance with the land use plans . . . when they are available. 43 U.S.C. § 1732(a)."

"Protection of wilderness has come into increasing conflict with another element of multiple use, recreational use of so-called off-road vehicles (ORVs), which include vehicles primarily designed for off-road use, such as lightweight, four-wheel 'all-terrain vehicles,' and vehicles capable of such use, such as sport utility vehicles. * * * The use of ORVs on federal land has negative environmental consequences, including soil disruption and compaction, harassment of animals, and annoyance of wilderness lovers. Thus, BLM faces a classic land use dilemma of sharply inconsistent uses, in a context of scarce resources and congressional silence with respect to wilderness designation."

In 1999, Southern Utah Wilderness Alliance (SUWA) sued BLM and the Secretary for declaratory and injunctive relief for BLM's alleged failure to act to protect public lands in Utah from damage caused by ORV use. SUWA claimed that BLM (1) had "violated its nonimpairment obligation under § 1782(c) by allowing degradation in certain WSAs"; (2) "had failed to implement provisions in its land use plans relating to ORV use"; and (3) had "failed to take a 'hard look' at whether, pursuant to the National Environmental Policy Act of 1969 (NEPA), 83 Stat. 852, 42 U.S.C. § 4321 *et seq.*, it should undertake supplemental environmental analyses for areas in which ORV use had increased." "SUWA contended that it could sue to remedy these three failures to act pursuant to the APA's provision of a cause of action to 'compel agency action unlawfully withheld or unreasonably delayed.' 5 U.S.C. § 706(1)."

The circuit court ruled that SUWA was entitled to judicial review for all three claims and that BLM failed to take action with respect to ORV use that it was required to take. **Justice Scalia**'s opinion for a unanimous Supreme Court reversed the lower court and held that the APA did not authorize judicial review for these failures to act.

"The APA authorizes suit by '[a] person suffering legal wrong because of agency action, or adversely affected or aggrieved by agency action within the meaning of a relevant statute.' 5 U.S.C. § 702. Where no other statute provides a private right of action, the 'agency action' complained of must be '*final* agency action.' § 704 (emphasis added). '[A]gency action' is defined in § 551(13) to include 'the whole or a part of an agency rule, order, license, sanction, relief, or the equivalent or denial thereof, *or failure to act*.' (Emphasis added.) The APA provides relief for a failure to act in § 706(1): 'The reviewing court shall . . . compel agency action unlawfully withheld or unreasonably delayed.'

"Sections 702, 704, and 706(1) all insist upon an 'agency action,' either as the action complained of (in §§ 702 and 704) or as the action to be compelled (in § 706(1)). The definition of that term begins with a list of five categories of decisions made or outcomes implemented by an agency—'agency rule, order, license, sanction [or] relief.' § 551(13). All of those categories involve circumscribed, discrete agency actions, as their definitions make clear: 'an agency statement of . . . future effect designed to implement, interpret, or prescribe law or policy' (rule); 'a final disposition . . . in a matter other than rule making' (order); a 'permit . . . or other form of permission' (license); a 'prohibition . . . or . . . taking [of] other compulsory or restrictive action' (sanction); or a 'grant of money, assistance, license, authority,' etc., or 'recognition of a claim, right, immunity,' etc., or 'taking of other action on the application or petition of, and beneficial to, a person' (relief). §§ 551(4), (6), (8), (10), (11).

"The terms following those five categories of agency action are not defined in the APA: 'or the equivalent or denial thereof, or failure to act.' § 551(13). But an 'equivalent . . . thereof' must also be discrete (or it would not be equivalent), and a 'denial thereof' must be the denial of a discrete listed action (and perhaps denial of a discrete equivalent).

"The final term in the definition, 'failure to act,' is in our view properly understood as a failure to take an *agency action*—that is, a failure to take one of the agency actions (including their equivalents) earlier defined in § 551(13). Moreover, even without this equation of 'act' with 'agency action' the interpretive canon of *ejusdem generis* would attribute to the last item ('failure to act') the same characteristic of discreteness shared by all the preceding items. * * * A 'failure to act' is not the same thing as a 'denial.' The latter is the agency's act of saying no to a request; the former is simply the omission of an action without formally rejecting a request—for example, the failure to promulgate a rule or take some decision by a statutory deadline. The important point is that a 'failure to act' is properly understood to be limited, as are the other items in § 551(13), to a *discrete* action.

"A second point central to the analysis of the present case is that the only agency action that can be compelled under the APA is action legally *required*. This limitation appears in § 706(1)'s authorization for courts to 'compel agency action *unlawfully* withheld.' (Emphasis added.) In this regard the APA carried forward the traditional practice prior to its passage, when judicial review was achieved through use of the so-called prerogative writs—principally writs of mandamus under the All Writs Act, now codified at 28 U.S.C. § 1651(a). The mandamus remedy was normally limited to enforcement of 'a specific, unequivocal command,' *ICC v. New York, N.H. & H.R. Co.*, 287 U.S. 178, 204 (1932), the ordering of a 'precise, definite act . . . about which [an official] had no discretion whatever,' *United States ex rel. Dunlap v. Black*, 128 U.S. 40, 46 (1888). * * * As described in the Attorney General's Manual on the APA, a document whose reasoning we have often found persuasive, * * * § 706(1) empowers a court only to compel an agency 'to perform a ministerial or non-discretionary act,' or 'to take action upon a matter, without directing *how* it shall act.'

"Thus, a claim under § 706(1) can proceed only where a plaintiff asserts that an agency failed to take a *discrete* agency action that it is *required to take*. These limitations rule out several kinds of challenges. The limitation to discrete agency action precludes the kind of broad programmatic attack we rejected in *Lujan v. National Wildlife Federation*, 497 U.S. 871 (1990). There we considered a challenge to BLM's land withdrawal review program, couched as unlawful agency 'action' that the plaintiffs wished to have 'set aside' under § 706(2). We concluded that the program was not an 'agency action':

> '[R]espondent cannot seek *wholesale* improvement of this program by court decree, rather than in the offices of the Department or the halls of Congress, where programmatic improvements are normally made. Under the terms of the APA, respondent must direct its attack against some particular 'agency action' that causes it harm.' *Id.* at 891 (emphasis in original).

The plaintiffs in *National Wildlife Federation* would have fared no better if they had characterized the agency's alleged 'failure to revise land use plans in proper fashion' and 'failure to consider multiple use,' in terms of 'agency action unlawfully withheld' under § 706(1), rather than agency action 'not in accordance with law' under § 706(2).

"The limitation to *required* agency action rules out judicial direction of even discrete agency action that is not demanded by law (which includes, of course, agency regulations that have the force of law). Thus, when an agency is compelled by law to act within a certain time period, but the manner of its action is left to the agency's discretion, a court can compel the agency to act, but has no power to specify what the action must be. For example, 47 U.S.C. § 251(d)(1), which required the Federal Communications Commission 'to establish regulations to implement' interconnection requirements '[w]ithin 6 months' of the date of enactment of the Telecommunications Act of 1996, would have supported a judicial decree under the APA requiring the prompt issuance of regulations, but not a judicial decree setting forth the content of those regulations."

Based upon this construction of the APA, the Court ruled that BLM acted within its discretionary authority to protect WSAs against nondegradation. Although BLM might have been subject to judicial review if it had ignored its duties, there was nothing in § 1782 to require BLM to exclude ORVs altogether. Likewise, Justice Scalia found no legally binding requirement to exclude ORVs in the land use plan's prospective aspirations for managing the wilderness areas. And he found no legal duty in NEPA for BLM to supplement its original environmental impact statement.

NOTES AND QUESTIONS ON THE NONREVIEWABILITY OF AGENCY INACTION

Contrast *Chaney* and *SUWA* doctrinally. In the former, a fractured Court created a presumption of nonreviewability for agency inaction, seemingly contrary to the text of the APA and *Bachowski*. In the latter, a unanimous Court hewed carefully to the text of the APA and disturbed no precedent to hold that the APA codifies the common law mandamus rule that an agency has policymaking discretion unless a statute specifically directs it to act. In *SUWA*, Justice Scalia also explicitly linked the Court's narrow view of the APA to the Court's Article III jurisprudence. *National Wildlife Federation*, for example, is a case where the Court denied Article III standing. Recall, from Chapter 3, § 1, our discussion of the Court's narrow view of standing in cases like *Allen v. Wright*. The Court justified such decisions on the ground that the constitutional separation of powers precludes the judiciary from interfering with the executive branch's enforcement of statutory duties. In *SUWA*, the Court opined that a court can require an agency to follow a statutory deadline, but it cannot tell the agency what the regulation subject to the deadline must say.

SUWA has had a dampening effect on lower court willingness to review Department of Interior land management policies and decisions. Even though federal land use statutes impose many duties on the Department, the duties are not sufficiently articulated to surmount the strong presumption against review laid out by *SUWA*. On the other hand, the Supreme Court has engaged in vigorous judicial review of agency failures to carry out their duties in cases such as *Brown v. Plata* (Chapter 3, § 1), albeit over the dissent of Justice Scalia. Consider the next case, also decided contrary to Justice Scalia's understanding of a strict separation of powers.

MASSACHUSETTS V. ENVIRONMENTAL PROTECTION AGENCY

United States Supreme Court, 2007.
549 U.S. 497, 127 S.Ct. 1438, 167 L. Ed. 2d 248.

JUSTICE STEVENS delivered the opinion for the Court

A well-documented rise in global temperatures has coincided with a significant increase in the concentration of carbon dioxide in the atmosphere. Respected scientists believe the two trends are related. For when carbon dioxide is released into the atmosphere, it acts like the ceiling of a greenhouse, trapping solar energy and retarding the escape of reflected heat. It is therefore a species—the most important species—of a "greenhouse gas."

Calling global warming "the most pressing environmental challenge of our time," a group of States, local governments, and private organizations alleged in a petition for certiorari that the Environmental Protection Agency (EPA) has abdicated its responsibility under the Clean Air Act to regulate the emissions of four greenhouse gases, including carbon dioxide. Specifically, petitioners asked us to answer two questions concerning the meaning of § 202(a)(1) of the Act: whether EPA has the statutory authority to regulate greenhouse gas emissions from new motor vehicles; and if so, whether its stated reasons for refusing to do so are consistent with the statute. * * *

[I] Section 202(a)(1) of the Clean Air Act, as added by Pub. L. 89–272, § 101(8), 79 Stat. 992, and as amended by, *inter alia,* 84 Stat. 1690 and 91 Stat. 791, 42 U.S.C. § 7521(a)(1), provides:

> "The [EPA] Administrator shall by regulation prescribe (and from time to time revise) in accordance with the provisions of this section, standards applicable to the emission of any air pollutant from any class or classes of new motor vehicles or new motor vehicle engines, which in his judgment cause, or contribute to, air pollution which may reasonably be anticipated to endanger public health or welfare. . . ."

The Act defines "air pollutant" to include "any air pollution agent or combination of such agents, including any physical, chemical, biological, radioactive . . . substance or matter which is emitted into or otherwise enters the ambient air." § 7602(g). "Welfare" is also defined broadly: among other things, it includes "effects on . . . weather . . . and climate." § 7602(h).

When Congress enacted these provisions, the study of climate change was in its infancy. In 1959, shortly after the U.S. Weather Bureau began monitoring atmospheric carbon dioxide levels, an observatory in Mauna Loa, Hawaii, recorded a mean level of 316 parts per million. This was well above the highest carbon dioxide concentration—no more than 300 parts per million—revealed in the 420,000-year-old ice-core record. By the time Congress drafted § 202(a)(1) in 1970, carbon dioxide levels had reached 325 parts per million.[10]

In the late 1970's, the Federal Government began devoting serious attention to the possibility that carbon dioxide emissions associated with human activity could provoke climate change. In 1978, Congress enacted the National Climate Program Act, 92 Stat. 601, which required the President to establish a program to "assist the Nation and the world to understand and respond to natural and man-induced climate processes and their implications," id., § 3. President Carter, in turn, asked the National Research Council, the working arm of the National Academy of Sciences, to investigate the subject. The Council's response was unequivocal: "If carbon dioxide continues to increase, the study group finds no reason to doubt that climate changes will result and no reason to believe that these changes will be negligible. . . . A wait-and-see policy may mean waiting until it is too late."

Congress next addressed the issue in 1987, when it enacted the Global Climate Protection Act, Title XI of Pub. L. 100–204, 101 Stat. 1407, note following 15 U.S.C. § 2901. Finding that "manmade pollution—the release of carbon dioxide, chlorofluorocarbons, methane, and other trace gases into the atmosphere—may be producing a long-term and substantial increase in the average temperature on Earth," § 1102(1), 101 Stat. 1408, Congress directed EPA to propose to Congress a "coordinated national policy on global climate change," § 1103(b), and ordered the Secretary of State to work "through the channels of multilateral diplomacy" and coordinate diplomatic efforts to combat global warming, § 1103(c). Congress emphasized that "ongoing pollution and deforestation may be contributing now to an irreversible process" and that "[n]ecessary actions must be identified and implemented in time to protect the climate." § 1102(4).

Meanwhile, the scientific understanding of climate change progressed. In 1990, the Intergovernmental Panel on Climate Change (IPCC), a multinational scientific body organized under the auspices of the United Nations, published its first comprehensive report on the topic. Drawing on expert opinions from across the globe, the IPCC concluded that "emissions resulting from human activities are substantially increasing the atmospheric concentrations of . . . greenhouse gases

---

[10] A more dramatic rise was yet to come: In 2006, carbon dioxide levels reached 382 parts per million, see Dept. of Commerce, National Oceanic & Atmospheric Administration, Mauna Loa CO_2 Monthly Mean Data, http://www.esrl.noaa.gov/gmd/ ccgg/ trends/ co 2_ mm_ mlo. dat (all Internet materials as visited Mar. 29, 2007, and available in Clerk of Court's case file), a level thought to exceed the concentration of carbon dioxide in the atmosphere at any point over the past 20 million years. See Intergovernmental Panel on Climate Change, Technical Summary of Working Group I Report 39 (2001).

[which] will enhance the greenhouse effect, resulting on average in an additional warming of the Earth's surface."

Responding to the IPCC report, the United Nations convened the "Earth Summit" in 1992 in Rio de Janeiro. The first President Bush attended and signed the United Nations Framework Convention on Climate Change (UNFCCC), a nonbinding agreement among 154 nations to reduce atmospheric concentrations of carbon dioxide and other greenhouse gases for the purpose of "prevent[ing] dangerous anthropogenic [*i.e.,* human-induced] interference with the [Earth's] climate system." S. Treaty Doc. No. 102–38, Art. 2, p. 5, 1771 U.N.T.S. 107 (1992). The Senate unanimously ratified the treaty.

Some five years later—after the IPCC issued a second comprehensive report in 1995 concluding that "[t]he balance of evidence suggests there is a discernible human influence on global climate"—the UNFCCC signatories met in Kyoto, Japan, and adopted a protocol that assigned mandatory targets for industrialized nations to reduce greenhouse gas emissions. Because those targets did not apply to developing and heavily polluting nations such as China and India, the Senate unanimously passed a resolution expressing its sense that the United States should not enter into the Kyoto Protocol. *See* S. Res. 98, 105th Cong., 1st Sess. (July 25, 1997) (as passed). President Clinton did not submit the protocol to the Senate for ratification.

[II] On October 20, 1999, a group of 19 private organizations filed a rulemaking petition asking EPA to regulate "greenhouse gas emissions from new motor vehicles under § 202 of the Clean Air Act." Petitioners maintained that 1998 was the "warmest year on record"; that carbon dioxide, methane, nitrous oxide, and hydrofluorocarbons are "heat trapping greenhouse gases"; that greenhouse gas emissions have significantly accelerated climate change; and that the IPCC's 1995 report warned that "carbon dioxide remains the most important contributor to [manmade] forcing of climate change." The petition further alleged that climate change will have serious adverse effects on human health and the environment. As to EPA's statutory authority, the petition observed that the Agency itself had already confirmed that it had the power to regulate carbon dioxide. In 1998, Jonathan Z. Cannon, then EPA's general counsel, prepared a legal opinion concluding that "CO_2 emissions are within the scope of EPA's authority to regulate," even as he recognized that EPA had so far declined to exercise that authority. Cannon's successor, Gary S. Guzy, reiterated that opinion before a congressional committee just two weeks before the rulemaking petition was filed.

Fifteen months after the petition's submission, EPA requested public comment on "all the issues raised in [the] petition," adding a "particular" request for comments on "any scientific, technical, legal, economic or other aspect of these issues that may be relevant to EPA's consideration of this petition." 66 Fed. Reg. 7486, 7487 (2001). EPA received more than 50,000 comments over the next five months. *See* 68 Fed.Reg. 52924 (2003).

Before the close of the comment period, the White House sought "assistance in identifying the areas in the science of climate change where there are the greatest certainties and uncertainties" from the National Research Council, asking for a response "as soon as possible." The result was a 2001 report titled Climate Change Science: An Analysis of Some Key Questions (NRC Report), which, drawing heavily on the 1995 IPCC report, concluded that "[g]reenhouse gases are accumulating in Earth's atmosphere as a result of human activities, causing surface air temperatures and subsurface ocean temperatures to rise. Temperatures are, in fact, rising." NRC Report 1.

On September 8, 2003, EPA entered an order denying the rulemaking petition. 68 Fed.Reg. 52922. The Agency gave two reasons for its decision: (1) that contrary to the opinions of its former general counsels, the Clean Air Act does not authorize EPA to issue mandatory regulations to address global climate change; and (2) that even if the Agency had the authority to set greenhouse gas emission standards, it would be unwise to do so at this time.

In concluding that it lacked statutory authority over greenhouse gases, EPA observed that Congress "was well aware of the global climate change issue when it last comprehensively amended the [Clean Air Act] in 1990," yet it declined to adopt a proposed amendment establishing binding emissions limitations. Congress instead chose to authorize further investigation into climate change. [*See* §§ 103(g) and 602(e) of the Clean Air Act Amendments of 1990, 104 Stat. 2652, 2703, 42 U.S.C. §§ 7403(g)(1) and 7671a(e)).] EPA further reasoned that Congress' "specially tailored solutions to global atmospheric issues"—in particular, its 1990 enactment of a comprehensive scheme to regulate pollutants that depleted the ozone layer, *see* Title VI, 104 Stat. 2649, 42 U.S.C. §§ 7671–7671q—counseled against reading the general authorization of § 202(a)(1) to confer regulatory authority over greenhouse gases.

EPA stated that it was "urged on in this view" by this Court's decision in *FDA v. Brown & Williamson Tobacco Corp.*, 529 U.S. 120 (2000) [Chapter 2, § 3]. In that case, relying on "tobacco['s] unique political history," we invalidated the Food and Drug Administration's reliance on its general authority to regulate drugs as a basis for asserting jurisdiction over an "industry constituting a significant portion of the American economy."

EPA reasoned that climate change had its own "political history": Congress designed the original Clean Air Act to address *local* air pollutants rather than a substance that "is fairly consistent in its concentration throughout the *world's* atmosphere," 68 Fed. Reg. 52927; declined in 1990 to enact proposed amendments to force EPA to set carbon dioxide emission standards for motor vehicles; and addressed global climate change in other legislation. Because of this political history, and because imposing emission limitations on greenhouse gases would have even greater economic and political repercussions than regulating tobacco, EPA was persuaded that it lacked the power to do so. In essence, EPA concluded that climate change was so important that unless Congress spoke with exacting specificity, it could not have meant the Agency to address it.

Having reached that conclusion, EPA believed it followed that greenhouse gases cannot be "air pollutants" within the meaning of the Act. The Agency bolstered this conclusion by explaining that if carbon dioxide were an air pollutant, the only feasible method of reducing tailpipe emissions would be to improve fuel economy. But because Congress has already created detailed mandatory fuel economy standards subject to Department of Transportation (DOT) administration, the Agency concluded that EPA regulation would either conflict with those standards or be superfluous.

Even assuming that it had authority over greenhouse gases, EPA explained in detail why it would refuse to exercise that authority. The Agency began by recognizing that the concentration of greenhouse gases has dramatically increased as a result of human activities, and acknowledged the attendant increase in global surface air temperatures. EPA nevertheless gave controlling importance to the NRC Report's statement that a causal link between the two " 'cannot be unequivocally established.' " Given that residual uncertainty, EPA concluded that regulating greenhouse gas emissions would be unwise.

The Agency furthermore characterized any EPA regulation of motor-vehicle emissions as a "piecemeal approach" to climate change, and stated that such regulation would conflict with the President's "comprehensive approach" to the problem. That approach involves additional support for technological innovation, the creation of nonregulatory programs to encourage voluntary private-sector reductions in greenhouse gas emissions, and further research on climate change—not actual regulation. According to EPA, unilateral EPA regulation of motor-vehicle greenhouse gas emissions might also hamper the President's ability to persuade key developing countries to reduce greenhouse gas emissions. * * *

[V] The scope of our review of the merits of the statutory issues is narrow. As we have repeated time and again, an agency has broad discretion to choose how best to marshal its limited resources and personnel to carry out its delegated responsibilities. That discretion is at its height when the agency decides not to bring an enforcement action. Therefore, in *Heckler v. Chaney*, we held that an agency's refusal to initiate enforcement proceedings is not ordinarily subject to judicial review. Some debate remains, however, as to the rigor with which we review an agency's denial of a petition for rulemaking.

There are key differences between a denial of a petition for rulemaking and an agency's decision not to initiate an enforcement action. *See American Horse Protection Assn., Inc. v. Lyng*, 812 F.2d 1, 3–4 ([D.C. Cir.] 1987). In contrast to nonenforcement decisions, agency refusals to initiate rulemaking "are less frequent, more apt to involve legal as opposed to factual analysis, and subject to special formalities, including a public explanation." *Id.*, at 4; *see also* 5 U.S.C. § 555(e). They moreover arise out of denials of petitions for rulemaking which (at least in the circumstances here) the affected party had an undoubted procedural right to file in the first instance. Refusals to promulgate rules are thus susceptible to judicial review, though such review is "extremely limited" and "highly deferential." *National Customs Brokers & Forwarders Assn. of America, Inc. v. United States*, 883 F.2d 93, 96 ([D.C. Cir.] 1989).

EPA concluded in its denial of the petition for rulemaking that it lacked authority under 42 U.S.C. § 7521(a)(1) to regulate new vehicle emissions because carbon dioxide is not an "air pollutant" as that term is defined in § 7602. In the alternative, it concluded that even if it possessed authority, it would decline to do so because regulation would conflict with other administration priorities. As discussed earlier, the Clean Air Act expressly permits review of such an action. § 7607(b)(1). We therefore "may reverse any such action found to be . . . arbitrary, capricious, an abuse of discretion, or otherwise not in accordance with law." § 7607(d)(9).

[VI] On the merits, the first question is whether § 202(a)(1) of the Clean Air Act authorizes EPA to regulate greenhouse gas emissions from new motor vehicles in the event that it forms a "judgment" that such emissions contribute to climate change. We have little trouble concluding that it does. In relevant part, § 202(a)(1) provides that EPA "shall by regulation prescribe . . . standards applicable to the emission of any air pollutant from any class or classes of new motor vehicles or new motor vehicle engines, which in [the Administrator's] judgment cause, or contribute to, air pollution which may reasonably be anticipated to endanger public health or welfare." 42 U.S.C. § 7521(a)(1). Because EPA believes that Congress did not intend it to regulate substances that contribute to climate change, the agency maintains that carbon dioxide is not an "air pollutant" within the meaning of the provision.

The statutory text forecloses EPA's reading. The Clean Air Act's sweeping definition of "air pollutant" includes "*any* air pollution agent or combination of such agents, including *any* physical, chemical . . . substance or matter which is emitted into or otherwise enters the ambient air. . . ." § 7602(g) (emphasis added). On its face, the definition embraces all airborne compounds of whatever stripe, and underscores that intent through the repeated use of the word "any." Carbon dioxide, methane, nitrous oxide, and hydrofluorocarbons are without a doubt "physical [and] chemical . . . substance [s] which [are] emitted into . . . the ambient air." The statute is unambiguous.

Rather than relying on statutory text, EPA invokes postenactment congressional actions and deliberations it views as tantamount to a congressional command to refrain from regulating greenhouse gas emissions. Even if such postenactment legislative history could shed light on the meaning of an otherwise-unambiguous statute, EPA never identifies any action remotely suggesting that Congress meant to curtail its power to treat greenhouse gases as air pollutants. That subsequent Congresses have eschewed enacting binding emissions limitations to combat global warming tells us nothing about what Congress meant when it amended § 202(a)(1) in 1970 and 1977. And unlike EPA, we have no difficulty reconciling Congress' various efforts to promote interagency collaboration and research to better understand climate change with the Agency's pre-existing mandate to regulate "any air pollutant" that may endanger the public welfare. *See* 42 U.S.C. § 7601(a)(1). Collaboration and research do not conflict with any thoughtful regulatory effort; they complement it.

EPA's reliance on *Brown & Williamson Tobacco Corp.*, is similarly misplaced. In holding that tobacco products are not "drugs" or "devices" subject to Food and Drug Administration (FDA) regulation pursuant to the Food, Drug and Cosmetic Act (FDCA), we found critical at least two considerations that have no counterpart in this case.

First, we thought it unlikely that Congress meant to ban tobacco products, which the FDCA would have required had such products been classified as "drugs" or "devices." Here, in contrast, EPA jurisdiction would lead to no such extreme measures. EPA would only *regulate* emissions, and even then, it would have to delay any action "to permit the development and application of the requisite technology, giving appropriate consideration to the cost of compliance," § 7521(a)(2). However much a ban on tobacco products clashed with the "common sense" intuition that Congress never meant to remove those products from circulation, there is nothing counterintuitive to the notion that EPA can curtail the emission of substances that are putting the global climate out of kilter.

Second, in *Brown & Williamson* we pointed to an unbroken series of congressional enactments that made sense only if adopted "against the backdrop of the FDA's consistent and repeated statements that it lacked authority under the FDCA to regulate tobacco." We can point to no such enactments here: EPA has not identified any congressional action that conflicts in any way with the regulation of greenhouse gases from new motor vehicles. Even if it had, Congress could not have acted against a regulatory "backdrop" of disclaimers of regulatory authority. Prior to the order that provoked this litigation, EPA had never disavowed the authority to regulate greenhouse gases, and in 1998 it in fact affirmed that it *had* such authority. *See* App. 54 (Cannon memorandum). There is no reason, much less a compelling reason, to accept EPA's invitation to read ambiguity into a clear statute.

EPA finally argues that it cannot regulate carbon dioxide emissions from motor vehicles because doing so would require it to tighten mileage standards, a job (according to EPA) that Congress has assigned to DOT. *See* 68 Fed.Reg. 52929. But that DOT sets mileage standards in no way licenses EPA to shirk its environmental responsibilities. EPA has been charged with protecting the public's "health" and "welfare," 42 U.S.C. § 7521(a)(1), a statutory obligation wholly independent of DOT's mandate to promote energy efficiency. *See* Energy Policy and Conservation Act, § 2(5), 89 Stat. 874, 42 U.S.C. § 6201(5). The two obligations may overlap, but there is no reason to think the two agencies cannot both administer their obligations and yet avoid inconsistency.

While the Congresses that drafted § 202(a)(1) might not have appreciated the possibility that burning fossil fuels could lead to global warming, they did understand that without regulatory flexibility, changing circumstances and scientific developments would soon render the Clean Air Act obsolete. The broad language of § 202(a)(1) reflects an intentional effort to confer the flexibility necessary to forestall such obsolescence. *See Pennsylvania Dept. of Corrections v. Yeskey*, 524 U.S. 206, 212 (1998) [Scalia, J.] ("[T]he fact that a statute can be applied in situations not expressly anticipated by Congress does not demonstrate ambiguity. It demonstrates breadth" (internal quotation marks omitted)). Because greenhouse gases fit well within the Clean Air Act's capacious definition of "air pollutant," we hold that EPA has the statutory authority to regulate the emission of such gases from new motor vehicles.

[In Part VII, Justice Stevens rejected EPA's argument that, even if it does have statutory authority to regulate greenhouse gases, it would be unwise to do so at this time.] If EPA makes a finding of endangerment, the Clean Air Act requires the Agency to regulate emissions of the deleterious pollutant from new motor vehicles. * * * EPA no doubt has significant latitude as to the manner, timing, content, and coordination of its regulations with those of other agencies. But once EPA has responded to a petition for rulemaking, its reasons for action or inaction must conform to the authorizing statute. Under the clear terms of the Clean

Air Act, EPA can avoid taking further action only if it determines that greenhouse gases do not contribute to climate change or if it provides some reasonable explanation as to why it cannot or will not exercise its discretion to determine whether they do. To the extent that this constrains agency discretion to pursue other priorities of the Administrator or the President, this is the congressional design. * * *

In short, EPA has offered no reasoned explanation for its refusal to decide whether greenhouse gases cause or contribute to climate change. Its action was therefore "arbitrary, capricious, . . . or otherwise not in accordance with law." 42 U.S.C § 7607(d)(9)(A). We need not and do not reach the question whether on remand EPA must make an endangerment finding, or whether policy concerns can inform EPA's actions in the event that it makes such a finding. We hold only that EPA must ground its reasons for action or inaction in the statute.

[We omit the dissenting opinion of CHIEF JUSTICE ROBERTS, joined by JUSTICES SCALIA, THOMAS, and ALITO. These dissenters objected that no party had Article III standing to challenge EPA's failure to act.]

JUSTICE SCALIA, with whom the CHIEF JUSTICE [ROBERTS], JUSTICE THOMAS, and JUSTICE ALITO join, dissenting.

[I.A]   The provision of law at the heart of this case is § 202(a)(1) of the Clean Air Act (CAA or Act), which provides that the Administrator of the Environmental Protection Agency (EPA) "shall by regulation prescribe . . . standards applicable to the emission of any air pollutant from any class or classes of new motor vehicles or new motor vehicle engines, which *in his judgment* cause, or contribute to, air pollution which may reasonably be anticipated to endanger public health or welfare." 42 U.S.C. § 7521(a)(1) (emphasis added). As the Court recognizes, the statute "condition[s] the exercise of EPA's authority on its formation of a 'judgment.'" There is no dispute that the Administrator has made no such judgment in this case. * * *

The question thus arises: Does anything *require* the Administrator to make a "judgment" whenever a petition for rulemaking is filed? Without citation of the statute or any other authority, the Court says yes. Why is that so? When Congress wishes to make private action force an agency's hand, it knows how to do so. *See, e.g., Brock v. Pierce County,* 476 U.S. 253, 254–255 (1986) (discussing the Comprehensive Employment and Training Act (CETA), 92 Stat. 1926, 29 U.S.C. § 816(b), which "provide[d] that the Secretary of Labor 'shall' issue a final determination as to the misuse of CETA funds by a grant recipient within 120 days after receiving a complaint alleging such misuse"). Where does the CAA say that the EPA Administrator is required to come to a decision on this question whenever a rulemaking petition is filed? The Court points to no such provision because none exists.

Instead, the Court invents a multiple-choice question that the EPA Administrator must answer when a petition for rulemaking is filed. The Administrator must exercise his judgment in one of three ways: (a) by concluding that the pollutant *does* cause, or contribute to, air pollution that endangers public welfare (in which case EPA is required to regulate); (b) by concluding that the pollutant *does not* cause, or contribute to, air pollution that endangers public welfare (in which case EPA is *not* required to regulate); or (c) by "provid[ing] some reasonable explanation as to why it cannot or will not exercise its discretion to determine whether" greenhouse gases endanger public welfare (in which case EPA is *not* required to regulate).

I am willing to assume, for the sake of argument, that the Administrator's discretion in this regard is not entirely unbounded—that if he has no reasonable basis for deferring judgment he must grasp the nettle at once. The Court, however, with no basis in text or precedent, rejects all of EPA's stated "policy judgments" as not "amount[ing] to a reasoned justification" effectively narrowing the universe of potential reasonable bases to a single one: Judgment can be delayed *only* if the Administrator concludes that "the scientific uncertainty is [too] profound." The Administrator is precluded from concluding *for other reasons* "that it would . . . be better not to regulate at this time." Such other reasons—perfectly valid reasons—were set forth in the Agency's statement.

> "We do not believe . . . that it would be either effective or appropriate for EPA to establish [greenhouse gas] standards for motor vehicles at this time. As described in detail below, the President has laid out a comprehensive approach to climate change that calls for near-term voluntary actions and incentives along with programs aimed at reducing scientific uncertainties and encouraging technological development so that the government may effectively and efficiently address the climate change issue over the long term. . . .

> "[E]stablishing [greenhouse gas] emission standards for U.S. motor vehicles at this time would . . . result in an inefficient, piecemeal approach to addressing the climate change issue. The U.S. motor vehicle fleet is one of many sources of [greenhouse gas] emissions both here and abroad, and different [greenhouse gas] emission sources face different technological and financial challenges in reducing emissions. A sensible regulatory scheme would require that all significant sources and sinks of [greenhouse gas] emissions be considered in deciding how best to achieve any needed emission reductions.

"Unilateral EPA regulation of motor vehicle [greenhouse gas] emissions could also weaken U.S. efforts to persuade developing countries to reduce the [greenhouse gas] intensity of their economies. Considering the large populations and growing economies of some developing countries, increases in their [greenhouse gas] emissions could quickly overwhelm the effects of [greenhouse gas] reduction measures in developed countries. Any potential benefit of EPA regulation could be lost to the extent other nations decided to let their emissions significantly increase in view of U.S. emissions reductions. Unavoidably, climate change raises important foreign policy issues, and it is the President's prerogative to address them." 68 Fed.Reg. 52929–52931 (footnote omitted).

The Court dismisses this analysis as "rest[ing] on reasoning divorced from the statutory text." "While the statute does condition the exercise of EPA's authority on its formation of a 'judgment,' . . . that judgment must relate to whether an air pollutant 'cause[s], or contribute[s] to, air pollution which may reasonably be anticipated to endanger public health or welfare.'" True but irrelevant. When the Administrator *makes* a judgment whether to regulate greenhouse gases, that judgment must relate to whether they are air pollutants that "cause, or contribute to, air pollution which may reasonably be anticipated to endanger public health or welfare." 42 U.S.C. § 7521(a)(1). But the statute says *nothing at all* about the reasons for which the Administrator may *defer* making a judgment—the permissible reasons for deciding not to grapple with the issue at the present time. Thus, the various "policy" rationales that the Court criticizes are not "divorced from the statutory text," except in the sense that the statutory text is silent, as texts are often silent about permissible reasons for the exercise of agency discretion. The reasons EPA gave are surely considerations executive agencies *regularly* take into account (and *ought* to take into account) when deciding whether to consider entering a new field: the impact such entry would have on other Executive Branch programs and on foreign policy. There is no basis in law for the Court's imposed limitation.

EPA's interpretation of the discretion conferred by the statutory reference to "its judgment" is not only reasonable, it is the most natural reading of the text. The Court nowhere explains why this interpretation is incorrect, let alone why it is not entitled to deference under *Chevron U.S.A. Inc. v. Natural Resources Defense Council, Inc.*, 467 U.S. 837 (1984). As the Administrator acted within the law in declining to make a "judgment" for the policy reasons above set forth, I would uphold the decision to deny the rulemaking petition on that ground alone. [Even the Court would defer to the EPA if it concluded that the science is too unclear to conclude that carbon dioxide is contributing to man-made global warming—yet, according to Justice Scalia, that is precisely what the EPA found.] * * *

[II.A]　　Even before reaching its discussion of the word "judgment," the Court makes another significant error when it concludes that "§ 202(a)(1) of the Clean Air Act *authorizes* EPA to regulate greenhouse gas emissions from new motor vehicles in the event that it forms a 'judgment' that such emissions contribute to climate change." (emphasis added). For such authorization, the Court relies on what it calls "the Clean Air Act's capacious definition of 'air pollutant.' "

"Air pollutant" is defined by the Act as "any air pollution agent or combination of such agents, including any physical, chemical, . . . substance or matter which is emitted into or otherwise enters the ambient air." 42 U.S.C. § 7602(g). The Court is correct that "[c]arbon dioxide, methane, nitrous oxide, and hydrofluorocarbons," fit within the second half of that definition: They are "physical, chemical, . . . substance[s] or matter which [are] emitted into or otherwise ente[r] the ambient air." But the Court mistakenly believes this to be the end of the analysis. In order to be an "air pollutant" under the Act's definition, the "substance or matter [being] emitted into . . . the ambient air" must also meet the *first* half of the definition—namely, it must be an "air pollution agent or combination of such agents." The Court simply pretends this half of the definition does not exist.

The Court's analysis faithfully follows the argument advanced by petitioners, which focuses on the word "including" in the statutory definition of "air pollutant." As that argument goes, anything that *follows* the word "including" must necessarily be a subset of whatever *precedes* it. Thus, if greenhouse gases qualify under the phrase following the word "including," they must qualify under the phrase preceding it. Since greenhouse gases come within the capacious phrase "any physical, chemical, . . . substance or matter which is emitted into or otherwise enters the ambient air," they must also be "air pollution agent[s] or combination[s] of such agents," and therefore meet the definition of "air pollutant[s]."

That is certainly one possible interpretation of the statutory definition. The word "including" can indeed indicate that what follows will be an "illustrative" sampling of the general category that precedes the word. Often, however, the examples standing alone are broader than the general category, and must be viewed as limited in light of that category. The Government provides a helpful (and unanswered) example: "The phrase 'any American automobile, including any truck or minivan,' would not naturally be construed to encompass a foreign-manufactured [truck or] minivan." The general principle enunciated—that the speaker is talking about *American* automobiles—carries forward to the illustrative examples (trucks and minivans), and limits them accordingly, even though in isolation they are broader. Congress often uses the word "including" in this manner. In 28 U.S.C. § 1782(a), for example, it refers to "a proceeding in a foreign or international tribunal, including criminal investigations conducted before formal accusation." Certainly this provision would not encompass criminal investigations underway in a *domestic* tribunal. * * *

In short, the word "including" does not require the Court's (or the petitioners') result. It is perfectly reasonable to view the definition of "air pollutant" in its entirety: An air pollutant *can* be "any physical, chemical, . . . substance or matter which is emitted into or otherwise enters the ambient air," but only if it retains the general characteristic of being an "air pollution agent or combination of such agents." This is precisely the conclusion EPA reached: "[A] substance does not meet the CAA definition of 'air pollutant' simply because it is a 'physical, chemical, . . . substance or matter which is emitted into or otherwise enters the ambient air.' It must also be an 'air pollution agent.'" 68 Fed. Reg. 52929, n.3. Once again, in the face of textual ambiguity, the Court's application of *Chevron* deference to EPA's interpretation of the word "including" is nowhere to be found. Evidently, the Court defers only to those reasonable interpretations that it favors. * * *

The Court's alarm over global warming may or may not be justified, but it ought not distort the outcome of this litigation. This is a straightforward administrative-law case, in which Congress has passed a malleable statute giving broad discretion, not to us but to an executive agency. No matter how important the underlying policy issues at stake, this Court has no business substituting its own desired outcome for the reasoned judgment of the responsible agency.

NOTES AND QUESTIONS ON MASSACHUSETTS V. EPA

1. *On Remand: The EPA's Carbon Dioxide Rules.* On remand, the EPA staff reportedly prepared a proposed rule regulating motor vehicle emissions—but EPA Administrator Stephen Johnson vetoed the rule and in 2008 issued an "Advance Notice of Proposed Rulemaking," a regulatory stall tactic. Meanwhile, the voters elected Barack Obama as President. President Obama appointed Lisa Jackson, an environmental activist, as EPA Administrator, and she moved swiftly to respond to the Court's invitation. First, EPA issued an Endangerment Finding, in which it determined that greenhouse gases may "reasonably be anticipated to endanger public health or welfare." See 42 U.S.C. § 7521(a)(1). Next, it issued the Tailpipe Rule, which set emissions standards for cars and light trucks. Finally, EPA determined that the Clean Air Act requires major stationary sources of greenhouse gases to obtain construction and operating permits.

The Supreme Court addressed the new rules in *Utility Air Regulatory Group v. EPA*, 134 S.Ct. 2427 (2014). The majority ruled that the Clean Air Act does not allow the EPA to impose greenhouse gas regulations on new stationary sources—but does allow the agency to regulate greenhouse-gas emissions from sources already emitting other kinds of pollution and thus subject to regulation anyway. Specifically, the Court held that the agency may require those sources to use the best available technology to control greenhouse gases. Although largely justified on the basis of the statutory text (for the plurality Justices), the Court's overall result represented an overall "win" for the agency, because most of the greenhouse gas emissions are from sources that are already regulated.

Massachusetts v. EPA may be an example of a forced dialogue between courts and an agency that has arguably been very productive—though the dialogue has been saturated by politics: If President Obama had not been elected in 2008, the EPA would not have moved to implement the Court's suggestions so aggressively.

2.   *Judicial Review of an Agency's Denial of a Petition for Rulemaking.* Before *Massachusetts*, the Supreme Court had never ruled on the question of whether an agency decision not to initiate rulemaking is subject to judicial review. Certainly, if Congress mandates agency rulemaking by a particular date, courts will be open to lawsuits compelling agency action once the deadline has passed—but there was no such deadline in *Massachusetts*. Why was this case not governed by the *Chaney* presumption of nonreviewability? Consider the different claims advanced in the two cases: the *Chaney* challengers were seeking review of an agency decision not to prosecute, while the *Massachusetts* challengers were seeking review of an agency decision not to initiate rulemaking. Does this adequately distinguish the two cases? The Court did not discuss *SUWA*: Why not? That is, even if Congress has not precluded judicial review altogether, why doesn't § 202(a)(1) vest the matter in the "judgment" (i.e., the discretion) of the EPA Administrator?

As Justice Stevens recognized, the D.C. Circuit has regularly entertained petitions for judicial review of an agency's decision not to initiate rulemaking proceedings. Judge Stephen Williams' decision in *American Horse* was one example—though his decision said that review would be "extremely limited" and the court would apply a "highly deferential" standard of review, namely, an examination of the agency's statement of reasons for not initiating the rulemaking process and remanding to the agency if its statement was illogical or did not address an important consideration or argument. (Notice the similarity to *Overton Park* and *Bachowski* review of an agency's statement of reasons.)

But the Supreme Court's review in *Massachusetts* was not "highly deferential." How could the Court justify this level of aggressive review? Notice that Justice Stevens' review was even more aggressive than is evident from the face of his opinion. Section 202(a)(1) requires EPA to regulate "air pollutants" that, in the judgment of its Administrator, may "endanger public health." Justice Stevens focused on EPA's erroneous judgment that carbon dioxide is not an air pollutant—but he gave less reason to reject EPA's "judgment" that carbon dioxide does not endanger public health.

After *Massachusetts*, are an agency's denials of petitions for rulemaking presumptively reviewable (the ordinary presumption)—or are they presumptively nonreviewable, but the statutory and factual record in *Massachusetts* trumped the presumption with its targeted statutory language and structure?

3.   *The Action-Inaction Issue? Massachusetts* looks a lot like *Chaney*: In both cases, the Court considered whether there should be judicial review for agency "inaction." But recall that APA § 553(e) entitles anyone to petition an agency for issuance, amendment, or repeal of a rule and requires a statement of reasons if the agency denies this (or any other) petition. Under the APA, then, was the Court reviewing agency "action"? Thereby rendering the *Chaney* presumption against judicial review inoperative? Or can a judge still consider EPA's denial to be "inaction" similar to the FDA's denial in *Chaney*? (Recall that Justice Marshall made the § 553(e) argument in *Chaney*, but no other Justice agreed.)

PROBLEM 7–4: DELAYED IMPLEMENTATION OF HEALTH REFORM

The Affordable Care Act of 2010 has kept the Department of Health & Human Services (HHS) busy. The 2,000-page statute requires HHS and other agencies to implement hundreds of provisions. Implementation delays are common, and usually do not cause much of a stir. The intense political opposition to health reform, however, has caused much attention to be paid to its delays in implementation. Part of the scrutiny comes from the fact that the provisions being delayed are central provisions in the law. Consider a few examples:

- The Internal Revenue Service (IRS) and the Treasury Department, through a final rule, have delayed implementation of the "employer mandate," the requirement that large employers offer health insurance or pay a tax;

- HHS, in a letter to state insurance commissioners, stated it would delay the deadline by more than a year for insurers to cancel insurance plans that do not comply with the statute;

- HHS, through an announcement, pushed back by one year the opening of the special insurance online marketplace for small businesses

The statute had deadlines written into it for all of the requirements, many of which were supposed to take effect in 2014. The IRS points to § 7805 of the Internal Revenue Code, which gives it the authority to "prescribe all needful rules and regulations for the enforcement of this title," as authorization for the delay, and a provision it has used to justify non-ACA delays in the past.

The ACA's opponents, and even some proponents, have questioned the legality of these delays. Assume you wish to challenge one (or more). How do you proceed? What are your strongest arguments? What is the strongest argument against you?

C. ADMINISTRATIVE GUIDANCES, INCLUDING POLICY STATEMENTS AND INTERPRETIVE RULES

In addition to legislative rules and adjudicated orders, the typical agency utilizes a host of other ways to communicate with the public that are much less formal. Generally grouped under the umbrella term "guidance," these communications include policy statements, interpretive rules, letters, "frequently asked questions," bulletins, and compliance guides and manuals. Understanding the status of guidance can be tricky. Legislative rules, orders resulting from agency adjudications, court judgments in favor of agency petitions, and administrative grants or denials of benefits or licenses are, generally speaking, directives that have the force of law. That is, they affect legal rights and duties and are immediately enforceable. But most guidance documents generally do not immediately affect legal rights, even when they suggest a new enforcement regime for the agency. The terms "policy statements" and "interpretive rules" appear in the APA—in § 553(b)(3)(A), which explicitly exempts this form of communication from notice-and-comment (a liberation from procedure that makes them attractive). The other types of guidance are not mentioned in the text of the statute.

These guidance documents are often interpretations with important legal consequences, and the D.C. Circuit treats some purportedly "interpretive" rules as, in effect, "legislative" rules with legally binding effect. E.g., *Syncor Int'l Corp. v. Shalala*, 127 F.3d 90, 96 (D.C. Cir. 1999); *American Mining Congress v. Mine Safety & Health Admin.*, 995 F.2d 1106, 1111 (D.C. Cir. 1993); John F. Manning, *Nonlegislative Rules*, 72 Geo. Wash. L. Rev. 893 (2004). In contrast to legislative rules, however, guidance documents (1) are not subject to the APA's procedural requirements for notice and comment and are usually not subject to immediate judicial review.[12] They must, however, be "separately state[d] and currently publish[ed] in the Federal Register for the guidance of the public." APA § 552(a)(1)(D); cf. Russell L. Weaver, *An APA Provision for Nonlegislative Rules?*, 56 Admin. L. Rev. 1179, 1188 (2004) (agencies usually ignore this requirement).

---

[12] For excellent introductions to guidance documents, see Robert A. Anthony, *Interpretive Rules, Policy Statements, Guidances, Manuals, and the Like—Should Federal Agencies Use Them to Bind the Public?*, 41 Duke L.J. 1311 (1992); Richard J. Pierce Jr., *Distinguishing Legislative Rules from Interpretive Rules*, 52 Admin. L. Rev. 547 (2000); Connor N. Raso, Note, *Strategic or Sincere? Analyzing Agency Use of Guidance Documents*, 119 Yale L.J. 782 (2010).

If legislative rules greatly outnumber statutes in the modern regulatory state, agency guidance documents like policy statements and interpretive rules are even more numerous than legislative rules, for a number of reasons. Congress has declined to grant legislative rulemaking authority to some agencies; the EEOC, for example, does not have legislative rulemaking authority to implement Title VII (Chapter 2), though it does have such authority to implement the Age Discrimination in Employment Act of 1967 and part of the Americans with Disabilities Act of 1990. The *most* the EEOC can do in Title VII cases is to issue policy statements and guidance documents, backed up by the threat of litigation. Even if an agency has legislative rulemaking authority, general regulations (like statutes) cannot anticipate all issues that might arise, and guidance documents can fill in the gaps left by rules and regulations—and the agency can promulgate guidance documents much more quickly and cheaply than it can create legislative rules.

Complicating matters is the fact that agencies often deploy guidance documents, no-action letters, and interpretive rules to explain how they intend to apply legislative rules. Does this characteristic transform an interpretive rule into a legislative rule that must go through the notice-and-comment process? Courts have been reluctant to transform purportedly interpretive rules into legislative ones, but will do so if they view the guidance as a veiled final action that makes an important change in a legislative rule or how it is applied. E.g., *American Mining Congress v. Mine Safety & Health Admin.*, 995 F.2d 1106 (D.C. Cir. 1993). Judge Stephen Williams in *American Mining Congress* opined that a rule is legislative if it has "legal effect," and suggested that a rule has legal effect if: (1) in the absence of the rule, no legislative basis would exist for an enforcement action; (2) "the agency has published the rule in the Code of Federal Regulations"; (3) the agency "explicitly invoked its general legislative authority" to pass the rule; or (4) "the rule effectively amends a prior legislative rule." Accord, *New York City Employees' Retirement Sys. v. SEC*, 45 F.3d 7 (2d Cir. 1995) (finding that an SEC no-action letter was an interpretive rule, even though it abandoned the agency's commitment to a published legislative rule). Conversely, guidance documents have legal bite as interpretive sources that federal courts take very seriously. Consider the following Supreme Court decision.

Jack Skidmore v. Swift & Co.
323 U.S. 134 (1944).

Seven employees of the Swift and Company packing plant at Fort Worth, Texas, brought an action under the Fair Labor Standards Act (FLSA), 29 U.S.C. § 201 *et seq.*, to recover overtime, liquidated damages, and attorneys' fees, totaling approximately $77,000. The daytime employment of these persons was working time within the FLSA. "Two were engaged in general fire hall duties and maintenance of fire-fighting equipment of the Swift plant. The others operated elevators or acted as relief men in fire duties. They worked from 7:00 a.m. to 3:30 p.m., with a half-hour lunch period, five days a week. They were paid weekly salaries."

"Under their oral agreement of employment, however, these employees undertook to stay in the fire hall on the Company premises, or within hailing distance, three and a half to four nights a week. This involved no task except to answer alarms, either because of fire or because the sprinkler was set off for some other reason. No fires occurred during the period in issue, the alarms were rare, and the time required for their answer rarely exceeded an hour. For each alarm answered the employees were paid in addition to their fixed compensation an agreed amount, fifty cents at first, and later sixty-four cents. The Company provided a brick fire hall equipped with steam heat and air-conditioned rooms. It provided sleeping quarters, a pool table, a domino table, and a radio. The men used their time in sleep or amusement as they saw fit, except that they were required to stay in or close by the fire hall and be ready to respond to alarms. It is stipulated that 'they agreed to remain in the fire hall and stay in it or within hailing distance, subject to call, in event of fire or other casualty, but were not required to perform any specific tasks during these periods of time, except in answering alarms.' "

The trial court ruled, as a matter of law, that the time the employees spent in the fire hall waiting for an alarm (which the court deemed to be "such pleasurable occupations or performing such personal chores") was not "time worked" for purposes of calculating overtime under the FLSA. The Supreme Court unanimously reversed the lower courts.

Justice Jackson's opinion for the Court rested in part on *Armour & Co. v. Wantock*, 323 U.S. 126 (1944), ruling that waiting time can, depending on the circumstances, be working time for purposes of the FLSA. "This involves scrutiny and construction of the agreements between the particular parties, appraisal of their practical construction of the working agreement by conduct, consideration of the nature of the service, and its relation to the waiting time, and all of the surrounding circumstances. Facts may show that the employee was engaged to wait, or they may show that he waited to be engaged. His compensation may cover both waiting and task, or only performance of the task itself. Living quarters may in some situations be furnished as a facility of the task and in another as a part of its compensation."

Although Congress vested ultimate authority for interpreting the FLSA with the federal judiciary, Justice Jackson observed that Congress also saw fit to "create the office of Administrator, impose upon him a variety of duties, endow him with powers to inform himself of conditions in industries and employments subject to the Act, and put on him the duties of bringing injunction actions to restrain violations. Pursuit of his duties has accumulated a considerable experience in the problems of ascertaining working time in employments involving periods of inactivity and a knowledge of the customs prevailing in reference to their solution. From these he is obliged to reach conclusions as to conduct without the law, so that he should seek injunctions to stop it, and that within the law, so that he has no call to interfere. He has set forth his views of the application of the Act under different circumstances in an interpretative bulletin and in informal rulings. They provide a practical guide to employers and employees as to how the office representing the public interest in its enforcement will seek to apply it. Wage and Hour Division, Interpretative Bulletin No. 13.

"The Administrator thinks the problems presented by inactive duty require a flexible solution, rather than the all-in or all-out rules respectively urged by the parties in this case, and his Bulletin endeavors to suggest standards and examples to guide in particular situations. In some occupations, it says, periods of inactivity are not properly counted as working time even though the employee is subject to call. Examples are an operator of a small telephone exchange where the switchboard is in her home and she ordinarily gets several hours of uninterrupted sleep each night; or a pumper of a stripper well or watchman of a lumber camp during the off season, who may be on duty twenty-four hours a day but ordinarily 'has a normal night's sleep, has ample time in which to eat his meals, and has a certain amount of time for relaxation and entirely private pursuits.' Exclusion of all such hours the Administrator thinks may be justified. In general, the answer depends 'upon the degree to which the employee is free to engage in personal activities during periods of idleness when he is subject to call and the number of consecutive hours that the employee is subject to call without being required to perform active work.' 'Hours worked are not limited to the time spent in active labor but include time given by the employee to the employer. . . .'

"The facts of this case do not fall within any of the specific examples given, but the conclusion of the Administrator, as expressed in the brief *amicus curiae* [filed in connection with the instant case], is that the general tests which he has suggested point to the exclusion of sleeping and eating time of these employees from the work-week and the inclusion of all other on-call time: although the employees were required to remain on the premises during the entire time, the evidence shows that they were very rarely interrupted in their normal sleeping and eating time, and these are pursuits of a purely private nature which would presumably occupy the employees' time whether they were on duty or not and which apparently could be pursued adequately and comfortably in the required circumstances; the rest of the time is different because there is nothing in the record to suggest that, even though pleasurably spent, it was spent in the ways the men would have chosen had they been free to do so.

"There is no statutory provision as to what, if any, deference courts should pay to the Administrator's conclusions. And, while we have given them notice, we have had no occasion to try to prescribe their influence. The rulings of this Administrator are not reached as a result of hearing adversary proceedings in which he finds facts from evidence and reaches conclusions of law from findings of fact. They are not, of course, conclusive, even in the cases with which they directly deal, much less in those to which they apply only by analogy. They do not constitute an interpretation of the Act or a standard for judging factual situations which binds a district court's processes, as an authoritative pronouncement of a higher court might do. But the Administrator's policies are made in pursuance of official duty, based upon more specialized experience and broader investigations and information than is likely to come to a judge in a particular case. They do determine the policy which will guide applications for enforcement by injunction on behalf of the Government. Good administration of the Act and good judicial administration alike require that the standards of public enforcement and those for determining private rights shall be at variance only where justified by very good reasons. The fact that the Administrator's policies and standards are not reached by trial in adversary form does not mean that they are not entitled to respect. This Court has long given considerable and in some cases decisive weight to Treasury Decisions and to interpretative regulations of the Treasury and of other bodies that were not of adversary origin.

"We consider that the rulings, interpretations and opinions of the Administrator under this Act, while not controlling upon the courts by reason of their authority, do constitute a body of experience and informed judgment to which courts and litigants may properly resort for guidance. The weight of such a judgment in a particular case will depend upon the thoroughness evident in its consideration, the validity of its reasoning, its consistency with earlier and later pronouncements, and all those factors which give it power to persuade, if lacking power to control." Hence, the Court reversed and remanded the case to the district court to reconsider its conclusions in light of *Armour* and the appropriate weight to be given the Administrator's views.

NOTES AND QUESTIONS ON JUDICIAL DEFERENCE TO LESS FORMAL AGENCY INTERPRETATIONS

In *Skidmore*, a unanimous Supreme Court deferred to the agency views, which were set forth in a general bulletin, which was, in turn, applied to the facts of this case by an *amicus* brief the agency filed with the Court. In an empirical study of 1014 Supreme Court decisions where there was an agency interpretation before the Court (see Chapter 9, § 2 of this coursebook), the authors found there are many more cases where the Supreme Court is influenced by agency views expressed in guidance documents or (especially) *amicus* briefs, than cases where the Court is relying directly on an agency regulation. Indeed, in more than 10% of the cases the authors examined, the Court considered (and almost always went along with) agency interpretations (usually in guidance documents or *amicus* briefs) of its own regulations. This raises a question that has bothered administrative law scholars and the D.C. Circuit: Are agencies making important policy moves through guidances rather than through the regular process of notice-and-comment rulemaking? E.g., Robert A. Anthony, *Interpretive Rules, Policy Statements, Guidances, Manuals, and the Like—Should Federal Agencies Use Them to Bind the Public?*, 41 Duke L.J. 1311 (1992).[13]

In an important empirical study of this phenomenon, Professors Hamilton and Schroeder found that agencies are most likely to use guidance documents when legislative rules are especially costly to promulgate, when Congress or the D.C. Circuit have monitored the agency more aggressively, or where a regulation imposes big costs on regulated parties who are likely to tie up agency rulemaking for years and years. See James T. Hamilton & Christopher H. Schroeder, *Strategic Regulators and the Choice of Rulemaking Procedures: The Selection of Formal vs. Informal Rules in Regulating Hazardous Waste*, Law & Contemp. Probs. 111 (Spring 1994); see also Connor N. Raso, Note, *Strategic or Sincere? Analyzing Agency Use of Guidance Documents*, 119 Yale L.J. 782 (2010) (more recent and more extensive empirical study of guidance documents, finding that agencies usually do not deploy them strategically in this way but that agencies do have strong reasons to use them in the situations identified by Hamilton and Schroeder).

Consider a judicial and then an administrative response to this phenomenon.

Alaska Professional Hunters Association v. Federal Aviation Administration
177 F.3d 1030 (D.C. Cir. 1999).

In January 1998, the Federal Aviation Administration (FAA) published a "Notice to Operators" aimed at Alaskan hunting and fishing guides who pilot light aircraft as part of their guiding service. The Notice required these guide pilots to abide by FAA regulations applicable to

---

[13] See also William Funk, *When Is a "Rule" a Regulation? Marking a Clear Line Between Nonlegislative Rules and Legislative Rules*, 54 Admin. L. Rev. 659 (2002); Peter L. Strauss, *The Rulemaking Continuum*, 41 Duke L.J. 1463 (1992), as well as H.R. Rep. No. 106–1009 (2000) (raising strong congressional concerns about this practice, with emphasis on the possibility of regulatory overreach without sufficient democratic participation in agency policy entrepreneurship).

commercial air operations. This was a new policy, and an association representing the guides challenged the policy as a violation of the APA.

Since 1963, the Alaskan Region of the Civil Aeronautics Board (CAB, the predecessor to the FAA) had consistently advised guide pilots that they were not governed by regulations dealing with commercial pilots. The advice stemmed from *Administrator v. Marshall*, 39 C.A.B. 948 (1963), a decision rejecting the CAB's attempt to sanction a registered Alaskan hunting and fishing guide and the holder of an FAA-issued private pilot's license. On a hunting trip, Marshall flew his customer out of Kotzebue, Alaska, searching for polar bears. Regulations then in effect said that a private pilot may pilot aircraft in connection with any business or employment if the flight is merely incidental thereto and does not involve the carriage of persons or property for compensation or hire. The CAB ruled that Marshall was not covered by the rule, because his piloting was "incidental" to his guide service and was not billed separately. Because substantially the same rule remained in effect, the Alaskan Region interpreted *Marshall* to exempt guides from the commercial pilot regulations.

Although the record was unclear, it appears that the CAB and, then, the FAA in Washington DC were not aware of the Alaskan Region's interpretation until the early 1990s, but even then there was no concerted effort by the central administration to correct the Region's longstanding interpretation of the FAA's legislative rules. But discussions apparently intensified, and the hunters association in 1997 asked the FAA to create a special regime for regulating Alaskan guide pilots. Rather than taking that approach, however, the FAA published its "Notice to Operators" in the Federal Register. See Compliance with Parts 119, 121 and 135 by Alaskan Hunt and Fish Guides Who Transport Persons by Air for Compensation or Hire, 63 Fed.Reg. 4 (1998).

Alaskan guides who transport customers by aircraft to and from sites where they provide guiding services, with transportation included in the package price of the trip, were instructed that they had to comply with the regulations of parts 119, 121 and 135, as applicable. In the future, the FAA would treat these guides as commercial operators or air carriers, transporting passengers for compensation or hire. The FAA acknowledged that the Alaskan Region had not enforced parts 121 or 135 against guide pilots in the past. But it attributed this to a misreading of the *Marshall* case. A guide's use of aircraft is, the FAA stated, integral to his business, and the customer pays for the transportation regardless whether there is or is not a separate charge for it. The Notice also stated that guide pilot operations would be safer if they were conducted pursuant to the stricter aviation standards of parts 119, 121 and 135.

The Association challenged the new guidance document on the ground that it was a significant modification of the agency's legislative rules and, as such, should have gone through the notice-and-comment process required by APA § 553. **Judge Randolph**'s opinion for the court agreed with the challengers on this point.

"Our analysis of these arguments draws on *Paralyzed Veterans of America v. D.C. Arena*, 117 F.3d 579, 586 (D.C. Cir.1997), in which we said: 'Once an agency gives its regulation an interpretation, it can only change that interpretation as it would formally modify the regulation itself: through the process of notice and comment rulemaking.' We there explained why an agency has less leeway in its choice of the method of changing its interpretation of its regulations than in altering its construction of a statute. 'Rule making,' as defined in the APA, includes not only the agency's process of formulating a rule, but also the agency's process of modifying a rule. 5 U.S.C. § 551(5). When an agency has given its regulation a definitive interpretation, and later significantly revises that interpretation, the agency has in effect amended its rule, something it may not accomplish without notice and comment. * * *

"The FAA thinks *Paralyzed Veterans* is inapposite because its January 1998 Notice to Operators did not fundamentally change any 'authoritative interpretation' of its regulations. *See Paralyzed Veterans* [accepting this argument and declining to overturn the agency's interpretation]. The FAA is confident that the Alaskan Region's advice to guide pilots for more than 30 years stemmed from a misreading of the *Marshall* decision and so could not have represented the view of the agency. The Notice to Operators put it this way: 'there appears to have been a misinterpretation of the scope and effect of a 1963 enforcement case involving a registered hunting guide, *Administrator v. Marshall*, 39 CAB 948 (1963) (decided on an extremely narrow set of facts that involved a registered guide's single flight from base camp to spot game from the air and return to base camp, with no landing at a point other than the point of takeoff).'

"We do not share the FAA's confidence that the ruling in *Marshall*—piloting was 'merely incidental to [the pilot's] business as a registered Alaska guide'—applied only to a guide pilot flying his customer from a base camp and returning to the camp without landing in between. The FAA believes these were the 'extremely narrow set of facts' in *Marshall* because the opinion stated: 'On the polar bear hunt respondent [the guide] utilizes his aircraft only to the extent of getting the hunter from the base camp out over the ice in order to spot the polar bear and return hunter to the camp.' According to the FAA, this means the pilot did not land his plane on the ice; the guide pilot and his passenger merely spotted the bear from the air and then turned for home.

"This reading of *Marshall* is, we suppose, possible but it is quite implausible. For one thing, the guide's client was not in Alaska for sightseeing. His objective was to hunt and kill a polar bear and the guide's objective was to help him do just that: 'in the event a polar bear was not killed, there was to be no payment of money made by [the customer] to the guides.' Why use a plane? The opinion explained: 'It is the general practice in Alaska to utilize aircraft in transporting hunters over the ice in the hunt of polar bears where formerly dog sleds were used.' The guide was not searching for a polar bear so that his customer could see what one looked like. He and his customer were hunting, and hunting involves killing the quarry. This must be why the opinion says several times * * * that the 'sole' purpose of the flight was 'hunting polar bear.' How could this be done without landing? The plane substituted for a dog sled. It would therefore be very unlikely for the hunter and guide, after spotting a bear from the air, to return to camp and then set out on foot over the ice to shoot it. Perhaps the customer could fire at the bear from the air (although Alaskan hunting regulations might have prohibited this). Even so, one would expect the hunter to want his 'trophy,' which he could only recover if the plane landed. If the FAA's current reading of *Marshall* were correct, the existence of a regulatory violation would depend on the success of the hunt, a senseless regulatory approach. * * * On the face of the *Marshall* opinion—all that the FAA in Washington had before it—we think it fairly implicit that a landing away from the camp was planned and contemplated. At the least, there is severe doubt that the FAA's Alaskan Region had been misinterpreting the *Marshall* decision and its import.

"We are unpersuaded by the FAA's additional claim that the Alaskan Region's interpretation * * * represented simply a local enforcement omission, in conflict with the agency's policy in the rest of the country. It is true that when a local office gives an interpretation of a regulation or provides advice to a regulated party, this will not necessarily constitute an authoritative administrative position, particularly if the interpretation or advice contradicts the view of the agency as a whole. * * * But the situation here is quite different. Agency officials in the Alaskan Region uniformly advised all guides, lodge managers and guiding services in Alaska that they could meet their regulatory responsibilities by complying with the requirements of part 91 only. FAA officials gave that advice for almost thirty years. As for the agency as a whole, the FAA noted in 1992 that its 'past policy' permitted guide pilots and lodge operators to operate aircraft under Part 91. And it acknowledged in 1997 that '[u]ntil recently, lodge/guide operators have been advised that Part 135 did not address their operation of aircraft.' This must be why the National Transportation Safety Board, in its 1995 Study of Aviation Safety in Alaska, described 'current FAA policy' as permitting guides to fly their customers 'as noncommercial operations under the general operating rules of 14 CFR Part 91, which are less restrictive than those in Part 135.'

"Even if the FAA as a whole somehow had in mind an interpretation different from that of its Alaskan Region, guides and lodge operators in Alaska had no reason to know this. Those regulated by an administrative agency are entitled to 'know the rules by which the game will be played.' *See* [Oliver Wendell Holmes Jr.], *Holdsworth's English Law*, 25 Law Quarterly Rev. 414 (1909). Alaskan guide pilots and lodge operators relied on the advice FAA officials imparted to them—they opened lodges and built up businesses dependent on aircraft, believing their flights were subject to part 91's requirements only. That advice became an authoritative departmental interpretation, an administrative common law applicable to Alaskan guide pilots. The FAA's current doubts about the wisdom of the regulatory system followed in Alaska for more than thirty years does not justify disregarding the requisite procedures for changing that system. Throughout this period, guide pilots and lodge operators had no opportunity to participate in the development of the part 135 regulations and to argue in favor of special rules for their operations. Air transportation regulations have evolved considerably since 1963 and part 135 has been the subject of numerous rule making proceedings. Had guides and lodge operators been able to comment on the resulting amendments and modifications to part 135, they could have suggested changes or exceptions that would have accommodated the unique circumstances of Alaskan air carriage. As the FAA pointed out in its brief, the agency's regulations have, in several respects, treated Alaska differently from the continental United States. * * * There is no reason to suppose that with the participation of Alaskan guide pilots and lodge operators, the regulations in part 135 would not have been affected. If the FAA now wishes to apply those regulations to these individuals, it must give them an opportunity to comment before doing so. The Notice to Operators was published without notice and comment and it is therefore invalid."

NOTES AND QUESTIONS ON GUIDANCE DOCUMENTS

Judge Randolph's opinion seems to give support to scholars' claims that agencies seeking to sneak in policy changes through guidance documents, without enduring the time-consuming but democracy-respecting notice-and-comment process, violate the APA. For the reception of Judge Randolph's decision in other circuits, see Brian J. Shearer, *Outfoxing Alaska Hunters: How Arbitrary and Capricious Review of Changing Regulatory Interpretations Can More Efficiently Police Agency Discretion*, 62 Am. U. L. Rev. 167, 180–81 (2012).

Nonetheless, *Paralyzed Veterans*, where the Court warned the agency against such sneakiness but still upheld its guidance, remains the majority practice in the D.C. Circuit. Indeed, Judge Randolph himself declined to extend *Alaskan Hunters* to a situation where the agency had not taken a direct and firm position on an issue for decades. See *MetWest Inc. v. Secretary of Labor*, 560 F.3d 506 (D.C. Cir. 2009). In *MetWest*, Judge Randolph indicated that the industry's longstanding and justifiable reliance interests (the guide industry in Alaska was built on the Region's construction of *Marshall*) made the earlier decision a special case. Leading administrative law scholars have warned that *Alaska Hunters* must not be read to mean that an agency's initial interpretation, "once informally adopted, freezes the state of agency law, which cannot subsequently be altered without notice-and-comment rulemaking." Peter L. Strauss, *Publication Rules in the Rulemaking Spectrum: Assuring Proper Respect for an Essential Element*, 53 Admin. L. Rev. 803, 844 (2001); see also William Funk, *A Primer on Nonlegislative Rules*, 53 Admin. L. Rev. 1321, 1329–30 (2001); Richard W. Murphy, *Hunters for Administrative Common Law*, 58 Admin. L. Rev. 917, 921–23 (2006). (Judge Randolph cited and relied on these works in footnote 4 of his *MetWest* opinion.)

On the other hand, the D.C. Circuit recently applied *Alaskan Hunters* in a case where the Department of Labor sought to change its application of the Fair Labor Standards Act to mortgage loan officers. See *Mortgage Bankers Association v. Harris*, 720 F.3d 966 (D.C. Cir. 2013). In a 2006 opinion letter, the Department had opined that such officers are not covered; when the Department withdrew that letter in 2010, the trade association sued, and the D.C. Circuit ruled that the new interpretation was invalid. The panel opinion rejected an interpretation of *MetWest* that the *Paralyzed Veterans/Alaskan Hunters* doctrine is inapplicable when there has not been private reliance; instead, the critical issue is whether the agency had issued a "definitive" interpretation that it was changing. The panel opinion suggested the possibility of en banc deliberation on this issue. If the D.C. Circuit were to consider how broadly to express the *Paralyzed Veterans/Alaskan Hunters* doctrine, does the Supreme Court's decision in *Fox I* have any bearing? Does *Mortgage Bankers* run the risk of ossifying agency policy? Or discourage "definitive" agency interpretations?

Executive Order 13,422 (Jan. 18, 2007)
72 Fed. Reg. 2763 (Jan. 18, 2007).

President George W. Bush issued this executive order to amend the Clinton Administration's Executive Order 12,866 (Appendix 5). Among other things, President Bush added a new § 9.1 to the previous order:

> Significant Guidance Documents. Each agency shall provide OIRA, at such times and in the manner specified by the Administrator of OIRA, with advance notification of any significant guidance documents. Each agency shall take such steps as are necessary for its Regulatory Policy Officer to ensure

the agency's compliance with the requirements of this section. Upon the request of the Administrator, for each matter identified as, or determined by the Administrator to be, a significant guidance document, the issuing agency shall provide to OIRA the content of the draft guidance document, together with a brief explanation of the need for the guidance document and how it will meet that need. The OIRA Administrator shall notify the agency when additional consultation will be required before the issuance of the significant guidance document.

"Guidance documents" and "significant guidance documents" are defined in the new executive order.

Two years later, in Executive Order 13,497, President Obama revoked President Bush's amendments to Executive Order 12,866. Such revocation deleted new § 9.1 from the executive order. But OMB Director Peter R. Orzag issued a Memorandum for the Heads and Acting Heads of Executive Departments and Agencies, "Guidance for Regulatory Review" (Mar. 4, 2009), http://www.regulationwriters.com/library/OMBMemo–030409–GuidanceRegReview.pdf. In that one-paragraph memorandum, the OMB Director said this about President Obama's executive order:

> Revocation of these [Bush era] amendments restored the regulatory review process to what it had been under Executive Order 12866 between 1993 and 2007. During this period, OIRA reviewed all significant proposed or final agency actions, including significant policy and guidance documents. Such agency actions and documents remain subject to OIRA's review under Executive Order 12866.

Progressives have denounced OMB's move as an aggressive "power grab."

In a letter to the President's counsel, the Center for Progressive Reform (CPR) claimed that OMB was defying the President, whose January 2009 executive order was a signal that OIRA's hard review of environmental regulations (and others) would be more responsive to congressional goals. See Letter from Professors Robert L. Glicksman et al., CPR, to Robert Bauer, White House Counsel, "Violation of Executive Order 13497 by the Office of Information and Regulatory Affairs" (Mar. 17, 2010), available at http://www.progressivereform.org/articles/WH_Counsel_re_OIRA_March2010.pdf. Citing examples where needed environmental guidances were being held up by OIRA, the CPR letter argued that OIRA review of guidance documents is unnecessary, discourages agencies from issuing guidances needed to inform the public, and slows down the guidance process considerably.

———————

OMB Director Rob Portman, Memorandum to Executive Departments and Agencies, "Agency Good Guidance Practices"
OMB, Jan. 18, 2007
(http://www.whitehouse.gov/sites/default/files/omb/memoranda/fy2007/m07-07.pdf)

On the same day that President Bush issued his executive order, the OMB Director promulgated this memorandum to executive branch agencies, in an ongoing Bush-Cheney Administration effort to regularize agency procedures and, effectively, to make it more expensive for agencies to take even gentle-nudge type regulatory action.

The OMB Director noted the utility of guidance documents to alert the citizenry to the agency's understanding of what the law required and to coordinate the advice given and action taken by agency officials themselves. But he also cautioned that guidance documents should not be considered substitutes for the regular notice-and-comment rulemaking process, a concern that had been repeatedly raised by the D.C. Circuit.

The main innovation of Director Portman's Good Guidance Practices was contained in Part IV(1):

[W]hen an agency prepares a draft of an economically significant guidance document, the agency shall:

a.   Publish a notice in the **Federal Register** announcing that the draft document is available;

b.   Post the draft document on the Internet and make it publicly available in hard copy (or notify the public how they can review the guidance document if it is not in a format that permits such electronic posting with reasonable efforts);

c.   Invite public comment on the draft document; and

d.   Prepare and post on the agency's website a response-to-comments document.

Part IV(2) provides that the OIRA Administrator can exempt some economically significant guidance documents from the notice-and-comment process.

We are not sure what effect the Portman memorandum continues to have after 2009, when the Bush-Cheney Administration ended, but a huge number of agency guidances are reproduced on the agency websites and some have been opened up to public comment as well.

QUERY ON AGENCY GUIDANCE

If an agency engages in notice-and-comment guidance-making, along the lines suggested in the Portman memorandum, ought the agency to have more leeway to alter its previous interpretations of its governing statute or legislative regulations? Recall that in *Alaska Hunters* the FAA had published its guidance in the Federal Register, but had not engaged in a notice-and-comment-and-response process. Do you think that might have made a difference in the guidance the FAA ultimately adopted? In the D.C. Circuit's treatment of the agency's guidance?

NOTE ON ADMINISTRATIVE WAIVERS

Another, increasingly important way that agencies exercise their implementation duties is through the process of granting *administrative waivers*. Congress often writes waiver provisions into its statutes—provisions that give the agency discretion to approve proposals for a different form of implementing the law than the one laid out in the statute. In the health reform legislation, for example, HHS has the discretion to exempt any state from the requirements of the law's insurance expansions if the state proposes a feasible, different plan to cover as many people. (ACA § 1332). As another example, in the context of the Clean Air Act, the EPA (after much political back and forth) approved a "waiver from preemption" that allowed California to enforce its greenhouse gas emissions standards. See Environmental Protection Agency, "California State Motor Vehicle Pollution Control Standards; Notice of Decision Granting a Waiver of Clean Air Act Preemption for California's 2009 and Subsequent Model Year Greenhouse Gas Emission Standards for New Motor Vehicles," 74 Fed. Reg. 32,744, 32,744 (July 8, 2009).

Waivers have been around for a long time. They have several important uses. Sometimes certain aspects of statutes are not feasible for certain implementers and waivers allow the lead agency to bend the statute to make its provisions work where they otherwise would not. At a broader level, more ambitious waivers have enabled federal-program implementers (often the states) to push federal policy in new directions, catalyzing experimentation. The health reform legislation was modeled on a program made possible by a Bush-Cheney Administration waiver to Massachusetts under the federal Medicaid Act. So understood, waivers might be a particularly modern expression of federalism for the statutory era: Waivers allow states to experiment and tailor programs to the particular needs of their states, both traditional federalism values, but here accomplished *through* federal legislation rather than apart from it.

Do waivers raise democracy concerns? Some object to executive agencies having so much discretion to reshape federal laws (or they object to congressional punting). There are also process concerns associated with waivers. There is no APA analogue for the waiver process and most of what occurs in behind-the-scenes negotiations between states and the federal government. Scholars divide on whether states have sufficient bargaining power for this process to be fair. E.g., Erin Ryan, *Negotiating Federalism*, 53 B.C. L. Rev. 1 (2011). In an ironic twist, some waivers in recent years have been used to *get around* Congress, rather than their original purpose of working as explicit delegation from Congress to the executive branch.

Consider the following problem and ask yourself whether this use of waivers is good or bad for democracy.

PROBLEM 7–5: WAIVERS AND NO CHILD LEFT BEHIND?

In 2011, President Obama announced that his Department of Education would grant waivers out of the federal No Child Left Behind (NCLB) Act to states that agreed to adopt what were, in the Administration's view, better education policies. The President specifically stated that the reason for the waivers was to get around congressional gridlock: Congress couldn't get the job done to fix the statute, the statute (in the President's view) needed fixing, and so he would use his executive power to do it. Earlier in his Administration, President Obama had presented his own blueprint for wholesale education reform to Congress and Congress had not acted on it.

Here is the relevant part of the waiver provision in the statute the Administration invoked:

SEC. 9401. WAIVERS   OF   STATUTORY   AND   REGULATORY
            REQUIREMENTS.

(a) IN GENERAL—* * * [T]he Secretary may waive any statutory or regulatory requirement of this Act for a State educational agency, local educational agency, Indian tribe, or school through a local educational agency, that—

> (1) receives funds under a program authorized by this Act; and

> (2) requests a waiver under subsection (b).

(b) REQUEST FOR WAIVER—

> (1) IN   GENERAL—A   State   educational   agency,   local educational agency, or Indian tribe that desires a waiver shall submit a waiver request to the Secretary that * * *

>> (B) describes which Federal statutory or regulatory requirements are to be waived and how the waiving of those requirements will—

>>> (i) increase the quality of instruction for students; and

>>> (ii) improve the academic achievement of students;

As of July 2014, more than thirty states have received such waivers, and some commentators have argued that they cast doubt on the continuing relevance of NCLB as originally conceived. "In just five months, the Obama administration has freed schools in more than half the nation from central provisions of the No Child Left Behind education law, raising the question of whether the decade-old federal program has been essentially nullified." Motoko Rich, *'No Child' Law 'Whittled Down' By White House*, N.Y. Times, Jul. 6, 2012. The waiver program was announced and implemented through a "Flexibility Policy Document" and a "Frequently Asked Questions" document called "a Guidance."

Are the waivers authorized by the statute? Are they legitimate? If you wanted to challenge them how would you go about it? What arguments would you make—and how would the Obama Administration respond? Would the Supreme Court be receptive to arguments challenging this aggressive waiver policy?

CHAPTER 8

DELEGATION, DEFERENCE, AND JUDICIAL TREATMENT OF AGENCY STATUTORY INTERPRETATIONS

■ ■ ■

In this chapter, we consider the doctrines and theories of delegation, deference, and "agency statutory interpretation." Congress delegates much statutory implementation to agencies, and agencies must interpret statutes to do that work. The courts have developed a broad continuum of doctrines to utilize and evaluate those administrative interpretations. At the same time, agencies and courts are very different institutions and it is not obvious that each does or should approach statutory interpretation in the same manner. This chapter introduces these questions and the legal regimes that have developed to address them.

Statutes are not the end of lawmaking, but often are only the beginning. In today's world, rare is the statute that enforces itself, and equally rare is the statutory text that contains all of the details necessary to effectuate a statute's mandates. Instead, as we have seen throughout this book, Congress typically enlists the help of expert implementers in the executive branch—federal agencies—to enforce and fill out the details of federal legislation.

What exactly does this mean? Consider the following directive in the recent health reform legislation: Congress provided that the Secretary of the Department of Health and Human Services "shall establish criteria for determining whether health insur[ers] * * * have discouraged an individual from remaining enrolled * * * based on that individual's health status," Patient Protection and Affordable Care Act of 2010, Pub. L. No. 111–148, § 1101(e)(1) (2010). You know well by now that the agency—the Department of Health and Human Services—has to abide by all of the limits on delegated authority that we saw in our study of the Administrative Procedure Act (APA) in Chapter 7. The agency must abide by court-imposed limits too, such as *State Farm*'s rule, from Chapter 7,

§ 2, that an agency cannot act based on insufficient evidence or for no reason (arbitrarily).

But you should never forget that what underlies every aspect of an agency's federal statutory implementation work is *statutory interpretation*. The agency cannot devise a rule to prevent insurers from using health status to discourage potential enrollees without interpreting what "health status" means, or what it means to "discourage" consumers. There are literally thousands of provisions just like this across the U.S. Code. The Dodd-Frank financial reform legislation alone has more than 330 rulemaking provisions.[1]

How agencies do, or should do, this interpretive work, and how "agency statutory interpretation"[2] gels with the courts' own role as federal statutory interpreters is where the rubber meets the road for federal statutory interpretation in the modern administrative state. Do or should agencies use canons like *exclusio unius* or the federalism canon when they interpret statutes? How about legislative history? And when it comes to judicial review, how should courts go about reviewing agency statutory interpretations? This question adds a whole new wrinkle to judicial review of agency action. Even after agency action has passed the threshold bar of the APA, the court still must review the way the agency interprets the statute itself. Thus, in the example of the health reform regulation, may HHS interpret "health status" to include obesity? This is the same type of inquiry that we have seen throughout this book in cases involving the Supreme Court's review of lower-court statutory interpretations, except now the interpreter being reviewed is an agency, not a lower court. The question is whether or how the existence of an agency interpreter changes that review process. The Court has spent at least the past eighty years working through that question, and this chapter provides the basic framework of these so-called "agency deference" regimes.

Two caveats before proceeding. First, remember that judicial review of agency action is a multilayered and often multi-step process. *State Farm* and the APA provide the framework that ensures the agency has passed the thresholds for evidence and procedure. Those questions come first. Judicial deference enters the analysis when the courts review the agency's statutory interpretations, but the court won't get there if they aren't satisfied first that the agency's processes were kosher. Most of the

---

[1] Curtis W. Copeland, Cong. Research Serv., R41472, *Rulemaking Requirements and Authorities in the Dodd-Frank Wall Street Reform and Consumer Protection Act* 6–7 (2010), available at http://www.law.umaryland.edu/marshall/crsreports/crsdocuments/R41472 11032010. pdf.

[2] Jerry L. Mashaw, *Exploring Agency Statutory Interpretation*, 31 Admin. & Reg. Law News (Spring 2006); see also Peter L. Strauss, *When the Judge Is Not the Primary Official with Responsibility to Read: Agency Interpretation and the Problem of Legislative History*, 66 Chi.-Kent L. Rev.321 (1990).

cases in this chapter are not APA/*State Farm* cases of the sort treated in Chapter 7: No one is challenging the agency's evidence or procedure. Instead, these cases involve challenges to the way in which the agency *read the statute*. But do not forget that all of these agency actions had to pass that APA/*State Farm* threshold first.

Second, do not forget that federal agencies are not the only game in town. Congress sometimes gives *non*-federal actors key roles in implementing—and so in interpreting—federal laws. States and, increasingly, private actors have important administrative duties in federal statutes ranging from the Clean Air Act to Medicare. These non-federal actors complicate the legal landscape, and we discuss them at the end of this chapter. For now, however, we keep our focus on the enormous landscape of federal agency statutory interpretation and the judicial response to it.

1.   THE EMERGENCE OF MODERN DEFERENCE PRACTICE

A. FOUNDATIONS OF THE CURRENT REGIME: *SKIDMORE* AND *CHEVRON*

Federal agencies existed long before Franklin Delano Roosevelt, see Jerry L. Mashaw, *Federal Administration and Administrative Law in the Golden Age*, 119 Yale L.J. 1362 (2010), but FDR's New Deal gave us the sprawling administrative state that we have today, and it laid the foundation for the kinds of complex federal statutes that now dominate our statute books. Subsequent decades saw the rise of faith in the bureaucracy—the idea that the success of government programs depends on a cadre of policy experts, working behind the scenes, often using scientific or other empirical data, to make statutes work.

Jack Skidmore v. Swift & Co.
323 U.S. 134 (1944).

One of the most important cases in the area of agency statutory interpretation was decided in the middle of this New Deal transformation. In *Skidmore* (also discussed in Chapter 7, § 3C), **Justice Jackson**'s opinion for the Court held that courts are not required to follow agency statutory interpretations, but rather should give them weight in accordance with their "power to persuade."

The case arose out of a lawsuit filed by employees of a Texas packing plant under the Fair Labor Standards Act, 29 U.S.C.A. § 201 et seq., to recover overtime pay for overnight time spent on call at work to answer fire alarms. The relevant section of the Act provided that "no employer shall employ any of his employees * * * for a workweek longer than forty hours unless such employee receives compensation for his employment in excess of the hours above specified at a rate not less than one and one-half times the regular rate at which he is employed." 29 U.S.C. § 207(a)(1). The dispute centered over whether the overnight time—which was typically very quiet, as alarms were rare—counted as "work" under the Act. The Department of Labor official charged with implementing the Act filed an *amicus* brief with the Supreme Court that described the flexible approach he had taken to the "inactive duty" issue. In his view, the on-call duty time spent sleeping and eating should not be included in "hours worked," but the remainder of the on-call time should be. The Court ultimately interpreted the statute in accordance with Labor's view, but made clear that Labor's recommendation did not "bind" the Court. Instead, the Court held that the Agency's views were entitled to "respect," because they "constituted a body of experience and informed judgment":

"The weight of such [an agency interpretation] in a particular case will depend upon the thoroughness evident in its consideration, the validity of its reasoning, its consistency with earlier and later pronouncements, and all those factors which give it power to persuade, if lacking power to control."

NOTES AND QUESTIONS ON SKIDMORE

1. *The Relationship Between* Skidmore *and Other Tools of Statutory Interpretation.* The Court in *Skidmore* recognized the expert knowledge of statutory administrators but still retained all of the interpretive power in the courts. The Court essentially held that an agency's understanding of what a federal statute means is useful for whatever it's worth—it all depends on factors like how much research the agency did and "all the factors which give [the interpretation] power to persuade."

This view of agency statutory interpretation should remind you of the canons of interpretation from Chapter 5. Under *Skidmore*, the agency interpretation is one more datum that a court might use—alongside dictionaries, textual canons, substantive canons, and legislative history—to determine a statute's meaning. Under *Skidmore*, the judiciary, not the agency, controls the meaning of the federal statute. But the agency's view is potentially a very important resource for courts to use, depending on how persuasive it is. For this reason the metaphor often accorded to the *Skidmore* standard is one of "gravity"—the agency's views can have "weight." See Peter L. Strauss, *"Deference" is too Confusing—Let's Call them "Chevron Space" and "Skidmore Weight,"* 112 Colum. L. Rev. 1143 (2012).

2. Skidmore's *Complexity.* Over the years, the *Skidmore* standard got quite messy. Colin S. Diver, in *Statutory Interpretation in the Administrative State*, 133 U. Pa. L. Rev. 549, 562 n.95 (1985), set forth a list of factors that

the Court had considered in deciding whether to accord agency interpretations weight under *Skidmore*, including:

- whether the agency construction was rendered contemporaneously with the statute's passage;

- whether the agency's construction is of longstanding application;

- whether the agency has maintained its position consistently;

- whether the public has relied on the agency's interpretation;

- whether the interpretation involves a matter of "public controversy";

- whether the interpretation is based on "expertise" or involves a "technical and complex" subject;

- whether the agency has rulemaking authority;

- whether agency action is necessary to set the statute in motion;

- whether Congress was aware of the agency interpretation and failed to repudiate it; and

- whether the agency has expressly addressed the application of the statute to its proposed action (internal citations omitted).

Notice that Professor Diver's "partial list"(!), drawn from the case law, demonstrates that courts were considering agency interpretations for many reasons *in addition to* the agency's relative expertise. Review the list. How many other normative justifications can you identify for going along with an agency interpretation beyond the agency's expertise? Why might the controversial nature of an issue (#5) be a reason to follow the agency? Why is the contemporaneousness of the agency construction (#1) important, or Congress's apparent acquiescence in the agency's view (#9)? Think about these and the other *Skidmore* factors, and then consider the following problem.

PROBLEM 8–1: SKIDMORE IN ACTION

The pregnancy discrimination case from Chapter 2, **General Electric Co. v. Gilbert**, 429 U.S. 125 (1976), provides an example of how this "totality of the circumstances" test from *Skidmore* worked. As you will recall, at issue in *Gilbert* was General Electric Co.'s decision to exclude pregnancy from its disability plan. Female employees challenged this decision as sex discrimination in violation of Title VII of the Civil Rights Act of 1964. The employees relied on a 1972 regulation issued by the Equal Employment Opportunity Commission (EEOC) supporting their view and urged the Court to defer to it.

Justice Rehnquist's opinion for the Court applied *Skidmore* and ruled that the EEOC regulation was not persuasive. The Court focused on the fact that the regulation was not a "contemporaneous interpretation of Title VII," since it was first promulgated eight years after the enactment of that Title," and also that the regulation "flatly contradicted the position which the agency had enunciated at an earlier date, closer to the enactment of the governing statute."

Justice Brennan (joined by Justice Marshall) dissented, finding the EEOC position worthy of respect under *Skidmore*, and arguing that the EEOC had moved slowly and deliberately toward a policy on pregnancy and maternity because the agency needed more information and study of this difficult issue. "[N]o one can or does deny that the final EEOC determination followed thorough and well-informed consideration. Indeed, realistically viewed, this extended evaluation of an admittedly complex problem and an unwillingness to impose additional, potentially premature costs on employers during the decision making stages ought to be perceived as a practice to be commended. It is bitter irony that the care that preceded promulgation of the 1972 guideline is today condemned by the Court as tardy indecisiveness, its unwillingness irresponsibly to challenge employers' practices during the formative period is labeled as evidence of inconsistency, and this indecisiveness and inconsistency are bootstrapped into reasons for denying the Commission's interpretation its due deference."

What exactly did the *Gilbert* majority object to? *Gilbert* provides a typical example of the Court's rather low tolerance for inconsistent agency statutory interpretations under its *Skidmore* jurisprudence. The *Gilbert* majority used the fact that the EEOC's view had evolved and changed over time as a reason *not* to follow it—as a reason that the EEOC interpretation of Title VII lacked the "power to persuade." Does that make sense? Do the reasons for the change matter? Agency positions often change, as a result not only of the agency's research and experience with the statute but also as a result of politics. In your view, does the presence of politics enhance or diminish the case for deference? As we have seen throughout this book, this adaptability of agencies and their responsiveness to Congress is a primary reason that Congress delegates work to agencies in the first place. *Skidmore* posed some difficulties for this kind of dynamic approach to agency statutory interpretation.

B. INTRODUCTION TO *CHEVRON*

The Court's next major statement on agency statutory interpretation was *Chevron U.S.A., Inc. v. Natural Resources Defense Council*, 467 U.S. 837 (1984), decided forty years after *Skidmore*. *Chevron* is the watershed opinion. It concerned a new interpretation of the Clean Air Act by the Reagan Administration's EPA that allowed companies to effectively shift pollution around a single plant without getting a new permit, as previously had been required, as long as the total amount of pollution emitted from the plant remained the same.

The relevant statutory provision of the Clean Air Act, § 172(b)(6), 42 U.S.C. § 7502(b), provided:

> "The [state] plan provisions required by [the statute] shall * * * (6) require permits for the construction and operation of new or modified major stationary sources."

And here is the Reagan Administration EPA's interpretation of that statutory provision, set forth in a regulation, 40 CFR §§ 51.18(j)(1)(i) and (ii) (1983):

> "(i) 'Stationary source' means any building, structure, facility, or installation which emits or may emit any air pollutant subject to regulation under the Act.

> (ii) 'Building, structure, facility, or installation' means all of the pollutant-emitting activities which belong to the same industrial grouping, are located on one or more contiguous or adjacent properties, and are under the control of the same person (or persons under common control) except the activities of any vessel."

Consider, as you read the case, the differences between the Court's approach here and in *Skidmore*, not only with respect to how agencies make policy but also with respect to the proper balance of power between courts and agencies as federal statutory interpreters.

CHEVRON, U.S.A., INC. v. NATURAL RESOURCES DEFENSE COUNCIL

United States Supreme Court, 1984.
467 U.S. 837, 104 S.Ct. 2778, 81 L.Ed.2d 694.

JUSTICE STEVENS delivered the opinion of the Court.

In the Clean Air Act Amendments of 1977, Pub. L. 95–95, 91 Stat. 685, Congress enacted certain requirements applicable to States that had not achieved the national air quality standards established by the Environmental Protection Agency (EPA) pursuant to earlier legislation. The amended Clean Air Act required these "nonattainment" States to establish a permit program regulating "new or modified major stationary sources" of air pollution. Generally, a permit may not be issued for a new or modified major stationary source unless several stringent conditions are met. The EPA regulation promulgated to implement this permit requirement allows a State to adopt a plantwide definition of the term "stationary source." Under this definition, an existing plant that contains several pollution-emitting devices may install or modify one piece of equipment without meeting the permit conditions if the alteration will not increase the total emissions from the plant. The question presented by these cases is whether EPA's decision to allow States to treat all of the pollution-emitting devices within the same industrial grouping as though they were encased within a single "bubble" is based on a reasonable construction of the statutory term "stationary source." * * *

[II] When a court reviews an agency's construction of the statute which it administers, it is confronted with two questions. First, always, is the question whether Congress has directly spoken to the precise question at issue. If the intent of Congress is clear, that is the end of the matter, for the court, as well as the agency, must give effect to the unambiguously expressed intent of Congress.[9] If, however, the court determines Congress has not directly addressed the precise question at issue, the court does not simply impose its own construction on the statute, as would be necessary in the absence of an administrative interpretation. Rather, if the statute is silent or ambiguous with respect to the specific issue, the question for the court is whether the agency's answer is based on a permissible construction of the statute.[11]

"The power of an administrative agency to administer a congressionally created * * *program necessarily requires the formulation of policy and the making of rules to fill any gap left, implicitly or explicitly, by Congress." If Congress has explicitly left a gap for the agency to fill, there is an express delegation of authority to the agency to elucidate a specific provision of the statute by regulation. Such legislative regulations are given controlling weight unless they are arbitrary, capricious, or manifestly contrary to the statute. Sometimes the legislative delegation to an agency on a particular question is implicit rather than explicit. In such a case, a court may not substitute its own construction of a statutory provision for a reasonable interpretation made by the administrator of an agency.

We have long recognized that considerable weight should be accorded to an executive department's construction of a statutory scheme it is entrusted to administer, and the principle of deference to administrative interpretations "has been consistently followed by this Court whenever decision as to the meaning or reach of a statute has involved reconciling conflicting policies, and a full understanding of the force of the statutory policy in the given situation has depended upon more than ordinary knowledge respecting the matters subjected to agency regulations." * * *

In light of these well-settled principles it is clear that the Court of Appeals misconceived the nature of its role in reviewing the regulations

---

[9] The judiciary is the final authority on issues of statutory construction and must reject administrative constructions which are contrary to clear congressional intent. If a court, employing traditional tools of statutory construction, ascertains that Congress had an intention on the precise question at issue, that intention is the law and must be given effect.

[11] The court need not conclude that the agency construction was the only one it permissibly could have adopted to uphold the construction, or even the reading the court would have reached if the question initially had arisen in a judicial proceeding.

at issue. Once it determined, after its own examination of the legislation, that Congress did not actually have an intent regarding the applicability of the bubble concept to the permit program, the question before it was not whether in its view the concept is "inappropriate" in the general context of a program designed to improve air quality, but whether the Administrator's view that it is appropriate in the context of this particular program is a reasonable one. Based on the examination of the legislation and its history which follows, we agree with the Court of Appeals that Congress did not have a specific intention on the applicability of the bubble concept in these cases, and conclude that the EPA's use of that concept here is a reasonable policy choice for the agency to make.

[The 1977 Amendments added a definition of "major stationary source," as "any stationary facility or source of air pollutants which directly emits, or has the potential to emit, one hundred tons per year or more of any air pollutant." Justice Stevens found this definition ambiguous. Examining the legislative history, he found only that Congress sought to accommodate both the "economic interest in permitting capital improvements to continue and the environmental interest in improving air quality." There was no clear evidence as to how Congress expected this balance to be carried out with regard to stationary sources.]

In these cases the Administrator's interpretation represents a reasonable accommodation of manifestly competing interests and is entitled to deference: the regulatory scheme is technical and complex, the agency considered the matter in a detailed and reasoned fashion, and the decision involves reconciling conflicting policies. Congress intended to accommodate both interests, but did not do so itself on the level of specificity presented by these cases. Perhaps that body consciously desired the Administrator to strike the balance at this level, thinking that those with great expertise and charged with responsibility for administering the provision would be in a better position to do so; perhaps it simply did not consider the question at this level; and perhaps Congress was unable to forge a coalition on either side of the question, and those on each side decided to take their chances with the scheme devised by the agency. For judicial purposes, it matters not which of these things occurred.

Judges are not experts in the field, and are not part of either political branch of the Government. Courts must, in some cases, reconcile competing political interests, but not on the basis of the judges' personal policy preferences. In contrast, an agency to which Congress has delegated policymaking responsibilities may, within the limits of that delegation, properly rely upon the incumbent administration's views of wise policy to inform its judgments. While agencies are not directly accountable to the people, the Chief Executive is, and it is entirely appropriate for this political branch of the Government to make such policy choices—resolving the competing interests which Congress itself either inadvertently did not resolve, or intentionally left to be resolved by the agency charged with the administration of the statute in light of everyday realities.

When a challenge to an agency construction of a statutory provision, fairly conceptualized, really centers on the wisdom of the agency's policy, rather than whether it is a reasonable choice within a gap left open by Congress, the challenge must fail. In such a case, federal judges—who have no constituency—have a duty to respect legitimate policy choices made by those who do. The responsibilities for assessing the wisdom of such policy choices and resolving the struggle between competing views of the public interest are not judicial ones: "Our Constitution vests such responsibilities in the political branches." *TVA v. Hill*, 437 U.S. 153, 195 (1978). * * *

NOTES AND QUESTIONS ON CHEVRON

1.   *Chevron's New Two-Step Test.* *Chevron's* approach to agency interpretation is more formal and, in some ways, simpler, than *Skidmore's*. Justice Stevens's opinion sets out a new two-step test. **Step One:** "First, always, is the question whether Congress has directly spoken to the precise question at issue. If the intent of Congress is clear, that is the end of the matter, for the court, as well as the agency, must give effect to the unambiguously expressed intent of Congress." Justice Stevens then identified a potential **Step Two:** "If, however, the court determines Congress has not directly addressed the precise question at issue, the court does not simply impose its own construction on the statute, as would be necessary in the absence of an administrative interpretation. Rather, if the statute is silent or ambiguous with respect to the specific issue, the question for the court is whether the agency's answer is based on a permissible construction of the statute."

What exactly does this mean? Under *Chevron*, statutory clarity is the ballgame. If Congress has specifically addressed the interpretive question—the question asked in *Chevron's* Step One—then Congress's command controls. In that instance, neither courts nor agencies have the power to replace Congress's clearly expressed mandates with their own. This is the same legislative supremacy idea that we already have seen in our study of the canons of interpretation: the courts will not substitute their own judgment for Congress's, if the statute is clear. The same goes in the agency interpretation context.

If, however, Congress is not clear—whether because the statute is ambiguous or because Congress simply did not address the issue at all—then *Chevron* tells courts to move to Step Two, which asks whether the agency's interpretation is "reasonable." Take note: Step Two is a highly deferential inquiry. The court does not ask whether the agency's interpretation is the "best" one. Instead, *Chevron* assumes that there is often a "zone of indeterminacy" within which Congress has authorized agencies to act, and the court does not substitute its judgment for that of the agency in deciding how that indeterminacy should be resolved. How is this different from *Skidmore*? Jot down your thoughts before proceeding to the next note.

2.   Chevron *versus* Skidmore. *Chevron* takes a different approach from *Skidmore* in at least three very important ways:

(A) Who "The Decider" Is. Under *Skidmore*, the courts retain ultimate interpretive authority. The agency's interpretation is a useful piece of information that might be given weight as merited. *Chevron*, however, works a massive transfer of interpretive authority *away* from courts and *to* agencies. *Chevron* says that as long as the statute is ambiguous and the agency's interpretation is reasonable, the agency can choose the interpretation, even if the courts, left to their own devices, might choose a different one. This is a "Wow!" moment. The cases you read in earlier chapters involved judicial disagreements about interpretation; *Chevron* changes the battlefield entirely, making agencies, not judges, the primary statutory interpreters.

(B) No "Right" Answer. *Chevron* also changes the nature of the inquiry. Under *Skidmore*, courts choose what, in their view, is the "best" interpretation. *Chevron*, in contrast, sees a "space" for interpretation—a zone of possible interpretations that all might be reasonable. The courts' job is not to pick the best one, but merely to confirm that the space exists and that the agency's choice is within it. See Peter L. Strauss, *"Deference" is too Confusing—Let's Call them "Chevron Space" and "Skidmore Weight"*, 112 Colum. L. Rev. 1143 (2012).

(C) A More Dynamic and Political Approach. *Chevron* is also an important recognition of dynamic statutory interpretation in the modern administrative state, because it recognizes that first-order statutory interpretation will usually be accomplished by politically accountable—and therefore politically protean—agencies; because it further recognizes that under general statutory language that does not target the interpretive issue (Step One) there may be several "reasonable" agency interpretations, any of which must be upheld (Step Two); and because it recognizes that agency interpretations may themselves change over time. "An initial agency interpretation is not carved in stone. On the contrary, the agency, to engage in informal rulemaking, must consider varying interpretations and the wisdom of its policy on a continuing basis." *Chevron*, 467 U.S. at 863–64. To illustrate how greatly this marks a departure from *Skidmore*, recall *Gilbert*, the pregnancy discrimination case. There, the Court relied on the dynamic, and perhaps politicized, nature of the agency's interpretation as a reason *not* to accord its views weight. But in *Chevron*, the Court took precisely the opposite view; namely, that the very politicized nature of the inquiry itself is a reason for a branch other than the judicial branch to decide such questions. By the way, would *Gilbert* have been decided differently under *Chevron*?

3.   *Chevron's Justifications.* How many justifications for *Chevron*'s new regime can you count in the Court's opinion? Which are most persuasive? Can you come up with any others?

(A) Congressional Intent. Many judges and scholars have justified *Chevron* on the ground that it approximates congressional intent, and many read the Court's opinion to rest on that proposition. The primary assumption of *Chevron* is that whenever there is statutory ambiguity, Congress intends to delegate the interpretive question to the agency. Justice Stevens' opinion is refreshingly frank about the reasons that statutory ambiguity might exist. He acknowledges both that sometimes Congress is deliberately vague—Congress punts questions to other branches because it may not know the answer, or cannot reach political agreement on a more specific resolution—and also that sometimes statutes are vague because Congress just didn't address the issue in question at all. Do both kinds of vagueness link to congressional intent in the same way? Justice Stevens's opinion says that "it matters not" what the reason is for the ambiguity, all that matters is that it exists. But isn't there a difference between assuming that Congress intends for agencies to resolve vague statutory provisions that Congress did write and assuming that Congress intends for agencies to resolve *any* statutory question that Congress failed to consider?

Chevron's critics have thus countered that the case's central assumption about congressional intent is a "fiction." They argue that not every instance of ambiguity signals an intent to delegate interpretive power to administrators and that *Chevron*'s court-to-agency transfer of authority is too broad if the goal is to effectuate congressional expectations. See Cynthia R. Farina, *Statutory Interpretation and the Balance of Power in the Administrative State*, 89 Colum. L. Rev. 452, 471 (1989); Thomas W. Merrill, *Judicial Deference to Executive Precedent*, 101 Yale L.J. 969, 995 (1992); Cass R. Sunstein, *Constitutionalism After the New Deal*, 101 Harv. L. Rev. 421, 468 (1987).

(B) Accountability and Democracy. Another important foundation of *Chevron*, and one less tethered to congressional intent, is democratic legitimacy. The Court in *Chevron* recognized the increasingly politicized nature of interpretive questions with which agencies have to grapple. The Court also recognized that agencies—which are politically accountable through the President—are better situated than courts to wade into those political waters, and to answer those difficult questions. See, e.g., Merrill, *Executive Precedent*, 978 (arguing that "democratic theory was important to [*Chevron*] because it supplied the justification for switching the default rule from independent judgment to deference"). The reason this justification is different from the congressional intent justification for *Chevron* is that *Chevron* seems to require deference even when the agency is responding to pressure from the *President* to move statutory policy in ways that the enacting Congress itself would not have adopted. As long as the statute is ambiguous, the agency in power at the relevant time can offer its preferred interpretation. This may have been the case in *Chevron* itself. The liberal Democratic House of Representatives would probably not have favored the bubble concept, but the Reagan Administration very much did. So understood, *Chevron* may be more about accountability than about effecting Congress's intent.

A different kind of democracy justification not mentioned by the *Chevron* Court—and one indeed more closely tied to Congress—is the idea that agencies may be more responsive to Congress than courts, and relatedly, that Congress and agencies may be speaking the same language much more so than Congress and courts are. The primacy of the Congress-agency relationship grows out of many connections, including ongoing interactions necessitated by congressional oversight of agency action; the fact that many agencies actively assist in statutory drafting; and the simple fact that both branches are immersed in the same world of politics in a way that courts are not. So understood, transferring interpretive power to agencies is democracy-enhancing, because it means that actors with closer, ongoing ties to Congress are at the forefront of statutory elaboration. See Abbe R. Gluck & Lisa Schultz Bressman, *Statutory Interpretation from the Inside—an Empirical Study of Congressional Drafting, Delegation, and the Canons: Part II*, 66 Stan. L. Rev. 725 (2014) (reporting congressional drafters' views of agencies as primary interpreters); Jerry L. Mashaw, *Norms, Practices and the Paradox of Deference: A Preliminary Inquiry into Agency Statutory Interpretation*, 57 Admin. L. Rev. 501 (2005).

(C) Institutional Competence. *Chevron* also rests on the idea that agencies are often more competent federal statutory interpreters than courts, especially when the matter is technical or complex. Most federal courts are legal generalists—agencies are policy specialists. On this view, with which many scholars agree, a strong agency-deference regime puts interpretive power in the hands of the actors (agencies) best situated to carry out Congress's demands and intentions. See, e.g., Lisa Schultz Bressman, *Reclaiming the Fiction of Congressional Delegation*, 97 Va. L. Rev. 2009 (2011); William N. Eskridge Jr., *Expanding* Chevron's *Domain: A Comparative Institutional Analysis of the Relative Competence of Courts and Agencies to Interpret Statutes*, 2013 Wis. L. Rev. 411; Cass R. Sunstein & Adrian Vermeule, *Interpretation and Institutions*, 101 Mich. L. Rev. 885 (2003).

(D) Uniformity and Coordination. A different type of justification for *Chevron* comes not from the Court's opinion but from Professor Strauss, who has argued that *Chevron* is a necessary court-organizing tool—a much-needed way to coordinate the enormous amount of agency statutory interpretation that takes place in the modern administrative state. Because the Supreme Court hears so few cases a year and so cannot possibly police all of the lower court cases reviewing agency statutory interpretation, Strauss argues, one way for the Court to ensure the uniformity of federal law is to come up with a clear decision rule—i.e., deference to the federal agency—that lower courts can employ. Under *Chevron*, instead of each lower court coming up with its own federal statutory interpretation, lower courts will all defer to a single decision maker (the federal agency), thereby making it more likely that federal statutes administered by agencies will mean the same thing in every Circuit even if those cases are never reviewed by the Supreme Court. Peter L. Strauss, *One Hundred and Fifty Cases Per Year: Some Implications of the Supreme Court's Limited Resources for Judicial Review of Agency Action*, 87 Colum. L. Rev. 1093, 1124 (1987).

4.   *Chevron's Initially Hostile Reception: A "Counter-*Marbury*" for the Administrative State? Chevron's* apparent transfer of power from courts to agencies did not meet an entirely friendly audience. Then-Judge Breyer objected that *Chevron* was inconsistent with the judicial role articulated both in *Marbury v. Madison*, 5 U.S. 137, 177–178 (1803)—that it is the province of the courts (not agencies!) to "say what the law is"—and in the APA. The APA has this to say about judicial review of agency action: "To the extent necessary to decision and when presented, the reviewing court shall decide all relevant questions of law, interpret constitutional and statutory provisions, and determine the meaning or applicability of the terms of an agency action." 5 U.S.C. § 706. The APA, like *Marbury*, thus requires courts to exercise independent judgment over legal questions. See Stephen G. Breyer, *Judicial Review of Questions of Law and Policy*, 38 Admin. L. Rev. 363, 370 (1986).[3] Breyer explained:

> [T]he present law of judicial review of administrative decision making, the heart of administrative law, contains an important anomaly* * *. The law (1) requires courts to defer to agency judgments about *matters of law*, but (2) it also suggests that courts conduct independent, 'in-depth' reviews of agency judgments about *matters of policy*. [E.g., *State Farm* (Chapter 7, § 2).] Is this not the exact opposite of a rational system? Would one not expect courts to conduct a stricter review of matters of law, where courts are more expert, but more lenient review of matters of policy, where agencies are more expert?

Breyer, *Judicial Review*, 397.

Chevron also creates some tension between appellate review of agency and lower-federal-court judicial interpretations. Federal appellate courts defer to decisions of fact by lower federal courts but review decisions of law *de novo*; that is, federal appellate courts begin "afresh" and do not defer to lower federal court decisions of law, including statutory interpretation decisions. As

---

[3]   See also Cynthia R. Farina, *Statutory Interpretation and the Balance of Power in the Administrative State*, 89 Colum. L. Rev. 452 (1989) (developing this objection in detail); Cass R. Sunstein, *Law and Administration After* Chevron, 90 Colum. L. Rev. 2071, 2075 (1990). *Cf.* Louis L. Jaffe, *Judicial Review: Question of Law*, 69 Harv. L. Rev. 239 (1955) (arguing that in the pre-*Chevron* era, the Court's approach had remained consistent with *Marbury* and APA § 706, because the Supreme Court had remained the expositor of what the law is but remained open to agency inputs).

the Breyer excerpt suggests, however, *Chevron* switches things around for agencies; courts defer on legal questions but apply closer review on factual ones. Does this make sense?

5.   *Was* Chevron *an Accident?* According to historical accounts, the *Chevron* doctrine did not emerge as the result of any premeditated consideration by the Court of how to handle agency statutory interpretation in the modern regulatory state or from a longstanding dissatisfaction with *Skidmore.* Instead, the "bubble concept" adopted by the EPA was twice rebuffed in the D.C. Circuit (by one panel that included then-D.C. Circuit Judge Ruth Bader Ginsburg), but the Department of Justice pressed it before the Supreme Court in an effort to reduce judicial interference with its deregulatory initiatives. In the process, DOJ advanced some of the arguments for deference that we saw in the case. Liberal Justice William Brennan was suspicious of DOJ's argument, but the Administration caught some lucky breaks as Brennan's allies dropped out of the case like flies in a hailstorm. Their biggest break, however, was that the legality of the bubble concept was impossibly complicated for the Court. Apparently the shakiest voice in the original 4–3 conference vote to reverse the D.C. Circuit, Justice Stevens explained his tentative willingness to side with the EPA: "When I am so confused, I go with the agency." (Justice Blackmun's Conference Notes for *Chevron.*)

Nor did the Court seem to realize that it was handing down the watershed opinion that *Chevron* would come to be. See Thomas W. Merrill, *The Story of* Chevron USA Inc. v. Natural Resources Defense Council, Inc.*: Sometimes Great Cases Are Made Not Born, in Statutory Interpretation Stories* 165 (Eskridge, Frickey & Garrett eds., 2011). Moreover, it was not clear that *Chevron* made a difference; long before *Chevron*, agency affirmance rates were on the rise in the federal courts, suggesting that there had been a tradition of deference already growing, even if not formalized as a doctrinal matter. See Peter Schuck & E. Donald Elliott, *To the* Chevron *Station: An Empirical Study of Federal Administrative Law*, 1990 Duke L.J. 984. Finally, *Chevron* did not take on immediate importance at the Supreme Court level after it was decided. Instead, it was the D.C. Circuit—which included then-Judges Scalia and Ginsburg—that embraced *Chevron* and was likely responsible for what Professor Merrill calls its "rise from obscurity." *Chevron* is now one of the most cited Supreme Court decisions in history. See e.g., Orin S. Kerr, *Shedding Light on* Chevron*: An Empirical Study of the* Chevron *Doctrine in the U.S. Courts of Appeals*, 15 Yale J. Reg. 1 (1998).

NOTE ON CHEVRON *AND THE TOOLS OF* STATUTORY INTERPRETATION

Statutory interpretation does not go away after *Chevron*. In fact, *Chevron* places the tools of interpretation that we already have studied front and center in Step One. *Chevron* held: "If the intent of Congress is clear, that is the end of the matter, for the court, as well as the agency, must give effect to the unambiguously expressed intent of Congress.[9]" In the opinion's now-famous footnote 9, the Court emphasized that this inquiry is one of statutory interpretation:

> [9] The judiciary is the final authority on issues of statutory construction and must reject administrative constructions which are contrary to clear congressional intent. If a court, employing traditional tools of statutory construction, ascertains that Congress had an intention on the precise question at issue, that intention is the law and must be given effect.

The Court in *Chevron* thus directs courts to use "traditional tools of statutory construction" to determine whether the statute is clear. This is a big deal for those tools, and they therefore remain highly relevant. *Chevron* tells us that tools like canons and (perhaps) legislative history themselves are devices that assist courts in determining statutory clarity. If application of those tools clarifies the statute, then there will be no ambiguity left for agencies to fill and no *Chevron* deference for the agency.

The problem, however, as you know well by now, is that there remains profound disagreement about which "traditional tools of construction" courts should employ and how they are employed. Thus, Chevron's two-step doesn't eliminate that judicial fight; it just shifts it from the question of how to decide the case to the preliminary question of whether the statute is clear (which sometimes has the same result). Judges continue to disagree over which tools—canons, dictionaries, legislative history, etc.—should be used in *Chevron* Step One to determine if the text is clear or ambiguous.

By way of illustration, consider the following hypothetical case:

PROBLEM 8–2: CHEVRON *AND THE TOOLS OF INTERPRETATION*

Assume that Congress passed the Internet Regulation Act of 2015 to extend many common features of the telecommunications regulatory landscape to entities that provide internet service. The statute includes some cumbersome paperwork and disclosure requirements, which many providers are eager to avoid. Here is the relevant provision in our hypothetical statute:

Internet Regulation Act § 1507

(A) All Internet Service Providers must file their customer lists and monthly rate plans with the Federal Communications Commission.

(B) "Internet Service Provider" is defined as any entity, whether operating for profit or not for profit, that provides internet service to residential or business entities, except for the Government.

In 2016, the State of New York buys Bell Atlantic Nynex Mobile's Internet Unit, makes it a state government agency, and begins providing free internet service to needy individuals across the state. Made aware of the Internet Regulation Act, New York sought and received guidance from the

FCC that New York's activities were not covered by § 1507, and so the state did not have to make the requisite filings. The FCC based its interpretation on the text of the statute, on the statute's purpose of lowering prices, and also on the longstanding presumption that telecommunications was an important government function traditionally carried out by the states.

A group of competing internet companies, however, contends otherwise, and has challenged the FCC's interpretation. Specifically, the competitors argue that Congress, by expressly exempting only one entity—"the Government," which competitors argue is a reference only to the federal government—made clear its intention not to make additional exceptions. The competitors also point to a Senate Committee Report that specifically mentioned states in a paragraph about potentially-covered providers under the Act.

How do you decide this case? First you must decide if the language of the statute is clear, using the traditional tools of statutory construction. Which canons do you see in the parties' arguments and which way do they cut? Will you use legislative history in your *Chevron* Step One? If so, does it trump a canon? (Do you see the federalism canon? Do you see *exclusio unius*?). Or does the canon trump the legislative history?

Be aware that the same debate over legislative-history use that we saw in earlier chapters carries over to the *Chevron* context too. While Justice Scalia usually declines to consult legislative history in the *Chevron* analysis, e.g., *INS v. Cardoza-Fonseca*, 480 U.S. 421 (1987), the Supreme Court repeatedly examines legislative history in its Step One analysis. See William N. Eskridge Jr. & Lauren E. Baer, *The Continuum of Deference: Supreme Court Treatment of Agency Statutory Interpretations from* Chevron *to* Hamdan, 96 Geo. L.J. 1083, 1135–36 (2008) (finding that the Court as a whole relies on legislative history *more* often in *Chevron* cases than in other statutory interpretation cases).

The Court also considers substantive canons as part of its Step One analysis. For example, in *INS v. St. Cyr*, 533 U.S. 289 (2001), the Court refused to accord *Chevron* deference to the agency's construction of an ambiguous deportation statute on the ground that the anti-retroactivity canon clarified the ambiguity: "Because a statute that is ambiguous with respect to retroactive application is construed under our precedent to be unambiguously prospective, [citing the canon] there is, for *Chevron* purposes, no ambiguity in such a statute for an agency to resolve." See also Kenneth A. Bamberger, *Normative Canons in the Review of Administrative Policymaking*, 118 Yale L.J. 64 (2008) (identifying the potential tension between *Chevron* and the substantive canons and providing examples).

Mayo Foundation for Medical Education and Research v. United States
131 S.Ct. 704 (2011).

A recent dispute over tax benefits for students provides an example of a relatively straightforward application (and expansion) of the *Chevron* framework. The question in *Mayo* was whether medical "residents"—young doctors in training—are "students" for purposes of tax exceptions under the Federal Insurance Contributions Act (FICA). FICA defines "employment" as "any service * * * performed * * * by an employee for the person employing him," but excludes from taxation any "service performed in the employ of * * * a school, college, or university * * * if such service is performed by a student who is enrolled and regularly attending classes at [the school]."

The problem was that, for medical residents, hours worked in the hospitals constitute an integral part of their training, even though they are also paid work. Until 2004, the Treasury Department had applied a case-by-case approach and generally applied the student exception to those who work for their schools "as an incident to and for the purpose of pursuing a course of study." In 2004, the Department instead adopted a bright-line rule: any employee working 40 hours or more per week could not be considered a student for purposes of the exemption. The rule specifically referenced medical residents as employees, not students, under the Department's interpretation.

Chief Justice Roberts's opinion for a unanimous Court applied *Chevron* and deferred to Treasury. "We begin our analysis with the first step of the two-part framework announced in *Chevron,* and ask whether Congress has 'directly addressed the precise question at issue.' We agree with the Court of Appeals that Congress has not done so. The statute does not define the term 'student,' and does not otherwise attend to the precise question whether medical residents are subject to FICA." (An important feature of the Chief Justice's opinion for the Court is that it announced that judges must apply *Chevron* to evaluate Treasury Department interpretations pursuant to a grant of lawmaking authority; those interpretations had previously been evaluated under the special standard of *National Muffler Dealers v. United States*, 440 U.S. 472 (1979), which was abrogated by *Mayo*.)

The Chief Justice's "traditional tools" inquiry considered dictionary definitions, practical questions, and the structure of the statute, before concluding that those tools did not clarify Congress's intent. "Mayo nonetheless contends that the Treasury Department's full-time employee rule must be rejected under *Chevron* step one. Mayo argues that the dictionary definition of 'student'—one 'who engages in 'study' by applying the mind 'to the acquisition of learning, whether by means of books, observation, or experiment'—plainly encompasses residents. * * *

"Mayo's reading does not eliminate the statute's ambiguity as applied to working professionals. In its reply brief, Mayo acknowledges that a full-time professor taking evening classes—a person who presumably would satisfy the statute's class-enrollment requirement and apply his mind to learning—could be excluded from the exemption and taxed because he is not 'predominant[ly]' a student. Medical residents might likewise be excluded on the same basis; the statute itself does not resolve the ambiguity.

"To the extent Congress has specifically addressed medical residents in [FICA], moreover, it has expressly excluded these doctors from exemptions they might otherwise invoke. *See* 26 U.S.C. §§ 3121(b)(6)(B), (7)(C)(ii) (excluding medical residents from exemptions available to employees of the District of Columbia and the United States). That choice casts doubt on any claim that Congress specifically intended to insulate medical residents from FICA's reach in the first place."

With this finding of ambiguity, the Court proceeded with the deferential Step Two analysis: "The full-time employee rule easily satisfies the second step of *Chevron,* which asks whether the Department's rule is a 'reasonable interpretation' of the enacted text. Regulation, like legislation, often requires drawing lines. Mayo does not dispute that the Treasury Department reasonably sought a way to distinguish between workers who study and students who work. Focusing on the hours an individual works and the hours he spends in studies is a perfectly sensible way of accomplishing that goal. The Department reasonably concluded that its full-time employee rule would 'improve administrability,' and it thereby 'has avoided the wasteful litigation and continuing uncertainty that would inevitably accompany any purely case-by-case approach.' "

PROBLEM 8–3: CHEVRON *STEP ONE—A HARDER CASE*

Now that you are more familiar with how *Chevron* is deployed, consider the facts of a more complicated case. The Clean Water Act makes it unlawful to discharge dredged or fill material into "navigable waters" without a permit. The Act, 33 U.S.C. §§ 1344, 1362, provides:

> The Secretary [of the Army Corps of Engineers] may issue permits, after notice and opportunity for public hearings for the discharge of dredged or fill material into the navigable waters at specified disposal sites * * *

> The term "navigable waters" includes the waters of the United States, including the territorial seas.

The Army Corps of Engineers (Corps), which issues the permits for the discharge of dredged or fill material into "navigable waters," has issued a regulation, 33 CFR § 323.3(a)(3), interpreting the statutory term "the waters of the United States" expansively to include not only traditional navigable waters which flow from point to point but also:

> All other waters such as intrastate lakes, rivers, streams (including intermittent streams), mudflats, sandflats, wetlands, sloughs, prairie potholes, wet meadows, playa lakes, or natural ponds, the use, degradation or destruction of which could affect interstate or foreign commerce.

The Corps also made a clarifying statement, known as the Migratory Bird Rule, 51 Fed. Reg. 412517, which provided:

> EPA has clarified that waters of the United States at 40 CFR 328.3(a)(3) also include the following waters: that § 404(a) extends to intrastate waters:
>
> a. Which are or would be used as habitat by birds protected by Migratory Bird Treaties; or
>
> b. Which are or would be used as habitat by other migratory birds which cross state lines; or
>
> c. Which are or would be used as habitat for endangered species; or
>
> d. Used to irrigate crops sold in interstate commerce.

Petitioners are a group of cities that want to use an abandoned mining site as a disposal site for waste. The site contains scattered permanent and seasonal ponds, at which some migratory bird species have been observed. They challenge the Corps' Migratory Bird Rule on two grounds: first, the agency had exceeded the powers Congress gave it with its interpretation of the CWA as covering nonnavigable, isolated, intrastate waters based upon the presence of migratory birds; second, in the alternative, if the Act could be read to extend to those intrastate waters, the Act exceeds Congress's power under the Commerce Clause.

Each side assembles a boatload of traditional tools of construction to support its view. All of the Justices agree that the text alone is not much help and that they need to consider some other interpretive aids. Study the chart below, which sets forth each side's arguments (and offers you a nice review, as a bonus). Should the Court give *Chevron* deference to the Corps' interpretation? Does the answer change if the Justice is a textualist or a purposivist?

Chevron Step One Arguments in the Migratory Bird Rule Case

Petitioners' Arguments	Corps' Arguments
Plain Text: The ordinary meaning of the term "navigable waters" does not extend to temporary ponds on an abandoned mining site. As a common law term, "navigable waters" does not come anywhere close to such a broad meaning.	*Super Strong* Stare Decisis *for Statutory Precedents:* The Court has previously held that Congress evinced its intent "to regulate at least some waters that would not be deemed 'navigable' under the classical understanding of that term," see *United States v. Riverside Bayview Homes, Inc.,* 474 U.S. 121 (1985), and the Court gives super-strong precedential weight to previous statutory interpretations (see *Flood*, Ch. 3, § 2)
Constitutional Avoidance: When the statutory text is unclear, the Court must interpret it to avoid "serious" constitutional questions (see *Skilling*, Ch.5, § 3B).	*Legislative History:* The CWA Conference Report stated that the conferees "intend that the term 'navigable waters' be given the broadest possible constitutional interpretation." S. Conf. Rep. No. 92–1236, p. 144 (1972)
Purpose and Federalism: The CWA's text contains the following statement of purpose: "[to] recognize, preserve and protect the primary responsibilities and rights of States to prevent, reduce and eliminate pollution." Plus, ambiguous statutes should be interpreted not to intrude on traditional state functions (see *Gregory*, Ch. 5, § 2C)	*Rejected Proposal Rule/Legislative Acquiescence:* In the 1977 CWA amendments, Congress rejected a proposal that would have narrowed the definition of "navigable waters" in the way petitioners suggest. Congress was clearly aware of the Corps' expansive definition and did not change it. (see *Bob Jones*, Ch. 5, § 3; *Johnson*, Ch. 3)
Rule of Lenity: Any ambiguity in the statute should be construed not to require a permit, since the CWA carries criminal penalties. (see *Muscarello*, Ch. 5, § 2A)	

For the debate within the Court, with all nine Justices applying the *Chevron* framework, see *Solid Waste Agency of Northern Cook County (SWANCC) v. U.S. Army Corp of Engineers*, 531 U.S. 159 (2001).

MCI TELECOMMUNICATIONS CORP. V. AT&T

United States Supreme Court, 1994.
512 U.S. 218, 114 S.Ct. 2223, 129 L.Ed.2d 182.

JUSTICE SCALIA delivered the opinion of the Court.

[The Communications Act of 1934 authorized the FCC to regulate the rates charged for communication services to ensure that they were reasonable and nondiscriminatory. The requirements of § 203 that common carriers file their rates with the Commission and charge only the filed rates were the centerpiece of the Act's regulatory scheme. For 40 years, AT&T had a virtual monopoly over the nation's telephone service, but in the 1970s new competitors emerged. During the 1980s, the Commission allowed, and briefly required, small carriers an exemption from the rate-filing requirements. AT & T's challenge to that agency rule resulted in this case.]

Section 203(a) of Title 47 of the United States Code requires communications common carriers to file tariffs with the Federal Communications Commission, and § 203(b) authorizes the Commission to "modify" any requirement of § 203. These cases present the question whether the Commission's decision to make tariff filing optional for all nondominant long-distance carriers is a valid exercise of its modification authority.

[II] Section 203 of the Communications Act contains both the filed rate provisions of the Act and the Commission's disputed modification authority. It provides in relevant part:

"(a) Filing; public display.

Every common carrier, except connecting carriers, shall, within such reasonable time as the Commission shall designate, file with the Commission and print and keep open for public inspection schedules showing all charges * * *, whether such charges are joint or separate, and showing the classifications, practices, and regulations affecting such charges* * *.

(b) Changes in schedule; discretion of Commission to modify requirements.

"(1) No change shall be made in the charges, classifications, regulations, or practices which have been so filed and published except after one hundred and twenty days' notice to the Commission and to the public, which shall be published in such form and contain such information as the Commission may by regulations prescribe.

(2) The Commission may, in its discretion and for good cause shown, modify any requirement made by or under the authority of this section either in particular instances or by general order applicable to special circumstances or conditions except that the Commission may not require the notice period specified in paragraph (1) to be more than one hundred and twenty days. * * * "

The dispute between the parties turns on the meaning of the phrase "modify any requirement" in § 203(b)(2). Petitioners argue that it gives the Commission authority to make even basic and fundamental changes in the scheme created by that section. We disagree. The word "modify"— like a number of other English words employing the root "mod-" (deriving from the Latin word for "measure"), such as "moderate," "modulate," "modest," and "modicum"—has a connotation of increment or limitation. Virtually every dictionary we are aware of says that "to modify" means to change moderately or in minor fashion. *See, e.g.,* Random House Dictionary of the English Language 1236 (2d ed. 1987) ("to change somewhat the form or qualities of; alter partially; amend"); Webster's Third New International Dictionary 1452 (1981) ("to make minor changes in the form or structure of: alter without transforming"); 9 Oxford English Dictionary 952 (2d ed. 1989) ("[t]o make partial changes in; to change (an object) in respect of some of its qualities; to alter or vary without radical transformation"); Black's Law Dictionary 1004 (6th ed. 1990) ("[t]o alter; to change in incidental or subordinate features; enlarge; extend; amend; limit; reduce").

In support of their position, petitioners cite dictionary definitions contained in, or derived from, a single source, Webster's Third New International Dictionary 1452 (1981) (Webster's Third), which includes among the meanings of "modify," "to make a basic or important change in." Petitioners contend that this establishes sufficient ambiguity to entitle the Commission to deference in its acceptance of the broader meaning, which in turn requires approval of its permissive detariffing policy. *See Chevron.* In short, they contend that the courts must defer to the agency's choice among available dictionary definitions, citing *National Railroad Passenger Corporation v. Boston & Maine Corp.,* 503 U.S. 407, 418 (1992). * * *

Most cases of verbal ambiguity in statutes involve * * * a selection between accepted alternative meanings shown as such by many dictionaries. One can envision (though a court case does not immediately come to mind) having to choose between accepted alternative meanings, one of which is so newly accepted that it has only been recorded by a single lexicographer. (Some dictionary must have been the very first to record the widespread use of "projection," for example, to mean "forecast.") But what petitioners demand that we accept as creating an ambiguity here is a rarity even rarer than that: a meaning set forth in a single dictionary (and, as we say, its progeny) which not only *supplements* the meaning contained in all other dictionaries, but *contradicts* one of the meanings contained in virtually all other dictionaries. Indeed, contradicts one of the alternative meanings contained in the out-of-step dictionary itself—for as we have observed, Webster's Third itself defines "modify" to connote *both* (specifically) major change *and* (specifically) minor change. It is hard to see how that can be. When the word "modify" has come to mean *both* "to change in some respects" *and* "to change fundamentally" it will in fact mean *neither* of those things. It will simply mean "to change," and some adverb will have to be called into service to indicate the great or small degree of the change.

If that is what the peculiar Webster's Third definition means to suggest has happened—and what petitioners suggest by appealing to Webster's Third—we simply disagree. "Modify," in our view, connotes moderate change. It might be good English to say that the French Revolution "modified" the status of the French nobility—but only because there is a figure of speech called understatement and a literary device known as sarcasm. And it might be unsurprising to discover a 1972 White House press release saying that "the Administration is modifying its position with regard to prosecution of the war in Vietnam"—but only because press agents tend to impart what is nowadays called "spin." Such intentional distortions, or simply careless or ignorant misuse, must have formed the basis for the usage that Webster's Third, and Webster's Third alone, reported.[3] It is perhaps gilding the lily to add this: In 1934, when the Communications Act became law—the most relevant time for determining a statutory term's meaning, *see Perrin v. United States,* 444 U.S. 37, 42–45 (1979)—Webster's Third was not yet even contemplated. * * *

Beyond the word itself, a further indication that the § 203(b)(2) authority to "modify" does not contemplate fundamental changes is the sole exception to that authority which the section provides. One of the requirements of § 203 is that changes to filed tariffs can be made only after 120 days' notice to the Commission and the public. § 203(b)(1). The *only* exception to the Commission's § 203(b)(2) modification authority is as follows: "except that the Commission may not require the notice period specified in paragraph (1) to be more than one hundred and twenty days." Is it conceivable that the statute is indifferent to the Commission's power to eliminate the tariff-filing requirement entirely for all except one firm in the long-distance sector, and yet strains out the gnat of extending the

---

[3] That is not an unlikely hypothesis. Upon its long-awaited appearance in 1961, Webster's Third was widely criticized for its portrayal of common error as proper usage. *See, e.g.,* Follett, *Sabotage in Springfield,* 209 Atlantic 73 (Jan. 1962); Barzun, *What Is a Dictionary?* 32 The American Scholar 176, 181 (spring 1963); Macdonald, *The String Unwound,* 38 The New Yorker 130, 156–157 (Mar. 1962).

waiting period for tariff revision beyond 120 days? We think not. The exception is not as ridiculous as a Lilliputian in London only because it is to be found in Lilliput: in the small-scale world of "modifications," it is a big deal. * * *

Bearing in mind, then, the enormous importance to the statutory scheme of the tariff-filing provision, we turn to whether what has occurred here can be considered a mere "modification." * * * It is not clear to us that the proportion of customers affected, rather than the proportion of carriers affected, is the proper measure of the extent of the exemption. * * * But even assuming it is, we think an elimination of the crucial provision of the statute for 40% of a major sector of the industry is much too extensive to be considered a "modification." What we have here, in reality, is a fundamental revision of the statute, changing it from a scheme of rate regulation in long-distance common-carrier communications to a scheme of rate regulation only where effective competition does not exist. That may be a good idea, but it was not the idea Congress enacted into law in 1934.

[JUSTICE O'CONNOR took no part in the consideration or decision of these cases.]

JUSTICE STEVENS, with whom JUSTICE BLACKMUN and JUSTICE SOUTER join, dissenting. * * *

In my view, each of the Commission's detariffing orders was squarely within its power to "modify any requirement" of § 203. Section 203(b)(2) plainly confers at least some discretion to modify the general rule that carriers file tariffs, for it speaks of "*any* requirement." * * * The FCC's authority to modify § 203's requirements in "particular instances" or by "general order applicable to special circumstances or conditions" emphasizes the expansive character of the Commission's authority: modifications may be narrow or broad, depending upon the Commission's appraisal of current conditions. From the vantage of a Congress seeking to regulate an almost completely monopolized industry, the advent of competition is surely a "special circumstance or condition" that might legitimately call for different regulatory treatment. * * *

According to the Court, the term "modify," as explicated in all but the most unreliable dictionaries, rules out the Commission's claimed authority to relieve nondominant carriers of the basic obligation to file tariffs. Dictionaries can be useful aids in statutory interpretation, but they are no substitute for close analysis of what words mean as used in a particular statutory context. Even if the sole possible meaning of "modify" were to make "minor" changes,[3] further elaboration is needed to show

---

[3]   As petitioner MCI points out, the revolutionary consent decree providing for the breakup of the Bell System was, per AT & T's own proposal, entitled "Modification of Final Judgment."

why the detariffing policy should fail. The Commission came to its present policy through a series of rulings that gradually relaxed the filing requirements for nondominant carriers. Whether the current policy should count as a cataclysmic or merely an incremental departure from the § 203(a) baseline depends on whether one focuses on particular carriers' obligations to file (in which case the Commission's policy arguably works a major shift) or on the statutory policies behind the tariff-filing requirement (which remain satisfied because market constraints on nondominant carriers obviate the need for rate filing). When § 203 is viewed as part of a statute whose aim is to constrain monopoly power, the Commission's decision to exempt nondominant carriers is a rational and "measured" adjustment to novel circumstances—one that remains faithful to the core purpose of the tariff-filing section. * * *

* * * A modification pursuant to § 203(b)(1), like any other order issued under the Act, must of course be consistent with the purposes of the statute. * * *The Court does not adequately respond to the FCC's explanations, and gives no reason whatsoever to doubt the Commission's considered judgment that tariff filing is altogether unnecessary in the case of competitive carriers; the majority's ineffective enforcement argument lacks any evidentiary or historical support. * * *

The filed tariff provisions of the Communications Act are not ends in themselves, but are merely one of several procedural *means* for the Commission to ensure that carriers do not charge unreasonable or discriminatory rates. The Commission has reasonably concluded that this particular means of enforcing the statute's substantive mandates will prove counterproductive in the case of nondominant long-distance carriers. Even if the 1934 Congress did not define the scope of the Commission's modification authority with perfect scholarly precision, this is surely a paradigm case for judicial deference to the agency's interpretation, particularly in a statutory regime so obviously meant to maximize administrative flexibility. Whatever the best reading of § 203(b)(2), the Commission's reading cannot in my view be termed unreasonable. It is informed (as ours is not) by a practical understanding of the role (or lack thereof) that filed tariffs play in the modern regulatory climate and in the telecommunications industry. Since 1979, the FCC has sought to adapt measures originally designed to control monopoly power to new market conditions. It has carefully and consistently explained that mandatory tariff-filing rules frustrate the core statutory interest in rate reasonableness. The Commission's use of the "discretion" expressly conferred by § 203(b)(2) reflects "a reasonable accommodation of

---

See United States v. American Telephone & Telegraph Co., 552 F.Supp. 131 (D.C. 1982), aff'd, 460 U.S. 1001 (1983).

manifestly competing interests and is entitled to deference: the regulatory scheme is technical and complex, the agency considered the matter in a detailed and reasoned fashion, and the decision involves reconciling conflicting policies." *Chevron*. The FCC has permissibly interpreted its § 203(b)(2) authority in service of the goals Congress set forth in the Act. We should sustain its eminently sound, experience-tested, and uncommonly well-explained judgment.

NOTES AND QUESTIONS ON DELEGATION, NEW TEXTUALISM, AND AGENCY DEFERENCE FOR MAJOR QUESTIONS

1. *The Implications of the New Textualism for* Chevron *Deference.* A textualist approach to *Chevron* might ultimately be less deferential than a purposive one. In *MCI*, the dissenters considered purpose to find more room for the agency's interpretation than did Justice Scalia's dictionary-focused opinion for the majority. Justice Scalia explains why this might be a common occurrence in *Judicial Deference to Administrative Interpretation of Law*, 1989 Duke L.J. 511, 521:

> * * * One who finds *more* often (as I do) that the meaning of a statute is apparent from its text and from its relationship with other laws, thereby finds *less* often that the triggering requirement for *Chevron* deference exists. It is thus relatively rare that *Chevron* will require me to accept an interpretation which, though reasonable, I would not personally adopt. Contrariwise, one who abhors a "plain meaning" rule, and is willing to permit the apparent meaning of a statute to be impeached by legislative history, will more frequently find agency-liberating ambiguity. * * *

Accord, Thomas W. Merrill, *Textualism and the Future of the Chevron Doctrine, 72 Wash. U. L.Q. 351 (1994).* Professor Merrill's empirical work supports Justice Scalia's view. He found that, in 1988–90 (the period of new textualist ascendancy), *Chevron*'s framework was applied in more cases than it had been in 1985–86 (51% to 32%) but that the agency view had prevailed much less often overall (59% to 72%). Thomas W. Merrill, *Judicial Deference to Executive Precedent*, 101 Yale L.J. 969, 992 (1992) (Table 3).

2. *"Ambiguity About Ambiguity."* It should be clear by now that ambiguity plays a starring role in our doctrinal landscape. In earlier chapters, we saw ambiguity as the necessary threshold that had to be crossed before the canons could be applied. Recall, for example, the gun "carrying" case, *Muscarello* (Chapter 5, § 2A), in which the Court divided over whether the statute was sufficiently ambiguous for the rule of lenity to be applied. Now, in the *Chevron* context, ambiguity is arguably even more central—a finding of no ambiguity defeats *Chevron* deference—but what counts as a statutory ambiguity remains as nebulously defined as ever. How would you define it? Some state courts have defined ambiguity as existing wherever opposing sides present reasonable arguments, see, e.g., *Jim's Auto Body v. Comm'r of Motor Vehicles*, 942 A.2d 305, 317 (Conn. 2008), a standard that

cannot possibly be taken literally or else every case with two honest opposing advocates—or a divided lower court panel!—would qualify. The federal courts have never settled—nay, never even tried to come up with—a standard definition. Is ambiguity really an objective enough concept to bear the weight that statutory interpretation doctrine places on it? Cf. Ward Farnsworth et al., *Ambiguity About Ambiguity*, 2 J. Leg. Analysis 257 (2010) (finding that ambiguity perceptions depend on the strength of one's policy preference and how the inquiry is framed).

3.   *Is Ambiguity Even the Right Signal?* A different question is whether ambiguity is even the right triggering signal for *Chevron* deference in the first place. The Gluck & Bressman empirical study of congressional drafting reported that committee counsels said that drafters are ambiguous for many different reasons and the intent is not always for agencies to fill those gaps. Ambiguity, in the counsels' view, is both too narrow and too broad a trigger: not all instances of ambiguity signal intent to defer, and sometimes drafters intend deference even when text is clear and signal that intent through different cues—like directives to agencies in legislative history. See Abbe R. Gluck & Lisa Schultz Bressman, *Statutory Interpretation from the Inside: An Empirical Study of Congressional Drafting, Delegation and the Canons: Part I and Part II,* 65 Stan. L. Rev. 901 (2013) & 66 Stan. Law Rev. 725 (2014).

4.   MCI *and the Presumption Against Delegation of Major Questions.* One reading of *MCI* is that it supports a presumption against excessive delegations to agencies. Recall from Chapter 1, § 2, that the Supreme Court will not enforce the nondelegation doctrine anymore—it will not strike down, as a constitutional violation, even extremely broad legislative delegations of lawmaking authority to administrative agencies. But that doesn't mean that the Court cannot give this "underenforced constitutional norm" some teeth through statutory interpretation. Scholars have identified a series of cases, including *MCI*, in which the Court seems to be objecting to the application of *Chevron*, even when the statute is ambiguous, when deferring per *Chevron* would mean that the agency would get to decide a major economic, political or policy question.

Some commentators have dubbed this presumption the "Major Questions Rule." Justice Scalia has described it more colorfully, as the presumption that "Congress does not hide elephants in mouse holes." *Whitman v. Am. Trucking Ass'ns*, 531 U.S. 457, 468 (2001). Underlying the rule is both an assumption about congressional intent and a concern about democratic accountability. The assumption is that Congress does not intend to give big-ticket questions to agencies, and so courts should not impute such congressional intent unless the text clearly delegates that authority. Some have argued this assumption is fictitious, given the anecdotal evidence that Congress in fact likes to "punt" the big questions, although recent empirical work lends some support to the Major Questions Rule. See Gluck & Bressman, *Statutory Interpretation from the Inside: Part I,* 65 Stan. L. Rev. at 1003–04 (finding that the majority of congressional counsels surveyed stated they do not intend for agencies to fill gaps in statutes involving major political, economic, or policy questions). Cf.

John F. Manning, *The Nondelegation Canon as a Canon of Avoidance*, 2000 Sup. Ct. Rev. 223 (2000) (arguing that broad delegations are often necessary for legislative compromise). The democratic accountability rationale underlying the Major Questions Rule is that Congress should not be able to shift big decisions onto agencies without taking some responsibility for it. The Major Questions Rule effectively requires Congress to be explicit if it intends to pass along big decisions in this manner.

One important question is how the Major Questions Rule can be reconciled with *Chevron*. The Court in *MCI* worked hard to find textual clarity, and so avoided the need to reconcile *Chevron* deference with a presumption against excessive delegations. But the Major Questions Rule seems to apply even where statutes might be ambiguous and so narrows *Chevron's* broad presumption of delegation wherever ambiguity exists by carving out an exception to it. *Chevron* might have been overbroad, but one thing its formalist approach had going for it was its simplicity and predictability. Deciding what questions are "too big" for agencies, as the Major Questions Rule requires, introduces significant judicial subjectivity into the *Chevron* inquiry and may unproductively complicate it.

It also is worth noting one particular irony of the Major Questions Rule. What happens when a court decides that a particular question is too big to assume that Congress delegated it implicitly? If the court does not let the agency interpret the question, *the court interprets the statute!* By preventing major delegations to agencies, the Major Questions Rule puts the interpretive power over big policy questions back in the hands of our generalist, non-expert and non-accountable judiciary. Which branch would you prefer decide such questions? Which do you think Congress or the President would prefer?

NOTE ON THE FDA TOBACCO CASE AS A CHEVRON CASE

Revisit the FDA Tobacco Case from Chapter 2, § 3. The excerpt we provided you there focused on the doctrines and sources—legislative history, other statutes, legislation inaction, and so on—that the Court used to infer that Congress did not intend to regulate tobacco as a "drug or device" under the Federal Drug and Cosmetic Act. But agency statutory interpretation was also central to the case. Specifically, it was an agency—President Clinton's FDA—that offered the statutory interpretation that was contested. In 1996, the FDA issued a regulation interpreting the FDCA to cover tobacco, thereby bringing that drug under the agency's regulatory jurisdiction. The hot politics of tobacco—combined with a Congress hostile to the President and leery of what seemed to be a major power grab by the agency—made the case obvious Supreme Court material. The following additional excerpt highlights the role of agency statutory interpretation in the case.

FOOD & DRUG ADMINISTRATION V. BROWN & WILLIAMSON TOBACCO CORP.

U.S. Supreme Court, 2000.
529 U.S. 120, 120 S.Ct. 1291, 146 L.Ed.2d 121.

JUSTICE O'CONNOR delivered the opinion of the Court.

This case involves one of the most troubling public health problems facing our Nation today: the thousands of premature deaths that occur each year because of tobacco use. In 1996, the Food and Drug Administration (FDA), after having expressly disavowed any such authority since its inception, asserted jurisdiction to regulate tobacco products. See 61 Fed. Reg. 44619–45318. The FDA concluded that nicotine is a "drug" within the meaning of the Food, Drug, and Cosmetic Act (FDCA or Act) and that cigarettes and smokeless tobacco are "combination products" that deliver nicotine to the body. Pursuant to this authority, it promulgated regulations intended to reduce tobacco consumption among children and adolescents.

[A]lthough agencies are generally entitled to deference in the interpretation of statutes that they administer, a reviewing "court, as well as the agency, must give effect to the unambiguously expressed intent of Congress." *Chevron.* In this case, we believe that Congress has clearly precluded the FDA from asserting jurisdiction to regulate tobacco products. * * * In light of this clear intent, the FDA's assertion of jurisdiction is impermissible.

[I]   The FDCA grants the FDA * * * the authority to regulate, among other items, "drugs" and "devices." See 21 U.S.C. §§ 321(g)–(h), 393 (1994 ed. and Supp. III). The Act defines "drug" to include "articles (other than food) intended to affect the structure or any function of the body." 21 U.S.C. § 321(g)(1)(C). It defines "device," in part, as "an instrument, apparatus, implement, machine, contrivance, * * * or other similar or related article, including any component, part, or accessory, which is * * * intended to affect the structure or any function of the body." § 321(h). The Act also grants the FDA the authority to regulate so-called "combination products," which "constitute a combination of a drug, device, or biological product." § 353(g)(1). The FDA has construed this provision as giving it the discretion to regulate combination products as drugs, as devices, or as both. See 61 Fed. Reg. 44400 (1996). * * * The FDA's assertion of jurisdiction to regulate tobacco products is founded on its conclusions that nicotine is a "drug" and that cigarettes and smokeless tobacco are "drug delivery devices." * * *

[Under *Chevron*], in determining whether Congress has specifically addressed the question at issue, a reviewing court should not confine itself to examining a particular statutory provision in isolation. The meaning—or ambiguity—of certain words or phrases may only become evident when placed in context. It is a fundamental canon of statutory construction that the words of a statute must be read in their context and with a view to their place in the overall statutory scheme. A court must therefore interpret the statute as a symmetrical and coherent regulatory scheme, and fit, if possible, all parts into an harmonious whole. Similarly, the meaning of one statute may be affected by other Acts, particularly where Congress has spoken subsequently and more specifically to the topic at hand. (quotation marks and citations omitted). In addition, we must be guided to a degree by common sense as to the manner in which Congress is likely to delegate a policy decision of such economic and political magnitude to an administrative agency. *MCI Telecommunications Corp.*

With these principles in mind, we find that Congress has directly spoken to the issue here and precluded the FDA's jurisdiction to regulate tobacco products.

[II.A]   [V]iewing the FDCA as a whole, it is evident that one of the Act's core objectives is to ensure that any product regulated by the FDA is "safe" and "effective" for its intended use. See 21 U.S.C. § 393(b)(2) (1994 ed., Supp. III) (defining the FDA's mission); More Information for Better Patient Care: Hearing before the Senate Committee on Labor and Human Resources, 104th Cong., 2d Sess., 83 (1996) (statement of FDA Deputy Comm'r Schultz) ("A fundamental precept of drug and device regulation in this country is that these products must be proven safe and effective before they can be sold"). This essential purpose pervades the FDCA. For instance, 21 U.S.C. § 393(b)(2) (1994 ed., Supp. III) defines the FDA's "[m]ission" to include "protect[ing] the public health by ensuring that . . . drugs are safe and effective" and that "there is reasonable assurance of the safety and effectiveness of devices intended for human use." The FDCA requires premarket approval of any new drug, with some limited exceptions, and states that the FDA "shall issue an order refusing to approve the application" of a new drug if it is not safe and effective for its intended purpose. §§ 355(d)(1)–(2), (4)–(5). If the FDA discovers after approval that a drug is unsafe or ineffective, it "shall, after due notice and opportunity for hearing to the applicant, withdraw approval" of the drug. 21 U.S.C. §§ 355(e)(1)–(3). The Act also requires the FDA to classify all devices into one of three categories. § 360c(b)(1). Regardless of which category the FDA chooses, there must be a "reasonable assurance of the safety and effectiveness of the device." 21 U.S.C. §§ 360c(a)(1)(A)(i), (B), (C) (1994 ed. and Supp. III); 61 Fed. Reg. 44412 (1996). Even the "restricted device" provision pursuant to which the FDA promulgated the regulations at issue here authorizes the agency to place conditions on the sale or distribution of a device specifically when "there cannot otherwise be reasonable assurance of its safety and effectiveness." 21 U.S.C. § 360j(e). Thus, the Act generally requires the FDA to prevent the marketing of any drug or device where the "potential for inflicting death or physical injury is not offset by the possibility of therapeutic benefit."

In its rulemaking proceeding, the FDA quite exhaustively documented that "tobacco products are unsafe," "dangerous," and "cause great pain and suffering from illness." 61 Fed. Reg. 44412 (1996). It found that the consumption of tobacco products presents "extraordinary health risks," and that "tobacco use is the single leading cause of preventable death in the United States." *Id.,* at 44398. It stated that "[m]ore than 400,000 people die each year from tobacco-related illnesses, such as cancer, respiratory illnesses, and heart disease, often suffering long and painful deaths," and that "[t]obacco alone kills more people each year in the United States than acquired immunodeficiency syndrome (AIDS), car accidents, alcohol, homicides, illegal drugs, suicides, and fires, combined."

[B]ased on these provisions, the FDA itself has previously taken the position that if tobacco products were within its jurisdiction, "they would have to be removed from the market because it would be impossible to prove they were safe for their intended us[e]." Public Health Cigarette Amendments of 1971: Hearings before the Commerce Subcommittee on S. 1454, 92d Cong., 2d Sess., 239 (1972) (hereinafter 1972 Hearings) (statement of FDA Comm'r Charles Edwards). See also Cigarette Labeling and Advertising: Hearings before the House Committee on Interstate and Foreign Commerce, 88th Cong., 2d Sess., 18 (1964) (hereinafter 1964 Hearings) (statement of Dept. of Health, Education, and Welfare (HEW) Secretary Anthony Celebrezze that proposed amendments to the FDCA that would have given the FDA jurisdiction over "smoking product[s]" "might well completely outlaw at least cigarettes").

Congress, however, has foreclosed the removal of tobacco products from the market. A provision of the United States Code currently in force states that "[t]he marketing of tobacco constitutes one of the greatest basic industries of the United States with ramifying activities which directly affect interstate and foreign commerce at every point, and stable conditions therein are necessary to the general welfare." 7 U.S.C. § 1311(a). More importantly, Congress has directly addressed the problem of tobacco and health through legislation on six occasions since 1965. See Federal Cigarette Labeling and Advertising Act (FCLAA), Pub.L. 89–92, 79 Stat. 282; Public Health Cigarette Smoking Act of 1969, Pub.L. 91– 222, 84 Stat. 87; Alcohol and Drug Abuse Amendments of 1983, Pub.L. 98–24, 97 Stat. 175; Comprehensive Smoking Education Act, Pub.L. 98– 474, 98 Stat. 2200; Comprehensive Smokeless Tobacco Health Education Act of 1986, Pub.L. 99–252, 100 Stat. 30; Alcohol, Drug Abuse, and Mental Health Administration Reorganization Act, Pub.L. 102–321, § 202, 106 Stat. 394. When Congress enacted these statutes, the adverse health consequences of tobacco use were well known, as were nicotine's pharmacological effects. * * * Nonetheless, Congress stopped well short of ordering a ban. Instead, it has generally regulated the labeling and advertisement of tobacco products * * * Congress' decisions to regulate labeling and advertising and to adopt the express policy of protecting "commerce and the national economy * * * to the maximum extent" reveal its intent that tobacco products remain on the market.

* * * The dissent contends that our conclusion means that "the FDCA requires the FDA to ban outright 'dangerous' drugs or devices," and that this is a "perverse" reading of the statute. This misunderstands our holding. The FDA, consistent with the FDCA, may clearly regulate many "dangerous" products without banning them. Indeed, virtually every drug or device poses dangers under certain conditions. What the FDA may not do is conclude that a drug or device cannot be used safely for any therapeutic purpose and yet, at the same time, allow that product to remain on the market. Such regulation is incompatible with the FDCA's core objective of ensuring that every drug or device is safe and effective.

[II.B]   In determining whether Congress has spoken directly to the FDA's authority to regulate tobacco, we must also consider in greater detail the tobacco-specific legislation that Congress has enacted over the past 35 years. At the time a statute is enacted, it may have a range of plausible meanings. Over time, however, subsequent acts can shape or focus those meanings.* * * As we recognized recently, a specific policy embodied in a later federal statute should control our construction of the [earlier] statute, even though it ha[s] not been expressly amended." (citations omitted).

Congress has enacted six separate pieces of legislation since 1965 addressing the problem of tobacco use and human health. Those statutes, among other things, require that health warnings appear on all packaging and in all print and outdoor advertisements, see 15 U.S.C. §§ 1331, 1333, 4402 [and]; prohibit the advertisement of tobacco products through "any medium of electronic communication" subject to regulation by the Federal Communications Commission (FCC), see §§ 1335, 4402(f) * * *.

In adopting each statute, Congress has acted against the backdrop of the FDA's consistent and repeated statements that it lacked authority under the FDCA to regulate tobacco absent claims of therapeutic benefit by the manufacturer. In fact, on several occasions over this period, and after the health consequences of tobacco use and nicotine's pharmacological effects had become well known, Congress considered and rejected bills that would have granted the FDA such jurisdiction. Under these circumstances, it is evident that Congress' tobacco-specific statutes have effectively ratified the FDA's long-held position that it lacks jurisdiction under the FDCA to regulate tobacco products. Congress has created a distinct regulatory scheme to address the problem of tobacco and health, and that scheme, as presently constructed, precludes any role for the FDA. * * *

Moreover, before enacting the FCLAA in 1965, Congress considered and rejected several proposals to give the FDA the authority to regulate tobacco. In April 1963, Representative Udall introduced a bill "[t]o amend the Federal Food, Drug, and Cosmetic Act so as to make that Act applicable to smoking products." H.R. 5973, 88th Cong., 1st Sess., 1. Two months later, Senator Moss introduced an identical bill in the Senate. S. 1682, 88th Cong., 1st Sess. (1963). In discussing his proposal on the Senate floor, Senator Moss explained that "this amendment simply places smoking products under FDA jurisdiction, along with foods, drugs, and cosmetics." 109 Cong. Rec. 10322 (1963). In December 1963, Representative Rhodes introduced another bill that would have amended the FDCA "by striking out 'food, drug, device, or cosmetic,' each place where it appears therein and inserting in lieu thereof 'food, drug, device, cosmetic, or smoking product.'" H.R. 9512, 88th Cong., 1st Sess., § 3 (1963). And in January 1965, five months before passage of the FCLAA, Representative Udall again introduced a bill to amend the FDCA "to make that Act applicable to smoking products." H.R. 2248, 89th Cong., 1st Sess., 1. None of these proposals became law.

[We have omitted numerous extra pages of Justice O'Connor's piling on of legislative history, other statutes and previous statements from the FDA supporting her argument. After her exhaustive survey, Justice O'Connor concluded that] it is clear that Congress' tobacco-specific legislation has effectively ratified the FDA's previous position that it lacks jurisdiction to regulate tobacco * * *.

Although the dissent takes issue with our discussion of the FDA's change in position, our conclusion does not rely on the fact that the FDA's assertion of jurisdiction represents a sharp break with its prior interpretation of the FDCA. Certainly, an agency's initial interpretation of a statute that it is charged with administering is not "carved in stone.". *Chevron* * * *. The consistency of the FDA's prior position is significant in this case for a different reason: It provides important context to Congress' enactment of its tobacco-specific legislation. Although not crucial, the consistency of the FDA's prior position bolsters the conclusion that when Congress created a distinct regulatory scheme addressing the subject of tobacco and health, it understood that the FDA is without jurisdiction to regulate tobacco products and ratified that position.

[II.C]   Finally, our inquiry into whether Congress has directly spoken to the precise question at issue is shaped, at least in some measure, by the nature of the question presented. Deference under *Chevron* to an agency's construction of a statute that it administers is premised on the theory that a statute's ambiguity constitutes an implicit delegation from Congress to the agency to fill in the statutory gaps. *See Chevron.* In extraordinary cases, however, there may be reason to hesitate before concluding that Congress has intended such an implicit delegation. *Cf.* Breyer, *Judicial Review of Questions of Law and Policy*, 38 Admin. L. Rev. 363, 370 (1986) ("A court may also ask whether the legal question is an important one. Congress is more likely to have focused upon, and answered, major questions, while leaving interstitial matters to answer themselves in the course of the statute's daily administration").

This is hardly an ordinary case. Contrary to its representations to Congress since 1914, the FDA has now asserted jurisdiction to regulate an industry constituting a significant portion of the American economy. * * * Owing to its unique place in American history and society, tobacco has its own unique political history. Congress, for better or for worse, has created a distinct regulatory scheme for tobacco products, squarely rejected proposals to give the FDA jurisdiction over tobacco, and repeatedly acted to preclude any agency from exercising significant policymaking authority in the area. Given this history and the breadth of the authority that the FDA has asserted, we are obliged to defer not to the agency's expansive construction of the statute, but to Congress' consistent judgment to deny the FDA this power.

Our decision in *MCI v. AT & T* is instructive. That case involved the proper construction of the term "modify" in § 203(b) of the Communications Act of 1934. The FCC contended that, because the Act gave it the discretion to "modify any requirement" imposed under the statute, it therefore possessed the authority to render voluntary the otherwise mandatory requirement that long distance carriers file their rates. We rejected the FCC's construction, finding "not the slightest doubt" that Congress had directly spoken to the question. In reasoning even more apt here, we concluded that "[i]t is highly unlikely that Congress would leave the determination of whether an industry will be entirely, or even substantially, rate-regulated to agency discretion—and even more unlikely that it would achieve that through such a subtle device as permission to 'modify' rate-filing requirements."

As in *MCI,* we are confident that Congress could not have intended to delegate a decision of such economic and political significance to an agency in so cryptic a fashion. * * * It is therefore clear, based on the FDCA's overall regulatory scheme and the subsequent tobacco legislation, that Congress has directly spoken to the question at issue and precluded the FDA from regulating tobacco products. * * *

JUSTICE BREYER, with whom JUSTICE STEVENS, JUSTICE SOUTER and JUSTICE GINSBURG join, dissenting. [We have provided a brief excerpt from Justice Breyer's lengthy dissent, but it is worth reading in its entirety.]

In my view, where linguistically permissible, we should interpret the FDCA in light of Congress' overall desire to protect health. That purpose requires a flexible interpretation that both permits the FDA to take into account the realities of human behavior and allows it, in appropriate cases, to choose from its arsenal of statutory remedies. A statute so interpreted easily "fit[s]" this, and other, drug- and device-related health problems.

* * * I now turn to the final historical fact that the majority views as a factor in its interpretation of the subsequent legislative history: the FDA's former denials of its tobacco-related authority.

Until the early 1990's, the FDA expressly maintained that the 1938 statute did not give it the power that it now seeks to assert. It then changed its mind. The majority agrees with me that the FDA's change of positions does not make a significant legal difference. Nevertheless, it labels those denials "important context" for drawing an inference about Congress' intent. In my view, the FDA's change of policy, like the subsequent statutes themselves, does nothing to advance the majority's position.

* * * What changed? For one thing, the FDA obtained evidence sufficient to prove the necessary "intent" despite the absence of specific "claims." This evidence, which first became available in the early 1990's, permitted the agency to demonstrate that the tobacco companies *knew* nicotine achieved appetite-suppressing, mood-stabilizing, and habituating effects through chemical (not psychological) means, even at a time when the companies were publicly denying such knowledge.

Moreover, scientific evidence of adverse health effects mounted, until, in the late 1980's, a consensus on the seriousness of the matter became firm* * *. Commissioners of the current administration simply took a different regulatory attitude. Nothing in the law prevents the FDA from changing its policy for such reasons* * *.

[O]ne might claim that courts, when interpreting statutes, should assume in close cases that a decision with "enormous social consequences," should be made by democratically elected Members of Congress rather than by unelected agency administrators. If there is such a background canon of interpretation, however, I do not believe it controls the outcome here.

Insofar as the decision to regulate tobacco reflects the policy of an administration, it is a decision for which that administration, and those politically elected officials who support it, must (and will) take responsibility. And the very importance of the decision taken here, as well as its attendant publicity, means that the public is likely to be aware of it and to hold those officials politically accountable. Presidents, just like Members of Congress, are elected by the public. Indeed, the President and

Vice President are the *only* public officials whom the entire Nation elects. I do not believe that an administrative agency decision of this magnitude—one that is important, conspicuous, and controversial—can escape the kind of public scrutiny that is essential in any democracy. And such a review will take place whether it is the Congress or the Executive Branch that makes the relevant decision. *** * ***

NOTES AND QUESTIONS ON BROWN & WILLIAMSON

1. Chevron *"Step One" in* Brown & Williamson. How many canons and other interpretive tools can you count in Justice O'Connor's Step One analysis? She argues that *Chevron* deference is not justified because Congress made its intentions clear to exclude tobacco from the FDA's purview. But her opinion goes far beyond the kind of textual analysis that Justice Scalia employed in *MCI* (the common carrier filing case), or that Chief Justice Roberts employed in *Mayo* (the medical residents tax case). By our count, her opinion for the Court invokes at least nine different canons or types of interpretive tools:

- the whole act rule (interpreting the FDA's jurisdiction in light of the FDCA's overall remedial structure);

- the whole code rule (interpreting the FDCA in light of other statutes in the U.S. Code);

- specific statutes (i.e., tobacco disclosure laws) trump general statutes (the FDCA);

- legislative acquiescence (presume congressional agreement when Congress does not overrule longstanding [here, agency] interpretations);

- the rejected proposal rule (presume against statutory interpretations that Congress has specifically rejected);

- legislative history (note that Justice Scalia still joins the opinion for the Court);

- statutory purpose;

- presumption against congressional delegation of major questions to agency determination; and

- consideration of pragmatic consequences of particular interpretations.

Are you persuaded by Justice O'Connor that all of these interpretive tools "clarified" the statute's meaning such that there was no ambiguity remaining that would justify *Chevron* deference?

2.   Brown & Williamson *as a "Major Questions" Case.* It may well be that the majority would have come out as it had regardless of how its *Chevron* Step One inquiry unfolded. The opinion did divide across partisan lines: the same five Justices who ended the 2000 presidential election in favor of Governor George W. Bush constituted the majority here, see *Bush v. Gore*, 531 U.S. 98 (2000), with the same four *Bush v. Gore* dissenting Justices in dissent here. Hence, one might read *Brown & Williamson* as a "result-oriented" case—the Supreme Court playing an active role in a big political debate. But another way to understand the majority's resistance to the FDA's move is through the lens of the "Major Questions Rule" that we introduced in our discussion of *MCI*. Justice O'Connor takes several opportunities to note the importance of the political issue and specifically references *MCI* more than once. "We are confident," she writes, "that Congress could not have intended to delegate a decision of such economic and political significance to an agency in so cryptic a fashion." In other words, without more express authorization, the Court wasn't going to let the FDA get away with such a major power grab (or let Congress get away with punting such a big question to an agency).

3.   *Different Types of "Major Questions."* Was the FDA's power grab a particularly offensive one? The Major Questions Rule has been applied inconsistently by the Court through the years, and it is not yet deeply entrenched in Supreme Court practice. Three types of Major Questions have received the most attention:

(A) Deference to agency interpretations about preemption of state law: Some commentators argue that agencies should not receive deference for statutory interpretations that go to the question of whether the statute they are interpreting preempts state law or otherwise infringes on federalism. See Nina Mendelsohn, Chevron *and Preemption*, 102 Mich. L. Rev. 737 (2004). The Supreme Court case most on point is **Wyeth v. Levine**, 555 U.S. 555 (2009), which involved the content of warning labels on the drug Phenergan. A Vermont jury found that Wyeth, the manufacturer of the drug, had failed to provide an adequate warning of the risk of harm from improper injection of the drug, in violation of Vermont tort law. But because the warnings on Phenergan's label had been deemed sufficient by the federal FDA when it approved Wyeth's new drug application in 1955 and when it later approved changes in the drug's labeling, Wyeth challenged the state tort verdict on the ground that it was preempted by the FDCA, which bars unsafe drugs and requires FDA approval of all drug labels. The agency—the FDA—agreed. The FDA had taken a similar position in a preface to a 2006 rule, in which it had opined that drug standards in the FDCA represented *both* a floor *and* a ceiling for manufacturers—meaning they did not have to worry about potentially conflicting state standards. The majority of the Court, in an opinion by Justice Stevens, refused to apply *Chevron* to the agency's interpretation. Justice Breyer concurred, but reserved judgment on the possibility that the FDA could in the future adopt a rule having preemptive force. See also William N. Eskridge Jr., *Vetogates,* Chevron, *Preemption*, 83

Notre Dame L. Rev. 1441 (2008) (comprehensive analysis of the Court's preemption cases, revealing skepticism when federal agencies seek interpretations preempting state law but deference to agencies when they opine that federal law does not preempt).

(B) Deference to agency interpretations of their own jurisdiction: Some also have argued that *Chevron* deference should not be given to agency interpretations that go to the question of an agency's own jurisdiction. See Cass R. Sunstein, *Law and Administration after* Chevron, 90 Colum. L. Rev. 2071 (1990); Thomas W. Merrill & Kristen Hickman, Chevron*'s Domain*, 89 Geo. L.J. 833 (2001). This type of potential power grab was at issue in *Brown & Williamson*—the FDA was trying to expand its jurisdiction to include tobacco—although the Court did not explicitly rule in that case on whether *Chevron* deference might ever be appropriate under such circumstances. The Court offered its first explicit statement on this point in ***Arlington, Texas v. FCC***, 133 S.Ct. 1863 (2013), in which it held that *Chevron* was, indeed, the deference regime of choice, even for jurisdictional questions. The Court split along unusual lines, with Justice Scalia writing for a majority that included Justices Thomas, Ginsburg, Sotomayor and Kagan. Justice Scalia's majority opinion argued that distinguishing between jurisdictional and nonjurisdictional matters in the agency context rests on a "false premise" because "[n]o matter how it is framed the question a court faces when confronted with an agency's interpretation of a statute it administers is always, simply, *whether the agency has stayed within the bounds of its statutory authority*." 133 S.Ct at 1864 (emphasis in original). In other words, *all Chevron* questions are in some sense jurisdictional because the question is always whether the agency has leeway to decide a particular issue. Justice Scalia thus refused the temptation to complicate *Chevron* further with a new exception for "jurisdictional questions."

(C) Deference to agency interpretations of their own regulations: Finally, sometimes agencies interpret their own, preexisting regulations. One year after *Skidmore*, in *Bowles v. Seminole Rock & Sand Co.*, 325 U.S. 410 (1945), the Supreme Court announced a highly deferential standard of review for these agency constructions of their own regulations: They receive "controlling weight unless it is plainly erroneous or inconsistent with the regulation." Accord, *Auer v. Robbins*, 519 U.S. 452 (1997) (making clear the deferential standard applies even where the regulation itself is ambiguous). Professor Manning has criticized *Seminole Rock* for creating the wrong incentives: Instead of encouraging agencies to add clarity to the statutes that they implement, *Seminole Rock* incentivizes them to pass vague regulations, because agencies can always fill in the details later by interpreting those same vague regulations (and get extra deference, to boot, for those later interpretations). John F. Manning, *Constitutional Structure and Judicial Deference to Agency Interpretations of Agency Rules*, 96 Colum. L. Rev. 612 (1996). Several Justices through the years have expressed discomfort with *Seminole Rock* for these and other reasons. Justice Scalia, long a proponent of this rule and the author of the Court's opinion in *Auer*, recently indicated he would be receptive to jumping ship. See *Talk Am., Inc. v. Mich. Bell Tel. Co.*, 131 S.Ct. 2254 (2011) (Scalia, J., concurring) ("[D]eferring to an agency's interpretation of its own rule encourages the agency to enact vague rules which give it the power, in future adjudications, to do what it pleases. This frustrates the notice and predictability purposes of rulemaking, and promotes arbitrary government.")

Do you agree that all (or any) of the above situations are particularly weak candidates for agency deference? Is the Court approaching these questions consistently? Why is the jurisdictional power grab sanctioned in *Arlington* less offensive than the federalism-related power grab blocked by the Court in *Wyeth?*

Those who oppose deference in these circumstances argue that agencies are subject-matter experts, not federalism/constitutional-structure/ jurisdictional experts. Each of these situations also involves some agency self-interest, too—i.e., their desire to increase their power relative to the states or to extend their own jurisdiction—which may undermine their credibility and cut against traditional arguments for deference. In *Arlington*, Chief Justice Roberts would have put a stop to this. His strongly worded dissenting opinion warns of the "danger posed by the growing power of the administrative state" and resists the idea of augmenting agencies' power "even further, to include not only broader power to give definitive answers to questions left to them by Congress, but also the same power to decide when Congress has given them that power." 133 S.Ct. at 1869 (Roberts, C.J., dissenting). Where would you draw the line?

C. WALKING *CHEVRON* BACK: *MEAD* AND A MORE TAILORED DEFERENCE REGIME

The Major Questions Rule can be viewed as an effort by the Court— although sporadically utilized—to walk the *Chevron* doctrine back a bit; a realization that *Chevron*'s bright-line rule that ambiguity justifies delegation may be overbroad in some circumstances. In 2001, just one year after *Brown & Williamson*, the Court was more explicit in this effort. In *United States v. Mead Corp.*, 533 U.S. 218 (2001), the Court much more dramatically and directly curtailed *Chevron*'s breadth. In the process, *Skidmore*—which left more interpretive power with the courts but whose precise status was unclear after *Chevron*—took on more explicit prominence.

In the sixteen years between *Chevron* and *Mead,* the relationship between *Chevron* and *Skidmore* was ambiguous. On the one hand, some commentators and judges claimed that *Chevron* rendered *Skidmore* obsolete. See *Christensen v. Harris County*, 529 U.S. 576, 589 (2000) (Scalia, J. concurring). Others maintained that *Skidmore* remained relevant. See Thomas W. Merrill & Kristin E. Hickman, Chevron's

Domain, 89 Geo. L.J. 833 (2001). In fact, the Court explicitly applied *Skidmore* deference in dozens of cases after *Chevron.* See William N. Eskridge Jr. & Lauren E. Baer, *The Continuum of Deference: Supreme Court Treatment of Agency Interpretations from* Chevron *to* Hamdan, 96 Geo. L.J. 1083, 1100, 1109–11 (2008).

At the same time, others were concerned that *Chevron* went too far—that it assumed too much: Congress did not intend to delegate every time a statute did not speak clearly on an issue. It also became apparent, as we saw in Chapter 7, that agencies do their statutory implementation work in many different ways. Some agency interpretation takes place through informal channels like *amicus* briefs or website summaries. Other interpretations utilize more formal processes, like notice-and-comment rulemaking or adjudication. Nor does Congress give every agency the same power to issue rules or regulations. The Court in *Skidmore* had implied that such differences might matter in terms of how much gravity the agency's interpretation would receive. *Chevron,* however, eschewed *Skidmore*'s balancing test with a simple but broad rule that did not take such variety into account.

The Court's next big move, *Mead,* changed the landscape dramatically and made clear the continuing importance of *Skidmore. Mead* is less formalist—and much less clear—than *Chevron.* At issue in *Mead* was the U.S. Customs Service's interpretation of the term "diaries" in a tariff statute to include day planners. Customs could have acted by notice-and-comment rulemaking but instead issued its interpretation through an informal ruling letter. Pay particular attention, as you read the opinion, to the Court's interest in both the *type* of interpretive authority delegated to the agency and the *process* by which the agency exercises that authority.

UNITED STATES V. MEAD CORP.
United States Supreme Court, 2001.
533 U.S. 218, 121 S.Ct. 2164, 150 L.ed 2d 292.

JUSTICE SOUTER delivered the opinion of the Court.

The question is whether a tariff classification ruling by the United States Customs Service deserves judicial deference. The Federal Circuit rejected Customs' invocation of *Chevron* in support of such a ruling, to which it gave no deference. We agree that a tariff classification has no claim to judicial deference under *Chevron*; there being no indication that Congress intended such a ruling to carry the force of law, but we hold that under *Skidmore,* the ruling is eligible to claim respect according to its persuasiveness. * * *

[II.A]   When Congress has "explicitly left a gap for an agency to fill," there is an express delegation of authority to the agency to elucidate a specific provision of the statute by regulation," *Chevron*, and any ensuing regulation is binding in the courts unless procedurally defective, arbitrary or capricious in substance, or manifestly contrary to the statute. See APA, 5 U.S.C. § 706(2)(A), (D). But whether or not they enjoy any express delegation of authority on a particular question, agencies charged with applying a statute necessarily make all sorts of interpretive choices, and while not all of those choices bind judges to follow them, they certainly may influence courts facing questions the agencies have already answered. "[T]he well-reasoned views of the agencies implementing a statute 'constitute a body of experience and informed judgment to which courts and litigants may properly resort for guidance,'" *Bragdon* v. *Abbott,* 524 U.S. 624, 642 (1998) (quoting *Skidmore*). * * *

The fair measure of deference to an agency administering its own statute has been understood to vary with circumstances, and courts have looked to the degree of the agency's care, its consistency, formality, and relative expertness, and to the persuasiveness of the agency's position, see *Skidmore*. * * * Justice Jackson summed things up in *Skidmore*:

"The weight [accorded to an administrative] judgment in a particular case will depend upon the thoroughness evident in its consideration, the validity of its reasoning, its consistency with earlier and later pronouncements, and all those factors which give it power to persuade, if lacking power to control."

Since 1984, we have identified a category of interpretive choices distinguished by an additional reason for judicial deference. This Court in *Chevron* recognized that Congress not only engages in express delegation of specific interpretive authority, but that "[s]ometimes the legislative delegation to an agency on a particular question is implicit." Congress, that is, may not have expressly delegated authority or responsibility to implement a particular provision or fill a particular gap. Yet it can still be apparent from the agency's generally conferred authority and other statutory circumstances that Congress would expect the agency to be able to speak with the force of law when it addresses ambiguity in the statute or fills a space in the enacted law, even one about which "Congress did not actually have an intent" as to a particular result. When circumstances implying such an expectation exist, a reviewing court has no business rejecting an agency's exercise of its generally conferred authority to resolve a particular statutory ambiguity simply because the agency's chosen resolution seems unwise, but is obliged to accept the agency's position if Congress has not previously spoken to the point at issue and the agency's interpretation is reasonable; *cf.* 5 U.S.C. § 706(2) (a reviewing court shall set aside agency action, findings, and conclusions found to be "arbitrary, capricious, an abuse of discretion, or otherwise not in accordance with law").

We have recognized a very good indicator of delegation meriting *Chevron* treatment in express congressional authorizations to engage in the process of rulemaking or adjudication that produces regulations or rulings for which deference is claimed. * * * It is fair to assume generally that Congress contemplates administrative action with the effect of law when it provides for a relatively formal administrative procedure tending to foster the fairness and deliberation that should underlie a pronouncement of such force. Thus, the overwhelming number of our cases applying *Chevron* deference have reviewed the fruits of notice-and-comment rulemaking or formal adjudication. That said, and as significant as notice-and-comment is in pointing to *Chevron* authority, the want of that procedure here does not decide the case, for we have sometimes found reasons for *Chevron* deference even when no such administrative formality was required and none was afforded. The fact that the tariff classification here was not a product of such formal process does not alone, therefore, bar the application of *Chevron*.

There are, nonetheless, ample reasons to deny *Chevron* deference here. The authorization for classification rulings, and Customs's practice in making them, present a case far removed not only from notice-and-comment process, but from any other circumstances reasonably suggesting that Congress ever thought of classification rulings as deserving the deference claimed for them here.

[II.B]   * * * On the face of the statute, to begin with, the terms of the congressional delegation give no indication that Congress meant to delegate authority to Customs to issue classification rulings with the force of law. We are not, of course, here making any global statement about Customs's authority, for it is true that the general rulemaking power conferred on Customs authorizes some regulation with the force of law." * * * It is true as well that Congress had classification rulings in mind when it explicitly authorized, in a parenthetical, the issuance of "regulations establishing procedures for the issuance of binding rulings prior to the entry of the merchandise concerned," 19 U.S.C. § 1502(a). The reference to binding classifications does not, however, bespeak the legislative type of activity that would naturally bind more than the parties to the ruling, once the goods classified are admitted into this country. * * *

It is difficult, in fact, to see in the agency practice itself any indication that Customs ever set out with a lawmaking pretense in mind when it undertook to make classifications like these. Customs does not generally engage in notice-and-comment practice when issuing them, and their treatment by the agency makes it clear that a letter's binding character as a ruling stops short of third parties; Customs has regarded a classification as conclusive only as between itself and the importer to whom it was issued, and even then only until Customs has given advance notice of intended change. Other importers are in fact warned against assuming any right of detrimental reliance.

Indeed, to claim that classifications have legal force is to ignore the reality that 46 different Customs offices issue 10,000 to 15,000 of them each year. Any suggestion that rulings intended to have the force of law are being churned out at a rate of 10,000 a year at an agency's 46 scattered offices is simply self-refuting. Although the circumstances are less startling here, with a Headquarters letter in issue, none of the relevant statutes recognizes this category of rulings as separate or different from others; there is thus no indication that a more potent delegation might have been understood as going to Headquarters even when Headquarters provides developed reasoning, as it did in this instance. * * *

[II.C]   To agree with the Court of Appeals that Customs ruling letters do not fall within *Chevron* is not, however, to place them outside the pale of any deference whatever. *Chevron* did nothing to eliminate *Skidmore*'s holding that an agency's interpretation may merit some deference whatever its form, given the "specialized experience and broader investigations and information" available to the agency, and given the value of uniformity in its administrative and judicial understandings of what a national law requires.

There is room at least to raise a *Skidmore* claim here, where the regulatory scheme is highly detailed, and Customs can bring the benefit of specialized experience to bear on the subtle questions in this case: whether the daily planner with room for brief daily entries falls under "diaries," when diaries are grouped with "notebooks and address books, bound; memorandum pads, letter pads and similar articles"; and whether a planner with a ring binding should qualify as "bound," when a binding may be typified by a book, but also may have "reinforcements or fittings of metal, plastics, etc." A classification ruling in this situation may therefore at least seek a respect proportional to its "power to persuade," *Skidmore*. Such a ruling may surely claim the merit of its writer's thoroughness, logic and expertness, its fit with prior interpretations, and any other sources of weight.

[II.D]   Underlying the position we take here, like the position expressed by Justice Scalia in dissent, is a choice about the best way to deal with an inescapable feature of the body of congressional legislation authorizing administrative action. That feature is the great variety of ways in which the laws invest the Government's administrative arms with discretion, and with procedures for exercising it, in giving meaning to Acts of Congress. Implementation of a statute may occur in formal adjudication or the choice to defend against judicial challenge; it may occur in a central board or office or in dozens of enforcement agencies dotted across the country; its institutional lawmaking may be confined to the resolution of minute detail or extend to legislative rulemaking on matters intentionally left by Congress to be worked out at the agency level.

Although we all accept the position that the Judiciary should defer to at least some of this multifarious administrative action, we have to decide how to take account of the great range of its variety. If the primary objective is to simplify the judicial process of giving or withholding deference, then the diversity of statutes authorizing discretionary administrative action must be declared irrelevant or minimized. If, on the other hand, it is simply implausible that Congress intended such a broad range of statutory authority to produce only two varieties of administrative action, demanding either *Chevron* deference or none at all, then the breadth of the spectrum of possible agency action must be taken into account. Justice Scalia's first priority over the years has been to limit and simplify. The Court's choice has been to tailor deference to variety. This acceptance of the range of statutory variation has led the Court to recognize more than one variety of judicial deference, just as the Court has recognized a variety of indicators that Congress would expect *Chevron* deference.

Our respective choices are repeated today. Justice Scalia would pose the question of deference as an either-or choice. On his view that *Chevron* rendered *Skidmore* anachronistic, when courts owe any deference it is *Chevron* deference that they owe. Whether courts do owe deference in a given case turns, for him, on whether the agency action (if reasonable) is "authoritative." The character of the authoritative derives, in turn, not from breadth of delegation or the agency's procedure in implementing it, but is defined as the "official" position of an agency, and may ultimately be a function of administrative persistence alone.

The Court, on the other hand, said nothing in *Chevron* to eliminate *Skidmore*'s recognition of various justifications for deference depending on statutory circumstances and agency action; *Chevron* was simply a case recognizing that even without express authority to fill a specific statutory gap, circumstances pointing to implicit congressional delegation present a particularly insistent call for deference.

We think, in sum, that Justice Scalia's efforts to simplify ultimately run afoul of Congress's indications that different statutes present different reasons for considering respect for the exercise of administrative authority or deference to it. Without being at odds with congressional intent much of the time, we believe that judicial responses to administrative action must continue to differentiate between *Chevron* and *Skidmore,* and that continued recognition of *Skidmore* is necessary for just the reasons Justice Jackson gave when that case was decided.

Since the *Skidmore* assessment called for here ought to be made in the first instance by the Court of Appeals for the Federal Circuit or the [Court of International Trade], we go no further than to vacate the judgment and remand the case for further proceedings consistent with this opinion.

JUSTICE SCALIA, dissenting.

Today's opinion makes an avulsive change in judicial review of federal administrative action. Whereas previously a reasonable agency application of an ambiguous statutory provision had to be sustained so long as it represented the agency's authoritative interpretation, henceforth such an application can be set aside unless "it appears that Congress delegated authority to the agency generally to make rules carrying the force of law," as by giving an agency "power to engage in adjudication or notice-and-comment rulemaking, or * * * some other [procedure] indicati[ng] comparable congressional intent," and "the agency interpretation claiming deference was promulgated in the exercise of that authority." What was previously a general presumption of authority in agencies to resolve ambiguity in the statutes they have been authorized to enforce has been changed to a presumption of no such authority, which must be overcome by affirmative legislative intent to the contrary. And whereas previously, when agency authority to resolve ambiguity did not exist the court was free to give the statute what it considered the best interpretation, henceforth the court must supposedly give the agency view some indeterminate amount of so-called *Skidmore* deference. We will be sorting out the consequences of the *Mead* doctrine, which has today replaced the *Chevron* doctrine, for years to come. I would adhere to our established jurisprudence, defer to the reasonable interpretation the Customs Service has given to the statute it is charged with enforcing, and reverse the judgment of the Court of Appeals.

[I.A]   As to principle: The doctrine of *Chevron*—that all *authoritative* agency interpretations of statutes they are charged with administering deserve deference—was rooted in a legal presumption of congressional intent, important to the division of powers between the Second and Third Branches. When, *Chevron* said, Congress leaves an ambiguity in a statute that is to be administered by an executive agency, it is presumed that Congress meant to give the agency discretion, within the limits of reasonable interpretation, as to how the ambiguity is to be resolved. By committing enforcement of the statute to an agency rather than the courts, Congress committed its initial and primary interpretation to that branch as well. * * *

The basis in principle for today's new doctrine can be described as follows: The background rule is that ambiguity in legislative instructions to agencies is to be resolved not by the agencies but by the judges. Specific congressional intent to depart from this rule must be found—and while there is no single touchstone for such intent it can generally be found when Congress has authorized the agency to act through (what the Court says is) relatively formal procedures such as informal rulemaking and formal (and informal?) adjudication, and when the agency in fact employs such procedures. [T]he Court's principal criterion of congressional intent to supplant its background rule seems to me quite implausible. There is no necessary connection between the formality of procedure and the power of the entity administering the procedure to resolve authoritatively questions of law. The most formal of the procedures the Court refers to— formal adjudication—is modeled after the process used in trial courts, which of course are not generally accorded deference on questions of law. The purpose of such a procedure is to produce a closed record for determination and review of the facts—which implies nothing about the power of the agency subjected to the procedure to resolve authoritatively questions of law.

As for informal rulemaking: While formal adjudication procedures are *prescribed* (either by statute or by the Constitution), informal rulemaking is more typically *authorized* but not required. Agencies with such authority are free to give guidance through rulemaking, but they may proceed to administer their statute case-by-case, "making law" as they implement their program (not necessarily through formal adjudication). Is it likely—or indeed even plausible—that Congress meant, when such an agency chooses rulemaking, to accord the administrators of that agency, *and their successors*, the flexibility of interpreting the ambiguous statute now one way, and later another; but, when such an agency chooses case-by-case administration, to eliminate all future agency discretion by having that same ambiguity resolved authoritatively (and forever) by the courts? Surely that makes no sense. It is also the case that certain significant categories of rules—those involving grant and benefit programs, for example, are exempt from the requirements of informal rulemaking. See 5 U.S.C. § 553(a)(2). Under the Court's novel theory, when an agency takes advantage of that exemption its rules will be deprived of *Chevron* deference, *i.e.*, authoritative effect. Was this either the plausible intent of the APA rulemaking exemption, or the plausible intent of the Congress that established the grant or benefit program? * * *

[II.B. In this portion of his dissent, Justice Scalia lamented the terrible "practical effects" of the Court's new rule.] (1) The principal effect will be protracted confusion. As noted above, the one test for *Chevron* deference that the Court enunciates is wonderfully imprecise: whether "Congress delegated authority to the agency generally to make rules carrying the force of law, * * * as by * * * adjudication[,] notice-and-comment rulemaking, or * * * some other [procedure] indicati[ng] comparable congressional intent." But even this description does not do justice to the utter flabbiness of the Court's criterion * * *. In the present case, it tells us, the absence of notice-and-comment rulemaking (and "[who knows?] [of] some other [procedure] indicati[ng] comparable congressional intent") is not enough to decide the question of *Chevron* deference, "for we have sometimes found reasons for *Chevron* deference even when no such administrative formality was required and none was afforded." The opinion then goes on to consider a grab bag of other factors—including the factor that used to be the sole criterion for *Chevron* deference: whether the interpretation represented the *authoritative* position of the agency. It is hard to know what the lower courts are to make of today's guidance.

(2) Another practical effect of today's opinion will be an artificially induced increase in informal [i.e., notice-and-comment] rulemaking. Buy stock in the [Government Printing Office]. Since informal rulemaking and formal adjudication are the only more-or-less safe harbors from the storm that the Court has unleashed; and since formal adjudication is not an option but must be mandated by statute or constitutional command; informal rulemaking—which the Court was once careful to make voluntary unless required by statute—will now become a virtual necessity. As I have described, the Court's safe harbor requires not merely that the agency have been given rulemaking authority, but also that the agency have *employed* rulemaking as the means of resolving the statutory ambiguity. (It is hard to understand why that should be so. Surely the mere *conferral* of rulemaking authority demonstrates—if one accepts the Court's logic—a congressional intent to allow the agency to resolve ambiguities. And given that intent, what difference does it make that the agency chooses instead to use another perfectly permissible means for that purpose?) * * *

(3) Worst of all, the majority's approach will lead to the ossification of large portions of our statutory law. Where *Chevron* applies, statutory ambiguities remain ambiguities subject to the agency's ongoing clarification. They create a space, so to speak, for the exercise of continuing agency discretion. As *Chevron* itself held, the Environmental Protection Agency can interpret "stationary source" to mean a single smokestack, can later replace that interpretation with the "bubble concept" embracing an entire plant, and if that proves undesirable can return again to the original interpretation. For the indeterminately large number of statutes taken out of *Chevron* by today's decision, however, ambiguity (and hence flexibility) will cease with the first judicial resolution. *Skidmore* deference gives the agency's current position some vague and uncertain amount of respect, but it does not, like *Chevron*, *leave* the matter within the control of the Executive Branch for the future. Once the court has spoken, it becomes *unlawful* for the agency to take a

contradictory position; the statute now *says* what the court has prescribed. * * *

One might respond that such ossification would not result if the agency were simply to readopt its interpretation, after a court reviewing it under *Skidmore* had rejected it, by repromulgating it through one of the *Chevron*-eligible procedural formats approved by the Court today. Approving this procedure would be a landmark abdication of judicial power. It is worlds apart from *Chevron* proper, where the court does not *purport* to give the statute a judicial interpretation—except in identifying the scope of the statutory ambiguity, as to which the court's judgment is final and irreversible. (Under *Chevron* proper, when the agency's authoritative interpretation comes within the scope of that ambiguity— and the court therefore approves it—the agency will not be "overruling" the court's decision when it later decides that a different interpretation (still within the scope of the ambiguity) is preferable.) By contrast, under this view, the reviewing court will not be holding the agency's authoritative interpretation within the scope of the ambiguity; but will be holding that the agency has not used the "delegation-conferring" procedures, and that the court must therefore *interpret the statute on its own*—but subject to reversal if and when the agency uses the proper procedures.

* * * I know of no case, in the entire history of the federal courts, in which we have allowed a judicial interpretation of a statute to be set aside by an agency—or have allowed a lower court to render an interpretation of a statute subject to correction by an agency * * *. There is, in short, no way to avoid the ossification of federal law that today's opinion sets in motion. What a court says is the law after according *Skidmore* deference will be the law forever, beyond the power of the agency to change even through rulemaking.

(4) And finally, the majority's approach compounds the confusion it creates by breathing new life into the anachronism of *Skidmore*, which sets forth a sliding scale of deference owed an agency's interpretation of a statute that is dependent "upon the thoroughness evident in [the agency's] consideration, the validity of its reasoning, its consistency with earlier and later pronouncements, and all those factors which give it power to persuade, if lacking power to control"; in this way, the appropriate measure of deference will be accorded the "body of experience and informed judgment" that such interpretations often embody. Justice Jackson's eloquence notwithstanding, the rule of *Skidmore* deference is an empty truism and a trifling statement of the obvious: A judge should take into account the well-considered views of expert observers.

It was possible to live with the indeterminacy of *Skidmore* deference in earlier times. But in an era when federal statutory law administered by federal agencies is pervasive, and when the ambiguities (intended or unintended) that those statutes contain are innumerable, totality-of-the-circumstances *Skidmore* deference is a recipe for uncertainty, unpredictability, and endless litigation. To condemn a vast body of agency action to that regime (all except rulemaking, formal (and informal?) adjudication, and whatever else might now and then be included within today's intentionally vague formulation of affirmative congressional intent to "delegate") is irresponsible.

[Justice Scalia also criticized the majority's approach as an important departure from the Court's post-*Chevron* precedents as well as *Chevron* itself.]

I dissent even more vigorously from the reasoning that produces the Court's judgment, and that makes today's decision one of the most significant opinions ever rendered by the Court dealing with the judicial review of administrative action. Its consequences will be enormous, and almost uniformly bad.

NOTES AND QUESTIONS ON MEAD

1.   Mead *as* Marbury*'s Revenge*? *Mead* has been called "*Marbury*'s Revenge" for a reason. Cass R. Sunstein, *Beyond* Marbury: *The Executive's Power to Say What the Law Is*, 115 Yale L.J. 2580, 2602 (2006). Much more explicitly than in the Major Questions Rule cases that we saw in the previous section, *Mead* aims to pull back the potentially massive transfer of interpretive power from courts to agencies that *Chevron* seemed to require. It also is an attempt to be more *realistic* about the way that Congress operates. *Chevron*'s broad presumption was that every instance of statutory ambiguity, and sometimes even statutory silence, signals congressional intent to delegate interpretive authority to agencies. *Mead* tells us that *Chevron* went too far—that, instead, there is a "great variety of ways in which the laws invest the Government's administrative arms with discretion, and with procedures for exercising it, in giving meaning to Acts of Congress" and not all of those should necessarily be accorded the same level of deference. *Mead*, in Justice Souter's words, is a move to "tailor deference to variety."

The main disagreement among the Justices in *Mead* is over the prudence of such a move. Justice Scalia favors *Chevron*'s bright line simplicity over the *Mead* majority's goal of making *Chevron* more reflective of congressional intent by looking for more concrete signals of delegation. As Justice Souter wrote: "If the primary objective is to simplify the judicial process of giving or withholding deference, then the diversity of statutes authorizing discretionary administrative action must be declared irrelevant or minimized. If, on the other hand, it is simply implausible that Congress intended such a broad range of statutory authority to produce only two varieties of administrative action, demanding either *Chevron* deference or none at all, then the breadth of the spectrum of possible agency action must be taken into account."

2.   Mead *as Shift Toward an Intent-Based Deference Regime.* Mead also appears to provide an answer from the Court about the best normative basis for deference to agency statutory interpretations. Recall that the Court in *Chevron* offered many justifications for its broad deference rule: namely, congressional intent to delegate, the need for technical expertise, political considerations, and democratic accountability. In contrast, *Mead* asks Congress for a very specific signal of intent to delegate—the giving to the agency of power to make rules with the force of law—and won't apply *Chevron* deference without it, even if those other factors like politics, expertise, and accountability still apply to the decision. As then-Professors Kagan and Barron wrote shortly after the decision: "*Mead* represents the apotheosis of a developing trend in *Chevron* cases: the treatment of *Chevron* as a congressional choice, rather than either a constitutional mandate or a judicial doctrine. * * * Congress [has] the power to turn on or off *Chevron* deference." Elena Kagan & David Barron, Chevron's *Nondelegation Doctrine*, 2001 Sup. Ct. Rev. 201, 212.

3.   *The Majority's Invocation of* Skidmore. Mead's rule effectively operates as a track switch between *Chevron* and *Skidmore*. One key holding of *Mead* is that the deference choice is not merely the binary choice between deference and no deference that *Chevron* prescribes, and that some had believed was the only choice after *Chevron*. See Kristin E. Hickman, *The Need for* Mead: *Rejecting Tax Exceptionalism in Judicial Deference*, 90 Minn. L. Rev. 1537, 1550–51 (2006). Instead, *Mead* creates something like a sliding scale: Some agency interpretations will merit *Chevron* deference and others won't but still will merit some weight, in accordance with *Skidmore*'s "power to persuade" standard. Courts thus must now begin their review of agency statutory interpretations by figuring out, using *Mead*'s framework, whether the interpretation at issue is eligible for *Chevron* deference in the first place. If it is, then the court should proceed with its *Chevron* inquiry. If it isn't, *Mead* tells us the court isn't done—it cannot simply decline deference and put in place its own preferred interpretation. Instead, the court must then ask itself whether the agency's interpretation nevertheless merits some weight under *Skidmore*. In this manner, *Mead* operates as the gateway to *Chevron* and *Skidmore*. This inquiry might be dubbed *Chevron* "Step Zero," the preliminary step preceding the possibility of performing the *Chevron* two-step dance in the first place. See Merrill & Hickman, Chevron's *Domain*, 89 Geo. L.J. at 836 (originating the term "Step Zero" to describe this preliminary *Chevron*-triggering inquiry).

4.   *Where Does* Mead *Draw Its Line?* As Justice Scalia notes, the Court was not entirely clear about where exactly *Mead* draws its new line. The Court put most of its emphasis on the idea that *Chevron*'s special deference regime is justified by congressional intent to delegate *lawmaking* authority to agencies. See Merrill & Hickman, Chevron's *Domain*; Thomas W. Merrill, *Rethinking Article I, Section 1: From Nondelegation to Exclusive Delegation*,

104 Colum. L. Rev. 2097 (2004). The Court lists circumstances in which "Congress delegated authority to the agency generally to make rules carrying the force of law, * * * as by * * * adjudication[,] notice-and-comment rulemaking, or * * * some other [procedure] indicati[ng] comparable congressional intent" as the quintessential examples. But see Thomas W. Merrill & Kathryn T. Watts, *Agency Rules with the Force of Law: The Original Convention*, 116 Harv. L. Rev. 467, 577–90 (2002) (arguing that historically only those rules that could be enforced by sanctions were understood to have the "force of law," a condition that *Mead* fails to impose). The Court in *Mead* did not spell out what those "other procedures indicating comparable congressional intent" might be, but did imply that there might have been some exceptional cases in which *Chevron* deference would still be justified "even when no such administrative formality was required and none was afforded." Justice Scalia's dissent correctly notes the imprecision of this standard and the potential doctrinal confusion it is likely to cause in the lower courts—a prediction that proved correct. See Lisa Schultz Bressman, *How* Mead *Has Muddled Judicial Review of Agency Action*, 58 Vand. L. Rev. 1443, 1465 (2005) (finding significant lower court uncertainty about how to apply *Mead*). What's more, the Court has added to the murkiness in subsequent cases, holding, for instance, that a particularly longstanding agency interpretation might be *Chevron*-worthy after *Mead*, even if it was not issued with the kinds of formal procedures that *Mead* seemed to require. See *Barnhart v. Walton*, 535 U.S. 212 (2002) (holding that the "expertise of the Agency, the importance of the question to administration of the statute * * * and the careful consideration that Agency has given the question over a long period of time all indicate that Chevron provides the appropriate legal lens through which to view the legality of the Agency interpretation here at issue" even though "the Agency previously raced its interpretation through means less formal than 'notice and comment' rulemaking").

5.   Mead *as an Administrative Due Process Case.* Justice Scalia also asks a good question about the Court's new rule: Why does the Court require the agency actually to *use* the lawmaking authority delegated? If the test is really about congressional intent, as the majority suggests, the mere *delegation* of the lawmaking authority arguably should be enough. Might *Mead* instead really be the Court's attempt to bring some more "due process" to the world of administrative law? The Court's opinion certainly seems to encourage agencies to use the more transparent and inclusive notice-and-comment procedures set out by the APA rather than proceeding with less formal processes. We have seen the Court discuss agency procedures before. Recall *Vermont Yankee, Nuclear Power Co. v. Natural Resources Defense Council, Inc.*, 435 U.S. 519 (1978) from Chapter 7, in which the Court held that federal courts could not impose additional procedures on agencies beyond those required by the APA. How does *Mead* fit with that holding? Is *Mead* a back-door attempt by the Court to encourage (but not require) administrative due process in a way the Court did not feel empowered to do directly in *Vermont Yankee*? So understood, *Mead* seems to play a role similar to some of the substantive canons of statutory construction that we already

have studied: a way for courts, through the lower-heat, often lower-visibility, mode of statutory interpretation, to advance constitutional norms it is not comfortable advancing through straight-up constitutional law.

6.   *More Subtle Modifications of* Chevron: *Deference by Subject Matter.* Although the Court has never explicitly said so, it does not apply *Chevron* equally across all statutes. In practice, the Court's decisions reveal a "continuum of deference"—different deference practices that often turn on the subject matter of the question at hand. See Eskridge & Baer, *Continuum of Deference,* 96 Geo. L.J. at 1098–1120. In other words, specialized deference regimes survived *Chevron.* For instance, the Court applies super-strong deference in foreign affairs areas, ordinary *Chevron* deference in cases involving the environment, energy, immigration, and labor, and sometimes even a presumption of "anti-deference" in some certain areas like criminal law. What might be the justification for these differences? Eskridge and Baer also note that, regardless of the Court's actual characterization, the Justices actually "go along with" agency interpretations almost all the time in cases involving energy, telecommunications, transportation, and intellectual property law (and often without citing any deference regime).

It is possible that things are now changing. The Court for years did not give *Chevron* deference to the Treasury Department's interpretation of the Tax Code, see *National Muffler Dealers v. United States,* 440 U.S. 472 (1979). But it recently reversed that practice in favor of basic *Chevron* in the medical residents tax case, *Mayo Foundation for Medical Education and Research v. United States,* 131 S.Ct. 704 (2011), following the suggestion made in Kristen E. Hickman, *The Need for* Mead: *Rejecting Tax Exceptionalism in Deference Cases,* 90 Minn. L. Rev. 1537 (2006). Although movement toward a more uniform deference regime may simplify matters for courts and litigants, it is not clear such a move is really consistent with *Mead*'s stated goal of "tailor[ing] deference to [the] variety" of ways in which Congress delegates. The Court's more subject-specific practice may have been closer to that mark. Indeed, congressional drafters do appear to approach deference differently depending on the subject matter. See Gluck & Bressman, *Statutory Interpretation from the Inside: Part I,* 65 Stan. L. Rev. at 1001–1002.

PROBLEM 8–4: MEAD *IN ACTION*

Return to *Wyeth v. Levine,* 555 U.S. 555 (2009), the drug labeling case discussed above, as an example of *Mead* in action. The issue in *Wyeth* was whether the drug labeling requirements of the Food, Drug, and Cosmetic Act (FDCA) preempted a state tort law cause of action alleging inadequate warnings on Wyeth's drug Phenergan. The FDA interpreted the FDCA as preempting the state law claims. Put yourself in the position of the Court and consider these two facts:

- The Court has never explicitly answered the question whether an agency is entitled to *Chevron* deference for its views on whether a federal statute should be interpreted to preempt state law.

- The FDA announced its position on preemption in a preamble to a rule that had gone through notice-and-comment, but the preamble itself and its substantive content had not been subject to that process.

How does *Mead* help you figure out what framework to apply to the agency's interpretation? Is it *Chevron? Skidmore?* Neither? Determine which regime you would apply before reading on.

A sharply divided Court in *Wyeth* found that *Mead* required the Court to apply *Skidmore*. The case had something of a "Major Questions Rule" flavor to it, in the sense that the Court focused less on whether the statute was ambiguous with respect to preemption and more on whether it could really be assumed that Congress intends to delegate, through statutory silence or ambiguity, these kinds of important federalism (i.e., preemption) questions to federal agencies. The majority refused to make that assumption. But it also clarified that, post-*Mead*, declining *Chevron* deference does not mean no deference. It means that *Skidmore*'s "persuasiveness" standard must be considered, as the Court held: "While agencies have no special authority to pronounce on pre-emption absent delegation by Congress, they do have a unique understanding of the statutes they administer and an attendant ability to make informed determinations about how state requirements may pose an 'obstacle' to the accomplishment and execution of the full purposes and objectives of Congress. The weight we accord the agency's explanation of state law's impact on the federal scheme depends on its thoroughness, consistency, and persuasiveness."

The Court also referenced the FDA's process, and implied that the inadequacy of that process was another reason to deny *Chevron* deference, *per Mead*: "The agency finalized the rule and, without offering States or other interested parties notice or opportunity for comment, articulated a sweeping position on the FDCA's pre-emptive effect in the regulatory preamble. The agency's views on state law are inherently suspect in light of this procedural failure. [Citing *Mead*.]"

Wyeth, like some of the other Major Questions Rule cases, divided the Justices in ways one might not expect. Why, for example, does federalism-loving Justice Scalia defer to the agency in *Wyeth*, which wanted to preempt rather than preserve state law? We suspect for the same reason that Justice Scalia recently wrote the majority opinion according *Chevron* deference to an agency's interpretation of a question concerning its own jurisdiction, see *Arlington v. FCC, supra*. The Court is engaged in a continuing debate over simplicity versus complexity when it comes to delegation doctrine. The Major Questions Rule, like *Mead*, complicates the bright-line simplicity that *Chevron* offers and that is championed by formalists like Justice Scalia. On the other side, the Court's efforts to refine the doctrine pose their own attractions for other Justices, like the Chief Justice, who are concerned about giving up too much judicial power, or like Justices Souter and Breyer, who hope for a doctrine more reflective of how Congress actually delegates.

NOTE ON EMPIRICAL STUDIES OF THE SUPREME COURT'S DEFERENCE REGIMES

Chevron and *Mead* in the Supreme Court: Empirical work paints a mixed picture of how well the courts are doing in their application of the deference regimes and whether the deference doctrines have any real effect on how cases are decided. The Supreme Court was highly deferential to agency rules and interpretations before *Chevron* and has continued to be deferential after *Chevron*. It thus remains unclear whether *Chevron* has had any real influence at the Supreme Court level—beyond creating the increasingly complicated legisprudence that we have presented in this chapter.

One question that continues to come up is whether *Chevron* does anything to temper ideological judicial voting. Cass Sunstein and Thomas Miles found pronounced ideological voting in *Chevron* cases (only those cases citing *Chevron*) in the Supreme Court. See Thomas J. Miles & Cass R. Sunstein, *Do Judges Make Regulatory Policy? An Empirical Investigation of* Chevron, 73 U. Chi. L. Rev. 823 (2006). More recently, William Eskridge and Lauren Baer conducted a study of all 1014 Supreme Court decisions between 1984 and 2006 where an agency statutory interpretation was presented to the Supreme Court. William N. Eskridge Jr. & Lauren E. Baer, *The Continuum of Deference: Supreme Court Treatment of Agency Statutory Interpretations from* Chevron *to* Hamdan, 96 Geo. L.J. 1083 (2008). Their study was not limited to decisions citing *Chevron,* and they found significant but less pronounced and fewer ideological effects than the Miles-Sunstein study. *Id.* at 1153–56. They also reported a wide variance of judicial willingness to go along with agency interpretations: Chief Justice Warren Burger and Justices Byron White and Lewis Powell were extremely deferential (with virtually no ideological preference for White and Powell), while William Brennan and Thurgood Marshall went against agency views most of the time. Surprisingly, John Paul Stevens, the author of *Chevron*, was one of the least deferential. On the current Court, Justice Breyer, a critic of *Chevron*, is easily the most agency-deferential in practice, while *Chevron*-loving Justice Scalia is much less deferential in practice.

Eskridge and Baer also found that the Court's deployment of *Chevron* was quite inconsistent, even in those cases where there had been an explicit grant of lawmaking authority, namely, the narrower trigger for *Chevron* deference announced in *Mead*. According to their analysis, the Court applied *Chevron* in 8.3% of those statutory case where there was an agency interpretation in play, even though almost 27% of those cases involved agency decisions pursuant to explicit grants of formal adjudicatory or legislative (substantive) rulemaking authority. Eskridge & Baer, *Continuum of Deference,* 96 Geo. L.J. at 1124–26. And about 10% of the *Chevron* cases involved very informal agency action clearly not derived from lawmaking grants—agency letters, interpretive guidances, and even opinions voiced in *amicus* briefs. *Id.* at 1128. The Eskridge and Baer study also confirmed the flourishing of *Skidmore* post-*Mead*, and the authors argue that *Skidmore* is now the dominant deference regime within the Supreme Court. *Id.* at 1109–16. At the same time, the authors found that "no deference" was the regime most often applied and that "the primary mechanism for agency success at the Supreme Court level is neither formal lawmaking delegation nor *Chevron* deference, but some combination of institutional acquiescence and statutory subject matter." *Id.* at 1100.

In fact, the particulars of the deference regime may not matter so much. Eskridge and Baer report that when the Court applies the *Chevron* framework, the agency wins 76.2% of the time, a very high agreement rate. But the agency win rate is also as high and sometimes higher when the Court invokes other deference regimes like *Skidmore* or *Curtiss-Wright*'s super-strong deference for national security decisions. *Id.* at 1100.

In the lower courts post-*Mead*, according to Kristin Hickman and Matthew Krueger, judges are not only frequently applying *Skidmore,* but they are also agreeing with agency interpretations in a majority of the *Skidmore* cases decided. See Kristin E. Hickman & Matthew D. Krueger, *In Search of the Modern* Skidmore *Standard*, 107 Colum. L. Rev. 1235 (2007). For environmental cases, Professor Revesz found that one does not see nearly as much ideological voting in deference cases in the District of Columbia Circuit Court of Appeals as in the Supreme Court so long as the three-judge panel has at least one judge from another party—in other words, *Chevron* may be doing more "real work" in those cases than it does at the Supreme Court. See Richard L. Revesz, *Environmental Regulation, Ideology, and the D.C. Circuit,* 77 Va. L. Rev. 1717 (1997). This finding raises the intriguing (and likely) possibility that the canons we have studied operate differently depending on the kind of court doing the interpreting. More research on lower court statutory interpretation would surely illuminate this terrain.

Finally, there is also some anecdotal, and in our view cogent, evidence that agencies themselves have internalized *Chevron* as freeing them up to make more decisions on policy or political ground. See E. Donald Elliott, Chevron *Matters: How the* Chevron *Doctrine Redefined the Roles of Congress, Courts, and Agencies in Environmental Law,* 16 Vill. Envtl. L.J. 1, 11–12 (2005).

Chevron and Mead in Congress: *Chevron* and *Mead* both have found their most common justifications in congressional intent. As we have discussed, however, *Chevron* was based on a generalized concept of intent—the assumption that when statutes don't answer a problem, Congress wants the agency to make the call. *Mead* refocused the deference inquiry and shows a Court in search of a "real" signal from Congress. *Mead* sent the message that we shall no longer make that generalized assumption about intent unless Congress gives agencies the power to interpret statutes with the force of law. So understood, *Mead* is a far more empirically ("real world") grounded test. But surprisingly, the empirical basis of *Mead* (or *Chevron*) was not tested by the Court or commentators for many years—despite the fact that how Congress works is ostensibly the linchpin.

In 2011–12, the Gluck-Bressman project surveyed 137 committee counsels in Congress about their knowledge and use of most important canons of statutory interpretation, including the deference regimes. See Abbe R. Gluck & Lisa Schultz Bressman, *Statutory Interpretation from the Inside: An Empirical Study of Congressional Drafting, Delegation, and the Canons: Part I*, 65 Stan. L. Rev. 901 (2013), and *Part II*, 66 Stan L. Rev. 725 (2014). The following findings are most relevant to our current discussion:

Signals of Delegation. Chevron was widely known to the Gluck & Bressman legislative drafters—82% knew of it, making it the best-known canon of all of the textual and substantive canons about which the authors inquired. But many of the counsels also told the authors that *Chevron* was both too broad and too narrow. Not every instance of statutory ambiguity indicates an intent to delegate; indeed more than 60% of the counsels validated the idea of the Major Questions Rule—that drafters do not intend to delegate big economic, policy or political question to agencies, even where statutes are ambiguous. In this sense, the Court seems right to have walked *Chevron* back through its Major Questions Rule, *Mead*, and other efforts to tailor deference. At the same time, the Gluck-Bressman study revealed that drafters use a lot of *other* signals of delegation—and ones the Court has not considered in its tailoring efforts. For example, many respondents pointed to statements in legislative history as relevant signals of congressional intent to delegate. The Court, however, fights over whether to use legislative history in *Chevron* Step One—to determine whether text is clear—but does not look in the legislative history itself to see whether there are any clues (like congressional directives to agencies) of congressional intent to delegate.

Step One and Traditional Tools. Chevron's canon-heavy reliance on the "traditional tools of statutory construction" also comes into tension with some of the Gluck-Bressman findings. Gluck and Bressman found that many congressional drafters do not know or use—and sometimes know but consciously reject—popular canons of interpretation, including the rule against superfluities, clear statement rules about federalism, presumptions of consistent usage and many others. *Chevron* assumes that Congress makes its intent to delegate evident through statutory clarity, and additionally instructs courts to use the canons of construction to determine whether statutory clarity exists. Does this test make sense if congressional drafters do not know the canons and do not draft with them in mind? If congressional drafters do not use the canons to clarify statutory meaning, how can *Chevron's* "traditional tools test" really be justified on the basis of effectuating congressional intent?

Mead *as a Decent Approximation.* The Gluck-Bressman study also contains two big revelations relevant to *Mead.* *Mead* has been explicitly justified on the ground that it better approximates congressional intent than *Chevron* does; that justification has been used to defend *Mead* as worth the additional doctrinal complexity that it imposes. As such, whether *Mead* lives up to that billing in the real world should really matter. Almost none of the congressional counsels whom Gluck and Bressman interviewed had heard of *Mead* by name. Thus, this does not appear to be a situation in which the Court and Congress are in any kind of interpretive dialogue, one in which the Court creates a new deference regime and transmits that regime to Congress, which then reacts accordingly. At the same time, *Mead*'s underlying assumption—that when drafters give agencies lawmaking authority they are signaling something about the agency's delegated interpretive authority— was overwhelmingly validated by 88% of the Gluck and Bressman respondents. Compare this to *Chevron*, which was better known but not as well supported. Which is more important? That Congress knows the rules or that the Court does a decent job, even if Congress remains in the dark, of approximating how Congress works?

2.   AGENCY DEFERENCE AND *STARE DECISIS*

In this section, we explore the relationship between agency statutory interpretation and *stare decisis.* When, if ever, should the Supreme Court allow agencies to alter rules that have been upheld by a precedent of the Court?

One touted benefit of *Chevron* over *Skidmore* is that *Chevron* provides space for agencies to change their positions. Justice Scalia's dissent in *Mead* laments that *Mead* will increase the *Skidmore*-type rigidity imposed by courts on the administrative process. Can you see why? Recall his explanation:

> [T]he majority's approach will lead to the ossification of large portions of our statutory law. Where *Chevron* applies, statutory ambiguities remain ambiguities subject to the agency's ongoing clarification. They create a space, so to speak, for the exercise of continuing agency discretion. As *Chevron* itself held, the Environmental Protection Agency can interpret "stationary source" to mean a single smokestack, can later replace that interpretation with the "bubble concept" embracing an entire plant, and if that proves undesirable can return again to the original interpretation. For the indeterminately large number of statutes taken out of *Chevron* by today's decision, however, ambiguity (and hence flexibility) will cease with the first judicial resolution. *Skidmore* deference gives the agency's current position some vague and uncertain amount of respect, but it does not, like *Chevron, leave* the matter within the control of the

Executive Branch for the future. Once the court has spoken, it becomes *unlawful* for the agency to take a contradictory position; the statute now *says* what the court has prescribed. * * *

One might respond that such ossification would not result if the agency were simply to readopt its interpretation, after a court reviewing it under *Skidmore* had rejected it, by repromulgating it through one of the *Chevron*-eligible procedural formats approved by the Court today. Approving this procedure would be a landmark abdication of judicial power. * * * I know of no case, in the entire history of the federal courts, in which we have allowed a judicial interpretation of a statute to be set aside by an agency—or have allowed a lower court to render an interpretation of a statute subject to correction by an agency * * * There is, in short, no way to avoid the ossification of federal law that today's opinion sets in motion. What a court says is the law after according *Skidmore* deference will be the law forever, beyond the power of the agency to change even through rulemaking.

Justice Scalia's argument turns on the important difference, from a "who controls the interpretation" perspective, between *Skidmore* and *Chevron*. *Chevron* transfers interpretive power to federal agencies; *Skidmore* does not. *Skidmore* leaves that power with courts, but counsels courts to take the agency's view into account. Think about what this tells us about *stare decisis* in this context. Recall the baseball antitrust case, *Flood v. Kuhn* (Chapter 3, § 2). The Court held there that judicial statutory interpretations get super-strong *stare decisis*. Putting *Flood* together with *Skidmore*, Justice Scalia's argument becomes clear. If *Mead* results in more cases being taken out of *Chevron* territory, it puts more cases into the world of *Skidmore* and so back into the hands of courts to interpret. Because those interpretations, per cases like *Flood*, receive super-strong *stare decisis*, one effect of *Mead* is to make the interpretive terrain less flexible, since more interpretation will now be controlled by courts.

Justice Scalia then asks: What happens if a Court reviews an agency interpretation, denies it *Chevron* deference under *Mead*, and so applies *Skidmore*—only to have the agency then go back and "re-do" its interpretation using the proper (e.g., notice-and-comment) procedures? Could that agency interpretation *then* get *Chevron* deference the next time around, now that it has used proper process—even if a court has already interpreted the statute? Justice Scalia thinks not ("I know of no case in the entire history of the federal courts, in which we have allowed a judicial interpretation of a statute to be set aside by an agency.") Justice Souter's opinion for the majority in *Mead* doesn't take on this argument.

Can you think of a counterargument to Justice Scalia? Brainstorm about this and decide for yourself before reading the next case.

NATIONAL CABLE & TELECOMMUNICATIONS ASSOCIATION V. BRAND X INTERNET SERVICES ET AL.
545 U.S. 967, 125 S.Ct. 2688, 162 L.Ed.2d 820 (2005).

JUSTICE THOMAS delivered the opinion of the Court.

Title II of the Communications Act of 1934 subjects all providers of "telecommunications servic[e]" to mandatory common-carrier regulation. In the order under review, the Federal Communications Commission concluded that cable companies that sell broadband Internet service do not provide "telecommunications servic[e]" as the Communications Act defines that term, and hence are exempt from mandatory common-carrier regulation under Title II. We must decide whether that conclusion is a lawful construction of the Communications Act under *Chevron*, and the Administrative Procedure Act, 5 U.S.C. § 551 *et seq*. We hold that it is. * * *

[II] At issue in these cases is the proper regulatory classification under the Communications Act of broadband cable Internet service. The Act, as amended by the Telecommunications Act of 1996, 110 Stat. 56, defines two categories of regulated entities relevant to these cases: telecommunications carriers and information-service providers. The Act regulates telecommunications carriers, but not information-service providers, as common carriers.

These two statutory classifications originated in the late 1970's, as the Commission developed rules to regulate data-processing services offered over telephone wires. That regime, the *Computer II* rules, distinguished between "basic" service (like telephone service) and "enhanced" service (computer-processing service offered over telephone lines). Basic service was subject to common-carrier regulation.

* * * By contrast to basic service, the Commission decided not to subject providers of enhanced service, even enhanced service offered via transmission wires, to Title II common-carrier regulation. The Commission explained that it was unwise to subject enhanced service to common-carrier regulation given the "fast-moving, competitive market" in which they were offered.

[Under the] 1996 [Telecommunications] Act * * * "Telecommunications service"—the analog to basic service—is "the offering of telecommunications for a fee directly to the public * * * regardless of the facilities used." 47 U.S.C. § 153(46). And "information service"—the analog to enhanced service—is "the offering of a capability for generating, acquiring, storing, transforming, processing, retrieving,

utilizing, or making available information via telecommunications* * * "
§ 153(20).

In September 2000, the Commission initiated a rulemaking
proceeding to, among other things, apply these classifications to cable
companies that offer broadband Internet service directly to consumers. In
March 2002, that rulemaking culminated in the *Declaratory Ruling* under
review in these cases. In the *Declaratory Ruling,* the Commission
concluded that broadband Internet service provided by cable companies is
an "information service" but not a "telecommunications service" under the
Act, and therefore not subject to mandatory Title II common carrier
regulation.

Numerous parties petitioned for judicial review, challenging the
Commission's conclusion that cable modem service was not
telecommunications service. By judicial lottery, the Court of Appeals for
the Ninth Circuit was selected as the venue for the challenge.

The Court of Appeals granted the petitions in part, vacated the
Declaratory Ruling in part, and remanded to the Commission for further
proceedings. Rather than analyzing the permissibility of that construction
under the deferential framework of *Chevron,* however, the Court of
Appeals grounded its holding in the *stare decisis* effect of *AT & T Corp. v.
Portland,* 216 F.3d 871 (C.A.9 2000). *Portland* held that cable modem
service was a "telecommunications service," though the court in that case
was not reviewing an administrative proceeding and the Commission was
not a party to the case. Nevertheless, *Portland's* holding, the Court of
Appeals reasoned, overrode the contrary interpretation reached by the
Commission.

[III] We first consider whether we should apply *Chevron's* framework
to the Commission's interpretation of the term "telecommunications
service." We conclude that we should. We also conclude that the Court of
Appeals should have done the same, instead of following the contrary
construction it adopted in *Portland.*

[III.A] The *Chevron* framework governs our review of the
Commission's construction. Congress has delegated to the Commission
the authority to "execute and enforce" the Communications Act, § 151,
and to "prescribe such rules and regulations as may be necessary in the
public interest to carry out the provisions" of the Act. *See Mead.*

Some of the respondents dispute this conclusion, on the ground that
the Commission's interpretation is inconsistent with its past practice. We
reject this argument. Agency inconsistency is not a basis for declining to
the agency's interpretation under the *Chevron* framework. Unexplained
inconsistency is, at most, a reason for holding an interpretation to be an
arbitrary and capricious change from agency practice under the
Administrative Procedure Act. See [*State Farm*]. For if the agency

adequately explains the reasons for a reversal of policy, change is not invalidating, since the whole point of *Chevron* is to leave the discretion provided by the ambiguities of a statute with the implementing agency. An initial agency interpretation is not instantly carved in stone. On the contrary, the agency * * * must consider varying interpretations and the wisdom of its policy on a continuing basis, for example, in response to changed factual circumstances, or a change in administrations.

[III.B]   The Court of Appeals declined to apply *Chevron* because it thought the Commission's interpretation of the Communications Act foreclosed by the conflicting construction of the Act it had adopted in *Portland*. It based that holding on the assumption that *Portland's* construction overrode the Commission's, regardless of whether *Portland* had held the statute to be unambiguous. That reasoning was incorrect.

A court's prior judicial construction of a statute trumps an agency construction otherwise entitled to *Chevron* deference only if the prior court decision holds that its construction follows from the unambiguous terms of the statute and thus leaves no room for agency discretion. This principle follows from *Chevron* itself. *Chevron* established a presumption that Congress, when it left ambiguity in a statute meant for implementation by an agency, understood that the ambiguity would be resolved, first and foremost, by the agency, and desired the agency (rather than the courts) to possess whatever degree of discretion the ambiguity allows. * * * Yet allowing a judicial precedent to foreclose an agency from interpreting an ambiguous statute, as the Court of Appeals assumed it could, would allow a court's interpretation to override an agency's. *Chevron's* premise is that it is for agencies, not courts, to fill statutory gaps. The better rule is to hold judicial interpretations contained in precedents to the same demanding *Chevron* step one standard that applies if the court is reviewing the agency's construction on a blank slate: Only a judicial precedent holding that the statute unambiguously forecloses the agency's interpretation, and therefore contains no gap for the agency to fill, displaces a conflicting agency construction.

A contrary rule would produce anomalous results. It would mean that whether an agency's interpretation of an ambiguous statute is entitled to *Chevron* deference would turn on the order in which the interpretations issue: If the court's construction came first, its construction would prevail, whereas if the agency's came first, the agency's construction would command *Chevron* deference. Yet whether Congress has delegated to an agency the authority to interpret a statute does not depend on the order in which the judicial and administrative constructions occur. The Court of Appeals' rule, moreover, would "lead to the ossification of large portions of our statutory law," *Mead* (Scalia, J., dissenting), by precluding agencies from revising unwise judicial constructions of ambiguous statutes. Neither *Chevron* nor the doctrine of *stare decisis* requires these haphazard results.

The dissent answers that allowing an agency to override what a court believes to be the best interpretation of a statute makes "judicial decisions subject to reversal by executive officers." It does not. Since *Chevron* teaches that a court's opinion as to the best reading of an ambiguous statute an agency is charged with administering is not authoritative, the agency's decision to construe that statute differently from a court does not say that the court's holding was legally wrong. Instead, the agency may, consistent with the court's holding, choose a different construction, since the agency remains the authoritative interpreter (within the limits of reason) of such statutes.

[In Part IV, the Court applies *Chevron,* finds the statute ambiguous, and therefore upholds the Commission's construction of the definition of "telecommunications service."]

JUSTICE STEVENS, concurring.

While I join the Court's opinion in full, I add this caveat concerning Part III–B, which correctly explains why a court of appeals' interpretation of an ambiguous provision in a regulatory statute does not foreclose a contrary reading by the agency. That explanation would not necessarily be applicable to a decision by this Court that would presumably remove any pre-existing ambiguity.

[We omit the concurring opinion of JUSTICE BREYER.]

JUSTICE SCALIA, with whom JUSTICE SOUTER AND JUSTICE GINSBURG join as to Part I, dissenting.

[In Part I, the dissent disputes that the statute is ambiguous and would affirm the Ninth Circuit on those grounds alone. Justice Scalia speaks for all three dissenters in Part I, but only for himself in the remainder of the opinion.]

[II] In Part III–B of its opinion, the Court continues the administrative-law improvisation project it began four years ago in *United States v. Mead Corp.*, to the extent it set forth a comprehensible rule. *Mead* drastically limited the categories of agency action that would qualify for deference under *Chevron.*

This meant that many more issues appropriate for agency determination would reach the courts without benefit of an agency position entitled to *Chevron* deference, requiring the courts to rule on these issues de novo. As I pointed out in dissent, this in turn meant (under the law as it was understood until today) that many statutory ambiguities that might be resolved in varying fashions by successive agency administrations would be resolved finally, conclusively, and forever, by federal judges—producing an "ossification of large portions of our statutory law." The Court today moves to solve this problem of its own creation by inventing yet another breathtaking novelty: judicial decisions subject to reversal by executive officers.

This is not only bizarre. It is probably unconstitutional. Article III courts do not sit to render decisions that can be reversed or ignored by executive officers.

NOTES AND QUESTIONS ON BRAND X

1.   Brand X *and Congressional Intent/Ambiguity as the Linchpin of Deference. Brand X* may seem jarring at first glance. Can you recall another area in which federal appellate legal interpretation gets displaced by the interpretations of other (non-Supreme Court) actors? Justice Scalia claims this is unconstitutional. For an interesting counter-argument, see Kenneth Bamberger, *Provisional Precedent: Protecting Flexibility in Administrative Policymaking*, 77 N.Y.U. L. Rev. 1272 (2002), and Strauss, *"Deference" is too Confusing*, 112 Colum. L. Rev. at 1147–48. These authors suggest a parallel that Justice Scalia missed: federal judicial interpretations of state law likewise are displaceable by other actors under the *Erie* doctrine. See Erie R. Co. v. Tompkins, 64 U.S. 304 (1938). (For *Erie* displacement, of course, the other actors are state courts, not administrative agencies.)

Isn't Justice Thomas faithful to the basic assumption underlying *Chevron*? If you buy into *Chevron*'s assumption that statutory ambiguity signals congressional intent to delegate to agencies, why should a "race to the courthouse" affect that delegation? Should litigants be permitted to hurry up and file suit before the agency finalizes its interpretation in order to have the court decide the issue first and so avoid the consequences of the agency rule?

2.   *How Exactly Does* Brand X *Work? Brand X* does not hold that *any* agency interpretation can displace a pre-existing judicial interpretation. The test is whether the question would have been *Chevron*-worthy in the first place, i.e., if it had never initially been interpreted by the federal appellate court. Thus, a judge must engage in something like imaginative reconstruction: "Had I received this statutory interpretation question with a relevant agency rule before I had interpreted the case myself, would I have deferred to the agency?" If so, *Chevron* applies now and displaces the earlier judicially-interpreted precedent. This process requires several tricky steps. First, as we just outlined, the judge must determine if the statute is sufficiently ambiguous to create a *Chevron*-worthy interpretive space—that process, always remember, involves reading the statute and applying the traditional tools of statutory interpretation as *Chevron* requires. Second, you can't forget *Mead*. Even if the statute does create the *Chevron* space (i.e., if the judge concludes, "Yes! Had I gotten the case first with an agency interpretation I would have found the statute sufficiently ambiguous to trigger the *Chevron* two step"), the judge must ask if the *way* in which the agency issued its rule is still *Chevron*-worthy under *Mead*. Did Congress

delegate the agency lawmaking power and did the agency use it here? If the agency, say, merely posts its interpretation on its website, the interpretation will fail *Mead*, and hence not merit *Chevron*, and therefore not displace the prior judicial interpretation, even if the statute is ambiguous. Third, assuming the statute is ambiguous and the agency interpretation was promulgated sufficiently formally for *Mead* purposes, you still need to do *Chevron* Step Two; that is, confirm the agency's interpretation is reasonable. If your head is spinning, you've probably got it right.

3.   Brand X *and the Supreme Court. Brand X* involved a decision by the Ninth Circuit, not the Supreme Court. Justice Stevens concurred specially in *Brand X* to suggest that there might be a difference when a previous statutory interpretation by the Supreme Court is involved. Consider how you would rule on that question, and why, before tackling the next problem.

PROBLEM 8–5: BRAND X AND THE SUPREME COURT

Taxpayer Jones has overstated the initial value of a piece of property—his "basis," to use the tax lingo—which led him to understate his taxable gains by more than 25% when he sold it. The relevant provision of the Tax Code provides as follows:

> The Government must assess a tax deficiency against a taxpayer within 3 years after the return was filed, unless the taxpayer omits from gross income an amount properly includible therein which is in excess of 25 percent of the amount of gross income stated in the return, in which case the period extends to 6 years.

The Government missed the three-year window, but claims (through its agency, the IRS) that the six-year window applies to this case; i.e., that the statutory reference to "omitting" gains should be interpreted to include "understating" them.

In 1958, the U.S. Supreme Court had interpreted a provision of the Tax Code that had nearly identical language to the statutory provision quoted above—but the Court interpreted the language in the opposite way as the IRS wishes to do now. The 1958 Court held:

> [T]axpayer misstatements, overstating the basis in property, do not fall within the scope of the statute. We recognize the Commissioner's contrary argument for inclusion. * * * [T]he Commissioner pointed out, an overstatement of basis can diminish the "amount" of the gain just as leaving the item entirely off the return might do. But the Commissioner's argument did not fully account for the provision's language, in particular the word "omit." The key phrase says "*omits* * * * an amount.*" The word "omits" (unlike, say, "reduces" or "understates") means " '[t]o leave out or unmentioned; not to insert, include, or name.' " (quoting Webster's New International Dictionary (2d ed. 1939)). Thus, taken literally, "omit" limits the statute's scope to situations in which specific

receipts or accruals of income are *left out* of the computation of gross income; to inflate the basis, however, is not to "omit" a specific item, not even of profit.

While finding this latter interpretation of the language the "more plausibl[e]," the Court also noted that the language was "not unambiguous."

The Court then examined various pieces of legislative history, notably congressional reports, discussing the relevant statutory language. It found in those reports:

> [P]ersuasive indications that Congress clearly had in mind failures to report particular income receipts and accruals, and did not intend the [extended] limitation to apply whenever gross income was understated* * *. The history shows * * * that the Congress intended an exception to the usual three-year statute of limitations only in the restricted type of situation already described. Congress manifested no broader purpose than to give the Commissioner an additional 3 years to investigate tax returns in cases where, because of a taxpayer's omission to report some taxable item, the Commissioner is at a special disadvantage * * * [because] the return on its face provides no clue to the existence of the omitted item* * *. [W]hen, *as here* [*i.e.,* where the overstatement of basis is at issue], the understatement of a tax arises from an error in reporting an item disclosed on the face of the return the Commissioner is at no such disadvantage * * * whether the error be one affecting 'gross income' or one, such as overstated deductions, affecting other parts of the return.

In 2010, the IRS had promulgated a regulation by notice-and-comment rulemaking taking the contrary position—that "omits" includes understatements. The IRS now contends the Court should defer to its 2010 interpretation in the new case, Taxpayer Jones's case, rather than apply the 1958 Supreme Court precedent. How do you decide? Come to your own conclusion before reading on.

———————

United States v. Home Concrete & Supply, LLC
132 S.Ct. 1836 (2012).

In *Home Concrete*, the Court tackled the issue set out in the above problem—and the jury is still out on what exactly the long-term effects of this decision will be. The Court in *Home Concrete* had to decide whether *Brand X* means that a later-coming agency interpretation could still get *Chevron* deference even if the judicial interpretation it would displace came originally from the U.S. Supreme Court itself. Recall Justice Stevens's *Brand X* concurrence rejecting that possibility—but Justice Stevens was retired by the time *Home Concrete* reached the Court.

Justice Breyer's opinion for the majority reveals a Court reluctant to relinquish its own interpretive power, now that it was the Supreme Court's power on the line. Instead, the Court found a loophole: It held that since the Court's earlier 1958 interpretation was pre-*Chevron*, its conclusion that the statute was "not unambiguous" should not be understood as an ambiguity finding in the post-*Chevron*, post-*Brand X* sense. The Court stated that the 1958 precedent used the traditional tools of statutory interpretation, including text and legislative history, to ultimately resolve the ambiguity, and so *Chevron* deference would likely not have been accorded had *Chevron* existed at the time. The Court's opinion seems to add yet another layer of complexity to the *Chevron*-meets-*stare-decisis* issue: a dichotomy between what a finding of ambiguity means in pre- and post-*Chevron* cases.

"*Chevron* and later cases find in unambiguous language a clear sign that Congress did not delegate gap-filling authority to an agency; and they find in ambiguous language at least a presumptive indication that Congress did delegate that gap-filling authority. * * * As the Government points out, the Court in *Colony* [the case decided in 1958] stated that the statutory language at issue is not 'unambiguous.' But the Court decided that case nearly 30 years before it decided *Chevron*. There is no reason to believe that the linguistic ambiguity noted by Colony reflects a post-*Chevron* conclusion that Congress had delegated gap-filling power to the agency. At the same time, there is every reason to believe that the Court thought that Congress had 'directly spoken to the question at hand,' and thus left '[no] gap for the agency to fill.' *Chevron*.

"For one thing, the Court said that the taxpayer had the better side of the textual argument. For another, its examination of legislative history led it to believe that Congress had decided the question definitively, leaving no room for the agency to reach a contrary result. * * * It may be that judges today would use other methods to determine whether Congress left a gap to fill. But that is beside the point. The question is whether the Court in *Colony* concluded that the statute left such a gap. And, in our view, the opinion (written by Justice Harlan for the Court) makes clear that it did not.

"Given principles of *stare decisis,* we must follow that interpretation. And there being no gap to fill, the Government's gap-filling regulation cannot change *Colony*'s interpretation of the statute. We agree with the taxpayer that overstatements of basis, and the resulting understatement of gross income, do not trigger the extended limitations period."

Justice Kennedy (joined by Justices Ginsburg, Sotomayor, and Kagan) dissented and would have deferred to the agency per *Brand X*. **Justice Scalia** concurred in most of the majority's analysis, not because he agreed with it, but because he disagreed with *Brand X* from the start and doesn't think an agency interpretation can displace a judicial holding, period.

NOTE ON ADMINISTRATIVE OVERRIDES OF SUPREME COURT STATUTORY INTERPRETATION DECISIONS

Recall *Flood v. Kuhn* and our discussion of the super-strong presumption of correctness for statutory precedents in Chapter 3, § 2. An important reason that the Supreme Court gives extra *stare decisis* effect to its statutory interpretation precedents is that *Congress*, not the Court, ought to have the primary institutional responsibility for overriding statutory precedents. Indeed, Congress did override *Flood v. Kuhn* in the Curt Flood Act of 1998, P.L. 105–297, § 2 (1998). Ironically, right after the 1998 Curt Flood Act (and, perhaps more importantly, the impeachment of President Clinton), congressional overrides substantially dried up, plummeting from dozens of decisions overridden in each Congress to only a handful.[4] Indeed, the override capacity of Congress has gotten worse in the 2010s than it was after the Clinton impeachment; the 113th Congress (2013–14), for example, has not only produced few if any overrides, but has been one of the most unproductive legislation sessions in American history.

Does the drying up of overrides mean that the Supreme Court's worst decisions will clog public policy without relief? Not necessarily. Matthew Christiansen and William Eskridge argue that some of the slack left by fewer congressional overrides can be picked up by a process of *administrative overrides* and *workarounds*.[4] Recall *TVA v. Hill* (Chapter 4, § 3A). The Court's ruling that the Interior Department could stop a costly public works project based upon its threat to the critical habitat of an endangered species still left enforcement of the Endangered Species Act to the Department of the Interior. That enforcement authority provided the executive several ways to work around or effectively override *TVA v. Hill* had it wanted to. For example, President Carter could have issued an executive order requiring interdepartmental consultation before a "major" public project could be terminated to protect endangered species—a move that would have replicated the first congressional override of *TVA v. Hill*. See Endangered Species Act Amendments of 1978, P.L. 95–632, § 7 (1978). Or the President could have directed the Department of Interior to review the project's threat to the snail darter and to identify possibilities for saving the fish even if the dam were completed—a move that would have replicated the second congressional override of *TVA v. Hill*. See Energy and Water Development Appropriation Act, 1980, P.L. 96–69 (1979).

---

[4]   See Matthew R. Christiansen & William N. Eskridge Jr., *Congressional Overrides of Supreme Court Statutory Decisions, 1967–2011*, 92 Tex. L. Rev. 1317 (2014) (documenting this phenomenon); see also Richard L. Hasen, *End of the Dialogue? Political Polarization, the Supreme Court, and Congress*, 86 S. Cal. L. Rev. 205 (2013) (first noticing a falloff in overrides in the new millennium).

[4]   The discussion in text is adapted from Christiansen & Eskridge, *Congressional Overrides, 1967–2011*, 92 Tex. L. Rev. at 1450–58, 1476–78.

In practice, administrative overrides of *TVA v. Hill* were unnecessary because Congress stepped in to remedy the problem. But if Congress continues to refrain from overriding harmful judicial decisions, we expect that the executive branch will, and often should, step into the gap and use its delegated authority to fix those statutes. But this authority extends beyond overriding court decisions. As Justice Scalia's *Brand X* dissent demonstrated, the Communications Act and other regulatory statutes create a huge policy space for agencies to update statutes in ways that are the functional equivalent to policy-updating overrides by Congress. If the current state of congressional gridlock continues, we also expect agencies to step in to update statutes that a generation ago might have instead undergone a legislative transformation. The Supreme Court's *Brand X* decision might create a significant space for these administrative moves.

Brand X can be understood to vest the executive with formal override authority when a court upholds an agency interpretation as reasonable under *Chevron* Step Two. Subsequently, the agency (perhaps not coincidentally part of a new presidential administration) decides to change its interpretation, overriding the earlier view (whether taken by court or agency). Under *Brand X*, a court ought to allow the agency to do this, so long as the new interpretation falls within the zone of reasonableness acceptable under *Chevron* Step Two. That is a significant power.

Brand X thus has the potential to fight statutory ossification in a number of important areas. The treatment of the Internet as an information service in *Brand X* is perhaps the best example. But there are also many narrower potential overrides that could prove excellent candidates for updating. Consider a recent example. In *Astrue v. Capato,* 132 S.Ct. 2021 (2012), the Supreme Court upheld the Social Security Administration's (SSA) interpretation of the Social Security Act that precluded survivor benefits for posthumously conceived children who could not inherit under state intestacy law. The groups most adversely affected by this decision—veterans, cancer patients (two groups that frequently utilize sperm banks), and children—would appear to be sympathetic parties capable of garnering Congress's attention and securing an override. But in the absence of an override, given recent congressional hyper-gridlock, a new interpretation by the SSA that reflects the evolving norms associated with the assisted reproduction could achieve many of the policy benefits associated with overrides. Because *Capato* found the statute ambiguous and therefore deferred to the agency under *Chevron* Step Two, the SSA has the discretion under *Brand X* to override its own interpretation.

In their recent study of congressional overrides (1967–2011), Christiansen and Eskridge worry that administrative overrides lack the "legitimacy bonus" of congressional overrides. But they can come close. "An administrative override adopted through notice-and-comment rulemaking can recreate some characteristics that produce the legitimacy bounce. Notice-and-comment rulemaking possesses many of the attributes of the open, deliberative, and pluralistic process that we find so admirable for most congressional overrides.[5] Through their statement of basis and purpose, agencies administering the process identify the goals of the statute and the impact of the new rule. In this respect, they function similarly to the committee reports and hearings that Congress uses to inform the public." Christiansen & Eskridge, *Congressional Overrides, 1967-2011,* 92 Tex. L. Rev. at 1456.

"The notice-and-comment process also requires the agency to engage in a conversation with affected parties, responding to the comments and concerns that they place in the record. And the rulemaking process frequently draws in numerous supporters and opponents of the proposed rule, endowing it with a pluralistic character. Indeed, because it is so much easier to submit comments than to secure precious time before a congressional committee (especially for opponents of the override), the rulemaking may provide superior access for some of the groups that we find underrepresented in the override process—consumers, prisoners, etc. And although critics complain that notice-and-comment may not deeply affect final rules, and thus provides a forum without effect, these are problems with the legislative process as well." *Id.* at 1456-57.

Do you agree with this analysis? Are there limits to the administrative override idea? For example, the Supreme Court retains the authority to trump new agency rules, either by characterizing previous decisions as Step One (by finding the statute unambiguous, as the Court did in *Home Concrete*), or by ruling that the agency went beyond its Step Two discretion (a move the Court rarely takes). But if Congress continues to default on its responsibility to legislate, might there be pressure on the Court to "go along" with more administrative overrides or workarounds?

3. MORE COMPLEX AGENCY INTERPRETATION QUESTIONS IN THE MODERN ADMINISTRATIVE STATE

A. MULTIPLE AGENCIES AND STATE AND PRIVATE IMPLEMENTERS OF FEDERAL LAW

Federal agencies are not the only administrative game in town—not by a long stretch. Just as the "textbook" legislative process is no more (if it ever was), see Chapter 6, the simple model of a single federal agency implementing and interpreting a federal statute does not accurately capture statutory administration in the modern regulatory state.

---

[5]   The authors cite See Henry S. Richardson, *Democratic Autonomy: Public Reasoning About the Ends of Policy* (2002) (arguing that notice-and-comment rulemaking provides a mechanism whereby democracy can be reconciled with the administrative state); Mark Seidenfeld, *A Civic Republican Justification for the Bureaucratic State,* 105 Harv. L. Rev. 1511, 1559–62 (1992) (similar).

As an initial matter, Congress often writes roles into federal statutes for *multiple* federal agencies. The Dodd-Frank financial reform legislation, for example, divides authority among at least seven agencies, and more than twenty provisions divide rulemaking authority among three or more at the same time. Curtis W. Copeland, Cong. Research Serv., R41472, *Rulemaking Requirements and Authorities in the Dodd-Frank Wall Street Reform and Consumer Protection Act* 6–7 (2010); see also Jody Freeman & Jim Rossi, *Agency Coordination in Shared Regulatory Space*, 125 Harv. L. Rev. 1131 (2012). *Chevron-Mead* tells us little about how courts should decide deference questions when several agencies are involved. The Court has held that when a statute includes two agencies, but only one of them is given lawmaking authority, *Mead* dictates that only the agency with lawmaking power is eligible for *Chevron* deference. See *Martin v. Occupational Safety and Health Review Comm'n,* 499 U.S. 144 (1991). But the Court has left open the question of what happens when multiple agencies are giving rulemaking authority, as is now common.

Professor Gersen has argued that courts should err on the side of deferring to multiple agencies, on the theory that interagency competition for deference will produce better administration. Jacob E. Gersen, *Overlapping and Underlapping Jurisdiction in Administrative Law*, 2006 Sup. Ct. Rev. 201. The Court, however, has hinted that it may favor the opposite position—that a multi-agency statute should be seen as a signal that Congress intended to delegate to *no* agency at all. See Thomas W. Merrill & Kristin E. Hickman, *Chevron's Domain* 89 Geo L.J. 833, 849 (2001).

Complicating the landscape further, *non*-federal administrators increasingly play a central role in federal statutory administration. State actors figure prominently here, as Congress has given states frontline administrative roles in statutes ranging from Medicaid, to the Clean Air Act to Dodd-Frank. States must devise standards for enforcing these federal laws, just as federal agencies do in statutes that they administer. But states operate within an entirely different set of rules than federal agencies. Some states have their own versions of administrative procedure acts, but others don't. Only about a third of the states apply something like *Chevron* to state agency interpretations. Many states do not employ a deference regime and leave all statutory interpretation to *de novo* state-court judicial review, even where an agency is in the picture. See Ann Graham, Chevron *Lite: How Much Deference Should Courts Give to State Agency Interpretation?*, 68 La. L. Rev. 1105, 1109 (2008) ("Existing state models range along a continuum from express adoption of the *Chevron* doctrine to outright rejection of *Chevron's* applicability."); Zachary Hudson, Comment, *A Case for Varying Interpretive Deference at the State Level*, 119 Yale L.J. 373, 374 (2009). Nor is there anything like a "typical" delegation to state actors. Some federal statutes give states little guidance and few restrictions concerning the content of the standards states must develop to implement the federal law; other federal statutes are very detailed in their prescriptions. Some federal statutes charge state and federal agencies, acting together, to implement the statute, and sometimes the federal agency must approve of the state agency's work.

How is the *Chevron-Mead* framework supposed to work in this context? If *Chevron* really turns on congressional intent, should federal courts give state agencies *Chevron* deference when Congress clearly delegates power to states to make standards to enforce federal law? The Gluck-Bressman study of congressional drafters found some support for the idea that, at least some of the time, Congress does intend to delegate to states in the same way as to federal agencies. See Gluck & Bressman, *Statutory Interpretation from the Inside: Part I,* 65 Stan. L. Rev. at 1011. But if you believe that *Chevron* is justified on grounds other than, or in addition to, congressional intent, then some of the other bases for *Chevron* do not hold up as well in the state implementation context. Consider, for example, the democracy justification for *Chevron*. State actors are politically accountable too, but at the state, not federal, level. Hence, voters are likely to be confused about whom to blame when state implementation of federal law goes awry. Or consider the uniformity/coordination justification for *Chevron*: According deference to state interpretation of federal law is likely to increase, not decrease, the variety of interpretations of a single federal statute simply because there are 50 state agencies that must interpret it. For arguments that courts should consider deferring to state implementers in some situations, see Abbe R. Gluck, *Intrastatutory Federalism and Statutory Interpretation: State Implementation of Federal Law in Health Reform and Beyond*, 121 Yale L.J. (2011); Philip J. Weiser, Chevron, *Cooperative Federalism, and Telecommunications Reform*, 52 Vand. L. Rev. 1 (1999).

Yet more complexity is created by the increasing number of *private* entities also charged with implementing federal statutes. Private entities run government prisons, administer parts of the federal Medicare program, enforce the securities laws, run welfare programs and provide public education. See Paul Verkuil, *Outsourcing Sovereignty* (2007); Sharon Dolovich, *State Punishment and Private Prisons*, 55 Duke L.J. 537 (2005); Jody Freeman, *The Private Role in Public Governance*, 75 N.Y.U. L Rev. 545 (2000); Gillian E. Metzger, *Privatization as Delegation*, 103 Colum. L. Rev. 1367 (2003); Jon D. Michaels, *Privatization's Progeny*, 101 Geo. L.J. 1022 (2013).[6] Anne Joseph O'Connell also describes a broad

---

[6]   For other relevant literature in this mushrooming field of inquiry, see also Matthew Diller, *The Revolution in Welfare Administration*, 75 N.Y.U. L. Rev. 1121 (2000); Matthew Diller, *Form and Substance in the Privatization of Poverty Programs*, 49 UCLA L. Rev. 1739, 1749 (2001); Kevin R. Kosar, *The Quasi-Government: Hybrid Organizations with Both Government and Private Sector Legal Characteristics*, Cong. Res. Serv., Jun. 22, 2011; Martha Minow,

world of what she calls "boundary organizations," which sit on the border of public and private (like the U.S. Postal Service), or state and federal (like the National Guard), and which likewise have central roles in administering federal laws. See Anne Joseph O'Connell, *Bureaucracy at the Boundary*, 162 U. Pa. L. Rev. 801 (2014).

Private entities are not subject to the same safeguards as government agencies—either constitutional or procedural (the Fourteenth Amendment and the APA do not apply to them except in special circumstances); nor must they be transparent or accountable. Is there any room for judicial deference to the interpretations or practices by private institutions to which Congress has delegated implementational authority? Does the Court's last major nondelegation decision preclude any kind of deference because Congress cannot delegate "lawmaking" authority to private institutions? See *A.L.A. Schechter Poultry Corp. United States,* 295 U.S. 495 (1935) (overturning congressional delegation of standard-creating authority to private trade associations, with presidential approval). Can you imagine situations in which *Chevron* or *Skidmore* might apply to these private implementers of federal law? See Aaron R. Cooper, Note, *Sidestepping* Chevron*: Reframing Agency Deference for an Era of Private Governance*, 99 Geo. L.J. 1431 (2011) (advocating a *Skidmore*-like standard).

The following case (and the last case we present in this chapter) presents this complexity in all its glory. The issue in *Gonzales v. Oregon* is the fit between Oregon's physician-assisted-suicide statute and the federal Controlled Substances Act as construed by Attorney General John Ashcroft, under a statutory scheme in which another agency—HHS—also is given a role. As you read the Justices' debate, think about the ways in which the various doctrines that we have studied come together to point to the outcome the majority reaches. What role does *Mead* play? Major Questions? Federalism? The traditional tools of statutory construction? The role of multiple statutory implementers?

ALBERTO R. GONZALES V. OREGON

United States Supreme Court, 2006.
546 U.S. 243, 126 S.Ct 904, 163 L. Ed. 2d 748.

JUSTICE KENNEDY delivered the opinion of the Court.

The question before us is whether the Controlled Substances Act allows the United States Attorney General to prohibit doctors from prescribing regulated drugs for use in physician-assisted suicide,

Outsourcing Power, 46 B.C. L. Rev. 989 (2005); Jon D. Michaels, *Deputizing Homeland Security*, 88 Tex. L. Rev. 1415 (2010); David A. Super, *Privatization, Policy Paralysis, and the Poor*, 96 Cal. L. Rev. 393 (2008); Benjamin Templin, *The Government Shareholder: Regulating Public Ownership of Private Enterprise*, 62 Admin. L. Rev. 1127, 1185 (2010).

notwithstanding a state law permitting the procedure. As the Court has observed, "Americans are engaged in an earnest and profound debate about the morality, legality, and practicality of physician-assisted suicide." *Washington v. Glucksberg,* 521 U.S. 702, 735 (1997). The dispute before us is in part a product of this political and moral debate, but its resolution requires an inquiry familiar to the courts: interpreting a federal statute to determine whether executive action is authorized by, or otherwise consistent with, the enactment.

In 1994, Oregon became the first State to legalize assisted suicide when voters approved a ballot measure enacting the Oregon Death With Dignity Act (ODWDA). Ore.Rev.Stat. § 127.800 *et seq.* (2003). ODWDA * * * exempts from civil or criminal liability state-licensed physicians who, in compliance with the specific safeguards in ODWDA, dispense or prescribe a lethal dose of drugs upon the request of a terminally ill patient.

The drugs Oregon physicians prescribe under ODWDA are regulated under a federal statute, the Controlled Substances Act (CSA or Act). 84 Stat. 1242, as amended, 21 U.S.C. § 801 *et seq.* The CSA allows these particular drugs to be available only by a written prescription from a registered physician. In the ordinary course the same drugs are prescribed in smaller doses for pain alleviation.

A November 9, 2001, Interpretive Rule issued by the Attorney General addresses the implementation and enforcement of the CSA with respect to ODWDA. It determines that using controlled substances to assist suicide is not a legitimate medical practice and that dispensing or prescribing them for this purpose is unlawful under the CSA. The Interpretive Rule's validity under the CSA is the issue before us.

[I.A] We turn first to the text and structure of the CSA. Enacted in 1970 with the main objectives of combating drug abuse and controlling the legitimate and illegitimate traffic in controlled substances, the CSA creates a comprehensive, closed regulatory regime criminalizing the unauthorized manufacture, distribution, dispensing, and possession of substances classified in any of the Act's five schedules.* * * Congress classified a host of substances when it enacted the CSA, but the statute permits the Attorney General to add, remove, or reschedule substances. He may do so, however, only after making particular findings, and on scientific and medical matters he is required to accept the findings of the Secretary of Health and Human Services (Secretary). * * *

The present dispute involves controlled substances listed in Schedule II, substances generally available only pursuant to a written, nonrefillable prescription by a physician. 21 U.S.C. § 829(a). A 1971 regulation promulgated by the Attorney General requires that every prescription for a controlled substance "be issued for a legitimate medical purpose by an individual practitioner acting in the usual course of his professional practice." 21 CFR § 1306.04(a) (2005).

To prevent diversion of controlled substances with medical uses, the CSA regulates the activity of physicians. To issue lawful prescriptions of Schedule II drugs, physicians must "obtain from the Attorney General a registration issued in accordance with the rules and regulations promulgated by him." 21 U.S.C. § 822(a)(2). The Attorney General may deny, suspend, or revoke this registration if, as relevant here, the physician's registration would be "inconsistent with the public interest." § 824(a)(4); § 822(a)(2).

The CSA explicitly contemplates a role for the States in regulating controlled substances, as evidenced by its pre-emption provision.

> "No provision of this subchapter shall be construed as indicating an intent on the part of the Congress to occupy the field in which that provision operates * * * to the exclusion of any State law on the same subject matter which would otherwise be within the authority of the State, unless there is a positive conflict between that provision * * * and that State law so that the two cannot consistently stand together." § 903.* * *

[I.C]   In 1997, Members of Congress concerned about ODWDA invited the DEA to prosecute or revoke the CSA registration of Oregon physicians who assist suicide. They contended that hastening a patient's death is not legitimate medical practice, so prescribing controlled substances for that purpose violates the CSA. * * * Attorney General Reno considered the matter and concluded that the DEA could not take the proposed action because the CSA did not authorize it to "displace the states as the primary regulators of the medical profession, or to override a state's determination as to what constitutes legitimate medical practice," Letter from Attorney General Janet Reno to Sen. Orrin Hatch, on Oregon's Death with Dignity Act (June 5, 1998), Hearing 5–6. * * * In 2001, John Ashcroft was appointed Attorney General. * * * On November 9, 2001, without consulting Oregon or apparently anyone outside his Department, the Attorney General issued an Interpretive Rule announcing his intent to restrict the use of controlled substances for physician-assisted suicide. [T]he Attorney General ruled:

> "[A]ssisting suicide is not a 'legitimate medical purpose' within the meaning of 21 CFR 1306.04 (2001), and that prescribing, dispensing, or administering federally controlled substances to assist suicide violates the Controlled Substances Act * * *."

[II] * * * [A]n administrative rule may receive substantial deference if it interprets the issuing agency's own ambiguous regulation. *Auer v. Robbins.* An interpretation of an ambiguous statute may also receive substantial deference. *Chevron.* Deference in accordance with *Chevron,* however, is warranted only "when it appears that Congress delegated authority to the agency generally to make rules carrying the force of law, and that the agency interpretation claiming deference was promulgated in the exercise of that authority." *Mead.* Otherwise, the interpretation is "entitled to respect" only to the extent it has the "power to persuade." *Skidmore.*

[II.A]   The Government first argues that the Interpretive Rule is an elaboration of one of the Attorney General's own regulations, 21 CFR § 1306.04 (2005), which requires all prescriptions be issued "for a legitimate medical purpose by an individual practitioner acting in the usual course of his professional practice." As such, the Government says, the Interpretive Rule is entitled to considerable deference in accordance with *Auer.*

In our view *Auer* and the standard of deference it accords to an agency are inapplicable here. * * * In *Auer,* the underlying regulations gave specificity to a statutory scheme the Secretary was charged with enforcing and reflected the considerable experience and expertise the Department of Labor had acquired over time with respect to the complexities of the Fair Labor Standards Act. Here, on the other hand, the underlying regulation does little more than restate the terms of the statute itself. The language the Interpretive Rule addresses comes from Congress, not the Attorney General, and the near equivalence of the statute and regulation belies the Government's argument for *Auer* deference.

[II.B]   [N]either does it receive deference under *Chevron.* If a statute is ambiguous, judicial review of administrative rulemaking often demands *Chevron* deference; and the rule is judged accordingly. All would agree, we should think, that the statutory phrase "legitimate medical purpose" is a generality, susceptible to more precise definition and open to varying constructions, and thus ambiguous in the relevant sense. *Chevron* deference, however, is not accorded merely because the statute is ambiguous and an administrative official is involved. To begin with, the rule must be promulgated pursuant to authority Congress has delegated to the official. *Mead.*

The Attorney General has rulemaking power to fulfill his duties under the CSA. The specific respects in which he is authorized to make rules, however, instruct us that he is not authorized to make a rule declaring illegitimate a medical standard for care and treatment of patients that is specifically authorized under state law.

The starting point for this inquiry is, of course, the language of the delegation provision itself. * * *The CSA gives the Attorney General limited powers, to be exercised in specific ways. * * * (1) "The Attorney

General is authorized to promulgate rules and regulations and to charge reasonable fees relating to the registration and control of the manufacture, distribution, and dispensing of controlled substances and to listed chemicals," 21 U.S.C. § 821 (2000 ed., Supp. V); and (2) "The Attorney General may promulgate and enforce any rules, regulations, and procedures which he may deem necessary and appropriate for the efficient execution of his functions under this subchapter," 21 U.S.C. § 871(b). As is evident from these sections, Congress did not delegate to the Attorney General authority to carry out or effect all provisions of the CSA. Rather, he can promulgate rules relating only to "registration" and "control," and "for the efficient execution of his functions" under the statute.

Turning first to the Attorney General's authority to make regulations for the "control" of drugs, this delegation cannot sustain the Interpretive Rule's attempt to define standards of medical practice. Control is a term of art in the CSA[:] "The term 'control' means to add a drug or other substance, or immediate precursor, to a schedule under part B of this subchapter, whether by transfer from another schedule or otherwise." § 802(5).

To exercise his scheduling power, the Attorney General must follow a detailed set of procedures, including requesting a scientific and medical evaluation from the Secretary. See 21 U.S.C. §§ 811, 812 (2000 ed. and Supp. V). * * *The Interpretive Rule now under consideration does not concern the scheduling of substances and was not issued after the required procedures for rules regarding scheduling, so it cannot fall under the Attorney General's "control" authority.* * *

We turn, next, to the registration provisions of the CSA. The CSA was amended in 1984 to allow the Attorney General to deny registration to an applicant "if he determines that the issuance of such registration would be inconsistent with the public interest." 21 U.S.C. § 823(f). Registration may also be revoked or suspended by the Attorney General on the same grounds. § 824(a)(4). In determining consistency with the public interest, the Attorney General must * * * consider five factors, including: the State's recommendation; compliance with state, federal, and local laws regarding controlled substances; and public health and safety. § 823(f).

The Interpretive Rule cannot be justified under this part of the statute. It does not undertake the five-factor analysis and concerns much more than registration. Nor does the Interpretive Rule on its face purport to be an application of the registration provision in § 823(f). It is, instead, an interpretation of the substantive federal law requirements.* * * It begins by announcing that assisting suicide is not a "legitimate medical purpose" under § 1306.04, and that dispensing controlled substances to assist a suicide violates the CSA. 66 Fed. Reg. 56608. Violation is a criminal offense, and often a felony, under 21 U.S.C. § 841 (2000 ed. and Supp. II). The Interpretive Rule thus purports to declare that using controlled substances for physician-assisted suicide is a crime, an authority that goes well beyond the Attorney General's statutory power to register or deregister.* * *

By this logic, however, the Attorney General claims extraordinary authority. If the Attorney General's argument were correct, his power to deregister necessarily would include the greater power to criminalize even the actions of registered physicians, whenever they engage in conduct he deems illegitimate. This power to criminalize—unlike his power over registration, which must be exercised only after considering five express statutory factors—would be unrestrained. It would be anomalous for Congress to have so painstakingly described the Attorney General's limited authority to deregister a single physician or schedule a single drug, but to have given him, just by implication, authority to declare an entire class of activity outside "the course of professional practice," and therefore a criminal violation of the CSA.

* * * The authority desired by the Government is inconsistent with the design of the statute in other fundamental respects. The Attorney General does not have the sole delegated authority under the CSA. He must instead share it with, and in some respects defer to, the Secretary [of HHS], whose functions are likewise delineated and confined by the statute. The CSA allocates decision making powers among statutory actors so that medical judgments, if they are to be decided at the federal level and for the limited objects of the statute, are placed in the hands of the Secretary. In the scheduling context, for example, the Secretary's recommendations on scientific and medical matters bind the Attorney General. * * *

The structure of the CSA, then, conveys unwillingness to cede medical judgments to an executive official who lacks medical expertise. In interpreting statutes that divide authority, the Court has recognized: "Because historical familiarity and policymaking expertise account in the first instance for the presumption that Congress delegates interpretive lawmaking power to the agency rather than to the reviewing court, we presume here that Congress intended to invest interpretive power in the administrative actor in the best position to develop these attributes." *Martin v. Occupational Safety and Health Review Comm'n,* 499 U.S. 144 (1991) (citations omitted). This presumption works against a conclusion that the Attorney General has authority to make quintessentially medical judgments.* * *

The idea that Congress gave the Attorney General such broad and unusual authority through an implicit delegation in the CSA's registration provision is not sustainable. "Congress, we have held, does not alter the fundamental details of a regulatory scheme in vague terms or ancillary provisions—it does not, one might say, hide elephants in mouse holes." *Whitman v. American Trucking Assns., Inc.,* 531 U.S. 457 (2001); see *FDA v. Brown & Williamson Tobacco Corp.,* 529 U.S. 120, 160 (2000) ("[W]e are confident that Congress could not have intended to delegate a decision of such economic and political significance to an agency in so cryptic a fashion").

The importance of the issue of physician-assisted suicide, which has been the subject of an "earnest and profound debate" across the country, *Glucksberg,* makes the oblique form of the claimed delegation all the more suspect.* * *

* * * Since the Interpretive Rule was not promulgated pursuant to the Attorney General's authority, its interpretation of "legitimate medical purpose" does not receive *Chevron* deference. Instead, it receives deference only in accordance with *Skidmore.* * * *The deference here is tempered by the Attorney General's lack of expertise in this area and the apparent absence of any consultation with anyone outside the Department of Justice who might aid in a reasoned judgment. In any event, under *Skidmore,* we follow an agency's rule only to the extent it is persuasive,; and for the reasons given and for further reasons set out below, we do not find the Attorney General's opinion persuasive.

[III] In deciding whether the CSA can be read as prohibiting physician-assisted suicide, we look to the statute's text and design. The statute and our case law amply support the conclusion that Congress regulates medical practice insofar as it bars doctors from using their prescription-writing powers as a means to engage in illicit drug dealing and trafficking as conventionally understood. Beyond this, however, the statute manifests no intent to regulate the practice of medicine generally. The silence is understandable given the structure and limitations of federalism, which allow the States great latitude under their police powers to legislate as to the protection of the lives, limbs, health, comfort, and quiet of all persons. [quotation marks and citation omitted]. * * *

[IV] The Government, in the end, maintains that the prescription requirement delegates to a single executive officer the power to effect a radical shift of authority from the States to the Federal Government to define general standards of medical practice in every locality. The text and structure of the CSA show that Congress did not have this far-reaching intent to alter the federal-state balance and the congressional role in maintaining it.

JUSTICE SCALIA, with whom CHIEF JUSTICE ROBERTS and JUSTICE THOMAS join, dissenting. [We provide only a brief excerpt of Justice

Scalia's lengthy dissent, which engages in some very impressive textual analysis of the CSA].

The Court does not take issue with the Solicitor General's contention that no alleged procedural defect, such as the absence of notice-and-comment rulemaking before promulgation of the Directive, renders *Chevron* inapplicable here. See Reply Brief for Petitioners 4 (citing *Barnhart v. Walton*, 535 U.S. 212, 219–222 (2002); 5 U.S.C. § 553(b)(3)(A) (exempting interpretive rules from notice-and-comment rulemaking)). * * *

[I] [T]he Directive's construction of "legitimate medical purpose" is a perfectly valid agency interpretation of its own regulation; and if not that, a perfectly valid agency interpretation of the statute. No one contends that the construction is "plainly erroneous or inconsistent with the regulation," *Bowles v. Seminole Rock & Sand Co.*, 325 U.S. 410, 414 (1945), or beyond the scope of ambiguity in the statute, see *Chevron*. In fact, as explained below, the Directive provides *the most natural* interpretation of the Regulation and of the statute. The Directive thus definitively establishes that a doctor's order authorizing the dispensation of a Schedule II substance for the purpose of assisting a suicide is not a "prescription" within the meaning of § 829.

[II] Even if the Directive were entitled to no deference whatever, the most reasonable interpretation of the Regulation and of the statute would produce the same result. Virtually every relevant source of authoritative meaning confirms that the phrase "legitimate medical purpose" does not include intentionally assisting suicide. "Medicine" refers to "[t]he science and art dealing with the prevention, cure, or alleviation of disease." Webster's Second 1527. The use of the word "legitimate" connotes an *objective* standard of "medicine," and our presumption that the CSA creates a uniform federal law regulating the dispensation of controlled substances means that this objective standard must be a federal one. As recounted in detail in the memorandum for the Attorney General that is attached as an appendix to the Directive (OLC Memo), virtually every medical authority from Hippocrates to the current American Medical Association (AMA) confirms that assisting suicide has seldom or never been viewed as a form of "prevention, cure, or alleviation of disease," and (even more so) that assisting suicide is not a "legitimate" branch of that "science and art." * * *

* * * [T]he Court argues that the statute cannot fairly be read to " 'hide elephants in mouseholes' " by delegating to the Attorney General the power to determine the legitimacy of medical practices in " 'vague terms or ancillary provisions.' " * * * The Attorney General's power to issue regulations against questionable uses of controlled substances in no way alters "the fundamental details" of the CSA. * * *

Finally, respondents argue that the Attorney General must defer to state-law judgments about what constitutes legitimate medicine, on the ground that Congress must speak clearly to impose such a uniform federal standard upon the States. But no line of our clear-statement cases is applicable here. The canon of avoidance does not apply, since the Directive does not push the outer limits of Congress's commerce power, compare *Solid Waste Agency of Northern Cook Cty. v. Army Corps of Engineers,* 531 U.S. 159, 172 (2001). * * * The clear-statement rule based on the presumption against pre-emption does not apply because the Directive does not pre-empt any state law. And finally, no clear statement is required on the ground that the Directive intrudes upon an area traditionally reserved exclusively to the States, * * * because the Federal Government has pervasively regulated the dispensation of drugs for over 100 years.

[IV] * * * [E]ven if explicit delegation were required, Congress provided it in § 821, which authorizes the Attorney General to "promulgate rules and regulations * * * relating to the *registration and control* of the manufacture, distribution, and dispensing of controlled substances * * *." (Emphasis added.) * * * Third, § 821 also gives the Attorney General authority to promulgate rules and regulations "relating to the * * * control of the * * * dispensing of controlled substances." As discussed earlier, it is plain that the *ordinary* meaning of "control" must apply to § 821, so that the plain import of the provision is to grant the Attorney General rulemaking authority over all the provisions of part C of the CSA, §§ 821–830 (main ed. and Supp.2005). Registering and deregistering the practitioners who issue the prescriptions necessary for lawful dispensation of controlled substances plainly "relat[es] to the * * * control of the * * * dispensing of controlled substances." § 821 (Supp.2005). * * *

It follows from what we have said that the Attorney General's authoritative interpretations of "public interest" and "public health and safety" in § 823(f) are subject to *Chevron* deference. * * * [I]n fact, the condemnation of assisted suicide by 50 American jurisdictions supports the Attorney General's view. The Attorney General may therefore weigh a physician's participation in assisted suicide as a factor counseling against his registration, or in favor of deregistration, under § 823(f). * * *

[We omit the separate dissenting opinion of JUSTICE THOMAS.]

NOTES AND QUESTIONS ON GONZALES

1. *How Many Canons Can You Count? Gonzales* offers you a great opportunity to review your command of the canons we have studied in this coursebook. How many canons can you spot? Which are used most persuasively? Notice how each side plays the canons like an orchestral conductor, creating a harmony through arrangement of canons, even while

trying to disrupt the harmony created by the other side. Do the canons, as a collection of interpretive principles, create any sense of limitation on interpreters and thereby contribute to the predictability of the rule of law? Or do the sheer number and malleability of the canons create room for interpretive discretion?

2. *Gonzales as a Step Zero Case?* The *Gonzales* majority opinion does not read like a typical *Chevron* opinion. The Court wastes little time engaging the question of whether the kind of procedures the Attorney General used met the *Mead* standard. One reason the Attorney General did not use the notice-and-comment process is that he saw himself as "merely interpreting" the 1971 Department of Justice Rule. The Attorney General expected his "interpretation" to receive the generous *Auer* deference typically offered to agency interpretations of their own regulations. Additionally, Attorney General Ashcroft, himself a former senator who had petitioned Attorney General Reno to enforce the CSA against Oregon, knew that this issue would have generated a firestorm of protest, and notice-and-comment rulemaking would have slowed down the process considerably. Be that as it may, the Court made nothing of the Department's failure to employ a more deliberative process for this important directive.

What is more, and also different from the usual flow of a *Chevron* opinion, the Court even diminishes the relevance of the statute's ambiguity. (Thus the Court says: "All would agree, we should think, that the statutory phrase 'legitimate medical purpose' is a generality, susceptible to more precise definition and open to varying constructions, and thus ambiguous in the relevant sense. *Chevron* deference, however, is not accorded merely because the statute is ambiguous and an administrative official is involved.") Why did Justice Kennedy write the opinion in this way? Perhaps Justice Kennedy was trying to make a bigger point—a Step Zero point—that regardless of whether the statute is ambiguous or whether lawmaking procedures were used, the Court was simply not going to defer to the Attorney General here. The questions at issue were too important, too politically divisive and implicated too many constitutional issues for the Court to give them to a single administrator—or to *this* single administrator—absent a clearer congressional signal.

See if you can formulate this argument using the language of the canons we have studied. We see arguments in the majority opinion based on the Major Questions Rule, federalism, constitutional avoidance, perhaps even lenity. Do you?

For bonus points, see if you can reconstruct these arguments as a *Chevron* Step One analysis. Take federalism as one example. That canon provides that when there are two possible meanings of statutory language, the Court should clarify the statute by choosing the interpretation that does not intrude on traditional state functions. Here, one of those traditional functions was the power traditionally accorded to the states over health law. In the *Chevron* Step One context, that argument goes like this: using the federalism canon, we can clarify any ambiguity in the statute by presuming Congress did not intend to intrude on the states' powers over health. Thus, the statute is now clear, and we do not apply *Chevron* deference to the Attorney General's interpretation. Try the others: does application of the avoidance or lenity canons—or other "traditional tools of construction"— clarify statutory meaning and so prevent *Chevron* deference to the Attorney General's interpretation?

3. Gonzales *as a Multiple-Agencies Case.* The majority places great emphasis on the role that Congress gave to the Secretary of Health and Human Services in the Controlled Substances Act and, relatedly, on the Secretary's superior expertise when it comes to questions involving the practice of medicine. Why is this relevant? The CSA is a multi-agency statute, like those discussed in the introductory note to this section. The *Gonzales* Court does not explicitly say so, but goes pretty far toward adopting an expertise-focused test for *Chevron* deference—perhaps even *Skidmore* too—in this context: Justice Kennedy makes clear that one reason he refuses to give any weight to the Attorney General's interpretation is because there is another agency in the statute more qualified to make medical judgments. The opinion does not tell us, however, whether the Court would have accorded *Chevron* deference to HHS, although it strongly suggests that HHS's views would have been at least accorded weight under *Skidmore.*

Do you agree with the Court's emphasis on expertise? Will it always be obvious which agency is more expert? As an example, consider one provision of the 2010 health reform statute that incentivizes a new form of medical-practice collaboration that previously might have raised antitrust concerns. Affordable Care Act § 3022 (authorizing "accountable care organizations"). Many different agencies—HHS, DOJ, the FTC, the IRS and the Centers of Medicare and Medicaid Services (CMS)—have issued guidance in conjunction with the implementation of this provision. Which agency is the expert? HHS, because of its expertise in the medical arena? DOJ or the FTC, each of which has different responsibilities when it comes to antitrust enforcement? CMS or the IRS, because the program is applied only to large Medicare providers?

The Gluck-Bressman empirical study uncovered some interesting alternatives to an expertise-based approach to the multiple-agencies question. These findings bring us back to the question of the relevance of legislative reality to our interpretation doctrines and the importance of understanding how Congress works. The congressional counsels interviewed reported that Congress often signals delegation in these multiple-agency statutes in ways that may have little to do with expertise. For example, the *jurisdiction of the committee* drafting the statute matters—drafters expect the agency within their committee's jurisdiction to be the lead agency regardless of whether that agency is expert. So, if the Senate Committee on Health, Environment, Labor and Pensions drafted the relevant provision in the health reform statute discussed above, those members would expect their agency—HHS—to take the lead. In contrast, the Judiciary Committee, which has jurisdiction over DOJ, might have a different expectation if it were the

Committee leading the drafting. This stems from the importance of *agency oversight* by Congress. The lead committee wants to be able to control the statute's implementation; it can do so only if the agencies leading the implementation are under the committee's jurisdiction.

The Gluck-Bressman respondents also identified certain *linguistic signaling conventions* that drafters use to signal their intent. For example, they told the authors that the phrase "The Secretary of X, in consultation with the Secretary of Y"—a phrase the authors then found in scattered throughout the U.S. Code—signals that "X" is the lead agency. Shouldn't courts take these conventions into account if their goal is really to be faithful to Congress?

In fact, some digging into the history of the statutory provisions at issue in *Gonzales* reveals just how important these factors were even there—and that Justice Kennedy likely got it right. It turns out that the provision in question was drafted by the committee with jurisdiction over the predecessor agency to HHS. A closer look at the CSA itself reveals that Congress utilized the same special linguistic signaling convention mentioned by the Gluck-Bressman respondents. In some provisions, including the joint-authority provision quoted by the Court, the Act provides that "the Secretary of [HHS] consultation with the Attorney General" shall make a decision, indicating that HHS should take the lead.

4. *Deference in Matters of Criminal Law.* The *Gonzales* majority was troubled that Ashcroft was expansively interpreting a statute imposing serious criminal liability. Recall from Chapter 5, § 2A, that the rule of lenity theoretically requires anti-deference—presumptive rejection of the agency's interpretation—when a criminal statute is ambiguous. Indeed, Justice Scalia is one of the few Justices who seems to apply the rule of lenity with rigor and even enthusiasm—but not in *Gonzales*. Why? Apparently, Justice Scalia views the notice and nondelegation policies underlying the rule of lenity to be satisfied by an open rule promulgated by the Attorney General pursuant to congressional authorization. See also Dan Kahan, *Is* Chevron *Relevant to Federal Criminal Law?*, 110 Harv. L. Rev. 469 (1996) (arguing that criminal law should move in precisely this direction).

5. *Deference to the Agency's Interpretation of Its Own Regulations.* The Attorney General in *Gonzales* didn't just interpret the CSA. He also interpreted DOJ's own earlier, 1971 administrative rule. Justice Scalia presents a typically powerful legal analysis in defense of the Attorney General's argument for according strong deference to agency interpretations of their own ambiguous regulations under the *Seminole Rock-Auer* framework we introduced in Section A. But, as we discussed in Section A, not everyone is a fan of the *Seminole Rock-Auer* deference rule. The concern is about "agency bootstrapping": that an agency will purposefully issue an exceedingly ambiguous regulation (that might itself not have been reasonable under *Chevron*) but then issue *another* interpretation clarifying that ambiguous regulation and so ultimately gain sneaky deference for the whole

ensemble. This is probably what worried Justice Kennedy, and it has certainly worried other Justices, e.g., *Thomas Jefferson Univ.*, 512 U.S. at 525 (Thomas, J., dissenting), and commentators, e.g., John F. Manning, *Constitutional Structure and Judicial Deference to Agency Interpretations of Agency Rules*, 96 Colum. L. Rev. 612 (1996).

As noted earlier in this chapter, Justice Scalia himself, in a 2011 concurring opinion issued after *Gonzales*, indicated a new receptiveness to overruling *Seminole Rock-Auer*. See *Talk Am., Inc. v. Mich. Bell Tel. Co.*, 131 S.Ct. 2254 (2011) (Scalia, J., concurring). The Eskridge and Baer survey of 1014 Supreme Court cases identified 155 cases where an agency said it was interpreting its own prior rules—yet the Court applied *Seminole-Auer* super-deference in only 12 of those cases, a surprisingly low number, perhaps because of the same concerns. See William N. Eskridge Jr. & Lauren E. Baer, *The Continuum of Deference: Supreme Court Treatment of Agency Statutory Interpretations from* Chevron *to* Hamdan, 96 Geo. L.J. 1083, 1103–04 (2008).

6.   *Ideological Voting.* Recall that commentators have found that ideology is often a better predictor of the Justices' voting patterns in agency deference cases than doctrine. *Gonzales* helps us see this. Notice the completely different linguistic as well as normative attitudes in the majority and chief dissenting opinions. The majority repeatedly cites to *Glucksberg* (the constitutional "right to die" case) and treats aid-in-dying as a matter for serious national debate. These and other bits of textual evidence suggest that the majority understands the matter as going to the heart of a possible privacy right of persons to choose "death with dignity." It is for this *normative* reason that the majority may think that aid-in-dying is an "elephant" that Congress cannot hide in a "mousehole"—it is just too important. Consider, in addition, the federalism argument that Oregon ought to have authority to decide the question of aid in dying without federal intervention. The dissenters, in contrast, rhetorically agree with Ashcroft that this is "assisted suicide," a half step away from murder. Because the matter has long been settled by religious doctrine, state law, and national policy, this is no "elephant," but is instead a mouse hiding in the mousehole. It is for this normative reason that the dissenters believe it outrageous for the majority to treat Oregon's law as a matter for state experimentation or deviation from settled national policy.

The process by which the Justices are voting their values more than their dictionaries is, by the way, probably unconscious in many cases. Social scientists would explain this phenomenon as an example of framing effects and cognitive dissonance: the way an interpreter frames the issue drives her thinking, and indeed she will filter evidence through the lens of this frame. Philosophers would cite this as an example of how interpretation is an activity by which we come to be who we are.

B. THE NEXT FRONTIER: STATUTORY INTERPRETATION BY AGENCIES

Our discussion of judicial review of agency statutory interpretation has been rather court-centric. We have looked to the tools that judges use to determine congressional delegation and textual clarity under *Chevron*, *Mead*, and the other doctrines we have studied. But what about agencies? Do agencies read statutes in the same ways that courts do? Do they use the same canons of construction (or *any* canons of construction)? Might there be a tension inherent in the entire enterprise of judicial deference to agency interpretations if agencies interpret statutes in ways that courts never would?

Jerry L. Mashaw, *Exploring Agency Statutory Interpretation*
31 Admin. & Reg. Law News (Spring 2006).[*]

Chevron v. Natural Resources Defense Council validated agency statutory interpretation as an autonomous enterprise over two decades ago. Yet since that time virtually no one has even asked, much less answered, some simple questions about agency statutory interpretation: As a factual matter, how do agencies interpret statutes? Are there distinctive interpretive methodologies that appeal to administrators? In what contexts? With what effects? And, on the normative side, how should administrative agencies approach their interpretive task?

Constitutional Demands

In some sense the position of agencies as "faithful agents" of the legislature has a constitutional clarity that exceeds that of the judiciary. Yet the meaning of "faithful agency" is never uncomplicated. What about agencies' relationship to the President? Presidents attempt to shape administration by a host of actions both formal and informal. And given the President's constitutional responsibility to see that the laws are "faithfully executed" (executive) agencies would seem bound to follow presidential direction to the extent that it is consistent with their statutory authority.

Much judicial statutory construction is based on principles of constitutional comity that counsel courts to avoid constructions of statutes that would raise serious constitutional questions. Agencies, by contrast, have no general responsibility for constitutional review of congressional action. Indeed, were agencies intensely attentive to

---

[*]   Reprinted with permission of the author.

The text is a summary version of Jerry Mashaw's important article, *Norms, Practices and the Paradox of Deference: A Preliminary Inquiry into Agency Statutory Interpretation*, 57 Admin. L. Rev. 501 (2005), which investigates about how agencies and courts might differ in their approach to statutory interpretation.

avoiding constitutional questions when interpreting the statutes entrusted to their care, they would often foreclose authoritative resolution of constitutional questions by the judiciary. And obviously administrators who fail to pursue implementation any time a constitutional issue looms on their horizon could not possibly carry out their legislative mandates effectively. Constitutionally timid administration both compromises faithful agency and potentially usurps the role of the judiciary in harmonizing congressional power and constitutional command.

Courts repeatedly suggest that interpretation designed to lend coherence to the general legal order is one of their most important responsibilities as custodians of the rule of law. But if we believe with Hamilton that the executive branch is meant to give energy to governance, we should also believe that an agency that seeks to harmonize its actions with the whole of the legal order risks forgetting that agencies are created precisely to carry out special purpose missions. Other legal institutions have responsibilities for coherence and balance.

In recent years, much controversy about statutory interpretation has centered on the evidentiary materials that should be relevant to the judicial task. But, whatever one thinks of judicial use of non-statutory, legislative material, Peter Strauss has argued persuasively that these materials are critical to the interpretive task of agencies. Agencies have a direct relationship with Congress that gives them insights into legislative purposes and meaning that are likely to be much more sure-footed than those available to courts in episodic litigation. For a faithful agent to forget this content, to in some sense ignore its institutional memory, would be to divest itself of critical resources in carrying out congressional designs.

Post enactment politics also matters. Agencies are subjected to both presidential and legislative oversight of their implementing activity. Indeed, agencies' continuous interaction with both executive branch offices and sub-parts of Congress provides us with constitutional security concerning the political accountability of our administrative institutions. Should not all of this political context be constitutionally relevant to administrators when pondering the appropriate interpretation of their statutory mandates?

Consider finally the matter of the constitutional status of judicial precedent. A judicial interpretation ignoring prior authoritative interpretations of higher courts would be considered constitutionally illegitimate and deeply inappropriate almost anywhere. Yet, there are numerous instances where non-acquiescence in judicial constructions may be necessary for the proper exercise of an agency's constitutional mandate. Agencies often confront conflicting interpretations of their statutes by district and circuit judges. In these situations there is no consistent judicial precedent to follow. More importantly, agencies are not inferior courts. They are a part of the executive branch. A court ruling is binding on the agency in the litigated case, but as a technical legal matter, not otherwise. The agency is legally free to maintain its prior position and litigate the matter further.

Prudential Considerations

Prudential approaches to statutory interpretation seem to have three major purposes: (1) increasing the interpreter's capacity to avoid error; (2) increasing or maintaining the legitimacy of the interpreter as an interpreter; and (3) enhancing the interpreter's capacity to make its interpretations effective. All of these prudential considerations are relevant with respect to agency interpretation of statutes as well.

For example, an agency that has been heavily involved in the negotiation of statutory language, privy both to formal and informal legislative debates, and is cognizant of the multiple motives that have prompted particular legislative utterances, may feel that its capacity to avoid error in statutory interpretation is enormously advanced by its utilization of pre- and even post-enactment legislative history.

Similarly, the question when interpreting is often not just how to avoid error, but in what direction to skew errors given irresolvable interpretive uncertainty. Considerations of institutional legitimacy may, however, reverse the interpretive default rules. Courts have long been viewed as rights-protecting, institutional brakes, while executive agencies are institutional accelerators. A prudent court may say to itself: "When in doubt protect the constitutional commitment to a government of limited powers." A prudent administrator might be better advised to adopt the counsel: "When in doubt make the statutory scheme effective." Judicial legitimacy is more often called into question by activism than by avoidance. Almost the opposite might be true for administrators.

Finally, agencies may have much more reason than courts to look at interpretation from the perspective of internal bureaucratic or hierarchical control. If the Social Security Administration is going to regulate the interpretive discretion of thousands of adjudicatory personnel, it had better have some hard-edged regulatory policy. "Rulishness" may not make a statute "the best that it can be," but it guards against the best defeating the good. Obviously, courts too are influenced by needs for hierarchical control over lower court judgments. But, courts can strive for the "best" interpretation with less risk that they will thereby drive out "good." * * *

[I]t seems fair to conclude that judges and administrators interpret, indeed should interpret, within divergent normative contexts. A set of "Canons of Responsible Interpretive Practice" would look different if addressed to administrators than if addressed to judges. Table 1 suggests, in an oversimplified bi-polar fashion, how great that divergence might be.

TABLE 1   Canons for Institutionally Responsible Statutory Interpretation

		Agency	Court
1.	Follow presidential directions unless clearly outside your authority.	+	-
2.	Interpret to avoid raising constitutional questions.	-	+
3.	Use legislative history as a primary interpretive guide	+	-
4.	Interpret to give energy and breadth to all legislative programs within your jurisdiction.	+	-
5.	Engage in activist lawmaking.	+	-
6.	Respect all judicial precedent.	-	+
7.	Interpret to lend coherence to the overall legal order.	-	+
8.	Pay particular attention to the strategic parameters of interpretive efficiency.	+	-
9.	Interpret to insure hierarchical control over subordinates.	+	-
10.	Pay constant attention to your contemporary political milieu.	+	-

NOTES AND QUESTIONS ON AGENCY STATUTORY INTERPRETATION

1.   *The "Paradox of Deference."* Mashaw concludes that, in light of these institutional differences, "there may be a paradox at the heart of *Chevron* deference." He asks:

> How can a court's determination of 'ambiguity' or 'reasonableness' at *Chevron's* famous two analytical "steps" be understood as deferential when that determination emerges from the normative commitments and epistemological presumptions of 'judging' rather than 'administering'? How could *Mead's* resuscitation of *Skidmore* deference make sense as deference at all when the discourse, to be

persuasive, would presumably have to be within the terms of a judicial conversation about meaning that ignores, if not falsifies, the grounds upon which much administrative interpretive activity is appropriately and responsibly premised?

The findings of the Gluck-Bressman empirical study extend Mashaw's point. The authors found that Congress uses many contextual cues beyond the tools of statutory interpretation to talk to agencies about deference. If Congress is not talking to agencies with *Chevron*'s traditional tools; if agencies also approach interpretation differently than courts do; and if, as Mashaw argues, canons like constitutional avoidance on which courts rely in the *Chevron* analysis would be inappropriate for agencies to apply, how can *Chevron*'s two-step really be understood as deferential to agency or congressional intent?

2. *Can Textualists Apply* Chevron *if Agencies Are Purposivists?* Kevin Stack likewise argues that agencies are, and ought to be, more purposive interpreters than judges. Kevin Stack, *Interpreting Regulations*, 111 Mich. L. Rev. 355 (2012). Does this pose a problem for textualists? Agencies are widely known to be frontline consumers of legislative history—a key source they consult to understand what Congress expects of them. And yet textualists like Justice Scalia staunchly defend *Chevron*, despite the fact that the interpretations that *Chevron* protects might reflect interpretive methods and philosophies entirely at odds with his own interpretive methodology. Mashaw puts this problem more provocatively, arguing that "to be comfortable with *Chevron* deference, we need to know much more about how agency interpretation works. If the results of that inquiry make us uncomfortable, then we must either rethink *Chevron*, or find ways to structure agency interpretive practice that comport with a better informed understanding of what it means to faithfully administer the law." Mashaw, *Norms, Practices and the Paradox of Deference*, at 542; see also Peter L. Strauss, *When the Judge Is Not the Primary Official with Responsibility to Read: Agency Interpretation and the Problem of Legislative History*, 66 Chi.–Kent L. Rev. 321 (1990) (exploring agency use of legislative history).

Consider a case that was decided by the Supreme Court just as this coursebook went to press. At issue in *Utility Air Regulatory Group v. EPA*, 134 S.Ct. 2427 (2014), was the Obama EPA's first major regulation on climate change (devised after President Obama announced in the State of the Union that he would regulate rather than wait for a gridlock-mired Congress). Following *Massachusetts v. EPA*, 549 U.S. 497 (2007), in which the Court held that greenhouse gases are "air pollutants" subject to regulation under the Clean Air Act, the EPA determined that its regulation of greenhouse gas emissions from new motor vehicles triggered certain permitting requirements under the CAA for stationary sources. The problem was that the statutory threshold for the relevant permitting requirement is 100 or 250 tons per year of a particular pollutant, but greenhouse gases by their nature are emitted in far greater volumes than other pollutants. Applying the statutory threshold would have opened the permitting floodgates in ways that the agency concluded would not be cost effective; that the permitting authorities could not handle; and that would harm other aspects of the Act's implementation.

The EPA, therefore, concluded that a "literal" application of the statutory threshold would bring about "absurd results" and frustrate congressional intent. Instead, the agency issued a "tailoring rule" designed to phase-in the applicability of the permitting requirements, beginning with the largest gas emitters. The EPA recognized that the Congress that enacted the CAA likely did not foresee global warming, but that "Congress drafted the CAA in broad terms 'to confer the flexibility necessary to forestall * * * obsolescence'" and that its approach "best implements Congress's purpose in enacting the program." Brief for Resp. (quoting *Massachusetts v. EPA*, 549 U.S. at 532). The alternative to the phase-in rule, the EPA concluded, would be not to regulate the greenhouse cases at all—a result at odds with both the CAA and the holding in *Massachusetts v. EPA*. The case presented an agency utilizing *dynamic* (updating) statutory interpretation, purposivism, pragmatism, and the rule against absurdities all at once—and asking for *Chevron* deference to back it up. In the end, the EPA's tailoring rule was too much for the Court, which held—through Justice Scalia—that "[a]n agency has no power to 'tailor' legislation to bureaucratic policy goals by rewriting unambiguous statutory terms." (As discussed in our Notes to *Massachusetts v. EPA*, in Chapter 7, § 3B, a majority of the *Utility Air* Court ruled that EPA could impose its greenhouse gas regulatory regime on sources already subject to regulation. Because that covered most production of greenhouse gases, the case as a whole was a "win" for the EPA.)

3. *Does the* Chevron-Mead-Skidmore-Brand X *Framework Make Sense?* What do you think of the deference framework we have developed in this chapter? Is it sufficiently useful to justify the sometimes befuddling doctrinal complexity that it imposes? Can it adequately capture the increasingly multi-party, multi-layered terrain of federal statutory administration? By now, we hope, you realize that agencies are essential partners in the interpretation and implementation of the modern administrative state. Negotiating these relationships and bringing coherence to the doctrines that govern them is the major challenge of modern judges, lawyers, and policymakers (you!).

CHAPTER 9

ADMINISTRATIVE CONSTITUTIONALISM

∎ ∎ ∎

A central theme of these materials is the importance of administrators and agencies in the creation and elaboration of public policy. In this concluding chapter, we invite the student to "think big" about public administration. When Congress enacts landmark statutes such as the Civil Rights Act of 1964, discussed in Chapter 1, or the Affordable Care Act of 2010, legislators transform public law in deeper ways than the Supreme Court does even in its groundbreaking decisions interpreting the U.S. Constitution. But the capacity of statutes to transform public policy or, even more ambitiously, public values, depends deeply on how those statutes are implemented, usually by agencies and their officials.

We agree with scholars who maintain that fundamental governance structures, public policies, and even individual rights often owe more to *administrative constitutionalism* than to judicial enforcement of the Constitution.[1] By "administrative constitutionalism" we do not mean agencies acting alone. Rather, we mean the iterative process of law-creation and elaboration by Congress and the federal, state, and even private implementers who put statutes into action. The courts have a role to play in this story, too, but not necessarily a central one. How is that possible? Section 1 of this chapter introduces administrative constitutionalism by briefly returning to a norm familiar to you from Chapters 1 and 2, the rule against pregnancy discrimination in the

---

[1] On "administrative constitutionalism" specifically, see William N. Eskridge Jr. & John Ferejohn, *A Republic of Statutes: The New American Constitution* ch. 1 (2010); Sophia Z. Lee, *Race, Sex, and Rulemaking: Administrative Constitutionalism and the Workplace, 1960 to the Present*, 96 Va. L. Rev. 799 (2010); accord, Elizabeth C. Fisher & Ronnie Harding, *The Precautionary Principle and Administrative Constitutionalism: The Development of Frameworks for Applying the Precautionary Principle*, in Elizabeth C. Fisher et al., editors, *Implementing the Precautionary Principle: Perspectives and Prospects* (2006).

For important work exploring the constitutional innovations of executive branch officials, see Stephen M. Griffin, *American Constitutionalism: From Theory to Politics* (1996); Jill Elaine Hasday, *Fighting Women: The Military, Sex, and Extrajudicial Constitutional Change*, 93 Minn. L. Rev. 96 (2008); Ming Hsu Chen, *Governing by Guidance: Civil Rights Agencies and the Emergence of Language Rights*, 49 Harv. C.R.-C.L. L. Rev. 201 (2014); Keith E. Whittington, *Extrajudicial Constitutional Interpretation: Three Objections and Responses*, 80 N.C. L. Rev. 773 (2001).

workplace. The Supreme Court has interpreted the Constitution's Equal Protection Clause to have nothing to say about pregnancy-based discrimination, and followed that position in its early Title VII jurisprudence—leading to a statutory response and agency implementation of an anti-discrimination norm that includes pregnancy.

Section 2 of this chapter will explore, in detail, the process by which legislators and administrators secured public acceptance—what political scientists call *entrenchment*—of one of the great and transformative norms of the twentieth century: the norm, entrenched through the federal Social Security Act of 1935, that a government-imposed saving system will secure retired workers in their old age.

The final section of this chapter will explore a dramatic recent episode of administrative constitutionalism, where the President and his administration upended the sweeping and formerly bipartisan policy excluding lesbian and gay couples from civil "marriage" and the hundreds of legal rights and duties entailed by that status. Section 3 will seek to encourage the student to think about why the President would engage in such norm entrepreneurship and why he was stunningly successful. Then, the question becomes: How does his Administration implement the new Large "C" Constitutional rule that it secured from the Supreme Court?

1. SUPER-STATUTES AND ADMINISTRATIVE CONSTITUTIONALISM

Reflect for a moment on figures in American history you consider to have been great "constitutional" entrepreneurs and innovators. The list is probably dominated by judges, such as Chief Justices John Marshall and Earl Warren, with perhaps a few Presidents, such as Abraham Lincoln and Franklin Delano Roosevelt. Although neglected by law schools, many legislators were also important constitutional innovators. Among them were Senators Henry Clay, Daniel Webster, John Calhoun (who towered over the presidents of the mid-nineteenth century), as well as more modern innovators such as Senators Hubert Humphrey, Jacob Javits, Edmund Muskie, and Edward Kennedy, as well as Representatives Emanuel Celler, Henry Hyde, and Newt Gingrich.

When you reflect on the great policy innovations that form the bedrock structure of modern governance, however, many of the primary innovators and implementers of bold new public norms were administrators. Among the most important administrative constitutionalists were antitrust innovators such as Thurman Arnold and William Baxter (each an Assistant Attorney General for the Antitrust Division); Secretary of Labor Frances Perkins and Social Security Commissioner Arthur Altmeyer, important parents of social security;

Sonia Pressman Fuentes and Susan Deller Ross, EEOC officials who pioneered the notion that sex discrimination law includes pregnancy discrimination; Rachel Carson of the Fish & Wildlife Service, an inspiration for the modern environmental movement, as well as William Ruckelshaus, the first Director of the Environmental Protection Agency (EPA); and Commissioner Paul Warburg, an important architect of the Federal Reserve System and an early member of the Federal Reserve Board that he helped create.[2]

You might find it odd to consider EEOC and EPA officials to have been "constitutional" figures; unlike Chief Justice Marshall, they did not author landmark decisions considered to be authoritative understandings of the U.S. Constitution. As we shall now suggest, foundational rules and norms include but are not limited to authoritative applications of the Constitution. What we call the Large "C" Constitution is a great and foundational document—but it is a document of limited guidance or compulsion as the modern administrative state confronts important issues. The Constitution has been a success in part because it establishes a creative and workable framework for government, and articulates a set of elastic rights and liberties enjoyed by the people against the government. As interpreted by the Supreme Court, as well as by legislators and executive officials, this Constitution has been a success.

But a limited success, for the Constitution answers very few important questions we have as a society about fundamental policies regarding the family, the market, public finance, national security, even about aspects of state-federal relations. Those matters have been addressed through state constitutional consensus and (increasingly) through federal "super-statutes"—major federal laws that trump the obsolescent common law regime with a new norm or structure, that is then entrenched through a process of administrative implementation and subsequent legislative confirmation. See William N. Eskridge Jr. & John Ferejohn, *Super-Statutes*, 50 Duke L.J. 1215 (2001). Super-statutes, enacted by Congress and implemented by administrators, are able to do things that judges cannot accomplish through Large "C" Constitutional interpretation. Unlike the U.S. Constitution, which—unlike some European constitutions—provides few positive rights (there is no right in the Constitution to, e.g., a sound education or good health) super-statutes can and do address positive needs of the citizenry and provide them the affirmative security that is the fundamental duty of the state.[3]

---

[2] For an account of the constitutional contributions of the administrative innovators listed in text, see Eskridge & Ferejohn, *Republic of Statutes*.

[3] Positive security assured by an aggressive, engaged government is the *sine qua non* of the state according to Thomas Hobbes, *The Leviathan* Review and Conclusion (1651); John Locke, *A Second Treatise of Government* ¶ 147 (1689); *Federalist* No. 1 (suggesting the relevance of this Hobbes-Locke idea to the proposed Constitution).

Also unlike the Constitution, super-statutes can and do target private as well as public threats to people's security. Super-statutes can and do mobilize public funds, programs, rules and even the diversity of the 50 states in a coordinated effort to attack the multiple sources of problems faced by modern citizens. Whereas, for example, the Constitution draws boundaries between state and federal governments, super-statutes can tailor the implementation of federal rights to the needs of a particular statutory scheme. Some major federal laws are implemented by the federal government alone; others put states on the front lines and allow them broad leeway to design local programs to implement new federal rights. This wide reach and poli-centricity are key virtues of statutory compared with Constitutional law. In turn, these multiple layers of implementation—for example, the ways in which they mobilize state governments as well as federal governments—help to entrench those statutes, and their norms, in our legal landscape.

The Civil Rights Act of 1964, including Title VII, is a classic super-statute. Title VII replaced the common law rule of employment at will with a regime whereby employers and unions cannot make workplace decisions based upon an employee's race, national origin, color, sex, or religion. The Constitution does not reach private employers, so this was an innovation not possible under the Equal Protection Clause, for example. Title VII also created an agency, the EEOC, to implement this new regulatory regime. Chapters 2 and 7 set forth the powers, and limits, of the EEOC as an organ implementing Title VII.

To implement a super-statute robustly, the energized agency must not only find ways to enforce its rules and norms in our society, but also must "sell" the super-statutory rules and norms to society, including employers and unions who are supposed to obey them. And, not least important, the agency must figure out how the super-statutory rules and norms apply to circumstances not contemplated during the process of congressional debate and enactment. One such issue was how Title VII's rule against "discrimination because of *sex*" should apply to employer policies discriminating because of *pregnancy*. The EEOC's internal deliberations on that topic are examined and reported in Problem 1–1 of Chapter 1 and in Chapter 3, § 3's Note on the EEOC's Pregnancy Discrimination Guideline.

Recall, from Chapter 3, § 3, that two staff attorneys, Sonia Pressman and Susan Ross, were the sources of pressure upon the agency to address and to discourage workplace pregnancy discrimination. These attorneys persuaded the agency to issue the 1972 Sex Discrimination Guidelines announcing the agency's view that Title VII barred pregnancy-discriminatory workplace policies, because they were discriminations "because of sex," in violation of § 703(a) of the Act. What kinds of arguments did Pressman and Ross have in mind? Consider three different kinds of normative foundations for their view that Title VII ought to regulate pregnancy-based discrimination:

- *Title VII's Purpose.* Pressman believed Title VII's purpose was to protect women's place in the job force and to provide individual women security against discrimination because they were having families. Reflecting ERA-style liberal feminism, Ross believed that Title VII's purpose was to eliminate an arbitrary and irrational trait (sex) from workplace decisions. Although they had different conceptions of the statutory purpose, Pressman and Ross worked together on the pregnancy issue and persuaded the agency that pregnancy discrimination fell within the statute for all these reasons.

- *Constitutional Equal Protection.* Ross, in particular, believed that the EEOC's interpretation of the statute ought to be informed by the proper construction of the Equal Protection Clause, which Ross read in light of the then-pending debate over whether to add the Equal Rights Amendment to the Constitution. Even though the agency did not have to interpret the Constitution to announce its statutory interpretation, Large "C" Constitutional ideas informed the staff discussions. Soon after the EEOC's Guidelines were issued, the Supreme Court ruled in *Geduldig v. Aiello* (1973) that pregnancy-based discrimination was **not** sex discrimination for purposes of the Equal Protection Clause. Neither Ross nor Pressman agreed with this interpretation in the least.

- *Legitimacy and America's Public Norms.* At the most general level, both Pressman and Ross were influenced by their understanding of America's public needs. From their own experiences and friendship networks, they understood that many women wanted careers and that pregnancy discrimination was a structural mechanism by which employers thwarted those careers. That was both intolerable and inefficient. Because neither Ross nor Pressman was a top EEOC official, they had to persuade male decisionmakers that they were right about this. After a great deal of internal deliberation, the EEOC endorsed the norm and sought to make it operational for American businesses.

In short, administrative constitutionalism entailed agency judgments about its statutory mission, its Constitutional responsibilities, and the overall welfare of the country. As to some of these judgments, especially the second, there was a great deal of public disagreement with the EEOC's position.

The Supreme Court in *Geduldig v. Aiello,* 417 U.S. 484 (1974) (excerpted in Chapter 3, § 3), refused to Large "C" Constitutionalize the EEOC's rule and allowed California to exclude pregnancy-related disabilities from the state fund compensating employees for work lost because of disabilities. In *General Electric Co. v. Gilbert,* 429 U.S. 125 (1976) (also Chapter 3, § 3), the Court interpreted Title VII to allow employers to discriminate on the basis of an employee's pregnancy. Responding swiftly, Congress overrode *Gilbert* through the Pregnancy Discrimination Act of 1978 (PDA), a transformative statute rich in historical and practical learning about the pervasive manner in which pregnancy discrimination impedes women's abilities to advance in the workplace. That statute was aggressively implemented by the EEOC, under the leadership of its Chair, Eleanor Holmes Norton, who promulgated Pregnancy Discrimination Guidelines in 1979 (Chapter 3, § 3).

This process is typical for administrative constitutionalism. Implementing super-statutes and applying them to unforeseen problems, administrators will consider the ambitious statutory purposes, relevant Large "C" Constitutional commitments, and small "c" constitutional norms as well as strategies that will help legitimize the statute and entrench its statutory values over time. This iterative process— legislative, to administrative, and then often to courts and back again to the implementers and legislators—is the typical mechanism for the evolution of America's fundamental normative commitments.

The recent health care reform legislation offers an example from a different context, and one we return to in Section 2. President Obama's Affordable Care Act of 2010 is not yet a "super-statute"; given intense opposition and implementational problems, "ObamaCare" is far from entrenched. But there is already a story of administrative constitutionalism underway. The statute's administrators—which include HHS, CMS, DOJ, FTC, the IRS and even more federal and state agencies—already have filled in important statutory gaps that have given meaning to what the right to health care means and helped to entrench the law. Administrators have defined what are "essential health benefits" (the benefits that every insurance plan must now carry, see 45 CFR Pts. 147, 155, & 156); they have interpreted the statute's requirement of women's preventative services to include contraception (a controversial move that the Supreme Court limited somewhat with respect to closely-held religious corporations in *Burwell v. Hobby Lobby Stores, Inc.,* 134 S.Ct. 2751 (2014)), see 78 Fed. Reg. 39870–99; and, when they determined parts of the statute were not working, they made changes. As one prominent example, administrators devised a new health insurance marketplace option that did not appear in the original statute—so-called hybrid insurance marketplaces—that allows states to implement the statute with significant federal administrative assistance. See HHS General Guidance on the FFE, http://www.cms.gov/cciio/index.html. This tactic may help entrench the law by bringing more states on board.

Nevada Department of Human Resources v. William Hibbs
538 U.S. 721 (2003).

In the PDA, Congress addressed systemic discrimination against female employees because of employer concerns about pregnancy; as an amendment to Title VII, the PDA applies to state employers because Title VII was amended in 1972 to include state employers. The Supreme Court had held in *Fitzpatrick v. Bitzer*, 427 U.S. 445 (1976), that the 1972 amendment was a valid action by Congress acting under its powers to enforce § 5 of the Fourteenth Amendment, under which it has the authority to abrogate state sovereign immunity. Meanwhile, in the 1980s, feminist allies in Congress sought to expand upon the PDA, to go beyond the simple anti-discrimination mandate. Between 1986 and 1993, Congress considered legislation requiring employers to accommodate family and medical needs of employees. Because the proposal required (affirmative) accommodation and not just nondiscrimination, employers objected to its cost, and President George H.W. Bush twice vetoed it. The voters turned him out of office in 1992 (partly because of this issue), and Congress promptly enacted the legislation in 1993.

The Family and Medical Leave Act of 1993 (FMLA), Public Law No. 103–3, 107 Stat. 6 (1993), codified at 29 U.S.C. §§ 2601 *et seq.*, entitles eligible employees to take up to 12 weeks of unpaid leave per year to care to a newly born or adopted child; to care for a family member with "a serious health condition"; or to attend to the employee's own serious health condition when the condition interferes with the employee's ability to perform at work. 29 U.S.C. § 2612(a)(1). In 1997, the Court handed down a case, *City of Boerne v. Flores*, 521 U.S. 507 (1997), which put limits on how far Congress could go in exercising its authority to remedy discrimination under § 5 of the Fourteenth Amendment. *Boerne* requires "congruence and proportionality between the injury to be prevented or remedied and the means adopted to that end." *Id.* at 519. Soon the question arose whether the FMLA had met that standard and could be constitutionally applied to state employers.

The Supreme Court upheld the application of the family-leave requirement, in an opinion by **Chief Justice Rehnquist**, who had authored *Gilbert* decades earlier. In *Hibbs,* the Chief Justice concluded that Title VII had not eradicated sex discrimination and that family-leave protections were necessary to supplement Title VII's original mandate—

an argument not unlike those that had been made by Sonia Pressmen and Susan Ross years earlier.

"According to evidence that was before Congress when it enacted the FMLA, States continue to rely on invalid gender stereotypes in the employment context, specifically in the administration of leave benefits. Reliance on such stereotypes cannot justify the States' gender discrimination in this area. The long and extensive history of sex discrimination prompted us to hold that measures that differentiate on the basis of gender warrant heightened scrutiny; here, as in *Fitzpatrick,* the persistence of such unconstitutional discrimination by the States justifies Congress' passage of prophylactic § 5 legislation.

"As the FMLA's legislative record reflects, a 1990 Bureau of Labor Statistics (BLS) survey stated that 37 percent of surveyed private-sector employees were covered by maternity leave policies, while only 18 percent were covered by paternity leave policies. S. Rep. No. 103–3, pp. 14–15 (1993). The corresponding numbers from a similar BLS survey the previous year were 33 percent and 16 percent, respectively. While these data show an increase in the percentage of employees eligible for such leave, they also show a widening of the gender gap during the same period. Thus, stereotype-based beliefs about the allocation of family duties remained firmly rooted, and employers' reliance on them in establishing discriminatory leave policies remained widespread.[3] * * *

"Finally, Congress had evidence that, even where state laws and policies were not facially discriminatory, they were applied in discriminatory ways. It was aware of the 'serious problems with the discretionary nature of family leave,' because when 'the authority to grant leave and to arrange the length of that leave rests with individual supervisors,' it leaves "employees open to discretionary and possibly unequal treatment." H.R. Rep. No. 103–8, pt. 2, pp. 10–11 (1993). Testimony supported that conclusion, explaining that "[t]he lack of uniform parental and medical leave policies in the work place has created an environment where [sex] discrimination is rampant." * * *

"The impact of the discrimination targeted by the FMLA is significant. Congress determined:

Historically, denial or curtailment of women's employment opportunities has been traceable directly to the pervasive

---

[3]   While this and other material described leave policies in the private sector, a 50-state survey also before Congress demonstrated that "[t]he proportion and construction of leave policies available to public sector employees differs little from those offered private sector employees." The Parental and Medical Leave Act of 1986: Joint Hearing before the Subcommittee on Labor-Management Relations and the Subcommittee on Labor Standards of the House Committee on Education and Labor, 99th Cong., 2d Sess., 33 (1986) (hereinafter Joint Hearing) (statement of Meryl Frank, Director of the Yale Bush Center Infant Care Leave Project).

presumption that women are mothers first, and workers second. This prevailing ideology about women's roles has in turn justified discrimination against women when they are mothers or mothers-to-be. [Quoting legislative history.]

"Stereotypes about women's domestic roles are reinforced by parallel stereotypes presuming a lack of domestic responsibilities for men. Because employers continued to regard the family as the woman's domain, they often denied men similar accommodations or discouraged them from taking leave. These mutually reinforcing stereotypes created a self-fulfilling cycle of discrimination that forced women to continue to assume the role of primary family caregiver, and fostered employers' stereotypical views about women's commitment to work and their value as employees. Those perceptions, in turn, Congress reasoned, lead to subtle discrimination that may be difficult to detect on a case-by-case basis.

"We believe that Congress' chosen remedy, the family-care leave provision of the FMLA, is 'congruent and proportional to the targeted violation.' Congress had already tried unsuccessfully to address this problem through Title VII and the amendment of Title VII by the Pregnancy Discrimination Act, 42 U.S.C. § 2000e(k)." [Because Congress confronted a "difficult and intractable proble[m]," *Kimel,* where previous legislative attempts had failed, the Court ruled that legislators could adopt "prophylactic measures" in response.]

POSTSCRIPT TO HIBBS: *LIMITS TO THE FMLA MANDATE*

Nine years later, the FMLA did not fare as well in Court. In *Coleman v. Court of Appeals of Maryland,* 132 S.Ct. 1327 (2012), the state employer challenged the applicability of the FMLA's provision authorizing leave for reasons due to one's own health conditions. 29 U.S.C. § 2612(a)(1)(D). A dissenter in *Hibbs,* Justice Kennedy delivered a plurality opinion in *Coleman,* ruling that the self-care provision was not congruent and proportional to the constitutional violations found by Congress and, therefore, not a valid exercise of Congress's Fourteenth Amendment authority that could abrogate state Eleventh Amendment immunity from damages lawsuits.

"When the FMLA was enacted, 'ninety-five percent of full-time state- and local-government employees were covered by paid sick leave plans and ninety-six percent of such employees likewise enjoyed short-term disability protection.' [Bureau of Labor Statistics.] The evidence did not suggest States had facially discriminatory self-care leave policies or that they administered neutral self-care leave policies in a discriminatory way. And there is scant evidence in the legislative history of a purported stereotype harbored by employers that women take self-care leave more often than men. Congress considered evidence that 'men and women are out on medical leave approximately equally.' [House Report.] Nothing in the record shows employers formulated self-care leave policies based on a contrary view.

"Without widespread evidence of sex discrimination or sex stereotyping in the administration of sick leave, it is apparent that the congressional purpose in enacting the self-care provision is unrelated to these supposed wrongs. The legislative history of the self-care provision reveals a concern for the economic burdens on the employee and the employee's family resulting from illness-related job loss and a concern for discrimination on the basis of illness, not sex. *See, e.g.,* [Senate and House Reports.] In the findings pertinent to the self-care provision, the statute makes no reference to any distinction on the basis of sex. See 29 U.S.C. § 2601(a)(4) ('[T]here is inadequate job security for employees who have serious health conditions that prevent them from working for temporary periods'). By contrast, with regard to family care Congress invoked concerns related to gender. See § 2601(a)(5) ('[D]ue to the nature of the roles of men and women in our society, the primary responsibility for family caretaking often falls on women, and such responsibility affects the working lives of women more than it affects the working lives of men')." **Justice Ginsburg** spoke for four Justices in dissent.

NOTES AND QUESTIONS ON HIBBS

1. *Social Movements and Constitutionalism.* Putting *Hibbs* and *Coleman* together, we now have the following policy: female state employees cannot bring damages actions for violations of the FMLA when they are pregnant—but they can bring such actions to enforce the FMLA after pregnancy, if they want to take care of their offspring. This dichotomy finds a parallel in the sameness-difference debate within feminist jurisprudence. Liberal feminists such as Justice Ginsburg say that women as workers are pretty much like men, and when they are treated differently that is subject to heightened scrutiny. Reflecting this point of view, *Hibbs* emphasized the tendency of employers to consider women as family caregivers first and employees second and reasoned that women's equality depends on protecting men as well as women against discriminatory rules.

Difference feminists say that women as workers are actually different from men as workers; as a descriptive matter, women tend to be caregivers even when they are also workers, and as a normative matter the state ought to be supporting their caregiving. *Coleman* seized upon women's differences from men to rule against the application of the FMLA's self-care provision to state employers. When the Supreme Court has agreed with difference feminists, it has typically used those "real differences" to deny rights. Judicial deployment of "real differences" jurisprudence provides a potential insight into *Coleman*. The majority Justices were unwilling to view employer pregnancy policies as a matter of "discrimination," perhaps because they viewed the matter as natural rather than social; it was not discrimination to treat different things differently, and pregnancy is different from anything else and so has its own distinctive jurisprudence. In contrast, Justice Ginsburg's dissenting opinion connected pregnancy with social practices of stereotyping and, hence, viewed it as deeply connected with the anti-discrimination project. Should it make a difference that Congress, the EEOC, and the President agreed with Justice Ginsburg? Note also that Justice Kennedy wrote the dissent in *Hibbs* but the plurality opinion in *Coleman*, the latter decision handed down after Chief Justice Rehnquist and Justice O'Connor had left the Court (their successors joined the new majority in *Coleman*).

2. *Legislative Constitutionalism.* When members of Congress deliberate on important legislation, they are often engaged in an enterprise reflecting their interpretation of the Constitution. This process may be invisible, because legislators and their staffs draft their statutes within the constitutional parameters laid out by the Supreme Court—though that is difficult when the Court itself is changing the parameters. Congress thought it was constitutionally regulating pregnancy discrimination by state employers when it adopted the PDA, and the social movement supporting that statute saw matters exactly the same way—but new Supreme Court doctrine (*Boerne* and *Coleman*) has brought that into sharper question today.

The FMLA story reflects a more aggressive legislative constitutionalism, where Congress believes the Supreme Court, perhaps out of institutional caution, has been too restrictive in recognizing constitutional equality rights for religious persons and for women. Under its § 5 authority to enforce the Fourteenth Amendment, Congress has expanded upon Supreme Court doctrine. The Supreme Court has set some limits to that exercise, see *Boerne*, 521 U.S. at 519, but *Hibbs* recognized that Congress might engage in more systematic factfinding and propound prophylactic rules that will head off unconstitutional state activities that would be hard for courts to remedy.

Praising *Hibbs* in particular, Dean Post and Professor Siegel maintain that constitutionalism ought to be "policentric," with multiple institutions vesting the Constitution with meaning. See Robert C. Post & Reva B. Siegel, *Legislative Constitutionalism and Section Five Power: Policentric Interpretation of the Family and Medical Leave Act*, 112 Yale L.J. 1943 (2003). Although Post and Siegel do not go so far, why not treat landmark statutes seriously and publicly deliberated as something like constitutional "precedents," to be followed or considered by courts applying the Constitution to an issue that has received extensive legislative deliberation? E.g., *Frontiero v. Richardson,* 411 U.S. 677 (1973) (plurality opinion, drawing from congressional statutes barring sex discrimination as support for heightened constitutional scrutiny for state sex discrimination). See generally Bruce Ackerman, *We the People, Volume 3: The Civil Rights Revolution* (2014); William N. Eskridge Jr. & John Ferejohn, *A Republic of Statutes: The New American Constitution* (2010).

If legislative constitutionalism has any bite, we should see it after the PDA, which was as thorough and complete a renunciation of a line of Supreme Court cases (i.e., *Geduldig* and *Gilbert*) as this country has ever seen. And the legislative record underlying the PDA documented the many ways in which footnote 20 of *Geduldig* was a Large "C" Constitutional blunder: not only is pregnancy-based discrimination flat-out sex discrimination because it disadvantages only one sex (i.e., women) and reflects core gender stereotypes (women are mothers, not workers), but such discrimination contributes centrally to women's fewer top job opportunities, the persistence of lower salaries for women doing the same work as men, and the perpetuation of gender ghettoes.

3. *Administrative Implementation and Constitutionalism.* As suggested at the beginning of this chapter, constitutional innovation finds its incubation among administrators more than among legislators or judges. Thus, the PDA might be understood as the vindication of the EEOC's normative vision for the role of women as workers and as citizens of the country. In the progression from the EEOC's 1972 Pregnancy Discrimination Guideline, to the Supreme Court decisions in *Geduldig* and *Gilbert*, to Congress's response in the PDA, the agency's constitutional vision was grand and good while the Supreme Court's Constitutional (and statutory) vision was too timid and was not even logical, and by confirming the agency's vision, Congress was helping entrench a public value.

Note that when agencies act in cases like the FDA Tobacco Case and the EEOC Pregnancy Discrimination Case, they may be entrepreneurial in a small "c" constitutional sense: it is likely that their constitutional position gives voice to large scale, but latent, majoritarian views held throughout the nation. As we have seen, the President's agents are likely to have an incentive to act in such circumstances, since the President is responsible to a national constituency. Once this national view comes out of the closet in response to the agency's position-taking, it is then possible for Congress to act in ways that it might not be able to without the electoral information provided by agency action. Reaction to the agency in the public is key information for congressional players who support the policy, giving them a leg up inside the Congress, and also for those who oppose the policy, suggesting they might have a reason to change their views. This is an example, then, of the ways in which the branches may act to catalyze other institutions, a dynamic form of the separation of powers.

So if Congress, the President, and agencies are constitutional entrepreneurs along lines of "policentric" constitutionalism, what distinct role is left for the Supreme Court? Think about that question in connection with the new norm against discrimination because of pregnancy. For example, should *Geduldig v. Aiello* be overruled?

2. ENTRENCHMENT OF SMALL "C" CONSTITUTIONAL NORMS THROUGH ADMINISTRATIVE CONSTITUTIONALISM (SOCIAL SECURITY)

Our account of pregnancy discrimination, above and in previous chapters, illustrates the rich interaction of legislative super-statutes, administrative constitutionalism, and judicial evaluation (and sometimes pushback). Although we think that legislators and administrators did most of the normative work on this issue, judges were major players. Most public law does not operate this way. For most public law issues, judges are not major players, and for many issues judges play no role at all. Consider an old landmark statute that continues to affect the lives and aspirations of most Americans, namely, the Social Security Act of 1935.[4]

Ida May Fuller was born on a farm outside Ludlow, Vermont on September 6, 1874. She attended school in Rutland, where she was a classmate of Calvin Coolidge, who would become the nation's thirtieth President. Her own ambitions were more modest; Fuller was a schoolteacher until 1905, when she became a legal secretary, a job which she performed diligently for several decades. Like many other Americans in the early twentieth century, she worried about how she would support herself when she grew old. Fuller never married and had no children, so she could not depend on family to care for her; a niece was her closest relative. The nation fell into the Great Depression in Fuller's fifty-fifth year. Although she was fortunate to retain her job in hard times, millions of other Americans were not. On January 31, 1940, Fuller was the nation's very first recipient of social security (check number 00–000–001), and that moment changed the rest of her life and those of countless others. What follows is a brief account of the origins of the Social Security of 1935, its new norm of old-age assistance, and its gradual entrenchment.

A. THE SOCIAL SECURITY ACT OF 1935

In the nineteenth and early twentieth centuries, European countries had experimented with various approaches to the problem of security for the elderly: (1) voluntary insurance programs, usually annuities offered by the government to provide income during old age; (2) compulsory insurance programs, where the government required wage earners and

---

[4] The account in text is largely taken from Eskridge & Ferejohn, *Republic of Statutes,* Ch. 3. Permission to reprint portions of this book has been granted by the authors. See also Social Security Administration, "Historical Background and Development of Social Security: Pre-Social Security Period," available on the Social Security Administration's website, www.ssa.gov/history/ briefhistory3.html (last visited January 2014); Martha Derthick, *Policymaking for Social Security* (1979).

their employers to contribute to a fund which would make guaranteed payments upon retirement; and (3) need-based public pensions, paid out of government funds. During the Great Depression, most states adopted some form of Option (3). One state was New York, whose Governor Franklin Roosevelt opined that Option (3) was not a viable long-term solution.

Soon after Governor Roosevelt became President, he told Congress that traditional safety nets failed to provide the minimal *security* that the American people needed to live their lives. "[S]ecurity was attained in the earlier days through the interdependence of members of families upon each other and of the families within a small community up each other. The complexities of great communities and of organized industry make less real these simple means of security. * * * We are compelled to employ * * * government in order to encourage a greater security for each individual who composes it." He went on to outline three kinds of security that had been provided through traditional institutions but which now needed governmental action as well. "[T]he security of the home, the security of livelihood, and the security of social insurance—are, it seems to me, a minimum of the promise that we can offer to the American people. They constitute a right which belongs to every individual and every family willing to work." Articulated and providing for such a right "does not require the creation of new and strange values. It is rather the finding of the way once more to known, but to some degree forgotten, ideals and values. If the means and details are in some instances new, the objectives are as permanent as human nature."[5]

Hence, Roosevelt established a cabinet-level Committee on Economic Security, with an interdepartmental technical staff, charged with studying "problems relating to the economic security of individuals" and asked to report recommendations and proposals to him by the end of the year. Chaired by Secretary of Labor Frances Perkins, the committee recommended a program for old age pensions that would combine all three of the approaches followed in Europe: (3) benefits for those currently retired or soon to retire (who could not be expected to work and contribute), (2) "compulsory contributory annuities" for those who could contribute during their working lifetimes, and (1) a voluntary annuity program for those who wanted to add to their retirement pensions. The committee's ten-volume report reached FDR's desk at the beginning of January 1935. On January 17, President Roosevelt forwarded most of the report and his recommended legislation to Congress.[6]

---

[5] The quotations in the text are taken from Message from President Franklin Delano Roosevelt to Congress, "Reviewing the Broad Objectives and Accomplishments of the Administration" (June 8, 1934).

[6] The Report of the Committee on Economic Security and related documents can be accessed on the SSA's website, http://www.ssa.gov/history/reports/ces.html (visited June 30, 2014).

The President urged Congress to create a structure permanently insuring "the security of men, women and children of the Nation against certain hazards and vicissitudes of life." The executive department's proposal insisted that the program be self-financed out of payroll taxes, rather than reliant on general revenues. This was inspired less by fiscal prudence than by the notion that benefit payments, when they began, would be given as a matter of right, as people had earned them through their contributions. If contributions were put into a designated trust fund, then as long as that fund maintained sufficient funds, payouts could naturally be understood as entitlements—giving back to people what was theirs as a matter of right. To be sure, this was a *political* tactic, as the President later admitted. "We put those payroll contributions there so as to give the contributors a legal, moral, and political right to collect their pensions. * * * With those taxes in there, no damn politician can ever scrap my social security program." In order to assure that the program remained solvent, it was to be put on an actuarially sound basis by basing judgments on coverage, taxes, and benefit levels on regularly produced seventy-five year projections of program finances. This insistence, too, was part of the political strategy. Program leaders, such as Arthur Altmeyer, who had invented Wisconsin's program for old-age security before joining the Roosevelt Administration, were convinced of the importance of fiscal soundness and worked hard to establish the system's reputation for caution. But they also had an almost religious belief that social security was an insurance program and that everyone had a basic right, a kind of property right, to receive their benefit checks.

FDR's proposals were considered in extensive hearings conducted by the House Ways and Means and Senate Finance Committees.[7] In the congressional hearings, Republicans and their business allies sharply questioned the proposed programs. Former President Hoover depicted the legislation as creating "a system of regimentation and bureaucratic domination in which men and women are not masters of government but are pawns and dependents of a centralized and potentially self-perpetuating government." Some Democrats privately harbored similar objections, and the Ways and Means Committee was originally not in favor of the old-age insurance program, because social security represented big government without any immediate political payoff. President Roosevelt personally intervened to save the old-age insurance program on the ground that it was essential to the New Deal and the long-term fate of the Democratic Party that controlled Congress. The congressional committees revised the social security bill to rely on state

---

[7]   On the behind-the-scenes difficulties faced by the social security bill, especially its old-age insurance title, see Arthur J. Altmeyer, *The Formative Years of Social Security* 31–42 (1968); Edward Berkowitz & Larry DeWitt, *Conservatives and American Political Development: The Case of Social Security, 1934–1956*, in Brian J. Glenn & Steven M. Teles, editors, *Conservatism and American Political Development* (2009).

implementation of its old-age assistance and unemployment programs and to severely restrict the categories of workers covered by the old-age insurance program (agricultural and domestic workers, the self-employed, and railroad workers were excluded, with different economic and political justifications for each exclusion). But only one major program was dropped, a voluntary pension system that would have operated alongside the compulsory one for those who wanted to enhance their retirement benefits. Congress as a whole approved the committee bills by overwhelming margins.

The structure of the Social Security Act itself exemplifies both its expansive vision and its modest beginnings. Most of the Act was aimed at providing immediate relief for those who could not protect themselves from the economic maelstrom: the blind (Title X), the elderly (Title I), dependent children (Titles IV and V), and the unemployed (Title III). These were people who could not easily pick themselves up and move or find other ways to earn something to keep body and soul together. From the vantage of the present, the most significant parts of the Act were contained in Titles II and VIII, which set up the compulsory insurance scheme that we know now as "social security." It was this part of the legislation that broke new ground by creating a new program of entitlement. The other sections picked up responsibilities that the states were already shouldering to some degree. The new pension program, however, was aimed at creating a secure basis for retirement for everyone—at least eventually—and so it drew the sharpest objections from conservatives and the Chamber of Commerce.

The original program was much more modest than the one we know today, consistent with a long tradition of *incrementalism* in American politics and legislation. See Charles E. Lindblom, *The Science of "Muddling Through,"* 2 Pub. Admin. Rev. 79 (1959). The original Act provided modest benefits only for retired workers in commerce and industry; today the benefits are much more substantial and extend to the vast majority of workers, as well as family members. As in the case of other major super-statutes, including the Clean Air Act, Medicare, and Medicaid, Congress took the long-term view when it enacted the original Social Security Act. It had universal aspirations, but the first goal was to entrench the basic framework of the law and then let future agencies and Congresses expand it.

America's Large "C" Constitutional traditions posed serious challenges to the new social security entitlement enshrined in Title II. In 1854, based upon the advice of Attorney General Caleb Cushing, President Franklin Pierce had vetoed a federal charitable relief measure, on the ground that it went beyond the specific authorities granted Congress by Article I of the Constitution. President Pierce's assumption remained the conventional Constitutional wisdom for three generations.

The Civil War created an exception for military pensions, which could be justified on the basis of Article I's explicit grant of authority for Congress to set rules for the governance of the armed forces. When Congressman William Wilson introduced the first congressional bill providing for old-age pensions a generation later, he feared that a general measure would be unconstitutional and so engaged in this subterfuge: his proposed law would have created an Old Home Guard, enlisting all elderly Americans for service to their country while simultaneously pensioning them. This oddball scheme died in committee.[8]

Consistent with this history, congressional, business, and media critics of the social security bill maintained that it was at war with "the fundamental principles of our form of Government embodied in our Constitution." The National Association of Manufacturers (NAM) maintained that Congress had no authority to create either welfare or social insurance programs. The Constitutional design was to grant Congress only limited powers, so that the states would retain the primary police powers, including the powers over welfare and social programs.

Supporters vigorously defended the validity of these proposals. The Taxing Clause in Article I of the Constitution authorizes Congress "[t]o lay and collect Taxes [etc.] to . . . provide for the common Defence and general Welfare." Republicans critical of big government read "general Welfare" as a limitation on Congress's authority, to be narrowly construed in light of the Constitution's federalist structure and, especially, the Tenth Amendment (which preserves to the states powers not delegated to Congress or retained by the People). Social security supporters read "general Welfare" more broadly, to allow Congress discretion to finance programs that "protect life and make it easier and happier" for the disadvantaged in society. The Department of Justice and other lawyers advising Congress opined that its taxing power was not limited to funding programs specifically enumerated in Article I.[9] These arguments are rich examples of administrative constitutionalism, where agencies develop their own interpretation of their powers and duties under the Constitution.

But administrative and legislative constitutionalism also entailed pre-Constitutional arguments about governmental responsibilities flowing from the social contract itself. Abraham Epstein, who had worked on the social security issue most of his professional career, went further

---

[8]   U.S. Constitution, Article I, § 8 (granting Congress authority to provide for and regulate the national armed forces but no specific authority to provide for old-age pensions); Abraham Epstein, *Insecurity: A Challenge to America* ch. XXVIII (1933) (describing early federal efforts to provide for old-age pensions, including Wilson's nutty Old Home Guard proposal).

[9]   House Committee on Labor, 71st Cong., 2d Sess., *Hearings on Old Age Pensions* 127 (1930) (statement of Representative Fiorello LaGuardia, New York); accord, H.C. Gilbert, Library of Congress, Legislative Research Service, *Constitutionality of Old Age Pension Legislation* 114–18 (February 12, 1930).

than the Department of Justice: "What is the whole purpose of our Government? Is it not in order to guarantee equal rights and making possible 'the pursuit of happiness'?" (Yes.) Epstein argued that Congress was *obliged* to consider the plight of poor people when it deliberates. Because he was not a lawyer, Epstein did not announce this obligation as a Large "C" Constitutional one; indeed, his best authority for an affirmative, obligatory view of "general Welfare" was the Declaration of Independence, not the Constitution. But even as a small "c" constitutional point, it had enormous normative force, grounded upon the purposes of government, the nature of a democracy, and the features of a good and just polity. (Closely following the Government's brief, which emphasized public necessity, a virtually unanimous Supreme Court upheld Title II of the Act in *Helvering v. Davis,* 301 U.S. 619 (1937).)

Ida May Fuller would not have been impressed by the Social Security Act of August 14, 1935, ch. 531, 49 Stat. 620 (1935), codified at 42 U.S.C. § 301 *et seq.,* or by the Supreme Court opinion upholding the program. The Act's preamble contained no ringing proclamation of a new basic liberty, aimed at assuring everyone the right to a dignified old age. The Act did aim "to make more adequate provision for aged persons, blind persons, dependent and crippled children, maternal and child welfare, public health, and the administration of their unemployment compensation laws." For the most part, it was intended to provide means-tested benefits to a rather special list of vulnerable and needy people, a class claiming many Americans in 1935, but not Fuller. Social security was a measure focused on alleviating dire but temporary conditions like unemployment, or chronic conditions that had been dealt with by families or localities in the past. Moreover, the various programs were to be administered by the states rather than the federal government (upheld in *Charles C. Steward Mach. Co. v. Davis,* 301 U.S. 548 (1937)), which meant that payments would vary widely, as would administrative standards. The limited ambitions of the original social security law, therefore, barely hinted that what was being established was a new right that would ultimately be underwritten by the federal government—a small "c" constitutional right.

B. ENTRENCHING SOCIAL SECURITY, 1936–1981

Notwithstanding the lopsided vote in Congress (1935), the landslide reelection of FDR (1936), and the Supreme Court's approval (1937), the social security idea was far from entrenched. Indeed, old-age insurance was highly vulnerable in the 1930s, because workers were paying taxes into the fund but were not collecting benefits. Yet within 15 years, social security moved from being a source of intense partisan disagreement and policy uncertainty, to being an entrenched policy.

How did this entrenchment occur? The success of the idea owes much to the law's implementation by determined New Dealers. Arthur Altmeyer, who was a member of the original Social Security Board and was then the first Social Security Commissioner until 1953, said that "[a]dministration consists of more than organization, procedures and personnel. * * * Administration also consists of interpreting social legislation in such a manner that it achieves its fundamental purpose most fully." Altmeyer, *The Formative Years of Social Security* 29 (1958). Altmeyer had no doubt as to what that purpose was and said so clearly in an early dispute with the accountants from the Government Accounting Office: "We had quite a time convincing them that this was a different kind of animal—that because of contributions there were certain rights, statutory rights, that had to be recognized and achieved, and that we had an obligation." *Id.* at 31.

Altmeyer's agenda was to protect the program in its early stages, mainly by administering it in the most economical way imaginable, thereby falsifying opponents' charges that social security would be a gross waste of money. Once benefits started to flow into the accounts of retired persons, Altmeyer was confident that the program would gradually become entrenched, because the beneficiaries would view their payments as vested rights and would rely on them for their retirement planning. Generally, his strategic vision worked the way he expected, but there were many twists and turns in the road to entrenchment.

The 1935 Act required the SSA to consult regularly with advisory councils that would have representatives from business and the insurance industry, as well as from organized labor and the general public. At the behest of Senator Arthur Vandenberg, a thoughtful Republican critic of social security, Congress appointed the 1937–38 Advisory Council on Social Security to review the program and make recommendations. The SSA viewed this process with suspicion: workers such as Ida May Fuller started paying into the program in 1937, but no one would start drawing benefits until 1942, so this was a point of extreme political vulnerability for the program, and the advisory council was viewed as a last chance for conservatives to undo FDR's great vision.

Instead, the opposite occurred. After research and investigation, carefully managed by Altmeyer and the agency's staff, as well as council member Edwin Witte (one of the key New Dealers behind the Act), the advisory council's 1938 report reaffirmed the social insurance idea and recommended a significant expansion. The council's biggest recommendation was that social insurance ought to be aimed at supporting *families*, and not just individual *workers*.[10] Hence, it

---

[10] Advisory Council on Social Security, Report (December 10, 1938), available on the SSA's website, www.ssa.gov/history/reports/38advise.html (last visited January 2014); Nancy Altman, *The Battle for Social Security* (2005).

recommended expanding social security to include benefits for surviving spouses and dependents (children) of workers who would contribute to the program but not live long enough to receive retirement benefits. It also recommended that retirees start receiving social security payouts in 1940, rather than 1942 as scheduled. Although rejecting its further proposals that would have expanded social security's coverage to include farm and domestic workers, Congress followed the advisory council on these other important matters when it adopted the Social Security Act Amendments of 1939, P.L. 76-379.

The 1937–38 Advisory Council and the 1939 Amendments were major events, rivaling the enactment of the original statute. One feature of the process was that it ultimately provided a mechanism whereby the experts in the SSA had an opportunity to educate and win over doubters. Social security administrators such as Arthur Altmeyer, Robert Ball, and Wilbur Cohen were effective strategizers and advocates for the social insurance idea. They and their technocrat colleagues (such as the chief actuaries, W. Rulon Williamson and Robert Myers) had an effective monopoly on information relevant to evaluating how the program operated and how it might be prudently changed. They insisted that this gave them a special responsibility to provide technical advice to congressional staff and even to interest groups, as well as to their bureaucratic superiors and to other executive branch appointees. For this reason and because these folks really did understand the economics and demography of the program, they came to be relied on by opponents and skeptics as well as proponents of the program. Moreover, they succeeded in persuading nearly everyone that social security was so technical that their advice was indispensable if any programmatic changes were contemplated. See Martha Derthick, *Policymaking for Social Security* (1979).

So the advisory council process offered persuasive opportunities for social security experts—but what was most notable about the process was how a bipartisan representative group of relevant interests worked together and ultimately propounded a *deep compromise* that combined legitimacy and some good ideas. The 1937–38 Advisory Council on Social Security was a body reflecting the range of interests concerned with the program. Its members were leaders from the business and labor communities as well as scholars with interests and expertise in social insurance. Because of the representation of the diverse set of politically salient interests, councils of this kind have come to play an important small "c" constitutional role: they have developed recommendations that express a consensus acceptable to business and labor interests as well as to the public. Through their service on the 1937–38 Advisory Council, Marion Folsom, Eastman Kodak's treasurer, and Edward Stettinius, Jr., U.S. Steel's chairman of the board, not only brought financial savvy to the oversight process but became effective ambassadors for social security in the business community and the Republican Party.

Although not a major policy proposal, of special political import was the council's recommendation that the SSA start paying benefits in January 1940, rather than 1942 as originally legislated. This was an important event in the lives of many Americans, as reflected by the experience of Ida May Fuller, who retired from her secretarial job in November 1939, shortly after her sixty-fifth birthday and after the Social Security Act Amendments had been enacted. While running an errand in Rutland, Vermont, she dropped by the Social Security Office. "It wasn't that I was expecting anything, mind you," ventured the cautious New Englander, "but I knew I'd been paying for something called Social Security, and I wanted to ask the people in Rutland about it." To her surprise, the "people in Rutland" told her she was now eligible for benefits and helped her file the necessary paperwork. On January 31, 1940, the agency issued Fuller its first old-age benefits check (number 00–000–001), which she received the same day. The amount was $22.54, and the recipient was delighted.

Fuller's experience was the beginning of the program's political ascendancy. People liked getting their checks, and everyone getting checks in the early days was getting back much more than he or she had contributed. Ida May Fuller, for example, had contributed less than twenty dollars in the two years before her retirement, an amount smaller than the first monthly check she received; she ultimately drew $22,888.92 in benefits, a spectacular return on the most modest of investments. Knowing that micro-events like this built political capital, program administrators such as Altmeyer and Ball urged Congress that it could safely increase the benefits paid out and enlarge the pool of eligible recipients, while postponing tax increases. The result was a period of slow program growth from the time of the 1939 Amendments to the much more expansionary amendments of 1950. Given the budgetary stringency of the war years, slow programmatic growth was perhaps to be expected, and the postwar boom and inflation probably inhibited any thirst for expansion. Social security remained smaller than the means-tested welfare programs and still excluded large fractions of the workforce (especially agricultural workers).

In 1944, President Roosevelt's State of the Union Address announced a "Second Bill of Rights" for the American people. The Constitution protected none of the fundamental rights identified by the President—but the Social Security Act of 1935 was the starting point for Right Number 7, namely, the "right to adequate protection from the economic fears of old age, sickness, accident, and unemployment."[11] By 1944, program leaders

[11] The Second Bill of Rights was presented in President Franklin D. Roosevelt, Message to the Congress on the State of the Union (January 11, 1944), reprinted in 13 *The Public Papers*

had cemented fairly strong support in Congress, especially in the finance committees, but social security had not yet fulfilled the ambitious administrative vision. For that to happen, its coverage would need to become universal and Congress would have to exhibit some willingness to accept its financial burdens.

The midpoint of the twentieth century marked another pivotal point for social security. The GOP-controlled Congress created another advisory council in 1948. As before, conservative critics assumed that a fair and balanced assessment would require some curtailment of the program. As before, the advisory council was composed of representatives from the business, labor, and academic communities. As before, the council's deliberations were strongly influenced by information provided through SSA staff member Robert Ball (playing the role in 1948 that Arthur Altmeyer played in 1938). As before, the council roundly endorsed the social security old-age insurance idea, recommended that eligibility for the program be expanded (and expanded much more than the 1938 council had recommended), and also recommended that benefits be increased. Although appointed during the Republicans' control of Congress, the council delivered its report to a Congress controlled by the Democrats, basking in the wake of their triumph in the 1948 presidential and congressional elections.[12]

Congress enthusiastically followed the council's recommendations. The Social Security Act Amendments of 1950, P.L. 81-734, expanded coverage by about ten million more workers (out of the twenty-five million not previously covered).[13] Through the efforts of the administrators and a friendly Congress, social security was coming close to the universal "right" prophesied in FDR's Second Bill of Rights. Additionally, the 1950 Amendments increased benefits an average of eighty percent, to reflect the cost of living increases since 1940. Like thousands of other beneficiaries, Ida May Fuller received a big social security increase on October 3, 1950—right before the off-year elections. Rather than the

---

and Addresses of Franklin D. Roosevelt: Victory and the Threshold of Peace, 1944–45, at 41 (1950). The small "c" constitutional rights identified by the President were rights [1] "to a useful and remunerative job"; [2] "to earn enough to provide adequate food and clothing and recreation"; [3] of a farmer "to raise and sell his products at a return which will give him and his family a decent living"; [4] of a businessman "to trade in an atmosphere of freedom from unfair competition and domination by monopolies"; [5] "to a decent home"; [6] "to adequate medical care" and "good health"; [7] "to adequate protection from the economic fears of old age, sickness, accident, and unemployment"; and [8] "to a good education."

[12] 1948–49 Advisory Council on Social Security, Report (October 1948), described and reprinted in the SSA's website, www.ssa.gov/history/reports/48advisegen.html (last visited June 2014); Edward D. Berkowitz, *Robert Ball and the Politics of Social Security* (2005) (describing the key informational role played by SSA staff representative Robert Ball).

[13] For excellent analyses of the 1950 Amendments, see Altman, *Battle for Social Security*, ch. 9; Altmeyer, *Formative Years of Social Security*, 169–208; Cohen & Meyers, "The Social Security Amendments of 1950."

monthly check of $22.54 that she had been receiving since 1940, Fuller received a check for $40.53; by the expression on her face, preserved for posterity on the SSA's website, she was even more delighted than she had been in 1940.

Egged on by administrators, members of Congress realized that this kind of legislation was electoral gold. For the next two decades, every Congress enacted cost-of-living increases in social security benefits. When the Republicans regained Congress and the Presidency (with Dwight D. Eisenhower) in 1953, there was a solid bipartisan majority that not only supported the social security idea, but also supported its expansion. Hard-line, reduce-the-size-of-government opponents of social security suffered one humiliating rebuff after another, culminating in President Eisenhower's 1954 State of the Union Address reaffirming the social security idea and urging its expansion to include farm workers and state and local employees, which the GOP Congress promptly enacted as the Social Security Amendments of 1954, P.L. 83-761.[14]

By the end of the Eisenhower Administration (1953–61), the federal government had delivered programs substantially fulfilling Right Number 7 in FDR's Second Bill of Rights. Old-age insurance was available to almost all workers by 1961, every state in the union had an unemployment compensation program funded in large part under Title III of the 1935 Act, and the Social Security Act Amendments of 1956, P,L. 84-80, funded a program providing income support to Americans who were disabled from working because of sickness or accident. Right Number 6 of the Second Bill of Rights assured Americans of a "right to adequate medical care and the opportunity to achieve and enjoy good health." This has proved to be a more difficult guarantee for the legislative process to deliver.

Thus, FDR's 1934–35 Committee on Economic Stabilization considered federally funded health insurance, a proposal that was met by determined opposition from the American Medical Association (AMA). The committee's report on public health was not even submitted to Congress, because President Roosevelt decided that including health insurance would imperil the already controversial social security bill. After the adoption of the 1935 Act, however, the new Social Security

---

[14] On the Eisenhower Administration's capitulation to the social security idea, see Altmeyer, *Formative Years of Social Security,* 209–55. Congress's practice of raising social security benefits in election years was made possible by the conservative method of making the 75-year projections that Robert Myers employed. His method guaranteed that actual revenues would always exceed the forecast, so that Congress could afford to use the unanticipated surplus to raise benefits. Then, following the elections, Congress would enact another bill that increased either the taxable base or the payroll tax rate. Allegedly, Robert Ball discovered this feature of Myers's projections while serving as staff chief for the Advisory Council in 1947–8 and conveyed that information to Ways and Means Committee staff. See Nancy J. Altman & Theodore R. Marmor, *Social Security in Transition: From the Mid 1950s to the Late 1970s,* in Glenn & Teles, eds., *Conservatism and American Political Development.*

Board and other agencies gathered information and episodically published reports on public health and possible federal responses to systemic problems. In 1937, Dr. Thomas Parran Jr. of the Public Health Service suggested, in an administrative memo, that health insurance could be limited to social security recipients.

World War II cut off serious political debate about national health insurance proposals (but did see the start of the employer-sponsored insurance program that became the foundation of our modern private health insurance system), but administrators kept Dr. Parran's idea alive. Congress in 1956 adopted a "military medicare" program, assuring medical care for the dependents of service personnel. The same year, Congress handed the AMA a rare defeat when it amended the Social Security Act to fund income-maintenance payments to disabled workers, over the medical profession's opposition. After that defeat, congressional reformers in 1957 introduced a medicare bill for the aged—for retirees such as Ida May Fuller, who was then eighty-three years old and still receiving her monthly social security check, augmented every two years by congressional increases. The Eisenhower Administration conceded that America's elderly (by then almost nine percent of the population, and growing) faced genuine problems of health care affordability. Fuller's Republican Senators, Ralph Flanders and George Aiken of Vermont, were strongly in favor of such federal legislation, and Flanders had introduced a weaker bill during the Truman Administration. With bipartisan support, Congress in 1960 enacted the Medical Assistance for the Aged Act (often referred to as "Kerr-Mills," after its sponsors), which funded assistance to elderly "medical indigents," people who were ill and could not afford standard medical treatment.

The 1960 presidential election saw both candidates criticize Kerr-Mills as only the first step, and the prevailing candidate, Senator John F. Kennedy, openly favored health insurance for the elderly. During President Kennedy's term (1961–63), however, medicare bills got nowhere in Congress, bottled up in the House Ways and Means Committee and defeated on the floor of the Senate in 1962. In the wake of President Kennedy's assassination in November 1963, Congress came within one vote of enacting a Medicare bill—but Ways and Means Chair Wilbur Mills killed the measure in conference committee.

The 1964 election provided a strong mandate for such legislation. President Lyndon Johnson was running for a full term; his opponent was Arizona Senator Barry Goldwater, the most articulate congressional critic of social security. Goldwater lost the election by one of the largest margins in American history, and congressional Democrats outnumbered Republicans two to one. After some brilliant political dealmaking, President Johnson won the enactment of both Medicare and Medicaid in 1965. See Social Security Amendments of 1965, P.L. 89-97. Like the original Social Security Act, Medicare and Medicaid began in more modest form, an incremental strategy based on entrenching the program through a focus on popular (the elderly in Medicare) and sympathetic (pregnant women and children in Medicaid) populations. Although we shall not provide a detailed account, the entrenchment of Medicare came more easily than the original social security idea, because Medicare swiftly won the loyalty of the medical community as well as America's aging population. Medicaid, an optional state-federal cooperative program, had a slower entrenchment process but was taken up by every state by 1982, and offers the paradigmatic story of state-led administrative constitutionalism. Through the years, progressive states used their flexibility under Medicaid to expand its categories in those states from the "deserving poor" to a means-tested program for all citizens—a series of moves that formed the template for the health care reform legislation of 2010.

By the time Richard Nixon became President (1969), social security was solidly entrenched in American public policy. Under the leadership of Commissioner Robert Ball (1962–73), the SSA was at its peak reputation, a universally respected agency. The figure below traces the process of entrenchment. Notice that entrenchment occurred over a period of time, fueled by smart public-regarding administrators and an expanding client group. The political process of entrenchment entailed both conflict, at times, and emerging consensus, driven by expert advice and positive results. The figure below provides a visual representation of this process of entrenchment.

Entrenchment of the Social Security Norm

Social Security Act of 1935 responds to both immediate and long-term problem of old-age destitution

⇩

Act survives early challenges: Supreme Court review and 1939 Amendments

⇩

Administrative implementation of new norm, with positive feedback from media, experts, public

⇩

Republican Congress tries to trim back social security coverage; President Truman defies Republicans and triumphs in 1948 election

⇩

Congress reaffirms social security norm and expands coverage, 1950 Amendments

⇩

Social security survives GOP control of Presidency and Congress, 1953–55, program flourishes and expands, 1950s

⇩

Social security norm is challenged by Senator Goldwater in 1964 election; American voters overwhelmingly endorse President Johnson, who expands social security with the Medicare Act of 1965

⇩

Social security norm is entrenched

Source: Eskridge & Ferejohn, *Republic of Statutes*, Figure 0.2.

C. SOCIAL SECURITY UNDER SIEGE, 1981–2007

The statutory and administrative entrenchment of a norm, such as social security, does not ensure that the norm will last forever—and certainly does not assure that the norm will not change over time and even degenerate. (Even Large "C" Constitutional norms change over time, as we have seen with the highly dynamic Equal Protection Clause, and often degenerate, as has been the fate of the Contracts Clause and perhaps also the Takings Clause.) Indeed, a new generation of agenda entrepreneurs may seek to "disentrench" an entrenched norm. (Slavery, for example, was a norm and practice entrenched in the Constitution of 1789, federal statutory law, and state property law in the first three generations of the republic. But the abolitionists engaged in a determined campaign to disentrench this norm, which was ultimately successful because of the Civil War.)

In 1972, Ways and Means Chair Wilbur Mills and President Richard Nixon (both tight-fisted fiscal conservatives) agreed to automatic cost-of-living adjustments to social security checks. On the one hand, this was a recognition that social security had become the center of the American version of the modern state, where the government assures every citizen of an economic and institutional structure allowing all of us the discretion to make life choices that satisfy us. But the Mills-Nixon compromise also meant that each Congress did not have an opportunity to take credit for increasing social security benefits. Program leaders had been divided on the wisdom of indexing, with Social Security Commissioner Robert Ball and analyst Richard Myers supporting the idea, and former HEW Secretary Wilbur Cohen opposing it. Cohen believed that, by requiring regular congressional action, the program would more effectively maintain political support. This debate illustrates how administrative constitutionalism is far from monolithic; program administrators sometimes disagreed among themselves as to the best course of action. Cohen was probably right. Even though beneficiaries such as Ida May Fuller (at age ninety-eight, still receiving her monthly check) appreciated indexing, it deprived the expanded social security program of political oomph in a decade when it faced a demographic dilemma.

Shortly after the 1972 Mills-Nixon deal, the economy entered into a long period of low-growth and double-digit inflation ("stagflation"). This was a double whammy for social security: with an automatic cost of living adjustment, benefits expanded rapidly with inflation, while tax revenue growth slowed with the economy. Even worse, the postwar baby boom had been followed by much smaller birth cohorts, so long-run financial projections became even less optimistic. The actuaries almost immediately began projecting deficits that extended far into the future. The 1976 projection, for example, was that the Social Security Trust Fund would be exhausted as early as 1979. In this time of increasing challenge, the program lost its most brilliant strategist, as President Nixon eased Commissioner Robert Ball out of office in 1973; the old generation of dedicated experts came to an end precisely as the program faced huge new challenges.

In 1975, the nation's first social security beneficiary, Ida May Fuller, died. She had been an invalid living with her niece before she passed away at age one hundred. Would social security follow her into the grave?

Presidents Gerald Ford and Jimmy Carter each proposed adjustments to benefit formulas, increases in the retirement age and payroll taxes, and expansion of the tax base. Congress went along with these initiatives. But neither presidents nor legislators had the courage to pursue any of these fixes far enough to do more than put off the problem for a few years. The program adjustments seemed to undermine, at least a little, the idea that social security was a basic right; the promises of the social security program began to look shaky. Indeed, public confidence that benefits would actually be paid fell sharply. Whereas sixty-three percent of survey respondents said they were confident in the future of Social Security in 1975, when Ida May Fuller died, that number fell to thirty-seven percent three years later.

As a result of these developments, the program became vulnerable to a new kind of objection. Traditionally, conservatives attacked social security either because it was compulsory or because it was a seductive road to big government. Both criticisms contained a great deal of truth—but their truth (the seductiveness of benefits coming exactly when an aging worker needed them) had little cogency for American workers. But once the program started to look like a bad deal for many Americans, conservatives came up with more appealing arguments: Americans could do better investing in their own retirement, or the government could make better use of the money in other programs. That social security survived these arguments is a testament to its enduring place (for better or for worse) in America's statutory constitution.

We do not detail this history here, but beginning in the Reagan Administration, political conservatives continued to see the social security deficit issue as a long term strategic advantage. At the very least, it would force social security onto the national agenda and, more importantly, would make people unsure that they would ever receive the benefits they had paid for. Indeed, at the very point when the deficit was gaining public attention, conservative think tanks Heritage Foundation (established in 1973) and the Cato Institute (1977) were developing sophisticated policy critiques of social security. This was an important development, for the imbalance between the information and data possessed by defenders of the modern administrative state and their conservative opponents undergirded the durability of liberal programs.[15]

Starting with Peter Ferrara's *Social Security: The Inherent Contradictions*, published by Cato in 1980, conservative intellectuals mounted a powerful assault on social security. They avoided the mistakes of the past. Rather than railing against "socialism security" and threatening to cut back on benefits, the new critics raised empirical doubts about the likelihood of future benefits, demonstrated that retirees

---

[15] Steven M. Teles, *Conservative Mobilization Against Entrenched Liberalism*, in Paul Pierson & Theda Skocpol, eds., *Transformations of the American Polity* (2007).

could obtain superior returns on their investments through private rather than public mechanisms, and developed concrete proposals for attractive alternatives. As Martha Derthick and Steven Teles put it, the new critics "recognized the need to move from 'normal' politics to a long-term strategy of disentrenchment. Disentrenchment required that conservatives weaken the public's certainty that they would receive benefits (thereby reducing their belief that future benefits were a right to which they were entitled) while simultaneously increasing their certainty in and experience with an alternative."[16]

Although intellectuals took the Cato critique seriously, it is not clear (in retrospect) that it moved public opinion very much. From 1984 to 2000, the percentage of respondents saying that either too little or about the right amount was spent on social security never fell below ninety percent in the NORC General Social Survey. This was true even as many people lost confidence that the program would continue to exist or pay benefits. Such a pattern suggests that the loss of confidence is not a simple prediction about the program, but is partly an implied criticism of those who would try to abolish it. As Lawrence Jacobs and Robert Shapiro wrote, "Super-majorities support Social Security but fear that politicians or an economic downturn will ruin it."[17] According to Jacobs and Shapiro, not only was the general level of support for social security stable over time, but the general public even opposes reductions in benefits to any recipients (including those with high incomes), reductions in the cost of living adjustments, and increases in the retirement age. While there is opposition to increasing payroll taxes, that disappears when there would be benefit cuts unless taxes are increased. In short, the American people have accepted the ideas that there is a basic right to retirement security that has been earned by paying payroll taxes, that this right should be available to everyone, and that it is a right worth paying for.

When in 1994–95 the Republicans gained control of Congress (for the first time since 1954–55), they moved cautiously on the matter of social security. Thus, the only mention of social security in House Speaker Newt Gingrich's Contract for America was a promise to expand the benefits that could be received by reducing taxes and earned income penalties on middle-income recipients. In 2000, Governor George W. Bush seized on the social security issue in his acceptance speech to the GOP's national convention on August 3, 2000:

---

[16] Martha Derthick & Steven M. Teles, *From Third Rail to Presidential Commitment—And Back? The Conservative Campaign for Social Security Privatization and the Limits of Long-Term Political Strategy*, in Glenn & Teles, eds., *Conservatism and American Political Development*.

[17] Lawrence R. Jacobs & Robert Y. Shapiro, *Myths and Misunderstandings About Public Opinion Toward Social Security: Knowledge, Support, and Reformism* (Century Foundation Report, 1999).

> Social security has been called the third rail of American politics, the one you're not supposed to touch because it might shock you. But if you don't touch it, you cannot fix it. And I intend to fix it. To the seniors in this country, you earned your benefits, you made your plans, and President George W. Bush will keep the promise of Social Security, no changes, no reductions, no way. * * * For younger workers, we will give you the option, your choice, to put part of your payroll taxes into sound, responsible investments. This will mean a higher return on your money in over 30 or 40 years, a nest egg to help your retirement or to pass on to your children.

This was, politically, a brilliant move—reassuring aging Americans that the Republicans had learned their lesson (don't mess with people's entitlements) but the Democrats had not learned theirs (social security needs to be modernized to reflect better consumer choices). With this kinder, gentler conservative message, Governor Bush defanged the social security reform issue and (kind of) won the presidency.

President Bush assumed office with a carefully articulated and rational social security reform proposal. But it had one huge problem: it would cost hundreds of billions of dollars to double fund the existing program *plus* the new accounts. Bush might have used the inherited budget surpluses for that purpose—but for political reasons the surpluses were spent on large tax cuts. And after September 11, 2001, the surpluses turned into large deficits to fund a series of foreign wars. These political decisions removed privatization from Bush's first term agenda, and in May 2001 the President followed the time-tested approach of appointing a bipartisan social security reform commission, this time headed by former Senator Moynihan and Time/Warner CEO Richard Parsons. Packed with Cato alumni and other avid privatizers, the commission predictably advocated privatization, which the President officially proposed for congressional enactment in 2005.

Notwithstanding his decisive 2004 reelection, President Bush's 2005 proposal was a train wreck. Social security prevailed and helped bring down the Bush Administration's second-term domestic agenda. According to Teles and Derthick, there were several reasons for the debacle: moderate Democrats supportive of privatizing reform died or left Congress, leaving the Bush proposal completely partisan and therefore ripe for attack rather than deliberation and compromise; labor unions and the American Association of Retired Persons unleashed ferocious public relations and lobbying campaigns against the proposal, while business groups remained quietly supportive at best; and burgeoning deficits from the tax cuts and the foreign wars dimmed the enthusiasm of fiscal conservatives, the group the President expected to beat the drums for his initiative. Perhaps the most important reason, however, was that the

American middle class considered social security an entrenched element in America's statutory constitution; although people recognized problems that needed addressing, they were never persuaded by the Cato-Bush case against social security.

NOTES ON ADMINISTRATIVE ENTRENCHMENT OF SUPER-STATUTES

1. *How Does the Process of Entrenchment Work?* For better or for worse, the social security idea is entrenched in American public law. What were the key variables that made this possible? Some ideas:

(A) Growing client group. How critical was the fact that a growing portion of the population benefited from social security and grew attached to it—such that any move to reverse those entitlements would have been politically suicidal? The primary critics of social security have been anti-big government conservatives, but much of the electoral base for such politicians is older voters, precisely the crowd that is most attached to social security.

(B) Smart, thrifty administration. Surely contributing to the success of social security was the fact that the administrators were very smart and practical. They got the program running without big problems or big costs, immediately falsifying the predictions of critics that the program would be wasteful. When social security administrators made projections, they turned out to be right most of the time, giving the program greater credibility.

(C) Utility of the underlying principle. Maybe social security got a normative boost because it is a good idea. Risk-averse people (i.e., most of us) like to have insurance. Almost all of us fear dependency or destitution in old age, and social security has proven to be a dependable insurance against destitution. Hundreds of millions of middle-class Americans have found social security to be an essential bulwark against poverty in old age.

The key question, of course, is whether such insurance can be provided in a more efficient manner. The Cato Institute and the Bush Administration maintained that individual retirement accounts would provide bigger checks in old age and therefore would be a superior way to do the same thing as social security. The financial collapse of 2008 discredited their approach in the short term, but over the long haul they might be right.

2. *Other Examples of Administrative Entrenchment.* Most areas of federal law provide further examples of administrative entrenchment of policy innovations introduced by super-statutes. Consider telecommunications law, military law and national security, intellectual property, energy law, federal income tax rules, transportation law, Indian law, and (perhaps the best example) environmental law. Reflecting traditional, and misguided, emphasis on judicial decisions as the best way to study a field, coursebooks covering these areas of law would be filled with cases. One theme of our coursebook is that you cannot understand any of these fields in any depth without understanding the norms, administrative

rules, and practices developed by legislators in statutes and elaborated upon by agencies, rather than by courts.

Chapter 3 of Eskridge and Ferejohn's *Republic of Statutes* provides a surprising example of where law schools focus on Supreme Court decisions to the detriment of students' understanding that area of law—namely, antitrust. The Sherman Act of 1891 is a classic super-statute nominally administered by courts, and so Supreme Court opinions have been the bread and butter of such courses. This is deeply unsatisfying, because almost everyone agrees that the Court's antitrust jurisprudence, taken as a whole, is a mess. A better way of understanding federal antitrust law is through an administrative lens, namely, the enforcement of the law by the Department of Justice's Antitrust Division. During the New Deal, Thurman Arnold updated the statute's original meaning, to protect small business, to reflect modern economics. William Baxter, during the Reagan Administration, tossed out the statute's original meaning and introduced a rigorous economic approach that has been religiously followed by the Supreme Court in the last generation.[18]

3. *How Super-Statutes Fail.* Perhaps it was far from inevitable that the Reagan or Bush Administration challenges to social security would fail. Indeed, in some areas of law it is putative super-statutes that are more likely to fail than to succeed. Perhaps the most critical arena for federal policy is public finance, an area where the federal government has often created more problems than it has solved. According to Eskridge and Ferejohn, the first great super-statute was the one creating the First Bank of the United States. See Act of Feb. 25, 1791, To Incorporate the Subscribers to the Bank of the United States, chap. 10, 1 Stat. 191 (1791). Although the Bank had many critics, it seemed entrenched after even its most thoughtful critics, President James Madison and his Democrat-Republican Party, revived it in 1816 after allowing its authorization to lapse in 1811. See Act of April 10, 1816, To Incorporate the Subscribers to the Bank of the United States, 3 Stat. 266 (1816) (authorizing the Second Bank).

However entrenched the Bank may have seemed during the founding generations, it disappeared under the democratizing Presidency of Andrew Jackson (1829–37). Furious with the Bank's high-handed dealings, President Jackson vetoed the Second Bank's reauthorization in 1832 and subsequently destroyed the Bank by withdrawing all federal funds from it.[19] Monetary

---

[18] See Eskridge & Ferejohn, *Republic of Statutes*, 120–64 (presenting an institutional history of the Sherman Act and demonstrating the dominance of the Department of Justice in setting antitrust policy, followed by the judiciary); Leah Brannon & Douglas H. Ginsburg, *Antitrust Decisions of the U.S. Supreme Court, 1967 to 2007*, Competition Pol'y Int'l, Autumn 2007, at 3, 17–20 (collecting empirical evidence demonstrating the complete dominance of the Department of Justice in setting antitrust policy and persuading the judiciary, 1967–2006).

[19] Veto Message of President Andrew Jackson of "A Bill to Modify and Continue the Act entitled 'An Act to Incorporate the Subscribers to the Bank of the United States' " (July 10, 1832), reprinted in 2 James D. Richardson, editor, *A Compilation of the Messages and Papers of the Presidents, 1789–1897* 1139 (1911); Jerry L. Mashaw, *Administration and 'The Democracy': Administrative Law from Jackson to Lincoln, 1829–1861*, 117 Yale L.J. 1568, 1587–98 (2008).

historians are highly critical of Jackson's action, which precipitated a financial crisis and depression in the short term and created many difficulties for public finance in the long term.[20] Between 1832 and 1914, the United States lurched from financial crisis to crisis, as the country had no rational system of public finance.

Many Americans believe that the Federal Reserve Act of 1913, P.L. 63–43, codified at 12 U.S.C. § 221 et al., solved these problems, but they forget that the Federal Reserve Board got off to a terrible start and, arguably, contributed to the Great Depression of 1929 through errors in financial judgment.[21] Arguably, too, the Federal Reserve Board under Chairman Alan Greenspan contributed to the financial panic of 2008. Be that as it may, the Board is probably the most successful federal financial agency in our history.

The cautionary tale of super-statutes in the field of public finance is that they fail more often than they succeed. One problem is that many solutions were poorly designed from the get-go, and so were doomed to fail. After President Jackson killed the Second U.S. Bank, his successors created a series of "pet banks" to manage the nation's financial policy and money supply—an experiment that never worked well and sometimes worked disastrously. Indeed, almost every structure for public finance that the federal government tried between 1836 and 1914 was disastrous.

Another problem is obsolescence: an administrative structure or regulatory principle that makes perfect sense in Time 0 makes less sense in Time 50. Thus, the Second U.S. Bank proved to be increasingly in tension with democratic principles, which left it vulnerable to the Jacksonian coup. See, e.g., *Shelby County, Alabama v. Holder,* 133 S.Ct. 2612 (2013) (performing a similar coup, striking down a portion of the Voting Rights Act of 1965 that imposed an administrative review mechanism for voting changes by "discriminatory" jurisdictions, on the ground that the covered jurisdictions had graduated from the "discriminatory" category as evidenced by excellent voting statistics).

Yet another problem for putative super-statutes is that even a well-designed law can die a quick death if its opponents gain the upper hand before it can be entrenched. After all the difficulties President Roosevelt and his advisers encountered in Congress, would the Social Security Act of 1935 have survived a Supreme Court decision striking it down, at least in part? This is a problem confronting the nation's most recent experiment in ensuring the well-being of its citizens, namely, the major health care law examined in the following problem.

---

[20] This is the critique advanced by the classic in the field, Bray Hammond, *Banks and Politics in America from the Revolution to the Civil War* (1957). Disputing this critique is Peter Temin, *The Jacksonian Economy* (1969), whose account is disputed in Peter L. Rousseau, *Jacksonian Monetary Policy, Specie Flows, and the Panic of 1837,* 62 J. Econ. Hist. 457 (2002).

[21] For a balanced but critical account of the Fed's early history, see Allan H. Meltzer, *A History of the Federal Reserve: Volume 1, 1913–1951* (2003). See also Neil Irwin, *The Alchemists: Three Central Bankers and a World on Fire* (2013) (an account of the conceptual and political process by which the Federal Reserve Act was crafted).

PROBLEM 9–1: ENTRENCHMENT STRATEGIES AND COUNTER-STRATEGIES FOR MODERN HEALTH CARE REFORM

Does our account of the entrenchment of the social security norm have any lessons for the public debate over the Patient Protection and Affordable Care Act of 2010 (ACA), P.L. 111–148?

In 2008, Senator Obama was elected President on a platform calling for comprehensive legislation to expand health insurance to many of the tens of millions of Americans who did not have coverage. Every President from Roosevelt to the second President Bush had attempted some type of health reform, but the most sweeping efforts Truman (1945–53) and Clinton (1993–2001) failed in part because of opposition from the health care and insurance industry, in part because of the massive administrative challenges posed by such a project, and in part because of a national, deep aversion to anything resembling "socialism."

In 2010, the President and his party delivered the ACA as a fulfillment of this promise. The Democrats in Congress supported the law, but not a single Republican in Congress voted for it. To secure the needed supermajority to break the GOP filibuster in the Senate, the measure that passed Congress was a compromise—not a single-payer approach like Medicare (where the government directly pays for covered health costs), but an approach that instead cobbled together and expanded upon the already-diverse and fragmented landscape American health care. The ACA expanded (but retained) Medicare and Medicaid and made important reforms to the private insurance market, the mechanism through which approximately half of Americans get their health insurance. Most important in this regard, the ACA provided subsidies to make insurance more affordable for the majority of those Americans who buy their insurance independently, and required insurers to cover any American desirous of coverage and not charge the sick more than the healthy. Most of the ACA survived a constitutional challenge in the Supreme Court, thanks to the Chief Justice's re-characterization of the Act as a tax-and-spend statute rather than as a Commerce Clause statute. See *National Federation of Independent Business v. Sebelius,* 132 S.Ct. 2566 (2012) (upholding the private insurance provisions but striking down the mandatory Medicaid expansion as unconstitutionally coercive to the states).

Passing Supreme Court review proved to be only the first of the ACA's many significant challenges. Perhaps even more than the 1935 Social Security Act, the ACA faced challenges from all directions. Its momentum was weakened by technological glitches that shut down the new web-based insurance marketplaces. Opponents continue to press legal challenges to discrete aspects of the Act—including the challenges to the ACA's contraception mandate, one of which was decided in 2014 in *Burwell v. Hobby Lobby,* as well as challenges to its insurance subsidies that were still being litigated at the time this coursebook went to press. Compare *Halbig v. Burwell,* 2014 WL3579745 (D.C. Cir. July 22, 2014) (invalidating IRS rule interpreting the ACA to permit subsidies in states where the federal, rather than state, government is operating health care exchanges), with *King v. Burwell*, 2014 WL 3582800 (4th Cir. July 22, 2014) (upholding the IRS rule and allowing subsidies in both federal and state exchanges). The House of Representatives has voted to repeal the ACA several dozen times, and we had a federal government shutdown over it. When, if ever, will this statute be entrenched? Are there any lessons that our social security story provides for the ACA? Consider some different perspectives:

(A) President Obama and the Democrats. Should the Democrats have followed a different legislative strategy? Was it a mistake to proceed without any GOP support? Should the Democrats have followed a different policy strategy? The single-payer approach of Social Security and Medicare, for example, likely would have headed off many of the current legal challenges, but most policy experts contend that such an approach would have been politically impossible. Might some smaller decisions have made a difference? For example, for reasons related to how the statute would cost out for budgetary purposes, the Democrats set the effective date of some of the ACA's most important benefits—including the new access to insurance and some quality improvements—for 2014. As such, it would be more than four years of fighting over the statute before the average American would experience its benefits. Most policy experts also criticized the Administration for terrible marketing of the statute. Polls continue to show that a majority of Americans do not understand the law, and that a substantial number of Americans do not even realize the law survived Supreme Court review. On the administrative side, the perception of things "not being ready" hasn't helped; in addition to the website fiasco, HHS has delayed several key aspects of the statute, such as the requirement that large employers provide health insurance or pay a tax, for at least a year.

(B) Senator McConnell and the Republicans. What might the Republicans have learned from the nation's experience with social security? If you were advising Senator McConnell (the GOP's Senate Leader), what strategic advice would you give him today? There is some evidence that the public was not pleased that the GOP shut down the federal government over this statute. In addition, a number of Republican-controlled states have refused to expand Medicaid (now optional after the Supreme Court ruling) in an effort to stymie the statute at any price, even one that leaves many state citizens out in the cold when it comes to health care access and insurance coverage. How will citizens in those states react to not having the same benefits as citizens in other states? How much opposition is too much?

(C) The States. Our social security story does not include a robust account of federalism, because the Social Security Act is administered by the federal government. The ACA is different. States' rights advocates in Congress insisted that the states be given prominent roles in the administration of the statute, and be left with substantial flexibility to tailor the new insurance marketplaces to the needs of individual states. From an entrenchment perspective, this seemed like smart politics: Giving the states a major role both diffused concerns about a federal takeover and also would get the states invested in the new law. Moreover, because new state government departments would be created and new state laws and regulations passed to implement the ACA, devolving the statute's administration down to the states would create an intricate (and perhaps irreversible) web of state law that would more deeply entrench the statute than federal administration alone. See Abbe R. Gluck, *Intrastatutory Federalism: State Implementation of Federal Law in Health Reform and Beyond*, 121 Yale L.J. 534 (2011).

Not all of this has worked out as planned. More than half the states (even those most concerned about the federal takeover) have refused to take the lead to implement the Act, leaving the federal government to run the marketplaces for those states. One view is that this is all the better for the feds, as it allows an even greater reach than initially assumed. Do you agree? At the same time, creative federal administrators have continued to devise new implementation models, including special "state partnership" marketplaces that incentivize the states to implement the law but offer substantial federal programmatic support.

(D) Chief Justice Roberts and the Supreme Court. Does our account of social security carry any lessons for the Court? Does it help explain why Chief Justice Roberts was willing to infuriate the Court's conservative wing and find a way to uphold most of the ACA, even as it required interpretive gymnastics (bolstered by the canon of constitutional avoidance, see Chapter 5, § 2A)? How much does the credibility of the Court—its legitimacy—depend on the Justices' not interfering with the ongoing entrenchment of a new potential super-statute? Acting strategically, which side do you think would have been more invigorated if the Court had struck the statute down?

3. DISENTRENCHMENT, ADMINISTRATIVE CONSTITUTIONALISM, AND THE LARGE "C" CONSTITUTION (MARRIAGE EQUALITY)

Consider the notion of statutory and administrative constitutionalism from another angle. At a deep level, federal super-statutes, such as the Civil Rights Act of 1964 and the Social Security Act of 1935, create what one of us has called a "Republic of Statutes" that transforms the legal regulatory baselines away from the common law regime—the judge-made landscape of law classically described in Sir William Blackstone, *Commentaries on the Laws of England* (1765). From a regulatory perspective, the Blackstonian common law regime left most activities to "private" ordering while aggressively structuring that ordering by "public" rules and baselines. For example, the Blackstonian regime protected the privacy of marriage and assured the marital partners freedom to order their affairs. But the regime also forced romantic couples into civil marriage, because its rules against fornication and adultery rendered procreative marriage the only legal form for romantic relationships and child rearing. Additionally, the Blackstonian regime created restrictive rules for the marital couple, including rules vesting legal rights in the husband (and leaving most wives without the ability to enter contracts or own property in their own names).[22] In the United States, state supreme courts applied these common law rules and read family law statutes in light of those rules.

The Blackstonian common law regime also focused marriage upon procreation. If the spousal couple were unable to consummate their marriage through successful procreative intercourse, the common law permitted them to annul their marriage. The common law recognized fornication (intercourse by unmarried persons), adultery (intercourse where at least one partner is married to someone else), and sodomy (nonprocreative anal sex) as serious crimes, punishable by death. A core assumption of the Blackstonian regime was that marriage was one man and one woman. Colonial and post-independence state statutes religiously followed and codified the Blackstonian regime. Sometimes, state law created new mechanisms to implement the Blackstonian norm, such as statutes criminalizing abortions as well as the sale or use of contraceptives.

For American family law, therefore, the baseline regime was the Blackstonian common law, as elaborated and enforced by state courts. There was no single federal super-statute that overturned the Blackstonian regime, as was the case for workplace nondiscrimination rules or social security. Instead, the new normative regime developed to meet the needs of a modern industrial society came about through state legislation and implementation. For example, nineteenth-century feminists assailed Blackstonian coverture, whereby wives lost their capacities to own property and enter into contracts. Although lacking the vote, feminists led by Elizabeth Cady Stanton persuaded the New York Legislature to enact a series of women's property and contract statutes. While judges undermined the new norm through narrow constructions, the norm of wives having legal rights gradually advanced, securing reaffirmation and expansion from the New York Legislature and adoption in other state legislatures.[23] The model below reflects the process by which a new constitutional norm may become entrenched through state experimentation, as occurred for the married women's property laws.

---

[22] On the Blackstonian foundations of American family law, and the evolution away from those premises, see Nancy F. Cott, *Public Vows: A History of Marriage and the Nation* (2000), Hendrik Hartog, *Man and Wife in America* (2000).

[23] New York was not the first to adopt married women's property laws, but it was the leading state, and the state whose success spurred others. See generally Norma Basch, *In the Eyes of the Law: Women, Marriage, and Property in Nineteenth-Century New York* (1982); Peggy A. Rabkin, *Fathers to Daughters: The Legal Foundations of Female Emancipation* (1980); Elizabeth Bowles Warbasse, *The Changing Legal Rights of Married Women, 1800–1861* (1987); Richard Chused, *Married Women's Property Laws: 1800–1850*, 71 Geo. L.J. 1359 (1983).

Model of State-Entrenched Small "c" constitutional Norms

State 1 responds to new socio-economic development/problem
by adopting statute embodying new statutory norm

Feedback from State 1's new statute

Within State 1

Implementation

Elaboration and ramifications

Legislative reaffirmation and
    expansion

Outside State 1

Inspiration

Legislative copying from State 1

Implementation and refinement
    for local needs

Ongoing implementation in these and other states

Further elaboration of the norm

Convergence of state legislation around a model statute,
reflecting new best practices for responding to the new phenomenon

National ramifications of the new norm

Source: Eskridge & Ferejohn, *Republic of Statutes*, Figure 3.1

Among the revolutionary developments advanced by state legislatures were laws vesting married women with rights to own property and enter contracts in their own names, statutes permitting divorce (and in the twentieth century allowing divorce without a showing of fault), acts permitting adoption of children not born within marriage, and new criminal codes decriminalizing consensual fornication and criminalizing rape within marriage.[24] Today, these reforms strike us as quite admirable, but not all statutes superseding the common law look to us like unequivocal "progress." Some small "c" constitutional, statutory regimes are quite terrible—and the goal of progressive social movements

---

[24] On these reforms, see the synthesis in Eskridge & Ferejohn, *Republic of Statutes,* ch. 5.

is to *disentrench* a bad super-statutory or state-consensus regime, and not just to *entrench* a new super-statute or state consensus.

Consider the following account. The account starts with the anti-homosexual constitution that dominated gay people's lives in the twentieth century, continues with the process of disentrenchment achieved by the gay rights social movement, and concludes with important issues of implementation created during the final transition to a gay-accepting constitution. At every point in the account that follows, the dominant players are *not* judges, but are administrators and legislators.

A. LEGISLATORS AND LAW ENFORCEMENT OFFICIALS: CREATING THE ANTI-HOMOSEXUAL CONSTITUTION, 1921–1961

Before the twentieth century, states had sodomy laws, but society had not used them against "homosexuals" (a term that did not exist until the 1890s). In the early twentieth century, state and municipal governments turned their attention to colonies of cross-dressing "fairies," gender-bending lesbians, and men who trained their attention onto minor girls and boys. Some citizens objected to *sodomites* who violated natural law and biblical admonitions against non-procreative sexuality; others expressed disgust with people that medical experts termed *inverts* or *degenerates* who had reverted to a more primitive evolutionary condition. Degenerates were considered threats to the fabric of society, corrupting the young. Racist medics linked "degenerate races" (people of color) with gender and sexual inversion. Sodomites, inverts, perverts, and degenerates (often lumped under the new term "homosexuals") were considered predatory threats against children, the family, and the social fabric.[25]

Reflecting new social attitudes, law enforcement officials began to target inverts and degenerates and invested more resources to expose or at least discipline them. The regime that law enforcement officials pieced together from various catch-all statutes (sodomy laws, public lewdness, and anti-solicitation bars, disorderly conduct and vagrancy prohibitions) was one where sexual and gender nonconformists were, at best, nuisances who needed to hide their orientations in the so-called "closet" and were, at worst, enemies of the state. The emerging regulatory state cut its teeth on surveillance, exposure, and harassment/abuse (and sometimes persecution) of sex workers, gender minorities, and sexual minorities.

---

[25] On the collective panic of middle-class society confronted with visible communities of sexual and gender "variants," see Lisa Duggan, *Sapphic Slashers: Sex, Violence, and American Modernity* (2002); Siobhan B. Somerville, *Queering the Color Line: Race and the Invention of Homosexuality in American Culture* (2000); Jennifer Terry, *American Obsession: Science, Medicine, and Homosexuality in Modern Society* (1999).

Once enterprising law enforcement officials "exposed" nonconformity as a big social "problem," legislators responded with new laws confirming and expanding administrative alarms.

In 1914, for an early example, the Long Beach, California police arrested thirty-one men for being part of a consensual oral sex ring. Because the state sodomy law did not include oral sex, most of the defendants went free. Responding to public outrage and law enforcement pressure, the California Legislature added to the penal code's list of serious felonies "fellatio" (oral sex on a man) and "cunnilingus" (oral sex on a woman), later recharacterized as "oral copulation." 1915 Calif. Stats., ch. 586; 1921 Calif. Stats., ch. 848. At the behest of concerned citizen groups and law enforcement officials, city councils and state legislatures created an array of other crimes to address same-sex intimacy and gender nonconformity. Thus, San Francisco made it a crime for anyone to appear in public "in a dress not belonging to his or her sex" in 1866, followed by Oakland in 1879 and Los Angeles in 1889. By 1930, most large California cities had laws criminalizing gender disguise or cross-gender attire. In 1903, the California Legislature made it a crime to be an "idle, lewd, or dissolute person." 1903 Calif. Stats., ch. 87. Local authorities used this "lewd vagrancy" statute to harass and arrest cross-dressing women, female impersonators, and effeminate male inverts looking for partners. In 1923, the Legislature made it a misdemeanor to engage in "any act . . . which openly outrages public decency," another vaguely worded law that was applied against gender and sexual nonconformists. 1923 Calif. Stats., ch. 69.[26]

Under these open-ended laws, almost any kind of activity deviating from standard sexual intercourse or gender presentation could be a crime in California. These crimes were enforced with increasing vigor after World War I. The pattern of arrests also took a turn, away from the focus on rape and abuse of minors, and toward greater enforcement against consenting adults of the same sex, "homosexuals."[27] To enforce the emerging anti-homosexual norms against consenting adults, police engaged in undercover stake-outs, posing as decoys in public restrooms and parks, and spying on people in their own homes. The consequences of being apprehended were potentially severe—long prison sentences for private activities between consenting adults, as well as sterilization of any person convicted of two or more sexual offenses if he showed evidence

---

[26] William N. Eskridge Jr., *Gaylaw: Challenging the Apartheid of the Closet* 27–29, app. A2 338–41 (1999) (municipal cross-dressing laws in California and other states); Lillian Faderman & Stuart Timmons, *Gay L.A.: A History of Sexual Outlaws, Power Politics, and Lipstick Lesbians* 30–37 (2006) (Long Beach raid and legislative response to acquittals); Louis Sullivan, *From Female to Male: The Life of Jack B. Garland* (1990) (evolving enforcement of cross-dressing ordinances).

[27] On sodomy law enforcement against consensual activities, see Eskridge, *Gaylaw*, 374 (app. C1) and 375 (app. C2); Faderman & Timmons, *Gay L.A.*, 71–104 (pervasive police harassment after World War II).

he was a "moral or sexual pervert." 1909 Calif. Stats., ch. 720, expanded by 1937 Calif. Stats., ch. 369, § 6624.[28]

California was not alone. Similar regimes were established in other states with large cities having noticeable communities of sexual and gender minorities: New York (New York City), Massachusetts (Boston), Illinois (Chicago), Ohio (Cleveland), Maryland (Baltimore), Oregon (Portland), and Washington (Seattle).[29] Southern states and the District of Columbia generally did not have visible subcultures of this sort and did not adopt explicit regimes before World War II. Although it did not regulate sex crimes as the states did, the federal government targeted sexual and gender "perverts" as well, banning homosexual literature from entering the country from abroad or being carried by the U.S. mail service and excluding degenerates from military service and from immigration into this country from abroad.

Engaging in either one-time homosexual liaisons or long-term homosexual relationships was not just a serious crime in California, as well as in every other state in the union, but excluded the suspected homosexual from a variety of rights and benefits. People who engaged in "immoral conduct," including sodomy and oral copulation, stood to lose teaching positions and state civil service jobs. The California Legislature in 1952 expanded the bases for revoking teaching certificates to include any conviction for "lewd vagrancy" and loitering at a public toilet, misdemeanor sex crimes enforced almost entirely against homosexuals. 1952 Calif. Stats., chs. 389–390. "Gross immorality" was a statutory basis for disciplinary action against a host of other licensed professionals, including lawyers, doctors, dentists, pharmacists, and embalmers and funeral directors. E. Carrington Boggan et al., *The Rights of Gay People: The Basic ACLU Guide to a Gay Person's Rights* 211–35 (1975) (listing licenses that could be lost). Many homosexual persons lost or left their teaching and other professional jobs because of these policies; some even had to leave college and terminate their educations because they were apprehended by the sexuality gendarmes.

---

[28] California State Department of Mental Hygiene, Sterilization Operations in California State Hospitals for the Mentally Ill, 1909–1960.

[29] For anti-homosexual regimes at the federal level before and right after World War II, see Eskridge, *Gaylaw*, 34–37. For anti-homosexual regimes at the state level, see generally George Painter, *The Sensibilities of Our Fathers: The History of Sodomy Laws in the United States*, available at www.sodomylaws.org/sensibilities (state-by-state survey). Municipal-level surveys can be found in *Report of the Vice Commission of Maryland* (1915) (Baltimore); The History Project, *Improper Bostonians: Lesbian and Gay History from the Puritans to Playland* (1998); The Vice Commission of Chicago, *The Social Evil in Chicago: A Study of Existing Conditions* (1911); George Chauncey Jr., *Gay New York: Gender, Urban Culture, and the Making of the Gay Male World, 1890–1940* (1994); Vice Commission of Philadelphia, *A Report of Existing Conditions, with Recommendations* (1913); Gary L. Atkins, *Gay Seattle: Stories of Exile and Belonging* (2003).

The reach of state legislative and administrative constitutionalism is not yet exhausted. After Prohibition ended, the California Legislature allowed alcohol sales at licensed establishments, with a statutory exclusion for bars and restaurants that regulators considered "disorderly" establishments. 1935 Calif. Stats., p. 1135. Postwar California considered homosexual hangouts per se "disorderly" and invested significant resources in monitoring such establishments, typically by sending undercover investigators to report excessive affection, sexual expression, and cross-dressing in places with liquor licenses.[30] Based upon reports of homosexual dancing, kissing, or hand-holding inside the premises, as well as solicitation for sexual activities outside, the state authorities could and did close down dozens bars by taking away their liquor licenses. In 1955, the Legislature ratified the administrative practices with a law allowing regulators to close down bars that had become a "resort for sex perverts." 1955 Calif. Stats., ch. 1217.

At the same time California was declaring war against homosexuals, the federal government and other state and municipal governments were following a similar aggressive philosophy.[31] Both the armed forces and federal civil service promulgated new and tougher rules against military service or federal employment by "homosexuals and other sex perverts," rules that were enforced by periodic witch hunts and purges of suspected homosexuals. Although known for its anti-Communist witch hunts, the McCarthy era actually uncovered very few Communists or genuine subversives, but disrupted the careers of thousands of lesbian or gay civil service employees and loyal soldiers each year in the 1950s. The most famous of the anti-homosexual crusaders were FBI Director J. Edgar Hoover (himself a closeted cross-dresser) and former Florida Governor Charley Johns, whose legislative investigating commission hounded lesbian and gay persons from the state's high schools and colleges, as well as the civil service.

The anti-homosexual caste regime was created in an era of increasing anxiety about nonmarital sexuality and the decline of traditional gender roles.[32] One concern that drove the pervasive discrimination was the view that lesbians and gay men are sex-obsessed predators who were a threat

---

[30] Nan Alamilla Boyd, *Wide-Open Town: A History of Queer San Francisco to 1965*, at 121–47 (2005) (describing draconian enforcement of licensing laws against gay bars).

[31] For detailed accounts of anti-homosexual campaigns, see Allan Bérubé, *Coming Out Under Fire: The History of Gay Men and Women in World War II* (1990) (armed forces); David K. Johnson, *The Lavender Scare: The Cold War Persecution of Gays and Lesbians in the Federal Government* (2004) (federal civil service); James T. Sears, *The Lonely Hunters: An Oral History of Lesbian and Gay Southern Life, 1948–1968*, at 48–108 (1997) (Florida).

[32] Eskridge, *Gaylaw*, 76–108; cf. Andrew Koppelman, *Why Discrimination Against Lesbians and Gay Men Is Sex Discrimination*, 69 N.Y.U. L. Rev. 197, 284–85 (1994) (anti-gay prejudice is centrally a revulsion based on gender role). See generally Rhonda R. Rivera, *Our Straight-Laced Judges: The Legal Position of Homosexual Persons in the United States*, 50 Hastings L.J. 1015 (1999) (reprinting 1979 article).

to the American family.[33] "[G]iven its concern for perpetuating the values associated with conventional marriage and the family as the basic unit of society, the state has a substantial interest in viewing homosexuality as errant sexual behavior which threatens the social fabric, and in endeavoring to protect minors from being influenced by those who advocate homosexual lifestyles." *Roberts v. Roberts*, 489 N.E.2d 1067, 1070 (Ohio Ct. App. 1985); accord, *Roe v. Roe*, 324 S.E.2d 691, 694 (Va. 1985); *In re Jane B.*, 380 N.Y.S.2d 848, 860 (Sup. Ct. 1976). Official public discourse was obsessed with the notion that homosexuality was the antithesis of monogamous marriage devoted to the well-being of children. Instead, "homosexuals have an insatiable appetite for sexual activities and find special gratification in the recruitment to their ranks of youth." Florida Legislative Investigation Comm'n, *Homosexuality and Citizenship in Florida* 10 (1964). "[H]omosexuality is unique among the sexual assaults . . . in that the person affected by the practicing homosexual is first a victim, then an accomplice, and finally himself a perpetrator of homosexual acts." *Id.*

Congressional investigators agreed: "[P]erverts will frequently attempt to entice normal individuals to engage in perverted practices. This is particularly true of young and impressionable people who come under the influence of a pervert." Subcomm. on Investigations of the Senate Comm. on Expenditures in the Executive Dep'ts, Interim Report, *Employment of Homosexuals and Other Sex Perverts in Government*, S. Doc. No. 241, 81st Cong, 2d Sess. 4 (1950). Federal officials maintained that "homosexuals" were not only anti-family, but anti-American. According to the Senate minority leader, "You can't hardly separate homosexuals from subversives," including Communists. See Johnson, *Lavender Scare* 30–38 (this quotation and many others linking homosexuality and subversion).

B. THE SUBSTANTIAL DISENTRENCHMENT OF THE ANTI-HOMOSEXUAL CONSTITUTION, 1961–2003

Inspired by black people's demands for equal treatment in the face of massive discrimination, a handful of gay and lesbian persons in the post-*Brown* civil rights era claimed that sexual and gender orientation ought not be the basis for discrimination or exclusion.[34] The Stonewall riots of June 1969 stimulated thousands of lesbians, gay men, and bisexuals to "come out of their closets" and become politically engaged at the local level. The many post-Stonewall gay rights groups were dedicated to

---

[33] Eskridge, *Gaylaw*, 76–84; Lillian Faderman, *Odd Girls and Twilight Lovers: A History of Lesbians in the United States* 130–50 (1997); Johnson, *Lavender Scare*, 55–64.

[34] The account in the text is largely taken from William N. Eskridge Jr., *Dishonorable Passions: Sodomy Law in America, 1861–2003* (2008), and Eskridge & Ferejohn, *Republic of Statutes*, ch. 8. See also Ellen Ann Andersen, *Out of the Closet & Into the Courts: Legal Opportunity Structure and Gay Rights Litigation* (2005).

disentrenching the small "c" anti-homosexual constitution. They realized that the first and most essential steps were challenging abusive police practices and decriminalizing consensual sodomy. Steady political pressure on police chiefs, district attorneys, and mayors in cities like San Francisco, New York, Los Angeles, Philadelphia, and Washington, D.C. made great headway toward the former goal.[35] Activists such as Frank Kameny in Washington DC and José Sarria in San Francisco formed small gay rights organizations devoted to persuading officials that they were wasting money and personnel when they targeted gay people posing no harm to others. Armed with civil rights and ACLU-affiliated allies, protesters started to make trouble for gay-bashers.

Increasingly, prosecutors, penologists, the medical/psychiatric community, and even police officials in these large cities came around to the notion that gay people were, in fact, no threat to public security or to other persons. As law enforcement experts and officials changed their attitudes toward homosexuality, law reform commissions pressed to decriminalize consensual sodomy.[36] With increased visibility and electoral cohesiveness on issues of concern to them, the lesbian, gay, bisexual, and transgender (LGBT) community attracted mainstream allies in the 1970s. In the California Legislature, Assemblyman Willie Brown and Senator George Moscone (both representing San Francisco and responsive to its gay voters) pledged their support for state sodomy reform. After a full-fledged public and legislative debate, Brown and Moscone in 1975 won enactment of a stand-alone sex crime reform statute that decriminalized consensual sodomy. 1975 Calif. Stats., ch. 71, § 7. The sponsors of the Brown-Moscone bill openly engaged opponents on the small "c" constitutional issue of the status of LGBT people in California. While opponents assailed sodomy reform on the ground that it would pollute public culture with selfish, sex-obsessed, predatory "homosexuals," Brown and Moscone defended it on the ground that lesbians and gay men were decent people who did not deserve to be criminals. The public was aware of the debate and joined it; legislators were flooded with letters, groups of all sorts engaged in lobbying, and the matter was hotly debated in the newspapers. Significantly, prosecutors and police groups supported the bill, on the ground that private consensual conduct posed no threat to public safety.

---

[35] On the ability of gay rights groups to bring pressure against abusive police practices at the local level, see Boyd, *Wide-Open Town*, 209–12 (San Francisco); Lillian Faderman & Stuart Timmons, *Gay L.A.: A History of Sexual Outlaws, Power Politics, and Lipstick Lesbians* (2006); Marc Stein, *City of Sisterly and Brotherly Loves: Lesbian and Gay Philadelphia, 1945–1972* (2000); Steven A. Rosen, *Police Harassment of Homosexual Women and Men in New York City 1960–1980*, 12 Colum. Human Rights Rev. 188 (1980–81).

[36] The discussion in this and the next paragraph is taken from Eskridge, *Dishonorable Passions*, chs. 6–8.

Official tolerance came more slowly elsewhere in the United States. At the height of the AIDS epidemic, for example, the U.S. Supreme Court ruled that it was, "at best facetious," for "homosexuals" to argue that the Constitution gave any protection to their private sexual expression the way that it did for heterosexuals. *Bowers v. Hardwick*, 478 U.S. 186 (1986) (rejecting a privacy challenge to a consensual sodomy law). Most municipal police forces and fire departments refused to admit openly gay persons into their service, as did the armed forces, a longstanding executive branch policy codified by statute in 1993.

By 1993, on the other hand, the world was already changing for gay people. *Bowers* fueled a pro-gay frontlash against the Court's discriminatory rhetoric and ignorant reasoning, and new images of lesbian couples raising children were replacing the old stereotypes of "vampire lesbians" and "predatory homosexuals" that dominated the old regime. All of these developments contributed to a modest sea change in Americans' attitudes about homosexuals and homosexual sodomy laws.[37] Opinion polls in the 1990s revealed that Americans still disapproved of homosexual activities (albeit at much lower rates), but no longer thought they should be illegal. Large and growing majorities of Americans told pollsters that gay people should not be subject to job discrimination, even in such traditional bastions of homo-exclusion as police forces, school teaching, and the armed forces. More Americans than before considered themselves liberals on matters of personal choice, but Americans who disapproved of sex outside of a committed relationship now found the situation more complicated, with the lesbian baby boom, the gay marriage movement, and the many stories of dedicated AIDS caregivers. Many thoughtful traditionalists rejected, for pragmatic reasons, the notion that an increasingly visible part of the community must be considered presumptive criminals.

The 1990s saw a decisive shift in America's small "c" constitution, away from the anti-homosexual terror of the postwar era, toward a constitution of tolerance for sexual and gender variation. California was a pioneer here as well, as the second state to bar (by executive order) anti-gay discrimination in state employment and the first state to prohibit private sexual orientation employment discrimination. Twelve other states and the District of Columbia had by 2003 also adopted statutes barring sexual orientation discrimination by private employers, and the Employment Non-Discrimination Act (barring private employment discrimination nationwide) came within one vote of passing the Senate in 1996. Twenty-two states and the District of Columbia had statutes or

---

[37] An excellent collection of public opinion polls regarding homosexuality and state policy is Karlyn Bowman et al., *Polls on Attitudes on Homosexuality & Gay Marriage* (AEI Studies in Public Opinion, updated June 2014), available at http://www.scribd.com/doc/229377762/Polls-on-Attitudes-on-homosexuality-and-gay-marriage (viewed July 1, 2014).

executive orders prohibiting sexual orientation discrimination in state employment; a presidential executive order barred sexual orientation discrimination in federal employment. Not a single anti-discrimination law or order had produced significant complaints from employers or even religious organizations, and most of the laws and orders had been greeted with approval by economists, humanitarians, and corporate executives.[38]

In a landmark decision, the U.S. Supreme Court gave its own nudge against the anti-homosexual constitution that had, seemingly, been endorsed in *Bowers v. Hardwick*. Reflecting the emerging legislative and administrative consensus that the modern regulatory state ought not persecute LGBT persons, the Court in *Romer v. Evans*, 517 U.S. 620 (1996), overturned a Colorado initiative that singled out gay people for exclusion from local or state anti-discrimination rules. Holding that anti-gay "animus" could not be the basis for governmental exclusions, the Court invalidated the discrimination as inconsistent with the Equal Protection Clause.

By the time a Large "C" Constitutional challenge to consensual sodomy laws returned to the Supreme Court in *Lawrence v. Texas,* 539 U.S. 558 (2003), the small "c" constitutional landscape had been transformed, as evidenced by state statutes and judicial opinions as well as opinion polls. The extent of its transformation was vividly illustrated by the briefs filed in *Lawrence*: Who really felt the country needed sodomy laws? Supporting the challengers to the Texas Homosexual Conduct Law were not just the usual liberal suspects (the ACLU, gay rights and feminist groups, the NAACP), but also a rainbow coalition of moderate and traditionalist perspectives. The conservative Cato Institute filed a powerful *amicus* brief urging the Court to overturn all consensual sodomy laws, as did the Republican Unity Coalition, former Wyoming Senator (1979–97) and Senate Republican Whip Alan Simpson, and the Log Cabin Republicans. There were no briefs supporting the law from the family-values-saturated Bush-Cheney Administration or even from the Texas Attorney General, a conservative Republican who declined the Court's request for a brief. Whereas twenty-nine churches and faith groups filed a brief supporting the challengers, no denomination filed in support of the Texas Homosexual Conduct Law—not the Roman Catholic Church, not the Southern Baptist Convention, not the Church of Jesus Christ of Latter-Day Saints.[39] When the Court struck down the Texas Homosexual Conduct Law in *Lawrence v. Texas* on June 26, 2003, few tears were shed for the obsolete statute.

---

[38] Employment discrimination bars are listed and discussed in Human Rights Campaign Foundation, *The State of the Workplace for Lesbian, Gay, Bisexual and Transgender Americans 2002* (2003); Nan D. Hunter, *Sexuality and Civil Rights: Re-Imagining Anti-Discrimination Laws*, 17 New York Law School Journal of Human Rights 565 (2000).

[39] The *amicus* briefs can be found and accessed at the end of the Westlaw display of the Court's opinions in *Lawrence v. Texas*, 539 U.S. 558 (2003) (Docket No. 02–102).

Lawrence nationalized a new constitution of tolerance for lesbian, gay, and bisexual persons. Tolerance, to be sure, did not mean full equality. Tolerating a practice or an idea is different from approval. If you are tolerant of my religious practices, you are not going to interfere with those practices, and implicitly you do not believe that they will harm innocent third parties. Also implicit in the concept of tolerance is that you do not find my religious practices completely acceptable for yourself and others, and you may think them not the best for me, but they are within the realm of acceptable ("tolerable") choices I can make.

In the 1990s and early 2000s, the issue that separated minority acceptance (Gay is Good) from tolerance (Gay is not a Threat) was civil marriage. After 1969, increasing numbers of lesbian and gay couples were asking local authorities to recognize their marriages. Even in tolerant California, this was going too far. In 1977, two years after sodomy reform, and after a few lesbian and gay couples asked the state to provide them with marriage licenses under the state's gender-neutral family code, the Legislature overwhelmingly reaffirmed the limitation of civil marriage to straight couples. 1977 Calif. Stats., ch. 339, §§ 1–2. A constitution of tolerance still allowed the state to favor heterosexuality, whose link with treasured marriage was reaffirmed.

Notwithstanding official reluctance, the couples kept coming, and some of them filed lawsuits. To the surprise of the entire country, the Hawaii Supreme Court opened the door for civil marriage recognition in *Baehr v. Lewin*, 852 P.2d 44 (Hawaii 1993). Writing for a plurality, Justice Steven Levinson interpreted the Hawaii Constitution to subject the exclusion of same-sex couples to strict scrutiny: on remand, the state would have to show a compelling public interest in excluding Ninia Baehr and Genora Dancel from civil marriage. Trial Judge Kevin Chang found all the state's arguments unsupported by factual evidence and in December 1996 ruled the discriminatory treatment unconstitutional.

When Americans learned about the Hawaii decision, many were appalled and alarmed. Associating line-crossing homosexual sodomy with the cherished institution of marriage disgusted many an American. Their disgust was exacerbated by the prospect of contagion—indeed, gay marriage activists themselves suggested that other states would potentially have to recognize Hawaiian gay marriages (a misunderstanding of the Full Faith and Credit Clause). The Republican Party seized upon this as an issue they could use to cement their status as America's new majority coalition, but the Democrats showed almost as much zeal in rebuking the Hawaii Supreme Court. Between 1995 and 2005, forty-three states adopted statutes or state constitutional amendments barring their judges from recognizing same-sex marriages in their jurisdictions; one of those states was California, whose citizens in

2000 voted by a big majority for the Knight Initiative, which prohibited out-of-state marriage recognition.[40]

States have a fair amount of discretion to refuse to recognize out-of-state marriages, but a bipartisan super-majority in Congress (85–14 in the Senate, 342–67 in the House) enacted the Defense of Marriage Act (DOMA) in 1996 to assure the states that they would not have to recognize such marriages. Public Law No. 104–199, § 2, 110 Stat. 2419 (1996), see Andrew Koppelman, *The Gay Rights Question in Contemporary American Law* (2002). Moreover, DOMA mandated that more than 1100 federal statutory and regulatory provisions using the terms "marriage" or "spouse" could never include same-sex couples married under state law. DOMA § 3. Heading off same-sex marriage and overriding the trial judge's injunction, gay-tolerant Hawaii in 1998 adopted a state constitutional amendment allowing the state to limit marriage to different-sex couples.

Endorsing DOMA and assuring Congress that its unprecedented level of discrimination was consistent with the Constitution, the Clinton Administration (1993–2001) reflected the new small "c" constitution of tolerance but explicit disapproval of gay people. "Some of my best friends [and cabinet members] are lesbians," President Clinton seemed to be saying, "but I wouldn't want my daughter to marry one." By our account, therefore, DOMA was not a super-statute, as it merely parroted the traditional exclusion of lesbian, gay, and bisexual persons from the foundational institutions of the polity (including also the armed forces, another exclusionary legacy from the Clinton era). But it was an important event, as it confirmed the second-class status of gay Americans—and the reasons given for that second-class status reflected the core stereotypes that had always stigmatized homosexuality. As DOMA sponsor (and thrice-married) Bob Barr put it, DOMA was needed, in order to extinguish the "flames of hedonism, the flames of narcissism, the flames of self-centered morality" that are "licking at the very foundation of our society: the family unit." 42 Cong. Rec. 17070 (July 12, 1996). Because LGBT people were the epitome of hedonism, narcissism, etc. that were undermining the altruistic ideal of family and marriage, the body politic itself would be endangered if "those people" were allowed to infect the institution and hasten its decline.

---

[40] For the public reaction in Hawaii and the rest of the country, see William N. Eskridge Jr., *Equality Practice: Civil Unions and the Future of Gay Rights* 22–42 (2002); David Orgon Coolidge, *The Hawaii Marriage Amendment: Its Origins, Meaning and Fate*, 22 Hawaii L. Rev. 19 (2000); Andrew Koppelman, *Interstate Recognition of Same-Sex Marriages and Civil Unions: A Handbook for Judges*, 153 U. Pa. L. Rev. 2143 (2005) (collecting statutes and constitutional provisions).

C. ADMINISTRATIVE CONSTITUTIONALISM AND MARRIAGE EQUALITY, 2003–2013

In a move Cassandra would have appreciated, Justice Scalia's dissenting opinion in *Lawrence* (the Texas sodomy case) lamented that Large "C" Constitutional protection for consensual sodomy meant that the Supreme Court was on the path toward imposing marriage equality upon an unwilling nation. The reasoning was that, once the Court rejected moral disapproval as a rational basis for state policy, there would ultimately be no defense for the traditional exclusion of same-sex couples from civil marriage.

LGBT rights activists had precisely the same idea, except that they thought it was a good thing. Since the 1970s, supporters of marriage equality had believed that such exclusions were vulnerable to question as inconsistent with the Constitution. On the one hand, the exclusion deprived LGBT persons of what the Supreme Court had deemed a "fundamental" right to marry. See *Loving v. Virginia*, 388 U.S. 1 (1967) (holding that the exclusion of different-race couples from civil marriage denied them a fundamental right); William N. Eskridge Jr., *The Case for Same-Sex Marriage* ch. 5 (1996) (applying that idea to argue for marriage equality). On the other hand, the exclusion was a discrimination because of sexual orientation, which progressives considered a suspect classification like race or a quasi-suspect classification like sex. See *id.* ch. 6.

As the Hawaii debacle and DOMA reflected, however, the nation as a whole was not ready for such arguments in 1996, but several states became central actors in the story of legislative and administrative constitutionalism that has culminated in significant federal action. In 1997, the Hawaii Legislature created a new institution, reciprocal beneficiaries, granting most rights and duties of marriage to same-sex couples; California's Legislature did the same thing, creating domestic partnerships in 1999. In 2000 the Vermont Legislature enacted a law recognizing civil unions, with all the legal rights and duties of marriage, for lesbian and gay couples. 2000 Vt. Acts & Resolves 72, responding to *Baker v. State,* 744 A.2d 864 (Vt. 1999).

In the next twelve years, advocates for marriage equality engaged in state-level campaigns to secure either marriage or civil union recognition.[41] The successful strategy for marriage equality advocates was

---

[41] For accounts of marriage equality activism, see Andersen, *Out of the Closet & Into the Courts,* 175–218; William N. Eskridge Jr. & Darren R. Spedale, *Gay Marriage: For Better or for Worse? What We've Learned from the Evidence* 21–31 (2006); Michael J. Klarman, *From the Closet to the Altar: Courts, Backlash, and the Struggle for Same-Sex Marriage* 48–155 (2012); Yuval Merin, *Equality for Same-Sex Couples: The Legal Recognition of Gay Partnerships in Europe and the United States* 217–27 (2002); Daniel R. Pinello, *America's Struggle for Same-Sex Marriage* 25–30, 41–45 (2006); Scott L. Cummings & Douglas NeJaime, *Lawyering for Marriage Equality,* 57 U.C.L.A. L. Rev. 1235 (2010).

a grassroots one, where advocates built upon local pro-gay public cultures to demonstrate that many lesbians and gay men were in committed relationships, with some raising children within those relationships.

The year 2003 was the *annus mirabilis* for marriage equality. That year, the California Legislature expanded the state domestic partnership law to include almost all the legal rights and duties of marriage. And the Gay and Lesbian Advocates and Defenders (GLAD) in Boston won recognition of marriage equality from the Massachusetts Supreme Judicial Court in *Goodridge v. Department of Public Health*, 798 N.E.2d 941 (Mass. 2003). Interpreting the Massachusetts Constitution, in an example of how courts (especially state courts) also sometimes assume the frontlines of social movements, Chief Justice Margaret Marshall ruled that the state did not have even a rational basis for excluding lesbian and gay couples from civil marriage.

Goodridge was the milestone advocates had been waiting for: Not only did a state for the first time issue legal marriage licenses to openly lesbian and gay couples, but equality advocates withstood the predicted backlash and persuaded the Massachusetts Legislature not to propound a constitutional override sought by Governor Romney. As the state handed out thousands of marriage licenses to lesbian and gay couples, it was remarkable that no harm befell the state. Contrary to the predictions of opponents of marriage equality, civil marriage actually flourished in Massachusetts in the decade after *Goodridge*.

In the next six years, six more states recognized marriage equality—two by state constitutional litigation (California and Iowa), three by legislative action (Vermont, New Hampshire, Maine), and one by both (Connecticut). Voters revoked marriage equality in California and Maine, but the movement gathered more momentum with marriage recognition from the New York Legislature and the District of Columbia City Council in 2010. In the next three years, eleven more states were added to the marriage equality list: two by state constitutional litigation (New Jersey, New Mexico), five by legislative action (Delaware, Hawaii, Illinois, Minnesota, and Rhode Island), two by legislative action followed by confirmatory referenda (Maryland, Washington), one by popular initiative (Maine), and one by federal constitutional litigation (California).

Relatedly, public opinion after *Goodridge* steadily shifted toward marriage equality. In light of that shift, gay rights lawyers launched major lawsuits challenging the constitutionality of DOMA § 3, which barred legitimately married couples from enjoying more than 1100 legal benefits and duties of marriage under federal law. In 2011, their cause received a big boost from the federal executive branch. In contrast with the Clinton Administration's Department of Justice, which endorsed DOMA and claimed it to be consistent with the Constitution, the

Department under President Obama announced a normative shift in the following document.

STATEMENT OF THE ATTORNEY GENERAL [ERIC HOLDER] ON LITIGATION INVOLVING THE DEFENSE OF MARRIAGE ACT

Press Release, Dep't Justice, Washington D.C., Feb. 11, 2011.

In the two years since this Administration took office, the Department of Justice has defended Section 3 of the Defense of Marriage Act on several occasions in federal court. Each of those cases evaluating Section 3 was considered in jurisdictions in which binding circuit court precedents hold that laws singling out people based on sexual orientation, as DOMA does, are constitutional if there is a rational basis for their enactment. While the President opposes DOMA and believes it should be repealed, the Department has defended it in court because we were able to advance reasonable arguments under that rational basis standard.

Section 3 of DOMA has now been challenged in the Second Circuit, however, which has no established or binding standard for how laws concerning sexual orientation should be treated. In these cases, [*Pedersen v. OPM* and *Windsor v. United States*], the Administration faces for the first time the question of whether laws regarding sexual orientation are subject to the more permissive standard of review or whether a more rigorous standard, under which laws targeting minority groups with a history of discrimination are viewed with suspicion by the courts, should apply.

After careful consideration, including a review of my recommendation, the President has concluded that given a number of factors, including a documented history of discrimination, classifications based on sexual orientation should be subject to a more heightened standard of scrutiny. The President has also concluded that Section 3 of DOMA, as applied to legally married same-sex couples, fails to meet that standard and is therefore unconstitutional. Given that conclusion, the President has instructed the Department not to defend the statute in such cases. I fully concur with the President's determination.

Consequently, the Department will not defend the constitutionality of Section 3 of DOMA as applied to same-sex married couples in the two cases filed in the Second Circuit. We will, however, remain parties to the cases and continue to represent the interests of the United States throughout the litigation. I have informed Members of Congress of this decision, so Members who wish to defend the statute may pursue that option. The Department will also work closely with the courts to ensure that Congress has a full and fair opportunity to participate in pending litigation.

Furthermore, pursuant to the President's instructions, and upon further notification to Congress, I will instruct Department attorneys to advise courts in other pending DOMA litigation of the President's and my conclusions that a heightened standard should apply, that Section 3 is unconstitutional under that standard and that the Department will cease defense of Section 3.

The Department has a longstanding practice of defending the constitutionality of duly-enacted statutes if reasonable arguments can be made in their defense. At the same time, the Department in the past has declined to defend statutes despite the availability of professionally responsible arguments, in part because—as here—the Department does not consider every such argument to be a "reasonable" one. Moreover, the Department has declined to defend a statute in cases, like this one, where the President has concluded that the statute is unconstitutional.

Much of the legal landscape has changed in the 15 years since Congress passed DOMA. The Supreme Court has ruled that laws criminalizing homosexual conduct are unconstitutional [2003]. Congress has repealed the military's Don't Ask, Don't Tell policy [2010]. Several lower courts have ruled DOMA itself to be unconstitutional. Section 3 of DOMA will continue to remain in effect unless Congress repeals it or there is a final judicial finding that strikes it down, and the President has informed me that the Executive Branch will continue to enforce the law. But while both the wisdom and the legality of Section 3 of DOMA will continue to be the subject of both extensive litigation and public debate, this Administration will no longer assert its constitutionality in court.

Postscript. Consistent with this announcement, the executive branch continued to apply the discriminatory rules mandated by DOMA § 3. The Department of Justice, however, filed briefs arguing that governmental discriminations because of sexual orientation violate the Constitution. In the Second Circuit cases, the Department made those arguments but still took an appeal when the Second Circuit ruled that the government had to compensate Edith Windsor for more than $500,000 in estate taxes that she had paid because the IRS could not recognize her as the spousal survivor when her marital partner died.

UNITED STATES V. EDITH WINDSOR
United States Supreme Court, 2013.
570 U.S. ___, 133 S.Ct. 2675, 126 L. Ed. 2d 808.

JUSTICE KENNEDY delivered the opinion of the Court.

* * * In 1996, as some States were beginning to consider the concept of same-sex marriage, and before any State had acted to permit it, Congress enacted the Defense of Marriage Act (DOMA). DOMA contains two operative sections: Section 2, which has not been challenged here,

allows States to refuse to recognize same-sex marriages performed under the laws of other States.

Section 3 is at issue here. It amends the Dictionary Act in Title 1, § 7, of the United States Code to provide a federal definition of "marriage" and "spouse." Section 3 of DOMA provides as follows:

> In determining the meaning of any Act of Congress, or of any ruling, regulation, or interpretation of the various administrative bureaus and agencies of the United States, the word 'marriage' means only a legal union between one man and one woman as husband and wife, and the word 'spouse' refers only to a person of the opposite sex who is a husband or a wife.

The definitional provision does not by its terms forbid States from enacting laws permitting same-sex marriages or civil unions or providing state benefits to residents in that status. The enactment's comprehensive definition of marriage for purposes of all federal statutes and other regulations or directives covered by its terms, however, does control over 1,000 federal laws in which marital or spousal status is addressed as a matter of federal law.

Edith Windsor and Thea Spyer met in New York City in 1963 and began a long-term relationship. Windsor and Spyer registered as domestic partners when New York City gave that right to same-sex couples in 1993. Concerned about Spyer's health, the couple made the 2007 trip to Canada for their marriage, but they continued to reside in New York City. The State of New York deems their Ontario marriage to be a valid one.

Spyer died in February 2009, and left her entire estate to Windsor. Because DOMA denies federal recognition to same-sex spouses, Windsor did not qualify for the marital exemption from the federal estate tax, which excludes from taxation "any interest in property which passes or has passed from the decedent to his surviving spouse." Windsor paid $363,053 in estate taxes and sought a refund. The Internal Revenue Service denied the refund, concluding that, under DOMA, Windsor was not a "surviving spouse." Windsor commenced this refund suit, [contending] that DOMA violates the guarantee of equal protection, as applied to the Federal Government through the Fifth Amendment.

While the tax refund suit was pending, the Attorney General of the United States notified the Speaker of the House of Representatives that the Department of Justice would no longer defend the constitutionality of DOMA's § 3. [See Holder Letter.] * * *

[The opinion first addressed the jurisdictional question under Article III that the Court had asked the parties to brief. As digested in Chapter

3, § 1 of this coursebook, the majority found the case properly before the Court].

It seems fair to conclude that, until recent years, many citizens had not even considered the possibility that two persons of the same sex might aspire to occupy the same status and dignity as that of a man and woman in lawful marriage. For marriage between a man and a woman no doubt had been thought of by most people as essential to the very definition of that term and to its role and function throughout the history of civilization. That belief, for many who long have held it, became even more urgent, more cherished when challenged. For others, however, came the beginnings of a new perspective, a new insight. Accordingly some States concluded that same-sex marriage ought to be given recognition and validity in the law for those same-sex couples who wish to define themselves by their commitment to each other. The limitation of lawful marriage to heterosexual couples, which for centuries had been deemed both necessary and fundamental, came to be seen in New York and certain other States as an unjust exclusion.

Slowly at first and then in rapid course, the laws of New York came to acknowledge the urgency of this issue for same-sex couples who wanted to affirm their commitment to one another before their children, their family, their friends, and their community. And so New York recognized same-sex marriages performed elsewhere; and then it later amended its own marriage laws to permit same-sex marriage. * * *

Against this background of lawful same-sex marriage in some States, the design, purpose, and effect of DOMA should be considered as the beginning point in deciding whether it is valid under the Constitution. * * * [DOMA's] operation is directed to a class of persons that the laws of New York, and of [Massachusetts, Iowa, Vermont, Connecticut, New Hampshire, Washington, Maine, Maryland, Delaware, Rhode Island, and the District of Columbia] have sought to protect. [Justice Kennedy emphasized the extent to which states, not the federal government, have traditionally defined and regulated marriage].

The States' interest in defining and regulating the marital relation, subject to constitutional guarantees, stems from the understanding that marriage is more than a routine classification for purposes of certain statutory benefits. Private, consensual sexual intimacy between two adult persons of the same sex may not be punished by the State, and it can form "but one element in a personal bond that is more enduring." *Lawrence v. Texas.* By its recognition of the validity of same-sex marriages performed in other jurisdictions and then by authorizing same-sex unions and same-sex marriages, New York sought to give further protection and dignity to that bond. For same-sex couples who wished to be married, the State acted to give their lawful conduct a lawful status.

This status is a far-reaching legal acknowledgment of the intimate relationship between two people, a relationship deemed by the State worthy of dignity in the community equal with all other marriages. It reflects both the community's considered perspective on the historical roots of the institution of marriage and its evolving understanding of the meaning of equality.

DOMA seeks to injure the very class New York seeks to protect. By doing so it violates basic due process and equal protection principles applicable to the Federal Government [citing the Fifth Amendment]. The Constitution's guarantee of equality "must at the very least mean that a bare congressional desire to harm a politically unpopular group cannot" justify disparate treatment of that group. In determining whether a law is motivated by an improper animus or purpose, " '[d]iscriminations of an unusual character' " especially require careful consideration (quoting *Romer*). DOMA cannot survive under these principles. The responsibility of the States for the regulation of domestic relations is an important indicator of the substantial societal impact the State's classifications have in the daily lives and customs of its people. DOMA's unusual deviation from the usual tradition of recognizing and accepting state definitions of marriage here operates to deprive same-sex couples of the benefits and responsibilities that come with the federal recognition of their marriages. This is strong evidence of a law having the purpose and effect of disapproval of that class. * * *

The history of DOMA's enactment and its own text demonstrate that interference with the equal dignity of same-sex marriages, a dignity conferred by the States in the exercise of their sovereign power, was more than an incidental effect of the federal statute. It was its essence. The House Report announced its conclusion that "it is both appropriate and necessary for Congress to do what it can to defend the institution of traditional heterosexual marriage. . . . H.R. 3396 is appropriately entitled the 'Defense of Marriage Act.' The effort to redefine 'marriage' to extend to homosexual couples is a truly radical proposal that would fundamentally alter the institution of marriage." H.R.Rep. No. 104–664, pp. 12–13 (1996). The House concluded that DOMA expresses "both moral disapproval of homosexuality, and a moral conviction that heterosexuality better comports with traditional (especially Judeo-Christian) morality." * * *

DOMA's operation in practice confirms this purpose. When New York adopted a law to permit same-sex marriage, it sought to eliminate inequality; but DOMA frustrates that objective through a system-wide enactment with no identified connection to any particular area of federal law. DOMA writes inequality into the entire United States Code. The particular case at hand concerns the estate tax, but DOMA is more than a simple determination of what should or should not be allowed as an estate tax refund. Among the over 1,000 statutes and numerous federal regulations that DOMA controls are laws pertaining to Social Security, housing, taxes, criminal sanctions, copyright, and veterans' benefits.

DOMA's principal effect is to identify a subset of state-sanctioned marriages and make them unequal. The principal purpose is to impose inequality, not for other reasons like governmental efficiency. Responsibilities, as well as rights, enhance the dignity and integrity of the person. And DOMA contrives to deprive some couples married under the laws of their State, but not other couples, of both rights and responsibilities. By creating two contradictory marriage regimes within the same State, DOMA forces same-sex couples to live as married for the purpose of state law but unmarried for the purpose of federal law, thus diminishing the stability and predictability of basic personal relations the State has found it proper to acknowledge and protect. By this dynamic DOMA undermines both the public and private significance of state-sanctioned same-sex marriages; for it tells those couples, and all the world, that their otherwise valid marriages are unworthy of federal recognition. This places same-sex couples in an unstable position of being in a second-tier marriage. The differentiation demeans the couple, whose moral and sexual choices the Constitution protects, see *Lawrence*, and whose relationship the State has sought to dignify. And it humiliates tens of thousands of children now being raised by same-sex couples. The law in question makes it even more difficult for the children to understand the integrity and closeness of their own family and its concord with other families in their community and in their daily lives.

Under DOMA, same-sex married couples have their lives burdened, by reason of government decree, in visible and public ways. By its great reach, DOMA touches many aspects of married and family life, from the mundane to the profound. It prevents same-sex married couples from obtaining government health care benefits they would otherwise receive. It deprives them of the Bankruptcy Code's special protections for domestic-support obligations. It forces them to follow a complicated procedure to file their state and federal taxes jointly. It prohibits them from being buried together in veterans' cemeteries.

For certain married couples, DOMA's unequal effects are even more serious. The federal penal code makes it a crime to "assaul[t], kidna[p], or murde[r] . . . a member of the immediate family" of "a United States official, a United States judge, [or] a Federal law enforcement officer," with the intent to influence or retaliate against that official. Although a "spouse" qualifies as a member of the officer's "immediate family," DOMA makes this protection inapplicable to same-sex spouses.

DOMA also brings financial harm to children of same-sex couples. It raises the cost of health care for families by taxing health benefits provided by employers to their workers' same-sex spouses. And it denies or reduces benefits allowed to families upon the loss of a spouse and parent, benefits that are an integral part of family security. * * *

The power the Constitution grants it also restrains. And though Congress has great authority to design laws to fit its own conception of sound national policy, it cannot deny the liberty protected by the Due Process Clause of the Fifth Amendment. * * *

The liberty protected by the Fifth Amendment's Due Process Clause contains within it the prohibition against denying to any person the equal protection of the laws. While the Fifth Amendment itself withdraws from Government the power to degrade or demean in the way this law does, the equal protection guarantee of the Fourteenth Amendment makes that Fifth Amendment right all the more specific and all the better understood and preserved.

The class to which DOMA directs its restrictions and restraints are those persons who are joined in same-sex marriages made lawful by the State. DOMA singles out a class of persons deemed by a State entitled to recognition and protection to enhance their own liberty. It imposes a disability on the class by refusing to acknowledge a status the State finds to be dignified and proper. DOMA instructs all federal officials, and indeed all persons with whom same-sex couples interact, including their own children, that their marriage is less worthy than the marriages of others.* * *By seeking to displace this protection and treating those persons as living in marriages less respected than others, the federal statute is in violation of the Fifth Amendment. This opinion and its holding are confined to those lawful marriages.

[We omit the dissenting opinion of CHIEF JUSTICE ROBERTS, as well as Part I of the dissenting opinion of JUSTICE SCALIA, which was joined by the Chief Justice and Justice Thomas.]

JUSTICE SCALIA, with whom Justice THOMAS joins, * * * dissenting.

[Justice Scalia strongly objected to the majority's coyness about precisely what constitutional principle required the invalidation of DOMA: Was it the equal protection guarantee? Substantive due process? Something else?] Some might conclude that this loaf could have used a while longer in the oven. But that would be wrong; it is already overcooked. The most expert care in preparation cannot redeem a bad recipe. The sum of all the Court's nonspecific hand-waving is that this law is invalid (maybe on equal-protection grounds, maybe on substantive-due-process grounds, and perhaps with some amorphous federalism component playing a role) because it is motivated by a " 'bare . . . desire to harm' " couples in same-sex marriages. * * *

As I have observed before [in *Lawrence* and other cases], the Constitution does not forbid the government to enforce traditional moral and sexual norms. I will not swell the U.S. Reports with restatements of that point. It is enough to say that the Constitution neither requires nor forbids our society to approve of same-sex marriage, much as it neither requires nor forbids us to approve of no-fault divorce, polygamy, or the consumption of alcohol.

However, even setting aside traditional moral disapproval of same-sex marriage (or indeed same-sex sex), there are many perfectly valid—indeed, downright boring—justifying rationales for this legislation.* * *

To choose just one of [the] defenders' arguments, DOMA avoids difficult choice-of-law issues that will now arise absent a uniform federal definition of marriage. *See, e.g.,* Baude, *Beyond DOMA: Choice of State Law in Federal Statutes*, 64 Stan. L. Rev. 1371 (2012). Imagine a pair of women who marry in Albany and then move to Alabama, which does not "recognize as valid any marriage of parties of the same sex." When the couple files their next federal tax return, may it be a joint one? Which State's law controls, for federal-law purposes: their State of celebration (which recognizes the marriage) or their State of domicile (which does not)? (Does the answer depend on whether they were just visiting in Albany?) Are these questions to be answered as a matter of federal common law, or perhaps by borrowing a State's choice-of-law rules? If so, *which* State's? And what about States where the status of an out-of-state same-sex marriage is an unsettled question under local law? DOMA avoided all of this uncertainty by specifying which marriages would be recognized for federal purposes. That is a classic purpose for a definitional provision.

Further, DOMA preserves the intended effects of prior legislation against then-unforeseen changes in circumstance. * * * DOMA's definitional section was enacted to ensure that state-level experimentation did not automatically alter the basic operation of federal law, unless and until Congress made the further judgment to do so on its own. That is not animus—just stabilizing prudence. Congress has hardly demonstrated itself unwilling to make such further, revising judgments upon due deliberation. See, *e.g.,* Don't Ask, Don't Tell Repeal Act of 2010.

The Court mentions none of this. * * * [T]he majority says that the supporters of this Act acted with *malice*—with the *"purpose"* "to disparage and to injure" same-sex couples. It says that the motivation for DOMA was to "demean,"; to "impose inequality,"; to "impose . . . a stigma,"; to deny people "equal dignity,"; to brand gay people as "unworthy,"; and to *"humiliat[e]"* their children (emphasis added). * * *

[T]o defend traditional marriage is not to condemn, demean, or humiliate those who would prefer other arrangements, any more than to defend the Constitution of the United States is to condemn, demean, or humiliate other constitutions. To hurl such accusations so casually demeans *this institution* * * *. It is one thing for a society to elect change; it is another for a court of law to impose change by adjudging those who oppose it *hostes humani generis,* enemies of the human race.

The penultimate sentence of the majority's opinion is a naked declaration that "[t]his opinion and its holding are confined" to those couples "joined in same-sex marriages made lawful by the State." I have heard such "bald, unreasoned disclaimer[s]" before. When the Court declared a constitutional right to homosexual sodomy, we were assured that the case had nothing, nothing at all to do with "whether the government must give formal recognition to any relationship that homosexual persons seek to enter." [Citing *Lawrence.*] Now we are told that DOMA is invalid because it "demeans the couple, whose moral and sexual choices the Constitution protects,"—with an accompanying citation of *Lawrence*. It takes real cheek for today's majority to assure us, as it is going out the door, that a constitutional requirement to give formal recognition to same-sex marriage is not at issue here—when what has preceded that assurance is a lecture on how superior the majority's moral judgment in favor of same-sex marriage is to the Congress's hateful moral judgment against it. I promise you this: The only thing that will "confine" the Court's holding is its sense of what it can get away with.

I do not mean to suggest disagreement with THE CHIEF JUSTICE'S view that lower federal courts and state courts can distinguish today's case when the issue before them is state denial of marital status to same-sex couples—or even that this Court could *theoretically* do so. Lord, an opinion with such scatter-shot rationales as this one (federalism noises among them) can be distinguished in many ways. And deserves to be. State and lower federal courts should take the Court at its word and distinguish away.

In my opinion, however, the view that *this* Court will take of state prohibition of same-sex marriage is indicated beyond mistaking by today's opinion. As I have said, the real rationale of today's opinion, whatever disappearing trail of its legalistic argle-bargle one chooses to follow, is that DOMA is motivated by " 'bare . . . desire to harm' " couples in same-sex marriages. How easy it is, indeed how inevitable, to reach the same conclusion with regard to state laws denying same-sex couples marital status. Consider how easy (inevitable) it is to make the following substitutions in a passage from today's opinion:

> "~~DOMA's~~ *This state law's* principal effect is to identify a subset of ~~state-sanctioned marriages~~ *constitutionally protected sexual relationships*, see *Lawrence*, and make them unequal. The principal purpose is to impose inequality, not for other reasons

like governmental efficiency. Responsibilities, as well as rights, enhance the dignity and integrity of the person. And ~~DOMA~~ *this state law* contrives to deprive some couples ~~married under the laws of their State~~ *enjoying constitutionally protected sexual relationships,* but not other couples, of both rights and responsibilities."

Or try this passage:

"~~[DOMA]~~ *This state law* tells those couples, and all the world, that their otherwise valid ~~marriages~~ *relationships* are unworthy of ~~federal~~ *state* recognition. This places same-sex couples in an unstable position of being in a second-tier ~~marriage~~ *relationship*. The differentiation demeans the couple, whose moral and sexual choices the Constitution protects, see *Lawrence, ...*"

Or this, which does not even require alteration, except as to the invented number:

"And it humiliates ~~tens of~~ thousands of children now being raised by same-sex couples. The law in question makes it even more difficult for the children to understand the integrity and closeness of their own family and its concord with other families in their community and in their daily lives."

* * * In sum, that Court which finds it so horrific that Congress irrationally and hatefully robbed same-sex couples of the "personhood and dignity" which state legislatures conferred upon them, will of a certitude be similarly appalled by state legislatures' irrational and hateful failure to acknowledge that "personhood and dignity" in the first place. * * *

As to that debate: Few public controversies touch an institution so central to the lives of so many, and few inspire such attendant passion by good people on all sides. Few public controversies will ever demonstrate so vividly the beauty of what our Framers gave us, a gift the Court pawns today to buy its stolen moment in the spotlight: a system of government that permits us to rule *ourselves*. Since DOMA's passage, citizens on all sides of the question have seen victories and they have seen defeats. There have been plebiscites, legislation, persuasion, and loud voices—in other words, democracy. * * *

A reminder that disagreement over something so fundamental as marriage can still be politically legitimate would have been a fit task for what in earlier times was called the judicial temperament. We might have covered ourselves with honor today, by promising all sides of this debate that it was theirs to settle and that we would respect their resolution. We might have let the People decide.

But that the majority will not do. Some will rejoice in today's decision, and some will despair at it; that is the nature of a controversy that matters so much to so many. But the Court has cheated both sides, robbing the winners of an honest victory, and the losers of the peace that comes from a fair defeat. We owed both of them better. I dissent.

JUSTICE ALITO, with whom JUSTICE THOMAS joins as to Parts II and III, dissenting.

[II] The family is an ancient and universal human institution. Family structure reflects the characteristics of a civilization, and changes in family structure and in the popular understanding of marriage and the family can have profound effects. Past changes in the understanding of marriage—for example, the gradual ascendance of the idea that romantic love is a prerequisite to marriage—have had far-reaching consequences. But the process by which such consequences come about is complex, involving the interaction of numerous factors, and tends to occur over an extended period of time. * * *

At present, no one—including social scientists, philosophers, and historians—can predict with any certainty what the long-term ramifications of widespread acceptance of same-sex marriage will be. And judges are certainly not equipped to make such an assessment. The Members of this Court have the authority and the responsibility to interpret and apply the Constitution. Thus, if the Constitution contained a provision guaranteeing the right to marry a person of the same sex, it would be our duty to enforce that right. But the Constitution simply does not speak to the issue of same-sex marriage. * * *

[III] Windsor and the United States are really seeking to have the Court resolve a debate between two competing views of marriage.

The first and older view, which I will call the "traditional" or "conjugal" view, sees marriage as an intrinsically opposite-sex institution. * * * [V]irtually every culture, including many not influenced by the Abrahamic religions, has limited marriage to people of the opposite sex. * * * While modern cultural changes have weakened the link between marriage and procreation in the popular mind, there is no doubt that, throughout human history and across many cultures, marriage has been viewed as an exclusively opposite-sex institution and as one inextricably linked to procreation and biological kinship.

The other, newer view is what I will call the "consent-based" vision of marriage, a vision that primarily defines marriage as the solemnization of mutual commitment—marked by strong emotional attachment and sexual attraction—between two persons. At least as it applies to heterosexual couples, this view of marriage now plays a very prominent role in the popular understanding of the institution. Indeed, our popular culture is infused with this understanding of marriage. Proponents of same-sex marriage argue that because gender differentiation is not relevant to this vision, the exclusion of same-sex couples from the institution of marriage is rank discrimination.

The Constitution does not codify either of these views of marriage (although I suspect it would have been hard at the time of the adoption of the Constitution or the Fifth Amendment to find Americans who did not take the traditional view for granted). The silence of the Constitution on this question should be enough to end the matter as far as the judiciary is concerned. Yet, Windsor and the United States implicitly ask us to endorse the consent-based view of marriage and to reject the traditional view, thereby arrogating to ourselves the power to decide a question that philosophers, historians, social scientists, and theologians are better qualified to explore. Because our constitutional order assigns the resolution of questions of this nature to the people, I would not presume to enshrine either vision of marriage in our constitutional jurisprudence. * * *

To the extent that the Court takes the position that the question of same-sex marriage should be resolved primarily at the state level, I wholeheartedly agree. I hope that the Court will ultimately permit the people of each State to decide this question for themselves. Unless the Court is willing to allow this to occur, the whiffs of federalism in the today's opinion of the Court will soon be scattered to the wind.

NOTE ON ADMINISTRATIVE VS. JUDICIAL CONSTITUTIONALISM

Notice that the executive and judicial branches reached the same result, but through a somewhat different analysis of the Constitution. Indeed, what is most striking is that the "political" branch (the executive) demanded greater Large "C" Constitutional protection for this minority than the "judicial" branch did. What institutional features of each branch might help explain the different paths the President and the Court took toward the precept that DOMA § 3 violates the Constitution?

Consider this angle. Many commentators have read the famous *Carolene Products* footnote 4 to support aggressive judicial review where a "discrete and insular minority" cannot turn to the political process for protection or assurances of basic governmental services and rights. See *United States v. Carolene Products Co.*, 304 U.S. 144, 158 n.4 (1938); John Hart Ely, *Democracy and Distrust: A Theory of Judicial Review* (1980). LGBT citizens, arguably, have at least access to the political process—they were a key group supporting and financing President Obama's 2008 election and his 2012 reelection—and that might explain why the executive branch was more gay-protective than the judicial branch. Do you accept the premise, though: Are LGBT people no longer "politically powerless"?

Another way of looking at the matter takes a longer strategic vision. When the Attorney General and the President announced their support for marriage equality, they were focused on DOMA and federal policy. But the Supreme Court knew that Large "C" Constitutional challenges to *state* as well as federal exclusions were on the horizon. (Indeed, a federal challenge to California's 2008 anti-marriage equality initiative was *Windsor's* companion case. The Court dismissed the appeal on Article III grounds and knew that more cases were on their way.) Any equal protection test announced in *Windsor* would be applicable to the challenges to state marriage exclusions, and so the Court had a strong incentive *not* to announce strict scrutiny in its first marriage case: Let the issue percolate in the lower courts, and see if the country moves toward a consensus before deciding whether all states need to recognize marriage equality.

Yet another way of looking at the matter is implementation. The Court announced that the federal government can no longer enforce DOMA § 3. But what does that mean for lesbian and gay couples who claim to be married? Do federal tax benefits (and burdens) now fall upon all couples who have been validly married under state law or in another country (Windsor's marriage was in Canada)? What if the couple is domiciled in a state that does not recognize the marriage? (Most states in 2014 do not recognize out-of-state lesbian and gay marriages.) What if the couple is joined in civil union? Does that count?

After *Windsor,* the Obama Administration immediately turned to issues of implementation. Indeed, within days of the decision, the Administration directed departments and agencies to make all spousal employment benefits available to federal employees who were married to a partner of the same sex. See Elaine Kaplan, Acting Director, Office of Personnel Management, Memorandum for Heads of Executive Departments and Agencies: *Guidance on the Extension of Benefits to Married Gay and Lesbian Federal Employees, Annuitants, and Their Families* (June 28, 2013). The Memorandum did not limit those benefits to employees living in states that recognized their marriages, nor did the Memorandum extend those benefits to employees joined in civil unions or domestic partnerships.

In the ensuing months, federal departments and agencies issued guidances indicating how they intended to apply *Windsor.* See generally Memorandum from the Attorney General to the President, *Implementation of* United States v. Windsor (June 20, 2014) (June 2014 Attorney General's Memo). For an important guidance, consider the IRS's document below.

REVENUE RULING 2013–17
Internal Revenue Service, Sept. 16, 2013.
http://www.irs.gov/irb/2013-38_IRB/ar07.html

[After the Supreme Court's decision in *Windsor,* the Internal Revenue Service expanded its analysis of what couples are "married" for purposes of the Internal Revenue Code. One issue the Service addressed in this revenue ruling was whether a marriage of same-sex individuals validly entered into in a state whose laws authorize the marriage of two individuals of the same sex even if the state in which they are domiciled does not recognize the validity of same-sex marriages. Another issue is whether the terms "spouse," "husband and wife," "husband," and "wife" include individuals (whether of the opposite sex or same sex) who have entered into a registered domestic partnership, civil union, or other similar formal relationship recognized under state law that is not denominated as a marriage under the laws of that state, and whether, for those same purposes, the term "marriage" includes such relationships.]

In Revenue Ruling 58–66, 1958–1 C.B. 60, the Service determined the marital status for Federal income tax purposes of individuals who have entered into a common-law marriage in a state that recognizes common-law marriages. The Service acknowledged that it recognizes the marital status of individuals as determined under state law in the administration of the Federal income tax laws. In Revenue Ruling 58–66, the Service stated that a couple would be treated as married for purposes of Federal income tax filing status and personal exemptions if the couple entered into a common-law marriage in a state that recognizes that relationship as a valid marriage.

The Service further concluded in Revenue Ruling 58–66 that its position with respect to a common-law marriage also applies to a couple who entered into a common-law marriage in a state that recognized such relationships and who later moved to a state in which a ceremony is required to establish the marital relationship.

The Service therefore held that a taxpayer who enters into a common-law marriage in a state that recognizes such marriages shall, for purposes of Federal income tax filing status and personal exemptions, be considered married notwithstanding that the taxpayer and the taxpayer's spouse are currently domiciled in a state that requires a ceremony to establish the marital relationship. Accordingly, the Service held in Revenue Ruling 58–66 that such individuals can file joint income tax returns under section 6013 of the Internal Revenue Code (Code).

The Service has applied this rule with respect to common-law marriages for over 50 years, despite the refusal of some states to give full faith and credit to common-law-marriages established in other states. Although states have different rules of marriage recognition, uniform nationwide rules are essential for efficient and fair tax administration. A rule under which a couple's marital status could change simply by moving from one state to another state would be prohibitively difficult and costly for the Service to administer, and for many taxpayers to apply. * * *

There are more than two hundred Code provisions and Treasury regulations relating to the internal revenue laws that include the terms "spouse," "marriage" (and derivatives thereof, such as "marries" and "married"), "husband and wife," "husband," and "wife." The Service concludes that gender-neutral terms in the Code that refer to marital status, such as "spouse" and "marriage," include, respectively, (1) an individual married to a person of the same sex if the couple is lawfully married under state law, and (2) such a marriage between individuals of the same sex. This is the most natural reading of those terms; it is consistent with *Windsor*, in which the plaintiff was seeking tax benefits under a statute that used the term "spouse"; and a narrower interpretation would not further the purposes of efficient tax administration.

[Interpreting "Husband and Wife" in the Code.] In light of the *Windsor* decision and for the reasons discussed below, the Service also concludes that the terms "husband and wife," "husband," and "wife" should be interpreted to include same-sex spouses. This interpretation is consistent with the Supreme Court's statements about the Code in *Windsor*, avoids the serious constitutional questions that an alternate reading would create, and is permitted by the text and purposes of the Code.

First, the Supreme Court's opinion in *Windsor* suggests that it understood that its decision striking down section 3 of DOMA would affect tax administration in ways that extended beyond the estate tax refund at issue. The Court observed in particular that section 3 burdened same-sex couples by forcing "them to follow a complicated procedure to file their Federal and state taxes jointly" and that section 3 "raise[d] the cost of health care for families by taxing health benefits provided by employers to their workers' same-sex spouses."

Second, an interpretation of the gender-specific terms in the Code to exclude same-sex spouses would raise serious constitutional questions. A well-established principle of statutory interpretation holds that, "where an otherwise acceptable construction of a statute would raise serious constitutional problems," a court should "construe the statute to avoid such problems unless such construction is plainly contrary to the intent of Congress." *Edward J. DeBartolo Corp. v. Fla. Gulf Coast Bldg. & Constr. Trades Council*, 485 U.S. 568, 575 (1988). "This canon is followed out of respect for Congress, which [presumably] legislates in light of constitutional limitations," *Rust v. Sullivan*, 500 U.S. 173, 191 (1991), and instructs courts, where possible, to avoid interpretations that "would raise serious constitutional doubts," *United States v. X-Citement Video, Inc.*, 513 U.S. 64, 78 (1994).

The Fifth Amendment analysis in *Windsor* raises serious doubts about the constitutionality of Federal laws that confer marriage benefits and burdens only on opposite-sex married couples. In *Windsor*, the Court stated that, "[b]y creating two contradictory marriage regimes within the same State, DOMA forces same-sex couples to live as married for the purpose of state law but unmarried for the purpose of Federal law, thus diminishing the stability and predictability of basic personal relations the State has found it proper to acknowledge and protect." Interpreting the gender-specific terms in the Code to categorically exclude same-sex couples arguably would have the same effect of diminishing the stability and predictability of legally recognized same-sex marriages. Thus, the canon of constitutional avoidance counsels in favor of interpreting the gender-specific terms in the Code to refer to same-sex spouses and couples.

Third, the text of the Code permits a gender-neutral construction of the gender-specific terms. Section 7701 of the Code provides definitions of certain terms generally applicable for purposes of the Code when the terms are not defined otherwise in a specific Code provision and the definition in section 7701 is not manifestly incompatible with the intent of the specific Code provision. The terms "husband and wife," "husband," and "wife" are not specifically defined other than in section 7701(a)(17), which provides, for purposes of sections 682 and 2516, that the terms "husband" and "wife" shall be read to include a former husband or a former wife, respectively, and that "husband" shall be read as "wife" and "wife" as "husband" in certain circumstances. Although Congress's specific instruction to read "husband" and "wife" interchangeably in those specific provisions could be taken as an indication that Congress did not intend the terms to be read interchangeably in other provisions, the Service believes that the better understanding is that the interpretive rule set forth in section 7701(a)(17) makes it reasonable to adopt, in the circumstances presented here and in light of *Windsor* and the principle of constitutional avoidance, a more general rule that does not foreclose a gender-neutral reading of gender-specific terms elsewhere in the Code.

Section 7701(p) provides a specific cross-reference to the Dictionary Act, 1 U.S.C. § 1, which provides, in part, that when "determining the meaning of any Act of Congress, unless the context indicates otherwise, . . . words importing the masculine gender include the feminine as well." The purpose of this provision was to avoid having to "specify males and females by using a great deal of unnecessary language when one word would express the whole." Cong. Globe, 41st Cong., 3d Sess. 777 (1871) (statement of Sen. Trumbull, sponsor of Dictionary Act). This provision has been read to require construction of the phrase "husband and wife" to include same-sex married couples. See *Pedersen v. Office of Personnel Mgmt.*, 881 F. Supp. 2d 294, 306–07 (D. Conn. 2012) (construing section 6013 of the Code).

The Dictionary Act thus supports interpreting the gender-specific terms in the Code in a gender-neutral manner "unless the context indicates otherwise." 1 U.S.C. § 1. " 'Context' " for purposes of the Dictionary Act "means the text of the Act of Congress surrounding the word at issue, or the texts of other related congressional Acts." *Rowland v. Cal. Men's Colony, Unit II Men's Advisory Council*, 506 U.S. 194, 199 (1993). Here, nothing in the surrounding text forecloses a gender-neutral reading of the gender-specific terms. Rather, the provisions of the Code that use the terms "husband and wife," "husband," and "wife" are inextricably interwoven with provisions that use gender-neutral terms like "spouse" and "marriage," indicating that Congress viewed them to be equivalent. For example, section 1(a) sets forth the tax imposed on "every married individual (as defined in section 7703) who makes a single return jointly with his spouse under section 6013," even though section 6013 provides that a "husband and wife" make a single return jointly of income. Similarly, section 2513 of the Code is entitled "Gifts by Husband or Wife to Third Party," but uses no gender-specific terms in its text. See also, e.g., §§ 62(b)(3), 1361(c)(1).

This interpretation is also consistent with the legislative history. The legislative history of section 6013, for example, uses the term "married taxpayers" interchangeably with the terms "husband" and "wife" to describe those individuals who may elect to file a joint return, and there is no indication that Congress intended those terms to refer only to a subset of individuals who are legally married. See, e.g., S. Rep. No. 82–781, Finance, Part 1, p. 48 (Sept. 18, 1951). Accordingly, the most logical reading is that the terms "husband and wife" were used because they were viewed, at the time of enactment, as equivalent to the term "persons married to each other." There is nothing in the Code to suggest that Congress intended to exclude from the meaning of these terms any couple otherwise legally married under state law.

Fourth, other considerations also strongly support this interpretation. A gender-neutral reading of the Code fosters fairness by ensuring that the Service treats same-sex couples in the same manner as similarly situated opposite-sex couples. A gender-neutral reading of the Code also fosters administrative efficiency because the Service does not collect or maintain information on the gender of taxpayers and would have great difficulty administering a scheme that differentiated between same-sex and opposite-sex married couples.

Therefore, consistent with the statutory context, the Supreme Court's decision in *Windsor*, Revenue Ruling 58–66, and effective tax administration generally, the Service concludes that, for Federal tax purposes, the terms "husband and wife," "husband," and "wife" include an individual married to a person of the same sex if they were lawfully married in a state whose laws authorize the marriage of two individuals of the same sex, and the term "marriage" includes such marriages of individuals of the same sex.

[Marital Status Based on the Laws of the State Where the Marriage Was Celebrated.] Consistent with the longstanding position expressed in Revenue Ruling 58–66, the Service has determined to interpret the Code as incorporating a general rule, for Federal tax purposes, that recognizes the validity of a same-sex marriage that was valid in the state where it was entered into, regardless of the married couple's place of domicile. The Service may provide additional guidance on this subject and on the application of *Windsor* with respect to Federal tax administration. Other agencies may provide guidance on other Federal programs that they administer that are affected by the Code.

Under this rule, individuals of the same sex will be considered to be lawfully married under the Code as long as they were married in a state whose laws authorize the marriage of two individuals of the same sex, even if they are domiciled in a state that does not recognize the validity of same-sex marriages. For over half a century, for Federal income tax purposes, the Service has recognized marriages based on the laws of the state in which they were entered into, without regard to subsequent changes in domicile, to achieve uniformity, stability, and efficiency in the application and administration of the Code. Given our increasingly mobile society, it is important to have a uniform rule of recognition that can be applied with certainty by the Service and taxpayers alike for all Federal tax purposes. Those overriding tax administration policy goals generally apply with equal force in the context of same-sex marriages.

In most Federal tax contexts, a state-of-domicile rule would present serious administrative concerns. For example, spouses are generally treated as related parties for Federal tax purposes, and one spouse's ownership interest in property may be attributed to the other spouse for purposes of numerous Code provisions. If the Service did not adopt a uniform rule of recognition, the attribution of property interests could change when a same-sex couple moves from one state to another with different marriage recognition rules. The potential adverse consequences could impact not only the married couple but also others involved in a transaction, entity, or arrangement. This would lead to uncertainty for both taxpayers and the Service.

A rule of recognition based on the state of a taxpayer's current domicile would also raise significant challenges for employers that operate in more than one state, or that have employees (or former employees) who live in more than one state, or move between states with different marriage recognition rules. Substantial financial and administrative burdens would be placed on those employers, as well as the administrators of employee benefit plans. For example, the need for and validity of spousal elections, consents, and notices could change each time an employee, former employee, or spouse moved to a state with different marriage recognition rules. To administer employee benefit plans, employers (or plan administrators) would need to inquire whether each employee receiving plan benefits was married and, if so, whether the employee's spouse was the same sex or opposite sex from the employee. In addition, the employers or plan administrators would need to continually track the state of domicile of all same-sex married employees and former employees and their spouses. Rules would also need to be developed by the Service and administered by employers and plan administrators to address the treatment of same-sex married couples comprised of individuals who reside in different states (a situation that is not relevant with respect to opposite-sex couples). For all of these reasons, plan administration would grow increasingly complex and certain rules, such as those governing required distributions under section 401(a)(9), would become especially challenging. Administrators of employee benefit plans would have to be retrained, and systems reworked, to comply with an unprecedented and complex system that divides married employees according to their sexual orientation. In many cases, the tracking of employee and spouse domiciles would be less than perfectly accurate or timely and would result in errors or delays. These errors and delays would be costly to employers, and could require some plans to enter the Service's voluntary compliance programs or put benefits of all employees at risk. All of these problems are avoided by the adoption of the rule set forth herein, and the Service therefore has chosen to avoid the imposition of the additional burdens on itself, employers, plan administrators, and individual taxpayers. Accordingly, Revenue Ruling 58–66 is amplified to adopt a general rule, for Federal tax purposes, that recognizes the validity of a same-sex marriage that was valid in the state where it was entered into, regardless of the married couple's place of domicile.

[Marriages Recognized, Not Domestic Partnerships, Civil Unions.] For Federal tax purposes, the term "marriage" does not include registered domestic partnerships, civil unions, or other similar formal relationships recognized under state law that are not denominated as a marriage under that state's law, and the terms "spouse," "husband and wife," "husband," and "wife" do not include individuals who have entered into such a formal relationship. This conclusion applies regardless of whether individuals who have entered into such relationships are of the opposite sex or the same sex.

PROBLEM 9–2: LESBIAN AND GAY MARRIAGES AND CIVIL UNIONS UNDER THE INTERNAL REVENUE CODE AND OTHER FEDERAL STATUTES

You are the White House Counsel in the wake of *Windsor*. President Obama has asked you for your legal advice regarding the IRS's Revenue Ruling and other rulings and guidances contemplated by other agencies. The President's position is that he wants to recognize lesbian and gay unions as much as the "law" allows; hence, he is not willing to recognize such unions where a statute constitutionally bars them. What advice do you give the President, in response to the following scenarios?

(A) Internal Revenue Code. At the request of the White House, the Treasury Department provides you with a preview of Revenue Ruling 2013–17. LGBT groups have also procured a copy of the proposed revenue ruling, and they have asked the White House why valid civil unions cannot be recognized as well. The IRS takes the position that couples in civil unions or domestic partnerships are not "spouses" or "married" for purposes of the Internal Revenue Code.

LGBT groups point to the Nevada domestic partnership statute, which says that "Domestic partners have the same rights, protections and benefits, and are subject to the same responsibilities, obligations and duties under law, whether derived from statutes, administrative regulations, court rules, government policies, common law or any other provisions or sources of law, as are granted to and imposed upon spouses." Nev. Rev. Stats. § 122A.200(1)(a). In Nevada, therefore, domestic partners have all the legal rights and duties as "spouses" and, hence, are similarly situated to Massachusetts married couples who have the legal rights and duties as "spouses."

What is the LGBT groups' best argument for inclusion of Nevada (and perhaps other) domestic partners in the revenue ruling? Under his directive, how should you advise the President? If you disagree with the IRS, what process would you recommend to the President?

(B) Veterans' Benefits. Veterans' benefits flow to a "spouse" or a "surviving spouse" of a person who served in the armed forces. Title 38 defines both terms as "a person of the 'opposite sex' who is a wife or a husband." 38 U.S.C. § 101(31) ("spouse"); *id.* § 101(3) ("surviving spouse"). These definitions exclude lesbian and gay spouses from the veterans' benefits law, and so the question is whether these definitions are unconstitutional in the wake of *Windsor*. What is the best argument that they survive *Windsor*? How do you advise the President as to their status? See Dep't of Justice, Office of the Att'y Gen., Letter from Att'y Gen. Eric Holder to The Honorable John Boehner (Sept. 4, 2013), http://www.justice.gov/iso/opa/resources/55720139415153091016.pdf (offering the Justice Department's opinion on the constitutional issue).

Assume that the veterans' benefits law now covers the spouses and surviving spouses of same-sex marriages. Would the statute cover a lesbian couple that was married in New York but is currently living in Ohio, a state that does not recognize marriage equality? The Ohio Const. § 15.11 says this:

> Only a union between one man and one woman may be a marriage valid in or recognized by this state and its political subdivisions. This state and its political subdivisions shall not create or recognize a legal status for relationships of unmarried individuals that

intends to approximate the design, qualities, significance or effect of marriage.

Hence, Ohio could not recognize the lesbian marriage, even if valid in the state of celebration (New York). But the controlling statute for determining a valid marriage for the purpose of veterans' benefits, 38 U.S.C. § 103(c), provides:

> In determining whether or not a person is or was the spouse of a veteran, their marriage shall be proven as valid for the purposes of all laws administered by the Secretary according to the law of the place where the parties resided at the time of the marriage or the law of the place where the parties resided when the right to benefits accrued.

VA regulations further define "marriage" in the adjudication of VA benefits to mean: "a marriage valid under the law of the place where the parties resided at the time of marriage, or the law of the place where the parties resided when the right to benefits accrued." 38 C.F.R. § 3.1(j). How should the White House Counsel analyze this provision?

Would it make a difference to your answer if the lesbian couple's "domicile" (the couple's permanent residence for purposes of voting, taxation, etc.) was Ohio at the time of the marriage as well as today? "Residence" and "domicile" are usually synonymous. Note, however, that the Secretary of Veterans Affairs has broad authority to "deem" a marriage valid for death benefits purposes even when there is a defect in the marriage or when the state of residence would disrespect the marriage. 38 U.S.C. § 103(a) provides:

> Whenever, in the consideration of any claim filed by a person as the widow or widower of a veteran for gratuitous death benefits under laws administered by the Secretary it is established by evidence satisfactory to the Secretary that such person, without knowledge of any legal impediment, entered into a marriage with such veteran which, but for a legal impediment, would have been valid * * * the purported marriage shall be deemed to be a valid marriage. * * *

This provision is intended to "alleviate hardships sometimes occasioned by the existing requirement that a widow of a veteran establish that she was his legal widow." See also Marjorie Dick Rombauer, *Marital Status and Eligibility for Federal Statutory Income Benefits: A Historical Survey,* 52 Wash. L. Rev. 227, 237 (1977). Deeming a marriage valid effectively *disregards* state laws, thereby finding a marriage exists for veterans' death benefits purposes even where a relevant state or states might refuse to recognize a marriage. Early cases set the standard for a broad interpretation of "legal impediment" as including "not only (1) particular substantive conditions for validity which may exist in certain jurisdictions such as those respecting age, race, mental capacity, marital status, and consanguinity, but also, with respect to one of the commonly accepted forms for creating a marriage (i.e., civil, religious, common-law, and tribal), (2) the special formalities, or external conduct required of the parties or of third persons, such as public officers, for the formation of a valid marriage by the laws of a particular jurisdiction." 1962 ADVA 979. See also 42 Op. Att'y Gen. 37 (1961).

As White House Counsel, of course, you cannot tell the Department of Veterans Affairs how it must interpret and apply these statutes—but you can advise the President, who can consult with the Secretary of Veterans Affairs (who serves at the pleasure of the President). Does the President have a legal basis for advising the Secretary that he or she has the authority to recognize the Ohio marriage? What advice might the President pass on with regard to administrative strategy? Would your advice also cover the lesbian couple if they were domestic partners under Nevada law and still living in Nevada?

(C) Social Security Benefits. Consider now whether the lesbian couple domiciled in Ohio but validly married in New York should be treated as "married" under the Social Security Act of 1935. The governing statutory provision is 42 U.S.C. § 416(h), "Determination of Family Status":

> (h)(1)(A)(i) An applicant is the wife, husband, widow, or widower of a fully or currently insured individual for purposes of this subchapter if the courts of the State in which such insured individual is domiciled at the time such applicant files an application, or, if such insured individual is dead, the courts of the State in which he was domiciled at the time of death, or, if such insured individual is or was not so domiciled in any State, the courts of the District of Columbia, would find that such applicant and such insured individual were validly married at the time such applicant files such application or, if such insured individual is dead, at the time he died.

> (ii) If such courts would not find that such applicant and such insured individual were validly married at such time, such applicant shall, nevertheless be deemed to be the wife, husband, widow, or widower, as the case may be, of such insured individual if such applicant would, under the laws applied by such courts in determining the devolution of intestate personal property, have the same status with respect to the taking of such property as a wife, husband, widow, or widower of such insured individual.

Is there a statutory basis for the Social Security Administration to provide survivors' benefits to the surviving spouse of the Ohio couple? How about the Nevada lesbian couple? Cf. Social Security Administration, GN 00210.400 Same–Sex Marriage—Benefits for Surviving Spouses (Dec. 16, 2013), https://secure.ssa.gov/apps10/poms.nsf/lnx/0200210400.

PROBLEM 9–3: IMPLICATIONS OF WINDSOR AND ADMINISTRATIVE CONSTITUTIONALISM FOR THE MARRIAGE EQUALITY MOVEMENT?

Assume that you are a legal adviser for Lambda Legal, the leading LGBT litigation group. Lambda Legal is handling several marriage cases and might file an *amicus* brief in other cases. As of July 1, 2014, nineteen states recognize marriage equality. Every other state is being sued to secure marriage equality for lesbian and gay couples, and in some cases marriage licenses have been issued. For example, a federal district court invalidated Utah's marital exclusion of lesbian and gay couples, *Kitchen v. Herbert,* Case No. 2:13–cv–217 (D. Utah, Dec. 20, 2013), and the Tenth Circuit refused to stay the court's injunction, so hundreds of lesbian and gay couples received marriage licenses in that state. On January 14, 2014, the Supreme Court issued a stay pending appeal, thereby terminating that process.

The Tenth Circuit has affirmed the District Court in *Kitchen,* and the Utah Attorney General is seeking review from the U.S. Supreme Court. Assume the Court takes the case for the 2014 Term. Lambda Legal will file an *amicus* brief that is certain to be read and considered by the Justices. As a matter of constitutional strategy, should Lambda Legal go for the **50 State Solution**, namely, a ruling that the Constitution requires marriage equality in all fifty states? How do *Windsor* and the Obama Administration's constitutionalism before and after *Windsor* affect your thinking about this issue?

* * *

CONCLUSION

No matter what courses you take as you progress through law school, we hope that you will carry with you the concepts developed in this coursebook—and indeed, carry them into the real world of practice, too. Whether you focus on tax, immigration, health care, bankruptcy, securities law, the environment, or virtually anything else, yours will be a world of statutes and regulations. This goes whether you are litigating the statutes, advocating policy solutions, or drafting contracts to help private entities comply with their legal rights. The doctrines of statutory law and administration are the bread and butter of modern lawyers, and most of the time the modern regulatory state is far ahead of the courts. It is up to you, the next generation of lawyers, to negotiate these modern interbranch relationships and to help give full effect to the rich legal landscape that describes our republic of statutes.

TABLE OF CONTENTS TO THE APPENDICES

■ ■ ■

APPENDIX 1

THE CONSTITUTION OF THE UNITED STATES

■ ■ ■

We the People of the United States, in Order to form a more perfect Union, establish Justice, insure domestic Tranquility, provide for the common defence, promote the general Welfare, and secure the Blessings of Liberty to ourselves and our Posterity, do ordain and establish this Constitution for the United States of America.

ARTICLE I

Section 1. All legislative Powers herein granted shall be vested in a Congress of the United States, which shall consist of a Senate and House of Representatives.

Section 2. [1] The House of Representatives shall be composed of Members chosen every second Year by the People of the several States, and the Electors in each State shall have the Qualifications requisite for Electors of the most numerous Branch of the State Legislature.

[2] No Person shall be a Representative who shall not have attained to the Age of twenty five Years, and been seven Years a Citizen of the United States, and who shall not, when elected, be an Inhabitant of that State in which he shall be chosen.

[3] Representatives and direct Taxes shall be apportioned among the several States which may be included within this Union, according to their respective Numbers, which shall be determined by adding to the whole Number of free Persons, including those bound to Service for a Term of Years, and excluding Indians not taxed, three fifths of all other Persons. The actual Enumeration shall be made within three Years after the first Meeting of the Congress of the United States, and within every subsequent Term of ten Years, in such Manner as they shall by Law direct. The Number of Representatives shall not exceed one for every thirty Thousand, but each State shall have at Least one Representative; and until such enumeration shall be made, the State of New Hampshire shall be entitled to chuse three, Massachusetts eight, Rhode Island and Providence Plantations one, Connecticut five, New York six, New Jersey four, Pennsylvania eight, Delaware one, Maryland six, Virginia ten, North Carolina five, South Carolina five, and Georgia three.

[4] When vacancies happen in the Representation from any State, the Executive Authority thereof shall issue Writs of Election to fill such Vacancies.

[5] The House of Representatives shall chuse their Speaker and other Officers; and shall have the sole Power of Impeachment.

Section 3.   [1] The Senate of the United States shall be composed of two Senators from each State, chosen by the Legislature thereof, for six Years; and each Senator shall have one Vote.

[2] Immediately after they shall be assembled in Consequence of the first Election, they shall be divided as equally as may be into three Classes. The Seats of the Senators of the first Class shall be vacated at the Expiration of the second Year, of the second Class at the Expiration of the fourth Year, and of the third Class at the Expiration of the sixth Year, so that one third may be chosen every second Year; and if Vacancies happen by Resignation, or otherwise, during the Recess of the Legislature of any State, the Executive thereof may make temporary Appointments until the next Meeting of the Legislature, which shall then fill such Vacancies.

[3] No Person shall be a Senator who shall not have attained to the Age of Thirty Years, and been nine Years a Citizen of the United States, and who shall not, when elected, be an Inhabitant of that State for which he shall be chosen.

[4] The Vice President of the United States shall be President of the Senate, but shall have no Vote, unless they be equally divided.

[5] The Senate shall chuse their other Officers, and also a President pro tempore, in the absence of the Vice President, or when he shall exercise the Office of President of the United States.

[6] The Senate shall have the sole Power to try all Impeachments. When sitting for that purpose, they shall be on Oath or Affirmation. When the President of the United States is tried, the Chief Justice shall preside: And no Person shall be convicted without the Concurrence of two thirds of the Members present.

[7] Judgment in Cases of Impeachment shall not extend further than to removal from Office, and disqualification to hold and enjoy any Office of honor, Trust or Profit under the United States: but the Party convicted shall nevertheless be liable and subject to Indictment, Trial, Judgment and Punishment, according to Law.

Section 4.   [1] The Times, Places and Manner of holding Elections for Senators and Representatives, shall be prescribed in each State by the Legislature thereof; but the Congress may at any time by Law make or alter such Regulations, except as to the Places of chusing Senators.

[2] The Congress shall assemble at least once in every Year, and such Meeting shall be on the first Monday in December, unless they shall by Law appoint a different Day.

Section 5. [1] Each House shall be the Judge of the Elections, Returns and Qualifications of its own Members, and a Majority of each shall constitute a Quorum to do Business; but a smaller Number may adjourn from day to day, and may be authorized to compel the Attendance of absent Members, in such Manner, and under such Penalties as each House may provide.

[2] Each House may determine the Rules of its Proceedings, punish its Members for disorderly Behavior, and, with the Concurrence of two thirds, expel a Member.

[3] Each House shall keep a Journal of its Proceedings, and from time to time publish the same, excepting such Parts as may in their Judgment require Secrecy; and the Yeas and Nays of the Members of either House on any question shall, at the Desire of one fifth of those Present, be entered on the Journal.

[4] Neither House, during the Session of Congress, shall, without the Consent of the other, adjourn for more than three days, nor to any other Place than that in which the two Houses shall be sitting.

Section 6. [1] The Senators and Representatives shall receive a Compensation for their Services, to be ascertained by Law, and paid out of the Treasury of the United States. They shall in all Cases, except Treason, Felony and Breach of the Peace, be privileged from Arrest during their Attendance at the Session of their respective Houses, and in going to and returning from the same; and for any Speech or Debate in either House, they shall not be questioned in any other Place.

[2] No Senator or Representative shall, during the Time for which he was elected, be appointed to any civil Office under the Authority of the United States, which shall have been created, or the Emoluments whereof shall have been encreased during such time; and no Person holding any Office under the United States, shall be a Member of either House during his Continuance in Office.

Section 7. [1] All Bills for raising Revenue shall originate in the House of Representatives; but the Senate may propose or concur with Amendments as on other Bills.

[2] Every Bill which shall have passed the House of Representatives and the Senate, shall, before it become a Law, be presented to the President of the United States; If he approve he shall sign it, but if not he shall return it, with his Objections to the House in which it shall have originated, who shall enter the Objections at large on their Journal, and proceed to reconsider it. If after such Reconsideration two thirds of that

House shall agree to pass the Bill, it shall be sent, together with the Objections, to the other House, by which it shall likewise be reconsidered, and if approved by two thirds of that House, it shall become a Law. But in all such Cases the Votes of both Houses shall be determined by yeas and Nays, and the Names of the Persons voting for and against the Bill shall be entered on the Journal of each House respectively. If any Bill shall not be returned by the President within ten Days (Sundays excepted) after it shall have been presented to him, the Same shall be a Law, in like Manner as if he had signed it, unless the Congress by their Adjournment prevents its Return, in which Case it shall not be a Law.

[3] Every Order, Resolution, or Vote to Which the Concurrence of the Senate and House of Representatives may be necessary (except on a question of Adjournment) shall be presented to the President of the United States; and before the Same shall take Effect, shall be approved by him, or being disapproved by him, shall be repassed by two thirds of the Senate and House of Representatives, according to the Rules and Limitations prescribed in the Case of a Bill.

Section 8.   [1] The Congress shall have Power To lay and collect Taxes, Duties, Imposts and Excises, to pay the Debts and provide for the common Defence and general Welfare of the United States; but all Duties, Imposts and Excises shall be uniform throughout the United States;

[2] To borrow money on the credit of the United States;

[3] To regulate Commerce with foreign Nations, and among the several States, and with the Indian Tribes;

[4] To establish an uniform Rule of Naturalization, and uniform Laws on the subject of bankruptcies throughout the United States;

[5] To coin Money, regulate the Value thereof, and of foreign Coin, and fix the Standard of Weights and Measures;

[6] To provide the Punishment of counterfeiting the Securities and current Coin of the United States;

[7] To establish Post Offices and post Roads;

[8] To promote the Progress of Science and useful Arts, by securing for limited Times to Authors and inventors the exclusive Right to their respective Writings and Discoveries;

[9] To constitute Tribunals inferior to the supreme Court;

[10] To define and punish Piracies and Felonies committed on the high Seas, and Offenses against the Law of Nations:

[11] To declare War, grant Letters of Marque and Reprisal, and make Rules concerning Captures on Land and Water;

[12] To raise and support Armies, but no Appropriation of Money to that Use shall be for a longer Term than two Years;

[13] To provide and maintain a Navy;

[14] To make Rules for the Government and Regulation of the land and naval Forces;

[15] To provide for calling forth the Militia to execute the Laws of the Union, suppress Insurrections and repel Invasions;

[16] To provide for organizing, arming, and disciplining, the Militia, and for governing such Part of them as may be employed in the Service of the United States, reserving to the States respectively, the Appointment of the Officers, and the Authority of training the Militia according to the discipline prescribed by Congress;

[17] To exercise exclusive Legislation in all Cases whatsoever, over such District (not exceeding ten Miles square) as may, by Cession of particular States, and the Acceptance of Congress, become the Seat of the Government of the United States, and to exercise like Authority over all Places purchased by the Consent of the Legislature of the State in which the Same shall be, for the Erection of Forts, Magazines, Arsenals, dock-Yards, and other needful Buildings;—And

[18] To make all Laws which shall be necessary and proper for carrying into Execution the foregoing Powers, and all other Powers vested by this Constitution in the Government of the United States, or in any Department or Officer thereof.

Section 9.   [1] The Migration or Importation of such Persons as any of the States now existing shall think proper to admit, shall not be prohibited by the Congress prior to the Year one thousand eight hundred and eight, but a Tax or duty may be imposed on such Importation, not exceeding ten dollars for each Person.

[2] The privilege of the Writ of Habeas Corpus shall not be suspended, unless when in Cases of Rebellion or Invasion the public Safety may require it.

[3] No Bill of Attainder or ex post facto Law shall be passed.

[4] No Capitation, or other direct, Tax shall be laid, unless in Proportion to the Census or Enumeration herein before directed to be taken.

[5] No Tax or Duty shall be laid on Articles exported from any State.

[6] No Preference shall be given by any Regulation of Commerce or Revenue to the Ports of one State over those of another: nor shall Vessels bound to, or from, one State, be obliged to enter, clear, or pay Duties in another.

[7] No Money shall be drawn from the Treasury, but in Consequence of Appropriations made by Law; and a regular Statement and Account of the Receipts and Expenditures of all public Money shall be published from time to time.

[8] No Title of Nobility shall be granted by the United States: And no Person holding any Office of Profit or Trust under them, shall, without the Consent of the Congress, accept of any present, Emolument, Office, or Title, of any kind whatever, from any King, Prince, or foreign State.

Section 10. [1] No State shall enter into any Treaty, Alliance, or Confederation; grant Letters of Marque and Reprisal; coin Money; emit Bills of Credit; make any Thing but gold and silver Coin a Tender in Payment of Debts; pass any Bill of Attainder, ex post facto Law, or Law impairing the obligation of Contracts, or grant any Title of Nobility.

[2] No State shall, without the Consent of the Congress, lay any Imposts or Duties on Imports or Exports, except what may be absolutely necessary for executing its inspection Laws: and the net Produce of all Duties and Imposts, laid by any State on Imports or Exports, shall be for the Use of the Treasury of the United States; and all such Laws shall be subject to the Revision and Controul of the Congress.

[3] No State shall, without the Consent of Congress, lay any Duty of Tonnage, keep Troops, or Ships of War in time of Peace, enter into any Agreement or Compact with another State, or with a foreign Power, or engage in War, unless actually invaded, or in such imminent Danger as will not admit of delay.

ARTICLE II

Section 1. [1] The executive Power shall be vested in a President of the United States of America. He shall hold his Office during the Term of four Years, and, together with the Vice President, chosen for the same Term, be elected, as follows:

[2] Each State shall appoint, in such Manner as the Legislature thereof may direct, a Number of Electors, equal to the whole Number of Senators and Representatives to which the State may be entitled in the Congress: but no Senator or Representative, or Person holding an Office of Trust or Profit under the United States, shall be appointed an Elector.

[3] The Electors shall meet in their respective States, and vote by Ballot for two Persons, of whom one at least shall not be an Inhabitant of the same State with themselves. And they shall make a List of all the Persons voted for, and of the Number of Votes for each; which List they shall sign and certify, and transmit sealed to the Seat of the Government of the United States, directed to the President of the Senate. The President of the Senate shall, in the Presence of the Senate and House of

Representatives, open all the Certificates, and the Votes shall then be counted. The Person having the greatest Number of Votes shall be the President, if such Number be a Majority of the whole Number of Electors appointed; and if there be more than one who have such Majority, and have an equal Number of Votes, then the House of Representatives shall immediately chuse by Ballot one of them for President; and if no Person have a Majority, then from the five highest on the List the said House shall in like Manner chuse the President. But in chusing the President, the Votes shall be taken by States, the Representation from each State having one Vote; a quorum for this Purpose shall consist of a Member or Members from two thirds of the States, and a Majority of all the States shall be necessary to a Choice. In every Case, after the choice of the President, the Person having the greatest Number of Votes of the electors shall be the Vice President. But if there should remain two or more who have equal Votes, the Senate shall chuse from them by Ballot the Vice President.

[4] The Congress may determine the Time of chusing the Electors, and the Day on which they shall give their Votes; which Day shall be the same throughout the United States.

[5] No person except a natural born Citizen, or a Citizen of the United States, at the time of the Adoption of this Constitution, shall be eligible to the Office of President; neither shall any Person be eligible to that Office who shall not have attained to the Age of thirty five Years, and been fourteen Years a Resident within the United States.

[6] In case of the removal of the President from Office, or of his Death, Resignation or Inability to discharge the Powers and Duties of the said Office, the Same shall devolve on the Vice President, and the Congress may by Law provide for the case of Removal, Death, Resignation or Inability, both of the President and Vice President, declaring what Officer shall then act as President, and such Officer shall act accordingly, until the disability be removed, or a President shall be elected.

[7] The President shall, at stated Times, receive for his Services, a Compensation, which shall neither be increased nor diminished during the Period for which he shall have been elected, and he shall not receive within that Period any other Emolument from the United States, or any of them.

[8] Before he enter on the execution of his Office, he shall take the following Oath or Affirmation: "I do solemnly swear (or affirm) that I will faithfully execute the Office of President of the United States, and will to the best of my Ability, preserve, protect and defend the constitution of the United States."

Section 2. [1] The President shall be Commander in Chief of the Army and Navy of the United States, and of the Militia of the several States, when called into the actual Service of the United States; he may require the Opinion, in writing, of the principal Officer in each of the executive Departments, upon any subject relating to the Duties of their respective Offices, and he shall have Power to grant Reprieves and Pardons for Offenses against the United States, except in Cases of Impeachment.

[2] He shall have Power, by and with the Advice and Consent of the Senate, to make Treaties, provided two thirds of the Senators present concur; and he shall nominate, and by and with the Advice and Consent of the Senate, shall appoint Ambassadors, other public Ministers and Consuls, Judges of the supreme Court, and all other Officers of the United States, whose Appointments are not herein otherwise provided for, and which shall be established by Law: but the Congress may by Law vest the Appointment of such inferior Officers, as they think proper, in the President alone, in the Courts of Law, or in the Heads of Departments.

[3] The President shall have Power to fill up all Vacancies that may happen during the Recess of the Senate, by granting Commissions which shall expire at the End of their next Session.

Section 3. He shall from time to time give to the Congress Information of the State of the Union, and recommend to their Consideration such Measures as he shall judge necessary and expedient; he may, on extraordinary Occasions, convene both Houses, or either of them, and in Case of Disagreement between them, with Respect to the Time of Adjournment, he may adjourn them to such Time as he shall think proper; he shall receive Ambassadors and other public Ministers; he shall take Care that the Laws be faithfully executed, and shall Commission all the Officers of the United States.

Section 4. The President and all civil Officers of the United States, shall be removed from Office on Impeachment for, and Conviction of, Treason, Bribery, or other high Crimes and Misdemeanors.

ARTICLE III

Section 1. The judicial Power of the United States shall be vested in one supreme Court, and in such inferior Courts as the Congress may from time to time ordain and establish. The Judges, both of the supreme and inferior Courts, shall hold their Offices during good Behaviour, and shall, at stated Times, receive for their Services, a Compensation, which shall not be diminished during their Continuance in Office.

Section 2. [1] The Judicial Power shall extend to all Cases, in Law and Equity, arising under this Constitution, the Laws of the United

States, and Treaties made, or which shall be made, under their Authority;—to all Cases affecting Ambassadors, other public Ministers and Consuls;—to all Cases of admiralty and maritime Jurisdiction;—to Controversies to which the United States shall be a Party;—to Controversies between two or more States;—between a State and Citizens of another State;—between Citizens of different States;—between Citizens of the same State claiming Lands under Grants of different States, and between a State, or the Citizens thereof, and foreign States, Citizens or Subjects.

[2] In all Cases affecting Ambassadors, other public Ministers and Consuls, and those in which a State shall be a Party, the supreme Court shall have original Jurisdiction. In all the other Cases before mentioned, the supreme Court shall have appellate Jurisdiction, both as to Law and Fact, with such Exceptions, and under such Regulations as the Congress shall make.

[3] The trial of all Crimes, except in Cases of Impeachment, shall be by Jury, and such Trial shall be held in the State where the said Crimes shall have been committed; but when not committed within any State, the Trial shall be at such Place or Places as the Congress may by Law have directed.

Section 3. [1] Treason against the United States, shall consist only in levying War against them, or in adhering to their Enemies, giving them Aid and Comfort. No person shall be convicted of Treason unless on the Testimony of two Witnesses to the same overt Act, or on Confession in open Court.

[2] The Congress shall have Power to declare the Punishment of Treason, but no Attainder of Treason shall work Corruption of Blood, or Forfeiture except during the life of the Person attainted.

ARTICLE IV

Section 1. Full Faith and Credit shall be given in each State to the public Acts, Records, and judicial Proceedings of every other State. And the Congress may by general Laws prescribe the Manner in which such Acts, Records and Proceedings shall be proved, and the Effect thereof.

Section 2. [1] The Citizens of each State shall be entitled to all Privileges and Immunities of Citizens in the several States.

[2] A Person charged in any State with Treason, Felony, or other Crime, who shall flee from Justice, and be found in another State, shall on demand of the executive Authority of the State from which he fled, be delivered up, to be removed to the State having Jurisdiction of the Crime.

[3] No Person held to Service or Labour in one State, under the Laws thereof, escaping into another, shall, in Consequence of any Law or

Regulation therein, be discharged from such Service or Labour, but shall be delivered up on Claim of the Party to whom such Service or Labour may be due.

Section 3.   [1] New States may be admitted by the Congress into this Union; but no new State shall be formed or erected within the Jurisdiction of any other State; nor any State be formed by the Junction of two or more States, or Parts of States, without the Consent of the Legislatures of the States concerned as well as of the Congress.

[2] The Congress shall have Power to dispose of and make all needful Rules and Regulations respecting the Territory or other Property belonging to the United States; and nothing in this Constitution shall be so construed as to Prejudice any Claims of the United States, or of any particular State.

Section 4.   The United States shall guarantee to every State in this Union a Republican Form of Government, and shall protect each of them against Invasion; and on Application of the Legislature, or of the Executive (when the Legislature cannot be convened) against domestic Violence.

ARTICLE V

The Congress, whenever two thirds of both Houses shall deem it necessary, shall propose Amendments to this Constitution, or, on the Application of the Legislatures of two thirds of the several States, shall call a Convention for proposing Amendments, which, in either Case, shall be valid to all Intents and Purposes, as part of this Constitution, when ratified by the Legislatures of three fourths of the several States, or by Conventions in three fourths thereof, as the one or the other Mode of Ratification may be proposed by the Congress; Provided that no Amendment which may be made prior to the Year One thousand eight hundred and eight shall in any Manner affect the first and fourth Clauses in the Ninth Section of the first Article; and that no State, without its Consent, shall be deprived of its equal Suffrage in the Senate.

ARTICLE VI

[1] All Debts contracted and Engagements entered into, before the Adoption of this Constitution, shall be as valid against the United States under this Constitution, as under the Confederation.

[2] This Constitution, and the Laws of the United States which shall be made in Pursuance thereof; and all Treaties made, or which shall be made, under the Authority of the United States, shall be the supreme Law of the Land; and the Judges in every State shall be bound thereby, any Thing in the Constitution or Laws of any State to the Contrary notwithstanding.

[3] The Senators and Representatives before mentioned, and the Members of the several State Legislatures, and all executive and judicial Officers, both of the United States and of the several States, shall be bound by Oath or Affirmation, to support this Constitution; but no religious test shall ever be required as a Qualification to any Office or public Trust under the United States.

ARTICLE VII

The Ratification of the Conventions of nine States shall be sufficient for the Establishment of this Constitution between the States so ratifying the Same.

Done in Convention by the Unanimous Consent of the States present the Seventeenth Day of September in the Year of our Lord one thousand seven hundred and Eighty seven and of the Independence of the United States of America the Twelfth.

ARTICLES IN ADDITION TO, AND AMENDMENT OF, THE CONSTITUTION OF THE UNITED STATES OF AMERICA, PROPOSED BY CONGRESS, AND RATIFIED BY THE LEGISLATURES OF THE SEVERAL STATES, PURSUANT TO THE FIFTH ARTICLE OF THE ORIGINAL CONSTITUTION

AMENDMENT I [1791]

Congress shall make no law respecting an establishment of religion, or prohibiting the free exercise thereof; or abridging the freedom of speech, or of the press; or the right of the people peaceably to assemble, and to petition the Government for a redress of grievances.

AMENDMENT II [1791]

A well regulated Militia, being necessary to the security of a free State, the right of the people to keep and bear Arms, shall not be infringed.

AMENDMENT III [1791]

No Soldier shall, in time of peace be quartered in any house, without the consent of the Owner, nor in time of war, but in a manner to be prescribed by law.

AMENDMENT IV [1791]

The right of the people to be secure in their persons, houses, papers, and effects, against unreasonable searches and seizures, shall not be violated, and no Warrants shall issue, but upon probable cause, supported by Oath or affirmation, and particularly describing the place to be searched, and the persons or things to be seized.

AMENDMENT V [1791]

No person shall be held to answer for a capital, or otherwise infamous crime, unless on a presentment of indictment of a Grand Jury, except in cases arising in the land or naval forces, or in the Militia, when in actual service in time of War or public danger; nor shall any person be subject for the same offence to be twice put in jeopardy of life or limb; nor shall be compelled in any criminal case to be a witness against himself, nor be deprived of life, liberty, or property, without due process of law; nor shall private property be taken for public use, without just compensation.

AMENDMENT VI [1791]

In all criminal prosecutions, the accused shall enjoy the right to a speedy and public trial, by an impartial jury of the State and district wherein the crime shall have been committed, which district shall have been previously ascertained by law, and to be informed of the nature and cause of the accusation; to be confronted with the witnesses against him; to have compulsory process for obtaining witnesses in his favor, and to have the Assistance of Counsel for his defence.

AMENDMENT VII [1791]

In Suits at common law, where the value in controversy shall exceed twenty dollars, the right of trial by jury shall be preserved, and no fact tried by a jury, shall be otherwise re-examined in any Court of the United States, than according to the rules of the common law.

AMENDMENT VIII [1791]

Excessive bail shall not be required, nor excessive fines imposed, nor cruel and unusual punishments inflicted.

AMENDMENT IX [1791]

The enumeration in the Constitution, of certain rights, shall not be construed to deny or disparage others retained by the people.

AMENDMENT X [1791]

The powers not delegated to the United States by the Constitution, nor prohibited by it to the States, are reserved to the States respectively, or to the people.

AMENDMENT XI [1798]

The Judicial power of the United States shall not be construed to extend to any suit in law or equity, commenced or prosecuted against one of the United States by Citizens of another State, or by Citizens or Subjects of any Foreign State.

AMENDMENT XII [1804]

The Electors shall meet in their respective states and vote by ballot for President and Vice-President, one of whom, at least, shall not be an inhabitant of the same state with themselves; they shall name in their ballots the person voted for as President, and in distinct ballots the person voted for as Vice-President, and they shall make distinct lists of all persons voted for as President, and of all persons voted for as Vice-President, and of the number of votes for each, which lists they shall sign and certify, and transmit sealed to the seat of the government of the United States, directed to the President of the Senate;—The President of the Senate shall, in the presence of the Senate and House of Representatives, open all the certificates and the votes shall then be counted;—The person having the greatest number of votes for President, shall be the President, if such number be a majority of the whole number of Electors appointed; and if no person have such majority, then from the persons having the highest numbers not exceeding three on the list of those voted for as President, the House of Representatives shall choose immediately, by ballot, the President. But in choosing the President, the votes shall be taken by states, the representation from each state having one vote; a quorum for this purpose shall consist of a member or members from two-thirds of the states, and a majority of all the states shall be necessary to a choice. And if the House of Representatives shall not choose a President whenever the right of choice shall devolve upon them, before the fourth day of March next following, then the Vice-President shall act as President, as in the case of the death or other constitutional disability of the President.—The person having the greatest number of votes as Vice-President, shall be the Vice-President, if such number be a majority of the whole number of Electors appointed, and if no person have a majority, then from the two highest numbers on the list, the Senate shall choose the Vice-President; a quorum for the purpose shall consist of two-thirds of the whole number of Senators, and a majority of the whole number shall be necessary to a choice. But no person constitutionally ineligible to the office of President shall be eligible to that of Vice-President of the United States.

AMENDMENT XIII [1865]

Section 1.   Neither slavery nor involuntary servitude, except as a punishment for crime whereof the party shall have been duly convicted, shall exist within the United States, or any place subject to their jurisdiction.

Section 2.   Congress shall have power to enforce this article by appropriate legislation.

AMENDMENT XIV [1868]

Section 1.   All persons born or naturalized in the United States, and subject to the jurisdiction thereof, are citizens of the United States and of the State wherein they reside. No State shall make or enforce any law which shall abridge the privileges or immunities of citizens of the United States; nor shall any State deprive any person of life, liberty, or property, without due process of law; nor deny to any person within its jurisdiction the equal protection of the laws.

Section 2.   Representatives shall be apportioned among the several States according to their respective numbers, counting the whole number of persons in each State, excluding Indians not taxed. But when the right to vote at any election for the choice of electors for President and Vice President of the United States, Representatives in Congress, the Executive and Judicial officers of a state, or the members of the Legislature thereof, is denied to any of the male inhabitants of such State, being twenty-one years of age, and citizens of the United States, or in any way abridged, except for participation in rebellion, or other crime, the basis of representation therein shall be reduced in the proportion which the number of such male citizens shall bear to the whole number of male citizens twenty-one years of age in such State.

Section 3.   No person shall be a Senator or Representative in Congress, or elector of President and Vice President, or hold any office, civil or military, under the United States, or under any State, who, having previously taken an oath, as a member of Congress, or as an officer of the United States, or as a member of any State legislature, or as an executive or judicial officer of any State, to support the Constitution of the United States, shall have engaged in insurrection or rebellion against the same, or given aid or comfort to the enemies thereof. But Congress may by a vote of two-thirds of each House, remove such disability.

Section 4.   The validity of the public debt of the United States, authorized by law, including debts incurred for payment of pensions and bounties for services in suppressing insurrection or rebellion, shall not be questioned. But neither the United States nor any State shall assume or pay any debt or obligation incurred in aid of insurrection or rebellion against the United States, or any claim for the loss of emancipation of any slave, but all such debts, obligation and claims shall be held illegal and void.

Section 5.   The Congress shall have power to enforce, by appropriate legislation, the provisions of this article.

AMENDMENT XV [1870]

Section 1. The right of citizens of the United States to vote shall not be denied or abridged by the United States or by any State on account of race, color, or previous condition of servitude.

Section 2. The Congress shall have power to enforce this article by appropriate legislation.

AMENDMENT XVI [1913]

The Congress shall have power to lay and collect taxes on incomes, from whatever source derived, without apportionment among the several States, and without regard to any census or enumeration.

AMENDMENT XVII [1913]

[1] The Senate of the United States shall be composed of two Senators from each State, elected by the people thereof, for six years; and each Senator shall have one vote. The electors in each State shall have the qualifications requisite for electors of the most numerous branch of the State legislatures.

[2] When vacancies happen in the representation of any State in the Senate, the executive authority of such State shall issue writs of election to fill such vacancies: Provided, That the legislature of any State may empower the executive thereof to make temporary appointments until the people fill the vacancies by election as the legislature may direct.

[3] This amendment shall not be so construed as to affect the election or term of any Senator chosen before it becomes valid as part of the Constitution.

AMENDMENT XVIII [1919]

Section 1. After one year from the ratification of this article the manufacture, sale, or transportation of intoxicating liquors within, the importation thereof into, or the exportation thereof from the United States and all territory subject to the jurisdiction thereof for beverage purposes is hereby prohibited.

Section 2. The Congress and the several States shall have concurrent power to enforce this article by appropriate legislation.

Section 3. This article shall be inoperative unless it shall have been ratified as an amendment to the Constitution by the legislatures of the several States, as provided in the Constitution, within seven years from the date of submission hereof to the States by the Congress.

AMENDMENT XVIX [1920]

[1] The right of citizens of the United States to vote shall not be denied or abridged by the United States or by any State on account of sex.

[2] Congress shall have power to enforce this article by appropriate legislation.

AMENDMENT XX [1933]

Section 1.   The terms of the President and Vice President shall end at noon on the 20th day of January, and the terms of Senators and Representatives at noon on the 3d day of January, of the years in which such terms would have ended if this article had not been ratified; and the terms of their successors shall then begin.

Section 2.   The Congress shall assemble at least once in every year, and such meeting shall begin at noon on the 3d day of January, unless they shall by law appoint a different day.

Section 3.   If, at the time fixed for the beginning of the term of the President, the President elect shall have died, the Vice President elect shall become President. If a President shall not have been chosen before the time fixed for the beginning of his term, or if the President elect shall have failed to qualify, then the Vice President elect shall act as President until a President shall have qualified; and the Congress may by law provide for the case wherein neither a President elect nor a Vice President elect shall have qualified, declaring who shall then act as President, or the manner in which one who is to act shall be selected, and such person shall act accordingly until a President or Vice President shall have qualified.

Section 4.   The Congress may by law provide for the case of the death of any of the persons from whom the House of Representatives may choose a President whenever the right of choice shall have devolved upon them and for the case of the death of any of the persons from whom the Senate may choose a Vice President whenever the right of choice shall have devolved upon them.

Section 5.   Sections 1 and 2 shall take effect on the 15th day of October following the ratification of this article.

Section 6.   This article shall be inoperative unless it shall have been ratified as an amendment to the Constitution by the legislatures of three-fourths of the several States within seven years from the date of its submission.

AMENDMENT XXI [1933]

Section 1. The eighteenth article of amendment to the Constitution of the United States is hereby repealed.

Section 2. The transportation or importation into any State, Territory, or possession of the United States for delivery or use therein of intoxicating liquors, in violation of the laws thereof, is hereby prohibited.

Section 3. This article shall be inoperative unless it shall have been ratified as an amendment to the Constitution by conventions in the several States, as provided in the Constitution, within seven years from the date of the submission hereof to the States by the Congress.

AMENDMENT XXII [1951]

Section 1. No person shall be elected to the office of the President more than twice, and no person who has held the office of President, or acted as President, for more than two years of a term to which some other person was elected President shall be elected to the office of the President more than once. But this Article shall not apply to any person holding the office of President when this Article was proposed by the Congress, and shall not prevent any person who may be holding the office of President, or acting as President, during the term within which the Article becomes operative from holding the office of president or acting as President during the remainder of such term.

Section 2. This article shall be inoperative unless it shall have been ratified as an amendment to the Constitution by the legislatures of three-fourths of the several States within seven years from the date of its submission to the States by the Congress.

AMENDMENT XXIII [1961]

Section 1. The District constituting the seat of Government of the United States shall appoint in such manner as the Congress may direct: A number of electors of President and Vice President equal to the whole number of Senators and Representatives in Congress to which the District would be entitled if it were a State, but in no event more than the least populous State; they shall be in addition to those appointed by the States, but they shall be considered, for the purposes of the election of President and Vice President, to be electors appointed by a State; and they shall meet in the District and perform such duties as provided by the twelfth article of amendment.

Section 2. The Congress shall have power to enforce this article by appropriate legislation.

AMENDMENT XXIV [1964]

Section 1. The right of citizens of the United States to vote in any primary or other election for President or Vice President, for electors for President or Vice President, or for Senator or Representative in Congress, shall not be denied or abridged by the United States or any State by reason of failure to pay any poll tax or other tax.

Section 2. The Congress shall have power to enforce this article by appropriate legislation.

AMENDMENT XXV [1967]

Section 1. In case of the removal of the President from office or of his death or resignation, the Vice President shall become President.

Section 2. Whenever there is a vacancy in the office of the Vice President, the President shall nominate a Vice President who shall take office upon confirmation by a majority vote of both Houses of Congress.

Section 3. Whenever the President transmits to the President pro tempore of the Senate and the Speaker of the House of Representatives his written declaration that he is unable to discharge the powers and duties of his office, and until he transmits to them a written declaration to the contrary, such powers and duties shall be discharged by the Vice President as Acting President.

Section 4. Whenever the Vice President and a majority of either the principal officers of the executive departments or of such other body as Congress may by law provide, transmit to the President pro tempore of the Senate and the Speaker of the House of Representatives their written declaration that the President is unable to discharge the powers and duties of his office, the Vice President shall immediately assume the powers and duties of the office as Acting President. Thereafter, when the President transmits to the President pro tempore of the Senate and the Speaker of the House of Representatives his written declaration that no inability exists, he shall resume the powers and duties of his office unless the Vice President and a majority of either the principal officers of the executive department or of such other body as Congress may by law provide, transmit within four days to the President pro tempore of the Senate and the Speaker of the House of Representatives their written declaration that the President is unable to discharge the powers and duties of his office. Thereupon Congress shall decide the issue, assembling within forty-eight hours for that purpose if not in session. If the Congress, within twenty-one days after receipt of the latter written declaration, or, if Congress is not in session, within twenty-one days after Congress is required to assemble, determines by two-thirds vote of both Houses that the President is unable to discharge the powers and duties of his office, the Vice President shall continue to discharge the same as Acting President; otherwise, the President shall resume the powers and duties of his office.

Amendment XXVI [1971]

Section 1. The right of citizens of the United States, who are eighteen years of age or older, to vote shall not be denied or abridged by the United States or by any State on account of age.

Section 2. The Congress shall have power to enforce this article by appropriate legislation.

Amendment XXVII [1992]

No law, varying the compensation for the services of the Senators and Representatives, shall take effect, until an election of Representatives shall have intervened.

APPENDIX 2

SELECTED RULES OF THE U.S. SENATE AND HOUSE OF REPRESENTATIVES (2013–2014)

■ ■ ■

This Appendix reprints relevant congressional rules from the House and the Senate. On many basic questions of sequence (committee consideration before debate, for example), the procedures of both bodies follow a similar outline at a very general level. In practice, however, procedures may differ substantially. The most significant difference between House and Senate procedure is in how debate is conducted. The Senate uses "unanimous consent" (UC) to conduct its business, making UC agreements at every point it proceeds to consider legislation. In the House, debate on the House floor is predetermined by the House Rules Committee, and subject to the large powers of the Speaker of the House.[1] The rules excerpted here are in no way intended to be a manual of parliamentary procedure, but instead, relevant for considering legislative and statutory history as they address voting, conference committees, cloture, authorization versus appropriations, and committee reports.

I. Voting

House Rule XX (1)(b): A recorded vote taken in the House under this paragraph shall be considered a vote by the yeas and nays.

House Rule XX (10): The yeas and nays shall be considered as ordered when the Speaker puts the question on passage of a bill or joint resolution, or on adoption of a conference report. . . .

Senate Rule VI: 1. A quorum shall consist of a majority of the Senators duly chosen and sworn. 2. No Senator shall absent himself from the service of the Senate without leave.

Senate Rule XII: When the yeas and nays are ordered, the names of Senators shall be called alphabetically; and each Senator shall, without debate, declare his assent or dissent to the question. . . .

---

[1] The House and Senate rules can be easily found online and are updated with each new Congress. Karen L. Haas, *Rules of the House of Representatives: One Hundred Thirteenth Congress* (Jan. 3, 2013), available at http://clerk.house.gov/legislative/house-rules.pdf; *Rules of the Senate*, http://www.rules.senate.gov/public/index.cfm?p=RulesOfSenateHome (last visited April 25, 2014).

II. Conference Committees

House Rule XXII (9): The introduction of any language presenting specific additional matter not committed to the conference committee by either House does not constitute a germane modification of the matter in disagreement.

House Rule XXII (10): A Member . . . may raise a point of order against nongermane matter . . . before the commencement of debate on . . . a conference report. . . .

Senate Rule XXVIII 2(a): Conferees shall not insert in their report matter not committed to them by either House, nor shall they strike from the bill matter agreed to by both Houses.

Senate Rule XXVIII 2(b): If matter which was agreed to by both Houses is stricken from the bill a point of order may be made against the report, and if the point of order is sustained, the report is rejected or shall be recommitted to the committee of conference if the House of Representatives has not already acted thereon.

Senate Rule XXVIII 2(c): If new matter is inserted in the report, a point of order may be made against the conference report and it shall be disposed of as provided under paragraph 4.

III. Cloture in the Senate (and post-cloture amendments)

Senate Rule XXII (2): [A]t any time a motion signed by sixteen Senators, to bring to a close the debate upon any . . . matter pending before the Senate . . . is presented to the Senate, the Presiding Officer, or clerk at the direction of the Presiding Officer, shall at once state the motion to the Senate, and one hour after the Senate meets on the following calendar day but one, he shall lay the motion before the Senate and direct that the clerk call the roll, and upon the ascertainment that a quorum is present, the Presiding Officer shall, without debate, submit to the Senate by a yea-and-nay vote the question: "Is it the sense of the Senate that the debate shall be brought to a close?" And if that question shall be decided in the affirmative by three-fifths of the Senators[2] duly chosen and sworn—except on a measure or motion to amend the Senate rules, in which case the necessary affirmative vote shall be two-thirds of the Senators present and voting—then said measure, motion, or other matter pending before the Senate, or the unfinished business, shall be the unfinished business to the exclusion of all other business until disposed of. . . . Except by unanimous consent, no amendment shall be proposed after the vote to bring the debate to a close, unless it had been submitted in writing to the Journal Clerk by 1 o'clock p.m. on the day following the filing of the cloture motion if an amendment in the first degree, and

---

[2]   Three-fifths of the Senate is 60 Senators.

unless it had been so submitted at least one hour prior to the beginning of the cloture vote if an amendment in the second degree.

IV. Authorizations Versus Appropriations Bills

House Rule XXI (2)(b): A provision changing existing law may not be reported in a general appropriation bill. . . .

House Rule XXI (2)(c): An amendment to a general appropriation bill shall not be in order if changing existing law. . . .

Senate Rule XVI (2): The Committee on Appropriations shall not report an appropriation bill containing amendments to such bill proposing new or general legislation. . . .

Senate Rule XVI (4): On a point of order made by any Senator, no amendment . . . which proposes general legislation shall be received to any general appropriation bill . . . and any such amendment or restriction to a general appropriation bill may be laid on the table without prejudice to the bill.

Senate Rule XVI (6): When a point of order is made against any restriction on the expenditure of funds appropriated in a general appropriation bill on the ground that the restriction violates this rule, the rule shall be construed strictly and, in case of doubt, in favor of the point of order.

V. Committee Reports

House Rule XI (2)(*l*): If at the time of approval of a measure or matter by a committee (other than the Committee on Rules) a member of the committee gives notice of intention to file supplemental, minority, or additional views for inclusion in the report to the House thereon, all members shall be entitled to not less than two additional calendar days after the day of such notice . . . to file such written and signed views with the clerk of the committee.

House Rule XIII (2)(a)(1): Except as provided in subparagraph (2), all reports of committees (other than those filed from the floor) shall be delivered to the Clerk for printing and reference to the proper calendar under the direction of the Speaker. . . . The title or subject of each report shall be entered on the Journal and printed in the Congressional Record.

House Rule XIII (2)(a)(2): A bill or resolution reported adversely . . . shall be laid on the table. . . .

House Rule XIII (2)(b)(1): It shall be the duty of the chair of each committee to report or cause to be reported promptly to the House a measure or matter approved by the committee and to take or cause to be taken steps necessary to bring the measure or matter to a vote.

House Rule XIII (2)(b)(2): In any event, the report of a committee on a measure that has been approved by the committee shall be filed within seven calendar days . . . after the day on which a written request for the filing of the report, signed by a majority of the members of the committee, has been filed by the clerk of the committee. . . . This subparagraph does not apply to a report of the Committee on Rules with respect to a rule, joint rule, or order of business of the House. . . .

House Rule XIII (2)(c): All supplemental, minority, or additional views . . . by one or more members of a committee shall be included in, and shall be a part of the report filed by the committee with respect to a measure or matter. . . . This clause . . . does not preclude the immediate filing or printing of a committee report in the absence of a timely request for the opportunity to file supplemental, minority or additional views. . . .

House Rule XIII (4)(a)(1): Except as specified in subparagraph (2), it shall not be in order to consider in the House a measure or matter reported by a committee until the third calendar day . . . on which each report of a committee on that measure or matter has been available to Members, Delegates, and the Resident Commissioner.

House Rule XIII (4)(b): A committee that reports a measure or matter shall make every reasonable effort to have its hearings thereon (if any) printed and available for distribution to the Members, Delegates, and the Resident Commissioner before the consideration of the measure or matter in the House.

Senate Rule XI (6): Every bill and joint resolution introduced or reported from a committee, and all bills and joint resolutions received from the House of Representatives, and all reports of committees, shall be printed, unless, for the dispatch of business of the Senate, such printing may be dispensed with.

Senate Rule XVII (5): Any measure or matter reported by any standing committee shall not be considered in the Senate unless the report of that committee upon that measure or matter has been available to Members for at least two calendar days (excluding Sundays and legal holidays) prior to the consideration of that measure or matter. If hearings have been held on any such measure or matter so reported, the committee reporting the measure or matter shall make every reasonable effort to have such hearings printed and available for distribution to the Members of the Senate prior to the consideration of such measure or matter in the Senate. This paragraph (1) may be waived by joint agreement of the Majority Leader and the Minority Leader of the Senate; and (2) shall not apply to (A) any measure for the declaration of war, or the declaration of a national emergency, by the Congress. . . .

Senate Rule XXVI (10)(c): If at the time of approval of a measure or matter by any committee (except the Committee on Appropriations), any member of the committee gives notice of intention to file supplemental, minority, or additional views, that member shall be entitled to not less than three calendar days in which to file such views, in writing, with the clerk of the committee. All such views so filed by one or more members of the committee shall be included within, and shall be a part of, the report filed by the committee with respect to that measure or matter. The report of the committee upon that measure or matter shall be printed in a single volume which (1) shall include all supplemental, minority, or additional views which have been submitted by the time of the filing of the report, and (2) shall bear upon its cover a recital that supplemental, minority, or additional views are included as part of the report. This subparagraph does not preclude (A) the immediate filing and printing of a committee report unless timely request for the opportunity to file supplemental, minority, or additional views has been made as provided by this subparagraph. . . .

APPENDIX 3

CIVIL RIGHTS ACT OF 1964, TITLE VII

■ ■ ■

(as printed in the Statutes at Large)

TITLE VII—EQUAL EMPLOYMENT OPPORTUNITY

DEFINITIONS

SEC. 701. For the purposes of this title—

(a) The term "person" includes one or more individuals, labor unions, partnerships, associations, corporations, legal representatives, mutual companies, joint-stock companies, trusts, unincorporated organizations, trustees, trustees in bankruptcy, or receivers. "Person."

(b) The term "employer" means a person engaged in an industry affecting commerce who has twenty-five or more employees for each working day in each of twenty or more calendar weeks in the current or preceding calendar year, and any agent of such a person, but such term does not include (1) the United States, a corporation wholly owned by the Government of the United States, an Indian tribe, or a State or political subdivision thereof, (2) a bona fide private membership club (other than a labor organization) which is exempt from taxation under section 501(c) of the Internal Revenue Code of 1954: *Provided,* That during the first year after the effective date prescribed in subsection (a) of section 716, persons having fewer than one hun- "Employer."

68A Stat. 163;
74 Stat. 534.
26 USC 501.

254   PUBLIC LAW 88-352–JULY 2, 1964   [78 STAT.

dred employees (and their agents) shall not be considered employers, and, during the second year after such date, persons having fewer than seventy-five employees (and their agents) shall not be considered employers, and, during the third year after such date, persons having fewer than fifty employees (and their agents) shall not be considered employers: *Provided further*, That it shall be the policy of the United States to insure equal employment opportunities for Federal employees without discrimination because of race, color, religion, sex or national origin and the President shall utilize his existing authority to effectuate this policy.

"Employment agency."

(c) The term "employment agency" means any person regularly undertaking with or without compensation to procure employees for an employer or to procure for employees opportunities to work for an employer and includes an agent of such a person; but shall not include an agency of the United States, or an agency of a State or political subdivision of a State, except that such term shall include the United States Employment Service and the system of State and local employment services receiving Federal assistance.

"Labor organization."

(d) The term "labor organization" means a labor organization engaged in an industry affecting commerce, and any agent of such an organization, and includes any organization of any kind, any agency, or employee representation committee, group, association, or plan so engaged in which employees participate and which exists for the purpose, in whole or in part, of dealing with employers concerning grievances, labor disputes, wages, rates of pay, hours, or other terms or conditions of employment, and any conference, general committee, joint or system board, or joint council so engaged which is subordinate to a national or international labor organization.

(e) A labor organization shall be deemed to be engaged in an industry affecting commerce if (1) it maintains or operates a hiring hall or hiring office which procures employees for an employer or procures for employees opportunities to work for an employer, or (2) the number of its members (or, where it is a labor organization composed of other labor organizations or their representatives, if the aggregate number of the members of such other labor organization) is (A) one hundred or more during the first year after the effective date prescribed in subsection (a) of section 716, (B) seventy-five or more during the second year after such date or fifty or more during the third year, or (C) twenty-five or more thereafter, and such labor organization—

61 Stat. 136.
29 USC 167.
44 Stat. 577;
49 Stat. 1189.
45 USC 151.

(1) is the certified representative of employees under the provisions of the National Labor Relations Act, as amended, or the Railway Labor Act, as amended;

(2) although not certified, is a national or international labor organization or a local labor organization recognized or acting as the representative of employees of an employer or employers engaged in an industry affecting commerce; or

(3) has chartered a local labor organization or subsidiary body which is representing or actively seeking to represent employees of employers within the meaning of paragraph (1) or (2); or

(4) has been chartered by a labor organization representing or actively seeking to represent employees within the meaning of paragraph (1) or (2) as the local or subordinate body through which such employees may enjoy membership or become affiliated with such labor organization; or

(5) is a conference, general committee, joint or system board, or joint council subordinate to a national or international labor organization, which includes a labor organization engaged in an

78 STAT.]   PUBLIC LAW 88-352—JULY 2, 1964   255

industry affecting commerce within the meaning of any of the preceding paragraphs of this subsection.

(f) The term "employee" means an individual employed by an employer. *"Employee."*

(g) The term "commerce" means trade, traffic, commerce, transportation, transmission, or communication among the several States; or between a State and any place outside thereof; or within the District of Columbia, or a possession of the United States; or between points in the same State but through a point outside thereof. *"Commerce."*

(h) The term "industry affecting commerce" means any activity, business, or industry in commerce or in which a labor dispute would hinder or obstruct commerce or the free flow of commerce and includes any activity or industry "affecting commerce" within the meaning of the Labor-Management Reporting and Disclosure Act of 1959. *"Industry affecting commerce."*   73 Stat. 519. 29 USC 401 note.

(i) The term "State" includes a State of the United States, the District of Columbia, Puerto Rico, the Virgin Islands, American Samoa, Guam, Wake Island, the Canal Zone, and Outer Continental Shelf lands defined in the Outer Continental Shelf Lands Act. *"State."*   67 Stat. 462. 43 USC 1331 note.

EXEMPTION

SEC. 702. This title shall not apply to an employer with respect to the employment of aliens outside any State, or to a religious corporation, association, or society with respect to the employment of individuals of a particular religion to perform work connected with the carrying on by such corporation, association, or society of its religious activities or to an educational institution with respect to the employment of individuals to perform work connected with the educational activities of such institution. *Religious organizations, etc.*

DISCRIMINATION BECAUSE OF RACE, COLOR, RELIGION, SEX, OR NATIONAL ORIGIN

SEC. 703. (a) It shall be an unlawful employment practice for an employer— *Unlawful practices.*   *Employers.*

(1) to fail or refuse to hire or to discharge any individual, or otherwise to discriminate against any individual with respect to his compensation, terms, conditions, or privileges of employment, because of such individual's race, color, religion, sex, or national origin; or

(2) to limit, segregate, or classify his employees in any way which would deprive or tend to deprive any individual of employment opportunities or otherwise adversely affect his status as an employee, because of such individual's race, color, religion, sex, or national origin.

(b) It shall be an unlawful employment practice for an employment agency to fail or refuse to refer for employment, or otherwise to discriminate against, any individual because of his race, color, religion, sex, or national origin, or to classify or refer for employment any individual on the basis of his race, color, religion, sex, or national origin. *Employment agency.*

(c) It shall be an unlawful employment practice for a labor organization— *Labor organization.*

(1) to exclude or to expel from its membership, or otherwise to discriminate against, any individual because of his race, color, religion, sex, or national origin;

(2) to limit, segregate, or classify its membership, or to classify or fail or refuse to refer for employment any individual, in any

way which would deprive or tend to deprive any individual of employment opportunities, or would limit such employment opportunities or otherwise adversely affect his status as an employee or as an applicant for employment, because of such individual's race, color, religion, sex, or national origin; or

(3) to cause or attempt to cause an employer to discriminate against an individual in violation of this section.

Training programs.

(d) It shall be an unlawful employment practice for any employer, labor organization, or joint labor-management committee controlling apprenticeship or other training or retraining, including on-the-job training programs to discriminate against any individual because of his race, color, religion, sex, or national origin in admission to, or employment in, any program established to provide apprenticeship or other training.

Exceptions.

(e) Notwithstanding any other provision of this title, (1) it shall not be an unlawful employment practice for an employer to hire and employ employees, for an employment agency to classify, or refer for employment any individual, for a labor organization to classify its membership or to classify or refer for employment any individual, or for an employer, labor organization, or joint labor-management committee controlling apprenticeship or other training or retraining programs to admit or employ any individual in any such program, on the basis of his religion, sex, or national origin in those certain instances where religion, sex, or national origin is a bona fide occupational qualification reasonably necessary to the normal operation of that particular business or enterprise, and (2) it shall not be an unlawful employment practice for a school, college, university, or other educational institution or institution of learning to hire and employ employees of a particular religion if such school, college, university, or other educational institution or institution of learning is, in whole or in substantial part, owned, supported, controlled, or managed by a particular religion or by a particular religious corporation, association, or society, or if the curriculum of such school, college, university, or other educational institution or institution of learning is directed toward the propagation of a particular religion.

(f) As used in this title, the phrase "unlawful employment practice" shall not be deemed to include any action or measure taken by an employer, labor organization, joint labor-management committee, or employment agency with respect to an individual who is a member of the Communist Party of the United States or of any other organization required to register as a Communist-action or Communist-front organization by final order of the Subversive Activities Control Board

64 Stat. 987.
50 USC 781
note.

pursuant to the Subversive Activities Control Act of 1950.

(g) Notwithstanding any other provision of this title, it shall not be an unlawful employment practice for an employer to fail or refuse to hire and employ any individual for any position, for an employer to discharge any individual from any position, or for an employment agency to fail or refuse to refer any individual for employment in any position, or for a labor organization to fail or refuse to refer any individual for employment in any position, if—

(1) the occupancy of such position, or access to the premises in or upon which any part of the duties of such position is performed or is to be performed, is subject to any requirement imposed in the interest of the national security of the United States under any security program in effect pursuant to or administered under any statute of the United States or any Executive order of the President; and

(2) such individual has not fulfilled or has ceased to fulfill that requirement.

(h) Notwithstanding any other provision of this title, it shall not be an unlawful employment practice for an employer to apply different standards of compensation, or different terms, conditions, or privileges of employment pursuant to a bona fide seniority or merit system, or a system which measures earnings by quantity or quality of production or to employees who work in different locations, provided that such differences are not the result of an intention to discriminate because of race, color, religion, sex, or national origin, nor shall it be an unlawful employment practice for an employer to give and to act upon the results of any professionally developed ability test provided that such test, its administration or action upon the results is not designed, intended or used to discriminate because of race, color, religion, sex or national origin. It shall not be an unlawful employment practice under this title for any employer to differentiate upon the basis of sex in determining the amount of the wages or compensation paid or to be paid to employees of such employer if such differentiation is authorized by the provisions of section 6(d) of the Fair Labor Standards Act of 1938, as amended (29 U.S.C. 206(d)). *77 Stat. 56. 29 USC 206.*

(i) Nothing contained in this title shall apply to any business or *Indians.* enterprise on or near an Indian reservation with respect to any publicly announced employment practice of such business or enterprise under which a preferential treatment is given to any individual because he is an Indian living on or near a reservation.

(j) Nothing contained in this title shall be interpreted to require *Preferential* any employer, employment agency, labor organization, or joint labor- *treatment.* management committee subject to this title to grant preferential treatment to any individual or to any group because of the race, color, religion, sex, or national origin of such individual or group on account of an imbalance which may exist with respect to the total number or percentage of persons of any race, color, religion, sex, or national origin employed by any employer, referred or classified for employment by any employment agency or labor organization, admitted to membership or classified by any labor organization, or admitted to, or employed in, any apprenticeship or other training program, in comparison with the total number or percentage of persons of such race, color, religion, sex, or national origin in any community, State, section, or other area, or in the available work force in any community, State, section, or other area.

OTHER UNLAWFUL EMPLOYMENT PRACTICES

SEC. 704. (a) It shall be an unlawful employment practice for an employer to discriminate against any of his employees or applicants for employment, for an employment agency to discriminate against any individual, or for a labor organization to discriminate against any member thereof or applicant for membership, because he has opposed any practice made an unlawful employment practice by this title, or because he has made a charge, testified, assisted, or participated in any manner in an investigation, proceeding, or hearing under this title.

(b) It shall be an unlawful employment practice for an employer, labor organization, or employment agency to print or publish or cause to be printed or published any notice or advertisement relating to employment by such an employer or membership in or any classification or referral for employment by such a labor organization, or relating to any classification or referral for employment by such an employment agency, indicating any preference, limitation, specification, or discrimination, based on race, color, religion, sex, or national origin, except that such a notice or advertisement may indicate a preference, limitation, specification, or discrimination based on religion, sex, or national origin when religion, sex, or national origin is a bona fide occupational qualification for employment.

EQUAL EMPLOYMENT OPPORTUNITY COMMISSION

Establishment.

SEC. 705. (a) There is hereby created a Commission to be known as the Equal Employment Opportunity Commission, which shall be composed of five members, not more than three of whom shall be members of the same political party, who shall be appointed by the President *Term of office.* by and with the advice and consent of the Senate. One of the original members shall be appointed for a term of one year, one for a term of two years, one for a term of three years, one for a term of four years, and one for a term of five years, beginning from the date of enactment of this title, but their successors shall be appointed for terms of five years each, except that any individual chosen to fill a vacancy shall be appointed only for the unexpired term of the member whom he shall succeed. The President shall designate one member to serve as Chairman of the Commission, and one member to serve as Vice Chairman. The Chairman shall be responsible on behalf of the Commission for the administrative operations of the Commission, and shall appoint, in accordance with the civil service laws, such officers, agents, attorneys, and employees as it deems necessary to assist it in the performance of its functions and to fix their compensation in *Post, p. 400.* accordance with the Classification Act of 1949, as amended. The *5 USC 1071* Vice Chairman shall act as Chairman in the absence or disability of *note.* the Chairman or in the event of a vacancy in that office.

(b) A vacancy in the Commission shall not impair the right of the remaining members to exercise all the powers of the Commission and three members thereof shall constitute a quorum.

(c) The Commission shall have an official seal which shall be judicially noticed.

Reports to the (d) The Commission shall at the close of each fiscal year report to *President and* the Congress and to the President concerning the action it has taken; *Congress.* the names, salaries, and duties of all individuals in its employ and the moneys it has disbursed; and shall make such further reports on the cause of and means of eliminating discrimination and such recommendations for further legislation as may appear desirable.

70 Stat. 736. (e) The Federal Executive Pay Act of 1956, as amended (5 U.S.C. *5 USC 2201* 2201–2209), is further amended— *note.*

(1) by adding to section 105 thereof (5 U.S.C. 2204) the following clause:

"(32) Chairman, Equal Employment Opportunity Commission"; and

70 Stat. 737. (2) by adding to clause (45) of section 106(a) thereof (5 *5 USC 2205.* U.S.C. 2205(a)) the following: "Equal Employment Opportunity Commission (4)."

(f) The principal office of the Commission shall be in or near the District of Columbia, but it may meet or exercise any or all its powers at any other place. The Commission may establish such regional or State offices as it deems necessary to accomplish the purpose of this title.

Powers. (g) The Commission shall have power—

(1) to cooperate with and, with their consent, utilize regional, State, local, and other agencies, both public and private, and individuals;

(2) to pay to witnesses whose depositions are taken or who are summoned before the Commission or any of its agents the same witness and mileage fees as are paid to witnesses in the courts of the United States;

(3) to furnish to persons subject to this title such technical assistance as they may request to further their compliance with this title or an order issued thereunder;

(4) upon the request of (i) any employer, whose employees or some of them, or (ii) any labor organization, whose members or some of them, refuse or threaten to refuse to cooperate in effectuating the provisions of this title, to assist in such effectuation by conciliation or such other remedial action as is provided by this title;

(5) to make such technical studies as are appropriate to effectuate the purposes and policies of this title and to make the results of such studies available to the public;

(6) to refer matters to the Attorney General with recommendations for intervention in a civil action brought by an aggrieved party under section 706, or for the institution of a civil action by the Attorney General under section 707, and to advise, consult, and assist the Attorney General on such matters.

(h) Attorneys appointed under this section may, at the direction of the Commission, appear for and represent the Commission in any case in court.

(i) The Commission shall, in any of its educational or promotional activities, cooperate with other departments and agencies in the performance of such educational and promotional activities.

(j) All officers, agents, attorneys, and employees of the Commission shall be subject to the provisions of section 9 of the Act of August 2, 1939, as amended (the Hatch Act), notwithstanding any exemption contained in such section.

53 Stat. 1148;
64 Stat. 475.
5 USC 118i.

PREVENTION OF UNLAWFUL EMPLOYMENT PRACTICES

Sec. 706. (a) Whenever it is charged in writing under oath by a person claiming to be aggrieved, or a written charge has been filed by a member of the Commission where he has reasonable cause to believe a violation of this title has occurred (and such charge sets forth the facts upon which it is based) that an employer, employment agency, or labor organization has engaged in an unlawful employment practice, the Commission shall furnish such employer, employment agency, or labor organization (hereinafter referred to as the "respondent") with a copy of such charge and shall make an investigation of such charge, provided that such charge shall not be made public by the Commission. If the Commission shall determine, after such investigation, that there is reasonable cause to believe that the charge is true, the Commission shall endeavor to eliminate any such alleged unlawful employment practice by informal methods of conference, conciliation, and persuasion. Nothing said or done during and as a part of such endeavors may be made public by the Commission without the written consent of the parties, or used as evidence in a subsequent proceeding. Any officer or employee of the Commission, who shall make public in any manner whatever any information in violation of this subsection shall be deemed guilty of a misdemeanor and upon conviction thereof shall be fined not more than $1,000 or imprisoned not more than one year.

(b) In the case of an alleged unlawful employment practice occurring in a State, or political subdivision of a State, which has a State or local law prohibiting the unlawful employment practice alleged and establishing or authorizing a State or local authority to grant or seek relief from such practice or to institute criminal proceedings with respect thereto upon receiving notice thereof, no charge may be filed under subsection (a) by the person aggrieved before the expira-

Legal proceedings.

260   PUBLIC LAW 88-352—JULY 2, 1964   [78 STAT.

tion of sixty days after proceedings have been commenced under the State or local law, unless such proceedings have been earlier terminated, provided that such sixty-day period shall be extended to one hundred and twenty days during the first year after the effective date of such State or local law. If any requirement for the commencement of such proceedings is imposed by a State or local authority other than a requirement of the filing of a written and signed statement of the facts upon which the proceeding is based, the proceeding shall be deemed to have been commenced for the purposes of this subsection at the time such statement is sent by registered mail to the appropriate State or local authority.

Time require-ments.

(c) In the case of any charge filed by a member of the Commission alleging an unlawful employment practice occurring in a State or political subdivision of a State, which has a State or local law prohibiting the practice alleged and establishing or authorizing a State or local authority to grant or seek relief from such practice or to institute criminal proceedings with respect thereto upon receiving notice thereof, the Commission shall, before taking any action with respect to such charge, notify the appropriate State or local officials and, upon request, afford them a reasonable time, but not less than sixty days (provided that such sixty-day period shall be extended to one hundred and twenty days during the first year after the effective day of such State or local law), unless a shorter period is requested, to act under such State or local law to remedy the practice alleged.

(d) A charge under subsection (a) shall be filed within ninety days after the alleged unlawful employment practice occurred, except that in the case of an unlawful employment practice with respect to which the person aggrieved has followed the procedure set out in subsection (b), such charge shall be filed by the person aggrieved within two hundred and ten days after the alleged unlawful employment practice occurred, or within thirty days after receiving notice that the State or local agency has terminated the proceedings under the State or local law, whichever is earlier, and a copy of such charge shall be filed by the Commission with the State or local agency.

(e) If within thirty days after a charge is filed with the Commission or within thirty days after expiration of any period of reference under subsection (c) (except that in either case such period may be extended to not more than sixty days upon a determination by the Commission that further efforts to secure voluntary compliance are warranted), the Commission has been unable to obtain voluntary compliance with this title, the Commission shall so notify the person aggrieved and a civil action may, within thirty days thereafter, be brought against the respondent named in the charge (1) by the person claiming to be aggrieved, or (2) if such charge was filed by a member of the Commission, by any person whom the charge alleges was aggrieved by the alleged unlawful employment practice. Upon application by the complainant and in such circumstances as the court may deem just, the court may appoint an attorney for such complainant and may authorize the commencement of the action without the payment of fees, costs, or security. Upon timely application, the court may, in its discretion, permit the Attorney General to intervene in such civil action if he certifies that the case is of general public importance. Upon request, the court may, in its discretion, stay further proceedings for not more than sixty days pending the termination of State or local proceedings described in subsection (b) or the efforts of the Commission to obtain voluntary compliance.

Courts. Jurisdiction.

(f) Each United States district court and each United States court of a place subject to the jurisdiction of the United States shall have jurisdiction of actions brought under this title. Such an action may be brought in any judicial district in the State in which the unlawful employment practice is alleged to have been committed, in the judicial district in which the employment records relevant to such practice are maintained and administered, or in the judicial district in which the plaintiff would have worked but for the alleged unlawful employment practice, but if the respondent is not found within any such district, such an action may be brought within the judicial district in which the respondent has his principal office. For purposes of sections 1404 and 1406 of title 28 of the United States Code, the judicial district in which the respondent has his principal office shall in all cases be considered a district in which the action might have been brought.

62 Stat. 937.
74 Stat. 912;
76A Stat. 699.

(g) If the court finds that the respondent has intentionally engaged in or is intentionally engaging in an unlawful employment practice charged in the complaint, the court may enjoin the respondent from engaging in such unlawful employment practice, and order such affirmative action as may be appropriate, which may include reinstatement or hiring of employees, with or without back pay (payable by the employer, employment agency, or labor organization, as the case may be, responsible for the unlawful employment practice). Interim earnings or amounts earnable with reasonable diligence by the person or persons discriminated against shall operate to reduce the back pay otherwise allowable. No order of the court shall require the admission or reinstatement of an individual as a member of a union or the hiring, reinstatement, or promotion of an individual as an employee, or the payment to him of any back pay, if such individual was refused admission, suspended, or expelled or was refused employment or advancement or was suspended or discharged for any reason other than discrimination on account of race, color, religion, sex or national origin or in violation of section 704(a).

(h) The provisions of the Act entitled "An Act to amend the Judicial Code and to define and limit the jurisdiction of courts sitting in equity, and for other purposes," approved March 23, 1932 (29 U.S.C. 101–115), shall not apply with respect to civil actions brought under this section.

47 Stat. 70.

(i) In any case in which an employer, employment agency, or labor organization fails to comply with an order of a court issued in a civil action brought under subsection (e), the Commission may commence proceedings to compel compliance with such order.

(j) Any civil action brought under subsection (e) and any proceedings brought under subsection (i) shall be subject to appeal as provided in sections 1291 and 1292, title 28, United States Code.

62 Stat. 929.
65 Stat. 726;
72 Stat. 348,
1770.
Costs, fees.

(k) In any action or proceeding under this title the court, in its discretion, may allow the prevailing party, other than the Commission or the United States, a reasonable attorney's fee as part of the costs, and the Commission and the United States shall be liable for costs the same as a private person.

SEC. 707. (a) Whenever the Attorney General has reasonable cause to believe that any person or group of persons is engaged in a pattern or practice of resistance to the full enjoyment of any of the rights secured by this title, and that the pattern or practice is of such a nature and is intended to deny the full exercise of the rights herein described, the Attorney General may bring a civil action in the appropriate district court of the United States by filing with it a complaint (1) signed by him (or in his absence the Acting Attorney General), (2) setting forth facts pertaining to such pattern or practice, and (3) requesting such relief, including an application for a permanent or temporary injunction, restraining order or other order against the

Suits by Attorney General.

person or persons responsible for such pattern or practice, as he deems necessary to insure the full enjoyment of the rights herein described.

(b) The district courts of the United States shall have and shall exercise jurisdiction of proceedings instituted pursuant to this section, and in any such proceeding the Attorney General may file with the clerk of such court a request that a court of three judges be convened to hear and determine the case. Such request by the Attorney General shall be accompanied by a certificate that, in his opinion, the case is of general public importance. A copy of the certificate and request for a three-judge court shall be immediately furnished by such clerk to the chief judge of the circuit (or in his absence, the presiding circuit judge of the circuit) in which the case is pending. Upon receipt of such request it shall be the duty of the chief judge of the circuit or the presiding circuit judge, as the case may be, to designate immediately three judges in such circuit, of whom at least one shall be a circuit judge and another of whom shall be a district judge of the court in which the proceeding was instituted, to hear and determine such case, and it shall be the duty of the judges so designated to assign the case for hearing at the earliest practicable date, to participate in the hearing and determination thereof, and to cause the case to be in every way expedited. An appeal from the final judgment of such court will lie to the Supreme Court.

In the event the Attorney General fails to file such a request in any such proceeding, it shall be the duty of the chief judge of the district (or in his absence, the acting chief judge) in which the case is pending immediately to designate a judge in such district to hear and determine the case. In the event that no judge in the district is available to hear and determine the case, the chief judge of the district, or the acting chief judge, as the case may be, shall certify this fact to the chief judge of the circuit (or in his absence, the acting chief judge) who shall then designate a district or circuit judge of the circuit to hear and determine the case.

It shall be the duty of the judge designated pursuant to this section to assign the case for hearing at the earliest practicable date and to cause the case to be in every way expedited.

EFFECT ON STATE LAWS

SEC. 708. Nothing in this title shall be deemed to exempt or relieve any person from any liability, duty, penalty, or punishment provided by any present or future law of any State or political subdivision of a State, other than any such law which purports to require or permit the doing of any act which would be an unlawful employment practice under this title.

INVESTIGATIONS, INSPECTIONS, RECORDS, STATE AGENCIES

SEC. 709. (a) In connection with any investigation of a charge filed under section 706, the Commission or its designated representative shall at all reasonable times have access to, for the purposes of examination, and the right to copy any evidence of any person being investigated or proceeded against that relates to unlawful employment practices covered by this title and is relevant to the charge under investigation.

Agreements, State and local agencies.

(b) The Commission may cooperate with State and local agencies charged with the administration of State fair employment practices laws and, with the consent of such agencies, may for the purpose of carrying out its functions and duties under this title and within the limitation of funds appropriated specifically for such purpose, utilize the services of such agencies and their employees and, notwithstanding any other provision of law, may reimburse such agencies and their employees for services rendered to assist the Commission in carrying out this title. In furtherance of such cooperative efforts, the Commission may enter into written agreements with such State or local agencies and such agreements may include provisions under which the Commission shall refrain from processing a charge in any cases or class of cases specified in such agreements and under which no person may bring a civil action under section 706 in any cases or class of cases so specified, or under which the Commission shall relieve any person or class of persons in such State or locality from requirements imposed under this section. The Commission shall rescind any such agreement whenever it determines that the agreement no longer serves the interest of effective enforcement of this title.

(c) Except as provided in subsection (d), every employer, employment agency, and labor organization subject to this title shall (1) make and keep such records relevant to the determinations of whether unlawful employment practices have been or are being committed, (2) preserve such records for such periods, and (3) make such reports therefrom, as the Commission shall prescribe by regulation or order, after public hearing, as reasonable, necessary, or appropriate for the enforcement of this title or the regulations or orders thereunder. The Commission shall, by regulation, require each employer, labor organization, and joint labor-management committee subject to this title which controls an apprenticeship or other training program to maintain such records as are reasonably necessary to carry out the purpose of this title, including, but not limited to, a list of applicants who wish to participate in such program, including the chronological order in which such applications were received, and shall furnish to the Commission, upon request, a detailed description of the manner in which persons are selected to participate in the apprenticeship or other training program. Any employer, employment agency, labor organization, or joint labor-management committee which believes that the application to it of any regulation or order issued under this section would result in undue hardship may (1) apply to the Commission for an exemption from the application of such regulation or order, or (2) bring a civil action in the United States district court for the district where such records are kept. If the Commission or the court, as the case may be, finds that the application of the regulation or order to the employer, employment agency, or labor organization in question would impose an undue hardship, the Commission or the court, as the case may be, may grant appropriate relief.

(d) The provisions of subsection (c) shall not apply to any employer, employment agency, labor organization, or joint labor-management committee with respect to matters occurring in any State or political subdivision thereof which has a fair employment practice law during any period in which such employer, employment agency, labor organization, or joint labor-management committee is subject to such law, except that the Commission may require such notations on records which such employer, employment agency, labor organization, or joint labor-management committee keeps or is required to keep as are necessary because of differences in coverage or methods of enforcement between the State or local law and the provisions of this title. Where an employer is required by Executive Order 10925, issued March 6, 1961, or by any other Executive order prescribing fair employment practices for Government contractors and subcontractors, or by rules or regulations issued thereunder, to file reports relating to his employment practices with any Federal agency or committee, and he is substantially in compliance with such requirements, the Commission shall not require him to file additional reports pursuant to subsection (c) of this section.

264   PUBLIC LAW 88-352—JULY 2, 1964   [78 Stat.

Prohibited disclosures.

(e) It shall be unlawful for any officer or employee of the Commission to make public in any manner whatever any information obtained by the Commission pursuant to its authority under this section prior to the institution of any proceeding under this title involving such information. Any officer or employee of the Commission who shall make public in any manner whatever any information in violation of this subsection shall be guilty of a misdemeanor and upon conviction thereof, shall be fined not more than $1,000, or imprisoned not more than one year.

INVESTIGATORY POWERS

Sec. 710. (a) For the purposes of any investigation of a charge filed under the authority contained in section 706, the Commission shall have authority to examine witnesses under oath and to require the production of documentary evidence relevant or material to the charge under investigation.

(b) If the respondent named in a charge filed under section 706 fails or refuses to comply with a demand of the Commission for permission to examine or to copy evidence in conformity with the provisions of section 709(a), or if any person required to comply with the provisions of section 709 (c) or (d) fails or refuses to do so, or if any person fails or refuses to comply with a demand by the Commission to give testimony under oath, the United States district court for the district in which such person is found, resides, or transacts business, shall, upon application of the Commission, have jurisdiction to issue to such person an order requiring him to comply with the provisions of section 709 (c) or (d) or to comply with the demand of the Commission, but the attendance of a witness may not be required outside the State where he is found, resides, or transacts business and the production of evidence may not be required outside the State where such evidence is kept.

Petitions.

(c) Within twenty days after the service upon any person charged under section 706 of a demand by the Commission for the production of documentary evidence or for permission to examine or to copy evidence in conformity with the provisions of section 709(a), such person may file in the district court of the United States for the judicial district in which he resides, is found, or transacts business, and serve upon the Commission a petition for an order of such court modifying or setting aside such demand. The time allowed for compliance with the demand in whole or in part as deemed proper and ordered by the court shall not run during the pendency of such petition in the court. Such petition shall specify each ground upon which the petitioner relies in seeking such relief, and may be based upon any failure of such demand to comply with the provisions of this title or with the limitations generally applicable to compulsory process or upon any constitutional or other legal right or privilege of such person. No objection which is not raised by such a petition may be urged in the defense to a proceeding initiated by the Commission under subsection (b) for enforcement of such a demand unless such proceeding is commenced by the Commission prior to the expiration of the twenty-day period, or unless the court determines that the defendant could not reasonably have been aware of the availability of such ground of objection.

(d) In any proceeding brought by the Commission under subsection (b), except as provided in subsection (c) of this section, the defendant may petition the court for an order modifying or setting aside the demand of the Commission.

NOTICES TO BE POSTED

SEC. 711. (a) Every employer, employment agency, and labor organization, as the case may be, shall post and keep posted in conspicuous places upon its premises where notices to employees, applicants for employment, and members are customarily posted a notice to be prepared or approved by the Commission setting forth excerpts from or, summaries of, the pertinent provisions of this title and information pertinent to the filing of a complaint.

(b) A willful violation of this section shall be punishable by a fine of not more than $100 for each separate offense.

VETERANS' PREFERENCE

SEC. 712. Nothing contained in this title shall be construed to repeal or modify any Federal, State, territorial, or local law creating special rights or preference for veterans.

RULES AND REGULATIONS

SEC. 713. (a) The Commission shall have authority from time to time to issue, amend, or rescind suitable procedural regulations to carry out the provisions of this title. Regulations issued under this section shall be in conformity with the standards and limitations of the Administrative Procedure Act.

60 Stat. 237.
5 USC 1001
note.

(b) In any action or proceeding based on any alleged unlawful employment practice, no person shall be subject to any liability or punishment for or on account of (1) the commission by such person of an unlawful employment practice if he pleads and proves that the act or omission complained of was in good faith, in conformity with, and in reliance on any written interpretation or opinion of the Commission, or (2) the failure of such person to publish and file any information required by any provision of this title if he pleads and proves that he failed to publish and file such information in good faith, in conformity with the instructions of the Commission issued under this title regarding the filing of such information. Such a defense, if established, shall be a bar to the action or proceeding, notwithstanding that (A) after such act or omission, such interpretation or opinion is modified or rescinded or is determined by judicial authority to be invalid or of no legal effect, or (B) after publishing or filing the description and annual reports, such publication or filing is determined by judicial authority not to be in conformity with the requirements of this title.

FORCIBLY RESISTING THE COMMISSION OR ITS REPRESENTATIVES

SEC. 714. The provisions of section 111, title 18, United States Code, shall apply to officers, agents, and employees of the Commission in the performance of their official duties.

62 Stat. 688.

SPECIAL STUDY BY SECRETARY OF LABOR

SEC. 715. The Secretary of Labor shall make a full and complete study of the factors which might tend to result in discrimination in employment because of age and of the consequences of such discrimination on the economy and individuals affected. The Secretary of Labor shall make a report to the Congress not later than June 30, 1965, containing the results of such study and shall include in such report such recommendations for legislation to prevent arbitrary discrimination in employment because of age as he determines advisable.

Report to
Congress.

266   PUBLIC LAW 88-352–JULY 2, 1964   [78 STAT.

EFFECTIVE DATE

SEC. 716. (a) This title shall become effective one year after the date of its enactment.

(b) Notwithstanding subsection (a), sections of this title other than sections 703, 704, 706, and 707 shall become effective immediately.

Presidential conferences.

(c) The President shall, as soon as feasible after the enactment of this title, convene one or more conferences for the purpose of enabling the leaders of groups whose members will be affected by this title to become familiar with the rights afforded and obligations imposed by its provisions, and for the purpose of making plans which will result in the fair and effective administration of this title when all of its provisions become effective. The President shall invite the participation in such conference or conferences of (1) the members of the President's Committee on Equal Employment Opportunity, (2) the members of the Commission on Civil Rights, (3) representatives of State and local agencies engaged in furthering equal employment opportunity, (4) representatives of private agencies engaged in furthering equal employment opportunity, and (5) representatives of employers, labor organizations, and employment agencies who will be subject to this title.

Membership.

APPENDIX 4

THE ADMINISTRATIVE PROCEDURE ACT OF 1946

■ ■ ■

**Codified as Amended through January 2014 at
Scattered Sections of 5 U.S.C.**

§ 551. Definitions

For the purpose of this subchapter—

(1) "agency" means each authority of the Government of the United States, whether or not it is within or subject to review by another agency, but does not include—

> **(A)** the Congress;
>
> **(B)** the courts of the United States;
>
> **(C)** the governments of the territories or possessions of the United States;
>
> **(D)** the government of the District of Columbia;

or except as to the requirements of section 552 of this title—

> **(E)** agencies composed of representatives of the parties or of representatives of organizations of the parties to the disputes determined by them;
>
> **(F)** courts martial and military commissions;
>
> **(G)** military authority exercised in the field in time of war or in occupied territory; or
>
> **(H)** functions conferred by sections 1738, 1739, 1743, and 1744 of title 12; subchapter II of chapter 471 of title 49; or sections 1884, 1891–1902, and former section 1641(b)(2), of title 50, appendix;

(2) "person" includes an individual, partnership, corporation, association, or public or private organization other than an agency;

(3) "party" includes a person or agency named or admitted as a party, or properly seeking and entitled as of right to be admitted as a party, in an agency proceeding, and a person or agency admitted by an agency as a party for limited purposes;

(4) "rule" means the whole or a part of an agency statement of general or particular applicability and future effect designed to implement, interpret, or prescribe law or policy or describing the organization, procedure, or practice requirements of an agency and includes the approval or prescription for the future of rates, wages, corporate or financial structures or reorganizations thereof, prices, facilities, appliances, services or allowances therefor or of valuations, costs, or accounting, or practices bearing on any of the foregoing;

(5) "rule making" means agency process for formulating, amending, or repealing a rule;

(6) "order" means the whole or a part of a final disposition, whether affirmative, negative, injunctive, or declaratory in form, of an agency in a matter other than rule making but including licensing;

(7) "adjudication" means agency process for the formulation of an order;

(8) "license" includes the whole or a part of an agency permit, certificate, approval, registration, charter, membership, statutory exemption or other form of permission;

(9) "licensing" includes agency process respecting the grant, renewal, denial, revocation, suspension, annulment, withdrawal, limitation, amendment, modification, or conditioning of a license;

(10) "sanction" includes the whole or a part of an agency—

(A) prohibition, requirement, limitation, or other condition affecting the freedom of a person;

(B) withholding of relief;

(C) imposition of penalty or fine;

(D) destruction, taking, seizure, or withholding of property;

(E) assessment of damages, reimbursement, restitution, compensation, costs, charges, or fees;

(F) requirement, revocation, or suspension of a license; or

(G) taking other compulsory or restrictive action;

(11) "relief" includes the whole or a part of an agency;—

(A) grant of money, assistance, license, authority, exemption, exception, privilege, or remedy;

(B) recognition of a claim, right, immunity, privilege, exemption, or exception; or

(C) taking of other action on the application or petition of, and beneficial to, a person;

(12) "agency proceeding" means an agency process as defined by paragraphs (5), (7), and (9) of this section;

(13) "agency action" includes the whole or a part of an agency rule, order, license, sanction, relief, or the equivalent or denial thereof, or failure to act; and

(14) "ex parte communication" means an oral or written communication not on the public record with respect to which reasonable prior notice to all parties is not given, but it shall not include requests for status reports on any matter or proceeding covered by this subchapter.

§ 552. Public information; agency rules, opinions, orders, records, and proceedings

[The Freedom of Information Act of 1967 is omitted.]

§ 552a. Records maintained on individuals

[The Privacy Act of 1974 is omitted.]

§ 553. Rule making

(a) This section applies, according to the provisions thereof, except to the extent that there is involved—

> **(1)** a military or foreign affairs function of the United States; or
>
> **(2)** a matter relating to agency management or personnel or to public property, loans, grants, benefits, or contracts.

(b) General notice of proposed rule making shall be published in the Federal Register, unless persons subject thereto are named and either personally served or otherwise have actual notice thereof in accordance with law. The notice shall include—

> **(1)** a statement of the time, place, and nature of public rule making proceedings;
>
> **(2)** reference to the legal authority under which the rule is proposed; and
>
> **(3)** either the terms or substance of the proposed rule or a description of the subjects and issues involved.

Except when notice or hearing is required by statute, this subsection does not apply—

> **(A)** to interpretative rules, general statements of policy, or rules of agency organization, procedure, or practice; or
>
> **(B)** when the agency for good cause finds (and incorporates the finding and a brief statement of reasons therefor in the rules issued) that notice and public procedure thereon are

impracticable, unnecessary, or contrary to the public interest.

(c) After notice required by this section, the agency shall give interested persons an opportunity to participate in the rule making through submission of written data, views, or arguments with or without opportunity for oral presentation. After consideration of the relevant matter presented, the agency shall incorporate in the rules adopted a concise general statement of their basis and purpose. When rules are required by statute to be made on the record after opportunity for an agency hearing, sections 556 and 557 of this title apply instead of this subsection.

(d) The required publication or service of a substantive rule shall be made not less than 30 days before its effective date, except—

(1) a substantive rule which grants or recognizes an exemption or relieves a restriction;

(2) interpretative rules and statements of policy; or

(3) as otherwise provided by the agency for good cause found and published with the rule.

(e) Each agency shall give an interested person the right to petition for the issuance, amendment, or repeal of a rule.

§ 554.   Adjudications

(a) This section applies, according to the provisions thereof, in every case of adjudication required by statute to be determined on the record after opportunity for an agency hearing, except to the extent that there is involved—

(1) a matter subject to a subsequent trial of the law and the facts de novo in a court;

(2) the selection or tenure of an employee, except a[1] administrative law judge appointed under section 3105 of this title;

(3) proceedings in which decisions rest solely on inspections, tests, or elections;

(4) the conduct of military or foreign affairs functions;

(5) cases in which an agency is acting as an agent for a court; or

(6) the certification of worker representatives.

(b) Persons entitled to notice of an agency hearing shall be timely informed of—

---

[1]   So in original.

(1) the time, place, and nature of the hearing;

(2) the legal authority and jurisdiction under which the hearing is to be held; and

(3) the matters of fact and law asserted.

When private persons are the moving parties, other parties to the proceeding shall give prompt notice of issues controverted in fact or law; and in other instances agencies may by rule require responsive pleading. In fixing the time and place for hearings, due regard shall be had for the convenience and necessity of the parties or their representatives.

(c) The agency shall give all interested parties opportunity for—

(1) the submission and consideration of facts, arguments, offers of settlement, or proposals of adjustment when time, the nature of the proceeding, and the public interest permit; and

(2) to the extent that the parties are unable so to determine a controversy by consent, hearing and decision on notice and in accordance with sections 556 and 557 of this title.

(d) The employee who presides at the reception of evidence pursuant to section 556 of this title shall make the recommended decision or initial decision required by section 557 of this title, unless he becomes unavailable to the agency. Except to the extent required for the disposition of ex parte matters as authorized by law, such an employee may not—

(1) consult a person or party on a fact in issue, unless on notice and opportunity for all parties to participate; or

(2) be responsible to or subject to the supervision or direction of an employee or agent engaged in the performance of investigative or prosecuting functions for an agency.

An employee or agent engaged in the performance of investigative or prosecuting functions for an agency in a case may not, in that or a factually related case, participate or advise in the decision, recommended decision, or agency review pursuant to section 557 of this title, except as witness or counsel in public proceedings. This subsection does not apply—

(A) in determining applications for initial licenses;

(B) to proceedings involving the validity or application of rates, facilities, or practices of public utilities or carriers; or

(C) to the agency or a member or members of the body comprising the agency.

(e) The agency, with like effect as in the case of other orders, and in its sound discretion, may issue a declaratory order to terminate a controversy or remove uncertainty.

§ 555.   Ancillary matters

(a) This section applies, according to the provisions thereof, except as otherwise provided by this subchapter.

(b) A person compelled to appear in person before an agency or representative thereof is entitled to be accompanied represented, and advised by counsel or, if permitted by the agency, by other qualified representative. A party is entitled to appear in person or by or with counsel or other duly qualified representative in an agency proceeding. So far as the orderly conduct of public business permits, an interested person may appear before an agency or its responsible employees for the presentation, adjustment, or determination of an issue, request, or controversy in a proceeding, whether interlocutory, summary, or otherwise, or in connection with an agency function. With due regard for the convenience and necessity of the parties or their representatives and within a reasonable time, each agency shall proceed to conclude a matter presented to it. This subsection does not grant or deny a person who is not a lawyer the right to appear for or represent others before an agency or in an agency proceeding.

(c) Process, requirement of a report, inspection, or other investigative act or demand may not be issued, made, or enforced except as authorized by law. A person compelled to submit data or evidence is entitled to retain or, on payment of lawfully prescribed costs, procure a copy or transcript thereof, except that in a nonpublic investigatory proceeding the witness may for good cause be limited to inspection of the official transcript of his testimony.

(d) Agency subpenas authorized by law shall be issued to a party on request and, when required by rules of procedure, on a statement or showing of general relevance and reasonable scope of the evidence sought. On contest, the court shall sustain the subpena or similar process or demand to the extent that it is found to be in accordance with law. In a proceeding for enforcement, the court shall issue an order requiring the appearance of the witness or the production of the evidence or data within a reasonable time under penalty of punishment for contempt in case of contumacious failure to comply.

(e) Prompt notice shall be given of the denial in whole or in part of a written application, petition, or other request of an interested person made in connection with any agency proceeding. Except in affirming a prior denial or when the denial is self-explanatory, the notice shall be accompanied by a brief statement of the grounds for denial.

§ 556. Hearings; presiding employees; powers and duties; burden of proof; evidence; record as basis of decision

(a) This section applies, according to the provisions thereof, to hearings required by section 553 or 554 of this title to be conducted in accordance with this section.

(b) There shall preside at the taking of evidence—

(1) the agency;

(2) one or more members of the body which comprises the agency; or

(3) one or more administrative law judges appointed under section 3105 of this title.

This subchapter does not supersede the conduct of specified classes of proceedings, in whole or in part, by or before boards or other employees specially provided for by or designated under statute. The functions of presiding employees and of employees participating in decisions in accordance with section 557 of this title shall be conducted in an impartial manner. A presiding or participating employee may at any time disqualify himself. On the filing in good faith of a timely and sufficient affidavit of personal bias or other disqualification of a presiding or participating employee, the agency shall determine the matter as a part of the record and decision in the case.

(c) Subject to published rules of the agency and within its powers, employees presiding at hearings may—

(1) administer oaths and affirmations;

(2) issue subpenas authorized by law;

(3) rule on offers of proof and receive relevant evidence;

(4) take depositions or have depositions taken when the ends of justice would be served;

(5) regulate the course of the hearing;

(6) hold conferences for the settlement or simplification of the issues by consent of the parties or by the use of alternative means of dispute resolution as provided in subchapter IV of this chapter;

(7) inform the parties as to the availability of one or more alternative means of dispute resolution, and encourage use of such methods;

(8) require the attendance at any conference held pursuant to paragraph (6) of at least one representative of each party who has authority to negotiate concerning resolution of issues in controversy;

(9) dispose of procedural requests or similar matters;

(10) make or recommend decisions in accordance with section 557 of this title; and

(11) take other action authorized by agency rule consistent with this subchapter.

(d) Except as otherwise provided by statute, the proponent of a rule or order has the burden of proof. Any oral or documentary evidence may be received, but the agency as a matter of policy shall provide for the exclusion of irrelevant, immaterial, or unduly repetitious evidence. A sanction may not be imposed or rule or order issued except on consideration of the whole record or those parts thereof cited by a party and supported by and in accordance with the reliable, probative, and substantial evidence. The agency may, to the extent consistent with the interests of justice and the policy of the underlying statutes administered by the agency, consider a violation of section 557(d) of this title sufficient grounds for a decision adverse to a party who has knowingly committed such violation or knowingly caused such violation to occur. A party is entitled to present his case or defense by oral or documentary evidence, to submit rebuttal evidence, and to conduct such cross-examination as may be required for a full and true disclosure of the facts. In rule making or determining claims for money or benefits or applications for initial licenses an agency may, when a party will not be prejudiced thereby, adopt procedures for the submission of all or part of the evidence in written form.

(e) The transcript of testimony and exhibits, together with all papers and requests filed in the proceeding, constitutes the exclusive record for decision in accordance with section 557 of this title and, on payment of lawfully prescribed costs, shall be made available to the parties. When an agency decision rests on official notice of a material fact not appearing in the evidence in the record, a party is entitled, on timely request, to an opportunity to show the contrary.

§ 557. Initial decisions; conclusiveness; review by agency; submissions by parties; contents of decisions; record

(a) This section applies, according to the provisions thereof, when a hearing is required to be conducted in accordance with section 556 of this title.

(b) When the agency did not preside at the reception of the evidence, the presiding employee or, in cases not subject to section 554(d) of this title, an employee qualified to preside at hearings pursuant to section 556 of this title, shall initially decide the case unless the agency requires, either in specific cases or by general rule, the entire record to be certified to it for decision. When the presiding employee makes an initial decision, that decision then becomes the decision of the agency without further proceedings unless there is an appeal to, or review on motion of, the agency within time provided by rule. On appeal from or review of the initial decision, the agency has all the powers which it would have in making the initial decision except as it may limit the issues on notice or by rule. When the agency makes the decision without having presided at the reception of the evidence, the presiding employee or an employee qualified to preside at hearings pursuant to section 556 of this title shall first recommend a decision, except that in rule making or determining applications for initial licenses—

> **(1)** instead thereof the agency may issue a tentative decision or one of its responsible employees may recommend a decision; or

> **(2)** this procedure may be omitted in a case in which the agency finds on the record that due and timely execution of its functions imperatively and unavoidably so requires.

(c) Before a recommended, initial, or tentative decision, or a decision on agency review of the decision of subordinate employees, the parties are entitled to a reasonable opportunity to submit for the consideration of the employees participating in the decisions—

> **(1)** proposed findings and conclusions; or

> **(2)** exceptions to the decisions or recommended decisions of subordinate employees or to tentative agency decisions; and

> **(3)** supporting reasons for the exceptions or proposed findings or conclusions.

The record shall show the ruling on each finding, conclusion, or exception presented. All decisions, including initial, recommended, and tentative decisions, are a part of the record and shall include a statement of—

> **(A)** findings and conclusions, and the reasons or basis therefor, on all the material issues of fact, law, or discretion presented on the record; and

> **(B)** the appropriate rule, order, sanction, relief, or denial thereof.

(d)

> **(1)** In any agency proceeding which is subject to subsection (a) of this section, except to the extent required for the disposition of ex parte matters as authorized by law—

(A) no interested person outside the agency shall make or knowingly cause to be made to any member of the body comprising the agency, administrative law judge, or other employee who is or may reasonably be expected to be involved in the decisional process of the proceeding, an ex parte communication relevant to the merits of the proceeding;

(B) no member of the body comprising the agency, administrative law judge, or other employee who is or may reasonably be expected to be involved in the decisional process of the proceeding, shall make or knowingly cause to be made to any interested person outside the agency an ex parte communication relevant to the merits of the proceeding;

(C) a member of the body comprising the agency, administrative law judge, or other employee who is or may reasonably be expected to be involved in the decisional process of such proceeding who receives, or who makes or knowingly causes to be made, a communication prohibited by this subsection shall place on the public record of the proceeding:

> **(i)** all such written communications;

> **(ii)** memoranda stating the substance of all such oral communications; and

> **(iii)** all written responses, and memoranda stating the substance of all oral responses, to the materials described in clauses (i) and (ii) of this subparagraph;

(D) upon receipt of a communication knowingly made or knowingly caused to be made by a party in violation of this subsection, the agency, administrative law judge, or other employee presiding at the hearing may, to the extent consistent with the interests of justice and the policy of the underlying statutes, require the party to show cause why his claim or interest in the proceeding should not be dismissed, denied, disregarded, or otherwise adversely affected on account of such violation; and

(E) the prohibitions of this subsection shall apply beginning at such time as the agency may designate, but in no case shall they begin to apply later than the time at which a proceeding is noticed for hearing unless the person responsible for the communication has knowledge that it will be noticed, in which case the prohibitions shall apply beginning at the time of his acquisition of such knowledge.

(2) This subsection does not constitute authority to withhold information from Congress.

§ 558.   Imposition of sanctions; determination of applications for licenses; suspension, revocation, and expiration of licenses

(a) This section applies, according to the provisions thereof, to the exercise of a power or authority.

(b) A sanction may not be imposed or a substantive rule or order issued except within jurisdiction delegated to the agency and as authorized by law.

(c) When application is made for a license required by law, the agency, with due regard for the rights and privileges of all the interested parties or adversely affected persons and within a reasonable time, shall set and complete proceedings required to be conducted in accordance with sections 556 and 557 of this title or other proceedings required by law and shall make its decision. Except in cases of willfulness or those in which public health, interest, or safety requires otherwise, the withdrawal, suspension, revocation, or annulment of a license is lawful only if, before the institution of agency proceedings therefor, the licensee has been given—

(1) notice by the agency in writing of the facts or conduct which may warrant the action; and

(2) opportunity to demonstrate or achieve compliance with all lawful requirements.

When the licensee has made timely and sufficient application for a renewal or a new license in accordance with agency rules, a license with reference to an activity of a continuing nature does not expire until the application has been finally determined by the agency.

§ 559.   Effect on other laws; effect of subsequent statute

This subchapter, chapter 7, and sections 1305, 3105, 3344, 4301(2)(E), 5372, and 7521 of this title, and the provisions of section 5335(a)(B) of this title that relate to administrative law judges, do not limit or repeal additional requirements imposed by statute or otherwise recognized by law. Except as otherwise required by law, requirements or privileges relating to evidence or procedure apply equally to agencies and persons. Each agency is granted the authority necessary to comply with the requirements of this subchapter through the issuance of rules or otherwise. Subsequent statute may not be held to supersede or modify this subchapter, chapter 7, sections 1305, 3105, 3344, 4301(2)(E), 5372, or 7521 of this title, or the provisions of section 5335(a)(B) of this title that relate to administrative law judges, except to the extent that it does so expressly.

§ 701.   Application; definitions

(a) This chapter applies, according to the provisions thereof, except to the extent that—

(1) statutes preclude judicial review; or

(2) agency action is committed to agency discretion by law.

(b) For the purpose of this chapter—

(1) "agency" means each authority of the Government of the United States, whether or not it is within or subject to review by another agency, but does not include—

(A) the Congress;

(B) the courts of the United States;

(C) the governments of the territories or possessions of the United States;

(D) the government of the District of Columbia;

(E) agencies composed of representatives of the parties or of representatives of organizations of the parties to the disputes determined by them;

(F) courts martial and military commissions;

(G) military authority exercised in the field in time of war or in occupied territory; or

(H) functions conferred by sections 1738, 1739, 1743, and 1744 of title 12; subchapter II of chapter 471 of title 49; or sections 1884, 1891–1902, and former section 1641(b)(2), of title 50, appendix; and

(2) "person", "rule", "order", "license", "sanction", "relief", and "agency action" have the meanings given them by section 551 of this title.

§ 702.   Right of review

A person suffering legal wrong because of agency action, or adversely affected or aggrieved by agency action within the meaning of a relevant statute, is entitled to judicial review thereof. An action in a court of the United States seeking relief other than money damages and stating a claim that an agency or an officer or employee thereof acted or failed to act in an official capacity or under color of legal authority shall not be dismissed nor relief therein be denied on the ground that it is against the United States or that the United States is an indispensable party. The

United States may be named as a defendant in any such action, and a judgment or decree may be entered against the United States: *Provided*, That any mandatory or injunctive decree shall specify the Federal officer or officers (by name or by title), and their successors in office, personally responsible for compliance. Nothing herein (1) affects other limitations on judicial review or the power or duty of the court to dismiss any action or deny relief on any other appropriate legal or equitable ground; or (2) confers authority to grant relief if any other statute that grants consent to suit expressly or impliedly forbids the relief which is sought.

§ 703.   Form and venue of proceeding

The form of proceeding for judicial review is the special statutory review proceeding relevant to the subject matter in a court specified by statute or, in the absence or inadequacy thereof, any applicable form of legal action, including actions for declaratory judgments or writs of prohibitory or mandatory injunction or habeas corpus, in a court of competent jurisdiction. If no special statutory review proceeding is applicable, the action for judicial review may be brought against the United States, the agency by its official title, or the appropriate officer. Except to the extent that prior, adequate, and exclusive opportunity for judicial review is provided by law, agency action is subject to judicial review in civil or criminal proceedings for judicial enforcement.

§ 704.   Actions reviewable

Agency action made reviewable by statute and final agency action for which there is no other adequate remedy in a court are subject to judicial review. A preliminary, procedural, or intermediate agency action or ruling not directly reviewable is subject to review on the review of the final agency action. Except as otherwise expressly required by statute, agency action otherwise final is final for the purposes of this section whether or not there has been presented or determined an application for a declaratory order, for any form of reconsideration, or, unless the agency otherwise requires by rule and provides that the action meanwhile is inoperative, for an appeal to superior agency authority.

§ 705.   Relief pending review

When an agency finds that justice so requires, it may postpone the effective date of action taken by it, pending judicial review. On such conditions as may be required and to the extent necessary to prevent irreparable injury, the reviewing court, including the court to which a case may be taken on appeal from or on application for certiorari or other writ to a reviewing court, may issue all necessary and appropriate process to postpone the effective date of an agency action or to preserve status or rights pending conclusion of the review proceedings.

§ 706. Scope of review

To the extent necessary to decision and when presented, the reviewing court shall decide all relevant questions of law, interpret constitutional and statutory provisions, and determine the meaning or applicability of the terms of an agency action. The reviewing court shall—

(1) compel agency action unlawfully withheld or unreasonably delayed; and

(2) hold unlawful and set aside agency action, findings, and conclusions found to be—

  (A) arbitrary, capricious, an abuse of discretion, or otherwise not in accordance with law;

  (B) contrary to constitutional right, power, privilege, or immunity;

  (C) in excess of statutory jurisdiction, authority, or limitations, or short of statutory right;

  (D) without observance of procedure required by law;

  (E) unsupported by substantial evidence in a case subject to sections 556 and 557 of this title or otherwise reviewed on the record of an agency hearing provided by statute; or

  (F) unwarranted by the facts to the extent that the facts are subject to trial de novo by the reviewing court.

In making the foregoing determinations, the court shall review the whole record or those parts of it cited by a party, and due account shall be taken of the rule of prejudicial error.

APPENDIX 5

EXECUTIVE ORDER 12,866 (CLINTON 1993) AND EXECUTIVE ORDER 13,563 (OBAMA 2011)

■ ■ ■

Federal Register
Vol. 58, No. 190
Monday, October 4, 1993

Presidential Documents

Title 3—

The President

Executive Order 12866 of September 30, 1993

Regulatory Planning and Review

The American people deserve a regulatory system that works for them, not against them: a regulatory system that protects and improves their health, safety, environment, and well-being and improves the performance of the economy without imposing unacceptable or unreasonable costs on society; regulatory policies that recognize that the private sector and private markets are the best engine for economic growth; regulatory approaches that respect the role of State, local, and tribal governments; and regulations that are effective, consistent, sensible, and understandable. We do not have such a regulatory system today.

With this Executive order, the Federal Government begins a program to reform and make more efficient the regulatory process. The objectives of this Executive order are to enhance planning and coordination with respect to both new and existing regulations; to reaffirm the primacy of Federal agencies in the regulatory decision-making process; to restore the integrity and legitimacy of regulatory review and oversight; and to make the process more accessible and open to the public. In pursuing these objectives, the regulatory process shall be conducted so as to meet applicable statutory requirements and with due regard to the discretion that has been entrusted to the Federal agencies.

Accordingly, by the authority vested in me as President by the Constitution and the laws of the United States of America, it is hereby ordered as follows:

Section 1. *Statement of Regulatory Philosophy and Principles.*

(a) *The Regulatory Philosophy.* Federal agencies should promulgate only such regulations as are required by law, are necessary to interpret the law, or are made necessary by compelling public need, such as material failures of private markets to protect or improve the health and safety of the public, the environment, or the well-being of the American people. In deciding whether and how to regulate, agencies should assess all costs and benefits of available regulatory alternatives, including the alternative of not regulating. Costs and benefits shall be understood to include both quantifiable measures (to the fullest extent that these can be usefully estimated) and qualitative measures of costs and benefits that are difficult to quantify, but nevertheless essential to consider. Further, in choosing among alternative regulatory approaches, agencies should select those approaches that maximize net benefits (including potential economic, environmental, public health and safety, and other advantages; distributive impacts; and equity), unless a statute requires another regulatory approach.

(b) *The Principles of Regulation.* To ensure that the agencies' regulatory programs are consistent with the philosophy set forth above, agencies should adhere to the following principles, to the extent permitted by law and where applicable:

(1) Each agency shall identify the problem that it intends to address (including, where applicable, the failures of private markets or public institutions that warrant new agency action) as well as assess the significance of that problem.

(2) Each agency shall examine whether existing regulations (or other law) have created, or contributed to, the problem that a new regulation is

Federal Register/Vol. 58, No. 190/Monday, October 4, 1993/Presidential Documents

intended to correct and whether those regulations (or other law) should be modified to achieve the intended goal of regulation more effectively.

(3) Each agency shall identify and assess available alternatives to direct regulation, including providing economic incentives to encourage the desired behavior, such as user fees or marketable permits, or providing information upon which choices can be made by the public.

(4) In setting regulatory priorities, each agency shall consider, to the extent reasonable, the degree and nature of the risks posed by various substances or activities within its jurisdiction.

(5) When an agency determines that a regulation is the best available method of achieving the regulatory objective, it shall design its regulations in the most cost-effective manner to achieve the regulatory objective. In doing so, each agency shall consider incentives for innovation, consistency, predictability, the costs of enforcement and compliance (to the government, regulated entities, and the public), flexibility, distributive impacts, and equity.

(6) Each agency shall assess both the costs and the benefits of the intended regulation and, recognizing that some costs and benefits are difficult to quantify, propose or adopt a regulation only upon a reasoned determination that the benefits of the intended regulation justify its costs.

(7) Each agency shall base its decisions on the best reasonably obtainable scientific, technical, economic, and other information concerning the need for, and consequences of, the intended regulation.

(8) Each agency shall identify and assess alternative forms of regulation and shall, to the extent feasible, specify performance objectives, rather than specifying the behavior or manner of compliance that regulated entities must adopt.

(9) Wherever feasible, agencies shall seek views of appropriate State, local, and tribal officials before imposing regulatory requirements that might significantly or uniquely affect those governmental entities. Each agency shall assess the effects of Federal regulations on State, local, and tribal governments, including specifically the availability of resources to carry out those mandates, and seek to minimize those burdens that uniquely or significantly affect such governmental entities, consistent with achieving regulatory objectives. In addition, as appropriate, agencies shall seek to harmonize Federal regulatory actions with related State, local, and tribal regulatory and other governmental functions.

(10) Each agency shall avoid regulations that are inconsistent, incompatible, or duplicative with its other regulations or those of other Federal agencies.

(11) Each agency shall tailor its regulations to impose the least burden on society, including individuals, businesses of differing sizes, and other entities (including small communities and governmental entities), consistent with obtaining the regulatory objectives, taking into account, among other things, and to the extent practicable, the costs of cumulative regulations.

(12) Each agency shall draft its regulations to be simple and easy to understand, with the goal of minimizing the potential for uncertainty and litigation arising from such uncertainty.

Sec. 2. *Organization.* An efficient regulatory planning and review process is vital to ensure that the Federal Government's regulatory system best serves the American people.

(a) *The Agencies.* Because Federal agencies are the repositories of significant substantive expertise and experience, they are responsible for developing regulations and assuring that the regulations are consistent with applicable law, the President's priorities, and the principles set forth in this Executive order.

Federal Register / Vol. 58, No. 190 / Monday, October 4, 1993 / Presidential Documents

(b) *The Office of Management and Budget.* Coordinated review of agency rulemaking is necessary to ensure that regulations are consistent with applicable law, the President's priorities, and the principles set forth in this Executive order, and that decisions made by one agency do not conflict with the policies or actions taken or planned by another agency. The Office of Management and Budget (OMB) shall carry out that review function. Within OMB, the Office of Information and Regulatory Affairs (OIRA) is the repository of expertise concerning regulatory issues, including methodologies and procedures that affect more than one agency, this Executive order, and the President's regulatory policies. To the extent permitted by law, OMB shall provide guidance to agencies and assist the President, the Vice President, and other regulatory policy advisors to the President in regulatory planning and shall be the entity that reviews individual regulations, as provided by this Executive order.

(c) *The Vice President.* The Vice President is the principal advisor to the President on, and shall coordinate the development and presentation of recommendations concerning, regulatory policy, planning, and review, as set forth in this Executive order. In fulfilling their responsibilities under this Executive order, the President and the Vice President shall be assisted by the regulatory policy advisors within the Executive Office of the President and by such agency officials and personnel as the President and the Vice President may, from time to time, consult.

Sec. 3. *Definitions.* For purposes of this Executive order: (a) "Advisors" refers to such regulatory policy advisors to the President as the President and Vice President may from time to time consult, including, among others: (1) the Director of OMB; (2) the Chair (or another member) of the Council of Economic Advisers; (3) the Assistant to the President for Economic Policy; (4) the Assistant to the President for Domestic Policy; (5) the Assistant to the President for National Security Affairs; (6) the Assistant to the President for Science and Technology; (7) the Assistant to the President for Intergovernmental Affairs; (8) the Assistant to the President and Staff Secretary; (9) the Assistant to the President and Chief of Staff to the Vice President; (10) the Assistant to the President and Counsel to the President; (11) the Deputy Assistant to the President and Director of the White House Office on Environmental Policy; and (12) the Administrator of OIRA, who also shall coordinate communications relating to this Executive order among the agencies, OMB, the other Advisors, and the Office of the Vice President.

(b) "Agency," unless otherwise indicated, means any authority of the United States that is an "agency" under 44 U.S.C. 3502(1), other than those considered to be independent regulatory agencies, as defined in 44 U.S.C. 3502(10).

(c) "Director" means the Director of OMB.

(d) "Regulation" or "rule" means an agency statement of general applicability and future effect, which the agency intends to have the force and effect of law, that is designed to implement, interpret, or prescribe law or policy or to describe the procedure or practice requirements of an agency. It does not, however, include:

(1) Regulations or rules issued in accordance with the formal rulemaking provisions of 5 U.S.C. 556, 557;

(2) Regulations or rules that pertain to a military or foreign affairs function of the United States, other than procurement regulations and regulations involving the import or export of non-defense articles and services;

(3) Regulations or rules that are limited to agency organization, management, or personnel matters; or

(4) Any other category of regulations exempted by the Administrator of OIRA.

(e) "Regulatory action" means any substantive action by an agency (normally published in the **Federal Register**) that promulgates or is expected to lead to the promulgation of a final rule or regulation, including notices

Federal Register / Vol. 58, No. 190 / Monday, October 4, 1993 / Presidential Documents

of inquiry, advance notices of proposed rulemaking, and notices of proposed rulemaking.

(f) "Significant regulatory action" means any regulatory action that is likely to result in a rule that may:

(1) Have an annual effect on the economy of $100 million or more or adversely affect in a material way the economy, a sector of the economy, productivity, competition, jobs, the environment, public health or safety, or State, local, or tribal governments or communities;

(2) Create a serious inconsistency or otherwise interfere with an action taken or planned by another agency;

(3) Materially alter the budgetary impact of entitlements, grants, user fees, or loan programs or the rights and obligations of recipients thereof; or

(4) Raise novel legal or policy issues arising out of legal mandates, the President's priorities, or the principles set forth in this Executive order.

Sec. 4. *Planning Mechanism.* In order to have an effective regulatory program, to provide for coordination of regulations, to maximize consultation and the resolution of potential conflicts at an early stage, to involve the public and its State, local, and tribal officials in regulatory planning, and to ensure that new or revised regulations promote the President's priorities and the principles set forth in this Executive order, these procedures shall be followed, to the extent permitted by law:

(a) *Agencies' Policy Meeting.* Early in each year's planning cycle, the Vice President shall convene a meeting of the Advisors and the heads of agencies to seek a common understanding of priorities and to coordinate regulatory efforts to be accomplished in the upcoming year.

(b) *Unified Regulatory Agenda.* For purposes of this subsection, the term "agency" or "agencies" shall also include those considered to be independent regulatory agencies, as defined in 44 U.S.C. 3502(10). Each agency shall prepare an agenda of all regulations under development or review, at a time and in a manner specified by the Administrator of OIRA. The description of each regulatory action shall contain, at a minimum, a regulation identifier number, a brief summary of the action, the legal authority for the action, any legal deadline for the action, and the name and telephone number of a knowledgeable agency official. Agencies may incorporate the information required under 5 U.S.C. 602 and 41 U.S.C. 402 into these agendas.

(c) *The Regulatory Plan.* For purposes of this subsection, the term "agency" or "agencies" shall also include those considered to be independent regulatory agencies, as defined in 44 U.S.C. 3502(10). (1) As part of the Unified Regulatory Agenda, beginning in 1994, each agency shall prepare a Regulatory Plan (Plan) of the most important significant regulatory actions that the agency reasonably expects to issue in proposed or final form in that fiscal year or thereafter. The Plan shall be approved personally by the agency head and shall contain at a minimum:

(A) A statement of the agency's regulatory objectives and priorities and how they relate to the President's priorities;

(B) A summary of each planned significant regulatory action including, to the extent possible, alternatives to be considered and preliminary estimates of the anticipated costs and benefits;

(C) A summary of the legal basis for each such action, including whether any aspect of the action is required by statute or court order;

(D) A statement of the need for each such action and, if applicable, how the action will reduce risks to public health, safety, or the environment, as well as how the magnitude of the risk addressed by the action relates to other risks within the jurisdiction of the agency;

(E) The agency's schedule for action, including a statement of any applicable statutory or judicial deadlines; and

Federal Register/Vol. 58, No. 190/Monday, October 4, 1993/Presidential Documents

(F) The name, address, and telephone number of a person the public may contact for additional information about the planned regulatory action.

(2) Each agency shall forward its Plan to OIRA by June 1st of each year.

(3) Within 10 calendar days after OIRA has received an agency's Plan, OIRA shall circulate it to other affected agencies, the Advisors, and the Vice President.

(4) An agency head who believes that a planned regulatory action of another agency may conflict with its own policy or action taken or planned shall promptly notify, in writing, the Administrator of OIRA, who shall forward that communication to the issuing agency, the Advisors, and the Vice President.

(5) If the Administrator of OIRA believes that a planned regulatory action of an agency may be inconsistent with the President's priorities or the principles set forth in this Executive order or may be in conflict with any policy or action taken or planned by another agency, the Administrator of OIRA shall promptly notify, in writing, the affected agencies, the Advisors, and the Vice President.

(6) The Vice President, with the Advisors' assistance, may consult with the heads of agencies with respect to their Plans and, in appropriate instances, request further consideration or inter-agency coordination.

(7) The Plans developed by the issuing agency shall be published annually in the October publication of the Unified Regulatory Agenda. This publication shall be made available to the Congress; State, local, and tribal governments; and the public. Any views on any aspect of any agency Plan, including whether any planned regulatory action might conflict with any other planned or existing regulation, impose any unintended consequences on the public, or confer any unclaimed benefits on the public, should be directed to the issuing agency, with a copy to OIRA.

(d) *Regulatory Working Group.* Within 30 days of the date of this Executive order, the Administrator of OIRA shall convene a Regulatory Working Group ("Working Group"), which shall consist of representatives of the heads of each agency that the Administrator determines to have significant domestic regulatory responsibility, the Advisors, and the Vice President. The Administrator of OIRA shall chair the Working Group and shall periodically advise the Vice President on the activities of the Working Group. The Working Group shall serve as a forum to assist agencies in identifying and analyzing important regulatory issues (including, among others (1) the development of innovative regulatory techniques, (2) the methods, efficacy, and utility of comparative risk assessment in regulatory decision-making, and (3) the development of short forms and other streamlined regulatory approaches for small businesses and other entities). The Working Group shall meet at least quarterly and may meet as a whole or in subgroups of agencies with an interest in particular issues or subject areas. To inform its discussions, the Working Group may commission analytical studies and reports by OIRA, the Administrative Conference of the United States, or any other agency.

(e) *Conferences.* The Administrator of OIRA shall meet quarterly with representatives of State, local, and tribal governments to identify both existing and proposed regulations that may uniquely or significantly affect those governmental entities. The Administrator of OIRA shall also convene, from time to time, conferences with representatives of businesses, nongovernmental organizations, and the public to discuss regulatory issues of common concern.

Sec. 5. *Existing Regulations.* In order to reduce the regulatory burden on the American people, their families, their communities, their State, local, and tribal governments, and their industries; to determine whether regulations promulgated by the executive branch of the Federal Government have become unjustified or unnecessary as a result of changed circumstances; to confirm that regulations are both compatible with each other and not

Federal Register/Vol. 58, No. 190/Monday, October 4, 1993/Presidential Documents

duplicative or inappropriately burdensome in the aggregate; to ensure that all regulations are consistent with the President's priorities and the principles set forth in this Executive order, within applicable law; and to otherwise improve the effectiveness of existing regulations: (a) Within 90 days of the date of this Executive order, each agency shall submit to OIRA a program, consistent with its resources and regulatory priorities, under which the agency will periodically review its existing significant regulations to determine whether any such regulations should be modified or eliminated so as to make the agency's regulatory program more effective in achieving the regulatory objectives, less burdensome, or in greater alignment with the President's priorities and the principles set forth in this Executive order. Any significant regulations selected for review shall be included in the agency's annual Plan. The agency shall also identify any legislative mandates that require the agency to promulgate or continue to impose regulations that the agency believes are unnecessary or outdated by reason of changed circumstances.

(b) The Administrator of OIRA shall work with the Regulatory Working Group and other interested entities to pursue the objectives of this section. State, local, and tribal governments are specifically encouraged to assist in the identification of regulations that impose significant or unique burdens on those governmental entities and that appear to have outlived their justification or be otherwise inconsistent with the public interest.

(c) The Vice President, in consultation with the Advisors, may identify for review by the appropriate agency or agencies other existing regulations of an agency or groups of regulations of more than one agency that affect a particular group, industry, or sector of the economy, or may identify legislative mandates that may be appropriate for reconsideration by the Congress.

Sec. 6. *Centralized Review of Regulations.* The guidelines set forth below shall apply to all regulatory actions, for both new and existing regulations, by agencies other than those agencies specifically exempted by the Administrator of OIRA:

(a) *Agency Responsibilities.* (1) Each agency shall (consistent with its own rules, regulations, or procedures) provide the public with meaningful participation in the regulatory process. In particular, before issuing a notice of proposed rulemaking, each agency should, where appropriate, seek the involvement of those who are intended to benefit from and those expected to be burdened by any regulation (including, specifically, State, local, and tribal officials). In addition, each agency should afford the public a meaningful opportunity to comment on any proposed regulation, which in most cases should include a comment period of not less than 60 days. Each agency also is directed to explore and, where appropriate, use consensual mechanisms for developing regulations, including negotiated rulemaking.

(2) Within 60 days of the date of this Executive order, each agency head shall designate a Regulatory Policy Officer who shall report to the agency head. The Regulatory Policy Officer shall be involved at each stage of the regulatory process to foster the development of effective, innovative, and least burdensome regulations and to further the principles set forth in this Executive order.

(3) In addition to adhering to its own rules and procedures and to the requirements of the Administrative Procedure Act, the Regulatory Flexibility Act, the Paperwork Reduction Act, and other applicable law, each agency shall develop its regulatory actions in a timely fashion and adhere to the following procedures with respect to a regulatory action:

(A) Each agency shall provide OIRA, at such times and in the manner specified by the Administrator of OIRA, with a list of its planned regulatory actions, indicating those which the agency believes are significant regulatory actions within the meaning of this Executive order. Absent a material change in the development of the planned regulatory action, those not designated as significant will not be subject to review under this section unless, within 10 working days of receipt

Federal Register / Vol. 58, No. 190 / Monday, October 4, 1993 / Presidential Documents

of the list, the Administrator of OIRA notifies the agency that OIRA has determined that a planned regulation is a significant regulatory action within the meaning of this Executive order. The Administrator of OIRA may waive review of any planned regulatory action designated by the agency as significant, in which case the agency need not further comply with subsection (a)(3)(B) or subsection (a)(3)(C) of this section.

(B) For each matter identified as, or determined by the Administrator of OIRA to be, a significant regulatory action, the issuing agency shall provide to OIRA:

(i) The text of the draft regulatory action, together with a reasonably detailed description of the need for the regulatory action and an explanation of how the regulatory action will meet that need; and

(ii) An assessment of the potential costs and benefits of the regulatory action, including an explanation of the manner in which the regulatory action is consistent with a statutory mandate and, to the extent permitted by law, promotes the President's priorities and avoids undue interference with State, local, and tribal governments in the exercise of their governmental functions.

(C) For those matters identified as, or determined by the Administrator of OIRA to be, a significant regulatory action within the scope of section 3(f)(1), the agency shall also provide to OIRA the following additional information developed as part of the agency's decision-making process (unless prohibited by law):

(i) An assessment, including the underlying analysis, of benefits anticipated from the regulatory action (such as, but not limited to, the promotion of the efficient functioning of the economy and private markets, the enhancement of health and safety, the protection of the natural environment, and the elimination or reduction of discrimination or bias) together with, to the extent feasible, a quantification of those benefits;

(ii) An assessment, including the underlying analysis, of costs anticipated from the regulatory action (such as, but not limited to, the direct cost both to the government in administering the regulation and to businesses and others in complying with the regulation, and any adverse effects on the efficient functioning of the economy, private markets (including productivity, employment, and competitiveness), health, safety, and the natural environment), together with, to the extent feasible, a quantification of those costs; and

(iii) An assessment, including the underlying analysis, of costs and benefits of potentially effective and reasonably feasible alternatives to the planned regulation, identified by the agencies or the public (including improving the current regulation and reasonably viable nonregulatory actions), and an explanation why the planned regulatory action is preferable to the identified potential alternatives.

(D) In emergency situations or when an agency is obligated by law to act more quickly than normal review procedures allow, the agency shall notify OIRA as soon as possible and, to the extent practicable, comply with subsections (a)(3)(B) and (C) of this section. For those regulatory actions that are governed by a statutory or court-imposed deadline, the agency shall, to the extent practicable, schedule rulemaking proceedings so as to permit sufficient time for OIRA to conduct its review, as set forth below in subsection (b)(2) through (4) of this section.

(E) After the regulatory action has been published in the **Federal Register** or otherwise issued to the public, the agency shall:

(i) Make available to the public the information set forth in subsections (a)(3)(B) and (C);

(ii) Identify for the public, in a complete, clear, and simple manner, the substantive changes between the draft submitted to OIRA for review and the action subsequently announced; and

Federal Register/Vol. 58, No. 190/Monday, October 4, 1993/Presidential Documents

(iii) Identify for the public those changes in the regulatory action that were made at the suggestion or recommendation of OIRA.

(F) All information provided to the public by the agency shall be in plain, understandable language.

(b) *OIRA Responsibilities.* The Administrator of OIRA shall provide meaningful guidance and oversight so that each agency's regulatory actions are consistent with applicable law, the President's priorities, and the principles set forth in this Executive order and do not conflict with the policies or actions of another agency. OIRA shall, to the extent permitted by law, adhere to the following guidelines:

(1) OIRA may review only actions identified by the agency or by OIRA as significant regulatory actions under subsection (a)(3)(A) of this section.

(2) OIRA shall waive review or notify the agency in writing of the results of its review within the following time periods:

(A) For any notices of inquiry, advance notices of proposed rulemaking, or other preliminary regulatory actions prior to a Notice of Proposed Rulemaking, within 10 working days after the date of submission of the draft action to OIRA;

(B) For all other regulatory actions, within 90 calendar days after the date of submission of the information set forth in subsections (a)(3)(B) and (C) of this section, unless OIRA has previously reviewed this information and, since that review, there has been no material change in the facts and circumstances upon which the regulatory action is based, in which case, OIRA shall complete its review within 45 days; and

(C) The review process may be extended (1) once by no more than 30 calendar days upon the written approval of the Director and (2) at the request of the agency head.

(3) For each regulatory action that the Administrator of OIRA returns to an agency for further consideration of some or all of its provisions, the Administrator of OIRA shall provide the issuing agency a written explanation for such return, setting forth the pertinent provision of this Executive order on which OIRA is relying. If the agency head disagrees with some or all of the bases for the return, the agency head shall so inform the Administrator of OIRA in writing.

(4) Except as otherwise provided by law or required by a Court, in order to ensure greater openness, accessibility, and accountability in the regulatory review process, OIRA shall be governed by the following disclosure requirements:

(A) Only the Administrator of OIRA (or a particular designee) shall receive oral communications initiated by persons not employed by the executive branch of the Federal Government regarding the substance of a regulatory action under OIRA review;

(B) All substantive communications between OIRA personnel and persons not employed by the executive branch of the Federal Government regarding a regulatory action under review shall be governed by the following guidelines: (i) A representative from the issuing agency shall be invited to any meeting between OIRA personnel and such person(s);

(ii) OIRA shall forward to the issuing agency, within 10 working days of receipt of the communication(s), all written communications, regardless of format, between OIRA personnel and any person who is not employed by the executive branch of the Federal Government, and the dates and names of individuals involved in all substantive oral communications (including meetings to which an agency representative was invited, but did not attend, and telephone conversations between OIRA personnel and any such persons); and

(iii) OIRA shall publicly disclose relevant information about such communication(s), as set forth below in subsection (b)(4)(C) of this section.

Federal Register/Vol. 58, No. 190/Monday, October 4, 1993/Presidential Documents

(C) OIRA shall maintain a publicly available log that shall contain, at a minimum, the following information pertinent to regulatory actions under review:

(i) The status of all regulatory actions, including if (and if so, when and by whom) Vice Presidential and Presidential consideration was requested;

(ii) A notation of all written communications forwarded to an issuing agency under subsection (b)(4)(B)(ii) of this section; and

(iii) The dates and names of individuals involved in all substantive oral communications, including meetings and telephone conversations, between OIRA personnel and any person not employed by the executive branch of the Federal Government, and the subject matter discussed during such communications.

(D) After the regulatory action has been published in the **Federal Register** or otherwise issued to the public, or after the agency has announced its decision not to publish or issue the regulatory action, OIRA shall make available to the public all documents exchanged between OIRA and the agency during the review by OIRA under this section.

(5) All information provided to the public by OIRA shall be in plain, understandable language.

Sec. 7. *Resolution of Conflicts.* To the extent permitted by law, disagreements or conflicts between or among agency heads or between OMB and any agency that cannot be resolved by the Administrator of OIRA shall be resolved by the President, or by the Vice President acting at the request of the President, with the relevant agency head (and, as appropriate, other interested government officials). Vice Presidential and Presidential consideration of such disagreements may be initiated only by the Director, by the head of the issuing agency, or by the head of an agency that has a significant interest in the regulatory action at issue. Such review will not be undertaken at the request of other persons, entities, or their agents.

Resolution of such conflicts shall be informed by recommendations developed by the Vice President, after consultation with the Advisors (and other executive branch officials or personnel whose responsibilities to the President include the subject matter at issue). The development of these recommendations shall be concluded within 60 days after review has been requested.

During the Vice Presidential and Presidential review period, communications with any person not employed by the Federal Government relating to the substance of the regulatory action under review and directed to the Advisors or their staffs or to the staff of the Vice President shall be in writing and shall be forwarded by the recipient to the affected agency(ies) for inclusion in the public docket(s). When the communication is not in writing, such Advisors or staff members shall inform the outside party that the matter is under review and that any comments should be submitted in writing.

At the end of this review process, the President, or the Vice President acting at the request of the President, shall notify the affected agency and the Administrator of OIRA of the President's decision with respect to the matter.

Sec. 8. *Publication.* Except to the extent required by law, an agency shall not publish in the **Federal Register** or otherwise issue to the public any regulatory action that is subject to review under section 6 of this Executive order until (1) the Administrator of OIRA notifies the agency that OIRA has waived its review of the action or has completed its review without any requests for further consideration, or (2) the applicable time period in section 6(b)(2) expires without OIRA having notified the agency that it is returning the regulatory action for further consideration under section 6(b)(3), whichever occurs first. If the terms of the preceding sentence have not been satisfied and an agency wants to publish or otherwise issue a

Federal Register / Vol. 58, No. 190 / Monday, October 4, 1993 / Presidential Documents

regulatory action, the head of that agency may request Presidential consideration through the Vice President, as provided under section 7 of this order. Upon receipt of this request, the Vice President shall notify OIRA and the Advisors. The guidelines and time period set forth in section 7 shall apply to the publication of regulatory actions for which Presidential consideration has been sought.

Sec. 9. *Agency Authority.* Nothing in this order shall be construed as displacing the agencies' authority or responsibilities, as authorized by law.

Sec. 10. *Judicial Review.* Nothing in this Executive order shall affect any otherwise available judicial review of agency action. This Executive order is intended only to improve the internal management of the Federal Government and does not create any right or benefit, substantive or procedural, enforceable at law or equity by a party against the United States, its agencies or instrumentalities, its officers or employees, or any other person.

Sec. 11. *Revocations.* Executive Orders Nos. 12291 and 12498; all amendments to those Executive orders; all guidelines issued under those orders; and any exemptions from those orders heretofore granted for any category of rule are revoked.

William J. Clinton

THE WHITE HOUSE,
September 30, 1993.

[FR citation 58 FR 51735]

Federal Register

Vol. 76, No. 14

Friday, January 21, 2011

Presidential Documents

Title 3—

The President

Executive Order 13563 of January 18, 2011

Improving Regulation and Regulatory Review

By the authority vested in me as President by the Constitution and the laws of the United States of America, and in order to improve regulation and regulatory review, it is hereby ordered as follows:

Section 1. *General Principles of Regulation.* (a) Our regulatory system must protect public health, welfare, safety, and our environment while promoting economic growth, innovation, competitiveness, and job creation. It must be based on the best available science. It must allow for public participation and an open exchange of ideas. It must promote predictability and reduce uncertainty. It must identify and use the best, most innovative, and least burdensome tools for achieving regulatory ends. It must take into account benefits and costs, both quantitative and qualitative. It must ensure that regulations are accessible, consistent, written in plain language, and easy to understand. It must measure, and seek to improve, the actual results of regulatory requirements.

(b) This order is supplemental to and reaffirms the principles, structures, and definitions governing contemporary regulatory review that were established in Executive Order 12866 of September 30, 1993. As stated in that Executive Order and to the extent permitted by law, each agency must, among other things: (1) propose or adopt a regulation only upon a reasoned determination that its benefits justify its costs (recognizing that some benefits and costs are difficult to quantify); (2) tailor its regulations to impose the least burden on society, consistent with obtaining regulatory objectives, taking into account, among other things, and to the extent practicable, the costs of cumulative regulations; (3) select, in choosing among alternative regulatory approaches, those approaches that maximize net benefits (including potential economic, environmental, public health and safety, and other advantages; distributive impacts; and equity); (4) to the extent feasible, specify performance objectives, rather than specifying the behavior or manner of compliance that regulated entities must adopt; and (5) identify and assess available alternatives to direct regulation, including providing economic incentives to encourage the desired behavior, such as user fees or marketable permits, or providing information upon which choices can be made by the public.

(c) In applying these principles, each agency is directed to use the best available techniques to quantify anticipated present and future benefits and costs as accurately as possible. Where appropriate and permitted by law, each agency may consider (and discuss qualitatively) values that are difficult or impossible to quantify, including equity, human dignity, fairness, and distributive impacts.

Sec. 2. *Public Participation.* (a) Regulations shall be adopted through a process that involves public participation. To that end, regulations shall be based, to the extent feasible and consistent with law, on the open exchange of information and perspectives among State, local, and tribal officials, experts in relevant disciplines, affected stakeholders in the private sector, and the public as a whole.

(b) To promote that open exchange, each agency, consistent with Executive Order 12866 and other applicable legal requirements, shall endeavor to provide the public with an opportunity to participate in the regulatory process. To the extent feasible and permitted by law, each agency shall afford the public a meaningful opportunity to comment through the Internet on any proposed regulation, with a comment period that should generally

3822 Federal Register/Vol. 76, No. 14/Friday, January 21, 2011/Presidential Documents

be at least 60 days. To the extent feasible and permitted by law, each agency shall also provide, for both proposed and final rules, timely online access to the rulemaking docket on regulations.gov, including relevant scientific and technical findings, in an open format that can be easily searched and downloaded. For proposed rules, such access shall include, to the extent feasible and permitted by law, an opportunity for public comment on all pertinent parts of the rulemaking docket, including relevant scientific and technical findings.

(c) Before issuing a notice of proposed rulemaking, each agency, where feasible and appropriate, shall seek the views of those who are likely to be affected, including those who are likely to benefit from and those who are potentially subject to such rulemaking.

Sec. 3. *Integration and Innovation.* Some sectors and industries face a significant number of regulatory requirements, some of which may be redundant, inconsistent, or overlapping. Greater coordination across agencies could reduce these requirements, thus reducing costs and simplifying and harmonizing rules. In developing regulatory actions and identifying appropriate approaches, each agency shall attempt to promote such coordination, simplification, and harmonization. Each agency shall also seek to identify, as appropriate, means to achieve regulatory goals that are designed to promote innovation.

Sec. 4. *Flexible Approaches.* Where relevant, feasible, and consistent with regulatory objectives, and to the extent permitted by law, each agency shall identify and consider regulatory approaches that reduce burdens and maintain flexibility and freedom of choice for the public. These approaches include warnings, appropriate default rules, and disclosure requirements as well as provision of information to the public in a form that is clear and intelligible.

Sec. 5. *Science.* Consistent with the President's Memorandum for the Heads of Executive Departments and Agencies, "Scientific Integrity" (March 9, 2009), and its implementing guidance, each agency shall ensure the objectivity of any scientific and technological information and processes used to support the agency's regulatory actions.

Sec. 6. *Retrospective Analyses of Existing Rules.* (a) To facilitate the periodic review of existing significant regulations, agencies shall consider how best to promote retrospective analysis of rules that may be outmoded, ineffective, insufficient, or excessively burdensome, and to modify, streamline, expand, or repeal them in accordance with what has been learned. Such retrospective analyses, including supporting data, should be released online whenever possible.

(b) Within 120 days of the date of this order, each agency shall develop and submit to the Office of Information and Regulatory Affairs a preliminary plan, consistent with law and its resources and regulatory priorities, under which the agency will periodically review its existing significant regulations to determine whether any such regulations should be modified, streamlined, expanded, or repealed so as to make the agency's regulatory program more effective or less burdensome in achieving the regulatory objectives.

Sec. 7. *General Provisions.* (a) For purposes of this order, "agency" shall have the meaning set forth in section 3(b) of Executive Order 12866.

(b) Nothing in this order shall be construed to impair or otherwise affect:

(i) authority granted by law to a department or agency, or the head thereof; or

(ii) functions of the Director of the Office of Management and Budget relating to budgetary, administrative, or legislative proposals.

(c) This order shall be implemented consistent with applicable law and subject to the availability of appropriations.

Federal Register / Vol. 76, No. 14 / Friday, January 21, 2011 / Presidential Documents   3823

(d) This order is not intended to, and does not, create any right or benefit, substantive or procedural, enforceable at law or in equity by any party against the United States, its departments, agencies, or entities, its officers, employees, or agents, or any other person.

THE WHITE HOUSE,
January 18, 2011.

[FR Doc. 2011–1385
Filed 1–20–11; 8:45 am]
Billing code 3195–W1–P

APPENDIX 6

THE SUPREME COURT'S CANONS OF STATUTORY INTERPRETATION (1986–2014)

■ ■ ■

This is a collection of canons invoked by the Supreme Court from the 1986 through the 2013 Terms and divided into categories that parallel the typology provided in Chapter 5 of the Casebook.[*]

TEXTUAL CANONS

- Plain meaning rule: follow the plain meaning of the statutory text,[1] except when textual plain meaning requires an absurd result[2] or suggests a scrivener's error.[3]

LINGUISTIC INFERENCES

- *Expressio* (or *inclusio*) *unius*: expression of one thing suggests the exclusion of others.[4] Inapplicable if context suggests listing is not comprehensive.[5]

- *Noscitur a sociis*: interpret a general term to be similar to more specific terms in a series.[6] *Noscitur* is often not helpful

---

[*] Diana Rusk, Yale Law School Class of 2009, provided invaluable assistance in the preparation of this appendix.

[1] Mohamad v. Palestinian Auth., 132 S.Ct. 1702 (2012); Bilski v. Kappos, 561 U.S. 593 (2010); Massachusetts v. EPA, 549 U.S. 497 (2007); Arlington Cent. Sch. Dist. Bd. of Educ. v. Murphy, 548 U.S. 291 (2006); Barnhart v. Thomas, 540 U.S. 20 (2003); West Virginia Univ. Hosps. v. Casey, 499 U.S. 83 (1991); United States v. Providence Journal Co., 485 U.S. 693, 700–01 (1988).

[2] Utility Air Regulatory Group v. EPA, 134 S.Ct. 2427 (2014) (plurality and concurring opinions); Brown v. Plata, 131 S.Ct. 1910, 1950–51 (2011) (Scalia, J., dissenting) (avoid "outrageous" and "absurd" results); Republic of Iraq v. Beaty, 556 U.S. 848, 861 (2009); Zuni Pub. Sch. Dist. No. 89 v. Department of Educ., 550 U.S. 81 (2007) (majority and concurring opinions); United States v. Wilson, 503 U.S. 329, 334 (1992); Green v. Bock Laundry Mach. Co., 490 U.S. 504, 509–11 (1989).

[3] United States Nat'l Bank v. Independent Ins. Agents, 508 U.S. 439, 462 (1993); Green v. Bock Laundry Mach. Co., 490 U.S. 504 (1989).

[4] POM Wonderful LLC v. Coca-Cola Co., 134 S.Ct. 2228, 2237-38 (2014); Hinck v. United States, 550 U.S. 501 (2007); TRW, Inc. v. Andrews, 534 U.S. 19 (2001); City of Chicago v. Environmental Def. Fund, 511 U.S. 328 (1994); United States v. Smith, 499 U.S. 160 (1991); Chan v. Korean Air Lines, Ltd., 490 U.S. 122, 133–34 (1989).

[5] Marrama v. Citizens Bank of Mass., 549 U.S. 365 (2007); Christensen v. Harris County, 529 U.S. 576, 583–84 (2000); Burns v. United States, 501 U.S. 129, 136 (1991); Sullivan v. Hudson, 490 U.S. 877, 891–92 (1989).

[6] Entergy Corp. v. Riverkeeper, Inc., 556 U.S. 208, 222 (2009); Gustafson v. Alloyd Co., 513 U.S. 561, 575 (1995); Beecham v. United States, 511 U.S. 368, 371 (1994); Dole v. United

when applied to a technical statute whose details were hammered out through a complex process, or to a statutory list that is too short or disparate to permit generalization.[7]

- *Ejusdem generis*: interpret a general term to reflect the class of objects reflected in more specific terms accompanying it.[8] *Ejusdem* might be trumped by other canons, such as the rule against redundancy.[9]

- Follow ordinary usage of terms, unless Congress gives them a specified or technical meaning.[10]

- Where Congress uses terms that have settled meaning, either by common usage or through the common law, interpreters should apply that settled meaning.[11]

- Defer to experts, including agencies, regarding the meaning of technical terminology.[12]

- Follow dictionary definitions of terms,[13] unless Congress has provided a specific definition.[14] Consider dictionaries of the era in which the statute was enacted.[15] For technical terms,

---

Steelworkers of Am., 494 U.S. 26, 36 (1990); Massachusetts v. Morash, 490 U.S. 107, 114–15 (1989).

[7] Bilski v. Kappos, 561 U.S. 593 (2010); Graham County Soil & Conserv. Dist. v. United States ex rel. Wilson, 559 U.S. 280 (2010); S.D. Warren Co. v. Maine Bd. of Environmental Prot., 547 U.S. 370 (2006).

[8] James v. United States, 550 U.S. 192 (2007); Circuit City Stores, Inc. v. Adams, 532 U.S. 105 (2001); Hughey v. United States, 495 U.S. 411, 419 (1990); Norfolk & Western Ry. Co. v. American Train Dispatchers' Ass'n, 499 U.S. 117, 129 (1991).

[9] Babbitt v. Sweet Home Chap. of Communities for a Great Or., 515 U.S. 687 (1995).

[10] Lopez v. Gonzales, 549 U.S. 47 (2006); Pasquantino v. United States, 544 U.S. 349, 355 (2005); Will v. Michigan Dep't of State Police, 491 U.S. 58, 64 (1989).

[11] CTS Corp. v. Waldburger, 134 S.Ct. 2175 (2014); Merck & Co. v. Reynolds, 539 U.S. 633 (2010); Stewart v. Dutra Constr. Co., 543 U.S. 481, 487 (2005); Scheidler v. NOW, Inc., 537 U.S. 393, 402 (2003); United States v. Wells, 519 U.S. 482, 491 (1997); Community for Creative Non-Violence v. Reid, 490 U.S. 730, 739 (1989).

[12] Zuni Pub. Sch. Dist. No. 89 v. Department of Educ., 550 U.S. 81 (2007).

[13] CTS Corp. v. Waldburger, 134 S.Ct. 2175 (2014) (*Black's*); Taniguchi v. Kan Pacific Saipan Ltd., 132 S.Ct. 1997 (2012) (many dictionaries); Mohamad v. Palestinian Auth., 132 S.Ct. 1702 (2012) (*Black's*); Kawashima v. Holder, 132 S.Ct. (2012) (*Webster's Third*); Limtiaco v. Comacho, 549 U.S. 483 (2007) (*Black's*); Rapanos v. United States, 547 U.S. 715 (2006) (plurality opinion of Scalia, J.) (*Webster's Second*); Muscarello v. United States, 524 U.S. 125 (1998) (*Oxford English*); Pittston Coal Group v. Sebben, 488 U.S. 105, 113 (1988) (*Webster's Third*).

[14] Babbitt v. Sweet Home Chap. of Communities for a Great Or., 515 U.S. 687 (1995).

[15] Bilski v. Kappos, 561 U.S. 593 (2010); Permanent Mission of India to the United Nations v. City of New York, 551 U.S. 193 (2007); Cook County v. United States ex rel. Chandler, 538 U.S. 119, 125–27 (2003); St. Francis College v. Al-Khazraji, 481 U.S. 604 (1987). But see New Process Steel L.P. v. NLRB, 130 S.Ct. 2635, 2642 (2010) (relying on dictionaries from era in which controversy arose); Metropolitan Life Ins. Co. v. Glenn, 554 U.S. 105, 112 (2008) (same).

consult specialized dictionaries.[16] Do not credit nonstandard, "idiosyncratic" dictionary definitions.[17]

- Rules of Construction (Dictionary) Act, 1 U.S.C. § 1 *et seq.*, contains default definitions that apply if Congress fails to define a particular term.[18]

- A statute has an ordinary meaning if you'd use its terminology at a cocktail party and "no one would look at you funny."[19]

GRAMMAR AND SYNTAX

- Punctuation rule: Congress is presumed to follow accepted punctuation standards, so that placements of commas and other punctuation are assumed to be meaningful.[20]

- Grammar rule: Congress is presumed to follow accepted standards of grammar.[21]

- Rule of the last antecedent: referential and qualifying words or phrases refer only to the last antecedent, unless contrary to the apparent legislative intent derived from the sense of the entire enactment.[22] Do not have to apply this rule if not practical.[23]

- "May" is usually precatory and connotes decisionmaking discretion,[24] while "shall" is usually mandatory and suggests less discretion.[25]

- "Or" means in the alternative.[26]

---

[16] Zuni Pub. Sch. Dist. No. 89 v. Department of Educ., 550 U.S. 81 (2007).

[17] MCI v. AT&T, 512 U.S. 218 (1994) (disrespecting *Webster's Third* for including colloquial as well as standard definitions).

[18] Burwell v. Hobby Lobby Stores, Inc., 134 S.Ct. 2751 (2014) (definition of "person" presumptively includes corporations); Mohamad v. Palestinian Auth., 132 S.Ct. 1702 (2012); Carr v. United States, 560 U.S. 438 (2010); Stewart v. Dutra Constr. Co., 543 U.S. 481 (2005).

[19] Johnson v. United States, 529 U.S. 694, 718 (2000) (Scalia, J., dissenting).

[20] Jama v. Immigration & Customs Enf., 543 U.S. 335, 344 (2005) (significance of periods); United States v. Ron Pair Enters., 489 U.S. 235, 241–42 (1989) (comma placement); San Francisco Arts & Athletics, Inc. v. United States Olympic Comm'n, 483 U.S. 522, 528–29 (1987).

[21] Carr v. United States, 560 U.S. 438 (2010); Limtiaco v. Camacho, 549 U.S. 483 (2007); Rapanos v. United States, 547 U.S. 715 (2006) (plurality opinion of Scalia, J.); Jama v. Immigration & Customs Enf., 543 U.S. 335 (2005).

[22] Jama v. Immigration & Customs Enf., 543 U.S. 335 (2005); Barnhart v. Thomas, 540 U.S. 20, 26 (2003); Nobelman v. American Savs. Bank, 508 U.S. 324, 330 (1993).

[23] Nobelman v. American Savs. Bank, 508 U.S. 324, 330–31 (1993).

[24] Jama v. Immigration & Customs Enf., 543 U.S. 335 (2005); Lopez v. Davis, 531 U.S. 230 (2001) ("may" vests wide discretion in agency).

[25] Mallard v. United States Dist. Ct., 490 U.S. 296, 302 (1989).

[26] Loughrin v. United States, 134 S.Ct. 2384, 2389–90 (2014); Hawaiian Airlines v. Norris, 512 U.S. 246, 253–54 (1994).

TEXTUAL INTEGRITY (WHOLE ACT RULE)

- Each statutory provision should be read by reference to the whole act.[27] Statutory interpretation is a "holistic" endeavor.[28]

- The statute's preamble may provide clues to statutory meaning,[29] as may the title.[30]

- Presumption against redundancy: avoid interpreting a provision in a way that would render other provisions of the statute superfluous or unnecessary.[31] This presumption must give way when offset by other evidence of statutory meaning, however.[32]

- Presumption of statutory consistency: interpret the same or similar terms in a statute the same way.[33] Presumption rebutted when other evidence suggests Congress was using the same term in different ways.[34]

- Presumption of meaningful variation: different statutory wording suggests different statutory meaning,[35] especially when Congress considered and rejected the alternate wording.[36] Presumption inapplicable when there is a

---

[27] Samantar v. Yousuf, 560 U.S. 305 (2010); Ricci v. DeStefano, 557 U.S. 557 (2009); Ledbetter v. Goodyear Tire & Rubber Co., 550 U.S. 618 (2007); Gonzales v. Oregon, 546 U.S. 243, 273–74 (2006); Doe v. Chao, 540 U.S. 614 (2004) (considering uncodified parts of the "whole act"); Clark v. Martinez, 543 U.S. 371 (2005); Babbitt v. Sweet Home Chapter of Communities for a Great Oregon, 515 U.S. 687 (1995); Pavelic & Leflore v. Marvel Entm't Group, 493 U.S. 120, 123–24 (1989); Massachusetts v. Morash, 490 U.S. 107, 114–15 (1989).

[28] Burwell v. Hobby Lobby Stores, Inc., 134 S.Ct. 2751 (2014); United Sav. Ass'n v. Timbers of Inwood Forest Assocs., Ltd., 484 U.S. 365, 371 (1988).

[29] Sutton v. United Airlines, Inc., 527 U.S. 471 (1999) (majority and concurring opinions).

[30] Almendarez-Torres v. United States, 523 U.S. 224, 234 (1998).

[31] Fifth Third Bancorp v. Didenhoeffer, 134 S.Ct. 2459 (2014); Ricci v. DeStefano, 557 U.S. 557 (2009); Circuit City Stores, Inc. v. Adams, 532 U.S. 105 (2001); United States v. Alaska, 521 U.S. 1 (1997); Walters v. Metropolitan Educ. Enters., Inc., 519 U.S. 202 (1997); Rake v. Wade, 508 U.S. 464 (1993); Kungys v. United States, 485 U.S. 759, 778 (1988) (plurality opinion by Scalia, J.).

[32] United States v. Home Concrete & Supply, LLC, 132 S.Ct. 1836 (2012); Gutierrez v. Ada, 528 U.S. 250 (2000); Landgraf v. USI Film Prods., 511 U.S. 240, 259–60 (1994).

[33] Robers v. United States, 134 S.Ct. 1854 (2014); Powerex Corp. v. Reliant Energy Servs., Inc., 551 U.S. 224 (2007); IBP, Inc. v. Alvarez, 546 U.S. 21, 34 (2005); Commissioner v. Lundy, 516 U.S. 235, 249–50 (1996); Gustafson v. Alloyd Co., 513 U.S. 561, 570 (1995); Sullivan v. Stroop, 496 U.S. 478, 484 (1990); United Sav. Ass'n v. Timbers of Inwood Forest Assocs., Ltd., 484 U.S. 365, 371 (1988).

[34] Utility Air Regulatory Group v. EPA, 134 S.Ct. 2427 (2014); Environmental Defense v. Duke Energy Corp., 549 U.S. 561 (2007); Robinson v. Shell Oil Co., 519 U.S. 337, 343–44 (1997); Dewsnup v. Timm, 502 U.S. 410, 417 & n.3 (1992).

[35] Burwell v. Hobby Lobby Stores, Inc., 134 S.Ct. 2751, 2772-74 (2014); Loughrin v. United States, 134 S.Ct. 2384, 2390-92 (2014); Pacific Operators Offshore, LLC v. Valladolid, 132 S.Ct. 680 (2012); Gross v. FBL Financial Services, Inc. 557 U.S. 167 (2009); Lawrence v. Florida, 549 U.S. 327 (2007); Lopez v. Gonzales, 549 U.S. 47 (2006); Lindh v. Murphy, 521 U.S. 320 (1997); Keene Corp. v. United States, 508 U.S. 200, 208 (1993); Gozlon-Peretz v. United States, 498 U.S. 395, 404–05 (1991). The leading case is Russello v. United States, 464 U.S. 16, 23 (1983).

[36] Hamdan v. Rumsfeld, 548 U.S. 557 (2006).

reasonable explanation for variation (e.g., different provisions are enacted at different times).[37]

- Avoid interpreting a provision in a way that is inconsistent with the overall structure of the statute[38] *or* with another provision[39] *or* with a subsequent amendment to the statute[40] *or* with another statute enacted by a Congress relying on a particular interpretation.[41]

- Presumption of purposive amendment: statutory amendments are meant to have real and substantial effect.[42]

- Avoid the implication of broad congressional delegation of agency authority when statute carefully limits agency authority in particular matters.[43]

- Avoid broad readings of statutory provisions if Congress has specifically provided for the broader policy in more specific language elsewhere.[44]

- Broad term is presumptively ambiguous if Congress has elsewhere used more targeted terminology.[45]

- Specific provisions targeting a particular issue apply instead of provisions more generally covering the issue.[46]

- Provisos and statutory exceptions should be read narrowly.[47]

- Do not create exceptions in addition to those specified by Congress.[48]

---

[37] Gutierrez v. Ada, 528 U.S. 250 (2000); Field v. Mans, 516 U.S. 59, 67–69 (1995).

[38] Abramski v. United States, 134 S.Ct. 2259 (2014); Samantar v. Yousuf, 560 U.S. 305 (2010); Ledbetter v. Goodyear Tire & Rubber Co., 550 U.S. 618 (2007); Beck v. PACE Int'l Union, 551 U.S. 96 (2007).

[39] Petrella v. MGM, Inc., 134 S.Ct. 1962 (2014); Ricci v. DeStefano, 557 U.S. 557 (2009); Babbitt v. Sweet Home Chapter of Communities for a Great Oregon, 515 U.S. 687 (1995); Gade v. National Solid Wastes Management Ass'n, 505 U.S. 88, 100–01 (1992); United Sav. Ass'n v. Timbers of Inwood Forest Assocs., Ltd., 484 U.S. 365, 371 (1988).

[40] Gonzales v. Oregon, 546 U.S. 243, 257–58 (2006).

[41] FDA v. Brown & Williamson Tobacco Corp., 529 U.S. 120, 144 (2000).

[42] Rumsfeld v. Forum for Academic & Institutional Rights, Inc., 547 U.S. 47 (2006); Babbitt v. Sweet Home Chapter of Communities for a Great Oregon, 515 U.S. 687 (1995).

[43] Gonzales v. Oregon, 547 U.S. 243, 262–63 (2006).

[44] Arlington Cent. Sch. Dist. Bd. of Educ. v. Murphy, 548 U.S. 291 (2006); Jama v. Immigration & Customs Enforcement, 543 U.S. 335 (2005); Custis v. United States, 511 U.S. 485, 491 (1994); West Virginia Univ. Hosps. v. Casey, 499 U.S. 83, 99 (1991).

[45] Zuni Pub. Sch. Dist. No. 89 v. Department of Educ., 550 U.S. 81 (2007).

[46] Green v. Bock Laundry Mach. Co., 490 U.S. 504, 524–26 (1989); Crawford Fitting Co. v. J.T. Gibbons, Inc., 482 U.S. 437, 444–45 (1987).

[47] Maracich v. Spears, 133 S.Ct. 2191, 2200 (2013); Cherokee Nation of Oklahoma v. Leavitt, 543 U.S. 631 (2005); City of Edmonds v. Oxford House, Inc., 514 U.S. 725, 732 (1995). The leading case is Commissioner v. Clark, 489 U.S. 726, 739 (1989). But see Republic of Iraq v. Beaty, 556 U.S. 848, 857–58 (2009) (acknowledging this general rule but applying proviso more liberally where Congress was granting the President needed foreign affairs flexibility).

[48] United States v. Smith, 499 U.S. 160, 166–67 (1991).

EXTRINSIC SOURCE CANONS

AGENCY INTERPRETATIONS

- *Skidmore* deference. Agency interpretations are entitled to respect to the extent that they have "power to persuade" based upon consistency, factual basis, and expertise.[49] Contrariwise, agency views that are shifting or insufficiently developed have little or no persuasive value.[50]

- Even informal and unsettled agency interpretations (such as those embodied in handbooks or litigation briefs) may be useful confirmations for the interpreter's interpretation of statutory language.[51]

- *Chevron* deference. "Reasonable" agency interpretations pursuant to congressional delegation of lawmaking authority are binding on courts unless Congress has directly addressed the issue,[52] or the Court has authoritatively resolved the issue in a binding precedent.[53] The agency's discretion is at its height when the agency decides not to enforce a statute.[54]

- For *Chevron* purposes, whether Congress has delegated the agency lawmaking authority is itself a matter of statutory interpretation.[55] Presumption against congressional delegation of authority for agency to make fundamental changes in the statute.[56] The Court often demands a clear statement authorizing agency constructions that press the envelope of constitutional validity or preempt state law.[57]

---

[49] Beck v. PACE Int'l Union, 551 U.S. 96 (2007); Gonzales v. Oregon, 546 U.S. 243, 255–56 (2006); United States v. Mead Corp., 533 U.S. 218, 226–27 (2001); EEOC v. Arabian Am. Oil Co., 499 U.S. 244 (1991). The leading case is Skidmore v. Swift & Co., 323 U.S. 134, 140 (1944).

[50] Burlington Northern & Santa Fe Ry. v. White, 548 U.S. 53 (2006).

[51] S.D. Warren Co. v. Maine Bd. of Envtl. Prot., 547 U.S. 370 (2006).

[52] Utility Air Regulatory Group v. EPA, 134 S.Ct. 2427 (2014) (plurality and concurring opinions); Scialabba v. Cuellar de Osorio, 134 S.Ct. 2191 (2014) (plurality and concurring opinions); Mayo Found. Med. Res. & Educ. v. United States, 131 S.Ct. 704 (2011) (overruling prior precedent in favor of *Chevron* deference for tax regulations); Zuni Pub. Sch. Dist. No. 89 v. Department of Educ., 550 U.S. 291 (2007) (majority and concurring opinions); National Cable & Telecommunications Ass'n v. Brand X Internet Servs., 545 U.S. 967 (2005); ABF Freight Sys., Inc. v. NLRB, 510 U.S. 317, 324 (1994); Sullivan v. Everhart, 494 U.S. 83, 88–89 (1990); K Mart Corp. v. Cartier, Inc., 486 U.S. 281, 291–92 (1988) The leading case is Chevron U.S.A., Inc. v. Natural Resources Defense Council, 467 U.S. 837 (1984).

[53] United States v. Home Concrete & Supply, LLC, 132 S.Ct. 1836 (2012). Cf. National Cable & Telecomm. Serv., Inc. v. Brand X Internet Services, 545 U.S. 967 (2005) (overruling a lower court's insistence that its own construction of a statute trumps that of an agency acting within its *Chevron* zone of discretion).

[54] Massachusetts v. EPA, 549 U.S. 497 (2007).

[55] Gonzales v. Oregon, 546 U.S. 243 (2006).

[56] Utility Air Regulatory Group v. EPA, 134 S.Ct. 2427 (2104) (plurality and concurring opinions); Gonzales v. Oregon, 546 U.S. 243 (2006); FDA v. Brown & Williamson Tobacco Corp., 529 U.S. 120 (2000); MCI v. AT&T, 512 U.S. 218 (1994).

[57] Bond v. United States, 134 S.Ct. 2077 (2014); Wyeth v. Levine, 555 U.S. 555, 576 (2009); Rapanos v. United States, 547 U.S. 715 (2006) (plurality opinion of Scalia, J.); Edward J.

- *Seminole Rock/Auer* deference. Agency interpretation of its own regulations is controlling unless "plainly erroneous or inconsistent with the regulation."[58] Rule does not apply when agency rule merely "parrots" the statute,[59] or where agency interpretation has been unstable over time.[60]

- *Curtiss-Wright* deference. In matters of foreign affairs and national security, presidential or executive statutory interpretations enjoy a super-strong presumption of correctness.[61] (The executive is still bound by statutory and treaty directives.[62]) Similar deference for executive branch views of federal jurisdiction over foreign states.[63]

- Courts accord great weight to executive department interpretation of treaties.[64]

CONTINUITY IN LAW

- Rule that statutes should be interpreted in light of binding precedents;[65] statutory precedents should rarely be overruled, as they enjoy a super-strong presumption of correctness.[66] The super-strong rule against overruling

---

Debartolo Corp. v. Florida Gulf Coast Building & Constr. Trades Council, 485 U.S. 568, 575 (1988).

[58] Pliva, Inc. v. Mensing, 131 S.Ct. 2567, 2575–76 (2011); Talk America, Inc. v. Michigan Bell Tel. Co., 131 S.Ct. 2254 (2011); Coeur Alaska, Inc. v. Southeast Alaska Conserv. Coun., 557 U.S. 261 (2009) (applying *Auer* deference to an internal EPA memorandum); Auer v. Robbins, 519 U.S. 452, 461–63 (1997); Thomas Jefferson Univ. v. Shalala, 512 U.S. 504, 512 (1994); Mullins Coal Co. v. Director, Office of Workers' Compensation Programs, 484 U.S. 135, 159 (1987). The leading case is Bowles v. Seminole Rock & Sand Co., 325 U.S. 410, 414 (1945).

[59] Gonzales v. Oregon, 546 U.S. 243, 257 (2006).

[60] Commissioner v. Schleier, 515 U.S. 323 (1995); Bowen v. Georgetown Univ. Hosp., 488 U.S. 204 (1988).

[61] Republic of Iraq v. Beaty, 556 U.S. 848, 856–57, 860 (2009); Hamdi v. Rumsfeld, 542 U.S. 507, 518 (2004) (plurality opinion of O'Connor, J.); id. at 580–81 (Thomas, J., concurring in part, with a stronger statement); Cheney v. U.S. Dist. Court, 542 U.S. 367 (2004); Crosby v. National Foreign Trade Council, 530 U.S. 363 (2000); Department of Navy v. Egan, 484 U.S. 518 (1988). The leading case is United States v. Curtiss-Wright Export Corp., 299 U.S. 304 (1936).

[62] Hamdan v. Rumsfeld, 548 U.S. 557 (2006).

[63] Republic of Austria v. Altmann, 541 U.S. 677, 689–90 (2004).

[64] Sanchez-Llamas v. Oregon, 548 U.S. 331 (2006); El Al Israel Airlines v. Tsui Yuan Tseng, 525 U.S. 155 (1999).

[65] United States v. Home Concrete & Supply, LLC, 132 S.Ct. 1836 (2012); Wal-Mart Stores, Inc. v. Dukes, 131 S.Ct. 2541 (2011); Global-Tech Appliances, Inc. v. SEB SA, 131 S.Ct. 2060 (2011); American Needle, Inc. v. National Football League, 560 U.S. 183 (2010); AT&T Corp. v. Hulteen, 556 U.S. 701 (2009).

[66] Halliburton Co. v. Erica P. John Fund, Inc., 134 S.Ct. 2398 (2014); Michigan v. Bay Mills Indian Community, 134 S.Ct. 2024 (2014); United States v. Home Concrete & Supply, LLC, 132 S.Ct. 1836 (2012); CSX Transp., Inc. v. McBride, 131 S.Ct. 2630, 2641 (2011); John R. Sand & Gravel Co. v. United States, 552 U.S. 130, 139 (2008); Hohn v. United States, 524 U.S. 236, 251 (1998); Neal v. United States, 516 U.S. 284 (1996); California v. FERC, 495 U.S. 490, 498–99 (1990); Patterson v. McLean Credit Union, 491 U.S. 164 (1989). See also Ledbetter v. Goodyear Tire & Rubber Co., 550 U.S. 618 (2007) (following precedent that had been largely overridden by Congress); Arlington Cent. Sch. Dist. Bd. of Educ. v. Murphy, 548 U.S. 291 (2006) (similar).

statutory precedents is inapplicable to the Sherman Act, which is a common law statute.[67]

- Wrongly decided precedents that are also inconsistent with recent legal developments can be overruled.[68]

- Where a Supreme Court decision follows an agency interpretation filling a gap in the law left by Congress (*Chevron*), a revised agency interpretation through rulemaking is not barred by *stare decisis*.[69]

- Presumption of continuity: Congress does not create discontinuities in legal rights and obligations without some clear statement.[70]

- Presumption against repeals by implication.[71] But where there is a clear repugnancy between a more recent statutory scheme and an earlier one, partial repeal will be inferred.[72]

- Presumption against hiding elephants in mouseholes: Congress usually does not alter the fundamental details of a regulatory scheme in vague or ancillary provisions.[73]

- Presumption that Congress uses same term consistently in different statutes and international agreements.[74]

- Presumption that statutes be interpreted consistent with international law and treaties.[75] But international

---

[67] Leegin Creative Leather Prods. v. PSKS, Inc., 551 U.S. 877 (2007); State Oil Co. v. Khan, 522 U.S. 3 (1997).

[68] Leegin Creative Leather Prods. v. PSKS, Inc., 551 U.S. 877 (2007); Bowles v. Russell, 551 U.S. 205 (2007); Rodriguez de Quijas v. Shearson/American Express, Inc., 490 U.S. 477, 480–81 (1989).

[69] National Cable & Telecomm. Serv. v. Brand X Internet Servs., 545 U.S. 967 (2005); Christensen v. Harris County, 529 U.S. 576, 589 (2000) (Souter, J., concurring); United States v. Watts, 519 U.S. 148 (1997) (Breyer, J., concurring); Central Laborers' Pension Fund v. Heinz, 541 U.S. 739, 751 (2004) (Breyer, J., concurring); Norfolk Southern Ry. v. Shankin, 529 U.S. 344 (2000) (Breyer, J., concurring); Christensen v. Harris County, 529 U.S. 576, 589 (2000) (Souter, J., concurring); United States v. Watts, 519 U.S. 148 (1997) (Breyer, J., concurring). This canon does not apply when it appears that a court has closed off agency discretion. United States v. Home Concrete & Supply, LLC, 132 S.Ct. 1836 (2012).

[70] POM Wonderful LLC v. Coca-Cola Co., 134 S.Ct. 2228 (2014); Green v. Bock Laundry Mach. Co., 490 U.S. 504, 521–22 (1989); Finley v. United States, 490 U.S. 545, 554 (1989). See also Pacific Operators Offshore, LLC v. Valladolid, 132 S.Ct. 680 (2012) (Scalia, J., concurring in the judgment) (presuming that Congress intended an easy-to-apply common law standard rather than a novel standard that would be harder to administer).

[71] POM Wonderful LLC v. Coca-Cola Co., 134 S.Ct. 2228 (2014); Hamdan v. Rumsfeld, 548 U.S. 557 (2006); Granholm v. Heald, 544 U.S. 460 (2005); Branch v. Smith, 538 U.S. 254, 273 (2003); Pittsburgh & Lake Erie R.R. v. Railway Labor Executives' Ass'n, 491 U.S. 490, 509 (1989); Traynor v. Turnage, 485 U.S. 535, 547–48 (1988). The leading case is Morton v. Mancari, 417 U.S. 535 (1974).

[72] Credit Suisse Securities (USA) LLC v. Billing, 551 U.S. 264 (2007).

[73] Gonzales v. Oregon, 546 U.S. 243, 267 (2006); Whitman v. American Trucking Ass'ns, Inc., 531 U.S. 457, 468 (2001); FDA v. Brown & Williamson Tobacco Corp., 529 U.S. 120, 160 (2000).

[74] Hawaiian Airlines v. Norris, 512 U.S. 246, 254 (1994); Smith v. United States, 508 U.S. 223, 234–35 (1993); Pierce v. Underwood, 487 U.S. 552 (1988).

agreements do not trump the plain meaning of federal statutes.[76]

- Borrowed statute rule: when Congress borrows a statute, it adopts by implication interpretations placed on that statute,[77] absent indication to the contrary.[78]

- *In pari materia* rule: when similar statutory provisions are found in comparable statutory schemes, interpreters should presumptively apply them the same way.[79]

- Re-enactment rule: when Congress re-enacts a statute, it incorporates settled interpretations of the re-enacted statute.[80] The rule is inapplicable when there is no settled standard Congress could have known.[81]

- Acquiescence rules: consistent agency or Supreme Court interpretation known to Congress is presumed correct.[82] Also, consider unbroken line of lower court decisions interpreting statute, but do not give them decisive weight.[83]

EXTRINSIC LEGISLATIVE SOURCES

- Statutory history (the formal evolution of a statute, as Congress amends it over the years) is always potentially relevant.[84]

- Consider legislative history (the internal evolution of a statute before enactment) if the statute is ambiguous.[85]

---

[75] Spector v. Norwegian Cruise Line Ltd., 545 U.S. 119 (2005); id. at 142 (Ginsburg, J., concurring in part and in the judgment); Hamdi v. Rumsfeld, 542 U.S. 507 (2004) (plurality opinion of O'Connor, J.); INS v. Cardoza-Fonseca, 480 U.S. 421 (1987) (strong presumption when statute is implementing an international agreement).

[76] Societe Nationale Industrielle Aerospatialle v. U.S. Dist. Ct., 482 U.S. 522, 538–39 (1987).

[77] Molzof v. United States, 502 U.S. 301, 307 (1992); Metropolitan Life Ins. Co. v. Taylor, 481 U.S. 58, 65–66 (1987).

[78] Shannon v. United States, 512 U.S. 573, 581 (1994).

[79] Hardt v. Reliance Standard Life Ins. Co., 560 U.S. 242 (2010); Ledbetter v. Goodyear Tire & Rubber Co., 550 U.S. 618 (2007) (finding NLRA but not EPA analogous to Title VII for limitations purposes).

[80] Merck & Co. v. Reynolds, 559 U.S. 633, 1794–96 (2010); Davis v. United States, 495 U.S. 472, 482 (1990); Pierce v. Underwood, 487 U.S. 552 (1988).

[81] Jama v. Immigration & Customs Enforcement, 543 U.S. 335 (2005).

[82] Michigan v. Bay Mills Indian Community, 134 S.Ct. 2024 (2014); CSX Transp., Inc. v. McBride, 131 S.Ct. 2630, 2641 (2011); Zuni Pub. Sch. Dist. No. 89 v. Department of Educ., 550 U.S. 81 (2007) (agency interpretation); FDA v. Brown & Williamson Tobacco Corp., 529 U.S. 120 (2000) (agency).

[83] CSX Transp., Inc. v. McBride, 131 S.Ct. 2630, 2641 (2011); Gonzalez v. Crosby, 545 U.S. 524 (2005); General Dynamics Land Sys., Inc. v. Cline, 540 U.S. 581 (2004); National Archives & Records Admin. v. Favish, 541 U.S. 157 (2004); Monessen Sw. Ry. Co. v. Morgan, 486 U.S. 330, 338–39 (1988).

[84] Burwell v. Hobby Lobby Stores, Inc., 134 S.Ct. ___ (June 30, 2014); Powerex Corp. v. Reliant Energy Servs., Inc., 551 U.S. 224 (2007) (Scalia, J.); Ballard v. Commissioner, 544 U.S. 40 (2005).

Additionally, legislative history (especially committee reports) can be useful confirmation of a perceived plain meaning of statutory language.[86]

- Committee reports (especially conference committee reports reflecting the understanding of both House and Senate) are the most authoritative legislative history,[87] but cannot trump a textual plain meaning,[88] and should not be relied on if they are themselves ambiguous or imprecise.[89]

- Committee report language that cannot be tied to a specific statutory provision cannot be credited.[90] House and Senate reports inconsistent with one another should be discounted.[91]

- Caution against interpretation considered and rejected by floor vote of a chamber of Congress or within committee.[92] Cautionary principle inapplicable when it is not clear why Congress rejected the proposal.[93]

---

[85] Bond v. United States, 134 S.Ct. 2077 (2014); Safeco Ins. Co. of Am. v. Burr, 551 U.S. 47 (2007); Zuni Pub. Sch. Dist. No. 89 v. Department of Educ., 550 U.S. 81 (2007); Gonzales v. Oregon, 546 U.S. 243, 257–58 (2006); Rumsfeld v. Forum for Academic & Institutional Rights, 547 U.S. 47 (2006); Koons Buick Pontiac GMC, Inc. v. Nigh, 543 U.S. 50, 62–64 (2004); id. at 65–66 (Stevens, J., concurring); FDA v. Brown & Williamson Tobacco Corp., 529 U.S. 120 (2000); Babbitt v. Sweet Home Chapter of Communities for a Great Oregon, 515 U.S. 687 (1995) (both majority and dissenting opinions); Wisconsin Pub. Intervenor v. Mortier, 501 U.S. 597, 610 n.4 (1991). But see Samantar v. Yousuf, 560 U.S. 305 (2010) (Scalia, J., concurring in the judgment) (arguing that legislative history is never useful and should not be invoked); James v. United States, 550 U.S. 192 (2007) (ignoring legislative history of a provision that was obsolete).

[86] Loughrin v. United States, 134 S.Ct. 2384 (2014); Samantar v. Yousuf, 560 U.S. 305, 316 & n.9 (2010); Carr v. United States, 560 U.S. 438, 456 (2010); Shinseki v. Sanders, 556 U.S. 396, 406–07 (2009); United States v. Ressam, 553 U.S. 272, 275–77 (2008); Zedner v. United States, 547 U.S. 489, 500–01 (2007).

[87] Brown v. Plata, 131 S.Ct. 1910, 1937 (2011); Tellabs, Inc. v. Makor Issues & Rights, Ltd., 551 U.S. 308 (2007); Rumsfeld v. Forum for Academic & Institutional Rights, 547 U.S. 47 (2006); Cherokee Nation of Oklahoma v. Leavitt, 543 U.S. 631 (2005); Intel Corp. v. Advanced Micro Devices, Inc., 542 U.S. 241 (2004); Jones v. R.R. Donnelley & Sons Co., 541 U.S. 369 (2004); Boeing Co. v. United States, 537 U.S. 437 (2003); Johnson v. DeGrandy, 512 U.S. 997, 1010–11 & n.9 (1994).

[88] Arlington Cent. Sch. Dist. Bd. of Educ. v. Murphy, 548 U.S. 291 (2006) (majority and concurring opinions); City of Chicago v. Environmental Def. Fund, 511 U.S. 328, 337 (1994); American Hosp. Ass'n v. NLRB, 499 U.S. 606, 613 (1991). This canon is controversial within the Court. See *Murphy*, 548 U.S. at 308–24 (Breyer, J., dissenting).

[89] Marrama v. Citizens Bank of Mass., 549 U.S. 365 (2007); Small v. United States, 544 U.S. 385 (2005).

[90] Shannon v. United States, 512 U.S. 573, 583 (1994).

[91] Moreau v. Klevenhagen, 508 U.S. 22, 26 (1993).

[92] Mohamad v. Palestinian Auth., 132 S.Ct. 1702 (2012) (relying on record of committee mark-up); Hamdan v. Rumsfeld, 548 U.S. 557 (2006); Doe v. Chao, 540 U.S. 614 (2004); F. Hoffmann-LaRoche, Ltd. v. Empagran S.A., 540 U.S. 1088 (2004); FDA v. Brown & Williamson Tobacco Corp., 529 U.S. 120, 144 (2000); Department of Revenue v. ACF Indus., 510 U.S. 332, 345–36 (1994).

[93] Safeco Ins. Co. of Am. v. Burr, 551 U.S. 47 (2007); Rapanos v. United States, 547 U.S. 715 (2006) (plurality opinion of Scalia, J.); Solid Waste Agency v. Army Corps of Eng'rs, 531 U.S. 159, 169 (2001).

- Floor statements, especially by statutory sponsors, can be used to understand what Congress meant by statutory language.[94]

- Public give-and-take between Members of Congress and executive department drafters or sponsors during committee hearings are relevant if they illuminate a shared meaning of statutory language by the participants closest to the process.[95]

- The "dog didn't bark" canon: presumption that prior legal rule should be retained if no one in legislative deliberations even mentioned the rule or discussed any changes in the rule.[96]

- Views of a subsequent Congress are a hazardous basis for inferring the intent of an earlier one,[97] but are sometimes relevant.[98] Subsequent legislation clearly incorporating these views is relevant and persuasive.[99]

SUBSTANTIVE POLICY CANONS

CONSTITUTION-BASED CANONS

- Avoidance canon: avoid interpretations that would render a statute unconstitutional *or* that would raise serious constitutional difficulties.[100] Inapplicable if statute would

---

[94] Entergy Corp. v. Riverkeeper, Inc., 556 U.S. 208, 230–35 (2009) (Breyer, J., concurring); Hamdan v. Rumsfeld, 548 U.S. 557 (2006); Department of Revenue v. ACF Indus., Inc., 510 U.S. 332, 345–46 (1994). But see Graham County Soil & Conserv. Dist. v. United States ex rel. Wilson, 130 S.Ct. 1396, 1408–09 (2010) (rejecting sponsor's statement as too generalized).

[95] General Dynamics Land Sys., Inc. v. Cline, 540 U.S. 581 (2004); FDA v. Brown & Williamson Tobacco Corp., 529 U.S. 120 (2000); Hagen v. Utah, 510 U.S. 399, 418 (1994); Darby v. Cisneros, 509 U.S. 137, 147–51 (1993).

[96] Zuni Pub. Sch. Dist. No. 89 v. Department of Educ., 550 U.S. 81 (2007); Chisom v. Roemer, 501 U.S. 380, 396 & n.23 (1991).

[97] Brusewitz v. Wyeth LLC, 131 S.Ct. 1068, 1081–82 (2011); Graham County Soil & Conserv. Dist. v. United States ex rel. Wilson, 559 U.S. 280, 296 (2010); Masschusetts v. EPA, 549 U.S. 497 (2007); Doe v. Chao, 540 U.S. 614 (2004); Solid Waste Agency v. Army Corps of Eng'rs, 531 U.S. 159, 170 (2001); Sullivan v. Finkelstein, 496 U.S. 617, 628 n.8 (1990).

[98] Musick, Peeler & Garrett v. Employers Ins. of Wassau, 508 U.S. 286, 293 (1993). This canon is controversial within the Court. Sullivan v. Finkelstein, 496 U.S. 617, 631–32 (1990) (Scalia, J., concurring in part).

[99] FDA v. Brown & Williamson Tobacco Corp., 529 U.S. 120, 144 (2000); Babbitt v. Sweet Home Chapter of Communities for a Great Oregon, 515 U.S. 687 (1995); Franklin v. Gwinnett County Pub. Sch., 503 U.S. 60 (1990); id. at 77–78 (Scalia, J., concurring in the judgment); Bowen v. Yuckert, 482 U.S. 137, 149–51 (1987).

[100] Bond v. United States, 134 S.Ct. 2077 (2014); Brown v. Plata, 131 S.Ct. 1910, 1928–29, 1937 (2011); Northwest Austin Mun. Utility Dist. No. 1 v. Holder, 557 U.S. 193 (2010); Rapanos v. United States, 547 U.S. 715 (2006) (plurality opinion of Scalia, J.); Cherokee Nation of Oklahoma v. Leavitt, 543 U.S. 631 (2005); Zadvydas v. Davis, 533 U.S. 678, 696–99 (2001); Public Citizen v. United States Dep't of Justice, 491 U.S. 440, 465–66 (1989); Edward J. Debartolo Corp. v. Florida Gulf Coast Building & Constr. Trades Council, 485 U.S. 568, 575 (1988).

clearly survive constitutional attack, or if statutory text is clear.[101]

1. *Separation of Powers*

- Super-strong rule against congressional interference with President's inherent powers, his executive authority.[102] Avoid interpretations whereby judges would interfere with foreign affairs.[103]

- Rule against review of President's core executive actions for "abuse of discretion."[104]

- Where Congress appropriates money without specific textual restrictions, the executive has leeway as to its expenditure, unlimited by more informal signals.[105]

- Rule of special treatment of President and Vice-President as litigants, affording them special privileges so as not to interfere with their official duties.[106]

- Rule against congressional curtailment of the judiciary's "inherent powers" or its "equity" powers.[107]

- Rule against congressional expansion of Article III injury in fact to include intangible and procedural injuries.[108]

- Presumption that Congress does not delegate authority without sufficient guidelines.[109]

- Presumption against "implying" causes of action into federal statutes.[110]

- Presumption that U.S. law conforms to U.S. international obligations.[111] Presumption that Congress takes account of

---

[101] Stern v. Marshall, 131 S.Ct. 2594, 2607–08 (2011); Peretz v. United States, 501 U.S. 923, 932 (1991); Rust v. Sullivan, 500 U.S. 173, 182 (1991).

[102] Department of Navy v. Egan, 484 U.S. 518, 527 (1988); Morrison v. Olson, 487 U.S. 654, 682–83 (1988); Carlucci v. Doe, 488 U.S. 93, 99 (1988); United States v. Johnson, 481 U.S. 681, 690–91 (1987).

[103] Sosa v. Alvarez-Machain, 542 U.S. 692 (2004).

[104] Franklin v. Massachusetts, 505 U.S. 788, 800–01 (1991).

[105] Cherokee Nation of Oklahoma v. Leavitt, 543 U.S. 631 (2005); Lincoln v. Vigil, 508 U.S. 182, 191 (1993).

[106] Cheney v. U.S. Dist. Court, 542 U.S. 367 (2004).

[107] Brown v. Plata, 131 S.Ct. 1910, 1928–29, 1936–37 (2011); Chambers v. Nasco, Inc., 501 U.S. 32, 43–44 (1991).

[108] Lujan v. Defenders of Wildlife, 504 U.S. 555, 557–61 (1992); id. at 579–80 (Kennedy, J., concurring in part).

[109] Mistretta v. United States, 488 U.S. 361, 373 n.7 (1989).

[110] Virginia Bankshares, Inc. v. Sandberg, 501 U.S. 1083, 1102–05 (1991); Thompson v. Thompson, 484 U.S. 174, 179 (1988).

[111] Hamdan v. Rumsfeld, 548 U.S. 557 (2006) (majority and concurring opinions); Sale v. Haitian Centers Council, 509 U.S. 155, 173–74 (1993).

the legitimate sovereign interests of other nations when it
writes American laws.[112]

- Rule against congressional abrogation of Indian treaty
  rights.[113]

- Presumption favoring severability of unconstitutional
  provisions.[114]

2. *Federalism*

- Super-strong rule against federal invasion of "core state
  functions."[115] Strong presumption against statutory
  interpretations that would alter the federal-state balance.[116]

- Super-strong rule against federal abrogation of states'
  Eleventh Amendment immunity from lawsuits in federal
  courts.[117] Eleventh Amendment rule does not apply to
  municipalities and counties.[118]

- Super-strong rule against inferring conditions on federal
  grants to the states under the Spending Clause; conditions
  must be expressed clearly and unambiguously.[119] Sometimes
  the Court will require less than targeted statutory language,
  so long as states are reasonably on notice of conditions, as
  through agency guidances to that effect.[120]

---

[112] Samantar v. Yousuf, 560 U.S. 305 (2010); Microsoft Corp. v. AT&T, 550 U.S. 437 (2007); F. Hoffmann-LaRoche Ltd. v. Empagran S.A., 542 U.S. 155, 164 (2004).

[113] South Dakota v. Bourland, 508 U.S. 679, 687 (1993).

[114] Executive Benefits Ins. Agency v. Arkison, 134 S.Ct. 2165 (2014); National Federation of Independent Business v. Kathleen Sebelius, 132 S.Ct. 2566 (2012) (plurality and concurring opinions). The leading case is Alaska Airlines, Inc. v. Brock, 480 U.S. 678, 684 (1987).

[115] Rapanos v. United States, 547 U.S. 715 (2006) (plurality opinion); Nixon v. Missouri Municipal League, 541 U.S. 125 (2004); BFP v. Resolution Trust Corp., 511 U.S. 531, 544 (1994); Gregory v. Ashcroft, 501 U.S. 452, 461–64 (1991).

[116] Bond v. United States, 134 S.Ct. 2077 (2014); Gonzales v. Oregon, 546 U.S. 243 (2006); Owasso Indep. Sch. Dist. v. Falvo, 534 U.S. 426 (2002); Raygor v. Regents of the Univ. of Minn., 534 U.S. 533 (2002); BFP v. Resolution Trust Corp., 511 U.S. 531, 544 (1994); Gregory v. Ashcroft, 501 U.S. 452, 461–64 (1991); Will v. Michigan Dep't of State Police, 491 U.S. 58, 65 (1989).

[117] Nevada Dep't of Human Resources v. Hibbs, 538 U.S. 721 (2003) (finding abrogation); Raygor v. Regents of the Univ. of Minn., 534 U.S. 533 (2001); Blatchford v. Native Village of Noatak, 501 U.S. 775, 779 (1991); Dellmuth v. Muth, 491 U.S. 223, 227–28 (1989); Pennsylvania v. Union Gas, 491 U.S. 1, 7 (1989) (finding abrogation). The leading case is Atascadero State Hosp. v. Scanlon, 473 U.S. 234, 241 (1985).

[118] Jinks v. Richland County, 538 U.S. 456 (2003).

[119] Arlington Cent. Sch. Dist. Bd. of Educ. v. Murphy, 548 U.S. 291 (2006); Barnes v. Gorman, 536 U.S. 181 (2002); Gonzaga Univ. v. Doe, 536 U.S. 273 (2002); Blessing v. Freestone, 520 U.S. 329 (1997); Suter v. Artist M., 503 U.S. 347 (1991). The leading case is Pennhurst State Sch. & Hosp. v. Halderman, 451 U.S. 1 (1981).

[120] Davis v. Monroe County Bd. of Educ., 526 U.S. 629 (1999); Franklin v. Gwinnett County Pub. Sch., 503 U.S. 60 (1992).

- Presumption against federal preemption of traditional state regulation.[121] Presumption trumped if clear statutory language or, sometimes, the statutory purpose requires preemption.[122]

- Presumption against federal regulation of intergovernmental taxation by the states.[123]

- Presumption against application of federal statutes to state and local political processes,[124] except when statutory plain meaning or other factors counsel in favor of such application.[125]

- Presumption against congressional derogation from state's land claims based upon its entry into Union on an "equal footing" with all other states.[126] Presumption that upon statehood, the new state acquires title to the land under navigable rivers.[127]

- Rule against federal habeas review of state criminal convictions unless prisoner has properly exhausted state remedies.[128] Rule against federal habeas review of state criminal convictions supported by independent state ground.[129]

- Strong presumption of correctness of state criminal convictions for purposes of federal habeas corpus review.[130]

- Narrow construction of federal laws to avoid any kind of interference with state court jurisdiction and judgments.[131]

---

[121] CTS Corp. v. Waldburger, 134 S.Ct. 2175, 2188-89 (2014); Wyeth v. Levine, 555 U.S. 555 (2008); Altria Group, Inc. v. Good, 555 U.S. 70, 77 (2008); Bates v. Dow Agrosciences LLC, 544 U.S. 431 (2005); Rush Prudential HMO v. Moran, 536 U.S. 355 (2002); Medtronic, Inc. v. Lohr, 518 U.S. 470 (1996); Hawaiian Airlines v. Norris, 512 U.S. 246, 252 (1994); BFP v. Resolution Trust Corp., 511 U.S. 531, 544 (1994); Cipollone v. Liggett Group, Inc., 505 U.S. 504 (1992); California v. ARC Am. Corp., 490 U.S. 93, 100–01 (1989); Rose v. Rose, 481 U.S. 619, 635–36 (1987) (O'Connor, J., concurring in part).

[122] FTC v. Phoebe Putney Health Sys., Inc., 133 S.Ct. 1003 (2013); National Meat Ass'n v. Harris, 132 S.Ct. 965 (2012); Riegel v. Medtronic, Inc., 552 U.S. 312 (2008); Geier v. Honda Motor Co., 529 U.S. 861 (2000).

[123] Davis v. Michigan Dep't of Treasury, 489 U.S. 803, 810 (1989).

[124] City of Columbia v. Omni Outdoor Advertising, Inc., 499 U.S. 365, 373 (1991); McCormick v. United States, 500 U.S. 257, 269 n.6 (1988); McNally v. United States, 483 U.S. 350, 361 n.9 (1987).

[125] National Meat Ass'n v. Harris, 132 S.Ct. 965 (2012) (explicit and broad preemption clause); Evans v. United States, 504 U.S. 255, 270–71 (1992).

[126] Utah Div'n of State Lands v. United States, 482 U.S. 193, 196 (1987).

[127] Idaho v. United States, 533 U.S. 262 (2001).

[128] O'Sullivan v. Boerckel, 526 U.S. 838, 845 (1999).

[129] Sanchez-Llamas v. Oregon, 548 U.S. 331 (2006); Massaro v. United States, 538 U.S. 500, 504 (2003); Wright v. West, 505 U.S. 277, 289 (1992); Coleman v. Thompson, 501 U.S. 722, 729 (1991).

[130] Felkner v. Jackson, 130 S.Ct. 1305 (2011) (per curiam); Hardy v. Cross, 132 S.Ct. 490 (2011) (per curiam); Brecht v. Abrahamson, 507 U.S. 619, 635–38 (1993).

- Rule against reading an ambiguous federal statute to authorize states to engage in activities that would violate the Dormant Commerce Clause.[132]

- Rule favoring concurrent state and federal court jurisdiction over federal claims.[133]

- Rule that Indian sovereignty is limited to Indian Tribe members and designated tribal territories.[134]

- Presumption that states can tax activities within their borders, including Indian tribal activities,[135] but also presumption that states cannot tax on Indian lands.[136]

- Principle that federal equitable remedies must consider interests of state and local authorities.[137]

- Presumption that Congress borrows state statutes of limitations for federal statutory schemes.[138]

3.   *Due Process*

- Rule of lenity: rule against applying punitive sanctions if there is ambiguity as to underlying criminal liability or criminal penalty.[139] Rule is trumped when Congress clearly intended to criminalize the conduct in question.[140]

- Rule of lenity may apply to civil sanction that is punitive or when underlying liability is criminal.[141]

---

[131] Smith v. Bayer Corp., 131 S.Ct. 2368 (2011) (stingy interpretation of exceptions to Anti-Injunction Act); Kokkonen v. Guardian Life Ins. Co. of Am., 511 U.S. 375, 377 (1994) (narrow construction of jurisdictional grants); Finley v. United States, 490 U.S. 545, 552–54 (1989).

[132] Granholm v. Heald, 544 U.S. 460 (2005); Wyoming v. Oklahoma, 502 U.S. 437, 458 (1992).

[133] Mims v. Arrow Financial Servs., LLC, 132 S.Ct. 740 (2012); Tafflin v. Levitt, 493 U.S. 455, 458 (1990); Yellow Freight Sys., Inc. v. Donnelly, 494 U.S. 820, 823 (1990).

[134] Michigan v. Bay Mills Indian Community, 134 S.Ct. 2024 (2014); Atkinson Trading Co. v. Shirley, 532 U.S. 645 (2001).

[135] Cotton Petroleum Corp. v. New Mexico, 490 U.S. 163, 174 (1989).

[136] Oklahoma Tax Comm'n v. Sac and Fox Nation, 508 U.S. 114 (1993); County of Yakima v. Confederates Tribes & Bands of the Yakima Indian Nation, 502 U.S. 251, 268 (1992).

[137] Raygor v. Regents of the Univ. of Minn., 534 U.S. 533 (2002); Spallone v. United States, 493 U.S. 265, 276 (1990).

[138] Wallace v. Kato, 549 U.S. 384 (2007); Lampf, Pleva, Lipkind, Prupis & Petigrow v. Gilbertson, 501 U.S. 350, 355–56 (1991).

[139] Burrage v. United States, 134 S.Ct. 881 (2014) (majority and concurring opinions); Skilling v. United States, 561 U.S. 358 (2010); Arthur Andersen LLP v. United States, 544 U.S. 696 (2005); Cleveland v. United States, 531 U.S. 12 (2000) (explaining both notice and nondelegation rationales); United States v. Aguilar, 515 U.S. 593 (1995); United States v. Granderson, 511 U.S. 39 (1994); United States v. Kozminski, 487 U.S. 931, 939 (1988).

[140] Abramski v. United States, 134 S.Ct. 2259 (2014); Robers v. United States, 134 S.Ct. 1854 (2014); Muscarello v. United States, 524 U.S. 125 (1998); Chapman v. United States, 500 U.S. 453, 463–64 (1991).

[141] Crandon v. United States, 494 U.S. 152, 158 (1990). The Court applies this canon very unevenly. E.g., Babbitt v. Sweet Home Chapter of Communities for a Great Oregon, 515 U.S. 687 (1995).

- Rule against criminal penalties imposed without showing of specific intent.[142] But willfulness requirement in civil sanction cases typically includes reckless conduct as well.[143]

- Super-strong rule against implied congressional abrogation or repeal of habeas corpus.[144]

- Rule against interpreting statutes to be retroactive,[145] even if statute is curative or restorative.[146]

- Rule against interpreting statutes to deny a right to jury trial.[147]

- Presumption in favor of judicial review,[148] especially for constitutional questions, but not for agency decisions not to prosecute.

- Presumption against pre-enforcement challenges to implementation.[149]

- Presumption against exhaustion of remedies requirement for lawsuit to enforce constitutional rights.[150]

- Presumption that judgments will not be binding upon persons not party to adjudication.[151]

- Presumption against national service of process unless authorized by Congress.[152]

- Presumption against foreclosure of private enforcement of important federal rights.[153]

- Presumption that preponderance of the evidence standard applies in civil cases.[154]

---

[142] Arthur Andersen LLP v. United States, 544 U.S. 696 (2005); Bryan v. United States, 524 U.S. 184, 191–92 (1998); Ratzlaf v. United States, 510 U.S. 135, 137 (1994); Cheek v. United States, 498 U.S. 192, 200–01 (1991).

[143] Safeco Ins. Co. of Am. v. Burr, 551 U.S. 47 (2007); McLaughlin v. Richland Shoe Co., 486 U.S. 128, 132–33 (1988).

[144] Demore v. Kim, 538 U.S. 510 (2003); INS v. St. Cyr, 533 U.S. 289 (2001).

[145] Vartelas v. Holder, 132 S.Ct. 1479 (2012); Fernandez-Vargas v. Gonzales, 548 U.S. 30 (2006); Landgraf v. USI Film Prods., 511 U.S. 244 (1994). See also Microsoft Corp. v. AT&T, 550 U.S. 437, 454–55 (2007) (rule against retroactivity especially strong in patent law).

[146] Rivers v. Roadway Express, 511 U.S. 298 (1994).

[147] Gomez v. United States, 490 U.S. 858, 863 (1989).

[148] Sackett v. EPA, 132 S.Ct. 1367 (2012); Demore v. Kim, 538 U.S. 510 (2003); Webster v. Doe, 486 U.S. 592 (1988).

[149] Thunder Basin Coal Co. v. Reich, 510 U.S. 200, 208–10 (1994).

[150] McCarthy v. Madigan, 503 U.S. 140, 146–49 (1992).

[151] Martin v. Wilks, 490 U.S. 755, 761–62 (1989).

[152] Omni Capital Int'l v. Rudolf Wolff & Co., 484 U.S. 97, 107–08 (1987).

[153] Wilder v. Virginia Hosp. Ass'n, 496 U.S. 498, 520–21 (1990). This presumption is probably no longer viable. See Gonzaga Univ. v. Doe, 536 U.S. 273 (2002).

[154] Grogan v. Garner, 498 U.S. 279, 286 (1991).

COMMON LAW–BASED CANONS

- Presumption in favor of following common law usage and rules where Congress has employed words or concepts with well-settled common law traditions.[155] Presumption inapplicable when Congress has directly addressed the issue[156] or when common law usage is inconsistent with statutory purpose.[157]

- Rule against extraterritorial application of U.S. law.[158] Presumption that Congress legislates with domestic concerns in mind.[159]

- American laws apply to foreign-flag ships in U.S. territory and affecting Americans, but will not apply to the "internal affairs" of a foreign-flag ship unless there is a clear statutory statement to that effect.[160]

- Super-strong rule against waivers of United States sovereign immunity: waivers must be "unmistakably expressed" by Congress.[161] Even if there is a waiver of immunity from suit, the scope of the immunity will be narrowly read.[162]

- Super-strong rule against congressional abrogation of state immunity from suit.[163] Common law rule does not apply to counties and other subdivisions created by the states.[164]

---

[155] CTS Corp. v. Waldburger, 134 S.Ct. 2175 (2014) (CERCLA); Wal-Mart Stores, Inc. v. Dukes, 131 S.Ct. 2541, 2557–58 (2011) (Federal Rules of Civil Procedure); Permanent Mission of India to the United Nations v. City of New York, 551 U.S. 193 (2007) (FSIA); Hamdan v. Rumsfeld, 548 U.S. 557 (2006) (UCMJ); Dura Pharmaceuticals, Inc. v. Broudo, 544 U.S. 336 (2005) (§ 10(b)); Stewart v. Dutra Constr. Co., 543 U.S. 481, 487 (2005) (LWHCA); United States v. Texas, 507 U.S. 529, 534 (1993) (Debt Collection Act); Nationwide Mut. Ins. Co. v. Darden, 503 U.S. 318 (1992) (ERISA); Kamen v. Kemper Fin. Servs., Inc., 500 U.S. 90, 98–99 (1991) (Investment Company Act); Community for Creative Nonviolence v. Reid, 490 U.S. 730, 739–40 (1989) (Copyright Act). See also Pacific Operators Offshore, LLC v. Valladolid, 132 S.Ct. 680 (2012) (Scalia, J., concurring in the judgment) (presuming that Congress intended an easy-to-apply common law standard rather than a novel standard that would be harder to administer).

[156] Pasquantino v. United States, 544 U.S. 349, 356 (2005).

[157] CSX Transp., Inc. v. McBride, 131 S.Ct. 2630 (2011); Taylor v. United States, 495 U.S. 575, 593–95 (1990).

[158] Morrison v. National Australia Bank Ltd., 561 U.S. 247 (2010); Microsoft Corp. v. AT&T, 550 U.S. 437 (2007); F. Hoffman-LaRoche, Ltd. v. Empangran S.A., 540 U.S. 1088 (2004); Sale v. Haitian Centers Council, 509 U.S. 155 (1993); EEOC v. Arabian Am. Oil Co., 499 U.S. 244, 248 (1991); Argentine Republic v. Amerada Hess Shipping Corp., 488 U.S. 428, 440 (1989).

[159] Morrison v. National Australia Bank Ltd., 561 U.S. 247 (2010); Small v. United States, 544 U.S. 385 (2005); Smith v. United States, 507 U.S. 197, 204 n.5 (1993).

[160] Spector v. Norwegian Cruise Line Ltd., 545 U.S. 119 (2005).

[161] Richlin Security Service Co. v. Chertoff, 553 U. S. 571, 589 (2008); United States v. White Mt. Apache Tribe, 537 U.S. 465, 472–73 (2003); United States v. Nordic Village, Inc., 503 U.S. 30 (1992); Ardestani v. INS, 502 U.S. 129 (1991); United States v. Dalm, 494 U.S. 596, 608 (1990).

[162] FAA v. Cooper, 132 S.Ct. 1441 (2012).

[163] Alden v. Maine, 527 U.S. 706, 713 (1999) (announcing that state immunity from suit was based on common law, not just Eleventh Amendment). This canon is controversial within the Court. See id. at 760 (Souter, J., dissenting).

[164] Northern Ins. Co. of N.Y. v. Chatham County, 547 U.S. 189 (2006).

- Rule that debts to the United States shall bear interest.[165]

- Presumption against conveyance of U.S. public lands to private parties.[166]

- Rule presuming against attorney fee-shifting in federal courts and federal statutes,[167] and narrow construction of fee-shifting statutes to exclude costs and other items that are not explicitly identified.[168]

- Presumption that jury finds facts, judge declares law.[169]

- Rule presuming that law takes effect on date of enactment.[170]

- Presumption that public (government) interest not be prejudiced by negligence of federal officials.[171]

- Presumption that federal agencies launched into commercial world with power to "sue and be sued" are not entitled to sovereign immunity.[172]

- Presumption favoring enforcement of forum selection clauses.[173]

- Presumption that federal judgment has preclusive effect in state administrative proceedings.[174]

- Presumption importing common law immunities into federal civil rights statutes.[175]

STATUTE-BASED CANONS

- Purposive construction: interpret ambiguous statutes so as best to carry out their statutory purposes.[176] Avoid

---

[165] United States v. Texas, 507 U.S. 529 (1993).

[166] Utah Div. of State Lands v. United States, 482 U.S. 193, 197–98 (1987).

[167] Hardt v. Reliance Standard Life Ins. Co., 560 U.S. 242 (2010); Key Tronic Corp. v. United States, 511 U.S. 809 (1994). The leading case is Alyeska Pipeline Serv. Co. v. Wilderness Society, 421 U.S. 240 (1975).

[168] Arlington Cent. Sch. Dist. Bd. of Educ. v. Murphy, 548 U.S. 291 (2006); West Virginia Univ. Hosps., Inc. v. Casey, 499 U.S. 83 (1991).

[169] Shannon v. United States, 512 U.S. 573 (1994).

[170] Gozlon-Peretz v. United States, 498 U.S. 395 (1991).

[171] United States v. Montalvo-Murillo, 495 U.S. 711, 717–18 (1990).

[172] Loeffler v. Frank, 486 U.S. 549, 554–55 (1988).

[173] Carnival Cruise Lines v. Shute, 499 U.S. 585, 589 (1991); Stewart Org. v. Ricoh Corp., 487 U.S. 22, 33 (1988) (Kennedy, J., concurring).

[174] Astoria Fed. Sav. & Loan Ass'n v. Solimino, 501 U.S. 104, 108 (1991).

[175] Rehberg v. Paulk, 132 S.Ct. 1497 (2012); Burns v. Reed, 500 U.S. 478, 484–85 (1991); Forrester v. White, 484 U.S. 219, 225–26 (1988).

[176] ABC, Inc. v. Aereo, Inc., 134 S.Ct. 2498 (2014); Clark v. Rameker, 134 S.Ct. 2242 (2014); Abramski, v. United States, 134 S.Ct. 2259 (2014); CSX Transp., Inc. v. McBride, 131 S.Ct. 2630 (2011); Wal-Mart Stores, Inc. v. Dukes, 131 S.Ct. 2541, 2557–58 (2011); AT&T Mobility (LLC) v. Concepcion, 131 S.Ct. 1740 (2011); Republic of Iraq v. Beaty, 556 U.S. 848, 864 (2009); Zuni Pub. Sch. Dist. No. 89 v. Department of Educ., 550 U.S. 81 (2007); Massachusetts v. EPA, 549 U.S. 497 (2007); Burlington Northern & Santa Fe Ry. v. White, 548 U.S. 53 (2006); Jones v. R.R.

"incongruous results."[177] Caution: no law pursues its purpose at all costs, and text-based limits on a law's scope are part of its "purpose."[178]

1. General Canons

- Presumption against repeals by implication.[179] But where there is a clear repugnancy between a more recent statutory scheme and an earlier one, partial repeal will be inferred.[180]

- *In pari materia*: similar statutes should be interpreted similarly,[181] unless legislative history or purpose suggests material differences.[182]

- Presumption *against* private right of action unless statute expressly provides one,[183] but once recognized a private right of action carries with it all traditional remedies.[184] Regulations cannot create a private cause of action not authorized by the statute.[185]

- A precisely drawn, detailed statute preempts or governs a more general statute or remedies.[186]

- When Congress enacts a specific remedy when no remedy was clearly recognized previously, the new remedy is regarded as exclusive.[187]

- Presumption against creating exemptions in a statute that has none.[188] Narrow interpretation of explicit exemptions.[189]

Donnelley & Sons Co., 541 U.S. 369 (2004); PGA Tour, Inc. v. Martin, 532 U.S. 661 (2001); Reves v. Ernst & Young, 494 U.S. 56, 60–61 (1990).

[177] Utility Air Regulatory Group v. EPA, 134 S.Ct. 2427 (2014) (plurality opinion); Ricci v. DeStefano, 557 U.S. 557 (2009); Winkelman v. Parma City Sch. Dist., 550 U.S. 516 (2007); Nixon v. Missouri Municipal League, 541 U.S. 125 (2004).

[178] Limelight Networks Inc. v. Akamai Technologies, Inc., 134 S.Ct. 2111 (2014); Rapanos v. United States, 547 U.S. 715 (2006) (plurality opinion of Scalia, J.).

[179] See sources in note 71 *supra*.

[180] Credit Suisse Securities (USA) LLC v. Billing, 551 U.S. 264 (2007).

[181] Powerex Corp. v. Reliant Energy Servs., Inc., 551 U.S. 224 (2007); Ledbetter v. Goodyear Tire & Rubber Co., 550 U.S. 618 (2007); John Hancock Mut. Life Ins. Co. v. Harris Trust & Sav. Bank, 510 U.S. 86, 101–06 (1993); Morales v. TWA, Inc., 504 U.S. 374 (1992); Communications Workers v. Beck, 487 U.S. 735, 750–52 (1988); Wimberly v. Labor & Indus. Relations Comm'n, 479 U.S. 511, 517 (1987).

[182] Ledbetter v. Goodyear Tire & Rubber Co., 550 U.S. 618 (2007); Fogerty v. Fantasy, Inc., 510 U.S. 517 (1994).

[183] Gonzaga Univ. v. Doe, 536 U.S. 273 (2002); Blessing v. Freestone, 520 U.S. 329 (1997); Suter v. Artist M., 503 U.S. 347 (1992).

[184] Franklin v. Gwinnett County Pub. Sch., 503 U.S. 60 (1992).

[185] Alexander v. Sandoval, 532 U.S. 275 (2001).

[186] Credit Suisse Securities (USA) LLC v. Billing, 551 U.S. 264 (2007); EC Term of Years Trust v. United States, 550 U.S. 429 (2007). The leading case is Brown v. General Serv. Admin., 425 U.S. 820, 834 (1976).

[187] Hinck, v. United States, 550 U.S. 501 (2007).

- Allow *de minimis* exceptions to statutory rules, so long as they do not undermine statutory policy.[190]

2. *Process Canons*

- Presumption that adjudicative bodies are vested with inherent authority to sanction abusive litigation practices.[191] Judges presumptively have discretion to raise procedural errors *sua sponte*.[192]

- Presumption that statutory exhaustion requirements entail implicit requirements that the petitioner follow the proper procedures; failing that, the petitioner has not met statutory exhaustion requirements.[193]

- Strict construction of statutes authorizing appeals.[194] Rule that Court of Claims is proper forum for Tucker Act claims against federal government.[195]

- Rule that "sue and be sued" clauses waive sovereign immunity and should be liberally construed.[196] Presumption that statute creating agency and authorizing it to "sue and be sued" also creates federal subject matter jurisdiction for lawsuits by and against the agency.[197]

- American rule: strong presumption that each side bears its own costs in adjudications.[198] Super-strong rule against finding statutory authorization of witness fees as costs unless the statute refers explicitly to witness fees.[199]

- Rule that the burden of proof is on the party requesting benefits or entitlements from the state.[200]

---

[188] Burwell v. Hobby Lobby Stores, Inc., 134 S.Ct. 2751 (2014); City of Chicago v. Environmental Def. Fund, 511 U.S. 328, 337 (1994).

[189] John Hancock Mut. Life Ins. Co. v. Harris Trust & Sav. Bank, 510 U.S. 86, 96–97 (1994); United States Dep't of Justice v. Landano, 508 U.S. 165 (1993); Citicorp Indus. Credit, Inc. v. Brock, 483 U.S. 27, 33–35 (1987).

[190] Wisconsin Dep't of Revenue v. William Wrigley, Jr., Co., 505 U.S. 214 (1992).

[191] Marrama v. Citizens Bank of Mass., 549 U.S. 365 (2007).

[192] Day v. McDonough, 547 U.S. 198 (2006).

[193] Woodford v. Ngo, 548 U.S. 81 (2006); see also O'Sullivan v. Boerckel, 526 U.S. 838, 845 (1999) (similar rule in habeas corpus law).

[194] Bowles v. Russell, 551 U.S. 205 (2007); Hohn v. United States, 524 U.S. 236, 247 (1998); California Coastal Comm'n v. Granite Rock Co., 480 U.S. 572, 579 (1987).

[195] Preseault v. ICC, 494 U.S. 1, 11–12 (1990).

[196] FDIC v. Meyer, 510 U.S. 471 (1994).

[197] American Nat'l Red Cross v. S.G., 505 U.S. 247 (1992).

[198] Buckhannon Bd. & Care Home, Inc. v. West Virginia Dep't Health & Human Resources, 532 U.S. 598 (2001). The leading case is Alyeska Pipeline Serv. Co. v. Wilderness Soc'y, 421 U.S. 240 (1975).

[199] Arlington Cent. Sch. Dist. Bd. of Educ. v. Murphy, 548 U.S. 291 (2006); Crawford Fitting Co. v. J.T. Gibbons, Inc., 482 U.S. 437, 445 (1987).

[200] NLRB v. Kentucky River Community Care, Inc., 532 U.S. 706 (2001).

- Rule that nonjurisdictional process objections (e.g., exhaustion of remedies, venue) are waived if not timely raised.[201]

3. *Specific Statutory Subject Areas*

- **Antitrust.** Sherman Act should be applied in light of its overall purpose of benefitting consumers.[202]

- Presumption against application of Sherman Act to activities authorized by states.[203]

- Exemption from antitrust liability should not be lightly inferred.[204] Principle that statutes should not be interpreted to create anti-competitive effects.[205]

- **Arbitration.** Federal court deference to arbitral awards, even where the Federal Arbitration Act is not by its terms applicable.[206]

- Strong presumption in favor of arbitration and of enforcing labor arbitration agreements.[207]

- Strong clear statement rule favoring arbitration of federal statutory claims unless Congress has clearly overridden Arbitration Act.[208]

- **Banking.** National Bank Act policy shielding national banks from "burdensome" state regulation.[209] But national banks are subject to state laws not conflicting with the NBA's purposes.[210]

- **Bankruptcy.** Bankruptcy Act should be construed in light of its overall purpose, to give a fresh start to the class of "honest but unfortunate debtors."[211]

- Presumption that the Bankruptcy Act of 1978 preserved prior bankruptcy doctrines.[212]

---

[201] Kontrick v. Ryan, 540 U.S. 443 (2004).

[202] Weyerhauser v. Ross-Simmons Hardwood Lumber, 549 U.S. 312 (2007).

[203] City of Columbia v. Omni Outdoor Advertising, Inc., 499 U.S. 365, 370 (1991).

[204] Credit Suisse Securities (USA) LLC v. Billing, 551 U.S. 264 (2007).

[205] Nautilus, Inc. v. Biosig Instruments, Inc., 134 S.Ct. 2120 (2014); Two Pesos, Inc. v. Taco Cabana, Inc., 505 U.S. 763 (1992).

[206] United Paperworkers Int'l Union v. Misco, Inc., 484 U.S. 29, 36–37 (1987).

[207] Howsam v. Dean Witter Reynolds, Inc., 537 U.S. 79, 83 (2002); Groves v. Ring Screw Works, Ferndale Fastener Div'n, 498 U.S. 168, 173 (1990).

[208] CompuCredit Corp. v. Greenwood, 132 S.Ct. 665 (2012); Circuit City Stores, Inc. v. Adams, 532 U.S. 105 (2001); Gilmer v. Interstate/Johnson Lane Corp., 500 U.S. 20, 26 (1991); Shearson/American Express, Inc. v. McMahon, 482 U.S. 220, 226–27 (1987).

[209] Watters v. Wachovia Bank, 550 U.S. 1 (2007); Beneficial Nat'l Bank v. Anderson, 539 U.S. 1, 10 (2003); Barnett Bank of Marion County, N.A. v. Nelson, 517 U.S. 25, 32–34 (1996).

[210] Atherton v. FDIC, 519 U.S. 213, 221–22 (1997).

[211] Marrama v. Citizens Bank of Mass., 549 U.S. 365 (2007).

[212] Dewsnup v. Timm, 502 U.S. 410 (1992).

- Where statute is ambiguous, courts should create gapfilling rules that are familiar, objective, and less expensive to administer.[213]

- **Civil Procedure and Jurisdiction.** Subject-matter jurisdictional rules will be strictly enforced and applied,[214] nor will jurisdictional provisions be inferred.[215]

- Article III baseline is that litigation involves claims by individuals (and not groups of people) aggrieved by a defendant's actions and presenting enough facts to warrant a plausible claim for legal relief.[216]

- Federal Rules of Civil Procedure apply in habeas cases, except to the extent they are inconsistent with the Habeas Corpus Rules.[217]

- Presumption that time-limitation periods, venue, and other nonjurisdictional requirements are waivable.[218]

- **Civil Rights.** Aspects of section 1983 not governed by state law are governed by federal rules conforming to common law tort principles.[219]

- Title VII of the Civil Rights Act should be interpreted to effectuate its goal of a workplace where individuals are not discriminated against because of their racial, ethnic, religious, or gender-based status.[220] But Title VII does not set forth a general code of workplace civility.[221]

- Voting Rights Act should be interpreted in light of its core purpose of preventing race discrimination in voting and fostering a transformation of America into a society no longer fixated on race.[222]

---

[213] Till v. CSC Credit Corp., 541 U.S. 465 (2004) (plurality opinion).

[214] Bowles v. Russell, 551 U.S. 205 (2007). Relatedly, courts will interpret even long-established jurisdictional exceptions narrowly. Marshall v. Marshall, 547 U.S. 293 (2006) (narrow interpretation of "probate exception"); Ankenbrandt v. Richards, 504 U.S. 689 (1992) (narrow interpretation of "domestic relations exception").

[215] Stern v. Marshall, 131 S.Ct. 2594, 2606–07 (2011); Henderson v. Shinseki, 131 S.Ct. 1197 (2011); Arbaugh v. Y & H Corp., 546 U.S. 500, 516 (2006).

[216] Wal-Mart Stores, Inc. v. Dukes, 131 S.Ct. 2541, 2550 (2011); Ashcroft v. Iqbal, 556 U.S. 662 (2009). Compare the majority and dissenting opinions in Brown v. Plata, 131 S.Ct. 1910 (2011).

[217] Woofard v. Garceau, 538 U.S. 202, 208 (2003).

[218] Stern v. Marshall, 131 S.Ct. 2594 (2011); Eberhart v. United States, 546 U.S. 12, 17–18 (2006) (per curiam).

[219] Wallace v. Kato, 549 U.S. 381 (2007).

[220] Burlington Northern & Santa Fe Ry. v. White, 548 U.S. 53 (2006).

[221] Oncale v. Sundowner Offshore Servs., Inc., 523 U.S. 75, 80 (1998); Faragher v. Boca Raton, 524 U.S. 775, 788 (1998).

[222] League of United Latin Am. Citizens v. Perry, 548 U.S. 399 (2006); Georgia v. Ashcroft, 539 U.S. 461, 490 (2003).

- **Criminal Law and Sentencing.** Rule of lenity: ambiguities in criminal statutes shall be decided in favor of the accused.[223] Likewise, ambiguous sentencing provisions should be interpreted against the government.[224]

- Failure of U.S. Attorneys to initiate criminal prosecutions in the past is evidence that the Attorney General's current reading of the statute is too broad.[225]

- Even when courts are not bound by Sentencing Commission interpretations, such interpretations may be considered.[226]

- **Environmental Law.** Environmental laws should be applied in light of their overall purpose of cleaning up the environment at a reasonable cost.[227]

- NEPA contains an implicit "rule of reason," relieving agencies of filing environmental impact statements that would serve no statutory purpose.[228]

- **Immigration.** Construe ambiguities in deportation statutes in favor of noncitizens.[229]

- **Indian Law.** Rule against state taxation of Indian tribes and reservation activities.[230]

- Presumption against national "diminishment" of Indian lands.[231]

- Longstanding assertion of state jurisdiction over Indian lands creates justifiable expectations of sovereign authority.[232]

- Presumption against criminal jurisdiction by an Indian tribe over a nonmember.[233]

- Presumption that party cannot invoke federal jurisdiction until she has exhausted her remedies in Indian tribal courts.[234]

---

[223] See sources in note 138 *supra*.

[224] United States v. R.L.C., 503 U.S. 291 (1992).

[225] Lopez v. Gonzales, 549 U.S. 47 (2006).

[226] James v. United States, 550 U.S. 192 (2007).

[227] Massachusetts v. EPA, 549 U.S. 497 (2007).

[228] Department of Transportation v. Public Citizen, 541 U.S. 752 (2004); Marsh v. Oregon Natural Resources Council, 490 U.S. 360, 373–74 (1989).

[229] INS v. St. Cyr, 533 U.S. 289, 320 (2001); INS v. Cardoza-Fonseca, 480 U.S. 421, 449 (1987). This canon is applied with an unusual level of unpredictability. Compare, e.g., INS v. Elias-Zacarias, 502 U.S. 478 (1992).

[230] California v. Cabazon Band of Mission Indians, 480 U.S. 202, 208 (1987). This canon seems to have had little bite in recent decades.

[231] Hagen v. Utah, 510 U.S. 399 (1994).

[232] City of Sherrill v. Oneida Indian Nation of N.Y., 544 U.S. 197 (2005); Hagen v. Utah, 510 U.S. 399, 421 (1994).

[233] Duro v. Reina, 495 U.S. 676, 693–94 (1990).

[234] Iowa Mut. Ins. Co. v. LaPlante, 480 U.S. 9, 15–17 (1987).

- **Labor Law.** Rule against statutory interference in labor-management discipline disputes.[235]

- **Patent Law.** Patent law should be applied liberally to encourage and reward ingenuity.[236]

- Practice and precedent of Patent Office are particularly persuasive evidence of statutory meaning in this area, given the much greater competence of that Office.[237]

- Strong presumption that abstract ideas and laws of nature are not patentable.[238]

- Strong presumption that inventor (and not her or his employer or grantor) is the party entitled to patent the invented product.[239]

- **Taxation.** Presumption that IRS tax assessments are correct.[240]

- Narrow interpretation of exemptions from federal taxation.[241] Presumption against taxpayer claiming income tax deduction.[242]

- Presumption that tax valuation statutes follow majority approach, and that departures from the majority approach would be signaled with clear statutory language.[243]

- **Veterans Benefits.** Principle that veterans' benefits statutes be construed liberally for their beneficiaries.[244]

---

[235] Eastern Associated Coal Corp. v. UMW Dist. 17, 531 U.S. 57 (2000).

[236] Bilski v. Kappos, 130 S.Ct. 3218 (2010).

[237] Festo Corp. v. Shoketsu Kinzoku Kogyo Kabushiki Co., 535 U.S. 722 (2002).

[238] Alice Corp. Pty. Ltd. v. CLS Bank Int'l, 134 S.Ct. 2347 (2014); Mayo Collaborative Servs., Inc. v. Prometheus Labs., Inc., 132 S.Ct. 1289 (2012).

[239] Board of Trustees, Leland Stanford Junior University v. Roche Molecular Sys., Inc., 131 S.Ct. 2254 (2011).

[240] Bilski v. Kappos, 561 U.S. 593 (2010).

[241] United States v. Burke, 504 U.S. 229 (1992) (Souter, J., concurring in the judgment); United States v. Wells Fargo bank, 485 U.S. 351, 357 (1988).

[242] INDOPCO, Inc. v. Commissioner, 503 U.S. 79 (1992).

[243] Limtiaco v. Camacho, 549 U.S. 483 (2007).

[244] King v. St. Vincent's Hosp., 502 U.S. 215 (1991).

INDEX

References are to Pages

SUPREME COURT

TEXTUALISM

VETOES